Marketing Management

Marketing editions work best when they are localized to bring in stories and ideas appropriate to those markets. Pearson Education's innovative global publishing program gives me the
advantage of working with highly regarded marketing coauthors in such countries as Canada,
France, Germany, Italy, India, China, Singapore and so on, because they each bring in new
relevant perspectives, some of which we incorporate into the US edition of *Marketing
Management*."

Philip Kotler
Kellogg School of Management, Northwestern University, USA

Today's students and marketers are learning about and managing marketing theory and
practice in a global marketplace. The global publishing concept enables marketing to 'leap
off the page'. It enables students and professionals to gain a firm understanding of how
marketing practice relates to the pursuit of customer value in both the familiar domestic
and often quite surprisingly different, international marketplaces."

Mairead Brady
Trinity College, University of Dublin, Ireland

Malcolm Goodman
Durham University, UK

Torben Hansen
Copenhagen Business School, Denmark

Introducing Pearson One

Each title in the Pearson One series is part of a collaborative global editorial development
process that aligns the talent and expertise of Pearson authors, editors,
and production people from all over the world. Titles in the Pearson One
series will offer students increased understanding of the global business
environment through content and cases, with both local and global
relevance.

PEARSON
One

The First in the Pearson One Series

Marketing Management is the first European adaptation of Philip Kotler and Kevin Keller's
international best seller. Their US title has been translated into 26 different languages and also
adapted into other English language editions for Canada, Asia, Africa, the Middle East, South
Asia, Australia and China. The current edition was simultaneously developed and produced to
launch around the world through an innovative publishing model that brought our authors and
editors together in a truly global endeavor.

Readers of the European edition will benefit from these local perspectives and
expertise through our international case studies, authored by our partners worldwide.
These cases will be identified by a marginal note in each chapter, linked to relevant
content and available through links on our Companion Website
www.pearsoned.co.uk/marketingmanagementeurope

PEARSON
Education

We work with leading authors to develop the
strongest educational materials in marketing
bringing cutting-edge thinking and best learning
practice to a global market.

Under a range of well-known imprints, including
Prentice Hall, we craft high-quality print and electronic
publications which help readers to understand and
apply their content, whether studying or at work.

To find out more about the complete range of our
publishing, please visit us on the World Wide Web at:
www.pearsoned.co.uk.

Philip
Kotler
Kevin Lane
Keller
Mairead
Brady
Malcolm
Goodman
Torben
Hansen

Marketing Management

PEARSON
Prentice
Hall

Harlow, England • London • New York • Boston • San Francisco • Toronto • Sydney • Singapore • Hong Kong
Tokyo • Seoul • Taipei • New Delhi • Cape Town • Madrid • Mexico City • Amsterdam • Munich • Paris • Milan

Pearson Education Limited
Edinburgh Gate
Harlow
Essex CM20 2JE
England

and Associated Companies throughout the world

Visit us on the World Wide Web at:
www.pearsoned.co.uk

First published 2009

ISBN 978-0-273-71856-7

British Library Cataloguing-in-Publication Data
A catalogue record for this book is available from the British Library

Library of Congress Cataloging-in-Publication Data
Marketing management / Philip Kotler . . . [et al.]. — 1st European ed.
      p. cm.
   Inspired by the American ed. of same title.
   Includes bibliographical references and index.
   ISBN 978-0-273-71856-7 (cased : alk. paper) 1. Marketing—Europe—Management.
2. Marketing—Management.   I. Kotler, Philip.   II. Kotler, Philip. Marketing management.
   HF5415.13.M35224 2009
   658.8—dc22

                                                                        2008053888

10 9 8 7 6 5 4
13 12 11

Typeset in 10/12 pt Garamond 3 by 73
Printed and bound in China (GCC/04)

Dedication

This book is dedicated to my wife and best friend, Nancy, with love. – PK

This book is dedicated to my wife, Punam, and my two daughters, Carolyn and Allison, with much love and thanks. – KLK

Many thanks to those who helped so much along the way especially Martin, Mum, Bernard and Cam. – MR

This work is dedicated to my wife, Jill, my daughter Abigail, son David and to the memory of my father. – MRVG

To Ulla and my parents. – TH

About the authors

Philip Kotler is one of the world's leading authorities on marketing. He is the S. C. Johnson & Son Distinguished Professor of International Marketing at the Kellogg School of Management, Northwestern University. He received his Master's degree at the University of Chicago and his PhD at MIT, both in economics. He did postdoctoral work in mathematics at Harvard University and in behavioural science at the University of Chicago.

Dr Kotler is the co-author of *Principles of Marketing* and *Marketing: An Introduction*. His *Strategic Marketing for Nonprofit Organizations*, now in its seventh edition, is the best seller in that specialised area. Dr Kotler's other books include *Marketing Models*; *The New Competition*; *Marketing Professional Services*; *Strategic Marketing for Educational Institutions*; *Marketing for Health Care Organizations*; *Marketing Congregations*; *High Visibility*; *Social Marketing*; *Marketing Places*; *The Marketing of Nations*; *Marketing for Hospitality and Tourism*; *Standing Room Only – Strategies for Marketing the Performing Arts*; *Museum Strategy and Marketing*; *Marketing Moves*; *Kotler on Marketing*; *Lateral Marketing: Ten Deadly Marketing Sins*; and *Corporate Social Responsibility*.

In addition, he has published more than one hundred articles in leading journals, including the *Harvard Business Review*, *Sloan Management Review*, *Business Horizons*, *California Management Review*, the *Journal of Marketing*, the *Journal of Marketing Research*, *Management Science*, the *Journal of Business Strategy*, and *Futurist*. He is the only three-time winner of the coveted Alpha Kappa Psi award for the best annual article published in the *Journal of Marketing*.

Professor Kotler was the first recipient of the American Marketing Association's (AMA) Distinguished Marketing Educator Award (1985). The European Association of Marketing Consultants and Sales Trainers awarded him their Prize for Marketing Excellence. He was chosen as the Leader in Marketing Thought by the Academic Members of the AMA in a 1975 survey. He also received the 1978 Paul Converse Award of the AMA, honouring his original contribution to marketing. In 1995, the Sales and Marketing Executives International (SMEI) named him Marketer of the Year. In 2002, Professor Kotler received the Distinguished Educator Award from The Academy of Marketing Science. He has received honorary doctoral degrees from Stockholm University, the University of Zurich, Athens University of Economics and Business, DePaul University, the Cracow School of Business and Economics, Groupe H.E.C. in Paris, the Budapest School of Economic Science and Public Administration, and the University of Economics and Business Administration in Vienna.

Professor Kotler has been a consultant to many major US and foreign companies, including IBM, General Electric, AT&T, Honeywell, Bank of America, Merck, SAS Airlines, Michelin, and others in the areas of marketing strategy and planning, marketing organisation, and international marketing. He has been Chairman of the College of Marketing of the Institute of Management Sciences, a Director of the American Marketing Association, a Trustee of the Marketing Science Institute, a Director of the MAC Group, a member of the Yankelovich Advisory Board and a member of the Copernicus Advisory Board. He was a member of the Board of Governors of the School of the Art Institute of Chicago and a member of the Advisory Board of the Drucker Foundation. He has travelled extensively throughout Europe, Asia and South America, advising and lecturing to many companies about global marketing opportunities.

Kevin Lane Keller is the E. B. Osborn Professor of Marketing at the Tuck School of Business at Dartmouth College. Professor Keller has degrees from Cornell, Carnegie-Mellon, and Duke universities. At Dartmouth, he teaches MBA courses on marketing management and strategic brand management and lectures in executive programmes on those topics.

Previously, Professor Keller was on the faculty of the Graduate School of Business at Stanford University, where he also served as the head of the marketing group. Additionally, he has been on the marketing faculty at the University of California at Berkeley and the University of North Carolina at Chapel Hill, been a visiting professor at Duke University and the Australian Graduate School of Management, and has two years of industry experience as Marketing Consultant for Bank of America.

Professor Keller's general area of expertise lies in marketing strategy and planning, and branding. His specific research interest is in how understanding theories and concepts related to consumer behaviour can improve marketing strategies. His research has been published in three of the major marketing journals – the *Journal of Marketing*, the *Journal of Marketing Research*, and the *Journal of Consumer Research*. He also has served on the Editorial Review Boards of those journals. With over 60 published papers, his research has been widely cited and has received numerous awards. Two of his articles, 'Consumer evaluations of brand extensions' and 'Conceptualizing, measuring, and managing customer-based brand equity' were named by INFORMS Society for Marketing Science in March 2007 to its list of Top 20 marketing science papers written in the past 25 years that have most affected the practice of marketing science. Professor Keller is acknowledged as one of the international leaders in the study of brands, branding and strategic brand management. Actively involved with industry, he has worked on a host of different types of marketing projects. He has served as a consultant and advisor to marketers for some of the world's most successful brands, including Accenture, American Express, Disney, Ford, Intel, Levi Strauss, Procter & Gamble and SAB Miller. Additional brand consulting activities have been with other top companies such as Allstate, Beiersdorf (Nivea), BlueCross BlueShield, Campbell's, Eli Lilly, ExxonMobil, General Mills, Goodyear, Kodak, Mayo Clinic, Nordstrom, Shell Oil, Starbucks, Unilever and Young & Rubicam. He has also served as an academic trustee for the Marketing Science Institute. A popular speaker, he has conducted marketing seminars to top executives in a variety of forums.

Professor Keller is currently conducting a variety of studies that address strategies to build, measure and manage brand equity. His textbook on those subjects, *Strategic Brand Management*, has been adopted at top business schools and leading firms around the world and has been heralded as the 'bible of branding'.

An avid sports, music and film enthusiast, in his so-called 'spare time', he has served as executive producer for one of Australia's great rock and roll treasures, The Church, as well as American power-pop legends Dwight Twilley and Tommy Keene. He is also on the Board of Directors for The Doug Flutie, Jr. Foundation for Autism. Professor Keller lives in Etna, New Hampsire with his wife, Punam (also a Tuck marketing professor), and his two daughters, Carolyn and Allison.

Mairead Brady is a lecturer in Marketing at the School of Business, Trinity College Dublin. She holds a PhD from the University of Strathclyde in Scotland, which she completed under the supervision of Professors Michael Saren and Nikolaos Tzokas.

She lectures at undergraduate to post-experience Masters level and supervises PhD students. She is a lead lecturer on the Master in International Business, a joint Trinity College and Enterprise Ireland programme targeted at high potential Irish businesses. She also lectures at the IMI (Irish Management Institute) to business practitioners. She provides marketing expertise to innovators and entrepreneurs within universities in Ireland through her work with the Innovation Centre at Trinity College.

As a sought-after consultant, Dr Brady provides consulting and marketing advice to multinational blue chip companies as well as small start-ups and Irish government agencies. Her clients range from Vodafone's Global Brand Academy to small start-ups supported by regional Enterprise boards.

Dr Brady's research focuses on the assimilation of information and communication technologies (ICT) into contemporary marketing practice (CMP) and along global supply networks (GSN). She is also interested in redesigning global services supply networks, understanding the level of preparedness for ICT innovations along GSN, and how consumers interface with the GSN technology and brands.

Dr Brady is also a member of an international research group, www.cmpnetwork. intranets.com, which includes researchers from the University of Nottingham, Cranfield School of Management, University of Auckland, Eindhoven University of Technology, Universidad Torcuato Di Tella, Argentina, and Georgia State University. This research group publishes comparative studies into marketing practice worldwide.

With over 70 publications including journal articles and international conference papers and presentations, Dr Brady is the author of many journal articles in publications like the *Journal of Marketing Management*, the *Journal of Business and Industrial Marketing*, *International Journal of Technology Marketing*, *Irish Marketing Review*, *Irish Journal of Management* and *Management Decision*. She has been guest editor of the *Creativity and Innovation Management Journal*, *Irish Journal of Management* and the *Journal of Business and Industrial Marketing*, which she jointly edited with Professor Rod Brodie of the University of Auckland.

She served as chair of the Irish Academy of Management Conference hosted by Trinity College Dublin in 2004, which attracted the highest ever delegate attendance. She was also on the organising committee of the 11th International Product Development Management Conference held at Trinity College in 2004. She is also a reviewer and/or track chair for the following conferences: European Marketing Academy Conference (EMAC), IEEE/INFORMS International Conference on Service Operations and Logistics, and Informatics, Academy of Marketing, The Irish Academy of Marketing, American Marketing Association and the American Academy of Management.

Additionally, Dr Brady regularly serves as reviewer for journals such as *European Journal of Marketing*, *Journal of Marketing Management*, *Qualitative Market Research: An International Journal*, *Journal of the Irish Academy of Management*, *Journal of Business and Industrial Marketing* and *Management Research News*. She has contributed book chapters to a selection of books including two chapters to *Marketing Graffiti* written by Professor Michael Saren.

Her many conference publications include the European Academy of Management (EURAM), American Academy of Management (AM), the British Academy of Management (BAM), the Irish Academy of Management, the Academy of Marketing (UK and Ireland), the European Academy of Marketing (EMAC), Australian and New Zealand Marketing Academy (ANZMAC), IEEE/Informs, the European Group in Organisational Studies (EGOS) and the Academy of International Business. She was the communications director for the technology and innovation special interest group of the American Marketing Association.

With a busy work and home life, Mairead still makes the time to enjoy travel and cooking. She particularly likes socialising with friends at dinner parties. She is actively involved with a range of charities and particularly enjoys her work with economically disadvantaged children in Dublin's inner city. Bringing educational and social support to these children through activities such as homework clubs and playgroups is both rewarding and fun.

Malcolm Robert Victor Goodman teaches both undergraduates and postgraduates at the University of Durham in the UK. His specialist subjects are business creativity, organisational change and marketing. He is an external examiner for the Edward de Bono Institute of Creativity at the University of Malta.

He graduated in economics after submitting a practical marketing study on the cricket bat and ball industries of Britain designed to explore the gap between theoretical knowledge and its application to the real world. This became the springboard for a lifetime interest in the practical application of marketing concepts and techniques. Professor Goodman also holds the Diploma from the UK's Chartered Institute of Marketing.

The paradigm change in many markets, both in Europe and further afield, from sellers' to buyers' markets sparked his fascination with the problems that many organisations face as they seek to come to terms with the challenges presented by mounting global competition. This has led to him developing a keen interest in business creativity and organisational change. The pursuit of business success now requires a holistic integration of creative management and marketing management skills and this challenges organisations to pursue and adopt new attitudes and skills.

Publications include original texts on *The Cricket Bat and Ball Industries of Britain* and *Creative Management*. He also contributed a chapter titled 'Managing in times of change: avoiding management myopia' in *Strategy and Performance: Achieving Competitive Advantage in the Global Market* edited by Abby Ghobadian, Nicholas O'Regan, David Gallear and Howard Viney, which has been translated into Chinese. Professor Goodman has produced several papers for academic, trade and industry publications. He has also authored and contributed to distance learning courses in marketing for Durham University Business School and tutored on the UK's Open University Creative Management course.

Before entering the academic profession, Professor Goodman gained experience in the practical application of creative management and marketing skills in executive posts in British Leyland (where he was market planner for British Leyland France); for General Motors; Lucas Industries and the Tube Investments Group. He also served as Marketing Director for Lindley Lodge, a charity charged with the provision of development training programmes for young people, which provided useful experience in getting results with a very small budget. Training courses run for the coal and steel industries were balanced by the pioneering of programmes for national retailers such as Boots and Marks & Spencer.

During his career, management briefs have covered both consumer and business-to-business assignments. These have included product and market planning posts that have provided a wealth of experience in working with outside professional agencies. Professor Goodman has worked on several international assignments and has conducted on-the-spot marketing surveys and management briefs in Europe (particularly France and Germany) and in the Far East (especially Indonesia, Malaysia, Singapore and Thailand).

He has been a consultant to and been involved in creative management and marketing training with many organisations including ICI, Lucas, Marks & Spencer, Price Waterhouse, Royal Navy, Sunderland Association Football Club and Uniroyal. He has also contributed to the UK Government inspired gifted and talented youth programme (NAGTY) by running two-week Summer School programmes in practical business skills at the University of Durham.

In his youth Professor Goodman played football and roamed the pitch for the London based Crystal Palace FC. A lifetime interest in sport – mainly football and cricket – has convinced him of the importance of taking a holistic and team-based approach to management tasks. His academic career began with an appointment to teach marketing and management skills on the Royal Navy Resettlement Programme and to run UK Government sponsored practical business courses for small businesses (SMEs) at the Portsmouth Management Centre. He also brought and further developed the retail oriented training programmes that he had pioneered at Lindley Lodge. His current activity is characterised by a strong desire to assist clients and students to practically apply creative management and marketing skills to enable them to make a difference in highly competitive global markets.

Outside of work he cites his main interests – other than sport – to be camping, creative thinking, current affairs, and classical music. He is happily married to Jill and has an adult daughter and son.

Source: Sine Fiig

Torben Hansen is a Professor at the Department of Marketing, Copenhagen Business School (CBS). He received his Bachelor and Master degrees from University of Southern Denmark and his PhD from Copenhagen Business School. His main fields of research are consumer behaviour and marketing research methods and his papers have appeared in various academic journals, examples include *International Journal of Consumer Studies, European Journal of Marketing, Journal of Consumer Behaviour, Journal of Foodservice Business Research, Journal of Product & Brand Management, Journal of International Consumer Marketing, Journal of Euromarketing, International Journal of Retail & Distribution Management, British Food Journal, The International Review of Retail Distribution and Consumer Research, Journal of Retailing and Consumer Services* and others, along with a number of chapters in scholarly books. He has authored or co-authored several books, including *New Perspectives in Retailing – A Study of the Interface between Consumers and Retailers*. He is a frequent speaker at national and international conferences and community forums.

Professor Hansen is Chairman of the *Consumer Research Group* at CBS, which he took the initiative to establish in 2003. Currently he leads a consumer food research project funded by the Danish Agency for Science, Technology and Innovation. Since 2007 Professor Hansen has served as Chairman of the *Danish Money and Pension Panel*. The Money and Pension Panel is a board established by the Danish Parliament with the purpose of improving consumers' knowledge of and interest in financial matters. Besides from the chairman the Panel comprises eight Danish consumer oriented and financial organisations. He is also a member of the Scientific Panel for *Center for Pension Law* at the University of Copenhagen. Professor Hansen has worked as a consultant for various companies and collaborates with several private organisations and public authorities, examples include *The Danish Chamber of Commerce, The Ministry of Science, Technology and Innovation, The Confederation of Danish Industry*, and *The Danish Consumer Council*. As a consumer behaviour expert, he is often called upon by the press, which relies on him for assessments of market trends and comments to consumer behaviour issues.

Professor Hansen has served as a reviewer for several leading marketing journals, including *Journal of the Academy of Marketing Science, The International Review of Retail, Distribution and Consumer Research, Journal of Consumer Psychology, Journal of Retailing and Consumer Services, International Journal of Retail and Distribution Management, British Food Journal* and *Journal of Marketing Management*. He is North Europe and UK editor of *Marketing Trends News*, which weekly provides news to academic and managerial Web community. Also, he is a member of the international scientific committee for the *Venice-Paris International Congress Marketing Trends*, a yearly conference sponsored by the Prime Minister of the French Republic. He has chaired, or been a member of, several assessment committees for various academic positions and has wide teaching experience, which also includes course coordinator and masters and PhD supervision activities.

Professor Hansen has a passion for food and wine and often experiments with exotic spices and new recipes, which with various successes he serves for people who visit his wife and him in their home. He has appeared on Danish television as a guest chef in a popular comedy, cook and talk show. In his spare time he often goes boating in his small but fast boat, which he also uses for fishing expeditions. Also, he enjoys do-it-yourself work on his old country house.

Brief contents

Contents

Guided tour

Chapter openers concisely introduce an at-a-glance list of **learning outcomes**, a visual representation of the **chapter journey** on which the reader is about to embark and a **brief introduction** that includes a prelude **company case example** relating to the themes discussed in the chapter.

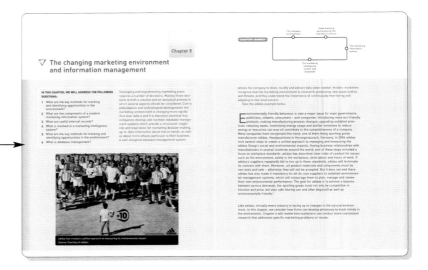

Video documentaries open each part of the book. They include interviews with top management teams from a variety of European and international organisations who discuss how their products or services are marketed. Access these documentaries online at **www.pearsoned.co.uk/marketingmanagementeurope**

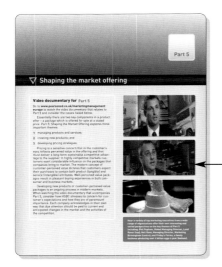

Marketing Insight boxes provide a valuable focus on the most important themes in each chapter and how they are applied in practice.

Readers of the European edition benefit from local perspectives and expertise through **international case studies**, authored by top academics around the world. Boxes with national flags appear in the margins of the text and refer readers to online sites where they can access the material.

Throughout the text you will find vivid, brief illustrations of chapter concepts using **real companies and situations.**

Breakthrough Marketing highlights innovative and astute marketing accomplishments by leading businesses and organisations.

Marketing Memos offer practical advice and direction when dealing with various decisions at all stages of the marketing management process.

Applications has two practical exercises to challenge the reader: **Marketing debate** suggests opposing points of view on an important marketing topic from the chapter and asks you to choose a side. **Marketing discussion** identifies provocative marketing issues and allows for a personal point of view.

At the end of each chapter, the **Summary** section recaps and reinforces the concepts put forth at the start of the chapter.

For students

The first European edition of *Marketing Management* is supported by a range of valuable online learning resources.
To make the most of your textbook, go to
www.pearsoned.co.uk/ marketingmanagementeurope

Watch eight brand new **video documentaries**, which expand on the key themes in each part of the book. In them you'll hear from top marketing managers from around the world at top multinational companies such as Tata, HSBC and IKEA, as well as smaller organisations such as the Voluntary Service Overseas (VSO) and St Paul's Cathedral.

Test your understanding of the subject matter by taking **online quizzes**. Every chapter is accompanied by an initial **Concept Check Quiz** that helps assess your understanding of the topics before you engage with the chapter. A **Concept Challenge Quiz**, which should be taken once you have finished your reading, reviews your understanding of the material covered in the chapter.

Explore **international perspectives** on marketing management by reading articles written by experts from around the world. In each chapter you'll find a brief description of a marketing challenge. For example, in the margin of page 205 there is a reference to Nokia and how it developed a mobile handset suited for Indian customers. Go to the website to read more.

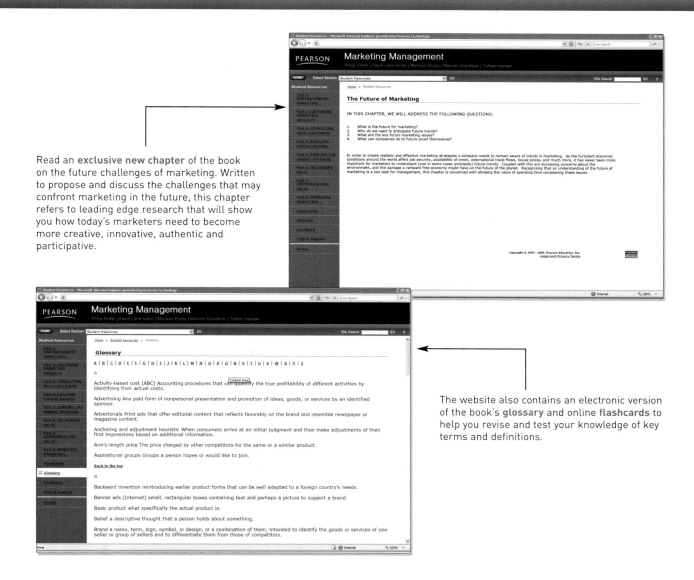

Read an **exclusive new chapter** of the book on the future challenges of marketing. Written to propose and discuss the challenges that may confront marketing in the future, this chapter refers to leading edge research that will show you how today's marketers need to become more creative, innovative, authentic and participative.

The website also contains an electronic version of the book's **glossary** and online **flashcards** to help you revise and test your knowledge of key terms and definitions.

For instructors

A full suite of lecturer support material is provided with this textbook. Developed with the overarching global scheme of this book in mind, the resource package includes:

- a DVD containing full versions of the video documentaries within the book;
- an Instructor's Manual with sample answers for all the question material in the book;
- media-rich PowerPoint slides, including animated figures from the book, video clips, audio and direct links on the web.

Contact your local Pearson Education sales consultant to obtain more details about these resources or to arrange a demonstration. Sales consultant details can be found at **www.pearsoned.co.uk/replocator.**

Preface

▽ What is *Marketing Management* all about?

The American edition of *Marketing Management* is the world's leading marketing text because its content and organisation consistently reflects changes in marketing theory and practice. This new European Edition of *Marketing Management* has been inspired by the American edition and explores the challenges facing European marketing practitioners. Increased global competition for business in European markets has led to a need for firms to develop market offerings that are especially tailored to meet the requirements of individual countries and customers. In the sellers' markets of yesteryear competition was less pronounced and many firms concentrated on becoming cost effective performers. This led to the formation of a mindset known as the *least-cost production paradigm*.

The paradigm change to and toward buyers' markets calls for marketers to provide customers with what they want and has become a challenge for supplying firms. It usually requires additional costs and may also involve substantial changes to their *modus operandi*. Additional costs are entailed as firms seek to meet customer-perceived value requirements. This normally entails offering a carefully tailored package of product and service benefits and places increased importance on relationship marketing. The task of marketers is to discover accurately what their targeted customers want and then to develop appropriate market offerings by effective applications of the marketing mix. The marketing of services has assumed a great importance in most developed western economies and increasingly so across the world as the leading emerging economies gather strength. Service benefits have become of greater importance as a means of increasing the customer-perceived value of offerings made by traditional product marketing firms.

The onward march of digital technology has had a profound effect on the practice of marketing. Firms now sell goods and services through a variety of direct and indirect channels. Mass advertising is increasingly giving way to new forms of communication as information and communication technologies (ICT) gather momentum. Communication has become truly two-way and customers are reporting more and more to other customers what they think of specific companies and market offerings using email, blogs, podcasts and other digital media to do so.

In response, companies are moving from managing product or service portfolios to relationship marketing. They do so by managing customer portfolios, compiling databases on individual customers in order to be able to fine tune their offerings and messages to meet bespoke needs. They are replacing traditional sellers' market product and service standardisation with more sophisticated marketing. The drive toward effectiveness (meeting the individual requirements of customers) is potentially expensive if pursued in an undisciplined fashion. Marketers are paying increased attention to efficiency and developing marketing metrics to measure their performance on key operative functions such as customer profitability and lifetime value. Monitoring payback on specific marketing decisions can be difficult due to the nature of the variables that influence customer buying behaviour and the contextual dynamics and complexities of individual markets. However, it is important for firms to seek improved methods to measure the return on their marketing investment and its impact on shareholder value.

As companies change their thinking in the light of emerging customer demands in buyers' markets, so they give increased attention to changing their marketing organisation. Marketing is increasingly being seen as a company-wide rather than a functional activity. It drives the company's vision, mission and strategic planning. Marketing is about identifying and consistently delivering appropriate customer-perceived value offerings to targeted customers. This involves a host of vital decisions such as who the company wants as its customers; which of their needs to satisfy; what products and services to offer; what process to design; what communications to send and receive; what channels of distribution to use; and what partnerships to develop. Marketing can only succeed when all functions in an organisation work in a holistic way as a team with the single aim of consistently pleasing or delighting their customers by balancing the concepts of effectiveness and efficiency.

Marketing management

In order to achieve this successfully marketers practice marketing management on a national, international and often a global scale. Marketing management is the development, design, and implementation of marketing programmes, processes, and activities that recognise the breadth and interdependencies of the business environment. Four key dimensions and operating attitudes define the task:

1 **Internal marketing**: ensuring everyone in the organisation consistently embraces appropriate marketing principles, especially senior management.
2 **Integrated marketing**: ensuring that the best possible way of utilising the marketing mix is employed to consistently deliver market offerings that continually delight customers.

3 **Relationship marketing**: developing sound and lasting relationships with all the members of the firm's value chain, customers and other marketing partners.
4 **Performance marketing**: the design and application of marketing metrics to gauge the costs and returns of marketing activities.

Marketing management recognises that 'everything matters' with marketing and that a broad, integrated perspective is often necessary. Therefore, these four dimensions are woven throughout the book.

Organisation

The text specifically addresses the following tasks that constitute the essence of modern marketing management in the 21st century:

1 understanding marketing management;
2 capturing marketing insights;
3 connecting with customers;
4 building strong brands;
5 shaping the market offering;
6 delivering value;
7 communicating value; and
8 managing marketing, implementation and control.

The most significant organisational changes in the first European edition are: all chapters provide a European focus and include illustrations drawn from European companies.

- The text argues the case for marketing management in Europe and explores its practice through the use of the expanded 7P marketing mix. The service dominant logic is explored in this capacity.
- The aim of marketing management is the provision of customer-perceived value offerings to both consumer and business-to-business customers.
- Modern technological developments have provided marketing management with an array of tools including Information and Communication Technology (ICT) and several digital advances that have revolutionised market research, product and service development, supply and communication practice.
- As marketing management becomes more crucial in Europe there is a need to make sure that marketing initiatives are both effective and efficient. The text devotes a whole chapter to exploring marketing metrics.
- To complement the use of digital technologies the book provides a window into the increasing use of creative marketing techniques as companies seek to develop and sustain innovatory products/services and processes.
- A selection of topic templates including formats to encourage readers to practise drawing up marketing plans are also included. A set of European videos, case studies and exercises are featured to help readers bridge the gap between knowledge and practice.

Chapter by chapter changes

Chapter 1 Introduction to marketing

- emphasis on the importance, scope and philosophy of marketing;
- focus on marketing management and understanding markets;
- an overview of marketing management using the contemporary marketing practice framework from transactions to relational and network marketing;
- understanding the European marketing environment: company and consumer challenges;
- a review of postmodern and retro marketing.

Chapter 2 Understanding marketing management

- understanding marketing management practices;
- the challenges for marketing managers;
- forces shaping marketing's role;
- the contemporary marketing management skills: introducing and managing information and communication technologies (ICT); networks, relationships and interactions and internal or cross departmental interactions;
- emphasis on the tasks of global marketing managers;
- marketing management in developing markets.

Chapter 3 Developing marketing strategies and plans

- importance of the business environmental paradigm change from sellers' to buyers' markets and the challenges that it presents to marketing management;
- the importance of the transformation in the concept of value and the need for firms to develop and deliver value to their customers;
- change today not tomorrow. Five key strategies for managing change;
- critique of conventional SWOT analysis;
- moving from know-what to know-how. Sample Euromart marketing plan enables readers to get to grips with the practical application of marketing concepts and reflects the eight major themes featured in the text;
- the Appendix contains a more detailed marketing planning example that is linked to key chapter assignments.

Chapter 4 Managing digital technology in marketing

- understanding the role and range of information and communication technologies (ICT)/digital technology in marketing practice;
- how to gain competitive advantage by using the Internet;

- comprehensive coverage of digital marketing within distribution and communication practice;
- consumer digital shopping behaviour;
- the use of ICT or digital technology within marketing decision making;
- future developments in technology.

Chapter 5 The changing marketing environment and information management

- the European macroenvironment;
- the European market population;
- European cultures;
- importance of green marketing in Europe.

Chapter 6 Managing market research and forecasting

- conducting market research in European markets;
- European ethnographic research;
- European market research case study;
- contacting market potential in Europe;
- the market potential in Europe.

Chapter 7 Analysing consumer markets

- three perspectives on the study of European consumer behaviour;
- European lifestyles and social groups;
- consumer emotions;
- consumer planned behaviour;
- means end chains.

Chapter 8 Analysing business markets

- the internationalisation of European firms;
- uncertainty in business relations;
- transaction cost economics;
- egovernement in Europe.

Chapter 9 Dealing with competition

- gaining competitive advantages in the European marketplace;
- balancing customer and competitive orientations;
- European blue-ocean thinking.

Chapter 10 Indentifying, analysing and creating target market differentiating and positioning strategies

- geodemographic market research agencies that operate in Europe;
- description of key trends in the social and cultural environment – youth and ethnic markets;
- forces shaping social change;
- perceptual or positioning mapping;
- the challenge of repositioning.

Chapter 11 Creating customer value, satisfaction and loyalty

- the pursuit of customer-perceived value;
- customer life-time value – a conceptual dream or real-time activity?
- the experience economy;

- co-creation;
- the empowered customer;
- emotional turn/mood management.

Chapter 12 Creating and managing brands and brand equity

- understanding and managing brands;
- managing and measuring brand equity;
- managing service brands;
- brand touch points;
- co-creation and customisation within branding.

Chapter 13 Devising a contemporary branding strategy

- understanding global brands, products and services;
- global, local and glocal strategies;
- global consumption issues: brand communities and brand tribes;
- understanding branding in an ICT digital-based environment;
- online gaming and branding;
- exploring branding in the developing world, country and place branding;
- celebrity branding.

Chapter 14 Designing, developing and managing market offerings

- the development of balanced product portfolios as product life cycles shorten;
- the challenge of high customer churn rates as market evolution gathers pace under the influence of dynamic competition and innovation;
- the ecological issues surrounding packaging in Europe;
- labels – their function and legal regulation in Europe.

Chapter 15 Introducing new market offerings

- many cultures, many markets – the importance of introducing new product offerings in Europe;
- the story told by EU surveys such as Innabarometer;
- examples of good new product development practice at Dyson, Reckitt Benckiser and Unilever.

Chapter 16 Developing and managing pricing strategies

- the power of pricing;
- the changing European pricing environment;
- customer-perceived value pricing;
- every-day low pricing practices in Europe.

Chapter 17 Designing and managing supply networks

- The importance of supply chains or network management;
- Exploring global networks;
- Designing demand driven supply networks: agility, adaptability and alignment;
- Emphasis on channel management and channel design decisions;
- The service supply network;
- Co-creation and prosumers;
- Understanding multichannels and multiple channels to market;
- The role of ICT or digital technology within distribution from self-service technologies to RFID.

Chapter 18 Managing the service process and the consumer interface

- the service mix elements (people, process and physical evidence);
- issues and challenges in service process design including a services process model showing relationships and interactions between service providers and customers;
- customer as the service provider; co-creation and variability;
- training customer service people;
- managing technology within the process and customer interface: self-service technologies, RFID and mobile;
- managing the physical evidence or experience environment;
- managing the five senses to create the physical or experience environment.

Chapter 19 Designing and managing marketing communications

- markets can be regarded as conversations – the rising importance of word-of-mouth communication;
- guerrilla marketing – getting noticed;
- generating media 'talkabout' as in the case of the groundbreaking Dove Comedy Tour;
- updating company images – a choice between evolution or revolution.

Chapter 20 Managing mass and personal communications

- the essentials of managing mass and personal communications;
- marketing communications – more a matter of reminding customers than informing them?
- the need to be innovative with press campaigns (Nissan Qashqai launch publicity);
- the increasing use of TV sponsorship for branded products and services.

Chapter 21 Implementing marketing management

- internal marketing critique – a dream or widespread practical activity?
- creative management and marketing practice;
- creativity – a mystical gift for some or something for all?
- the importance of leadership in creative marketing management;
- creative marketing;
- assessing marketing ethical standards;
- ethnic and green marketing;
- key tasks for marketing managers;
- key company marketing cultures (the transactional marketing, relationship marketing, customer relationship marketing and customer perceived-value marketing journey);
- getting started – a template to begin practising marketing.

Chapter 22 Managing marketing metrics

- the need for marketing metrics;
- what marketing metrics should do;
- the chain of marketing productivity;
- accounting-based metrics;
- outcome metrics;
- shareholder value;
- customer lifetime value;
- brand equity and financial performance;
- the Balanced Scorecard.

Acknowledgements

The first European edition of *Marketing Management* contains contributions from many people.

From Phil Kotler whose work, comments and guiding hand greatly assisted the development of text of the European edition.

From Kevin Lane Keller whose insights into marketing have also inspired the authors of this European Edition.

The text has been co-authored by Malcolm Goodman of Durham University, Torben Hansen of the Copenhagen Business School and Mairead Brady of Trinity College, Dublin. Our thanks are due to many academics in our own and other universities as well as contacts too numerous to detail.

We would like to thank the reviewers who have helped develop the content and perspective of this first European edition. We are very grateful for their insightful comments and recommendations. Our thanks go to:

Dr Ruth Ashford, Manchester Metropolitan University, Head of Marketing and Retail Division and Chartered Institute of Marketing Chief Examiner

Professor Douglas Brownlie, Department of Marketing, University of Stirling

Professor David Carson, Ulster Business School, University of Ulster

Christian Grönroos, Professor of Service and Relationship Marketing, Hanken Swedish School of Economics and Business Administration, Finland

Professor Evert Gummesson, Stockholm University School of Business, Sweden

Dr Paul Hewer, Department of Marketing, University of Strathclyde

Associate Professor Jan Møller Jensen, Department of Marketing and Management, University of Southern Denmark

AC Muir, Department of Management, University of Glasgow

Michael Saren, Professor of Marketing, University of Leicester

Dr Gary Warnaby, Management School, University of Liverpool

No publishing exercise on this scale can reach a satisfactory climax without the hard work and dedication of a host of people who work in support of the project. We wish to record our appreciation of the driving but encouraging and gentle hand of our acquisitions editor, David Cox; Oli Adams, marketing manager; Steven Jackson and Stephanie Poulter development editors and Matthew Smith, editorial director. We also wish to acknowledge the professional and creative contributions of Joe Vella, desk editor; Maggie Wells, text and cover designer; Hilary Luckcock, picture researcher; Jacqueline Twyman, copyeditor; Jonathon Price, proofreader; and Isobel Mclean, indexer.

In addition we all owe a lot to our families and close friends who have exercised patience and have supported us during the hectic authoring weeks. We have produced a fresh and modern text that we hope you will enjoy.

Mairead Brady

Malcolm Goodman

Torben Hansen

Publisher's acknowledgements

We are grateful to the following for permission to reproduce copyright material:

Figures

Figure 1.1: H. J. Schau, M. F. Smith and P. I. Schau (2005) The healthcare network economy: the role of Internet information transfer and implications for pricing, *Industrial Marketing Management*, 34, 147–56. Reproduced with permission conyed through the copyright clearance center; Figure 1.3: Michael Bauer Research (2007) European purchasing power in 2006: who's on top? 31 August (retrieved from www.english.mb-research.de/content /view/). Reproduced with permission; Figure 2.1: From J. Thomas and R. K. Gupta (2005) Marketing theory and practice: evolving through turbulent times, *Global Business Review*, 6(1), 95–112. Copyright © International Management Institute. All rights reserved. Reproduced with permission of the copyright holders and the publishers, Sage Publications India pvt Ltd., New Delhi; Figure 2.2: W. Frederick, A. Malter and S. Ganesan (2005) The decline and dispersion of the marketing competence, *MIT Sloan Management Review*, 46(4), 35–43. Copyright © 2005 Massachusetts Institute of Technology. All rights reserved. Reproduced with permission; Figure 2.3: From G. McGovern and J. A. Quelch (2004) The fall and rise of the CMO, *Strategy + Business*, 37, 3–8. Reproduced with permission from *strategy+business*, the award-winning management quarterly published by Booz & Company. www.strategy-business.com; Figure 3.3: From M. E. Porter (1985) *Competitive Advantage. Creating and Sustaining Superior Performance*, New York: Free Press. Copyright © 1985 by Michael E. Porter. Reproduced with permission from The Free Press, a division of Simon & Schuster Adult Publishing Group; Figure 3.4: From P. Kotler, D. C. Jain and S. Maesincee (2002) Formulating a market renewal strategy, in *Marketing Moves*, Boston: Harvard Business School Publishing, Figure 1.1, p. 29. Copyright © 2002 by the President and Fellows of Harvard College. All rights reserved. Reproduced wih permission; Figure 3.7: Adapted from I. Ansoff (1957) Strategies for diversification, *Harvard Business Review*, September–October. Copyright © 1957 by the President and Fellows of Harvard College. All rights reserved. Reproduced wih permission; Figure 4.1: Adapted from M. E. Porter (2001) Strategy and the Internet, *Harvard Business Review*, March, 62–78. Copyright © 2001 by the President and Fellows of Harvard College. All rights reserved. Reproduced with permission; Figure 4.2: M. Smihily (2007) Internet usage in 2007: households and individuals, in *Eurostat Data in Focus*, Luxembourg: Office for Official Publications of the European Communities (retrieved from http:// epp.eurostat.ec.europa.eu/cache/ITY_OFFPUB/KS-QA-07-023/EN/KS-QA-07-023-EN.PDF). Copyright © 2007 European Communities. Reproduced with permission;

Figure 4.3: Adapted from E. T. Brey, S.-l. (A.) So, D.Y. Kim and A. M. Morrison (2007) Web-based permission marketing: segmentation for the lodging industry, *Tourism Management*, 28, 1408–16. Copyright © Elsevier. Reproduced with permission; Figure 4.4: eMarketer (2008) The UK Internet boom: the British are going digital – fast, *eMarketer*, 19 February (retrieved from www.emarketer.com/Article.aspx?id=1005944&src=article_head_sitesearch). Copyright © eMarketer, Inc. Reproduced with permission; Figure 4.6: Screenshot of SalesLogic CRM system from Scientific Computers Ltd (www.scl.com) reprinted by permission from Sage Publications; Figure 5.1: Eurostat (2006) *EU Integration Seen Through Statistics. Key Facts of 18 Policy Areas, 2006 Edition*, Luxembourg: Office for Official Publications of the European Communities, p. 40. Copyright © 2006 European Communities. Reproduced with permission; Figure 5.2: J. A. Ottman, E. R. Stafford and C. L. Hartman (2006) Avoiding green marketing myopia, *Environment*, June, 22–36. Reproduced with permission from Helen Dwight Reid Educational Foundation; Figure 7.3: A. H. Maslow (1970) *Motivation and Personality*, 2nd edn, Upper Saddle River, New Jersey: Prentice Hall. Reproduced with permission of Pearson Education, Inc. Reproduced with permission; Figure 7.4: T. Klein-Reesink (2004) Conceptual brand mapping: a web-based approach to collect brand knowledge and its interpretation using network analysis, in A. J. Cañas, J. D. Novak and F. M. González (eds.) *Concept Maps: Theory, Methodology, Technology*, Proceedings of the First International Conference on Concept Mapping. Pamplona, Spain 2004, Figure 1, p. 3 (retrieved from http://cmc.ihmc.us/papers/cmc2004-177.pdf). Copyright © Dr Thomas Klein Reesink. Reproduced with permission; Figure 7.8: J. Jacoby, C. K. Berning and T. F. Dietvorst (1977) What about disposition?, *Journal of Marketing*, July, 23. Reprinted with permission of the American Marketing Association; Figure 7.9: I. Aizen (2006) TpB diagram (retrieved from www.people.umass.edu/aizen/tpb.diag.html). Copyright © 2006 Icek Aizen. Reproduced with permission; Figure 8.1: G. Urban (2005) *Where are you positioned on the trust dimensions?, in Don't Just Relate – Advocate. A Blueprint for Profit in the Era of Customer Power*, Indianapolis, Indiana: Wharton School Publishers, p. 99. Copyright © 2005. Reproduced with permission; Figure 9.1: From M. E. Porter (1985) *Competitive Advantage. Creating and Sustaining Superior Performance*, New York: Free Press. Copyright © 1985 by Michael E. Porter. Reproduced with permission from The Free Press, a division of Simon & Schuster Adult Publishing Group; Figure 9.2: W. Chan Kim and R. Mauborgne (2005) *Blue-Ocean Strategy: How to Create Uncontested Market Space and Make the Competition Irrelevant*, Cambridge, Massachusetts: Harvard Business School Press. Copyright © 2005 by the Harvard Business School Publishing Corporation. All rights reserved. Reproduced with permission; Figure 10.2: VALS™. Copyright © SRI Consulting Business Intelligence. Reproduced with permission; Figure 10.5: Adapted from D. F. Abell (1980) *Defining the Business: The Starting Point of Strategic Planning*, Upper Saddle River, NJ: Prentice Hall, Chapter 8, pp. 192–96. Copyright © 1980. Reproduced with permission from Pearson Education, Inc.; Figure 11.4: L. Selden and Y. S. Selden (2006) Profitable customer: the key to great brands, *Advertising Age*, 77(28), 7–9. Copyright © 2006 Crain Communications, Inc. Reproduced with permission; Figure 11.7: J. C. Anderson and J. A. Narus (2003) Selectively pursuing more of your customer's business, *MIT Sloan Management Review*, Spring, 45. Copyright © 2003 Massachusetts Institute of Technology. All rights reserved. Reproduced with permission; Figure 12.1: From J. von Kunde and B. J. Cunningham (2002) *Corporate Religion*, Harlow, England: Financial Times Prentice Hall. Copyright © 2002 Pearson Education Ltd. Reproduced with permission; Figure 12.3: From K. L. Keller (2008) *Strategic Brand Management*, 3rd edn, Upper Saddle River, NJ: Prentice Hall. Copyright © 2008 Pearson Education Inc. Reproduced with permission; Figures 12.4 and 12.5: K. L. Keller and D. R. Lehmann (2006) Brand and banding: research findings and future priorities, *Marketing Science*, 25(6), 740–59. Copyright © 2006 the Institute for Operations Research and the Management Sciences (INFORMS), 7240 Parkway Drive, Suite 300, Hanover, MD 21076 USA. Reprinted by permission of INFORMS and the authors; Figure 13.1: H&M (2006) *H&M Annual Report 2006*, Stockholm: H & M Hennes & Mauritz AB, p. 10. Copyright © 2006 H & M Hennes & Mauritz AB. Reproduced with permission; Figure 13.2: R. V. Kozinets, A. Hemetsberger and H. J. Schau (2008) The wisdom of consumer crowds: collective innovation in the age of networked marketing, *Journal of Macromarketing*. Copyright © 2008 Sage Publications, Inc. Reprinted with permission; Figure 14.9: B. P. Shapiro (2003) Industrial product policy: managing the existing product line. Cambridge, MA: Marketing Science Institute (Report No. 77-110). Copyright © 2003. Reproduced with permission from Marketing Science Institute and Benson P. Shapiro; Figure 15.2: Jerold Panas, Young & Partners. Reproduced with permission; Figure 15.7: Adapted from E. M. Rogers (1983) *Diffusion of Innovations*, New York: Free Press. Copyright © 1962, 1971, 1983 by The Free Press. All rights reserved. Reproduced with permission from The Free Press, a division of Simon & Schuster Adult Publishing Group; Figure 16.1: K. Heires (2006) Why it pays to give away the store, *Business 2.0*, October, 36–7. Reproduced with permission; Figure 16.7: N. Kumar (2006) Strategies to fight low-cost rivals, *Harvard Business Review*, December, 86–95. Copyright © 2006 by the President and Fellows of Harvard College. All rights reserved. Reproduced with permission; Figure 17.3: H. J . Schau, M. F. Smith and P. I. Schau. (2005) The healthcare network economy: the role of Internet information transfer and implications for pricing, *Industrial Marketing Management*, 34, 147–56. Reproduced with permission conveyed through the Copyright Clearance Center; Figure 17.4: M. de Lurdes, D.K. Velduo and S. Macbeth (2004) Partnering and relationships within an international network context, *European Journal of Marketing*,

21(2), 142–57. Copyright © 2004 Emerald Group Publishing Limited. Reproduced with permission; Figures 17.5, 17.6 and 17.7: H. Lee (2004) The three A's of supply chain excellence, *Electonics Supply and Manufacturing*, 1 October (retrieved from www.my-sm.com/showArticle.jhtml ?articleID=47903369). Reproduced with permission; Figure 17.9: D. Lambert and M. Cooper (2000) Issues in supply chain management, *Industrial Marketing Management*, 29, 65–83. Reproduced with permission conveyed through the Copyright Clearance Center; Figure 17.10: T. Baltacioglu, E. Ada, M. Kaplan, O. Yurt and Y. Kaplan (2007) A new framework for service supply chains, *The Service Industries Journal*, 27(2), 105–24. Reproduced with permission conveyed through the Copyright Clearance Center; Figure 17.12: Adapted from D. Schoenbachler and G. Gordon (2002) Multi-channel shopping: understanding what drives channel choice, *Journal of Consumer Marketing*, 19(1), 42–53. Reproduced with permission conveyed through the Copyright Clearance Center; Figure 17.14: R. T. Moriarty and U. Moran (1990) Marketing hybrid marketing systems, *Harvard Business Review*, November–December, 150. Copyright © 1990 by the President and Fellows of Harvard College. All rights reserved. Reproduced with permission; Figure 17.16: Adapted from Microsoft Corporation (2007) Microsoft® Customer Care Framework 2008: Redefining Customer Experience (retrieved from http://download.microsoft.com/ download/b/d/2/bd2a14b8-b64b-4191-a2d5-311d0dc9f0ce/ CCF_08_Brochure_web.pdf). Copyright © Microsoft Corporation. Reproduced with permission; Figure 17.17: C. Poirier and F. J. Quinn (2003) Calibrating supply chain management: findings from a survey jointly conducted by Computer Services Corporations (CSC) and *Supply Chain Management Review* magazine. Reproduced with permission; Figure 17.18: Adapted from P. Iskanius and H. Kilpala (2006) One step closer towards e-business – the implementation of a supporting ICT system, *International Journal of Logistics: Research and Applications*, 9(3) (September), 289. Reproduced with permission conveyed through the Copyright Clearance Center; Figure 18.1: H. Kasper, P. van Helsdingen and M. Gabbott (2006) *Services Marketing Management: A Strategic Perspective*, 2nd edn, Chichester, England: John Wiley & Sons. Copyright © 2006 John Wiley & Sons. Reproduced with permission; Figure 18.2: R. Johnston and C. Graham (2005) *Service Operations Management: Improving Service Delivery*, 2nd edn, Harlow, England: Prentice Hall. Copyright © 2005 Pearson Education Ltd. Reproduced with permission; Figure 18.3: R. Fisk, S. Grove and J. John (2004) *Interactive Service Marketing*, Boston, MA: Houghton Mifflin. Copyright © 2004 South-Western, a part of Cengage Learning, Inc. Reproduced by permission; Figure 18.4: H. Kasper, P. van Helsdingen and M. Gabbott (2006) *Services Marketing Management: A Strategic Perspective*, 2nd edn, Chichester, England: Wiley. Copyright © 2006 John Wiley & Sons. Reproduced with permission; Figure 18.5: E. Gummesson (2002) *Total Relationship Marketing*, 2nd edn, London: Elsevier, p. 68. Copyright © 2002 Elsevier. Reproduced with permission; Figure 18.6: Adapted from W. T. Gregor and E. M. Friars (1982) *Money Merchandising: Retail Revolution in Consumer Financial Service*. Cambridge, Massachusetts: The MAC

Group. Reproduced with permission; Figure 18.7: Adapted from L. Holman and G. Buzek (2008) *North American Self-Service Kiosks Market Study*, Franklin, Tennessee: IHL Group. Reproduced with permission; Figure 18.8: C. K. Prahalad and V. Ramaswamy (2003) The new frontier of experience innovation, *MIT Sloan Management Review*, 44(4), 12–18. Copyright © 2003 Massachusetts Institute of Technology. All rights reserved. Reproduced with permission; Figure 20.5: Rayport, J. F. and Jaworksi, B. J. (2001) *e-commerce*, New York: McGraw-Hill, p. 116. Copyright © 2001 McGraw-Hill Companies. Reproduced with permission; Figure 20.7: Zoltners, A., Sinha, P. and Lorimer, S. E. (2006) Match your sales-force structure to your business life cycle, *Harvard Business Review*, July-August, 81–9. Copyright © 2006 by the President and Fellows of Harvard College. All rights reserved. Reproduced with permission; Figure 22.1: Adapted from R. T. Rust, T. Ambler, G. S. Carpenter, V. Kumar and R. K. Srivastava (2004) Measuring marketing productivity: current knowledge and future directions, *Journal of Marketing*, 68, October, 77. Copyright © 2004 American Marketing Association. Reproduced with permission; Figure 22.2: Sales modelling carried out by BrandScience. Copyright © Omnicom Media Group. Reproduced with permission; Figures 22.3 and 22.4: Adapted from R. S. Kaplan and D. P. Norton (2007) Using the balanced scorecard as a strategic management system, *Harvard Business Review*, July–August, 150–161. Copyright © 2007 by the President and Fellows of Harvard College. All rights reserved. Reproduced with permission; Figure 22.5: Adapted from D. Schultz (2005) Chapter 13 in P. Kotler and A. Tybout (ed.) *Kellogg on Branding: The Marketing Faculty of the Kellogg School of Management*, New York: John Wiley & Sons. Copyright © 2005 John Wiley & Sons, Inc. Reproduced with permission; Figure 22.6: Adapted from P. LaPointe (2005) *Marketing by the Dashboard Light – How to Get More Insight, Foresight, and Accountability from Your Marketing Investments*. Copyright © 2005 Patrick LaPointe. Reproduced with permission.

Tables

Table 1.1: *Fortune* (2008) Fortune global 500: Europe's top 50 companies, 21 july 2008 (retrieved from http://money.cnn.com/magazines/fortune/global500/2007/europe/). Copyright © 2006 Time, Inc. Reproduced with permission; Table 1.2: United Nations World Tourism Organization (2007) International tourist arrivals by country of destination, *UNWTO World Tourism Barometer*, 5(2), June, p. 8. Copyright © UNTWO Publications. Reproduced with permission; Table 1.4: Modified from C. Gronroos (1991) The marketing strategy continuum: towards a marketing concept for the 1990s, *Management Decision*, 29(1), 7–13. Emerald Group Publishing Ltd. Copyright © 1991, MCB UP Ltd. Reproduced with permission; Table 1.5: From com-Score (2007) U.K. social networking site usage highest in Europe, comScore World Metrix, July (www.comscore.com/press/release.asp?press=1801). Reproduced with permission; Table 2.1: W. Frederick, A. Malter and S. Ganesan (2005) The decline and dispersion of the marketing competence, *MIT Sloan Management Review*, 46(4), 35–43. Copyright © 2005 Massachusetts Institute of Technology. All rights reserved. Reproduced with permission; Table 2.4: P. Kotler (1999) *Kotler on Marketing*, New York: Free Press,

pp. 21–22. Copyright © 1999 by Philip Kotler. Reprinted with permission of the Free Press, a division of Simon and Schuster Adult Publishing Group, All rights reserved; Table 2.5: G. Svensson (2002) Beyond global marketing and the globalization of marketing activities, *Management Decision*, 40(6), 574–83. Copyright © Emerald Group Publishing, Ltd. Reproduced with permission; Table 3.1: Source: G. S. Day and P. J. H. Schoemaker (2006) *Peripheral Vision: Detecting the Weak Signals That Will Make or Break Your Company*. Cambridge, MA: Harvard Business School Press. Reproduced with permission; Table 3.2: BP strategy; eBay, Inc mission statement; Oticon A/S mission statement; and Philips mission statement reproduced with permission from the companies; Table 3.4: M. Sawhney, R. C. Wolcott and I. Arroniz (2006) The 12 different ways for companies to innovate, *MIT Sloan Management Review*, 47(3), 78. Copyright © 2006 Massachusetts Institute of Technology. All rights reserved. Reproduced with permission; Table 3.5: 3M Company and 3M Innovative Properties Company mission statement copyright © 3M IPC, reproduced by courtesy of 3M. No further reproduction is permitted without 3M's prior written consent; Robert Bosch GmbH mission statement, Nokia mission statement; Siemens AG mission statement; Divine Chocolate Ltd mission statement all reproduced with permission; Table 4.2: Nielsen Games www.nielsen.com. Copyrighted information of The Nielsen Company, licensed for use herein; Table 5.1: Consumer Electronics Association's 'Eighth Annual Household & Teen CE ownership study' as reported in 'Special Report: Digital Media', *Advertising Age*, 5 June 2006, S-2. Copyright © Crain Communications Inc. Reprinted with permission; Table 7.1: from www.lohas.com. Copyright © LOHAS. Reproduced with permission; Table 7.2: Based on a list from G. Belch and M. Belch (2004) Advertising and Promotion: An Integrated Marketing Communications Perspective, 6th edn, Homewood, IL: Irwin. Copyright © 2004 McGraw-Hill Companies. Reproduced with permission; Table 8.1: From . Institute for the Study of Business Markets (2006) Know thy customer, Marketplace: The ISBM Review, Winter, Exhibit 1, p. 2 (www.smeal.psu.edu/isbm/documents/mktpw06.pdf). Reproduced with permission from ISBM, Smeal College, Pennsylvania State University; Table 9.3: J. H. Roberts (2005) Defensive marketing: how a strong incumbent can protect its position, *Harvard Business Review*, November, 156. Copyright © 2005 by the Harvard Business School Publishing Corporation; all rights reserved; Table 10.2: Table compiled by Peter Sleight and published in F. Brassington and S. Pettit (2003) *Principles of Marketing*, 3rd edn, Harlow, England: Prentice Hall, Chapter 5, p. 187. Copyright © Peter Sleight. Reproduced with permission; Table 10.3: F. Brassington and S. Pettit (2003) *Principles of Marketing*, 3rd edn, Harlow, England: Prentice Hall. Copyright © 2003 Pearson Education Ltd. Reproduced with permission; Table 10.4: L. Hasson (1995) Monitoring social change, *International Journal of Market Research*, 37(1) 1995 pp. 69–80. Copyright © 1995 Market Research Society (www.ijmr.com). Reproduced with permission; Table 10.6: Adapted from T. V. Bonoma and B. P. Shapiro (1983) Segmenting the Industrial Market, Lexington Books. Copyright © 1983 Lexington Books. Reproduced with permission; Table 10.7: Adapted from R. J. Best (2005) Market-Based Management, 5th edn,

Upper Saddle River, NJ: Prentice Hall. Copyright © 2005 Pearson Education, Inc. Reproduced with permission; Table 11.2: D. K. Rigby, F. F. Reichheld and P. Schefter (2002) Avoid the four perils of CRM, *Harvard Business Review*, February, 106. Copyright © 2002 by the President and Fellows of Harvard College. All rights reserved. Reproduced wih permission; Table 12.1 Adapted from by D. A. Aaker and E. Joachimsthaler (2000) *Brand Leadership*, New York: Free Press. Copyright © 2000 by David A. Aaker and Erich Joachimsthaler. Reprinted with the permission of The Free Press, a Division of Simon & Schuster, Inc.; Table 13.1: V. Griffith (2002) Welcome to Tesco, your global superstore: how the U.K. retailer won over the world, one market at a time, *Strategy+Business*, First Quarter 2002. Reprinted with permission from *Strategy+Business*, the award-winning management quarterly published by Booz & Company (www.strategy-business.com); Table 13.2: A. Buller (2007) Top 40 digital brands: customer service wins every time, Brand Republic, October (retrieved from www.brandrepublic.com/News/754399/Top-40-digital-brands-Customer-service-wins-every-time/). Reproduced with the permission of the copyright owner, Haymarket Business Publications Limited; Table 13.3: T. Khanna. (2007) CHINA + INDIA: the power of two, *Harvard Business Review*, 85(2) pp. 60–9. Copyright © 2007 by the Harvard Business School Publishing Corporation. All rights reserved. Reproduced with permission; Table 13.5: Institute of Practitioners in Advertising (IPA), IPA Effectiveness Awards databank www.ipaeffectivenessawards.co.uk email info@ipa.co.uk for further details; Table 15.3: D. Jain (2001) Managing new-product development for strategic competitive advantage, in D. Iacobucci (ed.) *Kellogg on Marketing*, New York: Wiley, Table 6.1, p. 131. Reproduced with permission from John Wiley & Sons, Inc.; Table 15.4: European Commission (2004) Flash Eurobarometer Report No. 144, p. 7 (www.estatisticas.gpeari.mctes.pt). Copyright © 2004 Office for Official Publications of the European Communities. Reproduced with permission; Table 16.1: Adapted from R. S. Winer (1988) Behavioral perspectives on pricing: buyers' subjective perceptions of price revisited, in T. Devinney (ed.) *Issues in Pricing: Theory and Research*, Lexington, Massachusetts: Lexington Books, pp. 35–57. Copyright © 1988 Lexington Books. Reproduced with permission; Table 16.2: D. Kiley (2004) U.S. automakers get a bum rap, USA Today, 15 January 2004. Copyright © 2004 USA Today. Reprinted with permission; Table 16.3: Adapted from T. T. Nagle and R, K. Holden (2001) *The Strategy and Tactics of Pricing*, 3rd edn. Upper Saddle River, NJ: Prentice Hall, Chapter 4. Copyright © 2001 Pearson Education, Inc. reproduced with permission; Table 16.4; V. Murphy Barret (2006) What the traffic will bear, *Forbes*, 3 July, pp. 69–70, Copyright © 2006 Forbes LLC. Reproduced with permission; Table 22.1: T. Ambler (2001) What does marketing success look like?, *Marketing Management*, 10(1), Spring, pp. 12–18. Reproduced with permission.

Photos

Page 2: Steven May / Alamy Images; 5: Sipa Press / Rex Features (left), David Pearson / Alamy (right); 7: Ralph A. Clevenger / Corbis; 10: Rex Features; 21: Luis Gene / AFP / Getty Images; 36: Jochen Tack / Alamy; 42: Courtesy of CCP Games; 45: Creatas / PunchStock; 56 (left): © 1997 Thomas Taylor / Courtesy of Bloomsbury Publishing; 56 (right): Courtesy of Bloomsbury Publishing; 61: Jim Mone / AP / PA Photos; 63: Sean Gallup / Getty Images; 71: Courtesy of the Fiat Group; 76: Courtesy of Siemens AG / Agency: Publicis-München; 81: Courtesy of Asda; 83: Dean Houlding / Rex Features; 87: The Advertising Archives; 93: Koji Sasahara / AP / PA Photos; 94: Alex Oliveira / Rex Features; 97: Adrian Sherratt / Alamy; 116: John James / Alamy; 131: Leagas Delaney; 140: © Inter IKEA Systems BV 2006; 144: Pasieka / Science Photo Library; 146: Courtesy of MasterCard / Agency: Weber Shandwick; 152: Courtesy of adidas; 155: Courtesy of Google, Inc.; 160: Courtesy of Phoenix CNE TV; 166: KNA-Bild Radtke / dpa / Corbis; 175: Courtesy of Ford Motor Company; 188: All Outdoor Ltd; 193: Anna G. Tufvesson / Nordicphotos / Alamy; 194: Imagebroker / Alamy; 195: Spencer Grant / PhotoEdit; 201: Courtesy of Norman H. Olson, Purdue University; 207: Courtesy of Gayot Publications; 211: Steven Moeder / IDEO; 222: Martin Keene / PA / PA Photos; 225: Courtesy of Fernandes Bottling Co. NV / Agency: Studio Prins; 228: The Advertising Archives; 229: Courtesy of Philips Consumer Electronics; 232: © Andy Warhol Foundation / Corbis; 234: Ulrich Baumgarten / vario images / Alamy; 235: Courtesy of Unilever Danmark AS; 245: Courtesy of Volvo Car Corporation; 254: Courtesy of Proctor & Gamble UK; 266: Studio Pons / Soitec SA; 269: Worth Canoy / Icon / Corbis; 272: © Profimedia International s.r.o./ Alamy; 276: Courtesy of Emerson Electric; 284: Courtesy of Rockwell Automation; 286: Courtesy of Lincoln Electric / Jenny Ogborn; 302: Lehtikuva Oy / Rex Features; 307: Bjorn Beheydt / www.photographersdirect.com; 313: Courtesy of Nokia / Agency: The Red Consultancy; 316: Stephen F. Faust / www.photographersdirect.com; 318: Dave Yoder / Polaris / eyevinearchive.com; 332: Steve Sant / Alamy; 337: Richard Levine / Alamy; 338: Gregory Wrona / Alamy; 339: Justin Kase / Alamy; 344: Sandro Campardo / AP / PA Photos; 345: Sara Krulwhich / The New York Times / Redux Pictures; 368: David Young-Wolff / PhotoEdit; 378: Simon Belcher / Alamy; 382: Serif; 384: Courtesy of Naoko; 385: Richard Leeney / DK Images; 388: Courtesy of Volvo Car Corporation / Agency: Arnold; 397: Text and artwork copyright © 1998 Yahoo! Inc. All rights reserved; 405: John G. Mabanglo / Corbis; 410: Phillipe Hays / Rex Features; 422: Courtesy of Procter & Gamble; 425: AFP / Getty Images; 428: KPA / Zuma / Rex Features; 430: The Advertising Archives; 435: Courtesy of the Kellogg Group; 437: Courtesy of Dyson; 422: Daniele La Monaca / Reuters / Corbis; 445: The Advertising Archives; 453: Courtesy of adidas; 458: Courtesy of the companies shown: Philips Consumer Electronics, SAP (UK) Limited, © Inter IKEA Systems BV, BP plc, UBS AG, Daimler AG / Agency: Cooney Bains, Prada S.p.A., Siemens AG / Agency: Publicis Müchen, ING Group N.V. and adidas group AG; 460: Sari Gustafsson / Rex Features; 476: J. O'Neill (2003) Dreaming with BRICS: the path to 2050, Goldman Sachs Global Economics Paper No. 99, October (www2.goldmansachs.com/ideas/brics/book/99-dreaming.pdf); 479: The Advertising Archives; 480: David Fisher / Rex Features (left); Most Wanted / Rex Features (centre); Carolyn Contino / BEV / Rex Features (right); 482: Courtesy of the organisations shown: By kind permission of South African Tourism 2008, Ministry of Tourism of the Dominican Republic, Jamaica Tourist Board / Agency: McClusky International, Polish National Tourist Office, St. Lucia Tourist Board, Turkish Culture and Tourism Office, Singapore Tourism Board; 483: Courtesy of IDA Ireland; 488: Douglas C. Pizac / AP Wide World Photos; 493: Mark Scheuern / Alamy; 508: © Jupiter Images / Brand X / Alamy; 512: Courtesy of Daimler AG; 513: John van Hasselt / Corbis; 522: Martin Meissner / AP Wide World Photos; 528: Bill Aron / PhotoEdit; 529: mediablitzimages UK ltd / Alamy; 536: Rex Features; 543 (top): Courtesy of Xerox Corporation; 543 (bottom) used by permission of Unilever; 544 (top): Paul Aresu / PunchStock; 544 (bottom) used by permission of Unilever; 549: Courtesy of Reckitt Benckiser; 552: image100 / Corbis; 553: Warner Brothers TV / Bright / Crane Pro / The Koball Collection / Chris Haston; 566: Justin Sullivan / Getty Images; 572: Marco Secchi / Rex Features; 574: Courtesy of E. C. Dewitt & Company Limited; 577: Steven May / Alamy; 579: Jeff Greenberg / Alamy; 581: Kazuhiro Hogia / AFP / Getty Images; 584: Reproduced under permission from V&S Vin & Sprit AB (publ); 595: Courtesy of eBay, Inc.; 612: Courtesy of Daimler AG; 629: Courtesy of Cadbury plc; 640: Justin Kase / zthreez / Alamy; 642: Courtesy of Kodak Ltd (UK); 643: © Marks & Spencer plc; 647: Redlink / Corbis; 654: Courtesy of Swiss International Air Lines; 660: David Paul Morris / Getty Images; 668: Erin Siegal / Reuters; 671: © Mike Baldwin / Cornered / CartoonStock Ltd; 675: Masatoshi Okauchi / Rex Features; 676: Phil Yeomans / Rex Features; 677: Ulrich Baumgarten / vario images / Alamy; 682: Rex Features; 688: used by permission of Unilever; 690: Serif; 693: Courtesy of Land Rover; 698: used by permission of Michelin, North America, Inc.; 700: Courtesy of Salton Europe; 705: Chris P. Batson / Alamy; 709: Courtesy of Ocean Spray; 720: The Advertising Archives; 725: The Advertising Archives; 726: Courtesy of Nissan / Agency: TBWA London; 730: Gareth Cattermole / Getty Images; 736: Reproduced with kind permission of Harveys Darlington; 740: Gaspar Risko / Getty Images; 747: Shawn Thew / epa / Corbis; 748: Lowe Brindfors AB; 768: Serif; 774: PunchStock / Digital Vision; 788: Ross Haily / Fort Worth Star Telegram / MCT / NewsCom; 790: Used by permission of Starbuck Corporation; 798: Courtesy of B&Q / Agency: The Red Consultancy; 801: Serif; 813: Serif; 824: Curt Pickens / iStockphoto; 833: The Advertising Archives.

Text

Page 26: Marketing memo: Marketing right and wrong adapted from P. Kotler (2004) *Ten Deadly Marketing Sins*, Hoboken, NJ: John Wiley & Sons, Inc. Copyright © 2004 John Wiley & Sons, Inc. Reprinted with permission; 38: Text extract 'five false business assumptions' from P. Drucker (2003) Future of management: start seeing change as a golden opportunity, *Executive Excellence*, 20 May; page 41: Marketing Insight: Web-based simulation for leadership adapted from B. Reeves, T. W. Malone and T. O'Driscoll (2008) Leadership's online labs, *Harvard Business Review*, July, 59–66. Copyright © 2008 by the Harvard Business School Publishing Corporation. All rights reserved; Page 111: Marketing memo: Getting started,

checklist adapted from K. Kashani and D. Turpin (1999) *Marketing Management: An International Perspective* (Section 1), IMD, Lusanne published by Macmillan Business and reproduced with permission of Palgrave Macmillan; Page 271: Based on M. Zineldin (2007) International business relationship and entry modes: a case of Swedish automotive industry Scania and Volvo in Mexico, *Cross Cultural Management: An International Journal*, 14(4), 365–86. Copyright © Emerald Group Publishing Limited. Reproduced with permission; Page 273: Marketing memo: maximising customer references based on a white paper by B. Lee (2004) Success stories: the top 5 mistakes. Copyright © 2004 Bill Lee, Customer Reference Forum, bill@customerreferenceforum.com. Reproduced with permission; Page 297: Marketing memo: Selling tech to the government from O. Thomas (2003) How to sell tech to the feds, *Business 2.0*, March, 111–12. Copyright © 2006 Time Inc. All rights reserved. Reproduced with permission; Page 277: SAS Institute, Inc. from B. Lamons (2005) Branding, B-to-B style, *Sales and Marketing Management Magazine*, 157(9), 46–50. Copyright © 2005 Nielsen Business Media. Reproduced with permission. Copyrighted information of The Nielsen Company, licensed for use herein; 416: Creatives Simon Morris, Patrick McLelland and Clive Pickering for a John Lewis plc. Full page advertisement published in *The Guardian*, 25 June 2008, p. 38 reproduced with permission; Page 445: Marketing memo: Twenty-first century branding adapted from S. Bedbury (2002) *A New Brand World*, New York: Viking Press. Copyright © 2001 by Scott Bedbury. Repoduced with permission of Viking Penguin, a division of Penguin Group (USA) Inc.; Page 498: Marketing insight: Competitive Category Dynamics reprinted from" by D. A. Aaker (2004) The relevance of brand relevance, *Strategy+Business*, 35, Summer, 1–10. Reprinted with permission from *Strategy+Business*, the award-winning management quarterly published by Booz & Company (www.strategy-business.com); Page 503: Marketing memo: How to build a breakaway brand adapted from F. J. Kelly, III and B. Silverstein (2005) *The Breakaway Brand*, New York: McGraw-Hill. Copyright © 2006 The McGraw-Hill Companies. Reproduced with permission; 548: Marketing memo: Ten ways to find great new product ideas adapted from R. Cooper (1998) *Product Leadership: Creating and Launching Superior New Products*, New York: Perseus Books. Copyright © 1998 Basic Books, a member of the Perseus Books Group. Reproduced with permission; Page 716: Marketing memo: How integrated is your IMC programme? From K. L. Keller (2007) *Strategic Brand Management*, 3rd edn, Upper Saddle River, NJ: Prentice Hall, pp. 268–71. Copyright © 2007 Pearson Education, Inc., Reproduced with permission; Page 798: Box adapted from S. Hawks (2008) B&Q rebuilds its image to top the eco-friendly shoppers, *The Times* 28 February. Copyright © 2008 NI Syndication Ltd. Reproduced with permission.

In some instances we have been unable to trace the owners of copyright material and we would appreciate any information that would enable us to do so.

▽ Understanding marketing management

Video documentary for Part 1

Go to **www.pearsoned.co.uk/marketingmanagementeurope** to watch the video documentary that relates to Part 1 and consider the issues raised below.

Marketing Management is designed to take both business practitioners and students on a journey to explore the marketing manager's world.

Part 1: Understanding Marketing Management provides an overview of this journey and addresses two essential themes:

1   What is marketing?

2   Selecting and targeting markets.

Despite being everyday terms, it is surprising how few people have a clear understanding of what is meant by the words 'marketing' and 'management'. Part 1 explores the world of the marketing manager from the point of view of *what* they do and rest of the book provides guidance as to *how* they do it.

The video documentary for Part 1 greatly assists our understanding of how real-life marketers from a range of European organisations perceive marketing, and why it is essential to their success. Marketing is a business activity that is relevant to all types of businesses whether private, public, charity or other not-for-profit organisations. It is about the identification and fulfilment of customer needs, and the establishment and maintenance of brand values.

As you watch the documentary, consider how in a highly competitive global market, companies need to exercise both vision and mission; identify what to do and where to go (*concept of market effectiveness*); and then seek to establish a suitable brand value image by carefully using company resources (*concept of efficiency*).

Hear a variety of top marketing executives from a wide range of organisations offer their own interesting and varied perspectives on the key themes of Part 1 including: Ashish Joshi, Director, Royal Enfield Motorcycles Europe (top); Colin Green, Director of Global Marketing, Land Rover (centre); and Voluntary Services Overseas, London, UK (bottom).

Chapter 1

▽ Introduction to marketing

IN THIS CHAPTER, WE WILL ADDRESS THE FOLLOWING QUESTIONS:

1 Why is marketing important and what is the scope of marketing?

2 How do we understand markets and customers?

3 How is marketing practised?

4 What are the European marketing realities, company and consumer challenges?

5 What is the philosophy of marketing?

6 How is marketing in a post modern world and retro marketing practised?

7 What is an overview of marketing management?

Marketing management is a challenging and rewarding career choice because it is a core management function central to all company efforts. Successful marketing of products and services both locally and globally in a dynamic, networked, demanding marketplace is a vital skill needed by every company. If we think about it marketing profoundly affects our day-to-day lives. It is embedded in everything we do – from the clothes we wear, to the food we eat, the restaurants we visit, the websites we click on, the advertisements we see, the service we receive, the price we pay and so on.

Marketing managers need to understand consumer needs and the effect all marketing mix variables have on their consumers. Low-cost airlines are a great example of companies that give the customer what they want – low-cost travel.

Source: Steven May / Alamy Images

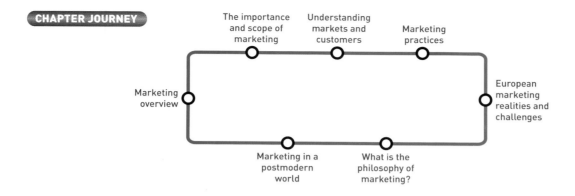

The importance and scope of marketing

Understanding markets and customers

Marketing practices

Marketing overview

European marketing realities and challenges

Marketing in a postmodern world

What is the philosophy of marketing?

Marketing managers oversee a wide range of internal and external activities to ensure business success and customer satisfaction, activities that will be covered in this text.

Take the Ryanair example below.

Ryanair is Europe's most successful low-cost airline, carrying over 65 million consumers, with 563 routes connecting 26 European countries. Ryanair and other low-cost airlines such as easyJet and German Wings have opened up the skies to more passengers and have completely revolutionised air travel. Since 1994, low-cost airlines have successfully matched a market need by capturing the imagination of overcharged Europeans travellers, tired of costly tickets but good service offered by national 'flag carriers' such as British Airways, Air France and Lufthansa. Consumers all over Europe are happy to have €1 flights to Riga or €5 flights to Warsaw or even free flights to the major European capitals such as London, Paris, Rome, Berlin, Barcelona, Amsterdam and Copenhagen.[1] Led by chief executive Michael O'Leary Ryanair focuses its company effort on its low-cost marketing strategy (Chapter 3), and uses a range of technologies both internally and externally (Chapter 4). It researches the market and understands its consumers, markets and competitors (Chapters 5–9). Ryanair understands the consumer segments, and chooses to target the price-conscious consumer (Chapter 10). It is positioned as the low-cost, low-service alternative to the full service airlines (Chapter 11). Marketing is designed to create the strong brand that is Ryanair in the minds of the European consumer (Chapters 12 and 13). To manage its brand image Ryanair uses the 7Ps of the marketing mix:

- **Product/service:** Ryanair's service offering is basic and low frills – an unassigned economy seat on an aircraft (Chapter 14).
- **Pricing:** It competes on rock-bottom prices (Chapter 16).
- **Place/global supply network and channels:** Ryanair operates from the lowest-cost airports, manages a network of suppliers and uses only one direct channel to market (Chapter 17).
- **Promotion/communication:** Promotion is minimal and inexpensive (Chapters 19 and 20), focusing on Internet marketing (Chapter 19);
- **Process:** Ryanair has eliminated all unnecessary service processes on board as well as for bookings and check in (Chapter 18);
- **Physical evidence:** Ryanair's planes have very basic and minimal interiors (Chapter 18).
- **People:** Ryanair's staff are focused on the low-cost, no frills marketing strategy (Chapter 18). It implements its marketing programme (Chapter 21) and manages its return to investors as a core focus (Chapter 22). In total, Ryanair is an excellent example of a company that understands both its consumers and the need for a total company marketing effort in creating a strong brand in a market dominated by major brands.

Marketing and a marketing department are critical ingredients for business success. It is the role of the marketing manager and the marketing department to plan, manage and execute the marketing strategy throughout the company with innovation, intuition and creativity. Marketing is organised effort, activity and expenditure designed first to acquire a customer and second to maintain and grow a customer at a profit. In this chapter, we lay the foundation for your study of marketing by providing an overview of the main marketing issues facing European companies in a rapidly changing marketing environment. This chapter also provides an overview of the book.

▽ The importance of marketing

Marketing is a significant dimension of any business in today's highly competitive environment and financial success is often dependent on marketing ability. Finance, operations, accounting, administration and other business functions will not really matter if companies do not understand consumer needs and identify sufficient demand for their products and services for them to make a profit.

Companies of all kinds – from consumer product manufacturers (such as Nokia or Ericsson in Sweden), to health care insurers (e.g. Bupa in the United Kingdom), from car manufacturers (e.g. BMW or Porsche in Germany) to banks (such as Société Générale in France or RaboBank in Holland), from non-profit organisations (Amnesty International, which was founded by a British lawyer) to industrial product manufacturers (e.g. Airbus – a French, German, English and Spanish conglomerate) – all have to use marketing to understand their core customers and grow their businesses. The 2007 survey of the 'Top Ten CEO Challenges' acknowledges the importance of marketing.[2] The CEOs cited excellence of strategy execution as their top challenge. The report highlighted the fact that marketing challenges differ globally, with European CEOs focusing on getting new, more responsive ideas out sooner. Therefore execution in terms of speed, flexibility and adaptability to change is a more dominant theme in Europe (3rd place) than in Asia (8th place) and the United States (10th place). All CEOs recognised the importance of marketing to building brands and a loyal customer base, two core assets that make up a large percentage of the value of a company.

Marketing is a complex set of tasks as well as a philosophy of business and it has been the Achilles heel of many formerly prosperous companies. Some companies had to confront new competitors: the Spanish clothing company Zara entered Benetton's target market, while H&M has been competing with Gap in many markets. There are also new consumer concerns. The Dutch company Philips, by being the first to focus on energy-efficient, environmentally friendly consumer and business lighting, has overtaken many national light bulb brands in Europe. Consumers also have more choice. The German discount supermarket Lidl has Euro 9 billion in non-domestic European sales, and now plans to target Hungary, Estonia, Lithuania, Croatia and Slovenia, where its main rival Aldi has no presence. Lidl has had a dramatic effect on established supermarkets such as Spar, Kaiser and Edeka in its domestic market. Its policies of 'hard discounting' – offering goods at prices even lower than normal discount stores, and supplying only own brands characterise its marketing strategy. Lidl has more than 400 stores in Britain, and a nationwide survey by the consumer magazine *Which?* in 2007 reported that British consumers rated Lidl and Aldi higher than Tesco, Asda, Morrison's and Sainsbury's. Marketing managers have to rethink and reorient their marketing efforts to deliver customer satisfaction within competitive markets.

Even market leaders such as Nokia, BMW and Carrefour recognise that they cannot afford to relax their marketing effort as their leadership is challenged by fast and agile competitors and changing consumer tastes. Just ask Ford or Gap, both of whom lost 19 per cent and 15 per cent of their brand value respectively, according to Business Week/Interbrands annual ranking of the 100 Best Global Brands 2008.[3] The big brand winners were Google, Zara and BMW, companies that really understand marketing and how to satisfy changing consumer needs.

As Rupert Murdoch, chief executive of the world's largest media company – News Corp, the owner of *The Times*, ITV and BSkyB in the UK and a host of TV stations across Europe including bTV in Bulgaria, B1 TV in Romania, Fox Televizija in Serbia, Fox Turkey, TV Puls in Poland and LNT in Latvia, noted: 'The world is changing very fast. Big will not beat small any more. It will be the fast beating the slow.' Take the example of Benetton, founded in Italy in 1965.

▽ Benetton

Benetton, which for years had enjoyed great success with a unique brand of clothing and provocative advertising, had to rethink its marketing strategy when new fast fashion competitors such as Zara and H&M entered the young fashion market and started capturing market share and brand loyalty through a comprehensive marketing strategy. Zara understood the new patterns of consumer behaviour of teenagers and young adults – markets that craved new styles quickly and cheaply and were happy with 'disposable clothing'. Zara studied the marketing mix variables and saw that global supply network management (Chapter 17), service process and physical evidence such as store layout and design (Chapter 18) were more important than traditional marketing expenditure on advertising (Chapters 19 and 20). Zara's advertising budget is 0.03 per cent of its revenues,[4] which is very different to Benetton that focused on creative advertising, spending €80 million on advertising alone. Benetton has now seen the errors of its ways, investing over €160 million in modernising its global supply chain. It can now deliver new styles to its worldwide stores once a week rather than once a month, which was its traditional delivery strategy. According to Vincenzo Scognamiglio, the head designer of Benetton, 'Time is my enemy.' Zara and H&M have very lean supply chains capable of replenishing shelves in days rather than months. Managing your supply network can be as important as style in the increasingly cut-throat business of mass market cloths.[5,6]

Marketing means understanding customer and consumer needs and making marketing choices to match these needs. Zara prospered due to its focus on rapid delivery of fashion styles to the market while Benetton floundered due to its over-focus on advertising. Advertising is not everything, marketers needs to use the full range of the marketing mix variables to succeed.

Source: Sipa Press/Rex Features (left); David Pearson/Alamy (right)

Awareness of changing consumer and business trends and the use of marketing expertise to react to and change before, or with these trends, is a major marketing skill set for the future generation of marketers. BMW prides itself on being the world's number one car manufacturer in the luxury niche market and also on its marketing ability to react to changing consumer lifestyle segments and match these segments with products. In 2000 BMW commissioned consumer research that identified four new market segments: Upper liberals; Postmoderns; Upper conservatives and Modern mainstreams, and then redesigned its product range to provide cars to match these predicted new segments. The strategy succeeded and in 2006 BMW had profits in excess of €4 billion. Changing a product range to match expected changes in future customer segments requires immense marketing skill. If BMW had got this wrong it could have been disastrous, but BMW was right and have the profits to reflect that.

Making the right decisions isn't always easy. Marketing managers must make major strategic or long-term decisions along with tactical or short-term decisions. *Strategically* they must consider which features to design into new services or products, what kind of price to offer customers, what channels to use to distribute their services and products, how much to spend on communications including advertising, sales, or the Internet, and which other media is most appropriate. *Tactically* they must also decide on details as diverse as the exact wording or colour for new packaging, managing ongoing research, the colour of the wallpaper in reception and the format for answering the phone. For many companies the role of the marketing department has being confined to tactical issues, ignoring the strategic role of marketing in the overall success of the company. This will be explored in more detail in Chapters 3 and 21. The companies at greatest risk are those that fail to carefully monitor their customers and competitors and who fail to continuously match their value offerings to customer needs. They take a short-term, sales-driven view of their business and ultimately they fail to satisfy their stockholders, employees, suppliers and supply network members and – most importantly – their customers. Skilful marketing is a never-ending pursuit. As Jay Conrad Levinson[7] author of *Guerrilla Marketing* noted: 'Marketing is not an event, but a process . . . It has a beginning, a middle, but never an end, for it is a process. You improve it, perfect it, change it, even pause it. But you never stop it completely.'

▽ The scope of marketing

To prepare to be a marketing manager, you need to understand what marketing is, how it works, what is marketed, and who does the marketing.

What is marketing?

Marketing is about identifying and meeting human and social needs. One of the shortest definitions of marketing is the process of 'meeting needs profitably'. This has been called balanced centricity – which is a focus on the customer but also on the company and its objectives.[8] When the Swedish company IKEA noticed that people wanted good furniture at a substantially lower price, they created well-designed, low-priced furniture. When Nokia realised that phone design was crucial and began to design its own range of clam shell phones the company captured part of a growing market. These companies demonstrated marketing savvy and expertise in turning a private or social need into a profitable business opportunity. Marketing is a revenue-generating function of a business, and the ultimate test of marketing success is a profit level that allows a company to prosper in the long run.[9]

There is much debate about a definition of marketing. A definition must be generic enough to cover a large variety of products and services in both consumer and business-to-business markets. It must be applicable to different marketing contexts and be able to change. In 2007 Professor Christian Gronroos, of the Hanken Swedish School of Economics in Finland, proposed a definition that encompasses recent research into customer value, relationship marketing, services marketing and the promise concept.[10]

Marketing is a customer focus that permeates organisational functions and processes and is geared towards marketing promises through value proposition, enabling the fulfilment of individual expectations created by such promises and fulfilling such expectations through support to customers' value-generating processes, thereby supporting value creation in the firm's as well as its customers' and other stakeholders' processes.[11]

Managing exchange processes between businesses and consumers and business-to-business calls for a considerable amount of work and skill. **Marketing management** is the art and science of choosing target markets and getting, keeping and increasing customers through creating, managing, communicating and delivering superior customer value.

We can distinguish between a *social* and a *managerial* definition of marketing. A social definition shows the role that marketing plays in society; for example, one marketer has said that marketing's role is to 'deliver a higher standard of living'. Here is a definition that reflects the role of marketing in society: Marketing is a *societal process* by which individuals and groups obtain what they need and want through creating, offering and freely exchanging products and services of value with others. **Social marketing** is an umbrella term used to describe how, in different ways, marketing can encourage positive social behaviour, and includes 'critical marketing', and 'green or sustainable marketing'.[12] This can be explained as follows. There are two dimensions to marketing and its role in society: 'On the one hand, social marketing encourages us to use our skills and insights as marketers to progress social good. On the other hand, it facilitates the control and regulation of conventional marketing through critical studies of its impact on the health and welfare of society'.[13] Social marketing is most often used to define the ways in which policy makers can use the techniques of marketing to change human behaviour for the better – whether it is concerned with obesity, gambling, smoking or drink-driving.

What is included in marketing?

Some business people who don't understand marketing think of marketing as 'the art of selling products', or simplistically equate it with advertising. Both of these are marketing tactics visible to the consumer. Many people are surprised when they hear that selling is *not* the most important part of marketing and that not all companies have large advertising budgets. Selling and advertising are only the tip of the marketing iceberg. Most of what occurs in marketing happens before the customer sees an advertisement (which is just the tangible representation of the marketing strategy), hears about a new product or service or meets a sales representative. Just like an iceberg, over 80 or 90 per cent of marketing occurs out of the sight of the consumer. Advertising, sales and so on are the final rather than the beginning stages of marketing.

The main focus of marketing is on what occurs below the waterline rather than above it. These are all the decisions that marketers make before the product or service comes to the market, and afterwards to maintain its position in the market. Non-marketers are inclined to think that marketing is only what occurs above the line.
Source: Ralph A. Clevenger / Corbis

Peter Drucker, a leading management theorist, describes the process of marketing this way: 'The aim of marketing is to know and understand the customer so well that the product or service fits him/her and sells itself.' Ideally, marketing should result in a customer who is ready to buy. All that should be needed then is to make the product or service available.[14]

When Sony designed its PlayStation 3 game system, when Apple launched its iPod, and when Toyota introduced its Prius hybrid car, these companies were swamped with orders because they had designed the 'right' product or service, based on executing and managing carefully designed and complete marketing programmes.

Innocent drinks has successfully marketed a product to customers who are looking for a healthier diet. Eight years after launching Innocent drinks the company has a turnover of £75 million. It has captured a 71 per cent share of the £169 million UK smoothie market, with over 2 million smoothies sold per week. Innocent drinks is expanding into other European countries including Ireland, Holland, France, Denmark and Belgium. Innocent's vision, in the words of co-founder Richard Reed, is 'to be Europe's favourite little juice company'.

Understanding markets

Marketing managers can market seven entities: services, products, events, experiences, people, places and ideas. Let's take a quick look at these categories.

Services A growing proportion of economic activity focuses on the provision of services. The current list of Fortune 500 companies contains more service companies and fewer manufacturers than in previous decades. The European economy, as a mature economy, consists of a 70–30 services-to-product GDP ratio. Services are everywhere. The top ten European companies and European service companies are shown in Table 1.1. Services include airlines, hotels, car hire, hairdressers and beauticians, maintenance and repair, accountants, bankers, solicitors, engineers, doctors, software programmers and management consultants to name but a few. Many market offerings consist of a variable mix of products and services. At a fast-food restaurant, for example, the customer consumes both a product and a service.

According to the World Trade Organisation (WTO), the services sector accounts globally for €1 trillion of world trade. Over two-thirds of the workforce in Europe are employed in services and between 60 and 70 per cent of the gross value-added figure achieved by European states can be attributed to services. Within Europe, an ageing population will have a future need for nurses, home health care, physical therapists and social workers. Double-income families need childcare, education, house cleaning and gardening services. There will also be an increased demand for business-to-business services that already account for over 55 per cent of total employment in Europe, equating to over 55 million people.

Table 1.1 The top European companies

The top 10 European firms (in terms of revenue)	The top 10 European service providers (in terms of revenue)
1 Royal Dutch Shell (Netherlands)	1 ING Group (Netherlands) [insurance]
2 BP (Britain)	2 AXA (France)
3 DaimlerChrysler (Germany)	3 Crédit Agricole [banking]
4 Total (France)	4 Allianz (Germany)
5 Volkswagen (Germany)	5 Fortis (Belgium/Netherlands) [banking]
6 ENI (Italy)	6 HBSC holdings
7 Siemens (Germany)	7 BNP Paribas (France) [banking]
8 Carrefour (France)	8 UBS (Switzerland) [banking]
9 E.ON (Germany)	9 Assicurazioni Generali (Italy) [insurance]
10 Tesco (Britain)	10 Deutsche Bank (Germany)

Current marketing thought argues that all companies are in fact service companies and that we need to use a services perspective for marketing as the main or dominant focus.[15, 16] This text takes a service-dominant logic perspective as an underlying concept. That means that the 7 Ps of the marketing mix – product/service, price, promotion, place; and the three extra service mix elements – process, physical evidence and people – are used for both products and services. In other words all businesses are considered service businesses using all 7Ps of the marketing mix. The 7Ps are used throughout this text as the default for both products and services. The service-dominant logic will be explored in greater detail throughout the text. This perspective acknowledges the importance of the customer experience of exchange, whether with a product or service. It also acknowledges that the company alone does not offer value to a consumer; value is in fact created when the company and the customer work together; often called **co-creation**.

Products The manufacture of physical products was the traditional cornerstone of economic activity in Europe. Marketing has always oriented towards the marketing of products, reflecting its historical development in the agricultural sector. European companies manufacture and market billions of fresh, canned, bagged and frozen food products, and millions of cars, refrigerators, television sets, machines and various other mainstays of a modern economy.

Services and products The service-dominant logic suggests that the separation between products and services is not a clear one. The 'servicisation' of products refers to the relative importance of the service dimension in a given product offering. Thinking in marketing has moved from a strategy that conceives of either a product or a service to one which sees both product and service dimensions in any market offering.[17] Many products have a service component and many services have product components. Take for example a physical product such as a car. We purchase a car, which provides the service of getting from one place to another. But the car comes with its own need for services such as insurance, finance, repairs and even a petrol station. The Swedish car manufacturer Volvo has built a service into its cars that alerts the driver if they are falling asleep. What a great service! Another example is a mobile phone provider such as Nokia. The company provides a product (mobile phone handsets) but also a service (networks). Nokia sees itself as a service or solutions provider – 'connecting people'.

Events Music shows such as the U2 Zoo tour, the Hurricane music festival in Germany, the Frankfurt book fair and major trade fairs or international summits, for example the global health conference, are all global marketing events that take months to plan and market. Global sporting events such as the Olympics and the World Cup Football are marketed to both companies and fans. Event marketing is big business, as evidenced by the estimated loss of £2 billion to the British economy when the England team failed to qualify for Euro 2008. The 2006 Football World Cup was one of the most watched events in television history, with over 26 billion viewers over the course of the tournament. The final attracted an estimated audience of 715.1 million people who watched Italy claim their fourth World Cup title.

Experiences By managing several services and products, a firm can create, stage and market experiences. Alton Towers – the most popular theme park in the United Kingdom – or Disneyland Resort Paris or Legoland in Denmark, Germany and England, all represent this kind of experiential marketing, allowing customers to visit a fairy kingdom, a pirate ship, a Lego town or a haunted house, complete with hotel accommodation and food. There is also a growing market for customised experiences, such as spending a week at a Samba Soccer camp, on a yoga retreat in Kitzbühel, Austria, or skiing on Mount Blanc in the Alps.[18]

People Celebrity marketing is a major business. Artists, musicians, chefs, CEOs, financiers and other professionals can all become celebrities through clever marketing. Some people have done a masterful job of marketing themselves and becoming global celebrities – think of David Beckham, Bono, Jordan and Carla Bruni. Within the United Kingdom, chefs such as Gordon Ramsay, Jamie Oliver and Nigella Lawson have all become household names, with their own brands of restaurants, cookbooks and kitchen utensils. Similarly, Spanish actors Penélope Cruz and

Celebrity: Kate Moss surrounded by a bevy of other models wearing her Topshop designs.

Source: Rex Features

Antonio Banderas, who were national celebrities in their native Spain, became global celebrities after working in Hollywood in English-speaking films. Celebrity culture is embedded in contemporary European culture, with nearly 3 million celebrity magazines sold each week in Britain, compared with 7.5 million in the United States, a country with five times the population.[19] Kate Moss, the English supermodel, launched her 5th line of clothing for Topshop in March 2008. Topshop credits the use of her name and designs with boosting Topshop sales by more than 10 per cent.[20] Another example is Virgin's CEO Richard Branson, who was famous as a CEO but became a global celebrity after he attempted to circumnavigate the globe in a hot air balloon. Management consultant Tom Peters, himself a master at self-branding, has advised each person to become a 'brand'.

Places Cities, states, regions and whole nations compete actively to attract tourists, factories, company headquarters and new residents.[21] Europe is the most visited region in the world.[22] Six European countries are in the world's top ten destinations for holiday makers, as can be seen from Table 1.2.

Place marketing includes a full marketing programme to attract both tourism and inward economic investment, often called foreign direct investment (FDI). Ireland's extraordinary economic growth in the past decade, leading the country to be called the 'Celtic Tiger', attracted an estimated 30 per cent of the global spend on FDI. The 'Cool Britannia' campaign tried to promote Britain as a cool place to visit and in which to invest.

Ideas Social marketing uses the tools and techniques of marketing to change people's behaviour. Whether it is to encourage people to drive slowly, to think about recycling, to stop smoking or eat healthily, marketing can be instrumental in getting people to think differently. In relation to campaigns against drink-driving in Europe, the European Safety Council runs the 'Safe and Sober' Campaign, while the UK's government body Drink Aware,[23] markets the idea

Table 1.2 Europe is the most popular tourist destination according to World Tourism Organization figures

Rank	Country	Continent	International tourist arrivals (2006) in millions	International revenues from tourism (2006) in € millions
1	France	Europe	54.4	29.57
2	Spain	Europe	40.29	35.22
3	United States	North America	35.19	59.7
4	China	Asia	34.16	23.36
5	Italy	Europe	28.30	26.26
6	United Kingdom	Europe	20.74	23.23
7	Germany	Europe	16.26	22.61
8	Mexico	North America	14.74	N/A
9	Austria	Europe	13.98	11.51
10	Russia	Europe	13.78	N/A

Source: United Nations World Tourism Organization (2007) International tourist arrivals by country of destination, *UNWTO World Tourism Barometer*, 5(2), June, p. 8. Copyright © UNWTO Publications. Reproduced with permission.

of alcohol restraint in its 'Respect alcohol, respect yourself' campaign. The '5 a day' campaign by the UK's Department of Health encourages consumers to think about eating five portions of fruit and vegetables a day. It has successfully encouraged supermarkets such as Marks & Spencer and Tesco to display a '5 a day' sign on products that contribute to this objective.

Marketing's role in creating demand

Marketers must have a variety of skills, one in particular being the ability to stimulate demand for their company's services and products. However, this is too limited a view of the tasks that marketers perform and the skills that they must have. Just as production and logistics professionals are responsible for supply management, marketers are responsible for demand management along with their other roles. Marketing managers seek to influence the level, timing, and composition of demand to meet the organisation's objectives. Eight states of market demand are possible:

1 **Full demand:** Consumers buy all services or products brought to market.

2 **Overfull demand:** There are more consumers demanding the service or product than can be satisfied.

3 **Irregular demand:** Consumer purchases vary on a seasonal, monthly, weekly, daily or even hourly basis.

4 **Declining demand:** Consumers begin to buy the service or product less frequently or not at all.

5 **Negative demand:** Consumers dislike the service or product and may even pay a price to avoid it.

6 **Nonexistent demand:** Consumers may be unaware of or uninterested in the product or service.

7 **Latent demand:** Consumers may share a strong need that cannot be satisfied by an existing product or service.

8 **Unwholesome demand:** Consumers may be attracted to services or products that have undesirable social consequences.

In each case, marketers must identify the underlying cause(s) of the demand state and then determine a plan of action to shift the demand to a more desirable state.

Figure 1.1 The health care market is an example of a contemporary network

Source: H. J. Schau, M. F. Smith and P. I. Schau (2005) The healthcare network economy: the role of Internet information transfer and implications for pricing, *Industrial Marketing Management*, 34, 147–56. Reproduced with permission.

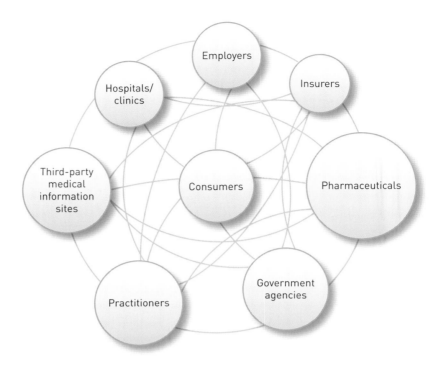

Markets Traditionally, a 'market' was a physical place where buyers and sellers gathered to buy and sell products and trade services. Economists describe a *market* as a collection of buyers and sellers who transact a particular service or product or product or service class (such as the housing market, the airline market or the gaming market).

Each nation's economy and the global economy in general consist of complex interacting sets of markets linked through exchange processes. This is referred to as the **network economy,** a term that will be used throughout this text. A network economy is driven by a dynamic and knowledge-rich technology dominant environment, meaning that the hierarchical stand-alone organisations of the twentieth century have changed into a variety of networks such as:

1 **internal networks:** are designed to reduce hierarchy and open firms to their environments;

2 **vertical networks:** maximize the productivity of serially dependent functions by creating partnerships among independent skill-specialised firms;

3 **intermarket networks:** seek to leverage horizontal synergies across industries; and

4 **opportunity networks:** are organised around customer needs and market opportunities and designed to search for the best solutions to them.

Marketing outcomes within the network economy are dependent on and face competition from a strategic network of companies rather than from competition among individual companies.[24] Marketing increasingly will be responsible for creating and managing new marketing knowledge, education, real-time market information systems, intrafirm integration, conflict resolution, technology forecasting, risk and investment analysis, transfer pricing of tangibles and intangibles, and the coordination of the network's economic and social activities. So managing a network of companies is a core marketing requirement explored further in Chapter 17. The health care network diagram (Figure 1.1) reflects not only the linkages between companies within the network but also the growing participation by the consumer in these networks.

Marketers often use the term **market** to describe various groupings of customers who buy their products or services. They view other companies with similar or substitute products and services as constituting the industry, and groups of buyers as constituting the market. They talk about need markets (the health food market), product or service markets (the shoe market or the holiday travel market), demographic markets (the youth market), and geographic markets (the French market).

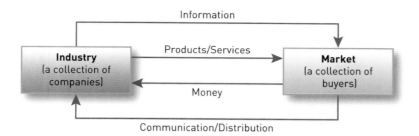

Figure 1.2 A simple marketing system

They extend the concept still further to describe other, not immediately obvious markets such as voter markets, labour markets and donor markets.

Figure 1.2 shows the relationship between the industry and the market. Companies and buyers are connected by four flows. The company distributes products and services to the market; and in return it receives money or payment and information, such as customer attitudes and sales data. The inner loop shows an exchange of money for products and services; the outer loop shows an exchange of information.

Consider the following key customer markets: consumer, business, global and non-profit.

Consumer markets Consumer purchases are generally made by individual decision makers or a decision-making unit, either for themselves or for others with whom they have relationships. The consumer market is made up of companies marketing consumer products and services as diverse as soft drinks (Red Bull), make-up (L'Oréal), air travel (AirFranceKLM), shoes (Clarks) and car insurance (the Automobile Association). The consumer market will be explored in greater detail in Chapter 7.

Consumer markets are enormous. Consumer purchasing power within the European Union has grown to the point where it is slightly larger than that of the United States.[25] Germany, with a population of 82 million, is Europe's largest consumer market with consumer purchasing power estimated to be €1495 billion, or 19.5 per cent of Europe's €7681 billion. A pan-European study by MB-Research ranked the United Kingdom second with €1180 billion and France third with €1076 billion, followed by Italy (€943 billion) and Spain (€536 billion).[26] (See Figure 1.3.)

There has been much debate about the high consumption levels in Europe and how this generation is the one 'born to consume' or what has been called the 'McLuxury Generation'. The champagne-growing region of Rheims in France has been expanded for the first time in over 80 years, as world consumption increased by 5 per cent in 2007, to a record 339 million bottles.[27] Consumers are smarter, they expect more, they approach purchase decisions with greater scrutiny and have access to more data for comparison. It is suggested that consumers are 'self-indulgent, pleasure-seeking individualists, dominated by marketers and advertisers, and sheeplike in their mimicking of others'. . . with the new religion of worshipping at the cathedral of the shopping mall'![28] Alternatively consuming can be seen as a sign of love and affection as we purchase for others to show affection and affiliation.[29]

In Tesco in the United Kingdom, the average number of product lines has exploded from 5000 in 1983 to over 40,000 in 2002. Only 20 years ago the average UK consumer could choose between three TV channels; now there are around 300 channels broadcasting to UK subscribers. The café chain Coffee Republic offers 11 different types of coffee, four added toppings, three types of milk and sugar, three types of cup size – in all 6000 different ways to have a cup of coffee. A visit to any chemist will yield 14 different types of dental floss and over 20 different toothpastes.[30] We live in a time of 'choice explosion'.[31]

Take the Internet. Customers can now log on to the Internet and choose from over 100,000 CDs rather than having to travel to a shop that can physically stock perhaps only 25,000 CDs. This changes choice, this changes distribution, this changes the service aspects and this changes the marketing programmes that marketers need to use. Information technology changes space–time–place relations; we have yet to grasp the scope of this disruption.[32] Take iTunes. As of January 2008, 50 million customers had downloaded over 4 billion songs since the service first launched in April 2003. This reflected an increase of 1 billion since July 2007 when there were

Figure 1.3 European purchasing power in 2007

Source: Michael Bauer Research (2007) European purchasing power in 2007: who's on top? 31 August (retrieved from www.english.mb-research .de/content/view/). Reproduced with permission.

Purchasing power in Europe 2007

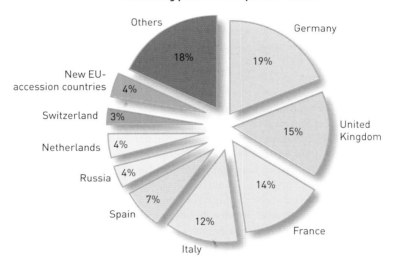

Purchasing power in Europe: €7.7 trillion

3 billion downloads.[33] A new single-day record was set when 20 million songs were downloaded on the 25 December 2007.

Business markets The term business, business-to-business or industrial marketing focuses on understanding business buying centres and on how businesses purchase in different ways to consumers – further explored in Chapter 8. Business markets are now networked organisations operating in a complex environment. Nowadays the focus is on neither consumer or business markets but on recognising that the lines between the two are blurring in four important ways:[34]

1   A blurring of value chains through outsourcing and other relationships that allows networks of companies and customers to operate (see Chapter 17). When Apple set up its iTunes online music store, it brought together recording companies with music and customers who wanted to download music tracks for €0.99 – a mix of consumer and business-to-business marketing for Apple.

2   A blurring of relationships with customers, as customers are invited to participate with companies in the design and delivery processes. The decline in travel agencies as customers book directly with airlines and hotels is an example.

3   A blurring of functions within the firm as marketing and other functions are more integrated through technology.

4 A blurring of products, services and customer experience, moving from an 'industrial' base to a knowledge-based society.

Pharmaceutical firms have long focused on business markets such as doctors, hospitals, clinics and insurance providers. In recent years, however, they have recognised the need to combine this approach with extensive campaigns to build consumer awareness and demand for new drugs and treatments. Rather than relying on channels to drive awareness, these companies work from the consumer side and the industrial side simultaneously to create sales in the middle.

Global markets Globalisation characterises the climate of business and society in the twenty-first century. This text is oriented towards global companies and each chapter explores both global and local marketing issues. We have more global organisations than at any other time in the history of the world. Singapore is ranked first in overall globalisation, followed by Hong Kong, with the Netherlands ranked third, followed by Switzerland, Ireland and Denmark. Global companies face unique and additional decisions and challenges that are introduced in Chapter 2. They must decide which countries to enter; how to enter each (as an exporter, licenser, joint venture partner, contract manufacturer or solo manufacturer); how to adapt their product and service features to each country; how to price their products and services in different countries; how to adapt their communications to fit different cultures; and how to manage their service process, people and technology across the globe and within a network of companies. They make these decisions in the face of different requirements for buying, negotiating, owning and disposing of products and services; different cultures, languages and legal and political systems; and currencies that might fluctuate in value. Yet the pay-off for doing all this additional marketing can be huge. Having a global mindset is important. The struggle is often summarised as the attempts of an organisation to be local while staying global – the concept of glocalisation – explored further in Chapter 2. Getting to a global mindset requires individual managers to demonstrate a glocal mentality, which features three components:[35]

1 Think globally.

2 Think locally.

3 Think globally and locally simultaneously.[36]

Many leading European football clubs – including Manchester United, Real Madrid and Juventus – have both a local and a global marketing strategy. They all have loyal local supporters but also a worldwide fan base. Both have to be managed well. Take Real Madrid:

> The popular Spanish football club Real Madrid became a global brand through the marketing expertise of Florentino Perez, the man who is credited with turning Real Madrid from an 'old-fashioned soccer club' into a star-studded global marketing brand when he took over the football club in 2000. He said that he wanted to be in every country in the world through their Real Madrid brand marketing and through sales of football shirts, club merchandise and image rights aligned with their leading players. Perez spent €316 million on 17 new players, including Zinedane Zidane, David Beckham, Christiano Ronaldo and Luis Figo, earning his collection of superstars the title of 'Los Galacticos'. Perez's pledge each season was that the world's best will play for Madrid. The club increased its revenue by 17 per cent to €327 million, particularly in the Asian market. During a 17-day tour of Asia in 2003 the club sold €135,000 worth of jerseys in Japan in one day of the club's promoted training sessions.[37]

Non-profit, voluntary and government markets Companies marketing their services and products to non-profit organisations such as churches, universities, charities and government agencies need to understand marketing as much as private, profit-making companies. There is no agreed definition for the non-profit sector, which has been called the third sector, as opposed to the public sector and the business sector. It is variously termed the independent sector in Scandinavian countries; civil society in central and eastern Europe; the charitable sector or voluntary sector in the United Kingdom and Ireland; or the 'économie sociale' in France. Whether these organisations are co-operatives, mutual societies, associations or foundations they are united in that they do not operate solely for financial gain but for some non-profit objective. For example Médecins Sans Frontières (MSF), founded in France, is an international humanitarian aid organisation that provides emergency medical assistance to populations in danger in more than 70 countries. MSF's objective is to provide aid to as many people as it can. In relation to government markets much government purchasing calls for bids or tenders as dictated by the European Union, and governments often favour the lowest bid in the absence of extenuating factors.

Marketplaces, marketspaces and metamarkets

The *marketplace* is physical, such as a shop you spend money in, the bank you visit or the restaurant you eat in.[38]

The *marketspace* is digital, as when you shop on the Internet, conduct your banking online or when you use an ATM or a kiosk for booking, ordering or confirming.[39]

The *metamarket*, proposed by Mohan Sawhney, describes a cluster of complementary products and services that are closely related in the minds of consumers, but spread across a diverse set of industries.[40] The car metamarket consists of car manufacturers, new and used car dealers, financing and insurance companies, mechanics, spare parts dealers, service shops, car magazines, classified car adverts in newspapers, and car sites on the Internet. In purchasing a car, a buyer will get involved in many parts of this metamarket, and this creates an opportunity for *metamediaries* to assist buyers in moving seamlessly through these groups, although they are disconnected in physical space. Metamediaries are intermediaries that bring together collections of companies or people. One example is Auto Trader, the world's largest car marketplace (www.autotrader.com), which provides a website where a car buyer can study the stated features and prices of different cars and easily click to other sites to search for the lowest price or nearest dealer, for financing, for car accessories, and for used cars at bargain prices. Auto Trader also has features that link to the car's history and links directly to classified advertisements or auction-style listings. Metamediaries also serve other metamarkets, such as the home ownership market, the parenting and baby care market, and the wedding market.

Autotrader.nl is a meta-intermediary website that helps prospective car buyers navigate the car metamarket.

Source: European Auto Trader BV

How is marketing practised?

Marketing practice can be viewed from many perspectives. The traditional view is the Kotlerian marketing management view of managing the marketing mix after selecting target market(s) and positioning.[41] The marketing mix was suggested by McCarthy, who classified marketing activities as *marketing mix* tools into four broad kinds, which he called *the 4Ps* of marketing: product, price, place and promotion.[42] It is worth noting that the first list had 52 marketing mix elements. The four marketing mix elements were expanded to 7Ps by Boden, which had a more services focus and included process (service process), physical evidence and people (participants). The marketing mix variables under each of the 7Ps are shown in Figure 1.4 and are explored in greater detail in Chapters 14–20. A study of European and UK academics highlighted the discontent with the 4Ps of the marketing mix and suggested that the use of the service marketing mix reflected the actual marketing environment.[43]

The marketing manager has a mix of short- and long-term marketing decisions to make once the company has selected the target market. They must also integrate all the marketing mix decisions together so that the distribution suits the product, or that the service process aligns to the pricing strategy and so on. The 7Ps of the marketing mix represent the company's view of the marketing tools available for influencing buyers. From a buyer's point of view, each marketing tool is designed to deliver a customer benefit. Winning companies satisfy customer needs and surpass their expectations economically and conveniently and with effective products or services, priced well, communicated interestingly and distributed in a timely manner or through a process and with people that create the right environment, all leading to a brand that customers support.

Value is a central marketing concept. We can think of marketing as the identification, creation, communication, delivery and monitoring of customer value. **Satisfaction** reflects a person's judgement of a service's or product's perceived performance (or outcome) in relationship to their expectations. If the performance falls short of expectations, the customer is dissatisfied and disappointed. If it matches expectations, the customer is satisfied. If it exceeds them, the customer is delighted.

In practice, marketing follows a logical process. The marketing *planning* process consists of analysing marketing opportunities; selecting target markets; designing positioning strategies; developing marketing mix programmes to reflect a brand that has loyal customers; and managing the marketing effort. After identifying market segments, the marketer then decides which present the greatest opportunity – which are its **target markets** (Chapter 10). For each target

Product/service
Service/product variety
Quality
Design
Features
Brand name
Packaging
Sizes
Services
Warranties
Returns

Target market

Marketing mix

People
Participants
Staff
Customers to customers
Co-creation

Process
Service blueprint
Process design
Self-service technologies
Online service provision

Price
List price
Discounts
Allowances
Payment period
Credit terms

Promotion
Sales promotion
Advertising
Sales force
Public relations
Direct marketing
Internet

Place
Global Channels
Coverage
Assortments
Locations
Inventory
Transport

Physical evidence
Service environment
Sound
Sight
Smell
Taste
Touch
Service evidence

Figure 1.4 The 7Ps components of the marketing mix.

market, the firm develops a *market* offering that it positions in the minds of the target buyers as delivering some central benefit(s) (Chapter 11). For example, with the car market we could say that BMW owns 'driving', Mercedes-Benz owns 'prestige', Volvo owns 'safety',[44] as the core positioning for their products in the eyes of the consumer. Companies do best when they choose their target market(s) carefully, choose suitable positioning and then use the full range of the marketing mix variables to develop a brand image and equity.

The challenge is that in highly competitive marketplaces, however, marketing planning and management is fluid and needs to be continually refreshed. Companies must always be moving forward with marketing programmes, innovating products and services, and staying in touch with customer needs, seeking new advantages rather than relying on past strengths. As Steve Jobs of Apple said, 'Innovation distinguishes between a leader and a follower.'

Transactional, relational and network marketing The Contemporary Marketing Practice Framework[45] shows that there are five main marketing practices depending on both the customer and the industry – explored in greater detail in Chapter 2. These are transactional, database, emarketing, interactive and network marketing, encompassing a transactional to relational perspective but with the full range of the marketing mix variables at your disposal for each. (see Table 1.3)

Transaction marketing (TM) is defined as attracting and satisfying potential buyers by managing the elements in the marketing mix, and actively manages communication 'to' buyers in the mass market in order to create discrete, arm's-length transactions.

Database marketing (DM) involves using database technology to create a relationship, thus allowing firms to compete in a manner different from mass transactional marketing. The intent is to retain identified customers, although marketing is still 'to' the customer, rather than 'with' the customer. Relationships per se are not close or interpersonal, and are facilitated and personalised through the use of database technology.

Emarketing (a term no longer in use) was used to describe 'the Internet and other interactive technologies to create and mediate dialogue between the firm and identified customers'.[46] Nowadays there is an extended view of emarketing or information and communication technologies (ICT) in marketing that shows their use across all marketing practices.[47] Chapter 4 will explore the role of ICT within marketing and the digital marketplace.

Interaction marketing (IM) implies face-to-face interaction between individuals. As such, it is truly 'with' the customer, as both parties in the dyad invest resources to develop a mutually beneficial and interpersonal relationship.

Similarly, *network marketing (NM)* is 'with' the customer but occurs across and among organisations. In this practice, managers commit resources to develop their firm's position in a network of various firm-level relationships.[48]

Table 1.3 Classifications of marketing practice by relational exchange dimensions

Transactional perspective				Relationship perspective
Transaction marketing	Database marketing	Emarketing	Interaction marketing	Network marketing

Marketing managers usually focus on one main marketing practice but most practise all the different types of marketing. For example Carrefour, the French supermarket chain, has many transactional customers who purchase from it but are not loyal or do not have a relationship with the company. It also has many customers who have developed a relationship with the company either through its loyalty card and database or through interactions in local stores. It also has a range of suppliers who Carrefour are networked to. This reflects the full range of marketing practices that a marketing manager would have to understand for different customer groups. Marketing managers must be aware of which practice suits which aspect of their network, channel members and customers. Some customers would prefer interactions with their bank and want to visit; others would prefer more arm's length contact through ICT or a

Table 1.4 Transaction to relationship marketing

Transaction marketing	←——————————→	Relationship marketing
One-off exchange, brand management	Focus	Ongoing exchanges, customer management
Short-term focus	Time perspective	Long-term focus
Mass communications	Primary communication	Personal communications
Isolated market research	Customer Feedback Mechanism	Ongoing dialogue
Mass markets or market segments	Market size	Market of one
Market share	Criterion for success	Mind share (share of customer)

Source: Modified from C. Gronroos (1991) The marketing strategy continuum: towards a marketing concept for the 1990s, *Management Decision*, 29(1), 7–13. Emerald Group Publishing Ltd. Copyright © 1991, MCB UP Ltd. Reproduced with permission.

database; while yet others want the bank networked to their organisation and to have a bank member on the board, which is popular in Germany.

Relationship marketing The concept of relationship marketing was developed by the Nordic School from northern Europe and developments from the United States. Relationship marketing in its simplest form is a progression from the dominant and often criticised traditional transactional 4P's focus.[49] It is a move away from the economic origins of marketing based on 'concepts such as exchange, profit maximization, utilities, specializations, the economic man and rationality'.[50] Relational is a focus on building long-term relationships with consumers rather than a focus on new customers as the growth potential. The contrast between transactional and relational marketing can be seen in Table 1.4.

▽ The European marketing environment: company and consumer challenges

The environment in which marketing takes place is crucial and will be explored in greater detail in Chapter 5. The marketing environment consists of the task environment and the broad environment. The *task environment* includes every company in the network engaged in producing, distributing and promoting the offering. These are the company, suppliers, distributors, dealers, and the target customers. In the supplier group are the material suppliers and service suppliers, such as marketing research agencies, advertising agencies, banking and insurance companies, transportation companies and telecommunications companies. Distributors and dealers include agents, brokers, manufacturing representatives and others who facilitate finding and creating a customer.

The *broad environment* consists of six components: demographic, economic, physical, technological, political–legal and the social-cultural environment. Marketers must pay close attention to the trends and developments in these environments and make timely adjustments to their marketing strategies.

The European environment As a European text it is imperative that the marketing environment in Europe is understood. The contemporary environment is a world of immense complexity, contradiction and change – from global conglomerates to stunning technological development; poverty amidst plenty; ongoing financial crises across the globe; the growth in the European Union to 27 member states, widespread ethnic conflict; and unprecedented stock growth and decline. The continued reign of many European monarchs with the development of the European Union; the post-industrial economies, with high-tech virtual organisational forms and service-dominated sectors; the shift from labour to consumption as the source of identity are some of the many changes.[51]

Externally, the EU has become a model for others to follow, maintaining peace and stability within Europe while pursuing closer political and economic union. From a group of six countries, it has expanded to its present 27. The EU is now the largest single market in the world and the largest player in world trade with a market of over 450 million people. In a book entitled, *The United States of Europe: From the Euro to Eurovision – the superpower nobody talks about*, Reid notes that

> Europe covers just 6 per cent of the Earth's total area and is home to just 12 per cent of the global population; yet Europe has 40 per cent of the world's wealth and accounts for more than half of all global commerce. European countries comprise five of the world's ten richest nations. The continent was the birthplace of 'Western values', the combination of individual rights, democratic governments and free markets that has spread around the world.[52]

A special issue of the *European Journal of Marketing* in 2007 portrayed the diversity of views existing on the complexity of marketing approaches in the enlarged European Union.[53] This is mainly due to the diversity of geography and culture, different levels of economic development, and disposable income.[54] Think of Romania versus France. The diversity in European markets has emerged with new dimensions defying embedded cultural, political, historical and geographical boundaries.[55] Current research suggests that European marketers have to address specific country contexts, issues, industries, cultures and geographic areas. So though the European trading environment is becoming increasingly standardised, national and individual wealth varies across the EU. There is a so-called 'Golden Triangle', a comparatively small area that includes Liverpool and Leeds at the top of the triangle, moving across through Oxford and London to include Paris to the bottom left of the pyramid and Rotterdam, Amsterdam, Dortmund and Dusseldorf to the right of the triangle. This triangle is serviced by a network of new fast trains and the Channel Tunnel, a massive infrastructural investment which clearly points to the fact that Britain and France wanted to move closer together and that Britain wanted to be physically attached to the rest of Europe. It is a much more potent symbol of the EU than the EU flag with its 12 gold stars, which we have been told will never change in number, irrespective of how many nations finally decide to join the EU.[56] Convergence has given rise not only to common consumer behaviour traits but has also created favourable conditions for leveraging marketing expertise across national borders.

There is a dominant position for many EU multinational companies (MNCs) within national and regional markets. For example, three EU MNCs control about 90 per cent of the brewing market in Bulgaria.[57] Many MNCs market global and regional brands at almost no price differential vis-à-vis domestic brands, to ensure market penetration. Similarly, Interbrew, Heineken and SABMiller control about 70 per cent of the Czech beer market and about 95 per cent of the beer market in Hungary. By contrast, the Slovenian brewery Lasko enjoys more than 57 per cent market share in the Slovene market. It exports 35 per cent of its output and has engaged in internationalisation.[58] Confectionery industries in Poland, Bulgaria and the Czech Republic are also dominated by global multinationals.

We can say with some confidence that 'the marketplace isn't what it used to be'. Marketers must attend and respond to a number of significant developments locally, globally and more specifically within the European Union.

Major societal forces

Today the marketplace is radically different as a result of major, and sometimes interlinking, societal forces that have created new behaviours, new opportunities and new challenges:

- **Heightened competition:** Companies are facing more intense competition from domestic and foreign brands, resulting in rising marketing costs and shrinking profit margins. Many strong brands are extending into related product or service categories. EasyJet now has over 17 easy products or services, including easyMobile, easyCinema and easyHotel. Tesco, the UK retailer, has also entered the mobile phone market; as has Italian fashion designer Prada – see the image on the next page. These are all entrants into an already competitive market. Another Italian fashion designer, Armani, has expanded into chocolates and a hotel!
- **Globalisation:** The increase in world trade, an increasing integration of the world's major economies, and the onward march of globalisation means that marketing will continue to have a more global orientation. This, coupled with technological advances in transportation,

Competition has intensified across most industries. The launch of a Prada mobile phone shows just how widespread is the competition.
Source: Luis Gene/AFP/ Getty Images

shipping and communication have made it easier for companies to market and easier for consumers to buy products and services from all over the world. We now consider it normal to ship kiwi fruit from New Zealand and oranges from South Africa, and in the services area we find it normal to access money from ATMs all over the world and to phone home from anywhere without any difficulty. In light of the oil and financial crises in 2008 these options may have to be reconsidered.

- **Increased range of information and communication technologies (ICT):** The marketplace has more ICT then ever before. Companies can communicate and connect globally in minutes and real time online information is becoming normal. The range of ICTs within the marketing domain is extensive – from internets to databases, from kiosks to planning software, from mobile phones to self-service technologies – all of which will be explored in Chapter 4. Marketing managers need to have the skills to understand and embrace a current range of ICTs both internally and externally and with an eye to new technologies ICT and a service perspective.

- **Industry convergence:** Industry boundaries are blurring at an incredible rate as companies are recognising that new opportunities lie at the intersection of two or more industries. The computing and consumer electronics industries are converging as the giants of the computer world release a stream of entertainment devices – from iPods and MP3 players to plasma TVs and camcorders. Nike and iPod have succeeded with a sports and music industry convergence. Nike has teamed with Apple iPod to offer a Nike-Apple workout experience. A sensor is placed in the runner or sports shoe and a receiver is attached to an iPod Nano. During training, the iPod will select music either in tune with the pace of the running or Nike 'sports music', while also recording the statistics of the run. Your iPod can record your running performance, and can coach you, encourage you, give you feedback on your performance and use your favourite music to motivate you.

- **Retail transformation:** Retailing in Europe has been transformed in four ways:

  1 **The growth of own brands:** Within the consumer goods sector powerful retailers now control limited shelf space and are putting out their own store brands in competition with national brands. By offering their own brand labels they can reap higher profit margins and, with the huge quantities they purchase, can bargain hard with their suppliers.

2 **Retail internationalisation:** This has occurred on a significant scale. The French chain Carrefour remains the continent's biggest food retailer, nearly twice the size of its nearest rivals, but Tesco has overtaken the other French retailer, Intermarche, to move into second place. European players dominate retail landscapes across other world regions, for example Carrefour dominates in Latin America.

3 **The retail market in Europe is still very fragmented:** Traditionally the European market has many small retailers but most areas are succumbing to the growing power of giant retailers and 'category killers'.

4 **Competition forces:** Competition from an explosion of retail outlets, out of town shopping centres and the Internet has all caused changes in retailing. In response, entrepreneurial retailers are building entertainment into their shops with bookshop–café combinations, lectures, demonstrations and in-store performances, marketing an 'experience' rather than a product assortment.

▽ MAC Cosmetics, Inc.

A division of French cosmetics giant Estée Lauder, MAC (which stands for Make Up Artist and Customer) Cosmetics is considered a significant reason for Lauder's 13 per cent net make-up sales increase. Yet MAC's 1000 stores worldwide don't simply sell Small Eye Shadow, Studio Fix, Lustreglass and Pro Longwear Lipcolour. Instead, they rely on highly paid 'artists' to bond with each customer during a free make-up consultation and application lesson. While this service process strategy (Chapter 18) is hardly new in the world of retail make-up, what is unique is that MAC's artists are not out there to bump up their commissions and load customers down with more products. Rather, they're trained to collaborate with customers so they'll leave the store with €50 or more of MAC products *and* the feeling, 'I can definitely do this at home.' The goal, says Matthew Waitesmith, MAC's head of 'artist training and development', is for each customer to feel she's had an authentically artistic experience 'that hopefully means they'll return to the place that makes them feel like an artist'.[59]

• **Disintermediation:** The amazing success of early online dot-coms such as Amazon, Yahoo! and eBay, and dozens of others created *disintermediation* in the delivery of products and services by intervening between the traditional flow of products and services through distribution channels. These so called 'pure-click' companies struck terror into the hearts of many established manufacturers and retailers. In response, many traditional companies engaged in *reintermediation* and became 'brick-and-click' retailers, adding online services to their existing offerings. Many brick-and-click competitors became stronger contenders than pure-click companies, since they had a larger pool of resources to work with and well-established brand names. Companies such as Ryanair and easyJet changed the intermediary model, completely bypassing the traditional travel agent and only allowing online bookings.

New consumer capabilities

Contemporary consumers and consumption patterns are changing.

• **Consumer sophistication:** The customer has become a more sophisticated consumer and marketers have to understand how to market to the marketing-savvy consumer. In some cases consumers have become more cynical about marketing efforts in general, are inundated with hundreds of advertising pitches a day, and are increasingly suspicious of expertise in a world where so many experts disagree.[60] Professor Stephen Brown from the University of Ulster, Northern Ireland, suggests that *'Today's* consumers *were trademarked at* *birth and brought up on branding* [author's italics]'.[61] Children as young as three can recognise brand logos, and the average child in the United Kingdom sees between 20,000 and 40,000 commercials a year.[62]

Consider what consumers have today that they didn't have in yesteryear:

- **A greater variety of available products and services:** As mentioned earlier the range of choice for consumers has grown. RaboBank, a Dutch bank founded over 100 years ago, now offers banking services in 34 countries that span all continents.

- **A great amount of information about practically anything:** People can read almost any newspaper in any language from anywhere in the world. They can access online encyclopedias, dictionaries, medical information, film ratings, consumer reports, and countless other information sources. Google runs the world's largest search engine, handling more than 100 million searches per day. Google Earth allows customers to zoom in on streets and even houses all over the world.

- **Greater ease in interacting and placing and receiving orders:** Today's buyers can place orders from home, office or mobile phone 24 hours a day, seven days a week, and quickly receive services and products at their home or office. Customers can also track and monitor their orders worldwide. DHL provides a tracking service online so that the customer knows where their parcel is at any time.

- **Tech savvy consumers:** Are you online, connected, iGeneration? Across Europe, around 60 per cent of Germans and Britons are online. More than seven in ten Dutch, Swedish and Danish households have a personal computer.[63] Many customers are now technology savvy, interactive, mouse clicking, engaged and intelligent consumers. We live in an era where many consumers are 'tech savvy' – technologically sophisticated, using technology in ways that marketers are only beginning to understand.

  Twenty years ago if you asked someone, 'Do you have a spare needle for my turntable?' most people would have understood. Many people nowadays would have no understanding of what that means. A more suitable sentence for our current level of technology assimilation would be, 'I downloaded a few podcasts to my iPod to share with you'!

  The Internet generation are people who have grown up with computer technology as a commonplace. They usually have no memory of (or nostalgia for) pre-Internet history. The iGeneration (a jocular allusion to the popular iPod boom, experienced by the Internet generation) takes the Internet for granted, accepting the utility of services such as Internet forums, email, Wikipedia, search engines, MySpace, Facebook, imageboards and YouTube. The term 'Generation Now' has been used as well, to reflect the urge for instant gratification that technology has imparted. This is the most wired or connected generation ever with several countries, including the United Kingdom, having more mobile phones than people.

- **Self-expression and interaction:** Rather than companies providing information to customers – what can be called top down – the Internet generation wants to discover new things for themselves and then share their discoveries. The 'me-to-we' generation wants to connect and share and has created an online world that operates beyond traditional boundaries. User-generated content allows customers to express themselves. YouTube or social networking sites such as Bebo and MyFace bring together people with a common interest but also allow consumers to share information. MySpace has had a dramatic impact on the way marketers have to define and interact with their customers. Young adults are moving away from other mediums to social networking. This has been driven by broadband penetration and also ubiquitous digital cameras and camera phones. Social networking sites within Germany reach 45 per cent of the country's online population with 14.8 million unique visitors, with MySpace as the most popular attracting 3.7 million and German site StudiVZals with strong traffic of 3.1 million.[64] These sites allow self-expression, discovery and interplay within a rich interactive environment, thus providing a close-knit neighbourhood and a truly global community. More that 162 million global profiles are registered on MySpace and the site has nearly 100 million unique monthly visits. Marketers need to interpose themselves into the dialogue and engage with customers on their terms. These issues are explored in more detail in Chapter 4 and throughout the text.

Table 1.5 European usage of social networking sites – selected countries

| Territory | Ranked by total unique visitors | | Age 15+ August 2007* | | |
	Total unique visitors (000)	% reach of country's total online population	Average hours per user	Average pages per user	Average visits per user
Europe	127,297	56.4	3.0	523	15.8
UK	24,857	77.9	5.8	839	23.3
Germany	15,475	46.9	3.1	423	13.8
France	13,332	49.6	2.0	476	16.8
Spain	8,828	61.5	1.8	251	14.9
Italy	8,736	49.3	1.8	346	12.6

*Age 15+, home and work locations; excludes traffic from public computers such as Internet cafés or access from mobile phones or PDAs.
Source: From comScore (2007) U.K. social networking site usage highest in Europe, comScore World Metrix, July (www.comscore.com/press/release.asp?press=1801). Reproduced with permission.

- **A substantial increase in buying power. An ability to compare notes on products and services:** The Internet and other technologies, such as mobile phones and palm pilots, fuel personal connections and user-generated content through social network sites such as MySpace, Wikipedia and YouTube.[65,66] Marketers are eyeing the success of these sites, given that 35 per cent of young, first-time car buyers consider the Internet their most important shopping tool.[67] Buyers are only a click away from comparing competitor prices and product and service attributes on the Internet. They can even name their price for a hotel room, airline ticket or mortgage. Business buyers can run a reverse auction in which sellers compete to capture their business. They can readily join with others to aggregate their purchases and achieve deeper volume discounts.

- **An amplified voice to influence peer and public opinion:** The Internet can be used as a vehicle to influence companies. In late 2004 Kryptonite, a company that makes high-priced bicycle locks, found itself in an awkward position when several blogs showed how the firm's U-shaped locks could be easily picked using only a Bic pen.[68] Many consumers were able to open the iPhone to any network despite the desire of the company to use one network in each European country, with the instructions posted to the web.

- **Co-creation:** Much of consumer experience with brands and companies now involves co-creation, where the consumer shapes their experience of the product or service. Volkswagen-UK now allows you to choose everything from colours, designs and specifications of your new Beetle.

  This also links to **customisation:** traditionally products and services were designed by companies, but now customers have an input into the design role, customising the product or service to suit themselves. Companies can produce individually differentiated products or services, whether they're ordered in person, on the phone or online, thanks to advances in factory customisation technology and the increased sophistication of databases, computers and the Internet. For a price, customers can buy M&M sweets with personalised messages on them and Heinz tomato ketchup bottles with customised messages.[69] BMW's technology now allows buyers to design their own models from among 350 variations, with 500 options, 90 exterior colours, and 170 trims. BMW says that 80 per cent of the cars bought by individuals in Europe are customised.

- **Self-service technologies:** More and more companies are choosing to provide self-service technology options for their customers. Self-service checkouts at supermarkets, self-check-ins at airports, and cinema ticket collection and online investment trading have all proliferated recently. Self-service should be a choice for customers rather than a cost-saving excerise by the company. Many self-service technologies have been designed without any marketing input. Take the ATM – what would it look like if it had been designed and managed by marketing rather than technologists?

▽ Understanding the philosophy of marketing

The marketing philosophy or concept is one of the most simple ideas but it is also one of the most important, and one that is often difficult for a company to embrace. At its very core is the customer and his or her satisfaction. The marketing concept and philosophy states that the organisation should strive to satisfy its customers' wants and needs while meeting the organisation's profit and other goals. In simple terms, 'the customer is king'. This marketing philosophy needs to be adopted by the whole company. From top management to the lowest levels and across all departments of the organisation, it is a philosophy or way of doing business. The customers' needs, wants and satisfaction should always be foremost in every manager's and employee's mind.[70]

Many companies have not progressed to a marketing philosophy but are challenged to move from the old-fashioned product or sales concept.

The production philosophy

The production concept is one of the oldest concepts in business and looks only to the product or service that the company has or wants to make or provide, rather than to a customer need. It is the idea of a product looking for a market. Managers of production-oriented businesses concentrate on achieving high production efficiency, low costs and mass distribution. The thinking is aligned to the product concept, which proposes that consumers prefer products that offer the most quality, performance or innovative features. Managers in these organisations focus on making superior products or services and improving them over time. However, these managers are sometimes caught up in a love affair with their products or services. They might commit the 'better mousetrap' fallacy, believing that a better mousetrap will lead people to beat a path to their door. A new or improved product or service will not necessarily be successful unless it is aligned to customer needs and then produced, priced, distributed, communicated and managed throughout its life. With this focus you often have a product looking for customers or a product that is way above what the customer wants.

The selling philosophy

The selling concept is a focus on making sales rather than really understanding the customers. The selling concept suggests businesses have to persuade or force customers to buy the organisation's products or services. The organisation must, therefore, undertake an aggressive selling and promotion effort.

Traditionally the selling concept was practised most aggressively with unsought products or services that buyers normally do not think of buying, such as insurance. Some companies also practise the selling concept when they have overcapacity. Their aim is to sell what they make, rather than make what the market wants. Company success based on hard selling carries high risks. It assumes that customers who are coaxed into buying a product or service will like it, and that if they don't, they will not return it or bad-mouth the company or complain to consumer organisations, but that they might even buy it again. The films *Tin Man* and *Glengarry Glen Ross* are very good examples of this concept within the windows and auctioneering areas where the characters put pressure on customers to order products they do not want or need in order to keep their own ugly jobs. These films and their hard-sell antics show clearly the dangers of an over focus on sales.

The marketing philosophy

The marketing philosophy emerged in the mid-1950s.[71] Instead of a product-centred and sales-oriented 'make-and-sell' philosophy, business shifted to a customer-centred, 'sense-and-respond' philosophy. The marketing task is not to find the right customers for your products or services, but to design the right services and products for your customers. Dell Computers doesn't prepare a perfect computer for its target market. Rather, it provides product platforms on which each person customises the features they desire in their computer.

The marketing concept holds that the key to achieving organisational goals is being more effective than competitors in creating, managing, delivering and communicating superior customer value to your chosen target markets.

Theodore Levitt of Harvard Business School explored the contrast between the selling and marketing philosophy and noted that:

Selling focuses on the needs of the seller; marketing on the needs of the buyer. Selling is preoccupied with the seller's need to convert his product into cash; marketing with the idea of satisfying the needs of the customer by means of the product or service and the whole cluster of things associated with creating, delivering and finally consuming it.[72]

To learn how mid-life companies such as Wal-Mart might benefit from a holistic marketing concept to combat stagnating growth, visit www.prenhall.com/kotler

Today's best marketers recognise the need to have a more complete, cohesive approach to marketing that moves beyond the production or selling approaches to business and really embraces the marketing philosophy. 'Marketing memo: Marketing right and wrong' suggests where companies go wrong – and how they can get it right – in their marketing.

Marketing memo

Marketing right and wrong

The ten deadly sins of marketing

1 The company is not sufficiently market focused and customer driven.

2 The company does not fully understand its target customers.

3 The company needs to better define and monitor its competitors.

4 The company has not properly managed its relationships with its stakeholders.

5 The company is not good at finding new opportunities.

6 The company's marketing plans and planning process are deficient.

7 The company's product and service policies need tightening.

8 The company's brand building and communications skills are weak.

9 The company is not well organised to carry on effective and efficient marketing.

10 The company has not made maximum use of technology.

The ten commandments of marketing

1 The company segments the market, chooses the best segments, and develops a strong position in each chosen segment.

2 The company maps its customers' needs, perceptions, preferences and behaviour and motivates its stakeholders to obsess about serving and satisfying the customers.

3 The company knows its major competitors and their strengths and weaknesses.

4 The company builds partners out of its stakeholders and generously rewards them.

5 The company develops systems for identifying opportunities, ranking them, and choosing the best ones.

6 The company manages a marketing planning system that leads to insightful long-term and short-term plans.

7 The company exercises strong control over its product and service elements.

8 The company builds strong brands by using the most relevant communication and promotion tools and techniques and other mix elements.

9 The company builds marketing leadership and a team spirit among its various departments.

10 The company constantly adds technology that gives it a competitive advantage in the marketplace.

Source: Adapted from P. Kotler (2004) *Ten Deadly Marketing Sins*, Hoboken, NJ: John Wiley & Sons, Inc.
Copyright © 2004 John Wiley & Sons, Inc. Reproduced with permission.

Marketing in a postmodern world and retro marketing

Postmodern marketing forces us to look at marketing and question some of our marketing beliefs. Postmodern consumption patterns are described as culturally diverse, fragmented, increasingly market-mediated, and performative. Whereas in modernity, the focus is on the individual, the market becomes the centre of all meaningful social activity in the post-modern era.[73] Postmodern marketing suggests that we critique or challenge some of the basic understandings of marketing. Professor Steven Brown, in an article entitled 'Torment your customer (they'll love it)', suggests that

> . . . everyone in business today seems to take it as a God-given truth that companies were put on this earth for one purpose alone: to pander to customers. Marketers spend all their time slavishly tracking the needs of buyers, then meticulously crafting products and pitches to satisfy them.'[74]

Brown further suggests that marketers need to tease, torment, tempt and tantalise the customer. The Spanish retailer Zara exemplifies this postmodernism. They do tempt, tease and tantalise the customer. Fashions arrive fast and leave the shop as quickly. If you don't buy now they will be gone. Some customers even monitor the delivery dates for stores and race in to be the first to buy. Average visits per store for fashion outlets are 3 to 4 a year yet Zara averages 14 a year as the consumer is enticed in to see what is there today and will be gone tomorrow. This relates to the customers' demand for high fashion, to the challenge of getting something great in the shop and engaging with the company in this marketing game. Zara really understands its customers and its customers understand the Zara system. According to *Marie Claire* magazine editor Marie O'Riordan, the formula works: 'With other high-street retailers, the risk in buying something is that you'll bump into somebody wearing the same thing, and it spoils the effect,' she says. 'With Zara, because the stock turnover is so fast, you have to get there on day one. It tends to sell out two days later so you have a real chance of being a little bit exclusive, which is quite unusual for a high street shop.'[75]

Postmodernism invites a unique perspective of how to manage marketing and how to understand the consumer. Postmodernism says that social experiences are an interplay of myths which produce regimes of truth and that much of what we understand or believe about the individual, self, freedom, structure and so on is arbitrary and short-lived, fleeting rather than essential and fixed. We need to change our views as the customer changes. Dove is a product that forces us to reconsider what we consider as beautiful and is a good example of a company changing perceptions. The Dove Campaign for Real Beauty is a global effort that is intended to serve as a starting point for societal change. The focus for Dove was on real women celebrating their very real body types, including fuller figures not typically portrayed in advertising. Six ordinary women were recruited off the street and chosen for their confidence and spark – baring all in their underwear without having been airbrushed or retouched in any way. The YouTube video of the Dove Evolution was popular because it challenged consumer thinking and by May 2008 had been viewed over 6 million times.

The main conditions of postmodern marketing are hyperreality, fragmentation, reversals of production and consumption, decentring of the subject, paradoxical juxtapositions (of opposites) and loss of commitment.[76]

- **Hyperreality:** Exemplified by the virtual worlds of cyberspace and the psuedo worlds of theme parks, hotels and heritage centres, hyperreality involves the creation of consumption sites and marketing phenomena that are 'more real then real'. Here the distinction between reality and fantasy is momentarily blurred.
- **Fragmentation:** Marketing in postmodernity is unfailingly fast, furious, frenetic, frenzied, fleeting and hyperactive.
- **Reversals of production and consumption:** Postmodern consumers are active in the production of meaning, of marketing, of consumption. They do rather than have 'done' to them.

- **Decentring of the subject:** Centredness is where individuals are defined by their occupation, social class, demographics, postcode, personalities and so on. Postmodernism suggests that this is not so, and that the harder marketers try to pin down the decentred consuming subject the less successful they will be. In the immortal words of Douglas Coupland, 'I am not a target market.' It is so much harder to market to consumers who cannot be classified.
- **Paradoxical juxtapositions (of opposites):** We have examples of the mixing and matching of opposites and the combination of contradictory styles in the world-famous Irish dance show – Riverdance or Lord of the Rings. The Riverdance show proved to be a huge success with its mixture of Irish, Scottish, Spanish and Russian dance, US tap, square dance, ballet and even break dancing. The musical grossed over €1 billion from performances in 32 countries.
- **Loss of commitment:** Growing disillusionment with the delivery of promises and the willingness to try different experiences has resulted in a *loss of commitment*. The postmodern consumer takes on multiple, sometimes even contradictory projects, to which s/he is marginally and momentarily committed. This is observed in all walks of life: in relationships, in professions, and consumption. Marketing managers experience this when consumer loyalties to brands (which they took for granted) change.

Table 1.6 explores the difference between the postmodern knowledge society and the modern industrial society. Many of these issues will be explored throughout the text but it is clear that markets and marketing practice is moving towards the right side of the table.

An over-focus on the customer can create problems when 'The truth is, customers don't know what they want. They never have. They never will. The wretches don't even know what they *don't* want!' Professor Brown suggests that, 'It's time to get back to an earlier era, to the time when marketers ruled the world with creativity and style. . . . It's time for retromarketing'[77] **Retromarketing** is based on tricksterism, exclusivity, amplification, secrecy and entertainment – TEASE:

Tricksterism – A little mischief adds intrigue and mystery.

Exclusivity – 'Retromarketing eschews the "here it is, come and get it, there's plenty for everyone" proposition – the modern marketing proposition – by deliberately holding back supplies and delaying gratification. You want it? Can't have it. Try again later, pal.' Minimise inventory. Customers as select few. The famous Beanie Babies were marketed as exclusive and only a certain number of each one was manufactured to create interest and demand. This is similar to the current Webkin craze with children logging on and registering their animals for points online.

Table 1.6 Contrasting the modern versus the postmodern marketing environment

Modern industrial society	Postmodern knowledge society
Mass markets, production and mass distribution and homogeneity and standardisation	Market fragmentation; services and ICT; pluralism and freedom of choice
Consumer as consumer; economic systems; value-creating production	Consumer as co-producer; symbolic system; value-creating consumption
Functional divisions; semi-qualified workforce; routine work	Cross-functional teams/projects; knowledge-based competences; learning, tacit processes
Authoritarian hierarchies, vertical communications; controlled ownership	Network, alliances and virtual organisations; horizontal communications; outsourcing

Source: A. O'Driscoll (2007) Advances in marketing theory: the post-modern perspective. Guest Lecture at Trinity College Dublin and A. O'Driscoll (1999) The postmodern condition, Samuel Beckett and marketing malady, Proceedings of the Marketing Paradiso Conclave, St Clement's, Belfast, September, pp. 96–103.

Amplify – 'Ensure that the ticket or cool item is talked about and, more important, that the talking is talked about.' WHO? Affrontery. Outrage. Surprise. Calvin Klein, Citroën Picasso.

Secrecy – Marketing (torment) of *Harry Potter*, where the books were delayed and then released at midnight to cause queues and demand and to create interest. Classic 'secret' recipes of many companies, such as the formula for Coca-Cola and the contents of the figroll.

Entertain – 'Marketing must divert. It must amuse. It must engage.' Imaginative quiz or competition. Marketing is fun.[78]

▽ Overview of marketing management

This section provides an overview of the textbook and of marketing management that the flow-chart in Figure 1.5 highlights.

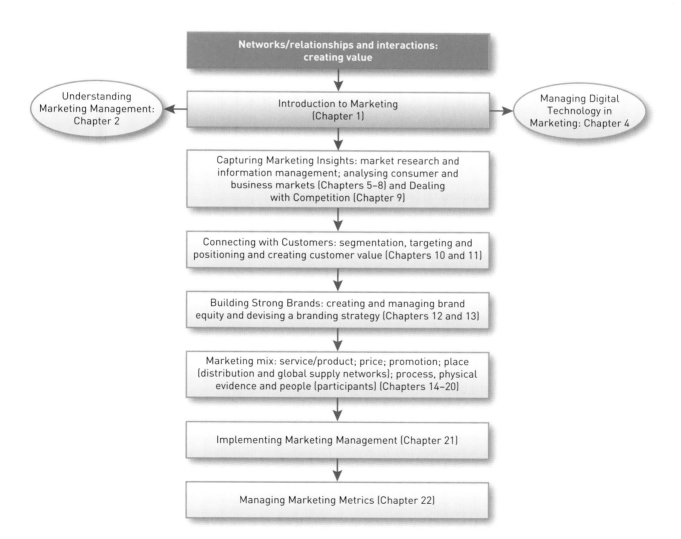

Figure 1.5 An overview of marketing management activities reflecting the main chapters in the text

The following case study provides a brief overview of each chapter and the main elements of marketing management.

Zeus, Inc. (name disguised), operates in several industries, including cameras, film and chemicals. The company is organised into strategic business units (SBUs). Corporate management is considering what to do with its Atlas camera division, which produces a range of 35 mm and digital cameras. Although Zeus has a sizeable market share and is producing good revenue, the 35 mm market itself is rapidly declining and Zeus's market share is slipping. In the faster-growing digital camera segment, Zeus faces strong competition and has been slow to gain sales. Zeus's corporate management wants Atlas's marketing management (Chapter 2) to produce a strong turnaround marketing plan for the division (Chapter 3).

Understanding marketing management

The marketing strategy should take into account changing global opportunities and challenges, changing customer perspectives and a variety of new challenges and marketing realities (see Chapter 1). To understand marketing is to understand management (Chapter 2) and the marketing team must understand the integrated marketing they will need to use throughout the organisation. Marketing management skills will be needed to change the direction of the organisation and to manage both an internally and externally challenging environment.

Developing marketing strategies and plans

The first task facing Atlas is to identify its potential long-run opportunities, given its market experience and core competences (see Chapter 3). Atlas needs to find the customer need and then it can design its cameras with better features. It can make a line of video cameras, or it can use its core competency in optics to design a line of binoculars and telescopes. Whichever direction it chooses, it must develop concrete marketing plans that specify the marketing strategy and tactics going forward.

Managing digital technology in marketing

Atlas needs to review the full range of information and communication technologies within their organisation and any they may need to acquire for their marketing task. It also needs to review the technological environment for its product in relation to other technologies and also the level of technology know-how its customers have (Chapter 4). Other camera manufacturers are embracing technology at the customer interface and have a range of self service devices both in shops and at home for customers. Digital picture frames that play rotating pictures are also becoming very popular. Depending on the target market, more of the communication spend could be linked to technologies, the Internet or digital channels and Atlas needs to understand how to use them innovatively (see Chapter 4).

Capturing marketing insights

Atlas needs a reliable marketing information system to closely monitor its marketing environment and also needs to understand their internal database information (Chapter 5).

Atlas also needs a dependable marketing research system. To transform marketing strategy into marketing programmes, marketing managers must measure market potential, forecast demand, and make basic decisions about marketing expenditures, marketing activities and marketing allocation – Chapter 6. Atlas must clearly understand its customers and to do so needs to understand consumer markets (see Chapter 7). Who buys cameras, and why do they buy? What are they looking for in the way of features and prices, and where do they shop? Atlas also sells cameras to business markets, including large corporations, professional firms, retailers and government agencies (see Chapter 8), where purchasing agents or buying committees make the decisions. Atlas needs to gain a full understanding of how organisational buyers buy. Atlas must also pay close attention to competitors (see Chapter 9), anticipating its competitors' moves and knowing how to react quickly and decisively. It may want to initiate some surprise moves, in which case it needs to anticipate how its competitors will respond.

Connecting with customers: segementation, targeting and positioning

Atlas must reconsider the segmentation in the market and how best to create value for its chosen target markets (Chapter 10). It must decide how to position in the market (Chapter 10). Suppose Atlas decides to focus on the consumer market and to develop a positioning strategy. Should it position itself as the 'Mercedes' brand, offering superior cameras at a premium price with excellent service and strong advertising – such as British Airways in the airline business? Should it build a simple, low-priced camera aimed at more price-conscious consumers such as those who travel on Ryanair or easyJet? Or something in between? It must look to develop strong, profitable, long-term relationships with customers (see Chapter 11).

Building strong brands

Atlas has a range of marketing mix elements that it must integrate and use to create and maintain its brand in the eyes of its consumers. Atlas must understand the strengths and weaknesses of the Zeus brand as customers see it (see Chapter 12). A **brand** is an offering from a known source. A brand name such as Virgin carries many associations in people's minds that make up the brand image. In the case of Virgin it could reflect fun and irreverence. For Nokia it could be modern and great phones. Atlas will have to build a strong, favourable and unique brand image within the mind of the consumer through the use of the marketing mix variables. It also has to manage this brand across many European markets and ultimately globally (see Chapter 13).

Shaping the market offerings

Once the target market and positioning have been selected the marketing managers now have the full range of the marketing mix to match to consumer needs. Aligned to its positioning and at the heart of the marketing programme is the product and service – the tangible offering to the market, which includes all the unique features of managing and marketing a service and also the product quality, design, features and packaging (see Chapter 14). Introducing new services and products regularly is a core marketing requirement covered in Chapter 15.

A critical marketing decision relates to price (see Chapter 16). Atlas has to decide on wholesale and retail prices, discounts, allowances and credit terms. Its price should match well with the offer's perceived value or positioning; otherwise, buyers will turn to competitors' products or services.

Delivering value

Atlas must also determine how to manage all aspects of product and service delivery properly in order to deliver to the target market the value embodied in its products and services. Nowadays companies are part of networks and channels making the product and aligned services accessible and available to target customers (see Chapter 17). Atlas must identify, recruit and link various intermediaries to supply its products and services efficiently to the target market. It must understand the various types of retailers, wholesalers and physical distribution firms and how they make their decisions as well as online Internet channels and other technology-based self-service or distribution systems (see Chapter 17). Atlas needs to understand the service process the customer will go through, any physical evidence they receive and also the impact of people during the customer–company encounter (see Chapter 18).

Communicating value

Atlas must also adequately communicate to the target market the value embodied by its products and services. It will need an integrated marketing communication programme that maximises the individual and collective contributions of all communication activities (see Chapter 19). Atlas needs to set up a communication plan that could consist of advertising, sales promotion, events and public relations and has to plan personal communications, in the form of direct and interactive marketing, as well as hire, train and motivate salespeople (see Chapter 20).

Implementing marketing management

Finally, Atlas must build a marketing organisation that is capable of implementing the marketing plan (see Chapter 21). Because surprises and disappointments can occur as marketing plans unfold, Atlas will need feedback and control mechanisms to understand the efficiency and effectiveness of its marketing activities and how it can improve them. Atlas also needs to report back to the corporate board, which will have allocated a budget to this marketing endeavour and will need to see the returns and measure the effectiveness of the marketing strategy and tactics (Chapter 22).

Marketing focuses on understanding the customer and honing in on their current (and more importantly their future) needs so that the total company effort is towards customer satisfaction at a profit. Marketing is all organised efforts, activities and expenditure designed to first acquire a customer and second to maintain and grow a customer at a profit.

▽ SUMMARY

1. Marketing is crucial for business success, focusing on understanding customers or 'meeting needs profitably'.

2. Marketing management is *the art and science of choosing target markets and getting, keeping and increasing customers through creating, managing, communicating and delivering superior customer value.*

3. Marketing can be used for services, products, events, experiences, persons, places and ideas.

4. There are many key markets, including consumer, business, global and non-profit, voluntary and government markets. Much of marketing takes place in a network of firms and customers. Marketing no longer competes against one company but against a network of companies.

5. Marketing has five main practices, including transactional, database, emarketing, interaction and network, each of which is used depending on the customer and the industry, but there is usually a dominant marketing practice. These reflect a transactional to relational perspective to marketing.

6. The European marketing environment presents some challenges for marketers. From a company perspective there is heightened competition, globalisation, increased ICT, industry convergence, disintermediation and retailer transformation. From a consumer perspective there is increased consumer sophistication and particularly a technology savvy customer who has greater choice, greater information and greater access to products and services 24/7.

7 Though a simple idea, the philosophy of marketing, which is customer focused, can be hard for companies to embrace. Many companies are stuck in a production or selling philosophy that overlooks the core needs of their customers. The marketing philosophy achieves organisational goals by being more effective than the competiton in creating, managing, delivering and communicating superior customer value to their choosen target market.

8 Postmodern marketing suggests that we should challenge marketing assumptions and tease, torment, tempt and tantilise customers. The move to postmodern marketing is reflective of a move to a more

knowledge society where the customer understands tricksterism, exclusivity, amplifications, secrecy and entertainment as core creative needs of marketing mix programmes.

9 The overview of marketing management sets out the core marketing tasks necessary for success to include developing marketing strategies and plans, capturing marketing insights, choosing target markets and positioning, creating long-term growth through building strong brands, and then using the marketing mix to connect with customers, shaping the market offerings, delivering and communicating value, implementing the marketing plan and managing marketing metrics.

▽ APPLICATIONS

Marketing debate

What is marketing? You have been asked by your managing director to justify an increased marketing budget. Explain the role of marketing within the organisation and discuss why an increased spend could benefit the company.

Take a position: Consumers are changing and so too must marketing. Discuss.

Marketing discussion

Select a low-cost airline (such as Ryanair, which was used in the introductory example to this chapter) and then choose a full service airline (e.g. Air France or Lufthansa). Compare and contrast the different marketing activities, from their choice of target markets through to all the variables in the marketing mix, following the chapter layout for this text.

▽ REFERENCES

[1]Adapted from *The Financial Times*, 21 June 2003, p. 16.

[2]The Conference Board (2007) The CEO challenge 2007 – top ten challenges, Research Report R-1380-05-RR (www.conference-board.org/UTILITIES/pressDetail.cfm?press_ID=3224).

[3]BusinessWeek/Interbrand (2008) Annual ranking of the 100 best global brands.

[4]K. Floor (2006) *Branding a Store: How to Build Successful Retail Brands in a Changing Marketplace*. London: Kogan Page.

[5]See www.allbusiness.com/marketing-advertising/branding-brand-development/4673704-1.html.

[6]S. Meichtry (2007) Benetton picks up the fashion pace: tracking trends with fast deliveries – the Italian brand makes a comeback, *Wall Street Journal* (eastern edition) 10 April, B1.

[7]J. C. Levinson (2007) *Guerrilla Marketing: Easy and Inexpensive Strategies for Making Big Profits from Your Small Business*, 4th edn, Boston, MA: Houghton Mifflin.

[8]E. Gummesson (2007) Exit services marketing: enter service marketing, *Journal of Consumer Behavior*, 6(2), 113–41.

[9]Ibid.

[10]C. Gronroos (2006) On defining marketing: finding a new roadmap for marketing, *Marketing Theory*, 6, 395–417.

[11]Ibid.

[12]J. Bakan (2004) *The Corporation*, London: Constable; N. Klein (2001) *No Logo*, London: Flamingo; G. Ritzer (2000)

The McDonaldization of Society, Thousands Oaks, CA: California: Pine Forge Press.

[13]R. Gordon, G. Hastings, L. McDermott, and P. Suiquier (2007) The critical role of social marketing, in M. Saren, P. Maclaran, C. Goulding, R. Elliot, A. Shankar and M. Catterall (eds) *Critical Marketing: Defining the Field*, London: Butterworth-Heinemann, pp. 159–73 (at p. 164).

[14]P. Drucker (1973) *Management: Tasks, Responsibilities, Practices*, New York: Harper and Row, pp. 64–5.

[15]S. Vargo and R. Lusch (2004) The four services marketing myths, *Journal of Service Research*, 6(4), 324–35.

[16]H. Winklhofer, R. Palmer and R. Brodie (2007) Researching the service dominant logic: normative perspective versus practice, *Australasian Marketing Journal*, 15(1), 76–83.

[17]C. Gronroos (1991) The marketing strategy continuum: towards a marketing concept for the 1990s, *Management Decision*, 29(1), 7–13.

[18]P. Kotler (1984) Dream vacations: the booming market for designed experiences, *The Futurist*, October, 7–13; B. J. Pine, II and J. Gilmore (1999) *The Experience Economy*, Boston, MA: Harvard Business School Press; B. Schmitt (1999) *Experience Marketing*, New York: Free Press.

[19]From Celebrity magazines, *The Economist*, 28 April 2005.

[20]See www.dailymail.co.uk/pages/live/articles/news/news.html?in_article_id=489645&in_page_id=1770.

[21]P. Kotler, I. J. Rein and D. Haider (1993) *Marketing Places: Attracting Investment, Industry, and Tourism to Cities, States, and Nations*, New York: Free Press; and P. Kotler, C. Asplund, I. Rein and D. H. Haider (1999) *Marketing Places in Europe: Attracting Investments, Industries, Residents and Visitors to European Cities, Communities, Regions, and Nations*, London: Financial Times Prentice-Hall.

[22]See http://ec.europa.eu/enterprise/services/tourism/index_en.htm.

[23]See http://drinkaware.co.uk/.

[24]R. Achrol and P. Kotler (1999) Marketing in the network economy, *Journal of Marketing* (special issue), 146–63.

[25]See www.prb.org.

[26]See www.english.mb-research.de/content/view/15/32/.

[27]C. Bremner (2008) Champagne region expanded to meet world demand, *The Times*, 14 March 2008 (http://www.timesonline.co.uk/tol/life_and_style/food_and_drink/wine/article3548465.ece).

[28]M. Moynagh and R. Worsley (2002) Tomorrow's consumer: the shifting balance of power, *Journal of Consumer Behavior*, 1(3), 293–301 (at 213).

[29]Ibid.

[30]Aquafresh varieties (online image) available at www.aquafresh.com/default.aspx?startPage=varieties, accessed on 5 March 2008.

[31]W. Nelson (2002) All power to the consumer? Complexity and choice in consumers' lives, *Journal of Consumer Behavior*, 2(2), 185–95.

[32]D. Hoffman and T. Novak (2000) How to acquire customers on the web, *Harvard Business Review*, May–June, 21–7.

[33]See http://en.wikipedia.org/wiki/ITunes.

[34]Y. (J.) Wind (2006) Blurring the lines: is there a need to rethink industrial marketing? *The Journal of Business & Industrial Marketing*, 21(7), 474–81.

[35]T. M. Begley and D. P. Boyd (2003) The need for a corporate global mind-set, *MIT Sloan Management Review*, 44(2), 25–32.

[36]Ibid.

[37]C. Vitzthum (2005) Real Madrid needs a new goal, *BusinessWeek*, 25 June (www.businessweek.com/magazine/content/05_26/b3939423.htm).

[38]J. Rayport and J. Sviokla (1994) Managing in the marketspace, *Harvard Business Review*, November–December, 141–50. Also see J. Rayport and J. Sviokla (1995) Exploring the virtual value chain, *Harvard Business Review*, November–December, 75–85.

[39]Ibid and W. Chan Kim and R. Mauborgne (1999) Creating new market space, *Harvard Business Review*, January–February, 1–14.

[40]M. Sawhney (2001) *Seven Steps to Nirvana*, New York: McGraw-Hill.

[41]N. H. Borden (1964) The concept of the marketing mix, *Journal of Advertising Research*, 4, 2–7. For another framework, see G. S. Day (1994) The capabilities of market-driven organizations, *Journal of Marketing*, 58(4), 37–52.

[42]E. J. McCarthy and W. D. Perreault (2002) *Basic Marketing: A Global-Managerial Approach*, 14th edn, Homewood, IL: McGraw-Hill/Irwin.

[43]M. Rafiq and P. K. Ahmed (1995) Using the 7Ps as a generic marketing mix: an exploratory survey of UK and European marketing academics, *Marketing Intelligence & Planning*, 13(9), 4–16.

[44]A. Ries (2006) Is it the end of the ultimate advertising slogan? *Advertising Age*, August (www.ries.com/iframes/articles-read.php?id=9).

[45]N. Coviello, R. Brodie and P. Danaher (2002) How firms relate to their markets: an empirical examination of contemporary marketing practices, *Journal of Marketing*, 66(3), 33–46.

[46]Ibid.

[47]M. Brady, M. Saren and N. Tzokas (2002) Integrating information technology into marketing practice: the IT reality of contemporary marketing practice, *Journal of Marketing Management*, 18(5-6), 555–77.

[48]Coviello et al. (2002) op. cit.

[49]C. Gronroos (1997) Keynote paper: from marketing mix to relationship marketing – towards a paradigm shift in marketing, *Management Decision*, 35, 322–39; E. Gummesson (1998) Implementation requires a relationship marketing paradigm, *Journal of the Academy of Marketing Science*, 26(3), 242–9; A. Payne, M. Christopher, M. Clark and H. Peck (1995) *Relationship Marketing for Competitive Advantage*, London: Butterworth-Heinemann; G. Day and D. Montgomery (1999) Charting new directions for marketing, *Journal of Marketing*, 63 (special issue), 3–13; M. Baker (2000) The future of marketing, in M. Baker (ed.) *Marketing Theory: A Student's Text*, Australia: Business Press Thomson Publishing.

[50]R. Heeler and E. Chung (2000) The economics basis of marketing? in M. Baker (ed.) *Marketing Theory: A Student's Text*, Australia: Business Press Thomson Publishing.

[51]L. Penaloza (2000) Consuming people: from political economy to theaters of consumption – a review, *Journal of Marketing*, 64(1), 106–111; A. Fuat Firat and N. Dholakia (1998) *Consuming People: From Political Economy to Theaters of Consumption*, London and New York: Routledge.

[52]T. Reid (2004) *The United States of Europe*, London: Penguin, p. 245.

[53]L. V. Kurylo and S. J. Maffei (2007) Understanding the legal status of the world's largest business market: the European Union, *Review of Business*, 27(3), 56–62.

[54]E. Kaynak and F. Jallat (2004) *Marketing in Western Europe: A Monolith or Multidimensional Market*, London: Hawthorne Press.

[55]R. Savitt (1998) This thing I call Europe, *International Marketing Review*, 15(6), 444–6.

[56]S. Paliwoda and S. Marinova (2007) The marketing challenges within the enlarged single European market, *European Journal of Marketing*, 41(3/4), 233–44.

[57]M. A. Marinov and S. Marinova (2002) Foreign direct investment in emerging markets of Central and Eastern Europe, *Journal of East-West Business*, 9(3/4), 27–52.

[58]J. Larimo, M. Marinov and S. Marinova (2006) The Central and Eastern European brewing industry since 1990, *British Food Journal*, 108(5), 371–84.

[59]D. Sacks (2006) MAC Cosmetics Inc., *Fast Company*, September, p. 62.

[60]Moynagh and Worsley (2001) op. cit.

[61]S. Brown (2003) Marketing to Generation®, Forethought, *Harvard Business Review*, June, 81(6), 2–3.

[62]M. Lindstrom (2003) Branding is no longer child's play! *The Journal of Consumer Marketing*, 21(213), 175–82.

[63]See http://russiatoday.ru/business/news/6776.

[64]J. Gavin (2008) German social networking community reaches 14.8 million, ComScore, Inc., (www.comscore.com/press/release.asp?press=1737).

[65]A. Kamenetz (2006) The network unbound, *Fast Company*, June, 69–73; see also M. Barrett (2007) The rise of social networking and the lessons for brands, content and all media business, Accenture Global Forum (www.accenture.com/global/services/by_industry/communications/acces_newsletter/articles_index/gcf07_barrett.html).

[66]See www.bikeforums.net/video/1.mov.

[67]D. Kiley (2006) Advertisers, start your engines, *BusinessWeek*, 6 March, p. 26.

[68]The blogs in the corporate machine, *The Economist*, 11 February 2006, 55–6.

[69]B. Horovitz (2006) In trend toward vanity food: it's getting personal, *USA Today*, 9 August.

[70]See www.enotes.com/management-encyclopedia/marketing-concept-philosophy.

[71]J. B. McKitterick (1957) What is the marketing management concept?, in F. M. Bass (ed.) *The Frontiers of Marketing Thought and Action*, Chicago: American Marketing Association, pp. 71–82; F. J. Borch (1957) The marketing philosophy as a way of business life, in *The Marketing Concept: Its Meaning to Management* (Marketing Series, No. 99), New York: American Management Association, pp. 3–5; R. J. Keith (1960) The marketing revolution, *Journal of Marketing*, January, 35–8.

[72]T. Levitt (1960) Marketing myopia, *Harvard Business Review*, July–August, 50–65.

[73]L. Penaloza (2000) op. cit.; A. Fuat Firat and N. Dholakia (1998) op. cit.

[74]S. Brown (2001) Torment your customers (they'll love it), *Harvard Business Review*, September–October, 82–91.

[75]See www.fashionunited.co.uk/news/archive/inditex1.htm.

[76]A. Fuat Firat, N. Dholakia and A. Venkatesh (1995) Marketing in a postmodern world, *European Journal of Marketing*, 29(1), 40–56.

[77]Brown (2001) op. cit., p. 84.

[78]A. O'Driscoll (1999) The postmodern condition, Samuel Beckett and marketing malady, Proceedings of the Marketing Paradiso Conclave, St Clement's, Belfast, September, pp. 96–103.

Chapter 2

▽ Understanding marketing management

IN THIS CHAPTER, WE WILL ADDRESS THE FOLLOWING QUESTIONS:

1 What is management?
2 What is marketing management?
3 How do we manage within a global environment; what is the role of a global marketing manager?
4 How do we manage within developing markets?

In a world where business is global, networked and technology based, marketing management is a challenging and rewarding career. Marketing managers have a broad responsibility, from managing new service designs, to research programmes, to planning promotional strategies, to managing global supply networks, to setting prices and ultimately managing a multitude of relationships both internally and externally. It is one discipline that has a real input into many other departments inside the organisation as well as managing the many networks, relationships and interactions outside the organisation. This chapter will help you to understand the marketing management role and support you in your effort to be a better marketer.

Zara, the Spanish clothing shop, provides very good insights into both the internal and external marketing management challenges.

Zara understands that listening to their customers is a core part of marketing management and provides their customers with fast fashion clothing.
Source: Jochen Tack/Alamy Images

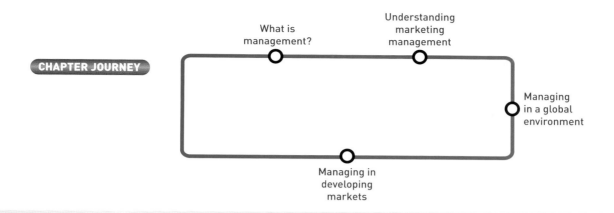

What is
management?

Understanding
marketing
management

Managing
in a global
environment

Managing in
developing
markets

The global success of Spain's best-known fashion house, Zara, relies on marketing expertise in understanding its target markets' need for fast fashion and also managing its internal operations to supply these needs at a profit. Under the management leadership of its founder Amancio Ortega Gaona, Zara has redefined the rules of retailing and has become a global market leader with over 1000 stores in 70 countries. Zara management maintain tight control of internal operations aligned with the outside needs of their target market for fast fashion. It manages along the length of the organisation from design to just-in-time production and on to the sales counter in the stores, all coordinated towards the customer need. Zara has built in more flexibility than its rivals to respond quickly to changing fashion trends and to deliver value to its customers. While its rivals focus on outsourcing much of their production to China and India and creating sophisticated advertising campaigns, Zara's 'fast fashion' strategy manages all operations in-house in its Spanish headquarters at La Coruna, where departments such as design, production and marketing all rub shoulders with each other. This allows the building of relationships between departments and an informal organisation that minimises bureaucracy and allows speedier reaction times, which is vital for serving its customers with the latest fashion trends. Zara can make a new line from start to finish in three weeks, against an industry average of six to nine months. Zara delivers value for its customers by offering quality and up-to-date fashion at reasonable prices. A combination of a strong marketing management team that listens to its customers, managing many supply chain operations in-house, and carefully developed information technology and marketing knowledge have built a small fashion chain located in Spain into a worldwide success.

With faster communication, transportation and financial flows, the world is rapidly shrinking. Products and services developed in one country are finding enthusiastic acceptance in others. A German business person may wear an Italian suit to meet an English friend at a Japanese restaurant, who later returns home to drink Russian vodka and watch a French film on a Korean TV. Countries across the world are experiencing the influence of large-scale multiculturalism. Marketing managers need to be able to cross boundaries within and outside their country and within and across companies all over the world.

▽ **What is management?**

It is apparent that we are living in times of tremendous change. When compared with the momentous changes that have taken place over the past 25 years in technology, communication, travel, lifestyle and geopolitics, the practice of management seems to have evolved at a slow pace, though with many changes occurring now.[1] Much of what we call 'management' was developed in the early or middle of the twentieth century. The traditional view of management is based on planning, organising, leading and controlling. Such a view is inherent in the hierarchies and the division of labour within companies, which results in the separation of departments rather than their integration. In many companies there are standardised job descriptions and work methods. There are strict protocols for production planning and scheduling. There is a strong focus on finance with cost accounting, profit analysis and financials as the dominant method of control within companies. Incentive-based compensation schemes and personnel or human resource departments to manage people are the norm. Lately, modern management has begun to address the importance of networks and teams, of collaboration and integration and processes rather than the defined roles and functions of the last 100 years. A marketing focus also suggests a focus on the customer, customer satisfaction and long-term growth rather than short-term financial controls.

In his article 'New trends in management'[2] Peter Drucker, one of the world's leading management experts, suggests that businesses often make five false assumptions that he attempts to redress:

1 **Old assumption**: That the company is the master, the employee the servant, the company owns the means of production without which people cannot make a living.

   New assumption: The means of production is knowledge that is owned by the knowledgeable employees and it is highly portable.

2 **Old assumption**: Most employees work full time for a company.

   New assumption: Many do but a lot of people will be part-time or temporary employees and contractors or employees of outsourcing firms.

3 **Old assumption**: Everything needs to be managed under the one management.

   New assumption: Integration is not necessarily best as the knowledge needed for many activity is specialised and deteriorates rapidly unless used consistently. Also the Internet and global communications mean that the physical cost of communication is eliminated so outsourcing can be one option for performing many tasks.

4 **Old assumption**: Suppliers and manufacturers have market power because they have information about a product or a service.

   New assumption: The customer has the information and the Internet and other technologies are making it easy to find out more. Whoever has the information has the power. Power is shifting to the consumer.

5 **Old assumption**: Any technology pertains to only one industry.

   New assumption: There are few unique technologies and the convergence of technologies and industries has resulted in major changes. The telephone can send email, hold text messages, and be an electronic organiser, a handheld computer and even a camera. The clear distinctions between products, services, channels, industries and companies are disappearing.

Management in a dynamic environment Management in today's business world is demanding and will continue to be so.[3] The globalisation of business, the massive increase in information and communication technologies, the development of supply chains spanning the globe, and the changing consumer faced with unprecedented access to personalisation, customisation, interaction, co-creation and choice all challenge the nature of managing. Managers have changed from managing domestic companies to managing global companies with products and services delivered all over the world. Ferrerro Rocher, founded in 1946 in Alba, a small town in Italy, now employs 19,000 people, has revenues of €5.6 billion and markets its chocolates in over 100 countries around the globe. What was once a small Italian company now purchases approximately 25 per cent of the world's supply of hazelnuts.

Change will continue to be focused on speed and innovations, expectations of the workforce, and an increasingly competitive world economy.[4] Managers have to balance the conflicting demands made by the need for short- and long-term results with the needs of various stakeholders including customers, shareholders, employees and communities.

Four core features of management

There are four core features of modern management: planning, organising, leading and controlling.[5] In many ways the nature of managerial work means that managers race around from task to task[6] and that 'brevity, variety and fragmentation' are better characteristics of managerial work.[7] These four core features will be introduced in this chapter and throughout the text though planning is also the focus of Chapter 3 and controlling is the focus of Chapter 22.

1. Planning The importance of planning cannot be overstated. As the saying goes: *If you don't have a plan to succeed, you* really have a *plan to fail*! Although business and marketing plans may overlap in some areas, what sets a marketing plan apart is its focus on the customer. According to Sir George Bull, chairman of J. Sainsbury, 'the marketing plan starts with the customer and works its way around the business'.[8] Therefore, the marketing manager must be able to effectively manage the design and implementation of a customer-focused marketing strategic plan for the organisation.

Despite the fact that strategic planning is centuries old it is still a problematic and unresolved issue. Strategy failures are uncomfortably high, even among well-schooled and experienced marketing managers.[9] Misguided marketing strategies have destroyed more shareholder value than shoddy accounting or shady fiscal practices.[10] Despite the enthusiasm for planning in textbooks, many companies operate without formal marketing plans. Evidence suggests that only one-fifth of companies have marketing planning processes.[11] There are many reasons for this. Some researchers contend that in today's extremely dynamic business environment, the formal business plan becomes obsolete for many companies before it is even printed. Others contend business plans are generated primarily to meet investors' requirements and are seldom used in day-to-day management.[12]

Plans must reflect the reality of the situation. As Henry Mintzberg, a leading management strategist once noted: 'Organizations differ as do animals, it makes no more sense to prescribe one kind of planning to all organizations than it does to describe one kind of housing for all animals.'[13]

▽ Swissair

Swissair, the once proud Swiss airline, filed for bankruptcy in 2001 after staggering losses of around €970 million *after successfully implementing a bad plan!*[14] The reason for the decline of this 70-year-old Swiss institution was a poorly conceived strategy that was designed in 1997. Eager to become an internationally renowned airline, the management board of the company decided to build its own partnership of airlines through acquisitions instead of joining an alliance such as One Alliance or Star Alliance. This was called the 'Hunter Strategy' and was drawn up by McKinsey Consultancy. Swissair proceeded to spend €2.65 billion buying stakes in dozens of smaller European airlines such as Sabena, LOT Polish airlines and Austrian Airlines, among others.[15] As fuel prices rose and profits fell, the debt piled up and by 2001 Swissair was in crisis. Their CEO Mario Conti acknowledged: 'Perhaps the expansionist strategy should have been underpinned by raising equity rather than debt.' Swissair never recovered from its disastrous Hunter Strategy. The company was renamed Swiss International Airlines and actually ended up joining the Star Alliance after being taken over by Lufthansa in 2007. A good news story is that it won European airline of the year in 2007, which shows that you can turn a situation around.

The lesson to learn is that planning may or may not suit certain organisations. Some industries are just too dynamic for formalised planning and it may be better for managers to make decisions as they experience issues or draw up a number of contingency plans.

2. Organising We will review organising from two perspectives:

1 How to organise a marketing department and
2 How to organise other staff and stakeholders: internal marketing.

How to organise a marketing department

Most companies follow the traditional pattern of setting up departments. Most departments work as stand-alone units reporting hierarchically to the top of the organisation. Such an organisational design is often called department silos or chimney stacking, which can separate rather than join departments. While there is a need for a separate marketing department, the philosophy of the company should be a marketing philosophy. It is not an either/or but a both/and perspective that is needed. If there is no marketing department that takes ownership for managing the full range of activities in a coordinated and integrated manner, a market-oriented attitude will be ad hoc, tactical, and often discontinuous. There must be a marketing department to integrate all departments, processes and activities towards the customer. In some instances the sales department and the marketing department share the one department but the relationship between the two then has to be managed very well. Sales could dominate and marketing could be regulated to a sales support function that would be detrimental to the long-term activities of the marketing department. There is increasingly worry about short-termism on the part of senior management instead of realising the long-term process of marketing and the possibilities that it brings.[16]

Owing to the importance of the marketing department as a key driver of business strategy, top management should focus attention on the work of this department above all.[17] There can be three key problems with marketing departments:

1 The marketing department lacks the organisation needed to get its primary job done.
2 The marketing staff do not have the skills or equipment to make maximum use of the range of technologies (ICT).
3 There is constant friction between marketing and other departments in the company.

Any combination of these three can spell doom for even the smallest of companies. The design of the marketing department is covered in Chapter 21.

The following are the steps that must be taken to ensure that a marketing department exists which can capitalise on market opportunities:

- **Assess the marketing manager's skill set**: Does the marketing manager have the ability to run a department, hire competent staff, set high standards for marketing planning and implementation and improve marketing staff's skills in research, forecasting, analytics, communication and so on? The marketing manager must also win the respect and confidence of the leaders of other departments such as finance, operations, purchasing and IT.
- **Building new marketing skills**: There are many aspects of modern marketing that need to be seen as an intrinsic part of the work of the marketing department. These include technology savvy customers, the increase in **globalisation**, the range of ICTs including the Internet, services marketing, the increasing demand for experiential consumption, integrated marketing communications, profitability analysis and finally market driving skills – that is, the ability to find needs and fill them.
- **Managing both day-to-day and strategic issues**: Much of management theory assumes that managers spend their time reading reports and analysing data. Though they do spend time in these areas, studies have revealed that much of management is involved with interpersonal and communication issues. Much of management time is spent as a figurehead, making speeches, interacting with people and getting and receiving information from conversations

and meetings. Managers spend a lot of time away from their desk running day-to-day operations rather than on the long-term strategic needs of the company.

3. Leadership: a core management requirement Leadership is crucial. According to management expert Peter Drucker, management operates successfully by aligning the work of people or by getting things done through people.[18] He likens leadership to running an opera. You have your star employees, and you can't give them orders; you have the supporting cast and the orchestra; you have the people who work behind the scenes and you have the audience. Each group has different needs but the leader has the score or music sheet and everyone should have the same score or music sheet. In management you need to ensure that all groups converge to produce the desired result.[19]

Training managers to lead can be quite a challenge. Not all leaders make great managers and not all managers make great leaders. Management leadership training needs to be cognisant of the changing world of business and train staff for the environment and challenges they will encounter. The Marketing insight below reflects how leading edge companies use technologies and management challenges to recreate environments that will help managers to learn and prosper under difficult circumstances.

Marketing insight

Web-based simulation for leadership

Tomorrow's business landscape could well be alien territory for today's business leaders. At many companies, important decision making will be distributed throughout the organisation to enable people to respond rapidly to change. A lot of work will be done by global teams – partly composed of people from outside the institution, over whom a leader has no formal authority – that are assembled for a single project and then disbanded. Collaboration within these geographically diverse groups will, by necessity, occur mainly through digital rather than face-to-face interaction. What will leadership look like in such a world – a world whose features have already begun to transform business?

'The answers may be found among the exploding space stations, grotesque monsters, and spiky-armored warriors of games such as Eve Online, EverQuest, and World of Warcraft. Despite their fantasy settings, these online play worlds – sometimes given the infelicitous moniker MMORPGs (for "massively multiplayer online role-playing games") – in many ways resemble the coming environment we have described and thus open a window onto the future of real-world business leadership.'

Reeves, Malone and O'Driscoll (2008) 59–60

Gamers have five key characteristics that are useful in a workforce: they are orientated towards the bottom line,

they understand the need for diversity; they understood that one cannot achieve something alone, they are excited by change, they see learning as something enjoyable and they think laterally.

'Leading 25 guild members in a six-hour raid on Illidan the Betrayer's temple fortress is hardly the same as running a complex global organization. For starters, the stakes are just a bit higher in business. But don't dismiss online games as mere play. The best ones differ from traditional video games as much as universities do from one-room schoolhouses. In fact, these enterprises are actually sprawling online communities in which thousands of players collaborate with and compete against one another in real time within a visually three-dimensional virtual world – one that persists and evolves even while a player is away.'

Reeves, Malone and O'Driscoll (2008) 60

Take Everet, a new web-based simulation which uses the dramatic context of a Mount Everest expedition to reinforce student learning in group dynamics and leadership. Players are assigned one of 5 roles on a team attempting to summit the mountain. The simulation lasts 6 rounds totaling about 1.5 hours of seat time. In each round, team members analyze information on weather, health conditions, supplies, goals, or hiking speed, and determine how much of that information to communicate to their team mates. They then collectively discuss whether to

► **Marketing insight** *(continued)*

MMORPG: massively multiplayer online role-playing game.

Source: Courtesy of CCP Games

attempt to reach the next camp en route to the summit. The team must decide how to effectively distribute supplies and oxygen bottles needed for the ascent—decisions which affect hiking speed, health, and ultimately the team's success in summiting the mountain. Failure to accurately communicate and analyze information as a team has negative consequences on team performance.'

Roberto and Edmondson (2007)

Sources: Adapted from B. Reeves, T. W. Malone and T. O'Driscoll (2008) Leadership's online labs, *Harvard Business Review*, July, 59–66; M. A. Roberto and A. C. Edmondson (2007) Leadership and team simulation: Everest, web-based simulation product, *Harvard Business Review*, September, 4; J. McGonigal (2008) Making alternative reality the new business reality, in HBR list 'breakthrough ideas for 2008', *Harvard Business Review*, February, 13–14; see also J. S. Brown and D. Thomas (2008) The gamer disposition, in HBR list 'breakthrough ideas for 2008', *Harvard Business Review*, February, 12–13.

It is impossible to define good leadership as a set of strategies that people can emulate; these strategies change from organisation to organisation, or even within organisations in different times. Roger Martin argues that the focus should be on how leaders think, rather than what they do. He argues that leaders demonstrate an ability to think integratively; that is, they understand that many ideas have conflicting elements in them, rather than being simple and certain. People who can tolerate this ambiguity make successful leaders.[20]

Management brings people together. As David Packard, the co-founder of HP noted,

A group of people get together and exist as an institution that we call a company so that they are able to accomplish something collectively that they could not accomplish separately – they make a contribution to society, a phase which sounds trite but is fundamental.

The Swedish company IKEA is a good example of a company with strong marketing management focus, with a strong leader.

▽ IKEA

IKEA is the world's most successful mass market retailer, selling Scandinavian-style home furnishings and other household goods in 230 stores in 33 countries and hosting 410 million shoppers per year.[21] The company designs its own furniture, which is made by about 1500 suppliers in more than 50 countries. Ingvar Kamprad has become the richest European in the world as the head of leading furniture retailer IKEA.[22] He recognises that his management style has to be people based in order for IKEA to succeed in its low-cost strategy. Despite being worth around €21 billion,[23] Kamprad practises leadership by example, enabling employees around the world to buy into IKEA's unique way of doing things. The Swedish billionaire drives a 15-year-old Volvo, flies economy class and encourages employees always to write on both sides of paper.[24] He even eats with his employees at IKEA stores to avail himself of cheap meals and to mix with his employees. As Kamprad says himself: 'If there is such a thing as good leadership, it is to give a good example. I have to do so for all the IKEA employees.'[25] Interestingly he named his company after himself, with IKEA being the anagram for Ingvar Kamprad, his name, and Elmtaryd Agunnaryd, the farm where he grew up (Elmtaryd), and his home county (Agunnaryd).[26]

4. Controlling This is a focus on monitoring and measuring the outcomes or returns from the marketing mix activities engaged in by the marketing manager. Controlling is explored in each chapter but in more depth in Chapter 22 on managing marketing metrics.

▽ Understanding marketing management

New paradigms of marketing management are emerging that shift the core focus of the field from firms to customers, from products to services or products and services and benefits, from transactions to relationships, from manufacturing to the co-creation of value with business partners and customers, and from physical resources and labour to knowledge resources and the firm's position in their supply network.[27] Thus, the focus of marketing has increasingly shifted away from sole emphasis on customers' needs to one of mutual dependence through networks and globalisation, based on skills and resources that the parties could bring to the relationship. Figure 2.1 reflects the changes that have occurred in marketing theory and practice.

Marketers must have a diverse skill set, an entrepreneurial attitude and a keen understanding of how marketing can create value within their organisation.[28] According to Sean Meehan, Professor of Marketing at the IMD Business School in Lausanne, Switzerland, 'the best companies are obsessed with detail, unforgiving of themselves, and genuinely upset when customers complain.' Results show that marketing in practice is about a logic of action, rather than the implementation of systemic theory. Marketing expertise is shown to consist of a broad range of skills, knowledge and experientially based judgements.[29]

Departmental boundaries are no longer the same – companies are making many efforts in team building and teamwork to ensure that departments work together well. New organisational forms are dissolving departmental boundaries, and blurring distinctions between firms and markets and between the company and its external environment. In a world of strategic partnerships, it is possible for a customer to be a competitor, supplier, partner, and even regulator. Therefore, the changing relationship structures surrounding organisations have a significant effect on reshaping the practice of marketing.

Like all management, marketing management could be said to include analysis, planning, implementation and control designed to achieve an efficient, coordinated actionable marketing mix programme and marketing plan. Therefore, the marketing management process can be viewed as an integrated sequence of four or five steps that feed back into each other.[30] As discussed in

To learn more about how the special ownership structure of Germany's Bosch Group guarantees the entrepreneurial freedom of the group, and makes it possible for the company to plan and invest over the long term, visit www.pearsoned.co.uk/marketingmanagementeurope

Figure 2.1
Environmental changes and developments in marketing theory and practice

Source: From J. Thomas and R. K. Gupta (2005) Marketing theory and practice: evolving through turbulent times, *Global Business Review*, 6(1), 95–112. Copyright © International Management Institute. All rights reserved. Reproduced with permission.

Chapter 1, marketing is also slightly different to other management disciplines as it is both a philosophy of business and a department. This means that an organisation which embraces a marketing philosophy understands that each department in the organisation should be oriented towards the consumer and their satisfaction. The marketing department is charged with managing this orientation and also all the other marketing tasks explored in this textbook.

Marketing management as a philosophy 'In a broad sense, marketing consists of activities designed to generate and facilitate exchange intended to satisfy human or organisational needs or wants.' A marketing philosophy or orientation, as studied in Chapter 1, is one where the company is oriented towards the customer, their needs and their wants. Many businesses try to force customers to like what they have rather than to ask the customer what they want and satisfy that need. The idea of a philosophy is that all staff believe it and that they live by it. *Marketing is a customer focus that permeates all organisational departments and processes.* Exploring this from a management perspective allows us to understand that marketing management can be a philosophy of business.

Marketing management as a department We can define marketing within the context of management as an organisational function or department and a set of practices for creating common rules for managing customer relations in a way that benefits the customer.[31] In many organisations, there is a department called the marketing department. This department has the responsibility for managing the customer focus of the company, and it is where all the

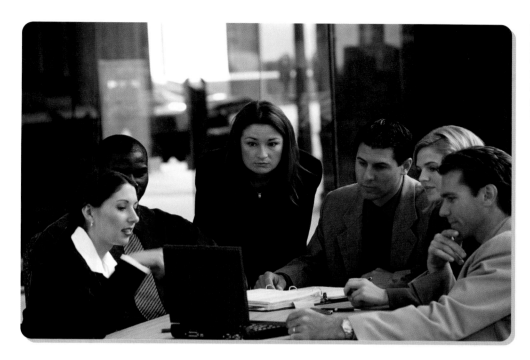

Marketing departments are challenged with bringing other department together to focus on the customer.
Source: Creatas/ PunchStock

aspects of this textbook are managed on a daily basis. Marketing involves an analysis of the market (Chapters 5 and 6), an analysis of the customer and/or business markets and the competition (Chapters 7 to 9), and the selection of the target markets and positioning within these markets (Chapters 10 and 11), creating and managing a brand (Chapters 12 and 13), the combination of all the marketing mix variables (Chapters 14–20) and then the implementation of the marketing mix variables (Chapter 21) within the profit criteria and other success measures of the company (Chapter 22). There are many types of models for how marketing departments operate within organisations (which will be explored in Chapter 21) but the major point is that there needs to be a marketing department to coordinate all marketing activities.

The perception of marketing The current status of marketing management is worrying. For many companies marketing is successful; the department is well defined and there is agreement on the scope and contribution of marketing to the business. Alternatively, despite the fact that marketing affects business and financial performance in many ways, it can have a poor image within organisations.[32] For some companies, marketing is underrepresented at board level and the financial rather than the marketing philosophy dominates.[33] Some of the reasons for this are highlighted in Figure 2.2, which reflects a range of issues facing marketing managers.

Marketing management in organisations can be at a disadvantage because of organisational and environmental pressures. These can include the following:

- uncertain definition of the term 'marketing' itself and the lack of understanding of marketing by some people;
- the tyranny of the profit and loss or financial focus of companies that often focus on short-term gain to the detriment of long-term sustained growth;
- the difficultly in directly measuring marketing productivity;
- shifts in channel power and the loss of manufacturing control;
- increased demands of customers;
- the limiting of marketing's role within top management;
- the shift of marketing to strategic business units.

There is an excellent quote from Michael Saren from the University of Leicester and Douglas Brownlie from the University of Stirling in Scotland that describes 'the high deeds of marketing

Figure 2.2 Forces shaping marketing's role

Source: W. Frederick, A. Malter and S. Ganesan (2005) The decline and dispersion of the marketing competence, *MIT Sloan Management Review*, 46(4), 35–43. Copyright © 2005 Massachusetts Institute of Technology. All rights reserved. Reproduced with permission.

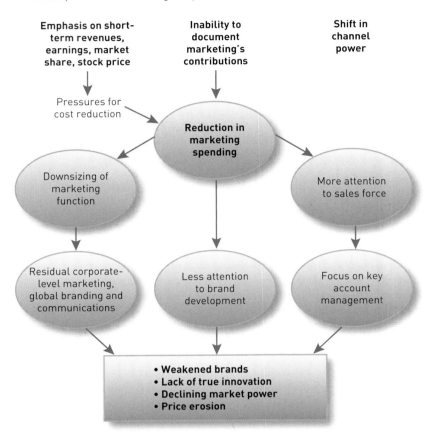

Forces shaping marketing's role

Financial pressures, a shift in channel power and marketing's inability to document its contribution to business results have combined to force reductions in marketing spending and influence – with significant consequences for marketing's impact.

theory and the low deeds of marketing practice'. This infers that there is often poor execution of marketing management in business. The marketing community worldwide clearly acknowledges a disconnect between marketing education and marketing practice. Ross Brennan, of the University of Middlesex in London, who was the guest editor for a recent special issue of *Marketing Intelligence & Planning*, entitled 'The academic/practitioner divide: myth or reality?' noted that 'nobody chose to submit a paper supporting the "myth" side of the argument'. In that issue Patrick McCole asserts that the 'academic/practitioner "gap" has now developed into a chasm', and that that there is a 'widespread and highly entrenched cultural prejudice, which does not recognize the professionalism and skills of marketing specialists', as noted from a study conducted by the UK Chartered Institute of Marketing.[34]

There are different characteristics of companies that embrace marketing and companies which are not greatly influenced by marketing – see Table 2.1.

For many, the Anglo-Saxon model of business with its finance orientation dominates. Finance and financial models are used to evaluate business, and as such decisions are often made through financial analysis only. Baker and Holt[35] noted that in many cases marketers are perceived to be 'unaccountable' by the rest of the organisation; they are seen as unable to demonstrate a return on investment in the activities over which they have control. Chapter 22 of this text addresses some of the lack of skills in this area of marketing. Marketing needs to have a

Table 2.1 Characteristics of companies at the two extremes of marketing's influence

The fact that marketing *does* continue to play an influential role in corporate strategy in some companies suggests that there is both an opportunity and a viable approach for building marketing competence as a source of competitive advantage.

Key dimensions	Characteristics when marketing is *not* influential in corporate decisions	Characteristics when marketing *is* influential in corporate decisions
Definition of marketing	Wide disagreement and ambiguity about the role and importance of marketing and customer orientation	Clear and shared understanding of the role of marketing: strong customer orientation in the corporate culture
Top-management objectives	Focused on current stock price, earnings per share (EPS), cost reduction, market share, sales volume	Focused on long-term growth in revenue, profitability, EPS and cash flow
Orientation and functional background of CEO	Little or no marketing experience; focused on financial community	Deep understanding of marketing; compelling vision of customer value. Advocate for the customer
Top-management priorities	Cost reduction and labour productivity	Customers, resellers and key accounts. Market information and tracking data are key management tools
Growth strategy	Growth achieved through mergers and acquisitions	Growth achieved through serious commitment to research and development, product innovation
Role of brands	Strong brands used as cash cows to fund acquisitions, growth strategy	Substantial investment to build and maintain brand equity
Focus of new product development	Product and technology focused	Customer analysis is hard-wired into product development
Portfolio strategy	Managed for cash flow; pricing used to achieve volume goals	Customer portfolio analysed and managed for loyalty, profitability

Source: W. Frederick, A. Malter and S. Ganesan (2005) The decline and dispersion of the marketing competence, *MIT Sloan Management Review*, 46(4), 35–43. Copyright © 2005 Massachusetts Institute of Technology. All rights reserved. Reproduced with permission.

match of more intuitive and creative ideas that can be tried and tested along with techniques which can be measured and monitored. Financial dominance can be successful, particularly during a period of growth, but challenging markets need marketing as well as financial focus to survive.

It is clear that marketing management is an evolving field of management practice. The overall marketing skills and competencies need to be retained and consciously developed and should be at the core of a company's management strategy.

Contemporary marketing management challenges

In a world where there are major challenges in the competitive landscape, including deregulation, ubiquitous connectivity and globalisation, the skills of marketing managers are more important than ever.[36] Managers are under overwhelming pressure to create value for shareholders, and none more so than marketing managers. Competition is intense across industries and profits are shrinking for many companies, though it can be said that successful companies have accrued unprecedented profit margins. The changing marketing environment places considerable demands on marketing management. There is no one established set of tasks or clearly defined role of the marketing manager. Marketing is not a 'one size fits all' discipline, and the variety and challenges of each situation are unique. Marketing managers need a range of skills to be able

Marketing insight

Marketing skills for an MBA

In a recent study of MBA graduates the following skills were recognised as being needed by marketing people.[37] The four most important skills were:

1 **Decision making under uncertainty**: Ability to adapt/change to new situations; ability to make decisions with imperfect information; ability to integrate information from a wide variety of sources.

2 **Communication skills**: Oral and written communications skills.

3 **Data collection and analysis**: Information-gathering skills; quantitative skills.

4 **Strategic/analytical thinking**: Ability to think strategically; ability to think analytically.

MBA alumni reported greatest usage of their interpersonal skills and oral and written communication skills. Integrating information from a wide variety of sources was also high, as were analytical thinking, creative problem-solving skills and strategic thinking. The skills used least involved financial analysis (conducting cost/benefit analyses of proposed changes and conducting financial analyses and preparing a budget) and direct staff management (recruiting, managing and maintaining staff).

> **Leadership skills**: 67 per cent of those recruiting for marketing identified leadership skills as attractive, contrasted with 65 per cent of those recruiting for non-marketing positions.

> **Ability to adapt/change to new situations**: 50 per cent of those recruiting for marketing identified the ability to adapt/change as attractive, contrasted with 54 per cent of those recruiting for non-marketing positions.

Initiative/risk-taking ability: 40 per cent of those recruiting for marketing identified initiative/risk-taking ability as attractive, contrasted with 38 per cent of those recruiting for non-marketing positions.

The future

In relation to the skills and abilities needed by marketing in the future, six underlying dimensions were suggested:

1 **Information analysis and strategic planning**: Developing a strategic plan; strategic thinking; developing creative problem-solving skills; integration of information from a wide variety of sources; analytical thinking.

2 **Communication skills**: Oral and written communication skills; interpersonal skills; leadership skills.

3 **Statistical and financial analysis**: Conducting financial analyses and preparing a budget; analysing, organising and interpreting statistical data; conducting cost/benefit analyses of potential changes.

4 **Organisation management**: Recruiting, managing and maintaining staff; stress management; managing change.

5 **Career management**: Managing your career, as well as networking skills.

6 **Marketing-specific skills**: Technical skills for marketing speciality, for example developing web-based marketing and designing and conducting market research.

---

to use the range of techniques available to them in creative and imaginative ways while always being cognisant of the financial outlays and returns needed. The Marketing insight above explores the core skills needed in marketing practitioners.

McGovern and Quelch suggest eight ways to improve marketing directors' success (see Figure 2.3).

The range of marketing tasks that the marketing manager has to manage is extensive. With a marketing philosophy as a backdrop, we can identify a specific set of tasks that comprise successful marketing management and marketing leadership. As you enter the field of marketing management, you will need to be an integrator, an organiser and a master of information. You will need to be familiar with a wide range of information and communication technologies and, most importantly, you will need to be a relationship manager.[38]

Because of the diversity of operations and situations across companies, the 'Marketing memo: Marketers' frequently asked questions' is a good checklist for the questions marketing managers ask, all of which we examine in this book.

1 Make the mission and responsibilities clear: Be certain that the case for having a marketing director is strong and the mission is well understood by leaders in the organisation, particularly the CEO, the board and line management. Without a clear need (real or perceived), the role will be rejected by the organisation.

2 Fit the role to the marketing culture and structure: Avoid having a marketing director in a marketing-led company that has many individual brands rather than a single corporate umbrella – unless the person appointed to the position is a well-connected insider.

3 Choose a marketing director who is compatible with the CEO: Beware the CEO who wants to hire a marketing director but doesn't want to relinquish any marketing control. Find a CEO who recognises his or her responsibility to be the cheerleader for marketing and the brand, but realises the need to be guided and coached by a marketing specialist.

4 Remember that showpeople don't succeed: The marketing director should work hard to ensure the CEO is successful at being the principal cheerleader for the brand.

5 Match the personality with the marketing director type: Be certain that the chief marketer has the right skills and personality for whichever of the three marketing director models he or she might fill (marketing director, marketing services; classic marketing director or 'super' marketing director). There is little tolerance for on-the-job training.

6 Make line managers marketing heroes: By stretching their marketing budgets, marketing directors can improve a division's marketing productivity and help business unit leaders increase their top-line revenues.

7 Infiltrate the line organisation: Have the marketing director support the placement of marketing professionals from the corporate marketing department into divisional marketing roles. Provide input from the marketing director into the annual reviews of line managers.

8 Require right-brain and left-brain skills: The most successful marketing director will have strong creative and technical marketing expertise, be politically savvy, and have the interpersonal skills to be a great leader and manager.

Figure 2.3
Improving marketing directors' success

Source: From G. McGovern and J. A. Quelch (2004) The fall and rise of the CMO, *Strategy+Business*, 37, 3–8. Reproduced with permission.

Marketing memo

Marketers' frequently asked questions

1 How can we spot and choose the right market segment(s)?

2 How can we differentiate our product or service offerings?

3 How should we respond to customers who buy on price?

4 How can we compete against lower-cost, lower-price competitors?

5 How far can we go in customising our offering for each customer?

6 How can we grow our business?

7 How can we build stronger brands?

8 How can we reduce the cost of customer acquisition?

9 How can we keep our customers loyal for longer?

10 How do we lose customers who are not within our target market?

11 How can we tell which customers are more important?

12 How can we measure the payback from advertising, sales promotion, public relations and our online activities?

13 How can we improve sales force productivity?

14 How can we establish multiple channels and yet manage channel conflict?

15 How can we get the other company departments to be more customer oriented?

16 How do we manage the service process?

17 How can we manage and improve the environment or any physical evidence?

18 How can we best manage and motivate the people who provide the service?

19 How can we align our target market needs and positioning with the marketing mix elements?

20 How can we integrate all elements of the marketing mix, from managing the service process to controlling the supply network?

21 How can we be consistently ahead of consumer needs and really understand the future?

Critical marketing management tasks include the following: Marketing is a total system of business activities designed to plan, price, process, design, manage people, promote and distribute satisfying services and products to target markets in order to achieve organisational objectives.

Contemporary marketing management skills

This section will explore the management challenges and skills and the core issues of which marketing managers must be aware.

1 managing the implementation of ICT and digital technology within marketing;

2 managing networks, relationships and interaction;

3 information handling and management;

4 understanding and managing change;

5 analytical and creative skills.

Managing the implementation of ICT and digital technology within marketing

Due to the explosion in technology both internally in organisations and at the customer interface, managing ICT means that managing the implementation process of ICT within marketing has become a core skill. These are not technical challenges but managerial challenges. There are three main responsibilities:[39]

1 **Information and communication technology selection:** Marketers must help select the best technology matched to the needs of their marketing strategy. They must focus on the capabilites of the ICT rather than on the ICT itself. The full range of ICTs will be discussed in Chapter 4. It is clear that ICT selection can be crucial to many businesses. The type of questions could include:

   - Which is the best database for our needs?

   - Which planning software should we use?

   - What supply chain management (SCM) software would be best?

   - What self-service technologies would be good for consumers and also for our needs?

2 **Support the ICT adoption:** Marketers must help and even lead the implementation process across the company to ensure that the ICT is implemented smoothly. Adoption can be challenging, especially where it crosses departments and changes work practices. Resistance to ICTs that change work practices or customer interactions need to be monitored and managed carefully. Preplanning how the key issues that may arise will be handled is crucial. Many staff and even customers have to be encouraged or forced to change their processes. Take for instance the 2008 opening of the new BA Terminal 5 in London Heathrow. The terminal was designed for maximum customer service but yet on the opening day many of the ICT systems did not work or staff had problems using them. All ICTs, particularly those at the customer interface, need to be supported prior to, during and after adoption.

3 **ICT exploitation:** Marketing must be able to extract the maximum benefit from ICTs. To exploit ICTs marketers must understand a range of ICTs and how they will develop. Take the phenomenal upsurge of blogging as a social activity among consumers. Blogging is similar to personal online diaries developed by people and posted on the web. As of December 2007, there were over 112 million blogs on the Internet.[40] To exploit this type of technological development marketing would have to understand the technology and how it could be used. Marketers can monitor blogs and other 'consumer-generated media' – such as chat groups, message boards and electronic forums – to analyse what is being said online about products and services, as well as follow the cult status that some blogging communities accord to brands. They can use blogs to communicate with their customers or they can use blogs as

knowledge management. They can also use web-tracking software to monitor each time their company is mentioned in a blog.

To manage ICT marketing managers must understand how companies adopt ICT. The most common view is that ICT assimilation into companies occurs in three stages – known as the Stages Theory[41] of ICT assimilation.

Automation This is where technology is used to replace previously automated tasks. The ATM machine is a very good example. This is used to replace the cashier in the bank. Check-in kiosks at airports also automate a process that previously involved a person checking each passenger in. Now the passenger does that themselves. These systems are designed to create efficiency – to make the process go faster.

Information This is when the information is used to improve the service supplied, so that rather than just going faster the system actually allows us to do something different which is more effective. The airport kiosk is also a good example here as passengers can choose their seating on the plane, making their trip more effective or better for them. British food retailer Tesco is thriving in large part due to its ability to mine the data generated by its Clubcard loyalty scheme, which monitors purchases and rewards frequent buyers with discounts. The company, which also solicits customer feedback through phone and written surveys, is considered by analysts to be top of the class at using the information it garners. Tesco detected that customers wanted more nutritional information. The marketing team then designed a new labelling system that gave shoppers more detailed information on the fat, salt and sugar content of hundreds of products.[42] This is an example of using information to be more effective.

Transformation This is where the technology transforms the industry or the process. The growth in ICT has created many opportunities but also challenges for companies worldwide. Managers need to know how to manage when technology changes the rules of the game. The music industry is a good example, where the downloading of music has changed how music is distributed. The technological impact on the music industry means that digital music sales are increasing all the time and affecting the sales of the physical CD.

These three stages have similarly been called inertia, application and change – each role reflects a different level of IT integration into the organisation.[43]

- The *inertia role* occurs when companies use ICTs to retain and preserve their existing ways of doing things and therefore they *reinforce* the status quo.
- The *application role* is when ICTs are used to augment and reinforce existing work practices and therefore *enhance* the status quo.
- The *change role* occurs when ICTs are treated as a philosophy, infusing and altering every business consideration, and therefore they *transform* the status quo.

A recent study suggests that within marketing, managers exhibit many responses, ranging from feelings of apparent disappointment, pessimism and scepticism when their organisations invest in ICTs which are perceived to be for reinforcement purposes, but that these feelings change to ones of anticipation, optimism and confidence when they see ICT investments which are largely for transformation purposes.[44]

Marketing managers can manage ICTs by reviewing ICTs in two categories:[45] information and interactions – see Table 2.2.

Information: Information technology has revolutionised the data gathering, processing and management of information enabling marketers to capture, analyse and distribute information more rapidly, more widely and more economically than ever before. Holland and Naude from the Manchester Business School and the University of Bath, respectively, have gone so far as to say that marketing should be called an 'information-handling' department.

Table 2.2 The information and interaction divide for ICTs in marketing

Information (Research, analysis and planning)	Interactions (Communications, connections and collaborations)
Analysis software	Communications
Planning software	Self-service technologies
Databases	Sales-related technologies
Research, tracking and monitoring technologies	Supply network management
Customer relationship management	Interactive products and service
Retailing systems	Sensor technologies
New product and service design technologies	Mobile technologies
(Others and general platform technologies)	

Interaction: Communication, connections and collaborations between the customer and companies abound and any technology at the customer interface could be classed as interaction technology. Many of these can be from the company to the customer but more and more communications and connections are initiated and controlled by the customer.

Marketing departments must make effective use of the range of ICTs available to them. They need both the technology and the training. Marketing departments may not see the full potential of many of the ICTs available to them due to a lack of ICT skills and vision.

Managing networks, relationships and interaction

With the move away from marketing at customers to a more relational and networked approach, that was introduced in Chapter 1, an enhanced skill set for marketing managers is required as they coordinate networks with suppliers, customers and service providers at a range and level never before witnessed in business history. The network school of management highlights that companies will have a multitude of relationships within a web of complex relationships. As supply network management and interfirm cooperation becomes crucial, information management between manufacturers, service providers and their suppliers need to become more efficient. Using the latest information and communication technologies to interconnect manufacturers, retailers and transporters, these companies can easily exchange information with others. However, the use of information technologies is not all that is necessary to enhance global supply competencies. It is even more important to effectively manage the relationships with all supply chain partners.[46]

The contemporary marketing practice (CMP) framework in Marketing insights on the next page highlights the different marketing practices and reviews the practices of relationship marketing and network marketing. Before marketers decide which marketing mix elements to use, they must understand relationships, networks and interactions that are a fundamental prerequisite to implementing the marketing mix.[47] The European market is particularly suited to network models of marketing and business because the European market has an interdependence view of markets where companies do not operate alone but rather in groups or networks.[48]

Understanding relationship marketing Many companies create separate offers, services and messages to *individual customers*, based on information about previous transactions, demographics, psychographics, media and distribution preferences. By focusing on their most profitable customers, products and channels, these firms hope to achieve profitable growth, capturing a larger share of each customer's expenditure by building high customer loyalty. They estimate individual customer lifetime value and design their market offerings and prices to make a profit over the customer's lifetime. The lifetime value of a customer to a pizza company, for example, is valued at between €2000 and €6000. This will be explored in more detail in Chapter 22 on marketing metrics.

Another goal of relationship marketing is to place a greater emphasis on customer retention. Attracting a new customer may cost five times as much as retaining an existing one. A bank aims

The contemporary marketing practice framework

As introduced in Chapter 1, the contemporary marketing practice framework[49] offers an interesting perspective on how we could view marketing's shift from transactional exchange to relational and networked relationships. This framework suggests that companies often have a dominant focus but that they practise marketing across the full range of transaction, database, emarketing interaction and network, and allow managers to study what core skills set they need depending on what is their dominant marketing practice. Remember that all of the practices can be in operation but that one usually dominates.

Taking network marketing, if a marketing manager was managing with network marketing as the dominant focus than the orientation would be towards all the aspects of column 6 of Table 2.3.

Table 2.3 Marketing as classified by relational exchange dimensions and managerial intention

	Transaction marketing	Database marketing	emarketing	Interactive marketing	Network marketing
Purpose of exchange	Economic transaction	Information and economic transaction	Information-generating dialogue between a seller and many identified buyers	Interpersonal relationships between a buyer and seller	Connected relationships between firms
Nature of communi-cation	Firm 'to' mass market	Firm 'to' targeted segment or individuals	Firm using technology to communicate 'with' and 'among' many individuals (who may form groups)	Individuals 'with' individuals (across organisations)	Firms 'with' firms (involving individuals)
Type of contact	Arm's length, impersonal	Personalised (yet distant)	Interactive (via technology)	Face to face, interpersonal	Impersonal – interpersonal (ranging from distant to close)
Duration of exchange	Discrete (yet perhaps over time)	Discrete and over time	Continuous (but interactivity occurs in real time)	Continuous (ongoing and mutually adaptive, short or long term)	Continuous (stable yet dynamic, may be short or long term)
Formality of exchange	Formal	Formal (yet personalised via technology)	Formal (yet customised and/or personalised via interactive technology	Formal and informal (i.e. at both a business and social level)	Formal and informal (i.e. at both a business and social level)
Managerial intent	Customer attraction	Customer retention	Creation of IT-enabled dialogue	Interaction	Coordination

▶ **Marketing insight** *(continued)*

Table 2.3 *(Continued)*

	Transaction marketing	Database marketing	emarketing	Interactive marketing	Network marketing
Managerial focus	Product or brand	Product/brand and customers (in a targeted market)	Managing IT-enabled relationships between the firm and many individuals	Relationships between individuals	Connected relationships between firms (in a network)
Managerial investment	Internal marketing assets	Internal marketing assets (emphasising information technology capabilities)	Internal operational assets (IT, website, logistics); functional systems integration	External market assets (focusing on establishing and developing a relationship with another individual)	External market assets (focusing on developing the firm's position in a network of firms)
Managerial level	Functional marketers (e.g. sales manager, product manager)	Specialist marketers (e.g. customer service manager, loyalty manager)	Marketing specialists (with) technology specialists, senior managers	Employees and managers (from across functions and levels in the firms)	Senior managers

Sources: Adapted from N. Coviello, R. Brodie and H. Munro (1997) Understanding contemporary marketing: development of a classification scheme, *Journal of Marketing Management*, 13(6), 501–22; N. Coviello, R. Brodie, P. Danaher et al. (2002) How firms relate to their markets: an empirical examination of contemporary marketing practices, *Journal of Marketing*, 66(3), 33–46; R. J. Brodie, H. Winklhofer, N. E. Coviello and W. J. Johnston (2007) Is e-marketing coming of age? an examination of the penetration of e-marketing and firm performance, *Journal of Interactive Marketing*, 21(1), 2–21.

to increase its share of the customer's wallet; the supermarket aims to capture a larger share of the customer's 'stomach' or purse. Companies build customer share by offering a larger variety of products or services to existing customers, and keeping their value offering relevant and worthwhile to the consumer.

Marketing must skilfully practise not only customer relationship management, but partner relationship management (PRM) as well. Companies have begun to nurture their partnering arrangements with key suppliers and distributors, thinking of these intermediaries not as customers but as partners in delivering value to final customers so everybody benefits.

This concept reflects a move from a 'one-to-many' approach to a 'one-to-one' approach: 'Mass marketing divides customers in markets, segments and niches while relationship marketing builds communities of individuals with similar needs and behaviour.'[50] 'Many-to-many marketing describes, analyses and exploits the network properties of marketing.'[51]

According to Professor Evert Gummesson relationships can be divided into three types:[52]

1 **Market relationships**: relationships that are primarily with customers, suppliers, intermediaries and competitors;

2 **Mega-relationships**: relationships with political connections, public opinion, large institutions such as the EU, academic scientific research institutions and so on;

3 **Nano-relationships**: intra-organisational relationships – namely how employees and departments interact – often called internal marketing.

All levels of relationships are interlinked. The mega-relationship impacts on what happens in the market relationship and also on the nano. In France in January 2008, politicians (mega-relationship) banned smoking in public and work places, which had an impact on many businesses. Many restaurants and cafés witnessed a change in customer behaviour as customers either chose to go to another place with a smoking garden or stayed at home. This is an example of how mega-relationships impact on market relationships. Many employees in French organisations have been affected and huddle outside in the cold having a cigarette. This is an example of how the mega-relationship impacts on nano-relationships. If you only consider the market relationships as a manager then you only concentrate on organisational tactics. If you study and manage all three you will be studying strategy, organisations and processes.

Network marketing Marketing now operates in a networked world and managing a network of people, companies, relationships, technologies and interactions is a core skill of marketing managers. Viewing companies as networks of relationships and interactions called virtual organisations is the suggested business model for today's business world, moving away from hierarchical entities to a more organic, integrative, network-based and process-oriented philosophy, with groups of separate enterprises linked through high-speed technologies. Networks are expected to have a profound, radical and pervasive effect on marketing.

Increasingly, a key goal of marketing is to develop deep, enduring relationships with people and organisations that could directly or indirectly affect the success of the companies' marketing activities. Network marketing aims to build mutually satisfying long-term relationships with key constituents in order to earn and retain their business.[53]

Four key constituents in network marketing are customers, employees, marketing partners (channels, suppliers, distributors, dealers, agencies) and members of the financial community (shareholders, investors, analysts). Marketers must respect the need to create prosperity among all these constituents and develop policies and strategies to balance the returns to all key stakeholders. To develop strong relationships with these constituents requires an understanding of their capabilities and resources, as well as their needs, goals and desires.

The ultimate outcome is a unique company asset called a **marketing network**. A marketing network consists of the company and its supporting stakeholders – customers, employees, suppliers, distributors, retailers, ad agencies, research companies, database company and others – with whom it has built mutually profitable business relationships. The operating principle is simple: build an effective network of relationships with key stakeholders, and profits will follow.[54] Using this reasoning, more companies are choosing to own and develop brands rather than actual physical assets. They are also increasingly subcontracting activities to outsourcing firms that can do them better and more cheaply, while retaining core activities. Marketing now operates complex networks and the interests of multiple parties have to be mediated, which can be seen clearly in Chapter 17 on designing and managing supply networks. Working in collaboration with partners is the focus of the next Marketing insight: Competent collaboration.

Marketing insight

Competent collaboration

Marketing management increasingly focuses on collaboration though close relationships with customers and partners to co-create solutions to complex problems or to jointly pursue marketplace opportunities. Collaboration is a strategy for managing a long-term relationship. For example, the publishers of the Harry Potter range of books, which are the third most popular book in the world, after the Bible and the *Red Book* by Mao, collaborated with printers, distributors, delivery companies and retailers and the media to ensure that the books went on sale at midnight on the same day across the globe. The books have been translated into 30 languages and are best sellers in over 120 countries.

Being able to collaborate successfully allows a firm to innovate, to respond to change and to achieve strategic marketing objectives. Successful collaboration requires:

- collaborative capability (the skills, capabilities and supporting processes);
- absorptive capability (the ability to learn and apply new knowledge);
- developing project-specific capability;
- selecting the right partner;
- managing the collaboration process;
- developing the right team.[55]

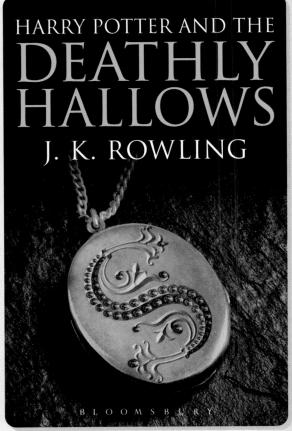

The Harry Potter marketing success relies on collaboration across a network of suppliers, distributors, publishers, retailers, the media and the consumer.

Source: © 1997 Thomas Taylor (left); Both courtesy of Bloomsbury Publishing

▶ **Marketing insight** *(continued)*

Marketing managers need to ask the following questions:

1 Can the company recognise when collaboration is needed on marketing projects?

2 Does the company have the commitment of senior management to invest the necessary time, resources and effort for marketing collaboration?

3 Can the company improve on whom they select as collaborators in marketing projects?

4 Does the company have the capabilities that allow them to learn from the collaboration partners?

5 Is the marketing manager committed to collaborating in ways that improve relationship quality with the partners?

Building relationships with other departments The relationships that the marketing department builds with other departments such as sales, production and finance are crucial to gaining the acceptance and enthusiasm of other departments towards the marketing mix programme. Take for example new product or service development engineers – they must work with marketing from the beginning rather than bringing marketing in after they have developed a new product or designed a new service. Some companies use marketing only for the promotional area and ignore all the rest of marketing. 'Tick-box' marketing is when marketing is brought in *after* the product or service has been developed and for promotions only – ticking off the promotional items such as brochures, point-of-sale displays and advertising without any understanding of the other aspects of marketing. Such a mindset contributes to product and service failure because there is no clear understanding of consumers and marketing needs.

The marketing department must have a strong leader who directs a well-organised team that can work with all the other departments company wide. A constant effort is needed to ensure that the marketing manager is able to provide the marketing skills needed to manage the company offering to the customer and identify opportunities, manage product and services to satisfy needs and expand brand awareness, loyalty and, ultimately, profitability.[56]

Integration: managing the cross-departmental aspects Companies generally establish a marketing department to be responsible for creating and delivering customer value. Many companies are moving to more innovative work practices and beginning to emphasise interdepartmental teamwork to manage key processes. They are also placing more emphasis on the smooth management of core business processes, such as new product or service realisation, customer acquisition and retention, and order fulfilment.

Companies are made up of departments, and interdepartmental cooperation is crucial. Marketing management must work in harmony with so many departments to try and integrate them towards a common goal of customer satisfaction at a profit. These departments can include the new service or product development department, the manufacturing or production department, the sales department, the purchasing department, the finance department and so on. When all departments know and understand their role and the importance of marketing or customer-focused processes, the company works better.

Marketing is involved with and needs to oversee many departments in which it has no input. Much of what occurs in marketing does not occur within the marketing department. The marketing department is responsible for certain tasks (Chapters 5–23) and also has a responsibility for planning and strategy (Chapter 3). Within the marketing department, the management of many aspects of the business is overviewed. The marketing manager may not be on the shop floor when the customer purchases a product or avails him- or herself of a service, but they are responsible for designing the process and researching it continuously to see if it needs changing. Marketing departments do not operate in isolation and need other employees in the company to understand the philosophy of a market-oriented business. The marketing concept means *'Total company effort towards customer satisfaction at a profit'*; a company-wide focus should be obvious but often it is not. Many employees do have roles that contribute to the overall marketing programme, such as repairs and maintenance, delivery, call centres and so on. Marketing needs to affect every aspect of the customer experience, meaning that marketers must properly manage all possible touch points with the consumer including store layouts, package designs, product functions, service employee training and distributors' methods.

To create a strong marketing organisation, marketers must think like executives in other departments, and executives in other departments must think more like marketers.[57] Many marketers lack an understanding of the cross-departmental role of marketing. Table 2.4 assesses which departments are customer minded and it can be used as a checklist within companies.

Integrated marketing mix elements The marketer's task is to devise marketing activities and assemble fully integrated marketing programmes to create, communicate, and deliver value for consumers. Thus much of their role is the coordination of activites spread throughout organisations.

Two key themes of integrated marketing are that: (1) many different marketing activities communicate and deliver value; and (2) when coordinated, marketing activities maximise their joint effects. In other words, marketers should design and implement any one marketing activity with all other activities in mind.

For example, using an integrated communication strategy means choosing communication options that reinforce and complement each other. A marketer might selectively employ television, radio and print advertising, public relations and events, and homepage communications, so that each contributes well on its own as well as improving the effectiveness of the others. Each communication must also deliver a consistent brand image to customers at every brand contact. Applying an integrated channel strategy ensures that direct and indirect channels, such as online and retail sales, work together to maximise sales and brand equity. Marketers must be able to deliver on promises made in advertising or delivery by being able to coordinate everything.

Information handling and management

Information and communication technologies supply much of the information for marketing. ICT-oriented marketing will rely less on experience, intuition and guesswork and much more on the information provided by ICT systems monitoring every stage of the product/service delivery through to consumption. The increased information provided by ICT must be matched with the skills of marketers to analyse the data supplied throughout the supply chain and across every facet of marketing. The marketing manager must manage huge amounts of information from multiple sources, channels and all members of networks, relationships and interaction.

Information abounds in marketing. There is 'almost limitless amounts of marketing data concerning customer details, buying patterns, channels of distribution and the performance of economic partners and so on.'[58] Our ability to store, process, analyse and transmit information far exceeds our ability to use this information. In many cases it is not a question of too little information, but too much. The real power base in marketing comes from its information power and not its sales power. Marketers who can analyse information and react to the knowledge that this information yields by creating innovative and creative products and services will be successful, not the company with the best sales force or advertising. Chapters 5–9 explore all these issues in greater detail.

Understanding and managing change

To survive and succeed, every business has to become a change agent. Marketing must be able to abandon what is not successful and continuously improve every product, service and process within the company.[59] This requires the exploitation of successes, especially those that are unexpected and unplanned for – and it requires systematic innovation. Change should be normal and expected rather than feared and avoided.

It is important to remember that innovation and creativity are marketing management skills. In many ways marketing departments need to be futurologists. They need to be at least a year or two ahead of the market and tell the company where the market is going. Contemporary companies imitate each other's structures and strategies resulting in decreased margins for all.[60] A solution to this is to build a capability in strategic innovation and imagination. The challenge is to

Table 2.4 Assessing which company departments are customer-minded

R&D

- They spend time meeting customers and listening to their problems.
- They welcome the involvement of marketing, manufacturing and other departments to each new project.
- They benchmark competitors' products and services and seek 'best of class' solutions.
- They solicit customer reactions and suggestions as the project progresses.
- They continuously improve and refine the product or service on the basis of market feedback.

Purchasing

- They proactively search for the best suppliers.
- They build long-term relationships with fewer but more reliable, high-quality suppliers.
- They don't compromise quality for price savings.

Manufacturing or service operations

- They invite customers to visit and tour their plants or visit their service operations.
- They visit customer plants or service operations.
- They willingly work overtime to meet promised delivery schedules.
- They continuously search for ways to produce products and services faster and/or at lower cost.
- They continuously improve product and service quality, aiming for zero defects or excellent service delivery models.
- They meet customer requirements for 'customisation' where possible.

Marketing

- They study customer needs and wants in well-defined market segments.
- They allocate marketing effort in relation to the long-run profit potential of the targeted segments.
- They develop winning offers for each target segment.
- They measure company image and customer satisfaction on a continuous basis.
- They continuously gather and evaluate ideas for new products and services and product and service improvements.
- They urge all company departments and employees to be customer centred.

Sales

- They have specialised knowledge of the customer's industry.
- They strive to give the customer 'the best solution'.
- They only make promises that they can keep.
- They feed back customers' needs and ideas to those in charge of product or service development.

Distribution

- They set a high standard for service delivery time and meet this standard consistently.
- They operate an efficient and effective global (local) supply network that delivers to the customer when and where they need it.
- They manage all the channel players in the network.

Accounting

- They prepare periodic 'profitability' reports by product/service, market segment, geographic areas (regions, sales territories), order sizes, channels and individual customers.
- They prepare invoices tailored to customer needs and answer customer queries courteously and quickly.

Finance

- They understand and support marketing expenditures that produce long-term customer preference and loyalty.
- They tailor the financial package to the customer's financial requirements.
- They make quick but accurate decisions on customer creditworthiness.

Customer service department

- They operate a knowledgeable and friendly customer service department that can answer questions, handle complaints and resolve problems in a satisfactory and timely manner.
- They try to solve the problem at source so that the same problem does not occur again.

create a marketing culture that values human capital and innovation, to provide a steady stream of innovation.[61] Innovation is about much more than new products and services. It is about reinventing business processes and building entirely new markets that meet untapped customer needs. As Peter Drucker noted, 'What was your winning formula for the last decade may be your losing formula for the next'. Virgin Atlantic, the UK-based airline, is a good example of an innovative company.

▽ Virgin Atlantic

Emerging out of the music-centred Virgin Group in 1984, Virgin Atlantic has led the journey of the Virgin brand from its counter-culture origins to pioneering customer-centric service innovation. Virgin Atlantic has been pre-eminent in delivering customer-centric, service-led innovation to the airline sector. Expanding from its original UK/US transatlantic base linking London with New York and Miami, Virgin has become a major international global airline, redefining economy and business-class travel experience along the way. Entering into a global partnership with Singapore Airlines in 1999, Virgin is now the second largest airline in the United Kingdom and has continued to lead innovation in the airline industry. Resembling a flying luxury hotel, Upper Class innovations have embraced limousine services, on-board massage and unique lounges. Having witnessed the roll-out of individual multichannel entertainment in economy class, the company introduced onboard SMS text messaging in 2003. In 2005, Virgin was the first airline to launch a pod-casting service.[62] Richard Branson, founder and CEO, Virgin Atlantic Airways, states that his focus is on 'Innovation, value for money, and the simple idea that flying should actually be fun'.[63]

The Marketing insight below highlights the dangers of becoming complacent.

Marketing insight

Marketing management successes and failures

Many firms that are deeply entrenched in their industry, where they have dominated for years, develop a particular mindset that leaves them vulnerable to aggressive and innovative competition. They forget to carry out marketing with an inside-out perspective and so miss the opportunities to change. They often suffer from the three Cs of:

Complacency: smugness, self satisfaction and contentment;

Conservatism: management which believes that the future will be the same as the past and adheres to tradition rather than market need;

Conceit: the belief that 'we are the best' and that no other company can better the organisation.

Staying marketing focused can be difficult when you are successful.[64] Take the example of Airbus, which has successfully competed with Boeing in their marketplace. In March 2008, the first flight of the 800-passenger aircraft Airbus A380 – designed and developed by

Airbus – took off from Singapore and landed successfully in London.[65] This airplane has more than double the capacity of a Boeing 747. For 35 years, Boeing's 747 aircraft set the standard for jumbo commercial aircraft and controlled this market, noting that 'our 747 jumbo jet is the largest that can be profitably used'.[66]

Airbus, which started as a European consortium of France and Germany and was later joined by Spain and Britain, decided to try and beat Boeing at their own game. The company, which is now controlled by a Dutch aerospace organisation, thinks its plane will create the blueprint for the next generation of airborne giants. 'It's the plane of the future, a cruise ship in the sky', said John Leahy, Airbus's top executive, who is credited with helping the company surpass Boeing as the world's largest aircraft maker. The A380 'will change the way we fly, just as the 747 did'.[67] As one passenger on the inaugural Singapore to London flight in March 2008 noted: 'First of all, well done to Airbus for making the biggest flying machine of mankind. It's awesome and unbelievable. Secondly, Airbus has made air travel so comfortable. I dread travelling in a 747 from now onwards, especially in economy class'.

▶ Marketing insight *(continued)*

The A380 provides customers with luxury and speed and for Airbus it cements its position as the world's leading manufacturer of civilian aircraft.
Source: Jim Mone/AP/PA Photos

Managing external suppliers Marketing departments within companies are often small but they avail themselves of and manage the services of a range of service providers for the marketing programme. These include but are not limited to advertising agencies, market research companies, Internet providers and database managers. There are also distributors, transportation companies, wholesaling and retailing services. So traditionally marketing is one area that is accustomed to outsourcing their requirements. Each marketing situation is unique, and marketing has to decide on which range of skills to keep in-house and which they should outsource to specialist companies.

Coordination of internal and external suppliers The following example highlights the coordination problem:

The marketing manager of a major European airline wants to increase the airline's traffic share. His strategy is to build up customer satisfaction by providing better food, cleaner cabins, better-trained cabin crews and lower fares, yet he has no authority in these matters. The catering department chooses food that keeps costs down; the maintenance department uses services that keep down cleaning costs; the human resources department hires people without regard to whether they are naturally friendly; the finance department sets the air-fares. Because these departments generally take a cost or production point of view, the director of marketing is held back in his efforts to create an integrated marketing mix.

Analytical and creative skills

Marketing managers need to be both analytical and creative. This is because marketing managers tend to think with the right side of the brain and forget that they can succeed in formulating the most ingenious marketing plan ever made and yet fail due to a lack of monitoring and control. One of the main failures of marketing today is an inability to make a demonstrated contribution to the company's financial performance.[68]

For a discipline that focused on the creative tasks of advertising, promotion, packaging, print and TV advertising, marketing has moved from an emphasis on solely creative activities to analytical ability and activities. The skill now needed is a move to left brain number crunchers who can understand modelling of information and analyse findings to produce innovative marketing mix programmes.[69] Much of marketing is now related to analysis: analysing computer models that can optimise everything from shelf space to sales representative allocations. For example, dynamic pricing models and yield management systems in airlines and hotels allow for seat and room allocation at the optimised rate. It is the marketing manager's role to ensure that they can monitor and utilise this information.

Marketing has long outsourced much of the creative right-brain marketing activities such as advertising and promotion campaigns but nowadays marketing departments also outsource many of the critical left-brain marketing activities such as customer database and database analysis.[70] As marketing has become more scientific and specialised, marketing practitioners are increasingly turning to advanced statistical techniques for dissecting segments, managing services and selecting prices and allocations. For example, Tesco outsourced its database management to a company called DunnHumby, which has been instrumental in the development and operation of Tesco's Clubcard, a modern form of loyalty scheme that has been a major influence for this retail giant over the past decade. When it first started working with DunnHumby, Tesco was the number two supermarket chain in the United Kingdom. Today, the company is one of the world's largest and most successful retailers. When Sony wanted to build a customer database and to develop an Internet store, *Sony Style*, it outsourced these tasks, knowing that it did not have the skills in-house. The most commonly outsourced tasks that must be monitored by marketing are call centres, website design and management, direct mail programmes and database management,[71] along with the more traditional advertising agencies and market research.

▽ Managing within a global marketing environment: the global marketing manager

Another aspect of marketing management is global management. Global firms, in both product and services, plan, operate and coordinate their activities worldwide in places such as Europe, North America and Asia. For example Nokia is a global company. Of the 900 million mobile phones sold worldwide in 2006, 320 million were made by Nokia. Otis Elevator uses door systems from France, small geared parts from Spain, electronics from Germany and motor drives from Japan; systems integration happens in the United States. Other firms are international companies operating in more than one country but are not global.

Marketing managers, deciding to go international or to go global, must make a series of management decisions (see Figure 2.4). We'll examine each of these decisions here.

Deciding whether to go abroad

Internationalisation is the process through which a firm moves from operating solely in its domestic marketplace to operating in international markets. Most companies now look to the global market rather than simply remain in their domestic market – a decision that creates management challenges. Outside the domestic market, managers need to learn other languages and laws, deal with volatile currencies, face political and legal uncertainties or redesign their products or services to suit different customer needs and expectations. Business could be easier if

Figure 2.4 Major decisions in international marketing

Nokia's global view motivates its broad product lines that appeal to all kinds of customers and price ranges all over the world.

Source: Sean Gallup/Getty Images

companies stayed within domestic markets but more and more companies go global. Several factors draw companies into the international arena:

- Some international markets present higher profit opportunities than the domestic market.
- The company needs a larger customer base to achieve economies of scale.
- It wants to reduce its dependence on any one market.
- The company decides to counterattack global competitors in their home markets.
- Customers are going abroad and require international service.

Before making a decision to go abroad, the company must be aware of and weigh up several risks:

- The company might not understand foreign preferences and could fail to offer a competitively attractive product or service.
- The company might not understand the foreign country's business culture even if they are geographically close.
- It might underestimate foreign regulations and incur unexpected costs.
- The company might lack managers with international experience.
- The foreign country might change its commercial laws, devalue its currency or undergo a political revolution and expropriate foreign property.

The *internationalisation process* typically has four stages:[72] Once a manager or company has success at one level – exporting – they may try and move on to foreign direct investment. Much of internationalisation links to networks and global supply networks which will be discussed in greater detail in Chapter 17. The four stages are:

1 No regular export activities – focus on the domestic market.
2 Export via independent representatives, distributor or agents.
3 Establishment of one or more subsidiaries.
4 Establishment of production and service facilities abroad – often called foreign direct investment.

As with much of marketing, a 'one size fits all' strategy does not work in all cases. Network theory suggests that the internationalisation process is far more complex and less structured than these four stages. The findings from a recent study of five small Norwegian computer software firms suggest that network relationships affect which foreign entry forms companies choose and, to some extent, which markets they decide to enter.[73] There is also a lack of consistency in companies' method of foreign market choice; companies look for competency, solidity and the ability to generate sales when searching for international partners rather than a uniform structure for all countries. This study also found that a company may choose one entry form in one market and a different one in another, similar market, very much depending upon the options available in terms of their network relationships. A key challenge is to balance the allocation of resources between expanding the network through current relationships and a focus on establishing new relationships and customers. The study's results illustrate the increasingly complex relationship between firms across national borders and supports the contention that the internationalisation process is driven by existing network relationships, often with major partners driving foreign market selection and also providing the mechanism for market entry.[74]

Many companies move from an export department to an international department and finally to a local presence. If markets are large and stable, or the host country requires local production or a local service operation, the company may locate production facilities in those markets or set up a service enterprise. Then it is operating as a multinational and is optimising its global sourcing, financing, manufacturing, service operations and marketing. According to some researchers, top management begins to pay more attention to global opportunities when over 15 per cent of revenues come from international markets.[75]

Deciding which markets to enter

In deciding to internationalise, the company needs to define its marketing objectives and policies. What ratio of international to total sales will it seek? Most companies start small when they venture abroad. Some plan to stay small; others have bigger plans.

The marketing manager must decide how many countries to enter and how fast to expand. Typical entry strategies follow the *waterfall* approach, that is, gradually entering countries in sequence, or the *sprinkler* approach, namely entering many countries simultaneously. Increasingly, firms – especially technology-intensive firms – are *born global* and market to the entire world from the outset.[76]

BMW, Benetton and The Body Shop followed the waterfall approach. It allows firms to carefully plan expansion and is less likely to strain human and financial resources. When first-mover advantage is crucial and a high degree of competitive intensity prevails, such as when Microsoft introduces a new version of Windows software, the sprinkler approach is better. The sprinkler effect allows the company to enter all markets quickly but the main risk is the substantial resources needed and the difficulty of planning entry strategies into many diverse markets at the same time.

The marketing manager must also decide on which countries to consider. Their attractiveness is influenced by the customer base, the product or service and by geography, income, population and political climate.

Evaluating potential markets

Although the world is becoming flatter for globalised organisations, there is still some 'uniqueness'. However much nations and regions integrate their trading policies and standards, each nation still has unique features. A country's readiness for different products and services, and its attractiveness as a market, depend on its economic, political, legal and cultural environments.

Suppose a marketing manager has assembled a list of potential markets to enter. How does it choose among them? Many companies prefer to market to neighbouring countries because they understand these countries better and can control their costs more effectively. It's not surprising that Germany's largest trading partner is France, but it is interesting to note that its second largest trading partner is the United States. Germany's other export partners are the United Kingdom (8.4 per cent), Italy (7.4 per cent), the Netherlands (6.2 per cent), Austria (5.3 per cent), Belgium (5.0 per cent), and Spain (4.9 per cent).[77] The two largest US export markets are Canada and Mexico, while Swedish companies often choose their Scandinavian neighbours – Finland and Norway.

At other times, *psychic proximity* determines choices. Many US firms prefer to sell in Canada, England, and Australia – rather than in larger markets such as Germany and France – because they feel more comfortable with the language, laws and culture. Companies should be careful, however, in choosing markets according to cultural distance. Besides overlooking potentially better markets, firms may perform superficial analysis of some very real differences among countries and adopt predictable marketing actions that put them at a disadvantage.[78] Disney overlooked European cultural issues when it first introduced EuroDisney to France. It did not serve wine at lunch; and it organised for lunch to be served at 11.00 or 14.00, but Europeans like to eat at 13.00–13.30. Disney also assumed that Europeans would plan a week's holidays to Disneyland but this was seen as a two-day visit event for many European guests. The company had to learn quickly and has now redeveloped most of its marketing, including its service process design, its staffing and pricing. EuroDisney now has more visitors than the Eiffel Tower in Paris.

It often makes sense to operate in fewer countries, with a deeper commitment and penetration in each. In general, a company prefers to enter countries: (1) that rank high on market attractiveness; (2) that are low in market risk; and (3) in which it possesses a competitive advantage.

Marketing insight

Understanding the European Union

The challenges of marketing management in Europe

A marketing manager must know and understand their market and customers. Within Europe, that means understanding the range of markets within the Continent.

A 2007 report, 'The single market: a vision for the 21st century' by the UK Treasury/DTI noted that Europe is now the largest free market in the world, with a population of over 490 million accounting for 20 per cent of world trade. After the 2004 enlargement, there are now around 20 official languages in the EU.[79] Unlike the United States, where there is one dominant language – English (though it must be noted that over 14 per cent or 41 million people actually speak Spanish) – the European Union has many languages, cultures and geographic diversity. This provides both unique opportunities and challenges for European marketing managers.

The multicultural aspects of contemporary Europe provide challenges for marketers. Marketing managers have to design marketing mix programmes that reflect these issues and address various unique national markets within Europe. For example, a study found that people in Italy – a country where society is based more on personal contacts with consumers – were much less likely to accept self-service and automatic machines for customer-level contacts than people in Northern Europe, where customers were more accepting of distance in the service process and welcome automated channels and self-service technologies.[80]

These challenges can be turned into opportunities. Consider the Proton car from Volkswagen, which will cater for a growing gap in the car market.

▶ **Marketing insight** *(continued)*

▽ **Volkswagen and the Islamic car**

The Malaysian national car manufacturer Proton, which is to become part of German automotive giant Volkswagen,[81] is building the world's first Islamic car for Muslim consumers. In 2006 the global population was 6.3 billion people, 1.7 billion of whom were Muslims.[82] It was estimated that the European Union's Muslim population in 2006 was 16 million people. The country with the largest percentage of Muslims in western Europe is France, whose population comprises 8–10 per cent Muslim people. The Islamic car has features such as a built-in compass that will allow occupants to determine the direction of Mecca in order to pray. It also has a special box for carrying a copy of the Koran and a separate compartment for headscarves. It will be produced for the European market in Turkey.[83] Within Europe, the cohort of potential consumers represents a large target market. While per capita car ownership is currently low in most Islamic countries it is predicted that there will be a significant increase by 2030. Turkey is one of the largest Muslim car-buying markets in the world.[84] Volkswagen's Proton marketing managers listened to their customers and perceived a religious/cultural gap in the market. They have tailored their product to meet the needs and wants of Muslim consumers not only in Europe, but around the world.

Companies marketing in Europe face 2000 years of historical and cultural differences, and a daunting mass of local rules. Italians eat chocolate for breakfast, the French croissants, the Germans cheese and ham, the Polish *chleb* (bread), and an assortment of *szinki* (cold meats), while the English often enjoy a fry-up with eggs, bacon, sausages and baked beans.

The EU creates an additional set of legal considerations for marketers. Essentially, firms are regulated by the EU and the member states in which they operate. From a marketing perspective EU legislation aims to impose uniform quality, safety and operating practices in the marketing process. It is important for marketers to be familiar with the decision-making processes in the EU and the different categories of legislation. EU law can affect marketers in many ways including market research, planning, product and service strategy, promotion and pricing among others. For example, Sweden and Norway do not permit any television advertising to be directed towards children under 12 and no advertisements at all are allowed during children's programmes. Austria does not permit advertising during children's

programmes, and in the Flemish region of Belgium, no advertising is permitted five minutes before or after programmes for children. Sponsorship of children's programmes is not permitted in Denmark, Finland, Norway and Sweden while in Germany and the Netherlands, although it is legal it is not used in practice. Britain has the highest level of advertising to children with no restrictions.[85]

Before engaging in strategic marketing planning, companies must examine the relevant EU policy. The EU has restrictions in relation to competition law, personal data, research and segmentation, product liability and product safety, metric labelling, promotion and communication, including online and web standards, as well as regulations relating to distribution and pricing.[86] In creating marketing and business objectives, marketers may unintentionally create marketing plans that run counter to legal and ethical standards. The high cost of failing to comply with competition law was evident when Dutch brewers Heineken, Grolsch and Bavaria were fined €273 million by the European Union for operating a beer cartel in Holland.[87]

Deciding on the marketing mix programme

Marketing managers must decide how much to adapt their marketing strategy to local conditions.[88] This will be explored in greater detail throughout the text. At one extreme are marketing managers that use a globally *standardised marketing mix* worldwide. Standardisation of the

Table 2.5 The differences between global and glocal marketing

Global marketing	Glocal marketing
Strategic level	Strategic, tactical and operative levels
Wider scope	Wide/narrow scope
Standardisation	Standardisation/adaptation
Homogenisation	Homogenisation/tailoring
Similarities	Similarities/differences
Concentration	Concentration/diffusion
Dependence	Dependence/independence
Synchronisation	Synchronisation/flexibility
Integration	Integration/separation

Source: G. Svensson (2002) Beyond global marketing and the globalization of marketing activities, *Management Decision*, 40(6), 574–83. Copyright © Emerald Publishing Group Ltd. Reproduced with permission.

product or service, communication, and distribution channels promises the lowest costs. Table 2.5 summarises some pros and cons of standardising versus glocalisation of the marketing mix programme. At the other extreme is an *adapted marketing mix,* where the producer or service provider, consistent with the marketing concept, holds that consumer needs vary and tailors marketing mix programmes to each target group.

As the table above illustrates, glocal marketing recognises that there needs to be a balance between local and global marketing activities. In other words glocal consumer segments are where consumers seek products and services of a global quality but which reflect local lifestyles – which have a 'local soul'.[89]

The development of the World Wide Web, the rapid spread of cable and satellite TV around the world, and the global linking of telecommunications networks have led to a convergence of lifestyles. Increasingly common needs and wants have created global markets for standardised products, particularly among the young middle class. When both forces prevail to some extent, a 'glocal' strategy that standardises certain elements and localises others can be the way to go (for instance with telecommunications). As this is often the case, many marketers seek a blend of centralised global control from corporate headquarters with input from local and regional marketers.

Although many companies have tried to launch their version of a world product or service, most products or service require at least some adaptation. Consumer behaviour can differ dramatically across markets. Toyota's Corolla car model will exhibit some differences in styling. European models were sold as the Corolla GT with DOHC engines and fixed Levin-style headlights. The Middle East received the same basic model as the North American market, with pop-up headlights and the regulated 5 mph (8 km/h) bumpers. Even Coca-Cola is sweeter or less carbonated in certain countries.

One of the lowest per capita consumers of carbonated soft drinks is Italy, but Italy is one of the highest per capita drinkers of bottled water, with 203 litres, whereas the United Kingdom consumes only 23 litres per person annually. When it comes to beer, Ireland and the Czech Republic lead the pack, with 157 and 131 litres per capita respectively, and France is among the lowest, consuming 36 litres per capita annually.[90]

▽ Managing in developing markets

One of the sharpest distinctions in global marketing is between developed and developing or less mature markets such as Brazil, Russia, India, China, (Bric countries) along with Indonesia and South Africa.[91] Many market leaders rely on developing markets to fuel their growth, and marketing managers must look to these markets for development potential.

Marketing insight

Spotlight on key developing markets

Brazil

The vast majority of people in Latin America have little to spend. According to the World Bank, 25 per cent live on less than €1.40 a day, and many millions more earn only a few hundred euros a month. In Brazil, the region's biggest market and the 12th largest economy in the world, low-income groups make up 87 per cent of the population, but earn only 53 per cent of the income. Marketers in the region are finding innovative ways to sell products and services to these poor and low-income residents.

Nestlé Brazil saw sales of Bono cookies jump 40 per cent after it shrank the package from 200 grams to 140 grams while lowering the price. Recognising that illiteracy is a problem, Unilever launched a brand of soap in north-east Brazil with the simple name, 'Ala'. Brazilian firms that have succeeded internationally include brewer and beverage producer AmBev, which merged with Interbrew to form Imbev; aircraft manufacturer Embraer; national airline Varig and sandal maker Havaianas. The world famous Rio Carnival and world champion football team have helped create an image of fun and physical fitness for Brazil.

Brazil has already experienced some 'go-go' growth years in the 1960s and 1970s, when it was the world's second-fastest-growing large economy. It also differs from other emerging markets in being a full-blown democracy, unlike Russia and China, and has no serious disputes with neighbours, unlike India. But Brazil's growth in recent years has been slower, and a number of obstacles exist that are popularly called *custo Brasil* (the cost of Brazil). For example, the cost of transporting products eats up nearly 13 per cent of Brazil's GDP, five percentage points more than in the United States. Most observers see Brazil's economic, social and political transformation as still a work in progress.

Russia

Russia has seen a recent rise in foreign investment and, importantly, not just in its traditionally strong markets in natural resources such as oil and gas. Dutch brewer Heineken, Swedish retailer IKEA, US banker Citibank and more than a dozen car manufacturers have ramped up operations in Russia. Their target is Russia's growing middle class, which expanded from 8 million in 2000 to 55 million in 2006 and now accounts for over one-third of the population. The mood in the country has become more upbeat too – the share of Russians who think life is 'not bad' has risen to 23 per cent in 2006 from just 7 per cent in 1999. Salaries are rising fast, savings are

comparatively low, and consumer credit is increasingly available even for small purchases.

But not everyone has participated in this increased prosperity. The average Russian earns €208 a month, about 10 per cent of the European average, and only a third own cars. Many elderly feel they have been left behind, as do those who live far from Moscow, the capital. Concerns about the business climate remain. Although the economy has produced 7 per cent annual growth in GDP, the Organisation for Economic Cooperation and Development (OECD) cautions that economic reforms have been stagnant, and ranks Russia as one of the most corrupt countries in the world. Many feel the government has been unpredictable and sometimes difficult to work with.

Motorola's experience in Russia is instructive. In 2006, 167,500 Motorola handsets were seized on arrival at Moscow airport, alleged to be smuggled and counterfeit, to violate a Russian patent, and to be a danger to public health. Around 50,000 were supposedly destroyed by the interior ministry, though some were later said to have turned up on the black market. Eventually most of the handsets were returned, but perhaps more telling was Motorola's reaction. With Russia being the company's third-biggest handset market in the world (behind the United States and China), Motorola takes a fairly sanguine attitude to the ups and downs inherent in doing business there and plans to stay the course.

India

India's recent growth rate has been as explosive as its neighbour China's. Reforms in the early 1990s that significantly lowered barriers to trade and liberalised capital markets have brought booming investment and consumption. But it's not all about demand. With its large numbers of low-cost, high-IQ, English-speaking employees, India is snapping up programming and call centre jobs once held by other workers in a wave of outsourcing that shows no signs of stopping. By 2008, IT services and back-office work in India will swell fivefold, to a €36 billion annual export industry employing 4 million people and accounting for 7 per cent of India's GDP.

While India's ascent inevitably means lost jobs for white-collar workers, it also means a larger market for Western goods – and pain for traditional Indian families. Along with training in accents and geography, India's legions of call centre employees are absorbing new ideas about family, material possessions and romance and questioning conservative traditions. They want to watch Hollywood movies, listen to western music, chat on mobile phones, buy on credit rather than save, and eat in restaurants or cafés. They are being targeted relentlessly by companies that have waited to see India develop a western-style consumer class.

India still struggles with poor infrastructure and highly restrictive labour laws. Its retail channel structure, although improving, still lags. The quality of public services – education, health, provision of water – is also often lacking. But all these obstacles have not prevented global firms such as Mittal, Reliance, Tata, WiPro and Infosys from achieving varying degrees of international success.

China

China's 1.3 billion people have marketers scrambling to gain a foothold there, and competition has been heating up between domestic and international firms. Initial gains in the Chinese market didn't necessarily spell long-term success for many international firms. After investing to establish the markets, foreign pioneers in television sets and motorcycles saw domestic Chinese firms emerge as rivals. In 1995, virtually all mobile phones in China were made by global giants Nokia, Motorola and Ericsson. Within ten years, their market share had dropped to 60 per cent. China's 2001 entry into the World Trade Organization has eased manufacturing and investment rules and modernised retail and logistics industries. Greater competition in pricing, products and channels have resulted.

Selling in China means going beyond the big cities to the 700 million potential consumers who live in small villages, towns and cities in the rural interior. About half of potential PC buyers live outside major cities; only one-third of overall retail revenues come from China's 24 largest cities. Rural consumers can be challenging though, as they have lower incomes, are less sophisticated buyers, and often cling to local cultural and buying habits.

Luxury cars, however, are the fastest-growing segment of the auto market thanks to China's growing ranks of millionaires and booming stock market and economy. China's emerging middle class consists of more active and more discerning consumers who demand higher-quality products.

South Africa

One of the toughest places in the world to do business is Africa. According to the World Bank, of the 35 least business-friendly countries, 27 are in sub-Saharan Africa. Sierra Leone imposes harsh taxes; in the Democratic Republic of Congo, registering a business takes 155 days and costs almost five times the average Congolese's annual income of €75; and in Angola, enforcing a contract takes over 1000 days. To avoid all the government red tape and restrictions, 42 per cent of the region's economy is informal, the highest proportion in the world. Bad roads – if there are roads at all – a lack of reliable electricity and volatile currency fluctuations add to the logistical and financial challenges. War, famine, AIDS and disaster are even more significant human difficulties.

But some successful businesses are emerging, especially in banking, retailing and mobile telephones, and many are using South Africa as a launch pad. Although many Africans are poor, they will still pay for what they need. Mobile phone operator Celtel invested in rural services by introducing the Me2U service, by which callers could send airtime credit to other mobile phones. Because most Africans don't have bank accounts, it has become a convenient and cheap way to transfer money, even replacing cash in some villages. South Africa's MTN, the largest mobile phone operator in the region, built its own microwave transmission backbone and power supplies in Nigeria, and the first solar payphone in Lake Victoria, Uganda. South Africa's Net 1 has built a customer base of 3.6 million accounts by issuing free smart cards to indigent people who have no bank accounts or credit cards, taking tiny percentages of their transactions for revenue.

The pay-off for companies willing to deal with the complications and risk associated with doing business in Africa is often large margins and a lack of competition. SABMiller, the world's second-largest brewer, enjoys its best operating margins (over 42 per cent) in Africa. Local knowledge is key, and South African companies are well placed to take advantage of opportunities. Finding a local partner can help in terms of expertise and contacts. SABMiller's African operations are joint ventures with locals, some of them government.

Sources: *Brazil:* A. Regalado (2007) Marketers pursue the shallow-pocketed, *Wall Street Journal*, 26 January; Land of promise, *The Economist*, 12 April 2007; M. Campanelli (2006) Marketing to Latin America? think Brazil, *DMNEWS*, 20 June. *Russia:* J. Bush (2006) Russia: how long can the fun last?, *BusinessWeek*, 18 December, pp. 50–1; Dancing with the bear, *The Economist*, 3 February 2007, pp. 63–4. *India:* M. Kripalani and P. Engardio (2003) The rise of India, *BusinessWeek*, 8 December, pp. 66–76; J. Slater (2004) Call of the west, *Wall Street Journal*, 2 January, p. A1; India on fire, *The Economist*, 3 February 2007, pp. 69–71. *China:* D. Roberts (2007) Cadillac floors it in China, *BusinessWeek*, 4 June, p. 52; B. Einhorn (2007) Grudge match in China, *BusinessWeek*, 2 April, pp. 42–3; R. Flannery (2007) Watch your back, *Forbes*, 23 April, pp. 104–5; D. Roberts (2007) Cautious consumers, *BusinessWeek*, 30 April, pp. 32–4; S.-H. Park and W. R. Vanhonacker (2007) The challenge for multinational corporations in China: think local, act global, *MIT Sloan Management Review*, May; D. Roberts (2007) Cadillac floors it in China, *BusinessWeek*, 4 June, p. 52; D. Roberts (2007) Scrambling to bring crest to the masses, *BusinessWeek*, 25 June, pp. 72–3. *South Africa:* The flicker of a brighter future, *The Economist*, 9 September 2006, pp. 60–2; H. Coster (2006) Great expectations, *Forbes*, 12 February, pp. 56–8; Going global, *The Economist*, 15 July 2006, pp. 59–60.

The unmet needs of the emerging or developing world represent huge potential markets for food, clothing, shelter, consumer electronics, appliances, and many other products and services. Eight out of ten people in the world now live in developing countries, a number that will increase to nine in less than 20 years. By 2025, the developing world will be home to 7.2 billion of a forecast global population of 8 billion. This so-called 'Bottom of the pyramid', includes more than 4 billion people, or about 60 per cent of the world's population. Many of these people have only about €1.40 a day in disposable income, but their sheer numbers translate into immense purchasing power, especially for the food industry.

▽ Nivea

Beiersdorf, the Hamburg-based cosmetics company that owns the Nivea brand, routinely undertakes market research on Chinese, Thai or Indonesian consumers so that they can form an impression of the way they live. Peter Kleinschmidt, a member of the executive board of Nivea, is convinced that 'Asia, as well as eastern Europe and South America, are among the most important engines of economic growth.'[92] He has seen Nivea products being sold from trees in Vietnam. In 2007, Beiersdorf's found that its Chinese operations grew by almost 50 per cent and its sales reached €90 million. It expects the Chinese market to grow by leaps and bounds in the future.[93] Beiersdorf's new factory near Shanghai will be opened in 2009, and will begin its operations at an initial annual capacity of 12,500 tons of personal care products. The German company also plans to move into the Asian hair care market and recently spent €270 million to acquire an 85 per cent stake in China's second-largest manufacturer of hair care products. 'It would be a sign of western arrogance to assume that consumers in China or Brazil have been waiting for generations to finally be blessed with our German products,' says Kleinschmidt. He speaks from experience. In Korea, for instance, Beiersdorf's attempt to introduce a face care product based on a western formula was a failure, and a skin care line containing rice and lotus ingredients, a big seller in Germany, where it is marketed as one of the secrets of Asian beauty, was met with derision by Asian focus groups.

Developed nations and the prosperous parts of developing nations account for about 20 per cent of the world's population. Can marketers serve the other 80 per cent, which has much less purchasing power, and living conditions ranging from mild deprivation to severe deficiency?[94] This imbalance is likely to get worse, as more than 90 per cent of future population growth is projected to occur in the less developed countries.

Successfully entering developing markets requires a special set of skills and plans. Consider how the following companies pioneered ways to serve these 'invisible' consumers:[95]

- The Fiat Palio is a supermini designed by the Italian manufacturer Fiat. Fiat developed this 'world' car, the Palio, which was designed as a low-cost, low-specification car for consumers in developing nations. The car is produced in Brazil, India, Turkey, South Africa and China, as well as in other countries.
- M-Banking is a promising service in countries such as Kenya where there are only 500 bank offices but 10 million mobile phones. Poor people in remote areas of the country have no access to banks and mobile phones now enable the transfer of money.
- Colgate-Palmolive tours Indian villages with video vans that show the benefits of toothbrushing.
- In India, German consumer products maker Henkel sells miniature packages of its 'Pril' dishwashing detergent for 1 rupee apiece, or a little less than 2 cents.[96]
- Another innovation is a mobile phone that, though lacking complex functions, contains a built-in flashlight – a valuable feature in countries where power outages are a daily occurrence.[97]

Many market-leading firms are relying on developing markets to fuel their future growth. Fiat, for example, sells its Palio car only in developing countries such as India.

Source: Courtesy of the Fiat Group

- Nokia has developed a mobile phone with a dust-resistant keypad for the Indian market.
- In Ghana, the Swiss company Nestlé sells shrimp-flavoured instant soup cubes for 2 cents apiece while other seasoning cubes have been reformulated to suit African palates. According to Nestlé, the flavour of fermented beans is in great demand in African countries.

These marketers capitalise on the potential of developing markets by changing their conventional marketing practices.[98] Marketing in developing areas can't be 'business as usual'. Economic and cultural differences abound; a marketing infrastructure may barely exist; and local competition can be surprisingly stiff.[99] In China, PC maker Lenovo, mobile phone provider TCL and appliance manufacturer Haier have thrived despite strong foreign competition. Besides their detailed understanding of Chinese tastes, these companies have vast distribution networks, especially in rural areas. Competition is also growing from other developing markets. China has exported cars to Africa, south-east Asia and the Middle East. Tata of India, Cemex of Mexico and Petronas of Malaysia have emerged from developing markets to become strong multinationals selling in many countries.[100]

Of consumers in emerging markets, 80 per cent buy their products from tiny bodegas, stalls, kiosks and small shops not much bigger than a closet, which Procter & Gamble calls 'high-frequency stores'. Smaller packaging and lower sales prices are often critical when incomes and housing space are limited. Unilever's 4-cent sachets of detergent and shampoo have been a big hit in rural India, where 70 per cent of the country's population still lives. When Coca-Cola moved to a smaller, 200 ml bottle in India, selling it for 10–12 cents in small shops, bus stop stalls and roadside eateries, sales jumped.[101]

▽ Danone

In Bangladesh, French food giant Danone recently partnered with Muhammed Yunus's Nobel prize-winning microcredit organisation, Grameen Bank, to make and market low-cost, nutrionally fortified yogurts under the brand name Shoktidoi. The joint venture will provide income to thousands of local farmers who supply the milk (and who raise cows by borrowing small amounts of money from Grameen), and to villagers who distribute the yoghurt. At 8 cents per 80 gram pot, Shoktidoi will not result in profits for Danone right now. Yet the firm is confident tangible returns will match the intangible returns of feeding the poor. Danone has transformed Bangladesh into a laboratory in which it develops new food products for malnourished children in very poor countries, but it could also churn out new products there for mature and richer markets, all at low cost.[102]

The challenge is to think creatively about how marketing can fulfil the dreams of most of the world's population for a better standard of living.

▽ Conclusion

Marketing management skills are diverse and challenging, ranging from managing relationships within and across companies and to those at the customer interface. The skill set needed ranges from technology and information management to leadership, planning and organising skills. Managing marketing nowadays often involves some level of international or global marketing and the ensuing challenges. The developing world offers unique challenges to marketing practitioners.

▽ SUMMARY

1 Management is a universal discipline that is only now beginning to change from the hierarchical focus of the past to the new networked, team-based organisation of the future.

2 The skills needed for marketing are diverse and are unique to each situation, though the move to more analytical marketing aligned to creative marketing and the need for innovation in marketing are core requirements.

3 Managing the external environment of networks, relationships and interactions is a core role of marketing. Marketers need to overview the core network of relationships that the firm has and to manage them for maximum benefit to all.

4 Marketing is not a task undertaken only by the marketing department. Marketing needs to affect every aspect of the customer experience. To create a strong marketing organisation, marketers must think like executives in other departments, and executives in other departments must think more like marketers.

5 In deciding to go abroad, a company needs to define its international marketing objectives and policies. The marketing manager must determine whether to market in a few countries or many countries. They must decide which countries to consider. In general, the candidate countries should be rated on three criteria: market attractiveness, risk and competitive advantage.

6 Once a company decides on a particular country, it must determine the best mode of entry. Its broad choices are indirect exporting, direct exporting, licensing, joint ventures and direct investment. Each succeeding strategy involves more commitment, risk, control and profit potential.

7 The developing world provides unique opportunities but also challenges for marketing managers who must be aware of local needs while operating globally.

▽ APPLICATIONS

Marketing debate

What are the core marketing management skills needed? Do these differ from the skills needed by other managers?

Marketing discussion

Global marketing produces unique management challenges. Critically evaluate the challenges of marketing globally and specifically in the developing world.

▽ REFERENCES

[1]G. Hamel (2007) Break free, *Fortune*, 1 October, 156(7), 119–24.

[2]P. Drucker (2003) New trends in management become grounded in basic principles, *Executive Excellence*, 20(8), 8–9.

[3]P. Drucker (2003) Future of management: start seeing change as a golden opportunity, *Executive Excellence*, 20(5), 3.

[4]Ibid.

[5]First described by Henri Fayol (1841–1925).

[6]S. Crainer and D. Dearlove (2004) *Financial Times Handbook of Management*, Harlow, England: Pearson Education.

[7]H. Mintzberg (1973) *The Nature of Managerial Work*, New York: HarperCollins College Division. See also H. Mintzberg (2007) *Mintzberg on Management*, New York: Free Press.

[8]M. B. Wood (2005) *The Marketing Plan: A Handbook,* 2nd edn, Harlow, England: Pearson Prentice Hall; W. Knight, Behind every successful product is a good marketing plan, themarketingsite.com (retrieved from www.themarketingsite.com/live/content.php?Item_ID=3849).

[9]D. Fodness (2005) Rethinking strategic marketing: achieving breakthrough results, *Journal of Business Strategy*, 26(3), 20–34.

[10]G. McGovern, D. Court, J. Quelch and B. Crawford (2004) Bringing customers into the boardroom, *Harvard Business Review*, November, 1–10.

[11]A. Greenyer (2006) Back from the grave: the return of modelled consumer information, *International Journal of Retail & Distribution Management*, 34(2/3), 212–19.

[12]B. Allred, K. Boal and W. Holstein (2005) Corporations as step-families: a new metaphor for explaining the fate of merged and acquired companies, *Academy of Management Executive*, 19(3), 23–37. M. McDonald (2002) *Marketing Plans: How to Prepare Them, How to Use Them,* London: Butterworth Heinemann.

[13]H. Mintzberg (1994) The fall and rise of strategic planning, *Harvard Business Review*, January, 397–405.

[14]See www.iht.com/articles/2001/03/16/swissair.2.php?page=2.

[15]See www.iwim.uni-bremen.de/publikationen/pdf/W028.pdf.

[16]F. E. Webster, Jr., A. J. Malter and S. Ganesan (2005) The decline and dispersion of marketing competence, *Sloan Management Review*, 46(4), 35–43.

[17]P. Kotler (2004) A three part plan for upgrading your marketing department for new challenges, *Strategy and Leadership*, 32(5), 5–9.

[18]P. Drucker (2003) Future of management: start seeing change as a golden opportunity, *Executive Excellence*, 20(5), 3.

[19]Ibid.

[20]R. Martin (2008) How successful leaders think, *Harvard Business Review*, June, 1–8.

[21]See http://fp05-527.web.dircon.net/ikea_company_profile.html.

[22]See http://www.forbes.com/lists/2007/10/07billionaires_The-Worlds-Billionaires_Rank_print.html.

[23]Ibid.

[24]See http://money.aol.com/forbes/general/most-frugal-billionaires?photo=3.

[25]See http://www.brainyquote.com/quotes/authors/i/ingvar_kamprad.html.

[26]See http://en.wikipedia.org/wiki/IKEA.

[27]As Webster (2005, p. 25) op. cit. stated.

[28]R. Rawlinson (2006) Beyond brand management, *Strategy+Business*, Summer (www.strategy-business.com/press/freearticle/06205).

[29]B. Ardley (2006) Situated learning and marketing; moving beyond the rational technical thought cage, *Marketing Intelligence & Planning*, 24(3), 202–17.

[30]O. Gok (2007) Marketing and marketing managers in the new era: a relational perspective, *Journal of American Academy of Business*, 10(2), 218–24.

[31]M. Baker (2007) Guest Lecturer, Trinity College Dublin; S. Dann (2006) Exploring the cross compatibility of the Andreasen (1995) definition of social marketing and the AMA (2004) definition of commercial marketing, www.philica.com (retrieved from http://philica.com/display_article.php?article_id=62);

S. Macaulay and G. Clark (1998) Creating a customer-focused culture: some practical frameworks and tools, *Managing Service Quality*, 8(3), 183–8.

[32]J. Egan (2006) Sidelined? the future of marketing in the contemporary organisation, *Irish Journal of Management*, 27(2), 99–119 and Webster et al. (2005) op. cit.

[33]McGovern et al. (2004) op. cit.

[34]P. McCole (2004) Refocusing marketing to reflect practice: the changing role of marketing for business, *Marketing Intelligence & Planning*, 22(5), 531–9; A. Tapp (2004) A call to arms for applied marketing academics, *Marketing Intelligence & Planning*, 22(5), 579–90.

[35]S. Baker and S. Holt (2004) Making marketers accountable: a failure of marketing education?, *Marketing Intelligence & Planning*, 22(5), 557–67.

[36]C. K. Prahalad and V. Ramaswamy (2003) The new frontiers of experience innovation, *MIT Sloan Management Review*, 44(4), 12–18.

[37]G. Bruce and G. Schoenfeld (2006) Marketers with MBAs: bridging the thinking-doing divide, *Marketing Intelligence & Planning*, 24(3), 257.

[38]Gok (2007) op. cit.

[39]A. McAfee (2006) Mastering the three worlds of information technology, *Harvard Business Review*, 84(11), 141–9.

[40]See http://en.wikipedia.org/wiki/Blog.

[41]R. Nolan (1973) Computer data bases: the future is now, *Harvard Business Review*, September–October, 98–112; R. Nolan (1985) Managing the advanced stage of computer technology: key research issues, in W. McFarlan (ed.) *Information System Research Challenges*, Boston, MA: Harvard Business School Press; R. Nolan (1998) Connectivity and control in the year 2000 and beyond, *Harvard Business Review*, July–August, 3–14. M. Brady, M. Sanan and N Tzokas (2002) Integrating information technology into marketing practice. The IT reality of Contemporary marketing practice, Journal of Marketing Management, 18 (5–6) 555–77.

[42]See www.businessweek.com/magazine/content/04_26/b3889402.htm.

[43]U. Schultze and W. Orliwinski (2004) A practice perspective on technology-mediated network relations: the use of internet-based self-serve technologies, *Information Systems Research*, 15(1), 87–106.

[44]R. Brodie, R. Brooks and M. Brady (2003) How information technologies impact on marketing practices: reinforcing versus enhancing and transforming. Proceedings of European Marketing Academy Conference (EMAC), University of Strathclyde, Scotland, CD-ROM.

[45]M. Brady and M. Saren (2005) A framework for ICT within contemporary marketing practice: the information and interaction dimensions, Academy of Marketing (UK) Conference, Dublin, July, CD-ROM, Paper No. 414.

[46]M. R. Fellenz and M. Brady (2008) Managing the innovative deployment of information and communication technologies (ICTs) for global service organisations, International Journal of Technology Marketing, 3(1), 39–55. L. Po-Chien and Bou-Wen Linb (2006) Building global logistics competence with Chinese OEM suppliers, *Technology in Society*, 28(3), 333–348.

[47]E. Gummesson (2007) *Total Relationship Marketing*, 2nd edn, Oxford: Butterworth Heinemann.

[48]L.-G. Mattsson and J. Johanson (2006) Discovering market networks, *European Journal of Marketing*, 40(3/4), 259–75.

[49]R. J. Brodie, N. E. Coviello and H. Winklhofer (2008) Contemporary marketing practices research program: a review of the first decade, *Journal of Business and Industrial Marketing*, 23(2), 84–94.

[50]Gummesson (2007) op. cit.

[51]Ibid.

[52]Ibid.

[53]E. Gummesson (1999) *Total Relationship Marketing*, Boston, MA: Butterworth-Heinemann; R. McKenna (1991) *Relationship Marketing*, Reading, MA: Addison-Wesley; M. Christopher, A. Payne and D. Ballantyne (1991) *Relationship Marketing: Bringing Quality, Customer Service, and Marketing Together*, Oxford: Butterworth-Heinemann.

[54]J.C. Anderson, H. Hakansson and J. Johanson (1994) Dyadic business relationships within a business network context, *Journal of Marketing*, October, 1–15.

[55]N. Nic, R. Lusch, Z. Zacharia and W. Bridges (2008) Competent collaborations, *Marketing Management*, March/April, 19–24.

[56]P. Kotler (2004) A three part plan for upgrading your marketing department for new challenges, *Stategy and Leadership*, 32(5), 4–9.

[57]C. von Hoffman (2006) Armed with intelligence, *Brandweek*, 29 May, 17–20.

[58]A. Lockett and I. Blackman (2004) Conducting market research using the Internet: the case of Xenon Laboratories, *Journal of Business & Industrial Marketing*, 19(3), 178–87.

[59]P. Drucker (2003) The future of management: start seeing change as a golden opportunity, *Executive Excellence*, 20(5), 3.

[60]M. Porter (1996) What is strategy?, *Harvard Business Review*, November–December, 61–78.

[61]L. Berry, V. Shankar, J. Turner Parish, S. Cadwallader and T. Dotzel (2006) Creating new markets through service innovation, *MIT Sloan Management Review*, 47(2), 56–63.

[62]See Innovation Leaders website, Profile: Virgin Atlantic (retrieved from http://fp05-527.web.dircon.net/va_company_profile.html).

[63]The Data Warehousing Institute™ (TDWI) (1999) Virgin Atlantic Airways: leveraging information to keep frequent flyers in their skies, *What Works*, 7, May (www.tdwi.org/research/display.aspx?ID=5483).

[64]R. H. Hartley (2006) *Marketing Mistakes and Successes*, 10th edn, Hoboken, NJ: John Wiley and Sons.

[65]P. Pae (2005) A plane as big as the globe, *Los Angeles Times*, 17 January.

[66]Hartley (2006) op. cit.

[67]Pae (2005) op. cit.

[68]In Webster's (2005) op. cit.

[69]G. McGovern and J. Quelch (2005) Outsourcing marketing, *Harvard Business Review*, 83(3), 22–6.

[70]Ibid.

[71]Ibid.

[72]J. Johanson and F. Wiedersheim-Paul (1975) The internationalization of the firm, *Journal of Management Studies*, October, 305–22.

[73]O. Moen, M. Gavlen and I. Endresen (2004) Internationalization of small, computer software firms: entry forms and market selection, *European Journal of Marketing*, 38(9/10), 1236–51.

[74]J. Bell (1997) A comparative study of the export problems of small computer software exporters in Finland, Ireland and Norway, *International Business Review*, 6(6), 585–604 and N. Coviello and H. Nunro (1997) Network relationships and the internationalisation process of small software firms, *International Business Review*, 6(4), 361–86.

[75]M. R. Czinkota and I. A. Ronkainen (1999) *International Marketing*, 5th edn, New York: Harcourt Brace Jovanovich.

[76]For a timely and thorough review of academic research on global marketing, see J. K. Johansson (2002) Global marketing: research on foreign entry, local marketing, global management, in B. Weitz and R. Wensley (eds.) *Handbook of Marketing*, London: Sage Publications, pp. 457–83. Also see J. K. Johansson (2003) *Global Marketing*, 2nd edn, New York: McGraw-Hill. For some global marketing research issues, see S. Douglas and S. R. Craig (2000) *International Marketing Research*, 2nd edn, Upper Saddle River, NJ: Prentice Hall.

[77]See http://en.wikipedia.org/wiki/Economy_of_Germany.

[78]Johansson (2002) op. cit.

[79]See http://ec.europa.eu/publications/booklets/move/45/en.doc.

[80]A. Lorenzon, P. J. Van Baaten and L. Pilotti (2005) Marketing knowledge management in strategic adoption of CRM solutions: global support of applications in Europe. Department of Economics, University of Milan, Italy, Departmental Working Paper No. 2005-03.

[81]See http://news.bbc.co.uk/1/hi/world/asia-pacific/7089707.stm.

[82]See www.islamicpopulation.com/world_islam.html.

[83]Reuters India (2007) Malaysia, Iran, Turkey plan 'Islamic' car – report, *Reuters India*, 11 November (http://in.reuters.com/article/businessNews/idINIndia-30439720071111).

[84]Lost compass, *The Economist*, 15 November, 2007 (www.economist.com/business/displaystory.cfm?story_id=10150353).

[85]Advertising to children; UK the worst in Europe, *Food Magazine* (UK), January–March 1997 (www.mcspotlight.org/media/press/food_jan97.html).

[86]D. Thorne LeClair (2000) Marketing planning and the policy environment in the European Union, *International Marketing Review*, 17(3), 193–207.

[87]Ibid.

[88]S. Zou and S. T. Cavusgil (2002) The GMS: a broad conceptualization of global marketing strategy and its effect on firm performance, *Journal of Marketing*, 66, 40–56; T. Levitt (1983) The globalization of markets, *Harvard Business Review*, May–June, 92–102; B. Wysocki, Jr. (1997) The global mall: in developing nations, many youths splurge, mainly on U.S. goods, *Wall Street Journal*, 26 June, p. A1; What makes a company great?, *Fortune*, 26 October 1998, pp. 218–226; D. M. Szymanski, S. G. Bharadwaj and P. R. Varadarajan (1993) Standardization versus adaptation of international marketing strategy: an empirical investigation, *Journal of Marketing*, October, 1–17; Burgers and fries a la francaise, *The Economist*, 17 April 2004, pp. 60–1; Johansson (2002) op. cit.

[89]T. Khanna and K. G. Palpeu (2006) Emerging giants: building world-class companies in developing countries, *Harvard Business Review*, October, 2–10.

[90]See www.beverageworld.com

[91]According to the *CIA World Factbook* (https://www.cia.gov/library/publications/the-world-factbook/index.html), there are 34 developed countries: Andorra, Australia, Austria, Belgium,

Bermuda, Canada, Denmark, Faroe Islands, Finland, France, Germany, Greece, Holy See, Iceland, Ireland, Israel, Italy, Japan, Liechtenstein, Luxembourg, Malta, Monaco, Netherlands, New Zealand, Norway, Portugal, San Marino, South Africa, Spain, Sweden, Switzerland, Turkey, United Kingdom and United States. They note that DCs are similar to the new International Monetary Fund (IMF) term 'advanced economies' that adds Hong Kong, Singapore, South Korea and Taiwan but drops Malta, Mexico, South Africa and Turkey.

[92]J. Bonstein (2008) European firms eye developing world, *BusinessWeek*, 16 January (www.businessweek.com/globalbiz/content/jan2008/gb20080116_886509.htm?campaign_id=rss_daily).

[93]Ibid.

[94]See www.populationmedia.org/issues/issues.htm.

[95]Adapted from V. Mahajan, M. V. Pratini De Moraes and J. Wind (2000) The invisible global market, *Marketing Management*, Winter, 31–5. See also Khanna and Palepu (2006) op. cit.

[96]Bonstein (2008) op. cit.

[97]Ibid.

[98]C. K. Prahalad (2005) *The Fortune at the Bottom of the Pyramid: Eradicating Poverty Through Profits*, Upper Saddle River, NJ: Wharton School Publishing; N. Dawar and A. Chattopadhyay (2002) Rethinking marketing programs for emerging markets, *Long Range Planning*, 35, 457–74.

[99]B. J. Bronnenberg, J.-P. Dubé and S. Dhar (2007) Consumer packaged goods in the United States: national brands, local branding, *Journal of Marketing Research*, 44, February, 4–13; B. J. Bronnenberg, J.-P. Dubé and S. Dhar (2007) National brands, local branding: conclusions and future research opportunities, *Journal of Marketing Research*, 44, February, 26–8; B. J. Bronnenberg, J.-P. Dubé and S. Dhar (2007) Market structure and the geographic distribution of brand shares in consumer package goods industries, Working Paper, UCLA Graduate School of Management.

[100]S. Hamm and D. Roberts (2006) China's first global capitalist, *BusinessWeek*, 11 December, pp. 52–7; B. Einhorn (2007) Grudge match in China, *BusinessWeek*, 2 April, pp. 42–3; R. Flannery (2007) Watch your back, *Forbes*, 23 April, pp. 104–5; The fast and the furious, *The Economist*, 25 November 2006, pp. 63–4.

[101]M. Kripalani (2003) Finally, Coke gets it right, *BusinessWeek*, 10 February, p. 47; M. Kripalani (2002) Battling for pennies in India's villages, *BusinessWeek*, 10 June, p. 22-E7.

[102] The bottom of the pyramid is where the real gold is hidden, *Marketing Week*, 8 February 2007, p. 18; A. Jones (2006) Danone and Yunus extend partnership food production, *Financial Times*, 19 December, p. 19; P. Betts (2007) Danone's taste for microfinance pays dividends, *Financial Times*, 30 March, p. 24.

Chapter 3

Developing marketing strategies and plans

IN THIS CHAPTER, WE WILL ADDRESS THE FOLLOWING QUESTIONS:

1   How does marketing affect customer value?
2   How is corporate and divisional strategic planning carried out?
3   How is business unit strategic planning carried out?
4   What is involved in developing a marketing plan?

Key ingredients of the marketing management process are insightful, creative marketing strategies and plans that can guide marketing activities. Developing the right marketing strategy over time requires a blend of discipline and flexibility. Firms must stick to a strategy but also constantly find new ways to improve it. Increasingly, marketing must also develop strategies to deliver customer value for a range of products and services (market offerings) within the organisation.

A highly successful business-to-business marketer, Siemens, for instance, must continually design and implement marketing activities at many levels and for many units of the organisation.

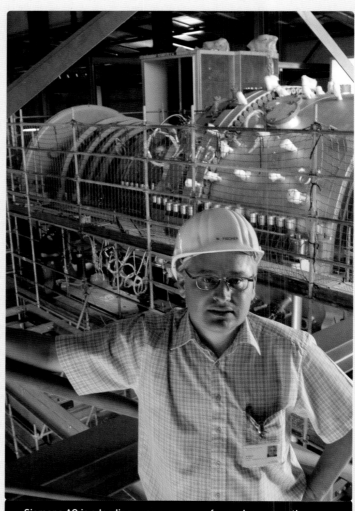

Siemens AG is a leading energy company focused on a growth strategy.
Source: Courtesy of Siemens AG / Agency: Publicis-München

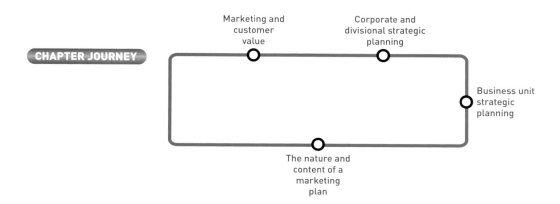

Siemens AG is one of the largest global electronics and engineering companies in the world, with 460,000 employees in 190 countries and worldwide sales of US $96 billion in fiscal year 2005. During 2005, Siemens grew organically through new product innovation and was the world's fifth largest corporate spender in research and development. Siemens also grew through strategic acquisition in the areas of medical imaging, clean-coal technology, pollution control, wind power and water technologies. New CEO Klaus Kleinfeld was faithful to his vow that problem businesses would be fixed, sold or closed, divesting the money-losing cellular handset unit to Taiwan's BenQ Corp. and realigning the ailing telecommunications network equipment unit in a joint venture with global handset supplier giant Nokia.[1]

This chapter begins by examining the main strategic marketing implications in creating customer value. This is followed by a review of the relationship between corporate strategy and divisional marketing strategy. Once the divisional marketing strategy has been set it is up to marketers in the operating parts or business units to develop marketing plans that will be both effective (in that they deliver the right customer value) and efficient in terms of resources. The chapter ends with some advice on how to draw up a formal marketing plan that is keyed into the architecture of the book.

▽ Marketing and customer value

Many in the United States, with notable exceptions, have tended to view marketing from a product oriented transactional standpoint. In Europe, practitioners have traditionally tended to place a greater emphasis on customer relationship concepts (see Chapter 1). Both viewpoints in basic economics terms emphasise the importance of satisfying customers' needs and wants. The UK's Chartered Institute of Marketing (CIM) defines marketing as 'the management process of anticipating, identifying and satisfying customer requirements profitably' (CIM, 2001). In today's European buyers' markets the task of any business is to form lasting relationships with customers by delivering customer-perceived value at a profit (see Chapter 11). In hyper-competitive economies with increasingly rational buyers faced with abundant choices, a company succeeds by fine tuning the value-delivery process and choosing, providing and communicating superior customer-perceived value (see Chapter 11).

Business environment paradigm change

The main consequences for organisations of the transition from sellers' to buyers' markets are:

- competition that really bites;
- customers usually demand more (perceived-value) for their money;
- customers have choice;
- a transformation in the concept of value which is now heavily influenced by the buyers;
- markets fragmenting into segments that appeal to customers who have distinct perceived-value requirements.

In sellers' markets (Figure 3.1) companies strive to increase the volume of goods and services supplied and to reduce costs as much as possible. This has been termed the *least-cost production paradigm* or the pursuit of *efficiency*. This understanding of the business process, however, will not be as successful in buyers' markets. Wise competitors seek to be *effective* by discovering through market research what customers value and then use their resources as efficiently as possible to supply it. Sensible competitors acknowledge the need to deliver customer-perceived value successfully. This realisation inspired a new view of business processes, which places marketing at the *beginning* of corporate planning. Instead of emphasising making and selling, companies now see themselves as part of a process that delivers personalised market offerings.

The value delivery process

A common view of marketing is that a firm makes something and then sells it. In this view, marketing takes place in the second sequence of the process. Companies that hold this belief have the best chance of succeeding in economies marked by goods shortages (sellers' markets), where consumers are not fussy about quality, features or style.

As Figure 3.2 shows the value delivery process involves four sequences. The first sequence, discovering the required value (see Parts 1, 2 and 3 of this text), represents the research marketing must do before any marketable value offering exists. Marketing practitioners segment the market, select the appropriate target market, and develop the offering's *customer-perceived value* positioning (see Chapter 10). The formula 'segmentation, targeting, positioning (STP)' is the essence of strategic marketing. Once the business unit has discovered the customer-perceived value (see Chapter 11), the second sequence involves developing a suitable customer offering (see Parts 4 and 5 of this text). Marketers put together a package of specific product

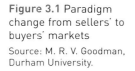

Figure 3.1 Paradigm change from sellers' to buyers' markets

Source: M. R. V. Goodman, Durham University.

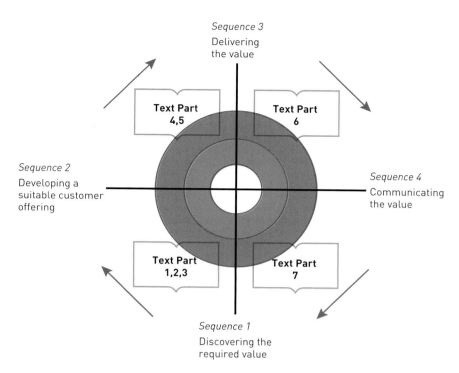

Sequence 3
Delivering
the value

Sequence 2
Developing a
suitable customer
offering

Sequence 4
Communicating
the value

Sequence 1
Discovering the
required value

Text Part
4,5

Text Part
6

Text Part
1,2,3

Text Part
7

Figure 3.2 Repetitive
sequences of the value
delivery process
Source: M. R. V. Goodman,
Durham University.

and service benefits at appropriate price levels. The third sequence concerns successfully delivering the value packages (see Part 7 of this text). The final sequence is about successfully communicating the value offerings to targeted customers. As buyers' markets are highly competitive these sequences need to be repeated continuously if a company is to achieve a market advantage. In this sense the sequences resemble the action that occurs in a four cylinder car engine.

Following nearly two generations of sellers' markets businesses have suddenly become exposed to buyers' markets. The stable conditions of sellers' markets (unsaturated markets) have given way to the challenging conditions posed by rampant buyer's markets.

▽ Nike

Critics of Nike often complain that its shoes cost almost nothing to make, yet cost the consumer so much. True, the raw materials and manufacturing costs of training shoes are relatively cheap, but marketing them to the consumer is expensive. Materials, labour, shipping, equipment, import duties and suppliers' costs are less than €25 a pair. Compensating the sales team, distributors, administration and endorsers, as well as paying for advertising and R&D, adds €15 or so to Nike's total. Nike sells to retailers to make a profit of say €7. The retailer therefore pays roughly €47 to put a pair of Nike's on the shelf. When we factor in the retailer's overhead (typically €30 covering human resources, lease and equipment), along with a €10 profit, the shoes cost the consumer over €80.

London Business School's Nirmalya Kumar has set forth a '3Vs' approach to marketing: (1) define the value segment or customers (and their needs); (2) define the value proposition; and (3) define the value network that will deliver the promised service.[2] Webster views marketing in terms of: (1) *value-defining processes* such as market research and company self-analysis; (2) *value-developing processes* including new product development, sourcing strategy and vendor selection; and (3) *value-delivering processes* such as advertising and managing distribution.[3] Gale[4]

Figure 3.3 The generic value chain

Source: From M. E. Porter (1985) *Competitive Advantage. Creating and Sustaining Superior Performance*, New York: Free Press. Copyright © 1985 by Michael E. Porter. Reproduced with permission from The Free Press, a division of Simon & Schuster Adult Publishing Group.

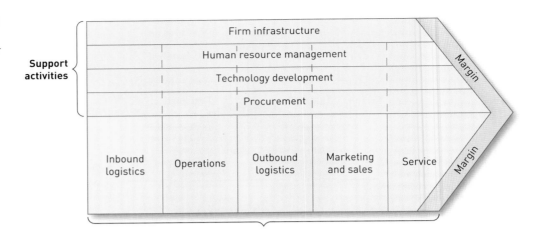

sees marketing as a business process that identifies and delivers high levels of *market-perceived value*, which he defines as *market-perceived quality* relative to *market-perceived price*. Kotler is in agreement with this view but refers to it as *customer-perceived value*. Marketing is ultimately about firms successfully answering the question: why should customers buy from them?

The value chain

Porter has proposed the **value chain** as a tool for identifying ways to create more customer-perceived value (see Figure 3.3).[5] According to this model, every firm is a synthesis of activities performed to design, produce, market, deliver and support its final market offering. The value chain identifies nine strategically relevant activities – five primary and four support activities – that create value and cost in a specific business.

The *primary activities* consist of inbound and outbound logistics. Inbound logistics refers to bringing materials into the business's operations and converting them into final saleable products and operations. Outbound logistics include shipping out final products, marketing them, and includes sales and servicing support activities. The *support activities* – procurement, technology development, human resource management and firm infrastructure – are handled in specialised departments. The firm's infrastructure covers the costs of general management, planning, finance, accounting, legal and government affairs.

The firm's task, whether large or small, is to examine its costs and performance in each value-creating activity and seek ways to make improvements. Managers should estimate their competitors' costs and performances as *benchmarks* against which to compare their own costs and performance. Additionally, they should go further and study the 'best practice' as exhibited by the world's best companies.[6]

▽ Toyota

Having become the leading automotive manufacturer in the world and on the eve of its 70th year Toyota unveiled its Global Vision 2020 in November 2007. The announced investment plan revealed Toyota's intention to invest heavily in cutting-edge technologies and to continue its policy of making its value chain ever more effective and efficient. Toyota has become an iconic manager of the modern *keiretsu* – a network of mutually supportive companies. The company's *keiretsu*, which comprises group companies, several large component manufacturers and many hundreds of smaller suppliers, sustains a relationship that would be hard to match elsewhere. The *keiretsu* corporate family creates an environment of trust that acts as a dynamic driver for constantly improving the value chain. Toyota continues to enjoy a strong sales performance in Europe.[7]

The firm's success depends not only on how well each functional department performs its work, but also on how well the company coordinates departmental activities to conduct *core business processes*.[8] These core business processes include:

- **The market sensing process:** All the activities in gathering market intelligence, disseminating it within the organisation, and acting on the information.
- **The new offering realisation process:** All the activities in researching, developing and launching new high-quality offerings quickly and within budget.
- **The customer acquisition process:** All the activities in defining target markets and prospecting for new customers.
- **The customer relationship management process:** All the activities in building deeper understanding, relationships and offerings for individual customers.
- **The fulfilment management process:** All the activities in receiving and approving orders, shipping the goods on time and collecting payment.

Strong companies are re-engineering their work flows and building cross-functional teams to be responsible for each process.[9] At Xerox, a Customer Operations Group links sales, shipping, installation, service and billing so these activities flow smoothly into one another. Winning companies are those that excel at managing core business processes through cross-functional teams. 3M's Technical Training organisation[10] has made cross-functional teamworking a part of its training curriculum for professional/technical employees involved in new product development. In the company's Industrial Specialties Division, the whole business is effectively managed by means of cross-functional teamworking. Each product family, for example adhesives, fasteners, urethane films is run by cross-functional teamworking that involves people from the laboratories, manufacturing and marketing. Motorola, Nissan and Polaroid provide further examples of well-known companies marketing in Europe that have reorganised their employees into cross-functional teams which are also found in both non-profit and government organisations (see Chapter 21).

To be successful, a firm also needs to look for competitive advantages beyond its own operations, in the value chains of suppliers, distributors and customers. Many companies today have partnered with specific suppliers and distributors to create a superior value delivery network (see Chapter 17).

Asda uses cross-functional teams to encourage and facilitate creativity and innovation.

Source: Courtesy of Asda

Core competencies

Traditionally, companies owned and controlled most of the factors of production that shaped their businesses – land, labour and capital. Prahalad and Hamel[11] have urged managers to look not only at their physical resources but also at the unique skills and knowledge embedded in their organisations and to stick to what they do best.[12] However, this efficiency argument was open to question soon after it entered the business arena as it failed to fully take into account the entire impact of emerging global buyers' markets and the Internet. This has led to a fundamental change in business architecture and companies and suppliers have increasingly begun to collaborate to form value chains to deliver researched customer value offerings (see Chapter 17).

One important key, then, is to own and nurture the resources and competencies that make up the *essence* of the business. Nike, for example, does not manufacture its own shoes, because Asian manufacturers are more cost efficient in this task. Instead it nurtures its superiority in shoe design and merchandising, which are its two core competencies. A **core competency** has three characteristics: (1) it is a source of competitive advantage in that it makes a significant contribution to customer-perceived value; (2) it has applications in a wide variety of markets; and (3) it is difficult for competitors to imitate.[13]

Competitive advantage also accrues to companies that possess distinctive capabilities such as Apple's iPhones, Dyson's vacuum cleaners and Telma's electronic braking retarders. Whereas 'core competencies' refers to areas of special technical and production expertise, *distinctive capabilities* describes excellence in broader business processes. The chief executive of Microsoft speaking at the annual financial analyst meeting in July 2007 stated that in today's fast paced business environment Microsoft would have 'to have multiple competencies and multiple business models all living in one body'.[14]

▽ ILVA – venture unfulfilled

When the Danish home store ILVA arrived in the United Kingdom it was billed as a furniture retailer that could potentially compete successfully with IKEA by offering a new purchasing experience. It was going to revolutionise the furniture market with its contemporary ranges and four upmarket shops. The company proudly proclaimed, 'We think that furniture should look good, cost less and last for ages.' It offered a wide range of furniture and accessories at affordable prices, and put its eclecticism down to its being 'inspired by cultures from around the world'. The 10,000-item strong range features such strange delights as cow-hide floor throws and authentic vinewood tables, with exclusive individual touches such as mosquito bites on the hide of some leather items. The merchandise is more expensive than IKEA but cheaper than that of Habitat.

ILVA was established in 1974 and, like IKEA, has its roots deep in Scandinavia. It now enjoys the popular prestige of being the second largest furniture and homeware retailer in Denmark. Stores in Sweden and Denmark have won civic architectural awards and been hailed as some of the most beautiful modern buildings in Northern Europe. However, initially the venture was a failure in the UK as the market was not researched effectively. ILVA's offerings were viewed by inquisitive customers who visited its stores as being too expensive, and much of its furniture was seen as too large to fit into many UK homes. Furthermore, early customers were badly let down by poor customer service.

In many respects it is reminiscent of Marks & Spencer's similar ill-fated venture that cost them more than £30 million. Even before the UK stores opened ILVA ran up losses of £11.5 million and in August 2007 the troubled retailer was sold to an Icelandic furniture group that owns rival UK furniture retailer The Pier.

Wise companies research the market, especially foreign ventures, before proceeding to realise a dream. Initially the dream fell flat in the United Kingdom but the new ownership repositioned the business and launched a new TV advertising campaign in the spring of 2008. However in June 2008, after running up huge losses, exacerbated by the decline in the UK furniture market – caused by a declining housing market and dwindling customer confidence – ILVA announced it had made a strategic withdrawal from the United Kingdom. The company will continue to operate stores in Denmark and Sweden.[15]

Furniture retailer ILVA ran up £11.5 million worth of losses before opening in the United Kingdom and after a revamping exercise went into administration in June 2008.
Source: Dean Houlding/Rex Features

How can companies avoid the disappointment suffered by ILVA? According to Day, market-driven organisations excel in three distinctive capabilities: market sensing, customer linking and channel bonding.[16] In terms of market sensing, he believes that tremendous opportunities and threats often begin as 'weak signals' from the 'periphery' of a business. He offers a systematic process for developing peripheral vision, and practical tools and strategies for building 'vigilant organisations' attuned to changes in the environment, by asking questions in three categories[17] (see Table 3.1).

Another important key is the extent to which competitive advantage results from how well the company has fitted its core competencies and distinctive capabilities into customer-perceived value offerings. Competitors have difficulty imitating companies such as Dell, IKEA, Red Bull and L'Oréal because they are unable to copy their activity systems.

Table 3.1 Becoming a vigilant organisation

- *Learning from the past*
  - What have been our past blind spots?
  - What instructive analogies do other industries offer?
  - Who in the industry is skilled at picking up weak signals and acting on them?
- *Evaluating the present*
  - What important signals are we rationalising away?
  - What are our mavericks, outliers, complainers and defectors telling us?
  - What are our peripheral customers and competitors really thinking?
- *Envisioning the future*
  - What future surprises could really hurt or help us?
  - What emerging technologies could change the game?
  - Is there an unthinkable scenario that might disrupt our business?

Source: G. S. Day and P. J. H. Schoemaker (2006) *Peripheral Vision: Detecting the Weak Signals That Will Make or Break Your Company*. Cambridge, MA: Harvard Business School Press. Reproduced with permission.

Business realignment may be necessary to maximise core competencies. It has three steps: (1) (re)defining the business concept or 'big idea'; (2) (re)shaping the business scope; and (3) (re)positioning the company's brand identity. Consider what Kodak is doing to realign its business.

▽ Kodak

With the advent of the digital era and consumers' new capacity to store, share and print photos using their PCs, Kodak faces more competition than ever, both in-store and online. In 2004, after being dumped from the Dow Jones Industrial Average Index, in which it had occupied a place for more than 70 years, the company started the painful process of transformation. It started off by expanding its line of digital cameras, printers and other equipment, and it also set out to increase market share in the lucrative medical imaging business. Making shifts is not without challenges, however. The company announced in the summer of 2006 that it would outsource the making of its digital cameras. Kodak also eliminated 15,000 jobs in 2006, with more layoffs projected for the rest of the decade, and it spent money acquiring a string of companies for its graphics communications unit. Not only must Kodak convince consumers to buy its digital cameras and home printers, but it must also become known as the most convenient and affordable way to process digital images. So far, the company faces steep competition from Sony, Canon and Hewlett-Packard.[18]

The final key to successfully applying core competencies in order to develop customer value offerings is the extent to which corporate attitudes have changed to reflect the importance of customer-perceived value. That is, to move from customisation of offerings to personalisation of customer offerings. As Professor Prahalad says 'this is not best practice, it is next practice'.[19]

A holistic marketing orientation and customer value

A holistic marketing orientation can also help capture customer-perceived value. One view of **holistic marketing** sees it as 'integrating the value exploration, value creation, and value delivery activities with the purpose of building long-term, mutually satisfying relationships and

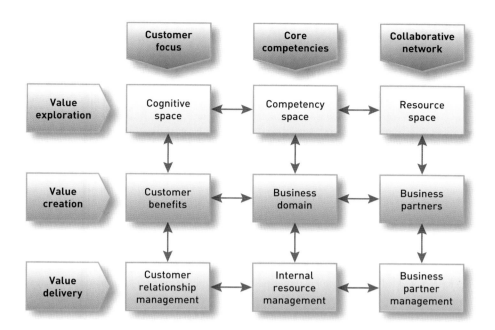

Figure 3.4 A holistic marketing framework

co-prosperity among key stakeholders'. According to this view, holistic marketers succeed by managing a superior value chain that delivers a high level of product quality, service and speed. Holistic marketers achieve profitable growth by expanding customer share, building customer loyalty and capturing customer lifetime value. Figure 3.4, a holistic marketing framework, shows how the interaction between relevant actors and value-based activities helps to create, maintain and renew customer-perceived value.

The holistic marketing framework is designed to address three key management questions:

1 **Value exploration**: How can a company identify new value opportunities?

2 **Value creation**: How can a company efficiently create more promising new value offerings?

3 **Value delivery**: How can a company use its capabilities and infrastructure to deliver the new value offerings more efficiently?

Marketing practitioners might approach these questions as follows.

Value exploration Finding new value opportunities is a matter of understanding the relationships between three spaces: (1) the customer's cognitive space; (2) the company's competence space; and (3) the collaborator's resource space. The customer's *cognitive space* reflects existing and latent needs and includes dimensions such as the need for participation, stability, freedom and change.[20] A company's *competency space* can be described in terms of breadth – broad versus focused scope of business; and depth – physical versus knowledge-based capabilities. The collaborator's *resource space* includes horizontal partnerships, with partners chosen for their ability to exploit related market opportunities, and vertical partnerships, with partners who can serve the firm's value creation (see Chapter 11).

Value creation Value-creation skills for marketers include identifying new customer benefits from the customer's viewpoint; utilising core competencies from its business domain; and selecting and managing business partners from its collaborative networks. To create new customer benefits, marketers must understand what customers think about, want, do, and worry about and observe who they admire and interact with, and who influences them (see Chapters 6–8).

Value delivery Delivering value often means making substantial investments in infrastructure and capabilities. The company must think about customer relationship management, internal resource management and business partnership management. *Customer relationship management* (CRM) allows the company to discover who its customers are, how they behave, and what they need or want. It also enables the company to respond appropriately, coherently and quickly to different customer opportunities. To respond effectively, the company requires *internal resource management* to integrate major business processes, such as order processing, general ledger, payroll and production, within a single family of software modules. Finally, *business partnership management* allows the company to handle complex relationships with its trading partners to source, process and deliver products (see Chapters 11, 17 and 18).

The central role of strategic planning

Successful marketing thus requires companies to have capabilities such as understanding customer-perceived value, creating customer-perceived value, delivering customer-perceived value, capturing customer-perceived value, and sustaining customer-perceived value. Only a select group of companies stand out as master marketers: Procter & Gamble, Nike, Disney, Starbucks, Wal-Mart, Enterprise Rent-A-Car, McDonald's, Ritz-Carlton, and several Asian (Canon, Nissan, Samsung, Sony, Toyota) and European (IKEA, Club Med, Bang & Olufsen, Electrolux, Nokia, Lego, Tesco and Virgin) companies. 'Breakthrough marketing: Intel' describes how that company created customer-perceived value and built a brand in a category for which most people thought branding impossible.

These companies focus on the customer and are organised to respond effectively to changing customer needs. They all have a strong commitment to marketing through their companies. However, it is just as important for small companies to contemplate these capabilities. All of them can also be scaled to further their fortunes, for sound marketing management is not the preserve of large corporations.

To ensure that they select and execute the right activities, marketers must give priority to strategic planning in three key areas: managing a company's businesses as an investment portfolio, assessing each business's strength by considering the market's growth rate and the company's position and fit in that market, and establishing a strategy. For each business, the company must develop a suitable strategy for achieving its long-run objectives.

Most large companies consist of four organisational levels (see Figure 3.5): the corporate level, the division level, the business unit level and the product level. Corporate headquarters is responsible for designing a corporate strategic plan to guide the whole enterprise; it makes decisions on the amount of resources to allocate to each division, as well as on which businesses to acquire or divest. Each division establishes a plan covering the allocation of funds to each of its constituent business units. Each business unit develops a strategic plan to carry that business unit into a profitable future. Finally, each product level (product line, brand) within a business unit develops a marketing plan for achieving its objectives in its own product market.

The **marketing plan** is the central instrument for directing and coordinating the marketing effort. The marketing plan operates at two levels: strategic and tactical. The **strategic marketing plan** lays out the target markets and the customer-perceived value offerings the firm will offer, based on an analysis of the best market opportunities. The **tactical marketing plan** specifies the marketing tactics, including product features, promotion, merchandising, pricing, sales channels and service.

Today cross-functional teams develop the marketing plan with inputs from every important business function. Management then implements these plans at the appropriate levels of the organisation, monitors results, and takes any necessary corrective action. The complete planning, implementation and control cycle is shown in the Euromart marketing plan at the end of this chapter.

Planning will now be discussed at each of the four levels of an organisation in turn.

Breakthrough marketing

Intel

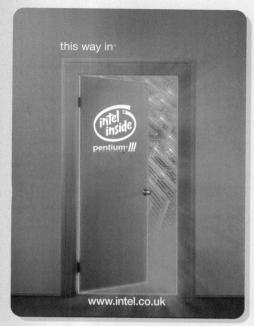

Advertisements such as this were part of Intel's strategy for building a brand in a product area where no brand name had existed before – microprocessors.

Source: The Advertising Archives

Intel makes the microprocessors that are found in 80 per cent of the world's personal computers. In the early days, Intel microprocessors were known simply by their engineering numbers, such as '80386' or '80486'. Intel positioned its chips as the most advanced. The trouble was, as Intel soon learned, numbers cannot be trademarked. Competitors came out with their own '486' chips and Intel had no way to distinguish itself from the competition. Worse, Intel's products were hidden from consumers, buried deep inside PCs. With a hidden, untrademarked product, Intel had a hard time convincing consumers to pay more for its high-performance products.

Intel's response was a marketing campaign that created history. The company chose the Pentium trademark and launched the 'Intel Inside' marketing campaign to build awareness of the brand and get its name outside the PC and into the minds of consumers.

Intel used an innovative cooperative scheme to extend the reach of the campaign. It would help computer makers who used Intel processors to advertise their PCs if the makers also included the Intel logo

in their advertisements. Intel also gave computer manufacturers a rebate on Intel processors if they agreed to place an 'Intel Inside' sticker on the outside of their PCs and laptops.

Intel continues its integrated ingredient campaigns to this day. For example, when launching its Centrino mobile microprocessor platform, Intel began with TV advertisements that aired in the United States and 11 other countries. These advertisements include the animated logo and now familiar five-note brand signature melody. Print, online and outdoor advertising followed shortly thereafter. Intel created eight-page inserts for major newspapers that urged the wired world to not only 'unwire', but also 'Untangle. Unburden. Uncompromise. Unstress.'

Intel even held a 'One Unwired Day' event that took place in major cities such as New York, Chicago, San Francisco and Seattle. In addition to allowing free trial wi-fi access, the company held festivals in each city that included live music, product demonstrations and prize giveaways.

The 'Unwired' campaign was another Intel success in marketing. The US$300 million total media effort for the Centrino mobile platform, which also included cooperative advertising with manufacturers, helped generate US$2 billion in revenue for Intel during the first nine months of the campaign.

Going forward, Intel launched a new brand identity in 2006, supported by a US$2 billion global marketing campaign. The company introduced a new logo with a different font and updated visual look and also created a new slogan: 'Leap Ahead'. In addition to the new logo and slogan, Intel developed a new microprocessor platform called Viiv (rhymes with 'five') aimed at home entertainment enthusiasts. These moves were designed to create the impression of Intel as a 'warm and fuzzy consumer company', with products that went beyond the PC. Intel remained one of the most valuable brands in the world, its US$32 billion brand valuation earning it fifth place in the 2006 Interbrand/*BusinessWeek* ranking of the best global brands.

Sources: C. Edwards (2004) Intel everywhere?, *BusinessWeek*, 8 March, 56–62; S. Van Camp (2004) ReadMe.1st, *Brandweek*, 23 February, 17; How to become a superbrand, *Marketing*, 8 January 2004, 15; R. Slavens (2003) Pam Pollace, VP-Director, Corporate Marketing Group, Intel Corp, *B to B*, 8 December, 19; K. Hein (2003) Study: new brand names not making their mark, *Brandweek*, 8 December, 12; H. Clancy (2003) Intel thinking outside the box, *Computer Reseller News*, 24 November, 14; C. L. Webb (2003) A chip off the old recovery?, *Washington Post*, 15 October (www.washingtonpost.com); Intel launches second phase of Centrino ads, *Technology Advertising & Branding Report*, 6 October; D. Kirkpatrick (2004) At Intel, speed isn't everything, *Fortune*, 9 February, 34; D. Clark (2005) Intel to overhaul marketing in bid to go beyond PCs, *Wall Street Journal*, 30 December.

Figure 3.5 The strategic planning, implementation and control processes

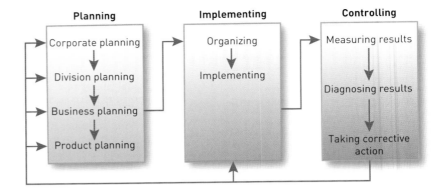

▽ Corporate and divisional strategic planning

Some corporations give their business units a great deal of freedom to set their own sales, profit goals and strategies. Others set goals for their business units but let them develop their own strategies. Still others set the goals and participate in developing individual business unit strategies.[21]

All corporate headquarters undertake four planning activities:

1   defining the corporate mission;

2   defining the business;

3   assigning resources to each **strategic business unit** (SBU);

4   assessing growth opportunities.

Defining the corporate mission

Organisations exist to accomplish their business interests by making cars, lending money, providing a night's lodging and so on. Over time the mission may change, to take advantage of new opportunities or respond to new market conditions. Amazon.com changed its mission from being the world's largest online bookstore to aspiring to become the world's largest online store. eBay changed its mission from running online auctions for collectors to running online auctions of all kinds of goods.

To define its mission, a company should address Drucker's classic questions:[22] What is our business? Who is the customer? What is of value to the customer? What will our business be? What should our business be? These simple-sounding questions are among the most difficult a company will ever have to answer. Successful companies continuously ask them and answer them thoughtfully and thoroughly.[23] An additional question for business to address in today's highly competitive markets is: Why should people bother to buy from them?

Organisations develop **mission statements** to share with managers, employees and (in many cases) customers. A clear, thoughtful mission statement provides employees with a shared sense of purpose, direction and opportunity. Mission statements are at their best when they reflect a vision, an almost 'impossible dream' that provides a direction for the company for the next 10–20 years. Sony's former president, Akio Morita, wanted everyone to have access to 'personal portable sound', so his company created the Walkman and portable CD player. Table 3.2 lists five sample mission statements.

Which of the mission statements opposite do you think would best impress their respective customers? Good mission statements have five major characteristics.

1   They focus on a limited number of goals. The statement 'We want to produce the highest-quality products, offer the most service, achieve the widest distribution and sell at the lowest prices' claims too much.

Table 3.2 Sample mission statements

BP

'We are taking action to close the competitive gap through a focused effort on our three priorities of safety, people and performance. We are determined to operate safely and reliably, to develop the capability of our people and to drive performance through restoring operational momentum.'

eBay

'We help people trade practically anything on earth. We will continue to enhance the online trading experiences of all – collectors, dealers, small businesses, unique item seekers, bargain hunters, opportunity sellers and browsers.'

Oticon

'Our mission

The professionals we work with across the globe and the specialists at Oticon share a common goal:

To assure that our hearing solutions provide the highest possible satisfaction.
To accomplish our mission, we continuously:

- Develop innovative and effective solutions
- Establish and build strong partnerships
- Share knowledge with professionals and hearing aid users.'

Philips

'We have a passion to improve the quality of people's lives through the timely introduction of meaningful technological innovations.'

Volvo

'To create the safest and most exciting car experience for modern families.'

Sources: Courtesy of BP, eBay, Oticon, Philips and Volvo. Reproduced with permission.

2 Mission statements stress the company's major policies, values and culture. They help employees to focus on the importance of working together to ensure that market offerings satisfy the company's customers.

3 They define the major competitive spheres within which the company will operate:

- **Industry:** Some companies will operate in only one industry; some only in a set of related industries; some only in industrial goods, consumer goods or services; and some in any industry. For example, DuPont prefers to operate in the industrial market, whereas ICI operates in both industrial and consumer markets.
- **Products and applications:** Firms define the range of products and applications they will supply. The mission of the crockery company Churchill is 'to be a leading provider to the tabletop market and deliver value through excellence in design, quality and customer service'.
- **Competence:** The firm identifies the range of technological and other core competencies it will master and leverage. Germany's Bosch cites its vision as 'creating value and sharing values' and its mission, 'as a leading technology and service company, we take advantage of our global opportunities for a strong and meaningful development. Our ambition is to enhance the quality of life with solutions that are both innovative and beneficial'.
- **Market segment:** The type of market or customers a company will serve is the market segment. Aston Martin makes only high-performance sports cars. Mothercare serves the baby and toddler market.
- **Vertical:** The vertical sphere is the number of channel levels, from raw material to final product and distribution, in which a company will participate. At one extreme are companies with a large vertical scope; at one time Ford owned its own rubber plantations, sheep farms, glass manufacturing plants and steel foundries. At the other extreme are 'hollow corporations' or 'pure marketing companies', such as some financial brokers who contract out or factor nearly everything.

- **Geographical:** The range of regions, countries or country groups in which a company will operate defines it geographical sphere. Some companies operate in a specific state. Others are multinationals such as Volkswagen and Unilever, which operate in almost every country in the world.

4 Mission statements take a long-term view. They should be enduring; management should change the mission only when it ceases to be relevant.

5 A good mission statement is ideally brief, flexible and distinctive. Good examples are Disney's 'to make people happy', 3M's 'to solve unsolved problems innovatively' and Wal-Mart's 'to give ordinary folk the chance to buy the same things as rich people'.

Compare the rather vague missions statements on the left with Google's mission statement and philosophy on the right.

To build total brand value by innovating.

To deliver customer value and customer leadership faster, better and more completely than our competition

We build brands and make the world a little happier by bringing our best to you

Google mission

To organise the world's information and
    make it universally accessible and useful

Google philosophy
Never settle for the best.

1 Focus on the user and all else will follow
2 It's best to do one thing really well
3 Fast is better than slow
4 Democracy on the Web works
5 You don't need to be at your desk to need an answer
6 You can make money without doing evil
7 There is always more information out there
8 The need for information crosses borders
9 You can be serious without a suit
10 Great just isn't good enough[24]

While few would argue with the prime purpose of a mission statement it is important for organisations to live up to the promises they declare. Avis's famous mission statement 'We try harder' provides a real challenge.[25]

Defining the business

Companies often define their businesses in terms of products: They are in the 'auto business' or the 'clothing business'. However, market definitions of a business are superior to product definitions. In other words, companies must see their business as a customer-satisfying process, not a goods-producing process. Products are transient; basic needs and customer groups endure forever. Transportation is a need: the horse and carriage, the automobile, the railroad, the airline and the truck are products that meet that need.

Viewing businesses in terms of customer needs can suggest additional growth opportunities. IBM redefined itself from a hardware and software manufacturer to a 'builder of networks'. Table 3.3 gives several examples of companies that have moved from a product to a market definition of their business. It highlights the difference between a target market definition and a strategic market definition.

Table 3.3 Product-oriented versus market-oriented definitions of a business

Company	Product definition	Market definition
BP	We sell fuels	We supply energy . . . beyond petroleum
Beiersdorf	We sell cosmetics (Nivea)	We sell beauty
EDF	We supply electricity	We supply energy
Renault	We sell automobiles	We supply personal and business transport vehicles
SNCF	We run a rail network	We are a people and goods mover
Xerox	We make copying equipment	We help improve office productivity

A target market definition tends to focus on selling a product or service to a current market. Pepsi could define its target market as everyone who drinks a cola beverage and competitors would therefore be other cola companies. A strategic market definition, however, focuses also on the potential market. If Pepsi considered everyone who might drink something to quench their thirst, their competition would also include non-cola soft drinks, bottled water, fruit juices, tea and coffee. To compete effectively, Pepsi might decide to sell additional beverages whose growth rate appears promising.

A business can define itself in terms of three dimensions: customer groups, customer needs and technology.[26] Consider a small company that defines its business as designing incandescent lighting systems for television studios. Its customer group is television studios; the customer's need is lighting; and the technology is incandescent lighting. The company might want to expand. It could make lighting for other customer groups, such as homes, factories and offices; or it could supply other services needed by television studios, such as heating, ventilation or air conditioning. It could design other lighting technologies for television studios, such as infrared or ultraviolet lighting.

Large companies normally manage quite different businesses, each requiring its own strategy. The Virgin Group has classified its businesses into seven strategic parts or strategic business units. An SBU has three characteristics:

1 It is a single business, or a collection of related businesses, that can be planned separately from the rest of the company.

2 It has its own set of competitors.

3 It has a manager responsible for strategic planning and profit performance, who controls most of the factors affecting profit.

The purpose of identifying the company's strategic business units is to develop separate strategies and assign appropriate funding. Senior management knows that its portfolio of businesses usually includes a number of 'yesterday's has-beens' as well as 'tomorrow's breadwinners'.[27]

Assigning resources to each SBU[28]

Once it has defined SBUs, management must decide how to allocate corporate resources to each. The 1970s saw several portfolio planning models introduced to provide an analytical means for making investment decisions. The American General Electric/McKinsey Matrix classifies each SBU according to the extent of its competitive advantage and the attractiveness of its industry. Management would want to grow, 'harvest' or draw cash from, or hold on to the business. Another model, the Boston Consulting Group's Growth-Market Share Matrix, uses relative market share and annual rate of market growth as criteria to make investment decisions.

Portfolio planning models such as these have fallen out of favour as oversimplified and subjective. More recent methods firms use to make internal investment decisions are based on shareholder value analysis, and whether the market value of a company is greater with an SBU or without it (whether it is sold or spun off). These value calculations assess the potential of a business based

Figure 3.6 The
strategic planning gap

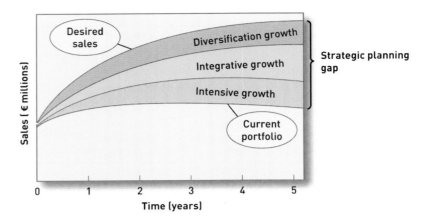

on potential growth opportunities from global expansion, repositioning or retargeting, and
strategic outsourcing. In layman's terms each SBU needs to make a positive contribution to the
perceived strength of the company. Unilever, for example, has over 100 SBUs and each one, such
as Dove, either does or is planned to (if it is a relatively new market offering such as Ben &
Jerry's) contribute positively to the corporate shareholder value.

Assessing growth opportunities

Assessing growth opportunities includes planning new businesses downsizing and terminating
older businesses. If there is a gap between future desired sales and projected sales, corporate management will have to develop or acquire new businesses to fill it.

Figure 3.6 illustrates this strategic planning gap for a major manufacturer of blank compact
disks called Musicale (name disguised). The lowest curve projects the expected sales over the next
five years from the current business portfolio. The highest curve describes desired sales over the
same period. Evidently, the company wants to grow much faster than its current businesses will
permit. How can it fill the strategic planning gap?

The first option is to identify opportunities to achieve further growth within current businesses
(intensive opportunities). The second is to identify opportunities to build or acquire businesses that
are related to current businesses (integrative opportunities). The third option is to identify opportunities to add attractive businesses unrelated to current businesses (diversification opportunities).

Intensive growth Corporate management's first course of action should be a review of opportunities for improving existing businesses. One useful framework for detecting new intensive
growth opportunities is called a 'product–market expansion grid' (Figure 3.7).[29]

The company first considers whether it could gain more market share with its current products in their current markets. Next it considers whether it can find or develop new markets for

	Current products	New products
Current markets	1 Market penetration strategy	3 Product development strategy
New markets	2 Market development strategy	(Diversification strategy)

Figure 3.7 Three intensive growth strategies: Ansoff's product–market expansion grid

Source: Adapted from I. Ansoff (1957) Strategies for diversification, *Harvard Business Review*, September–October.
Copyright © 1957 by the President and Fellows of Harvard College. All rights reserved. Reproduced with
permission.

its current products, in a market development strategy. Then it considers whether it can develop new products of potential interest to its current markets with a product development strategy. Later the firm will also review opportunities to develop new products for new markets in a diversification strategy.

▽ **Starbucks**

When Howard Schultz, Starbucks' CEO until 2000, came to the company in 1982, he recognised an unfilled niche for cafés serving gourmet coffee directly to customers. This became Starbucks' market penetration strategy and helped the company attain a loyal customer base in Seattle. The market development strategy marked the next phase in Starbucks' growth: it applied the same successful formula that had worked wonders in Seattle, first to other cities in the Pacific north-west, then throughout North America and, finally, across the globe. Once the company had established itself as a presence in thousands of cities internationally, Starbucks sought to increase the number of purchases by existing customers with a product development strategy that led to new in-store merchandise, including compilation CDs, a Starbucks Duetto Visa card that allows customers to receive points toward Starbucks purchases whenever they use it, and high-speed wireless Internet access at thousands of Starbucks 'HotSpots' through a deal with T-Mobile. Finally, Starbucks pursued diversification into grocery store aisles with Frappuccino® bottled drinks; Starbucks brand ice cream, and the purchase of tea retailer Tazo® Tea. Even a famous brand such as Starbucks cannot rest on its laurels in today's competitive buyers' markets. In February 2007 Howard Schultz was moved to accuse the company of losing their creativity. A survey in *Consumer Reports* magazine that February judged McDonald's coffee to be better than Starbucks.[30,31]

Howard Schultz of Starbucks waves after opening the company's first store outside North America in 1996. Today Starbucks' have stores across the globe.
Source: Koji Sasahara/AP/PA Photos

So how might Musicale use these three major intensive growth strategies to increase its sales? It could try to encourage its current customers to buy more by demonstrating the benefits of using compact disks for data storage in addition to music storage. Musicale could also try to attract competitors' customers if it noticed major weaknesses in competitors' products or marketing programmes. Finally, Musicale could try to convince non-users of compact disks to start using them.

How can Musicale use a market development strategy? First, it might try to identify potential user groups in the current sales areas. If Musicale has been selling compact disks only to consumer markets, it might go after office and factory markets. Second, it might seek additional distribution channels in its present locations. If it has been selling its disks only through stereo equipment dealers, it might add mass merchandising or online channels. Third, the company might consider selling in new locations in its home country or abroad. If Musicale sold only in Europe, it could consider entering the Middle Eastern market.

Management should also consider new product possibilities. Musicale could develop new features, such as additional data storage capabilities or greater durability. It could offer the CD at two or more quality levels, or it could research an alternative technology such as flash drives.

By examining these intensive growth strategies, managers may discover several ways to grow. Still, that growth may not be enough. In that case, management must also look for integrative growth opportunities.

Hit films offer opportunities for integrative growth. (In the movies, anything is possible!)
Source: Alex Oliveira/Rex Features

Integrative growth A business can increase sales and profits through backward, forward, or horizontal integration within its industry. For example, drug giant Merck has gone beyond just developing and selling ethical pharmaceuticals requiring a doctor's prescription. It purchased Medco, a mail-order pharmaceutical distributor, formed a joint venture with DuPont to establish more basic research, and began another joint venture with Johnson & Johnson to bring some of its ethical products into the over-the-counter market.

PepsiCo, the US-owned company, manufactures and markets a variety of carbonated and non-carbonated drinks, as well as salty or sweet grain-based snacks and other foods. The company has pursued a strategy of integral growth since its foundation in 1965. In Europe the company markets several well-known beverage brands including Pepsi Cola, 7 Up and Fiesta and in 1998 Tropicana was acquired. The company also has its own Bottling Group. Many consumers snack while refreshing themselves and the company has a wide portfolio of famous snack brands including Doritos, Quavers, The Smith's Snackfood Company, Walkers and Wotsits. In 2001 PepsiCo purchased Quaker Oats. The company has also formed partnerships with several brands to distribute these or to market them with their own brands.[32]

How might Musicale achieve integrative growth? The company might acquire one or more of its suppliers, such as plastic material producers, to gain more control or generate more profit through backward integration down the value chain. It might acquire some wholesalers or retailers, especially if they are highly profitable, in forward integration. Finally, Musicale might acquire one or more competitors, provided that the government does not bar this horizontal integration as part of its anti-monopoly policy. However, these new sources may still not deliver the desired sales volume. In that case, the company must consider diversification.

Diversification growth Diversification growth makes sense when good opportunities exist outside the present businesses – the industry is highly attractive and the company has the right mix of business strengths to be successful. For example, from its origins as an animated film producer, Walt Disney Company has moved into licensing characters for merchandised goods, entering the broadcast industry with its own Disney Channel as well as ABC and ESPN acquisitions, and developing theme parks and vacation and resort properties.

To understand how Group Danone has used internalisation to focus its growth strategy in the food products sector, visit www.pearsoned.co.uk/marketingmanagementeurope

▽ Diversification growth

Cisco Systems, Inc.

Known for years as a mass producer of rooters and switches, Cisco is attempting to diversify beyond these nuts and bolts products into the business of changing how consumers communicate and view television both in the United States and Europe. With its recent US$6.9 billion acquisition of Scientific-Atlanta, Inc., widely recognised for its expertise in video delivery, Cisco hopes to enter consumers' living rooms with items such as home-networking equipment, wirelessly networked DVD players, and services such as video on demand. The diversification move is already paying off: Scientific-Atlanta produced 7 per cent of Cisco's US$8 billion in revenue.[33]

Saltzgitter

Saltzgitter, the German steel group, is planning to diversify into a new area of business to be less dependent on the economic cycles of the steel industry. The company is particularly keen to add to their current operations in steel pipelines.[34]

PZ Cussons

PZ Cussons, the soap and detergents group, is transforming itself from a paternalistic Greek family-owned business into an international meritocracy. Rather than target global markets, the company tailors its products to local markets. It operates a completely different model to its main rivals such as Procter & Gamble and Unilever. It has a strong interest in the electrical goods market.

PZ Cussons sales in Africa rose from £211.8 million to £252.9 million boosted by a joint venture with Haier of China in the electrical goods market. The company has a plant in Nigeria to assemble goods such as refrigerators from parts made in China. It has now moved into flat-screen televisions, cookers and other goods. In June 2007 the company opened Hot Cool World, an electrical retailer mall in Lagos that is the first to offer Nigerians consumer credit facilities. This has countered a fall in sales in Asia from £113.9 million to £107.2 million, hurt by an decrease in the soap and detergent markets in Australia. Sales in Europe rose from £214.2 million to £217.8 million driven by a strong performance in the United Kingdom.[35]

Microsoft

Microsoft announced in July 2007 that it intended to diversify into new businesses such as advertising and consumer electronics as it believes that these will eventually grow to rival desktop and server software.[36]

Several types of diversification are possible for Musicale. First the company could choose a *concentric strategy*. This occurs when a company seeks to develop new products that have technological or marketing synergies with existing product lines, though the new products themselves may appeal to a different group of customers. Musicale might start a laser disk manufacturing operation as it knows how to make compact disks. Second, the company might use a *horizontal strategy* to search for new products that could appeal to current customers, even though the new products are technically unrelated to its current product line. For example, the company could produce compact disk cases, though they require a different manufacturing process. Finally, Musicale might decide to spread their risks by seeking new business opportunities that have no relationship to its current technology, products or markets (*a conglomerate strategy*) and review opportunities that may lie in markets such as, for example, application software or personal organisers.

Downsizing and divesting older businesses Weak businesses require a disproportionate amount of managerial attention. Companies must carefully prune, harvest or divest tired old businesses in order to release needed resources to other uses and reduce costs. In the face of serious difficulties Deutsche Telecom spun off its media and broadcast services business to a private equity-based European competitor in a deal worth €850 million. The German group has lost millions of fixed-line customers in recent years as rivals offered Internet-based telephone services and mobile phone services at prices Deutsche Telecom could not match. Telefonica, Spain's largest telecommunications group after three years of energetic activity, during which it paid €27 billion for O2 of the United Kingdom, has decided to consolidate its interests and develop its core business. Several of its non-core activities such as the television production business Endemol have been divested.[37]

▽ **Downsizing and divesting**

Danone

Paris-based Groupe Danone has grown by a series of acquisitions to become a leading player in the European food products sector. For some years the company's growth was the result of horizontal (market) and vertical (supply/value chain) acquisitions that did not seem to reflect a well-fashioned strategy. It embarked on a programme of internalisation. In the 1990s the incoming CEO sharpened the strategy and focused on the dairy, beverages and cereals sectors. End of year sales were up 5.9 per cent on 2006 and the group's consolidated net sales grow by 18.2 per cent from €6508 million in the first six months of 2007 to €7691 million for the first half of 2008.

PepsiCo

Over the last five decades PepsiCo has sold off several famous brands both in the United States and Europe, such as the fast-food restaurants Kentucky Fried Chicken, Pizza Hut and Taco Bell.[38]

Relationship between missions and visions

While missions are essentially concerned with what the company is about and how it behaves, visions are more associated with future corporate goals. Visions may be vague or precise but give the organisation a sense of purpose. Good business leaders create a vision for an organisation, articulate the vision, and motivate personnel to seek and achieve it (see also Chapter 6).

A vision and a mission can be one and the same but the concepts though related are not necessarily the same. Broadly speaking visions refer to future intentions and missions to delivering present ones. Both visions and missions are inspirational. Visions once achieved need to be restated. Missions, on the other hand, are continuous in that they encapsulate an organisation's purpose. A paradigm change from sellers' to buyers' markets challenges everything an organisation stands for and may require a complete and challenging evaluation of both vision and mission statements.

Organisation and organisational culture

(See also Chapters 15 and 21.)

Strategic planning happens within the context of the organisation. A company's organisation consists of its structures, policies and corporate culture, all of which can become dysfunctional in a rapidly changing business environment. Whereas managers can change structures and policies (with difficulty), the company's culture is very hard to change. Yet adapting the culture is often the key to successfully implementing a new strategy.

What exactly is a corporate culture? Most business people would be hard pressed to describe this elusive concept, which some define as 'the shared experiences, stories, beliefs and norms that characterise an organisation'. Yet, walk into any company and the first thing that strikes you is the corporate culture – the way people dress, talk to one another and greet customers.

A customer-centric culture can affect all aspects of an organisation. As one expert says,

> To me, being consumer centric is more a principle – the driving value of a company – than a process. It's in a company's DNA, top to bottom. It means you recognize the diversity across the face of consumers, and that you are open to observations and opinions other than your own; this allows you to be an advocate for the consumer – whether you are a leading innovator or packing boxes in the warehouse . . . The question is, do you see consumers as the driving life force of your company for as long as it exists, or do you see them as simply a hungry group of people that needs to be satisfied so your business will grow in the short term?[39]

Sometimes corporate culture develops organically and is transmitted directly from the CEO's personality and habits to the company employees. Sir James Dyson, the inventor of the Dual Cyclone bagless vacuum cleaner, and CEO of the company that carries his name, inspires his staff as he is a designer and an innovator in his own right[40] (see also Chapter 21).

Marketing innovation

Innovation in marketing is critical. The traditional view is that senior management hammers out the strategy and hands it down. Hamel offers the contrasting view that imaginative ideas on strategy exist in many places within a company.[41] Senior management should identify and encourage fresh ideas from three groups that tend to be under-represented in strategy making: employees with youthful

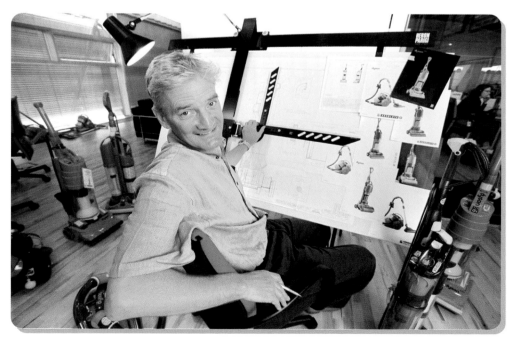

Research in Motion, the company that developed the Dyson Dual Cyclone bagless vacuum cleaner, fosters a culture of innovation that CEO Sir James Dyson carefully cultivates and values highly.
Source: Adrian Sherratt/ Alamy

perspectives; employees who are far removed from company headquarters; and employees who are new to the industry. Each group is capable of challenging company orthodoxy and stimulating new ideas. Jump Associates, a US innovative strategy firm, offers five key strategies for managing change in an organisation:[42]

1 **Avoid the innovation title:** Pick a name for the innovation team that won't alienate co-workers.
2 **Use the buddy system:** Find a like-minded collaborator within the organisation.
3 **Set the metrics in advance:** Establish different sets of funding, testing and performance criteria for incremental, experimental and potentially disruptive innovations.
4 **Aim for quick hits first:** Start with easily implemented ideas that will work to demonstrate that things can get done, before quickly switching to bigger initiatives.
5 **Get data to back up your gut feelings:** Use testing to get feedback and improve an idea. 'Marketing insight: Different approaches to innovative marketing' describes how some leading companies approach innovation.

For further discussion see Chapter 15.

Table 3.4 The 12 dimensions of business innovation

Dimension	Definition	Examples
Offerings (what)	Develop innovative new products or services	• Gillette Mach3Turbo razor • Apple iPod music player and iTunes music service
Platform	Use common components or building blocks to create derivative offerings	• General Motors OnStar telematics platform • Disney animated movies
Solutions	Create integrated and customised offerings that solve end-to-end customer problems	• UPS logistics services Supply Chain Solutions • DuPont Building Innovations for construction
Customers (who)	Discover unmet customer needs or identify underserved customer segments	• Enterprise Rent-A-Car focus on replacement car renters • Green Mountain Energy focus on 'green power'
Customer experience	Redesign customer interactions across all touch points and all moments of contact	• Washington Mutual Occasio retail banking concept • Cabela's 'store as entertainment experience' concept
Value capture	Redefine how company gets paid or create innovative new revenue streams	• Google paid search • Blockbuster revenue sharing with movie distributors
Processes (how)	Redesign core operating processes to improve efficiency and effectiveness	• Toyota Production System for operations • General Electric Design for Six Sigma (DFSS)
Organisation	Change form, function or activity scope of the firm	• Cisco partner-centric networked virtual organisation • Procter & Gamble front-back hybrid organisation for customer focus
Supply chain	Think differently about sourcing and fulfilment	• Moen ProjectNet for collaborative design with suppliers • General Motors Celta use of integrated supply and online sales
Presence (where)	Create new distribution channels or innovative points of presence, including the places where offerings can be bought or used by customers	• Starbucks music CD sales in coffee stores • Diebold RemoteTeller System for banking
Networking	Create network-centric intelligent and integrated offerings	• Otis Remote Elevator Monitoring service • US Department of Defense Network-Centric Warfare
Brand	Leverage a brand into new domains	• Virgin Group 'branded venture capital' • Yahoo! as a lifestyle brand

Source: M. Sawhney, R. C. Wolcott and I. Arroniz (2006) The 12 different ways for companies to innovate, *MIT Sloan Management Review*, 47(3), 78. Copyright © 2006 Massachusetts Institute of Technology. All rights reserved. Reproduced with permission.

Marketing insight

Different approaches to innovative marketing

In most markets there is too much sameness: too much safe differentiation between competitors. Go-ahead companies are constantly seeking ways to gain and sustain a strong market identity. This can be achieved by a commitment to the importance of new product development and by novel use of the tools of the marketing mix.

When IBM surveyed top CEOs and government leaders about their agenda priorities, their answers about innovation were revealing. Business-model innovation and coming up with unique ways of doing things scored high. IBM's own drive for business-model innovation led to much collaboration, both within IBM itself and externally with companies, governments and educational institutions. CEO Samuel Palmisano noted how the breakthrough Cell processor, based on the company's Power architecture, would not have happened without collaboration with Sony and Nintendo, as well as competitors Toshiba and Microsoft.

Procter & Gamble similarly has made it a goal for 50 per cent of the company's new products to come from outside the company's laboratories – from inventors, scientists and suppliers whose new product ideas can be developed in-house.

Similarly 3M, the US-based industrial and technology group whose products include Scotch tape and optical film, has been giving people 'tinkering time' for as long as anyone can remember. The reasoning is that 'exploring different areas is a very good way of keeping people inventive and keeping their imaginations fired up,' says the company's senior technical manager. One of 3M's most famous products, the Post-it note, was a result of tinkering.[43]

JCB

JCB have for several years developed an innovative marketing approach in a business-to-business industry that many would consider staid. It is famous for the use of events and stunts such as JCB dancing diggers. The tradition of innovative marketing continues today and the company promoted the launch of its JCB Dieselmax engine in August 2006 by using two high-performance versions of its new engine in a world record attempt for a diesel-powered vehicle in the United States. The JCB Dieselmax car reached 350.092 mph on the Bonneville Salt Flats in Utah. The company's marketing director, Chris Wright, says that supporting challenges such as the Dieselmax record not only raises the brand's profile but also helps to attract top engineers and puts a spotlight on British engineering.[44]

BMW (audio books)

To reach customers across the globe, the marketing department of BMW has decided to put less money and effort into traditional media such as television and newspapers. It is pioneering new ways of reaching customers, such as offering them the chance to download audio books and other material from the Internet.[45]

Facebook

In the fickle world of advertising trends, Facebook is enjoying the free marketing that comes from displacing MySpace and YouTube as the hippest online social network. However many people are starting to think that the program is starting to lose its appeal and in all likelihood will be replaced by a new online social network before long.[46]

Business writer C. K. Prahalad believes much innovation in industries, from financial and telecom services to health care and automobiles, can come from developments in emerging markets such as India. Forced to do more with less, Indian companies and foreign competitors are finding new ways to maximise minimal resources and offer quality products and services at low prices. Consider the money transfer company Western Union. On a visit to rural districts in Uttar Pradesh, India's most populous state, it discovered that many people were in receipt of remittances sent by relatives working in the oilfields of Saudi Arabia. This prompted Western Union to open branches in rural areas where people had huge difficulties in receiving money as most of the 65,000 bank branches in India are in urban areas, and about 80 per cent of India's population of 1.1 billion lack access to financial services. Significantly, India is the world's largest recipient of remittances, according to the World Bank. Inward remittances from Indians working overseas surged from $2.1 billion in 1990-91 to US$26.8 billion in 2006–07.[47]

Finally, to find breakthrough ideas, some companies find ways to immerse a range of employees in solving marketing problems. Samsung's Value Innovation Programme (VIP) isolates product development teams of engineers, designers and planners with a timetable and end date in the company's centre just south of Seoul, while 50 specialists help guide their activities. To help make tough trade-offs, team members draw 'value curves' that rank attributes such as a product's sound or picture quality on a scale from 1 to 5. To develop a new car, BMW similarly mobilises specialists in engineering, design, production, marketing, purchasing and finance at its Research and Innovation Centre or Project House.

Sources: S. Hamm (2006) Innovation: the view from the top, *BusinessWeek*, 3 April, 52–3; J. McGregor (2006) The world's most innovative companies, *BusinessWeek*, 24 April, 63–74; R. Karlgard (2006) Digital rules, *Forbes*, 13 March, 31; J. Rooney and J. Collins (2006) Being great is not just a matter of big ideas, *Point*, June, 20; M. Ihlwan (2006) Camp Samsung, *BusinessWeek*, 3 July, 46–7; M. Sawhney, R. C. Wolcott and I. Arroniz (2006) The 12 different ways for companies to innovate, *MIT Sloan Management Review*, 47(3), 75–85; P. Engardio (2006) Business prophet: how C.K. Prahalad is changing the way CEOs think, *BusinessWeek*, 23 January, 68–73.

Firms develop strategy by identifying and selecting from different views of the future. The Royal Dutch/Shell Group has pioneered scenario analysis, which consists of developing plausible representations of a firm's possible future that make different assumptions about forces driving the market and that include different uncertainties. Managers need to think through each scenario with the question: 'What will we do if this happens?' They need to adopt one scenario as the most probable and watch for signposts that might confirm or disconfirm it.[48]

Table 3.5 More sample mission statements

3M
'Our mission is to be innovative through product generations.'

Bosch
'Creating value – sharing values . . . Our ambition is to enhance the quality of life with solutions that are both innovative and beneficial.'

British Gas
'We are committed to providing the best value energy and the highest quality services expertise in the country. Our vision is clear and embedded to our management team to help us meet the challenges ahead.'

Fiat
'We don't just want to get you from A to B. We want to get you there with a smile on your face.'

L'Oréal
'At L'Oreal, we believe that everyone aspires to beauty. Our mission is to help men and women around the world realise that aspiration, and express their individual personalities to the full. This is what gives meaning and value to our business, and to the working lives of our employees. We are proud of our work.'

Michelin
'Our mission is to provide a service to people and their transportation.'

Nokia
'Nokia is about enhancing communication and exploring new ways to exchange information. Everyone has a need to communicate and share. Nokia helps people to fulfil this need and we help people feel close to what matters to them. We focus on providing consumers with very human technology – technology that is intuitive, a joy to use, and beautiful.'

Sainsbury's
'Our mission is to be the consumer's first choice for food, delivering products of outstanding quality and great service at a competitive cost through working "faster, simpler and together".'

Siemens
'Our knowledge and our solutions are helping to create a better world. We have a responsibility to the wider community and we are committed to environmental protection.'

Divine Chocolate Ltd
'To improve the livelihood of smallholder cocoa producers in West Africa by establishing their own dynamic branded proposition in the UK chocolate market, thus putting them higher up the value chain.'

Sources: Courtesy of 3M, Bosch, British Gas, Fiat, L'Oréal, Michelin, Nokia, Sainsbury's, Siemens and Divine Chocolate Ltd.

▽ Business unit strategic planning

The business unit strategic planning process consists of the steps shown in Figure 3.8. Each step is examined in the sections that follow.

Figure 3.8 The business unit strategic-planning process

The business mission

Each business unit needs to define its specific mission within the broader company mission. Thus, a television studio-lighting-equipment company might define its mission as, 'To target major television studios and become their vendor of choice for lighting technologies that represent the most advanced and reliable studio lighting arrangements.' Notice that this mission does not attempt to win business from smaller television studios, win business by being lowest in price, or venture into non-lighting products.

SWOT analysis

The overall evaluation of a company's strengths, weaknesses, opportunities and threats is called SWOT analysis. It is a way of monitoring the external and internal marketing environment.

Figure 3.9 Using SWOT analysis to monitor the internal and external position of an organisation

A business unit has to monitor key *macroenvironment forces* and significant *microenvironment actors* that affect its ability to earn profits. The business unit should set up a marketing intelligence system to track trends, important developments and any related opportunities and threats.

Good marketing is the art of finding, developing and profiting from these opportunities.[49] A **marketing opportunity** is an area of buyer need and interest that a company has a high probability of profitably satisfying. There are three main sources of market opportunities. The first is to supply something that is in short supply. This requires little marketing talent, as the need is obvious. The second is to supply an existing product or service in a new or superior way. There are several ways to uncover possible product or service improvements: the *problem detection method* asks consumers for their suggestions; the *ideal method* has them imagine an ideal version of the product or service; and the *consumption chain method* asks consumers to chart their steps in acquiring, using and disposing of a product. This last method often leads to a very new product or service.

Opportunities can take many forms, and marketers have to be good at spotting them. Consider the following:

- A company may benefit from converging industry trends and introduce hybrid products or services that are new to the market. At least five major cell phone manufacturers released phones with digital photo capabilities.
- A company may make a buying process more convenient or efficient. Consumers can now use the Internet to find more books than ever and search for the lowest price with a few clicks.
- A company can meet the need for more information and advice. Guru.com facilitates finding professional experts in a wide range of fields.
- A company can customise a product or service that was formerly offered only in a standard form. Timberland allows customers to choose colours for different sections of their boots, add initials or numbers to their boots, and choose different stitching and embroidery.
- A company can introduce a new capability. Consumers can now create and edit digital 'iMovies' with the new iMac and upload them to an Apple Web server or website such as YouTube to share with friends around the world.
- A company may be able to deliver a product or a service faster. DHL has discovered a way to deliver mail and packages much more quickly than the UK Post Office.
- A company may be able to offer a product at a much lower price. Pharmaceutical firms have created generic versions of brand-name drugs.

To evaluate opportunities, companies can use **market opportunity analysis (MOA)** to determine their attractiveness and probability of success by asking questions such as:

1 Can we articulate the benefits convincingly to a defined target market(s)?

2 Can we locate the target market(s) and reach them with cost-effective media and trade channels?

3 Does our company possess or have access to the critical capabilities and resources we need to deliver the customer benefits?

4 Can we deliver the benefits better than any actual or potential competitors?

5 Will the financial rate of return meet or exceed our required threshold for investment?

In the opportunity matrix in Figure 3.10(a), the best marketing opportunities facing the TV-lighting-equipment company are listed in the upper-left cell (no. 1). The opportunities in the lower-right cell (no. 4) are too minor to consider. The opportunities in the upper-right cell (no. 2) and lower-left cell (no. 3) are worth monitoring in the event that any improve in attractiveness and success probability.

(a) Opportunity matrix

Success probability

1 Company develops more powerful lighting system
2 Company develops device to measure energy efficiency of any lighting system
3 Company develops device to measure illumination level
4 Company develops software program to teach lighting fundamentals to TV studio personnel

(b) Threat matrix

Probability of occurrence

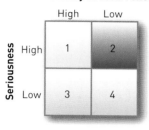

1 Competitor develops superior lighting system
2 Major prolonged economic depression
3 Higher costs
4 Legislation to reduce number of TV studio licences

Figure 3.10
Opportunity and threat matrices

An **environmental threat** is a challenge posed by an unfavourable trend or development that would lead, in the absence of defensive marketing action, to lower sales or profit. Figure 3.10(b) illustrates the threat matrix facing the TV-lighting-equipment company. The threats in the upper-left cell are major, because they can seriously hurt the company and they have a high probability of occurrence. To deal with them, the company needs contingency plans. The threats in the lower-right cell are minor and can be ignored. The firm will want to carefully monitor threats in the upper-right and lower-left cells in the event they grow more serious.

Internal environment (strengths/weaknesses) analysis It is one thing to find attractive opportunities, and another to be able to take advantage of them. Each business needs to evaluate its internal strengths and weaknesses.

 IBM

In the early 1980s IBM dominated the personal computer industry but its position was vulnerable. Many purchased from IBM at the time as the reliability of the IBM clones was unproven in use and thus risky. As the clones proved to be reliable the sales of IBM suffered when it failed to respond effectively, burdened as it was by a heavy bureaucracy.

Businesses can evaluate their own strengths and weaknesses by using a form such as the one shown in 'Marketing memo: Checklist for performing strengths/weaknesses analysis'.

Marketing memo

Checklist for performing strengths/weaknesses analysis

	Performance					Importance		
	Major strength	Minor strength	Neutral	Minor weakness	Major weakness	High	Medium	Low
Marketing								
1 Company reputation	___	___	___	___	___	___	___	___
2 Market share	___	___	___	___	___	___	___	___
3 Customer satisfaction	___	___	___	___	___	___	___	___
4 Customer retention	___	___	___	___	___	___	___	___
5 Product quality	___	___	___	___	___	___	___	___
6 Service quality	___	___	___	___	___	___	___	___
7 Pricing effectiveness	___	___	___	___	___	___	___	___
8 Distribution effectiveness	___	___	___	___	___	___	___	___
9 Promotion effectiveness	___	___	___	___	___	___	___	___
10 Sales force effectiveness	___	___	___	___	___	___	___	___
11 Innovation effectiveness	___	___	___	___	___	___	___	___
12 Geographical coverage	___	___	___	___	___	___	___	___
Finance								
13 Cost or availability of capital	___	___	___	___	___	___	___	___
14 Cash flow	___	___	___	___	___	___	___	___
15 Financial stability	___	___	___	___	___	___	___	___
Manufacturing								
16 Facilities	___	___	___	___	___	___	___	___
17 Economies of scale	___	___	___	___	___	___	___	___
18 Capacity	___	___	___	___	___	___	___	___
19 Able, dedicated workforce	___	___	___	___	___	___	___	___
20 Ability to produce on time	___	___	___	___	___	___	___	___
21 Technical manufacturing skill	___	___	___	___	___	___	___	___
Organisation								
22 Visionary, capable leadership	___	___	___	___	___	___	___	___
23 Dedicated employees	___	___	___	___	___	___	___	___
24 Entrepreneurial orientation	___	___	___	___	___	___	___	___
25 Flexible or responsive	___	___	___	___	___	___	___	___

Critique of conventional SWOT analysis

Over the years, SWOT analysis has been severely criticised as a sole and conventional tool for formulating strategy. While it can provide an indication of which listed items characterise a business and which do not it can tend to oversimplify critical issues, problems and themes as much as illuminate them. SWOT analyses are essentially descriptions of conditions whereas strategies define actions. Furthermore, they can present findings uncritically and without clear prioritisation so that, for example, weak opportunities may appear to balance strong threats. Consequently, they should be seen only as a basic initial review tool and used with caution.[50,51]

Clearly the business does not have to correct *all* its weaknesses, nor should it gloat about all its strengths. The big question is whether the firm should limit itself to those opportunities for which it possesses the required strengths, or consider those that might require it to find or develop new strengths. For example, managers at Texas Instruments (TI) were split between those who wanted TI to stick to industrial electronics, where it has clear strength, and those who wanted the company to continue introducing consumer products, where it lacks some required marketing strengths.

Sometimes a business does poorly not because its people lack the required strengths but because they fail to work together as a team. In one major electronics company, engineers look down on the salespeople as 'engineers who couldn't make it', and salespeople look down on the service people as 'salespeople who couldn't make it'. It is crucial to assess interdepartmental working relationships as part of the internal environmental audit.

Goal formulation

Once the company has performed a SWOT analysis it can proceed to develop specific goals for the planning period. This stage of the process is called **goal formulation**. Goals are objectives that are specific with respect to magnitude and time.

Most business units pursue a mix of objectives, including profitability, sales growth, market share improvement, risk containment, innovation and reputation. The business unit sets these objectives and then manages by objectives (MBO). For an MBO system to work, the unit's objectives must meet four criteria:

1   **They must be arranged hierarchically, from the most to the least important:** For example, the business unit's key objective for the period may be to increase the rate of return on investment. Managers can increase profit by increasing revenue and reducing expenses. They can grow revenue, in turn, by increasing market share and prices.

2   **Objectives should be quantitative whenever possible:** The objective 'to increase the return on investment (ROI)' is better stated as the goal 'to increase ROI to 15 per cent within two years'.

3   **Goals should be realistic:** Goals should arise from an analysis of the business unit's opportunities and strengths, not from wishful thinking.

4   **Objectives must be consistent:** It is not possible to maximise sales and profits simultaneously.

Other important trade-offs include short-term profit versus long-term growth, deep penetration of existing markets versus developing new markets, profit goals versus non-profit goals, and high growth versus low risk. Each choice calls for a different marketing strategy.[52]

Many believe that adopting the goal of strong market share growth may mean forgoing strong short-term profits. For years Compaq priced aggressively in order to build its share in the computer market. Compaq later decided to pursue profitability at the expense of growth. Yet management experts Charan and Tichy believe that most businesses can be growth businesses *and* grow profitably as, for example, BP, Bosch, IKEA, Nestlé and Tesco have done.[53]

Strategic formulation

Goals indicate what a business unit wants to achieve; **strategy** is a game plan for getting there. Every business must design a strategy for achieving its goals, consisting of a *marketing strategy*, and a compatible *technology strategy* and *sourcing strategy*.

Porter's generic strategies Porter has proposed three generic strategies that provide a good starting point for strategic thinking: overall cost leadership, differentiation and focus.[54]

• **Overall cost leadership:** Firms pursuing this strategy work hard to achieve the lowest production and distribution costs so they can price lower than their competitors and win a large market share. The problem with this strategy is that other firms will usually compete with still lower costs and hurt the firm that bases its whole future on cost alone.

- **Differentiation:** The business concentrates on uniquely achieving superior performance in an important customer benefit area valued by a large part of the market. Thus the firm seeking quality leadership, for example, must make products with the best components, put them together expertly, inspect them carefully and effectively communicate their quality.
- **Focus:** The business focuses on one or more narrow market segments. The firm gets to know these segments intimately and pursues either cost leadership or differentiation within the target segment.

▽ Belkin Corporation

For most people, a surge protector is a necessary item to avoid electrical surges damaging a personal computer. Yet one company decided to focus not on the utilitarian aspect of the surge protector but on its aesthetic aspect. An example of both focus and differentiation, Belkin Corporation's surge protectors organise consumers' workspaces and protect their equipment. Its Concealed Surge Protector organises cables and keeps them out of view with a unique closing cover. By differentiating itself from the average surge protector, Belkin can charge premium prices for its product.[55]

The online air travel industry provides a good example of these three strategies. British Airways is pursuing a differentiation strategy by offering the most comprehensive range of additional services to the traveller (executive airport lounges, optional onboard entertainment packs, etc.). On the other hand, Ryanair is pursuing a lowest-cost strategy; and LastMinute is pursuing a niche strategy in focusing on travellers who have the flexibility to travel at very short notice.

According to Porter, firms pursuing the same strategy directed to the same target market constitute a **strategic group**. The firm that carries out that strategy best will make the most profits. International Harvester went out of the farm equipment business because it did not stand out in its industry as lowest in cost, highest in perceived value or best in serving some market segments.[56]

Porter draws a distinction between operational effectiveness and strategy. Competitors can quickly copy the operationally effective company using benchmarking and other tools, thus diminishing the advantage of operational effectiveness. Porter defines strategy as 'the creation of a unique and valuable position involving a different set of activities'. A company can claim that it has a strategy when it 'performs different activities from rivals or performs similar activities in different ways'.

Strategic alliances Even giant companies – IBM, Philips, Nokia and Unilever – often cannot achieve leadership, either nationally or globally, without forming alliances with domestic or multinational companies that complement or enhance their capabilities and resources. The Dutch company Philips formed a strategic alliance with Dell to collaborate on the development of a range of electronic items such as computer monitors. The European aircraft manufacturers formed a strategic alliance to create the Airbus to compete successfully with their arch US rival Boeing. The Finnish company Nokia negotiated a strategic alliance with the German fixed-line company Siemens.

Just doing business in another country may require the firm to license its product, form a joint venture with a local firm or buy from local suppliers to meet local 'domestic content' requirements. As a result, many firms are rapidly developing global strategic networks, and victory is going to those who build the better global network. The Star Alliance, for example, brings together 18 airlines, including Lufthansa, United Airlines, Singapore Airlines, Air New Zealand

and South Africa Airways, into a huge global partnership that allows travellers to make nearly seamless connections to hundreds of destinations.

Many strategic alliances take the form of marketing alliances. These fall into four major categories.

1 **Product or service alliances:** One company licenses another to produce its product, or two companies jointly market their complementary products or a new product. The credit card industry is a complicated combination of cards jointly marketed by banks such as Royal Bank of Scotland, Crédit Lyonnais, credit card companies such as Visa, and affinity companies such as Virgin.

2 **Promotional alliances:** One company agrees to carry a promotion for another company's product or service. McDonald's, for example, teamed up with Disney for ten years to offer products related to current Disney films as part of its meals for children.

3 **Logistics alliances:** One company offers logistical services for another company's product. For example, BP has formed an alliance with the Russian company TNK to further oil exploration and extraction.

4 **Pricing collaborations:** One or more companies join in a special pricing collaboration. Hotel and car rental companies often offer mutual price discounts.

Companies need to give creative thought to finding partners that might complement their strengths and offset their weaknesses. Well-managed alliances allow companies to obtain a greater sales impact at less cost. To keep their strategic alliances thriving, corporations have begun to develop organisational structures to support them, and many have come to view the ability to form and manage partnerships as core skills called **partner relationship management (PRM)**.[57]

Programme formulation and implementation

Even a sound marketing strategy can be sabotaged by poor implementation. If the unit has decided to attain technological leadership, it must plan programmes to strengthen its R&D department, gather technological intelligence, develop leading-edge products, train the technical sales force and develop advertisements to communicate its technological leadership.

Once they have formulated marketing programmes the marketing people must estimate their costs. Is participating in a particular trade show worth it? Will a specific sales contest pay for itself? Will hiring another salesperson contribute to the bottom line? **Activity-based cost (ABC) accounting** can help determine whether each marketing programme is likely to produce sufficient results to justify its cost.[58]

Today's businesses are also increasingly recognising that unless they nurture other stakeholders – customers, employees, suppliers, distributors – they may never earn sufficient profits for the stockholders. For example, a company might aim to delight its customers, perform well for its employees and deliver a threshold level of satisfaction to its suppliers. In setting these levels a company must be careful not to violate any stakeholder group's sense of fairness about the treatment they receive relative to others.[59]

A dynamic relationship connects the stakeholder groups. A smart company creates a high level of employee satisfaction, which requires an increased effort, which leads to higher-quality products and services. This in turn creates higher customer satisfaction and leads to repeat business. This generates higher growth and profits and higher stockholder satisfaction, which results in more investment. This virtuous circle spells profits and growth. 'Marketing insight: Marketing's contribution to shareholder value' highlights the increasing importance of the proper bottom-line view to marketing expenditures.

According to McKinsey & Company, strategy is only one of seven elements – all of which start with the letter 's' – in successful business practice.[60] The first three – strategy, structure and systems – are considered the 'hardware' of success. The next four – style, skills, staff and shared values – are the 'software'.

Marketing insight

Marketing's contribution to shareholder value

Companies normally focus on maximising profits rather than shareholder value. Doyle argues that profit maximisation leads to short-term planning and under-investment in marketing, promoting a focus on building sales, market share and current profits. It also leads to cost cutting and shedding assets to produce quick improvements in earnings, and erodes a company's long-term competitiveness by eliminating investment in new market opportunities.

Companies normally measure their profit perform-ance using ROI (return on investment, calculated by dividing profits by investment). This method presents two problems:

1   Profits are arbitrarily measured and subject to manipulation. Cash flow is more important. As someone observed: 'Profits are a matter of opinion; cash is a fact.'

2   Investment ignores the real value of the firm. More of a company's value resides in its intangible market-ing assets – brands, market knowledge, customer relationships and partner relationships – than in its balance sheet. These assets are the drivers of long-term profits.

Doyle posits that marketing will not mature as a profession until it can demonstrate the impact of marketing on shareholder value, which is defined by the market value of a company minus its debt. The market value is the share price times the number of shares outstanding. The share price reflects what investors estimate is the present value of the future lifetime earnings of a company. When management is choosing a marketing strategy, Doyle wants it to apply shareholder value analysis (SVA) to see which alternative course of action will maximise shareholder value.

If Doyle's argument is accepted, instead of seeing marketing as a specific function concerned only with increasing sales or market share, senior management will see it as an integral part of the whole management process. It will judge marketing by how much it contributes to shareholder value by delivering consistently high levels of customer-perceived value.

Source: P. Doyle (2000) *Value-based Marketing: Marketing Strategies for Corporate Growth and Shareholder Value*, Chichester, England: John Wiley & Sons.

The first 'soft' element, *style*, means that company employees share a common way of think-ing and behaving. McDonald's employees smile at the customer, and IBM employees are very professional in their customer dealings. The second element, *skills,* means employees have the skills needed to carry out the company's strategy. *Staffing* means the company has hired able peo-ple, trained them well and assigned them to the right jobs. The fourth element, *shared values*, means employees share the same corporate culture values. When these elements are present com-panies are usually more successful at strategy implementation.[61]

Another study of management practices found that superior performance over time depended on flawless execution, a company culture based on aiming high, a structure that is flexible and responsive, and a strategy that is clear and focused.[62]

Feedback and control

See also Chapter 22.

A company's strategic fit with the environment will inevitably erode, because the market envi-ronment changes faster than the company's 7Ss. Thus, a company might remain efficient while it loses effectiveness. Peter Drucker pointed out that it is more important to 'do the right thing' – to be effective – than 'to do things right' – to be efficient. The most successful companies excel at both.

Once an organisation fails to respond to a changed environment it becomes increasingly hard to recapture its lost position. Consider how the fortunes of the Lotus Development Corporation have waned. Its Lotus 1-2-3 software was once the world's leading software program, and now its market share in desktop software has slipped so low that analysts largely ignore it.

Organisations, especially large ones, are subject to inertia. It is difficult to change one part without adjusting everything else. Yet organisations can be changed through strong leadership, preferably in advance of a crisis. The key to organisational health is willingness to examine the changing environment and adopt new goals and strategies.

Change today, not tomorrow

Here are some words of wisdom from John Whybrow, Chairman, Wolseley.

'Business leaders need to be alert to the changing landscape and respond swiftly to changing circumstances – today rather than tomorrow.'

'Managers and directors are generally slow to respond to change. We wait for tomorrow. The truth is, we shouldn't wait. We should do it now.'

'If only we'd looked at those issues ten or five years earlier, we wouldn't have had such a dramatic state of affairs to contend with.'

'The world is not going to be recreated in our image; the world will do what it wants to do. We must respond, and respond today, not tomorrow.'

Source: *Mastering Change* (2005), London: BBC Books.

▽ The nature and content of a marketing plan

Working within the plans set by the levels above them, product managers develop a marketing plan for individual products, lines, brands, channels or customer groups. Each product level, whether product line or brand, must develop a marketing plan for achieving its goals. A marketing plan is a written document that summarises what the marketer has learned about the marketplace and indicates how the firm plans to reach its marketing objectives.[63] It contains tactical guidelines for the marketing programmes and financial allocations over the planning period.[64] It is one of the most important outputs of the marketing process.

Marketing plans are becoming more customer- and competitor-oriented, and better reasoned and more realistic than in the past. They draw more inputs from all the functions and are team developed. Planning is becoming a continuous process in order to respond to rapidly changing market conditions.

Most marketing plans cover one year in 5–50 pages. The most frequently cited shortcomings of current marketing plans, according to marketing executives, are lack of realism, insufficient competitive analysis, and a short-run focus. (See 'Marketing memo: Marketing plan criteria' for some guideline questions to ask in developing marketing plans.)

What, then, does a marketing plan look like? What does it contain?

Contents of the marketing plan

- **Executive summary and table of contents:** The marketing plan should open with a brief summary for senior management of the main goals and recommendations. A table of contents outlines the rest of the plan and all the supporting rationale and operational detail.
- **Situation analysis:** This section presents relevant background data on sales, costs, the market, competitors, and the various forces in the macroenvironment. How do we define the market, how big is it, and how fast is it growing? What are the relevant trends? What is the product offering and what critical issues do we face? Firms will use all this information to carry out a SWOT (strengths, weaknesses, opportunities, threats) analysis.
- **Marketing strategy:** Here the product manager defines the mission, marketing and financial objectives, and groups and needs that the market offerings are intended to satisfy. The manager then establishes the product line's competitive positioning, which will inform the 'game plan' to accomplish the plan's objectives. All this requires inputs from other areas, such as purchasing, manufacturing, sales, finance and human resources.

Marketing memo

Marketing plan criteria

Here are some questions to ask in evaluating a marketing plan.

1 **Is the plan simple?** Is it easy to understand and act on? Does it communicate its content clearly and practically?

2 **Is the plan specific?** Are its objectives concrete and measurable? Does it include specific actions and activities, each with specific dates of completion, specific persons responsible, and specific budgets?

3 **Is the plan realistic?** Are the sales goals, expense budgets and milestone dates realistic? Has a frank and honest self-critique been conducted to raise possible concerns and objections?

4 **Is the plan complete?** Does it include all the necessary elements? Does it have the right breadth and depth?

_____

Source: Adapted from T. Berry and D. Wilson (2000) *On Target: The Book on Marketing Plans*, Eugene, OR: Palo Alto Software.

- **Financial projections:** Financial projections include a sales forecast, an expense forecast and a break-even analysis. On the revenue side, the projections show the forecast sales volume by month and product category. On the expense side, they show the expected costs of marketing, broken down into finer categories. The break-even analysis shows how many units the firm must sell monthly to offset its monthly fixed costs and average per-unit variable costs.
- **Implementation controls:** The last section of the marketing plan outlines the controls for monitoring and adjusting implementation of the plan. Typically, it spells out the goals and budget for each month or quarter, so management can review each period's results and take corrective action as needed. Firms must also take a number of different internal and external measures to assess progress and suggest possible modifications. Some organisations include contingency plans outlining the steps management would take in response to specific environmental developments, such as price wars or strikes.

▽ Sample marketing plan: Euromart

Introduction

The eight themes featured in the text reflect the key interests of marketing managers. In today's competitive business environment companies need to be constantly aware of the characteristics and developments in both domestic and international markets. This requires a commitment to carrying out both ad hoc and continuous market research. Resources are under increasing pressure as companies across the globe seek to find a place in the marketplace, so individual firms operating need to be able to harness new methods and technology to measure their cost, revenue and profit performances.

The ultimate task of marketers is to guide and assist their companies to secure satisfied or preferably delighted customers. This text explores the tasks facing marketing managers in the pursuit of meeting customers' perceived value requirements that emerge from a series of inputs from customers, value chain members and other stakeholders. The art/science of the successful company is to incorporate the detail of what customers really want and supply this efficiently and thus profitably in times of rampant global competition. Not an easy task.

The key tasks of marketers are outlined in the 'Marketing memo: Getting started'.

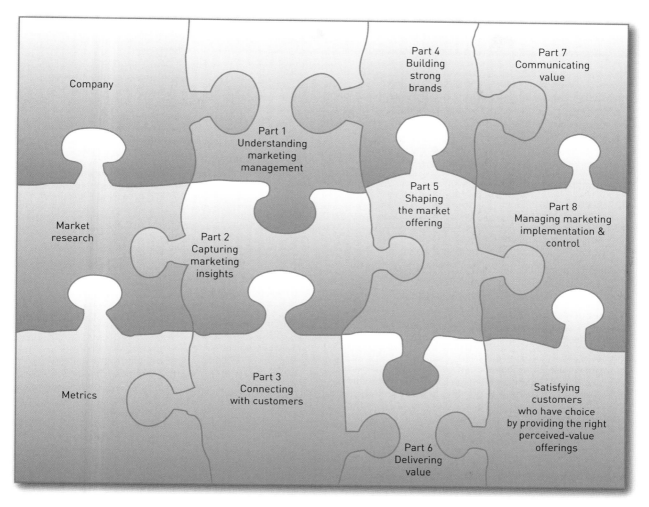

Figure 3.11 Snapshot of the text

Marketing memo

Getting started

The key tasks facing marketers are:

1 to have an understanding of marketing management (Part 1);

2 to capture marketing insights (Part 2);

3 to successfully connect with customers (Part 3);

4 to build strong brands (Part 4);

5 to shape the marketing offering (Part 5);

6 to deliver value (Part 6);

7 to communicate value (Part 7);

8 to successfully manage and control the implementation of marketing activity (Part 8).

Chapter 21 closes with the 'Marketing memo: Getting to grips with the practice of marketing', which is designed to assist marketers and students to bridge the sometimes troublesome gap between marketing theory and practice; between knowledge and the ability to put that into practice and thus develop *know-how*.

Wise companies and marketers set out to delight their customers – whether consumer or business-to-business – by successfully researching context (market situation); customer (requirements); competition (relevant competitive offers); cash implications (money in – revenue, and money out – expenditure, e.g. on market

▶ Marketing memo *(continued)*

research, offer development and supply); channels (distribution and marketing communications aspects). In addition they need to accept the underpinning marketing philosophy that in buyers' markets the customer needs to be a prime focus for the firm.

The next section presents a sample marketing plan featuring the fictional Euromart Company.

Euromart marketing plan

1 Executive summary
2 Contextual analysis
3 Customer analysis
4 Competition analysis
5 Company strategic approach
6 Channel analysis
7 Cash analysis
8 Marketing management implementation and control

1 Executive summary

Euromart is a new company that has recently been founded to provide books, computer hardware and software and electrical appliance offerings for students. The company is based in Copenhagen but rents premises on the mainstream university campuses in Eire, Netherlands, Norway, Sweden and the United Kingdom. Other branches are planned to open in 2009/10 in France, Germany, Russia and Spain. Euromart trades through its campus retail outlets and has developed a sophisticated online business.

Exhaustive market research has been carried out in both the mainstream university campuses where Euromart has shops and among its growing number of online customers. As a result there are ambitious plans under way to broaden the company's appeal by establishing new market offerings in the financial services and travel industries.

Euromart is run by a small, highly motivated management team who have all graduated from mainstream universities in the last five years. The company's mission is to provide quality offerings at prices that are affordable to students. Euromart sees its offerings as being a combination of customer-perceived value product and service attributes.

To maintain the company's initial early successes, net profits grew by 70 per cent in the first three years of operation. Euromart firmly believe in the benefits of sound medium- and long-range planning to prosper the business.

2 Contextual analysis

2.1 Market environment

    2.1.1 Euromart currently operates separate businesses in five European countries with plans to expand into four more in the next two years.

    2.1.2 The business environment in each operating country is constantly monitored by means of political, economic, socio-cultural, technological, legal and environmental profiling (PESTLE analysis).

    2.1.3 Each market is researched to identify whether it is a sellers' or a buyers' market. Buyers' markets (where supply exceeds demand, giving rise to fierce competition) are managed with a firm resolve to provide customers with the right customer-perceived value offerings.

2.2 Market entry

    2.2.1 All main means of entering new national markets are researched to determine the best method for the company. (e.g. own business, partnership, strategic alliance).

    2.2.2 All expansions of the existing business in each country are researched country by country so the range of offerings available in each country varies according to local requirements.

3 Customer analysis

3.1 Customer markets

    3.1.1 Euromart markets to individual student customers in its portfolio of national markets.

    3.1.2 The company also has a thriving business-to-business interest in its national market portfolios.

3.2 Segmentation, targeting and positioning

    3.2.1 Each national market is carefully segmented to reveal attractive target markets by means of demographics, geodemographics and behavioural factors.

    3.2.2 Euromart supplies offering portfolios for full-time, part-time, distance learning, executive and mature students.

    3.2.3 Each national market senior executive is responsible for meeting corporate headquarters' targets but does have some freedom to calculate the best positioning of resources that are released by the Copenhagen head office.

3.3 Branding

    3.3.1 Each national company is empowered to 'develop the Euromart brand'.

    3.3.2 Each national company is free to research and make a case to the Copenhagen head office for new market offering ventures.

4 Competition analysis

4.1 Identify major competitors.
4.2 Assess major competitors' strengths and weaknesses.
4.3 Select competitors to attack and avoid.

5 Company strategic approach

5.1 Mission

    5.1.1 To treat customers as Euromart's best friends and to deliver the best purchasing experience.

5.2 Marketing strategy

    5.2.1 Build the Euromart brand as the 'student's friend'.

    5.2.2 To grow the company profitably in existing countries and to expand into carefully selected countries on the back of a positive overall profit performance.

▶ **Marketing memo** *(continued)*

5.2.3 Maintain customer purchase standards and continuously monitor customer satisfaction to build Euromart's brand reputation.

5.2.4 Target markets – students, books, computers and electrical appliances.

5.2.5 Positioning – three market offering ranges – essential (market entry), value plus (mid-market) and premium (niche).

5.2.6 Develop customer awareness and then expand the target market offering portfolio.

5.2.7 Seek to maximise use of modern digital and Internet marketing strategies.

6 Channel analysis

6.1 Distribution

6.1.1 Design appropriate global and local supply networks for both consumer and business-to-business markets.

6.1.2 Continuously monitor performance of supply networks to secure efficiency and effectiveness of the Euromart customer-perceived value interface

6.2 Marketing communication

6.2.1 Design and implement suitable corporate marketing communications programme.

6.2.2 Design and implement suitable consumer (student) marketing communications programmes for all active national markets.

6.2.3 Design and implement suitable business-to-business marketing communications programmes for each active national market

6.2.4 Seek to maximise use of digital and Internet marketing communications.

7 Cash analysis

7.1 Control expenditure (money out)

7.1.1 Maintain tight but appropriate financial control.

7.1.2 Set budgets for headquarters activities (e.g. corporate marketing communications, staffing).

7.1.3 Set budgets for each national branch by market offering categories (i.e. books, computer items and electrical appliances) for both consumer (student) and business-to-business markets.

7.2 Revenue (money in)

7.2.1 Forecast sales in each national branch

7.2.2 Segment sales forecast in each national branch by market offering categories and consumer and business-to-business markets.

8 Marketing management implementation and control

8.1 Euromart supports a marketing-oriented culture to provide market offerings that meet customers' expectations by placing a strong emphasis on market research to discover market contextual data, customer requirements, the activities of competitors, the most appropriate way to run their channel operations (distribution and marketing communications). Market research is extended to staff, the supply/value chain and interested stakeholders. Euromart is characterised by a customer relationship approach to running its business.

8.2 Euromart headquarters has a minimal headcount.

8.3 All budget holders will be incentivised to hit and improve both their sales forecast and profit targets.

8.4 Headquarters management foster and encourage creativity and innovation throughout the business.

9 Contingency plans

9.1 This section describes actions to be taken by Euromart if specific threats or opportunities materialise during the planning period.

9.2 Actions to counter sudden changes in the business environment (e.g. the credit crunch, escalating fuel costs).

9.3 Actions to contain any invasive competitor's moves.

Source: Checklist adapted from K. Kashani and D. Turpin (1999), *Marketing Management* (Section 1), IMD: Lusanne, published by Macmillan Business, and reproduced with permission from Palgrave Macmillan.

▽ SUMMARY

1 The value delivery process involves choosing (or identifying), providing (or delivering) and communicating superior customer-perceived value. The value chain is a tool for identifying key activities that create value and costs in a specific business.

2 Strong companies develop superior capabilities in managing core business processes such as new product realisation, inventory management, and customer acquisition and retention. Managing these core processes effectively means creating a marketing network in which the company works closely with all parties in the production and distribution chain, from suppliers of raw materials to retail distributors. Companies no longer compete – marketing networks do.

3 According to one view, holistic marketing maximises value exploration by understanding the relationships between the customer's cognitive space, the company's competence space and the collaborator's resource space. It maximises value creation by identifying new customer benefits from the customer's cognitive space, utilising core competencies from its business domain, and selecting and managing business partners from its collaborative networks. It also maximises value delivery by becoming proficient at customer relationship management, internal resource management and business partnership management.

4   Market-oriented strategic planning is the managerial process of developing and maintaining a viable fit between the organisation's objectives, skills and resources and its changing market opportunities. The aim of strategic planning is to shape the company's businesses and products so that they yield target profits and growth. Strategic planning takes place at four levels: corporate, division, business unit and product.

5   The corporate strategy establishes the framework within which the divisions and business units prepare

their strategic plans. Setting a corporate strategy entails four activities: defining the corporate mission, establishing strategic business units (SBUs), assigning resources to each SBU based on its market attractiveness and business strength, and planning new businesses and downsizing older businesses.

6   Strategic planning for individual businesses entails the following activities: defining the business mission, analysing external opportunities and threats, analysing internal strengths and weaknesses, formulating goals, formulating strategy, formulating supporting programmes, implementing the programmes, and gathering feedback and exercising control.

7   Each product level within a business unit must develop a marketing plan for achieving its goals. The marketing plan is one of the most important outputs of the marketing process.

▽ APPLICATIONS

Marketing debate

What good is a mission statement? Virtually all firms have mission statements to help guide and inspire employees as well as signal what is important to the firm and to those outside the firm. Mission statements are often the product of much deliberation and discussion. At the same time, some critics claim that mission statements sometimes lack 'teeth' and specificity. Moreover, critics also maintain that in many cases mission statements do not vary much from firm to firm, and make the same empty promises.

Take a position: Mission statements are critical to a successful marketing organisation *versus* Mission statements rarely provide useful marketing value.

Marketing discussion

Consider Porter's value chain and the holistic marketing orientation model. What implications do they have for marketing planning? How would you structure a marketing plan to incorporate some of their concepts?

▽ REFERENCES

[1] J. Ewing (2005) Siemens's tough guy gets going, *Business Week*, 27 June; J. Ewing (2006) Nokia, Siemens plan to join and conquer, *BusinessWeek*, 20 June; A. Lustgarten (2006) Remaking a German giant with American-style tactics, *Fortune*, 7 August.

[2] N. Kumar (2004) *Marketing As Strategy: The CEO's Agenda for Driving Growth and Innovation*, Boston, MA: Harvard Business School Press.

[3] F. E. Webster, Jr. (1997) The future role of marketing in the organization, in edited by D. R. Lehmann and K. Jocz, *Reflections on the Futures of Marketing*, Cambridge, MA: Marketing Science Institute, pp. 39–66.

[4] B. T. Gale (1995) *Managing Customer Value*, New York: The Free Press.

[5] M. E. Porter (1985) *Competitive Advantage: Creating and Sustaining Superior Performance*, New York: The Free Press.

[6] R. Hiebeler, T. B. Kelly and C. Ketteman (1998) *Best Practices: Building Your Business with Customer-Focused Solutions*, New York: Simon and Schuster.

[7] L. Lewis (2007) Toyota sets out vision of greener future, *The Times*, 12 November.

[8] M. Hammer and J. Champy (1993) *Reengineering the Corporation: A Manifesto for Business Revolution*, New York: Harper Business.

[9] J. R. Katzenbach and D. K. Smith (1993) *The Wisdom of Teams: Creating the High-Performance Organization*, Boston, MA: Harvard Business School Press; Hammer and Champy (1993) op. cit.

[10] R. Rigby (2007) Trailblazers with tinkering time on their hands, *Financial Times*, 6 November.

[11] C. K. Prahalad and G. Hamel (1990) The core competence of the corporation, *Harvard Business Review*, May–June, 79–91.

[12] C. K. Prahalad and G. Hamel (1994) *Competing for the Future*, Cambridge, MA: Harvard Business School Press.

[13] C. K. Prahalad and V. Ramaswamy (2000) Co-opting customer competency, *Harvard Business Review*, 1 January, 79–90.

[14] R. Waters (2007) Microsoft defends its diversification, *Financial Times*, 27 July.

[15] E. Unsworth (2006) ILVA an IKEA beater?, *Manchester Evening News*, 28 August; R. Fletcher (2007) ILVA sold to Icelandic furniture group, *The Daily Telegraph*, 2 August; T. Braithwaite (2008) Backers pull the plug on ILVA UK, *Financial Times*, 26 June.

[16]G. S. Day (1994) The capabilities of market-driven organizations, *Journal of Marketing*, October, 38.

[17]G. S. Day and P. J. H. Schoemaker (2006) *Peripheral Vision: Detecting the Weak Signals That Will Make or Break Your Company*, Cambridge, MA: Harvard Business School Press.

[18]L. Lazaroff (2006) Kodak's big picture focusing on image change, *Chicago Tribune*, 29 January, pp. 5, 9.

[19]S. London (2002) The future means getting personal, *Financial Times*, 12 December.

[20]K. Ushikubo (1986) A method of structure analysis for developing product concepts and its applications, *European Research*, 14(4), 174–5.

[21]Y. J. Wind and V. Mahajan with R. E. Gunther (2002) *Convergence Marketing: Strategies for Reaching the New Hybrid Consumer*, Upper Saddle River, NJ: Prentice Hall.

[22]P. Drucker (1973) *Management: Tasks, Responsibilities and Practices*, New York: Harper and Row, Chapter 7.

[23]R. A. Oliva (2001) Nowhere to hide, *Marketing Management*, July/August, 44–46.

[24]*The Economist Miscellany* (2005) London: Profile Books, pp. 32–3.

[25]A. Sangera (2005) Too many mission statements, *Financial Times*, 22 July.

[26]J. F. Rayport and B. J. Jaworski (2001) *e-commerce*, New York: McGraw-Hill, p. 116.

[27]T. Kemmler, M. Kubicova, R. Musslewhite and R. Prezeau (2001) E-performance II: the good, the bad, and the merely average, *The McKinsey Quarterly* (mckinseyquarterly.com).

[28]This section is based on Chapter 16 of R. M. Grant (2005) *Contemporary Strategy Analysis*, 5th edn, Malden, MA: Blackwell Publishing.

[29]The same matrix can be expanded into nine cells by adding modified products and modified markets. See Johnson, S. J. and C. Jones (1957) How to organize for new products, *Harvard Business Review*, May–June, 49–62.

[30]See www.starbucks.com; H. Schultz (1997) *Pour Your Heart Into It*, New York: Hyperion; A. Serwer (2004) Hot Starbucks to go, *Fortune*, 26 January, pp. 60–74.

[31]A. Ward (2007) Why Schultz has caused a stir at Starbucks, *Guardian*, 26 February.

[32]PepsiCo company website (www.pepsico.com).

[33]B. White (2006) Expanding into consumer electronics, Cisco aims to jazz up its stodgy image, *Wall Street Journal*, 6 September, p. B1.

[34]M. Ruch (2006) Saltzgitter aims for diversification, *Financial Times*, 16 August.

[35]D. Blackwell (2007) Diversification bolsters Cussons, *Financial Times*, 1 August.

[36]R. Waters (2007) Microsoft defends its diversification, *Financial Times*, 27 July.

[37]M. Mulligan (2007) Alierta spells out Telefonica growth plans, *Financial Times*, 12 October.

[38]PepsiCo company website (www.pepsico.com).

[39]E. J. McCarthy (1996) *Basic Marketing: A Managerial Approach*, 12th edn, Homewood, IL: Irwin.

[40]Dyson Company website (www.dyson.co.uk).

[41]C. K. Prahalad and G. Hamel (1990) The core competence of the corporation, *Harvard Business Review*, May–June, 79–91.

[42]Jump Associates.

[43]Rigby (2007) op. cit.

[44]M. Gorman (2007) Icon celebrates its success, *Marketing Week*, 27 September.

[45]K. Jackson (2006) BMW benefits from audio books, *Automotive News Europe*, 11(20), 15.

[46]C. Grande (2007) Advertisers eye hip sites as testing ground, *Financial Times*, 29 June.

[47]A. Yee (2007) A cash lifeline for the rural poor, *Financial Times*, 12 June.

[48]P. J. H. Shoemaker (1995) Scenario planning: a tool for strategic thinking, *Sloan Management Review*, Winter, 25–40.

[49]P. Kotler (1999) *Kotler on Marketing*, New York: Free Press.

[50]T. Hill and R. Westbrook (1997) SWOT analysis it's time for a product recall, *Long Range Planning*, 30 (February), 46–52.

[51]E. K. Valentin (2001) SWOT analysis from a resource-based view, *Journal of Marketing Theory & Practice*, 9(2), 54–70.

[52]D. Dodd and K. Favaro (2006) Managing the right tension, *Harvard Business Review*, December, 62–74.

[53]R. Charan and N. M. Tichy (1998) *Every Business Is a Growth Business: How Your Company Can Prosper Year After Year*, New York: Time Business/Random House.

[54]M. E. Porter (1980) *Competitive A Strategy: Techniques for Analyzing Industries and Competitors*, New York: The Free Press, Chapter 2.

[55]S. C. Miller (2006) it protects electronic devices from power surges and gives dust bunnies no place to hide, *New York Times*, 14 September, p. C10; See also www.belkin.com/prssroom/release/uploads/08_15_06Concealed_CompactSurge.hml.

[56]M. E. Porter (1996) What is strategy?, *Harvard Business Review*, November–December, 61–78.

[57]For some readings on strategic alliances, see P. Lorange and J. Roos (1992) *Strategic Alliances: Formation, Implementation and Evolution*, Cambridge, MA: Blackwell; J. D. Lewis (1990) *Partnerships for Profit: Structuring and Managing Strategic Alliances*, New York: The Free Press; J. R. Harbison and P. Pekar (1998) *Smart Alliances: A Practical Guide to Repeatable Success*, San Francisco, CA: Jossey-Bass.

[58]R. Cooper and R. S. Kaplan (1991) Profit priorities from activity-based costing, *Harvard Business Review*, May–June, 130–35.

[59]As a tool for monitoring stakeholder satisfaction see R. S. Kaplan and D. P. Norton (1996) *The Balanced Scorecard: Translating Strategy into Action*, Boston, MA: Harvard Business School Press.

[60]T. J. Peters and R. H. Waterman, Jr. (1982) *In Search of Excellence: Lessons from America's Best-Run Companies*, New York: Harper Row, pp. 9–12.

[61]T. E. Deal and A. A. Kennedy (1982) *Corporate Cultures: The Rites and Rituals of Corporate Life*, Reading, MA: Addison-Wesley; Corporate culture, *BusinessWeek*, 27 October 1980, pp. 148–60; S. M. Davis (1992) *Managing Corporate Culture and Performance*, New York: The Free Press.

[62]N. Nohria, W. Joyce and B. Roberson (2003) What really works, *Harvard Business Review*, 81(7), 42–53.

[63]M. B. Wood (2003) *The Marketing Plan: A Handbook*, Upper Saddle River, NJ: Prentice Hall.

[64]D. R. Lehmann and R. S. Winer (2001) *Product Management*, 3rd edn, Boston, MA: McGraw-Hill/Irwin.

Chapter 4

▽ Managing digital technology in marketing

IN THIS CHAPTER, WE WILL ADDRESS THE FOLLOWING QUESTIONS:

1 What is digital technology in marketing?

2 How can companies gain competitive advantage from using digital marketing?

3 What is digital marketing communication?

4 What is consumer digital interactivity?

5 How can companies analyse and understand consumer digital shopping behaviour?

6 How do marketing managers use ICT and digital technologies to support internal marketing decisions?

Technology is all around us. Consumers live in a networked technology-based world with broadband, mobile phones, iPods, iTunes, online shopping, instant messaging and social networking as core parts of their lives. Marketing managers also operate with a range of technologies, from databases, internets, intranets, extranets, computer networks, planning software, CRM systems, personal digital assistants (PDA) and so on. As Chris Anderson, author of *The Long Tail* notes, 'we are in the new era of networked consumers and digital everything'.[1] IT (ICT) is so crucial to marketing that the spelling of marketing could be changed to MarkITing[2]

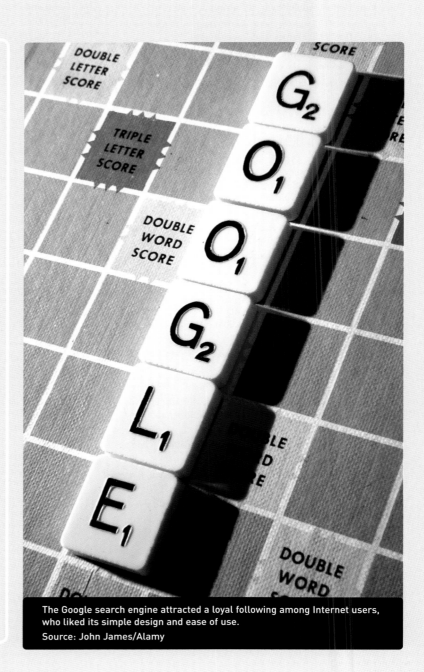

The Google search engine attracted a loyal following among Internet users, who liked its simple design and ease of use.
Source: John James/Alamy

CHAPTER JOURNEY

Understanding ICT and digital technology in marketing

ICT and digital marketing and multichannel marketing

Using digital technology to support decision making

What is consumer digital interactivity and digital shopping behaviour?

Understanding digital marketing communication

or even MarkIcTing! Technology is now embedded in business and the skills to manage it are core requirements for marketing managers now and into the future.
   Take Google.

Google has become the most popular Web search engine in the world, receiving several hundred million queries each day. It is so popular that it is now part of our language. You will hear people asking, 'Did you google that?' In July 2006 the verb 'to google' was officially added to the *Oxford English Dictionary*, meaning, 'to use the Google search engine to obtain information on the Internet'. Google, founded in 1996, now has an index of over 8 billion Web pages. Marketers know that consumers use Google for checking online and being on the first page of a Google search is crucial to many companies. Many marketers are eager to influence their website's Google rankings. They use search engine optimisation, which attempts to discern patterns in search engine listings, and then develop a methodology for improving rankings. Forrester Research, Inc. estimates that European marketers spent up to €4.5 billion in 2007 on search engine marketing, up from €856 million in 2004[3] and expected to reach €8.1 billion by 2012.[4]

Technological advances in the last ten years have fundamentally changed how we practise marketing and how business operates. Technology is a core part of customers' and marketers' lives and is covered throughout this text.

▽ Digital technology in marketing: The ICT Imperative

What is ICT? The term information technology was first coined by Leavitt and Whisler in 1985.[5] The extended term – ICT – encompasses information and also communication technologies, which are a core part of the technology choices available to marketing. What was once considered the technology of information has now become a technology of communication and information – ICT. The convergence of communication and information technologies has created possibilities that were unthinkable only a few years ago. Customers can now contact companies '24/7' and also provide much of the service themselves with home banking, holiday bookings and even stockbroking. The latest satellite navigation system can lead you to your nearest Spar or Dunkin' Donuts; it can even send an emergency message when your airbag is deployed.

To find out how Cadbury, a world leading confectionery company, used an online viral marketing campaign to generate buzz and to defend their dominant market share position in the UK, go to www.pearsoned.co.uk/marketingmanagementeurope

Digital marketing includes all ICTs emcompassing both Internet-based marketing activities and other kinds of activity (i.e. mobile phone communication, emails and interactive digital television) that are based on digital technology. The use of digital marketing is now an integrated and essential part of marketing efforts. For example, Canon iMage Gateway helps consumers share their digital photos with friends online, while L'Oréal's brand Lancôme uses email newsletters to stay in touch with customers and to strengthen brand loyalty.[6]

▽ The range of ICTs in marketing

There is no definitive list of ICTs in marketing but there are hundreds of ICTs targeted at the marketing department. Recent research has shown that ICT use in marketing has increased substantially over the last ten years, moving from 19 ICTS in 1999 to 56 in 2002 and over 106 in 2005.[7] Table 4.1 documents some of the main ICTs that a marketing manager may have to

Table 4.1 MarkITing: a framework for ICTs – the information and interactions dimensions

Information (Research, analysis and planning)	Interactions (Communications, connections and collaboration)
Analysis and planning	*Communications*
Marketing planning systems	Internet
Performance tracking software	• website design software: Photoshop
Executive support systems	• website security
Decision support systems	• interactive website applications
ERP (Enterprise resource planning)	• ecommerce applications
Knowledge management systems	Intranets
Pricing software	Extranets
Project management software	Electronic data interchange (EDI)
Promotion tracking software	Email
Media spend analysis packages	Video conferencing
Logistics systems	Call centre
Geographical information systems	CATI – computer-aided telephone interviewing
Customer profitability analysis	Automatic call distribution
PRISM clusters – databases	Computer telephony integration
Forecasting software	Mobile communication devices
Marketing modelling	Instant messaging
Information systems (SAP, PeopleSoft and i2)	Tracking devices – Bluetooth
	SMS – simple messaging service
Databases	Facsimile communications
Centralised customer database	Electronic markets
• integrated with sales	Helplines
• integrated with call centre	Voicemail
• integrated with Internet	Spam blocking systems
• integrated with point of sale	

Table 4.1 *(Continued)*

Information (Research, analysis and planning)	Interactions (Communications, connections and collaboration)
Data consolidation and display	Voice activated/recognition software
Data mining	Computer links with suppliers
Data warehousing	Computer links with customers
Data profiling	Web casting
Data visualisation and analysis packages	Web meetings: WebEx
GQL – graphical query language	Digital imaging software
SQL – standard query language	
	Self-service technologies
Research	Integrated TV and Internet – TIVO
Internet	Internet technology
Marketing information system	ATM
Data analysis packages	Automated vending machines
Geographic information systems	Handheld scanners
Demographic online systems	Biometrics
Internet survey – design and application	Mobile phones
Online mailing lists	Bluetooth technologies
Nielsen information database	Monitoring devices
Web analytical technologies	Customisation software
Website performance and activity tracking	Personalisation software
Monitoring and tracking software	
Searchable databases	*Sales related*
	Customer relationship management
Customer relationship management	Sales force automation packages
CRM software	Mobile phones
Customised front office/back office systems	Laptops
Marketing evaluation software	Telemarketing
Contact management software	Customised sales force systems
Personalisation technologies	Customised customer applications
Customisation technologies	Access databases
	Sales reporting software
Retailing system	
Electronic point of sale	*Supply chain management*
Planogram, Spaceman Category Management	Supply chain management software
Personalisation/customisations	Automated production
Bar codes – scanning	Internet marketplace emarketplace/ehub
New product and service development	Inventory management software
Product development and design software	Material planning and supply software
Simulation technologies	Electronic data interchange
Idea generation tool: Idea Garden – Imaginatik's Idea Central	QR/ECR (efficient customer response software)
Statistical tools	Eprocurement systems
CAD (Computer-aided design)	Online purchasing transactions
	RFID (radio frequency identification devices)
Others	Interactive products
Training and educational software	Biometric
	Bluetooth technologies

General underlying and platform technologies

Hardware: Personal computers, networked computers, mainframe, laptops, personal palm computers, CD ROM/DVD, mobile phones, digital assistants

Office packages: Word, PowerPoint, Excel

Internal communications: Groupware Systems Lotus Notes, wide/local area networks – WAN/LAN

Source: Adapted from M. Brady (2006) A holistic view of ICT within the marketing domain: challenges and issues, British Academy of Management Conference, Belfast, September.

engage with. Many of these ICTs are used not only by marketing but are shared and used by other departments throughout the organisation.

The framework shown in Table 4.1 allows marketers to view the range of ICTs available to them. Each marketing situation will demand a different set of ICTs. Some are similar across companies, such as the Internet and databases, while others are unique, for example Planogram software, which is designed to help retailers to manage their shelf space. This framework will continue to grow as more and more ICTs are introduced to the market.

Over the last two decades marketing has increasingly been shifting towards service, interactivity, connectivity and ongoing relationships.[8] Digital technology facilitates this shift and changes the way companies interact with, distribute to and analyse their customers as never before. For example, contacting customers via the Web or email can be much more cost efficient compared to communication media such as television and sales forces. In Norway, Sweden and the United Kingdom more than 10 per cent of advertising budgets are now spent on online activities. The relatively highest amount spent on online advertising is found in the United Kingdom, with an estimated share of 16.6 per cent in 2007 – a share that is expected to increase to more than 20 per cent in 2009.[9]

While digital technology opens the way to new opportunities (e.g. new modes of communication, new customers and new markets) it also imposes the threat that these opportunities will be exploited just because they are available and not because they are part of a deliberate marketing strategy. Thus, while digital technology in many ways has influenced and changed the way of practising marketing, digital technology itself should not be seen as an instrument that dominates other marketing instruments. Rather, digital marketing *complements* other marketing activities – with which it should be integrated.

Digital technology may support most business activities. Some scholars distinguish between **ecommerce**: digital technology supporting sales, distribution and customer service processes; **eprocurement**: digital technology supporting sourcing, procurement, tendering and order fulfilment processes; and **emanufacturing**: digital technology supporting demand and capacity planning, forecasting and internal supply chain integration.[10] By focusing on the various activities taking place in the company supply chain, this three-group classification relates to a supply chain management approach. The term **ebusiness** has been proposed as one that includes all activities taking place in the supply chain as well as the company's internal use of digital technology.[11]

This chapter explores a range of technologies you will encounter throughout the text from the technology savvy customer to the Internet (one of the most dominant marketing technologies), to mobile and self-service technologies, and concludes with some discussion of future technologies.

The Internet

Berners-Lee, an Englishman educated at Oxford University, invented the World Wide Web, HTML (Hypertext Mark-up Language), HTTP (Hypertext Transfer/Transport Protocol) and URLs (universal resource locators) in 1990 while he was based at CERN, an international scientific organisation, in Geneva. The growth of the Internet or the World Wide Web can be traced to 1992; when it has become a ubiquitous part of European life. From a marketing perspective we view the Internet as a service provider for communication, but also internally for research and monitoring, and for many network activities including extranets and intranets.

The Internet has had a major impact on how we practise marketing. Marketers use the Internet in a variety of ways, including as a powerful information channel, as a sales channel, as a delivery or distribution channel, as a promotional or communications channel and so on. The Internet can improve the geographical reach, inform customers and promote businesses, and can be used to distribute products and services worldwide. By establishing one or more websites, companies can interact with customers 24/7, portray their products and services, history, business philosophy, job opportunities and other information of interest to visitors.

In a six-month period European online shoppers made €1.3 billion purchases, spending an average of €747 each online.[12] A massive 80 per cent of European Internet users have bought a product or service online, up 3 per cent since 2006 and double the 2004 figure.[13] Interestingly

40 per cent of all European online shoppers have changed their minds about which brand to buy following research on the Web. A 2006 report highlights that European Internet users now spend over 11 hours a week online,[14] that broadband penetration is up 14 per cent across Europe year on year and social networking websites are used by nearly a quarter of online Europeans at least once a month.[15]

From a communications perspective, a study in 2006 of 13 countries suggested that the online advertising spend in Europe was €8.003 billion. The study covers spend on display, classified and directories, search and email advertising. The United Kingdom accounted for the largest share of European online adspend, at 39 per cent of the total (€3.101 billion), with Germany accounting for 22 per cent (€1.752 billion) and France 15 per cent (€1.179 billion). The Netherlands is Europe's fourth largest market at 7 per cent (€564.3 million), closely followed by Italy at 6 per cent (€480.2 million). Spain, Denmark, Belgium, Austria, Finland, Greece, Slovenia and Croatia account for the remaining 12 per cent (€927 million). Of online advertising spend in 2006, 31 per cent was on all forms of display advertising, 45 per cent search advertising, with 22 per cent on classifieds and directories and 1.6 per cent on email marketing.[16] Online advertising spend within Europe during 2007 was €11.5 billion.[17]

Gaining competitive advantage from using the Internet

The Internet is a low-cost, open standard and therefore everybody, and every company, can establish a website or otherwise make use of the possibilities for exchanging products and services, money and information in an online setting. As such the Internet, or in a broader perspective digital marketing, does not in itself offer companies competitive advantage; rather online success depends on companies' abilities to exploit online market opportunities for their market offerings. This is no different from an offline setting. Therefore, digital technology does not offer competitive advantages per se. Success depends on other factors, such as its actual integration into organisational routines and the management skills of the firm, co-specialisation with other organisational resources and the exploitation of networks.[18] We now review how companies may create competitive advantage by using the Internet.

Reducing transaction costs

The Internet can reduce transaction costs by reducing information asymmetries and by facilitating coordination of independent processes such as design and engineering. Transaction costs occur when products or services are transferred from one organisation to another and may include search costs, contracting costs, monitoring costs and enforcement costs (see Chapter 8 for a review of transaction costs).

Moreover, the Internet allows knowledge sharing within a partnership.[19] By utilising information and communication technologies for supporting supply chain integration, companies are able to control better flows of material, information and finance. ICT generally, and Internet and Web technologies in particular, are especially useful for supply chain management (see Chapter 17).

Reducing customer search costs

Search costs (i.e. the time, money and mental resources spent when searching for favourable products and services) are recognised as an important determinant of customers' decision-making processes in the marketplace (see also Chapter 7).[20] Digital technology enables customers to access more information about products and services while at the same time facilitating a larger choice due to the global reach of the Internet.

Many online retailers have attracted consumers by offering a reduction in search costs for products and product-related information.[21] Moreover, several websites are offering consumers easy access to comparison information about various products and services. For example www.Costameno.it, a leading shopping guide for the Italian market, has a website which compares products from over 1000 websites, listing up to 800,000 products divided into 2922 categories.

On the website Costameno.it, Italian consumers can compare 800,000 products.

Source: Display srl.

Other leading comparison sites serving European customers include Pricerunner, DealClick, Shopping.com, Bizrate and Pricegrabber, among others.

Ubiquitous

Digital technology is ubiquitous, allowing 24/7 communications with customers anywhere, whether at home or at work, at the point of purchase, when walking, on the road, etc. For example, sales force automation (SFA) has changed the role of the salesperson by providing new technological tools that make him/her accessible 24/7 via such communications technologies as mobile phones, beepers, car faxes, PDAs and the Internet.[22] Technology is not just about using digital technology, it also focuses on building long-term relationships with profitable business buyers and consumers. Sales managers may derive several benefits from *i*ntegrating the *I*nternet into the *s*elling *p*rocess (IISP). For example, IISP can assist salespeople in providing a faster and more complete service and at the same time reduce the time and effort that customers would have to invest in completing the transaction. In this way IISP may improve the perceived value that the buyer receives from the seller and thereby facilitate close and long-lasting seller–buyer relationships.

The influence of the Internet on industry structure and competition

Marketing professor Michael E. Porter has used his 'five forces' framework (see Chapter 9 for a review of this framework) to discuss how the Internet may influence industry structure.[23] Porter argues that gaining a competitive advantage through the Internet does not require a radically new approach to business. It requires building on the proven principles of effective strategy. In this respect, two underlying profitability drivers are fundamental: (1) *industry structure*, which determines the profitability of the average competitor; and (2) *sustainable competitive advantage*, which allows a company to outperform the average competitor. Since these vary widely across industries and companies, an analysis of potential profitability should be carried out by looking at individual industries and individual companies.

The general attractiveness of an industry is determined by five underlying forces of competition: the intensity of rivalry among existing competitors, the barriers to entry for new competitors, the threat of substitute products or services, the bargaining power of suppliers, and the bargaining power of buyers. Figure 4.1 suggests some implications of the Internet on industry attractiveness. Note that these are only general trends, and that variations may occur across industries. Some of these trends influence positively the attractiveness of an industry, whereas others negatively influence industry attractiveness.

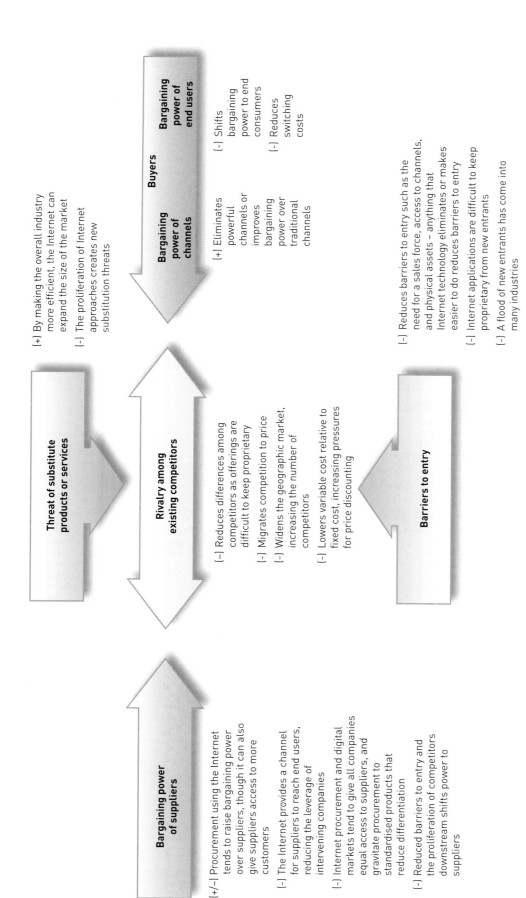

Figure 4.1 How the Internet influences industry structure

Source: Adapted from M. E. Porter (2001) Strategy and the Internet, *Harvard Business Review*, March, 62–78. Copyright © 2001 by the President and Fellows of Harvard College. All rights reserved. Reproduced with permission.

While the net effect of these trends – as looked upon from the company's perspective – seems negative, this is not true for all industries. Internet auctions provide an example of this. Here, customers and suppliers are fragmented and thus have little power. Substitutes, such as classified ads and flea markets, have less reach and are less convenient to use. Even though entry barriers are relatively modest, companies can build economies of scale by using the Internet – in particular because of many buyers and sellers.

However, since the Internet influences industry attractiveness in a way that might put average profitability under pressure, the pressure to reach and maintain competitive advantage also increases. Fundamentally, marketing managers can react to this pressure in two ways. They can seek to increase their operational effectiveness (doing the same things as their competitors but doing them better), and/or they can seek to increase their strategic positioning (doing things differently from their competitors in order to provide additional value to customers). The Internet, and other forms of digital technology, can be a powerful tool in increasing operational effectiveness. However, no matter how well digital technology supports the activities within an industry, companies can only build competitive advantage if they are able to improve and sustain operational effectiveness better than their competitors. With the digital revolution this task has become more difficult to accomplish. Because of the openness of the Internet, in combination with many companies relying on similar Internet applications, improvements in operational effectiveness tend to be broadly shared among companies in an industry.

▽ Digital marketing communication

Digital marketing communication (DMC) can be understood as 'communication and inter-action between a company or brand and its customers using digital channels (e.g., the Internet, email, mobile phones and digital TV) and information technology'.[24] Digital marketing facilitates interactivity, electronic word of mouth (eWOM) and the development of online communities.

Figure 4.2 displays the percentage of European individuals who have ever carried out specific Internet-related activities, including interactive messages to chatrooms, newsgroups, online discussions and peer-to-peer (P2P) file sharing. These interactive activities are considered next.

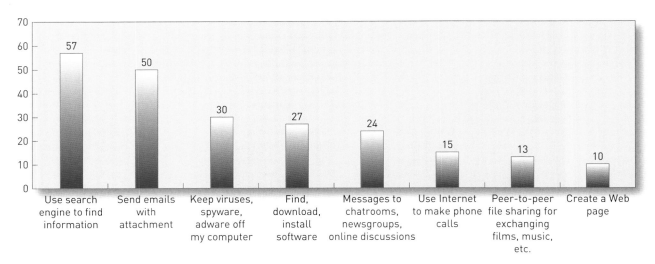

Figure 4.2 Individuals who have ever carried out specific Internet-related activities in the EU, 2007 (%)

Source: M. Smihily (2007) Internet usage in 2007: households and individuals, in *Eurostat Data in Focus*, Luxembourg: Office for Official Publications of the European Communities. Copyright © 2007 European Communities. Reproduced with permission.

Consumer digital interactivity and eWOM

Direct marketing, the idea of acting directly on the individual customer, was known long before the creation of the Internet. However, the Internet provides a new tool for supplier–customer interactivity that is less expensive and much more flexible than 'old' tools such as telephone marketing and reply-paid coupons. In spite of these advantages, digital marketing researchers John Deighton and Leora Kornfeld suggest that the revolution of direct marketing has been overshadowed by consumer online collaboration. Using digital media that lie beyond the control of marketers, consumers communicate among one another, responding to marketing's intrusions by disseminating counterargument, information sharing, rebuttal, parody and reproach. Globally the media of collaboration range from consumer review sites such as Epinions and Trip Advisor, to collaborative networking sites such as Bebo, Facebook, Orkut and Meetup, to trading sites such as Craigslist and eBay, and user-generated content sites such as YouTube, Cyworld, and blogs. As a consequence, future marketing may be less a matter of domination and control and more a matter of adapting and fitting into structures and platforms that are created outside managers' control.[25]

Word-of-mouth (WOM) between consumers has interested managers and researchers for a long time. WOM may have a significant impact on consumer choice as well as post-purchase perceptions and may even be more effective than the traditional marketing tools of personal selling and various types of advertising.[26] Until recently the interest in WOM has largely focused on interpersonal (or face-to-face) influence. However, the global nature of the Internet allows communication between people – even from different countries and cultures – who have never met. This sort of information – eWOM (electronic word of mouth) – often has higher credibility than marketer-created sources of information on the Internet, since no direct commercial interests interferes with the communication.[27]

Social networking

Social networking has revolutionised the way people communicate and share information with one another in today's society. Various social networking websites are being used by millions of people every day on a regular basis. The main types of social networking services are those that contain directories of some categories (such as former classmates), means to connect with friends (usually with self-description pages) and recommender systems linked to trust. Popular methods now combine many of these. Bebo, MySpace, Skyrock Blog, Facebook and Hi5 are the most popular sites in Europe. There are also more targeted social networking sites. For example BBC online – LINK website, targeting 13–16 year olds – gets over 1 million hits a day.[28]

Social networking is now in the fabric of young people's lives and this means that marketers need to understand this new use of the Internet. Though the Internet started off as a dominantly male preserve the advent of social networking has led to a female explosion in the use of the Web. A survey in the United Kingdom carried out by Hitwise showed that 55 per cent of all British users of social networking sites were women.[29] Whereas females are more suited to social networking, males are more likely to use YouTube and post videos to the site.

Offline and online social networks are compared across three dimensions: tie strength, online homophily and source credibility.

1 In general, *tie strength* refers to the strength of the dyadic interpersonal relationships in the context of a social network.[30] Strong ties are characterised by:

> (a) a sense that the relationship is intimate and special, with a voluntary investment in the tie and a desire for companionship with the partner; (b) an interest in frequent interactions in multiple contexts; and (c) a sense of mutuality of the relationship, with the partner's needs known and supported.[31]

In an online environment, individual-to-individual social ties seem less relevant than in an offline environment. Instead, individuals tend to use the websites themselves as proxies for individuals. Like brands, websites can have 'personalities' and therefore they can be treated as people with whom the individual can have personal relations. This notion receives support from social response theory, which states that consumers apply social rules to respond to computers on websites when these possess humanlike attributes, or social cues. That is, consumers may treat websites as social actors even though consumers are fully aware that websites are not humans.[32]

2 The likelihood of a tie usually depends on attributes of the actors. For example, for most social relations the likelihood of a relationship is a function of the age, gender, geography, lifestyle and status of the individuals. Also, ties are often more likely to occur between actors who have similar attributes than between those who do not. This tendency is called *homophily* by attributes.[33] However, in an online setting homophily can be thought of as the congruence between a user's psychological attributes and website content. That is, dominant dimensions of homophily are not gender or status but shared group interests and mindset.

3 *Source credibility* is always a key concern in communication efforts. Source credibility depends on a message source's perceived ability or motivation to provide accurate and truthful information concerning the issue under consideration. Source credibility is high if the source is perceived to have high expertise and high trustworthiness.[34] In an online social network setting, source credibility refers to the perceived competence of the website and its membership, and source credibility seems especially to be based on site trustworthiness and the expertise of the actors visiting the site.

Marketers are monitoring online social networks communication for information about consumers. Consumers participating in online communications may influence highly the opinions of other people. As an example of this, the 22-year-old Chinese activist Zeng Jinyan (who started a blog against the Chinese government and secret police as a protest against her husband's disappearance), little known outside of blogging circles, was included when *Time* magazine issued its list of the 100 most influential people in the world in May 2007. In China, television still reaches the single largest group of consumers – more than 700 million across the country – but the Internet has become a powerful unifying force, at least in urban areas. People discuss their opinions online more freely than they may in person and these discussions may obviously be of interest to managers. 'What are they talking about? 'What do they say? Are they talking about safety? About cost? About customer service?' asked Sam Flemming, co-founder of CIC, a company that tracks and analyses online chats on specific products. In China, there may be some 137 million people online – a relatively small number compared to the population of the country – but these are the same people who will buy cars and expensive Puma shoes.[35]

Brand communities

Branding is explored in Chapters 12 and 13 but the use of ICT and digital marketing has changed how marketing approaches and manages branding. An increase in global active brand communities can in many ways be attributed to the use of technology by consumers. A brand community is 'a specialised, non-geographically bound community, based on a structured set of social relations among admirers of a brand'.[36] While brand communities are found both online and offline, only virtual communities allow consumers to 'gather' independently of geographical location and time zones.[37] Nevertheless, brand communities may also meet outside the virtual world to enjoy their brands together in real life – be it cars, motorbikes, toys, books, games based on movies or even food products (such as Nutella) – which can create passionate feelings.[38] For example, on lovemarks.com – a site attributed to brands that are high in consumer respect and love – Enrico from Italy notes that

> eating Nutella is not only nourishing for my body but it also reignites, every morning, the inner flame in my soul. The simple act of spreading Nutella on a slice of bread puts the sun again in the sky, regardless of what the weather channel says!

Three kinds of brand communities can be detected: (1) exclusively consumer driven with no accepted interference from companies (e.g. fan clubs such as Star Trek); (2) company driven with input from consumers or customers (e.g. Saatchi & Saatchi's lovemarks.com); (3) consumer/customer-company 'joint ventures' (e.g. some of the LEGO community websites).[39] Virtual communities can be an effective tool for reaching a large number of consumers, segmenting the market with low promotional costs, or increasing consumer trust, among other benefits.[40]

Simply establishing a web-based brand community network does not guarantee a successful virtual community. Sustaining virtual communities depends on people visiting the site, facilitating social interaction among community members and, most significantly, enhancing the loyalty of community members.[41] Studies of offline and online brand communities reveal that much of the value gained by community members does not stem from the brand itself, but from the social links formed as a result of using the brand.[42]

Marketing professor Suzanne C. Beckmann from Copenhagen Business School, Denmark and Martin Gjerløff from DDB Needham Denmark suggest that companies seeking to communicate with brand communities may do so by following one or more of five approaches:

1 **Fight**: Many communities are positioning themselves as an opposition to another group: what would life be as a Real Madrid fan without Barcelona? The sense of 'us versus them' influences how community members think, feel and act. The Internet music file-sharing service Napster, one of the strongest – and first! – virtual brand communities, is an example of a fight strategy. Napster achieved its success by developing an ingenious anti-establishment attitude, not just by offering great technology. Napster later paved the way for decentralised peer-to-peer file-sharing programmes such as Kazaa, Limewire, iMesh, Morpheus, and BearShare.[43]

2 **Role models**: The main function for role models is to be both catalyst and backbone for a community: somebody to identify with, to be inspired by, and to aspire to. Role models can therefore be used to create unified feelings among community members. A typical example is communities based on information exchange, brought together by a prominent person such as Jamie Oliver (http://community.channel4.com/eve/forums/a/frm/f/4890059651).

3 **Exchange**: Exchange ranges from gift giving and knowledge sharing to strategic networks and alliances. Exchange, as a central driver of brand communities, is found in both consumer- and company-driven communities, and quite often results in a 'joint venture' between the two parties. An example of a primarily exchange-based community is the International LEGO Users Group Network 'Lugnet' (www.lugnet.com).

4 **Manifestation**: Manifestation builds on the human need for the traditions, rituals, symbols and icons around which groups gather. From a company perspective such human needs may be an attractive venue for relationship-marketing activities. The campaign by the British Columbia Dairy Foundation (BCDF, a not-for-profit organisation dedicated to increasing consumption of milk in British Columbia) provides an example of how manifestations may be used. Ads displayed people in daily situations, but only their head and feet were exposed in order to symbolise the impossibility of doing anything without a body. The pay-off was 'Don't take your body for granted. Drink milk'. The ads were used as a springboard for the young target group to start talking about milk in forums such as skating ramps, snowboard competitions and music events sponsored by BCDF.

5 **Progression**: Progression means looking forward, constantly striving for development and innovation. Second Life, an online 3D world imagined and created by residents, is an example of a progression site. Opened to the public in 2003, Second Life is today inhabited by millions of residents from around the globe.

Virtual worlds Millions of people have joined virtual worlds such as Second Life and There.com. These online games, known as 'massively multiplayer online games', allow people to inhabit alternative virtual worlds as a character of their choosing.

▽ Second Life

Second Life is an online, 3D virtual world imagined and created by its users, called residents. Launched in 2003, its popularity rocketed in 2006. The game currently has over 16.3 residents; 3 million users are considered regulars. Sixty per cent of Second Life's users come from the United Kingdom, the United States, Germany and France. There are currently about 500,000 residents who log into Second Life on a weekly basis. These 'residents' can explore, socialise and participate in activities and services using Second Life's currency, the Linden Dollar. Second Life is one of the biggest virtual worlds in existence and many major brands, including Coca-Cola, Vodafone, IBM, Toyota, Sony and Adidas, already have a presence there. Sweden and Estonia have both opened embassies on Second Life, designed to promote their country's image and culture, rather than providing any real or virtual services.[44] Second Life is becoming part of popular culture, with the Italian singer Irene Grandi using some scenes from Second Life in her music video 'Bruci la città'. St Patrick's Day – Ireland's national day – went virtual in 2008 with the largest ever viewing (by 12 million people) of the virtual St Patrick's Day Parade on Second Life. The availability of virtual classrooms on Second Life has been taken up my many universities including Delft University of Technology in Holland and Edinburgh University in Scotland. At Insead University in France, the first MBA class of the 2008 term was given on the Second Life campus. Professor Sarvary lectured on the evolution of modern media to a room full of students who had been invited by email.[45]

The St Patrick's Day Parade in Ireland received 12 million visitors on Second Life the virtual world on the Web.

Source: Linden Research, Inc.

Email marketing

People are most receptive to emails from companies with whom they already have a relationship but are really irritated by irrelevant communication messages. Indeed, most consumers can recognise the difference between 'spam' and legitimate direct marketing emails. A recent survey conducted by IPT Email Broadcasting revealed that nearly half of UK online consumers (46 per cent) believe that there is a difference between spam and direct marketing emails and can be expected to treat companies' messages accordingly.[46] Companies such as IPT, Email Reaction, iContact and RapidReach[TM] offer email broadcasting. Europe's largest email broadcaster, IPT Email Broadcasting, sends over 4 billion emails per year.

Managers considering an email marketing campaign must be aware that legal restrictions apply in this area. The EU Directive on privacy and electronic communications (2002/58/EC), often referred to as the 'spam directive' or the 'opt-in directive', states that sending commercial email messages is only allowed if recipients have given their prior consent. However, there are some exceptions to that rule. If there is an existing customer relationship, a seller of a product or a service has the right to market to the customer its own similar products or services. This right only applies if the customer has not initially refused commercial contact via email, and the sender also has to offer the recipient a free-of-charge and easy-to-use mechanism to say no to future emails.[47] Despite the opt-in directive, email marketing rules are not necessarily completely identical across EU member states. For example, business-to-business (B2B) emails require a mandatory opt-in in Austria, but may be sent to some companies on an opt-out basis in the United Kingdom. Thus, although the EU directive gives companies an overview of the base standard in Europe, each country's local email marketing laws still need to be checked on a case-by-case basis.[48]

Email marketing firm RapidReach[TM] (www.dnbRapidReach.com) recommends that the following five steps are taken when creating a commercial email:[49]

1 The email must be accurate and identify the person who initiated the email.

2 The subject line should not be misleading.

3 A return email address or an Internet-based response mechanism should be provided. Also, a facility allowing recipients to ask not to be sent future email messages must be included.

4 The physical address of the company must be included.

5 The message must contain clear and conspicuous notice that the message is an advertisement of solicitation.

Permission marketing

Introduced in 1999 by marketing consultant Seth Godin in his book of the same name,[50] permission marketing seeks permission in advance from consumers before they are sent marketing communications. In principle, such communications may be distributed through many media – including mobile phones, emails and interactive digital television. While commercial emails need permission from potential new customers before they are sent out, permission marketing is a broad term covering all kinds of permission seeking. Consumers provide interested marketers with information about the types of communication they would like to receive. This information enables marketing managers to target marketing communication to interested and involved consumers.[51] Seth Godin states that

> consumers are now willing to pay handsomely to save time, while marketers are eager to pay bundles to get attention . . . The alternative is permission marketing, which offers the consumer an opportunity to volunteer to be marketed to. By talking only to volunteers, permission marketing guarantees that consumers pay more attention to the marketing message (42–3).

Thus, permission marketing seeks to develop an interactive communication with customers and over time to establish trust and loyalty. When trust is established customers may subsequently increase the levels of permission, making permission marketing efforts an even more valuable

Figure 4.3 Levels in permission marketing

Source: Adapted from E. T. Brey, S.-l. (A.) So, D.Y. Kim and A. M. Morrison (2007) Web-based permission marketing: segmentation for the lodging industry, *Tourism Management*, 28, 1408–16. Copyright © 2007 Elsevier. Reproduced with permission.

- **Level 1:** *Situation permission* is a one-time or limited-time permission, which is the least potent of the five levels. This is given when consumers agree to receive sales or promotional messages from a company for a specified time.

- **Level 2:** *Brand trust* is the most common way managers practise their craft. With this permission, consumers have developed confidence in a product or service that carries a particular or well-known brand name.

- **Level 3:** *Personal relationship* uses individual relationships between the consumer and manager to temporarily refocus the attention or modify the consumer's behaviour. This approach is the best technique to sell customised or highly involving products.

- **Level 4:** At the level of *points permission*, points are a formalised, scalable approach to attracting and keeping the prospect's attention. This involves consumers allowing the company to collect personal data and to market its products and services to them on a points-based loyalty scheme.

- **Level 5:** *Intravenous* refers to the highest level of permission to be won from consumers. This involves customers trusting the marketer to make buying decisions for them.

---

asset.[52] Five levels of permission can be won from customers targeted by a permission-marketing campaign (see Figure 4.3).

Asking for permission could be beneficial to firms, even at times when permission is not strictly needed. Founded in 2004, Facebook is one of the most popular social utilities on the Internet. In 2007, Facebook decided to allow advertisers to display ads based on information users post on their profiles. With relative ease advertisers can now target under-age consumers, raising obvious ethical questions since no permission from parents is needed. Nevertheless, advertisers need to handle carefully this targeted marketing effort. Asking teenagers what ads they prefer might even be a beneficial strategy, as discovered by Flip.com. When Flip.com users register they are asked which ads they prefer to be displayed on their profiles. Asking for 'permission' before displaying ads gets teens to think about the products or service being offered, and lets them consciously choose to align themselves with a specific brand. Also, teens may have more respect for the service and for advertisers that they have chosen themselves since they can then get a feeling of control with regard to the information they are exposed to on the site. This in turn may lead to word-of-mouth recommendations, a major force behind teen purchasing decisions.[53]

Viral marketing

Viral marketing is an Internet adaptation of marketing using the word-of-mouth effect. Viral marketing can be understood as an advertising message spread by consumers among other consumers (see also Chapter 7). Viral marketing has been treated by many as an almost coincidental marketing instrument – as a 'funny instrument' that might add a little extra attention and colour to primary marketing efforts.

The number of new videos that are placed on the Internet is gigantic. For example, on YouTube more than 60,000 videos are uploaded every day and breaking through such an overwhelming stream of information is not an easy task. Therefore, the first and difficult task is to attract online attention among target segments.[54] In a viral marketing campaign, a company may use the influence of its own customers to promote a product or service to prospective customers but may also post its campaign material in a diversity of places. Seeding is the process of placing, posting and promoting the campaign material. It is important that the seeds match the characteristics and interests of the target group. For example, if you want to attract potential buyers of Rolls-Royce or Bentley cars it might not be a good idea placing your video on YouTube or Sharkle since people considering buying such cars may be unlikely to visit those sites. Also, the company needs to consider whether seeds should be framed to match local language and culture. Some viral marketing campaigns only manage to get 5 per cent of video recipients to forward the video to other customers, while the share for the more popular ones is usually around 30 per cent.[55] This emphasises the need for carefully targeting the company's viral marketing campaign.

Some marketing agencies, such as GoViral, have specialised in viral marketing campaigns.

▽ GoViral

Operating out of several European cities including London, Stockholm, Copenhagen and Hamburg, GoViral (http://www.goviral.com) launches user-driven marketing campaigns for leading creative agencies, media agencies and advertisers worldwide. GoViral's global Seed&Track™ solution helps marketers reach people globally in 27 countries. In all countries GoViral seeds content-based campaigns in local languages, on local sites and with local seeders. Communication materials, such as commercials, games, stories, etc. are placed on the Internet – seeking to create high-volume, targeted and cost-effective user-driven marketing campaigns.

In March 2006 tyre maker Goodyear launched a Europe-wide viral campaign. Consisting of three viral clips produced by Leagas Delaney, London, the campaign was launched by marketing agency GoViral in nine different languages with active seeding in five selected markets: Germany, France, the United Kingdom, Sweden and Denmark. In just nine months the videos were viewed more than 9 million times – with the major viewing in the five selected markets. The target for the campaign, which aimed to raise awareness of the Goodyear brand, was 700,000 views! From an expected average cost per view at €0.30, actual average cost per view turned out to be just €0.025.[56]
http://5x5m.com/files/goodyear

Goodyear viral marketing campaign: changing tyres can be dangerous.
Source: Leagas Delaney

In addition to email marketing, permission marketing and viral marketing, modern digital technology also offers several other communication channels, including mobile phone communication, banner ads and interactive television.

Other digital communication channels

Search engine optimisation

Search engine optimisation (SEO) is the process of improving the volume and quality of traffic to a website from search engines. Usually, the earlier a site is presented in the search results or the higher it 'ranks', the more searchers will visit that site. 'Paid searches' is a micromarketing technique unique to the Internet. If you type in a few words on a popular search engine, a column of paid advertisements, often called sponsored links, will appear on the right. Google is by far the most widely used search engine in European countries.

Wireless Internet access

Wireless Internet access is the ability to access the Internet without wires and is becoming a real growth area. Wireless connections to the Internet are growing with 'hot spots' in restaurants, train stations, airports, libraries, hotels, hospitals, coffee shops, bookstores, department stores, supermarkets and other public places. Many universities and schools have wireless networks on campus. City-wide Wi-Fi is available in nine cities in the United Kingdom, including Leeds, Manchester, Norwich and London, and also in the city of Luxembourg in continental Europe. Wi-Fi is the common name for a popular wireless technology used in home networks, mobile phones, video games and more. Wi-Fi is supported by nearly every personal computer operating system and most advanced game consoles. A Wi-Fi-enabled device such as a PC, games console, mobile phone, MP3 player or PDA can connect to the Internet over a wireless network.

A hot spot is one or more interconnected access points, which can comprise an area as small as a single room or as large as many square miles covered by overlapping access points. The public can use a laptop, Wi-Fi phone or other suitable portable device to access the Internet. Of the estimated 150 million laptops, 14 million PDAs and other emerging Wi-Fi devices sold over the last few years, most include the Wi-Fi feature. Wi-Fi is starting to be used in products and services, with the Toyota Camry using Autonet Mobile to introduce new product features that let passengers simultaneously store personalised content and media within the car, while accessing the Internet from any Wi-Fi-enabled device through its Autonet Mobile Wi-Fi Router.

Mobile phones

The mobile phone has become an indispensable item and a fashion totem for many consumers. Friedrich Joussen, head of Vodafone Germany notes that, 'Today, the mobile phone – next to keys and wallets – is the most important thing people carry with them when they leave the house.' From a marketing perspective its use will continue to grow. Marketing uses abound, from the sending of text messages such as Argos does to say your product has arrived for collection, to automatic payment using a mobile phone. Every time someone uses a phone they are leaving behind a few bits of information – where they are and what number they called – this has been called the trail of digital breadcrumbs.[57]

Mobile phones are now being used for multiple activities, including text messages (SMS), multimedia messaging services (MMS, allowing the sending of images, audio and video), emails and Internet browsing and video watching. With the introduction of 3G services (a technology that offers users a wider range of advanced services – for example broadband wireless data – while achieving greater network capacity (see also Chapter 6)) a convergence is expected of mobile and traditional Internet-based services.[58] 3G services were first introduced in March 2003 in the United Kingdom and Italy. The leading European '3G country' is Italy, with a third of its subscribers migrated to 3G (June 2007). Other leading countries by 3G migration include the United Kingdom, Austria and Singapore at the 20 per cent migration level.[59] Forrester Research estimates that 38 per cent of mobile phone users in western Europe will use mobile Internet by 2013. This equates to 125 million Europeans. In 2008, 42 million Europeans access the Internet regularly from their mobile phones.[60]

Moreover, mobile advertising has been named one of the most promising potential business areas.[61] By using mobile advertising companies can communicate directly with their consumers without location barriers. Top international companies such as Nike, BMW, Virgin and McDonald's are using mobile advertising campaigns to convey commercial content to customers.[62]

Mobile advertising campaigns should be aware that mobile consumers often regard their mobile phone as a private item and therefore are sensitive to receiving messages from companies if such messages have not been asked for in advance.[63] Mobile advertising researchers Ramin Vatanparast and Mahsa Asil suggest that 'mobile advertisements should be able to provide relevant information and rewards, be delivered by trusted organizations, and also give the viewer control over the message'.[64]

The real winner or killer application for the mobile phone is texting. Text messaging or texting is the common term for the sending of 'short' (160 characters or fewer) text messages from mobile phones using SMS. It is available on most digital mobile phones and some PDAs. SMS gateways exist to connect mobile SMS services with instant message services, the World Wide Web, desktop computers and even landline telephones (through speech synthesis).

The most common application of the service is person-to-person messaging, but text messages are also often used to interact with automated systems, such as ordering products and services from mobile phones, for example ringtones, or participating in contests. Ringtones are actually big business, with ringtone sales exceeding €800 million in 2006.[65] The ringtone market is now believed to be worth more than twice the value of CD single sales, excluding Internet downloads. Jamster's Crazy Frog ringtone was by far the year's bestseller, taking 31 per cent of the British ringtone market, now worth £133 million. Sweetie Chick's Tweet Tweet, another strange animal from Jamster, was the year's second-biggest selling ringtone. Novelty tracks are most popular with 5–15 year olds, who drive the ringtone market.

Some of the world's leading global search and content companies are currently redeploying their Internet content advertising model to fit the mobile industry.

▽ Peugeot's mobile Internet phone campaign

Using mobile text messaging helped marketing managers at Peugeot Ireland to communicate and promote the launch of the new Peugeot 207. Print advertisements encouraged consumers to text '207' to a given number in order to receive more information about the car and organise a test drive[66] . . . The campaign, which included billboard, mailing, press and radio advertising, encouraged target customers to download a link to a mobile Internet website that they could view on their handset. The company says that it has resulted in a large volume of responses, and with 40 per cent of respondents providing personal contact details, the campaign has proven to be very successful in generating test drives. Peugeot is one of the first in Ireland to use mobile Internet marketing and to integrate it across an entire campaign. Vincent Delettre, CRM manager, Peugeot Ireland said,

> The real advantage of mobile Internet marketing was being able to introduce much more creativity, colour, interactivity and fun to our marketing. The results have been very strong to date. They certainly justify our plan to allocate a larger proportion of our advertising budget to mobile.

Banner ads

Banner ads have dominated online advertising and have become the standard Web advertising format.[67] Now, banner ads are found on a huge number of Web pages, varying considerably in both appearance and subject matter. But they all share a basic function: if you click on them, you will be taken to the advertiser's website. Often a banner ad looks similar to the kinds of ads that are printed in newspapers or magazines. Banner ads may serve two objectives.[68] First, attracting visitors to the advertiser's website. Second, by placing banner ads on selected sites visitors may learn to associate the advertised brand with certain attributes or values. Banner advertising can thus be a useful branding instrument.

The way banner advertising is used can be expected to change in the years to come. Site visitors' attraction seems to be declining as banner ads are now part of thousands of websites. One good indicator of this tendency is HP, a global leading technology company that operates in more than 170 countries around the world. At the beginning of 2008 HP's Danish Department announced that it would downsize its banner advertising: 'I think that people are becoming immune to banner ads, there are simply too many banner ads out there,' sales manager Knud Ottosen said.[69]

Interactive television

Based on digital technology, interactive television (iTV) has the ability to individualise television viewing. Using iTV viewers already have (or will have in the near future) the opportunity of putting a show on hold, or even restarting a film if they have missed the beginning. Also, viewers can choose when they would like to see a TV programme (timeshifting). iTV also allows for personalisation in other ways. For example, much like Internet cookies, the television set will 'learn' the profile and interests of its user(s). When switching on the television set it will tell the viewer what programmes s/he has missed while being away (sorted in a prioritised order, of course) and it will suggest future programmes that might be of particular interest to the viewer(s).[70] There are over 180 TV channels across Europe. Interactive television provides additional features for television programmes, ranging from alternative soundtracks and camera views to additional information on the programmes. Digital television is available in Europe through all main platforms: terrestrial, satellite, cable and via the Internet (IPTV). Digital television differs considerably from one European country to the next. Digital TV penetration across the EU is around 25 per cent of households, and the United Kingdom is the leader with around 64 per cent.

iTV presents several possibilities to marketing managers. As part of iTV, the biggest commercial television network in the United Kingdom, ITV media (www.itvmedia.co.uk) offers a number of ways in which companies can communicate with TV viewers, such as red button advertising. By pressing the red button on the remote control handset viewers can choose to be actively involved with an advertised product or service and have the opportunity to create a return path, enabling a two-way dialogue between potential customers and the company. For example, viewers can read more about the product, request more information or make a purchase. Guinness and Unilever are both examples of companies utilising red button advertising. There is also red button programme sponsorship: it is possible to sponsor the interactive content of a programme and have the company name overlaid on the broadcast show. Again, viewers can go interactive using the remote control handset. Nokia, First Choice and Cobra are among the companies utilising interactive sponsorship.

Self-service technologies

Self-service technology (SST) means that the customer engages with technology-based systems rather than company personnel. So rather than visiting a bank we use the ATM, rather than going to a cashier in the supermarket customers choose the self-service option. Self-service checkouts are already successfully implemented in many supermarkets throughout Europe. Retail and business groups welcomed the use of the technology, which they say could prove appealing to customers looking to spend as little time as possible in stores. At the same time, they insisted that the technology would never replace the personal service offered by manned checkouts and would always be used alongside staff. In recent research 66 per cent of teenagers and 62 per cent of adults wanted self-checkout, but over 61 per cent of adults and 57 per cent of teenagers wanted staff to help with packing the bags.[71]

Technology allows customers access to what were traditionally back office functions private to the company. Log on to http://www.astonmartin.com/configurator to build your ideal Aston Martin car, the details of which go straight through to the production operation of Aston Martin. Alternatively, how about a customised M&M? Log on to the M&M sweets site and you can customise your own M&Ms with little messages such as 'Hello'. You can even select only certain colours, for example the colours of your favourite team.

In academic research, customers saw human contact as part of the service and 51 per cent wanted human contact at different stages of the buying process. The findings suggested that

The M&M website allows consumers to customise their M&Ms.
Source: Mars, Inc.

technology and human interaction should be complementary. What is really needed is for the technology to be designed around customer needs and preferences, but in reality much of the introduction of technology has meant that service has been diminished rather than enhanced.[72] The introduction of self-service technologies is often designed as a cost-cutting method. The use of automated voice answering machines can frustrate and annoy customers who wish to talk to a human being, especially when they have a problem. Another perspective is that the company is more productive, but is shifting work to consumers.

▽ Consumer digital shopping behaviour

The percentage of individuals aged 16–74 in the EU who purchased products or services over the Internet increased from 24 per cent in 2005 to 30 per cent in 2007. The highest proportions of Internet shoppers in 2007 were recorded in Denmark (55 per cent), the Netherlands (55 per cent), Sweden and the United Kingdom (both 53 per cent).[73] According to eMarketer, the United Kingdom will account for at least 40 per cent of 2008 online sales in western Europe. While this proportion is expected to decline slightly as ecommerce becomes better established elsewhere in Europe, the United Kingdom will still represent the greatest single share of the European market in 2011 (see Figure 4.4). 'A long tradition of catalogue and mail order shopping has contributed to the practice of online buying in the UK,' says eMarketer senior analyst Karin von Abrams. In 2006, 12 per cent of individuals aged 16–74 in the EU had not ordered products or services over the Internet in the preceding 12 months because of worries about giving credit card or personal details online. These security and privacy concerns were most common in Spain (27 per cent), Finland (26 per cent) and Cyprus (20 per cent).[74]

Of those individuals who use the Internet, 44 per cent now perform banking activities, making online banking the fastest-growing Internet activity in the EU. While online banking is perceived by many consumers as more convenient than visiting bank branches, the increasing speed of Internet connections is also an important reason for the fast growth. Other popular products include travel, theatre and concert tickets, clothing, books and magazines and software.[75] For the marketing manager it is important to gain insight into the factors that may influence consumer online shopping behaviour in order to match consumers' needs and wants. Five perspectives that consider such factors are reviewed below.

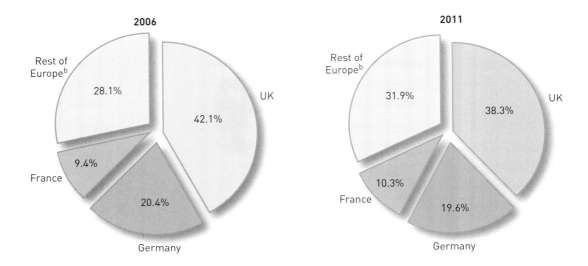

Figure 4.4 Distribution of B2C ecommerce sales[a] in Europe, 2006 and 2011 (% of total)
Notes: Numbers may not add up to 100% due to rounding.
[a]Includes online travel, event ticket and digital download sales.
[b]Includes Austria, Belgium, Denmark, Finland, Greece, Ireland, Italy, Luxembourg, the Netherlands,
Norway, Portugal, Spain, Sweden and Switzerland.
Source: eMarketer (2008) The UK Internet boom: the British are going digital – fast, *eMarketer*, 19 February.
Copyright © eMarketer, Inc. Reproduced with permission.

Perspectives on consumer digital shopping behaviour

Several models and theories can be applied for the purpose of understanding consumer digital shopping behaviour, that is, consumers' decisions on what to buy, in what amount and where – offline or online. We now consider five main perspectives on consumer digital behaviour:

1   the theory of reasoned action and the theory of planned behaviour;

2   the technology acceptance model;

3   the theory of adoption of innovations;

4   the trade-off/transaction costs perspective;

5   the perceived risk perspective.

The theory of planned behaviour

A consumer may be prevented from buying online if he or she perceives the purchase process as too complex or if the consumer does not possess the resources necessary to perform the considered behaviour. This may happen even if the consumer has a positive attitude towards online shopping. Such considerations are incorporated into the theory of planned behaviour (TPB) as perceived behavioural control (PBC).[76] PBC can be conceptualised as the consumer's subjective belief about how difficult it will be for that consumer to generate the behaviour in question. As an example, a consumer considering buying groceries over the Internet may hesitate to do so if he or she perceives the ordering process as too difficult. According to TPB the same consumer may, however, be persuaded that buying groceries is worth trying if one of the consumer's closest friends has already done so with success (social norm).

The technology acceptance model

The technology acceptance model (TAM) was developed to predict 'technology acceptance', which can be conceptualised as an individual's psychological state with regard to his or her voluntary or intended use of a particular technology. TAM proposes that the two most important variables in explaining attitude towards system-using intention are perceived ease of use (i.e., perceived complexity) and perceived usefulness. However, TAM can be modified to predict consumer digital shopping behaviour. For example, perceived usefulness can be conceptualised as the degree to which online shopping will provide the consumer with relative advantages in comparison to offline shopping.[77] Evidence, based on a modification of the TAM approach, suggests that both perceived usefulness and perceived ease of using the Internet for shopping purposes have positive effects on consumers' intentions to adopt online shopping. In addition, research suggests that attempts to understand consumer motivations for online shopping behaviour may benefit from taking into account the hedonic aspects (e.g., shopping enjoyment and/or fun) of the shopping experience along with perceived usefulness and perceived ease of use.[78]

The theory of adoption of innovations

Digital shopping could be regarded as an innovation, which like other innovations takes time to spread through the social system. The adoption of an innovation depends on various factors (including perceived compatibility, perceived relative advantage, perceived complexity, triability, and observability), that are related to the innovation itself and to the consumer.[79] Communicability is the ease with which the innovation can be observed or communicated among potential adopters. Triability or divisibility refers to the possibility of trying the innovation without huge investments. Complexity refers to the potential adopter's perceived complexity of the innovation or of using the innovation. Compatibility is the degree to which the innovation is consistent with existing values and past behaviour. Relative advantage is the degree to which consumers perceive the innovation as superior to existing alternatives. People in favour of online buying often point to the fact that this way of purchasing saves time and offers quality products at lower prices as compared to traditional shopping outlets.

Channel trade-offs and transactions costs

From the channel trade-offs and transaction costs perspective, an understanding of consumer online shopping behaviour needs to include considerations on how consumers will make choices relative to available retail alternatives. Often consumers are faced with trade-offs when deciding which retail alternative to use to make a purchase. When evaluating different shopping channel alternatives (including the Internet) the channel trade-offs and transaction costs perspective proposes that consumers are likely to choose the channel that minimises perceived transactions costs. Transactions costs (i.e., time, mental, money and physical costs) include costs for obtaining relevant information, costs for evaluating relevant products, order costs and costs for post-sales services. Consumers' perceived transaction costs may, among other factors, be affected by consumers' perceived uncertainty, which are costs associated with unexpected outcomes of the transaction and asymmetry of information, that is, the seller and buyer may not have the same amount of information.

The perceived risk perspective

The suggestion that a high level of uncertainty implies a higher transaction cost and therefore would be regarded negatively by consumers receives support from the perceived risk perspective. Perceived risk can be considered a multidimensional construct, which in a digital context can be conceptualised as a person's perception of the possibility of having negative outcome or suffering from harm or losses associated with ecommerce.[80] Consumers perceive risk because they face uncertainty and potentially undesirable outcomes or consequences as a result of their behavioural decisions.[81] For example, a high perceived risk might follow from not knowing the outcome (e.g. the delivered benefits) or the negative consequences (e.g. will digital shopping violate credit card security?) of carrying out online buying.

Synthesising the perspectives Based on the five perspectives on consumer digital shopping behaviour that we have reviewed, Figure 4.5 presents an overview of potential factors that in particular may influence consumer digital shopping behaviour (i.e., what to buy, in what amount and where – offline or online?).

Social norms and PBC have both been shown to affect intended consumer use of mobile advertising (advertising activities supported by mobile devices, which allows companies to directly communicate with their consumers without location or time barriers).[82] Other recent research

Figure 4.5 Potential determinants of consumer digital shopping behaviour

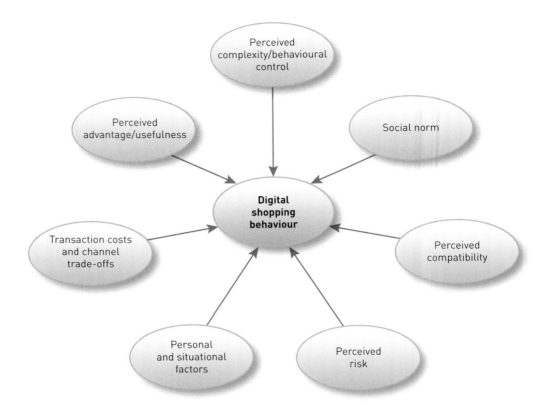

found that in relation to general Internet shopping behaviour PBC influenced consumer adoption of this shopping mode.[83] Research results have also demonstrated that perceived usefulness and perceived ease of use may affect digital shopping behaviour (i.e., the TAM perspective). One study found (along with another variable: perceived risk) that perceived usefulness and perceived ease of use explained more than 50 per cent of the consumers' intention to adopt online shopping of books and banking services. Another study revealed that perceived usefulness has a positive impact on consumers' attitudes towards a website and the perceived 'flow' (i.e., whether the experience is enjoyable and involving) of interacting with the website.[84] A study of Dutch households revealed that consumers' perception of relative advantage and compatibility positively influenced their intention to adopt online grocery shopping (i.e., the theory of adoption of innovations perspective). Consumers' perception of the complexity of online grocery shopping negatively influenced their intention to adopt online grocery shopping.[85] Another study has revealed that perceived complexity, perceived compatibility and perceived relative advantage highly influence Danish consumers' adoption of online grocery buying. Perceived transaction cost has been found to influence consumer choice between online and offline shopping channels (i.e., channel trade-offs and transactions costs perspective). In line with this finding, one study reported that saving time was reported as a primary reason for buying groceries online among already experienced online grocery buyers.[86] While these results concern the inter-channel trade-offs consumers may carry out when choosing among channels, online intra-channel trade-offs can also be considered. A study of German online consumers suggests that consumers value product-related information (at the expense of product breadth and product depth) and order fulfilment (at the expense of security and simplicity of the transaction process).[87] Research has also revealed that if consumers perceive potential losses or harm, that is, perceived risk, this may negatively influence their online buying intention. Yet, if consumers perceive high risk they may also respond by adopting risk reduction strategies such as information search prior to purchase.[88]

Personal and situational factors may moderate consumer online shopping behaviour. For example, in the online search process, the individual shopper is likely to be affected by her/his vocabulary and understanding of the subject area, as well as her/his ability to frame a query and to use a search engine.[89] Moreover, factors such as income, education, age, gender and lifestyle can also affect consumer online shopping behaviour.[90] For example, one recent study found that 15.3 per cent of Belgian Internet shoppers can be characterised as 'shopping lovers' – they love Internet shopping and all its facets (the convenience, the offer, and the possibility of window-shopping). These consumers frequently buy online, use the Internet for information, fun, and business, and find it enjoyable to explore millions of websites. Shopping lovers are of course a dream for any online retailer.[91] Another study indicates that while older online shoppers search for significantly fewer products than younger online shoppers, they actually purchase as much as younger consumers.[92] As considered in the next section, cultural differences may also influence digital shopping behaviour.

Cultural influence on digital shopping behaviour

Based on data collected from 8886 consumers from 23 countries on 30 consumer packaged goods, from websites in eight European countries (Belgium, France, Germany, Italy, the Netherlands, Spain, Sweden and the United Kingdom), marketing researchers Jan-Benedict E.M. Steenkamp (University of North Carolina, United States) and Inge Geyskens (Tilburg University, the Netherlands) found that relationships between consumer value and its drivers are systematically and predictably moderated by how and where consumers live.[93] The results revealed that perceived privacy/security and customisation have a greater effect in individualistic countries than in collectivistic countries. Moreover, cultural congruity (i.e., whether the website is adapted to the respondent's culture) weighs more heavily in countries that are high on national identity, and therefore websites in such countries should be adapted to the local context by using the local language, images, role models, symbols and so forth. As one example, at Beiersdorf's Nivea portal, visitors have access to more than 40 regional and country sites, which share the same look and feel. However, the sites are locally adapted with respect to language and the model used.

Within certain cultures a consumer's personal value may affect his or her digital shopping behaviour. See 'Marketing insight: Consumer online grocery shopping'.

The manager who is knowledgeable of customers' digital shopping behaviour stands a better chance of successfully interacting with them. The importance of online company–customer interactivity is considered in the next section.

Marketing insight

Consumer online grocery shopping

As predicted by several marketing scholars[94] a decade ago, products and services selected by consumers primarily on the basis of search attributes (e.g., books, computer products and travel) are now among the fastest-selling on the Internet due to low perceived search costs and because direct experience is not required. Other products, such as groceries, are still facing difficulties in being accepted by consumers. Although many consumers have adopted online grocery buying, and even though the online grocery market may expand in the future, there is still a large group of customers resisting this way of buying. In the United Kingdom, which can be considered among the leading

markets for online grocery sales, 11.7 per cent of consumers with online access have purchased groceries via the Internet at least once, of whom 2.5 per cent make online purchases at least once a week and 1.4 per cent two or three times a month.[95] Almost nine out of ten UK consumers still hesitate when buying groceries online, even though this shopping mode provides consumers with several advantages, including the ease and convenience of online shopping, the ability to search for products, compare prices and arrange delivery, usually at a time convenient for them. Studies from other countries show similar patterns.[96] As possible explanations for this, some consumers may find online grocery purchasing too complex, too risky, too expensive (e.g., delivery costs) and/or lacking personal attention from cashiers or floor staff.

Anna offers online guidance to IKEA customers.

Source: © Inter IKEA Systems BV 2006

Company-customer interactivity

Making the website more 'human'

Some people find that the lack of social interaction on the Internet is a barrier for them carrying out Internet shopping. In response, retailers are beginning to include personal characteristics on their websites, to provide consumers with the important feeling of being served when shopping online.[97] For example, on IKEA's website the 'human' assistant Anna can be found. When you turn on the sound, Anna even offers voice guidance to visiting customers.

Recent research suggests that social cues (i.e., cues based on human characteristics) can facilitate the development of website sociability.[98] Retailers can contribute to consumers' online experiences by adding social cues that enhance their flow, pleasure and arousal. Four online social cues should be considered potentially powerful marketing tools in retail website design:

1 **Language**: The language of a 'high-social' website should be written text *as well as* spoken language.

2 **Social role**: A tour guide may welcome visitors and thank customers when they log off.

3 **Voice**: The tour guide may give a brief summary of each web page and assist visitors navigating the website.

4 **Interactivity**: The tour guide may ask the visitor to indicate certain interests or needs and respond to them in a proper way. For example, the tour guide may ask, 'Are you looking for something specific?', and then provide a number of options.

Online personalisation

Online personalisation is 'the ability of a company to recognize and treat its customers as individuals through personalised products or service design, personal messaging, targeted banner ads, special offers on bills, or other personal transactions'.[99] Italian marketing researchers Gaetano 'Nino' Miceli, Francesco Ricotta and Michele Costabile have suggested a 'personalisation continuum' synthesising five different forms of personalisation strategies: product versioning, mass customisation, one-to-one personalisation, customerisation and reverse marketing.[100]

Product or service versioning The purpose of product versioning is to group consumers according to their willingness to pay. Consumers with high willingness to pay choose one version, while consumers with lower willingness to pay choose a different version.[101] Product or service versioning has for a long time been utilised by airlines. When booking a flight passengers can choose different service versions (first class, tourist class, and so on) of the same type of service: transportation. Software products (computer games, programs, etc.) are especially suited for product or service versioning. These offerings, which are capable of being distributed in digital form, are characterised by a distinctive cost structure: producing the first copy is often very expensive but producing subsequent copies is very cheap. The marginal cost of producing one extra unit is almost zero and therefore the price of the units cannot be set according to the price of producing them. Instead, the price should reflect the value that the individual customer attaches to the product or service. But since customers may attach different values, they are also willing to pay different prices for different versions. Moreover, producing many different versions of a certain product requires possible contact with many different customers, a condition that is especially fulfilled when distributing through digital channels.[102]

Mass customisation presents customers with a large amount of product and/or services from which the consumer can choose their 'made-to-order' customised product or service. This approach is well known in, for example, the car (Volkswagen, Fiat) and computer industries (Dell Computers). Mass customisation allows companies to tailor products to customers' individual needs while at the same time maintaining substantial economies of scale (i.e., the reduction in cost per unit that companies obtain when products are produced in high amounts). The negative side of mass customisation is that customers may be confused by the huge variety of offers and thus find it difficult to choose fully satisfying products. Dell is one of the pioneers of mass customisation. In fact, Dell has changed the competitive landscape by doing the following:[103]

- offering customised products directly to online customers on demand without premiums in either price or lead time;
- minimising inventory to unthinkable levels;
- being agile – quickly responding to market/technology changes;
- eliminating the cost and risk of finished goods inventory;
- successfully executing a mass customisation strategy quarter after quarter, year after year.

Although Dell CEO Michael Dell is widely acknowledged as the person who started the 'build-to-order' and 'mass customisation' wave, mass customisation was not planned but was born out of necessity. Michael Dell started his computer assembling business from his college bedroom and didn't have the space for mass production. That led to 'build-to-order' computers – where people pay first and get their computers later.[104]

One-to-one personalisation When using a one-to-one personalisation approach marketing provides content or recommendations that are relevant specifically to the individual user based on her/his individual characteristics and preferences. Web-based one-to-one personalisation is mainly focused on close communication within the company – customer relationship[105] and involves 'delivering customised content for the individual, through web pages, e-mail, or push technology'.[106] The first time a customer visits a personalised website he or she may be asked about his or her preferences for different kinds of services. By registration of user name and password it is possible later on to offer services that match these preferences. Customers may also be recognised by using cookies (i.e., short pieces of data used by Web servers to help identify Web users). Personalised websites help customers find the products and services they prefer and have even been compared to a dedicated assistant who knows your tastes well and makes your choice more effective.[107] For example, assist.com offers 'free personalised letters from Santa and the Easter Bunny', while time-frames.com offers 'personalised photo frames, baby's first year picture frames, through time children's frames with unique personalised custom story frame gifts for every occasion'.

Customisation Digital technology allows managers to cater to the needs of individual customers and to meet those needs.[108] Customisation means understanding customers' needs and preferences and other individual characteristics and then satisfying these needs and preferences by customised products and services. Customisation is different from one-to-one personalisation. Simply put, personalisation is essentially about using the right surname and associating, for example, an email with a recipient in a database. Customisation implies tracking and conditional content – content driven by data associated with the recipient. In other words, customisation implies personalisation – personalisation does not imply customisation.[109]

Reverse marketing Digital media may change the focus of marketing from a supplier perspective to a customer perspective. Traditional marketing has focused on the products and services that firms provide. Although managers for decades have carried out market analyses in order to determine customer needs and wants and thereby to estimate potential demand, emphasis has subsequently been on manufacturing and seeking orders. Reverse marketing means that manufacturing will only start when the customer orders. While Dell also provides an example of reverse marketing, the offline analogue is McDonald's and its transformation. McDonalds's traditional model was to produce burgers and keep them under heat lamps, serving them when the customer ordered. Due to competition, customer preferences and transformation in technologies, McDonald's later started assembling food only after it has been ordered.[110]

While some customers may find interactions with suppliers enjoyable and valuable, there is also the risk that other customers may become frustrated because they may not possess the necessary competencies and involvement for engaging in such interactions. Such customers may instead end up being dissatisfied. When companies design their personalisation programme it is therefore of utmost importance to realize that considerations concerning segmentation and targeting (see Chapter 10) should also be carried out in an online setting.

ICI and internal decision making

Marketing managers use digital marketing to support internal decision making

Much of the role of ICT in marketing focuses on digital technology at the customer interface, but the use of a wide range of ICTs within the marketing department of a company cannot be overlooked. These will be highlighted throughout the text and briefly introduced in this section ranging from databases to CRM software, marketing dashboards and biometrics, to name but a few.

Database, data mining and modelling customer data A core marketing requirement is the use of technology to manage information, which will be explored in Chapter 5. Marketing managers must also be able to combine information from a variety of channels – retail, online, phone, email, kiosks and so on. Call centres, database systems, website back office, data capture operations, document management and other systems now all have to have a data interchangeability among systems so that a full view of the customer is possible.[111] Database technologies and the manipulation of the information in them for tracking patterns of consumer behaviour and finding target markets is a normal part of marketing.

CRM software There has been much discussion in relation to customer relationship management. CRM systems are designed to gather information from the customer 'touch points' and then link to the internal operations to support better decision making. See Figure 4.6 for an example of a CRM software package.

CRM is software that is only as good as the information provided to it and the planned use of that information. Customer relationship management, data building and data mining are all ways in which marketing managers can use ICT to capture precise market insights that enable them to focus on meeting the individual needs of the consumer. Consider the Tesco example below.

Figure 4.6 CRM is a software for gathering and managing customer information to improve customer relationships and service provision.

Source: SalesLogic CRM system from Scientific Computers Ltd (www.scl.com). Reproduced by permission of Sage Publications.

▽ **Tesco**

Tesco, the £32 billion UK supermarket giant, is regarded by many academics and observers as being one of the top companies in the world for capturing new insights into their customers and their behaviour. Tesco partnered with data-mining experts DunnHumby and created an innovative loyalty card scheme that tracks the buying behaviour of 13 million customers, through recording and tracking consumption data from shopping bills. Using advanced ICT applications software, Tesco and DunnHumby are 'able to build, maintain and mine a rich customer database with information derived from all customer touch points'. Using this customer database, Tesco's marketing department is then able to manage changes in either individual or general consumption patterns and adapt their marketing strategies accordingly. For example, Tesco can track changes in demographic make-up in each store location. So, if Tesco can see that there has been a large increase in people of Polish or Afro-Caribbean origin shopping in its stores, it can adapt the service process and the product range sold in each store to better reflect this change in demographics. It also uses this information for targeted mailings and personalised communication, resulting in over 4 million versions of each mailing.[112]

Marketing dashboards A **marketing dashboard** is an on-screen easy to read summary of key marketing metrics[113] and is discussed in more detail in Chapter 22 on managing marketing metrics. A dashboard is a personalised view of all relevant marketing information needed by the marketing manager. Typical information contained in a marketing dashboard includes:

- Up-to-date overview of marketing budget (budget, planned, committed, spends)
- One click reports on all major views of marketing budget (by division/business unit, product, market segment, channel, cost centre break down, type of activity, cost category, etc.)
- Marketing calendar
- Overview of marketing campaigns and activities

- Overview of projects
- Tasks
- Marketing content (images, artworks, etc.)
- Compliance management
- Brand management
- Important links.[114]

▽ Future developments in digital technologies

Many exciting and potentially more fruitful technologies for marketing are in the development or adoption stage.

Biometrics

Biometrics is the science of fingerprint and retina recognition. For many people passport fingerprinting by the US government was their first real experience of biometrics. This technology is used to recognise individuals or things. Products and services are starting to use biometrics. For example there are cars fitted with fingerprint matching devices so that people can open them with their fingertip. See the Hitachi example on the next page.

There are two types of biometrics of interest.

1 **Physiological** (DNA and fingerprints, retina and handscans, pheromone signature): Amsterdam's Schiphol airport is claiming success in a biometric security system that scans eyes and allows passengers to bypass traditional passport control. Passengers register their personal details and then a picture is taken of their iris and recorded on a card, which looks like a credit card. Passengers pass through gates inserting the iris scan card and looking into a scanner where their eye is compared with the information on the card.

2 **Behavioural** (how you sign your name, or walk, or even type): Voice recognition is often categorised as 'behavioural', even though human voices are just as naturally unique as fingerprints.

The use of biometrics (fingerprint and retina recognition) is growing in both products and services.

Source: Pasieka/Science Photo Library

▽ **Hitachi**

Hitachi's finger vein authentication technology, which identifies individuals by the unique pattern of blood vessels in their fingers, has improved security in a range of devices ranging from ATMs and cardless payment systems to computers and automobile ignition systems. It is also being used in gyms. Fukui Computers has unveiled a new line of networked exercise machines, called *medimo*, that are equipped with Hitachi finger vein readers. When users identify themselves with a simple press of the finger, the machines respond by automatically adjusting the weight resistance and seat position based on the user's previously set preferences. The machines also connect to a remote server to retrieve the user's personal exercise data – including previous exercise records and stats, training regimes and calorie consumption data – which show up on a touch-screen display. Users can then do their workouts based on this data, which is updated each time a machine is used, or personal trainers can refer to it when providing exercise advice.

The cashless future

Technology is also impacting on payment and pricing. PayPass, pay and wave or touch point are just some of the terms for the ability to pay for items using your credit card and waving it at a reader. More than 10 million British commuters who use the Oyster card to pay fares to ride London's subway (tube) and bus system are already familiar with RFID technology used by PayPass.[115] MasterCard PayPass is now accepted at more than 80,000 shops in 20 countries.

A MasterCard global survey conducted in 13 countries in 2007 showed that a growing majority of consumers worldwide believe that one day there will be a cashless society. The survey also found that:

- A majority of respondents (56 per cent) believe that one day the world will be a cashless society where credit and debit cards will replace cash and cheques.
- 75 per cent of respondents believe that it is no longer necessary to have lots of cash on hand.
- Two-thirds of respondents (66 per cent) use cash to make purchases less often than five years ago.
- Only one-fifth (21 per cent) of consumers are willing to wait in line for more than ten minutes to make a purchase of less than €17.[116]

MasterCard, partnering with several UK-based banks, including Barclays, Citibank and HSBC, launched a campaign to introduce PayPass in the United Kingdom in September 2007 and plan to have issued 5 million PayPass cards by 2009. McDonald's, Coffee Republic, Krispy Kreme and Books Etc. are among the UK shops accepting the cards.[117] Attendees at the Brit Awards 2008 received virtual cash in their goodie bags, in the form of prepaid, RFID-enabled PayPass payment cards from MasterCard, the event's main sponsor.[118]

The next initiative will be use of mobile phones for payment. MasterCard Worldwide and Nokia have announced a mobile payments pilot programme using new Nokia mobile phones equipped with MasterCard PayPass payment functionality, allowing consumers 'to pay for purchases with a tap of their mobile phone, instead of sliding a card through a magnetic stripe reader, handing it over to the cashier, or fumbling for cash and coins.'[119] 'When it comes to ticketing, the mobile phone has huge advantages – everyone has one, first of all, and it's a great interface', says Friedrich Joussen, head of Vodafone Germany, which is working with German railroad operator Deutsche Bahn to deploy a ticketing system that uses RFID-enabled signs and mobile phones.[120] This Touch and Travel system will allow Germans to use mobile phones and RFID (radio frequency identification technology) technology to pay for train, subway, tram and bus fares.

The Paypass card from MasterCard used at the Brit Awards 2008.

Source: Courtesy of MasterCard / Agency: Weber Shandwick

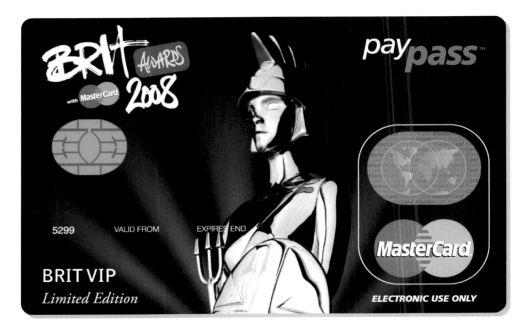

Gaming One hundred years ago entertainment might have consisted of playing games such as chess, reading Plato in the original Greek or enjoying Shakespeare's plays. Now we have gaming, including multiplayer online games. Twenty years ago, games such as Tetris or Pac-Man were simple exercises in motor coordination and pattern recognition. Today's games belong to another realm. The 'walk-throughs' for 'Grand Theft Auto III' – which are the informal guides that break down the games and help players navigate their complexities – is fifty-three thousand words long – about the length of a book. The contemporary video game involves a fully realised imaginary world, dense with detail and levels of complexity.[121] Though considered to be male dominated, a recent poll by GameVision found that there were more female owners of Nintendo's handheld DS console in the UK than men (54 per cent to 46 per cent).[122]

Table 4.2 Top ten PC game titles

Rank	Game title	Publisher	AU%*	Average minutes played per week
1	World of Warcraft	Blizzard Entertainment	0.87	837
2	Call of Duty 4: Modern Warfare	Activision	0.19	482
3	RuneScape	Jagex Ltd	0.14	615
4	Sims 2, The	Electronic Arts, Inc.	0.11	320
5	Sims, The	Electronic Arts, Inc.	0.10	274
6	Halo: Combat Evolved	Microsoft Game Studios	0.09	304
7	Counter-Strike: Source	Valve	0.08	434
8	Lord of the Rings Online: Shadows of Angmar, The	Midway Games	0.08	846
9	Madden NFL 08	Electronic Arts, Inc.	0.08	382
10	Civilization IV	2K Games	0.07	453

*AU% is the percentage of PC gamers playing a title in the average minute.

Source: Nielsen Games, February 2008 (www.nielsen.com). Reproduced with permission.

▽ SUMMARY

1 Digital marketing or ICT in marketing refers to digital technology in order to inform, interact with and/or distribute to their customers. Digital marketing includes both Internet-based marketing activities and other kinds of activities (i.e., mobile phone communication, emails and interactive digital television) that are based on digital technology.

2 By using the full range of over 100 ICTs, which can be classed as information and/or interaction technologies, marketing managers can reach, communicate and deliver as well as analyse and monitor customers and marketing programmes like never before.

3 Within the context of digital technology, market knowledge, once controlled by suppliers, is shifting towards consumers, since they can now more easily choose what they want and when they want it, on their own terms.

4 Digital marketing communication refers to 'communication and interaction between a company or brand and its customers using digital channels (e.g., the Internet, email, mobile phones and digital TV) and information technology'.

5 Electronic word of mouth has often higher credibility than marketer-created sources of information on the Internet since no direct commercial interests interfere with the communication.

6 Offline and online social networks are compared across three dimensions, tie strength, online homophily and source credibility.

7 Viral marketing is an Internet adaptation of marketing using word-of-mouth effects. Viral marketing can be understood as an advertising message spread by consumers to other consumers.

8 By using mobile advertising companies can communicate directly with their consumers without location or time barriers.

9 Banner ads serve two objectives. First, they attract visitors to the advertiser's website. Second, through banner ads on selected sites visitors may learn to associate the advertised brand with certain attributes or values.

10 Five main perspectives on consumer digital behaviour can be considered: the theory of reasoned action and the theory of planned behaviour, the technology acceptance model, the theory of adoption of innovations, the trade-off/transaction costs perspective, and the perceived risk perspective.

11 Online personalisation is 'the ability of a company to recognise and treat its customers as individuals through personal messaging, targeted banner ads, special offers on bills or other personal transactions'.

12 There are a wide range of ICTs that support marketers in their decision making including database and dashboards, CRM, pricing and planning software along with the Internet and other communication and research technologies.

13 Current and future technological developments, including social networking, virtual lives, biometrics and the cashless society all herald major changes in marketing practice.

▽ APPLICATIONS

Marketing debate

Ten years from now, digital shopping will be the primary shopping channel used by consumers *versus* digital shopping will never outperform offline shopping channels as there are simply too many problems associated with digital shopping.

Marketing discussion

Explore the range of ICTs available to marketers today both for internal and external use. What are the pros and cons of using so much technology in marketing?

▽ REFERENCES

[1] C. Anderson (2006) *The Long Tail: The New Economics of Culture and Communications*, London: Random House.

[2] M. Brady, M. Saren and N. Tzokas (2002) Integrating information technology into marketing practice – the It reality of contemporary marketing practice, *Journal of Marketing Management*, 18(5–6), 555–78.

[3] See www.crm2day.com/news/crm/113638.php.

[4] See www.forrester.com/Research/Document/Excerpt/0,7211,42707,00.html.

[5] H. Leavitt and T. Whisler (1985) Management in the 80s, *Harvard Business Review*, 63(1), 65–71.

[6]M. Merisavo (2006) The effects of digital marketing communication on customer loyalty: an integrative model and research propositions, Working Paper W-400, Helsinki School of Economics, February.

[7]M. Brady (2006) A holistic view of ICT within the marketing domain: challenges and issues, British Academy of Management, Belfast, September, CD-ROM.

[8]M.R. Fellenz and M. Brady (2008) Managing the innovative deployment of Information and Communication Technologies (ICTs) for global service organisations, International Journal of Technology Marketing 3(1), 39–55. Merisavo (2006) op. cit.; S. L. Vargo and R. F. Lusch (2004) Evolving to a new dominant logic for marketing, Journal of Marketing, 68(1), 1–17.

[9]See www.GoViral.com, D&AD Global Awards 2007, Goodyear&UK marketing fact sheet, www.goviral.com/newsletterArchive/upload/2007-05-01.da.pdf (accessed February 2008).

[10]See for example R. Cagliano, F. Caniato and G. Spina (2005) E-business strategy: how companies are shaping their supply chain through the internet, International Journal of Operations & Production Management, 25(12), 1309–27.

[11]D. Jobber (2007) Principles and Practice of Marketing, 5th edn, London: McGraw-Hill.

[12]See www.eiaa.net/research/research-details.asp?SID=1&id=382&lang=6&origin=media-consumption.asp.

[13]See www.eiaa.net/research/media-consumption.asp?lang=6.

[14]See www.e-consultancy.com/searchterms/internet-stats.html.

[15]See www.eiaa.net/research/research-details.asp?SID=1&id=307&lang=6&origin=media-consumption.asp.

[16]See www.iabuk.net/en/1/iabeuropeadspendfigures.mxs.

[17]http://www.eiaa.net/research/research-details.asp?SID=1&id=307&lang=6&origin=media-consumption.asp.

[18]Z. Fernández and M. J. Nieto (2005) The Internet: strategy and boundaries of the firm, Working Paper #05-01 (01) Business Economics Series, Universidad Carlos III de Madrid, January.

[19]Ibid.

[20]P. Rajan Varadarajan and Manjit S. Yadav (2002) Marketing strategy and the internet: an organizing framework, Journal of the Academy of Marketing Science, 30(4), 296–312.

[21]H. Lim and A. J. Dubinsky (2005) The theory of planned behavior in e-commerce: making a case for interdependencies between salient beliefs, Psychology & Marketing, 22(10), 833–55.

[22]M. M. Long, T. Tellefsen and J. D. Lichtenthal (2007) Internet integration into the industrial selling process: a step-by-step approach, Industrial Marketing Management, 36, 676–89.

[23]M. E. Porter (2001) Strategy and the Internet, Harvard Business Review, March, 62–78. See also: M. E. Porter (2008) The five competitive forces that shape strategy, Harvard Business Review, January, 79–93.

[24]M. Merisavo (2006) The effects of digital marketing communication on customer loyalty: an integrative model and research propositions, Working Paper W-400, Helsinki School of Economics, February.

[25]J. A. Deighton and L. Kornfeld (2007) Digital interactivity: unanticipated consequences for markets, marketing, and consumers, Harvard Business School Working Paper, No. 08-017, September.

[26]T. W. Gruen, T. Osmonbekov and A. J. Czaplewski (2006) eWOM: the impact of customer-to-customer online know-how exchange on customer value and loyalty, Journal of Business Research, 59, 449–56.

[27]J. Fong and S. Burton (2008) A cross-cultural comparison of electronic word-of-mouth and country-of-origin effects, Journal of Business Research, 61, 233–42.

[28]K. Spicer and A. Taher (2008) Girls and young women are now the most prolific web users, The Sunday Times, 9 March, p. 12.

[29]Ibid.

[30]R. B. Money, M. C. Gilly and J. L. Graham (1998) Explorations of national culture and word-of mouth referral behavior in the purchase of industrial services in the United States and Japan. Journal of Marketing, 62, 76–87.

[31]J. Walker, S. Wasserman and B. Wellman (1994) Statistical models for social support networks, in S. Wasserman and J. Galaskiewicz (eds.) Advances in Social Network Analysis, Thousand Oaks, CA: Sage, pp. 53–78.

[32]L. C. Wang, J. Baker, J. A. Wagner and K. Wakefield (2007) Can a retail web site be social?, Journal of Marketing, 71, 143–57.

[33]M. S. Handcock, A. E. Raftery and J. M. Tantrum (2007) Model-based clustering for social networks, Journal of the Royal Statistical Society: Series A (Statistics in Society), 170(2), 301–54.

[34]Z. L. Tormala and R. E. Petty (2004) Source credibility and attitude certainty: a metacognitive analysis of resistance to persuasion, Journal of Consumer Psychology, 14(4), 427–42.

[35]Based on: China: online marketing comes of age, BusinessWeek, 12 June 2007 (www.businessweek.com/globalbiz/content/jun2007/gb20070612_084967.htm?chan=search) (accessed March 2008).

[36]A. M. Muniz, Jr. and T. C. O'Guinn (2001) Brand community, Journal of Consumer Research, 27, 412–31.

[37]S. C. Beckmann and M. Gjerløff (2007) A framework for communicating with brand communities, 3Rs – reputation, responsibility and relevance, ANZMAC Conference 2007, Dunedin, 1710–1716.

[38]B. Cova and S. Pace (2005) Tribal branding on the net: the Nutella case. Paper presented at the 34th EMAC Conference: Rejuvenating marketing: contamination, innovation, integration, Milan.

[39]Beckmann and Gjerløff (2007) op. cit.

[40]C. Flavian and M. Guinalíu (2005) The influence of virtual communities on distribution strategies in the internet, International Journal of Retail & Distribution Management, 33(6), 405–42.

[41]H.-F. Lin (2007) The role of online and offline features in sustaining virtual communities: an empirical study, Internet Research, 17(2), 119–38.

[42]See J. Brown, A. J. Broderick and N. Lee (2007) Word of mouth communication within online communities: conceptualizing the online social network, Journal of Interactive Marketing, 21(3), 2–20.

[43]See http://en.wikipedia.org/wiki/Napster (accessed March 2008).

[44]See http://en.wikipedia.org/wiki/Second_Life.

[45]M. Sarvary (2008) The metaverse, TV of the future?, Harvard Business Review, February, 30.

[46]C. Costa, R. Eastman, C. Green and A. Vasey (2007) The power of online direct marketing, identifying the most important trends and market intelligence in online direct marketing today, IPT Research Report, July.

[47]M. Durnik (2005) New email marketing rules in the European Union: one year later, MarketingProfs, 28 June; Directive

2002/58/EC of the European Parliament and of the Council of 12 July 2002 concerning the processing of personal data and the protection of privacy in the electronic communications sector (Directive on privacy and electronic communications).

[48]Email marketing reports: Anti-spam laws and the EU, www.email-marketing-reports.com/canspam/eu/ (accessed March 2008).

[49]RapidReach™ Whitepaper, The basics of successful email marketing, available for free at www.dnbrapidreach.com/ (accessed March 2008).

[50]S. Godin (1999) *Permission marketing: Turning strangers into friends and friends into customers.* New York: Simon & Schuster.

[51]E. T. Brey, S.-I. (A.) So, D.-Y. Kim and A. M. Morrison (2007) Web-based permission marketing: segmentation for the lodging industry, *Tourism Management*, 28, 1408–16.

[52]Ibid; R. Kent and H. Brandal (2003) Improving email response in a permission marketing context, *International Journal of Market Research*, 45(4), 489–503.

[53]A. Goodstein (2007) Marketing to teens online, *BusinessWeek*, 7 November.

[54]B. Hauge, C. Moseholm and M. D. Svnedsen, Internettet anno 2006, www.marketmagzine.dk (accessed February 2008).

[55]Viral markedsføring er ved at miste pusten, *Business.dk*, 11 March 2008.

[56]www.GoViral.com; Successful tyre change for Goodyear www.goviral.com/articles/goviral_goodyear_runonflat_case_ 070228.pdf (accessed February 2008).

[57]K. Greene (2008) Reality mining, *Technology Review*, March/April, 54–6.

[58]P. E. Pedersen (2005) Adoption of mobile internet services: an exploratory study of mobile commerce early adopters, *Journal of Organizational Computing and Electronic Commerce*, 15(2), 203–22.

[59]See http://en.wikipedia.org/wiki/3G (accessed March 2008).

[60]eMarketer, Mobile Internet Grows in Europe, March 21, 2008, http://www.emarketer.com/Article.aspx?id=1006079&src=dp3_ home (accessed March 2008).

[61]R. Vatanparast and M. Asil (2007) Factors Affecting the Use of Mobile Advertising, *International Journal of Mobile Marketing*, 2(2), December, 21–34.

[62]Ibid.

[63]L. Fortunati (2001) The Mobile Phone: An Identity on the Move, *Personal and Ubiquitous Computing*, 5, 85–98.

[64]R. Vatanparast and M. Asil (2007) Factors affecting the use of mobile advertising, *International Journal of Mobile Marketing*, 2(2), 58–67.

[65]V. Shannon (2007) Global market for cellphone ring tones is shrinking, *New York Times*, 31 December.

[66]See Púca Technologies Ltd website, Case study: Peugeot Ireland (www.puca.ie/casestudies/cs_peugeot.html).

[67]C.-H. Cho (2003) Factors influencing clicking of banner ads on the WWW, *Cyberpsychology & Behavior*, 6(2), 201–15.

[68]T. Harris, How banner ads works, http://money.howstuffworks.com/banner-ad3.htm (accessed March 2008).

[69]H. El Hani (2008) HP Danmark ændrer annonce-strategi, *CRN*, 5 March.

[70]R. Langhoff (2008) TV ved en skillevej, *Berlingske Tidende*, 17 January, p. 8.

[71]Young shoppers want to pay with chip in skin, *The Daily Mail*, 11 October 2006.

[72]M. Howard and C. Worboys (2003) Self-service: a contradiction in terms or customer-led choice? *Journal of Consumer Behaviour*, 2(24), 382–92.

[73]Cf. Bulgarians, Romanians EU's staunchest e-shopping holdouts, www.news.dnevnik.bg (accessed March 2008).

[74]Ibid.

[75]www.ebusiness-watch.org/studies/sectors/banking/banking .htm (accessed March 2007).

[76]M. Fishbein and I. Ajzen (1975) *Belief, Attitude, Intention, and Behavior: An Introduction to Theory and Research*, Reading, MA: Addison Wesley.

[77]S. Al-Gahtani (2001) The applicability of TAM outside North America: an empirical test in the United Kingdom, *Information Resources Management Journal*, 14(3), 37–46.

[78]See T. Hansen (2006) Determinants of consumers' repeat online buying of groceries, *The International Review of Retail, Distribution and Consumer Research*, 16(1), 93–114.

[79]E. M. Rogers (1983) *Diffusion of Innovations*, 3rd edn, New York: The Free Press.

[80]Cf. X. Liu and K.-K. Wie (2003) An empirical study of product differences in consumers E-commerce adoption behaviour, *Electronic Commerce Research and Applications*, 2(3), 229–39.

[81]N. Lim (2003) Consumers' perceived risk: sources versus consequences, *Electronic Commerce Research and Applications*, 2(3), 216–28.

[82]R. Vatanparast and M. Asil (2007) Factors affecting the use of mobile advertising, *International Journal of Mobile Marketing*, 2(2), 21–34.

[83]M.-S. Wang, C.-C. Chen, S.-C. Chang and Y.-H. Yang (2007) Effects of online shopping attitudes, subjective norms and control beliefs on online shopping intentions: a test of the theory of planned behaviour, *International Journal of Management*, 24(2), 296–302.

[84]A. V. Hausman and J. S. Siekpe (2009) The effect of web interface features on consumer online purchase intentions, *Journal of Business Research*, 62(1), 5–13.

[85]P. C. Verhoef and F. Langerak (2001) Possible determinants of consumers' adoption of electronic grocery shopping in the Netherlands, *Journal of Retailing and Consumer Services*, 8, 275–85.

[86]M. A. Morganosky and B. J. Cude (2000) Consumer response to online grocery shopping, *International Journal of Retail & Distribution Management*, 28(1), 17–26.

[87]G. Odekerken-Schröder and M. Wetzels (2003) Trade-offs in online purchase decisions: two empirical studies in Europe, *European Management Journal*, 21(6), 731–39.

[88]S. M. Forsythe and B. Shi (2003) Consumer patronage and risk perceptions in Internet shopping, *Journal of Business Research*, 56, 867–75.

[89]A. D. Madden, N. J. Ford, D. Miller and P. Levy (2006) Children's use of the internet for information-seeking, *Journal of Documentation*, 62(6), 744–61.

[90]See N. F. Doherty and F. E. Ellis-Chadwick (2006) New perspectives in internet retailing: a review and strategic critique of the field, *International Journal of Retail & Distribution Management*, 34(4/5), 411–28.

[91]M. Brengman, M. Geuens, B. Weijters, S. M. Smith and W. R. Swinyard (2005) Segmenting Internet shoppers based on their web-usage-related lifestyle: a cross cultural validation, *Journal of Business Research*, 58(1), 79–88.

[92]P. Sorce, V. Perotti and S. Widrick (2005) Attitude and age differences in online buying, *International Journal of Retail & Distribution Management*, 33(2), 122–32.

[93]J.-B. E.M. Steenkamp and I. Geyskens (2006) How country characteristics affect the perceived value of web sites, *Journal of Marketing*, 70, 136–50.

[94]See for example: R.A. Peterson, S. Balasubramanian and B. J. Rosenberg (1997) Exploring the implications of the internet for consumer marketing, *Journal of the Academy of Marketing Science*, 25, 329–46; L. R. Klein (1998) Evaluating the potential of interactive media through a new lens, *Journal of Business Research*, 41, 195–203.

[95]Research and Markets (2006) E-commerce: the internet grocery market. *Market Assessment*, September, 143.

[96]K. Ramus and N. A. Nielsen (2005) Online grocery retailing: what do consumers think?, *Internet Research*, 15, 335–52.

[97]L. C. Wang, J. Baker, J. A. Wagner and K. Wakefield (2007) Can a retail web site be social?, *Journal of Marketing*, 71, 143–57.

[98]Ibid.

[99]C. Imhoff, L. Loftis and J. Geiger (2001) *Building the Customer-Centric Enterprise, Data Warehousing Techniques for Supporting Customer Relationship Management*, New York: Wiley.

[100]G. (N.) Miceli, F. Ricotta and M. Costabile (2007) Customizing customization: a conceptual framework for interactive personalization, *Journal of Interactive Marketing*, 21(2), 6–25.

[101]H. R. Varian (1997) Versioning information goods, Research Paper, University of California, Berkeley, 13 March.

[102]C. Shapiro and H. R. Varian (1998) Versioning: the smart way to sell information, *Harvard Business Review*, November–December, 106–14.

[103]D. J. Gardner, Profitability for small manufacturing companies: why 21st century manufacturers can't ignore mass customization, *The Business Forum Journal* (www.bizforum.org/Journal/www_journalDG003.htm).

[104]A. Kothari (2005) Mass customization, *Marketing eYe*, 24 January (/www.biztactics.com/blog/2005/01/mass-customization.php – accessed March 2008).

[105]J. Wind and A. Rangaswamy (2001) Customerization: the next revolution in mass customization, *Journal of Interactive Marketing*, 15(1), 13–32.

[106]D. Chaffey, R. Mayer, K. Johnston and F. Ellis-Chadwick (2000) *Internet Marketing*, Harlow, England: Financial Times Prentice-Hall, p. 299.

[107]H. Nysveen and P. E. Pedersen (2004) An exploratory study of customers' perception of company web sites offering various interactive applications: moderating effects of customers' Internet experience, *Decision Support Systems*, 37, 137– 50; W. Hanson (2000) *Principles of Internet Marketing*, South-Western College Publishing/Thompson Learning.

[108]T.S. Raghu, P.K. Kannan, H.R. Rao and A.B. Whinston (2001) Dynamic profiling of consumers for customized offerings over the Internet: a model and analysis, *Decision Support Systems*, 32, 117–134.

[109]T. Barnes (2004) RSS: marketing's next big thing, *MarketingProfs*, 7 September.

[110]A. Sharma and J. N. Sheth (2006) Web-based marketing: the coming revolution in marketing thought and strategy, *Journal of Business Research*, 57, 696–702; R. T. Rust and F. Espinoza (2006) How technology advances influence business research and marketing strategy, *Journal of Business Research*, 59, 1072–78.

[111]A. Greenyer (2006) Back from the grave: The return of modelled consumer information, *International Journal of Retail & Distribution Management*, 34(2/3), 212–19.

[112]C. Humby (2004) *Scoring Points: How Tesco Is Winning Loyalty*, London: Kogan page; see also www.tescocorporate.com/annualreview06/m/sumprofloss.html.

[113]G. McGovern, D., J. Quelch, and B. Crawford., (2004) Bringing the customers into the board room, *Harvard Business Review*, November, 1–10; T. Ambler and J. Roberts (2005) Beware the silver metric: marketing performance measurement has to be multidimensional, Working paper, No 05-709, The London Business School.

[114]http://www.themarketingleaders.com/articles/dec06/stephan_nobs.html.

[115]M. C. O'Connor (2007) MasterCard rolls out Contactless Carpet in the UK, *RFID Journal*, September (www.rfidjournal.com/article/articleview/3600/1/1/0).

[116]See www.paymentsnews.com/2007/12/mastercard-says.html.

[117]M. C. O'Connor (2008) RFID in the goodie bag, *RFID Journal*, 27 February (www.rfidjournal.com/article/articleprint/3942/-1/1).

[118]Ibid.

[119]U.S. bank, MasterCard launch mobile payments pilot in Spokane, see www.paymentsnews.com/2008/01/us-bank-masterc.html.

[120]A. Curry (2008) Deutsche Bahn launches Touch&Travel, *RFID Journal* (www.rfidjournal.com/article/articleview/3950/2/1/).

[121]S. Johnson (2006) *Everything Bad Is Good for You: How Today's Popular Culture Is Actually Making Us Smarter*, New York: Penguin/Riverhead.

[122]Spicer and Taher (2008) op. cit.

Part 2

▽ Capturing marketing insights

Video documentary for Part 2

Go to **www.pearsoned.co.uk/marketingmanagementeurope** to watch the video documentary that relates to Part 2 and consider the issues raised below.

In any competitive activity, marketing managers need to research the field of play and the strength of the competition carefully. Part 2: Capturing Marketing Insights explores the three broad themes of:

1 identifying and tracking;

2 researching the market; and

3 analysing the competition.

Macro trends, or the broad environmental factors that affect activity in markets, usually lie beyond the sphere of control of marketing managers. However, their influence is considerable and therefore research activity is needed to assess their strength and likely impact on both consumer and business markets. Key business variables such as an economic downturn as well as major market trends that affect purchasing activity need to be identified and tracked. Micro trends that can be managed by practitioners affect customer purchase preferences and include factors such as changing lifestyles, customer needs and purchase activity.

When watching the video documentary that accompanies Part 2, consider the broad macro and detailed micro trends that companies need to evaluate when judging their position in relation to the activities of their competitors. Hard quantitative data such as frequency, level, and degree of repeat spend requires continuous monitoring. Soft qualitative data, particularly on perceptions, need to be researched to ensure that companies can develop suitably differentiated market offerings for their customers. These key macro and micro trends can be researched effectively with modern digital marketing techniques.

Hear a variety of top marketing executives from a wide range of organisations offer their own interesting and varied perspectives on the key themes of Part 2 including: Dave Hodgson, Marketing Manager, Marketing Birmingham (top); Simon Topman, Managing Director, Acme Whistles (centre); a newly opened HSBC branch, Mumbai, India (bottom).

Chapter 5

▽ The changing marketing environment and information management

IN THIS CHAPTER, WE WILL ADDRESS THE FOLLOWING QUESTIONS:

1 What are the key methods for tracking and identifying opportunities in the environment?

2 What are the components of a modern marketing information system?

3 What are useful internal records?

4 What is involved in a marketing intelligence system?

5 What are the key methods for tracking and identifying opportunities in the environment?

6 What is database management?

Developing and implementing marketing plans requires a number of decisions. Making those decisions is both a creative and an analytical process in which several aspects should be considered. Due to globalisation and technological developments the marketing environment is changing more rapidly than ever before and it is therefore essential that companies develop and maintain database management systems which provide a structured insight into and inspiration for marketing decision making, up-to-date information about macro trends, as well as about micro effects particular to their business. A well-designed database management system

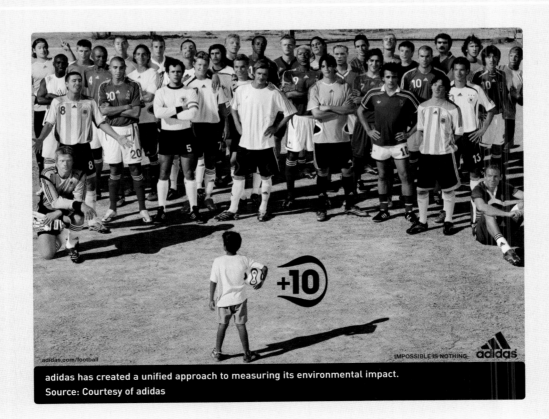

adidas has created a unified approach to measuring its environmental impact.
Source: Courtesy of adidas

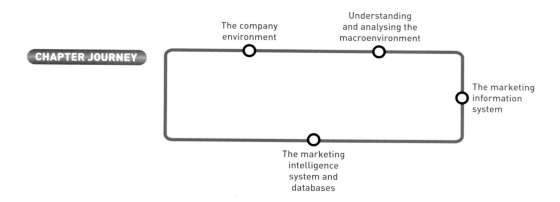
allows the company to store, modify and extract data when needed. Holistic marketers recognise that the marketing environment is constantly presenting new opportunities and threats, and they understand the importance of continuously monitoring and adapting to that environment.

Take the adidas example below.

Environmentally friendly behaviour is now a major issue for most governments, politicians, citizens, consumers – and companies. Introducing more eco-friendly products, making manufacturing process changes, upgrading outdated practices, reducing waste, minimising energy usage and similar initiatives to reduce energy or resources can now all contribute to the competitiveness of a company. Many companies have recognised this trend, one of them being sporting goods manufacturer adidas. Headquartered in Herzogenaurach, Germany, in 2006 adidas took several steps to create a unified approach to managing and measuring the adidas Group's social and environmental impacts. Having business relationships with manufacturers in several countries around the world, one of these steps included a focus on workplace standards. adidas has described clear rules of conduct for issues such as the environment, safety in the workplace, child labour and hours of work. If adidas's suppliers repeatedly fail to live up to these standards, adidas will terminate its contract with them. Moreover, all product materials and components must be non-toxic and safe – otherwise they will not be accepted. But it does not end there. adidas has also made it mandatory for all its core suppliers to establish environmental management systems, which will encourage them to plan, manage and review their own environmental performance. The goal for adidas is to achieve a balance between various demands: the sporting goods must not only be competitive in function and price, but also safe (during use and after disposal) as well as environmentally friendly.[1]

Like adidas, virtually every industry is facing up to changes in the natural environment. In this chapter, we consider how firms can develop processes to track trends in the environment. Chapter 6 will review how marketers can conduct more customised research that addresses specific marketing problems or issues.

▽ The company environment

Many companies are facing increasing global competition, faster flows of information and communication, increasing business complexity and rapidly changing customer needs and wants. Such dynamics reduce companies' ability to predict future marketplace changes and therefore add uncertainty to the decisions taken by marketing management. Since the marketing environment is constantly presenting new opportunities and threats, it is highly important that a company continuously monitors and adapts to changes in the marketing environment. In the first part of this chapter we will describe the salient aspects of the current marketing environment. In the second part, we will describe the systems for managing information about the changing marketing environment.

▽ The marketing environment

A company is surrounded by an immediate microenvironment of customers, suppliers, distributors, agencies and competitors that we will describe in later chapters of the book. The company is also surrounded by a macroenvironment of major forces impacting on all companies such as consumer trends, technological developments, and social, political and legal forces. These forces affect and moderate the behaviour of all the actors in a market including the company's competitors, suppliers, distributors and customers. Marketing scholars often organise the macro forces into five overall forces – political/legal, economic, ecological/physical, social/cultural and demographic, and technological. The acronym PEEST analysis is used to describe an analysis of the company's environment covering these five forces. We will describe and discuss these forces separately, but marketers must pay attention to their interactions, because these will lead to new opportunities and threats. For example, explosive population growth (demographic) leads to more resource depletion and pollution (natural), which leads consumers to call for more laws (political–legal), which stimulate new technological solutions and products (technological), which, if they are affordable (economic), may actually change attitudes and behaviour (social–cultural). 'Breakthrough marketing: Google' describes how that company has successfully capitalised on the new marketing environment.

Enterprising individuals and companies manage to create new solutions to unmet needs. For example, Interflora was created to meet the need for express delivery of flowers across country borders.[2] However, a new market opportunity doesn't guarantee success, even if the product is technically feasible. For example, some companies sell portable 'electronic books' or 'ebooks'; but there may not be a sufficient number of people interested in reading a book on a computer screen or willing to pay the required price. This is why market research is necessary to determine an opportunity's profit potential.

To help marketers spot cultural shifts that might bring new opportunities or threats, several firms offer social–cultural forecasts. Euromonitor International, for instance, offers (for a fee) access to internationally comparable statistics, market reports, articles and comments from expert industry and country analysts across the 205 countries researched. It has tracked consumer and market trends since 1972, and in a recent report outlines consumer trends such as 'enfranchisement through technology', 'entertainment on the move', 'media interactivity for consumers', 'the drive for fitness', 'fear of terrorism and crime', 'health with everything', 'personal enhancement', and 'kids get older younger'.[3] While reports, articles and other sources may provide valuable background information of the macroenvironment, each company also needs to analyse its macroenvironment to detect needs and trends of particular importance to the company.

Analysing the macroenvironment

Successful companies recognise and respond profitably to unmet needs and trends. We distinguish among fads, trends and megatrends. A **fad** is 'unpredictable, short-lived, and without social, economic, and political significance'. A company can cash in on a fad such as Tamagotchi,

Breakthrough marketing

Google

Google has become a business leader in the new marketing environment.

Source: Courtesy of Google, Inc.

Founded in 1998 by two Stanford University PhD students, search engine Google's name is a play on the word *googol* – the number represented by a 1 followed by 100 zeros – a reference to the massive quantity of data available online, which the company helps users make sense of. Google's stated corporate mission is 'To organize the world's information and make it universally accessible and useful.'

The company has become the global market leader for search engines through its business focus and constant innovation. As Google grew into a primary destination for Web users searching for information online, it attracted a host of online advertisers. These advertisers drove Google's revenue by buying what are called 'search ads', little text-based boxes shown alongside search results that advertisers pay for only when users click on them. Google's search ad program, called AdWords, sells space on its search pages to ads linked with specific keywords. AdWords displays a company's ads on Google and its advertising network. Google auctions off the keyword ads, with the prime key words and prime page locations going to the highest bidder.

In addition to offering prime online 'real estate' for advertisers, Google adds value to advertisers by providing them with a variety of means to better target their ads to users and better understand the effectiveness of their marketing. Google Analytics, which Google provides free to advertisers, provides advertisers with a custom report, or dashboard, detailing how Internet users found the site, what ads they saw and/or clicked on, how they behaved while at the site, and how much traffic was generated. Google client Discount Tire was able to identify where visitors to the site encountered problems that led them to abandon a purchase midstream. After modifying its site and updating its keyword search campaign, Discount Tire measured a 14 per cent increase in sales within a week.

With its ability to deploy data that enable up-to-the-minute improvements of a Web marketing program, Google supported a style of marketing where the advertising resources and budget could be constantly targeted, monitored and optimised. Google called this approach 'marketing asset management', implying that advertising should be managed in the same way as assets in a portfolio, with management marshalling certain resources at one time or place online and others at a different time or place, depending on the market conditions. Rather than follow a marketing plan that had been developed months in advance, companies could use the real-time data collected on their campaigns to optimise the campaign's effectiveness by making it more responsive to the market.

Google has augmented its search capabilities with additional services and features for Internet users, including Google Maps, Google Local, Google Finance, Gmail (a Google email service), and Google Video (which was bolstered by the €1.2 billion acquisition of video hosting site YouTube in 2006). These new efforts all offered opportunities for Google to grow by selling the additional targeted advertising space that was created.

Sources: www.google.com; C. P. Taylor (2006) Google flex, *Adweek*, 20 March (cover story); R. Karpinski (2006) Keywords, analytics help define user lifetime value, *Advertising Age*, 24 April, p. S2; D. Gorog (2005) Survival guide, *Herald Sun*, 29 March; J. Schlosser (2005) Google, *Fortune*, 31 October, pp.168–9; J. Graham (2005) Google's profit sails past expectations, *USA Today*, 31 October.

Pokemon, Build-a-Bear, or Polly Pocket, but getting it right is more a matter of luck and good timing than anything else.[4]

A **trend** is a direction or sequence of events that has some momentum and durability. Trends are more predictable and durable than fads. A trend reveals the shape of the future and provides many opportunities. For example, the percentage of people who value physical fitness and well-being has risen steadily over the years, especially in the under-30 group, young women, upscale consumers, and people living in the western world.

Megatrends have been described as 'large social, economic, political, and technological changes [that] are slow to form, and once in place, they influence us for some time — between seven and ten years, or longer'.[5]

Identifying the major forces

Companies and their suppliers, marketing intermediaries, customers, competitors and publics all operate in a macroenvironment of forces and trends, increasingly global, that shape opportunities and pose threats. These forces represent 'non-controllables', which the company must monitor and to which it must respond. Although the forces are non-controllable they differ, however, on how they may affect a company, see 'Marketing memo: Forces in the company environment'.

Marketing memo

Forces in the company environment

The forces in the environment differ in how they may affect a company. Some forces may have a direct and unavoidable impact on a company while others may just have a slight – and sometimes ignorable – effect. A company should continuously monitor its environment in order to detect possible changes and in order to estimate the possible impacts that such changes might have on the company. Systematising the environmental forces in the four kinds of groups described in the following can assist the company in performing these tasks.

1 **Deterministic forces** Some environmental forces have a direct and determining influence on a company since the company has no other options than to adapt to these forces. Consider the world market oil price. For companies dependent on oil, increasing oil prices have a direct and unavoidable influence on production and distribution costs. Another example is the tax that a company pays out of its profit. Tax rates are set by governments and paying taxes according to tax legislation is unavoidable. Appreciations and depreciations of currencies is one more example of a deterministic environmental force.

2 **Moderating forces** Moderating forces influence the company in several – but not entirely different – ways. As with determining forces, moderating forces often lead to a set of 'known' consequences for a company – but the company does not necessarily have to follow or adapt to changes in moderating forces. Fashion is one example of a moderating force. Fashion companies do not have to moderate their clothing programmes according to various market changes in fashion; nevertheless most fashion companies find it wise to do so in order to stay in business.

3 **Asymmetric forces** Asymmetric forces lead to a set of 'unknown' consequences for a company. Many political decisions are asymmetric forces; very often the possible outcomes of political decisions are heavily debated in national parliaments, in the press, at work places and among citizens. In Denmark, an ongoing debate is taking place concerning the law of store closing hours. At present, there are some restrictions on opening hours for large stores (Danish stores with a yearly revenue exceeding €7 million). The union of 'small supermarkets' claims that a full liberalisation of closing hours will ruin their businesses because most customers will find it easier to carry out their shopping in large supermarkets. Also, there will be a loss in welfare for old and handicapped people, who may find it difficult to overcome longer distances to their supermarkets. On the other hand, large supermarket chains claim that small supermarkets may even benefit from a liberalisation of opening hours if they change their business according to the new market opportunities – for example by becoming speciality shops and/or by offering extended services to their local communities (e.g., delivery services).

4 **Indeterministic forces** These forces are characterised by having only small and negligible – or no – consequences for the company. For example, changes in fashion hardly have noticeable consequences for a producer of steel. However, because business conditions may change rapidly, forces that at present are classified as indeterministic may not necessarily stay as such. The company should therefore continuously monitor its surroundings in order to determine which environmental forces may impose threats and/or opportunities to the company.

The early days of the twenty-first century brought a series of new challenges: the steep decline of the stock market, which affected savings, investment, and retirement funds; increasing unemployment; corporate scandals; and of course, the rise of terrorism. These dramatic events were accompanied by the continuation of existing trends that have already profoundly influenced the global landscape. In 2005, more transistors (semiconductor devices used to switch electronic signals) were produced (and at a lower cost) than grains of rice; 24 per cent of European readers considered blogs their most trusted information source, just behind newspapers with 30 per cent; and insatiable world oil consumption is expected to rise 50 per cent by 2030.[6]

The socio-cultural and demographic environment

There's little excuse for being surprised by demographic developments. The Singer Company should have known for years that its sewing machine business would be hurt by smaller families and more working wives, yet it was slow in responding.

The main demographic force that marketers monitor is *population*, because people make up markets. Marketers are keenly interested in the size and growth rate of the population in cities, regions and nations; age distribution and ethnic mix; educational levels; household patterns; and regional characteristics and movements.

> To learn about the challenges in conducting market research in China, visit www.pearsoned-asia.com/marketingmanagementchina

Worldwide population growth

The world population is showing explosive growth: it totalled 6.1 billion in 2000 and will exceed 7.9 billion by the year 2025.[7] Here is an interesting picture:

> If the world were a village of 1,000 people, it would consist of 520 females and 480 males, 330 children, 60 people over age 65, 10 college graduates and 335 illiterate adults. The village would contain 52 North Americans, 55 Russians, 84 Latin Americans, 95 Eastern and Western Europeans, 124 Africans and 584 Asians. Communication would be difficult because 165 people would speak Mandarin, 86 English, 83 Hindi/Urdu, 64 Spanish, 58 Russian and 37 Arabic, and the rest would speak one of over 200 other languages. There would be 329 Christians, 178 Moslems, 132 Hindus, 62 Buddhists, 3 Jews, 167 nonreligious, 45 atheists, and 84 others.[8]

The population explosion has been a source of major concern. Moreover, population growth is highest in countries and communities that can least afford it, such as African and Latin American countries. The less-developed regions of the world currently account for 76 per cent of the world population and are growing at 2 per cent per year, whereas the population in more developed countries is growing at only 0.6 per cent per year. In developing countries, the death rate has been falling as a result of modern medicine, but the birthrate has remained fairly stable. Feeding, clothing and educating children, although it can also raise the standard of living, is nearly impossible in these countries.

Explosive population growth has major implications for business. A growing population does not mean growing markets, unless these markets have sufficient purchasing power. Nonetheless, companies that carefully analyse their markets can find major opportunities.

Population age mix

National populations vary in their age mix. At one extreme is Mexico, a country with a very young population and rapid population growth. At the other extreme is Japan, a country with one of the world's oldest populations. Milk, nappies, school supplies and toys will be more important products in Mexico than in Japan. In general, there is a global trend toward an ageing population. In 2005, the population of people aged 60 or over surpassed the proportion of under-fives, and it is unlikely that there will ever again be more toddlers than seniors.[9]

The structure of the EU population will change in the years to come. Low fertility levels, combined with an extended longevity and the fact that the baby boomers will reach retirement age, results in a demographic ageing of the EU population. The share of the older generation is increasing, whereas that of working age is decreasing. For example, the share of European persons of 80 years and over is projected to grow from 4.0 per cent in 2004 to 14.1 per cent in 2050. If current trends prevail until 2050, anyone of working age might then have to provide for twice as many retired people as is usual today![10] This might be a threat to the future welfare of European citizens. By 2045, the EU is likely to have a significantly higher proportion of older persons than its main global competitors.[11] In Europe there are ongoing discussions on how these challenges should be met. Possible solutions may include more solidarity between generations (i.e., a more equal distribution of income across generations), increasing the birth rate, and other initiatives.[12]

The changing population has strong implications for marketers. For example, many suppliers may be considering offering special products and services designed for the elderly. Many travel agencies offer specially designed travel packages to senior citizens, including for example medical care and special training facilities.

Marketers generally divide the population into six age groups: pre-school children, school-age children, teens, young adults aged 20–40, middle-aged adults aged 40–65, and older adults aged 65 and upwards. Some marketers like to focus on cohorts. **Cohorts** are groups of individuals who are born during the same time period and travel through life together. The 'defining moments' they experience as they become adults can stay with them for a lifetime and influence their values, preferences and buying behaviour. 'Marketing insight: Friends for life' summarises one breakdown of generational cohorts in the US and UK markets.

Marketing insight

Friends for life

Isenberg School of Management marketing professor Charles D. Schewe and president and founder of consultant firm Lifestage Matrix Marketing Geoffrey Meredith have developed a generational cohort segmentation scheme based on the concept that the key defining moments (i.e., moments that define and redefine who a person is) which occur when a person comes of age (roughly between 17 and 24) imprint core values that remain largely intact throughout life. For generational cohorts to form on the basis of certain defining moments, individuals must know of these events. Today, both national and world events tend to be broadcast globally within minutes after they occurred. Thus, while different countries have various generational cohorts embedded within their societies, there are also striking similarities between cohorts on a global scale. The degree of similarity depends on which age group is considered and in which countries. For example, the United Kingdom and the United States share quite a few defining moments and cohort values, while other countries, such as Brazil and Russia, have very different cohort structures and values.

Schewe and Meredith divide the US adult population into seven distinct cohorts, each with its own unique value structure, demographic make-up and markers. In the following, we will look closer at each of these cohorts and the similarities and differences with their UK equivalents.

Depression cohort

Born from 1912–1921, aged 87–96 in 2008. This rapidly dwindling group's coming-of-age years were marked by economic strife and elevated unemployment rates. Financial security – what they most lacked when coming of age – rules their thinking. They are no longer in the workforce, but they have had a clear impact on many of today's management practices. Interestingly, the 1930s depression appears a stronger collective memory in the United States than in the United Kingdom.

World War II cohort

Born from 1922–1927, aged 81–86 in 2008. In the United States, sacrifice for the common good was widely accepted among members of the World War II cohort. This cohort was focused on defeating a common enemy during their coming-of-age years, and its members are team oriented and patriotic. Here, crucial differences in interpretations between the United States and the United Kingdom exist. Whereas many Americans of this cohort expressed associations with the prosperity that followed the war, of patriotism and a common spirit, the British reflections were more negative, focusing on the meaninglessness and tragedy of the war, and capturing the ever-present fear of destruction and death. According to Schewe and Meredith these differences can be explained by the fact that the war was actually fought on British soil. The sound of air raid sirens was often heard, making fear of bombings part of everyday life. Meanwhile, in the United States, except for the 450,000 who actually fought the battles, the war was more of a distant story.

Post-war cohort

Born from 1928–1945, aged 63–80 in 2008. These individuals experienced a time of remarkable economic growth and social tranquillity. In the United Kingdom, the Cold War and the threat of nuclear war set the agenda, and spurred early development towards European unity. At the same time, McCarthyism and the Korean conflict were important developments in the United States. People in this cohort were part of the rise of the middle class, sought a sense of security and stability, and expected prosperous times to continue indefinitely.

▶ Marketing insight *(continued)*

Leading-edge baby boomer cohort

Born from 1946–1954, aged 54–62 in 2008. The loss of John F. Kennedy and the onset of the Vietnam War had the largest influence on this cohort's values in the United States. Across the continents, the breakthrough in space exploration epitomised by Armstrong taking the first steps on the moon stood out as a very important historic event. Leading-edge boomers championed political, environmental and cultural causes (Greenpeace, civil rights, women's rights), yet were simultaneously hedonistic and self-indulgent (drugs, free love, sensuality).

Trailing-edge baby boomer cohort

Born from 1955–1965, aged 43–53 in 2008. This group witnessed the fall of Vietnam, Watergate, and Nixon's resignation. While these events were relatively more important in the United States, the energy crisis was equally severe in the minds of the American and the British. The economic downturn that followed the oil embargo with its raging inflation rate, stock market decline and rising unemployment led these individuals to be less optimistic about their financial future than the leading-edge boomers.

Generation X cohort

Born from 1966–1976, aged 32–42 in 2008. Many members of this cohort were latchkey children or have parents who divorced. They have delayed marriage and children, and

they don't take those commitments lightly. More than other groups, this cohort accepts cultural diversity and puts personal life ahead of work life. Members show a spirit of entrepreneurship unmatched by any other cohort. Common defining moments were the fall of the Berlin Wall, the dissolution of the Soviet Union and the Gulf War. In the United Kingdom, the Falklands War, the EU common market and the rise of Thatcherism were also epoch events.

Generation N cohort (or generation Y)

Born from 1977, aged 31 and under in 2008. The advent of the Internet is a defining and ongoing development for this group, and they will be the engine of growth over the next two decades. A very important historic memory held in common is likely to be the events of 11 September 2001. Although still a work in progress, their core value structure is different from that of Generation X. They are more idealistic and social-cause oriented, without the cynical, what's-in-it-for-me, free-agent mindset of many Xers.

Sources: C. D. Schewe and G. Meredith (2004) Segmenting global markets by generational cohort: determining motivations by age, *Journal of Consumer Behaviour*, 4, 51–63; G. E. Meredith and C. D. Schewe (2002) *Managing by Defining Moments: America's 7 Generational Cohorts, Their Workplace Values, and Why Managers Should Care*, New York: Wiley/Hungry Minds; G. E. Meredith, C. D. Schewe and J. Karlovich (2001) *Defining Markets Defining Moments*, New York: Wiley/Hungry Minds; J. Scott and L. Zac (1993) Collective memories in Britain and the United States, *Public Opinion Quarterly*, 57(3), 315–31.

The diversity of markets

Countries also vary in ethnic and racial make-up. At one extreme is Japan, where almost everyone is Japanese; at the other is the United States, where people come from virtually all nations. European countries lie somewhere between these extremes with large fluctuations between the countries. Ireland is one of the most globalised nations in Europe and, instead of mass emigration, the country now has significant immigration – 167 languages are spoken in Ireland today[13] similar to multicultural New York. Unlike the United States, the EU consists of independent nations, with different cultures and languages, cooperating in many areas (e.g., economic, legal, monetary) of mutual interest. The EU average of non-nationals in each country is around 6 per cent with Luxembourg having around 40 per cent and Romania, Slovakia and Bulgaria having less than 1 per cent. Fewer than half of the non-nationals in the EU are ethnic minorities. While the population of ethnic minorities is relatively low on EU average the group is nevertheless large enough to attract focus from companies, who cannot afford to neglect its purchasing power as well as its possible influence on other citizens.

A recent Datamonitor survey[14] revealed that 90 per cent of food industry experts believe ethnic minority consumers are a key group to target, with ethnic food sales rising at 14 per cent a year in Europe and 5 per cent in the United States. While minority consumers only form a small part of ethnic food spending, trends in the group drive mainstream ethnic food consumption. Marketers need to understand minority trends in order to grow sales of ethnic food products. Spending on ethnic food in the United States has grown at an average annual rate of 4.9 per cent over the last five years, and ethnic foods now account for 11.8 per cent of all retail food sales in the country. In Europe, the market is growing almost three times as fast – but total sales still account for less than 1 per cent of retail food spending.[15]

▽ Phoenix Chinese News and Entertainment Channel

Phoenix Television is a Hong Kong-based Mandarin Chinese television broadcaster providing Infotainment (a combination of the words *info*rmation and enter*tainment*) programmes with popular 'star' anchors and talk show hosts. It is one of the few non-government-related television broadcasters available to the mainland Chinese audience. It operates three domestic channels and two international services – Phoenix North America Chinese Channel and Phoenix Chinese News and Entertainment (PCNE) Channel. Phoenix CNE Channel is a 24-hour, London-based channel, catering to Chinese communities in Europe (encompassing around 1.7 million people in 2006) who are eager to stay in touch with what's happening back home. Shows such as *Good Morning China*, *The Asian Journal*, and *Taipei Tonight Live* are mixed with in-house programmes such as *Europe Today* and *Chinese in Europe Express*. The channel reaches 50 European and North African countries and regions and is available on mainstream satellite television networks such as Sky Digital and other cable networks in the United Kingdom, Ireland, France, Germany and the Netherlands.

Phoenix CNE Channel is a vivid example of how companies acknowledge the importance of cultural sensitivity and work to refine both their products and their marketing to reach such fastest-growing and important consumer groups as the European Chinese.

Source: Courtesy of Phoenix CNE TV

Several food, clothing and furniture companies have directed their products and promotions to one or more ethnic groups.[16] Yet marketers must be careful not to overgeneralise. Within each ethnic group are consumers who are quite different from each other. For example, each of the Asian consumer groups living in Europe has its own very specific market characteristics, speaks different languages, consumes different cuisines, practises different religions, and represents very distinct national cultures. During the years he spent working in advertising abroad, Shane McGonigle, managing director of advertising agency Leo Burnett and president of the Institute of Advertising Practitioners in Ireland, picked up a crucial piece of advice as regards multicultural marketing strategies: 'Look for the similarities and respect the differences,' McGonigle says.

This is highly relevant in regard to the European market, in which subsections are beginning to show themselves as divided as much by lifestyle and aspirations as by culture. For instance, a 2007 Euromonitor marketing study showed that segmenting consumers by demographic factors, such as age, gender or ethnicity, is becoming less exhaustive. Increasingly, consumers identify with people who lead similar lifestyles to themselves. According to Euromonitor, examples of lifestyles that companies could use as inspiration for new marketing concepts include 'retreat', 'escape' and 'indulge'. 'Retreat' is associated with the followers of the health and wellness trend, and this group is likely to be most receptive to natural and organic products. The 'escape' lifestyle broadly encompasses consumers who are nostalgic for more innocent times past, and tend to be attracted to vintage and home-grown brands. Finally, 'indulge' lifestylers see themselves as true connoisseurs and demand luxury and exclusivity from their brands.[17]

Diversity goes beyond ethnic, racial and national markets. Around 37 million consumers in the EU and 80 million in Greater Europe have disabilities, and they constitute a market for home delivery companies, such as British companies Ocado and Tesco, as well as for various medical services.[18]

Educational groups

The population in any society falls into five educational groups: illiterates, high school dropouts, high school diplomas, college degrees and professional degrees. Over two-thirds of the world's 785 million illiterate adults are found in only eight countries (India, China, Bangladesh, Pakistan, Nigeria, Ethiopia, Indonesia and Egypt); of all the illiterate adults in the world, two-thirds are women.[19] In the EU, more than 60 per cent of the population has completed at least upper secondary education.[20] The large number of educated people in the EU spells a high demand for quality books and magazines, and a high supply of skills.

Household patterns

The 'traditional household' consists of a husband, wife and children (and sometimes grandparents). While the number of households in the countries of the EU is growing, their average size is decreasing. There are, however, great differences between the various regions of the European Union. In the southern member states, larger and more complex households with more generations living together are more common, whereas the tendency for an increasing number of people to live alone is very pronounced in the northern member states.[21] In 2005, 49 per cent of the EU population living in private households lived in households that had dependent children. The highest percentages could be observed in Lithuania (66 per cent), Slovakia (63 per cent) and Romania (62 per cent) and the lowest ones in Finland (42 per cent) and Germany (43 per cent).

More people are divorcing or separating, choosing not to marry, marrying later or marrying without the intention of having children. In 2004 there were fewer than five marriages per 1000 inhabitants in the EU, compared with almost eight marriages per 1000 inhabitants in 1970. As well as a decrease in the rate of marriages, there was also an increase in the average age at which people got married. Every four out of ten marriages in the EU results in divorce, with relatively few divorces in Greece, Spain, Ireland, Italy, Cyprus and Malta and more than six divorces for each ten marriages in Belgium, the Czech Republic, Estonia and Lithuania.[22] Each group has a distinctive set of needs and buying habits. For example, people in the SSWD group (single, separated, widowed, divorced) need smaller apartments; inexpensive and smaller appliances, furniture and furnishings; and smaller-size food packages. Companies such as IKEA, Absolut, Procter & Gamble and Subaru have recognised the potential of this market and the non-traditional household market as a whole.

Yet, in focusing on the recently targeted 'metrosexual' – straight urban men with gay shopping styles (e.g., being highly involved in fashion, personal care products and so on) – marketers may miss out on other male markets just under their nose. For instance, millions of boomer dads shop a lot more than their fathers or grandfathers did. They married later and are much more involved in raising their children. For instance, many of today's dads actually push baby buggies, and they don't want to be seen behind some fussy-looking contraption of yesteryear. So the maker of the high-concept Bugaboo stroller designed one with a sleek design and tyres resembling those of a dirt bike.[23]

Geographical shifts in population

This is a period of great migratory movements into and within the European region. Over the past 45 years, the population of today's EU-27 countries has grown from 376 million (1960) to 460 million (2005). Until the end of the 1980s, the 'natural increase' (live births minus deaths) was by far the major component of population growth. Yet, falling birth rates in most EU member states has led to a steady decline of the 'natural increase', and migration has been the major force of population growth since the beginning of the 1990s (as illustrated in Figure 5.1). Thus, recent years have witnessed a significantly growing number of migrants coming into the EU, with net migration increasing from 590,000 persons in 1994 to 1.85 million by 2004. Migrants come from all parts of the world – but in particular from Africa, the Middle East and Asia.[24]

Regional analysis shows that in five areas of Europe more people have left than have arrived. For example, this was the case in the Baltic states, the Netherlands, Northern Ireland, Poland, and areas in the south of Italy and the north of France. Spain and Italy stood out as having by far the highest net inflows of migrants, whereas large areas of Scandinavia and western Germany experienced a just positive net migration. These waves of new immigration to Europe have meant that new ethnic groups are beginning to impact the economic, social and political scene – as consumers, workers and investors. Combined with growing numbers of EU residents moving between states, it has offset a gradual erosion of national boundaries and tastes, essentially changing the landscape for marketers, who are increasingly alert to where consumers are gathering, and focusing on the importance of targeting their products and advertising efforts towards specific consumer groups.[25]

In the new EU countries, such as Hungary, Poland, Romania and Bulgaria, this erosion of national tastes is particularly notable, as consumers are developing a strong taste for western lifestyles and brands. According to Euromonitor International, modern Europe's appetite for western lifestyles offers strong growth opportunities for food and drinks companies especially. For example, the introduction of breakfast cereals in Bulgaria has been extremely successful, and the packaged food market in Ukraine has seen double-digit growth over the past six years. On a similar note, forecasts suggest that the Bulgarian packaged food market will see

Figure 5.1
Components of EU (25) population change

Source: Eurostat (2006) *EU Integration Seen Through Statistics. Key Facts of 18 Policy Areas, 2006 Edition*, Luxembourg: Office for Official Publications of the European Communities, p. 40. Copyright © 2006 European Communities. Reproduced with permission.

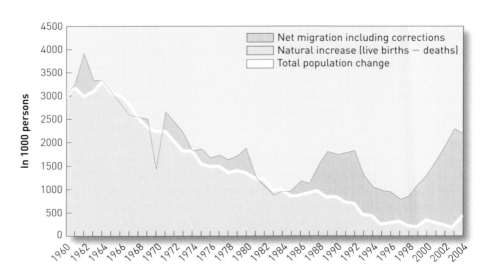

growth of 17 per cent and the Romanian soft drinks market of 33 per cent between 2006 and 2011.[26]

There are also regional developments in the 'old' EU member states: consumers in the United Kingdom eat more ready meals per capita (citizen) than people elsewhere in the EU, people in Italy prefer frozen soup, whereas the Germans buy more dehydrated soups, and the Spanish eat out more often than any other European nation. Spain also led the way with the highest per capita spending on health and wellness food in 2006, followed by the United Kingdom and Germany.[27] Clearly, marketers are learning how to cope with the changes brought about by current population developments in Europe.

The economic environment

The available purchasing power in an economy depends on current income, prices, savings, debt and credit availability. Marketers must pay careful attention to trends affecting purchasing power, because they can have a strong impact on business, especially for companies whose products are geared to high-income and price-sensitive consumers.

Income distribution

There are four types of industrial structure: *subsistence economies* such as Papua New Guinea, with 85 per cent of the population directly deriving their livelihood from farming, leaving few opportunities for marketers; *raw material exporting economies* such as Zaire (copper) and Saudi Arabia (oil), with good markets for equipment, tools, supplies and luxury goods for the rich; *industrialising economies* such as India, Egypt and the Philippines, where a new rich class and a growing middle class demand new types of goods; and *industrial economies* such as countries in western Europe, which are rich markets for all sorts of goods.

Marketers often distinguish countries using five different income-distribution patterns: (1) very low incomes; (2) mostly low incomes; (3) very low, very high incomes; (4) low, medium, high incomes; and (5) mostly medium incomes. Consider the market for Lamborghinis, an automobile costing more than €100,000. The market would be very small in countries with type (1) or (2) income patterns. One of the largest single markets for Lamborghinis turns out to be Portugal (income pattern 3) – one of the poorer countries in western Europe, but one with enough wealthy families to afford expensive cars.

Der Spiegel, one of Germany's major mainstream news magazines, recently noted: 'Not only is the number of poor people [in Germany] rising, the gap towards the wealthy in the Republic is growing too. In recent years the rich have grown richer and the poor poorer.'[28] Similar tendencies are detected throughout the EU. The inequality of income distribution (income quintile share ratio), measured as the ratio of total income received by the 20 per cent of the population with the highest income (top quintile) to that received by the 20 per cent of the population with the lowest income (lowest quintile), increased from 4.6 in 1998 to 4.9 in 2005 (EU25).[29] There is a risk that this trend, if it continues, may lead to a two-tier European market, with affluent people able to buy expensive goods and working-class people having to spend more carefully, shopping at discount stores and factory outlet malls, and selecting less expensive store brands.

Savings, debt and credit Consumer expenditure is affected by savings, debt and credit availability. For example, European consumers have a lower debt-to-income ratio than US consumers. For US consumers this slows down further expenditure on housing and high-cost items. Credit is readily available in the United States but at fairly high interest rates, especially to lower-income borrowers. An economic issue of increasing importance – not least to many unemployed European consumers – is the migration of manufacturers and service jobs offshore. From India, Infosys provides outsourcing services for many western companies. The 15,000 employees that the fast-growing €1.1 billion company hires every year receive training in Infosys's €85 million facility outside Bangalore. There they learn technical skills as well as 'softer' skills concerning team building, interpersonal communication, and the importance of being an ambassador for the brands they serve.[30]

The social–cultural environment

Society shapes the beliefs, values and norms that largely define consumer tastes and preferences (see Chapter 7). People absorb, almost unconsciously, a worldview that defines their relationship to themselves, to others, to organisations, to society, to nature, and to the universe.

- **Views of themselves:** At the turn of the millennium, a Eurobarometer survey looked into how Europeans viewed themselves and their lives. Overall, more than eight out of ten people felt positive about all things related to their lives, ranging from personal happiness, their health, their family, the economic situation and society in general. In addition, a majority of Europeans felt positive about the legacy passed on in terms of freedom, quality of life, equality, solidarity and welfare. On the other hand, people were most pessimistic when asked about employment, the environment, ethics and personal safety.

  While the question is often asked if a 'European' culture exists at all, this research shows that at least Europeans share a number of fundamental cultural values that guide their way of thinking and living. For instance, more than 90 per cent feel that it is extremely or very important to help others and to value people for who they are. To be involved in creating a better society and putting time and effort into personal development are also considered positive and crucial values by a majority.[31]

- **Views of others:** People are concerned about the homeless, crime and victims, and other social problems. At the same time, they seek out their 'own kind' for serious and long-lasting relationships and avoid strangers. These trends portend a growing market for social support products and services that promote direct relationships between human beings, such as health clubs, cruises and religious activity. They also suggest a growing market for 'social surrogates' such as television, video games and chatrooms on the Internet.

- **Views of organisations:** After a wave of company downsizings and corporate accounting scandals, there has been an overall decline in organisational loyalty.[32] Many people today see work not as a source of satisfaction but as a required chore to earn money to enjoy their non-work hours. Companies need to find new ways to win back consumer and employee confidence. They need to make sure they are good corporate citizens and that their consumer messages are honest.[33]

- **Views of society:** Some people defend society (preservers), some run it (makers), some take what they can from it (takers), some want to change it (changers), some are looking for something deeper (seekers), and still others want to leave it (escapers).[34] Consumption patterns often reflect social attitude. Makers tend to be high achievers who eat, dress and live well. Changers usually live more frugally, drive smaller cars and wear simpler clothes. Escapers and seekers are a major market for films, music, surfing and camping.

- **Views of nature:** People have woken up to nature's fragility and the finiteness of its resources. Business has responded to increased interest in being in harmony with and experiencing nature by producing wider varieties of camping, hiking, boating and fishing gear such as boots, tents, backpacks and accessories.

Other cultural characteristics of interest to marketers are the persistence of core cultural values and the existence of subcultures. Let's look at both.

High persistence of core cultural values Although divorce rates are high in many European countries most people in Europe still believe in work, in getting married, in giving to charity, and in being honest. *Core beliefs* and values are passed on from parents to children and reinforced by major social institutions – schools, churches, businesses and governments. *Secondary beliefs* and values are more open to change. Believing in the institution of marriage is a core belief; believing that people ought to get married early is a secondary belief.

Marketers have some chance of changing secondary values, but little chance of changing core values. Although core values are fairly persistent, cultural swings do take place. In the 1960s hippies, the Beatles, Elvis Presley and other cultural phenomena had a major impact on young people's hairstyles, clothing, sexual norms and life goals. Today's young people are influenced by new heroes and new activities such as Jamie Oliver or Victoria Beckham and social network services such as Facebook and MySpace.

Existence of subcultures Each society contains **subcultures**, groups with shared values, beliefs, preferences and behaviours emerging from their special life experiences or circumstances. There are sometimes unexpected rewards in targeting subcultures. Marketers have always loved teenagers because they are society's trendsetters in fashion, music, entertainment, ideas and attitudes. Besides being of similar age teenagers share on a global scale a youthful lifestyle that values growth and learning with an appreciation of future trends.[35] Marketers also know that if they attract someone as a teen, there's a good chance they will keep the person as a customer later in life. The Toyota Scion, which is clearly marketed to young drivers, is promoted through product placement in, for example, Whyville.net, an online interactive community populated primarily by 8–15 year olds. In this way, Toyota hopes to establish early brand presence, create positive associations and cultivate a new Toyota audience by building relationships with future car buyers.[36]

Having reviewed the socio-cultural and demographic environment we now turn to the ecological and physical component of the PEEST analysis.

The ecological and physical environment

The deterioration of the natural environment is a major global problem. There is great concern about 'greenhouse gases' in the atmosphere due to the burning of fossil fuels; about the depletion of the ozone layer due to certain chemicals and global warming; and about growing shortages of water. In western Europe, 'green' parties have vigorously pressed for public action to reduce industrial pollution.

New regulations hit certain industries very hard. Steel companies and public utilities have had to invest billions of euros in pollution-control equipment and more environmentally friendly fuels. The soap industry has increased its products' biodegradability. Great opportunities await companies and marketers who can create solutions that reconcile prosperity with environmental protection. Consider how the auto industry has adjusted to environmental concerns.[37]

▽ Toyota Prius

Some auto experts scoffed when Toyota launched its Prius saloons with hybrid gas-and-electric engines in 2001 and predicted sales of 300,000 cars within five years. But by 2004, the Prius was such a huge hit that it had a six-month waiting list. Toyota's winning formula consists of a powerful electric motor and the ability to quickly switch power sources – resulting in 55 miles per gallon for city and highway driving – with the roominess and power of a family saloon and an eco-friendly design and look, for a little over €14,000. The lesson? Products that consumers see as good for the environment and which are functionally successful can offer enticing options. Toyota is now rolling out hybrids throughout its auto line-up, and European automakers have followed suit – with Audi releasing the hybrid version of its Q7 in late 2008, hybrid cars are now found even in the up-scale sport utility vehicle (SUV) market.[38]

Consumers often appear confused about product decisions that affect the natural environment. An ACNielsen study shows that Latin American shoppers are the most likely to buy organic food, while the North Americans are the least likely. The Europeans place themselves in between.[39] The Europeans are willing to pay more for healthy and organic food, yet they are not willing to increase their overall food budget. Instead, they conduct a kind of food 'arbitrage': they spend more on fair trade or healthy products, but fund these purchases by buying certain staple products at discount shops. Actually increasing the number of green products they buy requires consumers to break such behavioural habits, overcome scepticism about the motives behind the introduction of the products and their quality level, and change their attitudes about the role such products play in environmental protection. (See 'Marketing insight: Green marketing'.)

Marketing insight

Green marketing

A Harris Interactive study reveals that the percentage of EU consumers who report that they consider environmental issues such as global warming the most important global challenge today range from 33 per cent in Spain to 54 per cent in France (2007). In this study, Europeans rated climate change as more personally relevant to them than other major global concerns, such as terrorism, religious fanaticism, viruses, war and famine. This sentiment is also reflected in a Eurobarometer survey, in which 63 per cent of European citizens said that the environment was the issue about which they worried most.

Environmental concerns may be manifested in many ways. In Europe, as well as in the United States, high proportions of consumers are willing to give up baths for showers to help save water, to use public transport, to buy a hybrid car or drive a smaller car as a means of reducing air pollution, to replace incandescent light bulbs with compact fluorescent bulbs or get solar panels installed at their homes to conserve energy. However, even if consumers are ready to change the way they wash themselves, only a small group is willing to shower less frequently or to pay a toll to drive their cars in city centres. Finally, between 16 and 37 per cent of respondents believe that industry and government are primarily responsible for global warming – and only between 7 and 12 per cent suggest that people in general share responsibility for climate change.

A new church built in Rome to commemorate the 2000th anniversary of Christianity was designed to take sustainability to new levels. US architect Richard Meier worked with the project's technical sponsor to develop a 'smart', anti-pollution material that essentially cleans itself and simultaneously helps destroy air pollutants found in car exhaust and heating emissions. Or, in more popular terms, a compound that not only enhances the sculptural forms of the building but also 'eats' surrounding smog.

Several companies are now developing 'smog-eating' products that can be used for the façades of buildings, as well as in paint, plaster and paving materials for roads. The new environment-friendly substances are being tried out in buildings, squares and highways in Europe as well as in Japan.

Taking sustainability to new levels, the Dives in Misericordia (Rich in Mercy) church in Rome contains a compound that minimises the need for maintenance of the building and helps reduce pollutants in the atmosphere.
Source: KNA-Bild Radtke/dpa/Corbis

▶ **Marketing insight** *(continued)*

From a branding perspective, however, 'green market-ing' programmes have not been entirely successful. Two main problems are that: (1) consumers may believe the product is of inferior quality as a result of being green; and (2) they may feel the product is not really that green to begin with. Sometimes consumers may even feel that the product has been 'greenwashed'. Greenwashing describes a situation in which a company deliberate mis-leads its customers about the company's environmental practices; that is, greenwashing appears when the com-pany's environmental claims are false or presented in a deceptive manner. In 2007, Boeing UK was bombarded with complaints about a print advertisement claiming its 747-8 international passenger plane produced 'less than 75 grams of CO_2 per passenger kilometre'. The problem was that Boeing UK based its figures on 100 per cent occupancy in contrast to the standard 79.9 per cent occu-pancy used by the British government in calculating air-liners' CO_2 emissions.[40]

Successful green products convincingly overcome both these concerns to persuade consumers they are acting in their own and society's long-run interest at the same time, such as with organic foods that are seen as healthier, tastier and safer, and energy-efficient appliances that cost less to run and last longer. Jacque-lyn A. Ottman – founder and president of J. Ottman Con-sulting – and her colleagues refer to the tendency to overly focus on a product's greenness as 'green market-ing myopia'. Figure 5.2 displays their recommendations for avoiding such myopia by following three key princi-ples: consumer value positioning, calibration of con-sumer knowledge, and the credibility of product claims.

Many top European companies are embracing sus-tainability and green marketing. Corporate Knights, Inc., with Innovest Strategic Value Advisors, Inc. a leading research firm specialising in analysing 'non-traditional' drivers of risk and shareholder value including companies' performance on social, environmental and

Consumer value positioning
- Design environmental products to perform as well as (or better than) alternatives.
- Promote and deliver the consumer-desired value of environmental products and target relevant consumer market segments (such as market health benefits among health-conscious consumers).
- Broaden mainstream appeal by bundling (or adding) consumer-desired value into environmental products (such as fixed pricing for subscribers of renewable energy).

Calibration of consumer knowledge
- Educate consumers with marketing messages that connect environmental product attributes with desired consumer value (for example, 'pesticide-free produce is healthier'; 'energy-efficiency saves money'; or 'solar power is convenient').
- Frame environmental product attributes as 'solutions' for consumer needs (for example, 'rechargeable batteries offer longer performance').
- Create engaging and educational Internet sites about environmental products' desired consumer value (for example, Tide Coldwater's interactive website allows visitors to calculate their likely annual money savings based on their laundry habits, utility source (gas or electricity), and postcode location).

Credibility of product claims
- Employ environmental product and consumer benefit claims that are specific, meaningful, unpretentious and qualified (i.e., compared with comparable alternatives or likely usage scenarios).
- Procure product endorsements or eco certifications from trustworthy third parties, and educate consumers about the meaning behind those endorsements and eco certifications.
- Encourage consumer evangelism via consumers' social and Internet communication networks with compelling, interesting, and/or entertaining information about environmental products (for example, Tide's 'Coldwater Challenge' website included a map of the United States so visitors could track and watch their personal influence spread when their friends requested a free sample).

Figure 5.2 Three keys to avoiding green marketing myopia

Source: J. A. Ottman, E. R. Stafford and C. L. Hartman (2006) Avoid-ing green marketing myopia, *Environment*, June, 22–36. Repro-duced with permission from Helen Dwight Reid Educational Foundation.

> ### ▶ Marketing insight *(continued)*

strategic governance issues, has initiated 'The Global 100 Most Sustainable Corporations in the World'. The list, which covers several European companies such as ABN Amro Holding NV (the Netherlands), Air France-KLM (France), BASF AG (Germany), Dexia (Belgium), Grupo Ferrovial SA (Spain), Kesko Corp. (Finland), Novo Nordisk A/S (Denmark), Pearson PLC (UK), Scania AB (Sweden) and Storebrand ASA (Norway), can be freely downloaded at www.global100.org. The Global 100 companies are sustainable 'in the sense that they have displayed a better ability than most of their industry peers to identify and effectively manage material environmental, social and governance factors impacting the opportunity and risk sides of their business' (www.global100.org).

Sources: J. Adler (2006) Going green, *Newsweek*, 17 July, 43–52; J. A. Ottman, E. R. Stafford and C. L. Hartman (2006) Avoiding green marketing myopia, *Environment*, June, 22–36; J. Meredith Ginsberg and P. N. Bloom (2004) Choosing the right green marketing strategy, *MIT Sloan Management Review*, Fall, 79–84; M. Gunther (2003) Tree huggers, soy lovers, and profits, *Fortune*, 23 June, 98–104; Roper ASW (2002) *Green Gauge Report 2002*, New York: Roper ASW; J. Ottman (1982) *Green Marketing: Opportunity for Innovation*, 2nd edn, Chicago: NTC/Contemporary Publishing Company; www.global100.org; T. Crampton (2007) More in Europe worry about climate than in US, poll shows, *International Herald Tribune*, 4 January (www.iht.com/articles/2007/01/04/news/poll.php?page=1); E. Povoledo (2006) Architecture in Italy goes green, *International Herald Tribune*, 22 November 2006 (www.iht.com/articles/2006/11/22/news/smog.php).

Corporate environmentalism is the recognition of the importance of environmental issues facing the firm and the integration of those issues into the firm's strategic plans.[41] Marketers practising corporate environmentalism need to be aware of the threats and opportunities associated with four major trends in the natural environment: the shortage of raw materials, especially water; the increased cost of energy; increased pollution levels; and the changing role of governments.

- The earth's raw materials consist of the infinite, the finite renewable, and the finite non-renewable. *Finite non-renewable resources* – oil, coal, platinum, zinc, silver – pose a particularly serious problem as the point of depletion approaches. Firms making products that require these increasingly scarce minerals face substantial cost increases. Firms engaged in research and development have an excellent opportunity to develop substitute materials.
- One finite non-renewable resource, oil, has created serious problems for the world economy. As oil prices soar to record levels, companies and governments are searching for practical means to harness solar, nuclear, wind, and other alternative forms of energy.
- Some industrial activity will inevitably damage the natural environment. A large market has been created for pollution-control solutions, such as scrubbers, recycling centres and landfill systems. Its existence leads to a search for alternative ways to produce and package goods.
- Governments vary in their concern for and efforts to promote a clean environment. Many less developed nations are doing little about pollution, largely because they lack the funds or the political will. It is in the richer nations' interest to help the poorer nations control their pollution, but even the richer nations today lack the necessary funds.

Environmental auditing

Environmental auditing offers a methodology to evaluate the environmental performance of companies and is likely to become increasingly widespread as more and more environmental regulations and codes of practice have to be adhered to in industry. The key objectives of the environmental audit are:[42]

- to determine the extent to which environmental management systems in a company are performing adequately;
- to verify compliance with local, national and European environmental and health and safety legislation;

- to verify compliance with a company's own stated corporate policy;
- to develop and promulgate internal procedures needed to achieve the organisation's environmental objectives;
- to minimise human exposure to risks from the environment and ensure adequate health and safety provision;
- to identify and assess company risk resulting from environmental failure;
- to assess the impact on the local environment of a particular plant or process by means of air, water and soil sampling; and
- to detect the environmental improvements a company can make.

Environmental auditing began in the 1980s. At first, industries and individual businesses created systems that suited their own needs. By the early 1990s there was growing support for the establishment of internationally recognised auditing procedures. In 1993, the European Community issued its Eco-Management and Audit Regulation (1836/93/EC). This regulation was set up as a voluntary management tool for industrial companies, to evaluate, report and improve their environmental performance.[43] An international system – ISO 14001 – was created by the International Standardisation Organisation (ISO) two years later.[44] While specifying a number of environmental management requirements for environmental management systems, ISO 14001 requires an environmental policy to be in existence within the company, fully supported by senior management, and outlining the policies of the company, not only to the staff but to the public. ISO 14001 is implemented voluntarily by the company and consists of six sections: General Requirements; Environmental Policy; Planning; Implementation and Operation; Checking and Corrective Action; Management Review. An increasing number of consultancies undertake environmental audits – examples include UL Europe, Auditeco, and Amberley. Being one of the UK's leading energy suppliers and part of E.ON, the world's largest investor-owned power and gas company with headquarters in Germany, E.ON UK runs environmental audits in areas where there is significant environmental risk. These are done by the company's internal audit department and external auditors, as part of the ISO 14001 certification process for E.ON businesses.

The technological environment

One of the most dramatic forces shaping people's lives is technology. Through the years, technology has released such wonders as penicillin, open-heart surgery, and the birth control pill, and such horrors as the hydrogen bomb, nerve gas, and the submachine gun. It has also given us such mixed blessings as mobile phones and video games.

Every new technology is a force for 'creative destruction'. Transistors hurt the vacuum-tube industry, xerography hurt the carbon-paper business, cars hurt the railways, and television hurts the newspapers. Instead of moving into the new technologies, many old industries fought or ignored them, and their businesses declined. Yet it is the essence of market capitalism to be dynamic and tolerate the creative destructiveness of technology as the price of progress.

The number of major new technologies we discover affects the economy's growth rate. Unfortunately, technological discoveries do not arise evenly through time – the railroad industry created a lot of investment, and then investment petered out until the car industry emerged. In the time between major innovations, an economy can stagnate. In the meantime, minor innovations fill the gap: freeze-dried coffee, combination shampoo and conditioner, anti-perspirants and deodorants, and so on. They require less risk, but they can also divert research effort away from major breakthroughs.

New technology also creates major long-run consequences that are not always foreseeable. The contraceptive pill, for example, helped lead to smaller families, more working wives, and larger discretionary incomes – resulting in higher expenditure on holiday travel, durable goods and luxury items. Mobile phones, video games and the Internet are not only reducing attention to traditional media, they are reducing face-to-face social interaction as people listen to music, watch a film on their mobile, and so on. Technologies also compete with each other. Consider the variety of means to view video material, as shown in Table 5.1.

Table 5.1 Video venues

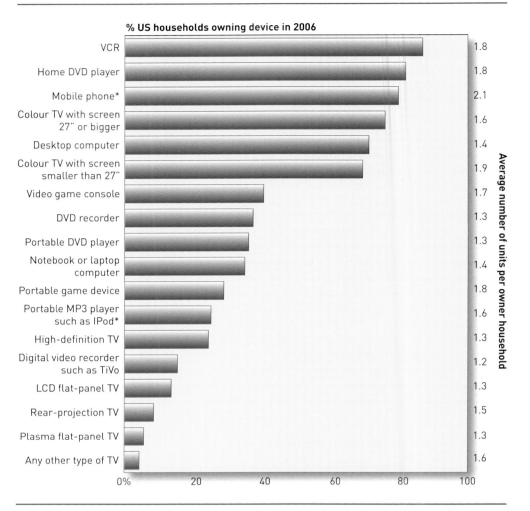

% US households owning device in 2006

Device	%	Average number of units per owner household
VCR		1.8
Home DVD player		1.8
Mobile phone*		2.1
Colour TV with screen 27" or bigger		1.6
Desktop computer		1.4
Colour TV with screen smaller than 27"		1.9
Video game console		1.7
DVD recorder		1.3
Portable DVD player		1.3
Notebook or laptop computer		1.4
Portable game device		1.8
Portable MP3 player such as IPod*		1.6
High-definition TV		1.3
Digital video recorder such as TiVo		1.2
LCD flat-panel TV		1.3
Rear-projection TV		1.5
Plasma flat-panel TV		1.3
Any other type of TV		1.6

*These numbers are for all mobile phones and MP3 players, not just those with video capability.

Source: Consumer Electronics Association's 'Eighth Annual Household & Teen CE Ownership Study' as reported in 'Special Report: Digital Media', *Advertising Age*, 5 June, 2006, S-2. Copyright © Crain Communications. Reproduced with permission.

Marketers should monitor the following four trends in technology: the accelerating pace of change, the unlimited opportunities for innovation, varying R&D budgets, and the increased regulation of technological change.

The accelerating pace of change Many of today's common products (computers, CD players, mobile phones, and so on) were not available 40 years ago. Electronics researchers are building smarter chips to make our cars, homes and offices connected and more responsive to changing conditions. More ideas than ever are in the works, and the time between the appearance of new ideas and their successful implementation is all but disappearing, as is the time between introduction and peak production. Apple quickly ramped up in a little over five years to sell 23.5 million iPods in 2006. In April 2007 the company announced that the 100 millionth iPod had been sold, making the iPod the fastest selling music player in history.[45]

The unlimited opportunities for innovation Some of the most exciting work today is taking place in biotechnology, computers, microelectronics, telecommunications, robotics and designer materials. The Human Genome project promises to usher in the Biological Century as biotech workers create new medical cures, new foods and new materials. Researchers are working on AIDS vaccines, totally safe contraceptives and non-fattening foods. They are designing robots for firefighting, underwater exploration and home nursing.

Varying R&D budgets A large portion of EU R&D expenditure is going into applied and basic research as opposed to experimental development. Hence, basic research is more important in the EU compared to the United States, Japan and China, and accounts for more than one-third of total R&D expenditure in many new member states.[46] To gain sustainable competitive advantage, many companies are no longer content just to put their money into copying competitors' products and making minor feature and style improvements. For instance, EU companies such as AstraZeneka, Roche, GlaxoSmithKline, Bayer and Solvay have increased their R&D investment in areas such as pharmaceuticals, biotechnology and chemicals.[47]

The increased regulation of technological change Many European governments have expanded their agencies' powers to investigate and ban potentially unsafe products. In the EU either the European Commission or the individual member state must approve all drugs before they can be legally sold. Safety and health regulations have also increased in the areas of food, automobiles, clothing, electrical appliances and construction.

The political–legal environment

The political and legal environment consists of laws, government agencies and pressure groups that influence and limit various organisations and individuals. Sometimes these laws also create new opportunities for business. For example, mandatory recycling laws have given the recycling industry a major boost and spurred the creation of dozens of new companies making new products from recycled materials. Two major trends in the political–legal environment are the increase in business legislation and the growth of special interest groups.

The increase in business legislation Business legislation has four main purposes: to protect companies from unfair competition, to protect consumers from unfair business practices, to protect the interests of society from unbridled business behaviour, and to charge businesses with the social costs created by their products or production processes. Although each new law may have a legitimate rationale, it may also have the unintended effect of sapping initiative and retarding economic growth.

Legislation affecting business has increased steadily over the years. The European Commission has been active in establishing a new framework of laws covering competitive behaviour, product standards, product liability and commercial transactions for the 27 member nations of the European Union.[48]

Several countries have passed strong consumer protection legislation. Norway bans several forms of sales promotion – trading stamps, contests, premiums – as inappropriate or 'unfair' instruments for promoting products. Thailand requires food processors selling national brands to market low-price brands also, so that low-income consumers can find economy brands. In India, food companies need special approval to launch brands that duplicate what already exists on the market, such as another cola drink or brand of rice.

Companies generally establish legal review procedures and promulgate ethical standards to guide their marketing managers, and as more business takes place in cyberspace marketers must establish new parameters for doing electronic business ethically.

The growth of special interest groups Political action committees (PACs) lobby government officials and pressure business executives to pay more attention to consumers' rights, women's rights, senior citizens' rights, minority rights and gay rights.

Many companies have established public affairs departments to deal with these groups and issues. An important force affecting business is the **consumerist movement** – an organised movement of citizens and government designed to strengthen the rights and powers of buyers in relationship to sellers. Consumerists have advocated and won the right to know the true interest cost of a loan, the true cost per standard unit of competing brands (unit pricing), the basic ingredients in a product, the nutritional quality of food as a percentage of their calorie allowance, the freshness of products and the true benefits of a product.

With consumers increasingly willing to swap personal information for customised products from firms – as long as they can be trusted – privacy issues will continue to be a public policy hot issue.[49] Consumers worry that they will be robbed or cheated; that private information will be used against them; that someone will steal their identity; that they will be bombarded by solicitations; and that children will be targeted.[50] Wise companies establish consumer affairs departments to help formulate policies and resolve and respond to consumer complaints.

Clearly, new laws and growing numbers of pressure groups have put more restraints on marketers. Marketers must clear their plans with the company's legal, public relations, public affairs and consumer affairs departments. Insurance companies directly or indirectly affect the design of smoke detectors; scientific groups affect the design of spray products. In essence, many private marketing transactions have moved into the public domain.

Although every manager in an organisation needs to observe the outside environment, the major responsibility for identifying significant marketplace changes falls to the company's marketers. Assisting with such tasks is the key purpose of the marketing information system.

▽ Managing the marketing information system

Components of a modern marketing information system

Marketers have two advantages: they have disciplined methods for collecting information, and they spend more time than anyone else interacting with customers and observing competition and other outside firms and groups. Marketers may be assisted by companies such as the Nielsen company, which specialise in delivering marketing information (information concerning buyer behaviour, market trends, brand and corporate image information, and so on) to business managers.

▽ The Nielsen Company

The Nielsen Company is a world-leading demographic, market segmentation research information and media company that includes ACNielsen, Nielsen Media Research, Spectra Marketing Systems and Scarborough Research, among others. Headquartered in both Europe (Haarlem, the Netherlands) and the United States (New York), Nielsen operates in more than 100 countries with a global team dedicated to 'helping clients compete more effectively and discover opportunity with more clarity than ever before'.[51]

Some firms have themselves developed marketing information systems that provide management with rich detail about buyer wants, preferences and behaviour.

▽ DuPont

Operating in more than 70 countries worldwide, including more than 30 European countries, DuPont commissioned marketing studies to uncover personal pillow behaviour for its Dacron Polyester unit, which supplies filling to pillow makers and sells its own Comforel brand. One challenge is that people don't give up their old pillows: 37 per cent of one sample described their relationship with their pillow as being like that of 'an old married couple', and an additional 13 per cent said their pillow was like a 'childhood friend'. Respondents fell into distinct groups in terms of pillow behaviour: stackers (23 per cent), plumpers (20 per cent), rollers or folders (16 per cent), cuddlers (16 per cent) and smashers, who pound their pillows into a more comfy shape (10 per cent). Women were more likely to plump, men to fold. The prevalence of stackers led the company to sell more pillows packaged as pairs, as well as to market different levels of softness or firmness.[52]

Marketers also have extensive information about how consumption patterns vary across countries. On a per capita basis within western Europe, for example, the Swiss consume the most chocolate, the Greeks eat the most cheese, the Irish drink the most tea and the Austrians smoke the most cigarettes.

Nevertheless, many business firms are not sophisticated about gathering information. Many do not have a marketing research department. Others have a department that limits its work to routine forecasting, sales analysis and occasional surveys (see Chapter 6). Some managers complain about not knowing how to get hold of critical information; getting too much information that they cannot use and too little that they really need; and getting important information too late. Companies with superior information enjoy a competitive advantage. They can choose their markets better, develop better offerings and execute better marketing planning.

Every firm must organise and distribute a continuous flow of information to its marketing managers. A **marketing information system (MIS)** consists of people, equipment and procedures to gather, sort, analyse, evaluate and distribute needed, timely and accurate information to marketing decision makers. A marketing information system relies on internal company records, marketing intelligence activities and marketing research. We will discuss the first two topics here, and the third one in the next chapter.

The company's marketing information system should be a cross between what managers think they need, what they really need and what is economically feasible. An internal MIS committee can interview a cross section of marketing managers to discover their information needs. Table 5.2 displays some useful questions.

Table 5.2 Information needs probes

---

1   What decisions do you regularly make?
2   What information do you need to make these decisions?
3   What information do you regularly get?
4   What special studies do you periodically request?
5   What information would you want that you are not getting now?
6   What information would you want daily? Weekly? Monthly? Yearly?
7   What magazines and trade reports would you like to see on a regular basis?
8   What topics would you like to be kept informed of?
9   What data analysis programs would you want?
10 What are the four most helpful improvements that could be made in the present marketing information system?

Internal records

Marketing managers rely on internal reports of orders, sales, prices, costs, inventory levels, receivables, payables, and so on. By analysing this information they can spot important opportunities and problems.

The order-to-payment cycle

The heart of the internal records system is the order-to-payment cycle. Sales representatives, dealers and customers send orders to the firm. The sales department prepares invoices, transmits copies to various departments, and back orders out-of-stock items. Shipped items generate shipping and billing documents that go to various departments.

Today's companies need to perform these steps quickly and accurately, because customers favour firms that can promise timely delivery. An increasing number of companies are using the Internet and extranets to improve the speed, accuracy and efficiency of the order-to-payment cycle.

Sales information systems

Marketing managers need timely and accurate reports on current sales. Tesco is the United Kingdom's national leader in the food sector, and a global player in retailing with outlets in Ireland, central Europe, Asia and the United States (here known as 'Fresh & Easy' stores). Tesco uses point-of-sale (POS) data (data available from the electronic cash register) to understand and anticipate customer behaviour, manage stock in individual stores and, above all, the speedy availability and accuracy of POS data makes a fundamental difference to a retailer's competitiveness and the strength of its supply chain. Simon Alcock, technical specialist, Tesco, says:

> Managing the supply chain is critical for Tesco in maintaining its leadership in the industry. If customers can't find the product they like on the supermarket shelves, then they can't buy it. The media has highlighted 'out of stocks' as an issue for some of our competitors, this solution will help us tackle the problem.[53]

Companies that make good use of 'cookies', records of website usage stored on personal browsers, are smart users of targeted marketing. Although the perception is that most people delete cookies out of concern for their privacy, the numbers tell a different story. A recent survey showed that only 8 per cent of people very frequently delete cookies, down from 18 per cent in 2004, and 24 per cent of respondents said they never delete cookies. Not only do customers *not* delete cookies, but they also expect customised marketing appeals and deals once they accept cookies. Technological gadgets are revolutionising sales information systems and allowing representatives to have up-to-the-second information. When visiting a golf shop, sales reps for TaylorMade used to spend up to two hours counting golf clubs in stock before filling new orders by hand. Since the company adopted handheld devices with bar-code readers and Internet connections, the reps simply point their handhelds at the bar codes and automatically tally inventory. By using the two hours they save to focus on boosting sales to retail customers, sales reps improved productivity by 20 per cent.[54]

Companies must carefully interpret the sales data so as not to draw the wrong conclusions. Founder of Dell computers Michael Dell gave this illustration:

> If you have three yellow Mustangs sitting on a dealer's lot and a customer wants a red one, the salesman may be really good at figuring out how to sell the yellow Mustang. So the yellow Mustang gets sold, and a signal gets sent back to the factory that, hey, people want yellow Mustangs.

The marketing intelligence system

The internal records system supplies *results* data, but the marketing intelligence system supplies *happenings* data. A **marketing intelligence system** is a set of procedures and sources managers use to obtain everyday information about developments in the marketing environment. Marketing managers collect marketing intelligence by reading books, newspapers and trade

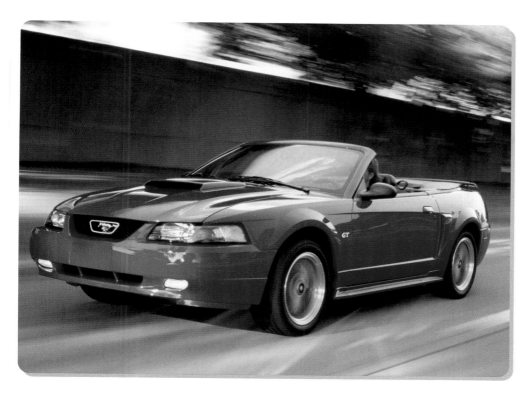

If customers want red Mustangs but buy yellow because red isn't available, marketers might draw an incorrect message from the sales data about what colour people really want.

Source: Courtesy of Ford Motor Company

publications; talking to customers, suppliers and distributors; monitoring 'social media' on the Internet via online discussion groups, emailing lists and blogs; and meeting with other company managers.

A company can take several steps to improve the quality of its marketing intelligence:

- **Train and motivate the sales force to spot and report new developments:** The company must 'sell' its sales force on their importance as intelligence gatherers. The front line people know and observe customer behaviour first hand, and their knowledge needs to be integrated into marketing strategy and tactics. Using a business intelligence system, a chain of chemists discovered that two of its stores, managed by the same person, had significantly higher sales in chocolate on Valentine's Day. They then discovered that instead of placing the lower-priced chocolates on a lower shelf and the more expensive chocolates higher up, this manager mixed shelf content. He knew that customers came in, reaching for the lower-priced items, but then stopped to revise their decision when they noticed the more expensive products; thinking 'she's worth it'. Communicating such practices and observations are extremely important for generating new business ideas.[55]

- **Motivate distributors, retailers and other intermediaries to pass along important intelligence:** Many companies hire specialists to gather marketing intelligence.[56] Service providers and retailers often send mystery shoppers, also known as 'secret shoppers', to their stores to assess cleanliness of facilities, product quality and the way employees treat customers. Health care facilities that use mystery shoppers say the reports have led to a number of changes in the patient experience, including improved estimates of waiting times, better explanations of medical procedures, and even less-stressful programming on the television in the waiting room.[57]

- **Network externally:** The firm can purchase competitors' products; attend open houses and trade shows; read competitors' published reports; attend stockholders' meetings; talk to employees, dealers, distributors, suppliers and freight agents; collect competitors' ads; and look up news stories about competitors. US software developer Cognos created an internal website called Street Fighter, where any of the firm's 3000 workers can submit scoops about competitors and win prizes.[58]

Of course, before the Internet, sometimes you just had to go out in the field, literally, and watch the competition. This is what Texas oil and gas entrepreneur T. Boone Pickens did. Describing how he learned about a rival's drilling activity, Pickens recalls,

> We would have someone who would watch [the rival's] drilling floor from a half-mile away with field glasses. Our competitor didn't like it but there wasn't anything they could do about it. Our spotters would watch the joints and drill pipe. They would count them; each [drill] joint was 30 feet long. By adding up all the joints, you would be able to tally the depth of the well.

Pickens knew that the deeper the well the more costly it would be for his rival to get the oil or gas up to the surface, and this information provided him with an immediate competitive advantage.[59]

Competitive intelligence gathering must be legal and ethical, however Procter & Gamble reportedly paid a multimillion-dollar settlement to Unilever when some external operatives (people from an outside firm) hired as part of a P&G corporate intelligence programme to learn about Unilever's hair care products were found to have engaged in such unethical behaviour as 'dumpster diving' (also known as 'rubbish archaeology') – including rummaging through skips on Unilever's property in search of unshredded documents containing key strategic plans.[60]

- **Set up a customer advisory panel:** Members might include representative customers, the company's largest customers or its most outspoken or sophisticated customers. Many business schools have advisory panels made up of alumni and recruiters who provide valuable feedback on the curriculum.
- **Take advantage of government data resources:** EUROSTAT, the Statistical Office of the European Communities, provides an in-depth look at the population swings, demographic groups, regional migrations and changing family structure of 491,011,000 people in the 27 EU member states. Acxiom Europe assists companies in maximising the value of information that already exists within the company or from external sources. Having acquired and now integrated Claritas Europe (including BPK and Altwood) and Consodata (the United Kingdom, France, Germany, Spain), Acxiom Europe represents one of Europe's leading sources of marketing and information management solutions.[61]
- **Purchase information from outside suppliers:** Well-known data suppliers include the AC Nielsen Company and Information Resources, Inc. These research firms gather consumer panel data at a much lower cost than the company could manage on its own. Biz360 has specialised databases to provide reports from 7000 sources on the extent and nature of print, broadcast and online media coverage, including blogs and message boards, that a company is receiving.[62]
- **Use online customer feedback systems to collect competitive intelligence:** Online customer review boards, discussion forums, chatrooms and blogs can distribute one customer's evaluation of a product or a supplier to a large number of other potential buyers and, of course, to marketers seeking information about the competition. Chatrooms allow users to share experiences and impressions, but their unstructured nature makes it difficult for marketers to find relevant messages. Thus some companies have adopted structured systems, such as customer discussion boards or customer reviews. See 'Marketing memo: Clicking on the competition' for a summary of the major categories of structured online feedback systems.[63]

▽ GlaxoSmithKline PLC

GlaxoSmithKline PLC, Kraft and Hewlett-Packard are learning how to use the Internet to harness customer input. They aren't going it alone but teaming up with Communispace Corp., a start-up that hosts private online communities. For instance, Glaxo sponsors an online community devoted to weight loss and says it is learning far more than it could have gleaned from focus groups on topics that range from advice on packaging its first weight-loss pill to where to place in-store marketing. Most importantly, members give Glaxo insights into their own battles with weight loss and dieting.[64]

Marketing memo

Clicking on the competition

There are five main ways marketers can find relevant online information about competitors' product strengths and weaknesses, as well as summary comments and overall performance ratings of a product, service or supplier.

- **Independent customer goods and service review forums** Independent forums include websites such as Epinions.com, Tripadvisor.com, Consumerreview.com and Bizrate.com. Bizrate.com is a consumer feedback network that collects millions of consumer reviews of stores and products each year from two sources: its 1.3 million members, who have volunteered to provide ratings and feedback to assist other shoppers; and survey results on service quality from stores that have agreed to allow BizRate.com to collect feedback directly from their customers as they make purchases. BizRate is operated by Shopzilla, which operates websites serving consumers and retailers in the UK, French, German and US markets.

- **Distributor or sales agent feedback sites** Feedback sites offer both positive and negative product or service reviews, but the stores or distributors have built the sites themselves. Amazon.com, for instance, offers an interactive feedback opportunity through which buyers, readers, editors and others may review all products listed on the site, especially books. Elance.com is an online professional services provider that allows contractors to describe their experience and level of satisfaction with subcontractors.

- **Combo sites** Combination sites (combo sites) offer both customer reviews and expert opinions. Combo sites are concentrated in financial services and high-tech products that require professional knowledge. Zdnet.com, an online adviser on technology products, offers customer comments and evaluations based on ease of use, features and stability, along with expert reviews. The advantage of this type of review site is that a product supplier can compare opinions from the experts with those from consumers.

- **Customer complaint sites** Customer complaint forums are designed mainly for dissatisfied customers. For instance, Planetfeedback.com allows customers to voice unfavourable experiences with specific companies. Another site, Complaints.com, is devoted to customers who want to vent their frustrations with particular firms or their offerings.

- **Public blogs** Tens of millions of blogs exist online and their numbers continue to grow. Firms such as JupiterResearch and NielsenBuzzMetrics, which operate in global markets, analyse blogs and social networks to provide firms with insights into consumer sentiment: pharmaceuticals want to know what questions are on patients' minds when they hear about problems with a medication; car companies are looking for better ways to spot defects and work out what to do about them.

Source: *The Economist* (2006) The blogs in the corporate machine, 11 February, 55–6; also adapted from R. T. Peterson and Z. Yang (2004) Web product reviews help strategy, *Marketing News*, 7 April, 18.

Some companies circulate marketing intelligence. The staff scan the Internet and major publications, abstract relevant news and disseminate a news bulletin to marketing managers. The competitive intelligence function works best when intelligence operations collaborate closely with key users in the decision-making process. In contrast, organisations where intelligence is seen as a distinct, separate function that only produces reports and doesn't get involved are less effective.[65]

The information gathered from the company's internal records and from the marketing intelligence system must be properly stored and managed in order for the company to take advantage of the obtained information. Databases, data warehousing and data mining may assist managers in performing these tasks.

Databases, data warehousing and data mining

Today companies organise their information into databases – customer databases, product databases, salesperson databases – and then combine data from the different databases. For example, the customer database will contain every customer's name, address, past transactions, and sometimes even demographics and psychographics (activities, interests and opinions). Instead of sending a mass 'carpet bombing' mailing of a new offer to every customer in its database, a company will rank its customers according to purchase recency, frequency and monetary value (RFM) and send the offer to only the highest-scoring customers. Besides saving on mailing expenses, this manipulation of data can often achieve a double-digit response rate.

Companies warehouse these data and make them easily accessible to decision makers. Furthermore, by hiring analysts skilled in sophisticated statistical methods, they can 'mine' the data and garner fresh insights into neglected customer segments, recent customer trends and other useful information. Managers can cross-tabulate customer information with product and salesperson information to yield still deeper insights. Using its own in-house technology, for example, US financial services company Wells Fargo has developed the ability to track and analyse every bank transaction made by its 10 million retail customers – whether at ATMs, bank branches or online. When transaction data are combined with personal information provided by customers, Wells Fargo can come up with targeted offerings to coincide with a customer's life-changing event. As a result, compared with the industry average of 2.2 products per customer, Wells Fargo sells 4.[66] Many other firms are also taking advantage of these new rich databases (see 'Marketing insight: The big dig').

Database marketing

Marketers must know their customers.[67] And in order to know the customer, the company must collect information and store it in a database from which to conduct database marketing. A **customer database** is an organised collection of comprehensive information about individual customers or prospects that is current, accessible and actionable for such marketing purposes as lead generation, lead qualification, sale of a product or service, or maintenance of customer relationships.

Marketing insight

The big dig

As companies gather more and more information, their ability to collect and analyse data to generate insights is more critical. Here is what several leading companies are doing.

Best Buy has assembled a 15+ terabyte database with seven years of data on 75 million households. The company captures information about every transaction and interaction – from phone calls and mouse clicks to delivery and rebate-check addresses – and then deploys sophisticated match-and-merge algorithms to classify over three-quarters of its customers, or more than 100 million individuals. Best Buy places its core customers into profiled categories, such as 'Buzz' (the young technology buff), 'Jill' (the suburban housewife), 'Barry' (the wealthy professional man), and 'Ray' (the family man). The firm also applies a customer lifetime value model that measures transaction-level profitability and factors in a host of customer behaviours that either increase or decrease the value of the relationship. Knowing so much about consumers allows Best Buy to employ precision marketing and customer-triggered incentive programmes with more favourable response rates.

Some companies have applied their database knowledge to drive media purchases. To assess the effectiveness of various advertising media a leading industry group, Interactive Advertising Bureau, conducted a series of tests over an 18-month period for 30 blue-chip companies. Analysing customer behaviour, the study concluded that Ford Motor Co. could have sold an additional US$625 million worth of trucks if it had increased its online budget from 2.5 per cent to 6 per cent. After seeing the results, Ford announced in August 2005 that it would shift up to 30 per cent of its $1 billion ad budget into media targeted to individual customers, half of it through online advertising.

Capturing online customer behaviour can yield a wealth of insights. A new customer signing up with Microsoft to get a free Hotmail email account is required to give the company his or her name, age, gender and postcode. Microsoft can then combine those facts with information such as observed online behaviour and characteristics of the area in which the customer lives, to help advertisers better understand whether, when and how to contact that customer. Although Microsoft must be careful to preserve consumer privacy – the company claims it won't purchase an individual's income history – it can still provide advertising clients with behavioural targeting information. For example, it can help takeaway stores to zero in on working parents aged 30–40 in a given neighbourhood with ads designed to reach them before 10 am when they are most likely to be planning their evening meal.

Sources: J. Zabin (2006) The importance of being analytical, *Brandweek*, 24 July, 21; S. Baker (2006) Math will rock your world, *BusinessWeek*, 23 January, 54–62; M. Kessler and B. Acohido (2006) Data miners dig a little deeper, *USA Today*, 11 July.

Database marketing is the process of building, maintaining and using customer databases and other databases (products, suppliers, resellers) to contact, transact and build customer relationships. The marketing database can assist marketing managers in tasks ranging from daily operation, resource allocation and budget planning to strategic decision processes.[68] Businesses increasingly have the capability to accumulate huge amounts of customer data in large databases. Many organisations have realised that the knowledge in these huge databases is key to supporting the various organisational decisions. In particular, the knowledge about customers from these databases is critical for the marketing function. However, many of the useful marketing insights into customer characteristics and their purchase patterns are largely hidden and untapped.[69]

The complexity of business markets is increasing. A shortened life cycle of many products, increasing globalisation as well as the emergence of the Internet are all examples of conditions that have contributed to the fact that the environment in which the company must plan and execute its market behaviour has become increasingly complex. Therefore, the transformation process (i.e., the exchange of information, goods and money between buyer and seller) has become still more complicated and market agents are facing increasing demands on their skills to communicate offerings, needs and expectations in the marketplace. In response to such challenges a growing interest for customer relationship management can be detected. CRM deals with the identification, attraction and retention of profitable customers by managing relationships with them[70] (an in-depth coverage of CRM is provided in Chapter 11). Also for that reason, customer knowledge is one of a company's most valuable resources. Over the last decade direct channels to the customer, such as ebusiness, call centres and loyalty programmes, have produced huge volumes of data. Many of these data are being channelled into CRM databases for use in targeted relationship management and statistical modelling of consumer behaviour. Such enhanced knowledge should provide improved business results. However, many companies are still at the data storing and explorative stages[71] and have thus not yet benefited from a complete database management system. Moreover, many companies confuse a customer mailing list with a customer database. A **customer mailing list** is simply a set of names, addresses and telephone numbers. A customer database contains much more information, accumulated through customer transactions, registration information, telephone queries, cookies, and every customer contact. Ideally, a customer database also contains the consumer's past purchases, demographics (age, income, family members, birthdays), psychographics (activities, interests and opinions), mediagraphics (preferred media), and other useful information. Ideally, a **business database** would contain business customers' past purchases; past volumes, prices, and profits; buyer team member names (and ages, birthdays, hobbies and favourite foods); status of current contracts; an estimate of the supplier's share of the customer's business; competitive suppliers; assessment of competitive strengths and weaknesses in selling and servicing the account; and relevant buying practices, patterns and policies.

For example, a Latin American unit of the Swiss pharmaceutical firm Novartis keeps data on 100,000 of Argentina's farmers, knows their crop protection chemical purchases, groups them by value, and treats each group differently. 'Breakthrough marketing: Tesco' describes how the UK supermarket giant has found ways to use its database to attract and engage customers.

Data warehousing and data mining

Savvy companies are capturing information every time a customer comes into contact with any of their departments. Touch points include a customer purchase, a customer-requested service call, an online query or a mail-in rebate card. Banks and credit card companies, telephone companies, catalogue marketers and many other companies have a great deal of information about their customers, including not only addresses and phone numbers but also transactions and enhanced data on age, family size, income and other demographic information. Companies with a well-functioning database system are capable of providing answers to the following questions:[72] (1) what data do we potentially have available?; (2) what data are needed to achieve our goals?; (3) what data are missing that we ought to have?; (4) what data will be necessary in the future in order to address the market?

Breakthrough marketing

Tesco

If you asked a customer of UK supermarket chain Tesco what the shopping experience there was like in the early 1980s, 'customer friendly' would probably not be the answer. Though it began upgrading its stores and product selection in 1983, Tesco continued to suffer from a reputation as a 'pile it high and sell it cheap' mass market retailer, lagging behind the more upscale market leader Sainsbury's. To gain share against Sainsbury's, Tesco needed to reverse the public perception of its stores. It decided to improve the shopping experience and highlight improvements with an image campaign to 'lift us out of the mould in our particular sector', as its 1989 agency brief put it.

Between 1990 and 1992, Tesco launched 114 separate initiatives to improve the quality of its stores, including adding baby-changing rooms, stocking speciality items such as French free-range chickens, and introducing a value-priced line of products. It developed a campaign entitled 'Every Little Helps' to communicate these improvements with 20 ads, each focusing on a different aspect of its approach – 'doing right by the customer'. As a result, between 1990 and 1995 Tesco attracted 1.3 million new customers, who pushed revenues and market share steadily upwards until Tesco surpassed Sainsbury's as the market leader in 1995.

Tesco then introduced an initiative that would make it a world-class example of how to build lasting relationships with customers: the Tesco Clubcard frequent-shopper programme. Essentially a loyalty card that offered discounts and special offers tailored to individual shoppers, the Clubcard was also a powerful data-gathering tool enabling Tesco to understand the shopping patterns and preferences of its customers better than any competitor. Using Clubcard data, Tesco created a unique 'DNA profile' for each customer based on shopping habits. To build this profile, it classified each product purchased by a customer on a set of up to 40 dimensions, including price, size, brand, ecofriendliness, convenience and healthiness. Based on their DNA profile, Tesco shoppers received one of 4 million different variations of the quarterly Clubcard statement, which contained targeted special offers and other promotions. The company also installed kiosks in its stores where Clubcard shoppers could get customised coupons.

The Clubcard data also helped Tesco run its business more efficiently. Tracking Clubcard purchases helped uncover price elasticities and set promotional schedules saving over £280 (€350) million. Tesco used customer data to determine the range of products and the nature of merchandising for each store, and even the location of new stores. Within 15 months of introduction, more than 8 million Clubcards had been issued, of which 5 million were used regularly. The customer focus enhanced by the Clubcard helped propel Tesco to even greater success than in the early 1990s. The company's market share in the United Kingdom rose to 15 per cent by 1999, and that year other British companies voted Tesco Britain's most admired company for the second year in a row.

In the following years, Tesco continued to apply its winning formula of using customer data to dominate the British retail landscape, moving beyond supermarkets to 'big-box' retailing of general merchandise, or non-food products. Not only was Tesco providing additional convenience to consumers who preferred shopping under one roof, it was also improving its profitability. The average margin of non-food products was 9 per cent, as opposed to 5 per cent for food. By 2003, nearly 20 per cent of Tesco's revenues came from non-food items, and the company was selling more CDs than Virgin Megastores, and its apparel line, Cherokee, was the fastest-growing clothing brand in the United Kingdom.

Tesco also undertook extensive customer research with telephone and written surveys and customer panels to extend its lead in the grocery market. By 2005, the company had a 35 per cent share of supermarket spending in the United Kingdom, almost twice that of its nearest competitor, and a 14 per cent share of total retail sales. Tesco used the same customer-centred strategy to expand overseas. In 2005, it had 648 stores outside the United Kingdom and was the supermarket leader in Poland, Hungary, Thailand, Ireland and Slovakia. In November 2007, Tesco began expanding into the US market with their new 'Fresh & Easy' convenience stores. The company expects to open 150 new US stores in 2008. 'We are very encouraged by the start Fresh & Easy has made. While it is still early days, the response of customers to our offer has surpassed our expectations,' Tesco said. In 2007, Tesco was Britain's largest company, the second largest retailer in Europe (the largest being French Carrefour Group) and the fourth-largest retailer in the world.

Sources: J. Hall (2008) Tesco's US adventure provides some cheer for British retailing, *The Telegraph*, 19 April; Tesco becomes fourth largest global retailer, overtakes Metro, www.freshplaze.com, 15 January 2008; R. Fletcher (2006) Leahy shrugs off talk of a 'brain drain', *Sunday Times* (London), 29 January; E. Rigby (2005) Prosperous Tesco takes retailing to a new level, *Financial Times*, 21 September, p. 23; L. Cohn (2003) A grocery war that's not about food, *BusinessWeek*, 20 October, 30; The Prime Minister launches the 10th Tesco Computers for Schools scheme, *M2 Presswire*, 26 January 2001; A. Sharpe and J. Bamford (2000) Tesco Stores Ltd., paper presented at Advertising Effectiveness Awards; H. Pringle and M. Thompson, *Brand Spirit*, New York: John Wiley & Sons.

Data are collected by the company's contact centre and organised into a **data warehouse** where marketers can capture, query and analyse them to draw inferences about an individual customer's needs and responses. Telemarketers can respond to customer enquiries about products and services based on a total picture of the customer relationship. Through **data mining** marketing statisticians can extract useful information about individuals, trends and segments from the mass of data. Using sophisticated statistical and mathematical techniques such as cluster analysis, automatic interaction detection, predictive modelling and neural networking,[73] data mining is a process of knowledge discovery and of distilling this knowledge into actionable information,[74] see 'Marketing insight: The CRISP-DM project'.

Marketing insight

The CRISP-DM project

With funding from the European Commission, the CRISP-DM (CRoss-Industry Standard Process for Data Mining) project developed a data-mining process model. Starting from the knowledge discovery processes used in early data-mining projects and responding directly to user requirements, this project defined and validated a data-mining process that is applicable in diverse industry sectors. CRISP-DM 1.0 (1999) is a methodology that aims to make data mining and predictive analytics projects more efficient, better organised, more reproducible, more manageable and more likely to yield business success.[75] Partners of the CRISP-DM Consortium include NCR Systems Engineering Copenhagen (the US and Denmark), DaimlerChrysler AG (Germany), SPSS, Inc. (the US) and OHRA Verzekeringen en Bank Groep B.V (the Netherlands). However, over 300 organisations have contributed to the process model and more than 200 organisations worldwide (including, e.g., AirTouch, DeloitteTouche, Capgemini and Lloyds Bank) are members of the CRISP-DM Special Interest Group (SIG). A main purpose for creating a standard data-mining process is to make the process reliable and repeatable even for companies with little data-mining background. While the CRISP-DM 1.0 user guide can be freely downloaded from www.crisp.com, the six-phase data-mining methodology is briefly considered here.[76]

1 **Business understanding**: This initial phase focuses on understanding the project objectives and requirements from a business perspective, and then converting this knowledge into a data-mining problem definition and a preliminary plan designed to achieve the objectives.

2 **Data understanding**: The data-understanding phase starts with an initial data collection and proceeds with activities in order to get familiar with the data, to identify data quality problems, to discover first insights into the data or to detect interesting subsets to form hypotheses for hidden information.

3 **Data preparation**: The data preparation phase covers all activities to construct the final dataset (data that will be fed into the modelling tool(s)) from the initial raw data. Data preparation tasks are likely to be performed multiple times, and not in any prescribed order. Tasks include table, record and attribute selection as well as transformation and cleaning of data for modelling tools.

4 **Modelling**: In this phase, various modelling techniques are selected and applied, and their parameters are calibrated to optimal values. Typically, there are several techniques for the same data-mining problem type. Some techniques have specific requirements on the form of data. Therefore, stepping back to the data preparation phase is often needed.

5 **Evaluation**: At this stage in the project you have built a model (or models) that appears to have high quality, from a data analysis perspective. Before proceeding to final deployment of the model it is important to evaluate the model more thoroughly, and review the steps executed to construct the model, to be certain it properly achieves the business objectives. A key objective is to determine if there is some important business issue that has not been sufficiently considered. At the end of this phase, a decision on the use of the data-mining results should be reached.

6 **Deployment**: Creation of the model is generally not the end of the project. Depending on the requirements, the deployment phase can be as simple as generating a report or as complex as implementing a repeatable data-mining process. In many cases it will be the customer, not the data analyst, who will carry out the deployment steps. However, even if the analyst will not carry out the deployment effort it is important for the customer to understand up front what actions will need to be carried out in order to actually make use of the created models.

The CRISP-DM consortium is planning on developing a CRISP-DM 2.0. As the role of data mining and predictive analytics continues to evolve so must the CRISP-DM methodology.

Figure 5.3 Examples of database marketing

Qwest: Twice a year Qwest sifts through its customer list looking for customers that have the potential to be more profitable. The company's database contains as many as 200 observations about each customer's calling patterns. By looking at demographic profiles, plus the mix of local versus long-distance calls or whether a consumer has voicemail, Qwest can estimate potential spending. Next, the company determines how much of the customer's likely telecom budget is already coming its way. Armed with that knowledge, Qwest sets a cut-off point for how much to spend on marketing to this customer.

Royal Caribbean: Royal Caribbean uses its database to offer spur-of-the-moment cruise packages to fill all the berths on its ships. It focuses on retired people and single people because they are more able to make quick commitments. Fewer empty berths mean maximised profits for the cruise line.

Fingerhut: The skilful use of database marketing and relationship building has made catalogue house Fingerhut one of the United States's largest direct mail marketers. Not only is its database full of demographic details such as age, marital status and number of children, but it also tracks customers' hobbies, interests and birthdays. Fingerhut tailors mail offers based on what each customer is likely to buy. Fingerhut stays in continuous touch with customers through regular and special promotions, such as annual sweepstakes, free gifts and deferred billing. Now the company has applied its database marketing to its websites.

Mars: Mars is a market leader not only in sweets, but also in pet food. In Germany, Mars has compiled the names of virtually every cat-owning family by contacting veterinarians and by advertising a free booklet titled 'How to Take Care of Your Cat.' Those who request the booklet fill out a questionnaire, so Mars knows the cat's name, age and birthday. Mars now sends a birthday card to each cat each year, along with a new cat-food sample or money-saving coupons for Mars brands.

American Express: It is no wonder that, at its secret location in Phoenix, security guards watch over American Express's 500 billion bytes of data on how its customers have used the company's 35 million green, gold and platinum charge cards. Amex uses the database to include precisely targeted offers in its monthly mailing of millions of customer bills.

Some observers believe that a proprietary (i.e., company-owned) database can provide a company with a significant competitive advantage. MCI Communications Corporation, the long-distance carrier, sifts through 1 trillion bytes of customer phoning data to create new discount calling plans for different types of customers. (See Figure 5.3 for additional examples.)

In general, companies can use their databases in five ways:

1 **To identify prospects**: Many companies generate sales leads by advertising their product or service. The ads generally contain a response feature, such as a business reply card or free-phone number, and the company builds its database from customer responses. It sorts through the database to identify the best prospects, then contacts them by mail, phone or personal call to try to convert them into customers.

2 **To decide which customers should receive a particular offer**: Companies are interested in selling, up-selling, and cross-selling their products and services. Companies set up criteria describing the ideal target customer for a particular offer. Then they search their customer databases for those who most closely resemble the ideal type. By noting response rates a company can improve its targeting precision over time. Following a sale, it can set up an automatic sequence of activities: one week later, send a thank-you note; five weeks later, send a new offer; ten weeks later (if customer has not responded), phone the customer and offer a special discount.

3 **To deepen customer loyalty**: Companies can build interest and enthusiasm by remembering customer preferences and by sending appropriate gifts, discount coupons and interesting reading material.

4 **To reactivate customer purchases**: Companies can install automatic mailing programs (automatic marketing) that send out birthday or anniversary cards, Christmas shopping reminders or off-season promotions. The database can help the company make attractive or timely offers.

5 **To avoid serious customer mistakes**: A major bank confessed to a number of mistakes it had made by not using its customer database well. In one case, the bank charged a customer a penalty for late payment on his mortgage, failing to note he headed a company that was a major depositor in the bank. He closed his account. In a second case, two different staff members of the bank phoned the same mortgage customer offering a home equity loan at different prices. Neither knew that the other had made the call. In a third case, the bank gave a premium customer only standard service in another country.

The downside of database marketing and CRM

Having covered the good news about database marketing, we also need to cover the bad news. Four problems can prevent a firm from using CRM effectively. The first is that building and maintaining a customer database requires a large investment in computer hardware, database software, analytical programs, communication links and skilled personnel. It is difficult to collect the right data, especially to capture all the occasions of company interaction with individual customers. Building a customer database would not be worthwhile in the following cases: (1) when the product is a once-in-a-lifetime purchase (a grand piano); (2) when customers show little loyalty to a brand (there is lots of customer brand switching); (3) when the unit sale is very small (a chocolate bar); and (4) when the cost of gathering information is too high.

The second problem is the difficulty of getting everyone in the company to be customer oriented and to use the available information. Employees find it far easier to carry on traditional transaction marketing than to practise customer relationship marketing. Effective database marketing requires managing and training employees as well as dealers and suppliers.

The third problem is that not all customers want a relationship with the company, and they may resent knowing that the company has collected so much personal information about them. Marketers must be concerned about customer attitudes toward privacy and security. Online companies would be wise to explain their privacy policies and to give consumers the right not to have their information stored in a database.

A fourth problem is that the assumptions behind CRM may not always hold true.[77] For example, it may not cost less to serve more loyal customers. High-volume customers often know their value to a company and can leverage it to extract premium service and/or price discounts. Loyal customers may expect and demand more from the firm and resent any attempt to charge full or higher prices. They may also be jealous of attention lavished on other customers. Loyal customers may not necessarily be the best ambassadors for the brand. One study found that customers who scored high on behavioural loyalty and bought a lot of a company's products were less active word-of-mouth marketers than customers who scored high on attitudinal loyalty and expressed greater commitment to the firm.

Thus, the benefits of database marketing do not come without heavy costs, not only in collecting the original customer data but also in maintaining them and mining them. When it works, a data warehouse yields more than it costs, but the data must be in good condition, and the discovered relationships must be valid.

Database marketing is most frequently used by business marketers and service providers (hotels, banks, airlines; and insurance, credit card and telephone companies) that normally and easily collect a lot of customer data. Other types of companies in the best position to invest in CRM are those that do a lot of cross-selling and up-selling (such as Amazon.com) or whose customers have highly differentiated needs and are of highly differentiated value to the company. Packaged-goods retailers and consumer packaged-goods companies use database marketing less frequently, though some (such as Kraft) have built databases for certain brands. Businesses with low customer lifetime value (CLV), high churn, and no direct contact between the seller and ultimate buyer may not benefit as much from CRM. Deloitte Consulting found that 70 per cent of firms found little or no improvement through CRM implementation. The reasons are many: the CRM system was poorly designed, it became too expensive, users didn't make much use of it or report much benefit, and collaborators ignored the system. One set of business commentators suggested the following as the four main perils of CRM:[78]

1 implementing CRM before creating a customer strategy;

2 rolling out CRM before changing the organisation to match;

3   assuming more CRM technology is better;

4   stalking, not wooing, customers.

Professor of marketing George Day concludes that one of the reasons many CRM failures occur is that companies concentrate on customer contact processes without making corresponding changes in internal structures and systems.[79] His recommendation? Change the configuration before installing CRM: 'Our findings confirm that a superior (customer-relating) capability is all about how a business builds and manages its organisation, and does not have much to do with CRM tools and technologies.'[80]

▽ SUMMARY

1   Marketers find many opportunities by identifying trends (directions or sequences of events that have some momentum and durability) and megatrends (major social, economic, political and technological changes that have long-lasting influence).

2   Within the rapidly changing global picture, marketers must monitor five major environmental forces: political/legal, economic, ecological/physical, social/cultural and demographic, and technological. The acronym PEEST analysis is used to describe an analysis of the company's environment covering these five forces.

3   In the economic arena, marketers need to focus on income distribution and levels of savings, debt and credit availability.

4   In the social–cultural and demographic arena, marketers must understand people's views of themselves, others, organisations, society, nature and the universe. They must market products that correspond to society's core and secondary values and address the needs of different subcultures within a society. Marketers must also be aware of worldwide population growth; changing mixes of age, ethnic composition and educational levels; the rise of non-traditional families; and large geographic shifts in population.

5   In the ecological/physical environment, marketers need to be aware of the public's increased concern about the health of the environment. Many marketers are now embracing sustainability and green marketing programmes that provide better environmental solutions as a result.

6   In the technological arena, marketers should take account of the accelerating pace of technological change, opportunities for innovation, varying R&D budgets, and the increased governmental regulation brought about by technological change.

7   In the political–legal environment, marketers must work within the many laws regulating business practices and with various special interest groups.

8   To carry out their analysis, planning, implementation and control responsibilities, marketing managers need a marketing information system. The role of the MIS is to assess the managers' information needs, develop the needed information and distribute that information in a timely manner.

9   An MIS has three components: (a) an internal records system, which includes information on the order-to-payment cycle and sales information systems; (b) a marketing intelligence system, a set of procedures and sources used by managers to obtain everyday information about pertinent developments in the marketing environment; and (c) a marketing research system that allows for the systematic design, collection, analysis and reporting of data and findings relevant to a specific marketing situation.

10   Today companies organise their information into databases – customer databases, product databases, salesperson databases – and then combine data from the different databases.

11   A customer database is an organised collection of comprehensive information about individual customers or prospects that is current, accessible and actionable for such marketing purposes as lead generation, lead qualification, sale of a product or service, or maintenance of customer relationships.

12   Database marketing is the process of building, maintaining and using customer databases and other databases (products, suppliers, resellers) to contact, transact and build customer relationships.

13   Data are collected by the company's contact centre and organised into a data warehouse where marketers can capture, query and analyse it to draw inferences about an individual customer's needs and responses.

14   Through data mining, marketing statisticians can extract useful information about individuals, trends and segments from the mass of data.

15 Customer relationship management deals with the identification, attraction and retention of profitable customers by managing relationships with them. Four problems can prevent a firm from effectively using CRM. Building a CRM-related customer database would not be worthwhile in the following cases:

(1) when the product is a once-in-a-lifetime purchase (a grand piano); (2) when customers show little loyalty to a brand (there is lots of customer churn); (3) when the unit sale is very small (a chocolate bar); and (4) when the cost of gathering information is too high.

▽ APPLICATIONS

Marketing debate

Is consumer behaviour more a function of a person's age? One of the widely debated issues in developing marketing programmes that target certain age groups is how much consumers change over time. Some marketers maintain that age differences are critical and that the needs and wants of a 25-year-old in 2009 are not that different from those of a 25-year-old in 1979. Others dispute that contention and argue that cohort and generation effects are critical, and that marketing programmes must therefore suit the times.

Take a position: Age differences are fundamentally more important than cohort effects *versus* Cohort effects can dominate age differences.

Marketing discussion

1 What brands and products do you feel successfully 'speak to you' and effectively target your age group? Why? Which ones do not? What could they do better?

2 What are the opportunities from database marketing and CRM? What are the pitfalls? How may the opportunities and pitfalls be moderated by company and market characteristics?

▽ REFERENCES

[1] Based on A. Corsano and A. Knitwear (2007) Going green, seeing green, 12 October, www.forbes.com; www.adidas.com.

[2] Interflora, http://www.interflora.dk/historie.php.

[3] Euromonitor, www.euromonitor.com.

[4] See www.badfads.com for examples of fads and collectables through the years.

[5] J. Naisbitt and P. Aburdene (1990) *Megatrends 2000*, New York: Avon Books.

[6] Indata (2006) *IN*, June 27; B. Craigie (2006) Brits don't buy the brand blog, *Marketing Week*, 29, 47, 38–9.

[7] World POPClock, U.S. Census Bureau, www.census.gov, September 1999.

[8] Although over ten years old, this breakdown provides a useful perspective. See D. H. Meadows, D. L. Meadows and Jorgen Randers (1993) *Beyond Limits*, White River Junction, VT: Chelsea Green, for some commentary.

[9] Survey: forever young (2004) *The Economist*, 27 March, 53–4.

[10] Eurostat/European Commission (2007) *Report: Living Conditions in Europe*, Luxembourg: Eurostat Pocketbooks, 2007, 112 pages.

[11] Eurostat/European Commission (2007) Report: Europe in figures, *Eurostat Yearbook 2006–07*, Luxembourg: Eurostat – European Commission, 357 pages.

[12] Ibid.

[13] GLEN – Gay and Lesbian Equality Network (2006) Civil marriage for gays should be next reform, *The Irish Times*, 3 April.

[14] Survey: Insights into tomorrow's ethnic food & drink consumers (2005) *Datamonitor*, 25 August.

[15] Ibid.

[16] For descriptions on the buying habits of and marketing approaches to African-Americans and Hispanics, see M. I. Valdes (2002) *Marketing to American Latinos: A Guide to the In-Culture Approach, Part II*, Ithaca, NY: Paramount Market Publishing and A. L. Schreiber (2001) *Multicultural Marketing*, Lincolnwood, IL: NTC Business Books.

[17] D. Dodson (2007) New cosmetics and toiletries global report highlights changes to the segmentation trend, *Euromonitor*, 16 July, http://www.euromonitor.com/New_Cosmetics_and_Toiletries_Global_Report_highlights_changes_to_the_segmentation_trend.

[18] Council of Europe (2007) Council of Europe hosts blindfolded lunch, café theatre and special film to mark International Day of Disabled Persons, 11 November, http://www.coe.int/t/dc/press/NoteRedac2006/20061130_handicap_en.asp and European Disability Forum, http://www.edf-feph.org/Page_Generale.asp?DocID=12534.

[19] The Central Intelligence Agency's World Factbook (www.cia.gov/library/publications/the-world-factbook/geos/xx.html) (accessed 10 September 2008).

[20] Eurostat – European Commission (2004) Report: The statistical guide to Europe, *Eurostat Yearbook 2004* (http://epp.eurostat.ec.europa.eu).

[21]*Report: Families in Germany – Facts and Figures, Federal Ministry for Family Affairs*, Senior Citizens, Women and Youth, Berlin, December 2004, 61 pages.

[22]Report: Europe in figures – Eurostat yearbook 2006–07, *Eurostat – European Commission*, 2007, 357 pages.

[23]N. Byrnes (2006) Secrets of the male shopper, *BusinessWeek*, 4 September, 44.

[24]C. Boswell (2005) Migration in Europe, A paper prepared for the Policy Analysis and Research Programme of the Global Commission on International Migration, Global Commission on International Migration, September; available at: http://www.gcim.org/attachements/RS4.pdf, accessed April 2008.

[25]I. Jakubowski (1995) Marketing in the New Europe, *British Food Journal*, 97, 6, 18–24 and F. A. Palumbo and I. Teich (2004) Market segmentation based on the level of acculturation (2004) *Marketing Intelligence & Planning*, 22(4), 472–84.

[26]M. Suggitt (2007) New Europe's hunger for western lifestyles means big business for food and drinks companies, *Euromonitor*, 17 March, http://www.euromonitor.com.

[27]O. Hofmann (2006) UK consumers eat the most ready meals, *Euromonitor*, 11 October, http://www.euromonitor.com and O. Hofmann (2007) Spanish manufacturers innovate in health and wellness food, *Euromonitor*, 6 March, http://www.euromonitor.com.

[28]*Der Spiegel*, Issue 34, 2004, p. 25.

[29]http://epp.eurostat.ec.europa.eu.

[30]J. Schlosser (2006) Infosys U, *Fortune*, 20 March, 41–2.

[31]European Commission (2001) How Europeans see themselves: looking through the mirror with public opinion surveys, European documentation series, Luxembourg: Office for Official Publications of the European Communities.

[32]P. Paul (2002) Corporate responsibility, *American Demographics*, May, 24–5.

[33]S. Baker (2006) Wiser about the Web, *BusinessWeek*, 27 March, 53–7.

[34]Clearing house suits chronology (2001) *Associated Press*, 26 January, and P. Wenske (1999) You too could lose $19,000!, *Kansas City Star*, 31 October.

[35]Cited from S. S. Hassan and L. P. Katsanis (1991) Identification of global consumer segments: a behavioural framework, *Journal of International Consumer Marketing*, 3(2), 11–28; for a good analysis of global youth cultural consumption see D. Kjeldgaard and S. Askegaard (2006) The Globalization of youth culture: the global youth segment as structures of common difference, *Journal of Consumer Research*, 33 (September), 231–47.

[36]J. Bosnan (2006) Advertising: hey, kid, you want to buy a Toyota scion?, *International Herald Tribune*, 15 June, http://www.iht.com/articles/2006/06/15/business/web.0616adcol.php?page=1.

[37]C. Chandler (2005) Full speed ahead, *Fortune*, 7 February, 78–84; What you can learn from Toyota, (2005) January–February, *Business 2.0*, 67–72; K. Naughton (2005) Red, white, and bold, *Newsweek*, 25 April, 34–6.

[38]http://www.hybridcars.com/vehicle/audi-q7-hybrid.html.

[39]R. Walzer (2007) At the supermarket, shopping for better health, *International Herald Tribune*, 14 December, http://www.iht.com/articles/2007/12/14/business/wbspot15.php.

[40]R. Lamb, How greenwashing works, http://www.howstuffworks.com/greenwashing.htm, accessed April 2008.

[41]S. B. Banerjee, E. S. Iyer and R. K. Kashyap (2003) Corporate enviromentalism: antecedents and influence of industry type, *Journal of Marketing*, 67, April, 106–22.

[42]R. Welford (1994) Improving corporate environmental performance, *Environmental Management and Health*, 5(2), 6–10.

[43]R. van Gestel (2005) Self-regulation and environmental law, *Electronic Journal of Comparative Law*, 9(1), 1–25.

[44]M. Watson and A. R. T. Emery (2004) Environmental management and auditing systems: the reality of environmental self-regulation, *Managerial Auditing Journal*, 19(7), 916–28.

[45]http://www.apple.com/pr/library/2007/04/09ipod.html, accessed April 2008.

[46]S. Frank (2006) R&D expenditure in Europe, *Statistics in Focus*, Luxembourg: Eurostat/European Communities, 6, 8 pages.

[47]The Commission of the European Communities (2007) The 2007 EU industrial R&D investment scoreboard, 5 October, http://iri.jrc.ec.europa.eu/research/scoreboard_2007.htm, accessed April 2008.

[48]See D. Cohen (1995) *Legal Issues on Marketing Decision Making*, Cincinnati, OH: South-Western.

[49]R. Gardyn (2001) Swap meet, *American Demographics*, July, 51–5.

[50]P. Paul (2001) Mixed signals, *American Demographics*, July, 45–9.

[51]www.nielsen.com.

[52]S. Warren (1998) Pillow talk: stackers outnumber plumpers – don't mention drool, *Wall Street Journal*, 8 January.

[53]http://download.microsoft.com.

[54]H. Green (2003) TaylorMade, *BusinessWeek*, 24 November, 94.

[55]N. Grossman (2007) How can they get that ability to make more informed decisions?, *Forbes*, 21 September, http://www.forbes.com/entrepreneurstechnology/2007/09/21/microsoft-oracle-amazon-ent-tech-cx_ng_0921bmightydatamining.html.

[56]S. Steindorf (2002) Shoppers spy on those who serve, *Christian Science Monitor*, 28 May and E. F. McQuarrie (1998) *Customer Visits: Building a Better Market Focus*, 2nd edn, Newbury Park, CA: Sage.

[57]S. S. Wang (2006) Health care taps Mystery Shoppers, *Wall Street Journal*, 10 August.

[58]K. Girard (2003) Strategies to turn stealth into wealth, *Business 2.0*, May, 66.

[59]L. M. Fuld (2006) Staying a step ahead of the rest, *Chief Executive*, 218, June, 32.

[60]A. Serwer (2001) P&G's covert operation, *Fortune*, 17 September 42–4.

[61]www.acxiom.com.

[62]Girard (2003) op. cit.

[63]R. T. Peterson and Zhilin Yang (2004) Web product reviews help strategy, *Marketing News*, 7 April, 18.

[64]H. Green (2006) It takes a Web village, *BusinessWeek*, 4 September, 66.

[65]American Productivity & Quality Center (2002) User-driven competitive intelligence: crafting the value proposition, 3–4 December.

[66]M. Der Hovanesian (2004) Wells Fargo, *BusinessWeek*, 24 November, 96.

[67]V. Kumar, R. Venkatesan and W. Reinartz (2006) Knowing what to sell, when, and to whom, *Harvard Business Review*, March, 131–7.

[68]Yu-Hui Tao and Chu-Chen Rosa Yeh (2003) Simple database marketing tools in customer analysis and retention, *International Journal of Information Management*, 23(4), 291–301.

[69]M. J. Shaw, C. Subramaniam, Gek Woo Tan and M. E. Welge (2001) Knowledge management and datamining for marketing, *Decision Support Systems*, 31(1), 127–37.

[70]D. Bradshaw and C. Brash (2001) Managing customer relationships in the e-business world: how to personalise computer relationships for increased profitability, *International Journal of Retail & Distribution Management*, 29(12), 520–30.

[71]D. Crié and A. Micheaux (2006) From customer data to value: what is lacking in the information chain?, *Database Marketing & Customer Strategy Management*, 13(4), 282–99.

[72]Ibid.

[73]C. R. Stephens and R. Sukumar (2006) An introduction to data mining in R. Grover and R. Vriens (eds) *Handbook of Marketing Research*, Thousand Oaks, CA: 455–86; Pang-Ning Tan, M. Steinbach and V. Kumar (2005) *Introduction to Data Mining*, Upper Saddle River, NJ: Addison Wesley; M. J. A. Berry and G. S. Linoff, *Data Mining Techniques: For Marketing, Sales, and Customer Relationship Management*, 2nd edn, Hoboken, NJ: Wiley Computer; J. Lattin, D. Carroll and P. Green (2003) *Analyzing Multivariate Data*, Florence, KY: Thomson Brooks/Cole.

[74]C. L. Gunnarsson, M. M. Walker, V. Walatka and K. Swann (2007) Lessons learned: a case study using data mining in the newspaper industry, *Database Marketing & Customer Strategy Management*, 14(4), 271–80.

[75]Adapted from www.crisp-dm.org/Process/index.htm.

[76]Adapted from www.crips-dm.org.

[77]W. Reinartz and V. Kumar (2002) The mismanagement of customer loyalty, *Harvard Business Review*, July, 86–94 and S. M. Fournier, S. Dobscha and D. G. Mick (1998) Preventing the premature death of relationship marketing, *Harvard Business Review*, January–February, 42–51.

[78]D. K. Rigby, F. F. Reichheld and P. Schefter (2002) Avoid the four perils of CRM, *Harvard Business Review*, February, 101–9.

[79]G. S. Day (2003) Creating a superior customer-relating capability, *Sloan Management Review* 44(3), 77–82; G. S. Day (2003) Creating a superior customer-relating capability, MSI Report No. 03–101, Cambridge, MA: Marketing Science Institute; Why some companies succeed at CRM (and many fail), *Knowledge at Wharton* (http://knowledge.wharton.upenn.edu) (accessed 15 January 2003).

[80]This quote is taken from G. Day (2002) Winning the competition for customer relationships, The Wharton School University of Pennsylvania, October, p. 6 (http://mktg-sun.wharton.upenn.edu/ideas/pdf/Day/Winning%20the%20Competition.pdf) (accessed 10 September 2008). (Note: parentheses not in original.)

Chapter 6

▽ Managing market research and forecasting

IN THIS CHAPTER, WE WILL ADDRESS THE FOLLOWING QUESTIONS:

1   What constitutes good marketing research?
2   What is the marketing research process?
3   How can marketers assess their return on investment of marketing expenditure?
4   How can companies more accurately measure and forecast demand?

Good marketers want insights to help them interpret past performance as well as plan future activities. They need timely, accurate, and actionable information about consumers, competition and their brands. They also need to make the best possible tactical decisions in the short run and strategic decisions in the long run. Discovering a consumer insight and understanding its marketing implications can often lead to a successful product launch or spur the growth of a brand.

See the SIGG Switzerland example.

Marketing research led to a doubling of SIGG Switzerland's US bottle sales.
Source: All Outdoor Ltd

CHAPTER JOURNEY

The marketing
research system

The marketing
research process

Marketing
productivity

Forecasting
and demand
measurement

For years, Swiss bottle producer SIGG Switzerland had been selling its aluminium water and fuel bottles to the US outdoor market. The company was counting on the Swiss reputation for quality to drive sales of the bottles with an average price twice as high as its closest competitors. However, sales were flat, as US customers didn't find the bottles to be worth a price premium. To gain insight into the underlying reasons for the low sales, the Swiss firm decided to conduct market research to uncover customers' perceptions and evaluations of the brand. Some surprising discoveries were made. US customers were worried that their water would taste like the metal container they carried it in, and they did not appreciate the variety of bottle designs. Also, they were worried about whether the bottle would leak. Based on the market research results, SIGG employed a variety of strategies, including an online contest encouraging customers to submit their preferred new bottle design and sponsorship of eco-design blog inhibit.com, where the advantages of using the bottles and the Swiss company's environmental friendly behaviour were promoted. The market research based strategy doubled bottle sales in just one year.[1]

In this chapter, we consider the marketing research system. We also review the steps involved in the marketing research process. Finally, we outline how marketers can develop good sales forecasts.

▽ The marketing research system

Marketing managers often commission formal marketing studies of specific problems and opportunities. They may request a market survey, a product-preference test, a sales forecast by region or an advertising evaluation. It's the job of the marketing researcher to produce insight into the customer's attitudes and buying behaviour. **Marketing insights** provide diagnostic information about how and why we observe certain effects in the marketplace, and what that means to marketers.[2] We define **marketing research** as the systematic design, collection, analysis and reporting of data and findings relevant to a specific marketing situation facing the company. Spending on marketing research topped €16 billion globally in 2006 with Europe accounting for 43 per cent of that amount (the United States accounts for 36 per cent), according to ESOMAR, the World Association of Opinion and Market Research Professionals. The global market research industry is expected to continue its growth in future years, due to increased global competition.[3]

Most large companies have their own marketing research departments, which often play crucial roles within the organisation. Telecommunications operator Orange, the key brand of France Telecom serving two-thirds of the company's 172 million customers, has developed a global innovation network called Orange Labs. It is made up of 5000 employees on four continents, and includes marketers, researchers and other professional groups. The international Orange Labs network reflects Orange's ambition to put innovation at the heart of its strategy, firmly focused on its clients. Thus, it is a main priority of the network to anticipate technological advances and changes in uses worldwide, for instance by conducting both internal and external survey research, and by designing customer analysis programs to identify where improvements can be made and to suggest appropriate responses.[4] Yet, marketing research is not limited to large companies with big budgets and marketing research departments. Often at much smaller companies everyone carries out marketing research – including the customers.

Companies normally budget marketing research at 1–2 per cent of company sales. A large percentage of that is spent on the services of outside marketing research firms, which falls into three categories:

1 **Syndicated-service research firms**: These firms gather consumer and trade information, which they sell for a fee. Examples: TNS Gallup, Business Monitor (Europe Service), Euromonitor.

2 **Custom marketing research firms**: These firms are hired to carry out specific projects. They design the study and report the findings. Example: The Hermelin Group (http://www.hermelin.se/company.aspx).

3 **Specialty-line marketing research firms**: These firms provide specialised research services. The best example is the field-service firm, which sells field interviewing services to other firms.

Small companies can hire the services of a marketing research firm or conduct research in creative and affordable ways, such as:

1 **Engaging students or professors to design and carry out projects**: Companies such as Mars, Hilton Hotels, IBM and Whirlpool engage in 'crowdcasting' and are sponsors of competitions such as the Innovation Challenge, where top MBA students compete in teams. The payoff to the students is experience and visibility; the pay-off to the companies is fresh sets of eyes to solve problems at a fraction of the costs that consultants would charge.[5]

2 **Using the Internet**: A company can collect considerable information at very little cost by examining competitors' websites, monitoring chatrooms and accessing published data.

3 **Checking out rivals**: Many small companies routinely visit their competitors. For example, many top restaurant managers and chefs regularly visit competing restaurants to stay updated and to bring back ideas.

Most companies use a combination of marketing research resources to study their industries, competitors, audiences and channel strategies.

▽ **The marketing research process**

Effective marketing research follows the six steps shown in Figure 6.1. We illustrate them with the situation shown in the example:[6]

> Hutchison Whampoa Limited (HWL) is a leading telecommunications and data services provider operating in a number of European countries including Austria, Denmark, Italy, Sweden and the United Kingdom. In 2003, HWL was the first to market an international 3G mobile service under the brand 3 (mobile phone network). 3G means third-generation mobile communication and can be viewed as wireless broadband for mobile phones. As illustrated in Figure 6.2 3G offers a number of multimedia services.
>
> Since then 3 has been first mover in many fields: in 2006 it was the first to introduce MSN Messenger as a mobile service and the first to launch High-Speed Downlink Packet Access (HSDPA) with a speed of 3.6 megabits per second (Mbps) (100 times as fast as global system for mobile communication [GSM]) in Denmark. Also, market research revealed that 3's customers wanted the opportunity to watch TV on their phones, so 3 responded by signing an exclusive deal to stream ITV1 to its UK customers. The company invested heavily to update and extend its network, as well as to develop new products and services, relying on its major strength in anticipating and meeting customers' needs. 3's market research was directed at investigating which consumer groups found 3G services appealing and which types of benefits were emphasised by these groups.[7]

Step 1: define the problem, the decision alternatives and the research objectives

Marketing managers must be careful not to define the problem too broadly or too narrowly for the marketing researcher. A marketing manager who says, 'Find out everything you can about mobile phone customers' needs' will collect a lot of unnecessary information. One who says,

Figure 6.1 The marketing research process

Figure 6.2 In the highly competitive mobile communication industry, marketing research is focusing on which new services customers might be willing to pay extra for, such as television viewing and music downloading

'Find out whether enough 3G customers would be willing to pay €30 a month for a mobile Internet service for 3 to break even in two years on the cost of offering this service' is taking too narrow a view of the problem. The marketing researcher might respond, 'Why does the mobile broadband connection have to be priced at €30 as opposed to €10, €50 or some other price? Why does 3 have to break even on the cost of the service, especially if it attracts new customers?' Another relevant question is: How important is it to be first mover in the market, and how long can the company sustain its lead?

Let's say that the marketing manager and marketing researcher agreed to define the problem as follows: 'Will offering a wireless Internet service for mobile phones create enough incremental preference and profit for 3 to justify its cost against other possible investments that Hutchison Whampoa might make?' To help in designing the research, management should first spell out the decisions it might face and then work backwards. Suppose management outlines these decisions: (1) Should 3 offer a mobile Internet service? (2) If so, should the offer be tailored to a specific consumer segment? (3) What price(s) should be charged? (4) What types of mobile phones, datacards, etc. should complement the service?

Now management and marketing researchers are ready to set specific research objectives: (1) What types of customers would respond positively to a mobile broadband service? (2) How many customers are likely to sign up for this service at different price levels? (3) How many additional customers might choose 3 over competitors because of this new service? (4) How much long-term goodwill will this service add to 3's image? (5) How important is a mobile Internet service to consumers relative to other services, such as a television viewing, video messaging or game playing?

Not all research projects can be this specific. Some research is *exploratory* – its goal is to shed light on the real nature of the problem and to suggest possible solutions or new ideas. Some research is *descriptive* – it seeks to quantify demand, such as how many customers would purchase a mobile broadband service at €30. Some research is *causal* – its purpose is to test a cause-and-effect relationship.

Step 2: develop the research plan

The second stage of marketing research is where we develop the most efficient plan for gathering the needed information and what that will cost. Suppose the company made a prior estimate that launching a mobile broadband service would yield a long-term profit of €500,000. If the manager believes that doing the marketing research will lead to an improved pricing and promotional plan and a long-term profit of €600,000, the company should be willing to spend up to €100,000 on this research. If the research will cost more than €100,000, it's not worth doing.[8]

To design a research plan we need to make decisions about the data sources, research approaches, research instruments, sampling plan and contact methods.

Data sources

The researcher can gather secondary data, primary data, or both. *Secondary data* are data that were collected for another purpose and already exist somewhere, such as in surveys or market reports from research organisations or government agencies. Secondary data may also take the form of internal company information, such as sales records or financial data. *Primary data* are data freshly gathered for a specific purpose or for a specific research project, such as identifying Norwegian consumers' preferences for various supermarket formats.

Researchers usually start their investigation by examining some of the rich variety of low-cost and readily available secondary data, to see whether they can partly or wholly solve the problem without collecting costly primary data. For instance, cosmetics companies wishing to reach out to new consumer groups might purchase a copy of Euromonitor's report on 'The world market for cosmetics and toiletries', a survey that provides insights into market trends and pinpoints future growth sectors.[9] Among the helpful findings they would discover in the report are:

- Young segments have received products designed especially for them very well, as exemplified by Bratz Mascara and the marykateandashley make-up line.
- Faster and improved application of make-up is a growing priority for women, along with convenience and portability.
- Make-up lines based on natural minerals are still growing rapidly, offering such benefits as chemical-free formulations, natural sunscreen, and suitability for sensitive skin types.

When the needed data don't exist or are dated, inaccurate, incomplete or unreliable, the researcher will need to collect primary data. Most marketing research projects do include some primary-data collection.

Research approaches

Marketers collect primary data in five main ways: through observation, focus groups, surveys, behavioural data, and experiments.

Observational research Researchers can gather fresh data by observing the relevant actors and settings,[10] unobtrusively observing as they shop or as they consume products. Sometimes they equip consumers with pagers and instruct them to write down what they're doing whenever prompted, or they hold informal interview sessions at a café or bar. Photographs can also provide a wealth of detailed information.

A picture is worth 1000 words to skilled marketing researchers, who can glean a number of insights from this photo of a Swedish kitchen.

Source: Anna G. Tufvesson/ Nordicphotos/Alamy

Ethnographic research is a particular observational research approach that uses concepts and tools from anthropology and other social science disciplines to provide deep understanding of how people live and work.[11] The goal is to immerse the researcher into consumers' lives to uncover unarticulated desires, meanings or behaviour that might not be captured in other forms of research. Firms such as IBM, Intel and Microsoft have embraced ethnographic research to design breakthrough products.

Pan-European supermarket chain Lidl, catering to the price-conscious, bottom end of the market found that data on the brand and its sector was scarce. It asked Ogilvy, an international advertising, marketing and public relations agency, to carry out an extensive audit of the shopping experience by talking to customers in the stores and filming them. The results proved an eye opener for Lidl. It underlined the retailer's strengths – its low prices and quality goods – but also its weaknesses, such as its limited and unfamiliar range – its 'foreignness' in many markets. However, when Ogilvy asked four consumers who usually value well-known, branded products to test shop in a Lidl supermarket, they were all positive in their evaluation of the actual experience. Today, Lidl focuses on simplicity in its brand offer and on its core strength in providing quality products at the lowest possible prices across the EU.[12]

Many other companies have benefited from ethnographic research.

- The global document management company Xerox was one of the first companies to use applied ethnography. In 1979, an anthropologist at Xerox conducted ethnographic fieldwork in the work place and summarised her findings in a film showing office workers struggling to do a copying job on a Xerox machine. After viewing the film, Xerox engineers began to think about designing Xerox machines differently. This ethnographic work led to the large green button we see on most copiers today that lets us walk up to the machine and easily make a copy.[13]
- Intel, the world's largest semiconductor company with its processors found in most personal computers, has also benefited from ethnographic research. Intel's ethnographic fieldwork played an important part in expanding its involvement in the health care market. In a study of health care providers, it was discovered that many doctors had time constraints, which prevented them from accessing the people, information and/or resources needed to provide patients with quality health care. Consequently, Intel developed a series of wireless devices that automate physician tasks such as prescribing medication and capturing billing information (Allscripts Healthcare Solutions).

Lidl benefited from ethnographic research.
Source: Imagebroker/ Alamy

- At Orange, ethnographic market research is applied to get to know the mindset of its consumers and as input in the product development process. 'For example, it can be difficult to ask consumers what they do in their "dead time", while commuting, between meetings and so on, because it is not in their particular language,' says research analyst Gino Zisa. 'So we thought it would be helpful to observe people in those circumstances in their own environment, rather than in a focus group.'

- Ethnographic research methods are also used by the motor industry in Germany, where – for part of the strategic development for the launch of a luxury sports car – Stephan Tun, managing director at Maritz Research Germany, spent time with owners driving on motorways, going to golf courses, shopping and in their homes. 'It gave us information that was vast and rich, providing a new understanding of a very specialised market,' he says. It fed into final product development, assisted positioning and contributed to the communication strategy.[14]

Ethnographic research is not limited just to consumer companies in developed markets. GE's ethnographic research into the plastic-fibre industry showed the firm that it wasn't in a commodity business driven by price as much as it was in an artisanal industry where production required the use of methods based on skills. Therefore, its customers wanted collaboration at the earliest stages of development. GE completely reoriented the way it interacted with the companies in the plastic-fibre industry as a result. Ethnographic research can be especially useful in developing markets, especially far-flung rural areas, where companies do not know consumers as well.[15]

Focus group research A **focus group** is a gathering of six to ten people carefully selected by researchers based on certain demographic, psychographic or other considerations and brought together to discuss various topics of interest at length. Participants are normally paid a small sum for attending. A professional research moderator provides questions and probes based on the marketing managers' discussion guide or agenda.

Moderators try to discern consumers' real motivations and why they say and do certain things. They typically record the sessions, and marketing managers often remain behind two-way mirrors in the next room. Focus-group research is a useful exploratory step, but researchers must avoid generalising from focus-group participants to the whole market, because the sample size is too small and the sample is not drawn randomly.

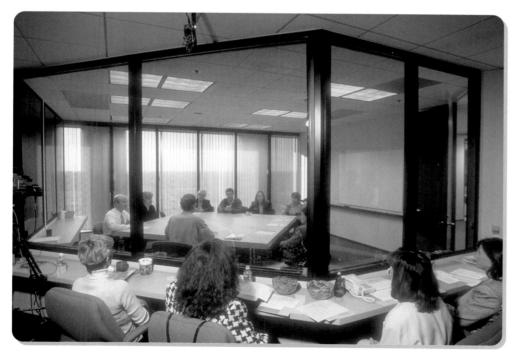

A focus group in session, with marketing people observing through a two-way mirror.

Source: Spencer Grant/PhotoEdit

In fact, an increasing number of marketers are relying on other means of collecting information that they believe are less artificial. 'Focus groups confirm what you already know,' says Eva Steensig, a sociologist at DDB Denmark. DDB, part of the Omnicom Group, introduced a new service called SignBank, which uses the Internet and the advertising agency's global office network to collect thousands of snippets of information about cultural change, identify trends within the data and advise clients about what it means to them. Consumers are not experts on their own consumption patterns, says Steensig, and this makes them easily led by focus group moderators. DDB and some other advertisers feel it is better to 'read the signs' of consumption than ask consumers to self-consciously comment on their own patterns. For instance, DDB's sign spotters in several markets noticed that dinner-party guests were bringing their hosts flowers instead of chocolates, in a nod to current concerns over obesity and health. Anthon Berg, a Danish chocolate company and DDB client, plans to use that information to more closely associate its chocolate with different social occasions.[16]

'Marketing insight: Conducting informative focus groups' offers some practical tips to improve the quality of focus groups. In 3's market research, the moderator might start with a broad question, such as, 'How do you feel about mobile phone services?' Questions then move to how people view the different providers, different existing services, different proposed services and, specifically, a mobile broadband service.

Marketing insight

Conducting informative focus groups

Focus groups allow marketers to observe how and why consumers accept or reject concepts, ideas, or any specific notion. The key to using focus groups successfully is to *listen and observe.* Marketers should eliminate their own biases as much as possible. Although many useful insights can emerge from thoughtfully run focus groups, questions can arise about their validity, especially in today's marketing environment.

Some researchers believe that consumers have been so bombarded with ads that they unconsciously (or perhaps cynically) parrot back what they have already heard instead of what they really think. There is always a concern that participants are just trying to maintain their self-image and public persona or have a need to identify with the other members of the group. Participants also may not be willing to admit in public – or may not even recognise – their behaviour patterns and motivations. And the 'loudmouth' or 'know-it-all' problem often crops up when one highly opinionated person drowns out the rest of the group. It may be expensive to recruit qualified subjects who meet the sampling criteria (€2000 to €3500 per group), but getting the right participants is crucial.

Even when marketers use multiple focus groups it may be difficult to generalise the results to a broader population. For example, within Europe, focus-group findings may vary from region to region because of differences in culture, shopping habits, economic welfare, etc. Also, within individual countries there could be lifestyle differences between people living in major cities and people living in the countryside. Participants must feel as relaxed as possible and strongly motivated to be truthful. Physical surroundings can be crucial to achieving the right atmosphere. At one agency an executive noted, 'We wondered why people always seemed grumpy and negative – people were resistant to any idea we showed them.' Finally in one session a fight broke out between participants. The problem was the room itself: cramped, stifling, forbidding: 'It was a cross between a hospital room and a police interrogation room.' To fix the problem, the agency gave the room a make-over. Other firms are adapting the look of the room to fit the theme of the topic – such as designing the room to look like a playroom when speaking to children.

Many firms are substituting observational research for focus groups, but ethnographic observation can be expensive and tricky: researchers must be highly skilled and participants on the level. Then there are the mounds of data to analyse. The beauty of focus groups, as one marketing executive noted, is that 'It's still the most cost-effective, quickest, dirtiest way to get information in rapid time on an idea.' In analysing the pros and cons, Wharton's Americus Reed might have said it best: 'A focus group is like a chain saw. If you know what you're doing, it's very useful and effective. If you don't, you could lose a limb.'

Sources: N. R. Henderson (2005) Beyond top of mind, *Marketing Research*, 1 September; R. Harris (2005) Do focus groups have a future?, *Marketing*, 6 June, 17; M. Gladwell (2005) *Blink: The Power of Thinking Without Thinking*, New York: Little, Brown; L. Tischler (2004) Every move you make, *Fast Company*, April, 73–5; A. S. Wellner (2003) The new science of focus groups, *American Demographics*, March, 29–33; D. Rook (2003) Out-of-focus groups, *Marketing Research*, 15(2), 11; D. W. Rook (2003) Loss of vision: focus groups fail to connect theory, current practice, *Marketing News*, 15 September, 40; S. J. Kasner (2001) Fistfights and feng shui, *Boston Globe*, 21 July.

Survey research Companies undertake surveys to learn about people's knowledge, beliefs, preferences and satisfaction and to measure these magnitudes in the general population. A company such as 3 might prepare its own survey instrument to gather the information it needs, or it might add questions to an omnibus survey that carries the questions of several companies (at a much lower cost). It can also put the questions to an ongoing consumer panel run by itself or another company. It may do a mall intercept study by having researchers approach people in a shopping mall and ask them questions.

As we'll discuss in more detail later in this chapter, many marketers are taking their surveys online where they can easily develop, administer and collect email and Web-based questionnaires. However they conduct their surveys – online, by phone or in person – companies must feel the information they're getting from the mounds of data makes it all worthwhile. Here are two that do:

- **TDC**: This major player on the Danish telecommunications market regularly surveys and interviews its customers on subjects such as needs, motivation and product satisfaction. Customer feedback has resulted in, for example, a low-priced broadband product (TDC Netway) tailored especially to young customers (between 18 and 28 years of age). This 'no nonsense' solution offers broadband Internet access and allows customers to call free of charge at all times on fixed-line connections in Denmark, but includes no technical support and can only be ordered online.[17]
- **Star Tour**: Scandinavian travel agency Star Tour continually collects surveys from customers at the end of their holiday (and at www.startour.dk). It uses customers' comments to obtain insights into customer experiences during their holiday and into their feelings about the company and its communications with them.

Of course, by putting out so many surveys, companies may run the risk of creating 'survey burnout' and seeing response rates plummet. Keeping a survey short and simple and avoiding contacting the same customers too often are two keys to drawing people into the data collection effort. Offering incentives is another way companies get consumers to respond. Companies such as UK-based StaTravel offer the chance to win cash prizes, gift certificates or computer equipment in exchange for taking part in their survey.

Behavioural data Customers leave traces of their purchasing behaviour in store-scanning data, catalogue purchases and customer databases. Marketers can learn much by analysing these data. Actual purchases reflect consumers' preferences and are often more reliable than statements they offer to market researchers. For example, grocery shopping data show that high-income people don't necessarily buy the more expensive brands, contrary to what they might state in interviews; and many low-income people buy some expensive brands. Clearly, companies such as 3 can learn many useful things about its customers by analysing mobile service purchase records and online behaviour.

Experimental research The most scientifically valid research is **experimental research**, designed to capture cause-and-effect relationships by eliminating competing explanations of the observed findings. If the experiment is well designed and executed, research and marketing managers can have confidence in the conclusions.

Experiments call for selecting matched groups of subjects, subjecting them to different treatments, controlling extraneous variables and checking whether observed response differences are statistically significant. If we can eliminate or control extraneous factors we can relate the observed effects to the variations in the treatments or stimuli. For instance, 3 might introduce a mobile Internet service in one of its mobile packages and charge €35 one week and €25 the next. If approximately the same number of potential customers visited 3's shops each week and the particular weeks were 'normal' and similar, the company could then relate a significant difference in the number of new customers to the difference in price charged.

Research instruments

In the last section you learned about the main research *approaches* that marketers use to collect primary data. Depending on the research problem and approach taken, marketing researchers can choose between a number of research *instruments* for collecting primary data. In this section, we will review three commonly used research instruments: questionnaires, qualitative measures, and technological devices.

Questionnaire A **questionnaire** consists of a set of questions presented to respondents. Because of its flexibility, it is by far the most common instrument used to collect primary data. Researchers need to carefully develop, test and de-bug questionnaires before administering them on a large scale. The form, wording and sequence of the question can all influence the response. *Closed questions* specify all the possible answers and provide answers that are easier to interpret and tabulate. *Open-ended questions* allow respondents to answer in their own words and often reveal more about how people think. They are especially useful in exploratory research, where the researcher is looking for insight into how people think rather than measuring how many people think a certain way. Table 6.1 provides examples of both types of questions; also see 'Marketing memo: Questionnaire dos and don'ts'.

Table 6.1 Types of questions

Name	Description	Example				
A. Closed questions						
Dichotomous	A question with two possible answers	In considering this service, did you personally contact 3? Yes No				
Multiple choice	A question with three or more answers	For whom are you considering purchasing this service? ☐ Myself ☐ Entire family ☐ Spouse ☐ Business associates/friends/relatives ☐ Children ☐ An organisation				
Likert scale	A statement with which the respondent shows the amount of agreement/ disagreement	Small mobile service providers generally give better service than large ones.				
		Strongly disagree	Disagree	Neither agree nor disagree	Agree	Strongly agree
		1___	2___	3___	4___	5___
Semantic differential	A scale connecting two bipolar words. The respondent selects the point that represents his or her opinion	3 Large _____Small Experienced _____Inexperienced Modern _____Old-fashioned				
Importance scale	A scale that rates the importance of some attribute	3G mobile service to me is				
		Extremely important	Very important	Somewhat important	Not very important	Not at all important
		1___	2___	3___	4___	5___
Rating scale	A scale that rates some attribute from 'poor' to 'excellent'	3 mobile service is				
		Excellent	Very good	Good	Fair	Poor
		1___	2___	3___	4___	5___

Table 6.1 *(Continued)*

Name	Description	Example
Intention-to-buy scale	A scale that describes the respondent's intention to buy	If a mobile Internet service was available, I would Definitely buy Probably buy Not sure Probably not buy Definitely not buy 1___ 2___ 3___ 4___ 5___

B. Open-ended questions

Name	Description	Example
Completely unstructured	A question that respondents can answer in an almost unlimited number of ways	What is your opinion of 3?
Word association	Words are presented, one at a time, and respondents mention the first word that comes to mind	What is the first word that comes to your mind when you hear the following? Mobile provider _____ 3 _____ Mobile _____
Sentence completion	An incomplete sentence is presented and respondents complete the sentence	When I choose a mobile service provider, the most important consideration in my decision is _____. _____.
Story completion	An incomplete story is presented, and respondents are asked to complete it	'I went to a 3 shop a couple of days ago. I noticed that the exterior and interior of the shop had very bright colours. This aroused in me the following thoughts and feelings . . .' Now complete the story.
Picture	A picture of two characters is presented, with one making a statement. Respondents are asked to identify with the other and fill in the empty balloon	
Thematic apperception test (TAT)	A picture is presented and respondents are asked to make up a story about what they think is happening or may happen in the picture.	

Marketing memo

Questionnaire dos and don'ts

1 **Ensure that questions are without bias** Don't lead the respondent into an answer.

2 **Make the questions as simple as possible** Questions that include multiple ideas or two questions in one will confuse respondents.

3 **Make the questions specific** Sometimes it's advisable to add memory cues. For example, be specific with time periods.

4 **Avoid jargon or shorthand** Avoid trade jargon, acronyms and initials not in everyday use.

5 **Steer clear of sophisticated or uncommon words** Only use words in common speech.

6 **Avoid ambiguous words** Words such as 'usually' or 'frequently' have no specific meaning.

7 **Avoid questions with a negative in them** It is better to say, 'Do you ever . . . ?' than 'Do you never . . . ?'

8 **Avoid hypothetical questions** It is difficult to answer questions about imaginary situations. Answers aren't necessarily reliable.

9 **Do not use words that could be misheard** This is especially important when administering the interview over the telephone. 'What is your opinion of sects?' could yield interesting but not necessarily relevant answers.

10 **Desensitise questions by using response bands** To ask people their age or ask companies about employee turnover rates, offer a range of response bands instead of precise numbers.

11 **Ensure that fixed responses do not overlap** Categories used in fixed-response questions should be distinct and not overlap.

12 **Allow for 'other' in fixed-response questions** Precoded answers should always allow for a response other than those listed.

Sources: Adapted from P. Hague and P. Jackson (1999) *Market Research: A Guide to Planning, Methodology, and Evaluation*, London: Kogan Page; see also H. Baumgartner and J.-B. E. M. Steenkamp (2001) Response styles in marketing research: a cross-national investigation, *Journal of Marketing Research*, May, 143–56.

Qualitative measures Some marketers prefer more qualitative methods for gauging consumer opinion, because consumer actions don't always match their answers to survey questions. *Qualitative research techniques* are relatively unstructured measurement approaches that permit a range of possible responses. Their variety is limited only by the creativity of the marketing researcher.

▽ LEGO

The Danish toy company LEGO, which offers creative and high-quality toys to children across the globe, has an ingenious way of conducting qualitative research on how to tailor their wide product portfolio to the needs of children of all ages. Over the years, LEGO has developed long-lasting relations with, for example, day care centres, which are invited (with parents' permission) to pick out a group of children that matches the target group of a specific product or product line to participate in a play session. Usually such sessions are arranged once a year, and it is essential that children play with LEGO toys in their usual surroundings. Video filming is used to capture important insights into how children play with particular products, what they find fun, what catches their interests and spurs their imagination, the functionality of toys and quality of play, etc.

This is just one of the many ways LEGO uses qualitative measures to stay up to date with how children play and how to challenge creative youngsters of particular age groups – an important element of LEGO's vision to inspire children to explore and challenge their own creative potential.[18]

Because of the freedom afforded both researchers in their probes and consumers in their responses, qualitative research can often be a useful first step in exploring consumers' brand and product perceptions, but it has its drawbacks. Marketers must temper the in-depth insights that emerge with the fact that the samples are often very small and may not necessarily generalise to broader populations. And different researchers examining the same qualitative results may draw very different conclusions. 'Marketing insight: Getting into consumers' heads with qualitative research' describes some popular approaches.

Marketing insight

Getting into consumers' heads with qualitative research

Here are some popular qualitative research approaches to getting inside consumers' minds and finding out what they think or feel about brands and products:

1 **Word associations**: Ask subjects what words come to mind when they hear the brand's name. 'What does the name Fiat mean to you? Tell me what comes to mind when you think of Fiat cars.' The primary purpose of free-association tasks is to identify the range of possible brand associations in consumers' minds. But they may also provide some rough indication of the relative strengths, favourability and uniqueness of brand associations.

2 **Projective techniques**: Give people an incomplete stimulus and ask them to complete it, or give them an ambiguous stimulus and ask them to make sense of it. One such approach is 'bubble exercises' in which empty bubbles, such as those found in cartoons, appear in scenes of people buying or using certain products or services. Subjects fill in the bubble, indicating what they believe is happening or being said. Another technique is comparison tasks, in which people compare brands to people, countries, animals, activities, fabrics, occupations, cars, magazines, vegetables, nationalities, or even other brands.

3 **Visualisation**: Visualisation requires people to create a collage from magazine photos or drawings to depict their perceptions of brands, experiences, ideas or other research topics. The ZMET technique asks participants in advance to select a minimum of 12 images from their own sources (magazines, catalogues, family photo albums) to represent their thoughts and feelings about the research topic. In a one-to-one interview the study administrator uses advanced interview techniques to explore the images with the participant and reveal hidden meanings. Finally, the participants use a computer program to create a collage with these images that communicates their subconscious thoughts and feelings about the topic. In one ZMET study about tights, some of the respondents' pictures showed fence posts encased in plastic wrap or steel bands strangling trees, suggesting that tights are

Drawings or other pictures that express consumers' feelings about products are part of ZMET studies. This vase demonstrated what one woman felt about wearing tights.
Source: Courtesy of Norman H. Olson, Purdue University

close fitting and inconvenient. Another picture showed tall flowers in a vase, suggesting that the product made a woman feel thin, tall and sexy. In this way, the technique seeks to unveil 'hidden knowledge' of underlying beliefs and feelings that influence the behaviour and reactions of consumers.

4 **Brand personification**: Ask subjects what kind of person they think of when the brand is mentioned: 'If the brand were to come alive as a person, what would it be like, what would it do, where would it live, what would it wear, who would it talk to if it went to a party (and what would it talk about)?' For example, the IKEA brand might make someone think of a straightforward Scandinavian female who is reliable and values quality at an affordable cost. The brand personality delivers a picture of the more human qualities of the brand.

▶ **Marketing insight** *(continued)*

5 **Laddering**: This technique involves asking a series of increasingly more specific 'why' questions that can reveal consumer motivation and consumers' deeper, more abstract goals. Think about how you might answer the following line (or ladder) of questions: 'Why does someone want to buy a Nokia mobile phone?' 'They look well built' (attribute). 'Why is it important that the phone be well built?' 'It suggests that the Nokia is reliable' (a functional benefit). 'Why is reliability important?' 'Because my colleagues or family can be sure to reach me' (an emotional benefit). 'Why must you be available to them at all times?'

'I can help them if they're in trouble' (brand essence). The brand makes this person feel like a Good Samaritan, ready to help others.

Sources: C. Marshall and G. B. Rossman (2006) *Designing Qualitative Research*, 4th edn, Thousand Oaks, CA: Sage; B. L. Berg (2006) *Qualitative Research Methods for the Social Sciences*, 6th edn, Boston, MA: Allyn & Bacon; N. K. Denzin and Y. S. Lincoln (eds.) (2005) *The Sage Handbook of Qualitative Research*, 3rd edn, Thousand Oaks, CA: Sage; L. Tischler (2004) Every move you make, *Fast Company*, April, 73–5; G. Zaltman (2003) *How Customers Think: Essential Insights into the Mind of the Market*, Boston, MA: Harvard Business School Press.

Technological devices Technological devices are occasionally useful in marketing research. Galvanometers can measure the interest or emotions aroused by exposure to a specific ad or picture. The tachistoscope flashes an ad to a subject with an exposure interval that may range from less than one-hundredth of a second to several seconds. After each exposure, the respondent describes everything he or she recalls. Eye cameras study respondents' eye movements to see where their eyes land first, how long they linger on a given item, and so on.

Technology has now advanced to such a degree that marketers can use devices such as skin sensors, brainwave scanners and full body scanners to get consumer responses.[19] TACODA, an advertising technology company, is studying the eye movements and brain activity of Web surfers to see which ads grab their attention.[20] 'Marketing insight: Understanding brain science' provides a glimpse into some new marketing research frontiers studying the brain.

Marketing insight

Understanding brain science

As an alternative to traditional consumer research, some researchers have begun to develop sophisticated techniques from neuroscience that monitor brain activity to better gauge consumer responses to marketing stimuli.

For example, Oxford-based neuro-marketing research firm Neurosense used functional magnetic resonance imaging (fMRI) to measure how consumers' brains responded to TV programming and ads. This study showed that ads generated activity in eight out of nine brain regions, indicating that consumers indeed register commercial content. Yet programming largely dominated the region of the brain that controls absorption, and hence occupied by far the largest part of consumers' attention. The study also confirmed that ads work best when they are in congruence with the programmes they accompany. Thus, more viewer interest was registered for an ad for the alcopop WKD than for a Red Cross appeal when these were aired during the anarchic cult comedy *South Park*.[21]

Although it can be more effective in uncovering inner emotions than conventional techniques, neurological research is costly, running to as much as €70,000 per project. One major finding to emerge from neurological consumer research is that many purchase decisions are characterised less by the logical weighing of variables than was previously assumed and more 'as a largely unconscious habitual process, as distinct from the rational, conscious, information-processing model of economists and traditional marketing textbooks'. Even basic decisions, such as the purchase of gasoline, are influenced by brain activity at the subrational level.

Neurological research can be used to measure the type of emotional response that consumers exhibit when presented with marketing stimuli. A group of researchers in England used an electroencephalograph (EEG) to monitor cognitive functions related to memory recall and attentiveness for 12 different regions of the brain as subjects were exposed to advertising. Brainwave activity in different regions indicated different emotional responses. For example, heightened activity in the left prefrontal cortex is characteristic of an 'approach' response to an ad and indicates an attraction to the stimulus. In contrast, a spike in brain activity in the right prefrontal cortex is indicative of a strong

> ► **Marketing insight** *(continued)*

revulsion to the stimulus. In yet another part of the brain, the degree of memory formation activity correlates with purchase intent. Other research has shown that people activate different regions of the brain in assessing the personality traits of people versus brands.

The term *neuro-marketing* has been used to describe brain research on the effect of marketing stimuli. By adding neurological techniques to their research arsenal, marketers are trying to move towards a more complete picture of what goes on inside consumers' heads. Given the complexity of the human brain, however, many researchers caution that neurological research should not form the sole basis for marketing decisions. These research activities have not been universally applauded,

however. Critics think that such a development will only lead to more marketing manipulation by companies.

Sources: C. Yoon, A. H. Gutchess, F. Feinberg and T. A. Polk (2006) A functional magnetic resonance imaging study of neural dissociations between brand and person judgments, *Journal of Consumer Research*, 33, 31–40; D. Travis (2006) Tap buyers' emotions for marketing success, *Marketing News*, 1 February, 21–2; D. L. Vence (2006) Pick someone's brain, *Marketing News*, 1 May, 11–13; L. Witt (2004) Inside intent, *American Demographics*, March, 34–9; S. M. McClure, J. Li, D. Tomlin, K. S. Cypert, L. M. Montague and P. R. Montague (2004) Neural correlates of behavioral preference for culturally familiar drinks, *Neuron*, 44, 379–87; M. Wells (2003) In search of the buy button, *Forbes*, 1 September 1.

Technology has replaced the diaries that participants in media surveys used to keep. Audiometers attached to television sets in participating homes now record when the set is on and to which channel it is tuned. Electronic devices can record the number of radio programmes a person is exposed to during the day or, using global positioning system (GPS) technology, how many billboards a person may walk by or drive by during a day. Technology is also used to capture consumer reactions to Internet and mobile services.

▽ Google in Japan

Internet giant Google tests its services, such as mobile search technologies, in many markets. However, it has found Japan's 100 million mobile subscribers represent perhaps the most diverse – and refined – test audience on the planet. The Japanese are often more critical in their assessment of mobile search technology because they are as likely to access the Internet with a high-tech phone as a PC and can do so at speeds rivalling fixed-line broadband.

To figure out what mobile Web surfers like, the company relies on research into user experience groups. Research participants are given phones with Internet access and asked to complete simple tasks, either in a company lab or out on the streets of Tokyo. Research may consist of asking participants to find the address of a particular restaurant or a timetable for a train, and then tracking and observing participants' search behaviour. At other times, Google conducts what it calls 1 per cent tests, in which a small portion of users see different layouts, fonts and other features on Google pages. The aim is to determine what changes make the service easier to use. Google's strategy, then, is to take market discoveries from Japan and apply them to other markets.[22]

Sampling plan

After deciding on the research approach and instruments, the marketing researcher must design a sampling plan. This calls for three decisions:

1 **Sampling unit: who should we survey?** In the 3 survey, should the sampling unit consist only of mobile broadband customers, 'regular' mobile service customers, or both? Should it include customers under the age of 15? Seniors, parents, children, teenagers? Once they have determined the sampling unit, marketers must develop a sampling frame so that everyone in the target population has an equal or known chance of being sampled.

Table 6.2 Probability and non-probability samples

(a) Probability sample

Simple random sample	Every member of the population has an equal chance of selection
Stratified random sample	The population is divided into mutually exclusive groups (such as age groups), and random samples are drawn from each group
Cluster (area) sample	The population is divided into mutually exclusive groups (such as city blocks), and the researcher draws a sample of the groups to interview

(b) Non-probability sample

Convenience sample	The researcher selects the most accessible population members
Judgement sample	The researcher selects population members who are good prospects for accurate information
Quota sample	The researcher finds and interviews a prescribed number of people in each of several categories

2 **Sample size: how many people should we survey?** Large samples give more reliable results, but it is not necessary to sample the entire target population to achieve reliable results. Samples of less than 1 per cent of a population can often provide good reliability, with a credible sampling procedure.

3 **Sampling procedure: how should we choose the respondents?** Probability sampling allows us to calculate confidence limits for sampling error and make the sample more representative. Thus we could conclude after choosing the sample that 'the interval five to seven trips per year has 95 chances in 100 of containing the true number of trips taken annually by first-class passengers flying between Stockholm and Rome'. Three types of probability sampling are described in Table 6.2 (a). When the cost or time to use probability sampling is too high, marketing researchers will take non-probability samples. Table 6.2(b). describes three types.

Contact methods

Now the marketing researcher must decide how to contact the subjects: by mail, by telephone, in person or online.

Mail questionnaire The *mail questionnaire* is the best way to reach people who would not give personal interviews or whose responses might be biased or distorted by the interviewers. Mail questionnaires require simple and clearly worded questions. Unfortunately, the response rate is usually low or slow.

Telephone interview *Telephone interviewing* is the best method for gathering information quickly; the interviewer is also able to clarify questions if respondents do not understand them. The response rate is typically higher than for mailed questionnaires, but interviews must be brief and not too personal. Telephone interviewing is getting more difficult because of consumers' growing antipathy toward telemarketers. In Sweden, for example, a registry known as 'Nix Telefon', through which consumers can request not to receive telemarketing calls, has been growing in popularity in recent years.[23] At the beginning of 2008, the share of Swedish telephone consumers who had registered was close to 10 per cent. While telemarketers are obligated by law to check the phone numbers they call against the 'Nix' registry, marketing research firms are so far exempt from this legislation. However, many think it spells the beginning of the end for telephone surveys as a marketing research method. In other parts of the world, such marketing customs and restrictive legislation do not exist. One in nine Africans now owns a phone, so mobile phones in Africa are used to convene focus groups in rural areas and to interact with text messages.[24]

Personal interview *Personal interviewing* is the most versatile method. The interviewer can ask more questions and record additional observations about the respondent, such as dress and body language. At the same time, however, personal interviewing is the most expensive method, is subject to interviewer bias, and requires more administrative planning and supervision. Personal interviewing takes two forms. In *arranged interviews,* marketers contact respondents for an appointment and often offer a small payment or incentive. In *intercept interviews,* researchers stop people at a shopping mall or busy street corner and request an interview on the spot. Intercept interviews must be quick, and they run the risk of including non-probability samples.

Online interview There are so many ways to use the Internet to do research. A company can embed a questionnaire on its website in different ways and offer an incentive to answer it, or it can place a banner on a frequently visited site such as Yahoo!, inviting people to answer some questions and possibly win a prize. Marketers can also sponsor a chatroom or bulletin board and introduce questions from time to time or host a real-time consumer panel or virtual focus group. The company can learn about individuals who visit its site by tracking how they *clickstream* through the website and move to other sites. It can post different prices, use different headlines, and offer different product features on different websites or at different times to learn the relative effectiveness of its offerings. Online product testing, in which companies float trial 'balloons' for new products, is also growing and providing information much faster than traditional new product marketing research techniques.

Yet, as popular as online research methods are, smart companies are choosing to use them to augment rather than replace more traditional methods. At Kraft Foods, online research is a supplement to traditional research, said Seth Diamond, director of consumer insights and strategy. 'Online is not a solution in and of itself to all of our business challenges,' he said, 'but it does expand our toolkit.' For example, insights from Kraft-sponsored online communities helped the company develop its popular line of 100-calorie snacks.[25]

'Marketing memo: Pros and cons of online research' outlines some of the advantages and disadvantages of online research thus far. Online researchers have also begun to use instant messaging in various ways – to conduct a chat with a respondent, to probe more deeply with a member of an online focus group, or to direct respondents to a website.[26] Instant messaging is also a useful way to get teenagers to open up on topics.

Step 3: collect the information

The data collection phase of marketing research is generally the most expensive and the most prone to error. Four major problems arise in surveys. Some respondents will not be at home and must be contacted again or replaced. Other respondents will refuse to cooperate. Still others will give biased or dishonest answers. Finally, some interviewers will be biased or dishonest. Data collection methods are rapidly improving thanks to computers and telecommunications. Some telephone research firms interview from a central location, using professional interviewers to read a set of questions from a monitor and type the respondents' answers into a computer. This procedure eliminates editing and coding, reduces errors, saves time, and produces all the required statistics. Other research firms have set up interactive terminals in shopping centres, where respondents sit at a terminal, read questions from the monitor and type in their answers.

> To learn how Nokia applied market research to develop a mobile handset especially suited for India, visit www.pearsoned.co.in/pkotler

One of the biggest obstacles to collecting information internationally is the need to achieve consistency.[27] Nan Martin, global accounts director for Synovate, Inc., a market research firm with offices in 46 countries, says:

> In global research, we have to adapt culturally to how, where and with whom we are doing the research . . . A simple research study conducted globally becomes much more complicated as a result of the cultural nuances, and it's necessary for us to be sensitive to those nuances in data collection and interpretation.

Marketing memo

Pros and cons of online research

Advantages

- **Online research is inexpensive** A typical email survey can cost between 20 per cent and 50 per cent less than what a conventional survey costs, and return rates can be as high as 50 per cent.

- **Online research is fast** Online surveys are fast because the survey can automatically direct respondents to applicable questions and transmit results immediately. One estimate says that 75–80 per cent of a survey's targeted response can be generated in 48 hours using online methods, compared to a telephone survey that can take 70 days to obtain 150 interviews.

- **People tend to be honest online** Britain's online polling company YouGov.com surveyed 250 people via intercom in a booth and the other half online, asking questions such as, 'Should there be more aid to Africa?' Online answers were deemed much more honest. People may be more open about their opinions when they can respond privately and not to another person who they feel might be judging them, especially on sensitive topics.

- **Online research is versatile** Increased broadband penetration offers online research even more flexibility and capabilities. For instance, virtual reality software lets visitors inspect 3-D models of products such as cameras, cars and medical equipment, and manipulate product characteristics. Even at the basic tactile level, online surveys can make answering a questionnaire easier and more fun than paper-and-pencil versions.

Disadvantages

- **Samples can be small and skewed** In the 27 EU member states, 54 per cent of households had access to the Internet during the first quarter of 2007, compared with 49 per cent during the first quarter of 2006. Household Internet access ranged from 19 per cent in Bulgaria to 83 per cent in the Netherlands. Although it is certain that more and more people will go online, online market researchers must find creative ways to reach population segments on the other side of the 'digital divide'. One option is to combine online and offline data collection instruments, for example by using both online and postal (offline) questionnaires. Providing temporary Internet access at locations such as shopping centres and leisure centres is another strategy. Some research firms use statistical models to fill in the gaps in market research left by offline consumer segments.

- **Online market research is prone to technological problems and inconsistencies** Because online research is relatively new, many market researchers have not got survey designs right. Others overuse technology, concentrating on the bells, whistles and graphics while ignoring basic survey design guidelines. Problems also arise because browser software varies. The Web designer's final product may look very different on the research subject's screen.

Sources: Eurostat (2007) News release, 3 December 3 166/2007; 'Survey: Internet should remain open to all, 25 January 2006, www.consumeraffairs.com; Highlights from the National Consumers League's survey on consumers and communications technologies: current and future use, www.nclnet.org, 21 July 2005; C. Arnold (2004) Not done net; new opportunities still exist in online research, *Marketing News*, 1 April, 17; L. Miles (2004) Online, on tap, *Marketing*, 16 June, 39–40; S. Bashford (2004) The opinion formers, *Revolution*, May, 42–6; N. M. Ray and S. W. Tabor (2003) Contributing factors; several issues affect e-research validity, *Marketing News*, 15 September 2003, 50; B. Lamons (2001) Eureka! future of b-to-b research is online, *Marketing News*, 24 September, 9–10.

Latin American respondents may be more uncomfortable with the impersonal nature of the Internet; they need interactive elements in a survey so they feel as if they are talking to a real person. On the other hand, in Asia, respondents may feel more pressure to conform and may therefore not be as forthcoming in focus groups as online.

Step 4: analyse the information

The next to last step in the process is to extract findings by tabulating the data and developing frequency distributions. The researchers now compute averages and measures of dispersion for the major variables and apply some advanced statistical techniques and decision models in the hope of discovering additional findings. They may test different hypotheses and theories, applying sensitivity analysis to test assumptions and the strength of the conclusions.

Step 5: present the findings

As the last step, the researcher presents findings relevant to the major marketing decisions facing management. Researchers increasingly are being asked to play a more proactive, consulting role in translating data and information into insights and recommendations.[28] They are also considering ways to present research findings in as understandable and compelling a fashion as possible.

For example, some researchers try to bring data to life for the marketers in their organisation. Marketing research consultancy Arnold + Bolingbroke uses a professional film crew and makes feature film presentations of its results, for instance in their work with European car brands Land-Rover and Jaguar. Bomme Komolafe, market research manager at Jaguar Cars says:

> These films are useful because they are accessible at all levels, even to very technically oriented audiences. And when a launch is seven years away, it is so valuable that they can be kept and referred to time and again, whenever we are debating issues as our designs evolve.[29]

Another way of organising and presenting complex and information-rich research findings, which may be difficult to express in verbal or linear form, is to create visual, artistic collages. The photos below visualise the many finer points of a Mercedes-Benz — exclusive and elegant, yet encompassing a vast amount of detail.

The many finer points of a Mercedes-Benz.
Source: Courtesy of Gayot Publications

Returning to the 3 case, the main survey findings might indicate that:

1   The chief reasons for having a mobile broadband connection are to browse the Web and download data files using your handset regardless of where the customer is. Also, constant access to information and staying in touch with others are essential consumer motivations.

2   At €35, about five out of ten 3 customers would choose a product package including mobile Internet service; about six would choose it at €25. Thus, a fee of €25 would produce less revenue (€150 = 6 × €25) than €30 (€175 = 5 × €35).

3   Offering high-speed mobile Internet service would strengthen the public's image of 3 as an innovative and progressive mobile provider. 3 would gain new customers and customer goodwill.

Step 6: make the decision

The managers who commissioned the research need to weigh the evidence. If their confidence in the findings is low, they may decide against introducing the mobile Internet service. If they are predisposed to launching the service, the findings support their inclination. They may even decide to study the issues further and do more research. The decision is theirs, but rigorously done research provides them with insight into the problem (see Table 6.3).

A growing number of organisations are using a marketing decision support system to help their marketing managers make better decisions. A **marketing decision support system (MDSS)** is a coordinated collection of data, systems, tools and techniques, with supporting software and hardware, by which an organisation gathers and interprets relevant information from business and environment and turns it into a basis for marketing action.[30]

Table 6.3 The seven characteristics of good marketing research

1 Scientific method	Effective marketing research uses the principles of the scientific method: careful observation, formulation of hypotheses, prediction and testing.
2 Research creativity	At its best, marketing research develops innovative ways to solve a problem: a clothing company catering to teenagers gave several young men video cameras, then used the videos for focus groups held in restaurants and other places teens frequent.
3 Multiple methods	Marketing researchers shy away from overreliance on any one method. They also recognise the value of using two or three methods to increase confidence in the results.
4 Interdependence of models and data	Marketing researchers recognise that data are interpreted from underlying models which guide the type of information sought.
5 Value and cost of information	Marketing researchers show concern for estimating the value of information against its cost. Costs are typically easy to determine, but the value of research is harder to quantify. It depends on the reliability and validity of the findings and management's willingness to accept and act on those findings.
6 Healthy scepticism	Marketing researchers show a healthy scepticism toward glib assumptions made by managers about how a market works. They are alert to the problems caused by 'marketing myths'.
7 Ethical marketing	Marketing research benefits both the sponsoring company and its customers. The misuse of marketing research can harm or annoy consumers, increasing resentment at what consumers regard as an invasion of their privacy or a disguised sales pitch.

An example is Dutch-based ABN AMRO bank, which is represented by more than 3000 branches in more than 60 countries and territories. ABN AMRO uses a decision support system to develop its consumer businesses in Asia. Via this system, regional headquarters in Hong Kong is able to view the region's total business as well as the performance of each individual country's business. The focus for ABN AMRO is on customer relationship management, customer revenue analysis and monitoring credit risk metrics.[31] Once a year, *Marketing News* lists hundreds of current marketing and sales software programs that assist in designing marketing research studies, segmenting markets, setting prices and advertising budgets, analysing media, and planning sales force activity.

Overcoming barriers to the use of marketing research

In spite of the rapid growth of marketing research, many companies still fail to use it sufficiently or correctly, for several reasons:[32]

- **A narrow conception of the research**: Many managers see marketing research as a fact-finding operation. They expect the researcher to design a questionnaire, choose a sample, conduct interviews and report results, often without their providing a careful definition of the problem. When fact-finding fails to be useful, management's idea of the limited usefulness of marketing research is reinforced.
- **Uneven calibre of researchers**: Some managers view marketing research as little more than a clerical activity and treat it as such. As a result of this view, they hire less competent, and perhaps less costly, marketing researchers, whose weak training and low creativity lead to unimpressive results. The disappointing results reinforce management's prejudice against marketing research, and low salaries perpetuate the basic problem.
- **Poor framing of the problem**: The famous failure of New Coke was largely due to a failure to set up the research problem correctly, from a marketing perspective. Coca-Cola's market share lead had been slowly declining for 15 consecutive years. And consumer awareness and preference was plummeting too. On this backdrop, Coca-Cola decided to change the secret formula and adopt a new taste preferred in taste tests of nearly 200,000 consumers. Nevertheless, the real issue turned out to be how consumers felt about Coca-Cola as a brand, not how they felt about its taste in isolation. The consumer upheaval that followed the introduction of New Coke ended with the return of the original formula, now called Coca-Cola Classic.
- **Late and occasionally erroneous findings**: Managers want results that are accurate and conclusive. They may want the results tomorrow. Yet good marketing research takes time and money. Managers are disappointed when marketing research costs too much or takes too much time.
- **Personality and presentational differences**: Differences between the styles of line managers and marketing researchers often get in the way of productive relationships. To a manager who wants concreteness, simplicity and certainty, a marketing researcher's report may seem abstract, complicated and tentative. Yet in the more progressive companies, marketing researchers are being included as members of the product management team, and their influence on marketing strategy is growing.

Failure to use marketing research properly has led to numerous gaffes, including this historic one.

▽ **Star Wars**

In the 1970s, a successful research executive left General Foods to try a daring gambit: bringing market research to Hollywood, to give film studios access to the same research that had spurred General Foods' success. A major film studio handed him a science fiction film proposal and asked him to research and predict its success or failure. His views would inform the studio's decision about whether to back the film.

The executive concluded the film would fail. For one, he argued, Watergate had made the United States less trusting of institutions and, as a result, its citizens in the 1970s prized realism and authenticity over science fiction. This particular film also had the word 'war' in its title; he reasoned that viewers, suffering from post-Vietnam hangover, would stay away in droves. The film was *Star Wars*. What this researcher delivered was information, not insight. He failed to study the script itself, to see that it was a fundamentally human story – of love, conflict, loss and redemption – that happened to play out against the backdrop of space. Since its release in 1977, *Star Wars* has won seven Academy Awards and influenced a generation of storytellers. It has sold hundreds of millions of dollars of tie-in merchandise, and more than 100 million home video units. Add to this the millions of DVDs recently welcomed into many a home theatre library.[33]

One company that has benefited from research-driven insights is IDEO. 'Breakthrough marketing: IDEO' shows how that company has used clever marketing research to come up with innovative product and service designs.

Breakthrough marketing

IDEO

IDEO is one of the leading industrial design firms in the world. The company has created some of the most recognisable design icons of the technology age, including the first laptop computer, the first mouse (for Apple), and more recently a gaming platform for the (infamous) N-Gage Nokia smartphones, and LCD monitors for Samsung. Beyond its high-tech wizardry, the company has designed household items such as the Swiffer Sweeper (Procter & Gamble) and high-performance, compact vacuum cleaners for Miele. IDEO's diverse roster of clients also includes Lufthansa, SAS, Philips, Nestlé, PepsiCo, Nike, Lilly, AT&T and Prada.

IDEO's success is predicated on its design philosophy of creating products that consumers actively want to use because they offer a superior experience. In order to achieve these consumer-friendly designs, IDEO tries to uncover deep insights through a variety of research methods to better understand how consumers purchase, interact with, use, and even dispose of products. This customer-focused approach has run counter to the prevailing wisdom of many high-tech firms, which focus more on their own capabilities when designing products. 'Tech companies design from the inside out, whereas we design from the outside in so that we can put customers first,' said David Blakely, head of IDEO's technology group.

For example, IDEO often uses observational research techniques to conduct 'deep dives' into consumer behaviour. The company's 'human factors' team shadows consumers, taking pictures or videos of them during product purchase or use occasions, and afterwards conducts in-depth interviews with them to further evaluate their experiences. For example, for apparel-maker Warnaco the company's designers shadowed eight women as they shopped for lingerie. The 'shop-alongs' revealed that most of their experience buying Warnaco's lingerie was negative. They had difficulty locating the lingerie section in the department store and finding the right size in the overcrowded display, plus the fitting rooms were too small. IDEO developed a new merchandising environment that included larger fitting rooms, 'concierges' to give shoppers information, and improved displays, which Warnaco worked with department stores to implement.

IDEO also employs a number of other observational methods. One such method is a 'behavioural mapping', that creates a photographic log of people within a certain area (e.g., an airline departure lounge, a hospital waiting room or a food court at a shopping centre) over a period of days to gauge how the experience can be improved. Another method is 'camera journals' that participants keep in which they record their visual impressions of a given product or category. A third such method is 'storytelling', where consumers are asked to share personal narratives about their experiences with a product or service.

▶ Breakthrough marketing *(continued)*

The innovative design process from IDEO uses a number of different techniques to understand the customer experience.

Source: Steven Moeder/IDEO

IDEO also encourages its clients, even senior executives, to participate in the research so they too get a sense for the actual consumer experience with their product or service. IDEO's novel consumer-led approach to design has led to countless success stories for its clients, and for the firm itself.

Sources: L. Chamberlain (2006) Going off the beaten path for new design ideas, *New York Times*, 12 March; C. Taylor (2005) School of bright ideas, *Time*, 14 March, Inside Business/Innovation, A8; S. Morrison (2005) Sharp focus gives design group the edge, *Financial Times*, 18 February, Business Life, 8; B. Nussbaum (2004) The power of design, *BusinessWeek*, 17 May, 86; www.ideo.com.

▽ Measuring marketing productivity

An important task of marketing research is to assess the efficiency and effectiveness of marketing activities.[34] Marketers are being held increasingly accountable for their investments and must be able to justify marketing expenditure to senior management.[35] Marketing research can help address this increased need for accountability. Two complementary approaches to measuring marketing productivity are: (1) *marketing metrics* to assess marketing effects; and (2) *marketing-mix modelling* to estimate causal relationships and measure how marketing activity affects outcomes. *Marketing dashboards* are a structured way to disseminate the insights gleaned from these two approaches within the organisation. Marketers employ a wide variety of measures to assess marketing effects.[36] **Marketing metrics** is the set of measures that helps them quantify, compare and interpret their marketing performance. Marketing metrics can be used by brand managers to justify and design marketing programmes and by senior management to decide on financial allocations.[37] The marketing-mix modelling approach is reviewed in this chapter, whereas the marketing metrics approach and marketing dashboards are considered in Chapter 22.

Marketing-mix modelling

Marketing accountability also means that marketers must more precisely estimate the effects of different marketing investments. *Marketing-mix models* analyse data from a variety of sources, such as retailer scanner data, company shipment data, pricing, media, and promotion spending data, to understand more precisely the effects of specific marketing activities.[38] To deepen understanding, marketers can conduct multivariate analyses, such as regression analysis, which are statistical procedures aiming at identifying relationships between a set of variables, such as price, quality and demand. These analytical tools will help estimate how each marketing element influences marketing outcomes such as brand sales or market share.[39]

Especially popular with packaged-goods marketers such as Procter & Gamble and Colgate, the findings from marketing-mix modelling help allocate or reallocate expenditure. Analyses explore which part of ad budgets are wasted, what optimal spending levels are, and what minimum investment levels should be.[40]

Although marketing-mix modelling helps to isolate effects, it is less effective at assessing how different marketing elements work in combination. Wharton's Dave Reibstein also notes three other shortcomings:[41]

1 Marketing-mix modelling focuses on incremental growth instead of baseline sales or long-term effects.

2 Despite their importance, the integration of metrics such as customer satisfaction, awareness and brand equity into marketing-mix modelling is limited, most likely due to the difficulty of establishing an explicit connection from investment to metric and to financial outcome.

3 Marketing-mix modelling generally fails to incorporate metrics related to competitors, the trade or the sales force (the average business spends far more on the sales force and trade promotion than on advertising or consumer promotion).

▽ Forecasting and demand measurement

One major reason for undertaking marketing research is to identify market opportunities. Once the research is complete, the company must measure and forecast the size, growth and profit potential of each market opportunity. Sales forecasts are used by finance departments to raise the needed cash for investment and operations; by the manufacturing department to establish capacity and output levels; by purchasing to acquire the right amount of supplies; and by human resources to hire the necessary number of workers. Marketing is responsible for preparing the sales forecasts. If its forecast is far off the mark, the company will face excess or inadequate inventory.

Sales forecasts are based on estimates of demand. Managers need to define what they mean by market demand. For example, Swedish Autoliv is a market leader in state-of-the-art automotive safety systems. However, Autoliv doesn't see itself as having more than a third of the €3 billion world market for airbags. Rather, the company evaluates the brand much more broadly in terms of the entire €11 billion automobile occupant restraint market.[42]

The measures of market demand

Companies can prepare as many as 90 different types of demand estimates for six different product levels, five space levels and three time periods (see Figure 6.3).

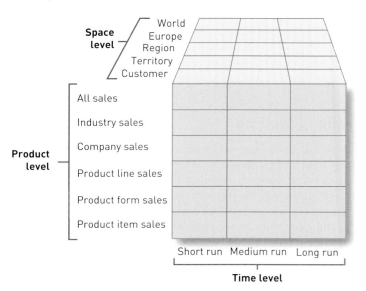

Figure 6.3 Ninety types of demand measurement (6 × 5 × 3)

Each demand measure serves a specific purpose. A company might forecast short-run demand for a particular product for the purpose of ordering raw materials, planning production and borrowing cash. It might forecast regional demand for its major product line to decide whether to set up regional distribution.

The size of a market hinges on the number of buyers who might exist for a particular market offer. But there are many productive ways to break down the market:

- The **potential market** is the set of consumers who profess a sufficient level of interest in a market offer. However, consumer interest is not enough to define a market for marketers unless they also have sufficient income and access to the product.
- The **available market** is the set of consumers who have interest, income *and* access to a particular offer. For some market offers, the company or government may restrict sales to certain groups. For example, a particular country might ban alcohol sales to anyone under 18 years of age. Eligible adults constitute the *qualified available market* – the set of consumers who have interest, income, access and qualifications for the particular market offer.
- The **target market** is the part of the qualified available market the company decides to pursue. The company might decide to concentrate its marketing and distribution effort in southern Europe.
- The **penetrated market** is the set of consumers who are buying the company's product.

These definitions are a useful tool for market planning. If the company isn't satisfied with its current sales, it can take a number of actions. It can try to attract a larger percentage of buyers from its target market. It can lower the qualifications for potential buyers. It can expand its available market by opening distribution elsewhere or lowering its price, or it can reposition itself in the minds of its customers.

A vocabulary for demand measurement

The major concepts in demand measurement are market demand and company demand. Within each, we distinguish among a demand function, a sales forecast and a potential.

Market demand

The marketer's first step in evaluating marketing opportunities is to estimate total market demand. **Market demand** for a product is the total volume that would be bought by a defined customer group in a defined geographical area in a defined time period in a defined marketing environment under a defined marketing programme.

Market demand is not a fixed number, but rather a function of the stated conditions. For this reason, we can call it the *market demand function*. The dependence of total market demand on underlying conditions is illustrated in Figure 6.4(a). The horizontal axis shows different possible levels of industry marketing expenditure in a given time period. The vertical axis shows the

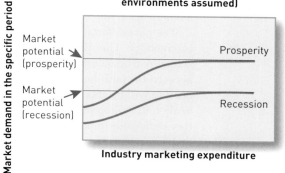

(a) Marketing demand as a function of industry marketing expenditure (assumes a particular marketing environment)

Market demand in the specific period

Market potential, Q_2

Market forecast, Q_F

Market minimum, Q_1

Planned expenditure

Industry marketing expenditure

(b) Marketing demand as a function of industry marketing expenditure (two different environments assumed)

Market demand in the specific period

Market potential (prosperity)

Market potential (recession)

Prosperity

Recession

Industry marketing expenditure

Figure 6.4 Market demand functions

resulting demand level. The curve represents the estimated market demand associated with varying levels of industry marketing expenditure.

Some base sales – called the *market minimum* and labelled Q_1 in the figure – would take place without any demand-stimulating expenditures. Higher levels of industry marketing expenditures would yield higher levels of demand, first at an increasing rate, then at a decreasing rate. Take fruit juices. Given all the indirect competition they face from other types of beverages, increased marketing expenditures would be expected to help fruit juice products stand out and increase demand and sales. Marketing expenditures beyond a certain level would not stimulate much further demand, thus suggesting an upper limit to market demand, called the *market potential* and labelled Q_2 in the figure.

The distance between the market minimum and the market potential shows the overall *marketing sensitivity of demand*. We can think of two extreme types of market, the expansible and the non-expansible. An *expansible market*, such as the market for badminton playing, is very much affected in size by the level of industry marketing expenditures. In terms of Figure 6.4(a), the distance between Q_1 and Q_2 is relatively large. A *non-expansible market* – for example, the market for weekly rubbish removal – is not much affected by the level of marketing expenditure; the distance between Q_1 and Q_2 is relatively small. Organisations selling in a non-expansible market must accept the market's size – the level of *primary demand* for the product class – and direct their efforts toward winning a larger **market share** for their product, that is, a higher level of selective demand for their product.

It pays to compare the current and potential levels of market demand. The result is called the **market penetration index**. A low market penetration index indicates substantial growth potential for all the firms. A high market penetration index suggests it will be expensive to attract the few remaining prospects. Generally, price competition increases and margins fall when the market penetration index is already high.

A company should also compare its current and potential market shares. The result is called the company's **share penetration index**. A low share penetration index indicates the company can greatly expand its share. The factors holding it back could be many: low brand awareness, low availability, benefit deficiencies and high price. A firm should calculate the share penetration increases that would occur if it removed each factor, to see which investments produce the greatest improvement.[43]

Remember that the market demand function is not a picture of market demand over time. Rather, the curve shows alternative current forecasts of market demand associated with possible levels of industry marketing effort.

Market forecast

At a given point in time, there can be only one actual level of industry marketing expenditure. The market demand corresponding to this level of expenditure is called the **market forecast**.

Market potential

The market forecast shows expected market demand, not maximum market demand. For the latter, we need to visualise the level of market demand resulting from a 'very high' level of industry marketing expenditure, where further increases in marketing effort would have little effect in stimulating further demand. **Market potential** is the limit approached by market demand as industry marketing expenditures approach infinity for a given marketing environment.

The phrase 'for a given market environment' is crucial. Consider the market potential for automobiles. This is higher during prosperity than during a recession. The dependence of market potential on the environment is illustrated in Figure 6.4(b). Market analysts distinguish between the position of the market demand function and movement along it. Companies cannot do anything about the position of the market demand function, which is determined by the marketing environment. However, they influence their particular location on the function when they decide how much to spend on marketing.

Companies interested in market potential have a special interest in the **product penetration percentage**, which is the percentage of ownership or use of a product or service in a population. Companies assume that the lower the product penetration percentage the higher the market potential, although this assumes that everyone will eventually be in the market for every product.

Company demand

Company demand is the company's estimated share of market demand at alternative levels of company marketing effort in a given time period. It depends on how the company's products, services, prices and communications are perceived relative to the competitors'. If other things are equal, the company's market share will depend on the relative scale and effectiveness of its market expenditures. Marketing model builders have developed sales response functions to measure how a company's sales are affected by its marketing expenditure level, marketing mix and marketing effectiveness.[44]

Company sales forecast

Once managers have estimated company demand, their next task is to choose a level of marketing effort. The **company sales forecast** is the expected level of company sales based on a chosen marketing plan and an assumed marketing environment.

We represent the company sales forecast graphically with sales on the vertical axis and marketing effort on the horizontal axis, as in Figure 6.4. We often hear that the company should develop its marketing plan on the basis of its sales forecast. This forecast-to-plan sequence is valid if 'forecast' means an estimate of national economic activity, or if company demand is non-expansible. The sequence is not valid, however, where market demand is expansible or where 'forecast' means an estimate of company sales. The company sales forecast does not establish a basis for deciding what to spend on marketing. On the contrary, the sales forecast is the result of an assumed marketing expenditure plan.

Two other concepts are important here. A **sales quota** is the sales goal set for a product line, company division or sales representative. It is primarily a managerial device for defining and stimulating sales effort. Generally, sales quotas are set slightly higher than estimated sales to stretch the sales force's effort.

A **sales budget** is a conservative estimate of the expected volume of sales, primarily for making current purchasing, production and cash flow decisions. It is based on the sales forecast and the need to avoid excessive risk and is generally set slightly lower than the sales forecast.

Company sales potential

Company sales potential is the sales limit approached by company demand as company marketing effort increases relative to that of competitors. The absolute limit of company demand is, of course, the market potential. The two would be equal if the company got 100 per cent of the market. In most cases, company sales potential is less than the market potential, even when company marketing expenditures increase considerably. Each competitor has a hard core of loyal buyers who are not very responsive to other companies' efforts to woo them.

Estimating current demand

We are now ready to examine practical methods for estimating current market demand. Marketing executives want to estimate total market potential, area market potential, and total industry sales and market shares.

Total market potential

Total market potential is the maximum amount of sales that might be available to all the firms in an industry during a given period, under a given level of industry marketing effort and environmental conditions. A common way to estimate total market potential is to multiply the potential number of buyers by the average quantity each purchases, times the price. The average quantity of buyer purchases may be estimated based on existing company sales data and/or on primary data collected for this purpose.

If 100 million people buy books each year, and the average book buyer buys three books a year, and the average price of a book is €20, then the total market potential for books is €6 billion (100 million × 3 × €20). The most difficult component to estimate is the number of buyers for the specific product or market. We can always start with the total population in the EU, which was 495 million people in 2007.[45]

Next we eliminate groups that obviously would not buy the product. Assume that illiterate people and children under 12 don't buy books and constitute 20 per cent of the population. This means 80 per cent of the population, or 396 million people, are in the potentials pool. We might do further research and find that people belonging to the 20 per cent of the EU population with the lowest income and/or with lower secondary education (or less) don't read books, and they constitute over 30 per cent of the potentials pool. Eliminating them, we arrive at a prospect pool of approximately 277.2 million book buyers. We use this number of prospective buyers to calculate total market potential.

A variation on this method is the *chain-ratio method*, which multiplies a base number by several adjusting percentages. Suppose a brewery is interested in estimating the market potential for a new light beer. It can make an estimate with the following calculation:

| Demand for the new light beer | = | Population | × | Average percentage of personal discretionary income per capita spent on food | × | Average percentage of amount spent on food that is spent on beverages | × | Average percentage of amount spent on beverages that is spent on alcoholic beverages | × | Average percentage of amount spent on alcoholic beverages that is spent on beer | × | Expected percentage of amount spent on beer that will be spent on light beer |

Area market potential

Because companies must allocate their marketing budget optimally among their best territories, they need to estimate the market potential of different cities, states and nations. Two major methods of assessing area market potential are the market-buildup method, used primarily by business marketers, and the multiple-factor index method, used primarily by consumer marketers.

Market-buildup method The **market-buildup method** calls for identifying all the potential buyers in each market and estimating their potential purchases. This method produces accurate results if we have a list of all potential buyers and a good estimate of what each will buy. Unfortunately, this information is not always easy to gather.

Consider a machine-tool company that wants to estimate the area market potential for its wood lathe in Greece. Its first step is to identify all potential buyers of wood lathes in the area, primarily manufacturing establishments that shape or ream wood as part of their operations. The company could compile a list from a directory of all manufacturing establishments in Greece. Then it could estimate the number of lathes each industry might purchase, based on the number of lathes per thousand employees or per €1 million of sales in that industry.

An efficient method of estimating area market potentials makes use of the statistical classification of economic activities in the European Community (NACE) consisting of a six-digit code. The first four digits of the code are the same in all European countries. The two last digits might vary from country to country. On 1 January 2008, the classification had changed considerably with the implementation of the NACE Regulation 1893/2006 (Rev. 2).[46]

The NACE classifies all manufacturing into 21 major industry sectors and further breaks each sector into a six-digit, hierarchical structure as illustrated.

C	Industry sector (manufacturing)
10	Industry subsector (food)
10.3	Industry group (fruit and vegetables)
10.3.2	Industry (fruit and vegetable juice)
10.3.2.00	(Country specific, the fruit and vegetable juice industry in this country has no sub-industries as illustrated by the last two digits, '00').

To use the NACE, the lathe manufacturer must first determine the NACE codes that represent products whose manufacturers are likely to require lathe machines. To get a full picture of NACE industries that might use lathes, the company can: (1) determine past customers' NACE codes; (2) go through the NACE manual and check off all the six-digit industries that might have an interest in lathes; (3) mail questionnaires to a wide range of companies enquiring about their interest in wood lathes.

The company's next task is to determine an appropriate base for estimating the number of lathes that each industry will use. Suppose customer industry sales are the most appropriate base. Once the company estimates the rate of lathe ownership relative to the customer industry's sales, it can compute the market potential.

Multiple-factor index method Like business marketers, consumer companies also need to estimate area market potentials, but the customers of consumer companies are too numerous to list. The method most commonly used in consumer markets is a straightforward index method. A drug manufacturer, for example, might assume that the market potential for drugs is directly related to population size. If Sweden has 1.83 per cent of the EU population, the company might assume that Sweden would be a market for 1.83 per cent of total drugs sold in the EU.

A single factor, however, is rarely a complete indicator of sales opportunity. Regional drug sales are also influenced by per capita income and the number of physicians per 10,000 people. Thus it makes sense to develop a multiple-factor index, with each factor assigned a specific weight. The numbers are the weights attached to each variable. For example, suppose Sweden has 2.50 per cent of the EU disposable personal income, 2.60 per cent of EU retail sales, and 1.83 per cent of the EU population, and the respective weights are 0.5, 0.3 and 0.2. The buying-power index for Sweden is then 2.40 [0.5(2.50) + 0.3(2.60) + 0.2(1.83)]. Thus 2.40 per cent of the EU drug sales (not 1.83 per cent) might be expected to take place in Sweden.

The weights in the buying-power index are somewhat arbitrary, and companies can assign others if appropriate. A manufacturer might also want to adjust the market potential for additional factors, such as competitors' presence in that market, local promotional costs, seasonal factors and local market idiosyncrasies.

Many companies compute other area indexes as a guide to allocating marketing resources. Suppose the drug company is reviewing the six cities listed in Table 6.4. The first two columns show its percentage of EU brand and category sales in these six cities. Column 3 shows the **brand development index (BDI)**, which is the index of brand sales to category sales. London, for example, has a BDI of 114 because the brand is relatively more developed than the category in that city. Paris has a BDI of 65, which means that the brand in Paris is relatively underdeveloped. Normally, the lower the BDI, the higher the market opportunity, in that there is room to grow the brand. However, other marketers would argue the opposite – that marketing funds should go into the brand's *strongest* markets, where it might be important to reinforce loyalty or more easily capture additional brand share.

Industry sales and market shares

Besides estimating total potential and area potential, a company needs to know the actual industry sales taking place in its market. This means identifying competitors and estimating their sales.

The industry trade association will often collect and publish total industry sales, although it does not usually list individual company sales separately. With this information, however, each company can evaluate its own performance against the whole industry. If a company's sales are increasing by 5 per cent a year, and industry sales are increasing by 10 per cent, the company is losing its relative standing in the industry.

Table 6.4 Calculating the brand development index (BDI)

Territory	(a) Percentage of EU brand Sales	(b) Percentage of EU category Sales	BDI (a ÷ b) × 100
London	3.09	2.71	114
Paris	6.74	10.41	65
Berlin	3.49	3.85	91
Madrid	.97	.81	120
Rome	1.13	.81	140
Amsterdam	3.12	3.00	104

Another way to estimate sales is to buy reports from a marketing research firm that audits total sales and brand sales. Nielsen Media Research audits retail sales in various product categories in supermarkets and drugstores and sells this information to interested companies. These audits let a company compare its performance to the total industry or to any particular competitor to see whether it is gaining or losing share either overall or on a brand-by-brand basis.

Because distributors typically will not supply information about how much of the competitors' products they are selling, business-goods marketers operate with less knowledge of their market share results.

Estimating future demand

The few products or services that lend themselves to easy forecasting generally enjoy an absolute level or a fairly constant trend and competition that is either non-existent (public utilities) or stable (pure oligopolies). In most markets, in contrast, good forecasting is a key factor to success.

Companies commonly prepare a macroeconomic forecast first, followed by an industry forecast, followed by a company sales forecast. The macroeconomic forecast calls for projecting inflation, unemployment, interest rates, consumer spending, business investment, government expenditures, net exports and other variables. The end result is a forecast of gross national product, which the firm uses (along with other environmental indicators) to forecast industry sales. The company derives its sales forecast by assuming that it will win a certain market share.

How do firms develop their forecasts? They may create their own or buy forecasts from outside sources such as marketing research firms, which interview customers, distributors and other knowledgeable parties. All forecasts are built on one of three information bases: what people say, what people do, or what people have done. Using what people say requires surveying the opinions of buyers or those close to them, such as sales people or outside experts, with surveys of buyers' intentions, composites of sales force opinions and expert opinion. Building a forecast on what people do means putting the product into a test market to measure buyer response. To use the final basis – what people have done – firms analyse records of past buying behaviour or use time-series analysis or statistical demand analysis.

Survey of buyers' intentions

Forecasting is the art of anticipating what buyers are likely to do under a given set of conditions. For major consumer durables such as appliances, several research organisations conduct periodic surveys of consumer buying intentions and ask questions such as: 'Do you intend to buy an automobile within the next six months?' and put the answers on a **purchase probability scale**:

0.00	0.20	0.40	0.60	0.80	1.00
No chance	Slight possibility	Fair possibility	Good possibility	High possibility	Certain

Surveys also inquire into consumers' present and future personal finances and their expectations about the economy. They combine various bits of information into a consumer confidence measure (e.g., European Commission Consumer Surveys, ACNielsen Consumer Confidence Index). The European Commission indicator is based on a monthly survey conducted across the countries of the European Union and those in the euro currency area (EA), with a total sample size of more than 32,000 consumers. It is based on answers to questions about expectations of the financial situation of households, the general economic situation, the unemployment situation and savings. The ACNielsen six-monthly survey is conducted online with 21,000 consumers across Europe.[47]

For business buying, research firms can carry out buyer-intention surveys regarding plant, equipment and materials. Estimates (of demand) are then based on buyers' *intentions*, meaning that some degree of deviance from actual behaviour will necessarily exist. Such estimates tend to fall within a 10 per cent error band around the actual level of demand/sales. Buyer-intention surveys are particularly useful in estimating demand for industrial products, consumer durables, product purchases where advanced planning is required, and new products. The value of a buyer-intention survey increases to the extent that buyers are few, the cost of reaching them is low, and they have clear intentions that they willingly disclose and implement.

Composite of sales force opinions

When buyer interviewing is impractical, the company may ask its sales representatives to estimate their future sales.

Few companies use sales force estimates without making some adjustments. Sales representatives might be pessimistic or optimistic, they might not know how their company's marketing plans will influence future sales in their territory, and they might deliberately underestimate demand so the company will set a low sales quota. To encourage better estimating, the company could offer incentives or assistance, such as information about marketing plans or past forecasts compared to actual sales.

Sales force forecasts bring a number of benefits. Sales reps might have better insight into developing trends than any other group, and forecasting might give them greater confidence in their sales quotas and more incentive to achieve them. Also, a 'grassroots' forecasting procedure provides detailed estimates broken down by product, territory, customer and sales rep.

Expert opinion

Companies can also obtain forecasts from experts, including dealers, distributors, suppliers, marketing consultants and trade associations. Dealer estimates are subject to the same strengths and weaknesses as sales force estimates. Many companies buy economic and industry forecasts from well-known economic-forecasting firms that have more data available and more forecasting expertise.

Occasionally, companies will invite a group of experts to prepare a forecast. The experts exchange views and produce an estimate as a group (*group discussion method*) or individually, in which case another analyst might combine them into a single estimate (*pooling of individual estimates*). Further rounds of estimating and refining follow (this is the Delphi method).[48]

Past sales analysis

Firms can develop sales forecasts on the basis of past sales. *Time-series analysis* breaks past time series into four components (trend, cycle, seasonal and erratic) and projects them into the future. *Exponential smoothing* projects the next period's sales by combining an average of past sales and the most recent sales, giving more weight to the latter. *Statistical demand analysis* measures the impact of a set of causal factors (such as income, marketing expenditure and price) on the sales level. Finally, *econometric analysis* builds sets of equations that describe a system and statistically derives the different parameters that make up the equations.

Market-test method

When buyers don't plan their purchases carefully, or experts are unavailable or unreliable, a direct-market test can help forecast new-product sales or established product sales in a new distribution channel or territory.

▽ SUMMARY

1 Knowing the market and its dynamics is at the heart of a truly market-oriented organisation. In this chapter, you have seen how marketing research spawns an informational foundation that is imperative to a company's efforts to make the best decisions possible, both tactically and strategically. And, since marketing information has come to be regarded as vital to company success, it is also an industry in rapid growth and development.

2 Some of the current trends in marketing research are: neuro-marketing research, online research – including data collection in social networking groups, such as MySpace or Facebook – and observational research. The latter type of research is furthered by technological advances, which makes it possible to accurately follow consumers' actual behaviour – in a still stronger focus on what consumers do and how they go about their daily lives.

3 Companies can conduct their own marketing research or hire other companies to do it for them. Good marketing research is characterised by the scientific method, creativity, multiple research methods, accurate model building, cost–benefit analysis, healthy scepticism, and an ethical focus.

4 The marketing research process consists of defining the problem, decision alternatives and research objectives, developing the research plan, collecting the information, analysing the information, presenting the findings to management, and making the decision.

5 In conducting research, firms must decide whether to collect their own data or use data that already exist. They must also decide which research approach (observational, focus group, survey, behavioural data or experimental) and which research instruments (questionnaire, qualitative measures or technological devices) to use. In addition, they must decide on a sampling plan and contact methods (by mail, by phone, in person or online).

6 Two complementary approaches to measuring marketing productivity are: (1) marketing metrics to assess marketing effects; and (2) marketing-mix modelling to estimate causal relationships and measure how marketing activity affects outcomes. Marketing dashboards are a structured way to disseminate the insights gleaned from these two approaches within the organisation.

7 There are two types of demand: market demand and company demand. To estimate current demand, companies attempt to determine total market potential, area market potential, industry sales and market share. To estimate future demand, companies survey buyers' intentions, solicit their sales force's input, gather expert opinions, analyse past sales or engage in market testing. Mathematical models, advanced statistical techniques and computerised data collection procedures are essential to all types of demand and sales forecasting.

▽ APPLICATIONS

Marketing debate

What is the best type of marketing research? Many market researchers have their favourite research approaches or techniques, although different researchers often have different preferences. Some researchers maintain that the only way to really learn about consumers or brands is through in-depth, qualitative research. Others contend that the only legitimate and defensible form of marketing research involves quantitative measures.

Take a position: The best marketing research is quantitative in nature *versus* qualitative.

Marketing discussion

When was the last time you participated in a survey? How helpful do you think was the information you provided? How could the research have been done differently to make it more effective?

▽ REFERENCES

[1]Based on L. Lande (2007) How a Swiss co. doubled US sales by convincing consumers that its product is hip and worth a premium, *MarketingProfs*, 9 November.

[2]See R. Schieffer (2005) *Ten Key Customer Insights: Unlocking the Mind of the Market,* Mason, OH: Thomson, for a comprehensive, in-depth discussion of how to generate customer insights to drive business results.

[3]ESOMAR (2007) 2007 Global Market Research Report. 17 September, Amsterdam: FSOMAR and ESOMAR (2006) Highlights 2006.

[4]http://www.orange.com/en_EN/.

[5]M. Haiken (2006) Tuned in to CrowdCasting, *Business 2.0,* November, 66–8.

[6]*The Economist* (2006) Would you fly in chattering class?, 9 September, 63.

[7]http://www.thetimes100.co.uk/index.php; J. Skouboe (2003) Se mig: Videotelefoni i virkeligheden, *Berlingske Tidende,* 7 April, Sektion 3, Business, 15; Messenger to go, press release from 3's website, 31 July, 2006; 3 først med Turbo 3G i Danmark,

press release from 3's website, 21 November 2006; K. Stensdal, 3 erklærer internetudbyderne krig, *Computerworld,* 4 April 2007.

[8]For a discussion of the decision-theory approach to the value of research, see D. R. Lehmann, S. Gupta and J. Steckel (1997) *Market Research,* Reading, MA: Addison-Wesley.

[9]D. Dodson (2008) Rapid innovation keeps the colour cosmetics category from stagnating in the mature markets, *Euromonitor,* 11 January.

[10]L. Tischler (2004) Every move you make, *Fast Company,* April, 73–5 and A. Stein Wellner (2003) Look who's watching, *Continental,* April, 39–41.

[11]For a detailed review of relevant academic work, see E. J. Arnould and A. Epp (2006) Deep engagement with consumer experience, in R. Grover and M. Vriens (eds) *Handbook of Marketing Research,* Thousand Oaks, CA: Sage, pp. 10–15. For a range of academic discussion, see the following special issue, Can ethnography uncover richer consumer insights?, *Journal of Advertising Research,* 46, September 2006. For some practical tips, see R. Durante and M. Feehan (2005) Leverage ethnography to improve strategic decision making, *Marketing Research,* Winter.

[12]L. Miles (2003) Market research: living their lives, *BrandRepublic*, 11 December; http://www.brandrepublic.com/bulletins/marketresearch/article/197919/market-research-living-lives/

[13]E. Sanders, Special section: ethnography in NPD research – how 'applied ethnography' can improve your NPD process, *PDMA*: http://www.pdma.org/visions/apr02/applied.html.

[14]http://www.brandrepublic.com.

[15]M. Fielding (2006) Shift the focus, *Marketing News*, 1 September, 18–20.

[16]E. Pfanner (2006) Agencies look beyond focus groups to spot trends, *New York Times*, 2 January.

[17]http://om.tdc.dk/.

[18]http://www.lego.com/eng/info/default.asp; http://www.ebst.dk/file/1599/daginst_virksomheder.pdf; Erhvervsfremme Styrelsen, BUPL, Samarbejde mellem daginstitutioner og virksomheder – M. Vanderbeeken (2006) Insights from the European market research event, 16 November; MarketingProfs Daily Fix: http://www.mpdailyfix.com/2006/11/post_14.html.

[19]L. Witt (2004) Inside intent, *American Demographics*, March, 34–9; A. Raskin (2003) A face any business can trust, *Business 2.0*, December, 58–60; G. Zaltman (1997) Rethinking market research: putting people back in *Journal of Marketing Research*, 34 November, 424–37; W. Wood. (1986) The race to replace memory, *Marketing and Media Decisions*, July, 166–7; R. D. Blackwell, J. S. Hensel, M. B. Phillips and B. Sternthal (1970), *Laboratory Equipment for Marketing Research*, Dubuque, IA: Kendall/Hunt.

[20]S. Baker (2006) Wiser about the Web, *BusinessWeek*, 27 March, 54–62.

[21]http://www.neurosense.com/; T. K. Grose (2006) Brain sells, *TIME*, 10 September; http://www.telegraph.co.uk/motoring/main.jhtml?xml=/motoring/exclusions/supplements/honda/nosplit/honda3switchedon.xml#1.

[22]http://www.businessweek.com/magazine/content/08_08/b4072055361150.htm?chan=top+news_top+news+index_businessweek+exclusives.

[23]http://www.mikab.se/index.php3?NodNummer=58&Poe_Session=adb9f75625f1462a6d81ef2ce5373d93.

[24]M. Fielding (2006) op. cit.

[25]B. Johnson (2006) Forget phone and mail: online's the best place to administer surveys, *Advertising Age*, 17 July, 23.

[26]D. L. Vence (2006) In an instant: more researchers use IM for fast, reliable results, *Marketing News*, 1 March, 53–5.

[27]C. Arnold (2004) Global perspective: Synovate exec discusses future of international research, *Marketing News*, 15 May, 43; M. Erard (2004) For technology, no small world after all, *New York Times*, 6 May; D. L. Vence (2003) Global consistency: leave it to the experts, *Marketing News*, 28 April, 37.

[28]M. Fielding (2006) Global insights: Synovate's Chedore discusses MR trends, *Marketing News*, 15 May, 41–2.

[29]www.brandrepublic.com; www.arnoldbolingbroke.com.

[30]Cf. J. D. C. Little (1979) Decision support systems for marketing managers, *Journal of Marketing*, Summer, 11. See also

Special issue on managerial decision making (1999) *Marketing Science* 18, 3 for some contemporary perspectives.

[31]D. Power (2006) What are examples of decision support systems in global enterprises?, http://dssresources.com, 26 October.

[32]R. Grover and M. Vriens (2006) Trusted advisor: how it helps lay the foundation for insight in *Handbook of Marketing Research*, Thousand Oaks, CA: Sage, 3–17; C. Moorman, G. Zaltman and R. Deshpandé (1992) Relationships between providers and users of market research: the dynamics of trust within and between Organizations, *Journal of Marketing Research*, 29, August, 314–28.

[33]Adapted from A. Shapiro (2004) Let's redefine market research, *Brandweek*, 21 June, 20; http://www.fromscripttodvd.com:80/star_wars_a_day_long_remembered.htm.

[34]R. Shaw and D. Merrick (2005) *Marketing Payback: Is Your Marketing Profitable?*, Harlow: FT Prentice Hall.

[35]J. McManus (2004) Stumbling into intelligence, *American Demographics*, April, 22–5.

[36]P. Farris, N. T. Bendle, P. E. Pfeifer and D. J. Reibstein (2006) *Marketing Metrics: 50+ Metrics Every Executive Should Master*, Upper Saddle River, NJ: Pearson Education; J. Davis (2005) *Magic Numbers for Consumer Marketing: Key Measures to Evaluate Marketing Success*, Singapore: John Wiley & Sons.

[37]B. Donath (2003) Employ marketing metrics with a track record, *Marketing News*, 15 September, 12.

[38]G. J. Tellis (2006) Modeling marketing mix, in R. Grover and M. Vriens (eds) *Handbook of Marketing Research*, Thousand Oaks, CA: Sage.

[39]J. Neff (2004) P&G, Clorox rediscover modeling, *Advertising Age*, 29 March, 10.

[40]L. Q. Hughes (2002) Econometrics take root, *Advertising Age*, 5 August, S–4.

[41]D. J. Reibstein (2005) Connect the dots, *CMO Magazine*, May.

[42]http://www.autoliv.com/alv/connect/Home/Who+We+Are/Our%20Market.

[43]For a good discussion and illustration, see R. J. Best, *Market-based Management*, 4th edn, Upper Saddle River, NJ: Prentice Hall.

[44]For further discussion, see G. L. Lilien, P. Kotler and K. S. Moorthy (1992) *Marketing Models*, Upper Saddle River, NJ: Prentice Hall.

[45]http://epp.eurostat.ec.europa.eu/portal/page?_pageid=2693,70381876,2693_70592044&_dad=portal&_schema=PORTAL.

[46]http://ec.europa.eu/environment/emas/documents/nace_en.htm.

[47]http://www.mrweb.com/drno/conf-euro.htm.

[48]For an excellent overview of market forecasting, see S. Armstrong (2001) (ed.) *Principles of Forecasting: A Handbook for Researchers and Practitioners*, Norwell, MA: Kluwer Academic Publishers and his website: http://fourps.wharton.upenn.edu/forecast/handbook.html; also see R. J. Best (1974) An experiment in Delphi estimation in marketing decision making, *Journal of Marketing Research*, November, 447–52; N. Dalkey and O. Helmer (1963) An experimental application of the Delphi method to the use of experts, *Management Science*, April 458–67.

Chapter 7

Analysing consumer markets

IN THIS CHAPTER, WE WILL ADDRESS THE FOLLOWING QUESTIONS:

1 How do consumer and situational characteristics influence buying behaviour?

2 What major psychological and behavioural processes influence consumer responses to the marketing programme?

3 How do consumers make purchasing decisions?

4 How do marketers analyse consumer decision making?

The aim of marketing is to meet and satisfy target customers' needs and wants better than competitors. Marketers are always looking for emerging customer trends that suggest new marketing opportunities.

Social network services are among the newest marketing frontiers for market communication.
Source: Martin Keene/PA/PA Photos

The emergence of the social web, especially with teens and young adults, has made marketers rethink their practices.

With annual growth rates of 65 per cent and higher in 2007, social network services such as Facebook, MySpace, Friendster and Tagged represent a major opportunity for marketers to enter into dialogue with their customers. Essentially, these services are websites dedicated to social networking, offering their members an easy and free way of creating personal profiles that may contain all sorts of content, such as photographs, music, blogs, and so on. Members can link their profile to those of their friends or can search for new friends who share their interests. In this way the social web takes form – and becomes a sphere for building and maintaining relationships between people.

These popular social networks accumulate a wealth of information about their members that marketers find valuable, and they have paved the way for new forms of communication between marketers and consumers. Facebook, one of the fastest growing popular social networks, has recently publicised its plans of how to share with marketers information posted by the 50 million+ people on the site worldwide. It is an advertising system that invites marketers to present ads to individual Facebook members, based on the details they share with friends on the site. This includes not only the types of data commonly available to marketers, such as demographic data, geographic location and content purchasing habits, but also much more personal information such as interests, preferences, attitudes and relationship status. The system provides a means for businesses to build profiles on Facebook to connect with their audiences; an ad system that facilitates the spread of brand messages virally; and an interface to gather insights into people's activity on Facebook that marketers care about. Examples of organisations and businesses joining Facebook range from small, local firms to multinational corporations such as Blockbuster, General Motors, Coca-Cola and Sony BMG.[1]

Successful marketing requires that companies fully connect with their customers. Adopting a holistic marketing orientation means understanding customers – gaining a 360-degree view of both their daily lives, their plans for the future and the changes that actually occur during their lifetimes so that the right products are marketed to the right customers in the right way. This chapter explores consumer buying dynamics; the next chapter explores the buying dynamics of business buyers.

▽ **The study of consumer behaviour**

Consumer behaviour is the study of how individuals or groups buy, use and dispose of goods, services, ideas or experiences to satisfy their needs and wants.[2] The needs and wants of consumers often vary across different cultures, situations and individual characteristics. The study of consumer behaviour can be divided into three interdependent dimensions: (1) the study of culture; (2) the study of social groups; (3) the study of the individual (Figure 7.1).

While it is possible to treat the three dimensions separately they also have a mutual influence on each other. In the following, each dimension will first be separately considered and then some possible interdependencies between the dimensions are discussed.

Culture

Culture, subculture and social class are particularly important influences on consumer buying behaviour. **Culture** is the fundamental determinant of a person's wants and behaviour. Culture can be conceptualised as the 'meanings that are shared by (most) people in a social group'[3] and can be thought of as the blueprint for human behaviour. In a culture values and norms are developed that serve as guidelines for human behaviour. Each culture consists of smaller **subcultures** that provide more specific identification and socialisation for their members. Subcultures include nationalities, religions, racial groups and geographic regions. When subcultures grow large and affluent enough, companies often design specialised marketing programmes to serve them. *Multicultural marketing* grew out of careful marketing research, which revealed that different ethnic and demographic niches did not always respond favorably to mass market advertising.

> To learn how Quebec's rich and diverse culture has led various multinational companies to adapt their campaigns, visit www.pearsoned.ca/marketingmanagementcanada

Companies have capitalised on well-thought-out multicultural marketing strategies in recent years, as illustrated in 'Marketing insight: Multicultural marketing in Europe'. As countries become more culturally diverse, however, marketing campaigns aimed at a specific cultural target can spill over and have a positive influence on other cultural groups.[4]

Virtually all human societies exhibit *social stratification*, most often in the form of **social classes**, relatively homogeneous and enduring divisions in a society, hierarchically ordered and with members who share similar values, interests and behaviour. One classic depiction of social classes in the EU is the EGP (Erikson-Goldthorpe-Portocarero) class schema – defined as 11 descending levels, as follows:

1 service class I (comprising higher-grade professionals, administrators and officials; managers in large industrial establishments; large proprietors);

Figure 7.1 The interaction of the cultural, the social and the individual level

Marketing insight

Multicultural marketing in Europe

Marketing targeted at national cultures: Comprising 47 independent countries,[5] Europe has had a tradition of national companies designing marketing programmes for specific national cultures. Many global corporations operating in the European market have followed this practice with success. Coca-Cola in Europe is a characteristic example of a global corporation with a local approach to marketing. During recent years, Coca-Cola has pursued a strategy of moving into niche markets by launching non-traditional soft drinks, such as Avra water in Greece, Cappy juice in Croatia, BURN (energy) in Poland, Fernandes sodas in the Netherlands and Fioravanti in Spain.

Fernandes sodas: a local approach to marketing.
Source: Courtesy of Fernandes Bottling Co. NV / Agency: Studio Prins

▶ **Marketing insight** *(continued)*

As the expansion of the EU has led to increasing numbers of immigrants, the market potential for ethnic drinks has grown. A case in point is Fernandes sodas, produced by Fernandes Concern Beheer NV, one of the oldest corporations in Suriname. Fernandes sodas is a sweet, lemonade-like drink that comes in several brightly coloured flavours such as red cherry bouquet and green punch.

For decades, many Dutch residents with ties to Suriname – a former Dutch colony in South America – had been bringing home cases of Fernandes in their luggage. But in the 1980s Coca-Cola Enterprises Nederland BV began bottling Fernandes under licence and selling the sodas in small ethnic grocery stories in big cities such as Amsterdam.

The South American soda soon become popular, and in 2003 Coca-Cola decided to introduce Fernandes to mainstream Dutch consumers through distribution in larger supermarket chains. Owing to the publicity of a new marketing campaign, featuring one of Amsterdam's hottest television comedians, and a switch from glass to plastic bottles, sales of Fernandes sodas rose by 20 per cent in 2007, to about 1 million cases. Marte van Esser, spokesperson for Coca-Cola in the Netherlands, commented on this success: 'Every country has its specific needs and Coca-Cola knows how to meet those needs . . . Although originally targeted at the Surinamese, the sodas really are for everyone.' As the roll-out of the no-calorie drink Coke Zero was also highly successful in Europe, Coca-Cola seems to be striking a balance between nurturing its roots and gaining new audiences by respecting the tastes of local consumers. This balance has resulted in steadily increasing profits in Europe (a 5 per cent increase in case volume in the European Union in the second quarter of 2007), helping to offset the company's more modest performance in North America.

Marketing targeted at minority groups: In recent years, however, Europe has also witnessed a trend towards multicultural strategies that go across traditional national lines of cultural identity, revolving around ethnic identities. In Ireland, foreign nationals constitute more than 10 per cent of the population, and companies are taking on new challenges in targeting and creating brand awareness among the growing ethnic communities. For instance, the Polish subsidiary of AIB, Bank Zachodni WBK, successfully ran a campaign in Ireland (in the summer of 2007) targeted at Poles who live and work in Ireland. Given the fact that around 120,000 Polish people live in Ireland and that Bank Zachodni had a strong affinity with Poland, AIB saw itself as well placed to serve this market segment. Another Irish example is phone companies, which are starting to commit to serving minority communities. Local phone company Meteor has tailored advertising campaigns and translated its website into Polish, Latvian, Mandarin and Lithuanian in order to optimise customer experiences.

In the United Kingdom, the need for companies to understand and communicate with ethnic groups has never been greater, as they represent a growing audience of around 5 million consumers with an expected spending power of €420 billion by 2010. Thus, corporations such as British Telecom have increased their investments targeting the ethnic minority market. In one of their campaigns, a black family was portrayed to reach out to ethnic minority customers as well as white customers. The aim of the campaign was to encourage overseas calling, a perfect example of targeting ethnic minority communities. Along similar lines of thought, health care chain Boots launched a range of halal baby food. They worked with the Muslim Food Board to develop it and make sure it was properly labelled and within Muslim law. The range featured in the *Muslim Food Guide*, which is distributed throughout the United Kingdom via mosques. Boots ensured its staff were up to speed on the new range to advise customers.

Finally, a number of non-profit and governmental organisations, such as hospitals and law enforcement agencies, have been very successful in developing recruitment campaigns aimed at individuals from under-represented groups, particularly women and those from minority ethnic communities. In both the United Kingdom and Denmark, such strategies have been employed to improve the diversity of the workforce so that it more closely reflects the diversity of the communities they serve. Despite these developments, researchers found that ethnic consumers in the United Kingdom often feel overlooked. At least one in two people from all ethnic groups – including the white population – believed that consumer brands often use ethnic faces in advertising as a token gesture. Also, more than three-quarters of Asian (77 per cent) and black (78 per cent) people and half (50 per cent) of Chinese people in the United Kingdom believed mainstream brands to be of no relevance to them. In addition, 75 per cent of black, 63 per cent of Asian and 50 per cent of Chinese people did not see marketers as knowledgeable of how to market to individuals from ethnically diverse backgrounds. These are important sentiments to bear in mind when designing strategies and campaigns intended for minority communities.

Sources: Based on S. Emling (2007) Coke goes local to win wider market in Europe, *Cox News Service*, 13 October (www.coxwashington.com/hp/content/reporters/stories/2007/10/13/BC_COKE_EUROPE13_COX.html); Firms target ethnic sector, *TCH Archives, Sunday Business Post*, 5 August 2007 (http://archives.tcm.ie/businesspost/2007/08/05/story25616.asp); L. MacDonald, W. Tanner and C. Wheeler, Advertising and ethnic minority communities: a report by the IPA Information Centre (www.ipa.co.uk/documents/Advertising&ethnic_minority_communities.pdf); Fokusgruppe hjælper politiet med etnisk rekruttering (www.politi.dk/da/aktuelt/nyheder/2006/etniskfokusgruppe_11102006.htm); The recruitment of black and minority ethnic groups to the MPS, Report 8, 1 September 2006 (www.mpa.gov.uk/committees/cop/2006/060901/08.htm); Understanding the multi-cultural market (www.webershand-wick.co.uk/features/understanding-the-multi-cultural-market).

2 service class II (comprising lower-grade professionals, administrators and officials; higher-grade technicians; managers in small industrial establishments; supervisors of non-manual employees);

3 routine non-manual;

4 routine non-manual employees;

5 self-employed with employees;

6 self-employed with no employees;

7 self-employed, farmers etc.;

8 manual supervisors;

9 skilled workers;

10 unskilled workers;

11 farm labour.[6]

Social classes have several characteristics. First, those within each tend to be more alike in dress, speech patterns and recreational preferences than persons from two different social classes. Second, persons are perceived as occupying inferior or superior positions according to social class. Third, a *cluster* of variables – for example occupation, income, wealth, education and value orientation – indicates social class, rather than any single variable. Fourth, individuals can move up or down the social class ladder during their lifetimes. How easily and how far depends on how rigid the social stratification is and on the level of equality in a society.

Social classes show distinct product and brand preferences in many areas, including clothing, home furnishings, leisure activities and automobiles. They also differ in media preferences, with upper-class consumers often preferring magazines and books and lower-class consumers often preferring television. Even within a category such as TV, upper-class consumers tend to prefer news and drama, and lower-class consumers tend to prefer soap operas and sports programmes. There are also language differences – advertising copy and dialogue must ring true to the targeted social class.

Social groups

Social factors such as reference groups, family, and social roles and statuses affect consumers' buying behaviour.

Reference groups

A person's **reference groups** are all the groups that have a direct (face-to-face) or indirect influence on their attitudes or behaviour. Groups having a direct influence are called **membership groups**. Some of these are **primary groups** with whom the person interacts fairly continuously and informally, such as family, friends, neighbours and co-workers. People also belong to **secondary groups**, such as religious, professional and trade union groups, which tend to be more formal and require less continuous interaction.

Reference groups influence members in at least three ways. They expose an individual to new behaviours and lifestyles, they influence attitudes and self-concept, and they create pressures for conformity that may affect product and brand choices. For instance, inspired by their friends and colleagues women may choose to buy high-quality branded products for their child in order to be perceived as a 'good mother'.[7] People are also influenced by groups to which they do *not* belong and by groups to which they do *not want* to belong. **Aspirational groups** are those a person hopes to join; **dissociative groups** are those groups to which a person does not belong and whose values, norms or behaviour an individual rejects; **disclaimant groups** are those groups to which a person belong but whose values, norms or behaviour an individual seeks to avoid.

Many ads play on the influence of reference groups on product and brand choice. The advertisement for Hugo Boss (page 228), for example, portrays two young, trendy, affluent and relaxed people, implying that choosing the Hugo Boss brand may help the consumer create a similar style or image.

Where reference group influence is strong, marketers must determine how to reach and influence the group's opinion leaders or other influential persons of the group. An **opinion leader** is the person who offers informal advice or information about a specific product or product category,

Choosing the Hugo
Boss brand helps
consumers to create a
relaxed style of living.
Source: The Advertising
Archives

such as which of several brands is best or how a particular product may be used.[8] Opinion leaders are often highly confident, socially active and involved with the category, and are often perceived by other consumers as highly credible information sources. **Market mavens** are also perceived by other consumers to offer credible advice, but in contrast to opinion leaders market mavens are not influential because of a specialised product or product category expertise. Instead, they possess a more broad expertise concerning many different products and decisions related to the marketplace.[9] Marketers try to reach opinion leaders and market mavens by identifying their demographic and psychographic characteristics, identifying the media they read, and directing messages at them. Today, important inroads into the lives of opinion leaders and market mavens are starting 'friendships' with them in social Web forums such as MySpace or Facebook, or offering sponsorships of popular personal blogs or communities based on interests or hobbies.

Family

The family is the most important consumer buying organisation in society, and family members constitute the most influential primary reference group.[10] There are two families in the buyer's life. The **family of orientation** consists of parents and siblings. From parents a person acquires an orientation toward religion, politics and economics and a sense of personal ambition, self-worth and love.[11] Even if the buyer no longer interacts very much with their parents, their influence on behaviour can be significant. Parents have been found to influence their children's future orientation towards areas as diverse as education, savings, food, smoking, drinking and driving, teen pregnancy, and even the choice of bank or insurance company.[12]

A more direct influence on everyday buying behaviour is the **family of procreation** – namely, one's spouse and children. In Europe, husband–wife involvement in purchases has traditionally varied widely by product category. The wife has usually acted as the family's main purchasing agent, especially for food, sundries and staple clothing items. Now traditional purchasing roles are changing, and marketers would be wise to see both men and women as possible targets. For expensive products and services such as cars, holidays or housing, the vast majority of husbands and wives engage in joint decision making.[13] And marketers are realising that women actually buy more technology than men do, but consumer electronics stores have been slow to catch on to this fact. Some savvy electronics stores are starting to heed women's complaints of being ignored, patronised or offended by sales people.

Nevertheless, men and women may respond differently to marketing messages.[14] One study showed that women valued connections and relationships with family and friends and placed a high priority on people. Men, on the other hand, related more to competition and placed a high priority on action. Marketers are taking more direct aim at women with products such as Kelloggs' Special K Brand or paint manufacturer Jotun's brand 'Lady'.[15] Recently Philips teamed up with Swarovski Crystal to design a new fashion line of electronic product – such as headphones and memory keys – targeted specifically at women.

Philips Swarovski Crystal: a new fashion line of electronic products targeted specifically at women.

Source: Courtesy of Philips Consumer Electronics

Another shift in buying patterns is an increase in the number of euros spent and the direct and indirect influence wielded by children and teens. Direct influence describes children's hints, requests and demands – 'I want to go to McDonald's.' Indirect influence means that parents know the brands, product choices and preferences of their children without hints or outright requests ('I think Tommy would want to go to McDonald's'). Research estimates that – in one-third of Danish households – more than 25 per cent of household food spending in 2006 is carried out as a direct result of children's stated requests.[16] On a similar note, recent studies found that English (UK) and Israeli children exercise quite strong influence on family decision making.[17] Children are highly involved and influential in regard to products of which they are primary users, such as toys, clothing, education and entertainment. Approximately 25 per cent of Israeli children, 40 per cent of English children, and a little over two-thirds of US children were reported to be involved in decision making regarding family consumption matters as well. Indeed, research has shown that teenagers are playing a more active role than before in helping parents choose a car, audio/video equipment or a holiday spot.[18] In fact, a J.D. Power study revealed that 62 per cent of parents say their child 'actively participated in the car-buying decision'. That's why car manufacturers are upping their marketing programmes for children as young as five.

Roles and status

A person participates in many groups – family, clubs, organisations. Groups are often an important source of information and help to define norms for behaviour. We can define a person's position in each group to which he belongs in terms of role and status. A **role** consists of the activities a person is expected to perform. Each role carries a **status**. A senior vice-president of marketing has more status than a sales manager, and a sales manager has more status than an office clerk. People choose products that reflect and communicate their role and actual or desired status in society. Marketers must be aware of the status symbol potential of products and brands.

Television can be powerful in reaching children, and marketers are using television to target children at younger ages than ever before. By the time children are around two years old they can often recognise characters, logos and specific brands. They can distinguish between advertising and programming by about the age of six or seven. A year or so later, they can understand the concept of persuasive intent on the part of advertisers. By nine or ten, they can understand the discrepancies between message and product.[19] Marketers are tapping into that audience with product tie-ins, placed at a child's eye level, on just about everything – from Bob the Builder Muffin Mix or biscuits to Spiderman Lunchboxes.[20]

Millions of kids under the age of 17 are also online. Marketers have jumped online with them, offering freebies in exchange for personal information. Many have come under fire for this practice and for not clearly differentiating ads from games or entertainment. Establishing ethical and legal boundaries in marketing to children online and offline continues to be a hot topic as consumer advocates decry the commercialism they believe such marketing engenders.

The individual consumer

A buyer's decisions are also influenced by personal characteristics. These include the buyer's age and stage in the life cycle; occupation and economic circumstances; personality and self-concept; and lifestyle and values. Because many of these characteristics have a very direct impact on consumer behaviour, it is important for marketers to follow them closely.

Age and stage in the life cycle

Our taste in food, clothes, furniture and recreation is often related to our age. For example, it is not at all uncommon for parents and teens to have different clothing preferences.[21] Consumption is also shaped by the *family life cycle* and the number, age and gender of people in the household at any point in time. Western households are increasingly fragmented – the traditional family of four with a husband, wife and two kids makes up a much smaller percentage of total households than it once did.[22] In addition, *psychological* life cycle stages may matter. Adults experience certain 'passages' or 'transformations' as they go through life.[23] Yet the behaviour people exhibit as they go through these passages, such as becoming a parent, is not necessarily fixed but changes with the times.

Marketers should also consider *critical life events or transitions* – marriage, childbirth, illness, relocation, divorce, career change, widowhood – as giving rise to new needs. These should alert service providers – banks, lawyers, and marriage, employment and bereavement counsellors – to ways they can help.[24]

Occupation and economic circumstances

Occupation also influences consumption patterns. A blue-collar worker will buy work clothes, work shoes and lunchboxes. A company president will buy lounge suits, air travel and country club membership. Marketers try to identify the occupational groups that have above-average interest in their products and services and even tailor products for certain occupational groups. Computer software companies, for example, design different products for brand managers, engineers, lawyers and physicians.

Product choice is greatly affected by economic circumstances: spendable income (level, stability and time pattern), savings and assets (including the percentage that is liquid), debts, borrowing power and attitudes toward spending and saving. Luxury goods makers such as Gucci, Prada and Burberry can be vulnerable to an economic downturn. If economic indicators point to a recession, marketers can take steps to redesign, reposition and reprice their products or introduce or increase the emphasis on discount brands so that they can continue to offer value to target customers.

Personality and self-concept

Each person has personality characteristics that influence his or her buying behaviour. By **personality**, we mean a set of distinguishing human psychological traits that lead to relatively consistent and enduring responses to environmental stimuli (including buying behaviour). We often describe it in terms of such traits as self-confidence, dominance, autonomy, deference, sociability, defensiveness and adaptability.[25] Personality can be a useful variable in analysing consumer brand choices. The idea is that brands also have personalities, and consumers are likely to choose brands whose personalities match their own. For example, some people may buy a BMW X5 (a large off-road vehicle) to signal self-confidence and dominance. We define **brand personality** as the specific mix of human traits that we can attribute to a particular brand.

Marketing professor Jennifer Aaker researched brand personalities and identified the following traits:[26]

- sincerity (down to earth, honest, wholesome and cheerful);
- excitement (daring, spirited, imaginative and up to date);
- competence (reliable, intelligent and successful);
- sophistication (upper class and charming);
- ruggedness (outdoorsy and tough).

She analysed some well-known brands and found that a number of them tended to be strong on one particular trait: Levi's with 'ruggedness'; MTV with 'excitement'; CNN with 'competence'; and Campbell's with 'sincerity'. The implication is that these brands will attract persons who are high on the same personality traits. A brand personality may have several attributes: Levi's suggests a personality that is also youthful, rebellious, authentic, and American.

A cross-cultural study exploring the generalisability of Aaker's scale found that three of the five factors applied in Japan and Spain, but a 'peacefulness' dimension replaced 'ruggedness' in both countries, and a 'passion' dimension emerged in Spain instead of 'competency'.[27] Research on brand personality in Korea revealed two culture-specifc factors – passive likeableness and ascendancy – reflecting the importance of Confucian values (i.e., respect for one's parents, humaneness and ritual) in Korea's social and economic systems.[28]

Consumers often choose and use brands that have a brand personality consistent with their own *actual self-concept* (how we view ourselves), although the match may instead be based on the consumer's *ideal self-concept* (how we would like to view ourselves) or even on *others' self-concept* (how we think others see us).[29] These effects may also be more pronounced for publicly consumed products than for privately consumed goods.[30] On the other hand, consumers who are high 'self-monitors' – that is, sensitive to how others see them – are more likely to choose brands whose personalities fit the consumption situation.[31] Finally, consumers often have multiple aspects of self (serious professional, caring family member, active fun lover) that may be evoked differently in different situations or around different types of people.

Levi's uses product features, services and image-making to transmit the brand's personality.

Source: © Andy Warhol Foundation/Corbis

Lifestyle and values

A **lifestyle** is a person's pattern of living in the world as expressed in activities, interests and opinions. It portrays the 'whole person' interacting with his or her environment. Marketers search for relationships between their products and lifestyle groups. For example, a computer manufacturer might find that most computer buyers are achievement oriented and then aim the brand more clearly at the achiever lifestyle. Here's an example of one of the latest lifestyle trends businesses are targeting:

▽ LOHAS

Consumers who worry about the environment, want products to be produced in a sustainable way, and spend money to advance their personal health, development and potential have been named 'LOHAS', an acronym standing for *lifestyles of health and sustainability.*

LOHAS consumers ('Lohasians') are interested in products covering a range of market sectors and subsectors, including alternative health care, organic clothing and food, energy-efficient appliances and solar panels, as well as social responsible investing, yoga tapes and ecotourism. While ethical consumerism, eco-consciousness and expectations of positive exchanges among companies and their stakeholders are global phenomena, Europeans are 50 per cent more likely than Americans to buy 'green' products – ranging from solar panels to hybrid cars, natural/organic foods, personal care to home products. Moreover, they are 25 per cent more likely to recycle and more than 30 per cent more likely to influence their friends and family about the environment than Americans. Researchers expect that differences in tax structures, subsidies and the longevity of the availability of LOHAS products induce these variations.[32]

Worldwide, this market segment is currently estimated to be worth €375 billion annually.[33] Table 7.1 breaks the LOHAS market into six segments, each with special product and service interests.[34]

Table 7.1 LOHAS market segments

Personal health	Natural lifestyles
Natural, organic products	Indoor and outdoor furnishings
Nutritional products	Organic cleaning supplies
Integrative health care	Compact fluorescent lights
Dietary supplements	Social change philanthropy
Mind, body, spirit products	Apparel
Green building	**Alternative transportation**
Home certification	Hybrid vehicles
Energy star appliances	Biodiesel fuel
Sustainable flooring	Car-sharing programmes
Renewable energy systems	
Wood alternatives	
Eco-tourism	**Alternative energy**
Eco-tourism travel	Renewable energy credits
Eco-adventure travel	Green pricing

Source: From www.lohas.com/. Copyright © LOHAS. Reproduced with permission.

Lifestyles are shaped partly by whether consumers are *money constrained* or *time constrained*. Companies aiming to serve money-constrained consumers will create lower-cost products and services. By appealing to thrifty consumers, Wal-Mart has become the largest company in the world. Its 'everyday low prices' have wrung tens of billions of dollars out of the retail supply chain, passing the larger part of savings along to shoppers in the form of rock-bottom bargain prices.[35] Another company focusing on offering low prices to consumers, and aiming to serve money-constrained consumers, is furniture retailer IKEA. 'Breakthrough marketing: IKEA' outlines IKEA's global success formula of appealing to price-conscious shoppers in the furniture market.

While IKEA may offer good value for money, the IKEA concept is not designed to serve time-constrained consumers. When shopping in IKEA consumers often have to queue to receive their chosen products from IKEA's storage and thereafter they must assemble the furniture on their own. Consumers who experience time famine are prone to **multitasking**, doing two or more things at the same time. They will also pay others to perform tasks because time is more important than money. Companies aiming to serve them will create convenient products and services for this group.

Breakthrough marketing

IKEA

Swedish furniture retailer IKEA excels at appealing to price-conscious shoppers around the world with stylish items carefully selected for each country's market.

Source: Ulrich Baumgarten/vario images/Alamy

IKEA was founded in 1943 by a 17-year-old Swede named Ingvar Kamprad. The company, which initially sold pens, Christmas cards and seeds from a shed on Kamprad's family farm, eventually grew into a retail titan in home furnishings and a global cultural phenomenon, what *BusinessWeek* called a 'one-stop sanctuary for coolness' and 'the quintessential cult brand'.

IKEA inspires remarkable levels of devotion from its customers, who visit in numbers that average 1.1 million per day. When a new location debuted in London in 2005, 6000 people arrived before the doors opened. A contest in Atlanta crowned five winners 'Ambassador of *Kul*' (Swedish for 'fun') who, in order to collect their prizes, had to live in the IKEA store for three full days before it opened, which they gladly did. In Norway, IKEA converted a part of a warehouse in Oslo in order to add a hostel to the store. In the IKEA Hostel, customers can stay overnight in case they haven't finished their shopping. Company spokesman Frode Ullebust explained:

'There will be the regular dormitory with lots of beds stacked up together. We will also have a bridal suite, with a round bed and a hanging chandelier and a luxury suite, where customers can enjoy breakfast in bed.'

IKEA achieved this level of success by offering a unique value proposition to consumers: leading-edge Scandinavian design at bargain prices. The company's fashionable bargains include Klippan sofas for €167, Billy bookcases for €80, and Lack side tables for €6. In Scandinavian markets, IKEA has even sold 2500 prefabricated homes for around €30,000, depending on local housing prices. The company is able to offer such low prices in part because most items come boxed and require complete assembly at home, meaning they are easier to transport, take up less shelf space and seldom require delivery, which reduces costs.

IKEA's mission of providing value is predicated on founder Kamprad's statement that 'People have very thin wallets. We should take care of their interests.' IKEA

▶ Breakthrough marketing *(continued)*

adheres to this philosophy by reducing the prices of its products by 2–3 per cent annually. Its focus on value also benefits the bottom line: IKEA enjoys 10 per cent margins, higher than competitors such as Target (7.7 per cent) and Pier 1 Imports (5 per cent).

Many of its products are sold uniformly throughout the world, but IKEA also caters to local tastes. In China, for example, it stocked 250,000 plastic place mats with Year of the Rooster themes, which quickly sold out after the holiday. When employees realised US shoppers were buying vases as drinking glasses because they considered IKEA's regular glasses too small, the company developed larger glasses for the US market.

IKEA managers visited European and US consumers in their homes and learned that Europeans generally hang their clothes, whereas US shoppers prefer to store them folded. Wardrobes for the US market were designed with deeper drawers. Visits to Hispanic households in California led IKEA to add seating and dining space in its California stores, brighten the colour palettes, and hang more picture frames on the walls.

IKEA evolved into a retail empire with 265 stores and revenues of €19.8 billion in 2007 and still had excellent growth opportunities. The company recently announced plans to offer a home measuring service for its kitchens, and to open new stores in Sweden, Finland and Denmark in the years ahead, as the Nordic market remains crucial to its success.

IKEA is famous for its pine furniture, and has teamed up with the Woodland Trust to plant a square foot of forest in the United Kingdom every time a customer uses its store card.

Sources: K. Capell (2005) IKEA: how the Swedish retailer became a global cult brand, *BusinessWeek*, 14 November, 96; Need a home to go with that sofa?, *BusinessWeek*, 14 November 2005, 106; www.ikea.com; IKEA gets hostel, *Retail Traffic*, 36(9), 1 September 2007; Sweden/Nordic: IKEA plans new establishments, *Esmerk Swedish News*, 26 October 2007; IKEA launches green initiative with Woodland Trust, *BrandRepublic*, 19 November 2007.

In some categories, notably food processing, companies targeting time-constrained consumers need to be aware that these very same people want to believe they're *not* operating within time constraints. Marketers call those who seek both convenience and some involvement in the cooking process the 'convenience involvement segment'.[36]

▽ Knorr Lasagne

The 'convenience involvement segment' of the food market is receptive to time savers such as Knorr Lasagne that still allows them to feel good about investing some time or effort in meal preparation.

Source: Courtesy of Unilever Danmark AS

Originally, the popular pasta-and-powdered mix Knorr Lasagne was designed to meet consumer demand for quick and easy preparation of a family meal. Knorr understood that consumers do not always have the time, energy or inspiration for cooking meals from scratch, and offered an easy way to prepare, for example, a lasagne that may also be spiced up with ingredients of the consumer's own choice.

With an increasing proportion of evening meals prepared in under 30 minutes and strong competition from fast-food drive-through windows, restaurant deliveries and pre-cooked grocery store dishes, the days of prosperity of products such as Knorr Lasagne might seem numbered. However, consumers don't always want the fastest solution possible – they also want to feel good about their meals and how they are prepared. Common requirements are that meals are tasty, healthy, nutritious, and made from quality produce. Thus, Knorr not only introduces new flavours to tap into the latest consumer taste trends, but is also introducing more healthy alternatives. Recently, a series of wholegrain/meal products such as Wholemeal Lasagnette was launched, as was the healthy Knorr Vie, which is a smoothie-like mixed fruit and vegetable drink. Also, Knorr offers a variety of recipes allowing consumers to choose between different tastes, ingredients and preparation times, acknowledging that the time available for cooking varies, as do people's mood, energy and inspiration for cooking.[37]

Sources: http://knorr.ebisu.dk/default.asp; J. Madsen (2007) Smid de traditionelle tøjler overbord, *Børsen*, 13 July 13, 2; M. Fischer Boel (2007) Godt nok er for ringe, *Børsen*, 11 January, 12; Knorr satser sundt med vie, *Mariager Avis*, 23 August 2008, 17.

Consumer decisions are also influenced by **core values**, the belief systems that underlie attitudes and behaviours. Core values go much deeper than behaviour or attitude and determine, at a basic level, people's choices and desires over the long term. In that sense, core values are trans-situational goals that serve the interests of individuals or groups and act as guiding principles in consumers' lives.[38] Marketers who target consumers on the basis of their values believe that with appeals to people's inner selves it is possible to influence their outer selves – their purchase behaviour.

The interaction between dimensions

As individuals we are not born with the value and norms that form a culture, we learn them gradually as we grow older. For this learning process to take place the individual does need to be in contact with other individuals. Such contacts can either be in the form of direct social contacts (e.g. communicating with other individuals) or indirect social contacts (e.g. observing the behaviour or communication carried out by other individuals). In this way the social dimension mediates the cultural and individual dimensions. Although the process of learning takes place within a certain cultural context that is saturated with ready-made knowledge of consumption,[39] individuals should not be seen as passive creatures who automatically adopt values and norms from other individuals – they also have independent thoughts and feelings. For example, values of individuality and uncertainty avoidance – dominant values in Sweden and Greece,[40] respectively – are not automatically transferred to new generations in those countries. Individuals' thoughts and feelings can be used for active construction and reconstruction of knowledge. Moreover, some thoughts and feelings may be shared with other individuals who have similar or different thoughts and feelings. Over time such interactions may even influence values and norms in a society; see 'Marketing insight: Changing cultural norms and values'.

While the individual interacts with the cultural and social settings, the starting point for understanding consumer behaviour is, however, the consumer her-/himself. Reflecting this, the next section reviews the key psychological processes that influence how an individual perceives, evaluates and responds to marketing stimuli.

Marketing insight

Changing cultural norms and values

An example of how values and norms may change over time as people interact in society is found in relation to safe driving. In Denmark, more lives are lost in traffic accidents than in other Northern European countries such as the United Kingdom, Sweden and Norway. As a result, the Danish Road Safety Council has as its objective a decrease in the number of serious traffic accidents in Denmark by 40 per cent by 2012. And one of the ways to achieve this goal is to motivate public debate and to influence people's values, norms and behaviour in relation to traffic safety. The council works to stir public debate on subjects such as speeding and drinking and driving and has been successful with a series of information campaigns renowned for their originality and strong appeals.

As an example, the Danish Road Safety Council launched a campaign called 'Speedbandits' (http://www.speedbandits.dk/) with the purpose of making young drivers aware of how fast they were driving. It had been found that although most young drivers knew the speed limits, many felt that there were 'legitimate' excuses not to remain within these – such as being in a hurry, knowing the road well, believing that they were in control of the situation and only risked their own lives, and so forth. In order to call attention to the notion that we should never speed in traffic, the council embarked upon a viral communication strategy, that is, an advertising message spread by consumers among other

consumers (see Chapter 4). The campaign consisted of a single video film that was distributed on the Internet, via links and Youtube.com. The video mimics a story on a make-believe TV newscast, and tells how the Danes developed new approaches to increasing safety in traffic. From now on, topless girls would stand by the side of the road holding speed signs, to remind drivers of their speed. The campaign was widely circulated and as such initiated communicative interaction between young people who forwarded the link to friends, who forwarded to their friends, and so forth.

The video caused some offence in other Nordic countries, where it was interpreted as a negative portrayal of women. In Denmark, however, Speedbandits was interpreted primarily as a humorous and self-ironic campaign. It remains to be seen how the behaviour of young Danish drivers will develop in future years. In another traffic-related area, however, the Danish Road Safety Council has observed a clear positive change over the years. This change relates to drinking and driving – an issue that is also a top priority for the council. Here, campaigns that encourage being a team player (e.g., by sticking to agreements about who should drive), and encourage intervention (e.g. removing a person's car keys if he or she intends to drive after drinking alcohol) have helped alter values and discourse among the Danes, in the sense that drinking and driving generally has come to be considered completely unacceptable.

Source: Based on: www.rfsf.dk/ (homepage of the Danish Road Safety Council); www.trafikklub.dk/db/files/hver_ulykke_er_en_for_meget_3.pdf.

▽ Key psychological processes

The starting point for understanding consumer behaviour is the stimulus-response model shown in Figure 7.2. Marketing and environmental stimuli enter the consumer's consciousness, and a set of psychological processes combine with certain consumer characteristics to result in decision processes and purchase decisions. The marketer's task is to understand what happens in the consumer's consciousness between the arrival of the outside marketing stimuli and the ultimate purchase decisions. Four key psychological processes – motivation, perception, learning and memory – fundamentally influence consumer responses.[41]

Motivation: Freud, Maslow, Herzberg

We all have many needs at any given time. Some needs are *biogenic*; they arise from physiological states of tension such as hunger, thirst or discomfort. Other needs are *psychogenic*; they arise from psychological states of tension such as the need for recognition, esteem or belonging. A need becomes a **motive** when it is aroused to a sufficient level of intensity to drive us to act in order to reach a desired goal. Motivation has both direction – we select one goal over another; intensity – the vigour with which we pursue the goal; and persistency – is the motivation situational or enduring?

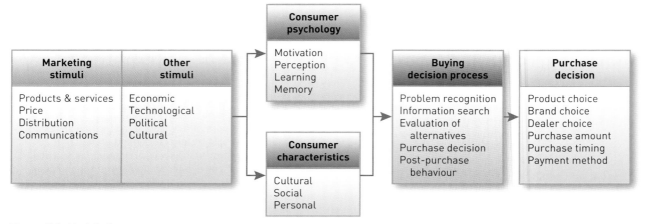

Figure 7.2 Model of consumer behaviour

Three of the best-known theories of human motivation – those of Sigmund Freud, Abraham Maslow and Frederick Herzberg – carry quite different implications for consumer analysis and marketing strategy.

Freud's theory

Sigmund Freud assumed that the psychological forces shaping people's behaviour are largely unconscious, and that a person cannot fully understand, or may not even be aware of, his or her own motivations. When a person examines specific brands, she or he will react not only to their stated capabilities, but also to other, less conscious cues such as shape, size, weight, material, colour and brand name. A technique called *laddering* lets us trace a person's motivations from the stated instrumental ones to the more terminal ones. Then the marketer can decide at what level to develop the message and appeal.[42]

Motivation researchers often conduct 'in-depth interviews' with a few dozen consumers to uncover deeper motives triggered by a product. They use various *projective techniques* such as word association, sentence completion, picture interpretation and role playing, many pioneered by Ernest Dichter, a Viennese psychologist who settled in the United States.[43]

Today motivational researchers continue the tradition of Freudian interpretation. Jan Callebaut identifies different motives a product can satisfy. For example, whisky can meet the need for social relaxation, status or fun. Different whisky brands need to be motivationally positioned in one of these three appeals.[44] Another motivation researcher, Clotaire Rapaille, works on breaking the 'code' behind a lot of product behaviour.[45]

Maslow's theory

Abraham Maslow sought to explain why people are driven by particular needs at particular times.[46] His answer is that human needs are arranged in a hierarchy from most to least pressing – (1) physiological needs, (2) safety needs, (3) social needs, (4) esteem needs, and (5) self-actualisation needs (see Figure 7.3). People will try to satisfy their most important needs first. When a person succeeds in satisfying an important need, he or she will then try to satisfy the next-most-important need. For example, a starving man (need 1) will not take an interest in the latest happenings in the art world (need 5), nor in how he is viewed by others (need 3 or 4), nor even in whether he is breathing clean air (need 2); but when he has enough food and water, the next-most-important need will become salient.

Herzberg's theory

Frederick Herzberg developed a two-factor theory that distinguishes *dissatisfiers* (factors that cause dissatisfaction) from *satisfiers* (factors that cause satisfaction).[47] The absence of dissatisfiers is not enough to motivate a purchase; satisfiers must be present. For example, a computer that does not come with a warranty would be a dissatisfier. Yet the presence of a product warranty

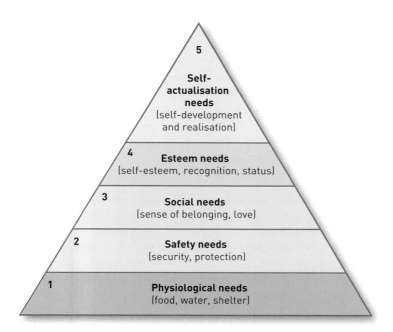

Figure 7.3 Maslow's hierarchy of needs

Source: A. H. Maslow (1970) *Motivation and Personality*, 2nd edn, Upper Saddle River, NJ: Prentice Hall. Reproduced with permission of Pearson Education, Inc.

would not act as a satisfier or motivator of a purchase, because it is not a source of intrinsic satisfaction. Ease of use would be a satisfier.

Herzberg's theory has two implications. First, sellers should do their best to avoid dissatisfiers (for example, a poor training manual or a poor service policy). Although these things will not sell a product, they might easily unsell it. Second, the seller should identify the major satisfiers or motivators of purchase in the market and then supply them. Support for Herzberg's two-factor theory was found in a Danish study investigating the effect of hygiene factors and motivators on visitors' experience and satisfaction with a visit to zoos and aquaria. Bad experiences with hygiene factors such as toilet facilities and eating or refreshment facilities created dissatisfaction with the visit as such, but positive experiences were obviously not capable of creating satisfaction by themselves.[48]

Perception

A motivated person is ready to act. *How* she acts is influenced by her view of the situation. In marketing, perceptions are more important than the reality, because it is perceptions that affect consumers' actual behaviour. **Perception** is the process by which we select, organise and interpret information inputs to create a meaningful picture of the world.[49] The key point is that it depends not only on the physical stimuli, but also on the stimuli's relationship to the surrounding field and on conditions within each of us. One person might perceive a fast-talking salesperson as aggressive and insincere; another, as intelligent and helpful. Each will respond differently to the salesperson. People can emerge with different perceptions of the same object because of three perceptual processes: selective attention, selective distortion and selective retention.

Selective attention

Attention is the allocation of processing capacity to some stimulus. Voluntary attention is something purposeful; involuntary attention is grabbed by someone or something. It is estimated that the average person may be exposed to over 1500 ads or brand communications a day. Because we have limited mental resources we cannot possibly attend to all these, we screen most stimuli out – a process called **selective attention**. Selective attention means that marketers must work hard to attract consumers' notice. The real challenge is to explain which stimuli people will notice. Here are some findings:

1   **People are more likely to notice stimuli that relate to a current need**: A person who is motivated to buy a computer will notice computer ads; he will be less likely to notice DVD ads.

2 **People are more likely to notice stimuli they anticipate**: You are more likely to notice computers than radios in a computer store because you don't expect the store to carry radios.

3 **People are more likely to notice stimuli whose deviations are large in relationship to the normal size of the stimuli**: You are more likely to notice an ad offering €5 off the list price of a bottle of wine than you are likely to notice an ad offering €5 off the list price of a computer. This phenomenon is also known as **Weber's law**.

Though we screen out much, we are influenced by unexpected stimuli, such as sudden offers in the mail, over the phone or from a salesperson. Marketers may attempt to promote their offers intrusively in order to bypass selective attention filters.

Selective distortion

Even noticed stimuli don't always come across in the way the senders intended. **Selective distortion** is the tendency to interpret information in a way that fits our preconceptions. Consumers will often distort information to be consistent with prior brand and product beliefs and expectations.[50]

For a stark demonstration of the power of consumer brand beliefs, consider that in 'blind' taste tests one group of consumers samples a product without knowing which brand it is, while another group knows. Invariably, the groups have different opinions, despite consuming *exactly the same product*.

When consumers report different opinions of branded and unbranded versions of identical products, it must be the case that their brand and product beliefs, created by whatever means (past experiences, marketing activity for the brand, something similar), have somehow changed their product perceptions. We can find examples with virtually every type of product.[51] When Coors changed its label from 'Banquet Beer' to 'Original Draft', consumers claimed the taste had changed even though the formulation had not.

Selective distortion can work to the advantage of marketers with strong brands when consumers distort neutral or ambiguous brand information to make it more positive. In other words, beer may seem to taste better, a car may seem to drive more smoothly, the wait in a bank queue may seem shorter, depending on the particular brands involved.

Selective retention

Most of us don't remember much of the information to which we're exposed, but we do retain information that supports our attitudes and beliefs. Because of **selective retention**, we are likely to remember good points about a product we like and forget good points about competing products. Selective retention again works to the advantage of strong brands. It also explains why marketers need to use repetition – to make sure their message is not overlooked.

Subliminal perception The selective perception mechanisms require consumers' active engagement and thought. A topic that has fascinated armchair marketers for ages is **subliminal perception**. They argue that marketers embed covert, subliminal messages in packaging or ads, for example 'buy it', 'try it', or by displaying an ambiguous image. Consumers are not consciously aware of them, yet they affect behaviour. Although it's clear that our mental processes include many subtle subconscious effects,[52] no evidence supports the notion that marketers can systematically control consumers at that level, especially in terms of changing moderately important or strongly held beliefs.[53]

Learning

When we act, we learn. **Learning** induces changes in our behaviour arising from experience. Most human behaviour is learned, although much learning is incidental. Learning theorists believe that learning is produced through the interplay of drives, stimuli, cues, responses and reinforcement. Two popular approaches to learning are classical conditioning and operant (instrumental) conditioning.

A **drive** is a strong internal stimulus impelling action. **Cues** are minor stimuli that determine when, where and how a person responds. Suppose you buy an HP computer. If your experience is rewarding, your response to computers and HP will be positively reinforced. Later on, when you want to buy a printer, you may assume that because HP makes good computers, it also makes good printers. In other words, you *generalise* your response to similar stimuli. A countertendency to generalisation is discrimination. **Discrimination** means we have learned to recognise differences in sets of similar stimuli and can adjust our responses accordingly; that is, the ability to notice even small differences in product attributes (e.g., taste, smell, freshness) between brands is learned.

Learning theory teaches marketers that they can build demand for a product by associating it with strong drives, using motivating cues, and providing positive reinforcement. A new company can enter the market by appealing to the same drives that competitors use and by providing similar cues, because buyers are more likely to transfer loyalty to similar brands (generalisation); or the company might design its brand to appeal to a different set of drives and offer strong cue inducements to switch (discrimination).

Some researchers prefer more active, cognitive approaches when learning depends upon the inferences or interpretations consumers make about outcomes (was an unfavourable consumer experience due to a bad product or did the consumer fail to follow instructions properly?). The **hedonic bias** says people have a general tendency to attribute success to themselves and failure to external causes. Consumers are thus more likely to blame a product than themselves, putting pressure on marketers to carefully explicate product functions in well-designed packaging and labels, instructive ads and websites, and so on.

Memory

All the information and experiences we encounter as we go through life can end up in our long-term memory. Cognitive psychologists distinguish between **short-term memory (STM)** – a temporary and limited repository of information – and **long-term memory (LTM)** – a more permanent, essentially unlimited repository.

Most widely accepted views of long-term memory structure assume we form some kind of associative model.[54] For example, the **associative network memory model** views LTM as a set of nodes and links. *Nodes* are stored information connected by *links* that vary in strength. Any type of information can be stored in the memory network, including verbal, visual, abstract and contextual. A spreading activation process from node to node determines how much we retrieve and what information we can actually recall in any given situation. When a node becomes activated because we are encoding external information (when we read or hear a word or phrase) or retrieving internal information from LTM (when we think about some concept), other nodes are also activated if they are strongly enough associated with that node.

In this model, we can think of consumer brand knowledge as a node in memory with a variety of linked associations. The strength and organisation of these associations will be important determinants of the information we can recall about the brand. **Brand associations** consist of all brand-related thoughts, feelings, perceptions, images, experiences, beliefs, attitudes, and so on that become linked to the brand node.

▽ Bahlsen

Germany's largest cookie company takes an unusual tack to embed cues in consumers' minds so that the next time they're in the cookie aisle, they'll reach for Bahlsen cookies. Bahlsen is concentrating on a mostly neglected aspect of the cookie-eating experience: sound. Steffen Heise, Bahlsen's director of R&D, says, 'Imagine, you would see a cookie on a plate and it looks very crunchy, it appears crunchy and when you eat it, you would find something very soft and unpleasant.' Bahlsen has hired a team of testers who use special microphones in their ears to record the crunching. Then Bahlsen adjusts the dough recipes to get just the right crunch. For cookies aimed at young people, Bahlsen aims for a loud, crisp, exciting sound. Elderly people, they have found, are not interested in noisy or stressful situations and prefer a softer crunch. While all this may sound a little far-fetched, sound design in other industries has been part of the brand experience for a long time. Engineers fiddle with everything from the buzz of an electric razor to the way a car door sounds when it slams – all to create a pleasing subconscious association for the consumer.

Source: K. James (2006) Getting that crunching sound just right, *Marketplace*, 15 December. American Public Media.

Figure 7.4 Brand beliefs among German students for the Internet auction site eBay

Source: T. Klein Reesink (2004) Conceptual brand mapping: a web-based approach to collect brand knowledge and its interpretation using network analysis, in A. J. Cañas, J. D. Novak and F. M. González (eds.) *Concept Maps: Theory, Methodology, Technology*, Proceedings of the First International Conference on Concept Mapping. Pamplona, Spain 2004, Figure 1, p. 3 Copyright © Dr Thomas Klein Reesink. Reproduced with permission.

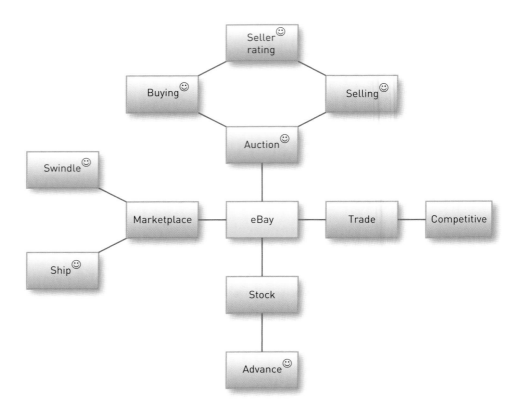

We can think of marketing as a way of making sure consumers have the right types of product and service experiences to create the right brand knowledge structures and maintain them in memory. Companies such as Procter & Gamble like to create mental maps (i.e., representations of how consumers' perceive the physical world) of consumers that depict their knowledge of a particular brand in terms of the key associations that are likely to be triggered in a marketing setting, and their relative strength, favourability and uniqueness to consumers. Figure 7.4 displays a simple mental map highlighting brand beliefs among German students for the popular Internet auction site eBay.[55]

Memory processes

Memory is a very constructive process, because we don't remember information and events completely and accurately. Often we remember bits and pieces and fill in the rest based upon whatever else we know.

Memory encoding describes how and where information gets into memory. The strength of the resulting association depends on how much we process the information at encoding (how much we think about it, for instance) and in what way.[56]

In general, the more attention we pay to the meaning of information during encoding, the stronger the resulting associations in memory will be.[57] When a consumer actively thinks about and 'elaborates' on the significance of product or service information, stronger associations are created in memory. It's also easier for consumers to create an association to new information when extensive, relevant knowledge structures already exist in memory. One reason personal experiences create such strong brand associations is that information about the product is likely to be related to existing knowledge.

The ease with which we can integrate new information into established knowledge structures also clearly depends on its simplicity, vividness and concreteness. Repeated exposures to information, too, provide greater opportunity for processing and thus the potential for stronger associations. Recent advertising research in a field setting, however, suggests that high levels of repetition for an uninvolving, unpersuasive ad are unlikely to have as much sales impact as lower levels of repetition for an involving, persuasive ad.[58]

Memory retrieval

Memory retrieval is the way information gets out of memory. According to the associative network memory model, a strong brand association is both more accessible and more easily recalled by 'spreading activation'. Our successful recall of brand information doesn't depend only on the initial strength of that information in memory. Three factors are particularly important.

First, the presence of *other* product information in memory can produce interference effects and cause us to either overlook or confuse new data. One marketing challenge in a category crowded with many competitors – for example airlines, financial services and insurance companies – is that consumers may mix up brands.

Second, the time between exposure to information and encoding matters – the longer the time delay, the weaker the association. The time elapsed since the last exposure opportunity, however, has been shown generally to produce only gradual decay. Cognitive psychologists believe memory is extremely durable, so that once information becomes stored in memory, its strength of association decays very slowly.[59]

Third, information may be *available* in memory but not be *accessible* (able to be recalled) without the proper retrieval cues or reminders. The particular associations for a brand that come to mind depend on the context in which we consider it. The more cues linked to a piece of information, however, the greater the likelihood that we can recall it. The effectiveness of retrieval cues is one reason marketing *inside* a supermarket or any retail store is so critical – the actual product packaging, the use of in-store minibillboard displays, and so on. The information they contain and the reminders they provide of advertising or other information already conveyed outside the store will be prime determinants of consumer decision making.

Memory can often be reconstructive, however, and consumers may remember an experience with a brand differently after the fact due to intervening factors or other events.[60]

▽ Perspectives on consumer behaviour

Understanding consumer behaviour may often be complicated since many different factors influence the behaviour and since many different forms of behaviour exist. Several perspectives on consumer behaviour can be considered.

The behaviourist perspective

The behaviourist perspective focuses on the impact of external influences on consumer behaviour. In the behaviourist perspective the consumer is viewed as a 'black box' in the sense that the consumer's behaviour is a conditioned response to marketing stimuli. The complex mental processes that a consumer may undertake in relation to a certain choice situation are not given much attention in the behaviourist perspective and therefore this perspective is also often referred to as an S (stimuli)–R (response) approach. Classical conditioning and operant conditioning are two main theories that have been developed to explain the stimuli–response mechanism.

In classical conditioning a stimuli with a 'known', or unconditioned, response (for example, a lightening is regarded by most people as something powerful, fresh and natural) is paired with a stimuli with a 'neutral' response (for example, a chewing-gum brand). After several exposures to the two stimuli paired together the consumer gradually learns to associate the chewing gum brand with – for a chewing gum producer – the very favourable characteristics of a lightening. Classical conditioning is very often used in advertising – an example is the advertising campaign for Ota Solgryn (a cereal), which is associated with the former and highly popular Danish football star Michael Laudrup. After a number of repetitions, it is hoped that the positive feelings for Michael Laudrup will transfer to the Ota Solgryn brand.

Operant conditioning presupposes that consumers are likely to repeat a behaviour for which they are positively rewarded (reinforced). For example, if a consumer receives a friendly smile when shopping at a retail outlet she may be more likely to shop there again than if she has been ignored or, even worse, been exposed to a rude employee. While classical and operant conditioning are both part of the behaviourist perspective they differ on when the learning takes place. In classical conditioning the learning of associations between stimuli takes place before the response, whereas learning in operant conditioning learning takes place after the response.

The information processing perspective

The information processing perspective emerged in consumer behaviour in the 1960s and 1970s and considers how consumers mentally process, store, retrieve and use marketing information in the decision process. The information processing perspective posits that the interaction between the consumer and marketing information is an ongoing cognitive process in which the consumer develops beliefs and attitudes towards the marketing offer. The information processing perspective presupposes that consumers behave as problem-solving cognitive individuals reaching for a reasoned decision.[61] The 'hierarchy of effects' information processing model[62] suggests that a stimuli is first processed at its most basic level and then at more abstract levels. Consumers are expected to use their cognitive resources in forming beliefs (cognitive component) about the attributes of a product, which in turn may result in the development of an overall feeling or attitude (affective component) in the sense of liking/disliking a product. Consumers with a positive attitude towards a product are expected to be more willing to consider buying it (conative component) than consumers with a less positive attitude towards the same product.

The direct marketing implication of the information processing perspective is that in order to sell their products and services, marketers should expose consumers to information about their offers. Consumers are assumed to use the information actively for the purpose of completing five decision-making activities, including problem recognition, information search, alternative evaluation, choice, and post-purchase evaluation in which problem recognition and information search relate to the cognitive component, alternative evaluation relates to the cognitive and the affective components, choice relates to the conative component, and post-purchase evaluation relates to the cognitive and affective components. The Volvo website shown in the photo opposite illustrates how market communication sometimes reflects the information processing perspective.

The emotional perspective

In contrast to the information processing perspective, the emotional perspective proposes that consumer affections, like emotional responses, should be included in the explanation of consumer decision making.[63] The consumer looks for new experiences via consumption. In this connection, the primary purpose is not to evaluate relations between attitude, beliefs and the environment, but to fulfil a desire and to obtain pleasure in life. Emotions are caused by consumers' exposure to specific stimuli. Surprise (an emotion) for instance may be caused by an unexpected gift. The emotional perspective complements the information processing perspective on consumer behaviour by taking into account consumers' affective responses, like the possible emotional responses to the perception and judgement of products and consumption experiences. Consumer emotions have been shown to have several significant effects. Positive emotions can make one kinder, more generous, more resistant to temptation and more willing to delay self-rewards.[64] Consumers' emotions may also lead to action. As an example, the experience of a rude employee of a service company may lead to some internal reactions, such as 'displeasure'. These internal reactions may lead to complaints by the consumer. Emotions are based on the appraisals (i.e., conscious or unconscious judgement and interpretation of stimuli) consumers make of stimuli in the environment.[65] A consumer who perceives a product to be of 'good quality' may form an affective response to this appraisal. It is not the product itself that may produce an emotional response, but the consumer's perception and

Marketing communication reflecting the information processing perspective.

Source: Courtesy of Volvo Car Corporation

judgement of the product. For example, a consumer may feel differently about a favourite food product after learning that this particular product contains higher levels of salt, sugar or fat than expected.

The cultural perspective

Over the last decades consumer researchers have been increasingly interested in the cultural aspects of consumer behaviour. In the cultural perspective, marketing is seen as a value transmitter that simultaneously shapes culture and is shaped by it. Marketing is then a channel through which cultural meanings are transferred to consumer goods.[66] In this way culture is the 'prism' through which consumers view products and try to make sense of their own and other people's consumer behaviour.[67] Products should therefore also be regarded as symbols – objects that represent beliefs, norms and values. While symbols may be used in this way for communication among social groups, marketing can also use symbols when positioning their products. Products are not bought just because they may deliver some wanted functional consequences – they are also bought because of their appearance, colour and name. The popularity of designer bags, sunglasses or shoes from, for example, Marc Jacobs, Dolce & Gabbana or Gucci is an example of this notion. However, the symbolic associations consumers attach to various appearances, colours and names may vary widely across cultures. To exemplify, the Starbucks brand was found to have very different meanings to local coffee shop patrons in Seattle, who felt a sense of pride in the success Starbucks has experienced in recent years, and to young Japanese coffee shop visitors, who tended to view Starbucks as a symbol of an exciting, fashionable, contemporary lifestyle contrasting restrictive local traditions.[68]

A multiperspective approach

Consumers do not have unlimited mental resources available for receiving, evaluating and using information.[69] Often therefore consumers do not undertake comparative evaluations of various brands and associated attributes for the purpose of reaching a reasonable decision as presupposed in the information processing perspective. Since the consumers' processing capacity is limited, consumers cannot process large amounts of cognitive information in relation to all choice situations and they may therefore seek to direct their use of mental resources at the information most easily available[70] or at the information offering the greatest relevant knowledge per used resource unit in the eyes of the consumer. Also, research results show that consumers might favour beliefs which are in accordance with a preferred conclusion.[71] Moreover, consumers who have strongly held preferences are likely to counter-argue preference-inconsistent information more than preference-consistent information.[72] These findings suggest that there is a resistance to devoting resources to change already established preferences and that consumers therefore may sometimes look for simple associations between product and expected benefit, which reinforce their established preferences or support their preferred conclusion. In this way, the behaviourist perspective complements the information processing perspective.

Also, the relationship between emotions and cognition remains an issue in psychology and in consumer behaviour. Most consumer researchers[73] believe that we do not become emotional about unimportant things, but about values, goals, intentions, plans, and so on. In other words, we cognitively perceive and evaluate what is happening in the environment and this 'knowledge' needs to be associated with personal relevant issues (e.g., personal well-being, well-being of relevant others, etc.) for an emotion to occur. Consumers' underlying evaluations of a situation combine to elicit specific emotions. For example, someone who has wrecked their car because they were talking on their mobile telephone and was therefore distracted may experience guilt, whereas someone whose car was wrecked by someone to whom they lent their car may be angry.[74] In other words, cognitions and emotions arise as a result of an interaction between consumers, objects and situations – and this interaction may differ across cultures and subcultures. When studying consumer behaviour it is therefore important that none of the different perspectives are excluded beforehand, but that the analyst keeps an open mind to various explanations for consumers' behaviour.

▽ The buying decision process: the five-stage model

Psychological processes play an important role in understanding how consumers actually make their buying decisions.[75] Table 7.2 provides a list of some key consumer behaviour questions in terms of 'who, what, when, where, how and why'.

Smart companies try to fully understand the customers' buying decision process – all their experiences in learning, choosing, using and even disposing of a product.[76] Bissel developed its Steam n' Clean vacuum cleaner based on the product trial experiences of a local PTA group near corporate headquarters in Grand Rapids, Michigan. The result was a name change, colour-coded attachments, and an infomercial highlighting its special features.[77]

Marketing scholars have developed a 'stage model' of the buying decision process (see Figure 7.5). The consumer passes through five stages: problem recognition, information search, evaluation of alternatives, purchase decision, and post-purchase behaviour. Clearly, the buying process starts long before the actual purchase and has consequences long afterwards.[78]

Table 7.2 Understanding consumer behaviour

Who buys our product or service?
Who makes the decision to buy the product?
Who influences the decision to buy the product?
How is the purchase decision made? Who assumes what role?
What does the customer buy? What needs must be satisfied?
Why do customers buy a particular brand?
Where do they go or look to buy the product or service?
When do they buy? Any seasonality factors?
How is our product perceived by customers?
What are customers' attitudes towards our product?
What social factors might influence the purchase decision?
Do customers' lifestyles influence their decisions?
How do personal or demographic factors influence the purchase decision?

Source: Based on list from G. Belch and M. Belch (2004) *Advertising and Promotion*, 6th edn, Homewood, IL: Irwin. Copyright © 2004 McGraw-Hill Companies. Reproduced with permission.

Figure 7.5 Five-stage model of the consumer buying process

```
        ┌─────────────────┐
        │    Problem      │
        │  recognition    │
        └─────────────────┘
                 │
                 ▼
        ┌─────────────────┐
        │   Information   │
        │     search      │
        └─────────────────┘
                 │
                 ▼
        ┌─────────────────┐
        │   Evaluation    │
        │  of alternatives│
        └─────────────────┘
                 │
                 ▼
        ┌─────────────────┐
        │    Purchase     │
        │    decision     │
        └─────────────────┘
                 │
                 ▼
        ┌─────────────────┐
        │  Post–purchase  │
        │    behaviour    │
        └─────────────────┘
```

Consumers don't always pass through all five stages in buying a product. They may skip or reverse some. When you buy your regular brand of toothpaste, you go directly from the need for toothpaste to the purchase decision, skipping information search and evaluation. The model in Figure 7.5 provides a good frame of reference, however, because it captures the full range of considerations that arise when a consumer faces a highly involving new purchase.[79]

Problem recognition

The buying process starts when the buyer recognises a problem or need triggered by internal or external stimuli. With an internal stimulus, one of the person's normal needs – hunger, thirst, sex – rises to a threshold level and becomes a drive; or a need can be aroused by an external stimulus. A person may admire a neighbour's new car or see a television ad for a Hawaiian holiday, which triggers thoughts about the possibility of making a purchase.

Marketers need to identify the circumstances that trigger a particular need by gathering information from a number of consumers. They can then develop marketing strategies that trigger consumer interest. Particularly for discretionary purchases such as luxury goods, holidays and entertainment options, marketers may need to increase consumer motivation so a potential purchase gets serious consideration.

Information search

Surprisingly, consumers often search for limited amounts of information. Surveys have shown that for durables, half of all consumers look at only one shop, and only 30 per cent look at more than one brand of appliance. We can distinguish between two levels of involvement with search. The milder search state is called *heightened attention.* At this level a person simply becomes more receptive to information about a product. At the next level, the person may enter an *active information search:* looking for reading material, phoning friends, going online and visiting shops to learn about the product.

Information sources

Major information sources to which consumers will turn fall into four groups:

- **Personal**: family, friends, neighbours, acquaintances;
- **Commercial**: advertising, websites, salespeople, dealers, packaging, displays;
- **Public**: mass media, consumer-rating organisations;
- **Experiential**: handling, examining, using the product.

The relative amount and influence of these sources vary with the product category and the buyer's characteristics. Generally speaking, the consumer receives the most information about a product from commercial – that is, marketer-dominated – sources. However, the most effective information often comes from personal sources or public sources that are independent authorities.

Each information source performs a different function in influencing the buying decision. Commercial sources normally perform an information function, whereas personal sources perform a legitimising or evaluation function. For example, doctors often learn of new drugs from commercial sources but turn to other doctors for evaluations.

Search dynamics

Through gathering information, the consumer learns about competing brands and their features. The first box in Figure 7.6 shows the *total set* of brands available to the consumer. The individual consumer will come to know only a subset of these brands, the *awareness set*. Some brands, the *consideration set,* will meet initial buying criteria. As the consumer gathers more information, only a few, the *choice set,* will remain strong contenders. The consumer makes a final choice from this set.[80]

Marketers need to identify the hierarchy of attributes that guide consumer decision making in order to understand different competitive forces and how these various sets get formed. This process of identifying the hierarchy is called **market partitioning**. Years ago, most car buyers first decided on the manufacturer and then on one of its car divisions (*brand-dominant hierarchy*). A buyer might favour General Motors' cars and, within this set, a Saab. Today, many buyers decide first on the nation from which they want to buy a car (*nation-dominant hierarchy*). Buyers may first decide they want to buy a Japanese car, then Toyota, and then the Corolla model of Toyota.

The hierarchy of attributes can also reveal customer segments. Buyers who first decide on price are price dominant; those who first decide on the type of car (sports, passenger, estate car) are type dominant; those who first decide on the car brand are brand dominant. Type/price/brand-dominant consumers make up a segment; quality/service/type buyers make up another. Each segment may have distinct demographics, psychographics and mediagraphics and different awareness, consideration and choice sets.[81]

Figure 7.6 makes it clear that a company must strategise to get its brand into the prospect's awareness, consideration and choice sets. As another example, if a food shop owner arranges yogurt first by brand (such as Danone and Yoplait) and then by flavour within each brand, consumers will tend to select their flavours from the same brand. However, if all the strawberry yogurts are

Figure 7.6
Successive sets involved in consumer decision making

together, then all the vanilla and so forth, consumers will probably choose which flavours they want first, and then choose the brand name they want for that particular flavour. Australian supermarkets arrange meats by the way they might be cooked, and shops use more descriptive labels, such as 'a 10-minute herbed beef roast'. The result is that Australians buy a greater variety of meats than US shoppers, who choose from meats laid out by animal type – beef, chicken, pork, and so on.[82]

The company must also identify the other brands in the consumer's choice set so that it can plan the appropriate competitive appeals. In addition, the company should identify the consumer's information sources and evaluate their relative importance. Asking consumers how they first heard about the brand, what information came later, and the relative importance of the different sources will help the company prepare effective communications for the target market.

Evaluation of alternatives

How does the consumer process competitive brand information and make a final value judgement? No single process is used by all consumers, or by one consumer in all buying situations. There are several processes, and the most current models see the consumer forming judgements largely on a conscious and rational basis.

Some basic concepts will help us understand consumer evaluation processes: first, the consumer is trying to satisfy a need. Second, the consumer is looking for certain benefits from the product solution. Third, the consumer sees each product as a bundle of attributes with varying abilities for delivering the benefits sought to satisfy this need. The attributes of interest to buyers vary by product – for example:

1   **Hotels**: location, cleanliness, atmosphere, price;

2   **Mouthwash**: colour, effectiveness, germ-killing capacity, taste/flavour, price;

3   **Tyres**: safety, tread life, ride quality, price.

Consumers will pay the most attention to attributes that deliver the sought-after benefits. We can often segment the market for a product according to attributes important to different consumer groups.

Beliefs and attitudes

Through experience and learning, people acquire beliefs and attitudes. These in turn influence buying behaviour. A **belief** is a descriptive thought that a person holds about something. Just as important are **attitudes**, a person's enduring favourable or unfavourable evaluations, emotional feelings and action tendencies towards some object or idea.[83] People have attitudes towards almost everything: religion, politics, clothes, music, food. Attitudes put us into a frame of mind: liking or disliking an object, moving towards or away from it. They lead us to behave in a fairly consistent way toward similar objects. Because attitudes economise on energy and thought, they can be very difficult to change. A company is often well advised to fit its product into existing attitudes rather than to try to change attitudes. For instance, Arla Foods ran an ad campaign with the slogan 'Good Food Deserves Lurpak' (a butter brand). To many, butter may not be interesting in itself, but because of what it does to the taste experience of a well-prepared meal. Hence, the basic idea was to remind consumers of an existing attitude, namely that Lurpak tastes better than competing brands and products.[84]

Here's another example of a campaign that reminds consumers of their attitudes.

▽ **Six a day**

The 'six-a-day' campaign was launched as a research and development project in 1999, based on research findings that eating more fruit and vegetables was preventive to such illnesses as cancer, heart disease, obesity and diabetes. The objective was to persuade Danish consumers to eat more fruit and vegetables – and the recommended amount was 600 g – or roughly six pieces of fruit or vegetables a day. Research had shown that most consumers were well aware of the health benefits of eating fruit and vegetables. However, research also showed that many consumers found previous health campaigns untrustworthy and irrelevant to them. So, the campaign's intention was to to increase relevance and influence behaviour by reminding consumers of their positive attitudes towards eating fruit and vegetables. This was done by:

- providing information on the health benefits of eating fruit and vegetables;
- communicating ideas of how to prepare and serve fruit and vegetables to ensure eating as close as possible to the recommended amount of 600 g each day;
- working to make it easier to get fruit and vegetables, for instance in schools.

The campaign was designed by a number of governmental agencies and non-profit organisations, including the Danish Cancer Society, the Danish Veterinary and Food Administration, the Danish Heart Foundation, among others, which joined forces to broaden knowledge and relevance of the 'six-a-day' recommendation through a number of different channels and strategies, such as the design of a shared logo, the creation of inspiring promotional material and active participation in events, meetings, presentations, and so on. As regards media coverage, this campaign employed the Internet, newsletters, trade journals and the popular press, but shied away from advertising in 'regular' media such as TV, radio and magazines.

In just five years, the 'six-a-day' campaign helped increase average consumption of fruit and vegetables per day by 100 g (to 379 g) for adults, and by 40 g (to 322 g) for children, and it is highly likely that the campaign will run at least until 2011.[85]

Expectancy-value model

The consumer arrives at attitudes towards various brands through an attribute evaluation procedure.[86] She develops a set of beliefs about where each brand stands on each attribute. The **expectancy-value model** of attitude formation posits that consumers evaluate products and services by combining their brand beliefs – the positives and negatives – according to importance.

Suppose Swedish student Helena Olsson has narrowed her choice set to four laptop computers (A, B, C, D). Assume she's interested in four attributes: memory capacity, graphics capability, size and weight, and price. Table 7.3 shows her beliefs about how each brand rates on the four attributes. If one computer dominated the others on all the criteria we could predict that Helena would choose it. But, as is often the case, her choice set consists of brands that vary in their appeal. If Helena wants the best memory capacity, she should buy A; if she wants the best graphics capability, she should buy B; and so on.

Table 7.3 A consumer's brand beliefs about laptop computers

Computer	Attribute			
	Memory capacity	Graphics capability	Size and weight	Price
A	10	8	6	4
B	8	9	8	3
C	6	8	10	5
D	4	3	7	8

Note: Each attribute is rated from 0 to 10, where 10 represents the highest level on that attribute. Price, however, is indexed in a reverse manner, with a 10 representing the lowest price, because a consumer prefers a low price to a high price.

If we knew the weights Helena attaches to the four attributes we could more reliably predict her computer choice. Suppose she assigned 40 per cent of the importance to the computer's memory capacity, 30 per cent to graphics capability, 20 per cent to size and weight and 10 per cent to price. To find Helena's perceived value for each computer, according to the expectancy-value model, we multiply her weights by her beliefs about each computer's attributes. This computation leads to the following perceived values:

Computer A = 0.4(10) + 0.3(8) + 0.2(6) + 0.1(4) = 8.0
Computer B = 0.4(8) + 0.3(9) + 0.2(8) + 0.1(3) = 7.8
Computer C = 0.4(6) + 0.3(8) + 0.2(10) + 0.1(5) = 7.3
Computer D = 0.4(4) + 0.3(3) + 0.2(7) + 0.1(8) = 4.7

An expectancy-model formulation predicts that Helena will favour computer A, which (at 8.0) has the highest perceived value.[87]

Suppose most computer buyers form their preferences the same way. Knowing this, the marketer of computer B, for example, could apply the following strategies to stimulate greater interest in brand B:

- **Redesign the computer:** This technique is called *real repositioning*.
- **Alter beliefs about the brand:** Attempting to alter beliefs about the brand is called *psychological repositioning*.
- **Alter beliefs about competitors' brands:** This strategy, called *competitive depositioning*, makes sense when buyers mistakenly believe a competitor's brand has more quality than it actually has.
- **Alter the importance weights:** The marketer could try to persuade buyers to attach more importance to the attributes in which the brand excels.
- **Call attention to neglected attributes:** The marketer could draw buyers' attention to neglected attributes, such as styling or processing speed.
- **Shift the buyer's ideals:** The marketer could try to persuade buyers to change their ideal levels for one or more attributes.[88] For example, changing buyers' opinion regarding the ideal size for a computer.

Purchase decision

In the evaluation stage, the consumer forms preferences among the brands in the choice set. The consumer may also form an intention to buy the most preferred brand. In executing a purchase intention, the consumer may make up to five subdecisions: brand (brand A), dealer (dealer 2), quantity (one computer), timing (weekend) and payment method (credit card).

Non-compensatory models of consumer choice

The expectancy-value model is a compensatory model, in that perceived good things for a product can help to overcome perceived bad things. But consumers often take 'mental short cuts' using simplifying choice heuristics. **Heuristics** are rules of thumb or mental short cuts in the decision process.

With **non-compensatory models** of consumer choice, positive and negative attribute considerations don't necessarily net out. Evaluating attributes in isolation makes decision making easier for a consumer, but it also increases the likelihood that he would have made a different choice if he had deliberated in greater detail. We highlight three such choice heuristics here.

1 With the **conjunctive heuristic**, the consumer sets a minimum acceptable cut-off level for each attribute and chooses the first alternative that meets the minimum standard for all attributes. For example, if Helena decided all attributes had to rate at least a 5, she would choose computer C. She would not chose computers A, B or D since computers A and B rate only 4 and 3, respectively, on price, and computer D rates only 4 on memory capacity and 3 on graphics capability.

2 With the **lexicographic heuristic**, the consumer chooses the best brand on the basis of its perceived most important attribute (i.e., memory capacity). With this decision rule, Helena would choose computer A, which has the highest rate on this attribute.

3 With the **elimination-by-aspects heuristic**, the consumer compares brands on an attribute selected probabilistically – where the probability of choosing an attribute is positively related to its importance – and eliminates brands that do not meet minimum acceptable cut offs.

Our brand or product knowledge, the number and similarity of brand choices and time pressure involved, and the social context (such as the need for justification to a peer or boss) may all affect whether and how we use choice heuristics.[89]

Consumers don't necessarily use only one type of choice rule. Sometimes they adopt a phased decision strategy that combines two or more. For example, they might use a non-compensatory decision rule such as the conjunctive heuristic to reduce the number of brand choices to a more manageable number, and then evaluate the remaining brands. One reason for the runaway success of the Intel Inside campaign in the 1990s was that it made the brand the first cut-off for many consumers – they would only buy a personal computer that had an Intel microprocessor. Personal computer makers such as IBM, Dell and Gateway had no choice but to support Intel's marketing efforts.

Intervening factors

Even if consumers form brand evaluations, two general factors can intervene between the purchase intention and the purchase decision (Figure 7.7).[90] The first is the *attitudes of others.* The extent to which another person's attitude reduces our preference for an alternative depends on two things: (1) the intensity of the other person's negative attitude toward our preferred alternative; and (2) our motivation to comply with the other person's wishes.[91] The more intense the other person's negativism and the closer the other person is to us, the more we will adjust our purchase intention. The converse is also true.

Related to the attitudes of others is the role played by suppliers of consumer and market information who publish their evaluations. Examples include *Consumer Reports,* which provides unbiased expert reviews of all types of products and services; J.D. Power, which provides consumer-based ratings of cars, financial services and travel products and services; professional film, book and music reviewers; customer reviews of books and music on Amazon.com; and the increasing number of chatrooms, bulletin boards, blogs, and so on where people discuss products, services and companies. Consumers are undoubtedly influenced by these evaluations, as evidenced by the success of a small-budget film such as *Napoleon Dynamite,* which cost only €270,000 to make but grossed over €30 million at the box office in 2004 thanks to a slew of favourable reviews by cinemagoers on many websites.

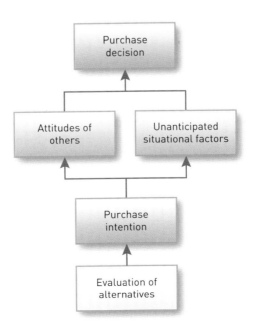

Figure 7.7 Steps between evaluation of alternatives and a purchase decision

The second factor is *unanticipated situational factors* that may erupt to change the purchase intention. Helena might lose her job, some other purchase might become more urgent, or a store salesperson may turn her off. Preferences and even purchase intentions are not completely reliable predictors of purchase behaviour.

A consumer's decision to modify, postpone or avoid a purchase decision is heavily influenced by *perceived risk*.[92] Consumers may perceive many types of risk in buying and consuming a product:

1 **Functional risk**: The product does not perform up to expectations.
2 **Physical risk**: The product poses a threat to the physical well-being or health of the user or others.
3 **Financial risk**: The product is not worth the price paid.
4 **Social risk**: The product results in embarrassment from others.
5 **Psychological risk**: The product does not conform to the consumer's perceived self-image.
6 **Time risk**: The failure of the product results in an opportunity cost of finding another satisfactory product.

The amount of perceived risk varies with the amount of money at stake, the amount of attribute uncertainty and the amount of consumer self-confidence. Consumers develop routines for reducing the uncertainty and negative consequences of risk, such as decision avoidance, information gathering from friends, and preferences for national brand names and warranties. Marketers must understand the factors that provoke a feeling of risk in consumers and provide information and support to reduce perceived risk.

Post-purchase behaviour

After the purchase, the consumer might experience dissonance that stems from noticing certain disquieting features or hearing favourable things about other brands and will be alert to information that supports his or her decision. Marketing communications should supply beliefs and evaluations that reinforce the consumer's choice and help them feel good about the brand.

The marketer's job doesn't therefore end with the purchase. Marketers must monitor post-purchase satisfaction, post-purchase actions and post-purchase product uses.

Post-purchase satisfaction

Satisfaction is a function of the closeness between expectations and the product's perceived performance.[93] If performance falls short of expectations, the consumer is *disappointed*; if it meets expectations, the consumer is *satisfied*; if it exceeds expectations, the consumer is *delighted*. These feelings make a difference in whether the customer buys the product again and talks favourably or unfavourably about it to others.

The larger the gap between expectations and performance, the greater the dissatisfaction. Here the consumer's coping style comes into play. Some consumers magnify the gap when the product isn't perfect and are highly dissatisfied; others minimise it and are less dissatisfied.[94]

Post-purchase actions

If the consumer is satisfied, she is more likely to purchase the product again. The satisfied customer will also tend to say good things about the brand to others. On the other hand, dissatisfied consumers may abandon or return the product. They may seek information that confirms its high value. They may take public action by complaining to the company, going to a lawyer or complaining to other groups (such as business, private or government agencies). Private actions include deciding to stop buying the product (*exit option*) or warning friends (*voice option*).[95]

Many companies seek to build long-term brand loyalty through CRM programmes. Post-purchase communications to buyers have been shown to result in fewer product returns and order cancellations. Computer companies, for example, can send a letter to new owners congratulating them on having selected a fine computer. They can place ads showing satisfied brand owners. They can solicit customer suggestions for improvements and list the location of available services.

Figure 7.8 How customers use or dispose of products

Source: J. Jacoby, C. K. Berning and T. F. Dietvorst (1977) What about disposition?, *Journal of Marketing*, July, 23. Reprinted with permission of the American Marketing Association.

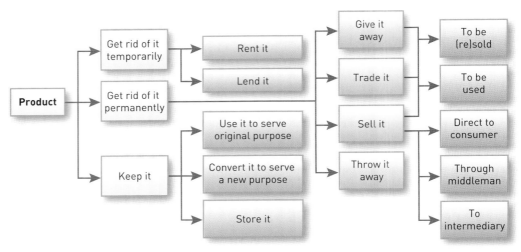

They can write intelligible instruction booklets. They can send owners a magazine containing articles describing new computer applications. In addition, they can provide good channels for speedy redress of customer grievances.

Post-purchase use and disposal

Marketers should also monitor how buyers use and dispose of the product (Figure 7.8). A key driver of sales frequency is product consumption rate – the more quickly buyers consume a product, the sooner they may be back in the market to repurchase it.

One opportunity to increase frequency of product use occurs when consumers' perceptions of their usage differ from reality. Consumers may fail to replace products with relatively short life spans soon enough because they overestimate its product life.[96] One strategy to speed up replacement is to tie the act of replacing the product to a certain holiday, event or time of year.

For example, Duracell has run battery promotions tied in with the springtime switch to daylight savings time. Another strategy is to provide consumers with better information about either: (1) when they first used the product or need to replace it; or (2) its current level of performance. Batteries have built-in gauges that show how much power they have left; toothbrushes have colour indicators to indicate when the bristles are worn; and so on. Perhaps the simplest way to increase usage is to learn when actual usage is less than recommended and persuade customers of the merits of more regular usage, overcoming potential hurdles.

If consumers throw the product away the marketer needs to know how they dispose of it, especially if – as with batteries, beverage containers, electronic equipment and disposable nappies – it can damage the environment. There is increasing pressure on companies to manage their businesses in an environmentally responsible way. Knowing consumers' disposal behaviour enables companies to be better informed about appropriate disposal behaviour.

One way to increase frequency of purchase is to remind consumers when it's time to replace batteries or toothbrushes.

Source: Courtesy of Procter & Gamble UK

▽ Other theories of consumer decision making

The consumer decision process may not always develop in a carefully planned fashion. Here are some other theories and approaches to explain it.

Level of consumer involvement

The expectancy-value model assumes a high level of involvement on the part of the consumer. We can define **consumer involvement** in terms of the level of engagement and active processing the consumer undertakes in responding to a marketing stimulus. A high-involved consumer is more likely to process a large amount of cognitive information. Celsi and Olson (1988: 211) conceptualise involvement as follows: 'like most consumer researchers, we view perceived personal relevance as the essential characteristic of involvement'.[97] Consumers may be involved in buying a product for various reasons, and different consumers may not be involved for the same reason. Consumers may purchase perfume because of its capacity to give pleasure, whereas consumers are more likely to focus on avoiding the negative consequences of a bad choice when buying a vacuum cleaner.[98] In general, factors such as high price, high perceived risk and high product heterogeneity are likely to increase the degree of consumer involvement.

Elaboration likelihood model

Psychologists Richard Petty and John Cacioppo's *elaboration likelihood model*, an influential model of attitude formation and change, describes how consumers make evaluations in both low- and high-involvement circumstances.[99] There are two means of persuasion in their model: the *central route*, where attitude formation or change stimulates much thought and is based on a diligent, rational consideration of the most important product information; and the *peripheral route*, where attitude formation or change provokes much less thought and results from the association of a brand with either positive or negative peripheral cues. *Peripheral cues* for consumers include a celebrity endorsement, a credible source, or any object that generates positive feelings.

Consumers follow the central route only if they possess sufficient motivation, ability and opportunity. In other words, consumers must want to evaluate a brand in detail, have the necessary brand and product or service knowledge in memory, and have sufficient time and the proper setting. If any of those factors is lacking, consumers tend to follow the peripheral route and consider less central, more extrinsic factors in their decisions.

Low-involvement marketing strategies

Many products are bought under conditions of low involvement and the absence of significant brand differences. Consider salt. Consumers have little involvement in this product category. If they keep reaching for the same brand, it's out of habit, not strong brand loyalty. Evidence suggests consumers have low involvement with most low-cost, frequently purchased products.

Marketers use four techniques to try to convert a low-involvement product into one of higher involvement. First, they can link the product to some involving issue, as when Crest linked its toothpaste to avoiding cavities. Second, they can link the product to some involving personal situation – for example, fruit juice makers began to include vitamins such as calcium to fortify their drinks. Third, they might design advertising to trigger strong emotions related to personal values or ego defence, as when cereal makers began to advertise to adults the heart-healthy nature of cereals and the importance of living a long time to enjoy family life. Fourth, they might add an important feature – as for example when Sony PlayStation and Microsoft Xbox launched options for multiplayer online gaming. These strategies at best raise consumer involvement from a low to a moderate level; they do not necessarily propel the consumer into highly involved buying behaviour.

If, regardless of what the marketer can do, consumers will have low involvement with a purchase decision, they are likely to follow the peripheral route. Marketers must pay special attention to giving consumers one or more positive cues to justify their brand choice. For instance, frequent ad repetition, visible sponsorships and vigorous PR are all ways to enhance brand familiarity.

Other peripheral cues that can tip the balance in favour of the brand include a beloved celebrity endorser, attractive packaging, and an appealing promotion.[100]

Variety-seeking buying behaviour

Some buying situations are characterised by low involvement but significant brand differences. Here consumers often do a lot of brand switching. Think about cookies. The consumer has some beliefs about cookies, chooses a brand without much evaluation, and evaluates the product during consumption. Next time, the consumer may reach for another brand out of a desire for a different taste. Brand switching occurs for the sake of variety rather than dissatisfaction.

The market leader and the minor brands in this product category have different marketing strategies. The market leader will try to encourage habitual buying behaviour by dominating the shelf space with a variety of related but different product versions, avoiding out-of-stock conditions, and sponsoring frequent reminder advertising. Challenger firms will encourage variety seeking by offering lower prices, deals, coupons, free samples, and advertising that tries to break the consumer's purchase and consumption cycle and presents reasons for trying something new.

The theory of planned behaviour

In contrast to the low-involvement, variety seeking situations, the theory of planned behaviour (Figure 7.9) is concerned with situations where consumers are involved and motivated to conduct an in-depth evaluation of the expected outcome of various choices before the purchase is made. TPB is an extension of its precursor the theory of reasoned action (TRA). TRA regards a consumer's behaviour as determined by the consumer's behavioural intention, where behavioural intention is a function of 'attitude towards the behaviour' (i.e., the general feeling of favourableness or unfavourableness for that behaviour) and 'subjective norm' (i.e., the perceived opinion of other people in relation to the behaviour in question).[101] The theory predicts intention to perform a behaviour by consumer's attitude towards that behaviour rather than by the consumer's attitude towards a product or service. In the model, attitude is based on the consumer's behavioural beliefs – a behavioural belief is the subjective probability that a certain behaviour will produce a given outcome. Also, a consumer's intention to perform a certain behaviour may be influenced by the normative social beliefs held by the consumer. As an example, a consumer might have a very favourable attitude towards having a drink before dinner at a restaurant. However, the intention to actually order the drink may be influenced by the consumer's beliefs about the appropriateness (i.e., the perceived social norm) of ordering a drink in the current situation (with friends for a fun meal or on a job interview) and her/his motivation to comply with those normative beliefs.[102] TRA is concerned with rational, volitional and systematic behaviour, that is, behaviours over which the individual has control.[103] This assumption has been widely

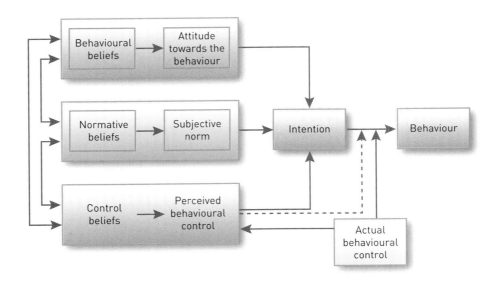

Figure 7.9 The theory of planned behaviour

Source: I. Aizen (2006) TpB diagram (retrieved from www.people.umass.edu/aizen/tpb.diag.html). Copyright © 2006 Icek Aizen. Reproduced with permission.

criticised. For example, a consumer may be prevented from buying groceries online if the consumer perceives the purchase process as too complex or if the consumer does not possess the resources necessary to perform the considered behaviour. Such considerations are incorporated into TPB.[104] In comparison with TRA, TPB adds 'perceived behavioural control' as a determinant of behavioural intention. TPB is therefore an extension of TRA. PBC can be conceptualised as the consumer's subjective belief about how difficult it will be for that consumer to generate the behaviour in question. PBC is determined by the total set of accessible control beliefs, that is, beliefs about the presence of factors that may facilitate or impede performance of the behaviour.[105] For instance, a consumer may be keen to go to a very popular concert yet, knowing that it will be difficult to get tickets, she may give up her intention without even trying to realise it.

Means end chains

In the means-end chain model (MEC model), products are not purchased for themselves or their characteristics, but rather for the meanings they engender in the mind of the consumer (e.g., buying this product would make me happy, would be good for my healthiness, or something similar). The MEC model explores the meanings a consumer attaches to a product through the construction of an associative network, which consists of attributes, functional consequences, psychosocial consequences and values. In this way, the MEC model proposes that consumer knowledge structures are hierarchically organised, referring to different levels of abstraction.[106] While attributes are the distinct characteristics of a product such as consistency, price, colour, size, ingredients, and so on, functional consequences are the tangible outcomes of using the product. For example, a new toothbrush might brush your teeth gently and effectively. Psychosocial consequences, in contrast, describe the psychological and social outcomes of the product. For example, having clean teeth might make you feel more attractive and comfortable. Values are centrally held cognitive elements that trigger motivation for behaviour, referring to more abstract concepts such as self-esteem, health or happiness. The means-end-approach assumes that consumers regard products as means to important ends. That is, the personal consequences produced by a product are more important (more self-relevant) than the characteristics of the product itself. A product is self-relevant to the extent a consumer sees it as instrumental in achieving important consequences or values.[107] As an example, a large (and growing) proportion of consumers view the Internet (and hence Internet access) as an indispensable and central component of their lives. To these consumers, Internet services have been integrated in daily routines and are seen as helping them to cope with everyday stress and difficulties.[108]

Decision heuristics and biases

We have seen that consumers don't always process information or make decisions in a deliberate, rational manner. 'Marketing insight: How consumers really make decisions' highlights some recent advances from the thriving academic study of how consumers make decisions.[109]

Behavioural decision theorists have identified many different heuristics (rules of thumb or mental short cuts in the decision process) and biases in everyday consumer decision making. They come into play when consumers forecast the likelihood of future outcomes or events.[110]

1 **Availability heuristic:** Consumers base their predictions on the quickness and ease with which a particular example of an outcome comes to mind; that is, an example that is easily brought to mind is considered as representative of future outcomes. However, if an example comes to mind too easily, consumers might overestimate the likelihood of its happening. For example, a recent product failure may lead a consumer to inflate the likelihood of a future product failure and make him more inclined to purchase a product warranty.

2 **Representativeness heuristic:** Consumers base their predictions on how representative or similar the outcome is to other examples. One reason that package appearances may be so similar for different brands in the same product category is that they want to be seen as representative of the category as a whole.

Marketing insight

How consumers really make decisions

One of the most active academic research areas in marketing is behavioural decision theory (BDT). Researchers have uncovered many fascinating influences and outcomes in consumer decision making, often challenging predictions from economic theory and assumptions about rationality.[109]

- Consumers are more likely to choose an alternative (a home bread maker) after a relatively inferior option (a slightly better but significantly more expensive home bread maker) is added to the choice set.

- Consumers are more likely to choose an alternative that appears to be a compromise in the particular choice set under consideration.

- The choices that consumers make influence their assessment of their own tastes.

- Shifting attention to one of two considered alternatives tends to enhance the perceived attractiveness and choice probability of that alternative.

- The manner in which consumers compare products that vary in terms of price and perceived quality (features, brand name) and the way those products are displayed in the shop (by brand or by model type) affect their willingness to pay more for additional features or a better-known brand.

- Consumers who think about the possibility that their purchase decisions will turn out to be wrong are more likely to choose better-known brands.

- Consumers for whom possible feelings of regret are made more relevant are more likely to choose a product that is currently on sale rather than wait for a better sale or buy a higher-priced item.

- Consumers' choices are influenced by subtle (and theoretically inconsequential) changes in the way alternatives are described.

- Consumers who make purchases for later consumption appear to make systematic errors in predicting their future preferences.

  - Consumer's predictions of their future tastes are not accurate – they do not really know how they will feel after consuming the same flavour of yogurt or ice cream several times.

  - Consumers often overestimate the duration of their overall emotional reactions to future events

(films, financial windfalls, outcomes of sporting events).

- Consumers often overestimate their future consumption, especially if there is limited availability (which may explain why Black Jack and other chewing gums have higher sales when availability is limited to several months per year than when they are offered year round).

- In anticipating future consumption opportunities, consumers often assume they will want or need more variety than they actually do.

- Consumers are less likely to choose alternatives with product features or promotional premiums that have little or no value, even when these features and premiums are optional (such as the opportunity to purchase a Collector's Plate) and do not reduce the actual value of the product in any way.

- Consumers are less likely to choose products selected by other consumers for reasons that they find irrelevant, even though these other reasons would not suggest anything positive or negative about the products' values.

- Consumers' interpretations and evaluations of past experiences are greatly influenced by the ending and trend of events. A positive event at the end of a service experience can colour later reflections and evaluations of the experience as a whole.

What all these and other studies reinforce is that consumer behaviour is very constructive and that the context of decisions really matters. Understanding how these effects show up in the marketplace can be crucial for marketers.

Sources: For an overview of some issues involved, see J. R. Bettman, M. F. Luce and J. W. Payne (1998) Constructive consumer choice processes, *Journal of Consumer Research*, 25, 187–217; I. Simonson (1993) Getting closer to your customers by understanding how they make choices, *California Management Review*, 35 (Summer), 68–84. For examples of classic studies in this area, see some of the following: D. Ariely and Z. Carmon (2000) Gestalt characteristics of experiences: the defining features of summarized events, *Journal of Behavioral Decision Making*, 13(2), 191–201; R. Dhar and K. Wertenbroch (2000) Consumer choice between hedonic and utilitarian goods, *Journal of Marketing Research*, 37 (February), 60–71; I. Simonson and A. Tversky (1992) Choice in context: tradeoff contrast and extremeness aversion, *Journal of Marketing Research*, 29 (August), 281–95; I. Simonson (1990) The effects of purchase quantity and timing on variety-seeking behavior, *Journal of Marketing Research*, 27 (May), 150–62.

3 **Anchoring and adjustment heuristic:** Consumers arrive at an initial judgement and then adjust it based on additional information. For services marketers, it is critical to make a strong first impression to establish a favourable anchor, so that subsequent experiences are interpreted in a more favourable light.

Note that marketing managers also may use heuristics and be subject to biases in their decision making. 'Marketing memo: Decision traps' reveals 10 common mistakes managers make in their decisions.

Mental accounting

Researchers have found that consumers use mental accounting when they handle their money.[111] **Mental accounting** refers to the way consumers code, categorise and evaluate financial outcomes of choices. Formally, it is

> the tendency to categorize *funds* or items of value even though there is no logical *basis* for the categorization, e.g., individuals often segregate their savings into separate accounts to meet different goals even though funds from any of the accounts can be applied to any of the goals.[112]

For example, assume you spend €35 to buy a ticket to see a concert.[113] As you arrive at the show, you realise you've lost your ticket. You may be unsure about purchasing another ticket for €35. Assume, on the other hand, that you realise you lost €35 on the way to buy the ticket in the first place. You might be much more likely to go ahead and buy the ticket anyway. Although you lost the same amount in each case – €35 – in the first case, you may have mentally allocated €35 for going to a concert. Buying another ticket would exceed your mental concert budget. In the second case, the money you lost did not belong to any account, so you had not yet exceeded your mental concert budget.

Marketing memo

Decision traps

In *Decision Traps*, Jay Russo and Paul Schoemaker reveal the ten most common mistakes managers make in their decisions.

1 **Plunging in** – beginning to gather information and reach conclusions without taking a few minutes to think about the crux of the issue you're facing or how you believe decisions like this one should be made.

2 **Allowing frame blindness** – setting out to solve the wrong problem because you've created a mental framework for your decision with little thought, causing you to overlook the best options or to lose sight of important objectives.

3 **Lacking frame control** – failing to consciously define the problem in more ways than one, or being unduly influenced by the frames of others.

4 **Being overconfident in your judgement** – failing to collect key factual information because you are too sure of your assumptions and opinions.

5 **Using shortsighted shortcuts** – relying inappropriately on 'rules of thumb' such as implicitly trusting the most readily available information or anchoring too much on convenient facts.

6 **Shooting from the hip** – believing you can keep straight all the information you've discovered, 'winging it'

rather than following a systematic procedure when making the final choice.

7 **Allowing group failure** – assuming that with many smart people involved, good choices will follow automatically, and therefore failing to manage the group decision-making process.

8 **Fooling yourself about feedback** – failing to interpret the evidence from past outcomes for what it really says, because you are protecting your ego or hindsight effects trick you.

9 **Not keeping track** – assuming that experience will make its lessons available automatically, and therefore failing to keep systematic records to track the results of your decisions and analyse them in ways that reveal their key lessons.

10 **Failing to audit your decision process** – failing to create an organised approach to understanding your own decision making, so you remain constantly exposed to all the other nine decision traps.

Sources: J. E. Russo and P. J. H. Schoemaker (1990) *Decision Traps: Ten Barriers to Brilliant Decision Making and How to Overcome Them*, New York: Doubleday; see also J. E. Russo and P. J. H. Schoemaker (2001) *Winning Decisions: Getting It Right the First Time*, New York: Doubleday.

According to professor of Behavioural Science and Economics, Richard H. Thaler, mental accounting is based on four key core principles:[114]

1 Consumers tend to *segregate gains.* When a seller has a product with more than one positive dimension, it is desirable to have the consumer evaluate each dimension separately. Listing multiple benefits of a large industrial product, for example, can make the sum of the parts seem greater than the whole.

2 Consumers tend to *integrate losses.* Marketers have a distinct advantage in selling something if its cost can be added to another large purchase. House buyers are more inclined to view additional expenditures favourably given the high price of buying a house.

3 Consumers tend to *integrate smaller losses with larger gains.* The 'cancellation' principle might explain why withholding taxes from monthly pay packets is less aversive than large, lump-sum tax payments – the smaller withholdings are more likely to be absorbed by the larger pay amount.

4 Consumers tend to *segregate small gains from large losses.* The 'silver lining' principle might explain the popularity of rebates on big-ticket purchases such as cars.

The principles of mental accounting are derived in part from prospect theory. **Prospect theory** maintains that consumers frame their decision alternatives in terms of gains and losses according to a value function. Consumers are generally loss averse. They tend to over-weight very low probabilities and under-weight very high probabilities.

Profiling the customer buying decision process

How can marketers learn about the stages in the buying process for their product? They can think about how they themselves would act, in the *introspective method.* They can interview a small number of recent purchasers, asking them to recall the events leading to their purchase, in the *retrospective method.* They can use the *prospective method* to locate consumers who plan to buy the product and ask them to think out loud about going through the buying process, or they can ask consumers to describe the ideal way to buy the product, in the *prescriptive method.* Each method yields a picture of the steps in the process.

Trying to understand the customer's behaviour in connection with a product has been called mapping the customer's *consumption system*,[115] *customer activity cycle*,[116] or *customer scenario.*[117] Marketers can do this for such activity clusters as doing laundry, preparing for a wedding or buying a car. The latter, for example, includes a whole cluster of activities – choosing the car, financing the purchase, buying insurance, buying accessories, and so on.

▽ SUMMARY

1 Consumer behaviour is influenced by three factors: cultural (culture, subculture and social class); social (reference groups, family, and social roles and statuses); and personal (age, stage in the life cycle, occupation, economic circumstances, lifestyle, personality and self-concept). Hence, the study of consumer behaviour can be divided into three interdependent dimensions: (1) the study of culture; (2) the study of social groups; (3) the study of the individual. Research into all these factors can provide marketers with clues to reach and serve consumers more effectively.

2 Virtually all human societies exhibit social stratification, most often in the form of social classes, relatively homogeneous and enduring divisions in a society, hierarchically ordered and with members who share similar values, interests and behaviour.

3 Social factors such as reference groups, family, and social roles and statuses affect consumers' buying behaviour.

4 The family is the most important consumer buying organisation in society, and family members constitute the most influential primary reference group.

5 While the individual interacts with the cultural and social settings, the starting point for understanding consumer behaviour is the consumer her-/himself. A consumer's decisions are influenced by several

personal characteristics including the buyer's age and stage in the life cycle; occupation and economic circumstances; personality and self-concept; and lifestyle and values.

6 Four main psychological processes affect consumer behavior: motivation, perception, learning and memory.

7 To understand how consumers actually make buying decisions, marketers must identify who makes and has input into the buying decision; people can be initiators, influencers, deciders, buyers or users. Different marketing campaigns might be targeted to each type of person.

8 The typical buying process consists of the following sequence of events: problem recognition, information search, evaluation of alternatives, purchase decision and post-purchase behaviour. The marketers' job is to understand the behaviour at each stage. The attitudes of others, unanticipated situational factors and perceived risk may all affect the decision to buy, as will consumers' levels of post-purchase product

satisfaction, use and disposal and actions on the part of the company.

9 Consumers are constructive decision makers and subject to many contextual influences. Consumers often exhibit low involvement in their decisions, using many heuristics as a result.

10 Understanding consumer behaviour may often be complicated since many different factors influence the behaviour and since many different forms of behaviour exist. Perspectives on consumer behaviour include the behaviourist perspective, the information processing perspective, the emotional perspective and the cultural perspective. When studying consumer behaviour it is therefore important that none of the different perspectives are excluded beforehand, but that the analyst keeps an open mind to various explanations for consumers' behaviour.

11 Researchers have found that consumers use mental accounting when they handle their money. Mental accounting refers to the way consumers code, categorise and evaluate financial outcomes of choices.

▽ APPLICATIONS

Marketing debate

Is target marketing ever bad? As marketers increasingly develop marketing programmes tailored to certain target market segments, some critics have denounced these efforts as exploitive. For example, the preponderance of billboards advertising cigarettes, alcohol and other vices in low-income urban areas is seen as taking advantage of a vulnerable market segment. Critics can be especially harsh in evaluating marketing programmes that target minority groups, claiming they often employ stereotypes and inappropriate depictions. Others counter that targeting and positioning is critical to marketing and that these marketing programmes are an attempt to be relevant to a certain consumer group.

Take a position: Targeting minorities is exploitative *versus* Targeting minorities is sound business practice.

Marketing discussion

What are your mental accounts? What mental accounts do you have in your mind about purchasing

products or services? Do you have any rules you employ in spending money? Are they different from what other people do? Do you follow Thaler's four principles in reacting to gains and losses?

Marketing exercises

- In your opinion what are the ten most important topics/issues to be learned from this chapter?
- Pick one of the companies mentioned in this chapter. For this company, investigate and discuss: (a) Do you think that any of the ten topics/issues you identified could be related to the problems, or opportunities, that the company – in your opinion – is currently facing or could expect to be facing in the near future? (b) Why?
- In your opinion, what should the company do to deal with the identified problems or to take advantage of the identified opportunities?

▽ REFERENCES

[1] Based on C. McCarthy (2007) ComScore's latest numbers: worldwide social-networking growth, 31 July (www.news.com/8301-13577_3-9752857-36.html); C. McCarthy (2007) Facebook ads makes a flashy debut in New York, 6 November (www.news.com/8301-13577_3-9811932-36.html); E. Barsky and M. Purdon (2006) Introducing web 2.0: social networking and social bookmarking for health librarians, *JCHLA/JABSC*, 27; R. Hof (2007) Facebook declares new era for advertising, *BusinessWeek*, 6 November (www.businessweek.com/the_thread/techbeat/archives/2007/11/facebook_declar.html); C. Holahan (2007) Facebook: marketers are your 'friends', *BusinessWeek*, 7 November (www.businessweek.com/technology/content/nov2007/tc2007116_289111.htm?chan=search)

[2] Input to this chapter from Duke University's Jim Bettman and John Lynch and Stanford University's Itamar Simonson is gratefully acknowledged. For an academic overview of the field of consumer research, see I. Simonson, Z. Carmon, R. Dhar, A. Drolet and S. M Nowlis (2001) Consumer research: in search of identity, *Annual Review of Psychology*, 52, 249–75.

[3] J. P. Peter, J. C. Olson and K. G. Grunert (1999) *Consumer Behaviour and Marketing Strategy*, European edn., Maidenhead, England: McGraw Hill, 264.

[4] S. A. Grier, A. Brumbaugh and C. G. Thornton (2006) Crossover dreams: consumer responses to ethnic-oriented products *Journal of Marketing*, 70 (April), 35–51.

[5] http://www.worldatlas.com/webimage/countrys/eu.htm.

[6] http://ess.nsd.uib.no/files/2003/ESS1SocialClassReport.pdf; http://www.iser.essex.ac.uk/esec/desc/steps/step4.6.php.

[7] T. U. Thomsen and E. B. Sørensen (2006) The first four-wheeled status symbol: pram consumption as a vehicle for the construction of motherhood identity, *Journal of Marketing Management*, 22(9–10), 907–27.

[8] L. G. Schiffman and L. L. Kanuk (2004) *Consumer Behavior*, 8th edn, Upper Saddle River, NJ: Pearson Prentice Hall.

[9] L. F. Feick and L. L. Price (1987) The market maven: a diffuser of marketplace information, *Journal of Marketing*, 51 (January), 83–97.

[10] J. M. Jensen (1991) Family purchase decisions: a buying centre approach, Proceedings of the 5th Biannual International Conference of The Academy of Marketing Science, Copenhagen, CBS, 332–7; E. S. Moore, W. L. Wilkie and R. J. Lutz (2002) Passing the torch: intergenerational influences as a source of brand equity, *Journal of Marketing*, April, 17–37; R. Boutilier (1993) Pulling the family's strings, *American Demographics*, August, 44–8; D. J. Burns (1992) Husband–wife innovative consumer decision making: exploring the effect of family power, *Psychology & Marketing*, May–June, 175–89; R. L. Spiro (1983) Persuasion in family decision making, *Journal of Consumer Research*, March, 393–402. For cross-cultural comparisons of husband–wife buying roles, see J. B. Ford, M. S. LaTour and T. L. Henthorne (1995) Perception of marital roles in purchase-decision processes: a cross-cultural study, *Journal of the Academy of Marketing Science*, Spring, 120–31.

[11] K. M. Palan and R. E. Wilkes (1997) Adolescent–parent interaction in family decision making, *Journal of Consumer Research*, 24, 2, March, 159–69; S. E. Beatty and S. Talpade (1994) Adolescent influence in family decision making: a replication with extension, *Journal of Consumer Research*, 21 (September), 332–41.

[12] P. E. Davis-Kean (2005) The influence of parent education and family income on child achievement: the indirect role of parental expectations and the home environment, *Journal of Family Psychology*, 19, 2, 294–304; P. Webley and E. K. Nyhus (2006) Parents' influence on children's future orientation and saving, *Journal of Economic Psychology*, 27, 1, 140–64; E. R. DeVore, R. B. Ginsburg (2005) The protective effects of good parenting on adolescents: adolescent medicine, *Current Opinion in Pediatrics*, 17(4), 460–5.

[13] Chenting Su, E. F. Fern and Keying Ye (2003) A temporal dynamic model of spousal family purchase-decision behavior, *Journal of Marketing Research*, 40, August, 268–81; C. Kwai-Choi Lee and B. A. Collins (2000) Family decision making and coalition patterns, *European Journal of Marketing*, 34, 9/10, 1181–98; Z. Mottiar and D. Quinn (2004) 'Couple dynamics in household tourism decision making: women as the gatekeepers?, *Journal of Vacation Marketing*, 10(2), 149–60.

[14] H. Chura (2002) Failing to connect: marketing messages for women fall short, *Advertising Age*, 23 (September), 13–14.

[15] http://www.kelloggs.dk/spk.aspx; http://www2.kelloggs.com/brand/brand.aspx?brand=215&cat=specialk; http://www.jotun.dk/www/dk/20030027.nsf!OpenDatabase&mt=&l=no.

[16] R. G. Westergaard (2006) Børnene bestemmer, *FoodCulture*, 28, p. 6.

[17] J. Tinson and C. Nancarrow; (2007) GROwing up: tweenagers' involvement in family decision making, *Journal of Consumer Marketing*, 24, 3, 160–70; A. Shoham and V. Dalakas (2005) 'He said, she said . . . they said: parents' and children's assessment of children's influence on family consumption decisions, *Journal of Consumer Marketing*, 3, 152–60.

[18] J. Bayot (2003) The teenage market; young, hip, and looking for a bargain, *New York Times*, 1 December

[19] D. R. John (1999) Consumer socialization of children: a retrospective look at twenty-five years of research, *Journal of Consumer Research*, December, 183–213; Lan Nguyen Chaplin and D. R. John (2005) The development of self-brand connections in children and adolescents, *Journal of Consumer Research*, June, 119–29.

[20] http://webshop.englishshop.se/en/article/205/mcdougalls_bob_the_builder_muffin_mix; http://www.heroesforkids.co.uk/erol.html#588X0.

[21] http://www.massgeneral.org/children/adolescenthealth/articles/aa_adolescent_clothing.aspx.

[22] http://epp.eurostat.ec.europa.eu/portal/page?_pageid=2173,45972494&_dad=portal&_schema=PORTAL&mo=containsall&ms=family&saa=&p_action=SUBMIT&l=dk&co=equal&ci=,&po=matchany&pi=1130671,0&an=product_type&ao=containsall&av=lTY_&as=0&ad=text&na=1&ob=41,0.

[23] R. Y. Du and W. A. Kamakura (2006) Household life cycles and lifestyles in the United States, *Journal of Marketing Research*, 48, February 121–32; L. Lepisto (1985) A life span perspective of consumer behavior, E. Hirshman and M. Holbrook (eds) in *Advances in Consumer Research*, vol. 12, Provo, UT: Association for Consumer Research, 47. Also see G. Sheehy (1995) *New Passages: Mapping Your Life across Time*, New York: Random House.

[24] See F. Herzberg (1966) *Work and the Nature of Man*, Cleveland, OH: William Collins; H. Thierry and A. M. Koopman-Iwerna, (1984) Motivation and satisfaction in P. J. Drenth (ed.), *Handbook of Work and Organizational Psychology*, New York: John Wiley & Sons, 141–2.

[25] P. C. M. Govers and J. P. L. Schoormans (2005) Product personality and its influence on consumer preference, *Journal of Consumer*

Marketing, 22, 4, 189–97; H. H. Kassarjian and M. J. Sheffet (1981) Personality and consumer behavior: an update in H. H. Kassarjian and T. S. Robertson (eds) *Perspectives in Consumer Behavior*, Glenview, IL: Scott, Foresman, 160–80.

[26]J. Aaker (1997) Dimensions of measuring brand personality, *Journal of Marketing Research*, 34 (August), 347–56.

[27]J. L. Aaker, V. Benet-Martinez and J. Garolera (2001) Consumption symbols as carriers of culture: a study of Japanese and Spanish brand personality constructs, *Journal of Personality and Social Psychology*, 81(3), 492–508.

[28]Yongjun Sung and S. F. Tinkham (2005) Brand personality structures in the United States and Korea: common and culture-specific factors, *Journal of Consumer Psychology*, 15(4) (December), 334–50.

[29]M. J. Sirgy (1982) Self concept in consumer behavior: a critical review, *Journal of Consumer Research*, 9 (December), 287–300.

[30]T. R. Graeff (1997) Consumption situations and the effects of brand image on consumers brand evaluations, *Psychology & Marketing*, 14, 1, January, 49–70; T. R. Graeff (1996) Image congruence effects on product evaluations: the role of self-monitoring and public/private consumption, *Psychology & Marketing*, 13(5) (August), 481–99.

[31]J. L. Aaker (1999) The malleable self: the role of self-expression in persuasion,' *Journal of Marketing Research*, 36(1), (February), 45–57.

[32]http://www.porternovelli.com/site/pressrelease.aspx?pressrelease_id=171&pgname=news.

[33]http://www.nuovon.com.au/LOHAS/tabid/53/Default.aspx [accessed October 2007].

[34]A. Cortese (2003) They care about the world (and they shop too), *New York Times*, 20 July.

[35]A. Banco and W. Zellner (2003) Is Wal-Mart too powerful?, *BusinessWeek*, 6 October, 100.

[36]T. Weber (2003) All three? Gee, *Wireless Review*, May, 12–14.

[37]N. C. Paul (2003) Meal kits in home, *Christian Science Monitor*, 9 June, 13.

[38]S. H. Schwartz and L. Sagiv (1995) Identifying culture-specifics in the content and structure of values, *Journal of Cross-Cultural Psychology*, 26, 92–116.

[39]F. Cram and Sik Hung Ng (1999) Consumer socialisation, *Applied Psychology: An International Review*, 48(3), 297–312.

[40]http://www.geert-hofstede.com/hofstede_greece.shtml; http://www.geert-hofstede.com/hofstede_sweden.shtml.

[41]For a review of current academic research on consumer behaviour, see Consumer psychology: categorization, inferences, affect, and persuasion, *Annual Review of Psychology*, 57, 2006, 453–95. To learn more about how consumer behaviour theory can be applied to policy decisions, see Special issue on helping consumers help themselves: improving the quality of judgments and choices, *Journal of Public Policy & Marketing*, 25(1), Spring 2006.

[42]T. J. Reynolds and J. Gutman (1988) Laddering theory, method, analysis, and interpretation, *Journal of Advertising Research*, February–March, 11–34.

[43]E. Dichter (1964) *Handbook of Consumer Motivations*, New York: McGraw-Hill.

[44]J. Callebaut, M. Janssens, D. Lorré and H. Hendrick (1994) *The Naked Consumer: The Secret of Motivational Research in Global Marketing*, Antwerp: Censydiam Institute.

[45]M. Wells (2003) Mind games, *Forbes*, 1 September, 70.

[46]A. Maslow (1954) *Motivation and Personality*, New York: Harper and Row, 80–106.

[47]See F. Herzberg (1966) *Work and the Nature of Man*, Cleveland, OH: William Collins; Thierry and Koopman-Iwerna (1984) op. cit.

[48]J. M. Jensen (2007) The relationships between hygiene factors, motivators satisfaction and response among visitors to zoos and aquaria', *Tourism Review International*, special issue on Zoos, Aquaria and other Captive Wildlife Attractions, 11(3), 307–16.

[49]B. Berelson and G. A. Steiner (1964) *Human Behavior: An Inventory of Scientific Findings*, New York: Harcourt Brace Jovanovich, 88.

[50]J. E. Russo, M. G. Meloy, and V. H. Medvec (1998) The distortion of product information during brand choice, *Journal of Marketing Research*, 35 (November), 438–52.

[51]L. de Chernatony and S. Knox (1990) How an appreciation of consumer behavior can help in product testing, *Journal of Market Research Society*, July, 333. See also C. Janiszewski and S. M. J. Osselar (2000) A connectionist model of brand–quality association, *Journal of Marketing Research*, August, 331–51.

[52]Florida's Chris Janiszewski has developed a fascinating research programme looking at preconscious processing effects. See C. Janiszewski (1993) Preattentive mere exposure effects, *Journal of Consumer Research*, 20, December, 376–92, as well as some of his earlier and subsequent research. For more perspectives, see also J. A. Bargh and T. L. Chartrand (1999) The unbearable automaticity of being, *American Psychologist*, 54, 462–79 and the research programmes of both authors. For lively academic debate, see Research dialogue, section of the July 2005 issue of the *Journal of Consumer Psychology*.

[53]See T. E. Moore (1982) Subliminal advertising: what you see is what you get, *Journal of Marketing*, 46, Spring, 38–47 for an early classic; and A. B. Aylesworth, R. C. Goodstein and A. Kalra (1999) Effect of archetypal embeds on feelings: an indirect route to affecting attitudes?, *Journal of Advertising*, 28(3), Fall, 73–81 for a more current treatment.

[54]R. S. Wyer Jr. and T. K. Srull (1989) Person memory and judgment, *Psychological Review*, 96, 1, January, 58–83; J. R. Anderson (1983) *The Architecture of Cognition*, Cambridge, MA: Harvard University Press.

[55]T. K. Reesink (2004) Conceptual brand mapping: a Web-based approach to collecting brand knowledge and its interpretation using network analysis, in A. J. Cañas, J. D. Novak and F. M. González (eds): Concept Maps: Theory, Methodology, Technology, Proceedings of the First Int. Conference on Concept Mapping, Pamplona, Spain.

[56]For additional discussion, see J. G. Lynch Jr. and T. K. Srull (1982) Memory and attentional factors in consumer choice: concepts and research methods, *Journal of Consumer Research*, 9, June, 18–36; and J. W. Alba, J. W. Hutchinson and J. G. Lynch Jr. (1992) Memory and decision making, in ed. H. H. Kassarjian and T. S. Robertson (eds) *Handbook of Consumer Theory and Research*, Englewood Cliffs, NJ: Prentice Hall, 1–49.

[57]R. S. Lockhart, F. I. M. Craik and L. Jacoby (1976) Depth of processing, recognition, and recall, in J. Brown (ed.) *Recall and Recognition*, New York: John Wiley & Sons; F. I. M. Craik and E. Tulving (1975) Depth of processing and the retention of words in episodic memory, *Journal of Experimental Psychology*, 104(3), September, 268–94; F. I. M. Craik and R. S. Lockhart (1972) Levels of processing: a framework for memory research, *Journal of Verbal Learning and Verbal Behavior*, 11, 671–84.

[58]L. M. Lodish, M. Abraham, S. Kalmenson, J. Livelsberger, B. Lubetkin, B. Richardson and M. E. Stevens (1995). How TV advertising works: a meta-analysis of 389 real world split cable

TV advertising experiments, *Journal of Marketing Research,* 32, May, 125–39.

[59]E. F. Loftus and G. R. Loftus (1980) On the permanence of stored information in the human brain, *American Psychologist,* 35, May, 409–20.

[60]K. A. Braun (1999) Postexperience advertising effects on consumer memory, *Journal of Consumer Research,* 25, March, 319–32.

[61]P. Østergaard and C. Jantzen (2000) Shifting perspectives in consumer research: from buyer behavior to consumption studies in S.C. Beckmann and R.H. Elliot (eds), *Interpretive Consumer Research: Paradigms, Methodologies and Applications*, Copenhagen: Handelshøjskolens Forlag, 9–23.

[62]R. Lavidge and G. A. Steiner (1961) A model for predictive measurements of advertising, *Journal of Marketing*, October, 59–62.

[63]F. Hansen and S. R. Christensen (2007) *Emotions, Advertising and Consumer Choice*, Copenhagen: Business School Press.

[64]W. R. Swinyard (1993) The effects of mood, involvement, and quality of store experience on shopping intentions, *Journal of Consumer Research*, 20, 271–80.

[65]R. P. Bagozzi, M. Gopinath and U. N. Prashanth (1999) The role of emotions in marketing, *Journal of the Academy of Marketing Science*, 27(2), 184–206.

[66]M. P. Pachauri (2002) Consumer behaviour: a literature review, *The Marketing Review*, 2, 319–55; G. McCracken (1988) *Culture and Consumption: New Approaches to the Symbolic Character of Consumer Goods and Activities*, Bloomington, IN: Indiana University Press.

[67]M. Solomon, G. Bamossy and S. Askegaard (2002) *Consumer Behaviour: A European Perspective,* 2nd eds, Harlow: Financial Times–Prentice Hall.

[68]C. J. Thompson and Z. Arsel (2004) The starbucks brandscape and consumers (anticorporate) experiences of glocalization, *Journal of Consumer Research,* 31 (December), 631–42.

[69]F. Hansen (1972) *Consumer Choice Behavior: A Cognitive Theory*, New York and London: Free Press/Macmillan; J. R. Bettman, M. F. Luce and J. W. Payne (1998) Constructive consumer choice processes, *Journal of Consumer Research*, 25 (December), 187–217.

[70]I. Simonson (1999) The effect of product assortment on buyer preferences, *Journal of Retailing*, 75(3), 347–70.

[71]Z. Kunda (1990) The case for motivated reasoning, *Psychological Bulletin*, 108(3), 480–98.

[72]S. P. Jain and D. Maheswaran (2000) Motivated reasoning: a depth-of-processing perspective, *Journal of Consumer Research,* 26, 358–71.

[73]See for example R. S. Lazarus (1991) Progress on a cognitive-motivational-relational theory of emotion, *American Psychologist,* 46, 8, 819–34; R. P. Bagozzi, M. Gopinath and U. N. Prashanth (1999) The role of emotions in marketing, *Journal of the Academy of Marketing Science*, 27(2), 184–206.

[74]L. Watson and M. T. Spence (2007) Causes and consequences of emotions on consumer behaviour: a review and integrative cognitive appraisal theory, *European Journal of Marketing*, 41(5–6), 487–511.

[75]For a comprehensive review of the academic literature on decision making see J. E. Russo and K. A. Carlson (2002) Individual decision making, in B. Weitz and R. Wensley (eds) *Handbook of Marketing*, London: Sage, 372–408.

[76]B. Shapiro, V. K. Rangan and J. Sviokla (1992) Staple yourself to an order, *Harvard Business Review*, July–August, 113–22. See also C. M. Heilman, D. Bowman and G. P. Wright (2000) The evolution of brand preferences and choice behaviors of consumers new to a market, *Journal of Marketing Research*, May, 139–55.

[77]A. S. Wellner (2001) Research on a shoestring, *American Demographics*, April, 38–9.

[78]Marketing scholars have developed several models of the consumer buying process. See M. F. Luce, J. R. Bettman and J. W. Payne (2001) *Emotional Decisions: Tradeoff Difficulty and Coping in Consumer Choice,* Chicago, IL: University of Chicago Press; J. F. Engel, R. D. Blackwell, and P. W. Miniard (1994) *Consumer Behavior*, 8th ed, Fort Worth, TX: Dryden; J. A. Howard and J. N. Sheth (1969) *The Theory of Buyer Behavior*, New York: John Wiley & Sons.

[79]W. P. Putsis Jr. and N. Srinivasan (1994) Buying or just browsing? the duration of purchase deliberation, *Journal of Marketing Research,* August, 393–402.

[80]C. L. Narayana and R. J. Markin (1975) Consumer behavior and product performance: an alternative conceptualization, *Journal of Marketing,* October, 1–6. See also L. G. Cooper and A. Inoue (1996) Building market structures from consumer preferences, *Journal of Marketing Research,* 33(3) (August), 293–306; W. S. DeSarbo and K. Jedidi (1995) The spatial representation of heterogeneous consideration dets, *Marketing Science,* 14(3), pt. 2, Summer, 326–42.

[81]For a market-structure study of the hierarchy of atrributes in the coffee market, see D. Jain, F. M. Bass and Yu-Min Chen (1990) Estimation of latent class models with heterogeneous choice probabilities: an application to market structuring, *Journal of Marketing Research*, February, 94–101. For an application of means-end chain analysis to global markets, see F. T. Hofstede, J.-B. E. M. Steenkamp and M. Wedel (1999) International market segmentation based on consumer–product relations, *Journal of Marketing Research*, February, 1–17.

[82]V. Postrel (2003) The lessons of the grocery shelf also have something to say about affirmative action, *New York Times,* 30 January.

[83]D. Krech, R. S. Crutchfield and E. L. Ballachey (1962) *Individual in Society,* New York: McGraw-Hill, Ch. 2.

[84]http://ameliatorode.typepad.com/life_moves_pretty_fast/2007/05/index.html.

[85]http://60mdagen.dk/; http://www.foedevarestyrelsen.dk/Ernaering/forside.htm.

[86]See L. McAlister (1979) Choosing multiple items from a product class, *Journal of Consumer Research,* December, 213–24; P. E. Green and Y. Wind, *Multiattribute Decisions in Marketing: A Measurement Approach*, Hinsdale, IL: Dryden, Ch. 2; R. J. Lutz (1991) The role of attitude theory in marketing, in H. Kassarjian and T. Robertson (eds.), *Perspectives in Consumer Behavior*, 317–39.

[87]This expectancy-value model was originally developed by M. Fishbein (1967) Attitudes and prediction of behavior, in M. Fishbein (ed.) *Readings in Attitude Theory and Measurement,* New York: John Wiley & Sons, 477–92. For a critical review see P. W. Miniard and J. B. Cohen (1981) An examination of the Fishbein-Ajzen behavioral-intentions model's concepts and measures, *Journal of Experimental Social Psychology*, May, 309–39.

[88]M. R. Solomon (2007) *Consumer Behavior: Buying, Having, and Being*, 7th edn, Upper Saddle River, NJ: Prentice Hall.

[89]J. R. Bettman, E. J. Johnson and J. W. Payne (1991) Consumer decision making, in *Handbook of Consumer Theory and Research,* ed. Kassarjian and Robertson, NJ: Prentice Hall, pp. 50–84.

[90]J. N. Sheth (1974) An investigation of relationships among evaluative beliefs, affect, behavioral intention, and behavior, in J. U. Farley, J. A. Howard and L. W. Ring (eds), *Consumer Behavior: Theory and Application*, Boston: Allyn & Bacon, 89–114.

[91]Fishbein (1967) op. cit.

[92]M. C. Campbell and R. C. Goodstein (2001) The moderating effect of perceived risk on consumers' evaluations of product incongruity: preference for the norm, *Journal of Consumer Research*, 28, December, 439–49; G. R. Dowling (1999) Perceived risk, in P. E. Ear and S. Kemp (eds) *The Elgar Companion to Consumer Research and Economic Psychology*, Cheltenham: Edward Elgar, 419–24; G. R. Dowling (1986) Perceived risk: the concept and its measurement, *Psychology and Marketing*, 3, Fall, 193–210; J. R. Bettman (1973) Perceived risk and its components: a model and empirical test, *Journal of Marketing Research*, 10, May, 184–90; R. A. Bauer (1967) Consumer behavior as risk taking, in D. F. Cox (ed.) *Risk Taking and Information Handling in Consumer Behavior*, Boston, MA: Division of Research, Harvard Business School.

[93]R. L. Oliver (2006) Customer satisfaction research, in R. Grover and M. Vriens (eds) *Handbook of Marketing Research*, Thousand Oaks, CA: Sage, 569–87.

[94]R. L. Day (1984) Modeling choices among alternative responses to dissatisfaction, *Advances in Consumer Research*, 11, 496–99. Also see P. Kotler and M. K. Mantrala (1985) Flawed products: consumer responses and marketer strategies, *Journal of Consumer Marketing*, Summer, 27–36.

[95]A. O. Hirschman (1970) *Exit, Voice, and Loyalty*, Cambridge, MA: Harvard University Press.

[96]J. D. Cripps (1994) Heuristics and biases in timing the replacement of durable products, *Journal of Consumer Research*, 21, September, 304–18.

[97]R. L. Celsi and J. C. Olson (1988) The role of involvement in attention and comprehension processes, *Journal of Consumer Research*, 15, 210–24.

[98]G. Laurent and J. N. Kapferer (1985) Measuring consumer involvement profiles, *Journal of Marketing Research*, February, 41–53.

[99]R. E. Petty (1986) *Communication and Persuasion: Central and Peripheral Routes to Attitude Change*, New York: Springer-Verlag; R. E. Petty and J. T. Cacioppo (1981) *Attitudes and Persuasion: Classic and Contemporary Approaches*, New York: McGraw-Hill.

[100]H. E. Krugman (1965) The impact of television advertising: learning without involvement, *Public Opinion Quarterly*, Fall, 349–56.

[101]M. Fishbein and I. Ajzen (1975) *Belief, Attitude, Intention, and Behavior: An Introduction to Theory and Research*, Reading, MA: Addison Wesley.

[102]Cf. D. I. Hawkins, R. J. Best and K. A. Coney (2001) *Consumer Behavior: Building Marketing Strategy*, 8th edn, New York: Irwin, McGraw-Hill.

[103]Cf. K. E. Thompson, N. Haziris and P. J. Alekos (1994) Attitudes and food choice behaviour, *British Food Journal*, 96(11), 9–17.

[104]I. Ajzen (1985) From intention to action: a theory of planned behavior, in J. Kuhl and J. Beckman (eds) *Action Control: From Cognitions to Behaviors*, New York: Springer; I. Ajzen (1991) The theory of planned behavior, *Organizational Behavior and Human Decision Processes*, 50, 179–211.

[105]http://www.people.umass.edu/aizen/, accessed October 2007.

[106]T. J. Reynolds, C. E. Gengler and D. J. Howard (1995) A means-end analysis of brand persuasion through advertising, *International Journal of Research in Marketing*, 12(3), 257–66.

[107]M. S. Mulvey and J. C. Olson (1994) Exploring the relationships between means-end knowledge and involvement, *Advances in Consumer Research*, 21(1), 51–7.

[108]D. L. Hoffman, T. P. Novak and A. Venkatesh (2004) Has the Internet become indispensable?, *Communications of the ACM*, 47, 7, 37–42.

[109]For a detailed review of the practical significance of consumer decision making, see I. Simonson (1993) Get close to your customers by understanding how they make their choices, *California Management Review*, 35 (Summer), 78–9.

[110]F. R. Kardes (2003) *Consumer Behavior and Managerial Decision Making*, 2nd edn, Upper Saddle River, NJ: Prentice Hall.

[111]See R. Thaler (1985) Mental accounting and consumer choice, *Marketing Science*, 4(3), Summer, 199–214 for a seminal piece; and R. Thaler (1999) Mental accounting matters, *Journal of Behavioral Decision Making*, 12(3), September, 183–206 for more contemporary perspectives.

[112]G. L. Gastineau and M. P. Kritzman (1999) *Dictionary of Financial Risk Management*, 3rd edn, New York: John Wiley & Sons.

[113]Example adapted from D. Kahneman and A. Tversky (1979) Prospect theory: an analysis of decision under risk, *Econometrica*, 47 (March), 263–91.

[114]Thaler (1985) op. cit.; Thaler (1999) op. cit.

[115]H. W. Boyd Jr. and S. Levy (1963) New dimensions in consumer analysis, *Harvard Business Review*, November–December, 129–40.

[116]S. Vandermerwe (1999) *Customer Capitalism: Increasing Returns in New Market Spaces*, London: Nicholas Brealey Publishing, Ch. 11.

[117]P. B. Seybold (2001) Get inside the lives of your customers, *Harvard Business Review*, May, 81–9.

▽ Analysing business markets

1 What is the business market, and how does it differ from the consumer market?

2 What buying situations do organisational buyers face?

3 Who participates in the business-to-business buying process?

4 How do business buyers make their decisions?

5 How can companies build strong relationships with business customers?

6 How do institutional buyers and government agencies do their buying?

Business organisations not only sell, they also buy vast quantities of raw materials, manufactured components, plant and equipment, supplies and business services. There are over 19 million businesses in Europe. To create and capture value, sellers in business markets need to understand their organisational customers' needs, resources, policies and buying procedures. In this chapter, you will learn more about the workings of business markets and how companies use this knowledge to market products and build relationships with their business customers.

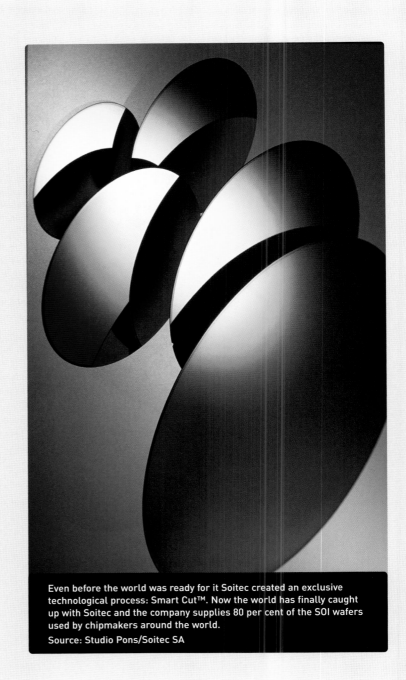

Even before the world was ready for it Soitec created an exclusive technological process: Smart Cut™. Now the world has finally caught up with Soitec and the company supplies 80 per cent of the SOI wafers used by chipmakers around the world.
Source: Studio Pons/Soitec SA

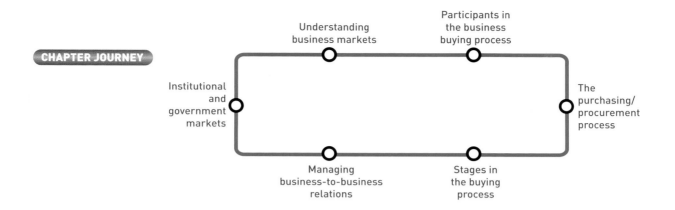

Institutional and government markets

Understanding business markets

Participants in the business buying process

The purchasing/ procurement process

Managing business-to-business relations

Stages in the buying process

In 1992 two researchers, André Auberton-Hervé and Jean-Michel Lamure from CEA-Léti (one of Europe's largest microelectronics research institutes) located in Grenoble, France, created Soitec. The name refers to the company's use of silicon-on-insulator technology. Soitec exploits and develops an exclusive technological process, Smart Cut™, which is protected by a portfolio of around 1000 patents. Smart Cut™ is used today mainly in SOI technology, which offers two major advantages: it considerably increases the speed of microprocessors built on it and cuts by three or four times the power that these microprocessors consume. Soitec's customers were allowed to capitalise (making faster, less energy-consuming chips) on these two advantages without investing in additional process equipment. Back in the early 1990s, Auberton-Hervé and Lamure were sure that the technology they had developed to boost the performance of microchips would be a winner – if only they could get it to work on a mass scale. 'We knew silicon-on-insulator technology could bring real value to the industry,' says Auberton-Hervé. Even though it took almost a decade to work out the kinks, their patience has paid off. Some of the most important semiconductor players worldwide, including, for example, Advanced Micro Devices, Inc., IBM Microelectronics, Philips Semiconductors, Sony and Toshiba, have now chosen to develop their major market applications – servers, PCs, watches, automotive sensors, game consoles, HTDV televisions, and so forth – on Soitec products. In fact, Soitec now supplies 80 per cent of the SOI wafers used by chipmakers around the world.[1]

Some of the world's most valuable brands belong to business marketers: ABB, Caterpillar, Hewlett-Packard, IBM, Intel, Maersk Line, Siemens and Vestas to name a few. Many principles of basic marketing also apply to business marketers. They need to embrace holistic marketing principles, such as building strong relationships with their customers, just like any marketer. But they also face some unique considerations in selling to other businesses. In this chapter, we will highlight some of the crucial similarities and differences for marketing in business markets.[2]

▽ What is organisational buying?

A company wanting to sell its products to other companies needs to understand organisational buying behaviour. In their seminal work on organisational buying behaviour, marketing researchers Webster and Wind define **organisational buying** as the decision-making process by which formal organisations establish the need for purchased products and services and identify, evaluate and choose among alternative brands and suppliers.[3]

The business market versus the consumer market

The **business market** consists of all the organisations that acquire goods and services used in the production of other products or services that are sold, rented or supplied to others. The major industries making up the business market are agriculture, forestry and fisheries; mining; manufacturing; construction; transportation; communication; public utilities; banking, finance and insurance; distribution; and services.

More euros and items change hands in sales to business buyers than to consumers. Consider the process of producing and selling a simple pair of shoes. Hide dealers must sell hides to tanners, who sell leather to shoe manufacturers, who sell shoes to wholesalers, who sell shoes to retailers, who finally sell them to consumers. Each party in the supply chain also buys many other goods and services to support their operations.

Business marketers face many of the same challenges as consumer marketers. In particular, understanding their customers (as this chapter relates to business markets the term 'customer' is used throughout the chapter) and what they value is of paramount importance to both.[4] Table 8.1 summarises the business-to-business challenges identified in the 2005–2007 ISBM Trends Study.

Business marketers, however, have several characteristics that contrast sharply with those of consumer markets:

- **Fewer, larger buyers**: The business marketer normally deals with far fewer, much larger buyers than the consumer marketer does, particularly in such industries as aircraft engines and defence weapons. The fate of Goodyear Tyre Company and other automotive parts suppliers depends on getting contracts from just a handful of major automakers. It's also true, however, that as a slowing economy has put a stranglehold on large corporations' purchasing departments, the small and midsize business market is offering new opportunities for suppliers.[5]

- **Close supplier–customer relationship**: Because of the smaller customer base and the importance and power of the larger customers, suppliers are frequently expected to customise their offerings to individual business customer needs. Business buyers often select suppliers who also buy from them. A paper manufacturer might buy from a chemical company that buys a considerable amount of its paper. See 'Marketing insight: Building business relationships in foreign markets' for more on the importance of creating business relationships.

To understand how Dome Coffee worked its business relationships to grow its operations from Australia to an international presence, visit www.pearsoned.com.au/marketingmanagementaustralia

Table 8.1 The top business marketing challenges for 2005–2007

1 Expand understanding of customer needs, market segments and the drivers of customer value
2 Compete globally as China and India reshape markets
3 Master analytical tools and improve quantitative skills
4 Reinstate innovation as an engine of growth
5 Create new organisational models and linkages
6 Improve return on marketing investment (ROMI) decision making
7 Demonstrate and document delivered customer value, and price accordingly

Source: From Institute for the Study of Business Markets (2006) Know thy customer. *Marketplace: The ISBM Review*, Winter, Exhibit 1, p. 2 (www.smeal.psu.edu/isbm/documents/mktpw06.pdf). Reproduced with permission from ISBM, Smeal College, Pennsylvania State University.

Goodyear Tyre Company exemplifies many suppliers that depend on a market of fewer, but larger, business buyers.

Source: Worth Canoy/Icon/ Corbis

▽ Texas Instruments Inc.

Texas Instruments is a maker of analogue- and digital-signal-processing chips that has learned it is worthwhile to pay attention to some of the smallest business customers. After reinventing itself as a more innovative company, TI is exploring sales leads for customers it used to ignore, such as tiny LifeSize Communications, which as a two-person start-up was too small for TI's attention ten years ago. Recently, TI took several engineers and sales people to LifeSize and spent half a day talking to its four employees and asking them what they wanted. The result is LifeSize Room, an €5400–8000 system that delivers high-definition video and CD quality sound over the Internet. LifeSize has sold over 1000 of the systems, with 75 TI components each, to customers such as a casting agency that allows actors on one coast to audition for roles on the opposite coast via teleconference.

Source: P. Lewis (2006) Texas Instruments' lunatic fringe, *Fortune*, 154(5), 4 September, 120.

Midsize businesses present a huge opportunity, and huge challenges. The market is large and fragmented by industry, size, and number of years in operation. Small business owners are notably averse to long-range planning and have an 'I'll buy it when I need it' decision-making style. Here are some guidelines for selling to small businesses:

- **Professional purchasing**: Business goods are often purchased by trained purchasing agents, who must follow their organisations' purchasing policies, constraints and requirements. Many of the buying instruments – for example requests for quotations, proposals and purchase contracts – are not typically found in consumer buying. Professional buyers spend their careers learning how to buy better. Some acquire their skills from the European Institute of Purchasing Management (EIPM), which seeks to train and educate professional business buyers, including buyers from, for example, IKEA, Unilever, LEGO and Electrolux. This means that business marketers must provide greater technical data about their product and its advantages over competitors' products.
- **Multiple buying influences**: More people typically influence business buying decisions. Buying committees consisting of technical experts and even senior management are common in the purchase of major goods. Business marketers need to send well-trained sales representatives and sales teams to deal with well-trained buyers.

Marketing insight

Big sales to small business

- **Don't lump small and midsize businesses together**: There's a big gap between €1 million in revenue and €50 million, or between a start-up with 10 employees and a more mature business with 100. IBM segments customers in its small and midsize business portal (www-ibm.com/businesscenter/us). Here, customers find a 'Small Business Resource Center' and an 'Express Advantage for Medium Business' service, each offering different products and services to these different market segments.

- **Don't waste their time**: That means no cold calls, entertaining sales shows, or sales pitches over long lavish lunches.

- **Do keep it simple**: Simplicity means one point of contact with a supplier for all service problems, or one bill for all services and products. AT&T corporation, which globally serves 3.9 million businesses with fewer than 100 employees, bundles data management, networking and other abilities into convenient single packages for this market. The AT&T network includes 38 Internet data centres on four continents across the globe.

- **Do use the Internet**: Hewlett-Packard found that time-strapped small-business decision makers prefer to buy, or at least research, products and services online. So it designed a site targeted to small and midsize businesses and pulls visitors through extensive advertising, direct mail, email campaigns, catalogues and events.

- **Don't forget about direct contact**: Even if a small business owner's first point of contact is via the Internet, you still need to offer phone or face-to-face time. In major metropolitan areas, global Internet carrier Sprint connects with small businesses through its Sprint Experience Centres, where Sprint reps or dealer reps can invite prospects to Interact with the technologies.

- **Do provide support after the sale**: Small businesses want partners, not pitchmen. When The DeWitt Company, a 100-employee landscaping products business, purchased a large piece of machinery from Moeller, a German company, the company's president paid DeWitt's CEO a personal visit and stayed until the machine was up and running properly.

- **Do your homework**: The realities of small or midsize business management are different from those of a large corporation. Microsoft created a small, fictional executive research firm, Southridge, and baseball-style trading cards of its key decision makers in order to help Microsoft employees tie sales strategies to small business realities.

Sources: Based on B. J. Feder (2003) When Goliath comes knocking on David's door, *New York Times*, 6 May; J. Greene (2003) Small biz: Microsoft's next big thing?, *BusinessWeek*, 21 April, 72–3; J. Gilbert (2004) Small but mighty, *Sales & Marketing Management*, January, 30–5; V. Kopytoff (2003) Businesses click on eBay, *San Francisco Chronicle*, 28 July; M. Krantz (2004) Firms jump on the eBay wagon, *USA Today*, 3 May.

- **Multiple sales calls**: A study by McGraw-Hill found that it takes four to four and a half calls to close an average industrial sale. In the case of capital equipment sales for large projects, it may take many attempts to fund a project, and the sales cycle – between quoting a job and delivering the product – is often measured in years.[6]

- **Derived demand**: The demand for business goods is ultimately derived from the demand for consumer goods. For this reason, the business marketer must closely monitor the buying patterns of ultimate consumers. Much of the boom in demand for steel-bar products is derived from the sustained growth in sales of minivans and other light trucks, which consume far more steel than cars. Business buyers must also pay close attention to current and expected economic factors, such as the level of production, investment, consumer spending and the interest rate. In a recession, they reduce their investment in plant, equipment and inventories. Business marketers can do little to stimulate total demand in this environment. They can only fight harder to increase or maintain their share of the demand.

- **Inelastic demand**: The total demand for many business goods and services is inelastic – that is, not much affected by price changes. Shoe manufacturers are not going to buy much more leather if the price of leather falls, nor will they buy much less leather if the price rises, unless they can find satisfactory substitutes. Demand is especially inelastic in the short run because producers cannot make quick changes in production methods. Demand is also inelastic for business goods that represent a small percentage of the item's total cost, such as shoelaces.

- **Fluctuating demand**: The demand for business goods and services tends to be more volatile than the demand for consumer goods and services. A given percentage increase in consumer demand can lead to a much larger percentage increase in the demand for plant and equipment necessary to produce the additional output. Economists refer to this as the *acceleration effect.*

Marketing insight

Building business relationships in foreign markets

An explosive growth in foreign direct investments across countries has contributed to the globalisation of markets. Given this growth the choice of mode of entry into a foreign market is a highly important issue for many companies, and the importance is further underlined by the fact that entry mode choices often involve massive investments, are irreversible and may influence the long-term performance of the company. When Scania, the Swedish bus and truck maker, entered the Mexican market in 1991 it chose to be represented by a local distributor but in 1995 Scania inaugurated a fully owned assembly plant as well as its own distribution office. The Mexican market is one of the most competitive car markets in the world and almost all the world's automakers are represented there.

While the truck market is presently dominated by US companies, the bus market is much more European oriented. Another difference is that in the buses segment, customers are buying products and parts but are themselves responsible for the necessary service, whereas in the trucks segment many customers request complete solutions, that is, trucks, parts and services. In the early phases of its operation in Mexico Scania was represented by a third party. However, the bus and truck maker discovered that it needed to develop more direct relationships with its customers in order to be able to fully comprehend and satisfy customer needs. In Mexico there are tight and well-structured car business networks.

In the buses segment Swedish carmakers have managed to acquire large market shares and to be market leaders with Volvo having 35 per cent and Scania 25 per cent. On the much more price-sensitive and US oriented trucks segment Scania has a market share of only 2 per cent. Since Scania is unable to press its prices to the same level as that of its competitors, this has created a constraint for the company in its effort to develop well-functioning networks. Scania must therefore seek to the change attitudes of potential truck customers and make them understand that the higher the price they pay the better quality and safety in their products.

Source: Based on M. Zineldin (2007) International business relationship and entry modes: a case of the Swedish automotive industry, Scania and Volvo in Mexico, *Cross Cultural Management*, 14(4), 365–86. Copyright © 2007 Emerald Group Publishing Limited. Reproduced with permission.

Sometimes a rise of only 10 per cent in consumer demand can cause as much as a 200 per cent rise in business demand for products in the next period; a 10 per cent fall in consumer demand may cause a complete collapse in business demand.

- **Direct purchasing**: Business buyers often buy directly from manufacturers rather than through intermediaries, especially items that are technically complex or expensive such as mainframes or aircraft.

Buying situations

The business buyer faces many decisions in making a purchase. The number depends on the buying situation: complexity of the problem being solved, newness of the buying requirement, number of people involved and time required. Three types of buying situations are the straight rebuy, modified rebuy and new task.[7]

Straight rebuy

In a straight rebuy, the purchasing department reorders supplies such as office supplies and bulk chemicals on a routine basis and chooses from suppliers on an approved list. The suppliers make an effort to maintain product and service quality and often propose automatic reordering systems to save time. 'Out suppliers' attempt to offer something new or to exploit dissatisfaction with a current supplier. Their goal is to get a small order and then enlarge their purchase share over time.

Modified rebuy

The buyer wants to modify product specifications, prices, delivery requirements or other terms. The modified rebuy usually involves additional participants on both sides. The in suppliers become nervous and want to protect the account. The out suppliers see an opportunity to propose a better offer to gain some business.

New task

A purchaser buys a product or service for the first time (an office building, a new security system). The greater the cost or risk, the larger the number of participants and the greater their information gathering – and therefore the longer the time to a decision.[8]

The business buyer makes the fewest decisions in the straight rebuy situation and the most in the new-task situation. Over time, new buy situations become straight rebuys and routine purchase behaviour.

New-task buying is the marketer's greatest opportunity and challenge. The process passes through several stages: awareness, interest, evaluation, trial and adoption.[9] Mass media can be most important during the initial awareness stage; sales people often have their greatest impact at the interest stage; and technical sources can be most important during the evaluation stage.

In the new-task situation, the buyer must determine product specifications, price limits, delivery terms and times, service terms, payment terms, order quantities, acceptable suppliers, and the selected supplier. Different participants influence each decision, and the order in which these decisions are made varies.

Because of the complicated selling involved, many companies use a *missionary sales force* consisting of their most effective sales people. The brand promise and the manufacturer's brand name recognition will be important in establishing trust and the customer's willingness to consider change.[10] The marketer also tries to reach as many key participants as possible and provide helpful information and assistance.

Once a customer is acquired, in suppliers are continually seeking ways to add value to their market offer to facilitate rebuys. Data storage leader EMC successfully acquired a series of computer software leaders to reposition the company to manage – and not just store – information, often by giving customers customised information.[11]

▽ Orica Ltd

Orica Ltd's success grew from its realisation that it could provide more than just explosives to its mining customers. Now it researches the efficiency of different kinds of explosions and manages the entire blast for its clients.

Source: © Profimedia International s.r.o./Alamy

Orica Ltd, formerly ICI Australia, competes in the cut-throat commercial explosives business. Its customers are quarries that use explosives to blast solid rock face into aggregate of a specified size. Orica is constantly trying to minimise the cost of explosives. The firm realised it could create significant value by improving the efficiency of the blast. To do this, company engineers identified over 20 parameters that influenced the success of the blast, such as the density and shape of the rock, and the chemistry of the explosive charge. Orica now began collecting data from customers on these parameters as well as the outcomes of individual blasts. By collating the data, Orica engineers came to understand the conditions that produced different outcomes. It could then offer customers a contract for 'broken rock' that would almost guarantee the desired outcome. The success of Orica's approach – of managing the entire blast for the quarry rather than simply selling explosives – entrenched the company as the world's leading supplier of commercial explosives.[12]

Customers considering dropping six or seven figures on one transaction for high-cost goods and services want all the information they can get. One way to entice new buyers is to create a customer reference programme in which satisfied existing customers act in concert with the company's sales and marketing department by agreeing to serve as references. Technology companies such as HP, Lucent and Unisys have all employed such programmes. 'Marketing memo: Maximising customer references' provides some tips for developing activities and programmes with impact.

Marketing memo

Maximising customer references

Many firms depend on the opinions and experiences of others in evaluating a new business proposal from a new company. Here is some industry wisdom as to what works and what doesn't when developing customer information and reference programmes to respond to these demands.

Five common mistakes in developing customer reference stories

1 **Failing to state the customer's need and its implications with specificity**: Clearly state why customers had a need and how the company's products would resolve it. Such detailed information can better allow sales people to assess whether a prospect has similar needs and could obtain similar pay-offs.

2 **Failing to quantify your customer's results**: Although outside companies may seem reluctant to share too much hard data, it may just reflect the fact that they don't have the information readily accessible. Assist them in getting it.

3 **Failing to describe business benefits of any kind (quantified or not)**: Don't focus on your expertise in various technologies and industries without saying how it specifically helped customers to enter or grow

markets. Make an obvious cause-and-effect link between the solution provided and the claims for your product.

4 **Failing to differentiate your offerings from the competition**: Make it clear why it was the case that not just any company's products or services could have led to the same solution.

5 **Failing to provide a concise, accessible summary of the story**: Make sure you package the customer reference story in a way that a prospect can easily and quickly understand. Here are seven ways to do so.

Seven keys to successfully developing customer reference stories

1 State the customer's needs in compelling terms.
2 Emphasise the barriers in satisfying customer needs.
3 Describe your company's solution in terms of value.
4 List quantified results, especially those that affect ROI.
5 Differentiate your offering from those of competitors.
6 Provide a brief comprehensive summary.
7 Include numerous customer quotes.

Systems buying and selling

Many business buyers prefer to buy a total solution to a problem from one seller. Called *systems buying,* this practice originated with government purchases of major weapons and communications systems. The government would solicit bids from *prime contractors,* who would enter into a contract with the government – the owner of the project or job – and assume full responsibility for its completion. The contractor who was awarded the contract would be responsible for bidding out and assembling the system's subcomponents from *second-tier contractors.* The prime contractor would thus provide a turnkey solution, so called because the buyer simply had to turn one key to get the job done.

Sellers have increasingly recognised that buyers like to purchase in this way, and many have adopted systems selling as a marketing tool. One variant of systems selling is *systems contracting,* where a single supplier provides the buyer with his entire requirement of MRO (maintenance, repair, operating) supplies. During the contract period, the supplier manages the customer's inventory. For example, Shell Oil manages the oil inventory of many of its business customers and knows when it requires replenishment. The customer benefits from reduced procurement and management costs and from price protection over the term of the contract. The seller benefits from lower operating costs because of a steady demand and reduced paperwork.

Systems selling is a key industrial marketing strategy in bidding to build large-scale industrial projects, such as dams, steel factories, irrigation systems, sanitation systems, pipelines, utilities, and even new towns. Project engineering firms must compete on price, quality, reliability and other attributes to win contracts. With systems selling, customers present potential suppliers with a list of project specifications and requirements. Suppliers, however, are not just at the mercy of these customer demands. Ideally, they're involved with customers early in the process to influence the actual development of the specifications. Or they can go beyond the specifications to offer additional value in various ways, as the following example shows.

Japan and Indonesia

The Indonesian government requested bids to build a cement factory near Jakarta. A western firm made a proposal that included choosing the site, designing the cement factory, hiring the construction crews, assembling the materials and equipment, and turning over the finished factory to the Indonesian government. A Japanese firm, in outlining its proposal, included all these services, plus hiring and training the workers to run the factory, exporting the cement through its trading companies, and using the cement to build roads and new office buildings in Jakarta. Although the Japanese proposal involved more money, it won the contract. Clearly, the Japanese viewed the problem not just as one of building a cement factory (the narrow view of systems selling) but as one of contributing to Indonesia's economic development. They took the broadest view of the customer's needs. This is true systems selling.

▽ Participants in the business buying process

Who buys the trillions of dollars' worth of goods and services needed by business organisations? Purchasing agents are influential in straight rebuy and modified rebuy situations, whereas other department personnel are more influential in new buy situations. Engineering personnel usually have a major influence in selecting product components, and purchasing agents dominate in selecting suppliers.[13,14]

The buying centre

Marketing researchers Webster and Wind call the decision-making unit of a buying organisation *the buying centre.* It consists of 'all those individuals and groups who participate in the purchasing decision-making process, who share some common goals and the risks arising from the decisions'.[15] The buying centre includes all members of the organisation who play any of seven roles in the purchase decision process.

1 **Initiators**: Users or others in the organisation who request that something be purchased.

2 **Users**: Those who will use the product or service. In many cases, the users initiate the buying proposal and help define the product requirements.

3 **Influencers**: People who influence the buying decision, often by helping define specifications and providing information for evaluating alternatives. Technical personnel are particularly important influencers.

4 **Deciders**: People who decide on product requirements or on suppliers.

5 **Approvers**: People who authorise the proposed actions of deciders or buyers.

6 **Buyers**: People who have formal authority to select the supplier and arrange the purchase terms. Buyers may help shape product specifications, but they play their major role in selecting vendors and negotiating. In more complex purchases, buyers might include high-level managers.

7 **Gatekeepers**: People who have the power to prevent sellers or information from reaching members of the buying centre. For example, purchasing agents, receptionists and telephone operators may prevent sales persons from contacting users or deciders.

Several people can occupy a given role such as user or influencer, and one person may occupy multiple roles.[16] A purchasing manager, for example, often occupies the roles of buyer, influencer and gatekeeper simultaneously: She can determine which sales reps can call on other people in the organisation; what budget and other constraints to place on the purchase; and which firm will actually get the business, even though others (deciders) might select two or more potential vendors that can meet the company's requirements.

The typical buying centre has a minimum of five or six members and often has dozens. Some may be outside the organisation, such as government officials, consultants, technical advisers and other members of the marketing channel. One study found that 3.5 more people on average were involved in making a purchase decision in 2005 than in 2001.[17]

Buying centre influences

Buying centres usually include several participants with differing interests, authority, status and persuasiveness and sometimes very different decision criteria. For example, engineering personnel may want to maximise the performance of the product; production personnel may want ease of use and reliability of supply; financial personnel focus on the economics of the purchase; purchasing may be concerned with operating and replacement costs; union officials may emphasise safety issues.

Business buyers also have personal motivations, perceptions and preferences that are influenced by their age, income, education, job position, personality, attitudes toward risk and culture. Buyers definitely exhibit different buying styles. There are 'keep-it-simple' buyers, 'own-expert' buyers, 'want-the-best' buyers and 'want-everything-done' buyers. Some younger, highly educated buyers are computer experts who conduct rigorous analyses of competitive proposals before choosing a supplier. Other buyers are 'toughies' from the old school who pit the competing sellers against one another and, in some companies, the purchasing powers-that-be are legendary.

▽ General Motors

Every year Bo I. Andersson, General Motors' VP of global purchasing, is charged with knocking a whopping €1.3 billion from GM's purchasing bill. As a former Swedish army officer, Andersson is a hands-on individual who buys €57 billion worth of wheels, axles, seats, bolts and other parts in a purchasing bill topped only by the US military. Yet he isn't focused so much on squeezing suppliers as he is on squeezing inefficiencies out of the system, such as getting GM's vehicles to share more parts. (GM currently makes 26 versions of seat frames, whereas Toyota makes 2.) Still, Andersson does not suffer inefficiency from suppliers. If they don't meet his standards, he will drop them even if it means forcing them into bankruptcy. In 2006, for instance, he decided to jettison 3200 suppliers. Perhaps that's why GM ranks last in an annual supplier satisfaction survey!

Source: D. Welch (2006) Renault-Nissan: say hello to Bo, *BusinessWeek*, 31 July, 56.

Webster cautions that ultimately individuals, not organisations, make purchasing decisions.[18] Individuals are motivated by their own needs and perceptions in attempting to maximise the rewards (pay, advancement, recognition and feelings of achievement) offered by the organisation. Personal needs motivate the behaviour of individuals, but organisational needs legitimate the buying decision process and its outcomes. People are not buying 'products'. They are buying solutions to two problems: the organisation's economic and strategic problem and their own personal need for individual achievement and reward. In this sense, industrial buying decisions are both 'rational' and 'emotional', as they serve both the organisation's and the individual's needs.[19]

For example, research conducted by one industrial component manufacturer found that although top executives at small and medium-sized companies stated they were comfortable in general with buying from other companies, they appeared to harbour subconscious insecurities about buying the manufacturer's product. Constant changes in technology had left them concerned about the internal effects within the company. Recognising this unease, the manufacturer retooled its selling approach to emphasise more emotional appeals and how its product line actually enabled the customer's employees to improve their performance, relieving management of the complications and stress of component use.[20]

Recognising these extrinsic, interpersonal influences, more industrial firms have put greater emphasis on strengthening their corporate brand. At one time Emerson Electric, global provider of power tools, compressors, electrical equipment and engineering solutions, was a conglomerate of 60 autonomous – and sometimes anonymous – companies. A new Chief Marketing Officer aligned the previously independent brands under a new global brand architecture and identity, allowing Emerson to achieve a broader presence so that

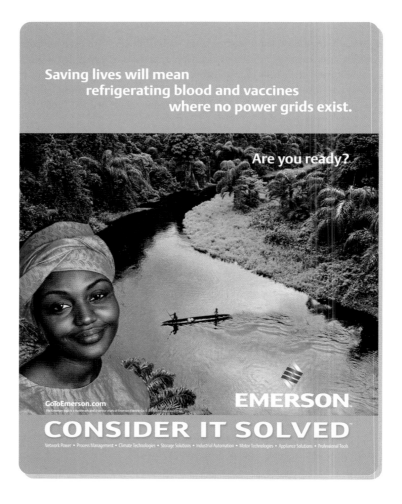

Recognisable brands are important to business buyers, as Emerson Electric found when it created a new global brand identity for its 60 autonomous companies.

Source: Courtesy of Emerson Electric

it could sell locally while leveraging its global brand name. Record sales and stock price highs soon followed.[21]

▽ SAS Institute, Inc.

With sales of more than €0.75 billion and a huge 'fan club' of IT customers, SAS, the business intelligence software firm, seemed to be in an enviable position in 1999. Yet its image was what one industry observer called 'a geek brand'. In order to extend the company's reach beyond IT managers with PhDs in maths or statistical analysis, the company needed to connect with high-ranking chief executives (also known as C-level executives) in the largest companies – the kind of people who either didn't have a clue what SAS's software was and what to do with it, or who didn't think business intelligence was a strategic issue. Working with its first outside ad agency ever, SAS emerged with a new logo, a new slogan, 'The Power to Know', and a series of TV spots and print ads in business publications such as *BusinessWeek* and *Forbes*. One TV spot that exemplifies SAS's rebranding effort ran like this:

> The problem is not harvesting the new crop of e-business information. It's making sense of it. With e-intelligence from SAS, you can harness the information. And put the knowledge you need within reach. SAS. The power to know.

Subsequent research showed that SAS had made the transition to a mainstream business decision-making support brand, both user friendly and necessary.

Source: B. Lamons (2005) Branding, B-to-B style, *Sales and Marketing Management*, 157(9), September, 46–50. Copyright © 2005 Nielsen Business Media. Reproduced with permission.

Buying centre targeting

To target their efforts properly, business marketers need to figure out the following: Who are the major decision participants? What decisions do they influence? What is their level of influence? What evaluation criteria do they use? Consider the following example.

> A company sells non-woven disposable surgical gowns to hospitals. The hospital personnel who participate in this buying decision include the vice-president of purchasing, the operating room administrator and the surgeons. The vice-president of purchasing analyses whether the hospital should buy disposable or reusable gowns. If the findings favour disposable gowns, then the operating room administrator compares various competitors' products and prices and makes a choice. This administrator considers absorbency, antiseptic quality, design and cost and normally buys the brand that meets the functional requirements at the lowest cost. Surgeons influence the decision retroactively by reporting their satisfaction with the particular brand.

The business marketer is not likely to know exactly what kind of group dynamics takes place during the decision process, although whatever information he or she can obtain about personalities and interpersonal factors is useful.

Small sellers concentrate on reaching the *key buying influencers*. Larger sellers go for *multilevel in-depth selling* to reach as many participants as possible. Their sales people virtually 'live' with high-volume customers. Companies must rely more heavily on their communications programmes to reach hidden buying influences and keep current customers informed.[22]

▽ Symantec Corporation

With research and development facilities located around the world, Internet security provider Symantec Corporation has moved from being primarily a provider of consumer software (under the Norton name) to a provider of enterprise security solutions for financial services, health care and utilities industries. To reach these new markets Symantec had to restructure its sales force to develop high-level relationships. So Symantec launched the Executive Sponsorship Program in 2003. The 13 Symantec executives enrolled in the programme are paired with vice-presidents or C-level executives within 19 key customer organisations in industries ranging from banking to telecommunications and manufacturing. The goal of the programme is to foster better understanding of Symantec's customers and their business concerns. So far the programme has enabled Symantec to be seen as a valued partner and has given its executives insights into how they can develop products that fit customers' needs.[23]

Business marketers must periodically review their assumptions about buying centre participants. For years, Kodak sold X-ray film to hospital lab technicians, but research indicated that professional administrators were increasingly making purchasing decisions. As a result, Kodak revised its marketing strategy and developed new advertising to reach out to these decision makers.

▽ The purchasing/procurement process

In principle, business buyers seek to obtain the highest benefit package (economic, technical, service and social) in relation to a market offering's costs. To make comparisons, they will try to translate all costs and benefits into monetary terms. A business buyer's incentive to purchase will be a function of the difference between perceived benefits and perceived costs.[24] The marketer's task is to construct a profitable offering that delivers superior customer value to the target buyers.

Supplier diversity is a benefit that may not have a price tag but that business buyers overlook at their risk. As the CEOs of many of the country's largest companies see it, a diverse supplier base is a business imperative. Minority suppliers are the fastest-growing segment of today's business landscape.

▽ Pfizer

One of the biggest names in pharmaceuticals, Pfizer views its supplier-diversity programme as an essential tool in connecting with customers. Gwendolyn Turner, manager of supplier diversity, says the company spent about €470 million with 2400 minority and women suppliers: 'Our business touches all kinds of customers, so it only makes sense that our supplier base represents a broad range of people as well.' Pfizer has even developed a mentoring programme that identifies the women and minority suppliers who need help growing, whether it's designing a better website or building a better business plan. Pfizer managers meet with the owners, often on site, to work out what they need.

Source: S. Caminiti (2006) Drivers of the economy, *Fortune*, 153(7), 17 April, C1–7.

Purchasing department perceptions

In the past, purchasing departments occupied a low position in the management hierarchy, in spite of often managing more than half the company's costs. Recent competitive pressures have led many companies to upgrade their purchasing departments and elevate administrators to vice-presidential rank. These new, more strategically oriented purchasing departments have a mission to seek the best value from fewer and better suppliers. Some multinationals have even elevated them to 'strategic supply departments' with responsibility for global sourcing and partnering. At Caterpillar, for example, purchasing, inventory control, production scheduling and traffic have been combined into one department. McDonald's is one company that has improved its business buying practices.

▽ McDonald's

As director of global technology supplier management for McDonald's, Joseph Youssef's mandate is to segment and measure suppliers and then manage them based on the measurements. And, be aware, Youssef oversees only one aspect of McDonald's huge supplier base – its IT services and equipment. As McDonald's began to see positive results from applying its supplier relationship management methods to one of its IT suppliers, it extended the strategy to its other IT contracts such as its network systems, Verizon and MCI, and its restaurant point-of-sale systems. McDonald's will now go on to apply supplier management strategies to its indirect materials suppliers.

Source: W. Forrest (2006) McDonald's applies SRM strategy to global technology buy, *Purchasing*, 135(12), 7 September, 16.

The upgrading of purchasing means that business marketers must upgrade their sales personnel to match the higher calibre of the business buyers.

Purchasing organisation and administration

Most purchasing professionals describe their jobs as more strategic, technical, team oriented and involving more responsibility than ever before. 'Purchasing is doing more cross-functional work than it did in the past,' says David Duprey, a buyer for Anaren Microwave, Inc., which supplies the world's leading Original Equipment Manufacturers with wireless infrastructures, wireless consumer products, satellites, defence electronics, among other things. Of buyers surveyed 61 per cent said the buying group was more involved in new product design and development than it was five years ago; and more than half the buyers participate in cross-functional teams, with suppliers well represented.[25]

Some companies have started to centralise purchasing. Headquarters identifies materials purchased by several divisions and buys them centrally, gaining more purchasing clout. For the business marketer, this development means dealing with fewer and higher-level buyers and using a national account sales group to deal with large corporate buyers. At the same time companies are decentralising some purchasing operations by empowering employees to purchase small-ticket items (such as special binders, coffee makers or Christmas trees) through corporate purchasing cards issued by credit card organisations.

We are now ready to describe the general stages in the business buying decision process.

▽ Stages in the buying process

Robinson and his associates identified eight stages in the business buying decision process and called them *buyphases*.[26] The model in Table 8.2 is the *buygrid* framework.

In modified rebuy or straight rebuy situations some stages are compressed or bypassed. For example, the buyer normally has a favourite supplier or a ranked list of suppliers and can skip the search and proposal solicitation stages. Here are some important considerations in each of the eight stages.

Table 8.2 Buygrid framework: major stages (buyphases) of the industrial buying process in relation to major buying situations (buyclasses)

			Buyclasses	
		New task	Modified rebuy	Straight rebuy
Buyphases	1 Problem recognition	Yes	Maybe	No
	2 General need description	Yes	Maybe	No
	3 Product specification	Yes	Yes	Yes
	4 Supplier search	Yes	Maybe	No
	5 Proposal solicitation	Yes	Maybe	No
	6 Supplier selection	Yes	Maybe	No
	7 Order-routine specification	Yes	Maybe	No
	8 Performance review	Yes	Yes	Yes

Problem recognition

The buying process begins when someone in the company recognises a problem or need that can be met by acquiring a good or service. The recognition can be triggered by internal or external stimuli. Internal stimuli might be that the company decides to develop a new product and needs new equipment and materials, or a machine breaks down and requires new parts. Or purchased material turns out to be unsatisfactory and the company searches for another supplier, or lower prices or better quality. Externally, the buyer may get new ideas at a trade show, see an ad or receive a call from a sales representative who offers a better product or a lower price. Business marketers can stimulate problem recognition by direct mail, telemarketing and calling on prospects.

General need description and product specification

Next, the buyer determines the needed item's general characteristics and required quantity. For standard items this is simple. For complex items the buyer will work with others – engineers, users – to define characteristics such as reliability, durability or price. Business marketers can help by describing how their products meet or even exceed the buyer's needs.

The buying organisation now develops the item's technical specifications. Often, the company will assign a product-value-analysis engineering team to the project. *Product value analysis* (PVA) is an approach to cost reduction that studies components to determine whether they can be redesigned, standardised or made by cheaper methods of production. The PVA team will identify overdesigned components, for instance, that last longer than the product itself. Tightly written specifications will allow the buyer to refuse components that are too expensive or that fail to meet specified standards. Suppliers can use product value analysis as a tool for positioning themselves to win an account.

Supplier search

The buyer next tries to identify the most appropriate suppliers through trade directories, contacts with other companies, trade advertisements, trade shows and the Internet.[27] The move to Internet purchasing has far-reaching implications for suppliers and will change the shape of purchasing for years to come.[28] Companies that purchase over the Internet are utilising electronic marketplaces in several forms:

- **Catalogue sites**: Companies can order thousands of items through electronic catalogues distributed by eprocurement software, such as Grainger's.
- **Vertical markets**: Companies buying industrial products such as plastics, steel, chemicals or services such as logistics or media can go to specialised websites (called ehubs). For example, Plastics.com allows plastics buyers to search for the best prices among thousands of plastics sellers.

- **'Pure Play' auction sites**: Online marketplaces such as eBay and Freemarkets.com could not have been realised without the Internet. Freemarkets.com provides online auctions for buyers and sellers of industrial parts, raw materials, commodities and services in over 50 product categories and has facilitated over €30 billion worth of commerce since 1995.
- **Spot (or exchange) markets**: A spot market is a market where commodities and cash are bought and sold immediately, with no time between trades. On spot electronic markets prices change by the minute. ChemConnect.com is an exchange for buyers and sellers of bulk chemicals such as natural gas liquids, aromatics, olefins and plastics, and it's a B2B success in an arena littered with failed online exchanges. ChemConnect's international community of members includes more than 9000 companies from over 150 countries worldwide. First to market, it is now the biggest online exchange for chemical trading, with an average of approximately 1 million barrels traded everyday in 2007. FizTrade.com is an instant trading site for physical metals offering both bid and ask, whereas Converge.com is a leading business-to-business global electronics trading exchange. Recognising the cost management advantages that this market can offer, manufacturers have been committing an increasing portion of their procurement budget to the spot market. Today, industry experts estimate that up to one-third of all procurement occurs outside of pre-arranged contracts.[29]
- **Private exchanges**: Hewlett-Packard and IBM operate private exchanges to link with specially invited groups of suppliers and partners over the Web.
- **Barter markets**: In barter markets, participants offer to trade goods or services.
- **Buying alliances**: Several companies buying the same goods, such as Transora and Covisint, join together to form purchasing consortia to gain deeper discounts on volume purchases.

Online business buying offers several advantages. It shaves transaction costs for both buyers and suppliers, reduces time between order and delivery, consolidates purchasing systems and forges more intimate relationships between partners and buyers. On the downside, it may help to erode supplier–buyer loyalty and create potential security problems. See 'Marketing insight: Alibaba.com in Europe' for an example of an online business marketplace.

Marketing insight

Alibaba.com in Europe

In October 2007 Alibaba.com opened its first European office in Geneva. Alibaba.com is the world's number one marketplace dedicated to small and medium-sized enterprises (SMEs), companies employing fewer than 250 people. From Geneva Alibaba.com will assist European SMEs to become more competitive by making their import and export business easier in a growing global market. Alibaba.com provides a platform where SME buyers and suppliers across the globe can connect and exchange raw materials, goods, manufactured products and even services. In just over eight years Alibaba.com has built a global community of more than 24 million members from over 200 countries and regions, covering some 30 industries and more than 5000 product categories. In Europe there are more than 19 million SMEs, who employ over 97 million people. The SMEs make up more than 99 per cent of the total number of companies and are the principal source of employment and wealth in the European Union. In fact, SMEs are responsible for 70 per cent of all private jobs in Europe's €9.3 trillion economy.

'The large concentration of SMEs is one of the reasons why, in just a few years, Europe has become one of the most important markets for Alibaba.com in terms of active members,' said Kenneth Liu, Alibaba.com vice-president of global operations. The success of Alibaba.com's marketplace is largely down to its efficiency and ease of use, enabling SMEs to save time by making global sourcing available 24/7 and removing barriers of geographies and time zones. Buyers use the site for free and have access to an active global supplier community and easy to use sourcing and communication tools. Sellers can also use the site for free, posting products to sell and searching for buyers. Premium fee-based packages are available for sellers who want to increase their exposure to potential buyers. Buyers and sellers meet online at Alibaba.com but transactions are completed offline.

Sources: Based on www.alibaba.com; Alibaba has $82 million password, *Private Equity Week*, 23 February 2004; J. Rossant (2004) Europe's hot growth companies, *BusinessWeek*, 25 October.

Eprocurement

Websites are organised around two types of ehubs: *vertical hubs* centred on industries (plastics, steel, chemicals, paper) and *functional hubs* (logistics, media buying, advertising, energy management).

In addition to using these websites, companies can use eprocurement in other ways:

- **Set up direct extranet links to major suppliers**: An extranet is a private computer network using Internet technology to which access is provided to select groups of vendors, suppliers or customers who need to access selected databases and processes. For example, a company can set up a direct eprocurement account at Dell or Office Depot, and its employees can make their purchases this way.
- **Form buying alliances**: A number of major retailers and manufacturers such as Ace Hardware, Coca-Cola, Colgate Palmolive, Johnson & Johnson, Kraft, Kroger, Lowe's, Nestlé, Office Depot, PepsiCo, Procter & Gamble, Sara Lee, Staples, Wal-Mart and Wegmans Food Markets are part of a data-sharing alliance called 1SYNC. Several car companies (GM, Ford, DaimlerChrysler) formed Covisint for the same reason. Covisint is the leading provider of services that can integrate crucial business information and processes between partners, customers and suppliers. The company has now also targeted health care to provide similar services.
- **Set up company buying sites**: General Electric formed the trading process network (TPN), where it posts *requests for proposals*, negotiates terms and places orders.

Moving into eprocurement means more than acquiring software; it requires changing purchasing strategy and structure. However, the benefits are many: aggregating purchasing across multiple departments yields larger, centrally negotiated volume discounts, a smaller purchasing staff and less buying of substandard goods from outside the approved list of suppliers.

Lead generation

The supplier's task is to ensure it is considered when customers are – or could be – in the market and searching for a supplier. Identifying good leads and converting them to sales requires the whole marketing and sales organisations to work in a coordinated, multichannel approach in the role of trusted adviser to prospective customers. Marketing must work together with sales to define what makes a 'sales-ready' prospect and cooperate to send the right messages via sales calls, tradeshows, online activities, PR, events, direct mail and referrals.[30]

To generate leads proactively, suppliers need to know about their customers. They can obtain background information from vendors such as EUbusiness.com, Business.com, Hoover.com and Dun & Bradstreet or information-sharing websites such as CSR Europe, Jigsaw and LinkedIn.[31]

Suppliers that lack the required production capacity or suffer from a poor reputation will be rejected. Those who qualify may be visited by the buyer's agents, who will examine the suppliers' manufacturing facilities and meet their personnel. After evaluating each company the buyer will end up with a shortlist of qualified suppliers. Many professional buyers have forced suppliers to change their marketing to increase their likelihood of making the cut.

Proposal solicitation

The buyer next invites qualified suppliers to submit proposals. If the item is complex or expensive the buyer will require a detailed written proposal from each qualified supplier. After evaluating the proposals the buyer will invite a few suppliers to make formal presentations.

Business marketers must be skilled in researching, writing and presenting proposals. Written proposals should be marketing documents that describe value and benefits in customer terms. Oral presentations must inspire confidence and position the company's capabilities and resources so that they stand out from the competition. Proposals and selling are often organised in teams, which may focus on a particular geographic region, industry or market concentration. Sales people can leverage the knowledge and expertise of co-workers instead of working in isolation.[32]

Table 8.3 An example of vendor analysis

Attributes		Rating scale			
	Importance weights	Poor (1)	Fair (2)	Good (3)	Excellent (4)
Price	.30				x
Supplier reputation	.20			x	
Product reliability	.30				x
Service reliability	.10		x		
Supplier flexibility	.10			x	
Total score: .30(4) + .20(3) + .30(4) + .10(2) + .10(3) = 3.5					

Supplier selection

Before selecting a supplier the buying centre will specify desired supplier attributes and indicate their relative importance. To rate and identify the most attractive suppliers buying centres often use a supplier-evaluation model such as the one shown in Table 8.3.

To develop compelling value propositions business marketers need to better understand how business buyers arrive at their valuations.[33] Researchers studying how business marketers assess customer value found eight different *customer value assessment* (CVA) methods. Companies tended to use the simpler methods, although the more sophisticated ones promise to produce a more accurate picture of customer-perceived value. (See 'Marketing memo: Developing compelling customer value propositions'.)

The choice and importance of different attributes varies with the type of buying situation. Delivery reliability, price and supplier reputation are important for routine-order products. As regards procedural-problem products, the customer may be uncertain of her/his ability to learn to use the product. Therefore, the three most important attributes are technical service, supplier flexibility and product reliability. For political-problem products that stir rivalries in the organisation (such as the choice of a computer system), the most important attributes are price, supplier reputation, product reliability, service reliability and supplier flexibility.

Overcoming price pressures and improving productivity

The buying centre may attempt to negotiate with preferred suppliers for better prices and terms before making the final selection. Despite moves toward strategic sourcing, partnering and participation in cross-functional teams, buyers still spend a large chunk of their time haggling with suppliers on price. The number of price-oriented buyers can vary by country depending on customer preferences for different service configurations and characteristics of the customer's organisation.[34]

Marketers can counter requests for a lower price in a number of ways. They may be able to show evidence that the 'total cost of ownership', that is, the 'life-cycle cost' of using their product, is lower than for competitors' products. They can cite the value of the services the buyer now receives, especially if they are superior to those offered by competitors. Research shows that service support and personal interactions, as well as a supplier's know-how and ability to improve customers' time to market, can be useful differentiators in achieving key-supplier status.[35]

While marketers may also improve their productivity to be able to deal with requests for better prices, such improvements may lead to other advantages as well. The Scandinavian metal packaging producer for food products, Glud & Marstrand, has recently invested in a new Warehouse Management System (WMS) delivered by Consafe Logistic.[36] The motive behind introduction of the new WMS was fourfold:

1 The system should enable the warehouse to improve its day-to-day operations while improving productivity and thereby reducing costs.

Marketing memo

Developing compelling customer value propositions

To command price premiums in competitive B2B markets firms must create compelling customer value propositions. The first step is to research the customer. Here are a number of productive research methods:

1 **Internal engineering assessment** Have company engineers use laboratory tests to estimate the product's performance characteristics. Weakness: ignores the fact that in different applications the product will have different economic value.

2 **Field value-in-use assessment** Interview customers about how costs of using a new product compare to those of using an incumbent. The task is to assess how much each cost element is worth to the buyer.

3 **Focus-group value assessment** Ask customers in a focus group what value they would put on potential market offerings.

4 **Direct survey questions** Ask customers to place a direct monetary value on one or more changes in the market offering.

5 **Conjoint analysis** Ask customers to rank their preferences for alternative market offerings or concepts. Use statistical analysis to estimate the implicit value placed on each attribute.

6 **Benchmarks** Show customers a 'benchmark' offering and then a new market offering. Ask how much more they would pay for the new offering or how much less they would pay if certain features were removed from the benchmark offering.

7 **Compositional approach** Ask customers to attach a monetary value to each of three alternative levels of a given attribute. Repeat for other attributes, then add the values together for any offer configuration.

8 **Importance ratings** Ask customers to rate the importance of different attributes and their suppliers' performance on each.

Having done this research you can specify the customer value proposition, following a number of important principles. First, clearly substantiate value claims by concretely specifying the differences between your offerings and those of competitors on the dimensions that matter most to the customer. For example, Rockwell Automation determined the cost savings customers would realise from purchasing its pump solution instead of a competitor's by using industry-standard metrics of functionality and performance: kilowatt-hours spent, number of operating hours per year and dollars per kilowatt-hour. Also, make the financial implications obvious.

Rockwell Automation's marketers quantified its customers' potential cost savings by applying industry-standard measures of performance to its products.
Source: Courtesy of Rockwell Automation

Second, document the value delivered by creating written accounts of costs savings or added value that existing customers have actually captured by using your offerings. Chemical producer Akzo Nobel conducted a two-week pilot study on a production reactor at a prospective customer's facility to document points of parity and points of difference of its high-purity metal organics product.

Finally, make sure the customer value proposition is well implemented within the company, and train and reward employees for developing a compelling one. Quaker Chemical conducts training programmes for its managers that include a competition to develop the best proposals.

Sources: J. C. Anderson, J. A. Narus and W. van Rossum (2006) Customer value propositions in business markets, *Harvard Business Review*, March, 2–10; J. C. Anderson and J. A. Narus, Business marketing: understanding what customers value, *Harvard Business Review*, November, 53–65; J. C. Anderson and J. A. Narus (1995) Capturing the value of supplementary services, *Harvard Business Review*, January, 75–83; J. C. Anderson, D. C. Jain and P. K. Chintagunta (1993) A customer value assessment in business markets: a state-of-practice study, *Journal of Business-to-Business Marketing*, 1(1), 3–29.

2 The system should provide the management and organisation with a valid system of data analysis for management of operations and capacity of the warehouse and line optimisation of picking work.

3 The system should provide the management board with an effective analysis tool for continuous evaluation of warehouse performance.

4 The system should provide online and real-time information on stock status.

Now, productivity has risen so much that the warehouse can operate to the same level with 22 employees as it did in 2005 with 34. There are also other advantages, such as the fact that today, internal sales people know exactly what the company holds in stock – important knowledge which they had difficulty in obtaining previously.

Some firms are using technology to devise novel customer solutions. With Web technology and tools, VistaPrint printers can offer professional printing to small businesses that previously could not afford it.[37] Some companies handle price-oriented buyers by setting a lower price but establishing restrictive conditions: (1) limited quantities; (2) no refunds; (3) no adjustments; and (4) no services.[38]

Solution selling can also alleviate price pressure and comes in different forms. Here are three examples.[39]

1 **Solutions to enhance customer revenues**: Through a sophisticated data management system, Hendrix Voeders helped farmers to monitor animals' feed consumption and weight gain. Farmers were now able to make microadjustments in nutrients and medicine, resulting in productivity gains such as animal weight gain of 5–10 per cent or increases of 4–5 per cent in live births.

2 **Solutions to decrease customer risks**: ICI Explosives formulated a safer way to ship explosives for quarries.

3 **Solutions to reduce customer costs**: W.W. Grainger employees work at large customer facilities to reduce materials-management costs.

More and more firms are seeking solutions that increase benefits and reduce costs enough to overcome any low price concerns. Consider the example of Lincoln Electric on the next page.

Risk and gain sharing can offset requested price reductions from customers. For example, a hospital supplier signs an agreement with a hospital promising €350,000 in savings over the first 18 months in exchange for a tenfold increase in the hospital's share of supplies. If the hospital supplier achieves less than this promised saving, it will make up the difference. If the hospital supplier achieves substantially more than promised, it participates in the extra savings. To make such arrangements work, the supplier must be willing to help the customer to build a historical database, reach an agreement for measuring benefits and costs, and devise a dispute resolution mechanism with directions on how any disagreements between the parties should be resolved.

Number of suppliers

As part of the buyer selection process, buying centres must decide how many suppliers to use. Companies are increasingly reducing the number of suppliers. Ford and Motorola have cut the number of suppliers by 20–80 per cent. These companies want their chosen suppliers to be responsible for a larger component system, they want them to achieve continuous quality and performance improvement, and at the same time they want them to lower prices each year by a given percentage. These companies expect their suppliers to work closely with them during product development, and they value their suggestions. There is even a trend toward single sourcing.

Companies that use multiple sources often cite the threat of a labour strike as the biggest deterrent to single sourcing. Another reason companies may be reluctant to use a single source is that they fear they will become too comfortable in the relationship and lose their competitive edge.

▽ Lincoln Electric

Lincoln Electric was founded in 1895 and today is the world leader in the design, development and manufacture of arc welding products, robotic welding systems, plasma and oxyfuel cutting equipment. While Lincoln is headquartered in Cleveland, Ohio, it also has a worldwide network of distributors and sales offices covering more than 160 countries, including more than 20 in Europe. Lincoln has a global workforce of more than 7000 and has a decades-long tradition of working with its customers to reduce costs through its Guaranteed Cost Reduction Program.

When a customer insists that a Lincoln distributor lowers prices to match competitors, the company and the particular distributor may guarantee that, during the coming year, they will find cost reductions in the customer's plant that meet or exceed the price difference between Lincoln's products and the competition's. For example, The Holland Binkley Company, a major manufacturer of components for tractor trailers including landing gear, suspension undercarriages and custom parts, had been purchasing Lincoln Electric welding wire for years. When Binkley began to shop around for a better price on wire, Lincoln Electric developed a package of reducing costs and working together that called for a €7000 saving but eventually led to a six-figure saving, a growth in business and a strong, long-term partnership between customer and supplier.[40]

Lincoln Electric is a successful industrial products company that works with its customers to build strong relationships by lowering their costs.

Source: Courtesy of Lincoln Electric/ Jenny Ogborn

Order-routine specification

After selecting suppliers, the buyer negotiates the final order, listing the technical specifications, the quantity needed, the expected time of delivery, return policies, warranties, and so on. Many industrial buyers lease heavy equipment such as machinery and trucks. The lessee gains a number of advantages: conserving capital, getting the latest products, receiving better service and gaining some tax advantages. The lessor often ends up with a larger net income and the chance to sell to customers who could not afford outright purchase.

In the case of maintenance, repair and operating items, buyers are moving towards blanket contracts rather than periodic purchase orders. A blanket contract establishes a long-term relationship in which the supplier promises to resupply the buyer as needed, at agreed-upon prices, over a specified period of time. Because the seller holds the stock, blanket contracts are sometimes called *stockless purchase plans*. The buyer's computer automatically sends an order to the seller when stock is needed. This system locks suppliers in tighter with the buyer and makes it difficult for out suppliers to break in unless the buyer becomes dissatisfied with the in supplier's prices, quality or service.

Companies that fear a shortage of key materials are willing to buy and hold large inventories. They will sign long-term contracts with suppliers to ensure a steady flow of materials. Ford and several other major companies regard long-term supply planning as a major responsibility of their purchasing managers. For example, General Motors wants to buy from fewer suppliers, which must be willing to locate close to its plants and produce high-quality components. Business marketers are also setting up extranets with important customers to facilitate and lower the cost of transactions. The customers enter orders directly on the computer that are automatically transmitted to the supplier. Some companies go further and shift the ordering responsibility to their suppliers in systems called *vendor-managed inventory*. These suppliers are privy to the customer's inventory levels and take responsibility for replenishing it automatically through *continuous replenishment programmes*.

Performance review

The buyer periodically reviews the performance of the chosen supplier(s) using one of three methods. The buyer may contact the end users and ask for their evaluations; the buyer may rate the supplier on several criteria using a weighted-score method; or the buyer might aggregate the cost of poor performance to come up with adjusted costs of purchase, including price. The performance review may lead the buyer to continue, modify or end a supplier relationship.

Many companies have set up incentive systems to reward purchasing managers for good buying performance, in much the same way that sales personnel receive bonuses for good selling performance. These systems lead purchasing managers to increase pressure on sellers for the best terms.

▽ Managing business-to-business relationships

The need for managing business-to-business relationships

To improve effectiveness and efficiency, business suppliers and customers are exploring different ways to manage their relationships.[41] Closer relationships are driven in part by supply chain management, early supplier involvement and purchasing alliances.[42] Cultivating the right relationships with business is paramount for any holistic marketing programme. A master at business-to-business marketing is GE, as chronicled in 'Breakthrough marketing: General Electric'.

The role of uncertainty in business relationships

Uncertainty refers to situations where the information available for decision making is too vague, or too imprecise, to calculate the probabilities of different outcomes of the decision.[43] Uncertainty can come in many forms and may relate to both institutional aspects (e.g., lack of formal institutional standards such as professionalisation, industry boundaries and product standards) and transactional aspects (e.g., lack of confidentiality of information and insufficient information).[44] Therefore, uncertainty has also to do with trust among business partners or in an industry.[45] Uncertainty can be highly damaging for the efficiency of business relations and should therefore be reduced. Uncertainty leads to unpredictable outcomes since it makes it difficult for business negotiators to anticipate the full impact – positive or negative – of a transaction or an agreement.[46] Hence, uncertainty may lead to irrational decisions. Uncertainty may even lead to a collective irrational outcome of a transaction between business partners, although each partner

Breakthrough marketing

General Electric

GE is made up of six recently reorganised major divisions that operate in areas as diverse as home appliances, jet engines, security systems, wind turbines and financial services. The company is so large (2005 revenues of €105 billion) that if each of its six business units were ranked separately, all would appear in the *Fortune* 500. If GE were a country, it would be one of the 50 largest, ahead of Finland, Israel and Ireland.

Founded by Thomas Edison as the Edison Electric Light Company in 1878, GE was an early pioneer in light bulbs and electrical appliances. It also served the electrical needs of various industries, such as transportation, utilities, manufacturing and broadcasting. It became the acknowledged pioneer in business-to-business marketing in the 1950s and 1960s when its tagline was 'Live Better Electrically'. As the company diversified its product lines, it created new campaigns, including 'Progress for People' and 'We Bring Good Things to Life'.

In 2003, GE faced a new challenge: how to promote its diversified brand globally with a unified message. Its major new campaign, called 'Imagination at Work', highlighted its renewed focus on innovation and new technology. The award-winning campaign promoted units such as GE Aircraft Engines, GE Medical Systems and GE Plastics, focusing on the breadth of GE's product offerings. GE spends some €105 million on corporate advertising – a large expenditure, but one that creates efficiencies by focusing on the core GE brand. The goal was to unify these divisions under the GE brand while giving them a voice. 'When you're a company like ours, with 11 different businesses, brand is really important in pulling the identity of the company together,' said former chief marketing officer Beth Comstock. 'Integration was important in communicating the brand across the organisation and to all of our constituents.'

The new integrated campaign got results. 'Research indicates GE is now being associated with attributes such as being high tech, leading edge, innovative, contemporary and creative,' said Judy Hu, GE's general manager for global advertising and branding. Just as encouraging, survey respondents still associate GE with some of its traditional attributes, such as being trustworthy and reliable.

In 2005, the company extended the campaign with its next initiative, 'Ecomagination', which highlighted the company's efforts to develop environmentally friendly 'green' technologies. It leveraged the 'Imagination' tagline again with a 2006 campaign called 'Health Care Re-Imagined' that featured innovative GE health care products for detecting, preventing and curing diseases.

While the campaign unites all GE business units, GE's success rests on its ability to understand the business market and the business buying process, putting itself in the shoes of its business customers. Consider its approach to pricing its aircraft engines. GE is aware that purchasing an aircraft engine is a multimillion-euro expenditure (€15 million for each large engine). And it doesn't end with the purchase of the engine – customers (airlines) face substantial maintenance costs to meet aviation authority guidelines and ensure reliability of the engines. So in 1999, GE pioneered a new pricing option. The concept, called 'Power by the Hour', gives customers an opportunity to pay a fixed fee each time they run the engine. In return, GE performs all the maintenance and guarantees the engine's reliability. When demand for air travel is uncertain, GE gives its customers a lower cost of ownership.

This kind of B2B marketing savvy helped GE cement its top position in the *Financial Times* 'World's Most Respected Companies' survey for six consecutive years. Its understanding of the business markets, its way of doing business and its brand marketing have kept GE's brand equity growing. Indeed, its brand equity was valued at €34 billion in the 2006 Interbrand/*BusinessWeek* ranking of the top 100 global brands, placing it fourth among all brands. 'The GE brand is what connects us all and makes us so much better than the parts,' chief marketing officer Comstock said.

Today, eastern Europe is growing at three times the global rate. GE has been a part of that growth, providing new technologies to build the region's infrastructure, and investing €36 million to build a Global Research Centre in Munich, Germany. Russia is one European country in which GE has made significant investments. GE is one of the largest foreign companies in Russia, operating multiple businesses including an equipment fleet with more than 1500 large units.

Sources: G. Colvin (2006) What makes GE great?, *Fortune*, 6 March, 90–104; T. A. Stewart (2006) Growth as a process, *Harvard Business Review*, June, 60–70; K. Kranhold (2006) The Immelt era, five years old, transforms GE, *Wall Street Journal*, 11 September; D. Fisher (2005) GE turns green, *Forbes*, 15 August, 80–5; J. A. Byrne (2005) Jeff Immelt, *Fast Company*, July, 60–5; www.ge.com.

individually performs rational behaviour. The famous example put forward by Akerlof[47] concerning the market for 'lemons' (i.e., used cars of poor quality) illustrates this point. A used car is mainly a 'credence good'[48] since the 'real' quality of a used car can usually not be determined by the potential buyer until after s/he has purchased it and driven it for a time. Because of a lack of information the buyer is motivated to pay only a low price for a used car, thereby minimising the potential risk of paying too much for poor quality. If the seller cannot justify a high price, which is difficult because there are no simple means of conveying the quality in a believable way, he will be motivated to sell only lemons. The consequence is that only low-quality cars will be sold and bought in the marketplace, a situation that hurts both sellers (lack of profit) and buyers (lack of quality). This example – although constructed – points to the need for reducing uncertainty in business relationships. As discussed in the next section, uncertainty is also one of the main concepts considered in the transaction cost economics approach.

Transaction cost economics

Within mainstream economic thinking all market agents can obtain perfect knowledge about products and prices at no cost. Business agents are fully informed about all products and business terms and no information asymmetric exists between suppliers and customers. Thus, rationality is assumed for all market agents. In transaction cost economics (TCE), market agents have limits on their ability to make truly rational decisions; they have limited mental resources and thus cannot deal with unlimited amounts of information. *Bounded rationality* can be seen either as the attempt to do as well as possible given the demands of the world – the notion of optimisation under constraints – or as the suboptimal outcome of the limited cognitive system.[49] The introduction of bounded rationality means that possible information asymmetry may exist between seller and buyer. Thus, a risk arises that market failure will occur due to opportunistic behaviour of the better-informed party.

When buyers cannot easily monitor supplier performance, the supplier might shirk or cheat and not deliver the expected value. *Opportunism* is 'some form of cheating or undersupply relative to an implicit or explicit contract'.[50] It may entail blatant self-interest and deliberate misrepresentation that violate contractual agreements. In creating the 1996 version of the Ford Taurus, Ford Corporation chose to outsource the whole process to one supplier, Lear Corporation. Lear committed to a contract that, for various reasons, it knew it was unable to fulfil. According to Ford, Lear missed deadlines, failed to meet weight and price objectives, and furnished parts that did not work.[51] A more passive form of opportunism might be a refusal or unwillingness to adapt to changing circumstances.

Opportunism is a concern because firms must devote resources to control and monitoring that they could otherwise allocate to more productive purposes. Contracts may become inadequate to govern supplier transactions when supplier opportunism becomes difficult to detect, when firms make specific investments in assets that they cannot use elsewhere, and when contingencies are harder to anticipate. Customers and suppliers are more likely to form a joint venture (instead of signing a simple contract) when the supplier's degree of asset specificity (asset specificity: whether the assets involved in business transactions are valuable in the context of one or more transactions) is high, monitoring the supplier's behaviour is difficult, and the supplier has a poor reputation.[52] When a supplier has a good reputation, it is more likely to avoid opportunism to protect this valuable intangible asset.

The presence of a significant future time horizon and/or strong solidarity norms typically causes customers and suppliers to strive for joint benefits. As a result, there is a shift in specific investments from expropriation (increased opportunism on the receiver's part) to bonding (reduced opportunism).[53]

According to TCE, companies may act in a self-interested way when possible, that is, they may exploit unforeseen circumstances even though the related actions taken may damage the other party. However, people will only act opportunistically some of the time and not all people are opportunists. The problem is to tell who is an opportunist at what time, which of course is not an easy task. The combination of bounded rationality (which may lead to information asymmetries) with the possibility of people acting opportunistically therefore introduces uncertainty in business relationships. Along with two other variables (frequency: the frequency of the business transaction and asset specificity) the level of uncertainty explains whether firms will deal with market agents or whether they will seek to integrate their activities vertically (for example, by taking over a supplier). Other things being equal, the higher the frequency, the uncertainty and the asset specificity the more likely it is that vertical integration will take place since this solution will result in the lowest transaction costs. *Transaction costs* occur when goods or services are transferred from one organisation to another and may include search costs, contracting costs, monitoring costs and enforcement costs.[54]

A certain amount of uncertainty can always be associated with a transaction since because of bounded rationality it is difficult and costly to determine all the possible effects a transaction might have.[55] In TCE theory, uncertainty therefore arises because of impenetrable complexity; and since 'objective' uncertainty can be difficult, or even impossible to estimate, focus is put on companies' perceived uncertainty. Companies are assumed to take action based on perceived uncertainty. Based on TCE a number of possible such perceived uncertainties can be detected within business relationships. Uncertainties may be related to differences between buyer and seller (e.g., language, culture, technology), trading procedures, contracting procedures and to the possibility that companies may act in an opportunist way when beneficial for just one of the parties. While TCE is useful in detecting the kinds of uncertainties that may be involved in transactions among business relationships, TCE has been criticised for focusing too much on agent opportunism and thereby neglecting the possibility of inter-firm trust and the evolvement of inter-firm relationships.[56] Network theory, however, introduces a view on business relationships that in many aspects deals with this criticism.

Network theory

Whereas TCE is based on analysis of the market behaviour of companies and views the results of that behaviour in terms of 'win–lose' outcomes, network theory emphasises the possibility that both sides can win simultaneously, that is, a win–win outcome. Basically, this possibility arises because of the introduction of 'trust' in network theory. While TCE can be considered an 'anti-trust' approach (people in companies are opportunists), network theory can be considered a 'trust' approach. Networking appears to be among the leading paradigms in the understanding and analysis of partnership between companies. A distinction can be made between strategic (governed) and industrial (non-governed) networks. The governed networks are those strategic networks where members strongly identify with the 'core firm'/network and where there are clear rules for participating in the network's knowledge-sharing activities.

Dyer and Nobeoka[57] have shown that Toyota's ability to effectively create and manage network-level knowledge-sharing processes at least partially explains the relative productivity advantages enjoyed by Toyota and its suppliers. Toyota's network: (1) motivates members to participate and openly share valuable knowledge (while preventing undesirable spillovers to competitors); (2) prevents free riders; and (3) reduces the costs associated with finding and accessing different types of valuable knowledge. Toyota has managed to do this by creating a strong network identity with rules for participation and entry into the network. In 2006 Toyota was the leading automaker in global sales with 8,808,000 units. In 2007, the Volkswagen group began working on a ten-year strategic plan that aimed to narrow the productivity and profit gap with Toyota. 'In the last five, six years, Toyota has pulled ahead of us, and what we plan to do is to reduce the lead they've got,' says CEO Martin Winterkorn. 'If we are approaching Toyota, we are approaching it in terms of productivity goals,' the VW spokesman added. 'The financial side is related. If you are highly productive, you are highly profitable.' In 2006 VW ranked fourth in global sales with 5,720,096 units.[58]

The strategic networks are managed by the hub, which sends signals to network members as to what actions, activities and structures are considered appropriate. In contrast, industrial networks are sets of interrelated agents performing interconnected activities by employing interdependent resources.[59] In industrial networks the relationships need therefore to be 'coped with' rather than controlled,[60] and in order to be able to manage these relationships a certain level of mutual trust and information sharing is needed. Thus, while emphasis in strategic networks is on coordination and control, emphasis in industrial networks is on trust and on exchange of 'sensitive/confidential' information. Shortcomings in coordination and/or in information sharing could therefore be a significant driver of uncertainty and transaction costs among the parties involved in the network.[61]

▽ SOI Industry Consortium

In November 2007, a group of electronics companies around the world launched the SOI (silicon-on-insulator) Industry Consortium. The consortium aims at accelerating SOI innovations, promoting the benefits of SOI technology and reducing the barriers to adoption. The SOI Consortium's goals are to reduce adoption costs, make SOI best practices available and facilitate design examples across the value chain. The most significant benefits demonstrated by SOI are performance enhancement and power consumption reduction. The founding membership roster includes: AMD, ARM, Cadence Design Systems, CEA-Leti, Chartered Semiconductor Manufacturing, Freescale Semiconductor, IBM, Innovative Silicon, KLA-Tencor, Lam Research, NXP, Samsung, Semico, Soitec, SHE Europe, STMicroelectronics, Synopsys, TSMC and UMC.

Source: Based on K. Nargi-Toth (2007) Silicon-on-Insulator Consortium, *Printed Circuit Design & Manufacture*, 24(11), November, 8.

In general – covering both types of networks – networks can be understood as long-term arrangements among organisations, which allow these organisations to get long-term sustainable advantages.[62] Network theory, developed first in the 1960s and 1970s, is based on the empirical observation that in many industrial markets stability of relations, exchange of information, interlacing of technologies and various forms of cooperation and contractual agreement is the rule rather than the exception.[63] In many producer markets, the selling firm has a limited number of highly important customers and the relationships to these customers are often complex, involving several people and functions on both sides. Because of the complexity and uncertainty associated with dealing with new partners both the selling and the buying company may find it useful to reduce the perceived distance between the companies. As transactions evolve successfully both parties may believe that the benefits of staying in the relationship outweigh the disadvantages of not operating 'freely' in the marketplace. This reduces opportunism, and increases trust, since both parties share an interest in nursing and maintaining the relationship.

However, building relationships also exposes companies to new uncertainties. In a network relationship the involved parties are 'selling' their independency for the purpose of attaining lower transaction costs. On the other hand, the closer the relationship the higher the uncertainty of being stuck and being caught with a single partner.[64] Thus, firms are in need of effective information tools, which not only fulfil intra-network demands for mutual information but also fulfil firms' need for information about alternatives. The higher the collaboration the higher the dependency, and thus the more difficult it is to change partner. Bringing 'external' market information into the collaboration may motivate each party to maximise short-term transactions in order to maintain long-term network advantages. Hence, because of an increased, collective insight into other market opportunities, costs and the uncertainties associated with not being able to operate 'freely' may decrease.

Much research has advocated greater vertical coordination between members of the distribution chain, or in other words stronger and more organised cooperation between, say, a company and its buyers and/or suppliers.

Vertical coordination

Through vertical coordination both buyers and sellers can transcend merely transacting and instead engage in activities that create more value for both parties.[65] Building trust is one prerequisite to healthy and well-coordinated long-term relationships. 'Marketing insight: Establishing corporate trust and credibility' identifies some key dimensions to such trust. Knowledge that is specific and relevant to a relationship partner is also an important factor in the strength of interfirm ties between partners.[66]

Marketing insight

Establishing corporate trust and credibility

Corporate credibility is the extent to which customers believe a firm can design and deliver products and services that satisfy their needs and wants. It reflects the supplier's reputation in the marketplace and is the foundation for a strong relationship.

Corporate credibility depends in turn on three factors:

1 **Corporate expertise**: the extent to which a company is seen as able to make and sell products or conduct services.

2 **Corporate trustworthiness**: the extent to which a company is seen as motivated to be honest, dependable and sensitive to customer needs.

3 **Corporate likeability**: the extent to which a company is seen as likeable, attractive, prestigious, dynamic, and so on.

In other words, a credible firm is good at what it does; it keeps its customers' best interests in mind and is enjoyable to work with.

Trust is the willingness of a firm to rely on a business partner. It depends on a number of interpersonal and interorganisational factors, such as the firm's perceived competence, integrity, honesty and benevolence. Personal interactions with employees of the firm, opinions about the company as a whole and perceptions of trust will evolve with experience. Figure 8.1 provides a summary of some core dimensions of trust.

Building trust can be especially tricky in online settings, and firms often impose more stringent requirements on their online business partners than on others. Business buyers worry that they won't get products of the right quality delivered to the right place at the right time. Sellers worry about getting paid on time – or at all – and how much credit they should extend. Some firms, such as the global

Figure 8.1 Trust dimensions

Source: G. Urban (2005) *Where are you positioned on the trust dimensions?*, in *Don't Just Relate – Advocate: A Blueprint for Profit in the Era of Customer Power*, Indianapolis, Indiana: Wharton School Publishers, p. 99. Copyright © 2005. Reproduced with permission.

▶ Marketing insight *(continued)*

transportation and supply chain management company Ryder System, use automated credit-checking applications and online trust services to determine the creditworthiness of trading partners. At the same time, Ryder System does not neglect that trust is a mutual thing. On the European part of its website (ryder.com) the company provides several reasons why it can be trusted as a business partner, including referring to the fact that, from Bristol to Budapest, over 1000 companies partner the company.

Sources: B. Violino (2002) Building B2B trust, *Computerworld*, 17 June, p. 32; R. E. Plank, D. A. Reid and E. Bolman Pullins (1999) Perceived Trust in business-to-business sales: a new measure, *Journal of Personal Selling and Sales Management*, 19(3), 61–72; K. L. Keller and D. A. Aaker (1998) Corporate-level marketing: the impact of credibility on a company's brand extensions, *Corporate Reputation Review*, 1 (August), 356–78; R. M. Morgan and S. D. Hunt (1994) The commitment–trust theory of relationship marketing, *Journal of Marketing*, 58(3), 20–38; C. Moorman, R. Deshpande and G. Zaltman (1993) Factors affecting trust in market research relationships, *Journal of Marketing*, 57 (January), 81–101; www.ryder.com.

Consider the mutual benefits from the following arrangement.

▽ Motoman, Inc. and Stillwater Technologies

Motoman, Inc., which along with its sister companies supports industry robotic solutions throughout the world, and Stillwater Technologies, a contract tooling and machinery company and a key supplier to Motoman, are tightly integrated. Not only do they occupy office and manufacturing space in the same facility, but their telephone and computer systems are linked, and they share a common lobby, conference room and employee cafeteria. Philip V. Morrison, chairman and CEO of Motoman, says it is like 'a joint venture without the paperwork'. Short delivery distances are just one benefit of the unusual partnership. Also key is the fact that employees of both companies have ready access to one another and can share ideas on improving quality and reducing costs. This close relationship has opened the door to new opportunities. Both companies had been doing work for Honda Motor Company, and Honda suggested that they work together on systems projects. The integration makes the two bigger than they are individually.[67]

One historical study of four very different business-to-business relationships found that several factors, by affecting partner interdependence and/or environmental uncertainty, influenced the development of a relationship between business partners.[68] The relationship between advertising agencies and clients illustrates these findings:

1 **In the relationship formation stage, one partner experienced substantial market growth**: Manufacturers capitalising on mass-production techniques developed national brands, which increased the importance and amount of mass media advertising.

2 **Information asymmetry between partners was such that a partnership would generate more profits than if the partner attempted to invade the other firm's area**: Advertising agencies had specialised knowledge that their clients would have had difficulty obtaining.

3 **At least one partner had high barriers to entry that would prevent the other partner from entering the business**: Advertising agencies could not easily become national manufacturers, and for years manufacturers were not eligible to receive media commissions.

4 **Dependence asymmetry existed such that one partner was more able to control or influence the other's conduct**: Advertising agencies had control over media access.

5 **One partner benefited from economies of scale related to the relationship**: Ad agencies gained by providing the same market information to multiple clients.

Research has found that buyer–supplier relationships differ according to four factors: availability of alternatives; importance of supply; complexity of supply; and supply market dynamism.

Based on these four factors, they classified buyer–supplier relationships into eight different categories:[69]

1 **Basic buying and selling**: These are simple, routine exchanges with moderate levels of cooperation and information exchange.

2 **Bare bones**: These relationships require more adaptation by the seller and less cooperation and information exchange.

3 **Contractual transaction**: These exchanges are defined by formal contract and generally have low levels of trust, cooperation and interaction.

4 **Customer supply**: In this traditional customer supply situation, competition rather than cooperation is the dominant form of governance.

5 **Cooperative systems**: The partners in cooperative systems are united in operational ways, but neither demonstrates structural commitment through legal means or adaptation.

6 **Collaborative**: In collaborative exchanges, much trust and commitment lead to true partnership.

7 **Mutually adaptive**: Buyers and sellers make many relationship-specific adaptations, but without necessarily achieving strong trust or cooperation.

8 **Customer is king**: In this close, cooperative relationship, the seller adapts to meet the customer's needs without expecting much adaptation or change in exchange.

Over time, however, the roles and nature of a relationship may shift and be activated depending on different circumstances.[70] Some needs can be satisfied with fairly basic supplier performance. Buyers then neither want nor require a close relationship with a supplier. Likewise, some suppliers may not find it worth their while to invest in customers with limited growth potential.

One study found that the closest relationships between customers and suppliers arose when the supply was important to the customer and there were procurement obstacles, such as complex purchase requirements and few alternative suppliers.[71] Another study suggested that greater vertical coordination between buyer and seller through information exchange and planning is usually necessary only when high environmental uncertainty exists and specific investments are modest.[72]

Researchers have noted that establishing a customer–supplier relationship creates tension between safeguarding and adaptation. Vertical coordination can facilitate stronger customer–seller ties but at the same time may increase the risk to the customer's and supplier's specific investments. *Specific investments* are those expenditures tailored to a particular company and value chain partner (investments in company-specific training, equipment and operating procedures or systems).[73] They help firms grow profits and achieve their positioning.[74] For example, Xerox has worked closely with its suppliers to develop customised processes and components that reduced its copier-manufacturing costs by 30–40 per cent. In return, suppliers received sales and volume guarantees, an enhanced understanding of their customer needs and a strong position with Xerox for future sales.[75]

Specific investments, however, also entail considerable risk to both customer and supplier. TCE maintains that because these investments are partially sunk, they lock the firms that make them into a particular relationship. Sensitive cost and process information may need to be exchanged. A buyer may be vulnerable to hold-up because of switching costs; a supplier may be more vulnerable to hold-up in future contracts because of dedicated assets and/or expropriation of technology/knowledge. In terms of the latter risk, consider the following example.[76]

An automobile component manufacturer wins a contract to supply an under-hood component to an original equipment manufacturer (OEM). A one-year, sole-source contract safeguards the supplier's OEM-specific investments in a dedicated production line. However, the supplier may also be obliged to work (non-contractually) as a partner with the OEM's internal engineering staff, using linked computing facilities to exchange detailed engineering information and coordinate frequent design and manufacturing changes over the term of the contract. These interactions could reduce costs and/or increase quality by improving the firm's responsiveness to marketplace changes. But they could also magnify the threat to the supplier's intellectual property.

Marketing memo

Electronic customer relationship management

Customer relationship management is a business approach or strategy that integrates all business functions which relate to the customer, namely marketing, sales, customer service and field support, through the integration of people, process and technology.[77] CRM can be considered a fraction of electronic customer relationship management (eCRM) as the latter approach expands CRM by integrating new technologies such as websites, wireless, voice technologies, email and information appliances into the traditional CRM approach. Moreover, management researchers Pan and Lee argue that a successful eCRM solution prerequisites that all customer-related information is consolidated into a single view. In this way, the eCRM concept facilitates suppliers' understanding of who their customers are and what products are of interest to them – only with such an understanding is it possible to provide customers with the products and services they want. Evidence suggests that businesses are increasingly taking advantage of eCRM to build relationships with customers.[78]

One of the main advantages of eCRM is that information technology makes it possible for a company to interact with a large numbers of customers, while treating them as individuals. A number of other potential advantages can also be detected:[79] eCRM (a) may reduce the cost of contacting customers; (b) may have the ability of transferring some administrative tasks to customers (e.g., product configuration, order tracking, online customers' details collection) and thereby reducing operational costs; (c) could be integrated with other systems such as production, finance and supply and thereby improve the workflow of the organisation; and (d) may improve sales by customer profiling and better market segmentation, automated campaign management, email marketing, and so on. Hence, eCRM has the potential of offering increased value to both the seller and the buyer by improving mutual understanding, by matching needs and requests and by providing more efficient workflows.

Our discussion has concentrated largely on the buying behaviour of profit-seeking companies, but much of what we have said also applies to the buying practices of institutional and government organisations. However, in the following section we want to highlight certain special features of these markets.

▽ Institutional and government markets

The **institutional market** consists of schools, hospitals, nursing homes, prisons and other institutions that must provide goods and services to people in their care. Many of these organisations are characterised by low budgets and captive clienteles; for example, hospitals must decide what quality of food to buy for patients. The buying objective here is not profit, because the food is provided as part of the total service package; nor is cost minimisation the sole objective, because poor food will cause patients to complain and harm the hospital's reputation. The hospital purchasing agent must search for institutional-food vendors whose quality meets or exceeds a certain minimum standard and whose prices are low. In fact, many food vendors set up a separate division to sell to institutional buyers because of these buyers' special needs and characteristics. Heinz produces, packages and prices its Ketchup differently to meet the requirements of hospitals, colleges and prisons.

In most countries government organisations are a major buyer of goods and services. They typically require suppliers to submit bids and often award the contract to the lowest bidder. In some cases the government unit will make allowance for superior quality or a reputation for completing contracts on time. Governments will also buy on a negotiated contract basis, primarily in the case of complex projects involving major R&D costs and risks, and in cases where there is little competition.

Public procurement is the process used by public authorities or bodies governed by public law to purchase products and services with tax money. Public procurement is a key sector of the EU economy, accounting for €1500 billion or about 16 per cent of gross domestic product (meaning the total market value of the goods and services produced by a nation's economy during a specific period of time).[80] A major complaint of multinationals operating in Europe was that each country showed favouritism toward its nationals despite superior offers from foreign firms. Although such practices are fairly entrenched, the European Union is attempting to remove this bias. For example, EU member states' contracting authorities need to wait for at least ten days after deciding who has won the public contract before the contract can actually be signed. The so-called 'standstill period' is designed to give bidders time to examine the decision and to assess whether it is appropriate to initiate a review procedure. If this standstill period has not been respected, the directive requires national courts under certain conditions to set aside a signed contract by annulling it. 'We need effective procedures for seeking review in all EU member states in order to make sure that public contracts ultimately go to the company which has made the best offer,' the EU internal market and services commissioner Charlie McCreevy said.[81]

▽ PublicOpportunity.com

PublicOpportunity.com is a government procurement consulting firm, formed by an American lawyer and a Danish MBA, to meet the needs of business in the global marketplace. With offices in the EU and the United States, PublicOpportunity.com provides its subscribers with the latest information and leads necessary for companies wanting to sell to government markets around the world. Once a company has decided which leads to follow up, which governments to target and what contracts to seek, PublicOpportunity.com helps complete the draft. PublicOpportunity.com offers three kinds of services:

1 **Subscription service**: providing companies with information and leads on current opportunities being offered by various governments that currently need their products or services.

2 **Consulting services**: offering companies consultation and assistance to understand any requirements companies must meet.

3 **Seminars**: conducting an ongoing series of seminars on current issues of interest to the public procurement sector, including designing special seminars and programmes to train companies' employees in dealing with government procurement, the World Trade Organization Agreement, the EU procurement rules and other international treaties and agreements.

Source: www.publicopportunity.com.

Because their spending decisions are subject to public review, government organisations require considerable paperwork from suppliers, which often complain about bureaucracy, regulations, decision-making delays and frequent shifts in procurement personnel. But the fact that the biggest market in the world is the government market makes it also the most potentially attractive customer in the world.

Government decision makers often think technology vendors have not done their homework. In addition, vendors do not pay enough attention to cost justification, which is a major activity for government procurement professionals. Companies hoping to be government contractors need to help government agencies see the bottom-line impact of products. The recent expansion of the EU to 27 countries further increased the opportunities for businesses to win such contracts across the EU and should also bring substantial savings for public bodies through increased competition among contractors. Just as companies provide government agencies with guidelines about how best to purchase and use their products, governments provide would-be suppliers with detailed guidelines describing how to sell to the government. Failure to follow the guidelines or to fill out forms and contracts correctly can create a legal nightmare.[82] Fortunately for businesses of all sizes, the EU has been trying to simplify the contracting procedure and make both bidding and procurement more attractive and effective.

▽ eGovernment in Europe

eGovernment is one of the priorities set by the eEurope 2005 action plan. It is a means of providing more efficient and better-quality public services, reducing waiting times for users and improving transparency and accountability in services. Public procurement is one area where use of ICT can be particularly advantageous. Traditional public procurement operations are complex, time consuming and resource intensive. Use of ICT in public procurement can therefore improve efficiency, quality and value for money in public purchases. Until now the absence of clear Community rules has been an obstacle to the take-up of electronic public procurement in Europe. The adoption of the new package of legislation on public procurement, which includes specific rules on electronic public procurement, should be a turning point for the spread of electronic public procurement in Europe.[83]

European legislation has encouraged competition between firms by means of transparent selection procedures. It also makes provision for redress procedures against awarding authorities who do not fulfil their obligations. European directives are continuously being reviewed with a view to simplifying the existing legal framework and encouraging the use of electronic procedures.[84] Recently the European Commission launched the SIMAP project,[85] which has as its objective the development of the information systems infrastructure needed to support the delivery of an effective public procurement policy in Europe, by providing contracting entities and suppliers with the information they need to manage the procurement process effectively. Initially the project aims to improve the quality of information about the EU procurement opportunities and ensure that the information is made known to all potentially interested suppliers. In the longer term it will address the whole procurement process, including bids, award of contracts, delivery, invoicing and payment.

Another large customer that is also attractive to European companies is the US government. 'Marketing memo: Selling tech to the government' provides some tips for attacking that multibillion-dollar market. The General Services Administration, for example, not only sells stocked merchandise through its website but also creates direct links between buyers and contract suppliers.

Marketing memo

Selling tech to the government

The US government was projected to spend $65.9 billion on IT in fiscal year 2006. A large chunk of this US government business, however, isn't contracted out at all. Through the General Services Administration (GSA) and other government organisations, companies can sell directly to agencies without formal bidding. Here are three tips for tapping into that market.

1 **Get in the government IT catalogue** The GSA runs an online catalogue of goods and services for government agencies. About 28 per cent of federal spending flows through the catalogue's Schedule 70, which includes more than 2000 tech vendors. Getting a business listed can be important. Apply electronically and remember to spell out pricing structure carefully.

2 **Work your way in** Small businesses – especially those owned by women and minorities – are often needed by large businesses to satisfy small business set-asides. To maximise that probability:

- *Make sure contractors can find you* Get listed on the Small Business Administration's Subcontracting Network (wed.sba.gov) or use the US Chamber of Commerce website.

- *Stay on top of key contracts* Several websites provide updates for the latest deals that might provide opportunities (www.fedbizopps.gov; www.dodbusopps.com; prod.nais.nasa.gov/pub/fedproc/home.hml).

- *Work the angles* Meet with prospective bidders and explain your qualifications.

3 **Network actively** Attend one of the large trade shows, such as FOSE, GSA Expo, or E-Gov.

Some companies have pursued government business by establishing separate government marketing departments. Companies such as Gateway, Rockwell, Kodak and Goodyear anticipate government needs and projects, participate in the product specification phase, gather competitive intelligence, prepare bids carefully, and produce strong communications to describe and enhance their companies' reputations.

▽ SUMMARY

1 Organisational buying is the decision-making process by which formal organisations establish the need for purchased products and services, then identify, evaluate and choose among alternative brands and suppliers. The business market consists of all the organisations that acquire goods and services used in the production of other products or services that are sold, rented or supplied to others.

2 Compared to consumer markets, business markets generally have fewer and larger buyers, a closer customer–supplier relationship, and more geographically concentrated buyers. Demand in the business market is derived from demand in the consumer market and fluctuates with the business cycle. Nonetheless, the total demand for many business goods and services is quite price inelastic. Business marketers need to be aware of the role of professional purchasers and their influencers, the need for multiple sales calls, and the importance of direct purchasing, reciprocity and leasing.

3 The buying centre is the decision-making unit of a buying organisation. It consists of initiators, users, influencers, deciders, approvers, buyers and gatekeepers. To

influence these parties, marketers must be aware of environmental, organisational, interpersonal and individual factors.

4 The buying process consists of eight stages, called buyphases: (1) problem recognition; (2) general need description; (3) product specification; (4) supplier search; (5) proposal solicitation; (6) supplier selection; (7) order-routine specification; and (8) performance review.

5 Business marketers must form strong bonds and relationships with their customers and provide them with added value. Some customers, however, may prefer more of a transactional relationship.

6 The institutional market consists of schools, hospitals, nursing homes, prisons and other institutions that provide goods and services to people in their care. Buyers for government organisations tend to require a great deal of paperwork from their vendors and to favour open bidding and domestic companies. Suppliers must be prepared to adapt their offers to the special needs and procedures found in institutional and government markets.

▽ APPLICATIONS

Marketing debate

How different is business-to-business marketing?
Many business-to-business marketing executives lament the challenges of business-to-business marketing, maintaining that many traditional marketing concepts and principles do not apply. For a number of reasons, they assert that selling products and services to a company is fundamentally different from selling to individuals. Others disagree, claiming that marketing theory is still valid and only involves some adaptation in the marketing tactics.

Take a position: Business-to-business marketing requires a special, unique set of marketing concepts and principles *versus* Business-to-business marketing is really not that different and the basic marketing concepts and principles apply.

Marketing discussion

Consider some of the consumer behaviour topics in Chapter 7. How might you apply them to business-to-business settings?

For example, how might non-compensatory models of choice work? Mental accounting?

Marketing exercises

- In your opinion what are the ten most important topics/issues to be learned from this chapter?
- Pick one of the companies mentioned in this chapter. For this company, investigate and discuss: (a) Do you think that any of the ten topics/issues you identified could be related to the problems, or opportunities, that the company – in your opinion – is currently facing or could expect to be facing in the near future? (b) Why?
- In your opinion, what should the company do to deal with the identified problems or to take advantage of the identified opportunities?

▽ REFERENCES

[1]Based on J. Rossant (2004) Europe's hot growth companies, *BusinessWeek*, 25 October; www.soitec.com.

[2]For a comprehensive review of the topic, see J. C. Anderson and J. A. Narus (2004) *Business Market Management: Understanding, Creating, and Delivering Value*, 2nd edn, Upper Saddle River, NJ: Prentice Hall. Comments on a draft of this chapter from Northwestern University's Jim Anderson and University of Wisconsin's Jan Heide are gratefully acknowledged.

[3]F. E. Webster Jr. and Y. Wind (1972) *Organizational Buying Behavior*, Upper Saddle River, NJ: Prentice Hall, 2. For a review of recent academic literature on the topic see H. Håkansson and I. Snehota (2002) Marketing in business markets in B. Weitz and R. Wensley (eds) *Handbook of Marketing*, London: Sage, 513–26.

[4]B. Donath (2005) Customer knowledge takes priority in study, *Marketing News*, 15 (December), 7.

[5]J. Gilbert (2004) Small but mighty, *Sales & Marketing Management*, January, 30–5.

[6]M. Collins (1996) Breaking into the big leagues, *American Demographics*, January, 24.

[7]P. J. Robinson, C. W. Faris and Y. Wind (1967) *Industrial Buying and Creative Marketing*, Boston, MA: Allyn & Bacon.

[8]M. D. Bunn (1993) Taxonomy of buying decision approaches, *Journal of Marketing*, 57, January, 38–56; D. H. McQuiston (1989) Novelty, complexity, and importance as causal determinants of industrial buyer behavior, *Journal of Marketing*, April, 66–79; P. Doyle, A. G. Woodside and P. Mitchell (1979) Organizational buying in new task and rebuy situations, *Industrial Marketing Management*, February, 7–11.

[9]U. B. Ozanne and G. A. Churchill Jr. (1971) Five dimensions of the industrial adoption process, *Journal of Marketing Research*, August, 322–8.

[10]To learn more about how business-to-business firms can improve their branding, see P. Kotler and W. Pfoertsch (2006) *B2B Brand Management*, Berlin: Springer.

[11]S. Hamm (2006) The fine art of tech mergers, *BusinessWeek*, 10 July, 70–1.

[12]N. Dawar and M. Vandenbosch (2004) The seller's hidden advantage, *MIT Sloan Management Review*, Winter, 83–8.

[13]J. E. Lewin and N. Donthu (2005) The influence of purchase situation on buying center structure and involvement: a select meta-analysis of organizational buying behavior research, *Journal of Business Research*, 58 (October), 1381–90; R. Venkatesh and A. K. Kohli (1995) Influence strategies in buying centers, *Journal of Marketing*, 59 (October), 71–82.

[14]D. W. Jackson Jr., J. E. Keith and R. K. Burdick (1984) Purchasing agents' perceptions of industrial buying center influence: a situational approach, *Journal of Marketing*, Fall, 75–83.

[15]Webster and Wind (1972) op. cit., 6.

[16]Anderson and Narus (2004) op. cit.; F. E. Webster Jr. and Y. Wind (1972) A general model for understanding organizational buying behavior, *Journal of Marketing*, 36, April, 12–19; Webster and Wind (1972) op. cit.

[17]A. Enright (2006) It takes a committee to buy into B-to-B, *Marketing News*, 15 February, 12–13.

[18]F. E. Webster Jr. and K. L. Keller (2004) A roadmap for branding in industrial markets, *Journal of Brand Management*, 11 (May), 388–402.

[19]S. Ward and F. E. Webster Jr. (1991) Organizational Buying Behavior in T. Robertson and H. Kassarjian (eds) *Handbook of Consumer Behavior*, Upper Saddle River, NJ: Prentice Hall, Ch. 12.

[20]B. Donath (2006) Emotions play key role in biz brand appeal, *Marketing News*, 1 June, 7.

[21]M. Krauss (2006) Warriors of the heart, *Marketing News*, 1 February, 7.

[22]Webster and Wind (1972) op. cit., 6.

[23]E. Strout (2003) Safe and sound, *Sales & Marketing Management*, September, 38.

[24]J. C. Anderson, J. A. Narus and W. van Rossum (2006) Customer value proposition in business markets, *Harvard Business Review*, March, 2–10; J. C. Anderson (2004) From understanding to managing customer value in business markets, in H. Håkansson, D. Harrison and A. Waluszewski (eds) *Rethinking Marketing: New Marketing Tools*, London: John Wiley & Sons, 137–59.

[25]T. Minahan (1998) OEM buying survey – Part 2: Buyers get new roles but keep old tasks, *Purchasing*, 16 July, 208–9.

[26]Robinson, Faris and Wind (1967) op. cit.

[27]R. Grewal, J. M. Comer and R. Mehta (2001) An investigation into the antecedents of organizational participation in business-to-business electronic markets, *Journal of Marketing*, 65 (July), 17–33.

[28]Knowledge@Wharton (2005) Open sesame? Or could the doors slam shut for Alibaba.com?, 27 July; J. Angwin (2004) Top online chemical exchange is unlikely success story, *Wall Street Journal*, 8 January; O. Kharif (2003) B2B, take 2, *BusinessWeek*, 25 November; G. S. Day, A. J. Fein and G. Ruppersberger (2003) Shakeouts in digital markets: lessons from B2B exchanges, *California Management Review*, 45(2), (Winter), 131–51.

[29]www.converge.com, About the spot market, accessed November 2007; http://www.chemconnect.com/market_info.html, accessed April 2008.

[30]B. J. Carroll (2006) *Lead Generation for the Complex Sale*, New York: McGraw-Hill.

[31]A. Enright (2006) It takes a committee to buy into B-to-B, *Marketing News*, 15 February, 12–13.

[32]R. Hiebeler, T. B. Kelly and C. Ketteman (1998) *Best Practices: Building Your Business with Customer-Focused Solutions*, New York: Arthur Andersen/Simon & Schuster, 122–24.

[33]D. J. Flint, R. B. Woodruff and S. F. Gardial (2002) Exploring the phenomenon of customers' desired value change in a business-to-business context, *Journal of Marketing*, 66 (October), 102–17.

[34]R. N. Bolton and M. B. Myers (2003) Price-based global market segmentation for services, *Journal of Marketing*, 67 (July), 108–28.

[35]W. Ulaga and A. Eggert (2006) Value-based differentiation in business relationships: gaining and sustaining key supplier status, *Journal of Marketing*, 70 (January), 119–36.

[36]www.consafelogistics.com: Glud & Marstrand improve productivity, quality and overview with new WMS, accessed November 2007.

[37]D. Kiley (2006) Small print jobs for peanuts, *BusinessWeek*, 17 July, 58.

[38]N. Kumar (2004) *Marketing as Strategy: Understanding the CEO's Agenda for Driving Growth and Innovation*, Boston, MA: Harvard Business School Press.

[39]Ibid.

[40]See W. Atkinson (2003) Now that's value added, *Purchasing*, 11 December, 26; J. A. Narus and J. C. Anderson (1986) Turn your industrial distributors into partners, *Harvard Business Review*, March–April, 66–71.

[41]For foundational material see L. M. Rinehart, J. A. Eckert, R. B. Handfield, T. J. Page Jr. and T. Atkin (2004) An assessment of buyer–seller relationships, *Journal of Business Logistics*, 25(1), 25–62; F. R. Dwyer, P. Schurr and S. Oh (1987) Developing buyer–supplier relationships, *Journal of Marketing*, 51, April, 11–28; and B. B. Jackson (1985) *Winning and Keeping Industrial Customers: The Dynamics of Customer Relations*, Lexington, MA: D. C. Heath.

[42]A. Buvik and G. John (2000) When does vertical coordination improve industrial purchasing relationships?, *Journal of Marketing*, 64 (October), 52–64.

[43]L. G. Epstein (1999) A definition of uncertainty aversion, *Review of Economic Studies*, 66, 579–608.

[44]J. Gluckler and T. Armbruster (2003) Bridging uncertainty in management consulting: the mechanisms of trust and networked reputation, *Organization Studies*, 24(2) (February), 269–97.

[45]A. Giddens (1990) *The Consequences of Modernity*, Stanford, CA: Stanford University Press.

[46]A. Le Flanchec (2004) How to reduce uncertainty in a context of innovation: the case of IBM's negotiation of its European Works Council, *International Negotiation*, 9(2), 271–89.

[47]G. A. Akerlof (1970) The market for 'Lemons': quality uncertainty and the market mechanism, *The Quarterly Journal of Economics*, 84(3), 488–500.

[48]M. M. Darby, and E. Karni (1973) Free competition and the optimal amount of fraud, *Journal of Law and Economics*, 16,1, 67–88.

[49]P. M. Todd and G. Gigerenzer (2003) Bounded rationality to the world, *Journal of Economic Psychology*, 24(2), 143–65.

[50]K. H. Wathne and J. B. Heide (2000) Opportunism in interfirm relationships: forms, outcomes, and solutions, *Journal of Marketing*, 64 (October), 36–51.

[51]M. Walton (1997) When your partner fails you, *Fortune*, 26 May, 151–4.

[52]M. B. Houston and S. A. Johnson (2000) Buyer–supplier contracts versus joint ventures: determinants and consequences of transaction structure, *Journal of Marketing Research*, 37, (February), 1–15.

[53]A. I. Rokkan, J. B. Heide and K. W. Wathne (2003) Specific investment in marketing relationships: expropriation and bonding effects, *Journal of Marketing Research*, 40 (May), 210–24.

[54]J. H. Dyer (1997) Effective interfirm collaboration: how firms minimize transaction costs and maximize transaction value, *Strategic Management Journal*, 18(5), 535–56.

[55]J. Hallikas, V. M. Virolainen and M. Tuominen (2002) Understanding risk and uncertainty in supplier networks: a transaction cost approach, *International Journal of Production Research*, 40, 15, 3519–31; E. Williamson (1987) *Antitrust Economics: Mergers, Contracting, and Strategic Behavior*, Oxford: Basil Blackwell.

[56]Wu, Wei-Ping and W. L. Choi (2004) Transaction cost, social capital and firms' synergy creation in Chinese business networks: an integrative approach, *Asia Pacific Journal of Management*, 21, 325–43; R. Gulati (1995) Does familiarity breed trust?, *Academy of Management Journal*, 38, 85–112.

[57]J. H. Dyer and K. Nobeoka (2000) Creating and managing a high-performance knowledge-sharing network: the Toyota case, *Strategic Management Journal*, 21, 345–67.

[58]T. Armitage (2007) VW chases Toyota productivity, profit with 10-year plan, *Automotive News*, 82, 16.

[59]A. Lundgren (1993) Technological innovation and the emergence and evolution of industrial networks: the case of digital image technology in Sweden, *Advances in International Marketing*, 5, 145–70.

[60]T. Ritter (1999) The networking company: antecedents for coping with relationships and networks effectively, *Industrial Marketing Management*, 28(5), 467–79.

[61]Hallikas, Virolainen and Tuominen (2002) op. cit.

[62]J. C. Jarillo (1988) On strategic networks, *Strategic Management Journal*, 9, 31–41.

[63]S. Laestadius, Staffan, Can Network Theory Explain Technological Change?, Working Paper 1995:2, Department of Industrial Economics and Management, Kungliga Tekniska Högskolan, Stockholm, May, 1995.

[64]Hallikas, Virolainen and Tuominen (2002) op. cit.

[65]D. Narayandas and V. K. Rangan (2004) Building and sustaining buyer–seller relationships in mature industrial markets, *Journal of Marketing*, 68 (July), 63–77.

[66]R. W. Palmatier, R. P. Dant, D. Grewal and K. R. Evans (2006) Factors influencing the effectiveness of relationship marketing: a meta-analysis, *Journal of Marketing*, 70 (October), 136–53; J. L. Johnson, R. S. Sohli and R. Grewal (2004) The role of relational knowledge stores in interfirm partnering, *Journal of Marketing*, 68, (July), 21–36; F. Selnes and J. Sallis (2003) Promoting relationship learning, *Journal of Marketing*, 67 (July), 80–95; P. M. Doney and J. P. Cannon (1997) An examination of the nature of trust in buyer–seller relationships, *Journal of Marketing*, 61 (April), 35–51; S. Ganesan (1994) Determinants of long-term orientation in buyer–seller relationships, *Journal of Marketing*, 58 (April), 1–19.

[67]J. H. Sheridan (1997) An alliance built on trust, *Industry Week*, 17 (March), 66–70.

[68]W. W. Keep, S. C. Hollander and R. Dickinson (1998) Forces impinging on long-term business-to-business relationships in the United States: an historical perspective, *Journal of Marketing*, 62 (April), 31–45.

[69]J. P. Cannon and W. D. Perreault Jr. (1999) Buyer–seller relationships in business markets, *Journal of Marketing, Research*, 36 (November), 439–60.

[70]J. B. Heide and K. H. Wahne (2006) Friends, businesspeople, and relationship roles: a conceptual framework and research agenda, *Journal of Marketing*, 70 (July), 90–103.

[71]Cannon and Perreault Jr. (1999) op. cit.

[72]T. G. Noordewier, G. John and J. R. Nevin (1990) Performance outcomes of purchasing arrangements in industrial buyer–vendor arrangements, *Journal of Marketing*, 54 (October), 80–93; Buvik and John (2000) op. cit.

[73]Rokkan, Heide and Wathne (2003) op. cit.

[74]K. H. Wathne and J. B. Heide (2004) Relationship governance in a supply chain network, *Journal of Marketing*, 68 (January), 73–89; D. Bowman and D. Narayandas (2004) Linking customer management effort to customer profitability in business markets, *Journal of Marketing Research*, 61 (November), 433–47; M. Ghosh and G. John (1999) Governance value analysis and marketing strategy, *Journal of Marketing*, 63 (Special issue), 131–45.

[75]S. Jap (1999) Pie expansion effects: collaboration processes in buyer–seller relationships, *Journal of Marketing Research*, 36 (November), 461–75.

[76]A. Buvik and G. John (2000), When does vertical coordination improve industrial purchasing relationships?, *Journal of Marketing* 64(4), 52–64.

[77]S. L. Pan and J.-N. Lee (2003) Using e-CRM for a unified view of the customer, *Communications of the ACM*, 46(4), 95–9.

[78]J. L. Harrison-Walker and S. E. Neeley (2004) Customer relationship building on the Internet in B2B marketing: a proposed typology, *Journal of Marketing Theory and Practice*, Winter, 19–34.

[79]D. Adebanjo (2003) Classifying and selecting e-CRM application: an analysis-based proposal, *Management Decision*, 41(6),

570–7; N. R. Ab Hamid (2005) E-CRM: are we there yet?, *The Journal of the American Academy of Business*, Cambridge, March, 51–7.

[80]Public Private Finance (2004) EU public procurement under review, 81, March, 2.

[81]Xinhua News Agency (2007) EU adopts new rules for public procurement, 15 November.

[82]M. Swibel and J. Novack (2003) The scariest customer, *Forbes*, 10 November, 96–7.

[83]www.europa.eu.

[84]www.europa.eu.

[85]www.simap.europe.eu.

Chapter 9

▽ Dealing with competition

IN THIS CHAPTER, WE WILL ADDRESS THE FOLLOWING QUESTIONS:

1 How do marketers identify primary competitors?

2 How should we analyse competitors' strategies, objectives, strengths and weaknesses?

3 How can market leaders expand the total market and defend market share?

4 How should market challengers attack market leaders?

5 How can market followers or nichers compete effectively?

World demand for cars is increasing and competition in the car industry is intense.
Source: Lehtikuva Oy/Rex Features

Balancing customer and competitor orientations

Competitive forces

Identifying competitors

Analysing competitors

Other competitive strategies

Competitive strategies for market leaders

Building strong brands requires a keen understanding of competitors, and competition grows more intense every year. New competition is coming from all directions – from global competitors eager to grow sales in new markets; from online competitors seeking cost-efficient ways to expand distribution; from private-label and store brands designed to provide low-price alternatives; and from brand extensions from strong megabrands leveraging their strengths to move into new categories. One good way to start to deal with competition is through creatively designed and well-executed marketing programmes.

Global car competition is changing rapidly. Company takeovers and various forms of company collaborations are seen still more often. Today, even honoured brands such as Ferrari, Bentley and Maserati that used to be autonomous/independent are now part of gigantic conglomerates. Thus, only a few carmakers are left, some of these earning a yearly revenue in excess of €65 billion. One example is Ford, which is being led by CEO Alan Mulally and now holds a broad brand portfolio including Swedish Volvo and Japanese Mazda, among others. Controlling seven different brands VW constitutes another example. However, due to intense price competition profit is scarce in the car business. Together the three conglomerates Ford, GM (marketing brands such as Cadillac, Chevrolet, Saab and Opel), and DaimlerChrysler (MercedesBenz, Jeep and Chrysler, among others) faced a loss of €1.5 billion in 2006 – out of total revenue of €390 billion. The intense competition in the car business has almost forced carmakers to create all kinds of joint ventures, cooperative agreements, and so on. For example, Peugeot, Citroën and Toyota manufacture their respective models 107, C1 and Aygo at the same Hungarian assembly plant. Experts expect that this is just the beginning. Intensified competition will increasingly force carmakers to share knowledge and to jointly improve technologies. Carmakers are facing a high European demand for small cars. However, developing new technical solutions are often just as expensive for small cars as for larger cars. As a result, selling a Nissan Micra simply does not provide the same kind of profit as selling a Mercedes or a BMW.

As you can tell from the development in the car market, companies must pay keen attention to their competitors in order to effectively devise and implement the best possible brand-positioning strategies. Markets have become too competitive to focus on the consumer alone. This chapter examines the role competition plays and how marketers can best manage their brands depending on their market position.[1]

▽ Competitive forces

In his now classic industry competition model Michael E. Porter, professor at Harvard Business School, has identified five forces that determine the intrinsic long-run attractiveness of a market or market segment: industry competitors, potential entrants, substitutes, buyers and suppliers. His model is shown in Figure 9.1. The threats these forces pose are as follows:

1 **Threat of intense segment rivalry:** A segment is unattractive if it already contains numerous, strong or aggressive competitors and if these competitors have high stakes in staying in the segment. It is even more unattractive if it's stable or declining, if economics or technology dictates that capacity can be increased only in large increments, or if fixed costs or exit barriers are high. Exit barriers keep companies competing in declining industries even though they are earning subnormal returns on investment. For example, a company may have invested in expensive fixed assets (e.g., specialised machinery) that may be non-transferable to another segment. When exit barriers are high, giving up a specific segment will impose high cost on the company. These conditions will lead to frequent price wars, advertising battles and new product introductions and will make it expensive to compete. The mobile phone market has seen fierce competition due to segment rivalry.

2 **Threat of new entrants:** The most attractive segment is one in which entry barriers are high and exit barriers are low.[2] Few new firms can enter the industry, and poorly performing firms

Figure 9.1 Five forces determining segment structural attractiveness

Source: From M. E. Porter (1985) *Competitive Advantage. Creating and Sustaining Superior Performance*, New York: Free Press. Copyright © 1985 by Michael E. Porter. Reproduced with permission from The Free Press, a division of Simon & Schuster Adult Publishing Group.

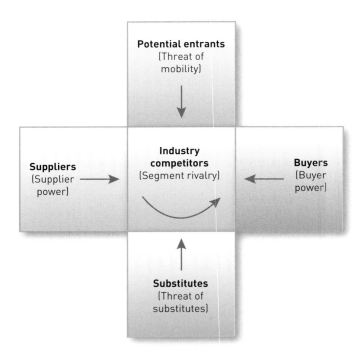

can easily exit. When both entry and exit barriers are high, profit potential is high, but firms face more risk because poorer-performing firms stay in and fight it out. When both entry and exit barriers are low, firms easily enter and leave the industry and the returns are stable and low. The worst case is when entry barriers are low and exit barriers are high: Here firms enter during good times but find it hard to leave during bad times. The result is chronic overcapacity and depressed earnings for all. The airline industry has low entry barriers but high exit barriers, leaving all carriers struggling during economic downturns.

3 **Threat of substitute products:** A segment is unattractive when there are actual or potential substitutes for the product. Substitutes place a limit on prices and on profits. If technology advances or competition increases in these substitute industries, prices and profits are likely to fall. Major music labels such as EMI, Warner Music Group and Universal Music Group have seen profitability threatened by the rise of digital music, which has triggered a steep decline in CD sales during recent years.[3]

4 **Threat of buyers' growing bargaining power:** A segment is unattractive if buyers possess strong or growing bargaining power. The strength of digital powerhouses such as Google has led some analysts to speculate that the potential power and profitability of marketing communication companies – such as the WPP Group, one of the world leaders in this line of business – may become curtailed.[4] Buyers' bargaining power grows when they become more concentrated or organised, when the product represents a significant fraction of the buyers' costs, when the product is undifferentiated, when buyers' switching costs are low, when buyers are price sensitive because of low profits, or when they can integrate upstream. To protect themselves, sellers might select buyers who have the least power to negotiate or switch suppliers. A better defence consists of developing superior offers that strong buyers cannot refuse. For example, WPP constantly works to improve the Group's understanding of digital markets and to provide their clients with access to superior experts in, for example, online and interactive marketing and media.

5 **Threat of suppliers' growing bargaining power:** A segment is unattractive if the company's suppliers are able to raise prices or reduce quantity supplied. Oil companies such as ExxonMobil, Shell, BP and Chevron-Texaco are at the mercy of the limited amount of oil reserves and the actions of oil-supplying cartels such as OPEC. Suppliers tend to be powerful when they are concentrated or organised, when there are few substitutes, when the supplied product is an important input, when the costs of switching suppliers are high, and when the suppliers can integrate downstream, that is, integrate the marketing- and sales-oriented activities directed to customers. The best defences are to build win–win relationships with suppliers or use multiple supply sources.

▽ Identifying competitors

It would seem a simple task for a company to identify its competitors. Microsoft Xbox knows that Sony PlayStation and Nintendo Wii are major games console competitors; Volkswagen knows that Peugeot is one of their key competitors; and British Airways knows that one of the major competitors in the air travel industry is Lufthansa. However, the range of a company's actual and potential competitors can be much broader than the obvious. And a company is more likely to be hurt by emerging competitors or new technologies than by current competitors, since companies tend to be more alert to known competitors' and their market activities.

In recent years, for instance, a number of new 'emerging giants' have arisen from developing countries, and these nimble competitors are not only competing with multinationals on their home turf but also becoming global forces in their own right. They have gained competitive advantage by exploiting their knowledge about local factors of production – capital and talent – and supply chains in order to build world-class businesses.

▽ Indian Software and services companies

Tata Consultancy Services, Infosys Technologies, Wipro and Satyam Computer Services, all of India, have succeeded in catering to the global demand for software and services. They have even triumphed against multinational software service providers such as Accenture and EDS, who have a hard time sorting out talent in a market where the level of people's skills and the quality of educational institutions vary dramatically. Indian companies know their way around the human resources market and are hiring educated, skilled engineers and technical graduates at salaries much lower than those that similar employees in developed markets earn. Even as the talent in urban centres such as Bangalore and Delhi gets scarce, the Indian companies will keep their competitive advantage by knowing how to find qualified employees in Indian's second-tier cities.[5]

▽ Inventec

Taiwan-based Inventec has become one of the world's largest manufacturers of notebook computers, PCs and servers, also by exploiting its knowledge of local factors of production. It makes products in China and supplies them to giants such as Hewlett-Packard and Toshiba and also makes mobile phones and MP3 players for other multinational customers. Inventec's customers get the low cost of manufacturing products in China without investing in factories there, and they can also use China's talented software and hardware professionals. It won't be long, however, before Inventec begins competing directly with its own customers; it has already started selling computers in Taiwan and China under its own retail brand name.[6]

We can examine competition from both an industry and a market point of view.[7] An **industry** is a group of firms that offer a product or class of products which are close substitutes for one another. Marketers classify industries according to number of sellers; degree of product differentiation; the number of new competitors entering the industry, mobility and exit barriers; cost structure; degree of vertical integration between a company and its suppliers and/or buyers; and degree of globalisation.

Using the market approach, we define *competitors* as companies that satisfy the same customer need. For example, a customer who buys a word-processing package really wants 'writing ability' – a need that can also be satisfied by pencils, pens or typewriters. Marketers must overcome 'marketing myopia', the risk of a company (or even an entire industry) taking a too narrow-minded, product-oriented view of itself and its role in the market. Marketers must define competition on the basis of market needs and opportunities rather than on traditional category and industry terms.[8] An example of such myopia is Coca-Cola, which focused on its soft drink business while failing to see the market for coffee bars and fresh fruit juice bars that eventually impinged on its core business.

The market concept of competition reveals a broader set of actual and potential competitors than competition defined in just product category terms. Rayport and Jaworski, who are influential thinkers in marketing and ecommerce, suggest profiling a company's direct and indirect competitors by mapping the buyer's steps in obtaining and using the product. This type of analysis highlights both the opportunities and the challenges a company faces.[9] 'Marketing insight: High growth through value innovation' describes how firms can tap into new markets that minimises competition from others.

Marketing insight

High growth through value innovation

INSEAD professors W. Chan Kim and Renée Mauborgne believe that too many firms engage in 'red-ocean thinking' – seeking bloody, head-to-head battles with competitors based largely on incremental improvements in cost, quality, or both. They advocate engaging instead in 'blue-ocean thinking' by creating products and services for which there are no direct competitors. Their belief is that instead of searching within the conventional boundaries of industry competition, managers should look beyond those boundaries to find unoccupied market positions that represent real value innovation.

The authors cite as one example Bert Claeys, a Belgian cinema operator, who was the first to introduce a megaplex cinema in Europe, in the city of Brussels. Despite an industry slump, the 25-screen, 7600-seat Kinepolis has thrived on a unique combination of features, such as ample, safe and free parking; large screens and state-of-the-art sound and projection equipment; and roomy, comfortable, oversized seats with unobstructed views. Through smart planning and economies of scale, Bert Claeys creates Kinepolis's unique cinema experience at a lower cost. Despite its success, the concept was not copied in Brussels, since the size of the city did not support a second megaplex cinema.

The Belgian Kinepolis cinema megaplex exemplifies 'blue-ocean thinking' – a competitive strategy that focuses on finding unoccupied market positions instead of battling head to head with established competitors. Here is an exterior shot of the megaplex in Antwerp, Belgium.

Source: Bjorn Beheydt/www.photographersdirect.com

This is classic blue-ocean thinking – designing creative business ventures to positively affect both a company's cost structure and its value proposition to consumers. Cost savings result from eliminating and reducing the factors affecting traditional industry competition; value to consumers comes from introducing factors the industry has never before offered. Over time, costs drop even more as superior value leads to higher sales volume, and that generates economies of scale.

We can offer other examples of marketers that exhibit unconventional, blue-ocean thinking:

- Novo Nordisk created the world's first insulin pen device, and is a world leader in production and distribution of these insulin delivery systems. Novo Nordisk created a blue ocean by shifting the industry's long-standing focus from doctors to the patients themselves.

- Nintendo developed the Wii gaming console that appealed to consumers who were looking for a different console experience. Instead of making a copycat console competing with the likes of Sony PS3 or Microsoft Xbox 360, Nintendo thought out of the box and created a new style of gaming, employing a wireless controller that worked with motion. In this way, players use the Wii almost as an extension of their own body, and this immersion seems to appeal to a diverse group of players, from 12-year-old boys to 40-year-old women.

- Philips solved the problem of lime scale accumulating in kettles as the water was boiled, later finding its way into consumers' freshly brewed tea. Philips designed a kettle having a spout filter that effectively captured the lime scale as the water was poured. Philips created a blue ocean by inducing people to replace their old kettles with the new filter kettles.

Kim and Mauborgne propose four crucial questions for marketers to ask themselves in guiding blue-ocean thinking and creating value innovation:

1. Which of the factors that our industry takes for granted should we eliminate?
2. Which factors should we reduce well *below* the industry's standard?
3. Which factors should we raise well *above* the industry's standard?
4. Which factors should we create that the industry has never offered?

They maintain that the most successful blue-ocean thinkers took advantage of all three platforms on which value innovation can take place: *physical product*; *service*, including maintenance, customer

▶ Marketing insight *(continued)*

Formulation principles

a) **Reconstruct market boundaries:**
- Look across alternative industries
- Look across strategic groups within industries
- Look across chain of buyers
- Look across complementary product and service offerings
- Look across functional or emotional appeal to buyers
- Look across time:

b) **Focus on the big picture not the numbers:**

c) **Reach beyond existing demand:**

d) **Get the strategic sequence right:**
- Is there buyer utility (customer value)?
- Is the price acceptable?
- Can we attain target cost?
- What are the adoption challenges?

Execution principles

a) **Overcome key organisational hurdles:**
- Cognitive hurdle (convincing employees of the need of a strategic shift)
- Resource hurdle (it is assumed that resources are needed to execute a strategic shift)
- Motivational hurdle (motivating key players)
- Political hurdle (organisational politics may stand in the way of change).

b) **Build execution into strategy.**

Figure 9.2 Key principles of blue-ocean strategy

Source: W. Chan Kim and R. Mauborgne (2005) *Blue-Ocean Strategy: How to Create Uncontested Market Space and Make the Competition Irrelevant*, Cambridge, Massachusetts: Harvard Business School Press. Copyright © 2005 by the Harvard Business School Publishing Corporation. All rights reserved. Reproduced with permission.

service, warranties and training for distributors and retailers; and *delivery*, meaning channels and logistics. Figure 9.2 summarises key principles driving the successful formulation and execution of blue-ocean strategy.

Sources: W. Chan Kim and R. Mauborgne (2005) *Blue-Ocean Strategy: How to Create Uncontested Market Space and Make the Competition Irrelevant*, Cambridge, MA: Harvard Business

School Press; W. Chan Kim and R. Mauborgne (1999) Creating new market space, *Harvard Business Review*, January–February, 83–93; W. Chan Kim and R. Mauborgne (1997) Value innovation: the strategic logic of high growth, *Harvard Business Review*, January–February, 103–12; www.novonordiskus.com/documents/promotion_page/document/diabetes_care.asp; www.blueoceanstrategy.com/about/lead/novo_nordisk.html; www.marketingweek.co.uk/item/58992/pg_dtl_art_news/pg_hdr_art/pg_ftr_art; www.blueoceanstrategy.com/about/lead/philips.html.

▽ Analysing competitors

Once a company identifies its primary competitors, it must ascertain their strategies, objectives, strengths and weaknesses.[10]

Strategies

A group of firms following the same strategy in a given target market is a **strategic group**.[11] Suppose a company wants to enter the major appliance industry. What is its strategic group?

Figure 9.3 Strategic groups in the major appliance industry

The company develops the chart shown in Figure 9.3 and discovers four strategic groups based on product quality and level of vertical integration (degree of organisational integration between a company and its suppliers and/or distributors and buyers). Group A has three competitors (Miele, SMEG, LG); group B has four (BSH, Electrolux, Indesit and Whirlpool); group C has three; and group D has three. Important insights emerge from this exercise. First, the height of the entry barriers differs for each group. Second, if the company successfully enters a group, the members of that group become its key competitors.

Objectives

Once a company has identified its main competitors and their strategies, it must ask: what is each competitor seeking in the marketplace? What drives each competitor's behaviour? Many factors shape a competitor's objectives, including size, history, current management and financial situation. If the competitor is a division of a larger company it is important to know whether the parent company is running it for growth, profits, or milking it.

It is useful to assume that competitors strive to maximise profits. However, companies differ in the relative emphasis they put on short-term and long-term profits. Many western firms have been criticised for operating on a short-run model, largely because current performance is judged by stockholders that might lose confidence, sell their stock, and cause the company's cost of capital to rise. Japanese firms operate largely on a market-share-maximisation model. They receive much of their funds from banks at a lower interest rate and in the past have readily accepted lower profits. So another reliable assumption is that each competitor pursues some mix of objectives: current profitability, market share growth, cash flow, technological leadership and service leadership.[12]

Finally, a company must monitor competitors' expansion plans. Figure 9.4 shows a product market battlefield map for the personal computer industry. Dell, which started out as a strong force in the sale of personal computers to individual users, is now a major force in the commercial and industrial market. Other incumbents may try to set up mobility barriers to Dell's further expansion.

Figure 9.4 A competitor's expansion plans

Strengths and weaknesses

A company needs to gather information about each competitor's strengths and weaknesses. Table 9.1 shows the results of a company survey that asked customers to rate its three competitors, A, B and C, on five attributes. Competitor A turns out to be well known and respected for producing high-quality products sold by a good sales force but is poor at providing product availability and technical assistance. Competitor B is good across the board and excellent in product availability and sales force. Competitor C rates poor to fair on most attributes. This result suggests that the company could attack Competitor A on product availability and technical assistance and Competitor C on almost anything, but should not attack B, which has no glaring weaknesses.

In general, a company should monitor three variables when analysing competitors:

1 **Share of market:** the competitor's share of the target market.

2 **Share of mind:** the percentage of customers who named the competitor in responding to the statement, 'Name the first company that comes to mind in this industry.'

3 **Share of heart:** the percentage of customers who named the competitor in responding to the statement, 'Name the company from which you would prefer to buy the product.'

There is an interesting relationship among these three measures. Table 9.2 shows them as recorded for the three competitors listed in Table 9.1. Competitor A enjoys the highest market share but is slipping. Its mind share and heart share are also slipping, probably because it's not providing good product availability and technical assistance. Competitor B is steadily gaining market share, probably due to strategies that are increasing its mind share and heart share. Competitor C

Table 9.1 Customers' ratings of competitors on key success factors

	Customer awareness	Product quality	Product availability	Technical assistance	Selling staff
Competitor A	E	E	P	P	G
Competitor B	G	G	E	G	E
Competitor C	F	P	G	F	F

Note: E = excellent, G = good, F = fair, P = poor.

Table 9.2 Market share, mind share and heart share

	Market share (%)			Mind share (%)			Heart share (%)		
	2006	2007	2008	2006	2007	2008	2006	2007	2008
Competitor A	50	47	44	60	58	54	45	42	39
Competitor B	30	34	37	30	31	35	44	47	53
Competitor C	20	19	19	10	11	11	11	11	8

Marketing memo

Benchmarking to improve competitive performance

Benchmarking is the art of learning from companies that perform certain tasks better than other companies. There can be as much as a tenfold difference between the quality, speed and cost performance of a world-class company and that of an average company. The aim of benchmarking is to copy or improve on 'best practices', either within an industry or across industries. Benchmarking has seven steps:

1 Determine which functions or processes to benchmark.

2 Identify the key performance variables (key factors contributing to corporate success) to measure.

3 Identify the best-in-class companies.

4 Measure the performance of best-in-class companies.

5 Measure the company's performance.

6 Specify programmes and actions to close the gap.

7 Implement and monitor results.

How can companies identify best-practice companies? A good starting point is consulting customers, suppliers, distributors, financial analysts, trade associations and magazines to see who they rate as doing the best job. Even the best companies can benchmark to improve their performance. To pursue its corporate vision to be 'a company that society wants to exist', Honda has even benchmarked its brand and its advertising against rivals from beyond the motor industry, such as Apple. With only 0.6 per cent market share, Italian kitchen furniture maker SPQ Cucine is a small player in the Italian market. Yet, through creative application of the data available to them, SPQ systematically benchmarks its 303 distributors. It uses the results to identify best practice and then disseminate it among the rest. At the same time, the company reviews the franchises of the worst performers. Thus, benchmarking is equally useful for small and medium-sized companies; its results can be an effective means of developing strategies in a key performance area.

Sources: www.benchmarking.org; P. O'Connell (2005) Bringing innovation to the home of six sigma, *BusinessWeek*, 1 August; J. E. Prescott, S. H. Miller and The Society of Competitive Intelligence Professionals (2001) *Proven Strategies in Competitive Intelligence: Lessons from the Trenches*, New York: John Wiley & Sons; R. Hiebeler, T. B. Kelly and C. Ketteman (1998) *Best Practices: Building Your Business with Customer-Focused Solutions*, New York: Arthur Andersen/Simon & Schuster; M. Hope (1997) Contrast and compare, *Marketing*, 28 August, 11–13; R. Lester (2006) The possible dream, *Marketing Week*, 26 October, 29(43), 24–5; J. Naylor, N. Hawkins and C. Wilson (2001) Benchmarking marketing in an SME: the case of an Italian kitchen furniture manufacturer, *The Marketing Review*, 1(3), 325–39.

seems to be stuck at a low level of market share, mind share and heart share, probably because of its poor product and marketing attributes. We could generalise as follows: *Companies that make steady gains in mind share and heart share will inevitably make gains in market share and profitability.* Firms such as Nokia, IKEA, L'Oréal, Philips, and Mercedes (Daimler AG) are all reaping the financial benefits of providing emotional, experiential, social and financial value to satisfy customers and all their constituents.[13]

To improve market share, many companies benchmark their most successful competitors as well as other world-class performers.[14] The technique and its benefits are described in 'Marketing memo: Benchmarking to improve competitive performance'.

Selecting competitors

After the company has conducted customer value analysis and examined its competitors carefully, it can focus its attack on one of the following classes of competitors: strong versus weak, close versus distant, and 'good' versus 'bad'.

- **Strong versus weak:** Most companies aim their shots at weak competitors, because this requires fewer resources per share point gained. Yet the firm should also compete with strong competitors to keep up with the best. Even strong competitors have some weaknesses.
- **Close versus distant:** Most companies compete with the competitors that resemble them the most. GM competes with Ford, not with Ferrari. Yet companies should also identify distant competitors. Coca-Cola recognises that its number one competitor is tap water, not Pepsi; Royal Dutch Shell increasingly worries about the development of more energy efficient fuels and technologies as well as competitors Exxon and BP; museums now worry about theme parks and malls.[15]

Table 9.3 Customer selection grid

	Vulnerable	**Not vulnerable**
Valuable	These customers are profitable but not completely happy with the company. Find out and address their sources of vulnerability to *retain them*.	These customers are loyal and profitable. Don't take them for granted but *maintain margins* and reap the benefits of their satisfaction.
Not valuable	These customers are likely to defect. Let them go or even *encourage their departure*.	These unprofitable customers are happy. Try to *make them valuable or vulnerable*.

Source: J. H. Roberts (2005) Defensive marketing: how a strong incumbent can protect its position, *Harvard Business Review*, November, 156. Copyright © 2005 by the Harvard Business School Publishing Corporation. All rights reserved.

- **'Good' versus 'Bad':** Every industry contains 'good' and 'bad' competitors.[16] Good competitors play by the industry's rules; they set prices in reasonable relationship to costs; and they favour a healthy industry. Bad competitors try to buy share rather than earn it; they take large risks; they invest in overcapacity; and they upset industrial equilibrium. A company may find it necessary to attack its bad competitors to reduce or end their dysfunctional practices.

Selecting customers

As part of the competitive analysis, a firm must evaluate its customer base and think about which customers it is willing to lose and which it wants to retain. One way to divide up the customer base is in terms of whether a customer is valuable and vulnerable, creating a grid of four segments as a result – see Table 9.3. Each segment suggests different competitive activities.[17]

Faced with formidable competition from its rival Optus (a joint subsidiary of UK-based Cable & Wireless and US company BellSouth), Australian telephone company Telstra conducted this type of segment analysis. Based on this analysis Telstra developed a series of 'Flex-Plan' products designed to retain the valuable/vulnerables but without losing the margin it realised on the valuable/not vulnerables. The Flex-Plans had a subscription fee but offered significant net savings. Because valuable/vulnerables were highly involved with the category, they were able to see how they could benefit from such plans, but valuable/not vulnerable regarded the plans as unnecessary. As a result, the plans achieved the desired goals.

▽ Competitive strategies for market leaders

Having identified and analysed its competitors, a company will decide on a competitive strategy. We can gain further insight into competitive behaviour by classifying firms by the roles they play in the target market: leader, challenger, follower or nicher. Suppose a market is occupied by the firms shown in Figure 9.5. Of the total 40 per cent market, is in the hands of a *market leader;* another 30 per cent is in the hands of a *market challenger;* another 20 per cent is in the hands of a *market follower*, a firm that is willing to maintain its market share and not rock the boat. The remaining 10 per cent is in the hands of *market nichers,* firms that serve small market segments not being served by larger firms.

Many industries contain one or two firms that are acknowledged market leaders. These firms have the largest market share in the relevant product market and usually lead the other firms in price changes, new product introductions, distribution coverage and promotional intensity. Some historical market leaders are Microsoft (computer software), Nestlé (food and beverages), Disney (entertainment), Reuters (news and data services), McDonald's (fast food), Sony (home electronics), Visa (credit cards) and Accenture (management consulting). 'Breakthrough marketing: Accenture' summarises how that firm has attained and maintained market leadership.

Although marketers assume well-known brands are distinctive in consumers' minds, unless a dominant firm enjoys a legal monopoly it must maintain constant vigilance. A product innovation may come along and hurt the leader; a competitor might unexpectedly find a fresh

Figure 9.5 Hypothetical market structure

new marketing angle or commit to a major marketing investment; or the leader might find its cost structure spiralling upward. One well-known brand and market leader that lost track of market trends for a while is Nokia.

▽ **Nokia**

Given its number five ranking on Interbrand's 2007 list of top 100 global brands, it may seem unlikely that the Finnish giant would recently have been in danger of losing out to competitors. Yet only a few years ago, Nokia found its stock stagnating and its market share declining. Nokia soon realised that its focus on marketing cheap handsets in emergent markets was hurting it in the United States and Europe, where consumers wanted ultra-thin, fashionable multimedia phones that played videos and surfed the Web. Nokia had missed design trends such as clamshell phones and the so-called 'candy-bar' phones that slide open and closed, and was starting to build a less attractive consumer image as unrelentingly un-cool. The Nokia brand retained trust among consumers, but was not seen as trendy. Nokia responded quickly, by releasing two series of high-end phones: the E-series aimed at corporate email users and the N-series equipped with multimedia capability. Also, it kept its focus on delivering on consumer expectations in terms of technology, design and brand identity, and is now showing strength in emerging and mature markets alike. As a result, its global market share rebounded and reached 38 per cent in 2007.[18]

The Nokia brand became diluted as mobile phones were turned into fashion statements and multimedia tools, yet the company was quick to develop new strategies to refocus it.
Source: Courtesy of Nokia / Agency: The Red Consultancy

Breakthrough marketing

Accenture

Accenture began in 1942 as Adminstrative Accounting Group, the consulting arm of accounting firm Arthur Andersen. In 1989, it launched as a separate business unit focused on IT consulting bearing the name Andersen Consulting. At that time, though it was earning €0.8 billion annually, Andersen Consulting had low brand awareness among information technology consultancies and was commonly mistaken for its accounting corporate parent. To build its brand and separate itself from the accounting firm with which it shared its name, Andersen Consulting launched the first large-scale advertising campaign in the professional services area. By the end of the decade it was the world's largest management and technology consulting organisation.

In 2000, following arbitration against its former parent, Andersen Consulting was granted its full independence from Arthur Andersen – but at the price of relinquishing the Andersen name. Andersen Consulting was given three months to find a name that was trademarkable in 47 countries, effective and inoffensive in over 200 languages, and acceptable to employees and clients – *and* that corresponded with an available URL. The effort that followed was one of the largest – and most successful – rebranding campaigns in corporate history.

As luck would have it, the company's new name came from a consultant at the company's Oslo office, who submitted 'Accenture' as part of an internal name generation initiative dubbed 'Brandstorming'. The consultant coined the Accenture name because it rhymed with 'adventure' and connoted an 'accent on the future'. The name also retained the 'Ac' of the original Andersen Consulting name (echoing the Ac.com website), which would help the firm retain some of its former brand equity, that is the attractiveness and familiarity of the Andersen Consulting brand in the market. On midnight, 31 December 2000, Andersen Consulting officially adopted the Accenture name and launched a global marketing campaign targeting senior executives at Accenture's clients and prospects, all Accenture partners and employees, the media, leading industry analysts, potential recruits and academia.

The results of the advertising, marketing and communications campaigns were quick and impressive. Overall, the number of firms considering purchasing Accenture's services increased by 350 per cent. Accenture's brand equity increased 11 per cent. Awareness of Accenture's breadth and depth of services achieved 96 per cent of its previous level. Globally, awareness of Accenture as a provider of management and technology consulting services was 76 per cent of its level before the change in brand name. These results enabled Accenture to successfully complete a €1.3 billion Initial Public Offering in July 2001.

In 2002, Accenture unveiled a new positioning to reflect its new role as a partner to aid execution of strategy, summarised succinctly by the tagline 'Innovation Delivered'. This tagline was supported by the statement, 'From innovation to execution, Accenture helps accelerate your vision.' Accenture surveyed senior executives from different industries and countries and confirmed that they saw inability to execute and deliver on ideas as the number one barrier to success.

Accenture saw its differentiator as the ability both to provide innovative ideas – ideas grounded in business processes as well as IT – and to execute them. Competitors such as McKinsey were seen as highly specialised at developing strategy, whereas other competitors such as IBM were seen as highly skilled with technological implementation. Accenture wanted to be seen as excelling at both. Ian Watmore, Accenture's UK chief, explained the need to have both strategy and execution: 'Unless you can provide both transformational consulting and outsourcing capability, you're not going to win. Clients expect both.'

In 2002, the global business climate changed. After the dot-com crash and the economic downturn, innovation was no longer enough. Executives wanted bottom-line results (improved financial performance). Accenture built on the 'Innovation Delivered' theme when it announced its new 'High Performance Delivered' tagline in late 2003, featuring golfer Tiger Woods as the spokesperson. As part of its new commitment to helping clients achieve their business objectives, Accenture introduced a policy whereby many of its contracts contained incentives that it realised only if specific business targets were met. For instance, a contract with British travel agent Thomas Cook was structured such that Accenture's bonus depended on five metrics, including a cost-cutting one. In 2004, 30 per cent of the company's contracts contained such incentives. The company's focus on improving the performance and results of its clients proved beneficial to the bottom line: 2006 revenues grew 13 per cent to €13.2 billion and profits rose 36 per cent to €720 million.

Sources: www.accenture.com; Lessons learned from top firms' marketing blunders, *Management Consultant International*, December 2003, 1; S. Callahan (2003) Tiger tees off in new Accenture campaign, *B to B*, 13 October, 3; Inside Accenture's biggest UK client, *Management Consultant International*, October, 1–3; Accenture's results highlight weakness of consulting market, *Management Consultant International*, October 2003, 8–10; Accenture re-branding wins UK plaudits, *Management Consultant International*, October 2002, 5.

In many industries, a discount competitor has entered and undercut the leader's prices. 'Marketing insight: when your competitor delivers more for less' describes how leaders can respond to an aggressive competitive price discounter.

Marketing insight

When your competitor delivers more for less

Companies offering the powerful combination of low prices and high quality are capturing the hearts and wallets of consumers all over the world. In the United States, more than half the population now shops weekly at mass merchants such as Wal-Mart and Target, up from 25 per cent in 1996. In the United Kingdom, premium retailers such as Boots and Sainsbury's are scrambling to meet intensifying price – and quality – competition from Asda and Tesco.

These and similar value players, such as Aldi, Dell, E*TRADE Financial, JetBlue Airways, Ryanair and Southwest Airlines, are transforming the way consumers of nearly every age and income purchase groceries, apparel, airline tickets, financial services and computers. As value-driven companies in a growing number of industries change the way they compete, traditional players are right to feel threatened. The formula these upstart firms often rely on includes focusing on one or a few consumer segments; providing better delivery of the basic product or one additional benefit; and matching low prices with highly efficient operations to keep costs down.

To compete with value-based rivals, mainstream companies must reconsider the perennial routes to business success: keeping costs in line, finding sources of differentiation and managing prices effectively. To succeed in value-based markets, companies need to infuse these timeless strategies with greater intensity and focus and then execute them flawlessly. Differentiation, for example, becomes less about the abstract goal of rising above competitive clutter and more about identifying opportunities left open by the value players' business models. Effective pricing means waging a transaction-by-transaction perception battle to win over those consumers who are predisposed to believe that value-oriented competitors are always cheaper.

Competitive outcomes will be determined, as always, on the ground – in product aisles, merchandising displays, reconfigured processes and pricing stickers. When it comes to value-based competition, traditional players can't afford to drop a stitch. Value-driven competitors have changed consumer expectations about the trade-off between quality and price. This shift is gathering momentum, placing a new premium on – and adding new twists to – the old imperatives of differentiation and execution.

Differentiation

To counter value-based players, marketers will need to focus on areas where their business models give other companies room to manoeuvre. Successful differentiation calls for marshalling multiple tactics to provide superior delivery of a highly desired consumer benefit. Instead of trying to compete with discounters and other value retailers on price, for example, Danish supermarket chain Irma emphasises high quality across all elements of its business. Embarking on its concept of high-quality products and premium prices, it has been highly successful at targeting customers who appreciate new and special grocery selections, luxury and ecological products, as well as expensive wines. The new management team overhauled Irma's product selections and in-store design to signal a cutting-edge, agenda-setting spirit, aiming to both meet and inspire consumer demand for high-quality and sustainable everyday lifestyle products. Today, around one-quarter of all products in Irma stores are ecological, and the chain has expanded rapidly in Denmark. In fact, this strategy of differentiation helped it to significantly increase its revenue to €10 million in 2006, which was close to a 40 per cent positive change in a single year.[19]

Execution

Value-based markets also place a premium on execution, particularly in prices and costs. Wal-Mart's disastrous experience in trying to compete head-on with the Metro Group and well-established discounters such as Aldi and Lidl in Germany highlights the difficulty of challenging value leaders on their own turf. Matching or even beating a value player's prices – as Wal-Mart did – won't necessarily win the battle of consumer perceptions against companies with already established reputations for the lowest prices.

To effectively compete against value-based players, firms may need to downplay or even abandon some target market segments. To compete with Ryanair and easyJet, British Airways has put more emphasis on its long–haul routes, where value-based players are not evident, and less on the highly competitive short-haul routes where low-cost carriers thrive.

Major airlines have also tried another competitive response, introducing their own low-cost airlines. But KLM Royal Dutch Airline's Buzz and SAS's Snowflake have both been unsuccessful. One school of thought is that companies should set up low-cost operations only if two conditions apply: (1) the firm's existing businesses will be made more competitive as a result; and (2) the new business will derive some advantages it would not have gained by being independent. The success of low-cost operations set up by HSBC, ING, Royal Bank of Scotland and IHG (InterContinental Hotels Group) – First Direct, ING Direct, Direct Line Insurance and Holiday Inn Express, respectively – is due in part to synergies between the old and new lines of business. Thus, success dictates that the low-cost operation must be designed and launched to be a moneymaker in its own right, not just as a defensive ploy.

Sources: Adapted from two insightful articles, N. Kumar (2006) Strategies to fight low-cost rivals, *Harvard Business Review*, December, 104–12; and R. J. Frank, J. P. George and L. Narasimhan (2004) When your competitor delivers more for less, *McKinsey Quarterly*, Winter, 48–59.

Staying the number one firm calls for action on three fronts. First, the firm must find ways to expand total market demand. Second, the firm must protect its current market share through good defensive and offensive actions. Third, the firm can try to increase its market share, even if market size remains constant. Let's look at each strategy.

Expanding the total market

To learn how retailer Lululemon uses grassroots marketing techniques to position itself in Canada, visit www.pearsoned.ca/marketingmanagementcanada

When the total market expands, the dominant firm usually gains the most. If western European consumers increase their consumption of tomato sauce, Heinz stands to gain the most because its is the top ranked brand of the sauce sold in this region, with a market share of 38 per cent (2006).[20] If it can convince more people to use tomato sauce, or to use it with more meals, or to use more sauce on each occasion, Heinz will benefit considerably. In general, the market leader should look for new customers or more usage from existing customers.

New customers Every product class has the potential to attract buyers who are unaware of the product or who are resisting it because of price or lack of certain features. A company can search for new users among three groups: those who might use it but do not *(market-penetration strategy)*, those who have never used it *(new-market segment strategy)*, or those who live elsewhere *(geographical-expansion strategy)*.

Starbucks Coffee is one of the best-known brands in the world. Starbucks is able to sell a cup of coffee for €2 while the coffee shop next door can only get less than €1. (And if you want the popular café latte, it's €3.) Starbucks has more than 7200 locations throughout Europe, North America, the Pacific Rim and the Middle East, and its annual revenue for 2007 topped €6.5 billion. Its corporate website (www.starbucks.com) gives a peek into its multipronged approach to growth.[21]

'Starbucks purchases and roasts high-quality whole bean coffees and sells them along with fresh, rich-brewed, Italian-style espresso beverages, a variety of pastries and confections, and coffee-related accessories and equipment – primarily through its company-operated retail stores. In addition, Starbucks sells whole-bean coffees through a speciality sales group and supermarkets. Additionally, Starbucks produces and sells bottled Frappuccino® coffee drinks and a line of premium ice creams through its joint venture partnerships and offers a line of innovative premium teas produced by its wholly

Among Starbucks' expansion efforts have been a new line of premium teas produced by Tazo Tea Company, a Starbucks' subsidiary.
Source: Stephen F. Faust/www.photographersdirect.com

owned subsidiary, Tazo Tea Company. The company's objective is to establish Starbucks as the most recognised and respected brand in the world. To achieve this goal, the company plans to continue to rapidly expand its retail operations, grow its speciality sales and other operations, and selectively pursue opportunities to leverage the Starbucks brand through the introduction of new products and the development of new distribution channels.'

More usage Marketers can try to increase the amount, level or frequency of consumption.

The *amount* of consumption can sometimes be increased through packaging or product redesign. Larger package sizes have been shown to increase the amount of product that consumers use at one time.[22] The usage of impulse consumption products such as soft drinks and snacks increases when the product is made more available.

Increasing *frequency* of consumption, on the other hand, requires either: (1) identifying additional opportunities to use the brand in the same basic way; or (2) identifying completely new and different ways to use the brand. Consumers may see the product as useful only in certain places and at certain times, especially if it has strong brand associations to particular usage situations or user types.

In the first case – where the marketer focuses on *additional opportunities to use the brand in the same basic way* – a marketing programme may communicate the appropriateness and advantages of using the brand more frequently in new or existing situations, or remind consumers to actually use the brand in those situations. Kellogg's Corn Flakes, for example, takes this approach when the company offers its customers inspiration for new ways to eat its cereal for breakfast and brunch. Another opportunity arises when consumers' perceptions of product usage differs from reality. Consumers may fail to replace a short-lived product when they should, because they over-estimate how long it stays fresh.[23]

One strategy to speed up product replacement is to tie the act of replacing the product to a holiday, event or time of year. Another might be to provide consumers with better information about either: (1) when they first used the product or need to replace it; or (2) the current level of product performance. Gillette razor cartridges feature coloured stripes that slowly fade with repeated use, signalling the user to move on to the next cartridge.

The second approach to increasing frequency of consumption is to *identify completely new and different applications*. For example, food product companies have long advertised recipes that use their branded products in entirely different ways. Toblerone and Daim (also known as Dime in the United Kingdom) are examples of chocolates that have become main components in delicious ice creams and cakes – Carte d'Or Toblerone and (home-made) Daim Ice Cream Cakes, respectively. On a similar note, sherry brand Tio Pepe has aimed at stretching consumer's associations and uses of the drink by promoting it as a special style of white wine. The brand encourages consumers to drink it just as they would a dry white wine – chilled and in a wine glass – and hence may increase the number of occasions in which Tio Pepe comes into consideration as an appropriate drink.[24]

Product development can also spur new uses. Chewing gum manufacturers such as Cadbury Schweppes, maker of Trident, are producing 'nutraceutical' products to strengthen or whiten teeth. Aquafresh has successfully launched dental chewing gums with health and cosmetic benefits.[25]

Defending market share

While trying to expand total market size, the dominant firm must continuously and actively defend its current business: Boeing against Airbus and Google against Yahoo! and Microsoft.[26] The success of online social network sites MySpace and Facebook has brought challenges from upstarts such as LinkedIn personal business network, Dogster for dog owners, Vox for sharing photos and videos, and blog posts for baby boomers and older consumers.[27]

What can the market leader do to defend its terrain? The most constructive response is *continuous innovation*. The leader should lead the industry in developing new products and customer services, distribution effectiveness and cost cutting. It keeps increasing its competitive strength and value to customers by providing comprehensive solutions.

▽ **Martelli Lavorazioni Tessili**

Consumers who wonder why it costs €140 or more to buy a pair of designer jeans might feel better about the high price tag if they strolled through a Martelli Lavorazioni Tessili factory in Vedelago, Italy. The market leader in the technology of 'distressing' denim, Martelli counts Gucci, Armani, Dolce & Gabbana, and Yves Saint Laurent among its clients on the high end and Levi-Strauss, Lee, Wrangler, and Gap on the low end. Martelli is uncontested in Europe; its only competitors are in the United States and Japan. The company stays on top by relentlessly innovating – investing at least €3.5 million a year to continually upgrade technology – and by finding cheap but skilled labour to carry out its bizarre but effective techniques. In its main factory with 900 workers, huge washing machines tumble jeans with pumice gravel. Workers wearing face masks put jeans legs over inflated balloons, which then are moved between sets of plastic brushes that scrub the denim. Some workers do painstaking hand work on individual jeans, applying discoloring chemicals with brushes, applying embroidered designs, or using handheld guns to blast jets of quartz sand. After experimenting with hiring workers from Africa and Romania, Martelli found that Chinese, legal immigrants are the most skilled, patient, and cost effective for the job of hand-crafting jeans.[28]

Italy's Martelli Lavorazioni Tessilli is a market leader in the technology of 'distressing' denim.
Source: Dave Yoder/Polaris/eyevinearchive.com

In satisfying customer needs, we can draw a distinction between responsive marketing, anticipative marketing and creative marketing. A *responsive* marketer finds a stated need and fills it. An *anticipative* marketer looks ahead into what needs customers may have in the near future. A *creative* marketer discovers and produces solutions customers did not ask for but to which they enthusiastically respond. Creative marketers are *market-driving firms,* not just market driven. Interactive ad agency, R/GA is one such market-driving firm.

▽ R/GA

The advertising business has been turned upside down by increasing consumer control, the ascendance of digital media and the fragmentation of one mass market into countless niche markets. Yet, rather than responding to trends in advertising, R/GA agency, headed by CEO Bob Greenberg and with offices in London and New York, has become a trendsetter by creating a totally different type of ad agency, one in which technology is considered equal to creativity. By blending pioneering technological applications – such as computer-assisted film-making, development of high-performance websites and an in-house digital studio – with 'big picture' creative strategies, R/GA expanded revenue over 35 per cent to an estimated €105 million in 2006 and was voted *Adweek*'s Interactive Agency of the Year. Clients include L'Oréal Interactive, Nike, Nokia, and Verizon.[29]

Market-driving firms become market leaders through superior value delivery of unmet – and maybe even unknown – consumer needs. Think of Sony. In the late 1970s Akio Morita, the Sony founder, was working on a pet project that would revolutionise the way people listened to music: a portable cassette player he called the Walkman. Engineers at the company insisted there was little demand for such a product, but Morita refused to part with his vision. By the 20th anniversary of the Walkman, Sony had sold over 250 million players in nearly 100 different models.[30]

Even when it does not launch offensives, the market leader must not leave any major flanks, or vulnerable areas, exposed. It must consider carefully which terrains are important to defend, even at a loss, and which can be surrendered. The aim of defensive strategy is to reduce the probability of attack, divert attacks to less-threatening areas, and lessen their intensity. The defender's speed of response can make an important difference in the profit consequences. A dominant firm can use the six defence strategies summarised in Figure 9.6.[31]

Position defence Position defence means occupying (and defending) a positive and superior standing in consumers' minds, including for example high-brand equity, customer satisfaction, customer loyalty, or a high repeat purchase rate. Holding this desirable market position can make the brand seem almost impregnable, as Procter & Gamble has shown with Ariel detergent (Tide in the United States), Crest toothpaste (marketed as Blend-a-Med in some European countries) for cavity prevention, and Pampers nappies for dryness.

Flank defence Although position defence is important, the market leader should also erect outposts to protect a weak front or possibly serve as an invasion base for counterattack. Flanking moves tend to occur in the periphery (or on the flanks) of a company's main activities. In marketing terms, this could include introducing new products or brands, repositioning existing products or launching promotional activities. When Europe's number two automaker, PSA Peugeot Citroën, was attacked by competitors Volkswagen and Renault in its core market of

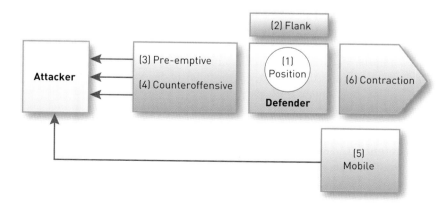

Figure 9.6 Six types of defence strategies

subcompacts, Peugeot's strategic response was a roll-out plan of 29 new models, including 5 entirely new concepts. The company decided to reposition some of its cars in more upscale markets, while steering clear of the race to engineer super cheap cars for emerging markets. Instead, Peugeot competes in these markets with lower-cost versions of existing models. This strategy protected Peugeot's flanks, although the competition remains fierce in the mature European car market.[32]

Pre-emptive defence A more aggressive manoeuvre is to attack *before* the enemy starts its offence. A company can launch a pre-emptive defence in several ways. It can wage guerrilla action across the market – hitting one competitor here, another there – and keep everyone off balance; or it can try to achieve a grand market envelopment. Electronic Arts has been experimenting with a radical new business model involving free online access to some of its popular games (FIFA soccer and Battlefield Heroes), while charging customers for so-called microtransactions and carrying in-game ads. In this way Electronic Arts establishes its position as a market leader and sends out market signals to dissuade competitors from attacking.[33]

Marketers can introduce a stream of new products, making sure to precede them with *preannouncements* – deliberate communications regarding future actions.[34] Preannouncements can signal to competitors that they will need to fight to gain market share.[35] If Microsoft announces plans for a new product development, smaller firms may choose to concentrate their development efforts in other directions to avoid head-to-head competition. Some high-tech firms have even been accused of engaging in selling 'vapourware' – preannouncing products that miss delivery dates or are never introduced.[36]

Counteroffensive defence When attacked, most market leaders will respond with a counterattack. In a *counteroffensive,* the leader can meet the attacker frontally or hit its flank or launch a pincer movement. An effective counterattack is to invade the attacker's main territory so that it will pull back to defend it. Swedish vodka brand Absolut faced an immense challenge as a crop of new 'super premium' brands such as Grey Goose, Chopin and Citadelle came along, questioning Absolut's position as 'coolness in a bottle'. To fight back, Absolut invested heavily in a new high-profile ad campaign, associating the brand with other classics that are 'absolutes' in popular culture, such as the Apollo moon landing and Marilyn Monroe.[37]

Another common form of counteroffensive is the exercise of economic or political clout. The leader may try to crush a competitor by subsidising lower prices for the vulnerable product with revenue from its more profitable products, or the leader may prematurely announce that a product upgrade will be available, to prevent customers from buying the competitor's product. Or the leader may lobby legislators to take political action to inhibit the competition. For instance, a leading pharmaceutical company might attempt to influence legislation regarding testing and marketing of a specific medical product category in order to make it more difficult for potential competitors to enter the market.

Mobile defence In mobile defence, the leader stretches its domain over new territories that can serve as future centres for defence and offence through market broadening and market diversification. *Market broadening* shifts focus from the current product to the underlying generic need. The company gets involved in R&D across the whole range of technology associated with that need. Thus 'petroleum' companies such as BP sought to recast themselves as 'energy' companies. Implicitly, this change demanded that they dip their research fingers into the oil, coal, nuclear, hydroelectric and chemical industries.

Market diversification shifts into unrelated industries. When Hochtief, the biggest construction firm in Germany, witnessed huge losses in the industry due to increasing costs of raw materials in 2007, it was not content with position defence or even with looking for substitute contracts. Instead they moved into the real estate market where steadier earnings and higher profit margins are expected.[38]

Contraction defence Large companies must sometimes recognise that they can no longer defend all their territory. The best course of action then appears to be *planned contraction* (also called *strategic withdrawal*): giving up weaker territories and reassigning resources to stronger territories. In 2006, Sara Lee phased out products that accounted for almost 40 per cent of the company's

Figure 9.7 The concept of optimal market share

revenues, including its strong Hanes hosiery brand, so it could concentrate on its well-known food brands.[39]

Expanding market share

In many markets, one share point is worth tens of millions of dollars. No wonder competition has turned fierce in so many markets. Gaining increased share in the served market, however, does not automatically produce higher profits – especially for labour-intensive service companies that may not experience many economies of scale. Much depends on the company's strategy.[40]

Because the cost of buying higher market share may far exceed its revenue value, a company should consider four factors before pursuing increased share:

1   **The possibility of provoking action from competition authorities:** Jealous competitors are likely to cry 'monopoly' if a dominant firm makes further inroads. This rise in risk would diminish the attractiveness of pushing market share gains too far. Microsoft and Intel are examples of companies that have faced great scrutiny for their market leadership and practices.

2   **Economic cost:** Figure 9.7 shows that profitability might *fall* with further market share gains after some level. In the illustration, the firm's *optimal market share* is 50 per cent. The cost of gaining further market share might exceed the value. Customers who have not been persuaded to try the product at this time may dislike the company, be loyal to competitive suppliers, have unique needs, or prefer dealing with smaller suppliers. And the costs of legal work, public relations and lobbying rise with market share. Pushing for higher share is less justified when there are few scale or experience economies, unattractive market segments exist, buyers want multiple sources of supply, and exit barriers are high. Some market leaders have even increased profitability by selectively *decreasing* market share in weaker areas.[41]

3   **Pursuing the wrong marketing activities:** Companies successfully gaining share typically outperform competitors in three areas: new product activity, relative product quality and marketing expenditures.[42] On the other hand, companies that attempt to increase market share by cutting prices more deeply than competitors typically don't achieve significant gains, because enough rivals meet the price cuts and others offer other values so buyers don't switch. Competitive rivalry and price cutting have been shown to be most intense in industries with high fixed costs, high inventory costs and stagnant primary demand, such as steel, cars, paper and chemicals.[43]

4   **The effect of increased market share on actual and perceived quality:**[44] Too many customers can put a strain on the firm's resources, hurting product value and service delivery. During the 2007 Christmas season, gaming company Nintendo experienced growing pains when its UK customer base expanded rapidly, forcing it to remove its advertisements for the Wii console as it was continuously sold out in shops for months.[45] Consumers may also infer that 'bigger is not better' and assume that growth will lead to a deterioration of quality. If 'exclusivity' is a key brand benefit, existing customers may resent additional new customers.

▽ Other competitive strategies

The previous section dealt especially with market leaders. However, most firms are not market leaders. Firms that occupy second, third and lower ranks in an industry are often called runner-up or trailing firms. Some, such as PepsiCo, Ford, Avis and Texas Instruments, are quite large in their own right. These firms can adopt one of two postures. As you will see from the following two sections, runner-up companies can either attack the leader and other competitors in an aggressive bid for further market share as *market challengers*, or they can play ball and not 'rock the boat' as *market followers*.

Market-challenger strategies

Many market challengers have gained ground or even overtaken the leader. Toyota today produces more cars than General Motors and AMD has been chipping away at Intel's market share.[46] Challengers set high aspirations, leveraging their resources while the market leader often runs the business as usual. Now let's examine the competitive attack strategies available to market challengers.[47]

Defining the strategic objective and opponent(s)

A market challenger must first define its strategic objective. Most aim to increase market share. The challenger must decide whom to attack:

- **It can attack the market leader:** This is a high-risk but potentially high-pay-off strategy and makes good sense if the leader is not serving the market well. It often has the added benefit of distancing the firm from other challengers. When the free newspaper '*20 Minutes*' attacked *Metro International* in the French (launched in 2002) and Spanish (launched in 2000)[48] markets, it focused on qualities such as vivid visuals and local content, and left traditional newspapers out of public debate on the subject.[49] *20 Minutes* is distributed to those travelling on public transport in major cities in, among others, Switzerland, France and Spain and has rapidly become the most read daily newspaper in France and Spain.[50] An alternative strategy is to out-innovate the leader across the whole segment. Xerox wrested the copier market from 3M by developing a better copying process. Later, Canon grabbed a large chunk of Xerox's market by introducing desk copiers.
- **It can attack firms of its own size that are not doing the job and are underfinanced:** These firms have ageing products, are charging excessive prices or are not satisfying customers in other ways.
- **It can attack small local and regional firms:** Several major banks grew to their present size by gobbling up smaller regional banks, or 'guppies'.

Choosing a general attack strategy

Given clear opponents and objectives, what attack options are available? We can distinguish among five attack strategies: frontal, flank, encirclement, bypass and guerrilla attacks.

Frontal attack In a pure *frontal attack,* the attacker matches its opponent's product, advertising, price and distribution. The principle of force says that the side with the greater resources will win. A modified frontal attack, such as cutting price, can work if the market leader doesn't retaliate, and if the competitor convinces the market that its product is equal to the leader's. Max Factor (P&G) is a master at convincing the market that its products – such as Masterpiece Mascara and Lipfinity lipstick – are equal in quality but a better value than higher-priced brands.

Flank attack An enemy's weak spots are natural targets. A *flank attack* can be directed along two strategic dimensions – geographic and segmental. In a geographic attack, the challenger spots areas where the opponent is underperforming. Although the Internet has siphoned away newspaper readers and advertisers in many markets, Independent News & Media, a 102-year-old Irish media company, sells a majority of its 175 newspaper and magazine titles in cities where the economy is strong but the Internet is still relatively weak – countries such as Ireland, South Africa, Australia, New Zealand and India.[51] The other flanking strategy is to serve uncovered market needs. Ariat International used this type of strategy to attain its position as a leading footwear and apparel brand for equestrian athletes around the world. Ariat discovered an opportunity to design riding boots that were every bit as luxurious and elegant as traditional English riding boots, but ergonomically designed to feel as comfortable as a running shoe – a totally new benefit in the category. Later, Ariat applied the same idea to casual footwear, cowboy boots, work boots and apparel.[52]

A flanking strategy is another name for identifying shifts in market segments that are causing gaps to develop, then rushing to fill the gaps and develop them into strong segments. Flanking is in the best tradition of modern marketing, which holds that the purpose of marketing is to discover needs and satisfy them. It is particularly attractive to a challenger with fewer resources than its opponent and much more likely to be successful than frontal attacks.

▽ Search engines

Given Google's 45 per cent share of the Internet search business, it might seem foolhardy for anybody to challenge it. A frontal attack on Google would mean building a better mousetrap – in this case a better search algorithm. Yet a handful of smaller search companies *are* mounting flank attacks on Google, and they are confident they'll be able to swipe some of the search giant's market share. The flank these small companies are attacking is the one missing element in Google's searches: human intelligence and its ability to reason and contextualise. Jim Wales, cofounder of Wikipedia, the collaborative Internet encyclopedia, plans to create an open-source search engine called Wikia that uses human deduction as well as a machine-driven algorithm. Wales figures that humans are better at weeding out spam search results. ChaCha, which is a free mobile answers service, employs a similar strategy and has thrived in Korea, where Google has made few inroads. ChaCha, founded by MIT research scientist Scott A. Jones, uses 25,000 part- and full-time employees who can offer guided searches in real time. Anyone who has ever 'Googled' a topic and come up with thousands of Web pages, only a handful of which are truly helpful, can see how guided search might be an attractive offering. ChaCha's human-guided searches can offer a smaller set of focused and relevant results. The expense of using human guides might be daunting, but ChaCha has managed to bring in 10,000 guides a month at €3 to €7 an hour; it offers them a financial incentive for bringing in others. For its part, Wikia plans to use thousands of volunteers, building on the model of its successful all-volunteer-run Wikipedia.[53]

Encirclement attack The *encirclement* manoeuvre is an attempt to capture a wide slice of the enemy's territory through a blitz. It means launching a grand offensive on several fronts. Encirclement makes sense when the challenger commands superior resources and believes a swift encirclement will break the opponent's will. In making a stand against archrival Microsoft, Sun Microsystems licensed its Java software to hundreds of companies and millions of software developers for all sorts of consumer devices. As consumer electronics products began to go digital, Java started appearing in a wide range of gadgets.

Bypass attack The most indirect assault strategy is *bypassing* the enemy altogether and attacking easier markets to broaden the firm's resource base. This strategy offers three lines of approach: diversifying into unrelated products, diversifying into new geographical markets, and leapfrogging into new technologies to supplant existing products. In the past decade, Pepsi has used a bypass strategy against Coke by: (1) aggressively rolling out Aquafina bottled water nationally in 1997 before Coke launched its Dasani brand; (2) purchasing orange juice giant Tropicana for €2.3 billion in 1998, which owned almost twice the market share of Coca-Cola's Minute Maid; and (3) purchasing The Quaker Oats Company, owner of market leader Gatorade sports drink, for €9.8 billion in 2000.[54]

Technological leapfrogging is a bypass strategy practised in high-tech industries. The challenger patiently researches and develops the next technology and launches an attack, shifting the battleground to its own territory where it has an advantage. Nintendo's successful attack in the video game market was precisely about wresting market share by introducing a superior technology and redefining the 'competitive space'. Then Sega/Genesis did the same with more advanced technology, and now Sony's PlayStation has grabbed the technological lead to gain almost half the video game market.[55] Google used technological leapfrogging to overtake Yahoo! and become the market leader in search.

Guerrilla warfare Guerrilla warfare consists of waging small, intermittent attacks to harass and demoralise the opponent and eventually secure permanent footholds. The guerrilla challenger uses both conventional and unconventional means of attack. These include selective price cuts, occasional legal action and intense promotional blitzes. For instance, phone operator 3 used guerrilla advertising around Dublin's Croke Park before the Six Nations rugby union clash between England and Ireland in 2007 – it used high-pressure hoses to clean three logos into the dirt/grub on the pavements around the stadium.[56]

Marketing memo

Making smaller better

Adam Morgan offers eight suggestions on how small brands can better compete:

1 **Break with your immediate past** Don't be afraid to ask 'dumb' questions to challenge convention and view your brand differently.

2 **Build a 'lighthouse identity'** Establish values and communicate who and why you are. Apple excels at projecting a strong sense of self that makes it relevant and salient to consumers. By wholeheartedly signifying its confidence and fortitude, it becomes a lighthouse brand that the consumer can navigate her life by, publicly or privately.[57]

3 **Assume thought leadership of the category** Break convention in terms of what you say about yourself, where you say it, and what you do beyond talk.

4 **Create symbols of re-evaluation** A rocket uses half its fuel in the first mile to break loose from Earth's gravitational pull – you may need to polarise people to get them to rethink your brand.

5 **Sacrifice** Focus your target, message, reach and frequency, distribution and line extensions, and recognise that less can be more.

6 **Overcommit** Although you may do fewer things, do 'big' things when you do them.

7 **Use publicity and advertising to enter popular culture** Unconventional communications can get people talking.

8 **Be idea centred, not consumer centred** Sustain challenger momentum by not losing sight of what the brand is about and can be, and redefine marketing support as the centre of the company to reflect this vision.

Sources: A. Morgan (1999) *Eating the Big Fish: How Challenger Brands Can Compete Against Brand Leaders*, New York: John Wiley & Sons. See also A. Morgan (2004) *The Pirate Inside: Building a Challenger Brand Culture Within Yourself and Your Organisation*, Chichester, England: John Wiley & Sons.

Choosing a specific attack strategy

The challenger must go beyond the five broad strategies and develop more specific strategies. Any aspect of the marketing programme can serve as the basis for attack, such as lower-priced or discounted products, new or improved products and services, a wider variety of offerings, and innovative distribution strategies. A challenger's success depends on combining several strategies to improve its position over time. 'Marketing memo: Making smaller better' provides some additional tips for challenger brands.

Market-follower strategies

Some years ago, legendary marketing scholar Theodore Levitt wrote an article entitled 'Innovative Imitation', in which he argued that a strategy of *product imitation* might be as profitable as a strategy of *product innovation*.[58] The innovator bears the expense of developing the new product, getting it into distribution, and informing and educating the market. The reward for all this work and risk is normally market leadership. However, another firm can come along and copy or improve the new product. Although it probably will not overtake the leader, the follower can achieve high profits because it did not bear any of the innovation expense.

▽ S&S Cycle

S&S Cycle is the biggest supplier of complete engines and major motor parts to more than 15 companies that build several thousand Harley-like cruiser bikes each year. These cloners charge as much as €21,000 for their customised creations. S&S has built its name by improving on Harley-Davidson's handiwork. Its customers are often would-be Harley buyers frustrated by long waiting lines at the dealers. Other customers simply want the incredibly powerful S&S engines. S&S stays abreast of its evolving market by ordering a new Harley bike every year and taking apart the engine to see what it can improve upon.[59]

Many companies prefer to follow rather than challenge the market leader, a strategy that allows a company to learn more about market needs and reactions or a technology before committing resources to market and product development. Patterns of 'conscious parallelism' are common in capital-intensive, homogeneous-product industries, such as steel, fertilisers and chemicals. The opportunities for product differentiation and image differentiation are low; service quality is often comparable; and price sensitivity runs high. The mood in these industries is against short-run grabs for market share because that strategy only provokes retaliation. Most firms decide against stealing one another's customers. Instead, they present similar offers to buyers, usually by copying the leader. Market shares show high stability.

That's not to say that market followers lack strategies. A market follower must know how to hold current customers and win a fair share of new ones. Each follower tries to bring distinctive advantages to its target market – location, services, financing. Because the follower is often a major target of attack by challengers, it must keep its manufacturing costs low and its product quality and services high. It must also enter new markets as they open up. The follower must define a growth path, but one that doesn't invite competitive retaliation. We distinguish four broad strategies:

1 **Counterfeiter:** The counterfeiter duplicates the leader's product and packages and sells it on the black market or through disreputable dealers. Music firms, Apple and Rolex have been plagued by the counterfeiter problem, especially in Asia.

2 **Cloner:** The cloner emulates the leader's products, name and packaging, with slight variations. For example, Danish Harboes Bryggeri A/S sells imitations of Coca-Cola Zero in look-alike bottles. Its Cola Minus sells for less than half the price of a Coca-Cola Zero.

3 **Imitator:** The imitator copies some things from the leader but maintains differentiation in terms of packaging, advertising, pricing or location. The leader doesn't mind the imitator as long as the imitator doesn't attack the leader aggressively. Fernandez Pujals grew up in Fort Lauderdale, Florida, and took Domino's home delivery idea to Spain, where he borrowed €56,000 to open his first store in Madrid. His TelePizza chain now operates almost 1000 stores in Europe and Latin America.

4 **Adapter:** The adapter takes the leader's products and adapts or improves them. The adapter may choose to sell to different markets, but often it grows into the future challenger, as many Japanese firms have done after improving products developed elsewhere.

What does a follower earn? Normally, less than the leader. For example, a study of food-processing companies showed the largest firm averaging a 16 per cent return on investment; the number two firm, 6 per cent; the number three firm, −1 per cent; and the number four firm, −6 per cent. In this case, only the top two firms have profits. No wonder Jack Welch, former CEO of GE, told his business units that each must reach the number one or two position in its market, or else! Followership is often not a rewarding path.

Market-nicher strategies

An alternative to being a follower in a large market is to be a leader in a small market, or niche (see also Chapter 10). Smaller firms normally avoid competing with larger firms by targeting small markets of little or no interest to the larger firms. But even large, profitable firms may choose to use niching strategies for some of their business units or companies. Firms with low share of the total market can become highly profitable through smart niching. Such companies tend to offer high value, charge a premium price, achieve lower manufacturing costs, and shape a strong corporate culture and vision. By delivering pre-packed boxes of the season's best ecological vegetables and groceries to customers' doorsteps, the Danish Web company Aarstiderne.com (*Aarstiderne* = 'Seasons') offers consumers the chance to spend their time and energy at the cooker and not at the shopping cart. Customers may choose between nine different vegetable and fruit boxes and a wide selection of special boxes, containing for example fish, meat, cheese, bread or processed foods. The boxes include recipes for delicious and easy-to-make everyday meals that are tailor-made to suit each week's box. This solution helps consumers avoid the 'what are we going to eat tonight' stress of a typical weekday. At the end of 2007, 44,000 Danish families received boxes from Aarstiderne every week.[60]

In a study of hundreds of business units, the Strategic Planning Institute found that the return on investment averaged 27 per cent in smaller markets, but only 11 per cent in larger markets.[61] Why is niching so profitable? The main reason is that the market nicher ends up knowing the target customers so well, it meets their needs better than other firms selling to this niche casually. As a result, the nicher can charge a substantial price over costs. The nicher achieves *high margin*, whereas the mass marketer achieves *high volume*.

Nichers have three tasks: creating niches, expanding niches and protecting niches. Niching carries a major risk in that the market niche might dry up or be attacked. The company is then stuck with highly specialised resources that may not have high-value alternative uses.

▽ Zippo

With smoking in steady decline Bradford, Pennsylvania-based Zippo Manufacturing is finding the market for its iconic metal cigarette lighter drying up. Zippo marketers now find themselves needing to diversify and to broaden their focus to 'selling flame'. With a goal of reducing reliance on tobacco-related products to 50 per cent of revenue by 2010, the company introduced a long, slender, multipurpose lighter for candles, grills and fireplaces in 2001; it has explored licensing arrangements with suppliers of flame-related outdoor products; and it has acquired Case Cutlery, a knifemaker, and DDM Italia, known throughout Europe for fine Italian leather goods.[62]

Because niches can weaken, the firm must continually create new ones. 'Marketing memo: Niche specialist roles' outlines some options. The firm should 'stick to its niching' but not necessarily to its niche. That is why *multiple niching* is preferable to *single niching*. By developing strength in two or more niches, the company increases its chances for survival.

Marketing memo

Niche specialist roles

The key idea in successful nichemanship is specialisation. Here are some possible niche roles:

- **End-user specialist**: The firm specialises in serving one type of end-use customer. For example, a *value-added reseller* (VAR) customises the computer hardware and software for specific customer segments and earns a price premium in the process.
- **Vertical-level specialist**: The firm specialises at some vertical level of the production–distribution value chain. A copper firm may concentrate on producing raw copper, copper components or finished copper products.
- **Customer-size specialist**: The firm concentrates on selling to either small, medium-sized or large customers. Many nichers specialise in serving small customers neglected by the majors.
- **Specific-customer specialist**: The firm limits its selling to one or a few customers. Many firms sell their entire output to a single company, such as Sears or General Motors.
- **Geographic specialist**: The firm sells only in a certain locality, region or area of the world.

- **Product or product-line specialist**: The firm carries or produces only one product line or product. A manufacturer may produce only lenses for microscopes. A retailer may carry only ties.
- **Product-feature specialist**: The firm specialises in producing a certain type of product or product feature. Streetcar's car-sharing services target people who live or work in several UK cities – people who need a car from time to time, but wish to save the time and hassle associated with owning a car (parking, insurance and maintenance).[63]
- **Job-shop specialist**: The firm customises its products for individual customers.
- **Quality–price specialist**: The firm operates at the low- or high-quality end of the market. Hewlett-Packard specialises in the high-quality, high-price end of the handheld calculator market.
- **Service specialist**: The firm offers one or more services not available from other firms. A bank might take loan requests over the phone and hand-deliver the money to the customer.
- **Channel specialist**: The firm specialises in serving only one channel of distribution. For example, a soft drinks company decides to make a very large-sized serving available only at gas stations.

Firms entering a market should initially aim at a niche rather than the whole market. The mobile phone industry has experienced phenomenal growth but is now facing fierce competition as the number of new potential users dwindles. An Irish upstart company, Digicel Group, has successfully tapped into one of the few remaining high-growth segments: poor people without mobiles.

▽ Digicel Group

In 2001, Digicel CEO Denis O'Brien heard that the government of Jamaica was opening up its local phone market, long monopolised by British telecom giant Cable & Wireless. O'Brien spent nearly €35 million for a licence, using money from the sale of his first telecom venture, Esat Telecom Group PLC. O'Brien took the plunge because he knew that Jamaicans had to wait over two years for a landline, and only 4 per cent of the population had mobile phones. Within 100 days, Digicel had signed on 100,000 subscribers, luring them with inexpensive rates and phones and with improved service. Five years later, 70 per cent of Jamaica's cell phone users – now 82 per cent of the country's 2.7 million citizens – are Digicel customers. O'Brien has also homed in on the rest of the Caribbean and boasts 3 million subscribers in 22 countries throughout the Caribbean, Latin America, and even the South Pacific. In an ambitious move, O'Brien now plans to target the United States, specifically US consumers who are young, poor or immigrants – the kind of customers that giants such as TMobile and Verizon don't court.[64]

▽ Balancing customer and competitor orientations

We have stressed the importance of a company's positioning itself competitively as a market leader, challenger, follower or nicher. Yet a company must not spend *all* its time focusing on competitors.

Competitor-centred companies

A *competitor-centred company* sets its course as follows:

Observed situation

- Competitor W is going all out to crush us in Portugal.
- Competitor X is improving its distribution coverage in Germany and hurting our sales.
- Competitor Y has cut its price in Italy, and we lost three share points.
- Competitor Z has introduced a new service feature in Greece, and we are losing sales.

Reactions

- We will withdraw from the Portuguese market because we cannot afford to fight this battle.
- We will increase our advertising expenditure in Germany.
- We will meet competitor Y's price cut in Italy.
- We will increase our sales promotion budget in Greece.

This kind of planning has some pluses and minuses. On the positive side, the company develops a fighter orientation. It trains its marketers to be on constant alert, to watch for weaknesses in its competitors' and its own position. On the negative side, the company is too reactive. Rather than formulating and executing a consistent, *customer-oriented* strategy, it determines its moves based on its competitors' moves. It does not move toward its own goals. It does not know where it will end up, because so much depends on what its competitors do.

Customer-centred companies

A *customer-centred company* focuses more on customer developments in formulating its strategies.

Observed situation

- The total market is growing at 4 per cent annually.
- The quality-sensitive segment is growing at 8 per cent annually.
- The deal-prone customer segment is also growing fast, but these customers do not stay with any supplier very long.
- A growing number of customers have expressed an interest in a 24-hour hot line, which no one in the industry offers.

Reactions

- We will focus more effort on reaching and satisfying the quality segment of the market. We will buy better components, improve quality control, and shift our advertising theme to quality.
- We will avoid cutting prices and making deals because we do not want the kind of customer that buys this way.
- We will install a 24-hour hot line if it looks promising.

Clearly the customer-centred company is in a better position to identify new opportunities and set a course that promises to deliver long-term profits. By monitoring customer needs it can decide which customer groups and emerging needs are the most important to serve, given its resources and objectives. Jeff Bezos, founder of Amazon.com, strongly favours a customer-centred orientation:

> Amazon.com's mantra has been that we were going to obsess over our customers and not our competitors. We watch our competitors, learn from them, see the things that they [are doing for customers] and copy those things as much as we can. But we were never going to obsess over them.[65]

▽ SUMMARY

1. To prepare an effective marketing strategy a company must study competitors as well as actual and potential customers. Marketers need to identify competitors' strategies, objectives, strengths and weaknesses.

2. A company's closest competitors are those seeking to satisfy the same customers and needs and making similar offers. A company should also pay attention to latent competitors, who may offer new or other ways to satisfy the same needs. A company should identify competitors by using both industry- and market-based analyses.

3. A market leader has the largest market share in the relevant product market. To remain dominant, the leader looks for ways to expand total market demand, attempts to protect its current market share, and perhaps tries to increase its market share.

4. A market challenger attacks the market leader and other competitors in an aggressive bid for more market share. Challengers can choose from five types of general attack; challengers must also choose specific attack strategies.

5. A market follower is a runner-up firm willing to maintain its market share and not rock the boat. A follower can play the role of counterfeiter, cloner, imitator or adapter.

6. A market nicher serves small market segments not being served by larger firms. The key to nichemanship is specialisation. Nichers develop offerings to fully meet a certain group of customers' needs, commanding a premium price in the process.

7. As important as a competitive orientation is in today's global markets, companies should not overdo the emphasis on competitors. They should maintain a good balance of consumer and competitor monitoring.

▽ APPLICATIONS

Marketing debate

How do you attack a category leader? Attacking a leader is always difficult. Some strategists recommend attacking a leader 'head-on' by targeting its strengths. Other strategists disagree and recommend flanking and attempting to avoid the leader's strengths.

Take a position: The best way to challenge a leader is to attack its strengths *versus* The best way to attack a leader is to avoid a head-on assault and to adopt a flanking strategy.

Marketing discussion

Pick an industry. Classify firms according to the four different roles they might play: leader, challenger, follower and nicher. How would you characterise the nature of competition? Do the firms follow the principles described in this chapter?

▽ REFERENCES

[1] For a detailed academic treatment of a number of issues on competition, see the Special Issue (2005) on Competitive Responsiveness, *Marketing Science*, 24, Winter.

[2] M. E. Porter (1980) *Competitive Strategy*, New York: Free Press, 22–3.

[3] M. Altberg and P. Cochelin (2007) EMI moves to non-DRM music: what's next?, *S & P Rating News*, 12 April.

[4] W. C. Taylor (2007) The new language of competition, *Harvard Business Online*, 25 September.

[5] T. Khanna and K. G. Palepu (2006) Emerging giants, *Harvard Business Review*, 84(10) (October), 60–9.

[6] Ibid.

[7] A. D. Shocker (2002) Determining the structure of product-markets: practices, issues, and suggestions in B. A. Weitz and R. Wensley, London: Sage, 106–25. *Handbook of Marketing*. See also B. H. Clark and D. B. Montgomery (1999) Managerial identification of competitors, *Journal of Marketing*, 63 (July), 67–83.

[8] What business are you in? Classic advice from Theodore Levitt (2006) *Harvard Business Review*, October, 127–37. See also Theodore Levitt's seminal article Marketing Myopia (1960) *Harvard Business Review*, July–August, 45–56.

[9] J. F. Rayport and B. J. Jaworski (2001) *e-Commerce*, New York: McGraw-Hill, 53.

[10] R. A. D'Aveni (2002) Competitive pressure systems: mapping and managing multimarket contact, *MIT Sloan Management Review*, Fall, 39–49.

[11] Porter (1980) op. cit. Ch. 7.

[12] For discussion of some of the long-term implications of marketing activities, see K. Pauwels (2004) How dynamic consumer response, competitor response, company support, and company inertia shape long-term marketing effectiveness, *Marketing Science*, 23 (Fall), 596–610; K. Pauwels, D. M. Hanssens and S. Siddarth (2002) The long-term effects of price promotions on category incidence, brand choice, and purchase quantity, *Journal of Marketing Research*, 34, November, 421–39; and M. Dekimpe and D. Hanssens (1999) Sustained spending and persistent response: a new look at long-term marketing profitability, *Journal of Marketing Research*, 36 (November), 397–412.

[13] R. S. Sisodia, D. B. Wolfe, and J. N. Sheth (2007) *Firms of Endearment: How World-Class Companies Profit from Passion and Purpose*, Upper Saddle River, NJ: Wharton School Publishing.

[14] For an academic treatment of benchmarking, see D. W. Vorhies and N. A. Morgan (2005) Benchmarking marketing capabilities for sustained competitive advantage, *Journal of Marketing*, 69(1), (January), 80–94.

[15] P. Maidment and D. Bigman (2005) Special report: Energy, *Forbes*, 16 November.

[16] Porter (1980) op. cit. Ch. 7.

[17] These taxonomy and the Telstra example come from the writings of Australian marketing academic John H. Roberts: J. H. Roberts (2005) Defensive marketing: how a strong incumbent can protect its position, *Harvard Business Review*, November, 150–7; J. Roberts, C. Nelson, and P. Morrison (2001) Defending the beachhead: Telstra vs. Optus, *Business Strategy Review*, 12 (Spring), 19–24.

[18] D. Kiley (2007) Nokia wins with wide-angle vision, *Businessweek*, 6 August; M. Scott (2007) Nokia: wired for profits, *Businessweek*, 2 August.

[19] C. Lindhardt (1999) FDB skal rettes op, *Politiken*, 11 Frebruary; P. F. Gammelby (2001) Irma vokser igen, *Jyllands-Posten*, 24 May; M. Zahle (2007) Bilka vil være billigst: men er det ikke, *Jyllandsposten*, 7 November; A. Bisgaard (2007) Odense får sin Irma tilbage, *Nyhedsavisen*, 27 June; J. Risom and N. Ostrynski (2007) Danmark fører det økologiske kapløb, *Berlingske Tidende*, 4 October; Bedste resultat i Irmas 120-årige historie (2007), *Ritzaus Bureau*, 14 February.

[20] M. Gehlhar, A. Regmi, S. E. Stefanou, and B. Zoumas (2006) Managing firm competitiveness in global markets, USDA and AIEA 2 International Meeting: Competitiveness in Agriculture and in the Food Industry: US and EU perspectives Bolegna, 15–16 June.

[21] www.starbucks.com/aboutus/overview.asp, accessed 7 March 2007.

[22] B. Wansink (1996) Can package size accelerate usage volume?, *Journal of Marketing*, 60 (July), 1–14. See also P. Raghubir and E. A. Greenleaf (2006) Ratios in proportion: what should the shape of the package be?, *Journal of Marketing*, 70 (April), 95–107; and V. Folkes and S. Matta (2004) The effect of package shape on consumers' judgments of product volume: attention as a mental contaminant, *Journal of Consumer Research*, 31 (September), 390–401.

[23] J. D. Cripps (1994) Heuristics and biases in timing the replacement of durable products, *Journal of Consumer Research*, 21 (September), 304–18.

[24] R. Gohlar (2007) Not just Granny's tipple, *Marketing Week*, 30 August, 28–9.

[25]Business Bubbles (2002) *The Economist,* 12 October.

[26]G. Stalk Jr. and R. Lachanauer (2004) Hardball: five killer strategies for trouncing the competition, *Harvard Business Review,* 82 (April), 62–71; R. D'Aveni (2002) The empire strikes back: counterrevolutionary strategies for industry leaders, *Harvard Business Review,* November, 66–74.

[27]R. D. Hof (2006) There's not enough 'me' in MySpace, *BusinessWeek,* 4 December, 40; P. Sellers (2006) MySpace cowboys, *Fortune,* 4 September, 66–74; A. Pressman (2006) MySpace for baby boomers, *BusinessWeek,* 16 October, 120–2.

[28]J. Tagliabue (2006) Yeah, they torture jeans. But it's all for the sake of fashion, *New York Times,* 12 July, C1. Copyright © 2006 *The New York Times.* Reprinted by permission.

[29]B. Morrissey (2007) R/GA, *Adweek,* 22 January, 20+.

[30]J. Glancey (1999) The private world of the Walkman, *Guardian,* 11 October.

[31]These six defence strategies, as well as the five attack strategies, are taken from P. Kotler and R. Singh (1981) Marketing warfare in the 1980s, *Journal of Business Strategy,* Winter, 30–41.

[32]G. Edmondson (2007) Peugeot Citroën's bold turnaround plan, *BusinessWeek,* 4 September.

[33]Porter (1980) op. cit. Ch. 4; J. Prabhu and D. W. Stewart (2001) Signaling strategies in competitive interaction: building reputations and hiding the truth, *Journal of Marketing Research,* 38 (February), 62–72; J. L. Schenker (2008) EA leaps into free video games, *BusinessWeek,* 22 January.

[34]R. J. Calantone and K. E. Schatzel (2000) Strategic foretelling: communication-based antecedents of a firm's propensity to pre-announce, *Journal of Marketing,* 64, January, 17–30; J. Eliashberg and T. S. Robertson (1988) New product preannouncing behavior: a market signaling study, *Journal of Marketing Research,* 25 (August), 282–92.

[35]T. S. Robertson, J. Eliashberg, and T. Rymon (1995) New-product announcement signals and incumbent reactions, *Journal of Marketing* 59 (July), 1–15.

[36]Yuhong Wu, S. Balasubramanian and V. Mahajan (2004) When is a preannounced new product likely to be delayed?, *Journal of Marketing,* 68 (April), 101–13; B. L. Bayus, S. Jain and A. G. Rao (2001) Truth or consequences: an analysis of vaporware and new-product announcements, *Journal of Marketing Research,* 38 (February), 3–13.

[37]K. Capell (2006) Absolut Makeover, *BusinessWeek,* 16 January; K. Kelleher (2003) Why FedEx is gaining ground, *Business 2.0,* October, 56–7; C. Haddad (2002) FedEx: gaining on ground, *BusinessWeek,* 16 December, 126–8.

[38]S. Haxel (2007) Movers: businesses in the news, *International Herald Tribune,* 6 September.

[39]Sara Lee cleans out its cupboards (2005) *Fortune,* 7 March, 38; J. Sassen (2006) How Sara Lee left Hanes in its skivvies, *BusinessWeek,* 18 September, 40.

[40]J. S. Armstrong and K. C. Green (2007) Competitor-oriented objectives: the myth of market share, *International Journal of Business,* 12(1) (Winter), 115–34; S. E. Jackson, *Where Value Hides: A New Way to Uncover Profitable Growth for Your Business,* New York: John Wiley & Sons.

[41]N. Kumar (2004) *Marketing as Strategy,* Cambridge, MA: Harvard Business School Press; P. Kotler and P. N. Bloom (1975) Strategies for high-market-share companies, *Harvard Business Review,* November–December, 63–72.

[42]R. D. Buzzell and F. D. Wiersema (1981) Successful share-building strategies, *Harvard Business Review,* January–February, 135–44.

[43]R. J. Dolan (1981) Models of competition: a review of theory and empirical evidence in B. M. Enis and K. J. Roering (eds) *Review of Marketing,* Chicago, IL: American Marketing Association 224–34.

[44]L. Hellofs and R. Jacobson (1999) Market share and customers' perceptions of quality: when can firms grow their way to higher versus lower quality? *Journal of Marketing,* 63 (January), 16–25.

[45]J. Harwood (2007) Nintendo pulls Wii ads due to demand, *Marketing Week,* 6 December, 4; R. Mortimer (2007) Nintendo gives Sony a bloody nose by refusing to play power games, *Marketing Week,* 13 December.

[46]J. Birger (2006) Second-mover advantage, *Fortune,* 20 March, 20–1.

[47]V. Shankar, G. Carpenter, and L. Krishnamurthi (1998) Late-mover advantage: how innovative late entrants outsell pioneers, *Journal of Marketing Research,* 35 (February), 54–70; G. S. Carpenter and K. Nakamoto (1996) The impact of consumer preference formation on marketing objectives and competitive second-mover strategies, *Journal of Consumer Psychology,* 5(4), 325–58; G. S. Carpenter and K. Nakamoto (1990) Competitive strategies for late entry into a market with a dominant brand, *Management Science* October, 1268–78.

[48]http://www.ejc.net/media_landscape/article/spain/.

[49]Free papers, costly competition (2007) *BusinessWeek,* 19 November.

[50]http://www.schibsted.com/eway/, accessed May 2008.

[51]M. Johnston (2006) The Ketchup strategy, *Forbes,* 13 November, 185.

[52]M. V. Copeland (2004) These boots really were made for walking, *Business 2.0,* October, 72–4.

[53]A. Klassen (2007) Search Davids take aim at Goliath Google, *Advertising Age,* 8 January, 1+; Anonymous (2007) Cha-Cha – CEO interview, *CEO Wire,* 9 January.

[54]K. Booker (2006) The Pepsi machine, *Fortune,* 6 February, 68–72.

[55]J. Last (2002) Setting the stage for another flop?, philly.com, 4 June; E. Brown (2002) Sony's big bazooka, *Fortune,* 30 December, 111–14.

[56]Team support, sponsorship deals, family – all is fair in love of sport (2007) *Marketing Week,* 19 April, 18.

[57]A. Morgan (1999) Eating the big fish: how challenger brands can compete against brand leaders, New York: John Wiley & Sons, Inc.

[58]T. Levitt (1966) Innovative lmitation, *Harvard Business Review,* September–October, 63. See also S. P. Schnaars (1994) *Managing Imitation Strategies: How Later Entrants Seize Markets from Pioneers,* New York: Free Press.

[59]S. F. Brown (1998) The company that out-Harleys Harley, *Fortune,* 28 September, 56–7; www.sscycle.com.

[60]J. E. Rasmussen (2007) IndKøbsvaner: Flere køber mad på nettet, *Jyllands-Posten,* 25 September, http://www.aarstiderne.com/omaarstiderne/English.

[61]Reported in E. R. Linneman and L. J. Stanton (1991) *Making Niche Marketing Work,* New York: McGraw-Hill.

[62]T. A. Fogarty (2003) Keeping Zippo's flame eternal, *USA Today,* 24 June, www.zippo.com.

[63]A. Mitchell (2006) They're talking about a convenience revolution, *Marketing Week,* 28 September, 24–5.

[64]K. Kingsbury (2006) The cell islands, *Time,* 20 November, G20.

[65]R. Spector (2000) *Amazon.com: get big fast,* New York: HarperBusiness, 151.

Connecting with customers

Video documentary for Part 3

Go to **www.pearsoned.co.uk/marketingmanagementeurope** to watch the video documentary that relates to Part 3 and consider the issues raised below.

Having gained essential insights into the structure and buying behaviour in both consumer and business markets, marketing managers should then turn to the task of successfully competing in those markets.

Part 3: Connecting with Customers explores the key themes of:

1 segmentation;
2 targeting; and
3 positioning.

Segmentation is a matter of dividing markets up into 'bite-sized' chunks so that their specific requirements and potential can be assessed and judged. Once attractive market segments have been identified, companies can apply suitable screening systems to select those that will become their centre of attention – or, their targets. Each targeted market – whether *niche, middle* or *entry* – requires separate marketing management attention to ensure that the appropriate mix of customer benefits are blended into suitable market offerings that meet customers' perceived value requirements.

When watching the video documentary that accompanies Part 3, pay close attention to the detailed needs of individual target markets described by the top European marketing managers being interviewed. This attention to detail enables each company to build strong value sets that can be distinctive, but also reflect the overall positive image characteristics of the corporate brand identity. Successful positioning enables companies to efficiently provide the right market offerings to the right target markets in order to secure a sustainable competitive advantage and acceptable degrees of profit.

Sujata Thakur
Regional Director, Incredible India

Hear a variety of top marketing executives from a wide range of organisations offer their own interesting and varied perspectives on the key themes of Part 3 including: Hans Stråberg, President for the Electrolux Group (top); Sujata Thakur, Regional Director, Incredible India (centre); The original IKEA outlet, Älmhult, Sweden (bottom).

▽ Identifying, analysing and creating target market differentiating and positioning strategies

IN THIS CHAPTER, WE WILL ADDRESS THE FOLLOWING QUESTIONS:

1   What are the different levels of market segmentation?

2   How can a company divide a market into segments?

3   How should a company choose the most attractive target markets?

4   What are the requirements for effective segmentation?

5   How can a firm create, develop and communicate a successful positioning strategy in the market?

Morgan Cars: have a long order book and continue to serve a niche market for handbuilt traditional sports cars for baby boomers.
Source: Steve Sant/Alamy

6 Why is the concept of positioning so important to marketing practitioners?

7 How can companies seek to positively differentiate their offerings in today's market conditions?

8 When might companies need to reposition their market offerings and what are the main inherent risks of such a strategy?

Companies cannot connect with all customers in large, broad or diverse markets. But they can divide such markets into groups of customers or segments with distinct needs and wants. A company then needs to identify which market segments it can serve effectively. This decision requires a keen understanding of customer behaviour and careful strategic thinking. To develop the best marketing plans, managers need to understand what makes each segment unique and different. Their next task is to explore specific ways companies can effectively position and differentiate their market offerings to achieve a competitive advantage.

One lucrative market segment is that of the people who were born in Europe between 1946 and 1964 who are often referred to as 'baby boomers'. In 2004 baby boomers held 80 per cent of the UK's wealth and bought 80 per cent of all top of the range cars, 80 per cent of cruises and 50 per cent of skin care products.[1] Throughout Europe this market has attracted the attention of marketers as it presents a distinct demographic sector that has provided a variety of marketing opportunities over the years. In the United Kingdom companies such as Saga and First Choice have tried to make the over-50s market trendy. However, as they approach the evening of their lives, many Baby Boomers have registered their displeasure at finding themselves on these companies' mailing lists.[2]

To compete more effectively many companies are now adopting target marketing. Instead of scattering their marketing efforts they are focusing on customers they have the greatest chance of satisfying.

Effective target marketing requires that marketers:

- Identify and profile distinct groups of buyers who differ in their needs and preferences (market segmentation).
- Select one or more market segments to enter (market targeting).
- For each target segment, establish and communicate the distinctive benefit(s) of the company's market offering (market positioning).

▽ Levels of market segmentation

(See also Chapter 6.)

The starting point for discussing segmentation is **mass marketing**. In mass marketing, the seller engages in the mass production, mass distribution and mass promotion of one item for all buyers. Henry Ford epitomised this strategy when he offered the Model-T Ford in one colour – black. Coca-Cola also practised mass marketing when it sold only one kind of Coke in a standard bottle.

The argument for mass marketing is that it creates the largest potential market, which leads to the lowest costs, which in turn can lead to lower prices or higher margins. This is the *least cost production paradigm* that has served many firms well for several decades. However, in contemporary buyers' markets, companies are faced with new challenges. Increasing levels of competition present customers with a wide choice of possible suppliers. This results in them wanting more for their money and there has been a transformation in the concept of value from a factor that was largely determined by suppliers to one that is now heavily influenced by buyers. Firms now have to provide market offerings that their customers perceive to possess the right value standard. Also many markets display an increasing trend to break up into several segments. Fewer standardised products and services can be offered to customers (standard customer-perceived value offerings). Thus the use of mass marketing is in decline and most companies are turning to *micromarketing* at one of four levels: segments, niches, local areas and individuals.

Segment marketing

A *market segment* consists of a group of customers who share a similar set of needs and wants. Rather than creating the segments, the marketer's task is to identify them and to decide which one(s) to target. Segment marketing offers key benefits over mass marketing. The company can offer a market offering that can be positively differentiated from the competition. If strategy is the art of allocating scarce resources, then segmentation – and the understanding it provides about your customer groups – is part of the science informing that allocation.

However, such a segment is partly a fiction, in that not everyone in the segment wants exactly the same offering. Business-to-business marketing experts Anderson and Narus have urged marketers to present flexible market offerings to all members of a segment.[3] A **flexible market-perceived value offering** consists of two parts: a *naked solution* containing the product and service elements that all segment members value and *discretionary value options* that some segment members require. Each quality option might carry an additional charge; for example, Siemens' Electrical Apparatus Division sells metal-clad boxes to small manufacturers at prices that include free delivery and a warranty, but it also offers installation, tests and communication peripherals as extra-cost options. Ryanair offers all economy passengers a seat and soft drinks and charges extra for alcoholic beverages, snacks and meals.

Market segments can be characterised in different ways. One approach is to identify *preference segments*. **Homogeneous preferences** exist when all customers have roughly the same preferences. At the other extreme, customers with **diffused preferences** vary greatly in their requirements. If several brands are in the market they are likely to provide offerings that appeal to identified specific consumer preferences. Finally, **clustered preferences** result when natural market segments emerge from groups of customers with shared preferences. Marketers should divide customers into groups based only on those needs and factors actually driving purchase decisions. A common mistake is to segment customers based on peripheral characteristics that, while interesting, provide no help in achieving the fundamental goal of segmentation: selling more product profitably.

Niche marketing

A niche is a more narrowly defined customer group seeking a distinctive mix of benefits or values. Marketers usually identify niches by dividing a market segment into subsegments. For example, while Hertz, Avis, Eurocar and others specialise in airport rental cars for business and leisure travellers, Enterprise has attacked the low-budget, insurance-replacement market by primarily renting to customers whose cars have been written off or stolen. By creating unique associations with low cost and convenience in an overlooked niche market, Enterprise has been highly profitable.

The objective of a niche competitor, such as The Body Shop, Porsche or Saab is to be a large fish in a small pool. The niche market customers have a distinct set of value requirements and they will pay a premium to the firm that provides the best market offering. Niche markets are generally fairly small in terms of volume but constitute a sufficiently attractive size, profit and growth potential. Also, they are less likely to attract many other powerful competitors and can benefit from focusing their resources to gain economies through specialisation. Some larger companies, such as IBM, have lost parts of their business to successful niche competitors. This market competitor has been colourfully termed 'guerrillas against gorillas'.[4] The same thing is also happening in the online social networking market, where MySpace is becoming a mature service provider.

▽ **MySpace**

Social networking sites such as MySpace show many of the characteristics of fads. They quickly become popular but they can just as quickly fall out of favour. These pioneering sites initially enjoy a wide appeal and are crucially reliant on advertising revenue. A sudden drop in traffic numbers can threaten their survival. As competition in current buyers' markets intensifies social networking sites too will disaggregate. Many upstart social networking nichers hope to capitalise on the tendency of individuals to want to congregate with others who share their own particular passions and values. For instance, there is now 1Up.com, a content-heavy social site where online gaming fanatics can trade tips, stories, opinions and gossip.[5]

Large companies are increasingly turning to niche marketing. The Anglo-Dutch company Unilever acquired the US premium ice cream maker, Ben & Jerry's, as it was perceived to have a distinctive business style that appealed to customers. Both firms enjoyed a good reputation for operating ethical and socially responsible operations as well as providing quality products.

As marketing efficiency increases, niches that were hitherto considered to be too small may become more profitable.[6] The low cost of setting up shop on the Internet has led to many small business start-ups aimed at niches. The recipe for Internet niching success: choose a hard-to-find product that customers don't need to see and touch. 'Marketing insight: Chasing the long tail' outlines how provocative are the implications of Internet niching.

Internet niching

After initial losses Amazon has come of age as an Internet shopping centre. Faced by the long-tail product life cycle curve that characterises many of today's businesses it has restructured its business and is now making profits.

Local marketing

Target marketing is leading to marketing programmes tailored to the needs and wants of local customer groups in trading areas, neighbourhoods, even individual stores. Retail firms such as Starbucks have all found great success emphasising local marketing initiatives, but other types

Marketing insight

Chasing the long tail

The advent of online commerce made possible by technology and epitomised by Amazon.com and iTunes has led to a shift in customer buying patterns, according to Chris Anderson, editor-in-chief of *Wired* magazine and author of *The Long Tail*.

In most markets, the distribution of product sales conforms to a curve weighted heavily to one side – the 'head' – where the bulk of sales is generated by a few products. The curve falls rapidly toward zero and hovers just above it far along the X-axis – the 'long tail' – where the vast majority of products generate very few sales. The mass market traditionally focused on generating 'hit' products that occupy the head, disdaining the low-revenue market niches comprising the tail.

Anderson asserts that as a result of consumers embracing the Internet as a shopping medium, the long tail harbours significantly more value than before. In fact, Anderson argues, the Internet has directly contributed to the shifting of demand 'down the tail, from hits to niches' in a number of product categories, including music, books, clothing, films and videos.

On his blog, Anderson states his argument as follows:

The Long Tail equation is simple: 1) The lower the cost of distribution, the more you can economically offer without having to predict demand. 2) The more you can offer, the greater the chance that you will be able to tap latent demand for minority tastes that was unreachable through traditional retail. 3) Aggregate enough minority taste, and you'll often get a big new market.

Anderson identifies two aspects of Internet shopping that contribute to this shift. First, greater choice is permitted by increased stock and variety. Given a choice between 10 hit products, consumers are forced to select one of them. If, however, the choice set is expanded to 1000, then the top 10 hits will be chosen less frequently. Second, the 'search costs' of finding relevant new products are lowered due to the wealth of information sources available online, the filtering of product recommendations based on user preferences that vendors can provide, and the word-of-mouth network of Internet users.

Anderson sees the long tail effect as particularly pronounced in media, a category that is historically hit driven but which benefits enormously from these two aspects of online shopping.

The long tail thesis was also supported by researchers Brynjolfsson, Yu 'Jeffrey' Hu and Smith, who conducted two studies to measure the tail in online versus offline book selling and clothing retail. The book-selling study concluded that the increased product variety offered by online bookshops increased customer choice substantially. In the case of online clothing retail, the study found that customers who used both online and catalogue channels purchased a more even distribution of products than would have been the case had they just used catalogue channels.

The same companies that compete in the business of creating hits are beginning to develop ways to evolve niche successes in the long tail. Others have countered that, especially in entertainment, the 'head' where the hits are concentrated is valuable to consumers, not only to the content creators. An arti-

Figure 10.1 Traditional and long-tailed product life cycles
Source: M. R. V. Goodman, Durham University.

▶ **Marketing insight** *(continued)*

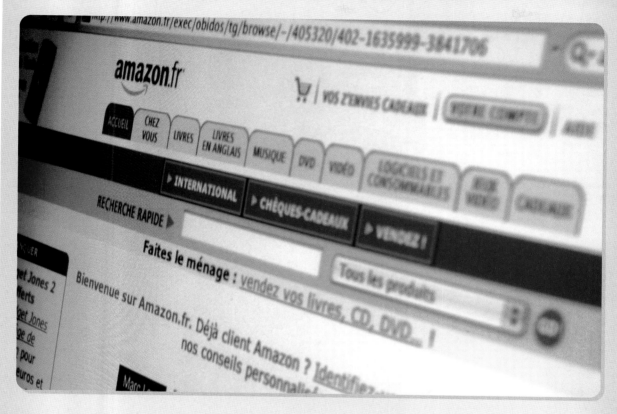

Amazing choice at Amazon.

Source: Richard Levine/Alamy

cle in *The Economist* argued that 'most hits are popular because they are of high quality' and a critique in the *New Yorker* notes that the majority of products and services making up the long tail originate from a small concentration of 'long-tail aggregators' – sites such as Amazon, eBay and iTunes. This observation challenges the premise that old business paradigms have changed as much as Anderson suggests.

Sources: C. Anderson (2006) *The Long Tail*, New York: Hyperion; 'Reading the Tail' interview with Chris Anderson, *Wired*, 8 July 2006, 30; Wag the dog: what the long tail will do, *The Economist*, 8 July 2006, 77; E. Brynjolfsson, Y. (J.) Hu and M. D. Smith (2006) From niches to riches: anatomy of a long tail, *MIT Sloan Management Review*, Summer, 67; J. Cassidy (2006) Going long, *The New Yorker*, 10 July; www.longtail.com.

of firms are also going local. Supermarkets vary the stock portfolios they carry to suit the locations of their stores. IKEA customises merchandise to match the perceived demand of local areas. The problems experienced in Europe by clothes retailer C&A that forced them to withdraw from several countries has been blamed on their Brussels-based central buying policy.

Local marketing reflects a growing trend called *grassroots marketing*. Marketing activities concentrate on getting as close and personally relevant to individual customers as possible. Much of Nike's initial success comes from engaging target customers through grassroots marketing such as sponsorship of local school teams, expert-conducted clinics, and the provision of shoes, clothing and equipment. 'Breakthrough marketing: HSBC' profiles another success story.

A Polish food shop opens to provide a taste of home for the large local Polish community in Darlington in the north of England.

Source: Gregory Wrona/Alamy

The risks associated with localised marketing include:

- a tendency to drive up manufacturing costs ansd so reduce economies of scale;
- a tendency to create logistical problems;
- a possibility that the overall image of the brand may be put at risk.

Those who advocate localised marketing see national advertising as wasteful because it is too 'arm's length' and fails to address local needs. Those against local marketing argue that it drives up manufacturing and marketing costs by reducing economies of scale and magnifying logistical problems. A brand's overall image might be diluted if the product and message are different in different localities. The advantages are all concerned with the capacity that is granted to firms to respond to local requirements more effectively than would otherwise be the case. Thus, the customer-perceived value of a firm's offering is enhanced. Overall, this advantage generally outweighs the disadvantages in contemporary buyers' markets.

Individual marketing

The ultimate level of segmentation results in 'segments of one', 'customised marketing' or 'one-to-one marketing'.[7] Today customers are taking a more individual initiative in determining what and how to buy. They log on to the Internet; look up information and evaluations of product or

Sainsbury's come to your neighbourhood to offer a convenient but relatively expensive local shopping opportunity.
Source: Justin Kase/Alamy

service offers; conduct dialogues with suppliers, users and product critics; and, in many cases, design the product they want.

Wind and Rangaswamy see a movement towards 'customerising' the firm.[8] Mass customisation introduces a *new paradigm* whereby companies seek to fragment the market through economies of scope.[9] Customers become integral to the product and service design processes, with more sophisticated customers undertaking simulations to answer 'what-if' questions. Products and services are assembled from valued components or attributes to develop unique products for individual needs.

Mass customisation, like one-to-one marketing, requires new organisational thinking. Every customer interaction provides an opportunity to learn more about the customer's needs and to adapt existing products or services to meet changing circumstances. True customer service leads to strong relationships and an enhanced lifetime value experience for customers. Every employee becomes a marketer as the whole firm networks to provide the right collection of value attributes or benefits for customers.

Customerisation combines operationally driven mass customisation with customised marketing in a way that empowers consumers to design the customer-perceived value offering of their choice. The firm no longer requires prior information about the customer, nor does the firm need to own manufacturing. The firm provides a platform and tools and 'rents' out to customers the means to design their own products. A company is customerised when it is able to respond to

Breakthrough marketing

HSBC

HSBC wants to be known as the 'world's local bank'. This tagline reflects HSBC's positioning as a globe-spanning financial institution with unique focus on serving local markets. Originally the Hong Kong and Shanghai Banking Corporation Limited, HSBC was established in 1865 to finance the growing trade between China and the United Kingdom. It is now the second-largest bank in the world. Despite serving over 100 million customers through 9500 branches in 79 countries, the bank works hard to maintain a local presence and local knowledge in each area. Its fundamental operating strategy is to remain close to its customers. As HSBC chairman Sir John Bond said, 'Our position as the world's local bank enables us to approach each country uniquely, blending local knowledge with a worldwide operating platform.' The bank's advertisements in its 'World's Local Bank' campaign depict the way different cultures interpret the same objects or events.

The bank pulls its worldwide businesses together under a single global brand with the 'World's Local Bank' slogan. The aim is to link its international size with close relationships in each of the countries in which it operates. HSBC spends $600 million annually on global marketing, which it consolidated in 2004 under the WPP group of agencies. Going forward, it will be seeking to leverage its position as 'The World's Local Bank' to improve on its $11.6 billion brand value, which placed it 28th on the 2006 Interbrand/*BusinessWeek* global brand rankings.

Sources: D. Orr (2004) New ledger, *Forbes*, 1 March, 72–3; HSBC's global marketing head explains review decision, *Adweek*, 19 January; Now your customers can afford to take fido to the vet, *Bank Marketing*, December 2003, 47; K. Hein (2003) HSBC bank rides the coattails of chatty cabbies, *Brandweek*, 1 December, 30; Sir J. Bond and S. Green (2003) HSBC strategic overview, presentation to investors, 27 November; Lafferty Retail Banking Awards 2003, *Retail Banker International*, 27 November 2003, 4–5; Ideas that work, *Bank Marketing*, November 2003, 10; HSBC enters the global branding big league, *Bank Marketing International*, August 2003, 1–2; N. Madden (2003) HSBC rolls out post-SARS effort, *Advertising Age*, 16 June, 12; K. Nicholson (2005) HSBC aims to appear global yet approachable, *Campaign*, 2 December, 15; C. Mollenkamp (2006) HSBC stumbles in bid to become global deal maker, *Wall Street Journal*, 5 October, A1, A12; www.hsbc.com.

individual customers by customising its products, services and messages on a one-to-one basis. In the United Kingdom Towels R Us offers customised towels, roller towels and dressing gowns. Customers can choose from a large range of logos and can add their own messages. Sanford Brands[10] offers to customise pens manufactured by Parker, Sharpie, Waterman, Papermate and Berol. Nike ID enables clients to design every aspect of a range of five Nike athletic shoes. Designing your own pair of Nike ID Pumas costs from £50–150 – about three times the cost of the standard shoes.[11]

Customerisation is particularly important in business-to-business markets. FAG Kugelfischer is a German manufacturer with sales of over €3 billion and Europe's second biggest maker of rolling bearings (devices essential to virtually all kinds of rotary motion) after SKF of Sweden. The company believes that customising bearings to suit individual tastes provides considerable untapped potential and will be a key determinant of future earnings growth.[12]

However, customerisation is not for every company. It may be very difficult to implement for some complex products but is now breaking through into the car market. Henry Ford launched mass production 88 years ago with his revolutionary assembly line for the Model T car. It proved a brilliant system – at least for as long as there were customers waiting at the end of the line to drive Ford's cars away. But it lost some of its shine when customers became harder to find, meaning that mass-produced cars remained expensively in car parks and showrooms. Now a new dream is at hand: to turn mass production on its head with the help of flexible systems and Internet ordering. Fiat has identified a strong trend in Europe towards customerisation and will be offering several ways for customers to personalise the latest version of their Punto model. The goal is to deliver precisely the car that a customer wants.

Customerisation can also raise the cost of goods by more than the customer is willing to pay. Some customers do not know what they want until they see actual items. In spite of this customerisation has worked well for some products. Mass customerisation harnesses these new technologies to bring customised and personalised products and services to customers at a mass production price.

One-to-one-marketing or customer-centric marketing was first developed in the late 1980s by the Boston Consulting Group.[13] It seeks to develop long-term relationships with individual customers to tailor responses to their needs.[14]

▽ Bases for segmenting consumer markets

Two broad groups of variables are used to segment consumer markets. Some researchers seek to define segments by looking at descriptive characteristics: geographic, demographic and psychographic. Then they examine whether these customer segments exhibit different needs or product responses. For example, they might examine the differing attitudes of 'professionals', 'blue-collars workers' and other groups towards, say, 'safety' as a customer-perceived benefit when considering purchasing a new car.

> To learn how BMW studies changing consumer lifestyles to match product development to segmentation, visit www.pearsoned.co.uk/marketingmanagementeurope

Other researchers try to define segments by looking at behavioural considerations, such as customer responses to benefits, use occasions or brands. The researcher then sees whether different characteristics are associated with each consumer-response segment. For example, do people who want 'quality' rather than 'low price' in a car purchase differ in their geographic, demographic and psychographic characteristics?

Regardless of which type of segmentation scheme is used, the key is adjusting the marketing programme to recognise customer differences. The major segmentation variables – geographic, demographic, psychographic, and behavioural segmentation for the United States – are summarised in Table 10.1.

Geographic segmentation

Geographic segmentation calls for dividing the market into different geographical units such as nations, states, regions, counties, cities or neighbourhoods. The company can operate in one or a few areas, or operate in all but pay attention to local variations. White goods manufacturers have to cater for variations in demand across European frontiers. Top-loading washing machines are needed for the French market, front loading for the UK market, slow spin speeds for the Italian market (as they have plenty of sunshine) and ecologically efficient machines for northern European markets. Tesco test marketed the new ultrastrong Dorset Naga chilli pepper in a north of England, Newcastle store as north-easterners have a known preference for stronger flavours. Geographic segmentation can also be used to assist marketers to study 'service' markets. In order to understand the different requirements of European visitors to the tourist attractions on the Danish island of Funen tourists were segmented by nationality.

More and more, regional marketing means marketing right down to a specific postcode. Many companies use mapping software to show the geographic locations of their customers. The software may show a retailer that most of his customers are within only a ten-mile radius of his shop, and further concentrated within certain postcode areas.

Some approaches combine geographic data with demographic data to yield even richer descriptions of customers and neighbourhoods. This has become known as geodemographic segmentation – 'the analysis of people by where they live'.[15] A number of specialist companies offer a variety of geodemographic databases. Table 10.2 presents some of the leading companies and classification systems that can be accessed in the United Kingdom.

An example of Experian's MOSAIC profile is given in Table 10.3.

All of these databases have numerous subsegment variations but they should be used with caution. There are many uncertainties such as reliability and validity of the data, and its freshness – CCI makes a selling point out of its claim to update its databases every two years. While this is to be welcomed these relational databases should be continually updated throughout the year. As strategic marketing planning poses ever stronger challenges wise companies take out online subscriptions with the database providers.

Geodemographic services are now available in a variety of microsegments for smaller firms because, as database costs decline, PCs proliferate, software becomes easier to use, data integration increases, and use of the Internet grows.[16]

Table 10.1 Major segmentation variables for consumer markets

US geographic region	Pacific Mountain, West North Central, West South Central, East North Central, East South Central, South Atlantic, Middle Atlantic, New England
City or metro size	Under 5000; 5000–20,000; 20,000–50,000; 50,000–100,000; 100,000–250,000; 250,000–500,000; 500,000–1,000,000; 1,000,000–4,000,000; 4,000,000 or over
Density	Urban, suburban, rural
Climate	Northern, southern
Demographic age	Under 6, 6–11, 12–19, 20–34, 35–49, 50–64, 64+
Family size	1–2, 3–4, 5+
Family life cycle	Young, single; young, married, no children; young, married, youngest child under 6; young; married, youngest child 6 or over; older, married, with children; older, married, no children under 18; older, single; other
Gender	Male, female
Income	Under $10,000; $10,000–$15,000; $15,000–$20,000; $20,000–$30,000; $30,000–$50,000; $50,000–$100,000; $100,000 and over
Occupation	Professional and technical; managers, officials and proprietors; clerical sales; craftspeople; forepersons; operatives; farmers; retired; students; homemakers; unemployed
Education	Grade school or less; some high school; high school graduate; some college; college graduate
Religion	Catholic, Protestant, Jewish, Muslim, Hindu, other
Race	White, black, Asian, Hispanic
Generation	Baby boomers, Generation Xers
Nationality	British, Chinese, French, German, Italian, Japanese, North American, South American
Social class	Lower lowers, upper lowers, working class, middle class, upper middles, lower uppers, upper uppers
Psychographic lifestyle	Culture oriented, sports oriented, outdoor oriented
Personality	Compulsive, gregarious, authoritarian, ambitious
Behavioural occasions	Regular occasion, special occasion
Benefits	Quality, service, economy, speed
User status	Non-user, ex-user, potential user, first-time user, regular user
Usage rate	Light user, medium user, heavy user
Loyalty status	None, medium, strong, absolute
Readiness stage	Unaware, aware, informed, interested, desirous, intending to buy
Attitude toward product	Enthusiastic, positive, indifferent, negative, hostile

Demographic segmentation

In demographic segmentation, the market is divided into groups on the basis of variables such as age, family size, family life cycle, gender, income, occupation, education, religion, race, generation, nationality and social class. One reason demographic variables are so popular with marketers is that they are often associated with customer needs and wants. Another is that they are easy to measure. Even when the target market is described in non-demographic terms (say by

Table 10.2 Geodemographic companies and classifications

Organisation	Classification system	Examples of data sources used
ABC Ltd/ISL	Residata	Housing types and structure; Risk indices; Insurance data; PAF; Unemployment statistics; Census
CACI	ACORN	Census data
	LifestylesUK	Lifestyle data; ER; Census; Share ownership
	PeopleUK	Lifestyle data; ER; Census; Census share ownership
Claritas Europe	PRIZM	Lifestyle data; Share ownership; Company directors; PAF; Unemployment statistics; Births and deaths
Euro Direct	CAMEO	Census data
Experian	MOSAIC	Census data; Credit card data; CCJs; PAF; ER; Company directors; Access to retail stores

Key: ACORN: A Classification of Residential Neighbourhoods; CCJs: County court judgments: consumers who have been taken to court for debt recovery; ER: Electoral register: gives names, addresses and number of adults in 95 per cent of UK households; PAF: Postcode address file: the Royal Mail's database of all addresses in the United Kingdom by postcode.

Source: Table compiled by Peter Sleight and published in F. Brassington and S. Pettitt (2003) *Principles of Marketing*, 3rd edn, Harlow, England: Prentice Hall, Chapter 5, p. 187. Copyright © Peter Sleight. Reproduced with permission.

Table 10.3 MOSAIC Group H: stylish singles

Nearly 1.3 million households, representing 5.5 per cent of all UK households:

- 2.8 million people in this group;
- students and young professionals;
- first-time openers of savings and mortgage accounts;
- frequent visitors to the cinema, concerts and exhibitions;
- like weekend breaks to European capital cities;
- prefer the *Guardian*, the *Independent* and the *Observer* newspapers;
- television viewing is light: current affairs and late films preferred;
- shop for food at convenience stores late in the day;
- convenience more important than price;
- prefer the city to the outer suburbs;
- enjoy living in diverse, cosmopolitan, multicultural environment;
- big spenders on mobile phones, music, sports equipment, audio and computer equipment.

Source: After F. Brassington and S. Pettitt (2003) *Principles of Marketing*, Harlow, England: Prentice Hall. Copyright © 2003 Pearson Education Ltd. Reproduced with permission.

personality type) it may be necessary to link back to demographic characteristics in order to estimate the size of the market and the media necessary to reach it efficiently.

Here's how certain demographic variables have been used to segment markets.

Age and life cycle stage Consumer wants and abilities change with age. Toothpaste brands such as Crest and Colgate offer three main lines of products to target children, adults and older consumers. Age segmentation can be even more refined. Pampers divides its market into pre-natal, new baby (0–5 months), baby (6–12 months), toddler (13–23 months), and pre-schooler (24 months+). LEGO divides its market into Duplo (pre-school), Lego (early mid-school age), and Legotechnic (mid-school to senior school). ClubMed and Club 18–30 are targeted to appeal to single or young couples and the Saga umbrella brand is designed to appeal to the over 50s.

Marketing memo

Gathering geodemographic data

PRIZM (trade name for a geodemographic index marketed by Claritas Europe) is an example of Pan-European lifestyle segmentation. This and other similar tools such as ACORN (trade name for A Classification of Residential Neighbourhoods) and MOSAIC (trade name for a geodemographic system that is popular in the UK and owned by the US-based Experian Group, a global services information company) function by assuming that residents of each postal unit form a distinct segment.

Claritas, which markets PRIZM, claims that it can be used to:

- assess market potential or demand for a given area;
- develop customer loyalty and value by identifying the most attractive customers;
- reveal emerging niche markets;
- identify and target customers most likely to defect in order to reduce customer turnover (churn).

Source: Adapted from F. Brassington and S. Pettitt (2003) *Principles of Marketing*, Harlow, England: Prentice Hall and Claritas Europe

Nevertheless, age and life cycle can be tricky variables. In some cases the target market for products may be the psychologically young. For example, the Mini Cooper appeals to several age groups.

Life stage

People in the same part of the life cycle may differ in their life stage. Life stage defines a person's major concern, such as going through a divorce, going into a second marriage, taking care of an older parent, deciding to cohabit with another person, deciding to buy a new home, and so on. These life stages present opportunities for marketers who can help people cope with their major concerns.

The growing proportion of retired people in the affluent European countries has created new market segments and new requirements in existing markets such as senior citizen banking.

Memories for baby boomers and a cool car for 20 year olds.
Source: Sandro Campardo/ AP/PA Photos

A marketing bonanza to the bridal industry and marketers targeting newlyweds, the popular Broadway show *The Wedding Singer* entered advertising partnerships with wedding websites and bridal magazines.

Source: Sara Krulwhich/ *The New York Times/* Redux Pictures

The trend toward single-adult households (i.e., the unmarried, divorced, widowed or single parent families) has stimulated the market for foodstuffs that are marketed in small portions. The trend towards more working women has stimulated the market sectors for time-saving items such as microwave ovens, catalogue shopping, easy-to-prepare foods and fast food restaurants. The wedding industry attracts marketers of a whole host of products and services who are keen to market to wedding guests as well as seeking to help newlyweds set up home.

Gender

Men and women have different attitudes and behave differently, based partly on genetic make-up and partly on socialisation.[17] For example, women tend to be more communal minded and men tend to be more self-expressive and goal directed; women tend to take in more of the data in their immediate environment; men tend to focus on things that will help them to achieve a goal. A research study examining how men and women shop found that men often need to be invited to touch a product, while women are likely to pick it up without prompting. Men often like to read product information; women may relate to a product on a more personal level.

In many European countries women are increasingly influencing consumer goods and services purchases and exercise a considerable influence in the purchase of new homes. Gender differentiation has long been applied in clothing, hairstyling, cosmetics and magazines. Avon has built a successful business selling beauty products to women. Some products have been positioned as more masculine or feminine. Gillette's Venus is the most successful female shaving line ever, with over 70 per cent of the market, and has appropriate product design, packaging and advertising cues to reinforce a female image.

However, it is not enough to present a product as masculine or feminine. Hyper-segmentation is now occurring within both male and female personal care segments. Nestlé markets its Yorkie chocolate bars in the United Kingdom to attract men and states on the packaging that 'It's not for girls'. Unilever earned kudos by targeting women who may be worried about ageing skin by stressing in their 'Dove Campaign for Real Beauty' that true beauty is timeless.

▽ Dove

Dove's Campaign for Real Beauty features women of all shapes, sizes and colours posing proudly in their underwear. The company claims that the advertising series, developed by Ogilvy & Mather, was not just a vehicle to sell more soap but 'aims to change the status quo and offer in its place a broader, healthier, more democratic view of beauty'. The springboard was a global study sponsored by Dove that researched women's attitudes towards themselves and beauty. Only 2 per cent of women in the study considered themselves beautiful, so not only women, but everyone, took notice when the pictures of beaming full-figured or average-looking women began appearing.[18]

Media have emerged to make gender targeting easier. Marketers can reach women more easily in celebrity, fashion and household women's magazines. Men can be targeted by advertisements on the sporting satellite channels and through popular male magazines.[19]

Some traditionally more male-oriented markets, such as the car industry, are beginning to recognise gender segmentation, and are changing the way they design and sell cars.[20] Women shop differently for cars than men; they are more interested in environmental impact, care more about interior than exterior styling, and view safety in terms of features that help survive an accident rather than handling to avoid an accident.[21] Men are usually more interested in 'go-fast' designs and performance statistics.

Income

Income segmentation is a long-standing practice in such categories as cars, clothing, cosmetics, financial services and travel. However, income does not always predict the best customers for a given product. Apparently blue-collar workers were among the first purchasers of colour television sets as it was cheaper for them to buy these sets than to go to the cinema and theatre.

Many marketers are deliberately targeting lower-income groups, in some cases discovering fewer competitive pressures or greater consumer loyalty.[22] Matalan and The Officers Club offer a range of cheap clothing lines and TK Maxx offers designer labels at bargain prices.

Yet, at the same time, other marketers are finding success with premium-priced products and services as is the case with Coutts Bank and Moët et Chandon champagne. The growing number of dual-income households commanding high levels of disposable income has boosted the sales of premium products such as innovative and expensive Dyson twin drum washing machines. Of particular note are the DINKYs (double income no kids yet). The growing number of dual-income households commanding high levels of disposable income have boosted the sales of premium products and services. The 'credit crunch' that erupted in 2008 caused many companies to suffer from loss of sales and hence profitability as consumer expenditure was pegged back by rising mortgage and credit costs.

Increasingly, companies are finding that their markets are becoming 'hourglass shaped' as middle-market consumers migrate towards both discount and premium products.[23] Companies that miss out on this new market risk being 'trapped in the middle' and seeing their market share steadily decline. General Motors was caught in the middle, between highly engineered German imports in the luxury market and high-value Japanese and Korean models in the economy class, and has seen its market share continually slide.[24] 'Marketing insight: Trading up (and down) – the new consumer' describes the factors creating this trend and what it means to marketers.

The new consumer

New consumers defy traditional marketing identification. In reaction to a synthetic, processed and packaged world, their main drive is for an 'authentic experience' used as a means for the individual to define him- or herself. According to them 'consumption is as much about services,

Marketing insight

Trading up (and down) – the new consumer

While the new consumer growth trends are stronger in the United States than in Europe, European countries are undergoing the same demographic changes.

A new pattern in consumer customer behaviour has emerged in recent years, according to Silverstein and Fiske, the authors of *Trading Up*. In unprecedented numbers, middle-market customers are periodically trading up to what Silverstein and Fiske call 'new luxury' products and services 'that possess higher levels of quality, taste, and aspiration than other goods in the category but are not so expensive as to be out of reach'. Customers might buy an expensive imported French wine, use a premium skin cream or stay in a luxury hotel.

As a result of the trading-up trend, new luxury goods sell at higher volumes than traditional luxury goods, while being priced higher than conventional mid-market items. The authors identify three main types of new luxury products:

1 **Accessible super-premium products**, such as designer label clothes. Kettle gourmet potato crisps carry a significant premium over middle-market

brands, yet consumers can readily trade up to them because they are relatively low-price items in affordable categories.

2 **Old luxury brand extensions** extend historically high-priced brands down market while retaining their cachet, such as the Mercedes-Benz C-class and Kenwood audio equipment.

3 **Prestige goods,** such as fine wines which are priced between average middle-market brands and super-premium old luxury brands. They are 'always based on emotions, and consumers have a much stronger emotional engagement with them than with other goods'.

The authors note that in order to trade up on the brands that offer these emotional benefits, customers often 'trade down' by shopping at discount stores such as Aldi and Lidl (for staple food items) and at TK Maxx (for goods that confer no emotional benefit but still deliver quality and functionality).

Sources: M. J. Silverstein and N. Fiske (2003) *Trading Up: The New American Luxury*, New York Portfolio; M. J. Silverstein (2006) *Treasure Hunt: Inside the Mind of the New Consumer*, New York Portfolio; J. Cioletti (2006) Moving on up, *BeverageWorld*, June, 20.

experiences, and citizenship as it is about the acquisition of goods.' These new consumers are a potent economic force and increasingly companies are adapting their standard products to meet their requirements.[25] Paradoxically, this aspirational consumption is not always making these new consumers any happier. The paralyzing effects of a marketplace that offers a bewildering and ultimately debilitating array of alternatives results in fuelling not greater satisfaction, but greater anxiety.[26]

Generation

Each generation is profoundly influenced by the age in which it is reared – the music, films, politics and defining events of that period. Demographers call these generational groups *cohorts*. Members share the same major cultural, political and economic experiences and have similar outlooks and values. Marketers often advertise to a cohort by using the icons and images prominent in its experiences. Citroën have used Transformer images in their advertising to attract male customers in the United Kingdom who have nostalgic memories of the popular Transformer toys of their childhood. 'Marketing insight: Marketing to "generation Y"' provides insight into that key age cohort.

Although distinctions can be made between the different generational cohorts they also influence each other. For instance, because so many members of generation Y – Echo boomers – are living with their boomer parents, parents are being influenced by what demographers are calling a 'boom-boom effect'. The same products that appeal to 21 year olds are appealing to youth-obsessed baby boomers. Noxon termed this the 'rejuvenile' mindset. Here are two examples of the rejuvenilisation phenomenon:

1 Adult gadgets, such as mobile phones, cars and even houseware, have been transformed from purely utilitarian to toy-like. Vacuums come in different primary colours. Cars in lemon yellow. Mini Coopers look as if they have been designed for the toddler set.

Marketing insight

Marketing to 'generation Y'

They are dubbed 'echo boomers' or 'generation Y'. They grew up amid economic abundance and will probably face years of economic recession. Their world has experienced little economic disturbance. They have been 'wired' almost from birth – playing computer games, navigating the World Wide Web, downloading music, and connecting with friends via instant messaging and mobile phones. They have a sense of entitlement and abundance from growing up during the economic boom and being pampered by their boomer parents. They are selective, confident and impatient. They want what they want when they want it – and they often get it by using credit cards.

The influences that shaped generation Y are incredibly important to marketers because this cohort will shape consumer and business markets for years to come. Born between 1977 and 1994, generation Y vastly outnumbers the post-Second World War baby boomers of generation X. They will command an awesome annual spending power and will probably live (barring any unforeseen catastrophe) well into their 80s.

It's not surprising, then, that market researchers and advertisers are actively seeking to understand generation Y's buying behaviour. As overt branding practices and 'hard sell' marketing are generally not welcomed by this cohort marketers have tried many different approaches to reach and persuade them.

1 **Online buzz**: Nike and Nokia advertise on Internet service providers (ISPs).
2 **Student ambassadors:** Red Bull enlists college students as Red Bull student brand managers to distribute samples, research drinking trends, design on-campus marketing initiatives and write stories for student newspapers.
3 **Unconventional sports:** Henkel sponsors the Men's European Handball Championships; Red Bull organises gliding races.
4 **Cool events:** Toyota sponsored a wheel-changing competition on a road-show truck and TDK have sponsored a dance marathon in Milan.
5 **Computer games:** Product placement is not restricted to movies or TV: firm are seeking display opportunities in electronic games from leading companies such as Activision.
6 **Videos:** Car companies make sure that their logos appear in film and video productions.
7 **Street teams:** Local pizza parlours support Danball, the fun street game in Belgium.

Sources: www.sponsorship.com.news; www.bslworld.com.news.

Marketing memo

Key trends in the social and cultural environment

Grey market

Marketers keep a close eye on the key trends in the social and cultural environment in the countries in which they do business. The changing environment causes a continuous change in social attitudes and perceived values. Improving living standards has a significant effect on the ways in which customers spend their disposable income.

In the developed west the so-called grey segment of the over 60s makes up over 20 per cent of the population and this figure is expected to rise to around 30 per cent by 2050. The segment constitutes an attractive target market for several perceived-value offerings. Increasingly it will become a significant target for marketing communications activities.

Youth market

As generation X, the *status quo* weary and cynical youth, gives way to generation Y the European youth market will change as they start to experience relatively declining levels of disposable income in the opening decades of the twenty-first century. This is because most of the developed European economies will experience relatively lower growth levels. The rebellious attitudes of generation X will mutate with the changing fortunes of this market. While fad and fashion will always be attractive to this segment, declining levels of purchasing power will impact on the offerings of the leading clothing companies such as Monsoon, Next and Hugo Boss, whose businesses will become increasingly price dependent.

Ethnic market

Following the rapid expansion of the European Union (which has been a marked feature since 2000), coupled with an increased tendency for ethnic migration, the developed west will be characterised by rising multiethnic societies. As the different cultures have distinct value sets marketers will develop a strong interest in ethnic marketing programmes. In the United Kingdom the Halifax Building Society's 'Harvey' character has pioneered the regular use of ethnic actors in TV advertising.

2 Half the adults who visit Disney World every day do so without children, and Noxon found that Disney enthusiasts return to the Magic Kingdom to recapture the safety and serenity of childhood.[27]

Social class

Social class can be classified using macrocriteria such as profession, education, family income and property value. In Europe the ESOMAR association, in an attempt to standardise many different national classifications, has developed a model that is based on property occupation, education and the principal earning power of the main contributor to the household income. Each social class tends to share a mix of common values that has a strong influence on purchasing decisions. Many companies target social class segments and design cars, clothing, home furnishings, leisure activities, and so on to suit their preferences. The tastes of these social classes change with the passing of the years. The 1990s were strongly characterised by consumerism and ostentation for the upper classes. Affluent tastes now run more conservatively, although luxury goods makers such as Burberry, Chanel, TAG Heuer and Louis Vuitton still successfully sell to those seeking the good life.

Psychographic segmentation

Psychographics is the science of using psychology and demographics to better understand consumer market consumers. In *psychographic segmentation* buyers are divided into different groups on the basis of psychological/personality traits, lifestyle or values. People within the same demographic group can exhibit very different psychographic profiles and thus display different lifestyles. Psychographic profiles are typically developed with reference to three variables known as the AIO factors that describe individual lifestyles:

1 activities;

2 interests;

3 opinions.

Lifestyle studies enhance basic socio-demographic descriptions and aid understanding of customer value preferences. The main psychographic profiles are general lifestyle studies and product-specific studies. The former classifies the total population into groups according to common characteristics such as 'receptivity to innovation', 'family centred', 'ecologically aware', etc. The latter specifies the importance of such characteristics in consumer purchasing decisions. The French International Research Institute on Social Change (RISC) has identified eight social-cultural variables that greatly influence the development of European society (see Table 10.4).

Table 10.4 The forces shaping social change

1 *Self-development* – affirming oneself as an individual.

2 *Hedonism* – giving priority to pleasure.

3 *Plasticity* – adapting to circumstances.

4 *Vitality* – exploiting one's energy.

5 *Connectivity* – relating to others, mixing cultures.

6 *Ethics* – searching for a sensitive and balanced social life.

7 *Belongings* – defining social links and cultural similarities.

8 *Inertia* – actively, or more often passively resisting change.

Source: L. Hasson (1995) Monitoring social change, *International Journal of Market Research*, 37(1), 69–80. Copyright © 1995 Market Research Society (www.ijmr.com). Reproduced with permission.

Table 10.5 SINUS typology

1   *Basic orientation*: traditional – to preserve.
2   *Basic orientation*: materialist – to have.
3   *Changing values*: hedonism – to indulge.
4   *Changing values*: post-materialism – to be.
5   *Changing values*: postmodernism – to have, to be and to indulge.

Another European typology has been developed by SINUS GmbH and identifies five social classes and value perspectives as shown in Table 10.5.

One of the most popular commercially available classification systems based on psychographic measurements is the Stanford Research Institute's Consulting Business Intelligence's (SRIC-BI) VALS™ framework. VALS, signifying values and lifestyles, classifies US adults into eight primary groups based on responses to a questionnaire featuring 4 demographic and 35 attitudinal questions. The VALS™ system is continually updated with new data from more than 80,000 surveys per year (see Figure 10.2).[28] Check your VALS™ classification by going to SRIC-BI's website.

The main dimensions of the VALS™ segmentation framework are customer motivation (the horizontal dimension) and customer resources (the vertical dimension). Customers are inspired by one of three primary motivations: ideals, achievement and self-expression. Those primarily motivated by ideals are guided by knowledge and principles. Those motivated by achievement look for products and services that demonstrate success to their peers. Customers whose motivation is self-expression desire social or physical activity, variety and risk. Personality traits such as energy,

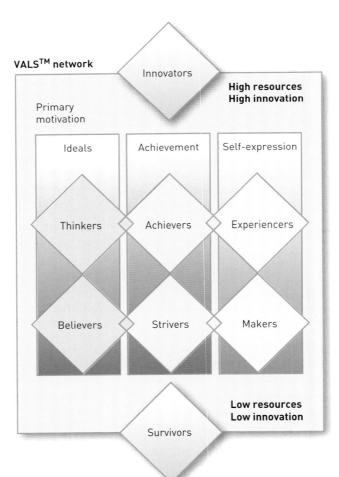

Figure 10.2 The VALS™ segmentation system: an eight-part typology

Source: VALS™. Copyright © SRI Consulting Business Intelligence. Reproduced with permission.

self-confidence, intellectualism, novelty seeking, innovativeness, impulsiveness, leadership and vanity – in conjunction with key demographics – determine an individual's resources. Different levels of resources enhance or constrain a person's expression of primary motivation.

The four groups with higher resources are:

1 **Innovators:** successful, sophisticated, active, 'take-charge' people with high self-esteem. Purchases often reflect cultivated tastes for relatively upscale, niche-oriented products and services.

2 **Thinkers:** mature, satisfied and reflective people who are motivated by ideals and who value order, knowledge and responsibility. They seek durability, functionality and value in products.

3 **Achievers:** successful goal-oriented people who focus on career and family. They greatly value products that demonstrate success to their peers.

4 **Experiencers:** young, enthusiastic impulsive people who seek variety and excitement. They spend a comparatively high proportion of income on fashion, entertainment and socialising.

The four groups with lower resources are:

1 **Believers:** conservative, conventional and traditional people with concrete beliefs. They prefer familiar, domestic products and are loyal to established brands.

2 **Strivers:** trendy and fun-loving people who are resource constrained. They like stylish products that emulate the purchases of those with greater material wealth.

3 **Makers:** practical, down-to-earth self-sufficient people who like to work with their hands. They seek domestic products with a practical or functional purpose.

4 **Survivors:** elderly, passive people who are concerned about change. They are loyal to their favourite brands.

Psychographic segmentation schemes are often customised by culture. The Japanese version of VALS™, Japan VALS™, divides society into ten consumer segments on the basis of two key concepts: life orientation (traditional ways, occupations, innovation and self-expression) and attitudes to social change (sustaining, pragmatic, adapting and innovating).

Marketers can apply their understanding of psychographic profiles to VALS™ to marketing planning. For example, Martini advertising has been targeted at individuals on the basis of what lifestyle they would like to have. It appeals to 'aspirational lifestyle segments'. While psychographic profiles can greatly assist marketers they do suffer from a number of drawbacks. They are expensive to maintain, update and develop and they can obscure the relationship between segment characteristics and brand performance.[29]

Behavioural segmentation

In behavioural segmentation, marketers place buyers into groups on the basis of their knowledge of, attitude towards, use of or response to a product.

Decision roles

It is easy to identify the buyer for many products. In Europe, men normally choose their shaving equipment and women choose their tights, but even here marketers must be careful in making their targeting decisions, because buying roles change. For example, in the United Kingdom Marks & Spencer found that it was women who usually purchased underpants for their men folk. When ICI, the giant British chemical company, discovered that women made 60 per cent of decisions on the brand of household paint, it decided to advertise its Dulux brand to women.

People play five roles in a buying decision: *initiator, influencer, decider, buyer* and *user.* For example, assume a wife initiates a purchase by requesting a modern coffee maker for her birthday. The husband may then seek information from many sources, including his best friend who has a Nespresso and is a key influencer in what models to consider. After presenting the alternative choices to his wife, he then purchases her preferred model which, as it turns out, is a Nespresso that ends up being used by the entire family. Different people are playing different roles, but all are crucial in the decision process and ultimate consumer satisfaction.

Behavioural variables

Many marketers believe behavioural variables – occasions, benefits, user status, usage rate, buyer-readiness stage, loyalty status and attitude – are the best starting points for constructing market segments.

Occasions Occasions can be defined in terms of the time of day, week, month, year, or in terms of other well-defined temporal aspects of a consumer's life. Buyers can be distinguished according to the occasions when they develop a need, purchase a product or use a product. For example, cereals have traditionally been marketed as a breakfast-related item. Kellogg's has always encouraged consumers to eat breakfast cereal on the 'occasion' of getting up. Recently, however, it has tried to extend the consumption of cereals by promoting them as an ideal 'anytime' snack food.

Marketers can also extend activities associated with certain holidays to other times of the year. While Christmas, Mother's Day and Valentine's Day are the major gift-giving holidays, these and other events account for just over half givers' budgets. That leaves the rest available throughout the year for occasions such as birthdays, weddings, anniversaries, house warming and new babies.[30]

Benefits Not everyone who buys a product wants the same benefits from it. This is recognised by the high street commercial banks that target their finance packages on the one hand to people who want a high return in the short term and on the other hand to those investors who are looking for an attractive return on their money over the longer term. Research in the toothpaste market has found four main 'benefit segments' – economic, medicinal, cosmetic and taste.

User status Every product has its non-users, ex-users, potential users, first-time users and regular users. Blood banks cannot rely only on regular donors to supply blood; they must also recruit new first-time donors and contact ex-donors, with a different marketing strategy for each. The key to attracting potential users, or even possibly non-users, is understanding the reasons they are not using the product in question. Do they have deeply held attitudes, beliefs or behaviours or just lack knowledge of the product or brand benefits and usage?

Included in the potential-user group are consumers who will become users in connection with some life stage or life event. Mothers-to-be are potential users who will turn into heavy users. Producers of infant products and services learn their names by maintaining close relationships with clinics and doctors and shower them with products and ads to capture a share of their future purchases. Market-share leaders tend to focus on attracting potential users because they have the most to gain. Smaller firms focus on trying to attract current users away from the market leader.

Usage rate Markets can be segmented into light, medium and heavy product users. Heavy users are often a small percentage of the market but account for a high percentage of total consumption. For example, heavy beer drinkers account for 87 per cent of the beer consumed – almost seven times as much as light drinkers. Marketers would rather attract one heavy user than several light users. A potential problem, however, is that heavy users are often either extremely loyal to one brand, or never loyal to any brand and always looking for the lowest price. They may also have less room to expand their purchase and consumption.

Buyer-readiness stage Some people are unaware of the product, some are aware, some are informed, some are interested, some desire the product, and some intend to buy. To help characterise how many people are at different stages and how well they have converted people from one stage to another, some marketers employ a marketing funnel. Figure 10.3 displays a funnel for two hypothetical brands, A and B. Brand B performs poorly compared to Brand A at converting one-time triers to more recent triers.

The relative numbers of customers at different stages make a big difference in designing the marketing programme. Suppose a health agency wants to encourage women to have an annual cervical smear to detect cervical cancer. At the beginning, most women may be unaware of the smear test. The marketing effort should go into awareness-building advertising using a simple message. Later, the advertising should dramatise the benefits of the test and the risks of not taking it.

Figure 10.3 Brand funnel

Loyalty status Marketers usually envision four groups based on brand loyalty status:

1 **Hard-core loyals:** consumers who buy only one brand all the time.
2 **Split loyals:** consumers who are loyal to two or three brands.
3 **Shifting loyals:** consumers who shift loyalty from one brand to another.
4 **Switchers:** consumers who show no loyalty to any brand.[31]

A company can learn a great deal by analysing the degrees of brand loyalty. Hard-core loyals can help identify the products' strengths; split loyals can show the firm which brands are most competitive with its own; and by looking at customers who are shifting away from its brand, the company can learn about its marketing weaknesses and attempt to correct them. One caution: what appear to be brand-loyal purchase patterns may reflect habit, indifference, a low price, a high switching cost or the unavailability of other brands.

Attitude Five attitudes about product purchase are: enthusiastic, positive, indifferent, negative and hostile. Door-to-door workers in a political campaign use voter attitude to determine how much time to spend with that voter. They thank enthusiastic voters and remind them to vote; they reinforce those who are positively disposed; they try to win the votes of indifferent voters; they spend no time trying to change the attitudes of negative and hostile voters.

Combining different behavioural bases can help to provide a more comprehensive and cohesive view of a market and its segments. Figure 10.4 depicts one possible way to break down a target market by various behavioural segmentation bases.

The Conversion Model

The Conversion Model measures the strength of customers' psychological commitment to brands and their openness to change.[32] To determine how easily a customer can be converted to another choice, the model assesses commitment based on factors such as customer attitudes towards, and satisfaction with, current brand choices in a category, and the importance of the decision to select a brand in the category.[33]

The model segments *users* of a brand into four groups based on strength of commitment, from low to high, as follows:

1 **Convertible:** (most likely to defect).
2 **Shallow:** (uncommitted to the brand and could switch – some are actively considering alternatives).
3 **Average:** (also committed to the brand they are using, but not as strongly – they are unlikely to switch brands in the short term).
4 **Entrenched:** (strongly committed to the brand they are currently using – they are highly unlikely to switch brands in the foreseeable future).

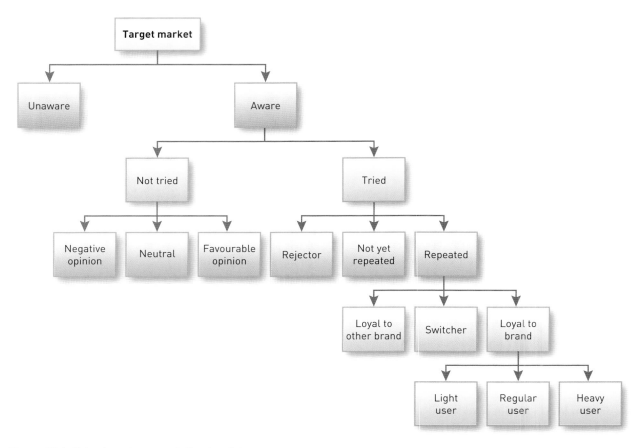

Figure 10.4 Behavioural segmentation breakdown

The model also classifies *non-users* of a brand into four other groups based on their 'balance of disposition' and openness to trying the brand, from low to high, as follows:

1 **Strongly unavailable:** (unlikely to switch to the brand – their preference lies strongly with their current brands).

2 **Weakly unavailable:** (not available to the brand because their preference lies with their current brand, although not strongly).

3 **Ambivalent:** (as attracted to the brand as they are to their current brands).

4 **Available:** (most likely to be acquired in the short run).

In an application of the Conversion Model, Lloyds TSB (a UK high street bank) discovered that the profitability of its 'least committed' clients had fallen by 14 per cent in a 12-month period, whereas for the 'most committed' it had increased by 9 per cent. Those who were 'committed' were 20 per cent more likely to increase the number of products they held during the 12-month period. As a result, the bank took action to attract and retain high-value committed customers, which resulted in increased profitability.

Finally, a related method of behavioural segmentation has recently been proposed that looks more at the expectations a customer brings to a particular kind of transaction and locates those expectations on a 'Gravity of decision spectrum'. At the shallow end of the spectrum, consumers seek products and services they think will save them time, effort and money, such as toiletries and snacks. Segmentation for these items would tend to measure customers' price sensitivity, habits and impulsiveness. At the other end of the spectrum, the deep end, are those decisions in which customers' emotional investment is greatest and their core values most engaged, such as deciding on a health care facility for an ageing relative or buying a new home. Here the marketer would seek to determine the core values and beliefs related to the buying decision. As the model suggests, focusing on customer's relationships and involvement with products and product categories can often be revealing as to where and how the firm should market to customers.[34]

▽ Bases for segmenting business markets

Business-to-business (see Chapter 8) markets can be segmented with variables that are used in consumer markets, such as geography, benefits sought and usage rate, together with some extra ones. As it is common to find a one-to-one relationship between buyer and seller, segmentations are closely fashioned to the needs of individual organisations. Table 10.6 shows one set of variables that can be applied to segment the business market. The demographic variables are the most important, followed by the operating variables – down to the personal characteristics of the buyer.

Table 10.6 Major segmentation variables for business markets

Demographic

1 *Industry*: Which industries should we serve?
2 *Company size*: What size companies should we serve?
3 *Location*: What geographical areas should we serve?

Operating variables

4 *Technology*: What customer technologies should we focus on?
5 *User or non-user status*: Should we serve heavy users, medium users, light users or non-users?
6 *Customer capabilities*: Should we serve customers needing many or few services?

Purchasing approaches

7 *Purchasing-function organisation*: Should we serve companies with highly centralised or decentralised purchasing organisation?
8 *Power structure*: Should we serve companies that are engineering dominated, financially dominated, and so on?
9 *Nature of existing relationship*: Should we serve companies with which we have strong relationships or simply go after the most desirable companies?
10 *General purchasing policies*: Should we serve companies that prefer leasing? Service contract? Systems purchases? Sealed bidding?
11 *Purchasing criteria*: Should we serve companies that are seeking quality? Service? Price?

Situational factors

12 *Urgency*: Should we serve companies that need quick and sudden delivery or service?
13 *Specific application*: Should we focus on a certain application of our product rather than all applications?
14 *Size of order*: Should we focus on large or small orders?

Personal characteristics

15 *Buyer-seller similarity*: Should we serve companies whose people and values are similar to ours?
16 *Attitude towards risk*: Should we serve risk-taking or risk-avoiding customers?
17 *Loyalty*: Should we serve companies that show high loyalty to their suppliers?

Source: Adapted from T. V. Bonoma and B. P. Shapiro (1983) *Segmenting the Industrial Market*, Lexington MA: Lexington Books. Copyright © 1983 Lexington Books. Reproduced with permission.

The table lists major questions that business marketers should ask in determining which segments and customers to serve. A tyre company for instance can sell tyres to manufacturers of cars, trucks, farm tractors, forklift trucks or aircraft. Within a chosen target industry, a company can further segment by company size. The company might set up separate operations for selling to large and small customers.

Within a given target industry and customer size, a company can segment further by purchase criteria. For example, government laboratories need low prices and service contracts for scientific equipment; university laboratories need equipment that requires little service; and industrial laboratories need equipment that is highly reliable and accurate.

Business marketers generally identify segments through a sequential process. Consider an aluminium company: the company first undertook macrosegmentation. It looked at which end-use market to serve: automobile, residential or beverage containers. It chose the residential market, and it needed to determine the most attractive product application: semi-finished material, building components or aluminium mobile homes. Deciding to focus on building components, it considered the best customer size and chose large customers. The second stage consisted of microsegmentation. The company distinguished among customers buying on price, service or quality. Because the aluminium company had a high-service profile, it decided to concentrate on the service-motivated segment of the market.

▽ Market targeting

There are many statistical techniques for developing market segments and targeting. Talent hits a target no one else can hit; genius hits a target no one else can see.[35] Once the firm has identified its market-segment opportunities, it has to decide how many and which ones to target. Marketers are increasingly combining several variables in an effort to identify smaller, better-defined target groups. Thus a bank may not only identify a group of wealthy retired adults, but within that group distinguish several segments depending on current income, assets, savings and risk preferences. This has led some market researchers to advocate a *needs-based market segmentation approach*. Best proposed the seven-step approach shown in Table 10.7.

Table 10.7 Steps in the segmentation process

		Description
1	*Needs-based segmentation*	Group customers into segments based on similar needs and benefits sought by customer in solving a particular consumption problem.
2	*Segment identification*	For each needs-based segment, determine which demographics, lifestyles and usage behaviours make the segment distinct and identifiable (actionable).
3	*Segment attractiveness*	Using predetermined segment attractiveness criteria (such as market growth, competitive intensity and market access), determine the overall attractiveness of each segment.
4	*Segment profitability*	Determine segment profitability.
5	*Segment positioning*	For each segment, create a 'value proposition' and product-price positioning strategy based on that segment's unique customer needs and characteristics.
6	*Segment 'acid test'*	Create 'segment storyboard' to test the attractiveness of each segment's positioning strategy.
7	*Marketing-mix strategy*	Expand segment positioning strategy to include all aspects of the marketing mix: product, price, promotion and place.

Source: Adapted from R. J. Best (2005) *Market-based Management*, 4th edn, Upper Saddle River, NJ: Prentice Hall. Copyright © 2005 Pearson Education, Inc. Reproduced with permission.

Effective segmentation criteria

Not all segmentation schemes are useful. For example, table salt buyers could be divided into blonde and brunette customers, but hair colour is undoubtedly irrelevant to the purchase of salt. Furthermore, if all salt buyers buy the same amount of salt each month, believe all salt is the same, and would pay only one price for salt, this market would be minimally segmentable from a marketing point of view.

To be useful, market segments must be capable of assessment on five key criteria:

1 **Measurable:** The size, purchasing power and characteristics of the segments can be measured.

2 **Substantial:** The segments are large and profitable enough to serve. A segment should be the largest possible homogeneous group worth pursuing with a tailored marketing programme. It would not pay, for example, for an automobile manufacturer to develop cars for people who are less than four feet tall.

3 **Accessible:** The segments can be effectively reached and served.

4 **Differentiable:** The segments are conceptually distinguishable and respond differently to different marketing-mix elements and programmes. If married and unmarried women respond similarly to a perfume sale they would not for this purpose constitute separate segments.

5 **Actionable:** Effective programmes can be formulated for attracting and serving the segments.

Evaluating and selecting the market segments

In evaluating different market segments, the firm must look at two factors: the segment's overall attractiveness and the company's objectives and resources. How well does a potential segment score on the five criteria? Does a potential segment have characteristics that make it generally attractive, such as size, growth, profitability, scale economies and low risk? Does investing in the segment make sense given the firm's objectives, competencies and resources? Some attractive segments may not be compatible with the company's long-run objectives, or the company may lack one or more necessary competencies to offer superior value.

After evaluating different segments, the company can consider five patterns of target market selection, shown in Figure 10.5. Each are now described in turn.

Single-segment concentration

Fiat and Volkswagen concentrate on the small-car market – and Porsche on the sports car market. Through concentrated marketing the firms gain a strong knowledge of the segment's needs and so can achieve a strong market presence. Furthermore, firms are able to enjoy operating economies through specialising their production, distribution and promotion. If firms can capture segment leadership they can earn a high return on investment.

However, there are risks. A particular market segment can turn sour or a competitor may invade the segment: when digital camera technology took off the earnings of Kodak (film) and Polaroid fell sharply. For these reasons many companies prefer to spread the risk and choose to operate in more than one segment. If selecting more than one segment to serve a company should pay close attention to segment interrelationships affecting costs, performance and technology. A company carrying fixed costs (sales force, retail outlets) can add products to absorb and share some costs. The sales force will sell additional products, and a fast-food outlet will offer additional menu items. Economies of scope can be just as important as economies of scale.

Companies can try to operate in super-segments rather than in isolated segments. A super-segment is a set of segments that share some significant exploitable similarity; for example, many symphony orchestras target people who have broad cultural interests rather than those who regularly attend concerts.

Single-segment concentration

Selective specialisation

Product specialisation

Market specialisation

Full market coverage

P = Product   *M* = Market

Figure 10.5 Five patterns of target market selection

Source: Adapted from D. F. Abell (1980) *Defining the Business: The Starting Point of Strategic Planning*, Upper Saddle River, NJ: Prentice Hall, Chapter 8, pp. 192–6. Copyright © 1980. Reproduced with permission from Pearson Education, Inc.

Selective specialisation

A firm selects a number of segments, each objectively attractive and appropriate. There may be little or no synergy among the segments, but each promises to be a moneymaker. This multi-segment strategy has the advantage of diversifying the firm's risk.

Product specialisation

The firm makes a certain product that it sells to several different market segments. A microscope manufacturer for instance sells to university, government and commercial laboratories. The firm makes different microscopes for the different customer groups and builds a strong reputation in the specific product area. The downside risk is that the product may be supplanted by an entirely new technology.

Market specialisation

The firm concentrates on serving many needs of a particular customer group. For instance a firm can sell an assortment of products only to university laboratories. The firm gains a strong reputation in serving this customer group and becomes a channel for additional products the customer group can use. The downside risk is that the customer group may suffer budget cuts or shrink in size.

Full market coverage

The firm attempts to serve all customer groups with all the products they might need. Only very large firms such as Microsoft (software market), General Motors (vehicle market), and Coca-Cola (non-alcoholic beverage market) can undertake a full market coverage strategy. Large firms can cover a whole market in two broad ways: through undifferentiated marketing or differentiated marketing.

In *undifferentiated marketing* the firm ignores segment differences and trades on the whole market with one offer. It designs a product and a marketing programme that will endow the product with a superior image and appeal to the broadest number of buyers, and it relies on mass distribution and advertising. Undifferentiated marketing is 'the marketing counterpart to standardisation and mass production in manufacturing'.[36] The narrow product line keeps down the costs of R & D, production, inventory, transportation, marketing research, advertising and product management. The undifferentiated advertising programme also reduces advertising costs. The company can turn its lower costs into lower prices to win the price-sensitive segment of the market.

In *differentiated marketing* the firm operates in several market segments and designs different products for each. Cosmetics firm Estée Lauder markets brands that appeal to women (and men) of different tastes. The flagship brand, the original Estée Lauder, appeals to older consumers; Clinique caters to middle-aged women; Hugo Boss to youthful hipsters; Aveda to aromatherapy enthusiasts; and The Body Shop to eco-conscious consumers who want cosmetics made from natural ingredients.[37]

▽ Nestlé

Nestlé provides a classic example of a highly differentiated marketing business. It operates The Nestlé Model, which is designed both to protect the house brand by spreading its activities across three broad interests – nutrition, health and wellness – and to seek business opportunities in markets that are consistent with the company's mission to build on its position as the world's leading nutrition, health and wellness company. In 2006 turnover was up by 8.1 per cent to SFr 98,458 million, with the food and beverages sub-brands the key drivers of growth and profitability. Nestlé has a brand portfolio that includes famous brands in bottled water, baby foods, dairy products, ice cream, nutrition, beverages, chocolate and confectionery, prepared foods, food services and pet care.

Sources: Nestlé Annual Report 2006; Nestlé website, www.nestlé.com; H. Simonian (2006) Nestlé enriches its choc value, *Financial Times*, 23 March.

Differentiated marketing typically creates more sales than undifferentiated marketing. However, it also increases the costs of doing business. Because differentiated marketing leads to both higher sales and higher costs, nothing general can be said about the profitability of this strategy. Companies should be cautious about oversegmenting their markets. If this happens, they may want to turn to *counter segmentation* to broaden the customer base. For example, Johnson & Johnson broadened its target market for its baby shampoo to include adults. SmithKline Beecham launched its Aquafresh toothpaste to attract three benefit segments simultaneously: those seeking fresh breath, whiter teeth and cavity protection. Kellogg's markets cereals as an evening snack as well as the traditional breakfast starter.

Additional considerations

Two other considerations in evaluating and selecting segments are segment-by-segment invasion plans and ethical choice of market targets.

Segment-by-segment invasion plans

A company would be wise to enter one segment at a time. Competitors must not know what segment(s) the firm will move to next. Segment-by-segment invasion plans are illustrated in Figure 10.6. Three firms, A, B and C, have specialised in adapting computer systems to the needs of airlines, railroads and trucking companies. Company A meets all the computer needs of airlines. Company B sells large computer systems to all three transportation sectors. Company C sells personal computers to trucking companies.

Where should company C move next? Arrows added to the chart show the planned sequence of segment invasions. Company C will next offer mid-size computers to trucking companies. Then, to allay company B's concern about losing some large computer business with trucking companies, C's next move will be to sell personal computers to railroads. Later, C will offer mid-size computers to railroads. Finally, it may launch a full-scale attack on company B's large computer position in trucking companies. Of course, C's hidden planned moves are provisional in that much depends on competitors' segment moves and responses.

Unfortunately, too many companies fail to develop a long-term invasion plan. PepsiCo is an exception. It first attacked Coca-Cola in the grocery market, then in the vending-machine market, then in the fast-food market, and so on. Japanese firms also plot their invasion sequence. They first gain a foothold in a market then enter new segments with products. Toyota began by introducing small cars (Corolla), then expanded into mid-size cars, and finally into luxury cars (Lexus).

A company's invasion plans can be thwarted when it confronts blocked markets. The invader must then find a way to break in, which usually calls for a mega-marketing approach. **Megamarketing** is the strategic coordination of economic, psychological, political and public relations skills, to gain the cooperation of a number of parties in order to enter or operate in a given market.

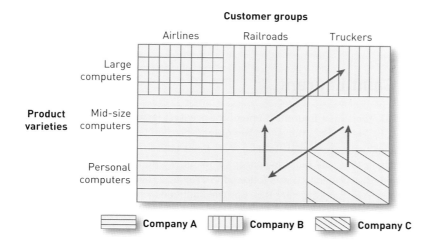

Figure 10.6 Segment-by-segment invasion plan

Ethical choice of market targets

Marketers must target segments carefully to avoid consumer backlash. Some consumers may resist being labelled. Single people may reject single-serve food packaging because they don't want to be reminded they are eating alone. Elderly consumers who don't feel their age may not appreciate products that identify them as 'old'.

Market targeting can also generate public controversy.[38] The public is concerned when marketers take unfair advantage of vulnerable groups (such as children)[39] or disadvantaged groups (such as inner-city poor people), or promote potentially harmful products. The cereal industry has been heavily criticised for marketing efforts directed towards children. Critics worry that high-powered appeals presented through the mouths of lovable animated characters will overwhelm children's defences and lead them to want sugared cereals or poorly balanced breakfasts. Parents, consumer associations and the EU are increasingly concerned about the impact of marketing on children with the Archbishop of Canterbury in the United Kingdom questioning 'a marketing culture that so openly feeds and colludes with obsession.' In the United Kingdom the government has forbidden schools to operate vending machines that offer confectionery and high-salt-content foods. Toy marketers have been similarly criticised. McDonald's and other chains have drawn criticism for pitching high-fat, salt-laden fare to low-income, inner-city residents.

Not all attempts to target children, minorities or other special segments draw criticism. Colgate-Palmolive's Colgate Junior toothpaste has special features such as coloured striped paste designed to get children to brush longer and more often. Other companies are responding to the special needs of minority segments.[40] Thus the issue is not *who* is targeted but rather *how* and *for what*. Socially responsible marketing calls for targeting that serves not only the company's interests but also the interests of those targeted. Many countries also place restrictions on the content and timing of advertising to children. Cadbury's dropped their 'Get Active' promotion that encouraged children to exchange chocolate packaging wrappers for school sports equipment when critics pointed out that 5440 wrappers would be needed to obtain one football goal.[41]

▽ Creating differentiation and positioning strategies

No company can be successful if its products and services resemble every other product and offering. As part of the strategic brand management process, each offering must represent a compelling, distinctive value offering in the mind of the target market.

A crucial pillar of marketing strategy is STP – *segmentation*, *targeting* and *positioning*. A company discovers different needs and groups in the marketplace (*segmentation*). It selects those *targets* it can satisfy in a competitive way, and then *positions* its offering so the *target* market recognises the company's distinctive offering and image. For market offerings to be successful in current buyers' markets they need to be developed and differentiated against competitive offerings if a company wants to achieve a sustained competitive advantage (SCA). The creation of a strong brand reputation to generate a lasting SCA involves an active consideration of one or a combination of cost leadership, differentiation and combined cost and brand acceptance opportunities.

▽ Yves Saint Laurent

Founded in 1961, Yves Saint Laurent is one of the greatest fashion names of the late twentieth century. Throughout the years, the ground-breaking designs of the couture house created innovative pieces of clothing. Yves Saint Laurent was the first couture house to launch, in 1966, the modern concept of luxury women's *prêt-à-porter*, in a collection called 'Rive Gauche'. It was followed in 1969 by a Rive Gauche men's ready-to-wear line. The Yves Saint Laurent Rive Gauche boutiques were soon opened throughout the world, allowing fashion-conscious working individuals to wear the

Yves Saint Laurent designs. This represented the first step in making luxury labels accessible to a wider public.

In 1999, the Gucci Group (the luxury division of the PPR Group, the official trading name of a French luxury goods company organised around six operating branches: Fnac, Redcats Group, Conforam, CFAO, Puma and Gucci Group)[42] acquired Yves Saint Laurent. Since then the brand has been repositioned at the top segment of the luxury goods market. Under the management of Valérie Hermann, appointed CEO in 2005, and Stefano Pilati, creative director since 2004, the brand has renewed the exceptional legacy of its founder while bringing a contemporary approach to its collections, which combine elegance, top-quality fabrics, refined and discreet but recognisable details.

Today Yves Saint Laurent's collections include women's and men's ready-to-wear, shoes, handbags, small leather goods, jewellery, scarves, ties and eyewear. They are designed for both modern women who have a keen sense of freedom and follow their instincts with assurance, captivating others with their elegance, as well as for men who prefer a non-conformist look and assert the different facets of their personality in a modern and sensitive way. The Yves Saint Laurent network currently has 63 directly operated shops, including flagship stores in Paris, New York, London, Milan, Hong Kong and Tokyo. The brand is also present in the most prestigious multibrand boutiques and department stores in the world and is likely to remain so even after the death of the famous designer in 2008, thus providing evidence of its success in developing and communicating an upmarket STP strategy.

Source: http://www.ysl.com

Positioning

Positioning is the act of designing the company's offering and image to occupy a distinctive place in the minds of the target market.[43] The goal is to establish the brand in the minds of consumers in order to maximise the potential benefit to the firm. Good brand positioning helps guide marketing strategy by clarifying the brand's essence, what goals it helps the consumer achieve (how it addresses their 'genes of meaning') and how it does so in a unique way.[44] Everyone in the organisation should understand the customer-perceived value that underlies the brand positioning and use it as context for making decisions.[45]

The result of positioning is the successful creation of a *customer-focused value proposition*, a cogent reason why the target market should buy the product. Table 10.8 shows how four

Table 10.8 Examples of value propositions

Company and market offering	Target customers	Benefits	Price premium (%)	Value proposition
Dornier (G)	Commercial weavers	High technology	20	High-quality, sophisticated weaving machines
Nivea (G)	Personal care-oriented people	Life and care	15	Quality skin and beauty care
Volvo (US/SW)	Safety conscious	Durability and safety	20	Safest car in which a family can travel
Wolford (A)	Women	Fashion and technology	30	High-fashion, high-tech seamless tights

(A) Austria; (G) Germany; (US/SW) USA/Sweden

Source: M. R. V. Goodman, Durham University.

companies – Dornier, Nivea, Volvo and Wolford – have defined their value proposition given their target customers, benefits and prices.

Positioning is a marketing concept that enables buyers and sellers to gain from being both effective and efficient. In Figure 10.6 an effective buying experience is realised as sellers provide the right market offering at an acceptable price. The seller gains as the right market offering is supplied cost efficiently. It requires that similarities and differences between brands be defined and communicated. Specifically, deciding on positioning requires determining a frame of reference by identifying the target market and the competition, and identifying the ideal points-of-parity and points-of-difference brand associations.

Breakthrough marketing

Orange looks for a brighter future

Tom Alexander, Virgin Mobile's co-founder, joined Orange in 2007 shortly after Virgin Mobile was taken over by NTL. His mission – to revive the brand after years of decline as mainstream competitors O2 and T-Mobile have stolen much of its customer appeal in terms of innovation and profile. Orange has 15 million users in the United Kingdom and is hardly in total disarray. Yet its current reputation pales in comparison to the company's image before it was acquired by France Telecom in 2000 for £25 billion. At that stage, Orange was considered a phenomenal UK success story with consumers flocking to sign up for its mobile services, tempted by effective advertising and catchy slogan: 'The Future's Bright, The Future's Orange'. Yet the future wasn't perhaps as bright as France Telecom had hoped. Orange's management has watched as its rivals have caught the public's imagination and its own initiatives failed to deliver expected results. The decline of Orange has often been attributed to a clash of cultures with its parent France Telecom.

While Orange maintains that its focus has been on moving more of its pre-pay users on to more lucrative long-term contracts, the perception has been that the company has struggled to keep pace with its rivals. Many of its major new initiatives have misfired – 3G services proved unpopular; its 'home-zone' converged fixed-mobile service failed to attract much attention and most recently its free broadband offer led to a flurry of customer service complaints. None of these innovations reignited its prospects in the way that T-Mobile's 'Flext' contract triggered a wave of customer additions. Orange has also been criticised for its efforts in marketing as various campaigns have failed to engage consumers, with the exception of its cinema advertisements based around celebrities pitching ideas to a board of product-obsessed businessmen.

The United Kingdom is arguably the most competitive mobile phone market in the world and Orange's malaise has been reflected in its financial results. The UK carrier's operating profit fell an alarming 17 per cent to €1.4 billion, and in the first six months of 2007 operating profit fell a further 7 per cent to €712 million. While Orange is not alone in struggling to cope with intensely competitive market conditions and an increasing regulatory burden in areas such as roaming, the performance has hardly inspired confidence. UBS, the investment bank, argued that radical action was needed after UK margins hit a nadir in 2006. However there are signs that things are starting to change. In August 2007, Olaf Swantee was appointed as head of Orange after Sanjiv Ahuja's decision to leave after four years at the helm. However the fact that Mr Swantee was appointed from outside the company – he joined from Hewlett-Packard where he was a high-level executive in charge of the IT giant's European sales and was a former head of customer services at Compaq – raised eyebrows.

Mr Swantee has immediately focused on Orange UK's problems and how to return it to its former glory. Bernard Ghillebaert, the incumbent head of the UK operation who has been frank about Orange's lack of progress against its peers over recent times, has been moved to a new role in charge of Orange's sales and customer service operations across Europe. The appointment of Mr Alexander suggests France Telecom has warmed to the idea of letting its subsidiaries have more control over their own destinies. According to Mr Swantee, the new team needs to focus first on improving customer service, although statistics suggest improvements are already being made in that area. He said that the company then needs to focus on becoming more efficient, which could include shaking up its tariff plans and product range. The third priority will be to bolster its sales channels to ensure that it is competing on equal footing with its rivals.

The new management team at Orange has already reignited interest in one of the UK's most well-known brands and appears to have the blessing of its French parent to do what is necessary to restore confidence – both internally and externally – in the mobile operator, which could spell bad news for its rivals.[46]

Competitive frame of reference

A starting point in defining a competitive frame of reference for a brand positioning is to determine **category membership** – the market offerings with which a brand competes and that function as close substitutes. Chapter 9 discussed competitive analysis and considered several factors – including the resources, capabilities and likely intentions of various other firms – in choosing those markets where consumers can be profitably served.

Deciding to target a certain type of consumer, in particular, can define the nature of competition, because certain firms have decided to target that segment in the past (or plan to do so in the future), or because consumers in that segment may already look to certain products or brands in their purchase decisions. To determine the proper competitive frame of reference, marketers need to understand consumer behaviour and the consideration factors that influence consumers' brand choices. In the United Kingdom, for example, the Automobile Association positioned itself as the fourth 'emergency service' – along with police, fire and ambulance – to convey greater credibility and urgency.

▽ Lindauer Dornier GmbH's weaving machines

The German company Lindauer Dornier GmbH emphasises its drive in technological progress. New developments cover the complete textile machine product line. The new performance generation of air-jet and rapier weaving machines, a new 540 cm wide air-jet weaving machine for technical fabrics and new machine models for specialist weaving complement decisive innovative advances in finishing machines for circular fabrics. Dornier found that its products were too sophisticated for most eastern European markets. Following an earlier initiative in Latin America, it started a second-hand machinery market for those customers, adapting used machines that the company had taken back from customers who had bought new more technologically advanced machines.

Source: www.lindauer-dornier.com

Points-of-parity and points-of-difference

Once marketers have fixed the competitive frame of reference for positioning by defining the customer target market and the nature of the competition, they can define the appropriate points-of-difference and points-of-parity associations.[47]

Points-of-difference **Points-of-difference (PODs)** are attributes or benefits consumers strongly associate with a brand, positively evaluate, and believe they could not find to the same extent with a competitive brand. Associations that make up points-of-difference may be based on virtually any type of attribute or benefit. Examples are IKEA (*affordable design*), Michelin (*performance*) and Bosch (*quality*). Creating associations that are strong, able and unique is a real challenge, but essential in terms of competitive brand positioning.

Points-of-parity **Points-of-parity (POPs)**, on the other hand, are associations that are not necessarily unique to the brand but may in fact be shared with other brands.[48] These types of associations come in two basic forms: category and competitive.

Category points-of-parity are associations consumers view as essential to a legitimate and credible offering within a certain product or service category. In other words, they represent necessary – but not sufficient – conditions for brand choice. Consumers might not consider a travel agency truly a travel agency unless it is able to make air and hotel reservations, provide advice about leisure packages and offer various ticket payment and delivery options. Category points-of-parity may change over time due to technological advances, legal developments or consumer trends, but they are the essential factors for marketers.

Competitive points-of-parity are associations designed to negate *competitors'* points-of-difference. If, in the eyes of consumers, a brand can 'break even' in those areas where the competitors are trying to find an advantage *and* achieve advantages in other areas, the brand should be in a strong – and perhaps unbeatable – competitive position. Consider the introduction of Nespresso.

▽ Nespresso

The actress Sharon Stone attended the grand opening in Paris of the Swiss multinational's lavish new coffee shop on the Champs-Elysées on 13 December 2007. Sales of Nespresso coffee machines and capsules have been growing during the past six years by an average of 30 per cent a year. In 2007, they increased by 42 per cent to SFr 1.16 billion and are expected to hit the SFr 2 billion mark by 2009. The Swiss food group is planning a massive expansion of Nespresso boutiques around the world. The idea is to turn Nespresso into a luxury brand that can sit alongside a Louis Vuitton or Harry Winston store. Nestlé's star brand risks facing the same dilemma as a pharmaceutical group's blockbuster drug. The Swiss company will lose the patent on its precious Nespresso coffee capsules in 2012. By then, it hopes to have developed such a cult for its coffee and boutiques that the patent expiry will make little difference to its continued success as a luxury brand. As Nespresso's lead promoter, George Clooney, would say, 'What else?'[49]

Points-of-parity versus points-of-difference For an offering to achieve a point-of-parity on a particular attribute or benefit, a sufficient number of consumers must believe the brand is 'good enough' on that dimension. There is a zone or range of tolerance or acceptance with points-of-parity. The brand does not literally have to be seen as equal to competitors, but consumers must feel that the brand does well enough on that particular attribute or benefit. If they do, they may be willing to base their evaluations and decisions on other factors potentially more amenable to the brand; for example, a light beer presumably would never taste as good as a full-strength beer, but it would have to taste close enough to be able to compete effectively.

With points-of-difference, however, the brand must demonstrate clear superiority. Consumers must be convinced that Louis Vuitton has the most stylish handbags, Duracell is the longest-lasting battery, and Crédit Lyonnais offers the best financial advice and planning. Often the key to positioning is not so much achieving a point-of-difference as achieving points-of-parity!

▽ Europcar – from car rental company to mobility provider

The company, an integral part of Volkswagen's mobility concept, claims to be the 'world's leading leisure car rental company' and to be highly committed to its customers: 'We promise to deliver the best car rental experience through excellent customer service and high quality vehicles.' Europcar has developed into a global provider of mobility services. This has resulted from the development of partnerships with airlines, railway operators, hotel groups, automobile clubs and roadside assistance services. Europcar thus integrates the business of renting cars within a consistent, global mobility concept.

Europcar offers its customers a wide variety of service solutions to the reservation process. The Internet has become an increasingly important tool for booking, alongside the telephone or travel agencies' Global Distribution Systems. As a matter of principle, Europcar does not promote any particular reservation channel, but offers customers the choice of all possible reservation methods to meet their individual needs. In an increasingly complex world, the freedom of each person to set individual priorities – whether in business-to-business or private consumer markets – is becoming more and more important. Europcar's strategy is to provide tailored mobility solutions to offer leading market-perceived value solutions.

Source: www.europcar.com

Establishing category membership

Target customers are aware that Chanel is a leading brand of cosmetics, Nestlé is a leading brand of cereal, Accenture is a leading consulting firm, and so on. Often, however, marketers must inform consumers of a brand's category membership. Perhaps the most obvious situation is the introduction of new products, especially when category identification itself is not apparent.

There are also situations where consumers know a brand's category membership, but may not be convinced that the brand is a valid member of the category; for example, consumers may be aware that Swatch produces watches, but they may not be certain whether they are in the same class as Casio, Seiko and Tissot. In this instance, Swatch might find it useful to reinforce category membership. With this approach, however, it is important not to be trapped between categories. Consumers should understand what the brand stands for, and not what it does not. The typical approach to positioning is to inform consumers of a brand's membership before stating its point-of-difference. Presumably consumers need to know what a market offering is and what function it serves before deciding whether it dominates the brands against which it competes. For new offerings, initial advertising often concentrates on creating brand awareness, and subsequent advertising attempts to craft the brand image.

Straddle positioning

Occasionally, a company will try to straddle two frames of reference.

 BMW

When BMW first made a strong competitive push into the UK market in the early 1980s, it positioned the brand as the only car that offered both luxury *and* performance. At that time, consumers saw luxury cars as lacking performance, and performance cars as lacking luxury. By relying on the design of its cars, its German heritage and other aspects of a well-conceived marketing programme, BMW was able to simultaneously achieve: (1) a point-of-difference on luxury and a point-of-parity on performance with respect to performance cars; and (2) a point-of-difference on performance and a point-of-parity on luxury with respect to luxury cars. The clever slogan 'The Ultimate Driving Machine' effectively captured the newly created umbrella category – luxury performance cars.

While a straddle positioning is often attractive as a means of reconciling potentially conflicting consumer goals and creating a 'best-of-both-worlds' solution, it also carries an extra burden. If the points-of-parity and points-of-difference with respect to both categories are not credible, the brand may not be viewed as a legitimate player in either category or ends up in 'no man's land'. Many early personal digital assistants that unsuccessfully tried to straddle categories ranging from pagers to laptop computers provide a vivid illustration of this risk.

Communicating category membership

There are three main ways to convey a brand's category membership:

1 **Announcing category benefits:** To reassure consumers that a brand will deliver on the fundamental reason for purchasing a category, marketers frequently use benefits to announce category membership. Thus industrial tools might claim to have durability and antacids might announce their efficacy. A cake mix might attain membership in the baked desserts category by claiming the benefit of great taste, and support this claim by including high-quality ingredients (performance) or by showing users delighting in its consumption (imagery).

2 **Comparing to exemplars:** Well-known, noteworthy brands in a category can also help a brand specify its category membership. When Stella McCartney was an unknown, advertising announced her membership as an up-and-coming UK designer by associating her with famous couturiers – recognised members of that category.

3 **Relying on the product descriptor:** The product descriptor that follows the brand name is often a concise means of conveying category origin. Ford Motor Co. invested more than US $1 billion on a radical new 2004 model called the X-Trainer, to build in its Land Rover plant in the United Kingdom, which combines the attributes of an SUV, a minivan and an estate car. To communicate its unique position – and to avoid association with its Explorer and Country Squire models – the vehicle (later called Freestyle) has been designated a 'sports wagon'.[50]

Choosing POPs and PODs

Points-of-parity are driven by the needs of category membership (to create category POPs) and the necessity of negating competitors' PODs (to create competitive POPs). Two important considerations in choosing points-of-difference are that consumers find the POD desirable and that the firm has the capabilities to deliver on it. As Table 10.9 shows, three criteria can judge both desirability and deliverability.

Table 10.9 Judging desirability and deliverability for points-of-difference

Desirability criteria	Deliverability criteria
Relevance Target consumers must find the POD personally relevant and important. • National Express, a UK train company serving the London to East Coast route advertised that all its trains had Wi-fi connections in each carriage. While of interest to some business travellers this was of little interest to most passengers.	*Feasibility* The product design and marketing offering must support the desired association. Does communicating the desired association require real changes to the offering itself, or just perceptual shifts in the way the consumer thinks of the offering or brand? The latter is typically easier. • Volkswagen in Germany has had to work hard to overcome public perceptions that Audi is not a youthful, contemporary brand.
Distinctiveness Target consumers must find the POD distinctive and superior. • Dyson gained a strong early niche market position by differentiating itself on the basis of its unique design and function.	*Communicability* Consumers must be given a compelling reason and understandable rationale as to why the brand can deliver the desired benefit. What factual, verifiable evidence or 'proof points' can ensure consumers will actually believe in the brand and its desired associations? • Substantiators often come in the form of patented, branded ingredients, such as Nivea Wrinkle Control Crème with Q10 co-enzyme or computers that have an Intel processor inside.
Believability Target consumers must find the POD believable and credible. A brand must offer a compelling reason for choosing it over the other options. • Red Bull may argue that it is more energising than other soft drinks and support this claim by noting that it has a higher level of safe stimulants. • Chanel No. 5 perfume may claim to be the quintessential elegant French perfume and support this claim by noting the long association between Chanel and haute couture.	*Sustainability* The firm must be sufficiently committed and willing to devote enough resources to create an enduring positioning. Is the positioning pre-emptive, defensible and difficult to attack? Can a brand association be reinforced and strengthened over time? • It is generally easier for market leaders such as Renault, Visa and Lindt, whose positioning is based in part on demonstrable product or service performance, to sustain their positioning than for market leaders such as H&M and Zara, whose positioning is based on fashion and is thus subject to the whims of a more fickle market.

Marketing memo

Writing a positioning statement

To communicate a company or brand positioning, marketing plans often include a *positioning statement*. The statement should follow the form: To *(target group and need)*, our *(Brand)* is *(the concept)* that *(what the point-of-difference is or does)*. For example: 'To *busy professionals who need to stay organised, Palm Pilot is an electronic organiser that allows you to back up files on your PC more easily and reliably than competitive products.'* Sometimes the positioning statement is more detailed:

> *Red Bull*: To young, active soft drink consumers who have little time for sleep, Red Bull is the soft drink that gives you more energy and allows you to push the margins further.

Red Bull

Note that the positioning first states the product's membership in a category (Red Bull is a soft drink) and then shows its point-of-difference from other members of the group (it has more caffeine). The product's membership in the category suggests the points-of-parity that it might have with other products in the category, but the case for the product rests on its points-of-difference. Sometimes the marketer will put the product in a surprisingly different category before indicating the points of difference.

Sources: Red Bull www.redbull.co.uk; www.cmwinteractive.com/ freewheel/RedBull-Consumer/Brochure.pdf; P. Bee (2001) So how safe are these energy drinks?, *Daily Mail*, 17 July; J. Cassey (2001) Enragingly ubiquitous, *Guardian*, 26 June.

Marketers must decide at which level(s) to anchor the brand's points-of-difference. At the lowest level are the *brand attributes,* at the next level are the *brand's benefits,* and at the top are the *brand's values.* Thus marketers of Dove soap can talk about its attribute of one-quarter cleansing cream, or its benefit of softer skin, or its value of being more attractive. Attributes are typically the least desirable level to position. First, the buyer is more interested in benefits. Second, competitors can easily copy attributes. Third, current attributes may become less desirable over time.

Brands can sometimes be successfully differentiated on seemingly irrelevant attributes, *if* consumers infer the proper benefit. Kenco differentiates its instant coffee by claiming that it harvests the best mountain-grown beans and then freeze dries them with a unique process to lock in the freshness. Saying that a brand of coffee is 'mountain grown' is irrelevant because most coffee is mountain grown. 'Marketing memo: Writing a positioning statement' outlines how marketers can express positioning formally.

Creating POPs and PODs

One common difficulty in creating a strong, competitive brand positioning is that many of the attributes or benefits that make up the points-of-parity and points-of-difference are negatively correlated. For example, it might be difficult to position a brand as 'inexpensive' and at the same time assert that it is 'of the highest quality'. Lidl and Matalan need to convince consumers that their merchandise is both cheap and of good quality. Table 10.10 displays some other examples of negatively correlated attributes and benefits. Moreover, individual attributes and benefits often have positive *and* negative aspects. For example, consider a long-lived brand such as Nestlé's KitKat chocolate biscuit finger bar. The brand's heritage could suggest experience, wisdom and expertise. On the other hand, it could also imply being old-fashioned and not up to date.[51]

Table 10.10 Examples of negatively correlated attributes and benefits

Low price vs high quality	Powerful vs safe
Taste vs low calories	Strong vs refined
Nutritious vs good tasting	Ubiquitous vs exclusive
Efficacious vs mild	Varied vs simple

▽ **Burberry Ltd**

In recent years the trademark Burberry plaid has become one of the world's most recognisable symbols. From its staid place on Burberry raincoats, the plaid began showing up on dog collars, taffeta dresses, bikinis, on gear worn by British soccer hooligans and, unfortunately, on an increasing number of counterfeit goods. This integral part of Burberry's heritage, called 'the check' by those in the fashion industry, had suddenly become a liability due to overexposure. Consequently Burberry's sales are sluggish and its CEO, Angela Ahrendt, is attempting to jump-start sales growth in numerous ways. For one, she has studied Burberry's 150-year history to create new brand symbols, such as an equestrian-knight logo that was trademarked by the company in 1901. Handbags will allude to the brand's tradition as a trench coat maker by featuring leather belt buckles or the quilt pattern that lined Burberry's outerwear. The other tactic Ms Ahrendt is pushing is to invest aggressively in selling Burberry accessories – handbags, shoes, scarves and belts – rather than apparel, which now accounts for 75 per cent of the company's sales. Not only do these accessories have higher profit margins, but they are also less exposed than clothing to changes in fashion.[52]

Unfortunately, consumers typically want to maximise *both* the negatively correlated attributes or benefits. Much of the art and science of marketing is dealing with trade-offs, and positioning is no different. The best approach clearly is to develop a product or service that performs well on both dimensions. BMW was able to establish its 'luxury and performance' straddle positioning due in large part to product design, and the fact that the car was in fact seen as both luxurious and high performance. Gore-Tex was able to overcome the seemingly conflicting product image of 'breathable' and 'waterproof' through technological advances.

Some marketers have adopted other approaches to address attribute or benefit trade-offs: launching two different marketing campaigns, each one devoted to a different brand attribute or benefit; linking themselves to any kind of entity (person, place or thing) that possesses the right kind of equity as a means to establish an attribute or benefit as a POP or POD; and even attempting to convince consumers that the negative relationship between attributes and benefits, if they consider it differently, is in fact positive.

A straddle brand positioning can help convince customers that the market offering can accomplish two or more seemingly conflicting benefits, such as Gore-Tex's promise to deliver both breathability and water protection.
Source: David Young-Wolff/ PhotoEdit

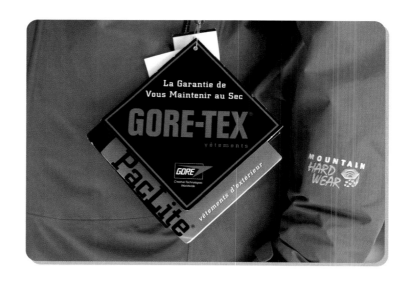

▽ Perceptual or positioning mapping

Perceptual or positioning mapping is a marketing tool that enables marketers to plot the position of their offering (product or service – but in buyers' markets it is best to see these as customer-perceived *value* offers (see Chapter 11)) against those of the competition.

What can positioning analysis do for a company's business?

To position market offerings/products/services in increasingly crowded markets, companies must understand the dimensions along which target customers perceive products in a category and how they view the firm's offer relative to competitive offers. To understand the competitive structure of their markets, firms need to ask these questions:

- How do customers (current or potential) view their brand?
- Which competitive brands do customers perceive to be their closest competitors?
- What market offering and company attributes are most responsible for these perceived differences?

Once marketers have answers to these questions they can assess how well or poorly their products are positioned in the market. They can then identify the critical elements of a positioning plan to differentiate their offerings from competitive products: are the brands in the market strongly or weakly differentiated? Which brand has the central position? What should be done to enable the company's target customer segments to perceive their brand offering as being significantly and positively different? Based on customer perceptions, which target segments are most attractive? How should the firm position new products (see Chapter 13) with respect to the company's existing products? What brand name (the company's or a competitor's) is most closely associated with attributes that the target segment perceives to be desirable?

Positioning maps

When a perceptual or positioning map is plotted two dimensions are commonly used. Figure 10.7 presents a very basic perceptual map of the UK chocolate block sector market.

The Belgian and Swiss and the UK's Green & Black brands are revealed as high quality and high price. Cadbury's Dairy Milk, Galaxy and Yorkie are low-quality and relatively high-price

Figure 10.7 Example positioning map of the UK chocolate block sector market

Source: M. R. V. Goodman, Durham University.

brands. Superior quality chocolate blocks are available from leading supermarket own brands and Fair Trade marked brands. It is clear that the leading mass brands in the United Kingdom need to launch chocolate bars with an improved quality specification as they are becoming increasingly likely to lose market share to the supermarket own brands and branded Fair Trade offerings.

Developing a positioning strategy

A company's positioning strategy depends on the existing strength or weakness of their brand and their competitive intent. If the market is under supplied – a sellers' market – then the volume competitors may be content to pursue the same positioning strategy. In buyers' markets it makes more sense to seek to positively differentiate their brands in the fastest-growing market segments. Ultimately positioning is about how they want consumers to perceive their market offerings and what strategies they select to achieve this goal.

▽ Repositioning

Today's markets are highly competitive and volatile so companies need to be prepared to make both proactive and reactive positioning decisions as market conditions dictate. Repositioning can become necessary for the following reasons:

- A competitor launches a market offering that is as good as or better than the existing company's brand, for example supermarkets now sell new chocolate bar products with superior specifications. Honda and Toyota have a well-earned reputation for continually updating their vehicles by such market-perceived value attributes as design, decor, performance and technological innovation.
- There is a marked consumer change in preference, for example for quality beers or for better quality overseas package holidays.
- New market categories appear, for example the market for energy drinks caused Lucozade marketers to reposition the brand from a drink for people recovering from illness to a high-energy sports drink for young people.
- An initial launch error, for example EuroDisney miscalculated the number of frugal visitors to the park and made several cultural errors such as not originally serving alcohol in the park nor providing appropriate menus in the restaurants.
- There is a need to change the perception of the firm in the eyes of existing and potential customers. Tesco is continuously using integrated marketing communications to emphasise that it is not a low-price retailer. Interestingly enough, they were advised to drop the brand name of Tesco, as it had become too closely associated with low quality and low price and replace it with another to boost their strategy of taking the stores upmarket. The senior executive refused and achieved a noteworthy success as Tesco enjoys a better 'quality' image.

▽ Skoda comes of age

Skoda was founded in what is now the Czech Republic in 1895 and started to produce cars in 1905 and trucks in 1924. It was bought by the Volkswagen Group in 1991 after the collapse of the Soviet Union. After being perceived as an unattractive, downmarket marque Skoda has been steadily repositioning itself in the car market as more of a value brand. Many now regard its vehicles as offering superior market-perceived value than those of its parent company. It is one of the Czech Republic's biggest employers, having more than 27,000 workers in its three factories. Skoda's own production, which includes some output from a factory in China, is set to exceed 640,000 vehicles this year. In 1994 the Czech company, which is more than 100 years old, produced only 173,000 vehicles. The car maker believes it can make one million cars in the foreseeable future. Skoda had revenues of €6.64 billion (£4.73 billion) and a workforce of nearly 27,000 in 2006.[53]

A major repositioning exercise can be an expensive and risky operation and success cannot be guaranteed. If a company feels the need to change the perceptions of its existing target market it has to find a way to change entrenched attitudes and views and this normally requires an immense investment in an integrated marketing communications initiative. It is easier to reposition by seeking to appeal to a different market category, as Lucozade did successfully until Red Bull intensified the competition in the energy drinks category. Overall repositioning is a complex marketing operation but may be the only way to rescue a brand that has faded badly. It may be better in the long run to abandon it and replace it with another in tune with the new positioning strategy. This seems to have been the conclusion of Accenture as it appears to be getting ready to commit to the history books long-standing brands it has acquired that have grown tired, such as Norwich Union.

▽ Developing and communicating a differentiation strategy

Cost leadership

Firms can gain a positive advantage in markets by developing and sustaining cost/efficiency gains. This cost-based approach can prove to be a winning strategy provided that a company offers an acceptable substitute to competitive offers from a reduced cost base. This gives a company the opportunity to benefit from offering a lower price; to offer the same price as their competitors or to improve market-perceived quality by offering additional market-perceived quality attributes for the ruling competitive price. The achievement of cost gains from operating scale economies, experience curve advantages, tight overhead controls and expenditure on R & D, production and marketing costs is a compound strategy practised skilfully by mass producing firms such as Philips, Siemens and Swatch.

▽ Swatch

Swatch overcomes crisis and leads to the survival of the Swiss watch industry

In the mid-1970s the Swiss watch industry was in the midst of its worst crisis ever. Technologically speaking, the Japanese competition had been outclassed in 1979 with the launch of the 'Delirium', the world's thinnest wristwatch with a limited number of components. But the event that marked the upturn in the industry's fortunes was the founding of SMH, the Swiss Corporation for Microelectronics and Watch Making Industries. And its answer to the crisis was Swatch – a slim plastic watch with only 51 components (instead of the usual 91 parts or more) that combined top quality with a highly affordable price. It first went on sale in 1983. Since then it has gone on to become the most successful wristwatch of all time, and The Swatch Group, the parent company, is the largest and most dynamic watch company in the world.

For many years, new developments have been taking place alongside the standard Swatch watch in plastic - from Irony (the metal Swatch) to the Swatch SKIN Chrono (the world's thinnest chronograph) to Swatch Snowpass (a watch with a built-in access control function that can be used as a ski pass at many ski resorts throughout the world), and Swatch Beat (featuring the revolutionary Internet Time). Outstanding technical capabilities and advances in the fields of science and technology were already proven by Swatch during its role as the official timekeeper in several Olympic Games and Ski and Snowboard World Cup competitions.

Source: http://www.swatch.com

An example of a smaller company successfully focusing on a special market to gain economies of scale is provided by Portugal's Corticeira Amorim, which controls around one-third of the country's cork manufacturing (see www.amorim.pt/mapa_site.php and www.amorimcork.com/.

To achieve maximum benefit from this strategy firms need to generate high market shares to enable them to maximise the benefits of low raw material, labour and overhead costs. The ability to realise high sales volumes at relative high market prices is of crucial importance. If market prices are squeezed downwards by fierce competition then this strategy can backfire and leave firms with large stocks of unsold market offerings. Ford and General Motors provide examples of two firms that attracted plaudits over the years for cost efficiency which have now become almost bankrupt as they have failed to generate and hold a sufficiently high market share in their target markets.

Distinctive superior quality

Companies can also seek a competitive advantage from successfully creating a strong market-perceived value for their market offerings. Such companies are providing the market with the right quality attributes (performance, reliability, design, novelty etc.) with the right transactional attributes (price, payment options). Thus a positive registration is made with prospective buyers as the companies meet and more than meet their purchase expectations and so bring about an enjoyable purchasing experience. This allows companies to command higher prices and therefore higher margins than they could achieve wholly by cost reduction activities.[54] Bang & Olufsen and Montblanc are differentiated on the basis of superior design; Duracell on superior durability and Miele on superior reliability.

▽ Montblanc Pen

The German company Montblanc has been known for generations as a maker of sophisticated, high-quality writing instruments. In the past few years the product range has been expanded to include exquisite writing accessories, luxury leather goods and belts, jewellery, eyewear and watches. Montblanc has thus become a purveyor of exclusive products that reflect the exacting demands made today for quality design, tradition and master craftsmanship. Montblanc is a truly international brand with operations in more than 70 countries. Montblanc sells its products exclusively through its international network of authorised retailers, jewellers and over 360 Montblanc boutiques worldwide.

Source: www.montblanc.com

Cost leadership and differentiation

The third option is to combine both cost reduction and quality advantages. Fulmer and Goodwin have shown that these strategies are not mutually exclusive, as have Buzzell and Gale.[55] Positive differentiation can be achieved by firms that are determined to offer high levels of market-perceived value (market-perceived quality relative to market-perceived price).

▽ Differentiation strategies

To avoid the commodity trap, marketers must start with the belief that you can differentiate anything. (See 'Marketing memo: How to derive fresh consumer insights to differentiate products and services.')

Marketing memo

How to derive fresh consumer insights to differentiate products and services

In 'Discovering new points of differentiation', MacMillan and McGrath argue that if companies examine customers' entire experience with a product or service – the consumption chain – they can uncover opportunities to position their offerings in ways that neither they nor their competitors thought possible. MacMillan and McGrath list a set of questions marketers can use to help them identify new, consumer-based points of differentiation:

- How do people become aware of their need for your product and service?
- How do consumers find your offering?
- How do consumers make their final selection?
- How do consumers order and purchase your product or service?

- What happens when your product or service is delivered?
- How is your product installed?
- How is your product or service paid for?
- How is your product stored?
- How is your product moved around?
- What is the consumer really using your product for?
- What do consumers need help with when they use your product?
- What about returns or exchanges?
- How is your product repaired or serviced?
- What happens when your product is disposed of or no longer used?

Source: I. C. MacMillan and R. G. McGrath (1997) Discovering new points of differentiation, *Harvard Business Review*, July–August, 133–45.

Competitive advantage is a company's ability to perform in one or more ways that competitors cannot or will not match. Porter urged companies to build a sustainable competitive advantage.[56] But few competitive advantages are sustainable. At best, they may be leverageable. A *leverageable advantage* is one that a company can use as a springboard to new advantages, much as Microsoft has leveraged its operating system to Microsoft Office and then to networking applications. In general, a company that hopes to endure must be in the business of continuously inventing new advantages. According to Seymour Tilley of the American Boston Consultancy Group, in considering differentiation it is important to include all of the conditions of the sale, as well as the tangible product itself. Service, reliability of vendor and delivery times are likely to be as important as inherent product characteristics. There are often highly differentiated suppliers in markets for commodity products.

Customers must see any competitive advantage as a *customer advantage*. For example, if a company delivers faster than its competitors, it won't be a customer advantage if customers don't value speed. The Stressless (www.stressless.com) company emphasises that its range of recliner chairs marketed in Europe allows consumers to find just the right comfort position for their body shape. Companies must also focus on building customer advantages.[57] Then they will deliver high customer value and satisfaction, which leads to high repeat purchases and ultimately to high company profitability. For example, German brewers make much of the purity of their beers that has resulted from the quality dictated by the historical German beer laws.

Marketers can differentiate brands on the basis of many variables. The obvious means of differentiation, and often the most compelling ones to consumers, relate to aspects of the product and service (reviewed in Chapters 12 and 13). Swatch offers colourful, fashionable watches. Subway differentiates itself in terms of healthy sandwiches as an alternative to fast food. In competitive markets, however, firms may need to go further. Consider these other dimensions, among the many that a company can use to differentiate its market offerings:

- **Personnel differentiation:** Companies can have better-trained employees. Singapore Airlines is well regarded in large part because of its flight attendants. The sales forces of such companies as Abbey National, BMW, British Gas, Cisco,[58] de Beers and Prudential enjoy an excellent reputation.

Figure 10.8 Two satisfied and happy people – perfect positioning

Seller

Supplies the
right offering

Buyer

Finds the
right offering

- **Channel differentiation:** Companies can more effectively and efficiently design their distribution channels' coverage, expertise and performance. The leading European supermarkets such as Carrefour and Tesco have developed highly effective and highly efficient distribution strategies.
- **Image differentiation:** Designer jewellery (Cartier). Even a seller's physical space such as international airports' shopping malls and departure lounge shops can be powerful image generators.

▽ The purpose of positioning

Professional positioning is of benefit to a supplier as it enables a company to invest its resources and skills in the right marketplace. As such it is both an *effective* and *efficient* strategy. The right market offering is being placed on the market and professional know-how is applied to achieving this cost effectively. As Figure 10.8 shows this is also an activity that results in advantages for customers as market offerings are *effective* in satisfying their requirements in dynamic market conditions when they have a choice of suppliers. Additionally they enjoy an *efficient* buying experience in the marketplace as they select the branded purchase that they perceive as representing the best value.

▽ SUMMARY

1 Target marketing includes three activities: market segmentation, market targeting and market positioning.

2 Markets can be targeted at four levels: segments, niches, local areas and individuals. Market segments are large, identifiable groups within a market. A niche is a more narrowly defined group. Globalisation and the Internet have made niche marketing more feasible to many. Marketers appeal to local markets through grassroots marketing for trading areas, neighbourhoods, and even individual stores.

3 More companies now practise individual and mass customisation. The future is likely to see more self-marketing, a form of marketing in which individual consumers take the initiative in designing products and brands.

4 There are two bases for segmenting consumer markets: consumer characteristics and consumer responses. The major segmentation variables for consumer markets are geographic, demographic, psychographic and behavioural. Marketers use them singly or in combination.

5 Business marketers use all these variables along with operating variables, purchasing approaches and situational factors.

6 To be useful, market segments must be measurable, substantial, accessible, differentiable and actionable.

7 A firm has to evaluate the various segments and decide how many and which ones to target: a single segment, several segments, a specific product, a specific market or the full market. If it serves the full market, it must choose between differentiated and undifferentiated marketing. Firms must also monitor segment relationships, and seek economies of scope and the potential for marketing to super segments.

8 Marketers must develop segment-by-segment invasion plans and choose target markets in a socially responsible manner at all times.

9 Deciding on positioning requires the determination of a frame of reference – by identifying the target market and the nature of the competition – and the ideal points-of-parity and points-of-difference brand associations. To determine the proper competitive frame of reference, one must understand consumer behaviour and the considerations consumers use in making brand choices.

10 Points-of-difference are those associations unique to the brand that are also strongly held and favourably evaluated by consumers. Points-of-parity are those associations not necessarily unique to the brand but perhaps shared with other brands. Category point-of-parity associations are associations consumers view as being necessary to a legitimate and credible product offering within a certain category. Competitive point-of-parity associations are those associations designed to negate competitors' points-of-difference.

11 The key to competitive advantage is relevant brand differentiation – consumers must find something unique and meaningful about a market offering. These differences may be based directly on the product or service itself or on other considerations related to factors such as personnel, channels or image.

12 As business conditions change and competitive activity varies, companies may need to reposition some or all of their brands in today's business world.

▽ APPLICATIONS

Marketing debate

Is mass marketing dead? With marketers increasingly adopting more and more refined market segmentation schemes – fuelled by the Internet and other customisation efforts – some critics claim that mass marketing is dead. Others counter that there will always be room for large brands which employ marketing programmes targeting the mass market.

Take a position: Mass marketing is dead *versus* Mass marketing is still a viable way to build a profitable brand.

Marketing discussion

Descriptive versus behavioural market segmentation schemes Think of various product categories. How would you classify yourself in terms of the various segmentation schemes? How would marketing be more or less effective for you depending on the segment involved? How would you contrast demographic versus behavioural segment schemes? Which ones do you think would be most effective for marketers trying to sell to you?

▽ REFERENCES

[1] D. Walker (2004) Live fast, die old, *BBC News Online Magazine*, 16 September (http://news.bbc.co.uk/1/hi/magazine/3659996.stm).

[2] D. Cowley (2004) Boomers turned off by attempts to make them belong to a group, *Financial Times*, 26 January.

[3] J. C. Anderson and J. A. Narus (1995) Capturing the value of supplementary service, *Harvard Business Review*, January–February, 75–83.

[4] T. Dalgic and M. Leeuw (1994) Niche marketing revisited: concept, applications, and some European cases, *European Journal of Marketing*, 28(4), 39–55.

[5] R. D. Hof (2006) There's not enough 'me' in MySpace, *Business Week*, 4 December, 4012, p. 40; A. Klaassen (2006) Niche-targeted social networks find audiences, *Advertising Age*, 6 November, 77(45), p. 15.

[6] R. Blattberg and J. Deighton (1991) Interactive marketing: exploiting the age of addressability, *Sloan Management Review*, 33(1), 5–14.

[7] D. Peppers and M. Rogers (2001) *One to One B2B: Customer Development Strategies for the Business-to-Business World*, New York: Doubleday; M. Rechtin (2005) Aston Martin woos customers one by one, *Automotive News*, 28 March.

[8] J. Wind and A. Rangaswamy (1999) Customerization: the second revolution in mass customization, Wharton School Working Paper, June.

[9] Anderson and Narus (1995) op. cit.

[10] See www.sanfordb2b.co.uk/Customisation.aspx.

[11] B. Cosgrave (2007) Sneakers for all occasions, *Financial Times*, 9 November.

[12] P. Marsh (2002) Mass customisation: make every one different, *Financial Times*, 21 May; see also J. B. Pine (1993) General review – Making mass customisation happen: strategy for new competitive realities, *Strategy and Leadership*, 21(5), 23–4.

[13]R. Winger and D. Edelman (1989) *Segment-of-One Marketing*, Boston, MA: Boston Consulting Group (available at: www.bcg.com/publications).

[14]P. Doyle and P. Stern (2006) *Marketing Management and Strategy*, 4th edn, Harlow, England: Prentice Hall, p. 418; I. Simonson (2005) Determinants of customer responses to customised offer: conceptual framework and research proposition, *Journal of Marketing*, 69 (January), 32–45.

[15]P. Sleight (2004) *Targeting Customers: How to Use Geodemographics: Lifestyle Data in Your Business*, 3rd edn, Henley-on-Thames, England: WARC (World Advertising Research Centre).

[16]M. J. Weiss (2000) *The Clustered World*, Boston: Little, Brown & Co.; A. Weinstein (2004) *Handbook of Market Segmentation: Strategic Targeting for Business and Technology Firms*, 3rd edn, Binghamton, NY: Haworth Press.

[17]For some consumer behaviour perspectives on gender, see J. Meyers-Levy and D. Maheswaran (1991) Exploring males' and females' processing strategies: when and why do differences occur in consumers' processing of ad claims, *Journal of Consumer Research*, 18 (June), 63–70; J. Meyers-Levy and B. Sternthal (1991) Gender differences in the use of message cues and judgments, *Journal of Marketing Research*, 28 (February), 84–96; R. J. Fisher and L. Dube 92005) Gender differences in responses to emotional advertising: a social desirability perspective, *Journal of Consumer Research*, 31 (March), 850–8; J. Cunningham and P. Roberts (2006) What woman want, *Brand Strategy*, December–January, pp. 40–1.

[18]Dove: 'celebrating curves', WARC Case Study, 2005, Henley-on-Thames, England: WARC (World Advertising Research Centre).

[19]T. Lowry (2003) Young man, your couch is calling, *BusinessWeek*, 28 July, pp. 68–9.

[20]D. Klingensmith (2006) Marketing gurus try to read women's minds, *Chicago Tribune*, 19 April.

[21]M. Barletta (2006) Who's really buying that car? Ask her, *Brandweek*, 4 September, p. 20; R. Craven, K. Maurey and J. Davis (2006) What women really want, *Critical Eye*, 15, pp. 50–3.

[22]C. Van Hoffman (2006) For some marketers, low income is hot, *Brandweek*, 11 September, p. 6.

[23]G. L. White and S. Leung (2002) Middle market shrinks as americans migrate toward the higher end, *Wall Street Journal*, 29 March, pp. A1, A8.

[24]L. Tischler (2003) The price is right, *Fast Company*, November, pp. 83–91.

[25]A. Frean (2007) Not just shopping: insights into the new consumer, *ESRC Society Today*, 21 September (www.esrc.ac.uk./ESRCInfoCentre/).

[26]K. Kress, N. Ozawa and G. Schmid (2000) The new consumer emerges, *Strategy and Leadership*, 28(5), 4–11.

[27]C. Noxon (2006) Toyification nation, *Brandweek*, 9 October; R. O'Connor (2006) Adulthood; are we there yet? – if you're still watching cartoons or playing kickball, then you, kiddo, just might be a 'rejuvenile', *Chicago Tribune*, 6 August, p. 1.

[28]See www.sric-bi.com.

[29]M. Schoenwald (2001) Psychographic segmentation: used or abused?, *Brandweek*, 22 January, pp. 34–8.

[30]P. Danziger (2004) Getting more for V-Day, *Brandweek*, 9 February, p. 19.

[31]This classification was adapted from G. H. Brown (1953) Brand loyalty: fact or fiction?, *Advertising Age*, June 1952–January 1953,

a series; see also P. E. Rossi, R. McCulloch and G. Allenby (1996) The value of purchase history data in target marketing, *Marketing Science*, 15(4), 321–40.

[32]C. Walker (1995) How strong is your brand, *Marketing Tools*, January/February, pp. 46–53.

[33]See www.conversionmodel.com.

[34]D. Yankelovich and D. Meer (2006) Rediscovering market segmentation, *Harvard Business Review*, February.

[35]For a review of many of the methodological issues in developing segmentation schemes, see W. R. Dillon and S. Mukherjee (2006) A guide to the design and execution of segmentation studies, in R. Grover and M. Vriens (eds.) *Handbook of Marketing Research*, Thousand Oaks, CA: Sage Publications; and M. Wedel and W. A. Kamakura (1997) *Market Segmentation: Conceptual and Methodological Foundations*, Boston, MA: Kluwer.

[36]W. R. Smith (1956) Product differentiation and market segmentation as alternative marketing strategies, *Journal of Marketing*, 4 July.

[37]See www.esteelauder.com.

[38]B. Macchiette and R. Abhijit (1994) Sensitive groups and social issues, *Journal of Consumer Marketing*, 11(4), 55–64.

[39]F. Lawrence (2004) Revealed: how food firms target children, *The Guardian*, 27 May.

[40]O.-B. Gonzalez and J.-B. Gonzalez (2005) The role of geodemographic segmentation in retail location strategy, *International Journal of Market Research*, 47(3), 295–316.

[41]C. Fill (2006) *Marketing Communications*, 4th edn, Harlow, England: Prentice Hall, see Chapter 3, pp. 85–6.

[42]PPR Group is an official trading name of a French Luxury Group which is organised around 6 operating branches: Fnac, Redcats Group, Conforam, CFAO, Puma and Gucci Group.

[43]A. Ries and J. Trout (2000) *Positioning: The Battle for Your Mind*, 20th Anniversary Edition, New York: McGraw-Hill.

[44]P. Marsden (2002) Brand positioning: meme's the word, *Marketing Intelligence and Planning*, 20(5), 307–12.

[45]S. Knox (2004) Positioning and branding your organisation, *Journal of Product and Brand Management*, 13(2), 1105–59; S. Jackson (2007) Market share is not enough: why strategic marketing positioning works, *Journal of Business Strategy*, 28(1), 18–25.

[46]A. Parker (2007) Orange shakes up UK business, *Financial Times*, 21 October; and www.orange.com.

[47]K. L. Keller, B. Stenthal and A. Tybout (2002) Three questions you need to ask your brand, *Harvard Business Review*, 80 (September), 80–9.

[48]T. A. Brunner and M. Wänke (2006) The reduced and enhanced impact of shared features on individual brand evaluations, *Journal of Consumer Psychology*, 16 (April), 101–11.

[49]P. Betts (2007) Nespresso, what else?, *Financial Times*, 13 December.

[50]K. Naughton (2001) Ford's 'perfect storm', *Newsweek*, 17 September, pp. 48–50.

[51]G. S. Carpenter, R. Glazer and K. Nakamoto (1994) Meaningful brands from meaningless differentiation: the dependence on irrelevant attributes, *Journal of Marketing Research*, 31 (August), 339–350; S. M. Broniarczyk and A. D. Gershoff (2003) The reciprocal effects of brand equity and trivial attributes, *Journal of Marketing Research*, 40 (May), 161–75.

[52]C. Rohwedder (2006) Playing down the plaid, *Wall Street Journal*, 7 July (http://online.wsj.com/article_print/SB115222828906800109.html).

[53]Adapted from C. Buckley (2007) Czech labour shortage forces Skoda to recruit workers from Vietnam, *The Times*, 29 November.

[54]B. Sharp and J. Dawes, (2001) What is differentiation and how does it work?, *Journal of Marketing Management*, 17, 739–59.

[55]W. E. Fulmer and J. Goodwin (1988) Differentiation: begin with the customer, *Business Horizons*, 31(5), 55–63;

R. D. Buzzell and B. T. Gale (1987) *The PIMS Principles*, New York: The Free Press.

[56]M. E. Porter (1980) *Competitive Strategy: Techniques for Analyzing Industries and Competitors*, New York: Free Press.

[57]P. Barwise (2004) *Simply Better: Winning and Keeping Customers by Delivering What Matters Most*, Cambridge, MA: Harvard Business School Press.

[58]N. Piercy and N. Lane (2003) Transformation of the traditional salesforce: imperatives for intelligence, interface and integration, *Journal of Marketing Management*, 19, 563–82.

Chapter 11

▽ Creating customer value, satisfaction and loyalty

IN THIS CHAPTER, WE WILL ADDRESS THE FOLLOWING QUESTIONS:

1   What are customer value, satisfaction and loyalty, and how can companies deliver them?

2   What is the lifetime value of customers and how can marketers maximise it?

3   How can companies cultivate strong customer relationships?

4   How can companies both attract and retain customers?

5   What is the Experience Economy and how does it relate to customer's perception of value?

Today, companies face their toughest competition ever. Moving from a product and sales, least-cost production philosophy to a holistic marketing philosophy, however, gives them a better chance of outperforming competition (see Chapter 10).

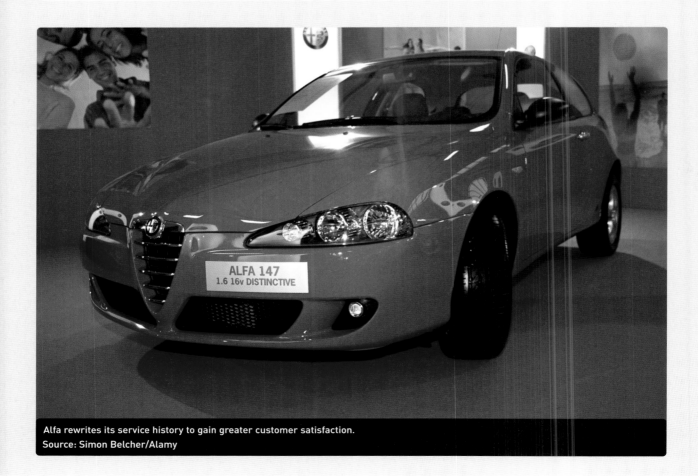

Alfa rewrites its service history to gain greater customer satisfaction.
Source: Simon Belcher/Alamy

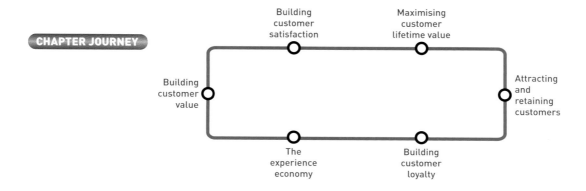

The cornerstone of a well-conceived marketing orientation is strong customer relationships. Marketers must connect with customers – informing, engaging, and maybe even energising them in the process. Customer-centred companies are adept at building customer relations.

Alfa-Romeo, Fiat Auto's premium brand, delivers high-quality workmanship and distinctive styling but has been plagued by poor service for which the brand has earned notoriety. The company, under the leadership of Sergio Marchionne, Fiat's chief executive since 2004, have decided to reposition Alfa as a luxury brand. This has required considerable attention to improving the overall customer-perceived value of this famous marque. Customer service standards had to be improved to provide a firm basis on which customer satisfaction could be improved to build lasting customer loyalty. Since February 2007 Fiat has been working with JDPower, the consumer ratings group, to emulate the best practice of top-end marques such as BMW and Toyota's Lexus. In the United Kingdom, JDPower has presented Alfa's management with its assessment of what was wrong. Car delivery times, spare parts delivery, and repair capability emerged as problems. Alfa's 'key performance indicators' were being met, but they had been incorrectly defined. For example, spare parts were deemed in service logs to be available – or even delivered – when they were still at the factory in Italy. Actual delivery and car repairs were not logged at all. Requests for parts from dealers in the United Kingdom were often being filled by other dealers or through an informal parts market. Alfa had also been notching up high warranty costs, with cars just delivered to customers being returned for minor alterations in areas such as finishing, trim and loose screws. Such problems are easily fixable but – as well as costing Alfa – they infuriated customers. Now Alfa is paying for pre-delivery inspections of cars in the UK while it works on improving production quality at factory level.[1]

As Alfa Romeo's experience shows, successful marketers are the ones that fully satisfy their customers profitably. This chapter explores the ways open to companies to win and retain customers and so secure a sustained competitive advantage. The solution lies largely in beating competition by doing a better job of meeting or exceeding customer expectations.

▽ Building customer value

According to Schieffer creating loyal customers is at the heart of every business.[2] Peppers and Rogers say:[3]

> The only value your company will ever create is the value that comes from customers – the ones you have now and the ones you will have in the future. Businesses succeed by getting, keeping, and growing customers. Customers are the only reason you build factories, hire employees, schedule meetings, lay fibre-optic lines, or engage in any business activity. Without customers, you don't have a business.

Dubois et al., Webster, and others echo these views and see effective marketing as being about the identification, design and delivery of customer-perceived value.[4] Managers who believe that the customer is the company's only true 'profit centre' consider the traditional organisation chart in Figure 11.1(a) – a pyramid with the CEO at the top, management in the middle, and front line people and customers at the bottom – obsolete.[5]

Successful marketing companies invert the chart (Figure 11.1(b)). At the top are customers; next in importance are front line people who meet, serve and satisfy customers; under them are the middle managers, whose job is to support the front line people so they can serve customers well; and at the base is top management, whose job is to hire and support good middle managers. Customers have been added along the sides of Figure 11.1(b) to indicate that at every level company staff must be personally involved in knowing, meeting and serving customers.

Some companies have been founded with the customer-on-top business model, and customer advocacy has been their strategy – and competitive advantage – all along. With the rise of digital technologies such as the Internet, today's increasingly informed consumers expect companies to do more than connect with them, more than satisfy them, and even more than delight them. They expect companies to *listen* to them.[6]

Many companies recognise the importance of satisfying their customers in order to develop brand reputations that can deliver a sustainable competitive advantage. Such communication is particularly important in retailing, where the vast majority of staff are either on the shop floor dealing with customers, or behind the scenes in areas such as the supply/value chain where they can feel divorced from central operations. Therefore, in order to attain this goal companies have developed a commitment to listening to their employees. Asda, the UK supermarket chain owned by Wal-Mart (see Chapter 3) have become renowned for listening to their staff. According to David Smith, Asda's director for people, the success enjoyed by the group in repeatedly winning employment plaudits has been hard won. Asda guards its reputation fiercely – evolving

Figure 11.1 Traditional organisation versus modern customer-oriented company organisation

its methods to keep staff happy: 'You have to keep changing. This success that we have around people has not occurred overnight. We have been working on this for ten years,' Smith comments. He believes that Asda's success with people comes down to a set of 'very simple mechanics' and has little time for companies with grandiose mission statements that fail to live up to their words. The key to Asda's success is communication. It not only involves filtering down the right messages from the top of the organisation, but also ensuring that feedback from the stores' staff is treated seriously and communicated back to the top.

It is also vitally important to listen to customers, and many companies are not as effective in this regard as they could be. A well-known UK BBC TV presenter, Jeremy Paxman, complaining about the declining quality of Marks & Spencer's underwear, criticised the company for not effectively listening to its customers. A correspondent to the *Financial Times* also complained about the arrogance and lack of customer service shown by the company to its loyal customer base. His question to Marks & Spencer was: How do you know what your customers feel about your products? It is commonly recognised within businesses that 95 per cent of UK customers with a perceived or genuine complaint will never voice it. If Marks & Spencer does not speak to its customers it will not know whether or not they are happy with the company's products and service standards.

Following a disappointing set of financial results in 2007 DSG International, the UK group that owns consumer electronics and white goods stores such as Curry's and PC World, appointed a new chief executive. The new incumbent told the UK press that he would spend his first few weeks walking the shop floor, listening to customers and staff, rather than adjusting strategy from his desk. 'Value, choice and service' was his mantra.[7]

In today's buyers' markets (see Chapter 10) customers can exercise considerable choice of supplier when they visit the marketplace. Listening to customers makes sense if a firm wishes to be both effective (produce what the customer wants) and efficient (do this cost efficiently). As the new chief executive at DSG International indicates 'value, choice and service' are of prime importance. The concept of customer-perceived value (CPV) enables marketers to discover what customers want through the medium of market research.

Customer-perceived value (CPV) is the difference between the prospective customer's evaluation of all the benefits and all the costs of an offering and the perceived alternatives. **Total customer benefit** is the perceived monetary value of the bundle of economic, functional and psychological benefits customers expect from a given market offering because of the products, services, personnel and image involved. **Total customer cost** is the perceived bundle of costs customers expect to incur in evaluating, obtaining, using and disposing of the given market offering, including monetary, time, energy and psychological costs.

The findings from this activity can be expressed as a customer-perceived value offering that will have both perceived quality and financial attributes. Once expressed as a specification it is the task of firms to translate the characteristics of such an offering to a value package that can be traded in the marketplace. The question is how? Many would infer that the answer lies in the application of the 4P marketing mix that is the primary means of securing a successful market offering.

As markets become more and more competitive so firms need to pay ever closer attention to supplying the right market offerings – which have the appropriate customer-perceived value rating. The pursuit of suitable CPV offerings calls into question the established status of the 4P marketing mix as being an approach of primary importance. A more useful, practical insight can be gained from consideration of the steps illustrated in Figure 11.3 and discussed below.

Practical, as opposed to many theoretical marketers, begin with a realistic appraisal of their firm's characteristic approach to business. Is this essentially a product/finance-oriented company or a market-oriented company? Many seem to view these positions as being mutually exclusive. However, in the real world, it is best to see these approaches as opposite ends of a continuum. So firms will be at some point between E1 (efficiency – least-cost production orientation) and E2 (effectiveness CPV market orientation). Firms determined to become truly market oriented (which entails moving closer to E2) will have accepted the need to formulate and adhere to a managing change programme that will transform their organisations. However, depending on the size and complexity of the firm, this transformation may take up to five to seven years to achieve and requires a consistent and steady hand on the tiller.

Figure 11.2
Determinants of customer-perceived value

Figure 11.3 The pursuit of customer-perceived value

Source: M. R. V. Goodman, Durham University.

The primary concern of firms in buyers' markets should be to face reality and seek to manage a strong and lasting positive differentiation with the intent of gaining a sustainable competitive advantage. The next concern is to gain the latest intelligence on the marketplace to discover the relative strength of buyers' choice opportunities and to acquire up-to-date information on the relative strength of the competition. The tertiary concern is for the firm then to design, develop and present a suitable set of CPV market offerings to place on the market. This involves consistently listening to customers to deliver a CPV package that meets with customers' approval.

It is rather simplistic to believe that this can be achieved solely by the conventional 4P or 7P marketing mixes. Such CPV offerings usually consist of a mix of tangible and intangible attributes. Conventional products (*tangibles*) usually form only a part of a CPV package which in buyers' markets normally includes many *services* (*intangibles*). That is why it is more useful to view marketing as being concerned with the provision of customer-perceived value circles rather than solely with products or services.

Value circles that make up CPV offerings can be viewed as a collection of ripple circles. Individual circles may be a tangible product value, an intangible service value or a collection of both.

Source: Serif

The emphasis should be placed on the provision of a series of value attributes (see Chapter 10). This is more practically achieved by attention to forming a deep understanding of marketplaces, customers, competition, costs, channels (distribution or place), marketing communications and the company strategic approach.

Customer-perceived value

An important consequence of the business environmental paradigm change from a sellers' to a buyers' market has been a subtle transformation in the concept of value (see Chapter 10). Value is heavily influenced by buyers as they have a choice of supplier and usually demand more for their money. The concept of *customer-perceived value* has become a matter of increasing concern in the marketing literature as it becomes imperative for suppliers to offer buyers in competitive markets what they want if they are to effectively generate profitable business. Several empirical studies have sought to explore it in practice. Gounaris *et al.* researched the relationships between value, satisfaction and purchase intentions.[8] Their research suggested that delivering superior customer value enables a firm to achieve favourable ('buy me') behavioural intentions. In contemporary buyers' markets the concept of CPV has become a vital concern for marketers.

How then do customers ultimately make choices? They tend to be perceived as value maximisers, within the bounds of search costs and limited knowledge, mobility and income. Customers estimate which market offering will deliver the most perceived value and act on it. A challenging task for market-oriented companies is to define, develop and deliver value when value itself is notoriously difficult to define. In many respects it is a matter of perception, like beauty.

▽ The truth about beauty creams

On 12 May 2008 a TV programme in the United Kingdom conducted an investigation into the beauty cream market with the intent of discovering whether anti-ageing creams really worked. Such market offerings promise eternal youth to women and the UK market is reputed to be worth €1 billion. As the regulating law stands at present companies competing in this market do not have to put their creams through accredited scientific tests as they are classed as cosmetics rather than medicines. Nonetheless, they do have to be careful as to the claims they make for their preparations. In 2007 L'Oréal was required by the UK Advertising Standards Authority to withdraw an advertisement campaign that claimed to reduce wrinkles in an hour.

Five creams were selected and given to five women to try for a month. At the start of the test each of the women was examined by a dermatologist and plastic surgeon to determine the start sate of their skin. Table 11.1 summarises the branded creams that were selected for testing.

After a month the women were re-examined by the dermatologist and the plastic surgeon and the performance of the competing cream was treatments was evaluated.

Table 11.1 Anti-ageing cream test brands

Brand	Price of total package
Boot's No. 7 Protect and Perfect	£70
Dior Capture XP Range	£252
Nivea Visage	£20
L'Oréal DermGenesis	£70
Olay Regenerist Range	£80
Simple Protect Moisturising Cream	£5

The Danish company Nanoko use cows' milk for its skin lotions.

Source: Courtesy of Nanoko

Despite using pseudo-scientific copy in their marketing efforts ('the science bit') no real change was observed in the state of the women's skin. While there was evidence of some slight surface improvement there was no evidence of significant deep skin improvement. There was little to choose between the cheapest and most expensive. The experts advised that the best way to look after skin was to stay out of the sun, use a sunblock, eat healthily, see that sufficient vitamin C was in their diet and avoid anti-wrinkle creams!

So value, like beauty, is highly prized and many women buy anti-wrinkle creams in pursuit of a promise and are captivated by slogans such as L'Oréal's 'Because you're worth it'.

There are many skin care products on the market and manufacturers are increasingly seeking to gain a market edge by searching for new ingredients. In Denmark, Nanoko has launched a skin lotion based on milk from cows. In Norway Bioforskning Skinscience Spermine cream is a crystal extracted from seminal fluid said to be 30 times stronger than vitamin E and able to repair sunburnt skin. Men too are now being targeted by the cosmetics companies in a market that sails close to the wind in terms of the scientifically questionable claims it makes.

Source: UK Channel 4 *TV Dispatches* programme screened on 12 May 2008; staff reporter, *Daily Telegraph*, 30 May 2008.

Whether the offer lives up to expectations affects customer satisfaction and the probability that the customer will purchase the product again.

Customer-perceived value is thus based on the difference between what the customer gets and what he or she gives for different possible choices. The customer gets benefits and assumes costs. The marketer can increase the value of the customer offering by some combination of raising economic, functional or emotional benefits and/or reducing one or more of the various types of costs. In line with the microeconomic concept of demand elasticity (a concept that measures how the level of customer demand changes as price changes) a customer, choosing between two value offerings, V1 and V2, will examine the ratio V1:V2. Offer V1 will be favoured if the ratio is larger than one. Offer V2 will be selected if the ratio is smaller than one. Lastly the customer will be totally indifferent if the ratio equals one.

Applying value concepts

Suppose a buyer for a large construction company wants to buy a backhoe low loader tractor from the UK's JCB or Japan's Komatsu. The competing sales people carefully describe their company's respective offers. The buyer wants to use the vehicle in residential construction work. The vehicle must deliver certain levels of reliability, durability, performance, and have resale value. The buyer evaluates the tractors and decides that the JCB offers greater product benefits and also perceives differences in the accompanying services – delivery, training and maintenance – and decides that the JCB offering provides better service as well as more knowledgeable and responsive personnel. He or she gains economic, functional and psychological benefits from these four sources – product, services, personnel and image – and so perceives JCB as delivering greater customer benefits.

Does this result in a purchase of the JCB tractor? Not necessarily, for the buyer also assesses and compares the total cost of transacting with JCB and Komatsu. This requires a consideration of more than money. As Adam Smith observed over two centuries ago, 'The real price of anything is the toil and trouble of acquiring it.'[9] Total customer cost includes not only the buyer's time, energy and psychological costs expended in product acquisition but also the costs incurred by usage, maintenance, ownership and disposal. The buyer evaluates these elements together with the monetary cost to form a total customer cost. He or she then considers whether the JCB's total customer cost is too high in relation to the total customer benefits Komatsu promises. If it is, the buyer might choose Komatsu. The buyer ultimately chooses the market offering that promises highest customer-perceived value. This is also the case with 'service industries'.[10]

When most people think of JCBs, the Backhoe Loader is the one that comes to mind. Loads of people have tried to copy it, but no one's been able to better it. It's the original and best! With that beefy bucket and arm on the back (that's the bit that's called the Backhoe) and the huge strong shovel on the front, they can do just about any job, anywhere!
Source: Richard Leeney/DK Images

Very often, managers conduct a **customer-perceived value analysis** to reveal the company's strengths and weaknesses relative to those of various competitors. The steps in this analysis are:

1 **Identify the major attributes and benefits that customers value**: Customers are asked what attributes, benefits and performance levels they look for in choosing a product and vendors.

2 **Assess the quantitative importance of the different attributes and benefits**: Customers are asked to rate the importance of the different attributes and benefits. If their ratings diverge too much, the marketer should cluster them into different segments.

3 **Assess the company's and competitors' performances on the different customer values against their rated importance**: Customers describe where they see the company's and competitors' performances on each attribute and benefit.

4 **Examine how customers in a specific segment rate the company's performance against a specific major competitor on an individual attribute or benefit basis**: If the company's offer exceeds the competitor's offer on all important attributes and benefits, the company can charge a higher price (thereby earning higher profits), or it can charge the same price and gain more market share.

5 **Monitor customer values over time**: The company must periodically repeat its studies of customer values and competitors' standings as the economy, technology and features change.

Choices and implications

Some marketers might argue that the process described above is too rational. Suppose the customer chooses the Komatsu tractor. How can this choice be explained? Here are three possibilities.

1 **The buyer might be under orders to buy at the lowest price**: The JCB salesperson's task is to convince the buyer's manager that buying on price alone will result in lower long-term profits and customer value.

2 **The buyer will leave before the company realises that the Komatsu tractor is more expensive to operate**: The buyer will look good in the short run; he is maximising personal benefit. The JCB's salesperson's task is to convince other people in the customer company that JCB delivers greater customer value.

3 **The buyer enjoys a long-term friendship with the Komatsu salesperson**: In this case, JCB's salesperson needs to show the buyer that the Komatsu tractor will draw complaints from the tractor operators when they discover its high fuel cost and need for frequent repairs.

The point of these examples is clear. Buyers operate under various constraints and in competitive markets make choices that give more weight to their personal benefit than to the company's benefit. So customer-perceived value is a useful concept and involves the following steps: First, the seller must assess the total customer benefit and total customer cost associated with each competitor's offer in order to know how his or her offer rates in the buyer's mind. Second, the seller who is at a customer-perceived-value disadvantage has two alternatives: to increase total customer benefit or to decrease total customer cost.

The former calls for strengthening or augmenting the economical, functional and psychological benefits of the offering's product, services, personnel and image. The latter calls for reducing the buyer's costs by reducing the price or cost of ownership and maintenance, simplifying the ordering and delivery process, or absorbing some buyer risk by offering a warranty.[11]

Delivering high customer value

Consumers have varying degrees of loyalty to specific brands, stores and companies. Oliver defines **loyalty** as 'A deeply held commitment to re-buy or re-patronise a preferred product or service in the future despite situational influences and marketing efforts having the potential to cause switching behaviour.'[12] As most markets have become increasingly competitive so it has become more difficult for companies to build brand reputations that command sustained customer loyalty. For example, many well-known brands of aspirin are finding it more and more difficult to succeed when generic or supermarket own brands are available at less than half the cost. Despite Intel's successful 'Intel Inside' promotion rival computer chip companies such as AMD and Cyrix are gaining ground on the market leader.

Many retailers are seeking to build lasting customer loyalty by offering loyalty card schemes (see the Tesco example in Chapter 5) of varying descriptions. Essentially what they are trying to do is to ensure that brand recognition (awareness) becomes brand preference (first choice if available) and preferably brand insistence (always first choice).

▽ Building customer satisfaction

Customers want loyalty, not perfection

With frustration verging on despair, marketing gurus and brand managers worldwide bemoan the erosion of customer loyalty. The global power of consumer brands is not what it used to be and marketers resent it. They think their customers fickle ingrates. In the dramatic phrase of an advertising agency executive, consumers today are 'brand sluts' who are most loyal to instant gratification. This 'consumer-as-slattern' attitude is a far cry from advertising grand master David Ogilvy's marketing admonition that: 'The consumer isn't a moron. She's your wife.'

In reality, the declared demise of brand loyalty is completely misunderstood. A review of the past decade reveals customers have not been cavalierly unfaithful to established brands; quite the opposite. Established brands have cheated on and betrayed their most loyal customers. They charge more and more for less and less; they chase after the youth market or the hot segment *du jour*; their 'innovations' frequently add more complexity than value; and their willingness to apologise and compensate for errors or mistakes is minimal. The more provocative marketing argument is that 'brand inertia', far more than 'brand loyalty', has kept so many customers for so many companies for so long.

Customers are neither sheep nor fools. They can sense when companies are consistently more loyal to investors, employees and regulators than to the people who buy their products and services. They behave accordingly. Customers are not being disloyal; they are being discriminating. The central marketing question confronting brand leaders therefore is not 'How can we radically increase customer loyalty?' but 'How can we radically increase our own loyalty to customers?'

The distinction is enormous. It is analogous to companies that say they promote a culture of 'employee loyalty' even as cutbacks and layoffs surge during economic slowdowns and mergers. Top management demands loyalty from below while regretfully declining to reciprocate. Yet the moral authority and value of loyalty comes from the courage to hold fast during difficult times. It is the defiant unwillingness of enterprises to be loyal to their best customers that has produced the promiscuous consumer behaviour they deplore. The real sin here is that companies, such as Alfa-Romeo and Marks & Spencer, have wilfully confused 'brand loyalty' with 'customer retention'. Just as with sullen employees, that is the perfunctory loyalty of compliance, not of pride or passion.

This challenge is not complex. Companies demonstrate loyalty to employees by investing in them, fairly compensating them, tapping their expertise and declining to throw them overboard when times get tough. Why should customers deserve any less?

This is where traditional marketing and brand advertising fail. Often it is not the brand attribute of flawless service but the act of rapidly recovering from a mistake that wins customer loyalty and return business. There are many examples: airline reservation clerks who waive 'change fees' for inadvertently misbooked flights or mobile telephone operators who politely and without complaint remove rightly disputed charges from the bill. These are less acts of 'customer service' than demonstrations of loyalty to customers. 'Brand value' comes not from promises of perfection but gracefully compensating for acknowledged weakness. The global luxury hotel chain Marriott and British Telecom have conducted customer research revealing that their most persuasive 'word-of-mouth' support comes more from individuals who have had an unpleasant problem happily resolved than those who simply enjoyed 'good' or 'excellent' service. The willingness and ability to see a difficult situation through to success despite cost and risk is what defines loyalty. Many companies already know this and invest accordingly.

To be fair, financial pressures, increasing transparency and the multiple demands of many corporate social responsibility movements make it more difficult than ever for companies to balance 'customer loyalty' with 'loyalty to customers'. Consumers are far quicker to see a brand as a mask the company hides behind.

However, this is where new technology creates new opportunities for reciprocal loyalty. Increasingly, cutting-edge companies such as Google and Apple – strong brands in their own right – create online spaces where customers can collaborate and interact around new features and technical problems. Established brands such as Procter & Gamble and the UK's BBC have used digital media to listen to customer ideas and shape new products. Customers know that these organisations have invested millions of dollars, pounds and euros into taking them seriously. In this millennium, brand value comes from investing as much in valued customers as in valuable products and services.[13]

The **value proposition** consists of the whole cluster of product and service attributes (benefits) the company promises to deliver; it is more than the core positioning of the offering. For example, Volvo's core positioning has been 'safety', but the buyer is promised more than just a safe car; other benefits include a long-lasting car, good service and a long warranty period. The value proposition is a statement about the experience customers will gain from the company's market offering and from their relationship with the supplier. The brand must represent a promise about the total experience customers can expect. Whether the promise is kept depends on the company's ability to manage its value delivery system.[14] The **value delivery system** includes all the experiences the customer will have on the way to obtaining and using the offering. At the

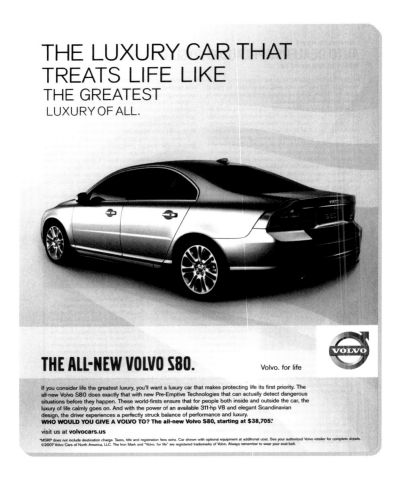

Safety is a leading, but not the only, benefit promised in Volvo's value proposition.

Source: Courtesy of Volvo Car Corporation / Agency: Arnold

heart of a good value delivery system is a set of core business processes that help to deliver distinctive consumer-perceived value to ensure that the customer has a pleasurable purchasing experience. Curiously Apple does not have a phone number for their Ipod queries but directs customers to a website. Many customers, however, prefer to contact a human voice. As a result some companies, for example service and insurance businesses, are promoting the 'personal approach' in TV advertisements.

Here's a company that is a master at delivering customer value.[15]

▽ Superquinn

Superquinn is Ireland's largest supermarket chain and its founder, Feargal Quinn, is Ireland's master marketer. A welcome message is posted at the store entrance to greet and help customers and even offers coffee, as well as providing a carry-out service to customers' cars and umbrellas in case of rain. Department managers post themselves in the aisles to interact with customers and answer questions. There is a high-quality salad bar, fresh bread baked every four hours, and indications of when produce arrived, including the farmers' pictures. Superquinn also operates a child care centre. It offers a loyalty programme that gives points for the amount purchased and for discovering anything wrong within the store, such as dented cans or bad tomatoes. A dozen other firms including a bank and petrol station that give points for purchases at their establishments recognise the loyalty card. Because everything is done to exceed normal customer expectations, Superquinn stores enjoy an almost cult-like following. In August 2006 Superquinn was sold to a consortium, Select Retail Holdings.

Total customer satisfaction

Whether the buyer is satisfied after purchase depends on the offer's performance in relationship to the buyer's expectations, and whether the buyer interprets any deviations between the two.[16] If the performance falls short of expectations, the customer is dissatisfied. If the performance matches the expectations, the customer is satisfied.[17] If the performance exceeds expectations, the customer is highly satisfied or delighted.[18] Customer assessments of product performance depend on many factors, especially the type of loyalty relationship the customer has with the brand.[19] Consumers often form more favourable perceptions of a product with a brand towards which they already feel positive.

Although the customer-centred firm seeks to create high customer satisfaction, that is not its ultimate goal. If the company increases customer satisfaction by lowering its price or increasing its services, the result may be lower profits. The company might be able to increase its profitability by means other than increased satisfaction (for example by improving manufacturing processes or investing more in R&D). Also, the company has many stakeholders, including employees, dealers, suppliers and stockholders. Spending more to increase customer satisfaction might divert funds from increasing the satisfaction of other 'partners'. Ultimately, the company must operate on the philosophy that it is trying to deliver a high level of customer satisfaction subject to delivering acceptable levels of satisfaction to the other stakeholders, given its total resources.[20]

How do buyers form their expectations? Expectations result from past buying experience; friends' and associates' advice; and marketers' and competitors' information and promises. If marketers raise expectations too high, the buyer is likely to be disappointed. However, if the company sets expectations too low, it will not attract enough buyers (although it will satisfy those who do buy).[21] Some of today's most successful companies are raising expectations and delivering performances to match. Korean automaker Kia found success in Europe by launching low-cost, high-quality cars offering six-year warranties.

A customer's decision to be loyal or to defect is the sum of many small experiences with the company. Many companies now strive to create a sustainable 'branded customer experience' and, like K.V.K., place a great emphasis on securing total customer satisfaction.

▽ **K.V.K.**

K.V.K. is the market leader in the mobile phone market in Turkey. K.V.K., together with the GSM operating services of Turkcell and its subsidiaries, distributes mobile telecommunication and data products for leading global brands including Nokia, Blackberry, HTC and accessories with the brand name of 'K.V.K. Tools'. K.V.K. also distributes SIM cards of Turkcell, the fifth fastest growing GSM operator in the world. With 3500 sales offices, K.V.K. has the widest distribution network in Turkey. The company also provides full after-sales support and technical services to its customers. Customer satisfaction takes precedence over all other issues and K.V.K. has made 'customer satisfaction first' its motto. All K.V.K. marketing strategies are structured according to this principle. Their mission is to provide leading and creative solutions in line with the changing needs of customers and their vision is to be a *brand* in mobile life with high quality products and service.

Source: www.kvk.com/AboutUsEnglish.asp

Monitoring satisfaction

Many companies are systematically measuring how well they treat their customers, identifying the factors shaping satisfaction, and making changes in their operations and marketing as a result.[22] For example IATA, the International Air Transport Association that represents some 240 airlines comprising 94 per cent of scheduled international air traffic, regularly monitors customer satisfaction in its Global Airport Monitor operation (http://www.iata.org/index.htm; www.bestransport.org).

Customer satisfaction

Companies should measure customer satisfaction regularly, because an important key to customer retention is customer satisfaction. A highly satisfied customer generally stays loyal longer and buys more as the company introduces new products and upgrades existing ones. They also promote the company by word of mouth and pay less attention to competing brands. They tend to be less sensitive to price and can proffer new product/service value-offering ideas to the company. They also cost less to serve than new customers because transactions can become routine.[23] Greater customer satisfaction has also been linked to higher returns and lower risk in the stock market.[24]

The link between customer satisfaction and customer loyalty, however, is not proportional. Suppose customer satisfaction is rated on a scale from one to five. At a very low level of customer satisfaction (level one), customers are likely to abandon the company and even criticise it. At levels two to four, customers are fairly satisfied but still find it easy to switch when a better value offering comes along. At level five, the customer is very likely to repurchase and actively promote the company. High satisfaction or delight creates an emotional bond with the brand or company, not just a rational preference. Xerox's senior management found out that its 'completely satisfied' customers were six times more likely to repurchase Xerox products over the following 18 months than its 'very satisfied' customers.

When customers rate their satisfaction with an element of the company's performance – say, delivery – the company needs to recognise that customers vary in how they define good performance.

Good delivery could mean early delivery, on-time delivery, order completeness, and so on. The company must also realise that two customers can report being 'highly satisfied' for different reasons. One may be easily satisfied most of the time and the other might be hard to please but was pleased on this occasion.

Measurement techniques

A number of methods exist to measure customer satisfaction. *Periodic surveys* can track customer satisfaction directly and also ask additional questions to measure repurchase intention and the respondent's likelihood or willingness to recommend the company and brand to others. Theme parks such as Legoland continuously conduct Web-based guest surveys of customers who have agreed to be contacted. A key purpose of this is to gather information on customer satisfaction with their theme park experience, including rides, dining, shopping, games and shows.

In the last two decades, it has been suggested that the marketing discipline is undergoing a paradigm shift from a transactional perspective to a relational perspective[25] (see Chapters 1, 3 and 10). At the same time, there has been a call for the discipline to focus on accurate measurement of the outcome of marketing activities[26] (see Chapter 22). Empirical research in this area has predominantly examined the sales and profitability of relationships through **customer** lifetime analysis or examined attitudinal measures such as satisfaction and loyalty. Sharma[27] attempted to combine both streams of research by examining the profitability, satisfaction and probability of switching associated with transactional customers, relationship customers (less than five years of relationship) and deep relationship customers (more than five years of relationship) in three business-to-business industries. The results demonstrated that the transactional customers were the most profitable, followed by the relationship and deep relationship customers. The probability of switching was in the reverse direction of profitability and there were no differences in satisfaction measures.

Besides conducting periodic surveys, companies can monitor their *customer loss rate* and contact customers who have stopped buying or who have switched to another supplier to find out why. Finally, companies can hire *mystery shoppers* to pose as potential buyers and report on strong and weak points experienced in buying the company's and competitors' products. Managers themselves can enter company and competitor sales situations where they are unknown and experience at first hand the treatment they receive, or they can phone their own company with questions and complaints to see how employees handle the calls.

In addition to tracking customer value expectations and satisfaction for their own firms, companies need to monitor their competitors' performance in these areas.

Marketing insight

Net promoter and customer satisfaction

Measuring customer satisfaction is a top priority for many companies, but a difference of opinion exists as to how they should go about doing it. Reichheld suggests that perhaps only one customer question really matters: 'How likely is it that you would recommend this product or service to a friend or colleague?' According to Reichheld, a customer's willingness to recommend to a friend results from how well the customer is treated by front line employees, which in turn is determined by all the functional areas that contribute to a customer's experience.[28]

Keiningham et al.[29] disputed Reichheld's assertions. Their results indicated that recommended intention alone would not suffice as a single predictor of customers' future loyalty behaviour. Use of a multiple indicator instead of a single predictor model performed better in predicting customer recommendations and retention. The practical implications of their research challenge assertions that regard intention as the primary, even sole gauge of customer loyalty.

Influence of customer satisfaction

For customer-centred companies, customer satisfaction is both a goal and a marketing tool. Companies need to be especially concerned today with their customer satisfaction level because the Internet provides a tool for consumers to quickly spread dissatisfaction – as well as satisfaction – to the rest of the world. Some customers even set up their own websites to air their grievances and dissatisfaction, targeting high-profile brands such as Mercedes-Benz.[30] Describing events and actions as being wronged by the company, these websites often attempt to galvanise consumer discontent and protest.

Companies that do achieve high customer satisfaction ratings, such as BMW, make sure that their target market knows it. Once they achieve number one status on, for example, market research agency JD Power's customer satisfaction ratings, companies stress this in their advertising copy.

Customer complaints

Some companies think they are getting a sense of customer satisfaction by recording the number of complaints, but studies of customer dissatisfaction show that customers are dissatisfied with their purchases about 25 per cent of the time but that only about 5 per cent complain. The other 95 per cent either feel complaining is not worth the effort, or they do not know how or to whom to complain, and they just stop buying.

Of the customers who register a complaint, between half and three-quarters will do business with the organisation again if their complaint is resolved. The figure goes up to almost 100 per cent if the customer feels the complaint was resolved *quickly*. Customers who have complained to an organisation and had their complaints satisfactorily resolved tell an average of 5 people about the good treatment they received. The average dissatisfied customer, however, complains to 11 people. If each of them tells still other people, the number of people exposed to this dissatisfaction may grow exponentially.

The fact is, no matter how perfectly designed and implemented a marketing programme is, mistakes will happen. The best thing a company can do is to make it easy for the customer to complain. Suggestion forms, free phone numbers, websites and email addresses allow for quick, two-way communication. The 3M Company, of *Post-it* note fame, claims that over two-thirds of its product improvement ideas come from listening to customer complaints.

Even companies that think they have done everything possible to ensure customers are happy may still not know what additional goods and services they could be marketing. Their customers may not have told them or may not have thought of them. A spokesperson for Volvo cars comments that companies can get into a rut of measuring the same things repeatedly without considering whether the information is still telling them anything useful.[31] Writing in the *MIT Sloan Management Review*, he says Volvo began to have doubts about its customer strategy; while its measures showed customers were happy with the cars, they appeared to feel less affection for the company. Customer satisfaction was increasing even as loyalty to the Volvo brand was falling.

Having set up ways to gauge customer satisfaction, companies become reluctant to question whether they are measuring the right things. Volvo believes that, 'Many factors influence satisfaction and how something is measured can begin to take precedence over *what* is measured.' For example, one Volvo manager insisted the company should concentrate on eliminating quality defects about which customers had complained. But, this 'fails to acknowledge that avoiding dissatisfaction might not necessarily generate satisfaction'.

The difference is easy to miss. As Volvo discovered, 'Many companies have fallen into a self-perpetuating pattern in which practices that are not truly customer-oriented are reinforced and those that are customer-centred remain undiscovered and unexplored, all while the company's distance from the customer gradually but inexorably increases.' So what should companies do? They need to find out more about what motivates their customers, about the way they live and use products. Nokia, one of the most successful innovators of recent years, sends researchers to sit at traffic lights, watching how drivers spend their time while they wait. This is a far more expensive and time-consuming way of collecting information. It is also harder to quantify – and makes it difficult to base people's remuneration on the results.

Given the potential disadvantage of having an unhappy customer, it is critical that marketers deal with the negative experience effectively.[32] Beyond that, the following procedures can help to recover customer goodwill:[33]

1 Set up a seven-day, 24-hour free phone 'hot line' (by phone, fax or email) to receive and act on customer complaints.

2 Contact the complaining customer as quickly as possible. The slower the company is to respond the more dissatisfaction may grow and lead to negative word of mouth.

3 Accept responsibility for the customer's disappointment; never blame the customer.

4 Use customer-service people who are empathetic.

5 Resolve the complaint swiftly and to the customer's satisfaction. Some complaining customers are not looking for compensation so much as a sign that the company cares.

Product and service quality

Customer satisfaction has a key quality dimension. Customer-perceived quality relative to customer-perceived price defines customer-perceived value. What exactly is quality? Various experts have defined it as 'fitness for use', 'conformance to requirements', 'freedom from variation', 'the purchase attributes that the customer perceives', and so on. In sellers' markets quality was usually seen to be a production concern but in the buyers' markets of today it is a vital concern of marketers. The American Society for Quality Control defines quality as 'the totality of features and characteristics of a product or service that bear on its ability to satisfy stated or implied needs'. This is a customer-centred definition. Thus a seller has delivered quality whenever the product/service offering meets or exceeds the customers' expectations. A company that satisfies most of its customers' needs most of the time is called a quality company. However, it is important to distinguish between *conformance* quality and *performance* quality (or grade). A Lexus provides higher performance quality than a Hyundai: the Lexus rides more smoothly, goes faster and lasts longer. Yet we can say that both a Lexus and a Hyundai deliver the same conformance quality if all the units deliver their respective promised quality.

Stockholm's smoothly running and exceptionally clean metro system, the *Tunnelbannen*, found in the late 1990s that cutting costs wasn't enough. Quality for customers had to be taken into account. It took a new direction and found a better balance between quality and price and adopted a new overall objective – to attract more passengers by offering higher quality.[34]

The drive to produce goods that are superior in world markets has led some countries – and groups of countries – to recognise or award prizes to companies that exemplify the best quality practices, such as the Deming Prize in Japan, the Malcolm Baldrige National Quality Award in the United States, and the European Quality Award.

Impact of quality

Product and service quality, customer satisfaction and company profitability are intimately connected. Higher levels of quality result in higher levels of customer satisfaction, which support higher prices and (often) lower costs as the volume of sales increases. Studies have shown a high correlation between relative product quality and company profitability.[35] Companies that have lowered costs to cut corners have suffered when the quality of the customer experience suffers; for example a local private dentist who fails to invest in improving the patients' experience by regularly updating equipment and the furnishings in the waiting room. Quality is clearly a vital key to customer-perceived value creation and customer satisfaction.

Total quality

Total quality is everyone's job, just as marketing is everyone's job. Marketers play several roles in helping their companies define and deliver high-quality goods and services to target customers:

• They bear the major responsibility for correctly identifying the customers' needs and requirements.
• They must communicate customer expectations properly to product designers.
• They must make sure that customers' orders are filled correctly and on time.

- They must check that customers have received proper instructions, training and technical assistance in the use of the product.
- They must stay in touch with customers after the sale to ensure that they are satisfied and remain satisfied.
- They must gather customer ideas for product and service improvements and convey them to the appropriate departments.

When marketers do all this, they are making substantial contributions to total quality management and customer satisfaction, as well as to customer and company profitability.

▽ Maximising customer lifetime value

Ultimately, marketing is the art of attracting and keeping profitable customers. Yet every company loses money on some of its customers. The well-known 20–80 rule says that the top 20 per cent of the customers often generates 80 per cent or more of the company's profits. In some cases the profit distribution may be more extreme – the most profitable 20 per cent of customers (on a per capita basis) may contribute as much as 150–300 per cent of profitability. The least profitable 10–20 per cent of customers, on the other hand, can actually reduce profits from 50–200 per cent per account, with the middle 60–70 per cent breaking even.[36] Figure 11.4 displays one customer profit distribution. The implication is that a company could improve its profits by losing its worst customers.

It's not always the company's largest customers who yield the most profit. The largest customers can demand considerable service and receive the deepest discounts. The smallest customers pay full price and receive minimal service, but the costs of transacting with them can reduce their profitability. The mid-size customers who receive good service and pay nearly full price are often the most profitable.

Customer profitability

What makes a customer profitable? A **profitable customer** is a person, household, or company that over time yields a revenue stream that exceeds by an acceptable amount the company's cost stream for attracting, selling and servicing that customer. Note that the emphasis is on the *lifetime* stream of revenue and cost, not on the profit from a particular transaction.[37] Marketers can assess customer profitability individually, by market segment or by channel.

Although many companies measure customer satisfaction, most companies fail to measure individual customer profitability.[38] Banks claim this is a difficult task, because each customer uses different banking services and the transactions are logged in different departments. However, the number of unprofitable customers in their customer base has appalled banks that have

Figure 11.4 The 150-20 rule: 'the 20 per cent most profitable customers generate as much as 150 per cent of the profits of a company; the 20 per cent least profitable lose 100 per cent of the profits'

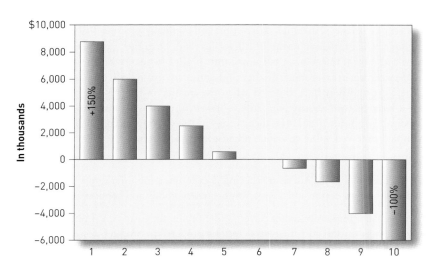

Customers

Products		C₁	C₂	C₃	
	P₁	+	+	+	Highly profitable product
	P₂	+			Profitable product
	P₃		−	−	Unprofitable product
	P₄			−	Highly unprofitable product
		High-profit customer	Mixed-bag customer	Losing customer	

Figure 11.5 Customer-product profitability analysis

succeeded in linking customer transactions. Some banks report losing money on over 45 per cent of their retail customers.

Customer profitability analysis

A useful type of profitability analysis is shown in Figure 11.5. Customers are arrayed along the columns and products along the rows. Each cell contains a symbol representing the profitability of selling that product to that customer. Customer 1 is very profitable; he buys three profit-making products (P1, P2 and P4). Customer 2 yields a picture of mixed profitability; he buys one profitable product and one unprofitable product. Customer 3 is a losing customer because he buys one profitable product and two unprofitable products.

What can the company do about customers 2 and 3? (1) it can raise the price of its less profitable products or eliminate them; or (2) it can try to sell customers 2 and 3 its profit-making products. Unprofitable customers who defect should not concern the company. In fact, the company should encourage these customers to switch to competitors.

Customer profitability analysis (CPA) is best conducted with the tools of an accounting technique called activity-based costing. The company estimates all revenue coming from the customer, less all costs. The costs should include not only the cost of making and distributing the products and services, but also of taking phone calls from the customer, travelling to visit the customer, paying for entertainment and gifts – all the company's resources that go into serving that customer.

When a company does this for each customer, it can classify customers into different profit tiers: *platinum customers* (most profitable), *gold customers* (profitable), *iron customers* (low profitability but desirable for volume) and *lead customers* (unprofitable and undesirable). The company can then move iron customers into the gold tier and gold customers into the platinum tier, while dropping the lead customers or making them profitable by raising prices or lowering the cost of serving them. More generally, marketers must segment customers into those worth pursuing and those potentially less lucrative customers that should receive little attention, if any at all.

Customer portfolios

Marketers are recognising the need to manage customer portfolios, made up of different groups of customers[39] defined in terms of their loyalty, profitability and other factors. One perspective is that a firm's portfolio consists of a combination of 'acquaintances', 'friends', and 'partners' that are constantly changing.[40] The three types of customers will differ in their product needs, their buying, selling and servicing activities, and their acquisition costs and competitive advantages.

Another perspective compares the individuals who make up the firm's customer portfolio to the stocks that make up an investment portfolio.[41] In marketing, as in investments, it is important to calculate the *beta*, or risk-reward value, for each portfolio item and then diversify accordingly. From this perspective, in order to maximise the portfolio's risk-adjusted lifetime value firms should assemble portfolios of negatively correlated individuals so that the financial contributions of one offset the deficits of another.

Customer lifetime value – conceptual dream or real-time activity?

As competition in buyers' markets intensifies it becomes increasingly important for companies to retain their customers as long as they can, and preferably for their lifetime. Winning new customers to replace lost ones is not an easy option. So why do customers defect? In short because they did not like what was on offer. The customer-perceived value package failed to satisfy. Generally speaking there are two main reasons why customers defect to a competitor.

The first is a breakdown in trust. Companies should not take their customers for granted but rather revere them and treat them with respect. While is was Mahatma Ghandi who was the first to coin the phrase 'The customer is king', today most marketers recognise its truth. The concept of customer-perceived value should be interpreted as a task to provide the right value package all the time. Mistakes will occur and then they need to be rectified promptly and effectively if customer loyalty is to be retained. Too often the horror stories seem to come from the same sectors: the financial sector, the utilities, satellite TV aerial companies, builders and garages, to name but a few of the cases aired in consumer TV programmes such as the BBC's *Watchdog*.

The second reason is a general failure of companies to interface successfully with their customers. The marketing culture should be recognised and practised by all in a company. The whole organisation represented by the brand either does its job well or badly. Modern times call for a coordinated team effort to ensure that customers do not experience any problems and are not just satisfied but delighted.[42]

'Chinmusic' is not enough!

Many companies claim to be deeply concerned about customer care. But several do not pay enough attention to delivering customer-perceived value constantly. While the sensitive use of loyalty programmes can prove useful they are no substitute for failing to constantly recognise the kingship of customers. Companies need to keep their eyes constantly on the alert to avoid becoming myopic in today's highly competitive global markets. Many have found that thinking about the long-term value or lifetime value and hence profitability of loyal customers helps to concentrate their strategy and actions.

The concept of customer lifetime value (CLV) and its associated metrics (see Chapter 22) has been developed to express the financial importance of long-term customer retention.[43] Several models have been devised to place a realistic assessment of the profitability of loyal customers but in reality comparatively few companies actively operate effective CLV metrics. So for many it remains a wonderful ambition but a pipe dream in most companies, for in practice too few are held accountable for maximising customers' overall value.[44]

▽ Cultivating customer relationships

Maximising customer-perceived value means cultivating long-term customer relationships. Companies are now moving away from wasteful mass marketing to precision marketing designed to build strong customer relationships[45] (see also Chapter 1). Today's economy is supported by information businesses. Information has the advantage of being easy to differentiate, customise, personalise and dispatch over networks at incredible speed.

But information cuts both ways. For instance, customers now have a quick and easy means of doing comparison shopping by using specialist Internet websites. The Internet also facilitates communication between customers. Websites such as Amazon.com enable customers to share information about their experiences with various products and services.

Customer empowerment has become a way of life for many companies that have had to adjust to a shift in the power with their customer relationships. 'Marketing insight: Company response to customer empowerment' describes some of the changes companies have made in their marketing practices as a result.

Marketing insight

Company response to customer empowerment

Often seen as the flag bearer for marketing best practices, Procter & Gamble's chairman, A. G. Lafley, created shock waves for marketers with his Association of National Advertisers' speech in October 2006. 'The power is with the consumer,' proclaimed Lafley, and 'marketers and retailers are scrambling to keep up with her.' Consumers are beginning in a very real sense to own our brands and participate in their creation. We need to learn to let go.' In support of his contention, Lafley pointed out how a teenager had created an animated spot for Pringles snacks that was posted on YouTube; how Pantene, the hair care products company, had created a campaign that encouraged women to cut their hair and donate the clippings to make wigs for cancer patients.

Other marketers have begun to advocate a 'bottom-up', grassroots approach to marketing, rather than the more traditional 'top-down' approach where the marketers feel they have an advantage. Burger King has launched campaigns on consumer-friendly new media such as YouTube, MySpace, video games and iPods. Allowing the customer to take charge just makes sense for a brand whose slogan is 'Have It Your Way' and whose main rival, McDonald's, already owns the more conservative family market.

To provide a little more control, Yahoo! engages in 'participation marketing' by contacting consumers who already like a particular brand, rather than just casting a wide net. Reflecting the company philosophy, Yahoo! commented that, 'Content is no longer something you push out; content is an invitation to engage with your brand.'

Perhaps the most compelling example of the new brand world comes from master marketer Nike. As part of its *Joga Bonito* (Portuguese for

Websites such as Yahoo! Music that empower visitors, allow them to post comments or pictures, or encourage the formation of active communities can benefit companies and customers alike.

'play beautiful') World Cup sponsorship, Nike spent U$100 million on a multilayered campaign. The centrepiece, however, was Joga.com, a social networking website available in 140 countries. One million members blogged, downloaded videos, created fan communities for their favourite players or teams, and expressed their passions on bulletin-board-type debates. Nike's CEO summed up the new marketing equation well, 'A strong relationship is created when someone joins a Nike community or invites Nike into their community.'

Sources: S. Elliott (2006) Letting consumers control marketing: priceless, *New York Times*, 9 October; L. Story (2006) Super bowl glory for amateurs with video cameras, *New York Times*, 27 September; T. Wasserman and J. Edwards (2006) Marketers' new world order, *Brandweek*, 9 October, 4–6; H. Green and R. D. Hof (2006) Your attention please, *BusinessWeek*, 24 July, 48–53; B. Sternberg (2006) The marketing maze, *Wall Street Journal*, 10 July.

Customer relationship management

Customer relationship management is the process of carefully managing detailed information about individual customers and all customer 'touch points' to maximise customer loyalty.[46] A *customer touch point* is any occasion on which a customer encounters the brand and product – from actual experience to personal or mass communications to casual observation. For a hotel, the touch points include reservations, check-in and checkout, room service, business services, exercise facilities, laundry service, restaurants and bars. For instance, customer-oriented hotels rely on personal touches, such as staff who always address guests by name and high-powered employees who understand the needs of sophisticated business travellers.[47]

Sometimes touch points are where you least expect, such as in customer billing. Microsoft's Global CRM product manager, Karen Smith, related what

> To find out how the Coles Group handles its customer relations and provides value to its customers with various loyalty programs and other perks, visit www.pearsoned.com.au/ marketingmanagementaustralia

happened when a telecommunications company converted to a unified billing system – one bill for all lines – to cut company costs. One of the customers requested a slightly modified version of unified billing to suit his expense submission purposes, but the service rep replied, 'No, Sir, we can't do that. We use unified billing.' The frustrated customer then switched his two business lines to another telecommunications company but lost his volume discount with the original provider, which still had his personal accounts. Even more frustrated, the customer then moved all his business to the new telecommunications company. Says Smith,

> We may think that something will be great to do for our customers, but before we take action we need to really step into their shoes. Companies often focus on CRM functionality and integration, but they forget about some of the most basic touch points.[48]

Customer relationship management enables companies to provide excellent real-time customer service through the effective use of individual account information. Based on what they know about each valued customer, companies can customise market offerings, services, messages and media. CRM is important because a major driver of company profitability is the aggregate value of the company's customer base.

One-to-one marketing

Some of the groundwork for customer relationship management was laid by Peppers and Rogers,[49] who outlined a four-step framework for one-to-one marketing that can be adapted to practising CRM marketing as follows:

1 **Identify your prospects and customers**: Do not go after everyone. Build, maintain and mine a rich customer database with information derived from all the channels and customer touch points.

2 **Differentiate customers in terms of (1) their needs and (2) their value to your company**: Spend proportionately more effort on the most valuable customers (MVCs). Apply activity-based costing and calculate customer lifetime value. Estimate net present value of all future profits coming from purchases, margin levels and referrals, less customer-specific servicing costs.

3 **Interact with individual customers to improve your knowledge about their individual needs and to build stronger relationships**: Formulate customised offerings that you can communicate in a personalised way.

4 **Customise products, services and messages to each customer**: Facilitate customer–company interaction through the company contact centre and website.

The practice of one-to-one marketing (see Chapter 5), however, is not for every company: the required investment in information collection, hardware and software may exceed the payout. It works best for companies that normally collect a great deal of individual customer information, carry a wide portfolio of market offerings which can be cross-sold, need periodic replacement or upgrading, and are of high customer perceived value.

Increasing the value of the customer base

A key driver of shareholder value is the aggregate value of the customer base. Winning companies improve the value of their customer base by excelling at strategies such as the following:

- **Reducing the rate of customer defection**: Selecting and training employees to be knowledgeable and friendly increases the likelihood that the inevitable shopping questions from customers will be answered satisfactorily.

- **Increasing the longevity of the customer relationship**: The more involved a customer is with the company, the more likely the customer will remain loyal. Some companies treat their customers as partners – especially in business-to-business markets – soliciting their help in the design of new products or improving their customer service.

- **Enhancing the growth potential of each customer by:**[50] increasing sales to existing customers with new offerings and opportunities. Football clubs across Europe market a range of products including clothing, scarves, souvenir watches and credit cards.

- **Making low-profit customers more profitable or ceasing to deal with them**: To avoid the direct need for termination, marketers can encourage unprofitable customers to buy more or in larger quantities, forgo certain features or services, or pay higher amounts or fees. Banks, phone companies and travel agencies are all now charging for once-free services to ensure minimum customer revenue levels.
- **Paying additional attention to high-value customers**: The most valuable customers can be treated in a special way. Thoughtful gestures such as birthday greetings, small gifts or invitations to special sports or arts events can send a strong positive signal to the customer. Volvo dealers, for example, have had a long tradition of placing a bouquet of flowers in every new car sold.

Attracting and retaining customers

Companies seeking to expand their profits and sales must spend considerable time and resources searching for new customers. To generate leads they develop advertisements and place them in media that will reach new prospects; send direct mail and make phone calls to possible new prospects; send their sales people to participate in trade shows where they might find new leads; purchase names from list brokers; and so on.

Reducing defection

It is not enough, however, to attract new customers; the company must keep them and increase their business.[51]

Too many companies suffer from high **customer churn** or defection. Adding customers here is like adding water to a leaking bucket. Mobile phone and cable TV operators, for example, are plagued with 'spinners', customers who switch carriers at least three times a year looking for the best deal. Many lose 25 per cent of their subscribers each year.

To reduce the defection rate, the company must:

1 Define and measure its retention rate. For a magazine, subscription renewal rate is a good measure of retention. For a college, it could be the first- to second-year retention rate, or the class graduation rate.

2 Distinguish the causes of customer attrition and identify those that can be managed better. Not much can be done about customers who leave the region or go out of business, but much can be done about those who leave because of poor service, badly made products or high prices.

3 Compare the lost profit equal to the customer's lifetime value from a lost customer to the costs to reduce the defection rate. As long as the cost to discourage defection is lower than the lost profit, the company should spend the money to try to retain the customer.

Capturing the heart of the serial switcher

In today's buyers' markets many companies are eagerly trying to build lasting relationships with their customers. However, many companies have been disappointed in the returns from their investment in CRM programmes. The blame for this is usually laid at the door of managers who allowed technology to dominate the corporate strategy, resulting in back office muddle and ill-coordinated approaches to customers. It is crucial that managers believe that customers should be won for life, but many companies failed to organise themselves around the customer. This meant consumer insight was held by individual employees and weakened when they moved on, although, thanks to new tools such as CRM software, many businesses are now building some semblance of corporate memory.

The drive for efficiency and cheaper production costs has led to customers being left out of many businesses' CRM strategies. 'In reality, the customer was never at the heart of CRM,' says Martin Hayward of Dunnhumby (www.dunnhumby.com/reading/customers-for-life.htm) the UK marketing and data analysis consultancy. 'It was simply about making the company machine as efficient as possible.'

Strategies such as farming out customer service to call centres have ended up undermining customer loyalty, which is why brand owners are now struggling to engage with a new generation of 20-something 'serial switchers'. 'These consumers have low brand loyalty and high confidence to move between rival brands at the drop of a hat,' Hayward adds. 'This new mindset is now the major challenge facing brand owners.'

Fast-moving consumer goods brand owners including Procter & Gamble and Unilever, for example, are working more closely with retailers such as Tesco to strengthen their relationship with their customers at point of sale. Meanwhile UK bank NatWest has bucked recent high street banking convention by acknowledging the importance of face-to-face customer relationships and maintaining rather than cutting local branches.

According to José Ferrão, president (Europe, Middle East and Africa) of Carlson Marketing,[52] many companies have been slow to address this challenge because of unwieldy organisational structures that restrict the ability to respond to customer needs and an overreliance on winning new consumers at the expense of holding on to and deepening their existing client base. Ferrão says,

> Telecoms businesses in particular have struggled with customer service levels as many have evolved from land-line business into mobile and cable through acquisitions, after which they continued to operate as separate units. Customers' services expectations from the brand owners they deal with are joined up; what they get from many, however, is anything but consistent.

Mr Hayward, however, concludes that both a customer-centric focus and low prices are viable brand strategies: 'Major brands currently struggling in national and international markets are those with neither a clear customer-service or price-led market positioning.' The riskiest place to be is somewhere in no man's land between the two.

Retention dynamics

Figure 11.6 shows the main steps in the process of attracting and retaining customers.[53] The starting point is everyone who might conceivably buy the product or service. These *potentials* are people or organisations that might conceivably have an interest in buying the company's product or service, but may not have the means or intention to buy. The next task is to identify which potentials are really good *prospects* – people with the motivation, ability and opportunity to make a purchase – by interviewing them, checking on their financial standing, and so on. Marketing efforts can then concentrate on converting the prospects into *first-time customers*, then into *repeat customers*, and then into *clients* – people to whom the company gives very special and knowledgeable treatment. The next challenge is to turn clients into *members* by starting a membership programme that offers benefits to customers who join, and then turning members into *advocates*, customers who enthusiastically recommend the company and its products and services to others. The ultimate challenge is to turn advocates into *partners*.

Unfortunately, much marketing theory and practice centres on the art of attracting new customers rather than on retaining and cultivating existing ones. The emphasis traditionally has been on making sales rather than on building relationships; on pre-selling and selling rather than on caring for the customer afterwards. More companies now recognise the importance of satisfying and retaining customers.

Satisfied customers constitute the company's *customer relationship capital*. If the company were to be sold, the acquiring company would pay not only for the plant and equipment and the brand name, but also for the delivered *customer base*, the number and value of the customers who would do business with the new firm. Here are some key issues that can influence customer retention:[54]

- Acquiring new customers can cost five times more than satisfying and retaining current customers. It requires a great deal of effort to induce satisfied customers to switch away from their current suppliers.
- The average company loses 10 per cent of its customers each year.
- A 5 per cent reduction in the customer defection rate can increase profits by 25 per cent to 85 per cent, depending on the industry.

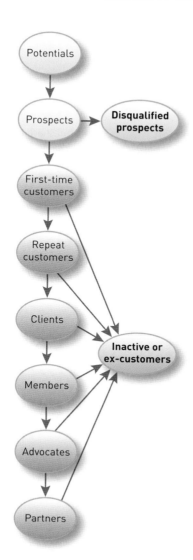

Figure 11.6 The customer-development process

Source: J. Griffin (1995) *Customer Loyalty: How to Earn It, How to Keep It*, New York: Lexington Books, p. 36. See also M. Raphel and N. Raphel (1995) *Up the Loyalty Ladder: Turning Sometime Customers Into Full-Time Advocates of Your Business*, New York: HarperBusiness.

• The customer profit rate tends to increase over the life of the retained customer due to increased purchases, referrals and price premiums, and reduced operating costs to service.

For example Enedesa, Spain's largest electricity company, is building a new customer relationship management system to help it to relate to its customers so that it does not lose them to its competitors.[55]

▽ Building customer loyalty

Improving loyalty

Creating a strong, tight connection to customers is the dream of any marketer and often the key to long-term marketing success. The Danish newspaper publishing company Dagbladet Borsen increases customer loyalty through relationship marketing. Companies that want to form strong customer bonds need to attend to a number of different considerations (see Figure 11.7). One set of researchers see retention-building activities as adding financial benefits, social benefits or structural ties.[56] The following sections explain four important types of marketing activities that companies are using to improve loyalty and retention.

Figure 11.7 Increasing customer share of requirements

Source: J. C. Anderson and J. A. Narus (2003) Selectively pursuing more of your customer's business, *MIT Sloan Management Review*, Spring, 45. Copyright © 2003 Massachusetts Institute of Technology. All rights reserved. Reproduced with permission.

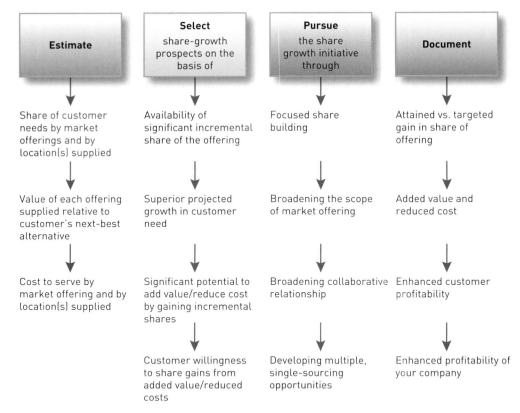

Estimate	**Select** share-growth prospects on the basis of	**Pursue** the share growth initiative through	**Document**
Share of customer needs by market offerings and by location(s) supplied	Availability of significant incremental share of the offering	Focused share building	Attained vs. targeted gain in share of offering
Value of each offering supplied relative to customer's next-best alternative	Superior projected growth in customer need	Broadening the scope of market offering	Added value and reduced cost
Cost to serve by market offering and by location(s) supplied	Significant potential to add value/reduce cost by gaining incremental shares	Broadening collaborative relationship	Enhanced customer profitability
	Customer willingness to share gains from added value/reduced costs	Developing multiple, single-sourcing opportunities	Enhanced profitability of your company

Interacting with customers

Listening to customers is crucial to customer relationship management. Some companies have created an ongoing mechanism that keeps senior managers permanently informed of front line customer feedback.[57]

- MBNA, the credit card giant, asks every executive to listen in on telephone conversations in the customer service area or customer recovery units.
- Deere & Company, which makes John Deere agricultural tractors and has a superb record of customer loyalty – nearly 98 per cent annual retention in some product areas – uses retired employees to interview defectors and customers.
- Once a quarter, 1.5 million copies of a glossy publication thud through letterboxes across Europe. Silky paper, striking photography and edgy design suggest the articles about travelling to Oman, Placido Domingo or the Bouroullec brothers – top French designers – could be from an architectural guide, an upmarket travel magazine or the latest lifestyle publication. The Mercedes magazine is all these – and more. Published in a dozen languages and as many distinct editions, the customer magazine for European Mercedes-Benz owners is part of a publishing phenomenon accelerating faster than one of the prestige German carmaker's convertibles.

Custom publishing – the business of devising and producing magazines under contract for big companies – has become one of the hottest corners in publishing, an industry not known for breakneck growth. According to the International Customer Publishing Federation, customer magazines are the fastest growing area of publishing, except the Internet, and employ about 20,000 people in Europe alone. Sak van der Boom, an industry consultant, says: 'Four of Sweden's top ten magazines by circulation are now customer products. In the UK, the figure is eight; while in the Netherlands customer magazines constitute the top five.'

Publishing for special interest groups is nothing new: guides and handbooks for clubs and associations have been around for years. But business has mushroomed as consumer-oriented companies, from carmakers to retailers, financial services to telecommunications groups, have discovered the appeal of publications delivered directly to customers as a way of marketing brands in a fiercely competitive media environment.

The general manager of Forum, a Munich-based corporate publishing company, who also acts as the federation's spokesman, says:

> The range of communications channels now available has forced advertisers to become more focused. Television viewers' choice has gone from terrestrial channels to countless alternatives on cable and satellite. Meanwhile, print media have been in decline. Traditional newspapers have suffered falling circulations – not always compensated for by freesheets – and magazines have been volatile.

Customer publishing is filling the gap. *BMW* – the 108-page customer magazine for that other German luxury carmaker – is every bit as glossy as its Mercedes equivalent and has a worldwide circulation of 3.2 million. *Waitrose Food Illustrated*, published monthly by the UK supermarket group, runs to 138 pages per issue.

'Custom publishing is a very effective marketing tool to position a brand among its customers' (Forum). The federation's research demonstrates, it says, declining demand for TV and traditional print media, with only customer magazines and the Internet on the ascendant. Julia Hutchinson, chief operating officer of the Association of Publishing Agencies, the UK trade association, says: 'UK customer publishing now accounts for about 5 per cent of companies' total marketing spending, with an annual growth rate of 16 per cent.' That compares with gradually falling rates for traditional print media and sharply declining ones for TV.

'Customer magazines are read on average for 25 minutes. That's a much longer attention span than many other media,' she adds. Such comments may sound odd for anyone recalling early customer publications. Uninspired content, unappealing design and crude photography often made such magazines embarrassing. Articles would be knocked out by company press officers, perhaps piggybacking on a foreign launch to produce an instant travel piece alongside a heavy-handed encomium to the group's latest product.

Today's customer magazines contain a mix of lifestyle, health, sport and travel, explains Wilfred Mons, the Dutchman who publishes nine national editions of Mercedes magazine outside the core German market. In an attempt to ensure that the magazine is read, building brand loyalty as a by-product, each edition is tailored to its national audience. In Mercedes' case, the Danish version takes about 75 per cent of its content from the core German edition, which is produced separately by a Munich-based group. By contrast, in the 100-page Italian edition, about 80 per cent of the material is originated locally.

The goal is to make such publications as attractive as paid-for magazines and many contain genuine advertising, which is a testament to their perceived effectiveness. Julia Hutchinson regards customer magazines as part of the marketing mix, no longer viewed as a sideline of PR. They are now produced as a joint effort between marketing, PR and advertising departments and include much more sophisticated content.

However, listening is only part of the story. It is also important to be a customer advocate and, as much as possible, to take the customers' side on issues, understanding their point of view.[58] The UK bank Lloyds TSB has established a reputation as being a listening bank. 'Marketing memo: Creating customer evangelists' describes six keys to creating customers who feel so strongly about companies and brands that they go way beyond just purchasing and consuming their products and services.

▽ Attracting and retaining customers

Developing loyalty programmes

Two popular customer loyalty programmes that companies can offer are frequency programmes and club marketing programmes. **Frequency programmes (FPs)** are designed to provide rewards to customers who buy frequently and in substantial amounts. They can help build long-term loyalty with high customer lifetime value customers, creating cross-selling opportunities in the process. Originally pioneered by the airlines, hotels, and credit card companies, FPs now exist in many other types of businesses. For example, today most supermarket chains offer price club cards, which provide member customers with discounts on particular items. However, perhaps their real value to the issuer is to provide data on customers' purchasing patterns.

Marketing memo

Creating customer evangelists

McConnell and Huba assert that *customer evangelists* not only buy a company's products or services but believe in them so much that they are compelled to spread the word and voluntarily recruit their friends and colleagues on the company's behalf. On their own 'church of the customer' blog site (www.churchofthecustomer.com) they offer six tips for marketing evangelism:

1 **Customer plus-delta** Understand what evangelists love by continuously gathering their input.

2 **Publicise your knowledge** Release your own knowledge, data or intellectual property into a fast-moving distribution network. Sharing knowledge freely makes it more accessible, reducing your biggest threat: obscurity. It's liable to fall into the hands of people who will tell others about it. People talking about your knowledge increases its perceived and actual value.

3 **Build the buzz** Keep customer evangelists talking by providing them with tools, programmes and features to demonstrate their passion.

4 **Create community** Give like-minded customers the chance to meet.

5 **Make bite-size chunks** Bite-size chunks of products and services reduce risk, improve sales cycles and offer upfront value. Even if a customer doesn't purchase, he or she may spread favourable word of mouth.

6 **Create a cause** Companies that strive for a higher purpose – such as supporting 'freedom', as Porsche and Air France do – often find that customers, vendors, suppliers and employees naturally root for their success. Customer evangelists crave emotional connection and validation; a well-defined cause generates emotional commitment. When your brand, product or service aspires to change the world, altruism and capitalism converge.

Sources: B. McConnell and J. Huba (2006) Learning to leverage the lunatic fringe, *Point*, July–August; M. Krauss (2006) Work to convert customers into evangelists, *Marketing News*, 15 December, 6; B. McConnell and J. Huba (2003) *Creating Customer Evangelists: How Loyal Customers Become a Volunteer Sales Force*, New York: Kaplan Business.

▽ Loyalty Management UK

On 16 September 2002 Loyalty Management UK (LMUK) launched the Nectar loyalty card. Unlike the majority of such cards, which have only one sponsor, the Nectar scheme now has 11 sponsors: Adams, Allsports, Barclaycard, BP, Debenhams, e-Energy, Ford, Sainsbury's, Thresher Group, Vodafone and – in Northern Ireland only – Winemark. With more than 13 million Nectar accounts set up since launch, the company deals with a huge volume of customer queries by telephone, email, and letter and through the scheme's website. 'When LMUK launched, we'd already implemented a CRM system [from Siebel Systems] at our multisite contact centres to track and manage customer inquiries,' says Gerard Whelan, LMUK's customer service manager. 'Following the success of the launch, however, customer contact volumes were higher than forecast, and the contact centres struggled to cope,' he adds. The company noticed that a high proportion of enquiries were fairly straightforward and related to the mechanics of the programme (such as questions about where the card could be obtained and used, and where points could be redeemed). It therefore decided that the best approach was to let customers find the answers to such questions themselves on the Nectar website.

The RightNow Loyalty Management Service is one of the new breed of on-demand (i.e., web-hosted) CRM systems. Greg Gianforte, RightNow's founder and chief executive, is emphatic that this is the way the CRM market is heading. 'On-demand CRM is transforming the way corporations consume enterprise software,' he says. 'This model eliminates 80 to 90 per cent of the total cost of ownership associated with traditional CRM software, and also eliminates all the headaches associated with infrastructure.'

Source: A. Stewart (2004) *Financial Times*, 12 February.

Typically, the first company to introduce an FP in an industry gains the most benefit, especially if competitors are slow to respond. After competitors respond, FPs can become a financial burden to all the offering companies, but some companies are more efficient and creative in managing FPs.

Many companies have created **club membership programmes**. Club membership programmes can be open to everyone who purchases a product or service, or can be limited to an affinity group or to those willing to pay a small fee. Although open clubs are good for building a database or capturing customers from competitors, limited membership clubs are more powerful long-term loyalty builders. Fees and membership conditions prevent those with only a fleeting interest in a company's products from joining. These clubs attract and keep those customers who are responsible for the largest portion of business. Some highly successful clubs include the following.

▽ Apple

Apple encourages owners of its computers to form local Apple-user groups. By 2001, there were over 600 such groups, ranging in size from fewer than 25 members to over 1000 members. The user groups provide Apple owners with opportunities to learn more about their computers, share ideas and get product discounts. They sponsor special activities and events and perform a community service. A visit to Apple's website will help a customer find a nearby user group.[59]

Local user groups have proliferated among Apple owners, thanks to links on the Apple website that help visitors locate them. The groups help executives such as Steve Jobs keep in close touch with the company's customers and their needs.
Source: John G. Mabanglo/Corbis

▽ Harley-Davidson

The world-famous motorcycle company sponsors the Harley Owners Group (HOG), which now numbers 650,000 members in over 1200 chapters. The first-time buyer of a Harley-Davidson motorcycle gets a free one-year HOG membership. HOG benefits include a magazine called *Hog Tales*, a touring handbook, emergency road service, a specially designed insurance programme, theft reward service, discount hotel rates and a Fly & Ride programme enabling members to rent Harley bikes while on vacation. The company also maintains an extensive website devoted to the HOG, which includes information on club chapters, events and a special members-only section.[60]

Personalising marketing

Company personnel can create strong bonds with customers by individualising and personalising relationships. In essence, thoughtful companies turn their customers into clients and then into advocates. One distinction that has been drawn is as follows:

> Customers may be nameless to the institution; clients cannot be nameless. Customers are served as part of the mass or as part of larger segments; clients are served on an individual basis. Customers are served by anyone who happens to be available; clients are served by the professional assigned to them.

An increasingly essential ingredient for the best relationship marketing today is the right technology. Table 11.2 highlights five imperatives of CRM and shows where technology fits in. Dell Computer could not customise computer ordering for its global corporate customers without advances in Web technology. Companies are using email, websites, call centres, databases and database software to foster continuous contact between company and customer.

Ecommerce companies looking to attract and retain customers are discovering that personalisation goes beyond creating customised information. The BBC, British archetype of an old media company, is reaping the benefits of customising its offerings, a practice that is taking it well beyond its commercial rivals in UK broadcasting.

▽ British Broadcasting Corporation

BBC iPlayer, now in trials, lets British users download current radio and TV programmes up to seven days after broadcast. Not only can viewers download content, they can also build on it and share it. One project, for instance, lets users download footage from BBC news and science shows, remix them, and eventually share them online. Even more radical is http://backstage.bbc.co.uk, which provides data, resources and support for Internet developers and designers – inside and outside the BBC – to share in order to build prototypes of new concepts using BBC material. One consumer-created prototype called Sport Map allows people to find the nearest soccer team on the map and get its latest news – a service bound to be popular in a country full of avid soccer fans.

Source: K. Capell (2006) BBC: step right into the telly, *BusinessWeek*, 24 July, 52; http://backstage.bbc.co.uk.

Table 11.2 Breaking down customer relationship management: what customer relationship really comprises

CRM imperative				
Acquiring the right customer	Crafting the right value proposition	Instituting the best processes	Motivating employees	Learning to retain customers
You get it when . . .				
• You've identified your most valuable customers. • You've calculated your share of their wallet for your goods and services.	• You've studied what products or services your customers need today and will need tomorrow. • You've surveyed what products or services your competitors offer today and will offer tomorrow. • You've spotted what products or services you should be offering.	• You've researched the best way to deliver your products or services to customers, including the alliances you need to strike, the technologies you need to invest in and the service capabilities you need to develop or acquire.	• You know what tools your employees need to foster customer relationships. • You've identified the HR systems you need to institute in order to boost employee loyalty.	• You've learned why customers defect and how to win them back. • You've analysed what your competitors are doing to win your high-value customers. • Your senior management monitors customer defection metrics.
CRM technology can help . . .				
• Analyse customer revenue and cost data to identify current and future high-value customers. • Target your direct-marketing efforts better.	• Capture relevant product and service behaviour data. • Create new distribution channels. • Develop new pricing models. • Build communities.	• Process transactions faster. • Provide better information to the front line. • Manage logistics and the supply chain more efficiently. • Catalyse collaborative commerce.	• Align incentives and metrics. • Deploy knowledge management systems.	• Track customer defection and retention levels. • Track customer service satisfaction levels.

Source: D. K. Rigby, F. F. Reichheld and P. Schefter (2002) Avoid the four perils of CRM, *Harvard Business Review*, February, 106. Copyright © 2002 by the President and Fellows of Harvard College. All rights reserved. Reproduced with permission.

At the same time, online companies need to make sure their attempts to create relationships with customers do not misfire, as when customers are bombarded by computer-generated recommendations that consistently miss the mark. Buy a lot of baby gifts on Amazon.com, and your personalised recommendations suddenly don't look so personal! Etailers need to recognise the limitations of online personalisation at the same time as they try harder to find technology and processes that really work.

Companies are also recognising the importance of the personal component to CRM and what happens once customers make actual contact. As the US business guru Jeffrey Pfeffer puts it, 'The best companies build cultures in which front line people are empowered to do what's needed to take care of the customer.' He cites examples of firms such as SAS, the Scandinavian airline, which engineered a turnaround based in part on the insight that a customer's impressions of a company are formed through myriad small interactions – checking in, boarding the plane, eating a meal.[61]

Creating institutional ties

The company may supply customers with special equipment or computer links that help customers manage orders, payroll and inventory. Customers are less inclined to switch to another supplier when this would involve high capital costs, high search costs or the loss of loyal-customer discounts.

Recapturing customers

Regardless of the nature of the category or how hard companies may try, some customers inevitably become inactive or drop out. The challenge is to reactivate dissatisfied customers through win-back strategies.[62] It's often easier to reattract ex-customers (because the company knows their names and histories) than to find new ones. The key is to analyse the causes of customer defection through exit interviews and lost-customer surveys and win back only those who have strong profit potential.[63]

Patronise or personalise?

Customer relationship marketing professionals, at the end of the day, have to navigate the narrow channel between earning customer favour and loyalty and irritating customers. They may be tempted to seek efficiency (to them) at the cost of becoming ineffective by irritating or patronising the customer. The challenge facing companies is to achieve the right balance between efficiency and effectiveness; between direct human communication and CRM automated systems. With banks in mind a frustrated customer might respond, 'Press 1 to make an appointment to see me; 2 to query a missing payment; 3 to transfer the call to my living room in case I'm there.' CRM can work, providing the goals are modest and there is some worthwhile benefit for customers. However, its capacity to irritate and repel is massive so it needs to be carried out sensitively.

▽ The experience economy

The value experience

The term 'experience economy' was first coined in 1999 by Pine and Gilmore[64] when they described an advanced service economy that began to market a 'mass customisation' of service offerings. Using theatre as a metaphor they argued that business should function in a similar way to a theatre that develops and presents a performance which it hopes will be appreciated by its audience. To achieve this requires the input of numerous attributes or benefits, some of which are tangible (such as props) and some intangible (such as acting and set expertise). If it all goes well on the night the audience leaves after having had a pleasurable 'experience'. This they claimed will produce repeat business and the 'transformation' that has occurred in their expectations will enhance the customer-perceived value of the company's brand. This in turn will enable it to charge a premium price. In experience terms, the memory itself is now the market offering. Although the concept was originally developed with business-to-business markets in mind Pine and Gilmore claimed that it could be applied effectively to other markets. Early examples included leisure, hospitality, tourism and urban planning.

The core concept at issue here is that of economic value. The concept of the 'experience economy' claims that customising a product turns it into a service. Customising a service turns it into an experience and customising an experience turns it into a transformation. This argument is essentially about customer-perceived value. As CPV attributes or benefits can be either tangible or intangible what determines an attractive purchase experience lies in the expertise with which a company undertakes the development and presentation of the final market offering.

Successful theatrical performances do deliver enjoyable experiences but for a company or theatre to establish a strong brand appeal the enjoyable outputs have to be sustained. 'Greatness' lasts only as long as someone fails to imagine something better. Successful companies know that their CPV offerings have to consistently improve. However, recent productivity, technology and transparency developments have placed increasing demands on their value offerings as product life cycles shorten under fierce pressure of global competition.

The Pine and Gilmore thesis, although elegantly expressed as a theatrical metaphor, has a serious flaw. Unconstrained customer expectations in rigorous buyers' markets are unrealistic for most suppliers who have to make a profit. Weissman and Mosby[65] believe that the solution to the problem of ever-escalating expectations lies in sustained effective market communications. It is a matter of convincing customers that a good company really does offer a better CPV package. However, what happens when the key distinguishing experience becomes increasingly difficult to discern?

Companies have long realised the necessity of building and sustaining brand reputations by satisfying their customers. However the experience economy notion implies something a lot more aspirational and personal. Peters[66] refers to this as 'dream fulfilment' – the next rung on the quality–service–experience ladder. Companies seeking to 'get up close and personal' to their customers often experience difficulty in knowing if their brand is sufficiently positively differentiated.

A key question for companies to think through is just what constitutes a business experience? What do they need to offer to succeed? Neither of these questions were addressed by Pine and Gilmore in their original text. For an experience to be effective it has to engage an individual in its delivery. It is a two-way event. It is an act that implies co-creation between a provider and the customer; the result is a memorable experience that has a high level of CPV. As a result customers will be prepared to pay a premium price.

According to Prahalad and Ramaswamy,[67] deregulation, emerging markets, new forms of regulation, convergence of technologies and industries and ubiquitous connectivity have changed many facets of the business world. These factors have changed the nature of consumers. Today they are informed, networked, active and global. These factors have also changed the nature of companies, which are now able to fragment their value chain in ways that were not possible in the past.

These contextual changes in markets are enabling a new form of value creation, co-creation, in which value is not created exclusively in the firm and then exchanged with the customer, but is co-created by the firm and the customer. As a result the world of business is moving away from a company- and product-centric view of value creation towards an experience-centric view of the co-creation of value. High-quality interactions that enable an individual customer to co-create unique experiences with the company are the key to unlocking new sources of competitive advantage. Products, or as this text argues, market offerings are merely artefacts around which compelling individual experiences are created.[68]

Marketing memo

Key steps in the co-creation process

1 Define clear objectives for the project.

2 Discover who are the right customers to involve in the process.

3 Work with customers to discover what they really want to include in a market offering.

4 Design market offerings-systems jointly to meet those customers' needs. This includes selecting the partners to be included in a company's network.

5 Decide how to share the customer-perceived value.

6 Overcome internal resistance to change – with seller, buyer and partner organisations.

Sources: www.onedegree.ca/2007/09/co-creation-1s.html; www.promisecorp.com.

Pret creates handmade natural foods avoiding the obscure chemical, additives and preservatives common to so much of the 'prepared' and 'fast' food on the market today

Source: Phillipe Hays/Rex Features

Hence companies such as Costa Coffee, Pret A Manger and Starbucks provide a value 'experience' as well as providing their key market offerings.

▽ Pret A Manger

Pret A Manger, the distinctive sandwich bar operator, is to be transformed into an international business following its sale to Bridgepoint Capital, the private equity firm, for an estimated £345 million. The company's co-founders, Julian Metcalfe and Sinclair Beecham, are expected to pocket at least £50 million in cash from the sale, which will see Goldman Sachs, Bridgepoint's adviser, take a minority stake of about 20 per cent in the company. However, the duo are thought to be leaving a similar amount in the company in a complex 'earnout' deal, which, depending on performance, could boost the headline price closer to the £400 million they had hoped for when they put it up for sale last year.

The private equity firm is expected to emerge with a stake of about 60 per cent from a total equity funding package of about £230 million. McDonald's, the US fast-food giant that bought into Pret A Manger in 2001, is selling its entire 33 per cent holding. The management team, led by Larry Billett, the chairman, and Clive Schlee, the chief executive, will stay with the business and with the co-founders will have a combined 20 per cent stake. The protracted sale of Pret, which has been handled by Rothschild, has been delayed by the credit crunch. The diverging interests of the shareholders are also said to have held things up.

The acquisition of Pret by Bridgepoint bolsters a portfolio of consumer-facing brands that includes Pets at Home, Fat Face, Molton Brown and Virgin Active. Metcalfe and Beecham, who were college friends, opened the first Pret outlet in 1986 to sell freshly prepared sandwiches using only natural, preservative-free ingredients.

The chain has 175 shops in Britain, 14 in New York , 11 in Hong Kong and a single outlet in Singapore. It employs almost 4000 people and had sales last year of £223 million, up from £194 million in 2007. Bridgepoint, which first tried to acquire Pret in 2001, said it planned to expand the shop estate by about 15 per cent a year, with 30 shops due to open in 2008, including 7 in New York. Metcalfe said: 'This is an exciting time for all of us at Pret. Bridgepoint shares our vision, understands our culture and will support our roll-out plan globally, while maintaining everything that makes Pret work for our customers and staff.'[69]

Kotler's concept of CPV, introduced earlier in this chapter, could now be extended to include an additional attribute input. Customer-perceived value is a function of customer-perceived quality attributes and customer-perceived pricing (i.e., transactional attributes) plus a positive experiential attribute. Poulsson and Kale argue that a positive experience should include the five elements in the 'experience scorecard' memo below:

1 **personal relevance**: the individual's internal state of arousal, activation and preparedness to engage in a specific experience;

2 **novelty**: an attractive change to regularly experienced stimuli;

3 **surprise**: the emotion generated by the appeal of something that is attractive and new;

4 **learning**: when an experience has been well received, the resultant learning becomes a positive influence on engagement with the provider;

5 **engagement**: the process by which providers seek to co-create CPV offerings with customers.

Source: S. H. G. Poulsson and S. H. Kale (2004) The experience economy and commercial experiences, *The Marketing Review*, 4, 267–77.

In general the best approach is to provide consumers with the opportunity to create their own story, as a successful market offering is part of the larger narrative of customers' lives. Harley-Davidson has achieved this effectively with its HOG website. However, not all purchasing 'experiences' need such a pronounced emphasis on the experiential attributes of a CPV offering. Commodity items such as bread, confectionery and salt are likely to require less perceived value in terms of quality and experiential attributes. Here the main emphasis will usually be on price but wise companies should not forget that a too cavalier approach towards commodity customers will result in desertion to the competition. The experience economy is a relationship marketing concept that needs to be interpreted by providers, in an appropriate way for their market activities. It is a matter of fine tuning market offerings in terms of customer effectiveness and provider efficiency and with regard to the wider societal implications of marketing activities as argued by the 'critical' movement.[70]

The empowered customer

As buyers' markets intensify so customers increasingly expect more value for their money. Wise companies seek to discover what their customers want and then attempt to deliver more than their customers expect if they intend to develop profitable brands.[71]

European Commission activity

The past US president John F. Kennedy[72] once said 'Consumers, by definition, include us all . . . yet they are the only important group . . . whose views are often not heard.' The European Commission is working hard to change this. Empowered consumers are viewed as good for Europe's economy as they encourage companies to work hard, compete and provide quality offerings in the marketplace. It is also seen as a way of breaking down the barriers between Europe's national markets. The internal market in Europe will offer empowered consumers more choice. The Commission has established a new system – the European Consumer Market Watch – to investigate whether various sectors of the economy were delivering the information, choice and value for money consumers deserved.

▽ EU cross-border initiatives

Legislation has been passed to cut charges for roaming – making calls from a mobile phone when abroad – to levels commensurate with the incurred costs. A Single European Payments Area has been set up to facilitate payments and transfers and the Commission has campaigned to make it easier for consumers to access, assess and compare banking services.

Market paradigm change

Most markets are characterised by an excess of providers, thus empowering consumers through the mechanism of their choice of supplier. Paradoxically, and reflecting the past sellers' market conditions, much of the literature on consumer empowerment focuses on consumers' efforts to regain control of their consumption processes from providers. However, many suppliers now set out to achieve success by seeking to empower consumers. The mechanism by which this takes place consists of researching and providing what consumers want – that is, the right mix of quality, price and experiential attributes. This provides many 'old school' suppliers with a conundrum as most traditional marketing techniques are market centric. Gross rating points, for example, define message delivery volume. Even the 4Ps, product, price, place and promotion, speak more to how a company wants to conduct business than about how consumers want to engage with the brand. Integrated marketing requires a deep knowledge of consumers' habits, needs and passions. Regular market research should be viewed by providers as an investment decision to enable them to know what mix of attributes to include in their offerings and not as a cost decision to be cut as soon as fortunes falter.

Marketing to the empowered consumer

Until recently there was an observable distinction between traditional brand and direct marketing activity. The former focused on creating awareness and share of mind mainly by means of TV, radio and print advertising. The latter concentrated on inspiring a specific action and share of wallet via mail, telemarketing and email. This distinction is rapidly fading as providers realise that both skill sets need to be integrated and directed to securing customer engagement. However most marketers are still organised around their traditional product lines, markets or technologies. As consumers take up the new technologies that give them fingertip control of how, when and if they want to be marketed to, marketers should seriously reconsider the traditional 4P mantra, and engage customers on their own terms.

   To achieve this requires the adoption by providers of a customer-centric organisational philosophy that really does put the customer at the centre of functional activity.[73] The new mantra should emphasise the question, 'Why should consumers buy from an organisation when they can favour several competitors?' It is surprising how many companies allow their agency partners to assume too great an influence over their marketing activity. Marketers need to take a more interactive, cross-disciplinary approach to campaign planning that integrates all the activities necessary to develop the required mix of customer-perceived value attributes.

Interactive marketing

(See also Chapters 4, 17 and 18)

The term 'interactive marketing' was first proposed by Deighton,[74] who described it as 'the ability to address the customer, remember what the customer says and address the customer again in a way that illustrates that we remember what the customer has told us'. (See Chapter 18 for more discussion of this channel.) It should be noted that interactive marketing is not the same thing as online marketing, although interactivity is facilitated by Internet technology. The ability to 'get up close and personal' with customers is boosted when it becomes possible to collect and analyse customer information over the Web. Amazon has developed interactive marketing to a fine art and suggests books that fit customers' purchasing profiles.

Cadbury/Schweppes (now demerged) used interactive marketing to raise awareness of its use of 100 per cent genuine flavours for their 7Up soft drink in the United States. Visitors to the brand name's website are able to personalise the rabbits who serve as the drink's TV advertising mascots. They can personalise the rabbits with an array of costumes and helpfully provided burps. Text-to-speech technology enables consumers to create custom messages to transmit to others by email. In the United Kingdom Britvic has held the 7Up franchise since 1987 but has not used sophisticated interactive marketing techniques.

Many companies are now starting to show an interest in how they could extend the benefits of information and communications technology in their marketing activities.[75] As more and more households sign up for broadband in the United Kingdom and TV advertising goes online, providers are starting to show a deep interest in Web 2.0, the second phase of the Internet, where consumers can move from information and search to content and user-generated interactivity (see Chapter 4). Problems remain, however, in relation to such issues as payment for the server capacity and bandwidth for commercial and free-to-air broadcasters.

Another interesting development is the use of mobile phones to revive coupon redemption. Procter & Gamble, Del Monte and Kimberly-Clark have joined up to explore the viability of a mobile marketing venture in selected supermarket stores. The companies offer marketing software that consumers can download to their mobile phones, which will present redeemable coupons for discounts on certain products.

Complexity of markets

Complexity has been one of the most frequently used terms for some time now. Managers talk about complex systems, complex interrelationships, complex problems, etc. There is hardly a presentation or discussion among executives without some reference to complexity – for instance, the complexity of markets, market offerings and processes.[76] In many respects management is the art and/or science of handling complexity. In today's fiercely competitive world companies are finding that complexity is becoming more difficult to manage. On the one hand it is necessary to bring a system under control but it is wise not to adopt too tight a management modus operandi as this can slow down the ability of a company to respond to important market movements. As business becomes an ever more dynamic activity so wise firms build in some degree of flexibility to respond to market forces. Thus loose/tight approaches hold the promise of getting the right balance between market effective and provider efficiency.

Market types

Economists describe markets as places where buyers and sellers gather to expedite exchange. As business became a world rather than a local, national or international affair so, in a sense, there is now one global market with many specialist sub-markets.

Figure 11.8 Structure of flows in a modern exchange economy

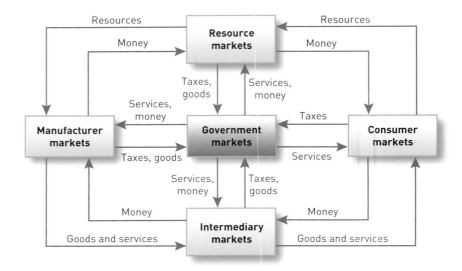

Communication between the selling and buying parties is a key characteristic of market trading but has greatly changed in nature as modern technological communication advances have made it possible for this to occur electronically. If the global market is viewed as a digital picture then each can usefully be regarded as a separate market. The global market is highly complex and this is further complicated by the challenging dynamics of modern buyers' markets in the world as a whole, but particularly in the developed nations.

To begin to understand this complexity five basic markets have traditionally been viewed to be a promising start. Figure 11.8 presents this basic structure and shows the flows in a modern exchange economy.

This is, of course, an oversimplification. The complexity of modern markets demands a deep and continuous understanding of the realities evident and emerging in every market of interest to companies. The suppliers' markets evident in most of the developed countries and the export potential that became available in the underdeveloped countries have led to a business approach that has been heavily supply oriented. The added complexity of widespread buyers' choice in most markets has brought many companies to deeply challenging times. So has marketing entered a mid-life crisis? This text has argued that marketing management is also a wide canvas. Theory and practice have their place but how to mix knowledge with effective market operations is a massive challenge for companies as there are no easy answers or quick fixes.

Emotional turn

Emotions matter as they can be fashioned to influence and change attitudes in marketing communications. They affect the way in which an audience can sense their past, present and future: all can seem bright, dull or darkened by emotional outlooks. Emotional Turn, or as it is sometimes known Affective Marketing (also Affective Economics), emphasises the emotional engagement that marketers seek to gain with their target audiences. Recent advances in the study of neurological and psychological insights – originating from brain scanning and neurological experiments – on basic emotional processes in the brain have led marketers to assess their application potential. Hansen and Christensen have brought together much of the theory and understanding of the role that emotion plays in advertising and marketing communications.[77] Their work provides a solid underpinning for all marketers who wish to understand the interactions between feelings, moods and emotionally based reactions to advertising, market offerings, brands, and hence consumer choice.

Today marketers influence people differently from the ways in which it was done in the heyday of sellers' markets, when companies tended to place the emphasis on rational messages to further their intentions. As consumer choice increased following the explosion of buyers' markets marketing practitioners have sought to connect with their targeted audiences by means of emotional communications.[78] As buyers' markets become ever more fiercely competitive marketers are now seeking to achieve customer engagement. Many might wonder what the practical difference is between engagement and connecting emotionally. The answer lies in the realisation that consumers have a lot more market power today. The concept of engagement recognises this power and seeks to share it between consumers and marketers. As a consequence consumers are key parties to co-creating their perceived value offerings. So leading marketers in the experience economy are seeking to engage all five senses in their brand building and are viewing this as the leading edge of their marketing.

Emotion triggers

Emotion lies at the acceptance and perception of many customer-valued brands. It can be expressed in many different forms in advertising. In the United Kingdom, Tesco have used celebrities in soap drama type advertisements to engage with their audience. These have included Prunella Scales and Jane Horrocks in a long-running series and The Spice Girls in late 2007 to take advantage of their twilight performances and to boost pre-Christmas shopping.

The main appeals designed to elicit emotional responses are as follows:[79]

- **Fear**: This is generally used in one of two ways. First to demonstrate the negativity and undesirability of certain behaviours that might put the individual and society in danger. Many governments brief marketers to help them with important messages such as the dangers inherent in drinking and driving. Financial firms sponsor TV dramas on the commercial channels and invite viewers to take care of their families in every advertising break. Second, to shame audiences. Examples here would include anti-dandruff shampoos and anti-ageing cream advertisements.
- **Humour**: This draws attention and stimulates interest and is widely used throughout Europe. Marketers, however, should always realise that what is amusing and funny in one culture may not transfer to another. The Walkers' series of TV advertisements featuring Gary Lineker, the ex-international footballer and current TV soccer presenter, in amusing situations did much to boost the company's sales of potato crisps.
- **Animation**: Recent and dramatic advances in animation technology provide the opportunity to register effectively both with child and adult audiences. Children appreciate mini-stories featuring their favourite TV and film characters. Adults laugh at the 'Ask Churchill the dog' screenings.
- **Sex**: The use of sex and sexual innuendo is both powerful and controversial as it usually attracts attention. Recent screenings in the United Kingdom include campaigns for fast-moving consumer goods – such as confectionery and cosmetics – and durables such as cars.
- **Music**: A powerful aid to re-call. Old screenings of lawn fertiliser advertisements can easily be reused every season and audiences warm to familiar jingles. Classical music is frequently used to suggest 'quality' in some shape or form.
- **Fantasy and surrealism**: To provide a distraction from expected or everyday life events and so create 'space' for a market offering message. The advertisements are different and either appeal or distract. Guinness has acquired a quality reputation over the years and increasingly car companies such as Citroën, Honda and Toyota are following suit.

Mood indigo

Literature research has shown that persuasive impact is greater if the target audience is in a happy, benevolent mood. A limitation of many studies concerning mood and advertising effectiveness, however, is that mood is manipulated under experimental, 'laboratory' conditions. As many authors state, these studies require replication under more realistic conditions. Research by Bonner et al.[80] has shown that target audiences are often in a better mood on Sundays.

▽ Mood management by John Lewis

COMPUTERS INSTALLED.

SOFAS COVERED.

A LITTLE FAITH IN HUMANITY RESTORED.

We're not about to suggest changing your sofa is going to change your life. But we do like to think the little added touches we do can make all the difference to your day.

It could simply be not feeling pressured into making a purchase. Or having a collection point where you'll find everything you've bought waiting for you. Or some free nursery advice at a time when you're a bit overwhelmed by what lies ahead. Or just simply your new television being guaranteed free for 5 years.

Because in a perfect world, we'd like everyone to leave us with something, even if they buy nothing. So for an unlimited time, an unlimited offer. A little bit of humanity. Free at John Lewis.

johnlewis.com

Source: Creatives Simon Morris, Patrick McLelland and Clive Pickering for John Lewis plc. Full page advertisement in the *Guardian*, 25 June 2008, 38. Reproduced with permission.

Creating customer value, satisfaction and loyalty to develop and sustain long-term advantage in highly competitive markets is the marketer's commission. Such a commission requires vision, mission and a determination to 'delight' customers for as César Ritz, the famous Swiss hotel proprietor quipped, 'Le client n'a jamais tort' (literally, 'The customer is never wrong'[81]).

▽ SUMMARY

1 Customers are value maximisers. They form an expectation of value and act on it. Buyers will buy from the firm that they perceive to offer the highest customer-delivered value, defined as the difference between total customer benefits and total customer cost.

2 A buyer's satisfaction is a function of the product's perceived performance and the buyer's expectations. Recognising that high satisfaction leads to high customer loyalty, many companies today are aiming for TCS – total customer satisfaction. For such companies, customer satisfaction is both a goal and a marketing tool.

3 Losing profitable customers can dramatically affect a firm's profits. The cost of attracting a new customer is estimated to be five times the cost of keeping a current customer happy. The key to retaining customers is relationship marketing.

4 Quality is the totality of features and characteristics of a product or service that bear on its ability to satisfy stated or implied needs. Marketers play a key role in achieving high levels of total quality so that firms remain solvent and profitable.

5 Marketing managers must calculate customer lifetime values of their customer base to understand their profit implications. They must also determine ways to increase the value of the customer base.

6 Companies are also becoming skilled in customer relationship management, which focuses on developing programmes to attract and retain the right customers and meet the individual needs of those valued customers.

7 Future marketing managers should be able to competently develop and maintain customer relations. In this respect, companies may not only be competing against other companies but may also belong to networks that are competing against other networks.

8 The world of business is moving away from a company- and product-centric view of value creation towards an experience-centric view of the co-creation of value.

9 The experience economy is a relationship marketing concept that needs to be interpreted by providers, in an appropriate way for their market activities. It is a matter of fine tuning market offerings in terms of customer effectiveness and provider efficiency and with regard to the wider societal implications of marketing activities as argued by the 'critical' movement.

10 Most markets are characterised by an excess of providers thus empowering consumers through the mechanism of their choice of supplier.

11 The added complexity of widespread buyers' choice in most markets has brought many companies to deeply challenging times.

▽ APPLICATIONS

Marketing debate

Online versus offline privacy As more and more firms practise relationship marketing and develop customer databases, privacy issues are emerging as an important topic. Consumers and public interest groups are scrutinising – and sometimes criticising – the privacy policies of firms and raising concerns about potential theft of online credit card information or other potentially sensitive or confidential financial information. Others maintain that the online privacy fears are unfounded and that security issues are every bit as much a concern in the offline world. They argue that the opportunity to steal information exists virtually everywhere and that it is up to the consumer to protect their interests.

Take a position: (1) Privacy is a bigger issue in the online than the offline world *versus* Privacy is no different online than offline. (2) Consumers on the whole receive more benefit than risk from marketers knowing their personal information.

Marketing discussion

Consider the lifetime value of customers (CLV). Choose a business and show how you would go about developing a quantitative formulation that captures the concept. How would that business change if it totally embraced the customer equity concept and maximised CLV?

▽ REFERENCES

[1]A. Michaels and J. Reed (2007) Alfa rewrites its service history, *Financial Times*, 1 January.

[2]R. Schieffer (2005) *Ten Key Consumer Insights*, Mason, OH: Thomson.

[3]D. Peppers and M. Rogers (2005) Customers don't grow on trees, *Fast Company*, July, pp. 25–6.

[4]P. L. Dubois, A. Jolibert and H. Mühlbacher (2007) *Marketing Management: A Value-Creation Process*, Basingstoke, England, pp. 1–28; see also F. E. Webster (1997) The future role of marketing in the organisation, in D. R. Lehmann and K. E. Jocz (eds.), *Reflections on the Futures of Marketing*, Cambridge, MA: Marketing Science Institute; G. Hooley, N. F. Piercy and B. Nicoulaud (2008) *Marketing Strategy and Competitive Positioning*, 4th edn, Harlow, UK, Prentice Hall, pp. 3–6; see also A. Payne and S. Holt (2001) Diagnosing customer value: integrating the

value process and relationship marketing, *British Journal of Management*, 12, 159–82.

[5]For discussion of some of the issues involved see G. Urban (2005) *Don't Just Relate: Advocate*, Upper Saddle River, NJ: Pearson Education / Wharton School Publishing.

[6]See G. L. Urban and J. R. Hauser (2004) 'Listening in' to find and explore new combinations of customer needs, *Journal of Marketing*, 68 (April), 72–87.

[7]A. Hill (2008) DSG's new year gift to Browett is a heavy one, *Financial Times*, 3 January.

[8]S. P. Gounaris, N. P. Tzempelikos and K. Chatzpagiotou (2007) The relationships of customer-perceived value, satisfaction and behavioural intentions, *Journal of Relationship Marketing*, 6(1), 63–87.

[9]A. Smith (1970 [1776]) *An Enquiry into the Nature and Causes of the Wealth of Nations*, A. Skinner (ed.), Harmondsworth, England: Pelican.

[10]J. C. Fandos Roig, J. Sanchez Garcia, M. A. Moliner Tena and J. Liorens Monzonis (2006) Customer perceived value in banking services, *International Journal of Bank Marketing*, 24(5), 266–83.

[11]For more on customer-perceived value, see D. C. Swaddling and C. Miller (2001) *Customer Power*, Dublin, OH: The Wellington Press.

[12]G. Hamel (1996) Strategy as revolution, *Harvard Business Review*, July–August, 69–82.

[13]M. Schrage (2007) Customers want loyalty not perfection, *Financial Times*, 2 May.

[14]M. J. Lanning (1998) *Delivering Profitable Value*, Oxford, England: Capstone.

[15]F. Crawford and R. Mathews (2001) *The Myth of Excellence: Why Great Companies Never Try to Be the Best of Everything*, New York: Crown Business, pp. 85–100.

[16]M. Tsiros, V. Mittal and W. T. Ross Jr. (2004) The role of attributions in customer satisfaction: a re-examination, *Journal of Consumer Research*, 31 (September), 476–83.

[17]For a succinct review, see R. L. Oliver (2006) Customer satisfaction research, in R. Grover and M. Vriens (eds.) *Handbook of Marketing Research*, Thousand Oaks, CA: Sage Publications, pp. 569–87.

[18]For some provocative analysis and discussion, see P. K. Kopalle and D. R. Lehmann (2006) Setting quality expectations when entering a market: what should the promise be?, *Marketing Science*, 25 (January–February), 8–24; and S. Fournier and D. Glenmick (1999) Rediscovering satisfaction, *Journal of Marketing*, October, 5–23.

[19]J. Aaker, S. Fournier and S. A. Brasel (2004) When good brands do bad, *Journal of Consumer Research*, 31 (June), 1–16; P. Aggrawal (2004) The effects of brand relationship norms on consumer attitudes and behavior, *Journal of Consumer Research*, 31 (June), 87–101.

[20]For in-depth discussion see M. D. Johnson and A. Gustafsson (2000) *Improving Customer Satisfaction, Loyalty, and Profit*, San Francisco: Jossey-Bass.

[21]For an interesting analysis of the effects of different types of expectations, see W. Boulding, A. Kalra and R. Staelin (1999) The quality double whammy, *Marketing Science*, 18(4), 463–84.

[22]N. A. Morgan, E. W. Anderson and V. Mittal (2005) Understanding firms' customer satisfaction information usage, *Journal of Marketing*, 69 (July), 131–51.

[23]See for example C. Homburg, N. Koschate and W. D. Hoyer (2005) Do satisfied customers really pay more? A study of the relationship between customer satisfaction and willingness to pay, *Journal of Marketing*, 69 (April), 84–96.

[24]C. Fornell, S. Mithas, F. V. Morgeson III and M. S. Krishnan (2006) Customer satisfaction and stock prices: high returns, low risk, *Journal of Marketing*, 70 (January), 3–14; see also T. S. Gruca and L. L. Rego (2005) Customer satisfaction, cash flow, and shareholder value, *Journal of Marketing*, 69 (July), 115–30.

[25]J. N. Sheth (2001) The future of relationship marketing, *Journal of Services Marketing*, 16(7), 590–2.

[26]R. T. Rust, T. Ambler, G. S. Carpenter, V. Kumar and K. Rajendra (2004) Measuring marketing productivity: current knowledge and future directions, *Journal of Marketing*, 68(4), 76–8.

[27]A. Sharma (2007) The metrics of relationships: measuring satisfaction, loyalty and profitability of relational customers, *Journal of Relationship Marketing*, 6(2), 33.

[28]F. K. Reichheld (2003) The one number you need to grow, *Harvard Business Review*, December, 46–54.

[29]T. L. Keigningham, B. Cooil, L. Ahsay, T. W. Andreassen and J. Weiner (2007) The value of different customer retention recommendation and share-of-wallet, *Managing Service Quality*, 17(14), 361–84.

[30]J. C. Ward and A. L. Ostrom (2006) Complaining to the masses: the role of protest framing in customer-created complaint sites, *Journal of Consumer Research*, 33 (September), 220–30; K. Hart (2006) Angry customers use web to shame firms, *Washington Post*, 5 July.

[31]F. Dahlsten (2003) Avoiding the customer satisfaction rut, *MIT Sloan Management Review*, 44(3) 73–7; see also S. Nambisan and P. Nambisan (2008) How to profit from a better virtual customer environment, *MIT Sloan Management Review*, 49(3), 53–61.

[32]C. Homburg and A. Fürst (2005) How organizational complaint handling drives customer loyalty: an analysis of the mechanistic and the organic approach, *Journal of Marketing*, 69 (July), 95–114.

[33]P. Kotler (1999) *Kotler on Marketing*, New York: The Free Press, pp. 21–2.

[34]R. Anderson (2007) Rail industry: performance targets raise the bar for quality, *Financial Times*, 18 May.

[35]E. Gummeson (1988) Service quality and product quality combined, *Review of Business*, Winter, Issue 3; R. D. Buzzell and B. T. Gale (1987) *The PIMS Principles: Linking Strategy to Performance*, New York: The Free Press, Chapter 6. (PIMS stands for Profit Impact of Market Strategy.)

[36]L. Aksoy, T. L. Keiningham and T. G. Vavra (2005) Nearly everything you know about loyalty is wrong, *Marketing News*, 1 October, pp. 20–1; T. L. Keiningham, T. G. Vavra, L. Aksoy and H. Wallard (2005) *Loyalty Myths*, Hoboken, NJ: John Wiley & Sons.

[37]W. J. Reinartz and V. Kumar (2003) The impact of customer relationship characteristics on profitable lifetime duration, *Journal of Marketing*, 67 (January), 77–99; W. J. Reinartz and V. Kumar (2000) On the profitability of long-life customers in a noncontractual setting: an empirical investigation and implications for marketing, *Journal of Marketing*, 64 (October), 17–35.

[38]R. Niraj, M. Gupta and C. Narasimhan (2001) Customer profitability in a supply chain, *Journal of Marketing*, July, 1–16.

[39]M. D. Johnson and F. Selnes (2005) Diversifying your customer portfolio, *MIT Sloan Management Review*, 46(3), 11–14.

[40]M. D. Johnson and F. Selnes (2004) Customer portfolio management, *Journal of Marketing*, 68(2), 1–17.

[41]R. Dhar and R. Glazer (2003) Hedging customers, *Harvard Business Review*, May, 86–92.

[42]J. Romaniuk and B. Sharp (2003) Brand salience and customer defection in subscription markets, *Journal of Marketing*, 19, 25–44; P. Verhoef (2003) Understanding the effect of customer relationship management efforts on customer retention and customer share development, *Journal of Marketing*, 67(4), 30–45.

[43]J. J. Jonker, N. Piersma and D. den Poel (2004) Joint optimization of customer segmentation and marketing policy to maximize long-term profitability, *Expert Systems with Applications*, 27(2), 159–68; H. Bauer and H. Hammerschmidt (2005) Customer-based corporate valuation – integrating the concept of customer equity and shareholder value, *Management Decision*, 43(3), 331–48.

[44]U. Werner (2008) Getting real about CLV, Marakon Associates, (www.marakon.com/ideas_pdf/id_031208_werner.pdf) (accessed on 1 March 2008).

[45]N. E. Coviello, R. J. Brodie, P. J. Danaher and W. J. Johnston (2002) How firms relate to their markets: an empirical examination of contemporary marketing Practices, *Journal of Marketing*, 66 (July), 33–46; A. Payne and P. Frow (2006) Customer relationship management: from strategy to implementation, *Journal of Marketing Management*, 22, 135–68.

[46]R. Siddle and D. Rigby (2001) What's the matter with CRM?, *European Business Forum* Autumn, 48–50. For an up-to-date view of academic perspectives, see the articles contained in the special section on Customer Relationship Management in *Journal of Marketing*, 69 (October), 2005. For a study of the processes involved, see W. Reinartz, M. Kraft and W. D. Hoyer (2004) The customer relationship management process: its measurement and impact on performance, *Journal of Marketing Research*, 61 (August), 293–305; A. Payne and P. Frow (2006) Customer relationship management: from strategy to implementation, *Journal of Marketing Management*, 22, 135–68.

[47]N. A. Aufreiter, D. Elzinga, and J. W. Gordon (2003) Better branding, *The McKinsey Quarterly*, 4, 29–39.

[48]Ibid.

[49]D. Peppers and M. Rogers (2001) *One-to-One B2B: Customer Development Strategies for the Business-To-Business World*, New York: Doubleday; D. Peppers and M. Rogers (1993) *The One-to-One Future: Building Relationships One Customer at a Time*, New York: Doubleday; D. Peppers and M. Rogers (1999) *The One-to-One Manager: Real-World Lessons in Customer Relationship Management*, New York: Doubleday; D. Peppers, M. Rogers and B. Dorf (1999) *The One-to-One Fieldbook: The Complete Toolkit for Implementing a One-to-One Marketing Program*, New York: Bantam; D. Peppers and M. Rogers (1997) *Enterprise One to One: Tools for Competing in the Interactive Age*, New York: Currency; L. G. Garber and M. J. Dotson (2002) A method for the selection of appropriate business-to-business integrated marketing communication mixes, *Journal of Marketing Communications*, 8(1), 1–18.

[50]T. Ostenon (2002) *Customer Share Marketing*, Upper Saddle River, NJ: Prentice-Hall; A. W. H. Grant and L. A. Schlesinger (1995) Realize your customer's full profit potential, *Harvard Business Review*, September–October, 59–72.

[51]W. Reinartz, J. S. Thomas and V. Kumar (2005) Balancing acquisition and retention resources to maximize customer profitability, *Journal of Marketing*, 69 (January), 63–79.

[52]See www.carlsonmarketing.com.

[53]M. Carter (2006) How to capture the heart of the 'serial switcher', *Financial Times*, 13 February.

[54]F. F. Reichheld (2001) *Loyalty Rules*, Boston, MA: Harvard Business School Press; F. F. Reichheld (1996) *The Loyalty Effect*, Boston, MA: Harvard Business School Press.

[55]G. Nairn (2006) Customer experience: Enedesa has to learn how to deal with the customer, *Financial Times*, 18 October.

[56]L. L. Berry and A. Parasuraman (1991) *Marketing Services: Computing Through Quality*, New York: The Free Press, pp. 136–42. For an academic examination in a business-to-business context, see R. W. Palmatier, S. Gopalakrishna and M. B. Houston (2006) Returns on business-to-business relationship marketing investments: strategies for leveraging profits, *Marketing Science*, 25 (September–October), 477–93.

[57]H. Simonian (2007) The glossy and growing world of customer magazines, *Financial Times*, 11 October.

[58]U. M. Dholakia (2006) How consumer self-determination influences relational marketing outcomes: evidence from longitudinal field studies, *Journal of Marketing Research*, 43 (February), 109–20.

[59]See www.apple.com.

[60]See www.hog.com.

[61]J. Pfeffer (2003) The face of your business, *Business 2.0*, December–January, p. 58.

[62]J. S. Thomas, R. C. Blattberg and E. J. Fox (2004) Recapturing lost customers, *Journal of Marketing Research*, 61 (February), 31–45.

[63]W. Reinartz and V. Kumar (2003) The impact of customer relationship characteristics on profitable lifetime duration, *Journal of Marketing*, 67(1), 77–99; W. Reinartz and V. Kumar (2002) The mismanagement of customer loyalty, *Harvard Business Review*, July, pp. 86–97.

[64]J. B. Pine II and J. H. Gilmore (1999) *The Experience Economy*, Boston, MA: Harvard Business School Press.

[65]D. Mosby and M. Weissman (2005) *The Paradox of Excellence*, San Francisco: Jossey-Bass.

[66]T. J. Peters and R. H. Waterman (2004) *In Search of Excellence*, London: Profile Books.

[67]C. K. Prahalad and V. Ramaswamy (2004) *The Future of Competition: Co-Creating Unique Value with Customers*, Boston, MA: Harvard Business School Press.

[68]Other noteworthy contributions to the exploration of the experience economy include: R. V. Kozinets, J. F. Sherry, B. DeBerry-Spence, A. Duhachek, K. Nuttavuthisit and D. Storm (2002) Themed flagship brand stores in the new millennium: theory, practice, prospect, *Journal of Retailing*, 78, 17–29; C. Mathwick, N. Malhotra and E. Rigdon (2001) Experiential value: conceptualization, measurement and application in the catalogue and Internet shopping environment, *Journal of Retailing*, 77, 39–56; R. Verma, J. Fitzsimmons, J. Heineke and M. Davis (2002) New issues and opportunities in service design research, *Journal of Operations Management*, 20(2), 117–20. In February 2008 the *Journal of Marketing Management*, Volume 24, Issue 1/2 devoted a whole issue to creating the service experience. Papers of particular interest include N. Koenig-Lewis, Experiential values over time, 69–85; S. Baron and H. Kim, Consumers as resource integrators, 113–30; T. M. Fernandes and J. F. Procenca, The blind spot of relationships in consumer markets: the consumer proneness to engage in relationships, 153–68; S. H. G. Poulsson and S. H. Kale (2004) The experience economy and commercial experiences, *The Marketing Review*, 4, 267–77.

[69]D. Walsh (2008) Pret A Manger to go global after £345m sale, *The Times*, 22 February.

[70]M. Saren (2007) Marketing is everything: the view from the street, *Marketing Intelligence and Planning*, 25(1), 11–16; M. Saren, P. Maclarun, C. Goulding, R. Elliott, A. Shankar and M. Cateral (2007) *Critical Marketing*, London: Butterworth Heinemann.

[71]C. Lawer and S. Knox (2006) Customer advocacy and brand development, *Journal of Product and Brand Management*, 15(2), 121–9.

[72]In his 1962 speech to the U.S Congress, President John F. Kennedy outlined four basic consumer rights: 1) the right to be informed, 2) the right to safety, 3) the right to choose, and 4) the right to be heard. These were endorsed by the United Nations as basic consumer rights in 1985.

[73]L. Tiu Wright, A. Newman and C. Dennis (2006) Enhancing consumer empowerment, *European Journal of Marketing*, 40(9/10), 925–35.

[74]J. A. Deighton (1996) The future of interactive marketing, *Harvard Business Review*, November/December, 151–60.

[75]M. Brady, M. R. Fellenz and R. Brookes (2008) Researching the role of information and communications technology (ICT) in contemporary marketing practices, *Journal of Business and Industrial Marketing*, 23(2), 108–14.

[76]F. Malik (2004) *Strategy for the Management of Complex Systems*, 8th edn, Berne, Stuttgart, Vienna: Verlaup Paul Haupt.

[77]F. Hansen and S. Riis Christensen (2007) *Emotions: Advertising and Consumer Choice*, Copenhagen: Copenhagen Business School Press.

[78]S. Robinette, C. Brand and V. Lenz (2001) *Emotion Marketing*, New York: McGraw-Hill.

[79]C. Fill (2006) *Marketing Communication: Engagement, Strategies and Practice*, 4th edn, Harlow, England: Pearson Education, pp. 541–5.

[80]F. E. Bonner, J. R. Bonner and J. H. Faasse (2007) In the mood for advertising, *International Journal of Advertising*, 26(3), 333–55.

[81]Slogan coined by C. Ritz and quoted in R. Nevill and C. E. Jerningham (1908) *Piccadilly to Pall Mall*, London: Duckworth & Co.

▽ **Building strong brands**

Video documentary for Part 4

Go to **www.pearsoned.co.uk/marketingmanagementeurope** to watch the video documentary that relates to Part 4 and consider the issues raised below.

In many respects the word brand can be used to encapsulate the achievement of marketing management. Well-regarded brands acquire strong customer acceptance and value – indeed, the word *brand* can be viewed as a mnemonic which summarises marketing activity, encouraging customers to **B**uy **R**egularly **A**nd **N**ever **D**esert in favour of a competitor's brand.

Part 4: Building Strong Brands explores two important themes:

1 the purpose of branding; and

2 how to create and sustain a strong well-regarded brand.

Successful marketing enhances the value of a brand or family of brands. A brand stands for the vision, mission and success of a company in developing and offering purchasing experiences that deliver high levels of customer-perceived value. Brands should seek to develop lasting and high confidence ratings with targeted customers. When watching the video documentary that accompanies Part 4, reflect on how Electrolux perfectly captures its role in the purchasing experience in their guiding mantra 'thinking of you'. Brands should fit their customers' needs like well-tailored clothes.

Once established, a brand is a standard that needs to be continually updated in the light of customer requirements. HSBC, for example, identifies five values that reflect the 'thoughtfulness' that underpins its success. Good brands are well perceived; progressive; responsive to changing customer expectations; respectful and seen to be ethical or fairly produced.

Chris Meares
Chief Executive Officer, Group Private Banking, HSBC

Hear a variety of top marketing executives from a wide range of organisations offer their own interesting and varied perspectives on the key themes of Part 4 including: Chris Meares, Chief Executive Officer, Group Private Banking, HSBC (top); Lucy Caldicott, Head of Fundraising, VSO (centre); and an example of Electrolux's high concept household goods (bottom).

Chapter 12

▽ Creating and managing brands and brand equity

IN THIS CHAPTER, WE WILL ADDRESS THE FOLLOWING QUESTIONS:

1 What do we understand by branding?

2 What are the key strategic brand management decisions?

3 How do we create and manage brand value or equity?

4 What are the crucial aspects of branding for services, co-creation and brand touch points?

A strong brand aims to command intense customer loyalty. The most successful brands in the world are worth billions to companies. For example Zara, the Spanish fashion retailer, has a brand valued at €3.34 billion. It also opens on average one new shop a day across the globe. IKEA, the Swedish furniture brand, is another successful European brand: IKEA is valued at €6.5 billion and it too has gone global with a move into both China and Japan in the last three years. How marketers create and manage brands is of the utmost importance.

One of the master marketers at creating brands is Procter & Gamble.[1]

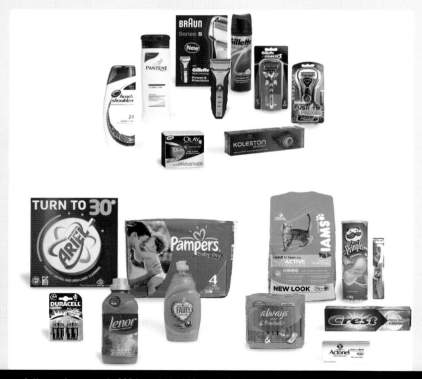

Procter & Gamble successfully markets nearly 300 brands in 160 countries by managing the totality of the marketing mix variables and focusing on the brand image of quality and innovation, aligned to excellent brand management and extension strategies.

Source: Courtesy of Procter & Gamble

Procter & Gamble (P&G) is one of the most skilful marketers of consumer packaged goods, owning many household brands such as Olay, Pampers, Braun, Pantene, Oral-B, Ariel, Crest and Gillette, to name but a few. The company's scope and accomplishments are staggering. It markets nearly 300 brands in more than 160 countries; is a global leader in 7 of the 12 different product categories in which it competes; and has total worldwide sales of more than €40 billion a year. Its sustained market leadership rests on a number of different capabilities and philosophies:

- **Customer knowledge:** P&G studies its customers – both end consumers and channel members – through continuous marketing research and intelligence gathering. It spends more than €100 million annually on more than 10,000 formal consumer research projects and generates more than 3 million consumer contacts via its email and call centre. It also puts more emphasis on getting its researchers out into the field, where they can interact with consumers and retailers in their natural environment.

- **Long-term outlook:** P&G takes the time to analyse each opportunity carefully and to prepare the best product. It then commits to making this product a success. It struggled with Pringles potato chips for almost a decade before achieving market success.

- **Product innovation:** P&G is an active product innovator, devoting €1.8 billion (3.5 per cent of sales) to research and development, an impressively high amount for a packaged goods company. It employs more science PhDs than Harvard, Berkeley and MIT combined and applies for roughly 3000 patents each year. Part of its innovation process is developing brands that offer new consumer benefits. Recent examples include Febreze, an odour-eliminating fabric spray, and Mr Clean Magic Eraser, an innovative cleaning sponge.

- **Product quality strategy:** P&G designs products of above-average quality and continuously improves them. When P&G says 'new and improved' it means it. Recent examples include Pantene Ice Shine shampoo, conditioner and styling gel; and Pampers BabyDry with Caterpillar Flex, a nappy designed to prevent leaks when babies' stomachs shrink at night.

- **Brand extension strategy:** P&G produces its brands in several sizes and forms. This strategy gains more shelf space and prevents competitors from moving in to satisfy unmet market needs. P&G also uses its strong brand names to launch new products with instant recognition and much less advertising outlay. The Mr Clean brand has been extended from a household cleaner to a bathroom cleaner, and even to a carwash system. Old Spice was successfully extended from men's fragrances to deodorant. Old Spice has toppled Right Guard to become the leading deodorant and antiperspirant for men.[2]

- **Multibrand strategy:** P&G markets several brands in the same product category, such as Luvs and Pampers nappies and Oral-B and Crest toothbrushes. Each brand meets a different consumer desire and competes against specific competitors' brands. At the same time, P&G has begun to prune carefully to reduce its vast array of products, sizes, flavours and varieties to assemble a stronger brand portfolio focused on the best products.

- **Communication pioneer:** P&G is one of the two top advertisers in the United Kingdom, spending about £180.3 million. A pioneer in using the power of television to create strong consumer awareness and preference, P&G is now taking a leading role in building its brands on the Web and through other digital technologies. It is also infusing stronger emotional appeals into its communications to create deeper consumer connections.

- **Aggressive sales force:** As part of its communication strategy P&G's sales force has been named one of the top 25 sales forces by *Sales & Marketing Management* magazine. A key to its success is the close ties its sales force forms with retailers.

- **Manufacturing efficiency and cost cutting:** P&G's reputation as a great marketing company is matched by its excellence as a manufacturing company. P&G spends large sums developing and improving production operations to keep its costs among the lowest in the industry, allowing it to reduce the premium prices at which some of its products sell.

- **Brand-management system:** P&G originated the brand-management system, in which one executive is responsible for each brand. The system has been copied by many competitors but not often with P&G's success. Recently P&G modified its general management structure so that each brand category is now run by a category manager with volume and profit responsibility. Although this new organisation does not replace the brand-management system, it helps to sharpen strategic focus on key consumer needs and competition in the category.

It is easy to see that P&G's success is based not on doing one thing well, but on successfully orchestrating the myriad factors that contribute to brand leadership.[3]

All the marketing mix variables are used to create, manage and maintain brand image, from how the product or service is designed, to pricing decisions, the communications you design, the management of your supply network, and so on. All are needed because with brands 'everything matters'.

Take the case of Louis Vuitton, a leading French fashion designer. When the company decided to build a fashion museum to reflect its brand it realised that the scaffolding and building works would look ugly and would not reflect their brand image. So it used the building to reflect its brand by covering the scaffold with a designed image of Louis Vuitton luggage – see the picture on the next page.

Rather than ugly scaffolding, the marketing manager of Louis Vuitton chose to use a design reflecting the brand to conceal the building work and to match the brand image.
Source: AFP/Getty Images

▽ Understanding branding

Perhaps the most distinctive skill of marketers is their ability to create, maintain, enhance and protect brands through their use of all the marketing mix variables. Building a brand is a very expensive and long-term development for companies and must be managed with great expertise.

What is a brand?

A **brand** is a name that is given to a particular product or service or range of products or services. It basically exists to distinguish a particular product or service from its competitors. A brand is the embodiment of customer goodwill accumulated during the lifetime of a service or product. It is a sustained effort by the company to encourage people to see its brand in the light in which it portrays it. Louis Vuitton, BMW, Vodafone, PlayStation and Ritz Carlton are all brands that command a price premium and elicit deep customer loyalty. Newer companies such as Google, Innocent, Red Bull and Zara capture the imagination of consumers and have quickly become major brands. Brands such as Ryanair and easyJet, Aldi and Lidl have all captured market share and brand loyalty in the low price, low service area.

A brand is a name, symbol, logo, design or image, or any combination of these, which is designed to identify the product or service. A successful brand is an identified product, service, person or place, augmented in such a way that the buyer or user perceives relevant unique, sustained added value that matches their needs most closely.[4] **Branding** has been around for centuries as a means to distinguish the products or services of one company from those of another.[5]

One of the earliest signs of branding in Europe was the medieval guilds, which required that craftspeople put trademarks on their products to protect themselves and their customers against inferior quality. In the fine arts, branding began with artists signing their works. The influence of brands in our society is huge, as seen by the fact that children as young as 3 can recognise brand logos.[6]

The Chartered Institute of Marketing (UK) defines a brand as a symbol that represents the consumers' experience with an organisation, product or services. A brand is a product or service whose dimensions differentiate it in some way from other products or services designed to satisfy the same need. Alternatively it can be viewed as a holistic, emotional and intangible experince – or both. A brand can be strong enough to evoke feelings of belonging, love and affection. Research has continually identified the emotional responses associated with brands, such as sensory pleasure, aesthetic beauty or excitement.[7] BMW's slogan for years has been 'Sheer Driving Pleasure', reflecting enjoyment and emotion.

Brands can play a functional, rational or tangible role – related to the performance of the product or service. Did the product work or provide the service wanted? They may also play a more symbolic, emotional or intangible role – related to what the brand represents to the consumer. The move away from functional to emotional branding is clear in much of European society. In a consumer culture people no longer consume for merely functional satisfaction but consumption becomes meaning based and brands are often used as symbolic resources for the construction and maintenance of identity.[8]

People express themselves through their brand choices. Take a look around you, look at how your fellow students brand themselves by the clothes they wear, the people they associate with, the places they go, what they consume, what music they listen to and by what they upload on to their online social networking site. This is all part of personal branding and shows how the concept of branding is so prevalent within our society that it permeates into the core of life.[9]

Let's distinguish between brand identity and image. Brand *identity* is the way a company aims to identify or position itself or its product or service. Brand *image* is the visual or verbal expressions of a brand which leads to the psychological or emotional associations that the brand aspires to maintain in the minds of the consumer.[10] **Brand image** is the way the consumer actually perceives this aim. For the right image to be established in the minds of consumers the marketer must convey brand identity through every available marketing mix variable. Brand identity should be diffused in everything the company does, from the way staff behave, to the design of annual reports, brochures, catalogues, packaging, company stationery and business cards, company decor, and so on. A **brand promise** is the marketer's vision of what the brand must be and do for consumers. The true value and future prospects of a brand rests with consumers, their knowledge about the brand and their likely response to marketing activity as a result of this knowledge. Understanding consumer **brand knowledge** – all the different things that become linked to the brand in the minds of consumers – is thus of paramount importance because it is the foundation of **brand equity** – which will be explored later in this chapter.

The power of the brand is in what resides in the mind of the consumer. Brand knowledge consists of all the thoughts, feelings, images, experiences, beliefs, and so on that become associated with the brand. In particular, brands must create strong, favourable and unique brand associations with customers. Think of Volvo (*safety*), Hallmark (*caring*) and Red Bull (*adventure*). **Emotions** play a powerful role in the customer's selection, satisfaction and loyalty towards brands. Marketers need to understand the emotional dynamics involved when a customer selects and decides to continue to use a product or service brand.[11] Research has confirmed that modern consumers no longer simply buy products and services, instead they buy the experiences around what is being sold.[12] **Emotional branding** is defined here as engaging the consumer on the level of senses and emotions; forging a deep, lasting, intimate emotional

Figure 12.1 Brand religion model

Source: From J. von Kunde and B. J. Cunningham (2002) *Corporate Religion*, Harlow, England: Financial Times Prentice Hall. Copyright © 2002 Pearson Education Ltd. Reproduced with permission.

connection to the brand that transcends material satisfaction; it involves creating a holistic experience that delivers an emotional fulfilment so that the customer develops a special bond with and unique trust in the brand.[13] The brand religion model – see Figure 12.1 – highlights the steps that customers can go through as they move forward in their beliefs about brands.

Kunde's Brand Religion model describes the evolution of the role of brands in consumers' lives as a five-stage process. Weak brands play the role of mere 'products or services' in people's lives; they have no meaning beyond their functionality. 'Concept brands' carry with them emotional values that resonate with consumers and call for increased involvement. 'Corporate concepts' are those brands which reflect the corporate strategy, expressing a wider philosophy that extends throughout the company. More valuable still are those brands that become 'brand cultures', seen by consumers as being fully embedded in their social lives. The most coveted place on this evolution is when a product or service achieves a status of a 'brand religion', when consumers view it as a total way of life.

For branding strategies to be successful and brand value to be created consumers must be convinced there are meaningful differences among brands in the product or service category. Brand differences are often related to attributes or benefits of the product or service itself. Some brands create competitive advantages through intangible image or non-product-related means. Gucci, Chanel, Louis Vuitton and others have become leaders in their product categories by understanding consumer motivations and desires and creating relevant and appealing images around their products. As Robert Pole, Chief Executive of the Gucci Group noted: 'We are not in the business of selling handbags. We are in the business of selling dreams!'[14]

Marketers can apply branding virtually anywhere a consumer has a choice. It is possible to brand a physical good (Pantene shampoo, BMW X5 series jeep), a service (France Telecom, Aviva general insurance), a shop (Les Galeries Lafayette; Carrefour), a person (David Beckham, Jamie Oliver), a place (Paris, a region of Spain – the Costa del Sol), an organisation (UNICEF, Automobile Association) a group (U2 or Coldplay), or an idea (free trade, freedom of speech).[15]

'Marketing insight: Brand cooking with Jamie Oliver' looks at how the popular English chef has become a brand in his own right.

Marketing insight

Brand cooking with Jamie Oliver

In 1997 Jamie Oliver got his start as a chef at London's River Café, when he was prominently featured in a TV documentary about the restaurant. His engaging personality led five different TV production companies to contact him the next day. His resulting television show on cooking, *The Naked Chef*, became a worldwide hit and a celebrity chef was born. Oliver has since leveraged his cooking fame and reputation to launch a number of successful new products and services:

- 7 books published internationally in 26 languages, with over 14 million sold worldwide;
- 11 different television series, with over 123 episodes shown in over 60 countries;
- 11 DVDs distributed in 25 countries;
- 2 UK-based newspaper columns syndicated in five countries;
- Jamie Oliver Professional Series of pots and pans, bakeware and kitchen accessories, licensed by Tefal and sold in department stores in 15 countries;
- porcelain tableware and serveware licensed by Royal Worcester;
- new products such as the Flavour Shaker, traditional Italian pasta sauces, antipasti, olive oils and vinegars;
- a web site, www.jamieoliver.com, that logs 250,000 unique visitors per month.

A celebrity endorser for UK supermarket giant Sainsbury's since 2000, Jamie Oliver is also credited with helping the chain's 'Recipe for Success' campaign deliver a staggering £1.12 billion of incremental revenue. The company believes the campaign has been 65 per cent more effective than any of its other campaigns.

Besides these commercial ventures, Oliver has a philanthropic side. For instance, he created the Fifteen Foundation, whose mission is to 'inspire young people'. An important activity was the introduction of the Fifteen restaurant in London in 2002 that trains 15 disadvantaged young people to work in the hospitality industry. Additional restaurants in Amsterdam, Melbourne and Cornwall have followed.

Jamie Oliver clearly has a strong brand. Like any strong brand, his has a well-defined brand image and appealing brand promise.

Jamie Oliver has skilfully managed his career as a brand with books, television shows and restaurants.
Source: KPA/Zuma/Rex Features

The role of brands

There are two perspectives to the role of branding: a consumer perspective and a channel members' perspective.

Brands perform many valuable roles for consumers:[16]

- Brands signal a certain level of quality so that satisfied buyers can easily choose the product or service again.[17] Brands assure expected levels of satisfaction.
- Brands facilitate purchase so that customers don't have high levels of indecisions as to what to buy.
- Brands reduce the perceived risk in the purchase situation and reduce the time needed to shop or purchase. As consumers' lives become more complicated, rushed, and time starved, the ability of a brand to simplify decision making and reduce risk is invaluable.[18]

Brands also perform valuable functions for companies:[19]

- A brand offers legal protection for unique features or aspects of the product or service.[20] The brand name can be protected through registered trademarks. These intellectual property rights ensure that the company can safely invest in the brand and reap the benefits of a valuable asset.

- Brands create greater customer loyalty, which provides predictability and security of demand for the company and creates barriers to entry that make it difficult for other companies to enter the market.
- Brand loyalty also means that companies are less vunerable to competitive marketing activities or to marketing crises.
- Brand loyalty can also translate into customer willingness to pay a higher price – often 20–25 per cent more than for competing brands.[21] Brand loyalty also ensures that customers are more favourable to price increases.
- Brands are hard to copy. Although competitors may duplicate product or service designs, they cannot easily match lasting impressions left in the minds of individuals and organisations by years of marketing activity and service or product experience. Take the example of bottled water – water is water is water, yet many companies have created brand images for their water for which they can charge premium price. Take Evian or San Pelliginos – these brand names carry the aura of quality.
- Branding can be a powerful means to secure a competitive advantage.[22] Brands help companies to differentiate their product or service from others. Think of the perception of the service provision from airlines such as Air France-KLM, British Airways and Lufthansa as opposed to Ryanair or easyJet. All offer the customer air travel, but the brands reflect different levels of service or different segments that have different values – in this case either service or price.
- Brands increase marketing communication efficiencies.
- Brands attract higher-quality employees.
- Brands elicit stronger support from channel and supply chain partners.
- Brands create growth opportunities through brand extensions and licensing.
- Brands help companies to segment their markets and have different products or services within the same market but aimed at different target markets.

▽ Strategic brand management

Strategic brand management can dramatically increase corporate success according to a study by Booz Allen Hamilton, who noted that 80 per cent of European companies that are managed with a strong brand focus have operating profits twice as high as the sector average.[23] The stock values for companies reflect a belief that strong brands result in better earnings and profit performance for companies, which, in turn, create greater value for shareholders.[24]

The most important issue is to have a brand vision that is a clear and consistent message about the value of the brand. This must be a clear value(s) proposition from the consumer perspective. The long-term brand vision is operationalised through both long- and short-term marketing endeavours. Marketers must provide a clear sense of direction for each employee within the company who appreciates how their role affects the brand values.

There are four processes for strategic brand management:

1 Ensure identification of the brand with customers and an association of the brand in customers' minds with a specfic product or service class or customer need.

2 Firmly establish the brand meaning in the minds of customers (by strategically linking a host of tangible and intangible brand associations).

3 Elicit the proper customer responses to this brand identity and brand meaning.

4 Convert brand response to create an intense, active loyalty relationship between the customer and the brand.

Different marketing activities have different strengths and can accomplish different objectives. Marketers should therefore engage in a mixture of marketing mix activities, each of which plays a specific role in building or maintaining brand equity. Sometimes marketers don't understand the real importance of all aspects of marketing to their brand until they change a crucial element of the brand and over time see the effects. Take Burberry, the British luxury brand.

▽ Burberry

Burberry changed its distribution and pricing to try and capture more market share, and also made its product available in more shops. Burberry found, to its cost, that this changed how the consumer viewed the company and the product went much further down market than expected. The familiar check pattern, synonymous throughout the world as the Burberry brand of luxury and elitism, began to appear on more and more people, on C-grade celebrities and even at football matches! The distinctive beige check, once only associated with A-listers, had become the uniform of a rather different social group within the United Kingdom called 'chavs'. A chav is a mainly derogatory slang term in the United Kingdom for a person fixated on low-quality or counterfeit goods and a group in society often associated with anti-social behaviour. Burberry had to react fast to the damage to its brand image. From a product perspective it removed the checked baseball caps from its product line and reduced the visibility of its distinctive check pattern on all its products. Burberry also cracked down on the fake goods, which allowed what it considered to be the wrong sort of people to look as if they were wearing the brand. Burberry also changed its own supply chain and again became available only in upmarket shops, reflecting its brand image.[25]

The 'chav' phenomenon in Britain damaged the Burberry brand while the image above profiles the brand image that Burberry would like to present.
Source: The Advertising Archives

▽ Creating and managing brand identities: names, logos, slogans and images

As more and more firms realise that the brand names associated with their products or services are among their most valuable assets, creating, maintaining and enhancing the strength of those brands has become a marketing management imperative.[26] From a marketing management perspective there are three main challenges to creating and managing brand identities:

1 **The initial choices for the brand elements or identities making up the brand. These include the brand names, logos, symbols, characters, slogans, accompanying music, websites, product design and features, packaging, and so on:** **Brand elements** are those trademarkable devices that identify and differentiate the brand. They are often the most tangible representation of the brand. In the United Kingdom and Ireland, Boots the chemist uses the 'Trust Boots' slogan to mirror the brand identity it wishes to create for its pharmacy outlets. Most strong brands employ multiple brand elements. Nike has the distinctive 'swoosh' logo, the empowering 'Just Do It' slogan, and the 'Nike' name based on the Greek winged goddess of victory.

2 **All accompanying marketing activities must support the brand:** The Juicy Couture label is one of the fastest-growing fashion labels, whose edgy, contemporary sportswear and accessories have a strong lifestyle appeal to women, men and children. Positioned as a luxury, the brand creates its exclusive image by limiting distribution, designing cutting-edge fashion and using a somewhat risqué name linked to a rebellious attitude.[27]

3 **Other associations indirectly transferred to the brand by linking it to some other entity (a person, place or thing):** French car manufacturer Renault has used footballer Thierry Henry and the *Sesame Steet* muppet 'Animal' to create a cooler, sexier image for its Clio model in its 'VaVaVoom' advertisements. This campaign brought the Renault Clio to a larger and more attentive audience and attracted more male audience attention rather than the traditional female consumer base. However, this is an example of where the star (and indeed the slogan) overshadows the product. Thierry Henry has since been referred to as 'Mr VaVaVoom himself', and the phrase has become more related to his persona than to the car.

Many brands create brand equity by linking the brand to other information in memory, which conveys meaning to consumers. These 'secondary' brand associations can link the brand to sources, such as the company itself (through branding strategies), to countries or other geographical regions (through identification of country origin), and to global supply chains or channels of distribution (through channel strategy); as well as to other brands (through ingredient or co-branding), characters (through licensing), spokespeople (through endorsements), sporting or cultural events (through sponsorship), or some other third-party sources (through awards or reviews).

To learn how Indian leather goods brand Hidesign has used a well-designed and creative branding strategy to distinguish itself as a leading name in leather goods, visit www.pearsoned.co.in/pkotler

For example, the coffee company Café Java has successful become linked in consumers' minds to protecting poorly paid coffee bean farmers all over the world. Figure 12.2 shows the range of secondary sources of brand knowledge.

Co-branding and ingredient branding

Co-branding

Marketers often combine their products with products from other companies in various ways. In **co-branding** – also called dual branding or brand bundling – two or more well-known brands are combined into a joint market offering or marketed together in some fashion. One form of co-branding is *same-company co-branding*, as when the Danone Group advertises Activia Yogurt and Actimel.

Figure 12.2 Secondary
sources of brand
knowledge

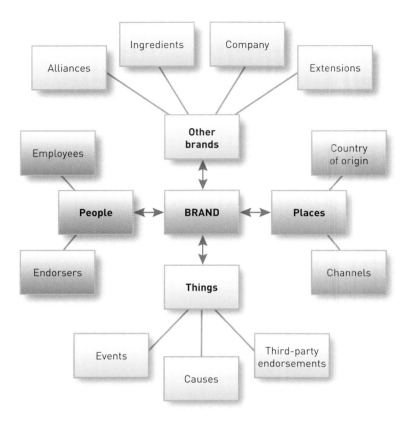

Still another form is *joint-venture co-branding*, such as British Gas energy and engineering and Bosch Worcester gas boilers in the United Kingdom. There is also *multiple-sponsor co-branding*, which is evident when football clubs grant after-match interviews with the media in a room full of sponsors' display logos. Finally, there is *retail co-branding*, where several retail establishments use the same location as a way to optimise both space and profits, as is the case in discount retail parks throughout Europe.

The main advantage of co-branding is that a market offering/product service may be convincingly positioned by virtue of the multiple brands. Co-branding can generate greater sales from the existing target market as well as opening additional opportunities for new consumers and channels. It can also reduce the cost of introducing a new market offer, because it combines two well-known images and speeds adoption. And co-branding may be a valuable means to learn about consumers and how other companies approach them. Companies within the motor industry have reaped all these benefits of co-branding.

The potential disadvantages of co-branding are the risks and lack of control in becoming aligned with another brand in the minds of consumers. Consumer expectations about the level of involvement and commitment with co-brands are likely to be high, so unsatisfactory performance could have negative repercussions for both brands. If the other brand has entered into a number of co-branding arrangements, overexposure may dilute the transfer of any association. It may also result in a lack of focus on existing brands.

For co-branding to succeed, the two brands must separately have brand equity – adequate brand awareness and a sufficiently positive brand image. The most important requirement is a logical fit between the two brands, such that the combined brand or marketing activity maximises the advantages of each while minimising their disadvantages. Research studies show that consumers are more apt to perceive co-brands favourably if the two brands are complementary rather than similar.[28]

Besides remembering these strategic considerations, managers must enter into co-branding ventures carefully. There must be the right kind of fit in values, capabilities and goals, in addition to an appropriate balance of brand equity. There must be detailed plans to legalise contracts, make financial arrangements and coordinate marketing programmes. The financial arrangement between brands may vary, although one common approach is for the brand more deeply involved in the production process to pay a licensing fee and royalty.

Brand alliances require a number of decisions.[29] What capabilities does a firm lack? What resource constraints is the firm facing (people, time, money, etc.)? What are the growth goals or revenue needs? In assessing a joint branding opportunity, a firm should satisfy itself that it is a profitable business venture. How might it help maintain or strengthen brand equity? Is there any risk of dilution of brand equity? Does the opportunity offer any extrinsic advantages such as learning opportunities?

Ingredient branding

Ingredient branding is a special case of co-branding. It creates brand equity for materials, components or parts that are necessarily contained within other branded products. Some successful ingredient brands include Dolby noise reduction, Gore-Tex water-resistant fibres, Intel processors and Scotchgard fabrics. Ingredient branding is growing in an area known as 'nutraceuticals', food products that have health benefit properties.

An interesting variation on ingredient branding is 'self-branding' in which companies advertise and even trademark their own branded ingredients. For instance, stately homes advertise crockery, foodstuffs and linen bearing their insignia in site-based shops and specialist magazines. If it can be done well, it makes much more sense to self-brand ingredients because you have more control and can develop the ingredient to suit your purposes.[30] Ingredient brands try to create enough awareness and preference for their market offerings so consumers will not buy a 'host' product that doesn't contain the brand badge.

Many manufacturers make components or materials that enter into final branded products but lose their individual identity. One of the few component branders that have succeeded in building a separate identity is Intel. Intel's consumer-directed brand campaign convinced many personal computer buyers to buy only computer brands with 'Intel Inside'. As a result, major PC manufacturers – IBM, Dell, Compaq – purchase their chips from Intel at a premium price rather than buy equivalent chips from an unknown supplier. Most component manufacturers, however, would find it difficult to create a successful ingredient brand. 'Marketing memo: Making ingredient branding work' outlines the characteristics of successful ingredient branding.

Marketing memo

Making ingredient branding work

What are the requirements for success in ingredient branding?

1 Customers must perceive that the ingredient matters to the performance and success of the end product. Ideally, this intrinsic value is easily seen or experienced.

2 Customers must be convinced that not all ingredient brands are the same and that the ingredient is superior.

3 A distinctive symbol or logo must clearly signal to customers that the host product contains the ingredient. Ideally, the symbol or logo would function like a 'seal' and would be simple and versatile and credibly communicate quality and confidence.

4 A coordinated 'pull' and 'push' programme must help customers understand the importance and advantages of the branded ingredient. Channel members must offer full support. Often this will require consumer advertising and promotions and – sometimes in collaboration with manufacturers – retail merchandising and promotion programmes.

Sources: K. L. Keller (2008) *Strategic Brand Management*, 3rd edn, Upper Saddle River, NJ: Prentice Hall; P. Kotler and W. Pfoertsch (2006) *B2B Brand Management*, New York: Springer; P. F. Nunes, S. F. Dull and P. D. Lynch (2003) When two brands are better than one, *Outlook*, January, 14–23.

Criteria for choosing brand names

There are six main criteria for choosing brand names. In general brand names should be short and simple, easy to spell and pronounce, pronounceable in only one way and one language and easy to recognise and remember. Many, such as BBC, Orange and Mastercard follow the above criteria while some very successful names do not. Think of Birkenstock, Adidas or even Stella Artois.

1 **Memorable:** How easily is the brand element recalled and recognised? Short names such as Virgin, Sky, Dove and Zara are memorable brand names.

2 **Meaningful:** Is the brand name credible and suggestive of the product or service? Does it suggest something about a product ingredient or service quality or the type of person who might use the brand? Consider the inherent meaning in names such as Crisp 'n Dry, Head and Shoulders, Fast Fit Exhausts, RightGuard deodorant or Sure Underarm Protection, Energeriser Batteries and Lean Cuisine low-calorie foods.

3 **Likeability:** How aesthetically appealing is the brand name? Is it likable visually, verbally, and in other ways? Concrete brand names such as Mr Muscle, Little Chef, and Shake and Vac are likeable names. Many characters associated with brands are also inherently likeable, such as the Michelin man and Chupa Chups.

4 **Transferable:** Can the brand element be used to introduce new products or services in the same or different categories? Does it add to brand equity across geographic boundaries and market segments? A great example is the 'Snap, Crackle and Pop' slogan that has been translated across Europe:[31]

- English: 'Snap! Crackle! Pop!'
- French: 'Cric! Crac! Croc!'
- Spanish: 'Pim! Pum! Pam!'
- German: 'Knisper! Knasper! Knusper!'
- Swedish: 'Piff! Paff! Puff!'
- Finnish: 'Riks! Raks! Poks!'
- Dutch: 'Pif! Paf! Pof!'

5 **Adaptable:** How adaptable and updatable is the brand name or slogan? The three Kelloggs' elf brothers made their debut in 1933 but Snap, Crackle and Pop, have since had several make-overs and still maintain their popularity with children all over the world. Bird's Eye also developed an image that remains relevant today – Captain Bird's Eye still sails the Bird's Eye ship. The 'Aero man' character is appealing to women aged 18–30 but alienates men from the brand. Nestlé offset this by targeting Yorkie directly at the male market to great effect. The slogan 'It's not for girls' uses humour to target the male market segment.

6 **Protectable:** How legally protectable is the brand name, image or slogan? Names that become synonymous with product or service categories can be difficult to manage. Brand names such as Kleenex, Hoover, Sellotape, Google, Xerox and Bandaid have all become known as the general title for the product or sevice and this can be difficult to manage. You will hear people saying 'Did you google that?' when they mean 'Did you do a search on the Internet?'

The first three – memorable, meaningful and likeable – are 'brand building'. The latter three – transferable, adaptable and protectable – are 'defensive' and deal with how to leverage and preserve the equity in a brand element in the face of challenges.

Brand elements can play a number of brand-building roles.[32] Brand elements should be easy to recognise and recall, and inherently descriptive and persuasive. The likeability and appeal of brand elements may also play a critical role in awareness and associations leading to high brand equity.[33] The Snap, Crackle and Pop characters from Kelloggs reinforce the sense of magic and fun for breakfast cereals. Many UK-based insurance companies have used symbols of strength

The Snap, Crackle and Pop slogan has been translated into many European languages.

Source: Courtesy of the Kellogg Group.

(the Rock of Gibraltar for Prudential and the stag for Hartford), security (the eagle of Eagle Star) and agility and strength (the horse for Lloyds bank).

Brand slogans or tag lines are an extremely efficient means to build brand equity. They can function as useful 'hooks' or 'handles' to help consumers grasp what the brand is and what makes it special, summarising and translating the intent of the total marketing programme. Think of the inherent brand meaning in slogans such as L'Oréal – 'Because you're worth it', 'Trust Boots', Gillette – 'The Best a Man Can Get' and 'We Try Harder' for Avis rental cars.

▽ **Avis car hire**

A classic example of a slogan that builds brand equity is Avis's 41-year-old 'We Try Harder', which is still used in their 3600 worldwide locations. In 1963, when the campaign was developed, Avis was losing money and was widely considered the number two car rental company next to market leader Hertz. When account executives from DDB advertising agency met with Avis managers, they asked: 'What can you do that we can say you do better than your competitors?' An Avis manager replied, 'We try harder because we have to.' Someone at DDB wrote this down and it became the heart of the marketing campaign in every aspect of their business. Avis was hesitant to air the campaign because of its blunt, break-the-rules honesty, but also because the company had to deliver on that promise. Yet, by creating buy-in on 'We Try Harder' from all Avis employees, especially its front line employees at the car rental desks, the company was able to create a company culture and brand image from a brand slogan that lives to this day. All the marketing activites from service process to pricing, to how staff interact with customers, is aligned with this brand slogan.[34]

Branding decisions: individual or house brands

The first branding strategy decision is whether to develop a brand name for a product or service. A brand element should provide a positive contribution to brand equity, for example it should convey certain value associations or responses. Based on its name alone, a consumer might expect ColorStay lipsticks to be long-lasting and Sunkist Orange Juice to be a healthy, natural orange juice full of vitamin C.

Four general strategies are often used:

1 **Individual names:** The British/Dutch company Unilever has many individually named brands within its company including many familiar brands such as Hellmann's, Knorr, Bird's Eye, Surf, Dove, Pond's, and Calvin Klein fragrances. L'Oréal, the French cosmetics company, also has many brands including Maybelline New York and the Garnier brand and – more recently – The Body Shop. A major advantage of an individual names strategy is that the company does not tie its reputation to the individual product or service. If a product or service fails or appears to have a brand image contrary to the company's, the other products or service are not damaged. Companies often use different brand names for different quality lines within the same product or service class. Lufthansa owns most of GermanWings but does not share a name with the low-cost airline, in part to protect the brand equity of its Lufthansa brand.

2 **Blanket corporate, family or house names:** Many companies use their corporate, family or house brand across their range of products or services.[35] Development costs are lower with blanket brand names because there's no need to run a 'name' search or spend heavily on advertising to create recognition. Heinz and Kelloggs are both good examples of this.

3 **Separate family or house names for all products and services:** Inditex, a company most people have probably never heard of, uses separate brand names for its retail shops, from the very familiar Zara and Massimo Dutti to the less familiar Pull & Bear, Stradivarius and Bershka. These are all very different brand names targeted at different segments with various levels of success. If a company produces quite different products such as these, one blanket name is often not desirable. Louis Vuitton and Moët Hennessy manage a whole portfolio of luxury brands under different brand names. They range from wines and spirits (Krug, Belvedere vodka) to jewellery (TAG Heuer, Chaumet) to fashion labels (Marc Jacobs, Donna Karan) and perfume (Gerlain, Parfums Givenchy).

4 **Corporate name combined with individual product names:** Kelloggs combines corporate and individual names in Kelloggs' Rice Krispies, Kelloggs' Bran Flakes and Kelloggs' Corn Flakes, as do Honda, Sony and HP for their products. The company name legitimises, and the individual name individualises, the new product or service.

Table 12.1 Selecting a brand relationship spectrum position

Toward a branded family	Toward a family of brands
Does the parent brand contribute to the offering by adding:	*Is there a compelling need for a separate brand because it will:*
– Associations enhancing the value proposition?	– Create and own an association?
– Credibility through organisational associations?	– Represent a new, different offering?
– Visibility?	– Retain/capture customer/brand bond?
– Communication efficiencies?	– Deal with channel conflict?
Will the master brand be strengthened by associating with the new offering?	**Will the business support a new brand name?**

Source: Adapted from D. A. Aaker and E. Joachimsthaler (2000) *Brand Leadership*, New York: Free Press, Figure 4.6, p. 120. Copyright © 2000 by David A. Aaker and Erich Joachimsthaler. Reprinted with permission from The Free Press, a division of Simon & Schuster, Inc.

Individual names and blanket family names are sometimes referred to as a 'house of brands' and a 'branded house' respectively, and they represent two ends of a brand relationship continuum – see Table 12.1. Separate family names come in between the two, and corporate-plus-individual names combine them. So, although companies rarely adopt a pure example of any of the four strategies, deciding which general strategy to emphasise depends on several factors, as evidenced by Table 12.1.

Most new products or services are in fact line extensions – typically 80–90 per cent of new products and services introduced in any one year are brand extensions. Moreover, many of the most successful new products and services are extensions. Examples include Mars extending its brand to ice cream, Caterpillar to shoes and watches, Michelin to a restaurant guide, Adidas to an aftershave and Dyson vacuum cleaners to hand dryers, Microsoft to gaming and Apple computers to the iPod digital music player.

Barbie, the very popular doll, is 97th in the list of the top brands in the world. Matel, which manages the Barbie brand, has had many marketing struggles to extend the Barbie brand to products that its customer base will use after they have grown out of playing with a doll. Matel has launched a range of Barbie-inspired teenage clothing and also Barbie make-up for teenagers, which it markets through the MAC make-up company.

The Dyson hand dryer is a brand extension from the Dyson vacuum cleaner which in itself was a revolution in vacuuming.

Source: Courtesy of Dyson

Deciding how to brand new services or products is especially critical. When a company introduces a new product or service marketers have three main choices:

1 They can develop new brand elements for the new product or service.
2 They can apply some of their existing brand elements.
3 They can use a combination of new and existing brand elements.

The existing brand is the parent of the brand extension. If the parent brand is already associated with multiple products through brand extensions, it can also be called a **family brand**. The Lucozade brand is now a family brand for the following sports products: Lucozade Sport, Lucozade Hydro Active and Lucozade Sport Nutrition.

Brand extensions fall into two general categories.[36] In a **line extension**, the parent brand covers a new product or service within a product or service category it currently serves, such as with new flavours, forms, colours, ingredients and package sizes. The French food company Danone has introduced several types of Danone yogurt line extensions over the years. These include Fruit on the Bottom, All Natural Flavours, and Fruit Blends.

▽ Magnum

Magnum is an ice cream brand that was owned by Swiss ice cream company Lusso but is now owned by the British/Dutch Unilever company, and is marketed as part of the Heartbrand line of products in most countries. The original 1990 Magnum Classic consisted of a thick bar of vanilla ice cream on a stick, covered with white or dark chocolate, with a weight of 86 grams (120 ml). In 1994 the company also started selling Magnum ice cream cones, and in 2002 an ice cream sandwich along with their Magnum Mint, Double Chocolate, and other flavours. Also in 2002 Magnum branched into frozen yogurt with their raspberry fruit swirl covered in milk chocolate. Late 2002 saw the launch of 'Magnum Intense' (a chocolate truffle centre enveloped in ice cream and covered with chocolate) and the limited edition '7 Deadly Sins' series of ice creams. The line extension 'Moments' was introduced in 2003 – these were bite-size ice cream treats with caramel, chocolate or hazelnut centres, followed later in the year by 'mini', 'crunchy' (with almonds) and 'light'. This was followed by another limited edition range in 2005 in which each flavour was named after one of the senses: Magnum Aroma, Magnum Touch, Magnum Sound, Magnum Taste and Magnum Vision. In 2008 Magnum brought out new variants in the United Kingdom – Mayan Mystica, which is a chocolate ice cream Magnum blended with cinnamon and honey flavours, and Magnum Minis, available in a variety of flavours.

In a **category extension**, the parent brand is used to enter a different product or service category from the one it currently serves. Honda, headquartered in Japan, is the fifth largest car manufacturer in the world as well as the largest engine-maker in the world, producing more than 14 million internal combustion engines each year. Honda has used its company name to cover such different products as cars, motorcycles, snowblowers, lawnmowers, marine engines and snowmobiles. This allows Honda to advertise that it can fit 'six Hondas in a two-car garage'. English entrepreneur Richard Branson has used his 'Virgin' brand to enter many different product and service markets, from the airline industry to the music business and soft drinks markets, all with varying degrees of success. His latest project is to enter the space aviation industry with Virgin Galactic: Virgin Galactic will be the world's first spaceline, giving customers the groundbreaking opportunity of being one of the world's first non-professional astronauts.

A **brand line** consists of all products or service – original as well as line and category extensions – sold under a particular brand. A **brand mix** (or brand assortment) is the set of all available brand lines from a company.

Many companies are now introducing **branded variants**, which are specific brand lines supplied exclusively to specific retailers or distribution channels. They result from the pressure retailers put on manufacturers to provide distinctive offerings. A camera company may supply its low-end cameras to large retailers while limiting its higher-priced items to speciality camera shops. Valentino, the Italian designer, designs and supplies different lines of suits and jackets to department stores compared to his own outlets.[37]

A **licensed product or service** is one whose brand name has been licensed to others. Marketers have seized on licensing to push their company name and image across a wide range of products – from bedding to shoes – making licensing a €33.36 billion business.[38] TinTin, the familiar French cartoon character's image, has been licensed to companies manufacturing a range of products from clocks to keyrings. The Harry Potter brand has had phenomenal success with licensing. Hallmark obtained the Harry Potter licence to design Harry Potter greeting cards, wrapping paper and partyware, while Warner Bros received the licence for Harry Potter clothing, ornaments and sweets.

Two key components of virtually any branding strategy are brand extensions and brand portfolios.

Brand extensions

Marketers must judge each potential brand extension by how effectively it leverages existing brand equity from the parent brand, as well as how effectively it contributes to the parent brand's equity.[39] Crest White Strips leveraged the strong reputation of Crest and dental care to provide reassurance in the teeth-whitening arena, while also reinforcing its dental authority image. The most important consideration with extensions is that there should be a 'fit' in the mind of the consumer, based on common attributes, usage situations or user types.

Figure 12.3 lists a number of academic research findings on brand extensions.[40]

One benefit of a successful extension is that it may also serve as the basis for subsequent extensions.[41]

Academics have studied brand extensions closely. Here is a summary of some of their key research findings.

- Successful brand extensions occur when the parent brand is seen as having favourable associations and there is a perception of fit between the parent brand and the extension product.
- There are many bases of fit: product-related attributes and benefits, as well as non-product-related attributes and benefits related to common usage situations or user types.
- Depending on consumer knowledge of the categories, perceptions of fit may be based on technical or manufacturing commonalities or more surface considerations such as necessary or situational complementarity.
- High-quality brands stretch farther than average-quality brands, although both types of brand have boundaries.
- A brand that is seen as prototypical of a product category can be difficult to extend outside the category.
- Concrete attribute associations tend to be more difficult to extend than abstract benefit associations.
- Consumers may transfer associations that are positive in the original product class but become negative in the extension context.
- Consumers may infer negative associations about an extension, perhaps even based on other inferred positive associations.
- It can be difficult to extend into a product class that is seen as easy to make.
- A successful extension can not only contribute to the parent brand image but also enable a brand to be extended even farther.
- An unsuccessful extension hurts the parent brand only when there is a strong basis of fit between the two.
- An unsuccessful extension does not prevent a firm from 'backtracking' and introducing a more similar extension.
- Vertical extensions can be difficult and often require subbranding strategies.
- The most effective advertising strategy for an extension emphasises information about the extension (rather than reminders about the parent brand).

Figure 12.3 Research insights on brand extensions

Source: From K. L. Keller (2008) *Strategic Brand Management*, 3rd edn, Upper Saddle River, NJ: Prentice Hall. Copyright © 2008 Pearson Education, Inc. Reproduced with permission.

Advantages of brand extensions As the costs of establishing a new brand name are so high it is understandable that brand extensions ae so popular. Extensions also can avoid the difficulty – and expense – of coming up with a new name. They also allow for many efficiencies across all the marketing mix variables including in distribution, inventory or stock, communications, packaging and labelling. Similar or identical packages and labels can result in lower production costs for extensions and, if coordinated properly, more prominence in the retail store via a 'bill-board' effect. For example, Bird's Eye offers a variety of frozen foods with similar packaging that increases their visibility when they are stocked together in the freezer. With a portfolio of brand variants within a product category, consumers who need a change – because of boredom, satiation, or whatever – can switch to a different product type without having to leave the brand family.

Using brand extensions can ensure positive expectations as extensions can reduce risk.[42] It may also be easier to convince retailers to stock and promote a brand extension because of increased customer demand. From a marketing communications perspective, an intro-ductory campaign for an extension doesn't have to create awareness of both the brand *and* the new product or service, but can concentrate instead on the new product or service itself.[43]

Business-to-business companies can use brand extensions as a powerful way to enter consumer markets, as these two rubber companies with strong brand names discovered.

▽ Michelin and Goodyear

Both French in origin, Michelin and Goodyear were known primarily for their rubber tyres, but have launched a number of brand extensions over the years.[44] Michelin's brand extensions have mainly been in the car accessories area – from inflation and pressure monitoring goods to car floor mats. So far its brand extensions fall into three categories: (1) car and cycle-related products; (2) footwear, clothing, accessories and equipment for work, sports and leisure; and (3) personal accessories – gifts and collectables. Its sports and leisure category now has the potential to overtake the car accessories line. Like Michelin, Goodyear has a category of products closely aligned to the car industry – such as jack stands and car repair tools – but it, too, has branched out into consumer areas. The company is marketing its own line of cleaning wipes for windows and upholstery, mechanics' gloves and garden hose nozzles, among other products. Interestingly, Goodyear and Adidas have become partners to create a series of driving shoes, prominently featuring the Goodyear 'Wingfoot' mark.[45]

Disadvantages of brand extensions On the downside, line extensions may cause the brand name to be less strongly identified with any one product.[46] Ries and Trout call this the 'line-extension trap'.[47] By linking its brand to mainstream food products such as mashed potatoes, powdered milk, soups and beverages, Cadbury ran the risk of losing its more specific meaning as a chocolates and sweet brand.[48] **Brand dilution** occurs when consumers no longer associate a brand with a specific or highly similar products or service and start thinking less of the brand.

If a company launches extensions consumers deem inappropriate, they may question the integrity of the brand or become confused and perhaps even frustrated: which version of the brand is the 'right one' for them? The company itself may become overwhelmed. When LEGO, the Danish toy manufacturer, decided to become a lifestyle brand and launch its own lines of clothes, watches and video games, as well as design programmes to attract more girls into the brand franchise, it neglected its core market of 5–9 year-old-boys. When plunging profits led to layoffs of almost half its employees in 2004, the company streamlined its brand portfolio to emphasise its core businesses.[49]

The worst possible scenario is for an extension not only to fail, but also to harm the parent brand image in the process. Fortunately, such events are rare. 'Marketing failures', where insufficient consumers were attracted to a brand, are typically much less damaging than 'product or service failures', where the brand fundamentally fails to live up to its promise. New products such as Virgin Cola, Levi's Tailored Classic suits, Fruit of the Loom washing powder, Bic Perfume, Capital Radio restaurant and Pond's toothpaste failed because consumers found them inappropriate extensions for the brand.[50] Even then, product or service failures dilute brand equity only when the extension is seen as very similar to the parent brand.

▽ Virgin challenges

At one stage the brand extension potential of Virgin was widely debated as Virgin entered a range of industries with brand extensions. It moved from aeroplanes to trains and from record stores to mobile phones. The UK newspaper *The Observer* explored the many brand moves in an article entitled 'The Virgin Life': 'Every morning you can wake up to Virgin Radio, put on Virgin clothes and make-up, drive to work in a car brought through Virgin using money from your Virgin bank account' and so on citing the Virgin gym, Virgin cinema and Virgin hotels. Despite this there have been some brand extension failures. Virgin Cola may have been a brand extension too far for the Virgin Group.[51] According to Matt Haig in his book *Brand Failures*, Virgin Cola failed because you must show a competitior's weakness, which Virgin did not do clearly. In addition, distribution is key in the soft drinks industry and Virgin struggled in this area. Virgin was also less than successful with its Virgin Vodka.

Brand switching Even if sales of a brand extension are high and meet targets, the revenue may be coming from consumers switching to the extension from existing parent-brand offerings – in effect *cannibalising* the parent brand. Intra-brand shifts in sales may not be a disadvantage if they are a form of *pre-emptive cannibalisation*. In other words, consumers might have switched to a competing brand instead of the line extension if the extension had not been introduced.

One easily overlooked disadvantage of brand extensions is that the company forgoes the chance to create a new brand with its own unique image and equity. Consider the advantages to Disney of having introduced more adult-oriented Touchstone films; to Levi's of creating casual Dockers pants; and to Black and Decker of introducing high-end Dewalt power tools.

Brand portfolios

The **brand portfolio** is the set of all brands and brand lines a particular company offers for sale in a particular category or market segment. Marketers often need multiple brands in order to pursue multiple segments.

▽ Armani

Armani has set out to create a product line differentiated by style, luxury, customisation and price to compete in three distinct price tiers. In the most expensive, Tier I, it sells Giorgio Armani and Giorgio Armani Privé, which are custom-made runway couture products that sell for thousands of pounds/euros. In the more moderately priced Tier II, it offers Emporio Armani, young and modern, as well as the informal A|X Armani. In the lower-priced Tier III the company sells the more youthful and street-savvy translation of Armani style, Armani Exchange, at retail locations in cities and shopping centres.

Armani's line of luxury clothing is differentiated to appeal to three distinct price tiers, each with different styles and levels of luxury, using the brand names Georgio Armani, Emporio Armani, A|X Armani and Armani Exchange.
Source: Daniele La Monaca/Reuters/Corbis

The hallmark of an optimal brand portfolio is the ability of each brand in it to maximise equity in combination with all the other brands. If a company can only increase profits by dropping brands, a portfolio is too big; if they can increase profits by *adding* brands, it is not big enough. The basic principle in designing a brand portfolio is to *maximise market coverage*, so that no potential customers are being ignored, but to *minimise brand overlap*, so company brands are not competing for customer approval. Each brand should be clearly differentiated and appealing to a sizeable enough market segment to justify its marketing and production costs.[52]

Brands can also play a number of specific roles as part of a portfolio.

Flankers Flanker or 'fighter' brands are positioned with respect to competitors' brands so that more important (and more profitable) *flagship brands* can retain their desired positioning. Procter & Gamble markets Luvs nappies in a way that flanks the more premium Pampers. Marketers walk a fine line in designing fighter brands, which must not be so attractive that they take sales away from their higher-priced comparison brands.

Cash cows Some brands may be kept around despite dwindling sales because they still manage to hold on to enough customers and maintain their profitability with virtually no marketing support. Companies can effectively 'milk' these 'cash cow' brands by capitalising on their reservoir of existing brand equity. For example, despite the fact that technological advances have moved much of its market to the newer Mach III brand of razors, Gillette still sells the older Trac II, Atra and Sensor brands. Withdrawing them may not necessarily move customers to another Gillette brand, so it is more profitable for Gillette to keep them in its brand portfolio for razor blades.

Low-end entry level The role of a relatively low-priced brand in the portfolio may often be to attract customers to the brand franchise. Retailers like to feature these 'traffic builders' because they are able to 'trade up' customers to a higher-priced brand. For example, BMW introduced a 3-series car in part as a means of bringing new customers into the brand franchise, with the hope of later 'moving them up' to higher-priced models.

High-end prestige The role of a relatively high-priced brand is often to add prestige and credibility to the entire portfolio. Mobile phone companies such as Nokia always have a high-end model in their range. Most Nokia customers will not buy this product but will buy its mid-range, flagship model. Nonetheless, it is often the case that it is the high-end model which attracts the consumers' attention.

Brand reinforcement and revitalisation

Brands need to be managed. As a company's major enduring asset, a brand needs to be carefully managed so that its value does not depreciate.[53]

Brand equity is reinforced by marketing actions that consistently convey the meaning of the brand in terms of:

1   What products and service the brand represents, what core benefits it supplies and what needs it satisfies. Nivea, one of Europe's strongest brands, has expanded its scope from a skin cream brand to a skin care and personal care brand through carefully designed and implemented brand extensions, reinforcing the Nivea brand promise of 'mild', 'gentle', and 'caring' in a broader arena.

2   How the brand makes service or products superior to others and which strong, favourable and unique brand associations should exist in the minds of consumers.[54] Ryanair has become the largest airline in Europe by focusing on its core brand value – providing cheap airline travel to over 49 million Europeans who prefer low cost to high service.

Reinforcing brand image requires innovation and relevance throughout the marketing programme. The brand must always be moving forward – but moving forward in the right direction, with new and compelling offerings and ways to market them.

▽ Apple Computers

The Apple brand is the story of a brand that has had to be managed well throughout its lifespan, which started on April Fool's Day 1976. This €77 billion company has some of the world's hottest consumer products and 82 per cent of the hard drive music market. The company's ability to delight consumers in a bland world of technological equipment and software makes it easy to see why it impacts on so many and across so many segments. From the student who loves their iPod, to the executives who worship their Mac, Apple has brought emotion to their brand and created a brand image and experience that endures and makes us 'Think Differently'.

Apple, Inc. is now a master at building a strong brand that resonates with customers across generations and national boundaries. It achieves incredible brand loyalty largely by delivering on its mission, as defined by CEO Steven Jobs: 'To create great things that change people's lives.' The company has created an army of Apple evangelists, not just because it produces great products that reflect consumer needs but also because everything it does and all its communcations reflect its brand values. Apple's innovative products combine superior design functionality and style, and many cite the wildly successful iPod music player as a prime example. Apple has also created 150 retail stores worldwide to fuel excitement for the brand. The rationale behind the move to retail is that the more people can see and touch Apple products, see what Apple can do for them, the more likely Apple is to increase its market share.[55] The launch and subsequent success of the Apple iPhone in 2008 created more hype and interest and allows Apple to maintain the image of an innovative company in tune with customer needs.

Brands that failed to move forwards – such as Benetton or Jaguar – find their market leadership dwindles or even disappears.

Brand revitalisation

Changes in consumer tastes and preferences, the emergence of new competitors or new technology, or any new development in the marketing environment can affect the fortunes of a brand. In virtually every product or service category, once-prominent and admired brands – such as Little Chef, Alitalia or British Airways – have fallen on hard times, struggled with their brand image or even disappeared.[56] The poor service image of the opening of Terminal 5 in Heathrow in early 2008 damaged the British Airways brand, which focuses on superior customer service. A number of brands have managed to make impressive comebacks in recent years, as marketers have breathed new life into them. Volkswagen and Dr Scholl's and Birkenstock are brands that have been revitalised, becoming popular with the youth market. In 2004 the Finnish mobile phone giant Nokia saw €3.8 billion wiped off its brand equity value as sales fell 13 per cent. In previous years it had focused on designing and marketing large volumes of 'basic handsets' in emerging markets such as China. Meanwhile rivals Samsung and Motorola had been overtaking Nokia in key product attributes such as technology and design in the main mature markets. Nokia refocused its marketing and redesigned its product to meet the market need and now has a brand value of €41.54 billion, up 12 per cent from 2006.

Often the first thing to do in revitalising a brand is to understand what the sources of brand equity are to begin with. Are positive associations losing their strength or uniqueness? Have negative associations become linked to the brand? Then it has to be decided whether to retain the same positioning or create a new one and, if so, which new one. Sometimes the actual marketing programme is the source of the problem, because it fails to deliver on the brand promise. In other cases, however, the old positioning is just no longer viable and a 'reinvention' strategy is necessary. Lucozade completely overhauled its brand image to become an energy drink powerhouse.

▽ Lucozade

The UK energy drinks market is predicted to reach €6 billion by 2010. In general, energy drinks account for £1 in every £5 spent on soft drinks in the United Kingdom. One of the main players, Lucozade is only in this market due to a successful rebranding that saw the company move the drink from a child-oriented, health-related tonic to an energy or sports drink. The original Lucozade, first manufactured in 1927, was available throughout the United Kingdom for use in hospitals. In 1983, a rebranding of Lucozade into an energy drink started with moving the slogan from 'Lucozade aids recovery' to 'Lucozade replaces lost energy', and an advertising campaign featuring the world and Olympic champion decathlete Daley Thompson. The effect of the rebranding was dramatic: the value of UK sales of the drink tripled to almost €95.87 million. During the 1990s it tapped into the sports market and introduced Lucozade Sport, which is now the market leader in sports drinks. Lucozade uses leading sports teams and personalities to keep the sports brand value in front of the consumer. Lucozade is the official drink of the FA and FA Premier League and also sponsors the England Rugby Football Union, the Irish Football Team, the London Marathon, Michael Owen, Steven Gerrard, Damien Duff and Jonny Wilkinson. The brand message is 'Lucozade Sport keeps top athletes going 33% longer', accompanied by the powerful tagline 'Hunger has a Thirst'.

These two campaigns show the use of advertising and product design to reposition the Lucozade brand from a tonic for sick children to an energy drink for leading athletes.

Source: The Advertising Archives

Managing a brand should be a top priority for any organisation. 'Marketing memo: Twenty-first-century branding' offers some contemporary perspectives on enduring brand leadership.

Marketing memo

Twenty-first-century branding

One of the most successful marketers of the last 15 years, Scott Bedbury played a key role in the rise of both Nike and Starbucks. In his insightful book, *A New Brand World*, he offers the following branding principles:

1 **Relying on brand awareness has become marketing fool's gold** – smart brands are more concerned with brand relevance and brand resonance.

2 **You have to know it before you can grow it** – most brands don't know who they are, where they've been, and where they're going.

3 **Always remember the Spandex rule of brand expansion** – just because you can, doesn't mean you should.

4 **Great brands establish enduring customer relationships** – they have more to do with emotions and trust than with footwear comfort or the way a coffee bean is roasted.

5 **Everything matters** – in marketing and therefore in branding it is the total offering – everything from the carpet in the hotel and to how the phone is answered, to product packaging; even colours and smells matter.

6 **All brands need good parents** – unfortunately, most brands come from troubled homes.

7 **Big is no excuse for being bad** – truly great brands use their superhuman powers for good and place people and principles before profits.

8 **Relevance, simplicity and humanity** – rather than technology, will distinguish brands in the future.

Source: S. Bedbury (2002) *A New Brand World*, New York: Viking Press. Copyright © 2002 by Scott Bedbury. Reproduced with permission from Viking Penguin, a division of the Penguin Group USA.

▽ Managing and measuring brand equity

Brand equity is the added value given to products and services. Brand equity and value is reflected in how consumers think, feel and act with respect to the brand, as well as the prices, market share and profitability that the brand commands for the company.

Brands play a major role in enhancing the **financial value** of companies. To companies, brands represent enormously valuable pieces of legal property that can influence consumer behaviour, be bought and sold, and provide the security of sustained future revenues. Companies have paid large sums of moneys for brands in mergers or acquisitions, often justifying the price premium on the basis of the extra profits to be extracted and sustained from the brands, as well as the tremendous difficulty and expense of creating similar brands from scratch. Although only founded in 1998, by 2008 Google was the most recognised and valuable brand in the world, valued at €11.51 billion.[57] A strong brand is a valuable asset, as can be seen from the Table 12.2, which highlights actual brand values for the top ten companies in Europe.[58]

As Rita Clifton, the author of *Brands and Branding* and the chairperson of Interbrand UK, puts it: 'Well-managed brands have extraordinary economic value and are the most effective and efficient creators of sustainable wealth.'[59] Malcolm Forbes described them as 'the best marketable investment a company can make'.[60] Brand value is typically over half the total company market capitalisation and so the importance of the brand to the company is clear. Brand value is increasingly included on balance sheets in countries such as the United Kingdom, Hong Kong and Australia. A recent Price-WaterhouseCoopers report of the US market revealed that 74 per cent of the average purchase prices of acquired companies was made up of intangible assets and goodwill – what is called brand value.[61]

Brand valuation

Marketers should distinguish brand equity from brand valuation, which is the job of estimating the total financial value of the brand.

For brand equity to perform a useful strategic function and guide marketing decisions, marketers need to fully understand: (1) the sources of brand equity and how they affect outcomes of interest; as well as (2) how these sources and outcomes change, if at all, over time. Brand audits are important for the former; brand tracking for the latter.

A **brand audit** is a consumer-focused procedure to assess the health of the brand, uncover its sources of brand equity and suggest ways to improve and leverage its equity. Conducting brand audits on a regular basis, such as annually, allows marketers to keep their fingers on the pulse of their brands so they can manage them more proactively and responsively. Brand audits are particularly useful background for marketing managers as they set up their marketing plans and select marketing mix variables, and when they are considering making changes.

Table 12.2 Top ten European brands 2007

European ranking	World ranking	Brand	Country of origin	Sector	Brand value (€ million)
1	5	Nokia	Finland	Consumer electronics	22,900
2	10	Mercedes	Germany	Automotive	15,813
3	13	BMW	Germany	Automotive	14,688
4	17	Louis Vuitton	France	Luxury	13,810
5	23	HSBC	UK	Financial services	9,217
6	24	Nescafé	Switzerland	Beverages	8,801
7	25	SAP	Germany	Computer software	7,373
8	38	IKEA	Sweden	Home furnishings	6,855
9	39	UBS	Switzerland	Financial services	6,686
10	42	Philips	Netherlands	Diversified	5,259

Source: Interbrand.

Marketing insight

The brand value chain

The **brand value chain** is a structured approach to assessing the sources and outcomes of brand equity and the manner in which marketing activities create brand value (see Figure 12.4). It is based on several premises.

First, the brand value creation process is assumed to begin when the firm invests in a marketing programme targeting actual or potential customers. Any marketing programme investment that can be attributed to brand value development, intentional or not, falls into this category – product research, development and design; trade or intermediary support; and marketing communications.

Next, customers' mindsets are assumed to change as a result of the marketing programme. The question is how. This change, in turn, is assumed to affect the way the brand performs in the marketplace through the collective impact of individual customers deciding how much to purchase and when, how much they'll pay, and so on. Finally, the investment community considers market performance and other factors such as replacement cost and purchase price in acquisitions to arrive at an assessment of shareholder value in general and the value of a brand in particular.

The model also assumes that a number of linking factors intervene between these stages and determine the extent to which value created at one stage transfers to the next stage. Three sets of multipliers moderate the transfer between the marketing programme and the subsequent three value stages – the programme multiplier, the customer multiplier and the market multiplier.

The *programme multiplier* determines the marketing programme's ability to affect the customer mindset and is a function of the quality of the programme investment. The *customer multiplier* determines the extent to which value created in the minds of customers affects market performance. This result depends on contextual factors external to the customer.

Three such factors are:

1 **Competitive superiority:** how effective the quantity and quality of the marketing investment of other competing brands are.

2 **Channel and other intermediary support:** how much brand reinforcement and selling effort various marketing partners are putting forth.

3 **Customer size and profile:** how many and what types of customers, profitable or not, are attracted to the brand.

The *market multiplier* determines the extent to which the value shown by the market performance of a brand is manifested in shareholder value. It depends, in part, on the actions of financial analysts and investors.

Sources: K. L. Keller and D. Lehmann (2003) How do brands create value?, *Marketing Management,* May–June, 27–31. See also M. J. Epstein and R. A. Westbrook (2001) Linking actions to profits in strategic decision making, *MIT Sloan Management Review,* Spring, 39–49; and R. K. Srivastava, T. A. Shervani and L. Fahey (1998) Market-based assets and shareholder value, *Journal of Marketing,* 62(1), January, 2–18.

Figure 12.4 The Brand Value Chain

Source: K. L. Keller, T. Aperia and M. Georgson, (2008) Strategic Brand Management: a European Perspective, Pearson education, FT Press, London; K. L. Keller, and D. R. Lehmann, (2003) How do Brands create value? Marketing Management, May/June, 12(3), 26–31.

Figure 12.5 A systems model of brand antecedents and consequences

Source: K. L. Keller and D. R. Lehmann (2006) Brand and banding: research findings and future priorities, *Marketing Science*, 25(6), 740–59. Copyright © 2006 The Institute for Operations Research and the Management Sciences (INFORMS). Reproduced by permission of INFORMS and the authors.

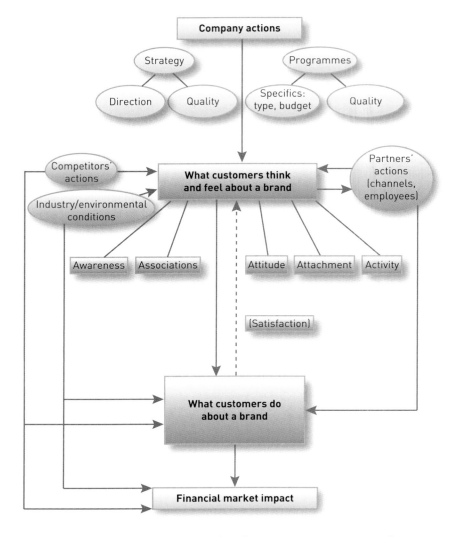

Brand tracking studies collect quantitative data from consumers on a routine basis over time to provide marketers with consistent, baseline information about how their brands and marketing programmes are performing on key dimensions. Tracking studies are a means of understanding where, how much, and in what ways brand value is being created, to facilitate day-to-day decision making.

Brand equity and brand performance

Marketing managers need a model to link brand equity and brand performance.[62] There are four major stages, as outlined in Figure 12.5.

What companies/marketing managers do The full marketing programme and other aspects of the company operations must be managed from both a quantitative (factors such as amount of marketing expenditure) and qualitative (clarity and consistency of the marketing programme) perspectives.

What customers think and feel Individual customer characteristics as well as competition and other aspects of the environment will influence how customers feel. What they think and feel is not under the sole control of the company. Personal experience and the experience of others will both affect what a customer thinks of a brand.

What customers do The main payoff is when the customer buys the product or service and so affects revenue, share and other metrics commonly used to judge brand success. Of course,

Marketing insight

The top ten traits of the world's strongest brands[63]

Devised by Kevin Keller, this brand report card is a systematic way for marketing managers to think about how to grade their brand's performance and also to grade their competitor brands.

1 The brand excels at delivering the benefits customers truly desire.

2 The brand stays relevant.

3 The pricing strategy is based on consumers' perception of value.

4 The brand is positioned properly.

5 The brand is consistent.

6 The brand portfolio makes sense.

7 The brand makes use of and coordinates a full range of marketing mix activities to build brand equity.

8 The brand managers understand what the brand means to consumers.

9 The brand is given proper support, and that support is sustained over the long run.

10 The company monitors sources of brand equity.

other things that customers do (especially word of mouth) impact on the future development of the brand.

How financial markets react Most brands are judged by how they perfom financially internally and also in relation to stock prices and market capitalisation (the value of the company if it was sold). This is called the bottom line and is what the chief executive will ask of marketing – that the brand provides a return to the company.

Measuring brand equity

There are various models used to study brand equity, which will be explored in Chapter 22. Marketers and researchers use various perspectives to study brand equity.[64]

Customer-based brand equity is the differential effect that brand knowledge has on consumer response to the marketing of that brand.[65] Customer-based approaches view the brand from the perspective of the consumer – either an individual or an organisation.[66] The premise of customer-based brand equity models is that the power of a brand lies in what customers have seen, read, heard, learned, thought and felt about the brand over time.[67] Customer-level brand equity can be characterised in terms of awareness, association, attitudes (or attraction) and activity.[68]

A brand has *positive* customer-based brand equity when consumers react more favourably to a product or service and the way it is marketed when the brand is *identified,* than when it is not identified. A brand has *negative* customer-based brand equity if consumers react less favourably to marketing activity for the brand under the same circumstances.

Another model used to measure brand equity is the brand asset valuator (BAV)

This model was based on research with almost 500,000 consumers in 44 countries. It provides comparative measures of the brand equity of thousands of brands across hundreds of different categories. There are five key pillars of brand equity, according to BAV:

1 **Differentiation:** measures the degree to which a brand is seen as different from others.

2 **Energy:** measures the brand's sense of momentum.

3 **Relevance:** measures the breadth of a brand's appeal.

4 **Esteem:** measures how well the brand is regarded and respected.

5 **Knowledge:** measures how familiar and intimate consumers are with the brand.

Differentiation, Energy and Relevance combine to determine *Energised Brand Strength.* These three pillars point to the brand's future value. Esteem and Knowledge together create *Brand Stature,* which is more of a 'report card' on past performance.

Figure 12.6 BAV
PowerGrid

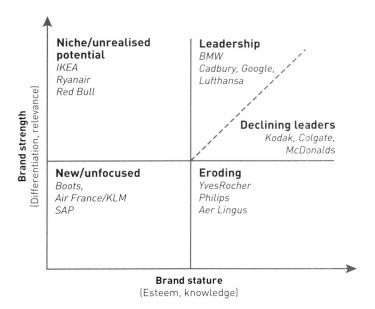

The relationships among these dimensions – a brand's 'pillar pattern' – reveal much about its current and future status. Energised Brand Strength and Brand Stature combined form the *PowerGrid,* depicting the stages in the cycle of brand development – each with characteristic pillar patterns – in successive quadrants (see Figure 12.6). Strong new brands show higher levels of Differentiation and Energy than Relevance, while both Esteem and Knowledge are lower still. Leadership brands show high levels on all pillars. Finally, declining brands show high Knowledge – evidence of past performance – a lower level of Esteem, and even lower Relevance, Energy and Differentiation.

Combining these factors, one can create a graphical approach to Brand Equity, as shown in Figure 12.6.

Top brand valuation company Interbrand defines brand equity or value as the net present value of the earnings a brand is expected to generate in the future. The following is a summary of the Interbrand model for evaluation of brand equity:

1 **Financial analysis:** Interbrand assesses purchase price, volume and frequency to help calculate accurate forecasts of future brand sales and revenues. Specifically, Interbrand performs a detailed review of the brand's equities, industry and customer trends, and historic financial performance across each segment. Once it has established branded revenues, it deducts all associated operating costs to derive earnings before interest and tax (EBIT).

2 **Role of branding:** Interbrand next attributes a proportion of intangible earnings to the brand in each market segment, by first identifying the various drivers of demand, then determining the degree to which the brand directly influences each. The role of branding assessment is based on market research, client workshops and interviews and represents the percentage of intangible earnings the brand generates.

3 **Brand strength:** Interbrand then assesses the brand's strength profile to determine the likelihood that the brand will realise forecast earnings. This step relies on competitive benchmarking, and a structured evaluation of the brand's market, stability, leadership position, growth trend, support, geographic footprint and legal protection. For each segment, Interbrand applies industry and brand equity metrics to determine a risk premium for the brand.

Increasingly, Interbrand uses brand value assessments as a dynamic, strategic tool to identify and maximise return on brand investment across a whole host of areas.

▽ Branding issues: branding of services, co-creation and brand touchpoints

Services branding

Though branding has traditionally focused on products, service branding is a skill that is crucial to marketing managers. Marketers can build strong service brands by creating and managing emotional brand experiences.[69] As leading services guru Leonard Berry notes:

> Branding plays a special role in service companies because strong brands increase customers' trust of the invisible purchase. Strong brands enable customers to better visualise and understand intangible services. Strong service brands are the surrogates when the company offers no fabric to touch, no trousers to try on, no watermelons or apples to scrutinize, no car to test drive.[70]

The best service brands are the ones that:

1 align their processes, organisational structures and service processes and environments to deliver a consistently superior brand experience;

2 harness the power of customer information to enhance the service experience;

3 leverage that information to expand their offerings into additional categories.[71]

In a study of four leading banks in the United Kingdom, Professor Leslie de Chernatony, Professor of Brand Marketing at the University of Birmingham, found that financial services brands that had not achieved 'greatness' tend to be rooted in the past.[72] They place emphasis on financial performance rather than brand success indicators, have inadequate leadership support for the brand, are poorly differentiated, exhibit a lack of understanding and confusion about branding issues, have service quality concerns, demonstrate HR activities that are not focused fully 'on the brand', and possess a culture and values which do not clearly and consistently reinforce the brand. From this example it is clear that every aspect of the service and marketing mix amplifies the brand's values.

Services businesses are increasingly the dominant form of business and are beginning to appear in the list of top global brands. Looking at Interbrand's 2007 top ten brands, three are considered to be services, however practically all the brands in this list have some element of service provision.[73] Can you review the list of top ten brands from Table 12.2 (on page 446) and select the three service companies?

Managing a service brand means focusing on four aspects, as portrayed in Figure 12.7.

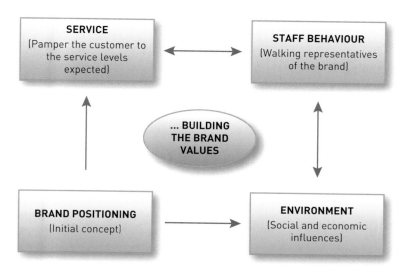

Figure 12.7 Managing the service brands

Service: how to pamper customers so that they achieve the service levels expected. Many customers accept low service in one aspect of their lives but expect great service in other aspects.

Staff behaviour: staff are the walking representatives of the brand and their behaviour must be managed at all times. Service branding and staff are crucial within services, as the perceived brand values can be based on the behaviour of employees. Brands are used symbolically in two different directions: inward and outward. Outwardly to communicate to others the kind of (company)/person we are; inwardly to bolster the sense of (*company*)/self.[74]

Marketers must ensure that all employees 'walk the walk and talk the talk' to deliver the brand promise. They must adopt an *internal* perspective to ensure employees and supply chain partners appreciate and understand the branding values, and how they can help – or hurt – brand equity.[75] It is often a member of the supply network or channels that delivers the brand to the consumer or who is aligned to the brand in the consumer's mind. These partners need to be managed too.

Brand positioning: this is the initial concept and the brand positioning as discussed in Chapter 10 is crucial for all brands.

Environment: the social and economic environments are influences that affect the brand. Often the brand is experienced at a distance from the company providing the brand.

Choosing brand elements for services

Because services are intangible, and because customers often make decisions and arrangements about them away from the actual service location itself (at home or at work), brand recall becomes critically important. So an easy-to-remember brand name is critical.

Other brand elements – logos, symbols, characters and slogans – can also help complement the brand name to build brand awareness and brand image. These brand elements often attempt to make the service and some of its key benefits more tangible, concrete, and real – for example, 'more than just flying' from Iberia Airlines or KLM: 'the reliable airline'. Because a physical product does not exist, the physical facilities of the service provider – its primary and secondary signage, environmental design and reception area, clothing, collateral material, and so on – are especially important. All aspects of the service delivery process can be branded, which is why UPS is concerned about the appearance of its drivers and why UPS has developed such strong equity with its brown trucks and brown uniforms.

Establishing image dimensions Given the human nature of services, it is no surprise that brand personality is an important image dimension for services. Starwood trains its hotel employees and call centre operators to convey different experiences for the firm's different hotel chains: Sheraton is positioned as warm, comforting and casual; Westin is positioned in terms of renewal and is a little more formal; Four Points by Sheraton is designed to be all about honest, uncomplicated comfort.[76]

Devising branding strategy Finally, services must also consider developing a brand hierarchy and brand portfolio that permits positioning and targeting of different market segments. Marketers can brand classes of service vertically on the basis of price and quality. Vertical extensions often require subbranding strategies that combine the corporate name with an individual brand name or modifier. In the hotel and airlines industries, brand lines and portfolios have been created by brand extension and introductions. Hilton Hotels has a portfolio of brands that includes Hilton Garden Inns to target budget-conscious business travellers and compete with the popular Courtyard by Marriott chain, as well as DoubleTree, Embassy Suites, Homewood Suites and Hampton Inn.

Co-creation and customisation

A major aspect of both products and services has been the move to **co-creation**, customisation or personalisation in the branding field. These concepts were introduced in Chapters 1 and 2 and will be expanded on in Chapter 18. Marketers are increasingly abandoning the mass market practices that built brand powerhouses in the 1950s, 1960s and 1970s for new approaches that are in fact a throwback to marketing practices from a century ago, when companies literally knew their customers by name and allowed them to design products and service themselves. Think of the traditional tailor or shoemaker. From a branding point of view, these different concepts are about getting consumers more actively involved with a brand by creating an intense, active relationship.

Co-creation

Marketers are now being urged to give up the steering wheel to a new breed of consumers who want more control over the brand for many products and services. This is the move from top-down marketing to bottom-up, grass-roots approaches that involve the consumer from the very beginning. Cammie Dunaway, chief marketing officer at Yahoo!, says you need to 'allow customers to help you shape the brand experience. Content is no longer something you push out. Content is an invitation to engage with your brand.' According to A. G. Lafley, chief executive at Procter & Gamble, the power is with the consumer, 'Marketers and retailers are scrambling to keep up with them.' Lafley cites P&G as an example of a company that attempts some co-creation with their customers. For example, an animated spot for Pringles snacks was created for the company by a teenager and put up on YouTube; a campaign for Pantene encouraged women to cut their hair and donate the clippings to make wigs for cancer patients.[77]

Customisation

The rapid expansion of the Internet and other technologies have created opportunities to personalise marketing offerings.[78] James L. McDowell, managing director at Mini BMW notes that the fact that so many customers choose to customise their cars shows executives that 'We'd never have complete control over the brand'. About 60 per cent of the estimated 40,000 Minis the company sells each year are customised. For instance, McDowell recalls how some Mini owners dress their cars in costumes for Halloween, and how two investment bankers mounted mock shark fins atop the roofs of their Minis.[79] Customers are now allowed or encouraged to personalise so many items, from their iPod to personalised adidas sports shoes.

mi adidas online shop allows customers to customise their sports shoes.
Source: Courtesy of adidas

Managing the brand touch points

Customers come to know a brand through a range of contacts and touch points, which will be discussed in Chapter 18. These can include personal observation and use, word of mouth, interactions with company personnel, online or telephone experiences and payment transactions. A **brand contact** is any information-bearing experience, whether positive or negative, which a customer has with the brand.[80] A moment of truth is defined as every opportunity that the customer has to experience and evaluate their relationship with a company. The aim of branding is to find a brand idea that will run through all the places and situation where consumers, employees, suppliers and investors experience the brand. Ashley Goodall, managing director of the UK-based Saatchi & Saatchi Design Agency identified Apple as a company that manages its brand touch points. From product to the Apple shop the whole identity, communication and design ethos pervades everything Apple does to create a unique and well-thought-out brand that is excuted at every touch point.

Nowadays the range of methods by which a consumer can make contact with a brand is immense. Whether by phone, fax, email, mail, Web, self-service or face to face in a purchase encounter the brand is embodied in all aspects of a consumer's contact with the company. Marketers must put as much effort into managing these experiences as into producing their advertisment or deciding on their price.[81] Non-marketing personnel may think that it is just advertising or slogans and brand names that create the brand, but it is always all the marketing mix elements working together that creates the brand and service process can be overlooked as a core requirement. Zara, the Spanish fashion retailer, is a company that uses only a tiny amount of advertising to build its brand. Compared to other companies it spends only .03 per cent of its revenues on advertising and only then for new stores. Zara focuses its marketing on the service process and store design and atmospherics – using the shopfront as the image of the company and the customer experience within the store as the crucial elements of its brand management. Zara also concentrates its spend on managing its distribution systems so that new styles hit the stores every week so that they always have the latest fashions. Zara's is one of the fastest-growing brands in Europe, growing 22 per cent in 2007.

▽ SUMMARY

1 A brand is a name, term, sign, symbol or design, or some combination of these elements, intended to identify the products and services of one company and to differentiate them from those of competitors. The different components of a brand – brand names, logos, symbols, package designs, and so on – are brand elements.

2 Brands offer a number of benefits to customers and companies. Brands are valuable intangible assets that need to be managed carefully. The key to branding is that consumers perceive differences among brands in a product or service category.

3 A branding strategy for a company identifies which brand elements a company chooses to apply across its various products or service. In a brand extension, the marketing manager uses an established brand name to introduce a new product. Potential extensions must be judged by how effectively they leverage existing brand equity as well as how effectively the extension, in turn, contributes to the equity of the existing parent brand.

4 Brands can play a number of different roles within the brand portfolio. Brands may expand coverage, provide protection, extend an image or fulfil a variety of other roles for the company. Each brand name must have a well-defined positioning. In that way, brands can maximise coverage, minimise overlap and thus optimise the portfolio.

5 Brand equity should be defined in terms of marketing effects uniquely attributable to a brand. That is, brand equity relates to the fact that different outcomes result from the marketing of a branded product or service when compared to the results if that same product or service was not branded.

6 Brand equity needs to be measured in order to be managed well. Brand audits measure 'where the brand has been', and tracking studies measure 'where the brand is now' and whether marketing programmes are having the intended effects.

7 Services branding, co-creation and brand touch points are all areas of branding that are growing and demanding marketing managers' attention.

▽ APPLICATIONS

Marketing debate

Are brand extensions good or bad? Some critics vigorously denounce the practice of brand extensions, as they feel that too often companies lose focus and consumers become confused. Other experts maintain that brand extensions are a critical growth strategy and source of revenue for the company. Discuss.

Take a position: Brand extensions can endanger brands *versus* Brand extensions are an important brand-growth strategy.

Marketing discussion

What are the main choices that marketing managers must decide on when managing their brands?

▽ REFERENCES

[1] M. Well (2004) Kid nabbing, *Forbes*, 2 February, p. 84; *P&G Fact Sheet*, August 2003; Chairman's Address, Annual Shareholder Meeting, 14 October, 2003; Ed Tazzia (2003) What's entertaining? *Brandweek*, 17 November, p. 40; N. O'Leary (2003) The new and improved P&G, *Brandweek*, 17 November, p. 44.

[2] R. Berner (2004) Old Spice extreme makeover, *BusinessWeek*, 1 November.

[3] A post-modern proctoid, *The Economist*, 15 April, p. 68; *P&G Fact Sheet*, December 2006; J. Galvin (2005) The world on a string, *Point*, February, pp. 13–24; J. Neff (2005) P&G kisses up to the boss: consumers, *Advertising Age*, 2 May, p. 18; R. Berner (2006) Detergent can be so much more, *BusinessWeek*, 1 May, pp. 66–8; www.pg.com; R. Berner (2004) op. cit.; A. Andrews (2006) Crazy Frog creator leaps up UK ad spending league, *The Times*, 4 January.

[4] L. deChernatony and M. McDonald (1998) *Creating Powerful Brands*, Oxford, England: Butterworth Heinemann.

[5] Interbrand Group, *World's Greatest Brands: An International Review*, New York: John Wiley & Sons; see also K. Moore and S. E. Reid (2006) The birth of a brand, Working Paper, Desautels Faculty of Management, McGill University.

[6] J. McNeal (1992) *Kids as Consumers: A Handbook for Marketing to Children*, New York: Lexington Books.

[7] D. Alleres (1990) *Luxe . . . Strategies Marketing*, Paris: Economica.

[8] R. Elliott and A. Davies (2005) Symbolic brands and authenticity of identity performance, in J. Schroeder and M. Salzer-Morling (eds.) *Brand Culture*, London: Routledge.

[9] M. Moynagh and R. Worsley (2002) Tomorrow's consumer: the shifting balance of power, *Journal of Consumer Behaviour*, 1(3), 293–301.

[10] W. Coop (2005) A question of identity, *Journal of Marketing*, 11(1), 36–7.

[11] S. Morrison and F. G. Crane (2007) Building the service brand by creating and managing an emotional brand experience, *Journal of Brand Management*, 14(5), 410–22.

[12] S. Morrison and F. G. Crane (2007) op. cit.; H. Brembeck and K. Ekstrom (2004) *Elusive Consumption*, Oxford, England: Berg Publishers; M. Gobe (2001) *Emotional Branding*, New York: Allworth Press; S. Ratneshwar and D. Mick (2005) *Inside Consumption*, London: Routledge.

[13] S. Morrison and F. G. Crane (2007) op. cit.; M. Gobe (2001) op. cit.

[14] P. Gumbel (2007) Luxury brands: the business of selling dreams, *European Business Review*, 26 October.

[15] For an academic discussion of how consumers become so strongly attached to people as brands, see M. Thomson (2006) Human brands: investigating antecedents to consumers' stronger attachments to celebrities, *Journal of Marketing*, 70 (July), 104–19; for some practical branding tips from the world of rock of roll, see R. Blackwell and T. Stephan (2004) *Brands That Rock*, Hoboken, NJ: John Wiley & Sons; and from the world of sports, see I. Rein, P. Kotler and B. Shields (2006) *The Elusive Fan: Reinventing Sports in a Crowded Marketplace*, New York, NY: McGraw-Hill.

[16] K. Keller (2001) Building customer-based brand equity, *Marketing Management*, 10(2), 14–19.

[17] T. Erdem (1998) Brand equity as a signaling phenomenon, *Journal of Consumer Psychology*, 7(2), 131–57.

[18] R. Suri and K. B. Monroe (2003) The effects of time pressure on consumers' judgments of prices and products, *Journal of Consumer Research*, 30 (June), 92–104.

[19] Rita Clifton and John Simmons (eds.) (2004) *The Economist on Branding*, New York: Bloomberg Press; R. Riezebos (2003) *Brand Management: A Theoretical and Practical Approach*, Harlow, England: Pearson Education Ltd; and P. Temporal (2002) *Advanced Brand Management: From Vision to Valuation*, Singapore: John Wiley & Sons.

[20] C. E. Bagley (2005) *Managers and the Legal Environment: Strategies for the 21st Century*, 3rd edn. Cincinnati, OH: Southwestern College/West Publishing; for a marketing academic point of view of some important legal issues, see J. Zaichkowsky (2006) *The Psychology Behind Trademark Infringement and Counterfeiting*, Philadelphia: LEA Publishing; and M. Morrin and J. Jacoby (2000) Trademark dilution: empirical measures for an elusive concept, *Journal of Public Policy & Marketing*, 19(2), 265–76.

[21] S. Davis (2000) *Brand Asset Management: Driving Profitable Growth Through Your Brands*, San Francisco: Jossey-Bass; D. C. Bello and M. B. Holbrook (1996) Does an absence of brand equity generalize across product classes?, *Journal of Business Research*, 34, 125–31; M. W. Sullivan (1998) How brand names affect the demand for twin automobiles, *Journal of Marketing Research*, 35, 154–65; A. J. Slywotzky and B. P. Shapiro (1993) Leveraging to beat the odds: the new marketing mindset, *Harvard Business Review*, September–October, 97–107.

[22]The power of branding is not without its critics, however, some of whom reject the commercialism associated with branding activities. See N. Klein (2000) *No Logo: Taking Aim at the Brand Bullies*, New York: Picador.

[23]G. Harter, A. Koster, M. Peterson and M. Stomberg (2005) Europe's brand-oriented companies almost twice as successful, *Booz, Allen, Hamilton* website (www.boozallen.com/publications/article/659562), 14 February.

[24]B. Lev (2001) *Intangibles: Management, Measurement, and Reporting*, Washington, DC: Brookings Institute; N. Mizik and R. Jacobson (2005) Talk about brand strategy, *Harvard Business Review*, October, p. 1.

[25]C. Bothwell (2005) Burberry versus the chavs, *BBC Money Programme*, 28 October (http://news.bbc.co.uk/1/hi/business/4381140.stm).

[26]K. L. Keller and S. Sood (2003) Brand equity dilution, *MIT Sloan Management Review*, 45(1), 12–15.

[27]R. Dodes (2006) From tracksuits to fast track, *Wall Street Journal*, 13 September, B1–2.

[28]C. W. Park, S . Y. Jun and A. D. Shocker (1996) Composite branding alliances: an investigation of extension and feedback effects, *Journal of Marketing Research*, 33, 453–66; L. Leuthesser, C. Kohli and R. Suri (2003) 2 + 2 = 5? A framework for using co-branding to leverage a brand, *Journal of Brand Management*, 2(1), 35–47.

[29]Based in part on a talk by N. Bailey (2000) Using licensing to build the brand, Brand Masters Conference, 7 December.

[30]K. K. Desai and K. L. Keller (2002) The effects of brand expansions and ingredients branding strategies on host brand extendibility, *Journal of Marketing*, 66 (January), 73–93; D.C. Denision (2002) Ingredient branding puts big names in the mix, *Boston Globe*, 26 May 26.

[31]See http://pal2pal.com/BLOGEE/index.php?/site/comments/left_wing_group_turns_cereal_killer/.

[32]A. Wheeler (2003) *Designing Brand Identity*, Hoboken, NJ: John Wiley & Sons.

[33]P. Fallon and F. Senn (2006) *Juicing the Orange: How to Turn Creativity into a Powerful Business Advantage*, Cambridge, MA: Harvard Business School Press.

[34]R. Salerno (2003) We try harder: an ad creates a brand, *Brandweek,* 8 September, 32–33.

[35]For comprehensive corporate branding guidelines, see J. R. Gregory (2004) *The Best of Branding: Best Practices in Corporate Branding*, New York, NY: McGraw-Hill; for some international perspectives, see M. Schultz, M. J. Hatch and M. H. Larsen (eds.) (2000) *The Expressive Organization: Linking Identity, Reputation and Corporate Brand*, Oxford, England: Oxford University Press; and M. Schultz, Y. M. Antorini and F. F. Csaba (eds.) (2005) *Corporate Branding: Purpose, People, and Process*, Copenhagen: Copenhagen Business School Press.

[36]P. Farquhar (1989) Managing brand equity, *Marketing Research*, 1 (September), 24–33.

[37]S. M. Shugan (1989) Branded variants, 1989 AMA Educators' Proceedings, Chicago: American Marketing Association, pp. 33–8; see also M. Bergen, S. Dutta, and S. M. Shugan (1996) Branded variants: a retail perspective, *Journal of Marketing Research*, 33 (February), 9–21.

[38]A. Bass (2004) Licensed extension: stretching to communicate, *Journal of Brand Management*, 12 (September), 31–8; see also D. Aaker (1995) *Building Strong Brands*. New York: Free Press.

[39]B. Loken and D. R. John (1993) Diluting brand beliefs: when do brand extensions have a negative impact?, *Journal of Marketing*, July, 71–84; D. Roedder John, B. Loken and C. Joiner (1998) The negative impact of extensions: can flagship products be diluted, *Journal of Marketing*, January, 19–32; S. M. Broniarcyzk and J. W. Alba (1994) The importance of the brand in brand extension, *Journal of Marketing Research*, May, 214–28 (note: the entire issue of JMR May 1994 is devoted to brands and brand equity); see also R. Ahluwalia and Z. Gürhan-Canli (2000) The effects of extensions on the family brand name: an accessibility-diagnosticity perspective, *Journal of Consumer Research*, 27 (December), 371–81; Z. Gürhan-Canli and M. Durairaj (1998) The effects of extensions on brand name dilution and enhancement, *Journal of Marketing Research*, 35, 464–73; S. J. Milberg, C. W. Park and M. S. McCarthy (1997) Managing negative feedback effects associated with brand extensions: the impact of alternative branding strategies, *Journal of Consumer Psychology*, 6, 119–40; C. Pullig, C. Simmons and R. G. Netemeyer (2006) Brand dilution: when do new brands hurt existing brands?, *Journal of Marketing*, 70 (April), 52–66.

[40]F. Völckner and H. Sattler (2006) Drivers of brand extension success, *Journal of Marketing*, 70 (April), 1–17.

[41]K. L. Keller and D. A. Aaker (1992) The effects of sequential introduction of brand extensions, *Journal of Marketing Research*, 29 (February), 35–50; for consumer processing implications see H. Mao and H. Shanker Krishnan (2006) Effects of prototype and exemplar fit on brand extension evaluations: a two-process contingency model, *Journal of Consumer Research*, 33 (June), 41–9.

[42]Keller and Aaker (1992) op. cit.; J. Milewicz and P. Herbig (1994) evaluating the brand extension decision using a model of reputation building, *Journal of Product & Brand Management*, 3(1), 39–47.

[43]D. C. Smith (1992) Brand extension and advertising efficiency: what can and cannot be expected, *Journal of Advertising Research*, November/December, 11–20; D. C. Smith and C. Whan Park (1992) The effects of brand extensions on market share and advertising efficiency, *Journal of Marketing Research*, 29 (August), 296–313; V. A. Taylor and W. O. Bearden (2003) Ad spending on brand extensions: does similarity matter?, *Journal of Brand Management*, 11 (September), 63–74; S. Bridges, K. L. Keller and S. Sood (2000) Communication strategies for brand extensions: enhancing perceived fit by establishing explanatory links, *Journal of Advertising*, 29 (Winter), 1–11.

[44]B. Meyer (2005) Rubber firms extend brands to gain customers, revenues, *Bnet Business Network,* October.

[45]J. Paisner, (2006) Goodyear and Michelin: on your feet, *CoreBrand*, 16 January (www.corebrand.com/index.php?option=com_content&task=view&id=47&Itemid=).

[46]J. A. Quelch and David Kenny (1994) Extend profits, not product lines, *Harvard Business Review*, September–October, 153–60; Perspectives from the editors: the logic of product-line extensions, *Harvard Business Review*, November–December, 53–62; M. Morrin (1999) The impact of brand extensions on parent brand memory structures and retrieval processes, *Journal of Marketing Research*, 36(4), 517–25.

[47]A. Ries and J. Trout (2000) *Positioning: The Battle for Your Mind, 20th Anniversary Edition*, New York: McGraw-Hill.

[48]D. A. Aaker (2004) *Brand Portfolio Strategy: Creating Relevance, Differentiation, Energy, Leverage, and Clarity*, New York: Free Press.

[49]Lego's turnaround: picking up the pieces, *The Economist*, 28 October, p. 76.

[50]M. Haig (2005) *Brand Failures: The Truth About the 100 Biggest Branding Mistakes of All Time*, London: Kogan Page.

[51]J. Doward, J. Arlidge and F. Islam (2000) Branson's big gamble, *The Observer*, 27 August (www.guardian.co.uk/society/2000/aug/27/lottery.observerfocus).

[52]J. Trout (2001) *Differentiate or Die: Survival in Our Era of Killer Competition*, New York: John Wiley & Sons.

[53]M. Sherrington (2003) *Added Value: The Alchemy of Brand-Led Growth*, Hampshire, England: Palgrave Macmillan.

[54]For an up-to-date discussion of what factors determines long-term branding success, see A. P. Adamson (2006) *Brand Simple*, New York: Palgrave Macmillan.

[55]A. Z. Cuneo (2003) Apple transcends as lifestyle brand, *Advertising Age*, 15 June, S2–S6.

[56]M. Speece (2002) Marketer's malady: fear of change, *Brandweek*, 19 August, p. 34; Haig (2005) op. cit.

[57]Interbrand/Business Week (www.interbrand.com/best_brands_2007.asp).

[58]Ibid.

[59]R. Clifton (2004) The future of brands, *Interbrand*, 23 April (www.brandchannel.com/papers_review.asp?sp_id=356).

[60]See http://www.brandwave.net/identity.html.

[61]T. Hadjiloucas and R. Winter (2005) Reporting the value of acquired intangible assets, PricewaterhouseCoopers Globe White Paper, London: PricewaterhouseCoopers.

[62]K. L. Keller and D. Lehmann (2006) Brand and branding: research findings and future priorities, *Marketing Science*, 25(6), 740–59.

[63]K. L. Keller (2000) The brand report card, *Harvard Business Review*, January–February, 147–57.

[64]Other approaches are based on economic principles of signaling, for example, T. Erdem (1998) Brand equity as a signaling phenomenon, *Journal of Consumer Psychology*, 7(2), 131–57; or for more of a sociological, anthropological, or biological perspective, for example, G. McCracken (2005) *Culture and Consumption II: Markets, Meaning, and Brand Management*, Bloomington, IN: Indiana University Press; or S. Fournier (1998) Consumers and their brands: developing relationship theory in consumer research, *Journal of Consumer Research*, 24 (September), 343–73.

[65]K. L. Keller (2007) *Strategic Brand Management. Building, Measuring, and Managing Brand Equity*, 3rd edn, Upper Saddle River, NJ: Prentice Hall.

[66]D. A. Aaker (1991) *Managing Brand Equity*, New York: Free Press; D. A. Aaker (1996) *Building Strong Brands*, New York: Free Press; D. A. Aaker and E. Joachimsthaler (2000) *Brand Leadership*, New York: Free Press; Keller (2008) op. cit.

[67]J.-N. Kapferer (1992) *Strategic Brand Management: New Approaches to Creating and Evaluating Brand Equity*, London: Kogan Page, p. 38; J. L. Aaker (1997) Dimensions of brand personality, *Journal of Marketing Research*, August, 347–56; S. M. Davis (2002) *Brand Asset Management: Driving Profitable Growth Through Your Brands*, San Francisco: Jossey-Bass; for an overview of academic research on branding, see K. L. Keller (2002) Branding and brand equity, in B. Weitz and R. Wensley (eds.) *Handbook of Marketing*, London: Sage Publications, pp. 151–78.

[68]Keller and Lehmann (2006) op. cit.

[69]S. Morrison and F. G. Crane (2007) Building the service brand by creating and managing an emotional brand experience, *Journal of Brand Management*, 14(5), 410–21.

[70]L. Berry, V. Shankar, J. Turner Parish, S. Cadwallader and T. Dotzel (2006) Creating new markets through service innovation, *MIT Sloan Management Review*, 47(2), 56–63.

[71]See www.bcg.com/publications/files/Master_Brands_Apr_01.pdf.

[72]L. de Chernatony and S. Cottam (2006) Why are all financial services brands not great?, *The Journal of Product and Brand Management*, 15(2), 88–97.

[73]Interbrand Group, *World's Greatest Brands: An International Review*, New York: John Wiley & Sons; see also K. Moore and S. E. Reid (2006) The birth of a brand, Working Paper, Desautels Faculty of Management, McGill University.

[74]P. Barwise, A. Dunham and M. Ritson (2000) Ties that bind: brands, consumers and business, in J. Pavitt (ed.) *Brand New*, London: V&A, pp. 70–97.

[75]S. Davis and M. Dunn (2002) *Building the Brand Driven Business*, New York: John Wiley & Sons; M. Dunn and S. Davis (2003) Building brands from the inside, *Marketing Management*, May/June, 32–7.

[76]M. Beirne and J. Benito (2006) Starwood uses personnel to personalize marketing, *Brandweek*, 24 April, p. 9.

[77]S. Elliott (2006) Letting consumers control marketing: priceless, *New York Times*, 9 October (www.nytimes.com/2006/10/09/business/media/09adcol.html).

[78]C. Locke, R. Levine, D. Searls and D. Weinberger (2000) *The Cluetrain Manifesto: The End of Business as Usual*, Cambridge, MA: Perseus Press.

[79]Elliott (2006) op. cit.

[80]D. E. Schultz, S. I. Tannenbaum and R. F. Lauterborn (1993) *Integrated Marketing Communications*, Lincolnwood, IL: NTC Business Books; D. Schultz and H. Schultz (2003) *IMC: The Next Generation*, New York: McGraw-Hill.

[81]M. Sawhney (2001) Don't harmonize, synchronize, *Harvard Business Review*, July–August, 101–8.

Chapter 13

Devising a contemporary branding strategy

IN THIS CHAPTER, WE WILL ADDRESS THE FOLLOWING QUESTIONS:

1 What are the challenges for managing global brands?

2 What are the contemporary global consumption issues including brand communities and brand tribes?

3 What is branding within an ICT-based or digital environment?

4 How is branding practiced in the developing world?

5 What is country/place branding and celebrity branding?

Global brands are crucial to business and the society we live in.

A range of European brands.
Source: Courtesy of the companies shown.

CHAPTER JOURNEY

Managing
global brands

Understanding
global communities
and brand tribes

Managing
branding in
a digital
environment

Branding in the
developing world,
country and
celebrity branding

Think about the start of your day and you'll begin to see how global the world has become. Your Nokia phone alarm goes off, you drink your Nescafé, eat a Danone Actimel yogurt before you open your Sony Vaio laptop to check your email on Google. You put on a pair of Diesel jeans, a jumper from Zara, adidas trainers and your Apple iPod is already in your H&M jacket pocket, while you sip your Evian water. On the bus into college you think about going for a drink of Guinness or a Heineken with friends that evening. These established global brands hail from cultures as diverse as Finland, Switzerland, Japan, Spain, the United States, Italy, France, the United Kingdom, the Netherlands and Ireland.

Look at the picture of a collage of European brands opposite. How many of the brands do you recognise? Probably most, if not all. These brands represent some of the most popular European brands with large global markets. The worth of these brands is valued at billions of euros. Considering that Nokia from Finland is worth €22 billion or BMW from Germany is worth €15 billion shows clearly how important branding is to companies and the challenges posed for marketing managers in managing such valuable assets.

▽ What is a global brand and how is it managed?

Almost all successful brands will consider going global or be actually born with the objective of becoming a global brand. More and more products and services are now global, from fast food to cars, from fashion to music, from banking to biking. Global brands are a reality and many marketers must manage their brands all around the world. With the regularity of consumer travel and the increasingly international distribution channels and media, more and more consumers expect brands to be available on a worldwide basis.

Global brands are brands that customers can find under the same name in multiple countries with generally similar and centrally coordinated marketing strategies.[1] When a brand is marketed around the world that fact alone can give it an aura of excellence and a set of obligations – to maximise the value of global brands marketers must manage both.[2] A **global brand** is one that in most countries shares the same strategic principle. The marketing mix elements may change but the substantial brand values are comparable across countries. So these global brands may make slight alterations to their logo or image depending on the market they are in but ultimately the brand image and values are *consistent* in all markets. 'A global brand is one that is available in many nations and, though it may differ from country to country, the localized versions have a common goal and a similar identity.'[3] For a brand to be judged as global it must achieve more than one-third of its sales from outside its home country and have a visible external marketing presence.[4] Alternatively the brands must be available in all four of the main regions of the world: Europe/the Middle East and Africa (EMEA), North America, Latin America and Asia.

Companies contemplating a global branding strategy need to be clear in their motives and ambitions. Any company wanting to develop international or global brands should have a clear idea of why and what they are trying to achieve. MasterCard – the global credit card company – has a vision 'to advance commerce globally'. Google's mission is 'to organise the world's information and make it universally accessible and useful'. Both have global visions.

Global branding is not new. Many companies have a deep-rooted history in global branding strategy. Many of Europe's top brands were developed over 100 years ago and still survive today. For example, Cadbury's was first introduced in 1905 and today sells over 250 million chocolate bars annually. BT is the world's oldest communications company, emanating from the Electric Telegraph Company that was established in 1846. Lyle's Golden Syrup, manufactured by British Company Tate & Lyle, is in the *Guinness Book of Records* as the world's oldest brand – founded in 1885. The dairy brand Friesche Vlag is an established brand in the Netherlands, originating in 1913.

▽ Guinness

The Guinness brewery at St James's Gate, Dublin, Ireland has been exporting Guinness around the world since 1811.

Source: Sari Gustafsson/Rex Features

Guinness is one of the world's most valuable and recognised brand names. Founded in Dublin over 250 years ago, Guinness is now brewed in 50 countries and sold in 100 countries across the globe. Over 10 million pints of Guinness are consumed globally everyday. Guinness was already creating global brand recognition in the early 1800s, with the first Guinness shipments in 1811 to Lisbon and later to Trinidad, Barbados and Sierra Leone. By 1870, 10 per cent of sales were foreign so Guinness appointed a 'global traveller' to monitor overseas markets in the Americas, Africa, Asia and Australia. In 1876 Guinness took another brand management measure by registering its harp logo as a trademark. Today, the importance of the global brand continues, as sales of Guinness in Africa are beginning to dwarf sales in the Irish market.

Often brands are 'born global'. This means that, from the start, they are created as global brands and do not focus on the domestic market. Many companies have no choice but to be born global in order to take global market share of an innovative but easily reproduced technology.[5] A good example of this is Google. Though founded by students in California, the Internet search company knows no geographic boundaries. The Google brand is now so entrenched in all the global markets it operates in that it is no longer considered a strictly US brand. This is an example of a brand with no geographic boundaries.

The sheer size of global companies

Many companies are now huge global networks with plants and operations all over the world. As Oxford Professor of Marketing Douglas Holt notes:

Many consumers are awed by the political power of companies that have sales greater than the GDP of small nations and that have a powerful impact on people's lives as well as the welfare of communities, nations and the planet itself.

The Swedish furniture store IKEA has 158 stores in 29 countries employing 118,000 staff and has sales of €5 billion. Over half a billion people (583,050,000) visited IKEA in 2007.

Take also the Swedish company H&M.

▽ H&M

H&M is a fashion retailer that prides itself on delivering fashionable clothing at a low price. Originally founded in Sweden, H&M now operates in 24 countries with 1345 shops all over the world.[6] Beginning with its first location in Stockholm, H&M has never lost sight of its core values of combining affordability and fashion. While its headquarters is still located in Sweden, H&M operates a global organisation, though all fashion designs are made in-house in Stockholm. However, H&M does not actually own any production facilities, and manufacturing is outsourced to lower-wage areas such as Bangladesh, China and Turkey, in order to reduce costs. Figure 13.1 shows the level of expansion of H&M over the world since 1974. H&M has been able to successfully market its brand values to many cultures by its ability to adapt to the differences in each new market.

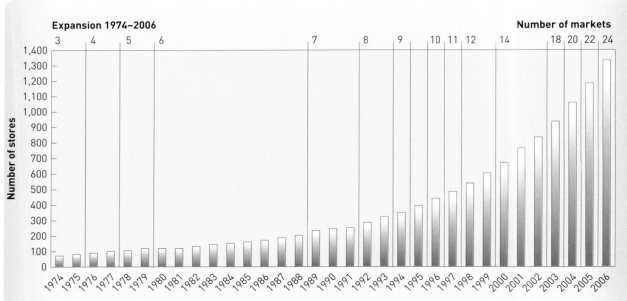

At the time of the IPO in 1974, H&M was present in Sweden, Norway and Denmark. In 1976 the company started to expand outside the Nordic region and today H&M is present in 24 countries with 1345 stores.

Figure 13.1 The expansion of Swedish fashion retailer H&M from 1974 to 2006

Source: H&M (2006) *H&M Annual Report 2006*, Stockholm: H&M Hennes & Mauritz AB, p. 10. Reproduced with permission.

Global services branding

Both product and service branding have expanded in recent years. The range of services that are now global service brands are increasing and are as diverse as major hotel chains, such as the Ritz Carlton, airlines – Lufthansa and banking – ING and UBS. Even the entertainment industry, which is the second largest industry in the world after military goods, is global. National TV shows such as the UK-based *Big Brother* reality show can go global. Countries all over the world have copied this format and there are *Big Brother* shows in all five continents.

Big Brother's global reach
- **Europe**: the Netherlands, the United Kingdom, Belgium, Spain, Denmark, Norway, France, Germany and Hungary;
- **the Americas**: the United States, Brazil and Argentina;
- **Asia-Pacific**: Australia;
- **Africa**: South Africa;
- **Middle East**: Bahrain.[7]

Some services adapt to global branding more easily than others. Food retailing is growing in globalisation despite the local nature of food.

▽ **Tesco**

Tesco is a good example of a service company going global. Of this traditional UK retailer's floor space, 37 per cent is located outside the UK market. Tesco, along with other European retailers, has decided to pursue a global strategy. Many of the big-name European retailers such as France's Carrefour SA and the Netherlands' Royal Ahold NV, are also expanding into foreign markets worldwide. Table 13.1 shows the

Table 13.1 Company-specific retailer profit from foreign stores

Company	Home country	Store locations	Annual sales (€ billions)	Foreign % of annual sales
Carrefour AS	France	Argentina, Belgium, Brazil, Chile, China, Columbia, Czech Republic, France, Germany, Greece, Indonesia, Italy, Japan, Malaysia, Mexico, the Netherlands, Poland, Portugal, Singapore, Slovakia, South Korea, Spain, Taiwan, Thailand, Turkey	35.1	48
Royal Ahold NV	the Netherlands	Argentina, Belgium, Brazil, Chile, Czech Republic, Denmark, El Salvador, Estonia, Guatemala, Honduras, Indonesia, Latvia, Lithuania, Malaysia, Netherlands, Norway, Paraguay, Peru, Poland, Portugal, Spain, Sweden, Thailand, US	29.3	69
Tesco PLC	the United Kingdom	Czech Republic, Hungary, Ireland, Poland, Slovakia, South Korea, Taiwan, Thailand, UK	21.08	13
Wal-Mart Stores Inc.	the United States	Argentina, Brazil, Canada, China, Germany, Mexico, Puerto Rico, South Korea, UK, US	12.2	17

Source: V. Griffith (2002) Welcome to Tesco, your glocal superstore: how the U.K. retailer won over the world, one market at a time, *Strategy+Business*, First Quarter (from www.strategy-business.com/press/16635507/11670). Reproduced with permission.

percentage of sales from foreign stores for four of the world's main retailers. For many retailers globalisation is uncharted territory. They had built their reputations and market share in home or domestic markets. Although the world has grown accustomed to the omnipresence of global brands such as the BBC, Volkswagen, Puma and Adidas, retailers, particularly those that cater to daily household needs, have been slow to reach out to consumers outside their own country. 'Retailing is still a very local business around the world,' says Allan Breese, international account director for Europanel, a firm that provides marketing information services based on consumer panels. 'Globalisation hasn't really happened, especially in the food side of the business, the way it has in other industries.'

Within the business-to-business domain many consultancy firms such as Ernst & Young, KMPG, and computer service companies, for example Cisco and SAP are global brands. As more and more companies move abroad many service providers go global with them, such as accountancy, management consultancies and computer services.

Iconic brands

Many of the major global brands are also predominantly the world's 'power brands'. Some brands become icons. Iconic brands are those brands that, according to Douglas Holt, customers 'regard with awe'. They are the brands that have conquered the world with ease and enthusiasm. Examples of European icons are Zara, Mercedes, Cartier, Rolex, Gucci and Hermès. The marketing managers of these companies understand and have a deep connection with the culture of the customer. These companies are totally focused on preserving and promoting their brands. When companies change these iconic brands customers can be very upset. British Airways found this out to their cost when they removed the British flag from their planes in an attempt to both modernise the brand and move to a more ethnic image. Customers were very angry and confused, sales fell, and British Airways had to replace the flags on the airplanes.

Becoming a brand icon is not something a marketing manager can prescribe – it requires *outperforming* everyone else to have the best brand and marketing around. There are five required aspects for a brand to gain iconic status:[8]

1 Target national contradictions – icons speak out to mass society by *challenging* anxieties and desires in society.

2 Create *myths* that lead culture – icons lead popular culture; this sets them apart from conventional branders, who tend to mimic it. *The Simpsons* show is a particularly good example of this unconventional view, forcing audiences to think differently about existing cultural material. It is not only consumer products and services that create myths or images, industries as diverse as information technology – Think Different – Think Apple, and oil with BP's 'Beyond Petroleum' slogans – create these images too.

3 Speak with a *rebel's voice*: iconic brands don't try to mimic their customers' tastes and feelings, instead they challenge them. The most successful icons rely on an intimate and credible relationship with a rebel world – such as Nike with the ghetto or Volkswagen with bohemian artists. Sony PlayStation's 'This is living' campaign and accompanying advertisement for 'Grand Theft Auto' video games are controversial because of their violent and explicit undertones that reflect some of the attitudes in society. The 'Wicked Vodka' commercial also has this rebel irreverent tone.

4 Draw on *political authority* to rebuild the myth: icons must be revitalised when ideology shatters; they can draw on the goodwill of the brand to rejuvenate ideas.

5 Draw on *cultural knowledge*, which is vital for building icons.

Marketers must understand how to develop these iconic brands, how to reinvent them when a cultural disruption occurs and how to anticipate new contradictions and align their brand with them. Some brands are seen as global icons as well as strong national brands. Take the Dutch drinks company Heineken. Heineken is both a strong local and a strong global brand. The same could be said for Guinness in Ireland. There are however other strong Dutch or Irish icons that do not have a strong global appeal – such as the Dutch peanut butter brand Calve or the Irish Tayto crisps – both strong local brands which are not well known abroad. Similarly Sony is seen as a global brand but is not an icon of Japanese culture.[9] To achieve iconic global status brands must stay close to the customer but explore and understand culture, and look far beyond consumers and where they are today.

Factors leading to increased global branding for European products and services

Many factors have encouraged the phenomenal growth in global brands, including increased communication, travel, technology and marketing skill. Some more specific factors are these:

- In the last 15 years, economic, cultural and media **globalisation** has become widespread, meaning that consumers have started to become more mentally similar to one another. Meaningful segments are developing around the world with consumers with similar needs and tastes. For decades media communications circulated within national boundaries but now this has become global and increasingly expanding due to the Internet and other media. Similarly, though supply chains have been in operation for centuries, the speed and agility now available to move products and services all over the world is phenomenal.

- Companies sought ways to expand out of their *oversaturated* markets in Europe. Even the strongest brands will face saturation in the markets in which they operate. It is for this reason that companies may embark on a global branding strategy in order to enhance their future prospects. Shareholder desire for growth can encourage a global marketing deployment.

- The *fall of Communism* meant that previously inaccessible markets in Russia, China and eastern Europe suddenly became much more available to marketers in the west. Better still, companies found consumers globally had been waiting for the chance to buy western products and services. India, China and growing consumer societies all over the world are hungry for western brands and now have the disposable income to buy them.

- The end of the twentieth century witnessed the global dissemination of popular culture. The growing love of *western popular culture* fuelled demand for brands from the west. People had to understand both Hollywood and Bollywood.

- The competitive environments meant that if *competitors* were going global, your organisation needed to be there too.[10] Intense competition in the home market can also encourage many companies to move abroad or go global.

- *Population explosions* and the increased *wealth* of nations. From 1950 to 2008 the population of the world increased from 2.5 billion in 1950 to over 6.6 billion. By 2042 the world population is expected to be 9 billion,[11] with 90 per cent of people living in developing countries.[12]

Understanding the global market

Brand managers must take into account many factors when deciding to 'go global' with their brand. However, David Aaker and Erich Joachimsthaler, in their article 'The lure of global branding',[13] decree that companies should not be focused so much on global branding, but instead the aim should be to cultivate global brand leadership. They define global brand leadership as: 'Using organizational structures, processes, and cultures to allocate brand-building resources globally, to create global synergies, and to develop a global brand strategy that coordinates and leverages country brand synergies'.

To understand how the UK enterprise Nice Group has used a positioning strategy to succeed in China, visit www.pearsoned-asia.com/marketingmanagementchina

There are five reasons why global brands work.[14]

1   Global brands have the *same positioning worldwide*: this allows the brand to be strong and have a consistent image in all of the brand's markets. IKEA is viewed as a high-style, low-cost furniture provider worldwide and Mercedes-Benz portrays a quality global image in all its markets.

2   There is a *focus on a single product or service category*: focusing on a single product or service means a brand can be instantly synonymous with the product or service. For example, if you think of Nokia do you need to ask what they do? The same is true in services, such as AXA or UBS.

3   The *company is the brand name*: because consumers recognise the company name, the release of new products or services have a better chance of success. Companies such as Nivea or BMW have expanded into many markets due to brand recognition.

4   *Consuming the brand gives membership of a club*: by owning the product or availing themselves of the service consumers became a member of a worldwide consumer group. This is a key component of the brand of almost all major football clubs in Europe, such as Real Madrid and Manchester United. Apple introduced the iPod and then the iPhone after the phenomenal success of their computer music software iTunes. There has been a growth in brand communities where consumers cluster around brands and form fan bases, mainly on the Internet.

5   Consumers expect global brands *to take action on corporate social responsibility*: this is particularly true in developing companies. The use of child labour by leading companies is a cause for concern, with many companies unaware that child labour was being used.[15]

Taking a brand global is a difficult step to reverse, and marketing or brand managers run the risk of damaging the brand's domestic image if they are unsuccessful in creating a global branding strategy. The risks of taking a brand into international markets are as follows: foreign markets can have different operating *environments*; foreign markets can have different cultural *histories and social institutions*; brands designed for global markets are not very *customer oriented* and thus they may not outclass other products or services to the extent they did in the home market.[16]

Introducing a brand into another country is a major achievement for a marketing manager. A structure needs to be in place to determine how best to introduce the brand locally while at the same time making sure that it does not diverge too much from the global standard. It is the marketer's role to ensure that local brand adaptations enhance rather than erode the brand core values. This is the concept of a glocal marketing strategy which was introduced in Chapter 2. A global brand must remain consistent, recognisable and unique the world over.

Analysis of the organisation

Is the organisation ready to go global? Marketers need to ask: 'Is the brand strategy *ready* to go global?' It is important to determine whether the brand strategy has potential to work abroad, or whether its origins in the home country have caused it to have some advantage that may mean its success is not as easily replicated in foreign markets. There are three main criteria that must be met before an organisation contemplates taking a brand global:[17]

1   The organisation needs to own a *valuable intangible asset* such as a specific technology, patents or brand proposition.

2   There should be adequate and solid *demand* in the new market(s) for the branded product or service to be offered.

3   The organisation needs to be able to reproduce the *consumer experience* in the new market(s).

Many questions will arise during this phase of analysis, such as:

* Are there *barriers to entry* that will make entry into the new market difficult? These could include sunk costs, market and legal barriers, and so on. Before the arrival of the Internet and other technologies, building a global banking brand would have been too expensive due to branch network costs, among others. Now technology allows banks to flourish all over the world, as witnessed by the Dutch bank Rabobank Group. RaboDirect is now available in over 100 countries with a purely Internet banking option that has been positioned as a low-cost, straight-talking, humorous and youthful bank.
* How do the *competitors* in the new market differ from those found in the home market?
* What are the *factors* that drive brand strategy into foreign markets?
* Are management and staff sufficiently *motivated* to make this move into new markets work?
* What are the *skills, talents and technologies* needed to make this move a success?

Global, local and glocal strategy

From a global perspective you need to ask whether there are aspects of the company and its culture that cannot be transferred from the home country to the new market. Examples of this include symbols, corporate culture, rituals, routines and control systems. Are there any aspects of the brand that would be offensive, not suitable or irrelevant to the target market's culture in the world market? Some classic examples are:

* The Vauxhall Nova car that is marketed all over Europe encountered problems in Spain. The brand name 'no va' translates as 'does not go' in Spanish!
* Gerber means 'to throw up' in colloquial French, creating problems for the baby food manufacturer of the same name.
* Nintendo's 'Wii' raised a few eyebrows in England and Ireland.
* Fridges in Spain were too small for the standard mineral bottles popular in the United Kingdom and new sized bottles had to be designed for that market.
* In France Hallmark cards do not have poems inside as the French prefer to write their own messages.

Similarly, brand communication campaigns do not always travel well:

- Germany's largest pharmaceutical manufacturer introduced a headache pill on billboards throughout the Middle East showing three photos: on the left, a picture of a grim-looking man with a bad headache; in the middle, a photo of the man taking a pill; on the right, a photo of the man smiling, looking relieved and happy. The campaign failed miserably. Why? Arabic is read from right to left, not left to right, as is the English language. So the message was reversed. Feeling good? Take our pills and get a really bad headache!
- '*Londres sur un coup de tête*' means (Go to) London on the spur of the moment, but it also means (Go to) London for a head-butt.

A key issue to be considered when devising a global branding strategy is how the core values of the brand are to be represented in different markets.[18] Quite often what works in one country won't work in another. Many global brands need to simultaneously project a global image and create localised empathy in targeted consumer segments. Marketers are often required to harmonise centralised global branding strategies and local market conditions.[19] Take the example of the BBC.

▽ The BBC

The BBC is synonymous with everything that is British. For decades BBC TV, Radio and, importantly, the BBC World Service have been broadcast around the globe and it is still a successful major global brand today. The BBC brand is the BBC service and the BBC strategy is the BBC brand. No matter where in the world, the BBC invokes a sense of no-nonsense quality that is very British – or the positive stereotypes of what Britishness symbolises.[20] The brand's primary success lies in consistency. All markets experience Britishness but it has been adapted to their taste. In India the BBC have an Indian *Mastermind* presenter, rather than John Humphrys and in Argentinian the news is presented by a Latin American, in English.

Brand managers need to decide whether the same kind of brand discrimination will be transferred from the home country to the new market or if a different approach should be taken. Brands often need to have some novelty feature to set them apart from other brands, particularly if consumers in the market demonstrate loyalty to local brands.

Global marketing strategies aim to maximise *standardisation*, *homogenisation* and *integration* of marketing activities across markets throughout the world.[21] However, global marketers must address a number of issues in their marketing strategy to ensure their brand will be successful worldwide. Examples of these issues include differences in economic environments, political environments and cultures around the world. While the theory of standardisation of marketing activities works on a strategic level, it is often not suitable for the richness of detail needed on operative and tactical levels. Most marketing activities will be more successful when *adapted* to local conditions and circumstances in the marketplace. In this way a pure global marketing strategy is not ideal as it does not take locally related issues into account. Marketers need to understand how their brand is meeting the needs of customers and how successful their marketing efforts are in individual countries.[22] The weakness of standardised global marketing is that it does not allow for the following differences:

- in consumer needs and wants;
- in consumer values, attitudes and behaviour;
- in economies, politics and cultures;
- in consumer responses to marketing mix elements.

A 'glocal strategy' standardises certain core elements and localises other elements. It is a compromise between global and domestic marketing strategies.[23] 'Glocal marketing' reflects both the ideal of a pure global marketing strategy and the recognition that locally related issues of marketing activities need to be considered. In other words, this concept prescribes that in order to be successful globally, marketing managers must act locally in the different markets they choose to enter. In a glocal strategy the corporate level gives strategic direction while local units focus on the local consumer differences.

Glocal marketing allows for local and global marketing activities to be optimised simultaneously. Continuing the Tesco example from earlier in the chapter, this UK retailer goes global by adapting its product range to local food requirements.

▽ Tesco

Tesco has expanded into central Europe and Asia, where it now has more than 139 stores. Tesco operates a glocal strategy. Shopping in the delicatessen aisle of Tesco's hypermarket in Warsaw is a strikingly Polish experience. Eight barrels of pickles stand at the end of one row, with all types of salami and sausages on display. It's not the sort of food you'd find in any of the UK shops, where Tesco is seen as a quintessential British store. Rather, Tesco in Warsaw is catering to local tastes. 'Deli foods are very important to us,' says an elderly Polish shopper appreciatively. 'This is what we want.'[24] Many scholars have emphasised the 'plan globally and act locally' concept and even extended it to 'think globally, act locally and manage regionally'.

Nowadays global companies understand that they often need to customise their products or services to a certain extent. Even McDonald's has adapted its global marketing and has beer in its product range in Germany, wine in France, mutton pies in Australia and McSpaghetti in the Philippines. Snow tyres designed by Pirelli are available on some car models in Scandinavia on account of the weather conditions in winter, and many come with an emergency blanket as standard.

The advantages of glocal marketing are as follows:

- Consumers feel that the brand is relevant to them and is tailored to their needs and wants.
- There is harmony and balance between the different levels of marketing activity: strategic, tactical and operative.
- Brands gain greater market share.

Glocal marketing or brand managers have the task of balancing demands from headquarters with those of local branches and taking full advantage of local expertise, knowledge and information.[25] Concentrating on a purely global strategy without adjusting the branding strategy for foreign markets has had embarrassing consequences for some brands, for example Mukk yogurt from Italy and Zit lemonade from Germany.

Many brand adoptions means altering the image of the brand to suit local conditions. There are four levels of adaptation:

1 A marketing manager can tailor the company's branding strategy to suit a *region*. For example, in Asia, Nivea adapted its product to cater for the demand for pale skin.

2 The marketing manager can tailor the branding strategy to suit a *country*. For example, in Russia, L'Oréal targets mothers and daughters with oil-based products focusing on red hair colouring – the most popular hair colour in Russia. Oil-based products would not be popular in Europe, where they would be considered greasy. Mr Clean, the household cleaner, becomes M. Propre in the French market.

3 The marketing manager can tailor the branding strategy to suit a *city*. For example, Bulmer's placed an advertisement over the River Liffey in Dublin that read 'North Cider or South Cider?', a question only Dubliners can relate to.[26]

4 The marketing manager can tailor the branding strategy to suit a *retailer*. For example, Stella McCartney Fashion label adjusted her luxury fashion brand to suit the pockets of H&M's customers.

Consumer culture should also be considered when adopting a 'glocal' marketing strategy as it is an important influence on consumer buying behaviour. 'Culture can be defined as the set of basic values, perceptions, wants and behaviours in a society.' Each country has its own *traditions, norms of behaviour and taboos*. For example, the Germans and the French eat more packaged, branded spaghetti than do Italians. Italian children like to eat chocolate bars between slices of bread as a snack – Nutella have a uniquely Italian website as Italians are huge fans of both chocolate and the brand. In Belgium, baby clothes for girls are trimmed with blue while baby clothes for boys are trimmed with pink. Marketers must understand how culture affects consumer reactions in each of the markets they enter in order for their brand to be successful in new markets. Building cultural empathy helps companies to avoid embarrassing mistakes and *optimise* their chances of being successful on a global scale.

By aligning brand image to the cultural ideals of a market, companies can become very successful. For example, L'Oréal has developed a formula for global success by conveying their understanding of different cultures through product design, their communication strategy and their targeting. Whether L'Oréal advertisements are evoking French beauty, Italian style or oriental elegance, the brand *attracts* consumers across borders and cultures. More and more global brands try to have a '*think local, act local*' strategy to make their brands more locally oriented in foreign markets. There is now a Barbie dressed in Muslim attire and a Volkswagen car with a compass for pointing towards Mecca and a shelf for the Koran. All of these help to customise and acknowledge other cultures and tastes. Fanta offers country-specific flavours. In Romania 'Fanta Shokata' is available, based on the Socata, which is a traditional Baltic cordial made from elderflower. In China consumers enjoy green apple Fanta, while Portugal and Spain have watermelon Fanta.

The brand expression

Another question is whether the original brand *expression* can be used in the new market or whether it needs to be changed to express something different. Global marketing or brand managers must ask several questions, such as:

- What is the desired brand *experience* that the brand expression is meant to achieve in the new market?
- Does *management* in the new market understand the brand as well as the home market management does? This is especially important when using local management to launch a brand.
- What is the *role* of the brand for the organisation in the new market?
- Does the brand expression in the new market need to be the *same* as the one in the home country?
- Is a new brand expression warranted by the brand *development* stages currently in progress?
- How does the brand expression *convert* into the actual marketing mix in the new market?
- Does local *alteration* of the brand expression require a variation of the marketing mix?
- Does *standardisation* of the brand expression lead to a standardised marketing mix?
- Should marketing managers use the *existing marketing mix* and implementation or create *a new one* that responds to the brand expression in the new market?

If the brand expression in the new market differs from the domestic expression it is likely that the marketing mix will need to be adapted. The marketing mix is the marketing activities used to create, communicate and deliver value to the customer. There were originally four marketing mix variables[27] expanded to seven to include the product/service, price, place, promotion, process, physical evidence and people.[28]

However, sometimes a similar brand expression will warrant a different marketing mix or conversely when the brand expression is changed the marketing mix may remain the same.

Using the seven variables from the marketing mix can highlight how changes to each may be needed globally.

- **Product**: The Danone product had to change quite fundamentally for entry into the Chinese market with the change to a less lactose-based yogurt because the Chinese are lactose intolerant. Swedish fashion retailer H&M had to change their product range in the United States, as the US male was less fashion conscious then his European counterparts.

- Price: The Spar brand is positioned as a low-cost supermarket in Germany while in the United Kingdom and Ireland there is greater service and store design as the shops are positioned as smaller, high-cost convenience stores.
- **Distribution**: Global supply network – French Louis Vuitton bags are sold from stands in shopping centres in Hong Kong because the market accepts this as a valid method of distribution. If Louis Vuitton did this in countries such as the United Kingdom and continental Europe it could damage the brand's luxury status. When H&M entered the US market it found that by locating in the suburbs it faced too much price competition and so it now locates its stores in more upscale and downtown locations where it continues to offer lower prices. Chemists in European countries such as France only sell medicines while in the United States 'chemists or drug stores', also sell make-up, food and toys.
- **Promotion/communications**: Most global brands see communication as the most easily standardised tool when going global. However, it is likely that marketing communications will need to be changed from the home country to the new market. Kinder chocolate – a confectionery product of the Italian chocolate manufacturer Ferrero – is popular all over Europe. Its TV adverts are standardised and it just changes the voice-over in each country. The original advertisements are poorly dubbed from country to country and the actors' lips are not synced with the advertisement. The Ronald McDonald clown with his white face denotes death in China and thus was not a good image to use for the Chinese launch.
- **Service process**: Service process changes are noticeable in EuroDisney where lunch is served at 13.30 rather than 11.00 and 14.00, which are the times in the United States. Self-service technologies are more accepted in Nordic countries then in the Mediterranean where they prefer the personal touch.
- **Physical evidence**: Some aspects of the physical environment that work well in one country do not work in another. Tablecloths are allowed on tables in McDonald's in France. The Mercedes is a symbol of wealth and elitism in many countries but in Germany it is the standard model of taxi.
- **People**: Though accepted in Disney Florida, when EuroDisney asked its staff in Paris to be clean shaven and not to wear personal jewellery these requests were offensive to some people. Disney withdrew them and accepted that both are normal for Europeans.

Maintaining a consistent global brand image lies at the *core* of a global brand management strategy. If brands are to succeed globally they must act accordingly by reacting to the various competitive and environmental forces that vary across each geographical boundary.

Most brands are adapted to some extent to reflect significant differences in consumer behaviour, brand development, competitive forces and the legal or political environment.[29] Even global brands undergo some changes in product features, service design, packaging, channels, pricing or communications in different global markets.[30] (See 'Marketing memo: The ten commandments of global branding'.) Marketers must make sure their message is relevant to consumers in every market.

Understanding global communities and tribes

Global consumer demand

It is said that companies do not choose to go global, rather that the market forces them to do so. One of the main reasons for growth in global brands is consumer and business demand. Certain consumer segments buy global brands as badges of membership to a 'global mall', and to reflect a cosmopolitan consumer culture.[31]

Global branding is about ensuring that people from different cultures, speaking different languages, recognise and want to purchase your brand.[32] Global brands are a way for people from different countries to connect with each other; the global brand is a key symbol in this **global community**.[33] A global community is where people around the world view themselves as potential partners or even family members in a vast increasingly interconnected human family.[34] Naomi Klein – the author of *No Logo* – suggests that 'Logos . . . have become the closest thing we have to an international language'.[35] This captures what marketers consider to be a positive

Marketing memo

The ten commandments of global branding

For many companies global branding has been both a blessing and a curse. A global branding programme can lower marketing costs, realise greater economies of scale in production and other variables and provide a long-term source of growth. If not designed and implemented properly, however, it may ignore important differences in consumer behaviour and/or the competitive environment in individual countries. The following ten suggestions can help a company retain the advantages of global branding while minimising potential disadvantages:

1 **Understand similarities and differences in the global branding landscape** International markets can vary in terms of brand development, consumer behaviour, consumer culture, competitive activity, legal restrictions, and so on.

2 **Do not take short cuts in brand building** Build a brand in new markets from the 'bottom up', both strategically (building awareness before brand image) and tactically (creating sources of brand equity in new markets).

3 **Establish a marketing team and infrastructure** A company must either build marketing infrastructure 'from scratch' or adapt to existing infrastructure in other countries.

4 **Embrace and integrate all the marketing mix variables** Marketers must consider the full range of the marketing mix variables to see where adaptations to the product, the services, the pricing, the promotion, the service process, and so on, may be needed.

5 **Establish brand partnerships** Most global brands have marketing partners in their international markets that help companies achieve advantages in distribution, profitability and added value.

6 **Balance standardisation and customisation** Some elements of a marketing programme can be standardised (packaging, brand name); others typically require greater customisation (distribution channels). A company must often use many forms of communication in overseas markets, not just advertising.

7 **Balance global and local control** Companies must balance global and local control within the organisation and distribute decision making between global and local managers.

8 **Establish global brand operable guidelines** Brand definition and guidelines must be established, communicated and properly enforced so everyone who is connected with the brand everywhere know what they are expected to do and not to do. The goal is to set rules for how the brand should be positioned and marketed.

9 **Implement a global brand equity measurement system** A global brand equity system is a set of research procedures designed to provide timely, accurate and actionable information for marketers so they can make the best possible short-run tactical decisions and long-run strategic decisions.

10 **Leverage brand elements** Proper design and implementation of brand elements (brand name and trademarked brand identifiers) can be an invaluable source of brand equity worldwide.

Source: Adapted from K. L. Keller and S. Sood (2001) The ten commandments of global branding, *Asian Journal of Marketing*, 8(2), 97–108.

reality – cross-cultural communication. To build a global brand is to build a brand that has a 'voice'. Brands talk. Global brands talk a lot. They talk to millions of people and are talked about by millions of people.

In a 2004 study in 12 countries across Europe and Asia, consumers were grouped into four separate segments:

1 **Global citizens**: 55 per cent of respondents rely on the global brands' success as a signal of quality and innovation. They also have some concerns for corporate socially responsible behaviour by global companies.

2 **Global dreamers**: 23 per cent of respondents consisted of consumers who are less discerning and really embrace the global brand images as portrayed by the companies.

3 **Anti-globals**: 13 per cent of respondents are sceptical about the higher quality and dislike brands that preach more global or in many cases US values. They do not trust global brands and try to avoid purchasing them.

4 **Global agnostics**: 8 per cent of respondents evaluate the global product or service by the same criteria as the local brand.

Consumers worldwide are seen to associate global brands with three main characteristics which account for 64 per cent of global brand preference:

1 **Quality signal (44 per cent)**: Most consumers equate global with quality and use the globalness of the brand rather than the country of origin as evidence of quality. For example consumers will pay a higher premium for a Renault car or L'Oréal shampoo due to their global brand equity.

2 **Global myths (12 per cent)**: Some consumers use global brands to create an imagined global identity that they share with like-minded people reflecting an attitude that 'local brands show what we are; global brands show what we want to be'. For example in Japan over 80 per cent of Japanese women between the ages of 18 and 24 own a piece of Louis Vuitton luggage.

3 **Social responsibility (8 per cent)**: Only a small number of customers expect companies they buy from to address social problems. This group dislikes the low levels of corporate social responsibility. Many consumers still remember Nestlé's baby formula sales in Africa or the Shell use of resources in Nigeria.

Cultural aspects of global branding

Cultural conventions are an intricate collection of rules that can affect a global brand. What is acceptable for one culture may not be acceptable for another.

- Numbers and colours have different meanings: four signifies death in China, as does white. Many European countries have metric while others still use the imperial measurement system.
- Time may mean different things in different cultures. A 'pace-of-life' study was carried out in 31 countries, ranking countries' concepts of time by using three measures: walking speed on urban pavements, how quickly a post office worker responds to a request for a stamp, and the accuracy of public clocks. Based on these variables, the five fastest-paced countries are Switzerland, Ireland, Germany, Japan and Italy. Because queuing, waiting, delivery and duration are intrinsically important to services, service marketers need to be especially aware of consumers' attitudes to time in designing a service in a foreign market.[36]
- Cultures hold different attitudes towards gender and race.

Many global brands are actually US brands, with only four European brands in the top 20 global brands according to the Interbrand survey of 'Top 100 Global Brands of 2007'. Of the world's top 100 global brands 51 were from the United States, even though that country accounts for only 21 per cent of global GDP.[37]

There is a status and prestige associated with global brands, with research showing that global brands have more cachet.[38] In recent research Johansson and Ronkainen found that global brands tend to have an 'esteem' dividend. This esteem is associated with familiarity that leads to comfort and feelings of prestige when buying or using the brand.[39]

Brands as cultural reflections and support for local cultures

Certain consumers use global brands to develop 'an imagined global identity that [is] shared with like-minded people'.[40] There is often conflict between supporting local brands and the desire for the global brand. Despite the advent of a global culture there is often still a desire for local culture. Studies have shown that many consumers like to support local products and services. By adapting and using brands to appeal to local consumers' appetite for imported or western products or services, a multinational can distinguish its products or services and could avoid competing directly with local groups that know the market better.

Global brand communities

Brand culture is the values and beliefs that people have about a brand in their hearts and minds. A shared culture is developed through popular culture like films, books, music, television and sports, which creates a common culture or stories that people can identify with.

In general, the following features characterise a brand community:[41]

- **Consciousness of kind**: The most important factor characterising a community, consciousness of kind refers to the feeling that binds every individual to the other community members and the community brand (e.g., admiration for Nelson Mandela, a passion for beer or red wine). Two factors determine consciousness of kind: legitimisation (distinguishing between true and false members) and opposition to other brands (a brand community is often defined in comparison with other brands) (e.g., BMW versus Mercedes).

- **Rituals and traditions**: These characteristics reproduce and transmit the community meaning in and out of the community. Members relate to each other with the memory of major events in the history of the brand and describe certain associate behaviours.
- **A sense of moral responsibility**: Concerning the creation of moral commitment among the community members, a sense of moral responsibility encourages conjoint behaviours (e.g., by sharing bad experiences suffered by individuals who have chosen different brands) and enables stronger group cohesion.

The behaviour of consumers driven by a similar passion or ethos to assemble into a group can become a subculture or tribe.[42] **A brand community concept**[43] refers more to a group of people who share their interest in a specific brand and create a parallel social universe ripe with its own values, rituals, vocabulary and hierarchy. It is a non-geographical community. Consumers often form brand communities, subcultures of consumers or even consumer tribes. For example Citroën in Greece – www.citroen.gr – includes a list of venues and dates where Citroën fans can meet, and an online forum to discuss different Citroën models, features and repairs. The Facebook social networking phenomenon and also the Apple iPod community are good examples. Online communities engage in a lot of work. They write new text, designing and reworking products and services, creating original artwork and music, disseminating podcasts, uploading video content, selling products and services, writing reviews and rating products and services, programming and debugging software, offering advice, editing photographs, setting up specialist blogs and vlogs to name but a few.[44]

Figure 13.2 describes a typology of the different ways consumers behave as participatory, creative collectives in online communities.

Crowds are large, organised groups that gather together for a specific competition or project.

Hives refers to members of a specialised community who have expert knowledge on a certain product or service.

Mobs are innovative and playful communities who have a specialist interest.

Finally, *swarms* are when large groups of members individually contribute something small to the community.

In summary, the four main distinguishing features of brand communities are:[45]

1 The members are consciousness of being in-group, that is, a sense of belonging to an in-group, thanks to a brand that is patronised by all of the group members.

2 The members have obligation of brand community – PlayStation gamers who give online community tips about different games.

3 There is evidence of rituals and traditions that surround the brand.

4 There is a sense of obligation to the community and its members that is often, but not always, shared by members of the group (e.g., in regard to product repairs or more personal services).

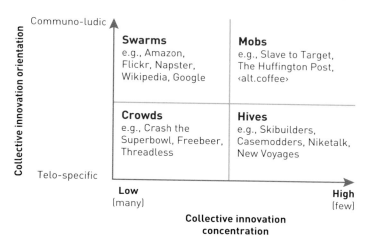

Figure 13.2 A typology of the different ways consumers behave as participatory, creative collectives in online communities

Source: R. V. Kozinets, A. Hemetsberger and H. J. Schau (2008) The wisdom of consumer crowds: collective innovation in the age of networked marketing, *Journal of Macromarketing*. Copyright © 2008 Sage Publications, Inc. Reprinted with permission.

▽ Understanding branding in an ICT-based environment

Information and communications technologies were introduced in Chapter 4 and have increased customers' knowledge and buying options by providing information, variety and lower prices. The increase in technology and consumer demands has led to increased quality standards and increased expectations and has intensified the competition between businesses for the brand loyalty of their target consumers. Competition for brand loyalties is also putting pressure on marketers to use the range of technologies available to them for branding.

Brand management needs to embrace a whole range of technologies. Take the Dove Campaign.

▽ Dove

One of the first instances of this to hit the marketplace was Ogilvy & Mather's 'The Campaign for Real Beauty' for Dove products. The campaign won the 2006 Grand Effie Award, and for good reason. Dove and O&M did a great job of finding a powerful brand attribute and then creating a highly inviting campaign around it that engaged their key audiences in a conversation. Evidence of this is the nearly 3000 blog entries about the campaign on Technorati and the 2 million viewers of their video on YouTube. By using YouTube Dove has engaged with the consumer in their technological domain. A worldwide marketing communications campaign positioned the Dove brand as a supportive, inclusive campaigner for a broader definition of physical beauty. In 2006, Dove also started the Dove Self-esteem Fund that campaigns to 'free the next generation from self-limiting beauty stereotypes'. The fund distributes money and resources to organisations battling with the consequences of distorted body image. It has also created prize-winning advertisements that celebrate physical diversity.

Innocent Smoothies encourages consumers to 'Buy 1, Grow 1 Tree'. On the back of the Smoothie carton is a promotional code. The consumer is encouraged to go to the Smoothie website and type the code in, in order to donate money that will plant a tree in India or Africa. It is an idea on the part of Innocent that also stimulates repeat purchase and social responsibility initiatives. Many marketing campaigns are starting to engage in 'split-ad' techniques, where a television-based advertisement ends with an invitation to visit an Internet site where the consumer can follow the story that is being told in the advertisement.

Digital branding online

Digital brand builders should care about all the consumers' technological and online experiences because all of them — good, bad or indifferent — influence consumer perceptions of a company's brand. Table 13.2 highlights the top online brands in the UK. Building successful online brands is a skill and marketers should consider how their online or technology-based initiative can build on the following brand promises:[46]

- **The promise of convenience**: making a purchase experience more convenient than the real world. Tesco online shopping and home delivery offers convenience and support to many customers, some who cannot go to the shops, whether through illness or old age, and for others who just like the convenience of home shopping.
- **The promise of achievement**: to assist consumers in achieving their goals.
- **The promise of fun and adventure**: creating a brand experience for the consumer that brings excitement and fun. Nike's website allows you to design your own trainers, you can also personalise your iPod and, if you feel like playing, the LEGO site allows you to build LEGO online and then order the bricks to be sent to you.
- **The promise of self-expression and recognition**: provided by personalisation services such as My Yahoo! where consumers can build their own website and express their own views through blogs.

Table 13.2 The top online brands in the UK

Reliability	Innovation	Recognition	Customer care	Longevity	Value
1 Amazon.co.uk	1 Google	1 Amazon.co.uk	1 Amazon.co.uk	1 Amazon.co.uk	1 Amazon.co.uk
2 Google	2 eBay	2 BBC	2 John Lewis	2 Google	2 Tesco.com
3 John Lewis	3 Amazon.co.uk	3 eBay	3 BBC	3 eBay	3 Argos.co.uk
4 BBC	4 YouTube	4 Google	4 Tesco.com	4 Wikipedia	4 eBay
5 Tesco.com	5 iTunes	5 Currys	5 Google	5 Tesco.com	5 Currys
6 HMV	6 Wikipedia	6 ITV	6 eBay	6 BBC	6 CD Wow
7 Argos.co.uk	7 Multimap	7 The *Sun*	7 The *Independent*	7 iTunes	7 uSwitch
8 Times Online	8 Facebook	8 Tesco.com	8 Argos.co.uk	8 Facebook	8 BBC
9 FT.com	9 Friends Reunited	9 Argos.co.uk	9 Guardian Unlimited	9 Yahoo!	9 Google
10 The *Independent*	10 BBC	10 Times Online	10 Ocado-	10 Money-supermarket	10 Play.com

Note: UK study into 1000 users, to find out which digital brands are most highly regarded online.

Source: A. Buller (2007) Top 40 digital brands: customer service wins every time, *Brand Republic*, October (www.brandrepublic.com/News/754399/Top-40-digital-brands-Customer-service-wins-every-time/). Reproduced with permission from Haymarket Business Publications Limited.

- **The promise of belonging**: this is provided by online communities and explains why social networking sites such as Facebook, StudioZ and Bebo are so popular. Brand communities online can be very powerful and marketers ignore them at their peril. On My Google consumers can send their homepage to Google, and personalise it with websites of their own interest that provide the latest local news, weather, horoscopes or joke of the day.

The Internet and the technology environment of computer games and interactive technologies provide global brands with an interactive medium through which they can deliver on their promises, quickly, reliably and rewardingly.[47] The Marketing insight below highlights the use of online and offline gaming by seven leading brands such as Evian, adidas and Red Bull.

Marketing insight

Gaming and branding

Interactive global game worlds are set to be the new way to reach future generations of consumers. Sony's online game EverQuest has millions of players, as does the game World of Warcraft with over 6 million paying subscribers. The most successful tabletop war game is Warhammer, a British brand that has reached global status.[48] adidas, Evian, Corona, Diesel and Sony are all brands that have recognised branding opportunities in these distinctively themed online communities. Branding in this territory is in its early, experimental stages; global brands still have to learn more about their new brand playgrounds.[49] Nike successfully incorporated its brand into the game *There*, selling its virtual trainers to allow avatars wearing them to outrun others.[50] Brand placement within these virtual worlds must take care not to burst the 'fantasy' bubble that virtual games offer users. As discussed in Chapter 4 the avatar 'represents a distinctly different "shadow" consumer, one able to influence its creator's purchase of real-world products and services and conceivably make its own real-world purchases in the virtual world'. 'Furthermore, many users of virtual worlds import real-world company logos as props or decorations. Coke machines are common. You can buy a Corona beer at a *Second Life* bar while listening to the hum of a neon Budweiser sign from the wall'.[51]

Red Bull, the Austrian energy drinks company, uses online gaming and virtual worlds that successfully gave its product virtual 'wings'. Since its launch it has kept its cool brand image by having a strong online presence and youth focus. A clever strategy, considering that it is an energy drink, and staying up for hours to play online requires that you stay awake. Red Bull teamed up with Sony PlayStation and the brand featured in their games, promoted as a way to 'rock out and relax' between the games' levels.[52] The virtual gaming world offers consumers and global brands opportunities to create new identities. For brands, computer games are a way to increase brand awareness on a global scale; for consumers, brands can enhance the realism of a game environment or their game character.[53] The subscribed players of virtual worlds such as *Second Life, EverQuest, There* and the *Sims Online* present marketers with highly invested, engaged, captive audiences for branded experiences.[54] Brands need to be well integrated into the game's landscape in order for it to be perceived as heightening the entertainment as opposed to being perceived as 'three-dimensional spam'.[55]

▽ The challenges of branding in developing economies

As more and more European companies enter the markets of the developing world – lured by their large populations, growing economies and the possibility of high returns – it is very important to understand how to manage brands effectively in these countries. Nowhere is this so true as in the so-called BRIC economies,[56] the rapidly growing economies of Brazil, Russia, India and China. These economies will become all the more important to brand managers in the future, as they continue to grow and become the world's dominant economies.

Table 13.3 explores the major countries of China and India. The sheer size of these markets makes them hard to ignore from a marketing perspective.

Developing countries are a highly diverse group, often with very different views and concerns. About two-thirds of the World Trade Organization's 150 members are developing countries. A developing country is a country that has a relatively low standard of living, an undeveloped industrial base and a moderate to low Human Development Index (HDI) score and per capita income, but is in a phase of economic development. Another way of looking at developing countries is that 14 per cent of the world live in countries with per captia gross national product of more than €15,000, while 86 per cent of the world live in areas with less than that.[57] According to a recent article in *Foreign Policy* by the University of Michigan Business School Professor C. K. Prahalad, and Allen Hammond of the World Resources Institute, the 18 largest developing nations are home to some 680 million families earning €3845 a year or less.[58]

Vital branding tools such as market research, technology links, supply networks and media development are still in their infancy in the developing world. Although the markets of developing countries have grown rapidly in recent years, companies still struggle to get reliable information about consumers, particularly about those consumers with low incomes. It can be difficult to find the deep databases on consumption patterns that allow the segmentation of consumers in more developed markets. Marketers also need to change their view of consumers based on disposable income and reinvent consumer value propositions when looking to the developing world.

- In Brazil, fast-moving consumer goods giant Unilever has developed Ala, a brand of detergent created specifically to meet the needs of low-income consumers who want an affordable yet effective product for laundry that is often washed by hand in river water.
- In India, Unilever successfully markets Sunsil and Lux shampoo sachets sold in units of 2–4 cents; Clinic All Clear anti-dandruff shampoo sachets at 2.5 rupees each; and 16-cent Rexona deodorant sticks. In Tanzania, Key soap is sold in small units for a few cents.
- Whirlpool is cashing in on its line of inexpensive yet stylish washing machines in Brazil, India and China. In Brazil, customers want to see the machine operate, so Whirlpool made

The term BRIC was first prominently used by Jim O'Neill, head of global economic research at Goldman Sachs in his 2003 thesis, Dreaming with BRICs.

Source: J. O'Neill (2003) Dreaming with BRICS: the path to 2050, Goldman Sachs Global Economics Paper No. 99, October (www2.goldmansachs.com/ideas/brics/book/99-dreaming.pdf).

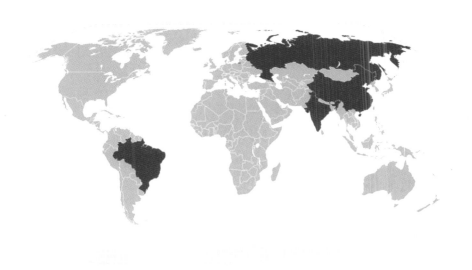

Table 13.3 A comparison of India and China: the markets of the future

India	China
Area 3,287,590 sq km (2007)	Area 9,596,960 sq km (2007)
Population 1.13 billion (2007)	Population 1.32 billion (2007)
GDP real growth rate 9.4%	GDP real growth rate 11.1%
GDP per capita (ppp)* €2,736	GDP per capita (ppp)* €5,616
Unemployment 7.8% (2006)	Unemployment 4.2% (2005)
Population below poverty line 25% (2002)	Population below poverty line 10% (2004)
Exports €80.6 billion	Exports $974 billion
Imports €135.9 billion	Imports €560 billion
Imports from China, U.S., Germany, Singapore	Imports from Japan, S. Korea, U.S., Germany
Exports to U.S., UAE, China, UK	Exports to U.S., Japan, S. Korea, Germany
Literacy rate 61% (2001)	Literacy rate 90.9% (2000)
Life expectancy 68.59 years (2007)	Life expectancy 72.88 years (2007)

*purchasing power parity

Source: T. Khanna (2007) CHINA + INDIA: the power of two, *Harvard Business Review*, 85(2), 60–3. Copyright © 2007 by the Harvard Business School Publishing Corporation. All rights reserved. Reproduced with permission.

a transparent acrylic lid. In China, where washing machines are considered status symbols and are often placed in living rooms due to lack of space, extra attention was paid to sleek looks. Wash cycles were named on a by-country basis (in India, the delicate cycle is called the 'sari' cycle).

The acceptance of local and global brands and the country of origin of a brand can be very important in developing countries. Brands coming from the west are generally held in high esteem, especially in developing countries where status is important culturally.[59] Research carried out in 2005 in each of the BRIC economies, compared to those in the EU and the United States found brand preferences differ across the world – see Table 13.4.

Similar to the decisions to enter any new market, marketing managers looking to enter developing economy markets have three strategy choices:[60]

1 **Adapt the strategy**: The company can adapt their business model to countries while keeping their core value propositions constant. They must start by identifying the value propositions that they will not modify whatever the context. If the company changes its brand too radically, it will lose its advantage of global scale and global branding.

2 **Change the contexts**: Some multinationals are powerful enough to change the context in which they operate.

3 **Stay away**: In some cases it is just impractical or uneconomical for a brand to enter the emerging market(s). Sometimes it is just that the time is not right.

Table 13.4 Brand perceptions by global region[61]

Europe/US: markets are mature and have strong local and global brands. The profusion of brands clutters consumer choice.

Brazil: consumers accept both local and global brands.

Russia: consumers prefer global brands in cars and high tech. Local brands thrive in the food and beverage sectors.

India: consumers buy both local and global brands.

China: consumers prefer to buy products from US, European and Japanese companies.

Take the case of Danone.

▽ **Danone**

China has a long history and its complex culture is still unfamiliar to many in the west. Danone is a good example of a company that succeeded in entering the Chinese market after an initial failure. The Danone Group (DG) is a global French company founded in 1919. Danone is the brand name in most of Europe but it is called Doanonino in Latin America and Dannon and Danimals in the United States.[62] In 1987 when DG entered the Chinese market with their Yogurt brand, it applied an ethnocentric strategy of offering an almost identical product to the one in its home market. This caused problems as very few Chinese had a fridge and they eat using chop sticks (very difficult to eat yogurt that way!). Also, reflecting their non-dairy diet, they tend to be lactose intolerant. Having reviewed these issues, a new marketing programme was introduced. Danone began by creating multiple joint ventures with local firms, buying local dairy facilities and entering the market by paying attention to China's idiosyncratic distribution networks. It also offered free fridges, attached spoons to the yogurt pots and developed products with reduced lactose to suit the Chinese biological condition. Following these changes, which show a better understanding of the consumer and the market, the Danone Group is now in second place in the Chinese dairy market and yogurt sales have increased 100 per cent since 2000.

▽ **Celebrity branding**

Celebrities with worldwide popularity and recognition can help *overcome cultural barriers* in global marketing communications. The universal appeal of celebrities is key to their successful use as brand ambassadors. *Manchester United* has completed several pre-season tours to exploit the lucrative markets of the United States and the Far East. Through the marketing of their world-famous players, the Manchester United brand has become a hugely successful global brand. Many football players now endorse brands, from sunglasses to cars.

Celebrity endorsement is not new. In the 1800s Pope Leo XIII endorsed a Vin Mariani, a sparkling red wine made with cocaine. He even honoured the wine with a gold medal.[63]

What is novel about celebrity endorsements is that they have become so commonplace in society. This leads to a growing role for celebrities in global branding decisions. Nowadays, approximately 25 per cent of TV advertisements feature celebrities.[64] In a memorable incident during the 2006 World Cup, one commercial break featured top celebrity and soccer player David Beckham in four separate advertisements.[65] The *longevity* of celebrity endorsements is not surprising given that their correct use has many advantages for the brand.

How to use celebrities successfully

The celebrity should have high recognition. In other words, the endorser must have a *clear and popular image.*[66] Madonna has high recognition, as does Oprah Winfrey, who is top of the 2007 Forbes top 100 celebrities list. Donnatella Versace and Jordan are European examples. The celebrity's perceived *credibility* must be high in consumers' minds. Consumers must trust a celebrity's motives for endorsing a product or service in order for the advertisement to be believed. The celebrity's image and that of the brand he or she endorses should be appropriate to each other, that is, *they must match up*. Former Ireland football manager Jack Charlton was considered to be an appropriate endorser for fishing products because of his widely known fishing hobby.[67] As a top model and high fashion icon, Kate Moss's endorsement for UK high-street clothing company TopShop is very successful.

EMILE ZOLA
The Well-Known French Writer.

EMILE ZOLA Writes:

Vin Mariani--The Elixir of Life, which combats human debility, the one real cause of every ill--a veritable scientific fountain of youth, which, in giving vigor, health and energy, would create an entirely new and superior race.
EMILE ZOLA.

Never has anything been so highly and so justly praised as

MARIANI WINE, the FAMOUS FRENCH TONIC for BODY, NERVES and BRAIN
FOR OVERWORKED MEN, DELICATE WOMEN SICKLY CHILDREN
Vin Mariani is indorsed by the medical faculty all over the world. It is specially recommended for Nervous Troubles, Throat and Lung Diseases, Dyspepsia, Consumption, General Debility.

MALARIA, WASTING DISEASES AND LA GRIPPE.
Sold at all Druggists.   Refuse Substitutions.

VIN MARIANI GIVES STRENGTH.
SPECIAL OFFER.—To all who write mentioning LESLIE'S WEEKLY, we send a book containing portraits and indorsements of EMPERORS, EMPRESS, PRINCES, CARDINALS, ARCHBISHOPS and other distinguished personages.
MARIANI & CO., 52 WEST 15TH STREET, NEW YORK.
Paris—41 Boulevard Haussmann; London—83 Mortimer Street; Montreal—28-30 Hospital Street.

In the 1800s Pope Leo XIII and Emile Zola (pictured left) both endorsed a wine tonic. Celebrity endorsement is now a global phenomenon.

Source: The Advertising Archives

The advantages of celebrity endorsements

- They *enhance both the company image and brand attitudes*.
- Celebrities help *breathe new life* into a company's advertising for a particular brand. Furthermore, successful personalities add character to a brand. As the British Post Office tries to modernise its brand image it selected the image of boy band Westlife, which is designed to make the Post Office more appealing to a 'prime-time' audience. The point of using Westlife was to 'uncover the essence of the Post Office' and show it is 'on the people's side'.
- Above all, celebrity endorsements can lead to *increased profits and sales*. Table 13.5 highlights the many successful celebrity endorsed campaigns.
- A new and important way in which brands use celebrities to endorse their products is by sending them gifts or loans of their products to wear to premieres, press interviews, television interviews, weddings, or just to use on a daily basis. The popularity and voyeuristic nature of celebrity magazines means that images of these celebrities are dissected to investigate which brands they wear and use, thus endowing the brand with credibility and authenticity.
- They make the advertising campaigns *stand out from the clutter* and draw increased attention from the audience.[68]

Celebrity endorsements of products and services is a major branding development. European stars who have become global brands are Germany's Claudia Schiffer, Spain's Penelope Cruz and from Wales, Catherine Zeta-Jones.

Source: David Fisher/Rex Features (left); Most Wanted/Rex Features (centre); Carolyn Contino/BEV/Rex Features (right)

Table 13.5 Most successful celebrity campaigns in the United Kingdom

Celebrity	Company	ROI	Incremental value £
Prunella Scales and Jane Horrocks	Tesco	2.25:1	£2.2 billion
Jamie Oliver	Sainsbury's	27:1	£1.12 billion
Stephen Fry and Hugh Laurie	Alliance & Leicester	30:1	£656 million
Bob Hoskins	BT	6:1	£297 million
Vic Reeves and Bob Mortimer	FirstDirect	18:1	£223 million
Ian Wright, Martin Luther King, Kate Moss, Elvis Presley, John McCarthy, Yuri Gagarin	One2One	5.4:1	£199 million
Martin Clunes, Caroline Quentin, Jonah Lomu, Caprice, Jonathan Ross	Pizza Hut	3:1	£55 million
Pauline Quirke and Linda Robson	Surf	2:1	£42 million
George Best, Chris Eubank, Rolf Harris, Prince Naseem	The Dairy Council	2:5	£21 million
The Simpsons	Domino's Pizza	5:3	£13 million

Source: Institute of Practitioners in Advertising (IPA), IPA Effectiveness Awards databank (www.ipa.co.uk/databank). Reproduced with permission.

Issues arising from celebrity branding

Multiple brand celebrity endorsers

Many celebrities are now shared by the same company, that is, they are promoting more than one brand. Research shows that the endorsement of four or more products and services negatively influences the credibility of the celebrity endorser. This weakens the message of the advertisement and the projection of the brand's image to the consumer. Victoria's Secret bombshell Gisele Bundchen is the highest-paid model in the world, with 20 fashion contracts including Ebel watches, Vogue Eyewear and Dolce & Gabbana. Can she truly embody one particular brand?

Celebrity image considerations

In a society becoming increasingly obsessed with celebrity culture, the lives of celebrities have been placed under a microscope. Europe has a profusion of magazines devoted to chronicling even the smallest activities of celebrities, from ¡Hola! in Spain to OK! and Heat in the United Kingdom. Under such constant examination it is easy for the image of the celebrity to be negatively portrayed or reported. If the celebrity's image is negatively portrayed then so is the brand associated with it. Brand managers must be reactive and wary of this. Most celebrity endorsement contracts now contain a 'morality clause' that allows the company to drop the celebrity if warranted by inappropriate behaviour. Supermodel Kate Moss's public dismissal from campaigns with H&M, Chanel and Burberry after being photographed alledgedly using cocaine is a reflection of the risks of linking brands and celebrities. Reviled for having money but no taste, the wives and girlfriends (WAGs) of the England football team can kill a brand with a single approving nod. Being 'Wagged' can *damage* the brand's credibility. According to one source, the images of Chloe and Jimmy Choo have been tarnished through the WAGs' public use of them.

Celebrities as brands

Many celebrities have completed the journey from featuring in advertising campaigns to being the 'face' of a brand to becoming brands themselves. In today's fame-obsessed culture, celebrities exist in the mind of the consumer in the same way packaged goods' brands do. Brand managers must be careful that they are not creating future competition for themselves through the immediate benefits of utilising celebrity endorsements. For example within the perfume industry *celebrity scents* have increased 2000 per cent since 2004. Actress Elizabeth Taylor was the first to launch a celebrity perfume with White Diamonds in 1991. She has been joined by the Beckhams, Christina Aguilera, Britney Spears, Kate Moss and many others – celebrity brand scents are everywhere. Now, 40 per cent of the £638 million UK women's fragrance market is accounted for by celebrity fragrances.[69] Celebrity brands have become competition for established brands.

Perhaps the most famous celebrity brand is 'Brand Beckham', which is a joint branding effort between David and Victoria Beckham. At 17 years of age, Posh was asked what she would like to be when she grew up and she said, 'I would like to be more famous than Persil.'[70] This statement shows her desire to become a global brand, and she understood that.

▽ Countries and places as brands

In the world in which we now live every place has to compete with every other place for share of mind, share of income, share of voice. The idea of considering a *country* from a brand perspective only took hold in the last two decades.[71] There are now many *deliberately managed* country brands. This type of marketing is often called place marketing, or tourism marketing.

Many countries have strong associations, such as Scotland with Scotch Whisky, Germany with cars, Italy with fashion, France with cosmetics and perfumery, Switzerland with banking, the Czech Republic with beer, Germany with sausages, Russia with vodka and Thailand for massage. Even places such as Cambridge for the university, Waterford for Crystal, Evian Water and Parma

The branding of countries is a contemporary branding challenge.
Source: Courtesy of the organisations shown

for ham have strong associations. For effective country brand management, brand managers must agree what the country stands for, ensure *consistency of communication* in delivering the brand message and plan for the long term.

▽ Ireland

Ireland can claim to be one of the first countries to consciously manage its brand image with country brand management dating back over 50 years.[72] As a tourist destination Ireland's brand values have been built over time, reflecting a land that has beautiful scenery, engaging people and a traditional rural, isolated, relaxed pace of life, evoking images of green fields and beautiful countryside.

From a business-oriented stance, the Irish Development Authority (IDA) began branding Ireland as a location for overseas investment. There was a high level of dissonance between the tourist-oriented brand message and the business-oriented brand message. The tourist brand message emphasised the traditional rural Ireland while the business message emphasised a modern, industrialised Ireland. Instead of an emphasis on the underdeveloped wilderness, a new modern Ireland, which at the same time is rich in culture, was strategically positioned. Tourists could still find rural Ireland but they could also find modern sophistication. This move towards sophistication complemented Ireland's 'we are modern and industrial' business message. The Irish brand now encompasses a vibrant literary and cultural tradition with an educated, innovative workforce and this has helped Ireland economically.[73]

Some of the print advertisements used to change the brand image of Ireland.

Source: Courtesy of IDA Ireland

More specifically, effective country brand management requires the following:[74]

- carrying out an analysis to determine the country's chief strengths, weaknesses, opportunities and threats;
- selecting some industries, personalities, natural landmarks and historical events that could provide a basis for strong branding and storytelling;
- developing an umbrella concept of the country brand that covers, and is consistent with, all of its separate branding activities;
- allocation of sufficient national funds to carry out the branding strategy;
- through export controls, making sure that every exported product or service is reliable and delivers the promised level of performance.

▽ SUMMARY

1 A global brand is a brand that in most countries shares the same strategic principles even though some of the marketing mix elements might change.

2 Some brands become iconic brands or power brands regarded with awe around the world.

3 Marketing managers must be sure that the company is ready to go global and that they are motivated and have the skills and technologies to manage a global brand.

4 Glocal strategies are changing some aspects of the brand to reflect the market in which it is operating. Think global but act local.

5 A brand community refers to a group of people who share their interest in a specific brand and create a parallel social universe with its own values, rituals, hierarchy and vocabulary; it is non-geographical.

6 Digital branding is a core area as brand image can be creating using technologies and online.

7 Due to the lack of vital branding tools in developing countries marketing managers face many branding challenges.

8 Celebrity branding using the worldwide popularity and recognition of a celebrity can help to overcome cultural barriers in global marketing communications.

9 There are many deliberately managed country and place brands all reflecting different positions in the global market.

▽ APPLICATIONS

Marketing debate

Celebrity branding can add value to a brand but can also damage the brand. Critically evaluate and debate this issue using examples to support your answer.

Marketing discussion

Comment on some of the global brands with which you are familiar. Have they created global brand communities? What strategies have they followed to ensure a global brand following?

▽ REFERENCES

[1] J. B. Steenkamp, R. Batra and D. Alden (2003) How perceived brand globalness creates brand value, *Journal of International Business Studies*, 34, 53–63.

[2] D. B. Holt, J. A. Quelch and E. L. Taylor (2004) How global brands compete, *Harvard Buisness Review*, 82(9), 68–75.

[3] Interbrand (2006) Lessons learned from global brands, *Best Global Brands*, (www.brandchannel.com/papers_review.asp?sp_id=1260).

[4] Ibid.

[5] J. Walker (2006) Born to be global, *Australasia Business Intelligence*, 28(34), 94.

[6] J. Johansson and I. Ronkainen (2004) The brand challenge, *Marketing Management*, 13(2), 54–5.

[7] G. Wyner (2008) A changing climate, *Marketing Management*, January–February, 8–9.

[8] Holt, Quelch and Taylor (2004) op. cit.

[9] Steenkamp, Batra and Alden (2003) op. cit.

[10] Holt, Quelch and Taylor (2004) op. cit.

[11] See www.worldometers.info/population/.

[12] See www.unfpa.org/pds/facts.htm.

[13] D. Aaker and E. Joachimsthaler (1999) The lure of global branding, *Harvard Business Review*, November–December, 137–44.

[14] J.A. Quelch (2007) Why global brands work, Harvard Business School Working Knowledge Report, 17 October, p. 1.

[15] M. Skapinker (2004) How baby milk marketing fed a long-life campaign, *Financial Times*, 26 May.

[16] T. C. Melewar and C. Walker (2003) Global corporate brand building: guidelines and case studies, *Journal of Brand Management*, 11(2), 157–70.

[17] V. K. Rangan, J. A. Quelch, G. Herrero and B. Barton (2007) (eds.) *Business Solutions for the Global Poor*, Boston, MA: John Wiley & Sons.

[18] M. Desbordes (2006) *Marketing and Football: An International Perspective*, Boston, MA: Elsevier.

[19] J. Barron and J. Hollingshead (2004) Brand globally, market locally, *Journal of Business Strategy*, 25(1), 9–15.

[20] Melewar and Walker (2003) op. cit.

[21]G. Svensson (2002) Beyond global marketing and the globalization of marketing activities, *Management Decision*, 40(5/6), 574–84.

[22]G. McGovern, D. Court, J. Quelch and B. Crawford (2004) Bringing customers into the boardroom, *Harvard Business Review*, November, 1–10.

[23]Svensson (2002) op. cit.

[24]V. Griffith (2002) Welcome to Tesco, your glocal superstore: how the U.K. retailer won over the world, one market at a time, Strategy + Business Case Study (www.strategy-business.com/press/16635507/11670).

[25]C. Macrae and M. D. Uncles (1997) Rethinking brand management: the role of brand chartering, *Journal of Product & Brand Management*, 6(1), 64–77.

[26]J. Fanning (2006) *The Importance of Being Branded: An Irish Perspective*, Dublin: Liffey Press.

[27]E. J. McCarthy and W. D. Perreault (2002) *Basic Marketing: A Global-Managerial Approach*, 14th edn, Homewood, IL: McGraw-Hill/Irwin.

[28]S. L. Vargo and R. F. Lusch (2004) The four service marketing myths, *Journal of Service Research*, 6(4), 324–35.

[29]For some recent treatments of branding in Asia in particular see M. Roll (2006) *Asian Brand Strategy: How Asia Builds Strong Brands*, New York: Palgrave MacMillan; P. Temporal (2001) *Branding in Asia: The Creation, Development and Management of Asian Brands for the Global Market*, Singapore: John Wiley & Sons; S. R. Kumar (2007) *Marketing & Branding: The Indian Scenario*, Delhi: Pearson Education.

[30]P. Ghemawat (2003) Globalization: the strategy of differences, Harvard Business School Working Knowledge, 10 November; P. Ghemawat (2003) The forgotten strategy, *Harvard Business Review*, 81 (November), 76–84.

[31]N. Klein (2000) *No Logo*, London: Flamingo Books.

[32]M. Neumeier (2006) *The Brand Gap: How to Bridge the Distance Between Business Strategy and Design: A Whiteboard Overview*, Berkeley, CA: New Riders; London: Pearson Education.

[33]Holt, Quelch and Taylor (2004) op. cit.

[34]C. L. Borgman (2003) *From Gutenberg to the Global Information Infrastructure: Access to Information in the Networked World*, Boston, MA: The MIT Press.

[35]N. Klein as quoted by K. Viner (2000) Hand-to-brand-combat, *The Guardian*, 23 September (www.guardian.co.uk/books/2000/sep/23/society.politics).

[36]C. Ezzell (2002) Clocking cultures, *Scientific American* (special edition), 287(3), 56–8.

[37]J. Quelch (2003) The return of the global brand, *Harvard Business Review*, August, 22–3.

[38]J. Johansson and I. Ronkainen (2005) The esteem of global brands, *Journal of Brand Management*, 12(5), 339–54.

[39]Ibid.

[40]B. Cova, S. Pace and D. J. Park (2007) Global brand communities across borders: the Warhammer case, *International Marketing Review*, 24(3), 313–29.

[41]C. Flavián and M. Guinalíu (2005) The influence of virtual communities on distribution strategies in the internet, *International*

Journal of Retail & Distribution Management, 33(6), 405–25; A. Muniz and T. C. O'Guinn (2001) Brand community, *Journal of Consumer Research*, 27 (March), 412–32.

[42]M. Maffesoli (1996), *The Time of the Tribes: The Decline of Individualism in Mass Society*, Thousand Oaks, CA: Sage Publications.

[43]Muniz and O'Guinn (2001) op. cit.; A. Wipperfürth (2005) Brand *Hijack: Marketing Without Marketing*, London: Portfolio Hardcover.

[44]R. V. Kozinets, A. Hemetsberger and H. J. Schau (2008) The wisdom of consumer crowds: collective innovation in the age of networked marketing, *Journal of Macromarketing*, 28(4), 339–54.

[45]Muniz and O'Guinn (2001) op. cit.

[46]S. Dayal, H. Landesberg and M. Zeisser (2000) Building digital brands, *The McKinsey Quarterly*, 2, 42–51.

[47]Ibid.

[48]Cova, Pace and Park (2007) op. cit.

[49]P. Hemp (2006) Avatar-based marketing, *Harvard Business Review*, June, 48–57.

[50]Ibid.

[51]Ibid.

[52]M. Lindstrom (2004) Branding is no longer child's play!, *Journal of Consumer Marketing*, 21(3), 175–82.

[53]M. Nelson (2002) Recall of brand placements in computer/video games, *Journal of Advertising Research*, 42(2), 80–92.

[54]Ibid.

[55]Hemp (2006) op. cit.

[56]J. O'Neill (2003) Dreaming with BRICS: the path to 2050, Goldman Sachs Global Economics Paper No. 99, October (www2.goldmansachs.com/ideas/brics/book/99-dreaming.pdf).

[57]G. Wyner, (2008) A changing climate, *Marketing Management*, January–February, 8–9.

[58]C. K. Prahalad and A. Hammond (2004) Selling to the poor, Foreign Policy, May–June (www.ckprahalad.com/2006/01/29/selling-to-the-poor-by-allen-l-hammond-ck-prahalad/).

[59]R. Batra, V. Ramaswamy, D. L. Alden, J.-B. E. M. Steenkamp and S. Ramachander (2000) Effects of brand local and nonlocal origin on consumer attitudes in developing countries, *Journal of Consumer Psychology*, 9(2), 83–5.

[60]Ibid.

[61]T. Khanna, K. G. Palepu and J. Sinha (2005) Strategies that fit emerging markets, *Harvard Business Review*, 83(6), 63–81.

[62]T. Melewar, E. Badal and J. Small (2006) Danone branding stategy in China, *Brand Management*, 13(6), 407–17.

[63]D. Cave (2005) How breweth Java with Jesus?, *New York Times*, 23 October.

[64]T. Shimp (2000) *Advertising and Promotion: Supplemental Aspects of Integrated Marketing Communications*, Fort Worth, TX: Dryden Press.

[65]S. Moon (2006) Beckham the world brand, *This Is Money* (*Daily Mail*), 8 June (www.thisismoney.co.uk/news/special-report/article.html?in_article_id=409642&in_page_id=108).

[66]M. R. Solomon (1999) *Consumer Behavior*, 4th edn, Englewood Cliffs, NJ: Prentice Hall.

[67]S. M. Choi, L. Wei-Na and K. Hee-Jung (2005) Lessons from the rich and famous, *Journal of Advertising*, 34(2) 85–98.

[68]Ibid.

[69]Celebrity-endorsed perfumes on the rise, *The Economic Times*, 24 October 2007 (http://economictimes.indiatimes.com/articleshow/2484543.cms).

[70]Extract from V. Beckham (2001) *Learning to Fly*, (www.wpp.com/wpp/marketing/branding/articles_poshspice.htm).

[71]P. Kotler and D. Gertner (2002) Country as brand, product, and beyond: a place marketing and brand management perspective, *Journal of Brand Management*, 9(4/5), 249–61.

[72]Fanning (2006) op. cit.

[73]Fanning (2006) op. cit.

[74]Kotler and Gertner (2002) op. cit.

▽ Shaping the market offering

Video documentary for Part 5

Go to **www.pearsoned.co.uk/marketingmanagementeurope**
to watch the video documentary that relates to Part 5 and
consider the issues raised below.

Essentially there are two key components in a product
offer – a *package* which is offered for sale at a stated
price.

Part 5: Shaping the Market Offering explores three
important themes:

1 managing products and services;

2 creating new products; and

3 developing pricing strategies.

Pricing is a sensitive concern that in the customer's
eyes reflects perceived value in the offering and that
must deliver a long-term sustainable competitive advantage to the supplier. In highly competitive markets customers exert considerable influence on the packages that
companies bring to market. The modern concept of
customer-perceived value dictates that customers expect
their purchases to contain both product (tangible) and
service (intangible) attributes. Well-perceived value
packages result in pleasant buying experiences in both
consumer and business markets.

Developing new products or customer-perceived value
packages is an ongoing process in modern markets.
When watching the video documentary that accompanies
Part 5, consider how HSBC stresses its concern for
customer's expectations and how they are of paramount
importance. Each company acknowledges in their own
way that due attention should be paid to current and
anticipated changes in the market and the activities of
the competition.

Hear a variety of top marketing executives from a wide
range of organisations offer their own interesting and
varied perspectives on the key themes of Part 5
including: Phil Popham, Global Managing Director, Land
Rover (top); Neil Rami, Managing Director, Marketing
Birmingham (centre); and Friday's Farms, a family
business producing over 4 billion eggs a year (bottom).

Chapter 14

▽ Designing, developing and managing market offerings

IN THIS CHAPTER, WE WILL ADDRESS THE FOLLOWING QUESTIONS:

1 What marketing strategies are appropriate at each stage of the product life cycle?

2 What are the implications of market evolution for marketing strategies?

3 What are the characteristics of market products and how do marketers classify products?

4 How can companies differentiate products and manage their product mix and product lines?

5 How can companies use packaging, labelling, warranties, and guarantees as marketing tools?

Marketing begins with formulating an offering to meet target customers' needs or wants. The offer will be judged in terms of the relative degree of customer-perceived value the offering delivers. This chapter examines how successful companies design, develop and manage their CPV portfolio offerings.

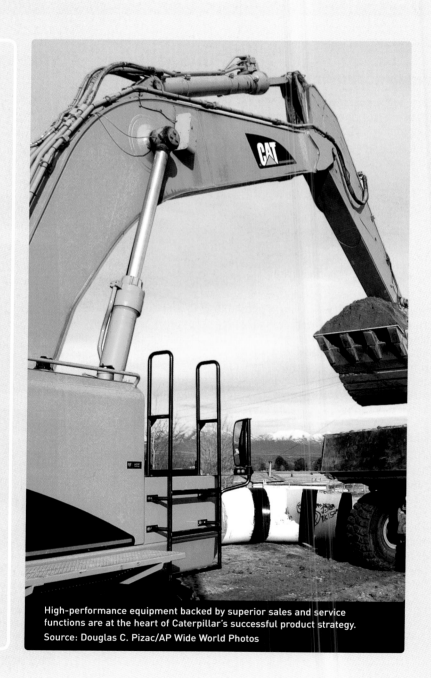

High-performance equipment backed by superior sales and service functions are at the heart of Caterpillar's successful product strategy.
Source: Douglas C. Pizac/AP Wide World Photos

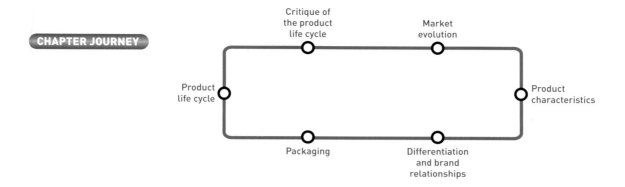

Product
life cycle

Critique of
the product
life cycle

Market
evolution

Product
characteristics

Packaging

Differentiation
and brand
relationships

Caterpillar has become a leading firm by maximising total customer-perceived value in the construction equipment industry, despite challenges from a number of able competitors such as John Deere, J. I. Case, Komatsu, Volvo and Hitachi. First, Caterpillar produces high-performance equipment known for its reliability and durability – key purchase considerations in the choice of heavy industrial equipment. The firm also makes it easy for customers to find the right product by providing a full line of construction equipment and offering a wide range of financial terms. Caterpillar maintains the largest number of independent construction equipment dealers in the industry. These dealers all carry a complete line of Caterpillar products and are typically better trained and perform more reliably than competitors' dealers. Caterpillar has also built an impressive worldwide parts and service system. As the company offers CPV packages it is able to command a premium price in the marketplace.[1]

Markets are becoming increasingly dynamic. As a result product life cycles shorten dramatically.

▽ Product life-cycle marketing strategies

A company's positioning and differentiation strategy must change as the product (market offering – a term that includes both tangible products and intangible services), market and competitors change over the *product life cycle* (PLC). To say that a product (offering) has a life cycle is to assert four things:

1 Products (market offerings) have a limited life.

2 Sales pass through distinct stages, each posing different challenges, opportunities and problems to the seller.

3 Profits rise and fall at different stages of the product life cycle.

4 Products require different marketing, financial, manufacturing, purchasing and human resource strategies in each life cycle stage.

Product life cycles

Most product life cycle curves are portrayed as bell-shaped (see Figure 14.1). This curve is typically divided into four stages: introduction, growth, maturity and decline.

1 **Introduction**: A period of slow sales growth as the product (market offering) is introduced into the market. Profits are non-existent because of the heavy expenses associated with market introduction.

2 **Growth**: A period of rapid market acceptance and substantial profit improvement.

3 **Maturity**: A slowdown in sales growth because the product (market offering) has achieved acceptance by most potential buyers. Profits stabilise or decline because of increased competition.

4 **Decline**: Sales show a downward drift and profits erode.

The PLC concept can be applied to analyse a product category (alcohol), a product form (white alcohol), a product (vodka) or a brand (Smirnoff). Not all products exhibit a bell-shaped PLC. Three common alternative patterns are shown in Figure 14.2.

Figure 14.2(a) shows a *growth-slump-maturity pattern*, often characteristic of small kitchen appliances such as handheld mixers and breadmakers. Sales grow rapidly when the item is first introduced and then fall to a residual level that is sustained by late adopters buying for the first time and early adopters replacing it.

The *cycle-recycle pattern* in Figure 14.2(b) often describes the sales of new drugs. The pharmaceutical company aggressively promotes its new drug, and this produces the first cycle. Later, sales start declining and the company gives the drug another promotion push, which produces a second cycle (usually of smaller magnitude and duration).

Another common pattern is the *scalloped PLC* in Figure 14.2(c). Here sales pass through a succession of life cycles based on the discovery of new product/market offering characteristics, uses or users. The sale of nylon, for example, shows a scalloped pattern because of the many new uses – parachutes, hosiery, shirts, carpeting, boat sails, car tyres – that continue to be discovered over time.

Figure 14.1 Long range product market expansion strategy (P1 = product 1; M1= market 1)

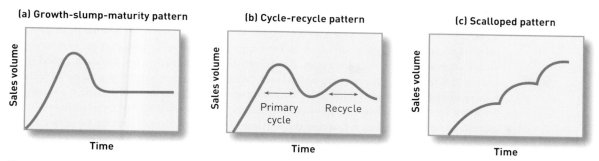

Figure 14.2 Common product life-cycle patterns

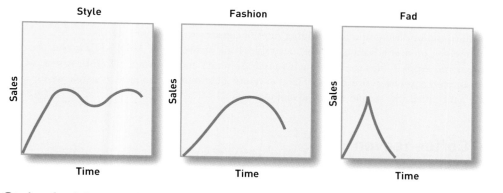

Figure 14.3 Style, fashion and fad life cycles

Style, fashion and fad life cycles

Three special categories of product life cycles – styles, fashions and fads – can be distinguished. (Figure 14.3). A *style* is a basic and distinctive mode of expression. Styles appear in homes (French, Italian, Scandinavian and Spanish); clothing (formal, casual); and art (realistic, surrealistic, abstract). A style can last for generations and go in and out of vogue. A *fashion* is a currently accepted or popular style in a given field. Fashions pass through four stages: distinctiveness, emulation, mass fashion and decline.[2]

The length of a fashion cycle is hard to predict. One point of view is that fashions end because they represent a purchase compromise, and consumers start looking for the missing attributes. For example, as cars become smaller, they become less comfortable, and then a growing number of buyers start wanting larger cars. Another explanation is that too many consumers adopt the fashion, thus turning others away. Still another is that the length of a particular fashion cycle depends on the extent to which the fashion meets a genuine need, is consistent with other trends in the society, satisfies societal norms and values, and keeps within technological limits as it develops.

Fads are fashions that come quickly into public view, are adopted with great zeal, peak early, and decline very fast. Every Christmas in the United Kingdom certain toys are all the rage: Buzz Lightyear, Cabbage Patch dolls and Rubik's cube have all been at the top of children's wish lists in recent years. Generally speaking fads are characterised by a short life cycle and tend to attract only a limited following, those who are searching for excitement or want to distinguish themselves from others. Fads fail to survive because they don't normally satisfy a strong need. The marketing winners are those who recognise fads early and leverage them into products (market offerings) with staying power. For example successful rock bands such as Abba, the Beatles and the Police.

Marketing strategies: the introduction stage and the pioneer advantage

Because it takes time to roll out a new product/market offering, work out the technical problems, fill dealer pipelines and gain consumer acceptance, sales growth tends to be slow in the introduction stage. Profits are negative or low, while promotional expenditures are at their highest ratio to sales because of the need to: (1) inform potential consumers; (2) induce customers to trial the market offering; and (3) secure distribution in retail outlets.[3] Firms focus on those buyers who are the most ready to purchase. Prices tend to be high because costs are high.

Companies that plan to introduce a new market offering must decide when to enter the market. To be first can be rewarding, but risky and expensive. To come in later makes sense if the firm can bring superior technology, quality or brand strength. Speeding up innovation time is essential in an age of shortening product life cycles. Being early has been shown to pay. Nokia is a good illustration of a fast-track innovator. In many cases the market pioneer gains the greatest advantage. Companies such as Amazon, Nintendo, Sony and Swatch developed sustained market dominance.

What are the sources of the pioneer's advantage? Early users will recall the pioneer's brand name (as in the case of Hoover, whose brand name became the generic term for vacuum cleaners for several years in the United Kingdom) if the product satisfies them. The pioneer's brand also establishes the attributes the product class should possess. The pioneer's brand normally aims at the middle of the market and so captures more users. Customer inertia also plays a role; and there are producer advantages: economies of scale, technological leadership, patents, ownership of scarce assets, and other barriers to entry. Furthermore, pioneers can benefit from effective marketing communications and enjoy higher rates of consumer repeat purchases.

However, pioneer advantage is not inevitable. Look at the fate of Amstrad (low-cost personal computers), Apple's Newton (personal digital assistant) and Netscape (Web browser), which were all market pioneers overtaken by later entrants. First movers also have to watch out for what some have called the 'second mover advantage'.

▽ Coffeeheaven

Quick to plug gap in Europe's café society

Richard Worthington was in Warsaw for a business deal when he went in search of a good cup of coffee. He could not find one, which gave him a great business idea. Seven years later the business he founded, Coffeeheaven, is the largest modern branded coffee shop chain in central Europe, with 59 outlets across the region, 39 of them in Poland. 'To me it was just a question of time before coffee bars appeared here. When we looked around central Europe, we saw fragmented markets, unfriendly staff, women-unfriendly restaurants and bad coffee. It was an enormous opportunity,' says the British entrepreneur.

For the moment, Coffeeheaven is more or less alone in a region with 140 million consumers. Older, more established coffee operations have skipped central Europe, jumping from Germany to oil-booming Moscow. Worthington's idea was not particularly ground breaking. Anyone walking down a North American or British street in the past decade would have noticed the trend to smart coffee bars that serve food, in a pleasant atmosphere that encourages lounging with a book or a laptop.

Central Europe is still fertile ground for adopting well-established western business models wholesale for increasingly wealthy customers, who are familiar with offerings in western Europe. The trick was to see that central Europe would rapidly become much more like western Europe in its tastes, in its expectations of service and quality, and eventually in its spending patterns.

The model Worthington chose was Britain's Café Nero, which stresses its food as well as its coffee. The first Coffeeheaven opened in 2000, followed in 2001 by an outlet in Galeria Mokotow, a new high-end shopping mall in southern Warsaw. That branch recouped its initial investment in 37 weeks. Since then the chain has grown by setting up in Warsaw's airport, main railway station as well as in cinemas. It is also looking at closer cooperation with Empik, a leading bookseller that is also a shareholder. In 2007, the chain reported sales of £6.4 million and a loss of about £700,000. It expects to make its first profit in 2008, as it continues to expand in the Czech Republic, Slovakia, Bulgaria, Romania and Latvia. It is listed on the Alternative Investment Market (AIM) in London.

But Coffeeheaven's unchallenged expansion throughout the region is coming to an end. Costa Coffee, the coffee chain owned by Britain's Whitbread, announced recently that it will be moving into Romania, Bulgaria and Poland, with the aim of opening 200 shops over the next five years. Other large coffee chains are also taking a second look at central Europe. However, late entrants will face several hurdles. The first is that Coffeeheaven already has choice locations in most of the region's new shopping malls. 'We have a first-mover advantage,' says Worthington. 'The action here is in the malls, and outsiders will have to buy someone out if they want to get in.'

Coffeeheaven has avoided the fate of many other pioneers entering new markets which take advantage of their status to make quick profits with an inferior offering. Even if the competition does make an appearance in a region where people drink only about half as much coffee as in western Europe, the company should be able to sustain fairly robust rivalry. There are also plans to expand into the Ukraine.

Source: J. Cienski (2006) Jan Cienski in Warsaw, *Financial Times*, 20 December.

▽ Jaguar

Premium sports car

Jaguar was looking to replace the flagship of its range, the XK8/XKR high-performance sports car. It was imperative that the new model strongly communicated the core brand values of beauty, luxury and sportiness. The specialist agency Innovia was asked to create ideas for new features and attributes that would be worthy of the pedigree and would keep the trade press buzzing. Innovia explored the different associations of luxury and sportiness in the consumer's mind, and then created concepts that exploited the synergies and overcame the contradictions. It identified emerging technologies and created a range of features that could help the new model build a leading market position.

The new car was launched to widespread acclaim in March 2006 and won the UK's BBC *Top Gear*'s 'Car of the Year' Award in 2007.

Jaguar's XK8/XKR high-performance sports car.
Source: Mark Scheuern/Alamy

Source: www.innoviatech.com/projects/articles/9/premium-sports-car.

If a company wants to win it needs to be the first, surely? The first mover advantage theory states that the first company entering a certain market will gain massive market share and, thanks to the competitive advantages developed, it will also be able to defend its leadership position from new entrants. The reasoning behind it is quite intuitive, it goes a long way with conventional wisdom and, if that was not enough, the principle has also been proposed by academics and managers around the world. Andrew Grove, Intel's ex-CEO, defended that 'the first mover and only the first mover, the company that acts while others dither, has a true opportunity to gain time over its competitors; and time advantage, in this business, is the surest way to gain market share'.[4]

There is a lot of theoretical evidence supporting the model, but does this evidence emerge empirically as well? Not quite. Consider the markets for safety razors, disposable nappies, photographic film, laser printers, games consoles, VCRs, energy drinks, personal computers, Internet browsers, operating systems, search engines, online bookstores, online auctions, VoIP (a protocol optimised for the transmission of the voice through the Internet) services – and the list goes on. In each and every one of these markets the leader position is held by a company that was a late entrant to the market.

The question then becomes: Why, despite the lack of empirical evidence, do people still embrace the idea that being the first to enter a market is extremely important? There are three main reasons: the industrial age environment, natural monopolies and the bias towards winners.

Industrial age environment

Until the 1980s the pace of change in some industries was much slower. Being the first to enter a market characterised by stability and predictable incremental changes could actually yield significant advantages. In the information age, however, discontinuities and market innovations are becoming the norm. As a consequence, success often comes no longer from being the first to market but from rapidly evolving the product to become the dominant design. JVC's VHS recording technology came to the market almost two years after Sony's Betamax. Nonetheless by licensing out the technology to other producers, creating alliances with content creators and adapting the features to address the needs of customers and rental stores JVC managed to establish the VHS as the standard for video recording, driving Betamax out of the market.

Natural monopolies

Some markets present predominant capital costs and infrastructure constraints, meaning that the first mover can actually build a strong competitive position by merely entering the market before other players. This is the case for oil and gas distribution, water services and electricity. Natural monopolies represent exceptions in most countries. In modern economies being able to understand customers, manage innovation and adapt quickly to market discontinuities is much more important than being the first to enter a market. The most evident example is the Internet. Google was not the first search engine. Amazon was not the first online bookstore. eBay was not the first online auction site. All these companies were focused on understanding their customers, innovating and adapting their strategies to reflect market changes, thus enabling them to build strong leadership positions.

Bias towards winners

Over the long term there is a natural tendency to forget failures and to overcelebrate successes. It is not surprising, therefore, that people wrongly associate long-term market leaders with the first to enter a certain segment. Consider the case of laser printers. In 1971 Xerox developed the first working model. IBM on the other hand was the first company to commercialise it in 1976. Hewlett-Packard entered the market almost ten years later, developed laser printers rapidly to suit mass market requirements and managed to become the clear winner. Hewlett-Packard has sold more than 100 million units – no wonder people think it was the first company to commercialise laser printers.

Entering a new market too early can prove to be disappointing. Many companies have found that it pays to learn from the experience of first movers and then enter the market before a dominant branded design emerges. Contrary to what most people think King Gillette was not the first to market safety razors. They were invented in 1880 by the Kampfe brothers, and a decade before King Gillette opened his company there were already commercial safety razors being sold. Gillette, however, evolved the product rapidly both by improving the design and by creating a business model where the profits would be made with the disposable blades. Neatly crafted business strategy, good understanding of customer needs and marketing enabled Gillette to dominate the safety razor market for a long period, after being a late market entrant.

Schnaars studied 28 industries where the imitators surpassed the innovators.[5] He found several weaknesses among the failing pioneers, including new products that were too crude, were improperly positioned or appeared before there was strong demand; product development costs that exhausted the innovator's resources; a lack of resources to compete against entering larger firms; and managerial incompetence or unhealthy complacency. Successful imitators thrived by offering lower prices, improving the product more continuously or using brute market power to overtake the pioneer. None of the companies that now dominate in the man-ufacture of personal computers – including Dell, Packard-Bell and Compaq – were first movers.[6]

Golder and Tellis raise further doubts about the pioneer advantage.[7] They distinguish between an *inventor,* first to develop patents in a new product category; a *product pioneer,* first to develop a working model; and a *market pioneer,* first to sell in the new product category. They also include non-surviving pioneers in their sample. They conclude that although pioneers may still have an advantage, a larger number of market pioneers fail than has been reported, and a larger number of early market leaders (though not pioneers) succeed. Examples of later entrants over-taking market pioneers are IBM over Sperry in mainframe computers and Matsushita over Sony in VCRs.

In a more recent study, Tellis and Golder identify the following five factors as underpinning long-term market leadership: vision of a mass market, persistence, relentless innovation, finan-cial commitment and asset leverage.[8] Other research has highlighted the importance of the nov-elty of product innovation.[9] When a pioneer starts a market with a really new product, as was the case with the Dyson Cyclone vacuum cleaner, survival can be very challenging. In contrast, when the market is started by an incremental innovation, as was the case with MP3 players with video capabilities, pioneers' survival rates are much higher.

The pioneer should visualise the various product markets it could initially enter, knowing it cannot enter all of them at once. Suppose market-segmentation analysis reveals the product market segments shown in Figure 14.4. The pioneer should analyse the profit potential of each product market singly and in combination and decide on a market expansion path. Thus the pioneer in Figure 14.4 plans first to enter product market P_1M_1, then move the product into a second market (P_1M_2), then surprise the competition by developing a second product for the second market (P_2M_2), then take the second product back into the first market (P_2M_1), and then launch a third product for the first market (P_3M_1). If this game plan works the pio-neer firm will own a good part of the first two segments and serve them with two or three products.

Marketing strategies: the growth stage

The growth stage is marked by a rapid climb in sales. Early adopters like the market offering, and new consumers start purchasing from the firm. New competitors enter, attracted by the opportunities. They introduce new product features (and market offering value attributes) and expand distribution.

Prices remain where they are or fall slightly, depending on how quickly demand increases. Companies maintain their promotional expenditures at the same or at a slightly increased level to meet competition and to continue to educate the market. Sales rise much faster than promo-tional expenditures, causing a welcome decline in the promotion–sales ratio. Profits increase dur-ing this stage as promotion costs are spread over a larger volume and unit manufacturing costs

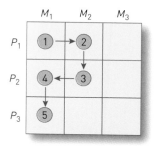

Figure 14.4 Long-range product market expansion strategy (p_i = product i; m_j = market j)

fall faster than price declines owing to the producer learning or experience curve effect. Firms have to watch for a change from an accelerating to a decelerating rate of growth in order to prepare new strategies. The European Internet service provider market has grown rapidly since 2001 and by late 2007 showed signs of moving into the mature stage.

▽ ISP UK market

Consumers are highly fickle with their choice of Internet provider, with nearly one in four people switching companies every year. People are far more likely to change their Internet company than their power supplier, bank or mortgage provider, according to research from Group 1 Software, a division of the Pitney Bowes office technology group. Customer churn rates among Internet service providers are about 24 per cent each year, far higher than a cross-industry average of about 19 per cent. Power utilities and mortgage lenders have a customer churn rate of less than 14 per cent, while banks see about 20 per cent of customers swap each year. The only sector with a higher churn rate is the mobile phone industry, where about one-third of customers change providers every year. Increasing customer disloyalty in the Internet service market comes as competition, especially over price, intensifies. The Carphone Warehouse delivered the latest shakeup to the market when it announced an offer of 'free' high-speed Internet access for customers who signed up to its landline telephone service.

Competition in the United Kingdom has increased, in particular after Ofcom, the communications regulator, ruled that the British Telecom Group should open its telecommunications exchanges to competitors, giving them control over the entire telephone line direct to the customer's home. This has made it easier for British Telecom's rivals to offer higher-speed Internet connections at a lower cost. As a result the United Kingdom has become one of Europe's largest broadband markets, with more than 10 million connections, and about 70,000 new customers signing up every week. Brian Ahearne, of the Internet Service Providers' Association, said: 'We have a very competitive industry now with a wide variety of packages and contracts tailored to different needs. This is making people shop around.' Ofcom is also keeping a close watch to ensure that customers can easily change their ISP. More than 40 UK Internet companies have signed up to a voluntary code that helps make customer migration easier and Ofcom periodically investigates its effectiveness.

Though good for consumer choice, high churn rates are proving a headache for Internet service companies, which have to spend increasing amounts of money to attract and retain customers. A number of them, such as AOL and Tiscali, have begun running loyalty reward schemes, where customers can win CDs, DVDs and gadgets if they stay with the same provider. Softpoint Multimedia, a firm that runs loyalty schemes for companies in a number of sectors, says Internet service providers have become their single biggest client group, driving annual revenue growth of about 68 per cent.[10]

During the growth stage, the firm uses several strategies to sustain rapid market growth:

- It improves product quality and adds new product features and improved styling.
- It adds new models, accessory items and personalising options (i.e., products of different sizes, flavours, and so forth that protect the main product).
- It enters new market segments.

- It increases its distribution coverage and enters new distribution channels.
- It shifts from product-awareness advertising to product-preference advertising.
- It lowers prices to attract the next layer of price-sensitive buyers.

These market expansion strategies strengthen the firm's competitive position. Consider how Yahoo! has fuelled growth.

▽ **Yahoo!**

Founded in 1994 by Web-surfing Stanford University postgraduate students, Yahoo! has become the number one place to be on the Web, averaging 129 million unique visitors a month, representing almost 80 per cent of the online population. The company grew into more than just a search engine; it became a portal, offering a full-blown package of information and services, from email to online shopping centres. Yahoo!'s revenues, which exceeded US $6 billion in 2005, come from a number of sources – banner ads, paid search, subscriptions for services such as personals, and a broadband partnership with SBC Communications. Yahoo!'s US $1.6 billion acquisition of Overture Services in 2003, a key paid search competitor of Google, helped strengthen its claim as a one-stop shop for advertisers. Subsequent years have seen many additional acquisitions to expand the company's online capabilities and services, including online social event calendar Upcoming.org, online video editing site Jumpcut, and online social contest site bix.com. Yahoo! also continued to grow globally with strong emphasis on Europe and Asia, helped in part by the acquisition of Kelkoo, a European comparison shopping site, for US $579 million and 46 per cent of Alibaba, a Chinese ecommerce company, for US $1 billion in cash in 2005. Increasingly aware that they were losing ground to Google in the computer search engine market, Microsoft announced its interest in merging with Yahoo! in February 2008 but on 1 May withdrew its offer after failing to agree terms.

A firm in the growth stage faces a trade-off between high market share and high current profit. By spending money on product improvement, promotion and distribution it can capture a dominant position. It forgoes maximum current profit in the hope of making even greater profits in the next stage.

Marketing strategies: the maturity stage

At some point the rate of sales growth will slow, and the product will enter a stage of relative maturity. This stage normally lasts longer than the previous stages and poses big challenges to marketing management. Most market offerings are in the maturity stage of the life cycle.

The maturity stage divides into three phases: growth, stable and decaying maturity. In the first phase, the sales growth rate starts to decline. There are no new distribution channels to fill. New competitive forces emerge (see 'Marketing insight: Competitive category dynamics'). In the second phase, sales flatten on a per capita basis because of market saturation. Most potential consumers have tried the product (market offering), and future sales are governed by population growth and replacement demand. In the third phase, decaying maturity, the absolute level of sales starts to decline, and customers begin switching to other market offerings.

Marketing insight

Competitive category dynamics

One of marketing's most astute observers, Professor David Aaker notes that because new categories can represent strategically important threats or opportunities, marketers have to be very attentive to the forces that drive their emergence. He cites seven such dynamics that result in new categories:

1   **A new product or service dimension expands the boundaries of an existing category**: As exemplified by the introduction of 'new' healthy yogurt derivatives such as Danone's Actimel yogurt drink.

2   **A new product or set of products carves out a fresh niche in an existing category**: Red Bull took the energy drinks market by storm and rapidly assumed market leadership in the United Kingdom.

3   **A new competitor devises a way to bundle existing categories into a super category**: In the late 1990s, Siebel created Internet-based customer relationship management software by pulling together a host of applications, including customer loyalty programmes, customer acquisition, call centres, customer service, customer contact, and sales force automation. In doing so, Siebel rendered irrelevant, for some customers, the more specialised application programmes of competitors.

4   **A new competitor repositions existing products or services to create an original category**: In the United Kingdom, Ford positioned its Galaxy minivan in relation to first-class air travel – comfortable enough to be suitable for busy executives. By highlighting attributes far different from those that would appeal to a buyer looking for a family vehicle, the car maker created a new minivan subcategory.

5   **Customer needs propel a new product category or subcategory**: Dual trends – wellness and the use of herbs and natural supplements – have supported a huge new beverage category, healthy refreshment drinks. It now contains a host of subcategories, including enhanced teas, fruit drinks, soya-based drinks and speciality waters.

6   **A new technology leads the development of a product category or subcategory**: The introduction of a low cost, manual, battery-powered toothbrush by Oral-B Pulsar extended the product life cycle of the conventional manual toothbrush market. The new technology pulses the brush bristles to produce a deep-cleaning action that removes plaque and food particles from between teeth.

7   **A company exploits changing technologies to invent a new category**: Nintendo created a whole new market in portable entertainment with its DS Lite and Wii electronic gaming equipment.

Source: From D. A. Aaker (2004) The relevance of brand relevance, *Strategy Business*, 35, Summer, 1–10. Reproduced with permission. See also D. A. Aaker (2004) *Brand Portfolio Strategy: Creating Relevance, Differentiation, Energy, Leverage, Clarity*, New York: Free Press.

The third phase of maturity poses the most challenges. The sales slowdown creates overcapacity in the industry, which leads to intensified competition. Competitors scramble to find niches. They engage in frequent price reductions and sales promotions. They increase advertising and trade and consumer promotion. They increase R&D budgets to develop product (market offering) improvements and line extensions. They make deals to supply private brands and weaker competitors withdraw. The industry eventually consists of well-entrenched competitors whose basic drive is to gain or maintain market share to build a sustainable competitive advantage in the market.

Dominating the industry are a few giant firms – perhaps a quality leader, a service leader and a cost leader – that serve the whole market and make their profits mainly through high volume and lower costs. Surrounding these dominant firms is a multitude of market nichers, including market specialists, product specialists and customising firms. The issue facing a firm in a mature market is whether to struggle to become one of the 'big three' and achieve profits through high volume and low cost, or to pursue a niching strategy and achieve profits through low volume and a high margin. Sometimes, however, the market will become polarised between low- and high-end segments and the firms in the middle see their market share steadily erode. Here is how Swedish appliance manufacturer, Electrolux, has coped with this situation.

▽ Electrolux AB

In 2002 Electrolux began facing a rapidly polarising appliance market. At one end, low-cost Asian companies such as Haier, LG and Samsung were applying downward price pressure. At the other end, premium competitors such as Bosch, Sub-Zero and Viking were continuing to grow at the expense of the middle-of-the-road brands. Electrolux's new CEO Hans Stråberg, who took over the reins just as the middle was dropping out of the market, decided to escape the middle by rethinking Electrolux's customers' wants and needs. For instance, rather than accept the stratification between low and high, Stråberg segmented the market according to the lifestyle and purchasing patterns of about 20 different types of consumers – '20 product positions' as he calls them. Electrolux now successfully markets its steam ovens to health-oriented consumers, for example, and its compact dishwashers, originally developed for smaller kitchens, to a broader consumer segment interested in washing dishes more often. To companies finding themselves stuck in the middle of a mature market, Stråberg offers these words of advice:

> Start with consumers and understand what their latent needs are and what problems they experience . . . then put the puzzle together yourself to discover what people really want to have. Henry Ford is supposed to have said, 'If I had asked people what they really wanted, I would have made faster horses' or something like that. You have to figure out what people really want, although they can't express it.[11]

Some companies abandon weaker products to concentrate on more profitable and new products. Yet they may be ignoring the high potential many mature markets and old products still have. Industries widely thought to be mature – cars, motorcycles, televisions, watches, cameras – were proved otherwise by the Japanese, who found ways to offer new value to customers. Seemingly moribund brands such as Lucozade have achieved sales revivals by repositioning the brand as an isotonic sports drink aimed at young people.

Three potentially useful ways to change the course for a brand are market, item and marketing programme modifications.

Market modification

A company might try to expand the market for its mature brand by working with the two factors that make up sales volume: volume = number of brand users × usage rate per user, as in Table 14.1.

Table 14.1 Alternative ways to increase sales volume

Expand the number of brand users	Increase the usage rates among users
• *Convert non-users.* The key to the growth of air freight service is the constant search for new users to whom air carriers can demonstrate the benefits of using air freight rather than ground transportation.	• *Have consumers use the product on more occasions.* Serve yogurt for a snack.
• *Enter new market segments.* The major super-market chains across Europe are increasingly placing more and higher value non-food lines on their shelves.	• *Have consumers use more of the product on each occasion.* Drink a larger glass of orange juice.
• *Attract competitors' customers.* Shops on garage forecourts generate profitable sales in food and non-food items as drivers pay for their petrol.	• *Have consumers use the product in new ways.* Use washing-up liquid to clean windows.

Product modification

Managers also try to stimulate sales by modifying the product characteristics through quality improvement feature improvement or style improvement.

Quality improvement aims at increasing functional performance. A manufacturer can often overtake its competition by launching a 'new and improved' product. Grocery manufacturers call this a 'plus launch' and promote a new additive or advertise something as 'stronger', 'bigger', or 'better'. This strategy is effective to the extent that the quality is improved, buyers accept the claim, and a sufficient number will pay for it. In the case of the tinned coffee industry, manufacturers are using 'freshness' to better position their brands in the face of fierce competition from premium rivals, such as store brands that let customers grind their own beans in the store. Coffee brands are increasingly becoming available in 'seal-easy' packaging to keep the beans fresh.

Feature improvement aims at adding new features such as size, weight, materials, additives and accessories that expand the product use performance, versatility, safety or convenience. This strategy has several advantages. New features build the company's image as an innovator and win the loyalty of market segments that value these features. They provide an opportunity for free publicity and they generate sales force and distributor enthusiasm. The chief disadvantage is that feature improvements are easily imitated; unless the marketer realises a permanent gain from being first, the feature improvement might not pay off in the long run.

Style improvement aims at increasing aesthetic appeal. The periodic introduction of new car models is largely about style competition, as is the introduction of new packaging for consumer goods. A style strategy might give the product (market offering) a unique market identity. Yet style competition has problems. First, it is difficult to predict whether people – and which people – will like a new style. Second, a style change usually requires discontinuing the old style, and the company risks losing customers.

Regardless of the type of improvement, marketers must beware of a possible backlash. Customers are not always willing to accept an 'improved' product, as the now-classic tale of New Coke illustrates.

▽ Coca-Cola

Battered by competition from the sweeter Pepsi-Cola, Coca-Cola decided in 1985 to replace its old formula with a sweeter variation, dubbed New Coke. Coca-Cola spent US $4 million on market research. Blind taste tests showed that Coke drinkers preferred the new, sweeter formula, but the launch of New Coke provoked a national uproar. Market researchers had measured the taste but had failed to measure the emotional attachment consumers had to the original Coca-Cola. There were angry letters, formal protests, and even lawsuit threats, to force the retention of 'The Real Thing'. Ten weeks later, the company withdrew New Coke and reintroduced its century-old formula as 'Classic Coke', giving the old formula even stronger status in the marketplace.

Marketing programme modification

Marketing managers might also try to stimulate sales by modifying other marketing programme elements. They should ask the following questions:

- **Prices**: Would a price cut attract new buyers? If so, should the list price be lowered, or should prices be lowered through price specials, volume or early purchase discounts, freight cost absorption or easier credit terms? Or would it be better to *raise* the price, to signal higher quality?
- **Distribution**: Can the company obtain more product support and display in existing outlets? Can it penetrate more outlets? Can the company introduce the product into new distribution channels?

- **Advertising**: Should advertising expenditure be increased? Should the message or advertising copy be improved? Or the media mix? Or the timing, frequency or size of advertisements?
- **Sales promotion**: Should the company step up sales promotion – trade deals, money-off coupons, rebates, warranties, gifts and contests?
- **Personal selling**: Should the number or quality of sales people be increased? Should sales force duties be changed? Or sales territories and sales force incentives be revised? Can sales-call planning be improved?
- **Services**: Can the company speed up delivery? Can more technical assistance or better credit deals be given to customers?

Marketing strategies: the decline stage

Sales decline for a number of reasons, including technological advances, shifts in consumer tastes and increased domestic and foreign competition. All can lead to overcapacity, increased price cutting and profit erosion. The decline might be slow, as in the case of sewing machines; or rapid, as in the case of floppy disks. Sales may plunge to zero, or they may stagnate at a low level. As sales and profits decline, some firms withdraw from the market. Those remaining may reduce the number of items they offer. They may withdraw from smaller market segments and weaker trade channels, and they may cut their promotion budgets and reduce prices further. Unfortunately, most companies have not developed a policy for handling ageing products.

Unless strong reasons for retention exist, carrying a weak product is very costly to the firm – and not just by the amount of uncovered overhead and profit: there are many hidden costs. Weak products often consume a disproportionate amount of management's time; require frequent price and inventory adjustments; incur expensive set-up for short production runs; draw both advertising and sales force attention that might be better used to make healthy products more profitable; and cast a shadow on the company's image. The biggest cost might well lie in the future. Failing to eliminate weak products delays the aggressive search for replacement products. The weak products create a lopsided product mix, long on yesterday's breadwinners and short on tomorrow's.

In handling ageing products, a company faces a number of tasks and decisions. The first task is to establish a system for identifying weak market offerings. Many companies appoint a product-review committee with representatives from marketing, R&D, manufacturing and finance who, based on all available information make a recommendation for each product – leave it alone, modify its marketing strategy or drop it.[12]

Some firms abandon declining markets earlier than others. Much depends on the height of exit barriers in the industry.[13] The lower the exit barriers, the easier it is for firms to leave the industry, and the more tempting it is for the remaining firms to stay and attract the withdrawing firms' customers. For example, Procter & Gamble stayed in the declining liquid soap business and improved its profits as others withdrew.

The appropriate strategy also depends on the industry's relative attractiveness and the company's competitive strength in that industry. A company that is in an unattractive industry but possesses competitive strength should consider shrinking selectively. A company that is in an attractive industry but has competitive strength should consider strengthening its investment. Companies that successfully reposition or rejuvenate a mature product often do so by adding value to the original offering.

If the company were choosing between harvesting and divesting, its strategies would be quite different. *Harvesting* calls for gradually reducing a product or business's costs while trying to maintain sales. The first step is to cut research and development costs and plant and equipment investment. The company might also reduce product quality, sales force size, marginal services and advertising expenditure. It would try to cut these costs without letting customers, competitors and employees know what is happening. Harvesting is difficult to execute. Yet many mature products warrant this strategy. It can substantially increase the company's current cash flow.[14]

When a company decides to drop a product it faces further decisions. If a product has strong distribution and residual goodwill, the company can probably sell it to another firm. In 2008

Ford sold on the famous UK car marques of Jaguar and Land-Rover to Tata Steel of India. If the company cannot find any buyers, it must decide whether to liquidate the brand quickly or slowly. It must also decide on how much inventory and after-sales service support to maintain for past customers.

▽ Evidence on the product life cycle concept

Based on the above discussion, Table 14.2 summarises the characteristics, marketing objectives and marketing strategies of the four stages of the PLC. The PLC concept helps marketers interpret product and market dynamics, conduct planning and control, and perform forecasting. One recent research study of 30 product categories unearthed a number of interesting findings concerning the PLC.[15]

- New consumer durables show a distinct take-off, after which sales increase by roughly 45 per cent a year, but also show a distinct slow-down, when sales decline by roughly 15 per cent a year.
- Slow-down occurs at 34 per cent penetration on average, well before the majority of households own a new product.
- The growth stage lasts a little over eight years and does not seem to shorten over time.
- Informational cascades exist, meaning that people are more likely to adopt over time if others have bought, instead of by making careful product evaluations. One implication, however, is that product categories with large sales increases at take-off tend to have larger sales decline at slow-down.

Table 14.2 Summary of product life cycle characteristics, objectives and strategies

	Introduction	Growth	Maturity	Decline
Characteristics				
Sales	Low sales	Rapidly rising sales	Peak sales	Declining sales
Costs	High cost per customer	Average cost per customer	Low cost per customer	Low cost per customer
Profits	Negative	Rising profits	High profits	Declining profits
Customers	Innovators	Early adopters	Middle majority	Laggards
Competitors	Few	Growing number	Stable number beginning to decline	Declining number
Marketing Objectives				
	Create product awareness and trial	Maximize market share	Maximize profit while defending market share	Reduce expenditure and milk the brand
Strategies				
Product	Offer a basic product	Offer product extensions, service, warranty	Diversify brands and items models	Phase out weak products
Price	Charge cost-plus	Price to penetrate market	Price to match or best competitors'	Cut price
Distribution	Build selective distribution	Build intensive distribution	Build more intensive distribution	Go selective: phase out unprofitable outlets
Advertising	Build product awareness among early adopters and dealers	Build awareness and interest in the mass market	Stress brand differences and benefits	Reduce to level needed to retain hard-core loyals
Sales Promotion	Use heavy sales promotion to entice trial	Reduce to take advantage of heavy consumer demand	Increase to encourage brand switching	Reduce to minimal level

Sources: C. R. Wasson (1978) *Dynamic Competitive Strategy and Product Life Cycles*, Austin, TX: Austin Press; J. A. Weber (1976) Planning corporate growth with inverted product life cycles, *Long Range Planning*, October, 12–29; P. Doyle (1976) The realities of the product life cycle, *Quarterly Review of Marketing*, Summer.

▽ Critique of the product life cycle concept

PLC theory has its share of critics. Crawford argued that what had traditionally been recognised as the PLC was actually a special case of the new, broader product evolutionary cycle.[16] The evolutionary concept borrowed from biology is useful in solving problems in the fixed cycle sequence: but still no simple solutions exist.[17]

The critics claim that life cycle patterns are too variable in shape and duration to be generalised, and that marketers can seldom tell what stage their product is in. A product may appear to be mature when actually it has reached a plateau prior to another upsurge. They also charge that, rather than an inevitable course that sales must follow, the PLC pattern is the self-fulfilling result of marketing strategies, and that skilful marketing can in fact lead to continued growth. 'Marketing memo: How to build a breakaway brand' provides ten rules for long-term marketing success.

Marketing memo

How to build a breakaway brand

Marketing experts Kelly and Silverstein define a *breakaway brand* as one that stands out, not just in its own product category, but from all other brands, and which achieves significant results in the marketplace. Here is a summary of their ten tips for building a breakaway brand:

1 **Make a commitment** The entire organisation, from the top down, needs to make a commitment to build and support a breakaway brand and to develop new products that have breakaway attributes.

2 **Get a 'chief' behind it** Few breakaway branding initiatives have a chance of success without the enthusiastic support of the company's CEO, Chief Operations Officer (COO) or Chief Marketing Officer (CMO). A senior executive must play the role of brand visionary, brand champion and brand architect.

3 **Find your brand truth** Ultimately, the DNA of a breakaway brand is its brand truth. It is what defines and differentiates every breakaway brand. It is the single most important weapon a brand will ever have in the battle for increased awareness, profitability, market share, and even share price.

4 **Target a winning mindset** The winning mindset is the potent, aspirational, shared 'view of life' among all core audience segments. It should inspire all of the company's advertising and promotional activities.

5 **Create a category of one** To be a breakaway brand, your brand needs not only to stand apart from others in its own category but also to transcend categories and open a defining gap between itself and its competitors. Then it becomes a category of one.

6 **Demand a great campaign** Great campaigns are a team sport – they require a partnership between the company and its agencies to create a campaign that breaks away. Never compromise on a campaign, because without a great campaign, the potential breakaway brand is likely to fail to take off.

7 **Tirelessly integrate** Integration is the name of the game. Depending on the audience a company is trying to reach, the campaign might feature an integrated marketing communication with both network and cable TV, print and online advertising, direct mail, email, radio and non-traditional media – from street marketing to publicity stunts to contests.

8 **Take risks** Today, 80 per cent of brands are just about holding their own. Only 20 per cent are doing well.

9 **Accelerate new product development** Nothing is more important than differentiating a product in the marketplace – but the only way to rise above me-too branding is to innovate and do something different and unique with the product. It may mean throwing away an old brand and reinventing it. Or it may mean introducing a new branded product.

10 **Invest as if the brand depends on it** Building a breakaway brand is serious business, so it takes a serious business investment. Invest in the product, of course – but also in the packaging and a smart, integrated marketing campaign. Invest wisely . . . as the brand depends on it.

Source: Adapted from F. J. Kelly III and B. Silverstein (2005) *The Breakaway Brand*, New York: McGraw-Hill. Copyright © 2005 The McGraw-Hill Companies. Reproduced with permission.

▽ **Market evolution**

Because the PLC focuses on what is happening to a particular product or brand rather than on what is happening to the overall market, it yields a product-oriented picture rather than a market-oriented picture. Firms also need to visualise a *market's* evolutionary path as it is affected by new needs, competitors, technology, channels and other developments.[18] In the course of a product's or brand's existence, its positioning must change to keep pace with market developments. Like products, markets evolve through four stages: emergence, growth, maturity and decline.

Emergence

Before a market materialises, it exists as a latent market. For example, for centuries people have wanted faster means of calculation. The market satisfied this need with abacuses, slide rules and large adding machines. Suppose an entrepreneur recognises this need and imagines a technological solution in the form of a small, handheld electronic calculator. He now has to determine the product attributes, including physical size and number of mathematical functions. Because he is market oriented, he interviews potential buyers and finds that target customers vary greatly in their preferences. Some want a four-function calculator (adding, subtracting, multiplying and dividing) and others want more functions (calculating percentages, square roots and logarithms). Some want a small hand calculator and others want a large one. This type of market, in which buyer preferences scatter evenly, is called a *diffused-preference market.*

The entrepreneur's problem is to design an optimal product package for this market. He or she has three options:

1   Design the new product to meet the preferences of one of the corners of the market – *a single-niche strategy.*

2   Launch two or more products simultaneously to capture two or more parts of the market – *a multiple-niche strategy.*

3   Design the new product for the middle of the market – *a mass-market strategy.*

A small firm does not have the resources for capturing and holding the mass market, so a single-niche market strategy makes the most sense. A large firm might aim for the mass market by designing a product that is medium in size and number of functions. Assume a pioneer firm is large and designs its product for the mass market. Once it has launched the product, the *emergence* stage begins.

Growth

If the new product sells well, new firms will enter the market, ushering in a *market-growth stage.* Where will a second firm enter the market, assuming the first firm established itself in the centre? If the second firm is small, it's likely to avoid head-on competition with the pioneer and to launch its brand in one of the market corners. If the second firm is large, it might launch its brand in the centre against the pioneer. The two firms can easily end up sharing the mass market. Or a large second firm can implement a multiple-niche strategy and surround and box in the pioneer.

Maturity

Eventually, the competitors cover and serve all the major segments and the market enters the *maturity stage.* In fact, the competitors go further and invade each other's segments, reducing everyone's profits in the process. As market growth slows down, the market splits into finer segments and high *market fragmentation* occurs. This situation is illustrated in Figure 14.5(a) where the letters represent different companies supplying various segments. Note that two segments are unserved because they are too small to yield a profit.

Market fragmentation is often followed by a *market consolidation*, caused by the emergence of a new customer-perceived value attribute that has strong appeal. This situation is illustrated in Figure 14.5(b) and the expansive size of the X territory.

(a) Market fragmentation stage

(b) Market consolidation stage

Figure 14.5 Market fragmentation and market consolidation strategies

However, even a consolidated market condition will not last. Other companies will copy a successful brand, and the market will eventually splinter again. Mature markets swing between fragmentation brought about by competition, and consolidation brought about by innovation. Consider the evolution of the paper towel market.

▽ Paper towels

Originally, homemakers used cotton and linen dishcloths and towels in their kitchens. A paper company, looking for new markets, developed paper towels. This development crystallised a latent market, and other manufacturers entered. The number of brands grew and created market fragmentation. Industry overcapacity led manufacturers to search for new features. One manufacturer, hearing consumers complain that paper towels were not absorbent, introduced 'absorbent' towels and increased its market share. This market consolidation didn't last long because competitors came out with their own versions of absorbent paper towels. The market fragmented again. Then another manufacturer introduced a 'super strength' towel. It was soon copied. Another manufacturer introduced a 'lint-free' paper towel, which was subsequently copied. Thus paper towels evolved from a single product to one with various absorbencies, strengths and applications. Market evolution was driven by the forces of innovation and competition.

Decline

Eventually, demand for the current products will begin to decrease, and the market will enter the *decline stage*. Either society's total need level declines, or a new technology replaces the old. For example, shifts in tradition and a trend toward cremation have caused coffin makers and funeral homes to reconsider how to conduct their business.[19]

▽ Product characteristics and classifications

The traditional term **product** is a confusing one in today's highly competitive global markets. Many people think a product is a single, tangible offering – but it is more than that. Broadly, a product is anything that can be offered to a market to satisfy a want or need and consists of a set of

Figure 14.6
Components of the
market offering

attributes, including physical goods, services, experiences, events, persons, places, properties, organisations, information and ideas (see Figure 14.6). In current buyers' markets, where customers have a wide choice of suppliers, it is usually insufficient to provide tangible goods alone. As most markets are fiercely competitive, firms have to surround their core product with a set of carefully selected additional tangible (e.g. attractive design, packaging) and intangible attributes or benefits (e.g. prompt polite and efficient service). This mix of benefits makes up the desirable customer offering.

Product levels: the customer-perceived value hierarchy

In planning its customer offering, the marketer needs to address five CPV benefit levels (see Figure 14.7).[20] Each level adds more customer-perceived value that results in the appropriate market offering.

1 The fundamental level is the **core benefit**: the benefit the customer is really buying. A hotel guest is buying 'rest and sleep'. The purchaser of a drill is buying 'holes'. Marketers must see themselves as benefit providers.

2 At the second level, the marketer must turn the core benefit into a **basic product**. Thus a hotel room includes a bed, bathroom, towels, desk and wardrobe.

3 At the third level, the marketer prepares an **expected product**, a set of attributes and conditions buyers normally expect when they purchase this product. Hotel guests expect a clean bed, fresh towels, working lamps, and a relative degree of quiet.

4 At the fourth level, the marketer prepares an **augmented product** that exceeds customer expectations. A hotel provides a Wi-fi connection and a flat-screen TV.

5 At the fifth level stands the **potential product**, which encompasses all the possible augmentations and transformations the product or offering might undergo in the future. Here is where companies search for new ways to satisfy customers and distinguish their offering. The hotel staff provide a free fruit bowl and petit four tray every night.

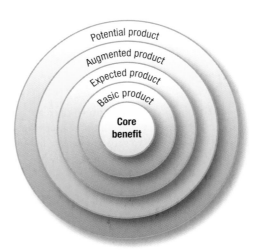

Figure 14.7 Five
product levels

Marketing insight

Metamarkets and metamediaries

There are some products whose purchase necessitates other product purchases. The new car market is a good example of a 'metamarket'. The customer chooses a car but then also needs to buy insurance from an insurance company and often has to get a loan from a bank. A smart car company or dealer would make all three purchases easy for the buyer by partnering with an insurance company and a bank, thus acting as a 'metamediary'.

The wedding market is also a metamarket. The bride and groom need a bridal gown and suit respectively, a venue for the marriage and wedding reception, a caterer, and possibly a wedding consultant. Here the wedding dress seller or the wedding consultant could well act as a wedding metamediary.

Metamarkets are the result of marketers observing the total consumption system and 'packaging' a collection of CPV offerings that simplifies the purchase process. A metamarket has been defined as 'a set of products and services that consumers need to perform a *cognitively related* set of activities'. Other metamarkets that are organised around major assets or major life events include:

- buying a home
- giving birth to a child
- getting a divorce
- planning a holiday
- planning funeral arrangements.

Source: Adapted from M. Sawhney (1999) Rethinking marketing and mediation in the networked economy, Winning strategies for ecommerce lecture at the Kellogg School of Management, 7–10 April.

Differentiation arises and competition increasingly occurs on the basis of the additional augmented and potential benefit attributes that comprise market offerings. This stimulates marketers to look at the user's total **consumption system**: the way the end customer obtains and uses such CPV offerings. Each augmentation and potential additional benefit attribute raises the supplier's cost. As customers strive to increase their perceived value for their money, augmented and potential benefits soon become expected necessary points-of-parity. Today's hotel guests expect cable or satellite television with a remote control and high-speed Internet access or two phone lines. This means competitors must search continually for still other features and benefits in order to gain a market edge.

As some companies raise the price of their augmented and potential product offerings, others offer a lower, less expensive, version. Thus, alongside the growth of five-star hotels there is a demand in many locations for modest hotels and motels such as Novatel.

▽ Sultzer Pumps

The company is a subsidiary of the Swiss engineering group, and makes heavy-duty pumps for oil and gas pipelines, individually designed to meet the needs of customers operating in adverse environments. 'We offer differentiation – highly engineered products. We focus on engineered solutions and on demonstrating that they will work in arduous conditions,' says the company's managing director.[21]

Product classifications

Marketers have traditionally classified products or market offerings on the basis of durability, tangibility and use (consumer or industrial). Each type of offering has an appropriate marketing mix strategy.

Durability and tangibility

Marketers classify products or CPV offerings into three categories on the basis of durability and tangibility:

1 **Non-durable goods**: offerings, usually termed fast-moving consumer goods (fmcgs), are normally consumed in one or a few uses. They include offerings such as beer and soap. Because these offerings are purchased frequently, the appropriate strategy is to make them available in many locations, charge only a small mark-up, and advertise heavily to induce trial and build preference.

2 **Durable goods**: are product offerings that have a longer use lifetime, such as refrigerators, machine tools and clothing. These offerings require more personal selling and service, command a higher margin, and require more seller guarantees.

3 **Services**: are traditionally viewed as intangible, inseparable, variable and perishable offerings. As a result, they normally require more quality control, supplier credibility and adaptability. Examples include haircuts, legal advice and appliance repairs. In reality service offerings contain both tangible and intangible benefit attributes so are best considered as CPV packages.

Consumer goods classification

The array of market offerings consumers buy can be classified on the basis of shopping habits.

Consumers usually purchase **convenience goods** frequently, immediately, and with a minimum of effort. Examples include soft drinks, soaps and newspapers. Convenience goods can be further segmented. *Staples* are goods consumers purchase on a regular basis. A buyer might routinely purchase bread, toothpaste and yogurt. *Impulse goods* are purchased without any planning or search effort. Confectionery and magazines can be impulse goods. *Emergency goods* are purchased when a need is urgent – umbrellas during a rainstorm, boots and shovels during the first winter snow. Manufacturers of impulse and emergency goods will place them in those outlets (e.g., petrol stations) where consumers are likely to make an impulse purchase.

Shopping goods are goods that consumers characteristically evaluate on such criteria as suitability, quality, price and style. Examples include furniture, clothing, used cars and major appliances. *Homogeneous shopping goods* are similar in quality but different enough in price to justify shopping comparisons. *Heterogeneous shopping goods* differ by offering high customer-perceived value and a strong brand association, for example offerings stocked by quality department stores. The seller of heterogeneous shopping goods carries a wide assortment to satisfy individual tastes and must have well-trained sales people to inform and advise customers.

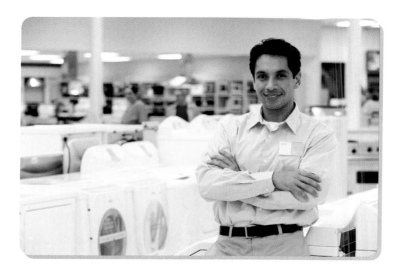

Marketers rely on well-trained sales people to help customers compare quality and features of shopping such as home appliances.

Source: © Jupiter Images/ Brand X/Alamy

Speciality products have unique characteristics or brand identification for which a sufficient number of buyers are willing to make a special purchasing effort. Examples include cars, stereo components, photographic equipment and men's suits. A Mercedes is a speciality product because interested buyers will travel far to buy one.

Unsought goods are those the customer does not know about or does not normally think of buying, such as smoke detectors. The classic examples of unsought products include life insurance and gravestones. Unsought goods require advertising and personal selling support.

Industrial goods classification

Industrial products can be classified in terms of their relative cost and how they enter the production process: materials and parts, capital items, and supplies and business services.

Materials and parts are goods that become part of a complete manufacturer's product offering. They fall into two classes: raw materials, and manufactured materials and parts. *Raw materials* fall into two major groups: *farm products* (wheat, cotton, livestock, fruit and vegetables) and *natural products* (fish, lumber, crude petroleum, iron ore). Farm products are supplied by many producers, who turn them over to marketing intermediaries, who provide assembly, grading, storage, transportation and selling services. Their perishable and seasonal nature gives rise to special marketing practices, whereas their commodity character results in relatively little advertising and promotional activity, with some exceptions. At times, commodity groups will launch campaigns to promote their product – potatoes, cheese and beef. Some producers such as Chiquita bananas and Jaffa oranges brand their products.

Natural products are limited in supply. They usually have great bulk and low unit value and must be moved from producer to user. Fewer and larger producers often market them directly to industrial users. Because users depend on these materials, long-term supply contracts are common. The homogeneity of natural materials makes it more difficult for suppliers to raise the value level of their products.

Manufactured materials and parts fall into two categories: component materials (iron, yarn, cement and wire) and component parts (small motors, tyres, castings). *Component materials* are usually fabricated further – pig iron is made into steel, and yarn is woven into cloth. The standardised nature of component materials usually means that price and supplier reliability are key purchase factors. *Component parts* enter the finished product offering with no further change in form, as when small motors are put into vacuum cleaners, and tyres are put on vehicles. Most manufactured materials and parts are sold directly to industrial users. Price and service are major marketing considerations, and branding and advertising tend to be less important.

Capital items are long-lasting goods that facilitate developing or managing the finished CPV offering. They include two groups: installations and equipment. *Installations* consist of buildings (factories, offices) and heavy equipment (generators, drill presses, mainframe computers, lifts). Installations are major purchases. They are usually bought directly from the producer, whose sales force includes technical personnel, and a long negotiation period precedes the typical sale. Producers must be willing to design to specification and to supply after-sales services. Advertising is much less important in these markets than personal selling.

Equipment includes portable factory equipment and tools (hand tools, lift trucks) and office equipment (personal computers, desks). These do not become part of a finished product. They have a shorter life than installations but a longer life than operating supplies. Although some equipment manufacturers sell direct, more often they use intermediaries, because the market is geographically dispersed, the buyers are numerous and the orders are small. Quality, price and service standards are major considerations. The sales force tends to be more important than advertising, although advertising can be used effectively.

Supplies and business services are short-term goods and services that facilitate developing or managing the finished product. Supplies are of two kinds: *maintenance and repair items* (paint, nails and brooms) and *operating supplies* (lubricants, coal, writing paper, pencils). Together, they go under the name of MRO goods. Supplies are the equivalent of convenience; goods that are usually purchased with minimum effort on a straight rebuy basis. They are normally marketed through intermediaries because of their low unit cost and the great number and geographic dispersion of customers. Price and service are important considerations, because suppliers are standardised and brand preference is not high.

Business services include *maintenance and repair services* (window cleaning, copier repair) and *business advisory services* (legal, management consulting and advertising). Maintenance and repair services are usually supplied under contract by small producers or are available from the manufacturers of the original equipment. Business advisory services are usually purchased on the basis of the supplier's reputation and staff.

▽ Differentiation

Branding enables market offerings to be positively differentiated. This is possible with every market offering that has a preferred CPV. The humble aspirin can be as positively branded by a generic firm as it can by a strongly branded firm such as Bayer. Firms often offer a portfolio of market offerings to cover many market segments. Procter & Gamble and Unilever offer a variety of detergents, each with a separate brand identity. Some products such as cars, commercial buildings and furniture are capable of high differentiation. This is achieved by the seller developing a rich mix of customer perceived benefit attributes. These can include such attributes as form, features, customisation, performance quality, conformance quality, durability, reliability, repairability and style. Over the last decade design has become an increasingly important means of differentiation.

Product (market offering) differentiation

Form

Many market offerings can be differentiated in **form** – the size, shape or physical structure of an offering. Consider the many possible forms taken by items such as aspirin. Although aspirin is essentially a commodity, it can be differentiated by dosage size, shape, colour, coating or action time.

Features

Most market offerings can be marketed with varying benefit attributes that supplement their basic function. A company can identify and select appropriate new attributes by surveying recent buyers and then assessing the package of *customer benefits* versus *company cost* for each potential featured value attribute. The company should also consider how many people want each attribute feature, how long it would take to introduce it, and whether competitors could easily copy it. To avoid 'feature fatigue' the company must also be careful to prioritise those attributes that are included and find unobtrusive ways to provide information about how consumers can use and benefit from them.[22] Companies must also think in terms of several product bundles or packages. Car manufacturers offer cars at several CPV 'trim levels'. Each company must decide in which market segment to compete and use market research techniques to discover the appropriate value-offering specifications.

Customisation

Marketers can differentiate products by customising. As companies have grown proficient at gathering information about individual customers and business partners (suppliers, distributors, retailers), and as their factories are being designed more flexibly, they have increased their ability to individualise products, messages and media. For example, publishers of academic texts customise books for selected college and university courses. **Mass customisation** is the ability of a company to meet each customer's requirements – to prepare on a mass basis individually designed products, services, programmes and communications.[23]

Although Levi's and Lands' End were among the first clothing manufacturers to introduce custom jeans, other players have introduced mass customisation into other markets. BMW customises over half the Minis it markets in Europe.[24] LEGO has customised its offering from the beginning.

▽ LEGO

In a sense, LEGO of Billund, Denmark, has always been mass customised. Every child who has ever had a set of the most basic LEGO has built his or her own unique and amazing creations, brick by plastic brick. Many wrongly believe that the name LEGO stems from the Latin word for 'I put together'. In reality it comes from *leg godt*, Danish for 'play well'. However, in 2005, Lego set up The Lego Factory, which, as it says on the company website, 'lets you design, share, and build your very own custom LEGO products'. Using LEGO's freely downloadable Digital Designer Software, customers can create any structure. The creations can exist – and be shared with other enthusiasts – solely online or, if customers want to build them, the software tabulates the pieces required and sends an order to its nearest LEGO warehouse. The employees there put all the pieces into a box and send it back to the customer. LEGO Factory customers have the pride of building their own creations, but they can also earn royalties if LEGO decides the design is good enough to include in its own catalogue. In 2006, The LEGO Factory initiated a design competition in which eight contestants competed to be profiled on the LEGO Factory website along with their creations.[25]

Performance quality

Most market offerings are established at one of four performance levels: low, average, high or superior. **Performance value** is the level at which the market offering's primary characteristic attributes operate. Customer-perceived quality is becoming an increasingly important dimension for differentiation as companies seek to meet and preferably exceed customers' expectations in the marketplace. Continuously improving the product offering can produce high returns and market share; failing to do so can have negative consequences.

▽ Mercedes-Benz

From 2003 to 2006 Mercedes-Benz endured one of its most painful periods in its 127-year history, as its quality reputation took a beating in independent quality reviews. BMW surpassed it in global sales. As a consequence, DaimlerChrysler's chief executive Dieter Zetsche and his new management team initiated a major restructuring, organising the company around functional elements of the car – motors, chassis and electronic systems – instead of by model lines. To improve customer perceived quality, the company also made a number of changes in product development. Engineers begin testing electronic systems a year earlier than in the past. Laboratory workers put each new model's electronic system through a battery of 10,000 tests that ran 24 hours a day for three weeks. Trying to uncover even the most unlikely event, Mercedes found over

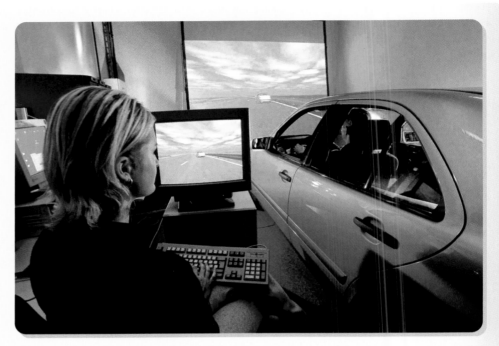

Performance quality is such a critical part of Mercedes-Benz's product strategy that the company undertook a series of sweeping changes in its quality control processes to reduce errors and flaws when its quality ratings slipped.

Source: Courtesy of Daimler AG

1000 errors in the new S-Class. Mercedes now uses three times as many prototypes of new designs, allowing engineers to drive a new model 3 million miles before it goes into production. As a result of these and other changes, the number of flaws in the cars has dropped 72 per cent from its peak in 2002 and warranty costs have also decreased by 25 per cent.[26]

Conformance quality

Buyers expect products to have a high **conformance quality**, which is the degree to which all the produced units are identical and meet the promised specifications. Suppose a Porsche 911 is designed to accelerate to 60 miles per hour within ten seconds. If every Porsche 911 coming off the assembly line does this, the model is said to have high conformance quality. If the model fails to perform as claimed the low performance quality will disappoint some buyers.

Durability

Durability, a measure of the market offering's expected operating life under natural or stressful conditions, is a key value attribute in some markets. Customers will generally pay more for vehicles and kitchen appliances that have a reputation for being long-lasting. However, this rule is subject to some qualifications.

Reliability

Buyers will normally pay a premium for more reliable products. **Reliability** is a measure of the probability that a key benefit or valued attribute will not malfunction or fail within a specified time period. Bosch, which manufactures major home appliances, has an outstanding reputation for creating reliable appliances. 'Breakthrough marketing: Toyota' describes how that company has excelled at making and selling high-quality, dependable motor vehicles.

Breakthrough marketing

Toyota

Toyota may have begun making cars by being a fast follower, but it is now a leading innovator. Toyota offers a full line of cars covering the market, from family cars to 4 x 4s to trucks and minivans. The company offers cars in the entry, middle and niche markets. Designing these different products (market offerings) entails listening to different customers, building the cars they want and then customising them to reinforce each model's image.

Toyota's marketing strategy for the Lexus line focuses on perfection. The tagline for the global strategy is 'Passionate Pursuit of Perfection'. Toyota markets Lexus globally and understands that each country defines perfection differently. In Europe, luxury means attention to detail and brand heritage. Therefore, although the core of Lexus marketing is similar (a consistent Lexus visual vocabulary, logo, font and overall communication), the advertising varies by country.

One big reason behind Toyota's success is its manufacturing. Toyota's combination of manufacturing speed and flexibility is world class. It is the master of lean manufacturing and continuous improvement. Its plants can make as many as eight different models at the same time, which brings Toyota huge increases in productivity and market responsiveness. It is also a continuous innovator. A typical Toyota assembly line makes thousands of operational changes in the course of a single year. Toyota employees see their purpose as threefold: making cars, making cars better, and teaching everyone how to make cars better. The company encourages creative problem solving, always looking to improve its thinking to enable it to improve its operational processes.

Toyota is integrating its assembly plants around the world into a single giant network. The plants will customise cars for local markets and be able to shift production quickly to satisfy any surges in demand from markets worldwide. With a manufacturing network, Toyota can build a wide variety of models much more inexpensively. That means Toyota will be able to fill market niches as they emerge without building whole new assembly operations. As buyers' markets are characterised by consumers who demand high levels of customer-perceived value in a car Toyota's ability to meet individual country and customer requirements gives it a distinctly powerful competitive edge.

In the first quarter of 2007 Toyota edged past General Motors to become the world's largest carmaker.

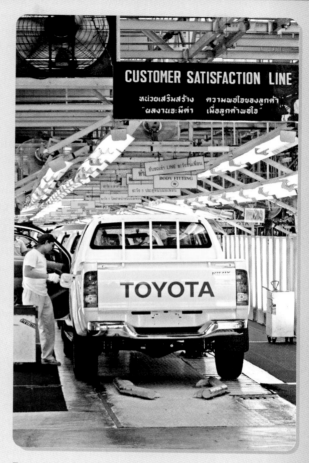

Toyota's product strategy is built on innovation and agility and has recently placed the firm into the number one spot in the industry for the first time.

Source: John van Hasselt/Corbis

Sources: M. Zimmerman (2007) Toyota's frst quarter global sales beat GM's preliminary numbers, *Los Angeles Times*, 24 April; C. Fishman (2006) No satisfaction at Toyota, *Fast Company*, December–January, 82–90; S. F. Brown (2004) Toyota's global body shop, *Fortune*, 9 February, 120; J. B. Treece (2004) Ford down; Toyota aims for no. 1, *Automotive News*, 2 February, 1; B. Bemner and C. Dawson (2003) Can anything stop Toyota?, *BusinessWeek*, 17 November, 114–22; and www.toyota.com.

Repairability

Repairability is a measure of the ease of putting right a market offering when it malfunctions or fails. Ideal repairability would exist if users could fix the problem themselves with little cost in money or time. Some products include a diagnostic feature that allows service people to correct a problem over the telephone or advise the user how to correct it. Many computer hardware and software companies offer technical support over the phone, by fax or email, or by real-time 'chat' online.

Style

Style describes the market offering's look and feel to the buyer. Car buyers pay a premium for Jaguars as they value their unique design. Aesthetics also play a key role in such brands as Absolut vodka, Apple computers, Montblanc pens, Lindt chocolate, and Harley-Davidson motorcycles. Style has the advantage of creating distinctiveness that is difficult to copy. On the negative side, strong style does not always mean high-use performance. A car may look sensational but spend a lot of time in a dealer's garage.

Design

As competition intensifies, design offers a potent way to differentiate and position a company's products and services.[27] In increasingly fast-paced markets, design is the attribute that will often give a company its competitive edge. **Design** is the mix of features that affect how a market offering looks, feels and functions in terms of customer requirements.

Design is particularly important in making and marketing retail services, clothes and shoes, packaged goods and durable equipment. The designer decides how much to invest in attributes such as form, feature development, performance, conformance, durability, reliability, repairability and style. To the company, a well-designed market offering is one that is easy to manufacture and distribute. To the customer, a well-designed market offering is one that is pleasant to look at and easy to open, install, use, repair and dispose of. The designer must take all these benefit value attribute factors into account.

The arguments for good design are particularly compelling for smaller consumer companies and start-ups operating in consumer markets such as upmarket 'real-wood' furniture firms such as the English Ercol hand-crafted furniture company.

Certain countries and companies are design leaders: Italian design in clothing and furniture; Scandinavian design for functionality, aesthetics and environmental consciousness. Finland's Nokia was the first to introduce user-changeable covers for mobile phones, the first to have elliptical shaped, soft and friendly forms, and the first with big screens, all contributing to its remarkable market success. Braun, a German division of Gillette, has elevated design to a high art in its electric shavers, coffee makers, hair dryers and food processors. The company's design department enjoys equal status with engineering and manufacturing. The Danish firm Bang & Olufsen has received considerable recognition for the design of its stereos, TV equipment and telephones.

Firms should seek new designs to create differentiation and establish a more complete connection with consumers. Holistic marketers recognise the emotional power of design and the importance to consumers of how things look and feel. In an increasingly visually oriented culture, translating brand meaning and positioning through design is critical. A bad design can also ruin a product's prospects.

Service differentiation

When a market offering cannot easily be differentiated, the key to competitive success may lie in adding to the service attributes that comprise the value package. Rolls-Royce PLC ensures that its aircraft engines are in high demand by continuously monitoring the health of its 3000 engines for 45 airlines through live satellite feeds. Under its TotalCare programme, airlines pay a fee for every hour an engine is in flight, and the company assumes responsibility for downtime and repairs expenses.[28]

The main service benefit attributes differentiators are: ordering ease, delivery, installation, customer training, customer consulting, and maintenance and repair.

Ordering ease

Ordering ease refers to how easy it is for the customer to place an order with the company. Many financial service institutions offer secure online sites to help customers obtain information and complete transactions more efficiently.

Delivery

Delivery refers to how well the market offering is brought to the customer. It includes speed, accuracy and care throughout the process. Today's customers have grown to expect delivery speed: pizza delivered in half an hour, film developed in one hour, spectacles made in one hour, cars lubricated in 15 minutes. Levi Strauss, and Benetton, have adopted computerised *quick response systems* (QRS) that link the information systems of their suppliers, manufacturing plants, distribution centres and retailing outlets.

Installation

Installation refers to the work done to make a product operational in its planned location. Buyers of heavy equipment expect good installation service. Differentiating at this point in the consumption chain is particularly important for companies with complex products. Ease of installation becomes a true selling point, especially when the target market contains many technological novices as is frequently the case in the home PC market.

Customer training

Customer training refers to training the customer's employees to use the vendor's equipment properly and efficiently. One example is McDonald's, which requires its new European franchisees to attend its Hamburger University in the United States for a two-week franchise management training course.

Customer consulting

Customer consulting refers to data, information systems and advice services that sellers offer buyers.

Maintenance and repair

Maintenance and repair describes the service programme for helping customers keep purchased market offerings in good working order. Hewlett-Packard offers online technical support, or 'esupport', for its customers. In the event of a service problem, customers can use various online tools to find a solution. Those aware of the specific problem can search an online database for solutions; those unaware can use diagnostic software that finds the problem and searches the online database for an automatic repair. Customers can also seek online help from a technician.

Returns

Although returns are undoubtedly a nuisance to customers, manufacturers, retailers and distributors alike, they are also an unavoidable reality of doing business, especially with online purchases. Although the average return rate for online sales is relatively small – roughly 5 per cent – return and exchange policies are estimated to serve as a deterrent for one-third to one-half of online customers. The cost of processing a return can be two to three times that of an outbound shipment.

Returned items can be considered in two ways:[29]

- **Controllable returns**: result from problems, difficulties or errors of the seller or customer and can mostly be eliminated with proper strategies and programmes by the company or its value chain partners. Improved handling or storage, better packaging and improved transportation and forward logistics can eliminate problems before they happen.
- **Uncontrollable returns**: cannot be eliminated by the company in the short run through any of these means.

One basic returns strategy that companies can adopt is to attempt to eliminate the root causes of controllable returns while at the same time developing processes for handling uncontrollable product returns. The goal of a product return strategy is to have fewer items returned and a higher percentage of returns that can go back into the distribution pipeline to be sold again.

▽ Product and brand relationships

Each market offering can be compared to competitive ones to ensure that a firm is performing effectively in the marketplace.

The product hierarchy

The hierarchy stretches from basic needs to particular value attributes that satisfy those needs. Six hierarchy levels can be identified, using life insurance as an example:

1 **Need family**: The core need that underlies the existence of a family policy. Example: security.

2 **Product family**: All the product classes that can satisfy a core need with reasonable effectiveness. Example: savings and income.

3 **Product class**: A group of products within the product family recognised as having a certain functional coherence. Also known as a product category. Example: financial instruments.

4 **Product line**: A group of products within a product class that are closely related because they perform a similar function, are sold to the same customer groups, are marketed through the same outlets or channels, or fall within given price ranges. A product line may consist of different brands, or a single family brand, or individual brand that has been developed from a line extension. Example: house and property insurance.

5 **Product type**: A group of items within a product line that share one of several possible forms of the market offering. Example: life insurance.

6 **Item** (also called *stock keeping unit* or *product variant*): A distinct unit within a brand or product line distinguishable by size, price, appearance or some other attribute. Example: renewable life insurance.

Product systems and mixes

A **product system** is a group of diverse but related items that function in a compatible manner. For example, the PalmOne handheld and smart phones come with attachable items including headsets, cameras, keyboards, presentation projectors, ebooks, MP3 players and voice recorders. A **product mix** (also called a **product assortment**) is the complete set of all products and items that a company brings to the marketplace.

To read about French carmaker Renault and its strategy for pursuing international growth, visit www.pearsoned.co.uk/ marketingmanagementeurope

A product mix consists of various product lines. Seagate now makes 29 kinds of drives that are essential to servers, PCs and consumer electronic products such as video games, DVRs and cameras. Michelin has three product lines: tyres, maps and restaurant-rating services. A company's product mix has a certain width, length, depth and consistency.

- The *width* of a market of a product mix refers to how many different product lines the company carries. Table 14.3 shows the four lines that make up Nivea's Sun Care range.
- The *length* of a product mix refers to the total number of items in the mix. Nivea has four items in its Children's Protection line

Table 14.3 Product-mix width and product line length for Nivea Sun Care

	Product-mix width			
	Protection	**Children's Protection**	**After Sun**	**'Sunntouch' Self-Tan**
PRODUCT LINE LENGTH	Light Feeling Sun Lotion	Baby Sun Lotion 50+	Cooling After Sun Spray	Quick & Easy Tan Spray (Fair Skin)
	Firming Sun Lotion	Children's Lotion	Regenerating After Sun Balm	Self-Tan Spray
	Moisturising Sun Spray	Children's Sun Spray	Tan Prolonging After Sun Lotion	Self-Tan Lotion
	Oil Spray	Moisturising After Sun Lotion		Self-Tan Cream

Source: Beiersdorf GmbH.

- The *depth* of a product mix refers to how many variants there are in the market offering/product mix portfolio. Nivea has fifteen in its Sun Care portfolio.
- The *consistency* of the product mix refers to how closely related the various lines are in end use, production requirements, distribution channels, or in some other way. Nivea's product lines are consistent so far as they are consumer goods that go through the same distribution channels.

The four product-mixed dimensions enable the company to expand its business in four ways. It can add new product lines, thus widening its product mix. It can lengthen each line. It can add more variants to each product and deepen its product mix. Finally, a company can pursue more product-line consistency. To make these product and brand decisions, it is useful to conduct product-line analysis.

Product-line analysis

When designing a product line, companies normally develop a basic platform and modules that can be added to meet different customer requirements. Car manufacturers build their cars around a basic platform. Homebuilders show a model home to which buyers can add additional features. This modular approach enables the company to position itself optimally by offering variety (to exhibit effectiveness in the marketplace) and to lower production costs (to become effective with its resources).

Product-line managers need to know the sales and profits of each market offering in their line in order to determine which items to build, maintain, harvest or divest.[30] They also need to understand each market offering/product line's market profile.

Sales and profits

Figure 14.8 shows a sales and profit report for a five-item market offering product line. The first item accounts for 50 per cent of total sales and 30 per cent of total profits. The first two items account for 80 per cent of total sales and 60 per cent of total profits. If these two items were suddenly attacked by a competitor, the line's sales and profitability could collapse. These items must be carefully monitored and protected. Finally, the last item delivers only 5 per cent of the line's sales and profits. The firm may consider dropping this item unless it has strong growth potential.

Every company's product portfolio contains offers with different margins. Supermarkets make almost no margin on bread and milk; reasonable margins on tinned and frozen foods; and better margins on flowers, ethnic food lines and freshly baked goods. A telephone company makes different margins on its core telephone, call waiting, caller ID and voicemail services.

A company can classify its products into four types that yield different gross margins, depending on sales volume and promotion. To illustrate with laptop computers:

1 **Core product offerings**: Basic laptop computers that produce high sales volume and are heavily promoted but with low margins because they are viewed as undifferentiated commodities.

2 **Staples**: Items with lower sales volume and no promotion, such as faster central processing units (CPUs) or bigger memories. These yield a somewhat higher margin.

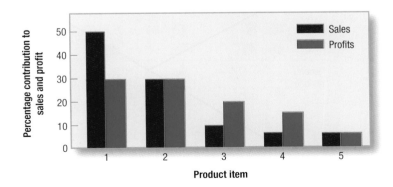

Figure 14.8 Product-item contributions to a product line's total sales and profits

3 **Specialities**: Items with lower sales volume but that might be highly promoted, such as digital film-making equipment; or which might generate income for services, such as personal delivery, installation or on-site training.

4 **Convenience items**: Peripheral items that sell in high volume but receive less promotion, such as carrying cases and accessories, top quality video or sound cards, and software. Consumers tend to buy them where they buy the original equipment because it is more convenient than making further shopping trips. These items can carry higher margins.

The main point is that companies should recognise that these items differ in their potential for being priced higher or advertised more as ways to increase their sales, their margins or both.[31]

Market profile

The product-line manager must review how the line is positioned against competitors' lines. Consider Paper Company X with a paperboard product line.[32] Two paperboard attributes are weight and finish quality. Paper is usually offered at standard levels of 90, 120, 150 and 180 g/m^2 weight. Finish quality is offered at low, medium and high levels. Figure 14.9 shows the location of the various product-line items of company X and four competitors, A, B, C and D. Competitor A sells two product items in the extra-high weight class ranging from medium to low finish quality. Competitor B sells four items that vary in weight and finish quality. Competitor C sells three items in which the greater the weight, the greater the finish quality. Competitor D sells three items, all lightweight but varying in finish quality. Company X offers three items that vary in weight and finish quality.

The **product map** shows which competitors' items are competing against company X's items. For example, company X's low-weight, medium-quality paper competes against competitor D's and B's papers, but its high-weight, medium-quality paper has no direct competitor. The map also reveals possible locations for new items. No manufacturer offers a high-weight, low-quality paper. If company X estimates a strong unmet demand and can produce and price this paper at low cost, it could consider adding this item to its line.

Another benefit of market offering/product mapping is that it identifies market segments. Figure 14.9 shows the types of paper, by weight and quality, preferred by the general printing industry, the point-of-purchase display industry and the office supply industry. The map shows that company X is well positioned to serve the needs of the general printing industry but is less effective in serving the other two industries.

Product-line analysis provides information for two key decision areas – product-line length and product-mix pricing.

Product-line length

Company objectives influence market offering/product-line length. One objective is to create a line to induce customers to trade up. Thus General Motors would like to move customers up

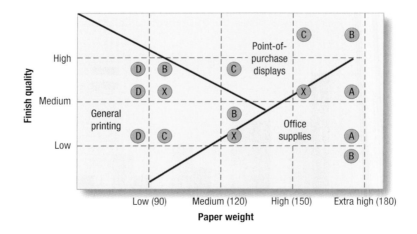

Figure 14.9 Product map for a paper-product line

from their entry market Chevrolet to an Opel or Vauxhall. A different objective is to create a line that facilitates cross-selling: Hewlett-Packard sells printers as well as computers. Still another objective is to create a product line that protects against economic cycles; Electrolux offers white goods such as refrigerators, dishwashers and vacuum cleaners under different brand names in the discount, middle-market and niche segments.[33] Companies seeking high market share and market growth will generally carry longer lines. Companies that emphasise high profitability will carry shorter lines consisting of carefully chosen items.

Product lines tend to lengthen over time. Excess manufacturing capacity puts pressure on firms to develop new items. The sales force and distributors also pressure the company for a more complete portfolio of market offerings to satisfy customers. However as items are added, costs rise: design and engineering costs, inventory-carrying costs, manufacturing-changeover costs, order-processing costs, transportation costs and new item promotional costs. Eventually, someone calls a halt: top management may stop development because of insufficient funds or manufacturing capacity. The controller may call for a study of money-losing items. A pattern of market offering/product-line growth followed by massive pruning may repeat itself many times. Increasingly, consumers are growing weary of dense market offering/product lines, overextended brands and feature-laden market offerings (see 'Marketing insight: When less is more').

A company lengthens its product line in two ways: line stretching and line filling.

Line stretching

Every company's product line covers a certain part of the total possible range. For example, Mercedes cars are located in the upper price niche segment of the car market. **Line stretching** occurs when a company lengthens its line beyond its current range. The company can stretch its line down market, up market, or both ways.

Marketing insight

When less is more

Although many customers find the notion of having more choices appealing, the reality is that customers can sometimes be overwhelmed by the choices involved. With thousands of new products introduced each year, customers find it harder and harder to successfully navigate shop aisles. Although customers with well-defined preferences may benefit from more differentiated offers with specific benefits to better suit their needs, too much choice may be a source of frustration, confusion and regret for other customers. Product proliferation has another disadvantage. Exposing the customer to constant offer changes and introductions may nudge them into reconsidering their choices, resulting in their switching to a competitor as a result.

Also, not all the new choices may be winners anyway, as Nestlé found out with its KitKat bars, among the best-selling confectionery bars in the United Kingdom since they were invented there in the 1930s. To increase sales in 2004, the company rolled out a vast array of new flavours. The summer saw the launch of strawberries and cream, passion fruit and mango, and red berry versions; with winter came Christmas pudding, tiramisu (with real wine and mascarpone), and low-carbohydrate versions. The new flavours were a disaster – the tastes

were too sweet and unusual for many – and even worse, some consumers couldn't find the classic KitKat bars among all the new varieties. An ill-timed switch from the classic slogan, 'Have a Break, Have a KitKat', didn't help, and sales dropped 18 per cent as a result. The new flavours were then discontinued.

Perceptive marketers are also realising that it's not just the lines that are confusing customers – many items are just too complicated for the average consumer. Royal Philips Electronics learned its lesson when the company asked 100 top managers to take various Philips electronic products home one weekend and see whether they could make them work. The number of executives who returned frustrated and angry spoke volumes about the challenges the ordinary consumer faced.

Sources: D. Ball (2006) Flavor experiment for KitKat leaves Nestlé with a bad taste, *Wall Street Journal*, 6 July; B. Schwartz (2004) *The Paradox of Choice: Why More Is Less*, New York: HarperCollins Ecco; F. Endt (2004) It is rocket science, *Newsweek*, 18 October, E8; A. Chernev (2003) When more is less and less is more: the role of ideal point availability and assortment in choice, *Journal of Consumer Research*, 30 September, 170–83; S. S. Iyengar and M. R. Lepper (2000) When choice is demotivating: can one desire too much of a good thing?, *Journal of Personality and Social Psychology*, 79(6), 995–1006; R. Dhar (1997) Consumer preference for a no-choice option, *Journal of Consumer Research*, 27 September, 233–48.

Down-market stretch A company positioned in the middle market may want to introduce a lower-priced line for any of three reasons:

1 The company may notice strong growth opportunities as mass retailers such as Carrefour and others attract a growing number of shoppers who want lower priced goods.

2 The company may wish to tie up lower-end competitors that might otherwise try to move up market. If the company has been attacked by a low-end competitor it often decides to counterattack by entering the low end of the market.

3 The company may find that the middle market is stagnating or declining.

A company faces a number of naming choices in deciding to move a brand down market:

- Use the parent brand name on all its offerings. Sony has used its name on products in a variety of price tiers.
- Introduce lower-priced offerings using a sub-brand name, such as General Motors's Chevrolet models in Europe.
- Introduce the lower-priced offerings under a different name, such as VW did with Seat and Skoda. This strategy is expensive to implement, and consumers may not accept a new brand that lacks the equity of the parent brand name.

Moving down market carries risks. Kodak introduced Kodak Funtime film to counter lower-priced brands, but it did not price it low enough to match the lower-priced film. It also found some of its regular customers buying Funtime, so it was cannibalising its core brand. Kodak withdrew the product and may also have lost some of its quality image in the process. On the other hand, Mercedes successfully introduced its C-class cars without injuring its ability to sell other top-priced Mercedes cars. In these cases, consumers may have been better able to compartmentalise the different brand offerings and understand and rationalise functional differences between offerings in higher and lower price tiers.

Up-market stretch Companies may wish to enter the high end of the market to achieve more growth, either to realise higher margins or simply to position themselves as full-line manufacturers. Many markets have spawned surprising upmarket segments: Starbucks in coffee, Häagen-Dazs in ice cream, and Evian in bottled water. However other companies have included their own name in moving up market as is evidenced by supermarket premium lines.

Two-way stretch Companies serving the middle market might decide to stretch their line in both directions. Pet food companies have stretched up and down to create a portfolio to offer varieties in the entry, middle and niche market segments.

▽ Holiday Inn

Holiday Inn Worldwide has also performed a two-way stretch of its hotel product line. The hotel chain segmented its domestic hotels into five separate chains to tap into five different benefit segments – the upscale Crowne Plaza, the traditional Holiday Inn, the budget Holiday Inn Express, and the business-oriented Holiday Inn Select and Holiday Inn Suites & Rooms. Different branded chains received different marketing programmes and emphasis. Holiday Inn Express has been advertised with a humorous advertising campaign. By basing the development of these brands on distinct consumer targets with unique needs, Holiday Inn is able to ensure against overlap between brands.

The relative position of a brand and its competitor context will also affect consumer acceptance. Research has shown that a high-end model of a low-end brand is favoured over a low-end model of a high-end brand, even when information about competing categories is made available.[34]

Line filling

A firm can also lengthen its product line by adding more items within the present range. There are several motives for *line filling*: reaching for incremental profits, trying to satisfy dealers who complain about lost sales because of missing items in the line, trying to utilise excess capacity, trying to be the leading full-line company, and trying to plug holes to keep out competitors.

▽ **BMW AG**

In four years BMW has evolved from a one-brand, five-model carmaker into a three-brand, ten-model powerhouse. Not only has the carmaker expanded its product range downward with Mini Coopers and its compact 1-series models, but it has also built it upward with Rolls-Royce and filled the gaps in between with its X3 and X5 sports activity vehicles, the Z3 and Z4 roadsters, and a 6-series coupé. The company has used line filling successfully to boost its appeal to the rich, the super-rich, and the 'wannabe-rich', all without departing from its pure premium positioning.[35]

Line filling is overdone if it results in self-cannibalisation and customer confusion. The company needs to differentiate each item in the consumer's mind with a *just-noticeable difference*. The company should also check that the proposed product meets a market need.

Line modernisation, featuring and pruning

Product lines need to be modernised. The issue is whether to overhaul the line piecemeal or all at once. A piecemeal approach allows the company to see how customers and dealers take to the new style. It is also less draining on the company's cash flow, but it allows competitors to see changes and to start redesigning their own lines.

In rapidly changing product markets, modernisation is continuous. Companies plan improvements to encourage customer migration to higher-valued, higher-priced items. Microprocessor companies such as Intel and AMD, and software companies such as Microsoft and Sage, continually introduce more advanced versions of their products. A major issue is *timing* improvements so they do not appear too early (damaging sales of the current line) or too late (after the competition has established a strong reputation for more advanced equipment).

Firms must periodically review the line for products that are depressing profits.[36] The weak items can be identified through sales and cost analysis. One study found that for a big Dutch retailer, a major assortment reduction led to a short-term drop in category sales, caused mainly by fewer category purchases by former buyers, but it also attracted new category buyers at the same time. These new buyers partially offset the sales losses among former buyers of the delisted items.[37]

In 1999, Unilever announced its 'Path to Growth' programme designed to get the most value from its brand portfolio by eliminating three-quarters of its 1600 distinct brands by 2003.[38] More than 90 per cent of its profits came from just 400 brands, prompting Unilever co-chairman Niall FitzGerald to liken the brand reduction to weeding a garden, so 'the light and air get in to the blooms which are likely to grow the best'. The company retained global brands such as Lipton, as well as regional brands and 'local jewels' such as Persil, the leading detergent in the United Kingdom.

Multibrand companies all over the world are attempting to optimise their brand portfolios. In many cases, this has led to a greater focus on core brand growth and to concentrating energy and resources on the biggest and most established brands.

Pruning slow-selling brands from product lines often benefits the brands that are left, such as Unilever's global best-sellers including Lipton worldwide or Persil in the United Kingdom.

Source: Martin Meissner/ AP Wide World Photos

▽ VW

VW has four different brands to manage in its European portfolio. Initially, Audi and Seat had a sporty image and VW and Skoda had a family-car image. Audi and VW were in a higher price-quality tier than their respective counterparts. Skoda and Seat, with their basic spartan interiors and utilitarian engine performance, were clearly differentiated. With the goal of reducing costs, streamlining parts/systems designs and eliminating redundancies, Volkswagen upgraded the Seat and Skoda brands. Once viewed as below-par products by European consumers, Skoda and Seat have captured market share with attractive interiors, a full array of safety systems and reliable power-trains borrowed from Volkswagen. The danger, of course, is that by borrowing from its upper-echelon Audi and Volkswagen products Volkswagen may have diluted their cachet. Frugal European car buyers may convince themselves that a Seat or Skoda is almost identical to a VW, but it is several thousand euros cheaper.[39]

Product-mix pricing

Chapter 16 discusses pricing concepts in detail, but a short summary of some basic market offering/ product-mix pricing issues is given here. Marketers must modify their price-setting logic when the offering is part of a product mix. In **market offering/product-mix pricing**, the firm searches for a set of prices that maximises profits on the total mix. Pricing is difficult because the various products have demand and cost interrelationships and are subject to different degrees of competition. Six situations calling for market offering/product-mix pricing can be categorised: product-line pricing, optional-feature pricing, captive-product pricing, two-part pricing, by-product pricing and product-bundling pricing.

Product-line pricing

Companies normally develop product lines rather than single products, and introduce price steps. In many lines of trade, sellers use well-established price points for the products in their line. A men's clothing store might carry men's suits at three price levels: €200, €400 and €600. Customers will associate low-, average- and high-quality suits with the three price points. The marketer's task is to establish customer-perceived quality differences that justify the price differences.

Optional-feature pricing

Many companies offer optional products, features and services along with their main product. The car buyer can order power window controls, remote adjustable mirrors, a sunroof, an electronic parking aid and theft protection. Pricing is a serious problem, because companies must decide which items to include in the standard price and which to offer as options.

Restaurants face a similar pricing problem. Many charge premium prices for their wine and alcoholic drinks. The food revenue covers costs, and the drinks produce the profit. This explains why waiters and waitresses often press hard to get customers to order drinks. Other restaurants offer low-price drinks and charge premium prices for their food.

Captive-product pricing

Some products require the use of ancillary products, or **captive products**. Manufacturers of razors, cameras and computer printers often price them low and set high mark-ups on razor blades, film and ink cartridges.

▽ Hewlett-Packard

In 1996, Hewlett-Packard (HP) began drastically cutting prices on its printers, by as much as 60 per cent in some cases. HP could afford to make such dramatic cuts because customers typically spend twice as much on replacement ink cartridges, toner and speciality paper as on the actual printer over the life of the product. As the price of printers dropped, printer sales rose, as did the number of after-market sales. HP now owns about 40 per cent of the worldwide printer business. Its inkjet supplies command a 35 per cent profit margin and generated US $2.2 billion in operating profits in 2002 – over 70 per cent of the company's total.[40]

There is a danger in pricing the captive product too high in the after market, however. If parts and service are too expensive, counterfeiting and substitutions can erode sales. Consumers can now buy cartridge refills for their printers from discount suppliers and save 20–30 per cent of the price of the manufacturer's cartridges.

Two-part pricing

Firms in service sectors engage in **two-part pricing**, consisting of a fixed fee plus a variable usage fee. Mobile telephone users pay a monthly fee plus additional tariffs for different calls, and

Internet plans. Amusement parks charge an admission fee plus fees for rides over a certain minimum. The service firm faces a problem similar to captive-product pricing – namely, how much to charge for the basic service and how much for the variable usage. The fixed fee should be low enough to induce purchase of the service; the profit can then come from the usage fees.

By-product pricing

The production of certain goods – meats, petroleum products and other chemicals – often results in by-products. If the by-products have value to a customer group, they should be priced to reflect customer-perceived value. Any income earned on the by-products will make it easier for the company to charge a lower price on its main product if competition forces it to do so.

Product-bundling pricing

Sellers often bundle products and features. **Pure bundling** occurs when a firm offers its products only as a bundle. Many computer software companies do this with the twin aims of attracting additional custom through a sales promotion and running down excess stocks. In **mixed bundling**, the seller offers goods both individually and in bundles. When offering a mixed bundle, the seller normally charges less for the bundle than if the items were purchased separately. A car manufacturer might offer an option package at less than the cost of buying all the options separately. A magazine publisher will price an annual subscription at less than the cost of buying 12 issues.[41]

Some customers will want less than the whole bundle. Suppose a medical equipment supplier's offer includes free delivery and training. A particular customer might ask to forgo the free delivery and training in exchange for a lower price. The customer is asking the seller to 'unbundle' or 'rebundle' its offer. If a supplier saves €100 by not supplying delivery and reduces the customer's price by €80, the supplier has kept the customer happy while increasing its profit by €20.

Experience has shown that as promotional activity increases on individual items in the bundle, buyers perceive less saving and so are less likely to be attracted by the offer. This research suggests the following guidelines for correctly implementing a bundling strategy:[42]

- It is unwise to promote individual products in a package as frequently and cheaply as the bundle. The bundle price should be much lower than the sum of individual products or the consumer will not perceive its attractiveness.
- It is best to limit promotions to a single item in the mix if the company wants to promote individual products. Another option: alternate promotions, one after another, in order to avoid running conflicting promotions.
- If firms offer large rebates on individual products, it is best to do so with discretion and make them the sole exception. Otherwise, the consumer uses the price of individual products as an external reference for the bundle, which then loses value.

Co-branding and ingredient branding

Co-branding

Marketers often combine their products with products from other companies in various ways. In **co-branding** – also called dual branding or brand bundling – two or more well-known brands are combined into a joint market offering or marketed together in some fashion. One form of co-branding is *same-company co-branding*, as when the Danone Group advertises Activia Yogurt and Actimel. Still another form is *joint-venture co-branding*, such as British Gas energy and engineering and Bosch Worcester gas boilers in the United Kingdom. There is also *multiple-sponsor co-branding* that is evident when football clubs grant after-match interviews with the media in a room full of sponsors' displayed logos. Finally, there is *retail co-branding* where several retail establishments use the same location as a way to optimise both space and profits, as is the case in discount retail parks throughout Europe.

The main advantage of co-branding is that a market offering/product may be convincingly positioned by virtue of the multiple brands. Co-branding can generate greater sales from the existing target market as well as opening additional opportunities for new consumers and channels. It can also reduce the cost of introducing a new market offer, because it combines two well-known images and speeds adoption. And co-branding may be a valuable means to learn about consumers and how other companies approach them. Companies within the motor industry have reaped all these benefits of co-branding.

The potential disadvantages of co-branding are the risks and lack of control in becoming aligned with another brand in the minds of consumers. Consumer expectations about the level of involvement and commitment with co-brands are likely to be high, so unsatisfactory performance could have negative repercussions for both brands. If the other brand has entered into a number of co-branding arrangements, overexposure may dilute the transfer of any association. It may also result in a lack of focus on existing brands.

For co-branding to succeed, the two brands must separately have brand equity – adequate brand awareness and a sufficiently positive brand image. The most important requirement is a logical fit between the two brands, such that the combined brand or marketing activity maximises the advantages of each while minimising their disadvantages. Research studies show that consumers are more apt to perceive co-brands favourably if the two brands are complementary rather than similar.[43]

Besides remembering these strategic considerations, managers must enter into co-branding ventures carefully. There must be the right kind of fit in values, capabilities and goals, in addition to an appropriate balance of brand equity. There must be detailed plans to legalise contracts, make financial arrangements and coordinate marketing programmes. The financial arrangement between brands may vary, although one common approach is for the brand more deeply involved in the production process to pay a licensing fee and royalty.

Brand alliances require a number of decisions. What capabilities does a firm lack? What resource constraints is the firm facing (people, time, money, etc.)? What are the growth goals or revenue needs? In assessing a joint branding opportunity, a firm should satisfy itself that it is a profitable business venture. How might it help maintain or strengthen brand equity? Is there any risk of dilution of brand equity? Does the opportunity offer any extrinsic advantages such as learning opportunities?

Ingredient branding

Ingredient branding is a special case of co-branding. It creates brand equity for materials, components or parts that are necessarily contained within other branded products. Some successful ingredient brands include Dolby noise reduction, Gore-Tex water-resistant fibres,[44] Intel processors and Scotchgard fabrics. Ingredient branding is growing in an area known as 'nutraceuticals' – food products that have health benefit properties.

An interesting variation on ingredient branding is 'self-branding', in which companies advertise and even trademark their own branded ingredients. For instance, stately homes advertise crockery, foodstuffs and linen bearing their insignia in site-based shops and specialist magazines. If it can be done well, it makes much more sense to self-brand ingredients because you have more control and can develop the ingredient to suit your purposes.[45] Ingredient brands try to create enough awareness and preference for their market offerings so consumers will not buy a 'host' product that doesn't contain the brand badge.

Many manufacturers make components or materials that enter into final branded products but lose their individual identity. One of the few component branders that have succeeded in building a separate identity is Intel. Intel's consumer-directed brand campaign convinced many personal computer buyers to buy only computer brands with 'Intel Inside'. As a result, major PC manufacturers – IBM, Dell, Compaq – purchase their chips from Intel at a premium price rather than buy equivalent chips from an unknown supplier. Most component manufacturers, however, would find it difficult to create a successful ingredient brand. 'Marketing memo: Making ingredient branding work' outlines the characteristics of successful ingredient branding.

Marketing memo

Making ingredient branding work

What are the requirements for success in ingredient branding?

1 Customers must perceive that the ingredient matters to the performance and success of the end product. Ideally, this intrinsic value is easily seen or experienced.

2 Customers must be convinced that not all ingredient brands are the same and that the ingredient is superior.

3 A distinctive symbol or logo must clearly signal to customers that the host product contains the ingredient. Ideally, the symbol or logo would function like a 'seal', be simple and versatile and credibly communicate quality and confidence.

4 A coordinated 'pull' and 'push' programme must help customers understand the importance and advantages of the branded ingredient. Channel members must offer full support. Often this will require consumer advertising and promotions and – sometimes in collaboration with manufacturers – retail merchandising and promotion programmes.

Sources: K. L. Keller (2008) *Strategic Brand Management*, 3rd edn, Upper Saddle River, NJ: Prentice Hall; P. Kotler and W. Pfoertsch (2006) *B2B Brand Management*, New York: Springer; P. F. Nunes, S. F. Dull and P. D. Lynch (2003) When two brands are better than one, *Outlook*, January, 14–23.

▽ Packaging, labelling, warranties and guarantees

Most physical items must be packaged and labelled. Some packages – such as the Coke bottle and the L'eggs ladies' tights egg-shaped pack – are world famous. Many marketers have called packaging a fifth P, along with price, product, place and promotion. Most marketers, however, treat packaging and labelling as an important element of product strategy. It could also be seen as an important part of marketing communications and distribution. Cost is an important consideration too. So it is best to see packaging as part of the overall activity of companies that seeks to develop highly regarded customer-perceived value offerings which enable businesses to achieve a sustainable competitive advantage. Warranties and guarantees can also be an important part of the market offering as they often appear on the packaging.

Packaging

Packaging is traditionally defined as all the activities of designing and producing the container for a product or market offering. Packages might include up to three levels of material – beer comes in a bottle or can (*primary package*) in a cardboard box (*secondary package*) and in a palette box (*shipping package*).

Well-designed packages can build brand equity and drive sales. The package is the customers' first encounter with the item and either impresses or disinterests them. Absolut vodka and Coca-Cola are world famous for their distinctive bottles. Toblerone confectionery is well known for its famous triangular shape and packaging. Expensive cereals feature see-through plastic windows in packaging to emphasise the quality of the contents. Packaging also affects consumers' later product experiences – good packaging, for example, protects the item after first opening and keeps it in good condition for subsequent use. Various factors have contributed to the growing use of packaging as a marketing tool:

- **Self-service**: An increasing number of product items are sold on a self-service basis. In an average supermarket, which stocks 15,000 items, the typical shopper passes by some 300 items per minute. Given that 50–70 per cent of all purchases are made in the shop, the effective package must perform many of the sales tasks: attract attention, describe the product's features, create consumer confidence and make a favourable overall impression.

- **Consumer affluence**: Rising consumer affluence means consumers are willing to pay a little more for the convenience, appearance, dependability and prestige of the better packaged items.
- **Company and brand image**: Packages contribute to instant recognition of the company or brand. In a shop they can effectively advertise the item.
- **Innovation opportunity**: Innovative and unique packaging design can bring large benefits to consumers and profits to producers. Companies are incorporating materials and features such as tamper-proof packs.

From the perspective of both the firm and consumers, packaging must achieve a number of objectives:[46]

1 identify the brand in an attractive way;
2 convey descriptive and persuasive information;
3 provide protection to facilitate transportation;
4 assist at-home storage;
5 aid product consumption;
6 be environmentally friendly on disposal.

To achieve the marketing objectives for the brand and satisfy the desires of consumers, marketers must choose the aesthetic and functional components of packaging correctly. Aesthetic considerations relate to a package's size and shape, material, colour, text and graphics. Blue is cool and serene, red is active and lively, yellow is medicinal and weak, pastel colours are feminine, dark colours are masculine. Functionally, structural design is crucial. For example, innovations with food products over the years have resulted in packages that are re-sealable, tamper-proof, and more convenient to use (easy to hold, easy to open, or squeezable). The packaging elements must harmonise with each other and with pricing, advertising and other parts of the marketing programme.

Packaging changes can have an immediate impact on sales. A good example is the book publishing industry, where customers often quite literally choose a book by its cover: Penguin Books has repackaged most of its titles and promoted them under the banner, 'Classic Books, Fresh Looks'.[47] Packaging changes can come in all forms. Kleenex tissues' seasonally themed oval-shaped boxes and Crest toothpaste's beauty-product-inspired Vivid White packaging all led to sales increases.[48]

After the company designs its packaging, it must test it. *Engineering tests* ensure that the package stands up under normal conditions; *visual tests*, that the script is legible and the colours harmonious; *dealer tests*, that dealers find the packages attractive and easy to handle; and *consumer tests*, that buyers will respond favourably. Eye tracking by hidden cameras can assess how much consumers notice and examine packages.[49]

Although developing effective packaging may be expensive and take several months to complete, companies must pay attention to growing environmental and safety concerns to reduce packaging. Increasingly many companies are recognising the importance of going 'green' and are finding new ways to develop their packaging. Disposal of used packaging is rapidly becoming a major concern in many countries as landfill sites come under strain and as the EU fines for poor re-cycling practices begin to bite. In the United Kingdom many supermarkets either choose not to supply plastic carrier bags or sell temporary shopping bags at a slight penalty cost. Most, however, also promote the sales of environmentally friendly multiple-use bags, often sourced in underdeveloped economies.

Plastic packaging: an ecological disaster?

The overuse of plastic materials in packaging is stimulating passionate debate as they are not easily biodegraded. Many cardboard packs have plastic lids or spouts. Few drinks such as milk and fruit juice seem to be offered in glass bottles that are biodegradable. Most of the popular mineral waters such as Evian and Volvic are supplied in plastic bottles and even the niche brands such as San Pellegrino and Perrier seem to be abandoning their glass bottles. All is not doom and gloom, however, as some ecologically sensitive companies are starting to experiment with the use of reusable packaging. Danone, for example, is now supplying supermarkets in Belgium with yogurts in small brown earthenware pots that can be washed out and reused.[50]

In 2008 the UK produced around 2 million tonnes of plastic waste, twice as much as in the early 1990s. The very qualities of plastic – its cheapness, its indestructible aura – make it hubristic, perhaps a reproachful symbol of an unsustainable way of life. However, plastics do have their plus points. There are more than 20 types of polymers to choose from and many can be blended to offer designers and manufacturers a limitless variety of options. There is the clarity of polyethylene terephthlate (PET), used in most plastic bottles and trays; the strength of high-density polyethylene (HDPE), the cloudier polymer that is used in milk bottles; and easy-sealing polypropylene (PP), which is used to make bags and films.

Plastics even have an important positive ecological advantage – a little of the material goes a long way. Furthermore plastic materials are light and while they encase over 50 per cent of the items that are bought they only account for 20 per cent by weight of the packaging that is consumed. Thus less energy is needed to transport plastic-packed goods. This is the main reason why it remains the packaging material of choice for many product offerings. It is actually good for the environment as it reduces the carbon footprint – a classic case of their being two sides to every story! Now the righteous indignation of the ecologists may begin to look irrational.

Might it be possible to gain the benefits of plastic packaging without its associated recycling problems? Curiously enough the answer is yes. Cellulose, the most abundant organic compound on earth, is the main ingredient of cellophane, which was first used in Switzerland after its invention there in 1908. So why not consider abandoning oil-based plastics in favour of biodegradable ones? Research into environmentally renewable polymers has been gathering pace since the 1980s. Polyactic acid (PLA) and other starch-based polymers from sugar cane, potatoes, corn and wheat have emerged as the likeliest packaging materials. Worldwide polymer production increased from 20,000 tons a year in 1996 to 400,000 tons in 2006.[51]

However, there is a real problem with biodegradable plastic packaging – it looks the same as oil-based plastic packaging and so presents an insurmountable recycling problem. Perhaps this could be solved by households all over Europe being supplied with a separate recycling bin and for biodegradable plastic packaging to carry a distinctive image on the label.

▽ ## Cordier Mestrezat breaks with tradition and packages Bordeaux in plastic cartons

Purists have been challenged by a French fine wine brand to sip their wine through a straw rather than pour it from a bottle into a wine glass. In June 2008 Cordier began supplying the new packs to supermarkets in a determined effort by the company to boost wine consumption among young urbanites. The new packs are biodegradable and come with a 'sensory straw' to send a spray of wine around the palate and to 'ensure that customers enjoy the same sensations as with a wine glass'. Wine experts have expressed their horror, as the wine's bouquet and colour will not be able to be appreciated in the conventional way. Cordier responded to the purists' protests by emphasising the serious state of the wine industry in France, where consumption is falling from 100 litres per person to 54 litres, and the need to move with the times.

Source: A. Sage (2008), Is Bordeaux in cartons the last straw for French wine?, *The Times*, 16 May.

Cardboard packaging is more ecologically friendly

The fast food burger chain McDonald's has franchised many restaurants across Europe and this has generated a considerable amount of packaging. The company has gone to considerable trouble to see that its packaging is biodegradable and recycled.

McDonald's burger and fries cardboard packaging is environmentally friendly.

Source: mediablitzimages UK Ltd/Alamy

Packaging power

Special packs are often designed for low-risk trial. The UK Dulux paint company offers mini-pots to enable potential customers to see what the paint colours and textures will look like in the at-home situation. Multiple packs are increasingly found in supermarkets across Europe and seek to sell more and more alcoholic and non-alcoholic drinks. As a fully integrated marketing communications campaign is usually expensive (see Chapter 19) many companies pay particular attention to developing effective and efficient packaging. At certain times during the year the pack assumes a great deal of importance. In the United Kingdom chocolate Easter eggs are presented in elaborately designed packaging; and high-value items such as expensive jewellery and watches usually feature expensive packaging.

Distinctive packaging is usually protected in European countries by law to prevent pirating. In the United Kingdom packaging is covered by the 1994 Trade Marks Act. To convey value to the buyer some companies place their offerings in over-size boxes, which is a practice that can be challenged in the EU.

Labelling

The label may be a simple tag attached to the item or an elaborately designed graphic that is part of the package. It might carry only the brand name, or a great deal of information. Even if the seller prefers a simple label, the legal regulations may require more.

Labels perform several functions:[52]

1 The label *identifies* the product or brand – for instance, the name Jaffa stamped on oranges. It also states the ingredients.

2 The label might also *grade* the item.

3 The label might *describe* the item: who made it, where it was made, when it was made, what it contains, how it is to be used, and how to use it safely. Cigarette packs in the United Kingdom warn buyers that smoking can damage their health.

4 The labels on food items increasingly *carry messages* about healthy eating.

5 The label might *promote* the product through attractive graphics. New technology allows for 360-degree shrink-wrapped labels to surround containers with bright graphics and accommodate more on-pack product information, replacing paper labels glued on to cans and bottles.

Quality labels usually indicate a quality market offering. Eventually they become outmoded and need freshening up. Companies with labels that have become icons need to tread very carefully when initiating a redesign.

▽ The Campbell Soup Company

The Campbell Soup Company has estimated that the average shopper sees its familiar red-and-white can 76 times a year, creating the equivalent of millions of dollars worth of advertising. Its label is such an icon that pop artist Andy Warhol immortalised it in one of his silk screens in the 1960s. The original Campbell's Soup label – with its scripted name and signature red and white – was designed in 1898, and the company did not redesign it until more than a century later, in 1999. With the goal of making the label more contemporary and making it easier for customers to find individual soups, Campbell made the famous script logo smaller and featured a photo of a steaming bowl of the soup flavour. In addition to the new graphic, the company put nutritional information on the packaging, with serving suggestions, quick dinner ideas and coloured bands that identify the six subgroups of condensed soup, that is, creams, broths, and so on.[53]

While attractive and clear labelling reinforces a company's brand it can also be used to mislead potential customers. Some firms claim that their wares are made in the home country whereas they may be made elsewhere and merely packaged in the domestic market. Some food packs are deliberately scented in order to provide a pleasurable experience when the package is opened. Foods may carry evocative claims such as 'country fresh' or make questionable health claims. In the United Kingdom the Food Standards Agency keeps a wary eye on labelling practice. Throughout Europe national and EU laws protect consumers from the worst labelling practices.

Warranties and guarantees

Even the best businesses are sometimes faced with a customer who isn't satisfied with the goods they have bought or who simply wants their money back. Alongside improved consumer protection legislation, awareness of consumer rights has increased dramatically over the last 30 years – and so have people's expectations of the sort of redress they can expect when the market offerings aren't up to an acceptable standard.. Anyone in business who provides market offerings should be aware of their obligations to customers.

All sellers are legally responsible for fulfilling a buyer's normal or reasonable expectations. **Warranties** are formal statements of expected product/market offering performance by the manufacturer. Products under warranty can be returned to the manufacturer or designated repair centre for repair, replacement or refund. Whether expressed or implied, warranties are legally enforceable. Wise companies will extend their warranties if there are good reasons do so. In some cases they are obliged to do so to retain market credibility if they have been unfavourably exposed by a consumer body. Samsung decided to extend the warranty on their R21 refrigerator in the United Kingdom in May 2008 after a fault was exposed in the popular BBC-TV consumer affairs programme *Watchdog*. Similarly, when several viewers complained of skin irritation (subsequently found to be caused by a fungicide sachet) after buying leather sofas manufactured by Linkwise, retailers Argos, Land of Leather and the high street chain Walmsley's eventually agreed to return customers' money and to stop trading with Linkwise.

▽ Extended warranties – are they all they claim to be?

The UK government's Consumer Direct Unit urges people to think carefully about the value for money they are offered by an extended warranty because it is likely to be expensive compared with the amount customers could normally pay out in repair costs. Some people forget that the goods they buy new have a manufacturer's guarantee which usually lasts for one year, so there is no need to buy an extended warranty when they buy the goods.

If consumers decide that they would like a warranty, they do not have to buy one at the shop where they bought the goods. There are a number of firms – including insurance companies and the manufacturers themselves – that sell extended warranties on everyday household goods, from toasters to computers. In some cases they may be cheaper and more comprehensive than retailers' extended warranties. It is now also possible to buy warranties that cover a number of appliances, such as all the electrical equipment in the kitchen. So it is certainly a good idea to shop around for some quotes before signing up to a warranty.

The law also requires retailers to provide certain information on warranties they are selling, and consumers may get rights to cancel their extended warranty if they choose to do so. Contact Consumer Direct for advice.

Source: Consumer Direct: www.consumerdirect.gov.uk/contact

Extended warranties can be extremely lucrative for manufacturers and retailers. Despite being regularly challenged as to their real worth in the United Kingdom many retailers still attempt to market them robustly. Electrical appliance stores and home computer shops have become infamous for pushing (bullying!) customers into purchasing additional 'peace of mind' cover. Many sellers offer either general guarantees or specific guarantees. A company such as Procter & Gamble promises general or complete satisfaction without being more specific – 'If you are not satisfied for any reason, return for replacement, exchange or refund.' Other companies offer specific and in some cases extraordinary guarantees:

- The John Lewis Partnership promises that it is 'never knowingly undersold' and if challenged on price will investigate. If the customer is right it will immediately lower its price.
- Marks & Spencer will exchange clothing items that are found to be the wrong size provided the goods are returned in good condition with the appropriate invoice.
- British Gas guarantees its domestic central heating installations and promises prompt and efficient service if anything goes wrong.

Guarantees reduce the buyer's perceived risk. They suggest that the product is of high quality and that the company and its service performance are dependable. They can be especially helpful when the company or product (market offering) is not that well known or when the product's quality is superior to competitors.

▽ SUMMARY

1 Because economic conditions change and competitive activity varies, companies normally find it necessary to reformulate their marketing strategy several times during a product's life cycle. Technologies, product forms and brands also exhibit life cycles with distinct stages. The general sequence of stages in any life cycle is introduction, growth, maturity and decline. The majority of products today are in the maturity stage.

2 Each stage of the product life cycle calls for different marketing strategies. The introduction stage is marked by slow growth and minimal profits. If successful, the product enters a growth stage marked by rapid sales growth and increasing profits. There follows a maturity stage in which sales growth slows and profits stabilise. Finally, the product enters a decline stage. The company's task is to identify the truly weak products, develop a strategy for each one, and phase out weak products in a way that minimises the hardship to company profits, employees and customers.

3 Like products, markets evolve through four stages: emergence, growth, maturity and decline. This necessitates coordinated decisions on product mixes, product lines, brands, and packaging and labelling.

4 In planning its market offering, the marketer needs to think through the five levels of the product: the core benefit, the basic product, the expected product, the augmented product and the potential product, which encompasses all the augmentations and transformations the product might ultimately undergo.

5 Products can be classified in several ways. In terms of durability and reliability, products can be non-durable goods, durable goods or services. In the consumer goods category, products are convenience goods (staples, impulse goods and emergency goods), shopping goods (homogeneous and heterogeneous), speciality goods or unsought goods. In the industrial goods category, products fall into one of three categories: materials and parts (raw materials and manufactured materials and parts) capital items (installations and equipment), or supplies and business services (operating supplies, maintenance and repair items, maintenance and repair services, and business advisory services).

6 Brands can be differentiated on the basis of a number of different product or service dimensions: product form, features, performance, conformance, durability, reliability, repair ability, style and design, as well as such service dimensions as ordering ease, delivery, installation, customer training, customer consulting, and maintenance and repair.

7 Most companies sell more than one product. A product mix can be classified according to width, length, depth and consistency. These four dimensions are the tools

for developing the company's marketing strategy and deciding which product lines to grow, maintain, harvest and divest. To analyse a product line and decide how many resources should be invested in that line, product-line managers need to look at sales and profits and market profile.

8 A company can change the product component of its marketing mix by lengthening its product via line stretching (down market, up market, or both) or line filling, by modernising its products, by featuring certain products, and by pruning its products to eliminate the least profitable.

9 Brands are often sold or marketed jointly with other brands. Ingredient brands and co-brands can add value, assuming they have equity and are perceived as fitting appropriately.

10 Physical products must be packaged and labelled. Well-designed packages can create convenience value for customers and promotional value for producers. In effect, they can act as 'five-second commercials' for the product. Warranties and guarantees can offer further assurance to consumers.

▽ APPLICATIONS

Marketing debate

With products, is it form or function? The 'form versus function' debate applies in many arenas, including marketing. Some marketers believe that product performance is the be all and end all. Other marketers maintain that the looks, feel, and other design elements of products are what really make the difference.

Take a position: Product functionality is the key to brand success *versus* Product design is the key to brand success.

Marketing discussion

Can products be totally differentiated from services? Can products (i.e. tangible items) and services (intangible items) really be separated from customer-perceived value offerings in contemporary sellers' markets? (See argument in Chapters 3, 10 and 11.)

▽ REFERENCES

[1] B. Upton (1999) Sharpening the claws, *Forbes*, 26 July, 102–5.

[2] R. Reed (1987) 'Fashion life-cycles and extension theory, *European Journal of Marketing*, 21(3), 52–62.

[3] R. J, Chandy, G. J. Tellis, D. J. MacInnis and P. Thaivanich (2001) What to say when: advertising appeals in evolving markets, *Journal of Marketing Research*, November, 399–414.

[4] C. Nuttall (2005) Intel ventures beyond PCs, *Financial Times*, 12 November; C. Edwards (2006) Inside Intel, *BusinessWeek*, 9 January, pp. 52–3; C. Edwards (2006) AMD: chipping away at Intels's lead, *BusinessWeek*, 12 June, 72–3.

[5] S. P. Schnaars (1994) *Managing Imitation Strategies*, New York: Free Press. See also J. K. Han, N. Kim and H. B. Kin (2001) Entry barriers: a dull-, one-, or two-edged sword for incumbents? Unravelling the paradox from a contingency perspective, *Journal of Marketing*, January, 1–14.

[6] V. Kegan (2002) Second sight: second movers take all, *The Guardian*, 10 October.

[7] P. N. Golder (2000) Historical method of marketing research with new evidence on long-term of marketing share stability, *Journal of Marketing Research*, 37 (May), 156–72.

[8] G. Tellis and P. Golder, *Will and Vision: How Latecomers Can Grow to Dominate Markets*, New York: McGraw-Hill; R. K. Chandy and G. J. Tellis (2000) The incumbents' curse? Incumbency, size, and radical product innovation, *Journal of Market Research*, July, 1–17.

[9] S. Min, M. U. Kalwani and W. Robinson (2006) Market pioneer and early follower survival risks: a contingency analysis of really new versus incrementally new product-markets, *Journal of Marketing*, 70 (January), 15–35. See also R. Srinwasan, G. L. Lilien and A. Rangaswamy (2004) First in, first out? The effects of network externalities on pioneer survival, *Journal of Marketing*, 68 (January), 41–58.

[10] M. Palmer (2006) Internal provider loyalty hard to find, *Financial Times*, April.

[11] R. B. Trond (2006) Escaping the middle–market trap: an interview with the CEO of Electrolux, *McKinsey Quarterly*, 4, 72–9.

[12]P. Kotler (1965) Phasing out weak products, *Harvard Business Review*, March–April, 107–18; G. J. Avlenitis (1985) Product elimination decision making: Does formality matter?, *Journal of Marketing*, Winter 41–52; G. J. Avlonitis (1990) 'Project Dropstrat' product elimination and the PLC, *European Journal of Marketing*, 24(9), 55–67; R. Varadarajan, M. P. DeFanti and P. S. Busch (2006) Brand portfolio, corporate image, and reputation: managing brand deletions, *Journal of the Academy of Marketing Science*, 34 (Spring), 195–205; N. Kumar (2003) Kill a brand, keep a customer, *Harvard Business Review*, 81 (December), 86–95.

[13]K. R. Harrigan (1980) The effect of exit barriers upon strategic flexibility, *Strategic Management Journal*, 1, 165–76.

[14]P. Kotler (1978) Harvesting strategies for weak products, *Business Horizons*, August, 15–22; L. P. Feldman and A. L. Page (1985) Harvesting: the misunderstood market exit strategy, *Journal of Business Strategy*, Spring, 79–85.

[15]P. N. Golder and G. J. Tellis (2004) Growing, growing, gone: cascades, diffusion, and turning points in the product life cycle, *Marketing Science*, 23 (Spring), 207–18

[16]C. Crawford (1992) Business took the wrong life cycle from biology, *Journal of Product and Brand Management*, 1, 51–7; L. M. Grantham (1997) The validity of the product life cycle in the high-tech industry, *Journal of Marketing Intelligence and Planning*, 15 (1), 4–10.

[17]Y. Moon (2005) Break free from the product life cycle, *Harvard Business Review*, May, 87–94.

[18]R. D. Buzzell (1999) Market functions and market evolution, *Journal of Marketing*, 63 (Special Issue) 61–3; H. Gatignon and David S. (2002) Competitive response and market evolution, in B. A. Weitz and R. Wensley) *Handbook of Marketing*, (eds) (London: Sage (126–47).

[19]D. Fisher (2003) Six feet under, *Forbes*, 7 July, 2003, 66–8.

[20]This discussion is adapted from T. Levitt (1980) Marketing success through differentiation: of anything, *Harvard Business Review*, January–February, 83–91. The first level, core benefit, has been added to Levitt's discussion.

[21]J. Willman and W. MacNamara (2007) An uplifting experience, *Financial Times*, 6 September.

[22]P. Kedrosky (2005) Feature fatigue: when product capabilities become too much of a good thing, *Journal of Marketing Research*, 42 (November), 431–42.

[23]J. H. Gilmore and B. J. Pine (2000) *Markets of One: Creating Customer-unique Value through Mass Customization*, Boston, MA: Harvard Business School Press.

[24]S. Elliott (2006) Letting consumers control marketing: priceless, *New York Times*, 9 October.

[25]P. Grimaldi (2006) Consumers design products their way, *Knight Rider Tribune Business News*, 25 November; M. A. Prospero (2005) *Fast Company*, September, 35.

[26]G. Edmundson (2006) Mercedes gets back up to speed, *BusinessWeek*, 12 November, 46–7.

[27]B. Nussbaum (2004) The power of design, *BusinessWeek*, 17 May, 88–94; P. Kotler (1984) Design: a powerful but neglected strategic tool, *Journal of Business Strategy*, Fall, 16–21.

[28]S. Reed (2005) Rolls-Royce at your service, *BusinessWeek*, 15 November, 92–3.

[29]This section is based on a comprehensive treatment of product returns: J. Stock and T. Speh (2006) Managing product returns for competitive advantage, *MIT Sloan Management Review*, Fall, 57–62.

[30]R. Bordley (2003) Determining the appropriate depth and breadth of a firm's product portfolio, *Journal of Marketing Research*, 40, February, 39–53: P. Boatwright and J. C. Nunes (2001) Reducing assortment: an attitude-based approach, *Journal of Marketing*, 65, July, 50–63.

[31]Adapted from a Hamilton Consultants White Paper, 1 December 2000.

[32]This illustration is found in B. P. Shapiro (1977) *Industrial Product Policy: Managing the Existing Product Line*, Cambridge, MA: Marketing Science Institute, 3–5, 98–101.

[33]Brand challenge (2002) *The Economist*, 6 April, 68.

[34]F. Leclerc, C. K. Hsee and J. C. Nunes (2005) Narrow focusing: why the relative position of a good in its category matters more than it should, *Marketing Science*, 24 (Spring), 194–205.

[35]N. E. Boudette (2005) BMW's push to broaden line hits some bumps in the road, *Wall Street Journal*, 25 January; A. Taylor III (2004) The ultimate fairly inexpensive driving machine, *Fortune*, 1 November, 130–40.

[36]N. Kumar (2003), Kill a brand, keep a customer, *Harvard Business Review*, December, 86–95; B. Stone (2003) Back to basics, *Newsweek*, 4 August, 42–4.

[37]L. M. Sloot, D. Fok and P. Verhoef (2006) The short- and long-term impact of an assortment reduction on category sales, *Journal of Marketing Research*, 43 (November), 536–48.

[38]P. O'Connell (2001) A chat with Unilever's Niall Fitzgerald, *BusinessWeek* Online, 2 August; J. Willman (2000) Leaner, cleaner and healthier is the stated aim, *Financial Times*, 23 February, 2000; Unilever's goal: power brands, *Advertising Age*, 3 January, 2000.

[39]G. Radler, J. Kubes and B. Wojnar (2006) Skoda auto: from 'no-class' to world-class in a decade, *Critical EYE*, 15 July.

[40]B. Elgin (2003) Can HP's printer biz keep printing money?, *BusinessWeek*, 14 July, 68–70.

[41]D. Soman and J. T. Gourville (2001) Transaction decoupling: how price bundling affects the decision to consumer, *Journal of Marketing Research*, 38 (February), 30–44.

[42]Adapted from G. Wuebeker (2002) Bundles effectiveness often undermined, *Marketing News*, 18 March, 9–12; S. Stremersch and G. J. Trellis (2002) Strategic bundling of products and prices, *Journal of Marketing*, 66 (January), 55–72.

[43]L. Leuthesser, C. Kohli and R. Suri (2003) 2 + 2 = 5? A framework for using co-branding to leverage a brand, *Journal of Brand Management*, 2(1), 35–47.

[44]WL Gore and Associates: GoreTex manufacturer (2007), *The Sunday Times*, 11 March.

[45]K. K. Desai and K. L. Keller (2002) The effects of brand expansions and ingredient branding strategies on host brand extendibility, *Journal of Marketing*, 66 (January), 73–93.

[46]P. Dart (1999) Packaging and design, in R. J. Baker (ed.) *Encyclopedia of Marketing*, London: International Business Press (368–75); R. Underwood, N. Klein and R. Burke (2001) Packaging Communication: attentional effects of product imagery, *Journal of Product and Brand Management*, 10(7), 403–22.

[47]K. Springen (2004) Nancy's still nice, *Newsweek*, 16 February; J. Rosen (2003) Classics' strategies: classics' sales, *Publishers Weekly*, 6 October, 16–18; O. Ampuero and N. Vila (2006) Consumer perceptions of product packaging, *Journal of Consumer Marketing*, 23(2), 100–12.

[48]S. Hamner (2006) Packaging that pays, *Business 2.0*, July, 68–9.

[49]M. Frazier (2006) How can your package stand out? Eye tracking looks hard for answers, *Advertising Age*, 16 October, 14.

[50]N. Tait (2008) I gave up plastic for Lent, *Financial Times*, 26 April.

[51]S. Knight (2008) Plastic: the elephant in the room, *Financial Times Arts & Weekend Magazine*, 25 April.

[52]R. Opie (1987) *The Art of the Label*, London: Chartwell.

[53]K. Novack (2004) Tomato soup with a side of pop art, *Time*, 10 May; Campbell Soup Co. changes the look of its famous cans, (1999) *Wall Street Journal*, 26 August.

Chapter 15

▽ Introducing new market offerings

IN THIS CHAPTER, WE WILL ADDRESS THE FOLLOWING QUESTIONS:

1 What challenges does a company face in developing new products and services?

2 What organisational structures and processes do managers use to manage new product development?

3 What are the main stages in developing new products and services?

4 What is the best way to manage the new product development process?

5 What factors affect the rate of diffusion and consumer adoption of newly launched products and service market offerings?

Firms all over the world are trying to come up with creative ways to develop even better new products faster and more efficiently. Marketers are playing a key role in the development of new products by identifying and evaluating new product ideas and working with R&D personnel and other functional areas in every stage of development. Companies need to grow their revenue over time by developing new products and expanding into new markets. New product development shapes the company's future. Improved or replacement products and services can maintain or build sales;

Dyson knows the value of innovation and new-product development. The company's engineers are continuously seeking to innovate and see the establishment of the new design and engineering school in 2010 as a major part of the Dyson mission.
Source: Rex Features

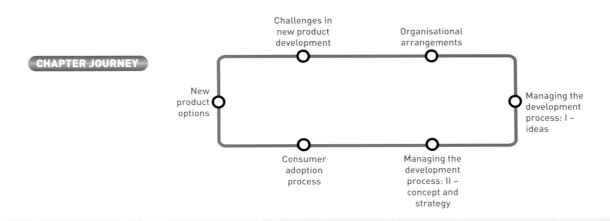

New product options — Challenges in new product development — Organisational arrangements — Managing the development process: I – ideas — Consumer adoption process — Managing the development process: II – concept and strategy

new-to-the-world products and services can transform industries and companies and change lives. However, the low success rate of new products and services points to the many challenges involved. More and more companies are doing more than just talking about innovation. They are fundamentally changing the way they develop their new market offerings.

Look how Sir James Dyson has and is approaching this all-important task.

To encourage and to improve the speed of development of new product innovations Sir James Dyson, who invented the 'bagless' vacuum cleaner, is building a design and engineering school in the spa city of Bath in the United Kingdom. The dual cyclone 'bagless' cleaner took five years to develop and a further two before Sir James managed to obtain financial backing in Japan. Using income from the Japanese licence he began to manufacture a new model under his own name in the United Kingdom in 1993. The new concept and colourful design of his cleaners resulted in much popular acclaim and his 'bagless' vacuum cleaners now have 46 per cent of the UK market. In addition to the cleaners Sir James has a number of other inventions carrying his name including the Sea Truck, award-winning Ballbarrow, as well as the Trolleyball, a trolley that makes it easier to launch boats and the less successful Wheelboat which can travel at speeds of up to 64 km/h on both land and water. To revive falling sales in the vacuum cleaner business in 2005 Sir James incorporated his Dyson Ball™ technology into a new version of the Dyson vacuum cleaner principle to create the more manoeuvrable DC25 model. This offers the tried and trusted benefits from Root Cyclone™ technology and is easy to operate as it has no wheels and can pivot easily round awkward corners as it cleans. However, Dyson has suffered several setbacks on its way to becoming an iconic company. Sir James advises companies to 'Enjoy failure and learn from it. You can never learn from success.' The most notable was the early failure of the company's venture into the washing machine market. After making heavy losses the company pulled out of the market but has recently announced a determination to re-enter it. Sir James hopes that his new design and engineering school, which is due to open in 2010, will do much to reclaim some of the lost appeal following the company's decision for economy reasons to move its manufacturing base from the United Kingdom to Malaysia.[1,2]

▽ **New product options**

The following sections review several ways in which companies develop new products as they strive to achieve an evolving portfolio of new products. Is there one best way to manage this process that involves specific managers and executives? Or perhaps the creation of new products is really about a coordinated effort involving all within the company as well as key organisations in the company's value chain and stakeholders?

The celebrated guru Peter Drucker believed that a continual determination to develop new products was a crucial matter for all organisations.

> If the prime purpose is to create a customer, the business has two – and only two – functions: marketing and innovation. Marketing and innovation produce results. Everything else is a cost.[3]

Make or buy?

A company can add new products through acquisition or by innovative development. The acquisition route can take three forms. The company can buy other companies, it can acquire patents from other companies, or it can buy a licence or franchise from another company.

However, firms can make only so many acqusitions successfully. At some point, there becomes a pressing need for *organic growth* – the development of new products from within the company. New products can evolve in its own organisation or it can contract with independent researchers or specialist agencies to develop specific new products or provide new technology. Many firms have engaged consultants to provide fresh insights and different points of view.[4]

Types of new products

New products range from completely new items that create an entirely new market at one end, to minor improvements or revisions of existing products at the other. Most new offering activity is devoted to improving existing products. At Sony, over 80 per cent of such activity is modifying and improving existing products. Some of the most successful new consumer products in recent years have been brand extensions.

In many categories, it is becoming increasingly difficult to identify high potential products that will transform a market. However, continuous innovation to improve customer satisfaction can force competitors to retaliate.[5] Continually launching new products as brand extensions into related offering categories can also broaden the brand meaning. Nike started as a running-shoe manufacturer but now competes in the sports market with all types of athletic shoes, clothing and equipment. Armstrong World Industries moved from selling floor coverings to selling finishes for ceilings and to total interior surface decoration. Product innovation and effective marketing programmes have allowed these firms to expand their 'market footprint'. (See also Chapters 12 and 13.)

Comparatively few new products are truly innovative and really new. These incur the greatest cost and risk because they are new to both the company and the marketplace.[6] Radical innovations can strain the company's profit performance in the short term, but their successful addition to a company's portfolio of products can create a greater sustainable competitive advantage than existing conventional products. Companies typically must create a strong R&D and marketing partnership to achieve radical innovations.[7] Few reliable techniques exist for estimating demand for these innovations. Focus groups will provide some perspectives on customer interest and need, but marketers may need to use a probe and learn approach based on observation and feedback of early users' experiences and other suitable means.[8]

Many high-tech firms strive for radical innovation.[9] High-tech covers a wide range of industries – telecommunications, computers, consumer electronics, biotech and software. High-tech marketers face a number of challenges in launching their products: high technological uncertainty; high market uncertainty; high competitive volatility; high investment costs; short product life cycles; and difficulty in finding funding sources for risky projects.[10]

▽ Challenges in new product development

New product introductions have accelerated in recent years. In many industries, such as retailing, consumer goods, electronics and cars, among others, the time it takes to introduce new products has been halved.[11] Luxury leather-goods maker Louis Vuitton implemented a new factory format dubbed Pégase so that it could ship fresh collections to its boutiques every six weeks – more than twice as frequently as in the past – giving customers more new looks to choose from.[12]

The innovation imperative

In strong buyers' markets many products fall into decline – as a result of technological developments, severe competition, changing market and societal factors and customer purchase experiences – making innovation a necessity. Highly innovative firms are able to identify and quickly seize new market opportunities. In a Special Report published by *BusinessWeek*, featuring the top 25 most innovative companies in the world just three (Nokia at 13; BMW at 16 and Virgin at 18) were based in Europe[13] (see Table 15.1). Innovative firms, such as Vodafone, which have a special business unit solely devoted to increasing innovation, create a positive attitude towards innovation and risk taking, streamline the innovation process, practise teamwork and allow their people to experiment and even fail.

Table 15.1 The world's top 25 most innovative companies

2007 Rank	2006 Rank	Company name	HQ city	HQ country	HQ continent	Stock returns 2001–2006	Revenue growth 2001–2006	Margin growth 2001–2006	Patent citation index
1	1	APPLE	Cupertino, CA	United States	North America	50.60	29.21	NA	34
2	2	GOOGLE	Mountain View, CA	United States	North America	NA	NA	NA	1
3	4	TOYOTA MOTOR	Tokyo	Japan	Asia	20.50	8.30	5.21	361
4	6	GENERAL ELECTRIC	Fairfield, CT	United States	North America	1.11	5.06	1.36	155
5	5	MICROSOFT	Redmond, WA	United States	North America	0.83	11.85	−3.04	174
6	7	PROCTER & GAMBLE	Cincinnati, OH	United States	North America	12.20	11.69	3.70	105
7	3	3M	St. Paul, MN	United States	North America	7.77	7.35	5.49	57
8	43	WALT DISNEY CO.	Burbank, CA	United States	North America	11.71	6.29	7.35	8
9	10	IBM	Armonk, NY	United States	North America	−3.48	1.26	4.97	94
10	13	SONY	Tokyo	Japan	Asia	−2.62	0.60	1.14	418
11	20	WAL-MART	Bentonville, AR	United States	North America	−3.35	9.79	3.54	0
12	23	HONDA MOTOR	Tokyo	Japan	Asia	13.61	7.40	0.38	377
13	8	NOKIA	Espoo	Finland	Europe	−9.24	5.68	4.37	287
14	9	STARBUCKS	Seattle, WA	United States	North America	30.04	24.07	1.51	2
15	22	TARGET	Minneapolis, MN	United States	North America	7.55	8.32	4.23	0
16	16	BMW	Munich	Germany	Europe	4.30	4.96	−1.23	84
17	12	SAMSUNG ELECTRONICS	Seoul	South Korea	Asia	36.24	4.60	8.07	1000
18	11	VIRGIN GROUP	London	United Kingdom	Europe	Private	Private	Private	0
19	17	INTEL	Santa Clara, CA	United States	North America	−7.57	5.92	12.55	216
20	21	AMAZON.COM	Seattle, WA	United States	North America	29.53	27.96	NA	0
21	70	BOEING	Chicago, IL	United States	North America	19.91	1.12	−4.23	59
22	14	DELL	Round Rock, TX	United States	North America	−1.59	12.87	−5.24	16
23	27	GENENTECH	South San Francisco, CA	United States	North America	24.50	34.85	32.40	4
24	18	EBAY	San Jose, CA	United States	North America	12.45	51.47	4.91	1
25	28	CISCO SYSTEMS	San Jose, CA	United States	North America	8.58	5.02	205.04	20

Source: The World's Fifty Most Innovative Companies (2007), Special Report, *BusinessWeek*, 9 May.
Note: The *BusinessWeek*-Boston Consulting Group 2007 rankings are based on a senior management survey about innovation distributed electronically to executives worldwide in October 2006. Surveys were sent to their top ten executives in charge of innovation at the 1500 largest global corporations, determined by market capitalisation in US dollars. Surveys were also distributed to senior management members of the *BusinessWeek* Market Advisory Board, an online panel consisting of *BusinessWeek* readers, and via the Knowledge@Wharton email newsletter. Survey participation was voluntary and anonymous, and the survey closed in March 2007. The survey consisted of 20 general questions on innovation and an optional 12 questions focused on innovation metrics. A total of 2468 executives answered the survey. Of those indicating their location, 77 per cent were from North America, 12 per cent were from Europe, and 9 per cent were from Asia or the Pacific region.

▽ **W. L. Gore**

W. L. Gore, best known for its durable Gore-Tex outdoor fabric, has innovated breakthrough new products in a number of diverse areas – guitar strings, dental floss, medical devices and fuel cells. It has adopted several principles to guide its new product development. First, it works with potential customers. Its thoracic graft, designed to combat heart disease, was developed in close collaboration with physicians. Second, it lets employees choose projects and appoints few of its actual product leaders and teams. Gore likes to nurture 'passionate champions' who convince others a project is worth their time and commitment. The development of the fuel cell rallied over 100 of the company's 6000 research associates. Three, Gore gives employees 'dabble' time. All research associates spend 10 per cent of their work hours developing their own ideas. Promising ideas are pushed forward and judged according to a 'Real, Win, Worth' exercise: Is the opportunity real? Can we win? Can we make money? Fourth, it knows when to let go. Sometimes dead ends in one area can spark an innovation in another. Elixir acoustic guitar strings were a result of a failed venture into bike cables. Even successful ventures may need to move on. Glide shred-resistant dental floss was sold to Procter & Gamble because Gore-Tex knew that retailers would want to deal with a company selling a whole family of health care products.[14]

Companies that fail to develop new products put themselves at risk. Their existing products are vulnerable to changing customer needs and tastes, new technologies, shortened product life cycles and increased domestic and foreign competition. New technologies are especially threatening. Kodak has worked hard to develop a new business model and product-development processes that work well in a digital photography world. Its new goal is to do for photos what Apple does for music by helping people to organise and manage their personal libraries of images. Table 15.2 displays the company's philosophy of innovation and transformation.

New product success

Most established companies focus on *incremental innovation*. Incremental innovation can allow companies to enter new markets by adapting existing market offerings for new customers, use variations on a core product to stay one step ahead of the market, and create interim solutions for industry-wide problems.[15]

Newer companies create *disruptive technologies* that are cheaper and more likely to alter the competitive space. Established companies can be slow to react or to invest in these disruptive technologies because they threaten their existing business. As a result they may find themselves facing formidable new competitors, and many fail.[16] To avoid this trap, firms must carefully

Table 15.2 Kodak CEO Antonio Perez's seven notions of innovation

1 See the future through the eyes of your customer.
2 Intellectual property and brand power are key assets.
3 Use digital technology to create tools for customers.
4 Build a championship team, not a group of champions.
5 Innovation is a state of mind.
6 Speed is critical, so push your organisation.
7 Partner up if you're not the best in something.

Source: S. Hamm and W. C. Symonds (2006) Mistakes made on the road to innovation, *BusinessWeek IN Inside Innovation*, November, 27–31.

monitor the preferences of both customers and potential customers to discover new viable market opportunities.[17]

What else can a company do to develop successful new products? In a study of US industrial products, the new products specialist agency Cooper & Kleinschmidt found that the main success factor was a unique, superior product. Another key factor is a well-defined product concept. The company carefully defines and assesses the target market, product requirements and benefits before proceeding. Other success factors are technological and marketing synergy, quality of execution in all stages, and market attractiveness.

The study also found that products designed solely for the domestic market tend to show a high failure rate, low market share and low growth. On the other hand products designed for foreign markets achieved significantly better profits. Yet few of the new products in their study were designed specifically for export markets. A study of small and medium-sized firms in Finland, Germany, Japan, South Korea and South Africa found that committed management leadership resulted in significant success in foreign markets. The implication is that companies should adopt an international focus in designing and developing new products.[18]

New product failure

New product development can be risky. New products continue to fail at a disturbing rate. Recent studies put the rate as high as 50 per cent and potentially as high as 95 per cent in the United States and 90 per cent in Europe.[19] Failure can result for many reasons: ignored or misinterpreted market research; overestimates of market size; high development costs; poor design; incorrect positioning, ineffective advertising or wrong pricing; insufficient distribution support; and competitors who retaliate fiercely. Some additional factors hindering new product development are:

- **Shortage of important ideas in certain areas**: There may be few ways left to improve some basic market (such as steel or detergents).
- **Fragmented markets**: Companies must aim their new products at smaller market segments, and this can mean lower sales and profits for each product.

Table 15.3 Causes of new product failure

1 Market/marketing failure
- Small size of the potential market
- No clear product differentiation
- Poor positioning
- Misunderstanding of customer needs

2 Financial failure
- Low return on investment

3 Timing failure
- Late in the market
- 'Too early' – market not yet developed

4 Technical failure
- Product did not work
- Bad design

5 Organisational failure
- Poor fit with the organisation's culture
- Lack of organisational support

6 Environmental failure
- Government regulations
- Macroeconomic factors

Source: D. Jain (2001) Managing new-product development for strategic competitive advantage, in D. Iacobucci (ed.) *Kellogg on Marketing*, New York: Wiley, Table 6.1, p. 131. Reproduced with permission.

- **Social and governmental constraints**: New products must satisfy consumer safety and environmental concerns.
- **Cost of development**: A company typically must generate many ideas to find just one worthy of development and often faces high R&D, manufacturing, and marketing costs.
- **Capital shortages**: Some companies with good ideas cannot raise the funds needed to research and launch them.
- **Shorter required development time**: Companies must learn how to compress development time by using new techniques, strategic partners, early concept tests and advanced marketing planning.
- **Shorter product life cycles**: When a new product is successful, rivals are quick to copy it. Sony used to enjoy a three-year lead on its new products. Now Matsushita will copy the product within six months, barely leaving time for Sony to recoup its investment.
- **Hostile reception by the media**: Coca-Cola successfully launched a new brand of mineral water in the United States called Dasani but failed to gain any success in the United Kingdom and was forced to withdraw the product from all distribution outlets. The media criticised Dasani as being 'rebottled tap water' following the broadcast of an episode of the UK TV hit comedy programme *Only Fools and Horses*, which featured the lead character filling bottles from tap water and branding the product as 'Peckham Springs'.

Failure comes with the task, and truly innovative firms accept it as part of what is required to be successful. (See chapter opening vignette.) Many Web companies are the result of failed business ventures and experience numerous failed initiatives as they evolve their products and services.

Initial failure is not always the end of the road for an idea. Recognising that 90 per cent of experimental drugs fail, ethical pharmaceutical companies have established a corporate culture that looks at failure as an inevitable part of discovery, and its scientists are encouraged to look for new uses for compounds that fail at any stage in a human clinical trial.[20]

▽ Organisational arrangements

(See also Chapters 3 and 21.)
Many companies use *customer-driven engineering* to design new market offerings. This strategy attaches high importance to incorporating customer value preferences in the final design.

▽ Xerox

Xerox traditionally developed new products as many firms did in the past: come up with an idea, develop a prototype, and get some consumer feedback. When Xerox researchers first came up with the idea for a dual-engine commercial printer, it decided to first go straight to the consumer to collect feedback before even developing any prototypes. Lucky it did. Although the Xerox team thought customers would want a second engine for special purposes, the fact that the second engine would be a back-up if the main engine failed turned out to be the biggest draw. In introducing the dual-engine Nuvera 288 Digital Perfecting System in April 2007, 'customer-led innovation' was cited as a critical driver. Xerox now believes in brainstorming, or 'dreaming with the customer', by combining company experts who know technology with customers who know the problem areas and what the most valuable product features can be. In addition, scientists and engineers are encouraged to meet face to face with customers, in some cases working on-site for a few weeks to see how customers interact with products.[21]

Xerox's popular new dual-engine printer was a response to customers' feedback on the value of a commercial printer with a back-up engine.
Source: Courtesy of Xerox Corporation

▽ Unilever

Unilever champions innovation to widen consumer choice and thus give it a consistent competitive edge. Unilever's R&D test kitchen in the Netherlands is one of its centres of culinary expertise. Its chefs create ideas for new products, recipes and product demonstrations for its Foodsolutions professional catering business, as well as providing culinary training for employees. The company aims to provide consumers with choice in terms of product varieties, such as low-fat and low-sugar versions of its ice creams, and low-fat versions of its margarines. Unilever also invests in developing new products with added health and nutrition benefits.

The work is led by the Unilever Food and Health Research Institute, which employs around 450 scientific staff and collaborates with external experts on product innovation and enhancement. The Institute is part of the company's wider commitment to research and development across both its Foods and Home and Personal Care categories. Around 6000 Unilever scientists and product developers work on the discovery and development of new ingredients and processes for products that provide proven benefits in nutrition, hygiene and personal care for consumers while minimising environmental impacts. In 2007, Unilever invested €868 million in R&D, equivalent to 2.2 per cent of sales.

Here are some examples of recent innovations.

Knorr Vie – increasing fruit and vegetable intake

People the world over do not eat enough fruit and vegetables. The World Health Organization and the UN Food and Agriculture Organization recommend a minimum intake of 400 g/day, but the average is only 100 g/day in developing countries and around 300 g/day in the western world. In 2005 Unilever launched Knorr Vie in Europe, a smoothie-style shot made from concentrated vegetable and fruit juices without any additives. In a 100 ml bottle, it provides half the recommended daily intake of fruit and vegetables. Sales of Knorr Vie fruit and vegetable shots continue to grow, increasing by 67 per cent with around 162 million bottles sold in Europe in 2007.

Source: Used by permission of Unilever

Source: Paul Aresu/PunchStock

Ice cream – a choice

Unilever invests around €50 million in ice cream R&D each year, and 40 per cent of this is now devoted to opportunities in the fast-growing health and wellness sector. Ice cream is primarily about pleasure and indulgence, but eaten sensibly it can form part of a nutritionally balanced diet. The company provides a broad range of options, with light, low-fat and no-sugar-added versions. Many brands, such as Cornetto and Magnum, are available in snack size, too, to help with calorie control. Moo is a range of children's ice creams based on the goodness of milk, with each ice cream containing as much calcium as in 100 ml of milk. Since 2006, most of Unilever's ice creams have been labelled with the values for eight nutrients, including energy, protein, fat and sugars.

After successful test marketing in Belgium and Ireland in 2006, Frusì, Unilever's frozen yogurt brand, has been rolled out in France, Italy, the United Kingdom and the Netherlands. Frusì contains 110 calories or less per 100 ml pot and just 2.4 g of fat. Each pot also provides 50 per cent of the recommended daily allowance of Vitamin C. The Solero range of products is made with fruit juice and fruit pieces and has a maximum of 99 kilo calories per product.

The company has also developed non-dairy alternatives for ice cream, such as Carte d'Or, Soy and Ades ice creams.

Source: Used by permission of Unilever

Becel/Flora pro-activ – improving heart health

According to the World Health Organization, heart disease is the principal cause of premature death worldwide. Reducing cholesterol is key to minimising the risks of heart disease. Since 2003 the company has worked in partnership with the World Heart Federation and national groups to promote heart health. Becel/Flora's Love your Heart campaign focuses on raising awareness and has distributed 4.5 million heart health leaflets to consumers and health professionals. It also offers free cholesterol testing, for example in Greece, where 25,000 people have been tested. Becel/Flora pro-activ was originally launched as a spread to help people reduce cholesterol levels – it is proven to lower blood cholesterol levels by 10–15 per cent. The healthy heart foods market is growing fast and the pro-activ range has been extended to include milk drinks and yogurt products. Between 2003 and 2005 sales of pro-activ grew by 40 per cent and it now reaches over 13 million households.

Source: Adapted from Unilever website: www.unilever.com/ourvalues/environment-society/sustainable development-report/nutrition-hygiene-wellbeing/nutrition/innovation.asp?print=true.

New product development requires senior management to define business domains, product categories and specific criteria for success. Most importantly they need to be willing to devote significant financial and management support over the medium to long term. For example Siemens VAI, one of the largest metallurgical firms in the world, took 12 years to develop COREX, a direct reduction technology for iron production that cuts costs and improves the production environment.

Budgeting for new product development

Senior management also need to decide how much to budget for new product development. R&D outcomes are so uncertain that it is difficult to use normal investment criteria. Some companies solve this problem by financing as many projects as possible, hoping to achieve a few winners. Other companies apply a conventional percentage-of-sales figure or spend what the competition spends. Still other companies decide how many successful offerings they need and work backwards to estimate the required investment. In either case new product development is an expensive activity as several ideas need to be generated and screened for their potential in order to identify one strong runner.

Success rates vary. Inventor Sir James Dyson claims he made 5127 prototypes of his bagless, transparent vacuum cleaner before finally achieving success. However, he does not regret his failures: 'If you want to discover something that other people haven't, you need to do things the wrong way . . . watching why that fails can take you on a completely different path.' Toshiba had great expectations of leading the way when it launched its cutting edge TV high definition player in 2007 but by early 2008 that had been comprehensively outsold by the Sony-developed Blu-ray system.[22]

Organising new product development

Companies handle the organisational aspect of new product development in several ways. Many assign responsibility for new ideas to *product managers*. However product managers are often so busy managing existing lines that they give little thought to new projects other than line extensions.[23] They also lack the specific skills and knowledge needed to develop and critique potential new products. Some companies have a *high-level management committee* charged with reviewing and approving proposals. Large companies often establish a new product development department headed by a executive who has direct access to top management. The department's major responsibilities include generating and screening new ideas, working with the R&D department, and carrying out field testing and final marketing.

▽ Adobe Systems, Inc.

A developer of software solutions for graphic designers and publishers, Adobe established a task force in 2004 to identify all the obstacles company innovators faced in trying to develop new products. The team found the corporate hierarchy resisted ideas needing a new sales channel, new business model, or even new packaging, and the company had grown so large that ideas originating in branch offices were not getting a fair hearing. The company then established a New Business Initiatives Group that holds quarterly Adobe Idea Champion Showcases. About 20 product managers and other employees (except top executives, who are barred from the proceedings) watch as potential employee-entrepreneurs give brief presentations and Q&A sessions. The ideas are vetted by Adobe entrepreneurs-in-residence, but even one that is turned down can still get a hearing on the company's brainstorming site. Since the new initiative was formed, the event has become extremely popular within Adobe.[24]

Some companies assign new product development work to **venture teams,** cross-functional groups charged with developing a specific product or business. These 'intrapreneurs' are relieved of their other duties and given a budget, time frame and 'skunkworks' setting. (*Skunkworks* are informal workplaces, sometimes garages, where intrapreneurial teams attempt to develop new products.)

Cross-functional teams can collaborate and use concurrent new offering development to push new offerings to market.[25] Concurrent product development resembles a football match, with team members passing the new market offering back and forth as they head towards the goal.

Many top companies use the *stage-gate system* to manage the innovation process.[26] The system enables companies to strike a considered balance between entrepreneurial creativity and business acumen. They divide the process into stages, at the end of each being a gate or checkpoint. The project leader, working with a cross-functional team, must bring a set of known deliverables to each gate before the project can pass to the next stage. To move from the business plan stage into offering development requires a convincing market research study of consumer needs and interest, a competitive analysis and a technical appraisal. Senior managers review the criteria at each gate to make one of four decisions: *go*, *kill*, *hold* or *recycle*. Stage-gate systems make the innovation process visible to all involved and clarify the project leader's and team's responsibilities at each stage.[27]

The stages in the new product development process are shown in Figure 15.1. Many firms have parallel sets of projects working through the process, each at a different stage. Think of the process as a *funnel*: a large number of initial new product ideas and concepts are winnowed down to a few high-potential products that are ultimately launched. But the process is not always linear. Many firms use a *spiral development process* that recognises the value of returning to an earlier stage to make improvements before moving forward.[28]

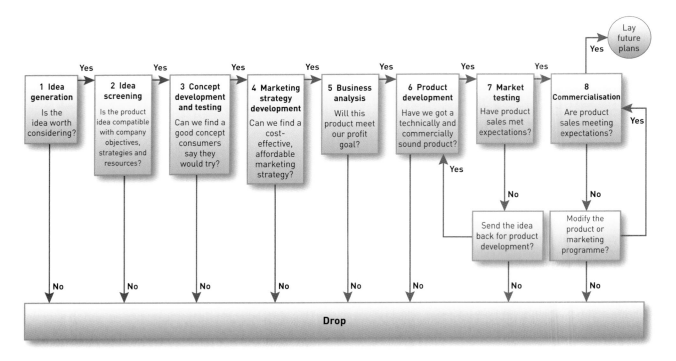

Figure 15.1 The new product development decision process

▽ Managing the development process I: ideas

Process stages

Introducing a new product to the marketplace requires a firm to manage three process activities:

1 managing idea generation and screening;

2 managing activities as selected ideas develop from concepts to strategy, paying particular attention to concept development and timing, marketing strategy development and business analysis;

3 managing the introduction of the new product to the marketplace with particular reference to product development, market testing and commercialisation.

To learn more about the extension of Richard's Branson's Virgin umbrella brand into Virgin Media, set up as rival to Rupert Murdoch's BSkyB, visit www.pearsoned.co.uk/ marketingmanagementeurope

Idea generation

The new product development process starts with the search for ideas. Some marketing experts believe the greatest opportunities and best advantages with new products are found by uncovering the best possible set of unmet customer needs or technological innovations.[29]

Inventions and innovations

The term invention traditionally refers to turning money into ideas; innovation is turning ideas into money. There is a fine line between these two essential new product activities. Patent offices provide a testimony to the creative activity of individuals. Some are just interesting ideas that inventors have filed; for example, the US actress Jamie Lee Curtis filed an early idea for a disposable nappy featuring a sealed pocket on the outside containing one or more wet wipes. She was granted a US patent in 1988. Inventions that are taken up by businesses and developed from ideas to products that are capable of being marketed have to meet real customer needs if they are to become innovations. Innovation is the first practical application of a new mode of thought that can generate a better solution to an existing need (for example, the invention and subsequent commercialisation of electric washing machines revolutionised domestic clothes washing) or completely transform traditional practices (in the way mobile phones have done).

In many ways the days of the mad inventor have given way to the age of innovation and existing ideas are being improved and applied more efficiently to meet known and perceived customer needs. New presentations of existing technology through clever design is increasingly capturing customers' attention and becoming 'must-have' items. The technology behind the Apple iPod is not that new. What makes it a successful new product is how the technology is packaged – in other words the design and the marketing skills.

Ideas can come from interacting with various groups and using creativity-generating techniques. (See 'Marketing memo: Ten ways to find great new product ideas.')

Interacting with others

Encouraged by the *open innovation* movement, many firms are increasingly going outside the company to gather sources of new ideas,[30] including customers, employees, scientists, engineers, channel members, marketing agencies, top management, and even competitors.

A true innovation is a product, a service or a concept, that is, a product which brings a new solution to consumers' problems by offering more customer-perceived value than the usual solution or by offering a totally different conceptual solution. A better conventional vacuum cleaner or the Dyson DC25 roller ball model? The Dyson engineers are seeking to make the company's vacuum machines smaller and easier to handle while keeping and if possible improving on their performance. The Gallup Organisation has produced a series of audits or Innobarometers to assist the EU civil service and politicians to audit the degree of innovation evident within the EU member states. The Innobarometer 2004 researched 'the experience of European managers in innovative activities'. It sought to discover the

Marketing memo

Ten ways to find great new product ideas

1 Run informal sessions where groups of customers meet with company engineers and designers to discuss problems and needs and brainstorm potential solutions.

2 Allow time off – scouting time – for technical people to discuss their own pet projects.

3 Make a customer brainstorming session a standard feature of plant tours.

4 Survey your customers: find out what they like and dislike in your and your competitors' products.

5 Encourage spontaneous ideas and hold idea-generating away-day meetings with key customers.

6 Use iterative rounds: a group of customers in one room, focusing on identifying problems; and a group of technical people in the next room, listening and brainstorming solutions. Immediately test proposed solutions with the group of customers.

7 Set up a keyword search that routinely scans trade publications in multiple countries for new offering announcements.

8 Treat trade shows as intelligence missions, where you view all that is new in your industry under one roof.

9 Have your technical and marketing people visit your suppliers' labs and spend time with their technical people – find out what's new.

10 Set up an ideas workshop, and make it open and easily accessed. Allow employees to review the ideas and add constructively to them.

Source: Adapted from R. Cooper (1998) *Product Leadership: Creating and Launching Superior New Products*, New York: Basic Books. Copyright © 1998 Basic Books. Reproduced with permission.

degree of 'innovative readiness in Europe'. Table 15.4 shows the percentage of turnover resulting from the introduction of new products and services (market offerings) between 2002 and 2004.

The research shows that only 10 per cent of the EU15 companies surveyed were deemed to be 'highly innovative' with over half of their turnover being generated by new products and services. Twice this percentage were found to be 'non-innovator' companies. A country-by-country comparison reveals Portugal, the United Kingdom and Spain as having the highest proportion of innovative companies while Belgium, Greece and France have the most non-innovator companies.

The latest Innobarometer survey looked at active innovators in clustered environments and was carried out in June 2006. Table 15.5 summarises the key findings.

Customer needs and wants are the logical place to start the search for new ideas. One-to-one interviews and focus group discussions can explore needs and reactions. Griffin and Hauser suggest that conducting 10–20 in-depth experiential interviews per market segment often uncovers the vast majority of customer needs.[31] But many additional approaches can be profitable. (See 'Marketing memo: Seven ways to draw new ideas from your customers'.)

The traditional company-centric approach to innovation is giving way to a world in which companies co-create products with customers.[32] Companies are increasingly turning to 'crowd sourcing' to generate new ideas and to create consumer-generated marketing campaigns. Crowd sourcing means inviting the Internet community to help create content or software, often with prize money or a celebratory moment involved. This strategy has helped create new offerings and companies such as Wikipedia and Google's popular video website YouTube.

Regular users of a product can be a good source of input when they innovate without the consent or even the knowledge of the companies that produce them. Mountain bikes developed as a result of young people taking their bicycles up to the top of a mountain and riding down. When the bicycles broke, the young riders began building more durable machines and adding such things as motorcycle brakes, improved suspension and accessories. The young cyclists, not the companies, developed these innovations. Some companies, particularly those that want to appeal to young consumers, bring the lead users into their product design process.[33]

Technical companies can learn a great deal by studying customers who make the most advanced use of the company's products and who recognise the need for improvements before other customers do. Employees throughout the company can be a source of ideas for improving

Marketing insight

Reckitt Benckiser connect-and-develop approach to innovation

Reckitt Benckiser . . . finding the 'I didn't know I needed that' opportunities

Since its creation in 1999 through the merger of the UK's Reckitt & Colman and Benckiser of the Netherlands, profits almost doubled by 2004 and the share price has more than doubled since the start of the millennium. In 2006 revenues of €6.5 billion were achieved together with profits of €910 million. The company has achieved this by fostering an innovative approach which has developed several new products that customers never knew they needed. So where do these ideas come from? According to the company's chief executive, Bart Brech:

> Consumers will generally not come up with the next innovation. So we try to have ideas that target consumers in specific areas. Then we screen them. We go through literally thousands of ideas every quarter. Then we ask consumers about the ideas.

This relentless quest to find and exploit new market offering/product ideas has generated over 35 per cent of the company's sales between 2004 and 2007. To ensure that consumers know about these ideas Reckitt Benckiser spends over 12 per cent of its entire revenue on marketing. The company aims to double its sales by 2012 and double its profit margins to more than 30 per cent.

The key phrase, never omitted from any Reckitt Benckiser presentation, is 'power brands'. In February 2008 there were 18 such brands – the best known in Britain being Veet hair remover, Dettol, Nurofen, Strepsils, Calgon, Vanish, Woolite, Cillit Bang, Harpic, Finish, Airwick, Lemsip and Gaviscon.

An important contributor to the company's success has been its development of a strong innovative culture across all of its branded offerings. The company seeks to generate 40 per cent of its revenues from market offerings/products launched in the previous three years. Its culture values swift decision making, innovation and a focus on financial results. Managers' pay is closely linked to individual performance and – to foster teamwork – to that of their colleagues.

Cillit Bang is a good example of well-known technology that has been given a new set of clothes and a clever slogan which most people remember.

Two of Reckitt Benckiser brands that are markedly imaginative: Cillit Bang ' . . . and the dirt is gone!' and 'Dettol kills all known germs stone dead!'
Source: Courtesy of Reckitt Benckiser

Sources: M. Urry (2008) Reckitt's strongly flavoured essence, *Financial Times*, 21 January; Cleaning up, *The Economist*, 14 February 2008; B. Laurence (2008) Reckitt Benckiser cleans up with research to boost global sales, *The Sunday Times*, 17 February.

Table 15.4 Innovation in Europe: percentage of turnover resulting from new products or services 2000–04

Country	Sample	0%	1–5%	6–10%	11–20%	21–50%	51%+
Germany	286	14	25	17	16	16	11
Denmark	185	15	17	24	16	22	6
Ireland	95	19	14	19	17	19	12
Italy	294	21	22	22	16	13	7
Sweden	172	21	24	21	13	10	11
Portugal	87	22	14	15	17	17	15
Austria	172	22	23	21	14	11	9
Finland	90	23	34	17	10	12	5
the UK	282	23	13	20	14	16	14
Spain	287	23	15	11	19	19	13
the Netherlands	198	23	34	19	12	9	3
Luxembourg	92	24	32	16	18	8	2
France	286	27	26	17	12	11	7
Greece	94	32	21	15	12	13	8
Belgium	188	34	20	20	11	8	7
EU15	**2849**	**20**	**22**	**18**	**15**	**14**	**10**

Source: European Commission (2004) *Flash Eurobarometer Report*, No. 144, p.7 (from www.estatisticas.gpeari. mctes.pt/archive/doc/f_innobarometer_report_en_2003.pdf). A Gallup Organisation survey requested by the Directorate of General Enterprise and Industry and Co-ordinated by the Directorate of General Communication. Copyright © 2004 Office for Official Publications of the European Communities. Reproduced with permission.

Table 15.5 Active innovators in cluster-like environments

Country	Percentage
The UK, Ireland	50–99
Austria, Italy, Turkey	25–49
Belgium, Portugal, Sweden, Norway	20–24
France, Holland, Germany	10–19
Spain, Switzerland, Poland, Denmark	1–9

Source: European Commission (2006) *Flash Eurobarometer Report*, No. 187, p.7. A Gallup Organisation survey requested by the Directorate of General Enterprise and Industry and Co-ordinated by the Directorate of General Communication.

production, products and services. Toyota claims its employees submit 2 million ideas annually (about 35 suggestions per employee), over 85 per cent of which are implemented. Many firms, such as Kodak and Oticon, the Danish hearing aid company, give monetary, holiday or other recognition awards to employees who submit the best ideas. Nokia inducts engineers with at least ten patents into its 'Club 10', recognising them each year in a formal awards ceremony hosted by the company's CEO.[34]

A company can motivate its employees to submit new ideas to an *idea manager* whose name and phone number are widely circulated or by means of the traditional *suggestion box*. Internal brainstorming sessions also can be quite effective – if they are conducted correctly. 'Marketing memo: How to run a successful creative problem-solving session' provides some brainstorming guidelines.

Companies can find good ideas by researching the market offerings of competitors and other companies. They can find out what customers like and dislike about competitors' products. They can buy their competitors' products, take them apart, and build better ones. Company sales representatives and intermediaries are a particularly good source of ideas. These groups have first-hand exposure to customers and are often the first to learn about competitive developments.

Top management can be another major source of ideas. Some company leaders, such as the former CEO of Intel, take personal responsibility for technological innovation in their companies. Ideas can come from inventors, patent lawyers, university and commercial laboratories, industrial consultants, advertising agencies, marketing research firms and industrial publications. However, although ideas can flow from many sources, their chances of receiving serious attention often depend on whether the company has a formal screening system and new offering responsibility.

Marketing memo

Seven ways to draw new ideas from your customers

1 Observe how your customers are using your products.

2 Ask your customers about their problems with your products.

3 Ask your customers about their dream goods. Ask your customers what they want your product to do, even if the ideal sounds impossible.

4 Use a customer advisory board to comment on your company's ideas.

5 Use websites for new ideas. Companies can use specialised search engines to find blogs and postings relevant to their businesses.

6 Form a brand community of enthusiasts who discuss your offerings. Sony engaged in collaborative dialogues with consumers to co-develop Sony's PlayStation 2. LEGO draws on children and influential adult enthusiasts for feedback on new product concepts in the early stages of development.

7 Encourage or challenge your customers to change or improve your products. BMW posted a toolkit on its website to let customers develop ideas using telematics and in-car online services.

Source: From an unpublished paper, P. Kotler (2007) Drawing new ideas from your customers.

Marketing memo

How to run a successful creative problem-solving session

Group creative problem-solving (CPS) sessions have much to recommend them, but also some drawbacks. If carried out incorrectly, they can frustrate and antagonise participants; if carried out correctly, however, they can create insights, ideas and solutions that would have been impossible without everyone's participation. To ensure success, experts recommend the following guidelines:

1 There should be a trained facilitator to guide the session.

2 Participants must feel that they can express themselves freely.

3 Participants must see themselves as collaborators working towards a common goal.

4 Rules need to be set up and followed, so conversations do not stray.

5 Participants must be given proper background preparation and materials so that they can get into the task quickly.

6 Individual sessions before and after the CPS workshop can be useful to think and learn about the topic ahead of time as well as reflect afterwards on what happened.

7 CPS sessions must lead to a clear plan of action and implementation, so the ideas that materialise can provide tangible value.

8 CPS sessions can do more than just generate ideas – they can help build teams and leave participants better informed and energised.

Source: L. Tischler (2007) Be creative: you have 30 seconds, *Fast Company*, May, 47–50.

Creativity techniques

The following list is a sampling of techniques for stimulating creativity in individuals and groups.[35]

- **Attribute listing**: List the attributes of an object, such as a screwdriver. Then modify each attribute, such as replacing the wooden handle with plastic, providing torque power, adding different screw heads, and so on.

- **Forced relationships**: List several ideas and consider each in relation to each other one. In designing new office furniture, for example, consider a desk, bookcase and filing cabinet as separate ideas. Then imagine a desk with a built-in bookcase or a desk with built-in files or a bookcase with built-in files.

A cyber café: cafeteria + Internet

Source: image100/Corbis

'I've got a great idea!'

'It won't work here.'

'We've tried it before.'

'This isn't the right time.'

'It can't be done.'

'It's not the way we do things.'

'We've done all right without it.'

'It will cost too much.'

'Let's discuss it at our next meeting.'

Figure 15.2 Forces fighting new ideas

Source: Jerold Panas, Young & Partners. Reproduced with permission.

- **Morphological analysis**: Start with a problem, such as 'getting something from one place to another via a powered vehicle'. Now think of dimensions, such as the type of platform (cart, chair, sling, bed), the medium (air, water, oil, rails), and the power source (compressed air, electric motor, magnetic fields). By listing every possible combination, many new solutions can be generated.
- **Reverse assumption analysis**: List all the normal assumptions about an entity and then reverse them. Instead of assuming that a restaurant has menus, charges for and serves food, reverse each assumption. The new restaurant may decide to serve only what the chef bought that morning and cooked; it may provide some food and charge only for how long the person sits at the table; or it may design an exotic atmosphere and rent out the space to people who bring their own food and beverages.
- **New contexts**: Take familiar processes, such as people-helping services, and put them into a new context. Imagine helping dogs and cats instead of people with day care service, stress reduction, psychotherapy, animal funerals, and so on. As another example, instead of sending hotel guests to the front desk to check in, greet them at kerb side and use a wireless device to register them.
- **Mind mapping**: Start with a thought, such as a car, write it on a piece of paper, then think of the next thought that comes up (say Mercedes); link it to car, then think of the next association (Germany); and do this with all associations that come up with each new word. Perhaps a whole new idea will materialise.

Increasingly, offering ideas arise from *lateral marketing* that combines two value concepts or ideas to create a new offering. Here are some successful examples:

- petrol station shops = petrol stations + food
- cyber cafés = cafeteria + Internet
- cereal bars = cereal + snacking
- Kinder Surprise = confectionery + toy
- Sony Walkman = audio + portable.

Idea screening

In screening ideas the company must avoid two types of error. A *DROP-error* occurs when the company dismisses a good idea. It is extremely easy to find fault with other people's ideas (see Figure 15.2). Some companies shudder when they look back at ideas they dismissed or breathe sighs of relief when they realise how close they came to dropping what eventually became a huge success. This was the case with the hit television show *Friends*.

▽ Friends

An idea that did not get off the storyboard was the pilot for *Friends*, one of the longest-running hit comedies on television. Dismissing an idea that later proves successful is a marketer's nightmare and is called a DROP error.
Source: Warner Brothers TV/Bright/Crane Pro/The Kobal Collection/Chris Haston

The US NBC situation comedy *Friends* enjoyed a ten-year run from 1994 to 2004 as a perennial ratings powerhouse. But the show almost did not see the light of day. According to an internal NBC research report, the pilot episode was described as 'not very entertaining, clever or original' and was given a failing grade, scoring 41 out of 100. Ironically, the pilot for an earlier hit sit-com,

Seinfeld, was also rated 'weak', although the pilot for the medical drama *ER* scored a healthy 91. Courtney Cox's Monica was the *Friends* character who scored best with test audiences, but characters portrayed by Lisa Kudrow and Matthew Perry were deemed to have marginal appeal, and the Rachel, Ross and Joey characters scored even lower. Adults 35 and over in the sample found the characters as a whole 'smug, superficial and self-absorbed'.[36]

Friends was a substantial success in the United Kingdom but another US comedy import, *Pushing Daisies,* while a success in the United States obtained poor viewing figures elsewhere.

A *GO-error* occurs when the company permits a poor idea to move into development and commercialisation. An *absolute product failure* loses money; its sales do not cover variable costs. A *partial product failure* loses money, but its sales cover all its variable costs and some of its fixed costs. A *relative product failure* yields a profit lower than the company's target rate of return.

The purpose of screening is to drop poor ideas as early as possible. The rationale is that development costs rise substantially with each successive development stage. Most companies require ideas to be described on a standard form for a review. The description states the idea, the target market and the competition and roughly estimates market size, product price, development time and costs, manufacturing costs and rate of return.

The executive committee then reviews each idea against a set of criteria. Does the product meet a need? Would it offer superior in-use value? Can it be distinctively advertised? Does the company have the necessary know-how and capital? Will the new product deliver the expected sales volume, sales growth and profit? Consumer input may be necessary to tap into marketplace realities.[37]

Management can rate the surviving ideas using a weighted-index method such as that in Table 15.6. The first column lists factors required for successful product launches, and the second column assigns importance weights. The third column scores the product idea on a scale from 0 to 1.0, with 1.0 the highest score. The final step multiplies each factor's importance by the product score to obtain an overall rating. In this example, the product idea scores 0.69, which places it in the 'good idea' level. The purpose of this basic rating device is to promote systematic evaluation and discussion. It is not supposed to make the decision for management.

As the idea moves through development, the company will constantly need to revise its estimate of the product's overall probability of success, using the following formula:

$$
\begin{array}{ccc}
\text{Overall} & \text{Probability} & \text{Probability of} & \text{Probability of} \\
\text{probability of} \;=\; & \text{of technical} \;\times & \text{commercialisation} \;\times & \text{economic} \\
\text{success} & \text{completion} & \text{given technical} & \text{success given} \\
& & \text{completion} & \text{commercialisation}
\end{array}
$$

Table 15.6 Product–idea rating device

Product success requirements	Relative weight (a)	Product score (b)	Product rating (c = a × b)
Unique or superior product	.40	.8	.32
High performance-to-cost ratio	.30	.6	.18
High marketing euro support	.20	.7	.14
Lack of strong competition	.10	.5	.05
Total	1.00		.69[a]

[a]Rating scale: .00–.30 poor; .31–.60 fair; .61–.80 good. Minimum acceptance rate: .61

For example, if the three probabilities are estimated as 0.50, 0.65 and 0.74, respectively, the overall probability of success is 0.24. The company then must judge whether this probability is high enough to warrant continued development.

▽ Managing the development process II: concept to strategy

Attractive ideas must be refined into testable market offer concepts. An *idea* is a possible product the company might introduce to the market. A *product concept* is an elaborated version of the idea expressed in customer terms.

Concept development and testing

Concept development

This can be illustrated by considering concept development with the following situation: a large food-processing company has the idea of producing a powder to add to milk in order to increase its nutritional value and taste. This is a product *idea*, but customers do not buy such ideas; they buy product *concepts*.

A product idea can be turned into several concepts. The first question is: who will use this product? The powder can be targeted at infants, children, teenagers, young or middle-aged adults or older adults. Second, what primary benefit should this product provide? Taste, nutrition, refreshment, energy? Third, when will people consume this drink? Breakfast, mid-morning, lunch, mid-afternoon, dinner, late evening? By answering these questions, a company can form several concepts:

- **Concept 1**: An instant breakfast drink for adults who want a quick, nutritious breakfast without preparation.
- **Concept 2**: A tasty snack for children to drink as a midday refreshment.
- **Concept 3**: A health supplement for older adults to drink in the late evening before they go to bed.

Each concept represents a *category concept* that defines the product's competition. An instant breakfast drink would compete against bacon and eggs, breakfast cereals, coffee and pastry, and other breakfast alternatives. A tasty snack drink would compete against soft drinks, fruit juices, sports drinks and other thirst quenchers.

Suppose the instant-breakfast-drink concept looks best. The next task is to show where this powdered product would stand in relationship to other breakfast offerings. *Perceptual maps* are a visual way to display consumer perceptions and preferences (see Chapter 10). They provide quantitative portrayals of market situations and how consumers see different market products, services and brands. By overlaying consumer preferences with brand perceptions, marketers can reveal 'holes' or 'openings' that suggest unmet customer needs.

Figure 15.3(a) uses the two dimensions of cost and preparation time to create a *product-positioning map* for the breakfast drink. An instant breakfast drink offers low cost and quick preparation. Its nearest competitor is cold cereal or breakfast bars; its most distant competitor is bacon and eggs. These contrasts can help communicate and promote the concept to the market.

Next, the product concept becomes a *brand concept* (see Chapters 12 and 13). Figure 15.3(b) is a *brand-positioning map*, a perceptual map showing the current positions of three existing brands of instant breakfast drinks (A–C), as seen by consumers. It can also be useful to overlay consumer preferences on to the map in terms of their current or desired preferences. Figure 15.3(b) also shows that there are four segments of consumers (1–4) whose preferences are clustered around the points displayed on the map.

The brand-positioning map helps the company to decide how much to charge and how calorific to make its drink. Three segments (1–3) are well served by existing brands (A–C). The company would not want to position itself next to one of those existing brands, unless that brand is weak or inferior or market demand was high enough to be shared. As it turns out, the new brand would be distinctive in the medium-price, medium-calorie market or in the high-price, high-calorie market. There is also a segment of consumers (4) clustered fairly near the medium-price, medium-calorie market, suggesting that it may offer the greatest opportunity.

(a) Product-positioning map (breakfast market)

(b) Brand-positioning map (instant breakfast market)

Figure 15.3 Product and brand positioning

Concept testing

Concept testing means presenting the product idea concept, symbolically or physically, to target consumers and getting their reactions. The more the tested concepts resemble the final offering or experience, the more dependable concept testing is. Concept testing of prototypes can help avoid costly mistakes, but it may be especially challenging with radically different, innovative products.[38] In the past, creating physical prototypes was costly and time consuming, but today firms can use *rapid prototyping* to design products on a computer, and then produce outline models of each to show potential customers for their reactions. Companies are also using *virtual reality* to test product concepts. Virtual reality programmes use computers and sensory devices (such as gloves or goggles) to simulate reality.

Concept testing presents customers with an elaborated version of the concept. Here is the elaboration of concept 1 in the milk example:

> The market product idea is a powdered mixture added to milk to make an instant breakfast that gives the person all the day's needed nutrition along with good taste and high convenience. The product comes in three flavours (chocolate, vanilla and strawberry) and individual packets, six to a box, at €5 a box.

After receiving this information, researchers measure product dimensions by getting customers to respond to the following types of questions:

1 **Communicability and believability**: Are the benefits clear and believable? If the scores are low, the concept must be refined or revised.

2 **Need level**: Does the proposed product solve a problem or fill a need? The stronger the need, the higher the expected customer and consumer interest.

3 **Gap level**: Do any other products currently meet this need and are they satisfactory? The greater the gap, the higher the expected customer interest. Marketers can multiply the need level by the gap level to produce a *need-gap score*. A high score means the customer sees the proposed product as filling a strong need not satisfied by available alternatives.

4 **Perceived value**: Is the potential benefit of the proposed product (using the term 'product' to mean a market offering that is a mix of tangible and intangible benefits) acceptable? The higher the value, the higher is the expected customer and consumer interest.

5 **Purchase intention**: Would the respondents (definitely, probably, probably not, definitely not) buy the product? Customers who answered the first three questions positively should answer 'Definitely' here.

6 **User targets, purchase occasions, purchasing frequency**: Who would use this product, when and how often?

Respondents' answers indicate whether the concept has a broad and strong customer and consumer appeal, what rival market products it competes against, and which customers are the best targets. The need-gap levels and purchase-intention levels can be checked against norms for the market category to see whether the concept appears to be a winner, a long shot, or a loser.

Conjoint analysis

This is a scaling technique method for deriving the use benefit values that consumers attach to varying levels of a product's value attributes. It is also called trade-off analysis as it models the relative customer-perceived value of competing products and throws light on how customers decide what value attributes (quality or transaction) can be traded off. The technique has become one of the most popular concept development and testing tools. With conjoint analysis, respondents see different hypothetical products formed by combining varying levels of the attributes, then rank them. Management can then identify the most appealing product and its estimated market share and profit.

Suppose the new product marketer is considering five attribute benefit design elements:

Figure 15.4 Vacuum cleaner samples for conjoint analysis

1 three package designs (A, B, C – see Figure 15.4);

2 three brands (Euro 1, Euro 2 and Euro 3);

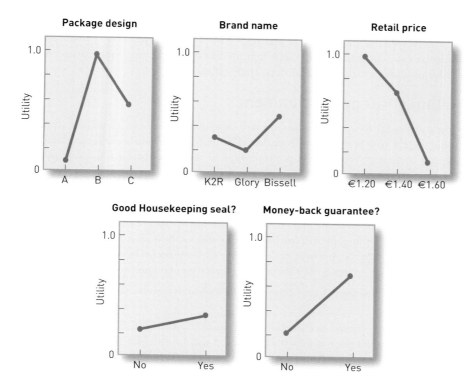

Figure 15.5 Utility functions based on conjoint analysis

3   three retail prices (€1.20, €1.40 and €1.60);
4   a possible seal of approval such as *Good Housekeeping* magazine in the United Kingdom (yes, no)
5   a possible money-back guarantee (yes, no).

Although the researcher can form 108 possible product concepts ($3 \times 3 \times 3 \times 2 \times 2$), it would be too much to ask customers to rank 108 concepts. A sample of, say, 18 contracting product concepts is feasible, and customers would rank them from the most to the least preferred.

The marketer can then use a statistical software program to derive the customer's preferred utility functions for each of the five attributes (see Figure 15.5). Utility ranges between zero and one; the higher the utility, the stronger the consumer's preference for that level of the attribute. Looking at packaging it is clear that package B is the most favoured, followed by C and then A, which has hardly any perceived utility. The preferred brands are Bissell, K2R and Glory, in that order. The consumer's utility varies inversely with price. A *Good Housekeeping* Seal is preferred, but it does not add that much utility and my not be worth the effort to obtain it. A money-back guarantee is strongly preferred.

The consumer's most desired offer is package design B, brand name Bissell, priced at €1, with a *Good Housekeeping* Seal and a money-back guarantee. It is also possible to determine the relative importance of each attribute to this consumer – the difference between the highest and lowest utility level for that attribute. The greater the difference, the more important the attribute. Clearly this consumer sees price and package design as the most important attributes, followed by money-back guarantee, brand name and a *Good Housekeeping* Seal.

Preference data from a sufficient sample of target consumers helps the company to estimate the market share any specific offer is likely to achieve, given any assumptions about competitive responses. Still, the organisation may not launch the market offer that promises to gain the greatest market share, because of cost considerations. The most customer-appealing product (in terms of customer-perceived value) is not always the most profitable one to bring to market.

Under some conditions, researchers will collect the data without a full-profile description of each product, by presenting two factors at a time. For example, respondents may see a table with three price levels and three package types and indicate which of the nine combinations they would like most, second best, and so on. A further table consists of trade-offs between two other variables. The trade-off approach may be easier to use when there are many variables and possible offers. However, it is less realistic in that respondents are focusing on only two variables at a time. Adaptive conjoint analysis (ACA) is a 'hybrid' data collection technique that combines self-explicated importance ratings with pair-wise trade-off tasks.[39]

Marketing strategy development

Following a successful concept test, the firm will develop a preliminary three-part strategy plan for introducing the new product to the market. The first part describes the target market's size, structure and behaviour; the planned positioning; and the sales, market share and profit goals sought in the first few years:

> The target market for the instant breakfast drink is families with children who are receptive to a new, convenient, nutritious and inexpensive form of breakfast. The company's brand will be positioned at the higher-price, higher-quality end of the instant breakfast drink category. The company will initially aim to sell 500,000 cases or 10 per cent of the market, with a loss in the first year not exceeding €1.5 million. The second year will aim for 700,000 cases or 14 per cent of the market, with a planned profit of €2.2 million.

The second part outlines the planned price, distribution strategy and marketing budget for the first year:

> The product will be offered in chocolate, vanilla and strawberry in individual packets of six to a box, at a retail price of €2.49 a box. There will be 48 boxes per case, and the case price to distributors will be €24. For the first two months, dealers will be offered one case free for every four cases bought, plus cooperative advertising allowances. Free samples will be distributed door to door. Money-off coupons will appear in newspapers. The total sales promotional budget will be €2.9 million. An advertising budget of €6 million will be split 50:50 between national and local. Two-thirds will go into television and one-third into newspapers. Advertising copy will emphasise the benefit concepts of nutrition and convenience. The advertising execution concept will revolve around a small boy who drinks instant breakfast and grows strong. During the first year, €100,000 will be spent on marketing research to buy store audits and consumer-panel information to monitor market reaction and buying rates.

The third part of the marketing strategy plan describes the long-run sales and profit goals and marketing mix strategy over time:

> The company intends to win a 25 per cent market share and realise an after-tax return on investment of 12 per cent. To achieve this return, product quality will start high and be improved over time through technical research. Price will initially be set at a high level and lowered gradually to expand the market and meet competition. The total promotion budget will be boosted each year about 20 per cent, with the initial advertising–sales promotion split of 65:35 evolving eventually to 50:50. Marketing research will be reduced to €60,000 per year after the first year.

Business analysis

After management develops the product concept and marketing strategy, it can evaluate the proposal's business attractiveness. Management needs to prepare sales, cost and profit projections to determine whether they satisfy company objectives. If they do, the concept can move to the development stage. As new information comes in, the business analysis will undergo revision and expansion.

Estimating total sales

Total estimated sales are the sum of estimated first-time sales, replacement sales and repeat sales. Sales estimation methods depend on whether the product is purchased once (such as an engagement ring or retirement home), infrequently, or often. For one-time products, sales rise at the beginning, peak, and approach zero as the number of potential buyers is exhausted (see Figure 15.6(a)). If new buyers keep entering the market, the curve will not go down to zero.

Infrequently purchased products – such as cars, toasters and industrial equipment – exhibit replacement cycles dictated by physical wear or obsolescence associated with changing styles, features and performance. Sales forecasting for this category calls for estimating first-time sales and replacement sales separately (see Figure 15.6(b)).

Frequently purchased products, such as consumer and industrial non-durables, have product life cycle sales resembling Figure 15.6(c). The number of first-time buyers initially increases and then decreases as fewer buyers are left (assuming a fixed population). Repeat purchases occur soon, providing the product satisfies some buyers. The sales curve eventually falls to a plateau representing a level of steady repeat-purchase volume; by this time, the product is no longer a new product.

In estimating sales, the manager's first task is to estimate first-time purchases of the new product in each period. To estimate replacement sales, management researches the products' *survival-age distribution* – that is, the number of units that fail in year one, two, three, and so on. The low end of the distribution indicates when the first replacement sales will take place. Because replacement sales are difficult to estimate before the product is in use, some manufacturers base the decision to launch a new offering solely on the estimate of first-time sales.

For a frequently purchased new product, the seller estimates repeat sales as well as first-time sales. A high rate of repeat purchasing means customers are satisfied; sales are likely to stay high even after all first-time purchases take place. The seller should note the percentage of repeat purchases in each repeat-purchase class: those who rebuy once, twice, three times, and so on. Some products and brands are bought a few times and then dropped.[40]

Estimating costs and profits

Costs are estimated by the R&D, manufacturing, marketing, and finance departments. Table 15.7 illustrates a five-year projection of sales, costs, and profits for a company marketing an instant breakfast drink.

Row 1 shows projected sales revenue over the five-year period. The company expects to sell €11,889,000 (approximately 500,000 cases at €24 per case) in the first year. Behind this projection is a set of assumptions about the rate of market growth, the company's market share, and the ex-factory price. *Row 2* shows the cost of goods sold, which hovers around 33 per cent of sales revenue. This cost is calculated by estimating the average cost of labour, ingredients and packaging per case. *Row 3* shows the expected gross margin, the difference between sales revenue and cost of goods sold.

Row 4 shows anticipated development costs of €3.5 million, including product development costs, marketing research costs and manufacturing development costs. *Row 5* shows the estimated marketing costs over the five-year period to cover advertising, sales promotion and marketing research and an amount allocated for sales force coverage and marketing administration. *Row 6*

(a) One-time purchased product

(b) Infrequently purchased product

(c) Frequently purchased product

Figure 15.6
Product life cycle sales for three types of products

Table 15.7 Projected five-year cash-flow statement (in €000)

	Year 0	Year 1	Year 2	Year 3	Year 4	Year 5
1 Sales revenue	0	11,889	15,381	19,654	28,253	32,491
2 Cost of goods sold	0	3,981	5,150	6,581	9,461	10,880
3 Gross margin	0	7,908	10,231	13,073	18,792	21,611
4 Development costs	−3,500	0	0	0	0	0
5 Marketing costs	0	8,000	6,460	8,255	11,866	13,646
6 Allocated overhead	0	1,189	1,538	1,965	2,825	3,249
7 Gross contribution	−3,500	−1,281	2,233	2,853	4,101	4,716
8 Supplementary contribution	0	0	0	0	0	0
9 Net contribution	−3,500	−1,281	2,233	2,853	4,101	4,716
10 Discounted contribution (15%)	−3,500	−1,113	1,691	1,877	2,343	2,346
11 Cumulative discounted cash flow	−3,500	−4,613	−2,922	−1,045	1,298	3,644

shows the allocated overhead to this new product to cover its share of the cost of executive salaries, heat, light, and so on.

Row 7, the gross contribution, is gross margin minus the preceding three costs. *Row 8,* supplementary contribution, lists any change in income to other company products caused by the new product introduction. *Dragalong income* is additional income to them, and *cannibalised income* is reduced income. Table 15.7 assumes no supplementary contributions. *Row 9* shows net contribution, which in this case is the same as gross contribution. *Row 10* shows discounted contribution – that is, the present value of each future contribution discounted at 15 per cent per annum. For example, the company will not receive €4,716,000 until the fifth year. This amount is worth only €2,345,000 today if the company can earn 15 per cent on its money through other investments.[41]

Finally, *row 11* shows the cumulative discounted cash flow, the accumulation of the annual contributions in row 10. Two things are of central interest. The first is the maximum investment exposure, the highest loss the project can create. The company will be in a maximum loss position of €4,613,000 in year 1. The second is the payback period, the time when the company recovers all its investment, including the built-in return of 15 per cent. The payback period here is about three and a half years. Management must decide whether to risk a maximum investment loss of €4.6 million and a possible payback period of three and a half years.

Companies use other financial measures to evaluate the merit of a new product proposal. The simplest is **breakeven analysis**, which estimates how many units the company must sell (or how many years it will take) to break even with the given price and cost structure. If management believes sales could easily reach the break-even number, it is likely to develop the new offering.

A more complex method of estimating profit is **risk analysis**. Here three estimates are obtained (optimistic, pessimistic and most likely) for each uncertain variable affecting profitability, under an assumed marketing environment and marketing strategy for the planning period. The computer simulates possible outcomes and computes a distribution showing the range of possible rates of returns and their probabilities.

▽ Managing the development process III: development to commercialisation

Up to now, the offering has existed only as a word description, a drawing or a prototype. The next step represents a jump in investment that dwarfs the costs incurred so far. The company will determine whether the new idea can translate into a technically and commercially feasible CPV market offering. If not, the accumulated project cost will be lost, except for any useful information gained in the process.

Product and market development

The job of translating target customer requirements into a working prototype is helped by a set of methods known as *quality function deployment* (QFD). The methodology takes the list of desired *customer attributes* (CAs) generated by market research and turns them into a list of *engineering attributes* (EEs) that engineers can use. For example, customers of a proposed truck may want a certain acceleration rate (CA). Engineers can turn this into the required horsepower and other engineering equivalents (EEs). The methodology measures the trade-offs and costs of meeting customer requirements. A major contribution of QFD is improved communication between marketers, engineers and manufacturing people.[42]

Physical prototypes

The R&D department will develop one or more versions of the core offer product concept. Its goal is to find a prototype that embodies the key attributes described in the product concept statement, which performs safely under normal use and conditions, and that the firm can produce within budgeted manufacturing costs. In the past, developing and manufacturing a successful prototype could take days, weeks, months, or even years. The Web now permits more rapid prototyping and more flexible development processes.[43] Sophisticated virtual-reality technology is also speeding up the process. By designing and testing product designs through simulation, for example, companies achieve the flexibility to respond to new information and to resolve uncertainties by quickly exploring alternatives.

▽ **Boeing**

Boeing designed its 777 aircraft on a totally digital basis. Engineers, designers and more than 500 suppliers designed the aircraft on a special computer network without ever making a blueprint on paper. Project partners were connected by an extranet enabling them to communicate, share ideas, and work on the design at a distance. A computer-generated 'human' could climb inside the three-dimensional design on-screen to show how difficult maintenance access would be for a live mechanic. Such computer modelling allowed engineers to spot design errors that otherwise would have remained undiscovered until a person began to work on a physical prototype. Avoiding the time and cost of building physical prototypes reduced development time, wastage and rework by 60 per cent to 90 per cent.[44]

Laboratory scientists must not only design the new offering's functional characteristics, but also communicate its psychological aspects and brand image through physical cues. How will consumers react to different colours, sizes and weights? Marketers need to supply lab people with information about what attributes consumers seek and how consumers judge whether these attributes are present.

Customer tests

When the prototypes are ready, they must be put through rigorous functional tests and customer tests before they enter the marketplace. *Alpha testing* is testing the product within the firm to see how it performs in different applications. After refining the prototype further, the company moves to *beta testing* with customers.[45] Consumer testing can take several forms, from bringing consumers into a laboratory to giving them samples to use in their homes. Procter & Gamble has on-site labs such as a nappy-testing centre where dozens of mothers bring their babies to be studied. In-home placement tests are common for products ranging from ice cream flavours to new appliances.

How are customer preferences measured? The *rank-order* method asks the consumer to rank the options. The *paired-comparison* method presents pairs of options and asks the consumer which one is preferred in each pair. The *monadic-rating* method asks the consumer to rate each product on a scale so marketers can derive the individual's preference order and levels.

Market testing

After management is satisfied with functional and psychological performance, the new product is ready to be dressed up with a brand name and packaging and put into a market test. In an authentic setting, marketers can learn how large the market is and how consumers and dealers react to handling, using and repurchasing the product.

Not all companies undertake market testing. Many companies, however, believe market testing can yield valuable information about buyers, dealers, marketing programme effectiveness, and market potential. The main issues are: how much market testing should be done, and what kind(s)?

The amount of market testing is influenced by the investment cost and risk on the one hand, and the time pressure and research cost on the other. High-investment–high-risk products, where the chance of failure is high, must be market tested; the cost of the market tests will be an insignificant percentage of total project cost. High-risk products – those that create new product categories (first instant breakfast drink) or have novel features (first gum-strengthening toothpaste) – warrant more market testing than modified products (another toothpaste brand).

The amount of market testing may be severely reduced if the company is under great time pressure because the season is just starting, or because competitors are about to launch their brands. The company may prefer the risk of a product failure to the risk of losing distribution or market penetration on a highly successful product.

Consumer goods market testing

Consumer products tests seek to estimate four variables: *trial*, *first repeat*, *adoption* and *purchase frequency*. The company hopes to find all these variables at high levels. Many consumers may try the product but few rebuy it; or it might achieve high permanent adoption but low purchase frequency (e.g., gourmet frozen foods).

Here are four major methods of consumer goods market testing, from least to most costly.

1 Sales-wave research In *sales-wave research* consumers who initially try the product at no cost are reoffered it, or a competitor's product, at slightly reduced prices. The offer may be made as many as five times (sales waves), while the company notes how many customers selected that product again and their reported level of satisfaction. Sales-wave research can also expose consumers to one or more advertising concepts to measure the impact of that advertising on repeat purchase.

Sales-wave research can be implemented quickly and conducted with a fair amount of security. It can be carried out without final packaging and advertising. However, it does not indicate trial rates the product would achieve with different sales promotion incentives as the consumers are pre-selected to try the product. Nor does it indicate the brand's power to gain distribution and favourable shelf position.

2 Simulated test marketing Simulated test marketing calls for finding 30–40 qualified shoppers and questioning them about brand familiarity and preferences in a specific product category. These consumers attend a brief screening of both well-known and new TV commercials or print advertisements. One advertisement promotes the new product but is not singled out for attention. Consumers receive a small amount of money and are invited into a store where they may buy any items. The company notes how many consumers buy the new brand and competing brands. This provides a measure of the advertisement's relative effectiveness against competing advertisements in stimulating customer trials. Consumers are asked the reasons for their purchases or non-purchases. Those who did not buy the new brand are given a free sample. Some weeks later, they are interviewed by phone to determine product attitudes, usage, satisfaction and repurchase intention and are offered an opportunity to repurchase any products.

This method gives fairly accurate results on advertising effectiveness and trial rates (and repeat rates if extended) in a much shorter time and at a fraction of the cost of using real test markets. The results are incorporated into new product forecasting models to project ultimate sales levels. Marketing research firms have reported surprisingly accurate predictions of sales levels of products that are subsequently launched in the market.[46] In a world where media and channels have become highly fragmented, however, it will become increasingly harder for simulated test marketing to truly simulate market conditions with only traditional approaches.

3 Controlled test marketing In controlled test marketing, a research firm manages a panel of stores that will carry new products for a fee. The company with the new product specifies the number of stores and geographic locations it wants to test. The research firm delivers the product to the participating stores and controls shelf position; number of facings, displays and point-of-purchase promotions; and pricing. Electronic scanners measure sales at checkout. The company can also evaluate the impact of local advertising and promotions.

Controlled test marketing allows the company to test the impact of in-store factors and limited advertising on buying behaviour. A sample of consumers can be interviewed later to give their impressions of the product. The company does not have to use its own sales force, give trade allowances or 'buy' distribution. However, controlled test marketing provides no information on how to persuade the trade to carry the new product. This technique also exposes the product and its features to competitors' scrutiny.

4 Test markets The ultimate way to test a new consumer product is to put it into full-scale test markets. The company chooses a few representative cities, and the sales force tries to persuade the trade to carry the product and give it good shelf exposure. The company puts on a full advertising and promotion campaign similar to the one it would use in national marketing. Test marketing also measures the impact of alternative marketing plans by varying the marketing programme in different cities: a full-scale test can cost over €1 million, depending on the number of test cities, the test duration, and the amount of data the company wants to collect.

Management faces several decisions:

1 **How many test cities?** Most tests use two to six cities. The greater the possible loss, the greater the number of contending marketing strategies, the greater the regional differences, and the greater the chance of test-market interference by competitors, the more cities management should test.

2 **Which cities?** Each company must develop selection criteria such as having good media coverage, cooperative chain stores and average competitive activity. How representative the city is of other markets must also be considered.

3 **Length of test?** Market tests last anywhere from a few months to a year. The longer the average repurchase period, the longer the test period.

4 **What information to collect?** Warehouse shipment data will show gross stock buying but will not indicate weekly sales at the retail level. Store audits will show retail sales and competitors' market shares but will not reveal buyer characteristics. Consumer panels will indicate which people are buying which brands and their loyalty and switching rates. Buyer surveys will yield in-depth information about consumer attitudes, usage and satisfaction.

5 **What action to take?** If the test markets show high trial and repurchase rates, the marketer should launch the product nationally; if a high trial rate and low repurchase rate, redesign or drop the product; if a low trial rate and high repurchase rate, develop marketing communications to convince more people to try it. If trial and re purchase rates are both low, abandon the product. Many managers find it difficult to kill a project that created much effort and attention even if they should, resulting in an unfortunate (and typically unsuccessful) escalation of commitment.[47]

In spite of its benefits, many companies today do not do any test marketing and rely on faster and more economical testing methods. Absolut vodka and Colgate-Palmolive often launch a new product in a set of small 'lead countries' and keep rolling it out if it proves successful.

Business-goods market testing

Business goods can also benefit from market testing. Expensive industrial goods and new technologies will normally undergo alpha testing (within the company) and beta testing (with outside customers). During beta testing, the company's technical people observe how test customers use the product, a practice that often exposes unanticipated problems of safety and servicing and alerts the company to customer training and servicing requirements. The company can also observe how much value the equipment adds to the customer's operation as a clue to subsequent pricing.

The company will ask test customers to express their purchase intention and other reactions after the test. Companies must interpret beta test results carefully, because only a small number of test customers are used, they are not randomly drawn, and tests are somewhat customised to each site. Another risk is that test customers who are unimpressed with the product may leak unfavourable reports about it.

A second common test method for business goods is to introduce the new product at trade shows. The company can observe how much interest buyers show in the new product, how they react to various features and terms, and how many express purchase intentions or place orders.

New industrial products can be tested in distributor and dealer display rooms, where they may stand next to the manufacturer's other products and possibly competitors' products. This method yields preference and pricing information in the product's normal selling atmosphere. The disadvantages are that the customers might want to place early orders that cannot be filled, and those customers who come in might not represent the target market.

Industrial manufacturers come close to using full test marketing when they give a limited supply of the product to the sales force to sell in a limited number of areas that receive promotion support and printed catalogue sheets.

Commercialisation and new product launch

If the company goes ahead with commercialisation, it will face its largest costs to date.[48] It will need to contract for manufacture or build or rent a full-scale manufacturing facility. Another major cost is marketing. To introduce a major new consumer packaged good into the national market can cost from €25 million to as much as €100 million in advertising, promotion and other communications in the first year. In the introduction of new food products, marketing expenditures typically represent 57 per cent of sales during the first year. Most new product campaigns rely on a sequenced mix of marketing communication tools.

When (timing)

In commercialising a new product, market-entry timing is critical. Suppose a company has almost completed the development work on its new product and learns that a competitor is nearing the end of *its* development work. The company faces three choices:

1 **First entry**: The first firm entering a market usually enjoys the 'first mover advantages' of locking up key distributors and customers and gaining leadership. But if the product is rushed to market before it is ready, the first entry can backfire.

2 **Parallel entry**: The firm might time its entry to coincide with the competitor's entry. The market may pay more attention when two companies are advertising the new product.[49]

3 **Late entry**: The firm might delay its launch until after the competitor has entered. The competitor will have borne the cost of educating the market, and its product may reveal faults the late entrant can avoid. The late entrant can also learn the size of the market.

The timing decision requires additional considerations.[50] If a new product replaces an older product, the company might delay the introduction until the old product's stock is drawn down. If the product is seasonal, it might be delayed until the right season arrives; often a product waits for a 'killer application' to occur. Complicating new product launches, many companies are encountering competitive 'design-arounds' – rivals are imitating inventions but making their own versions just different enough to avoid patent infringement and the need to pay royalties.

Where (geographic strategy)

The company must decide whether to launch the new product in a single locality, a region, several regions, the national market or the international market. Most will develop a planned market roll-out over time. Company size is an important factor here. Small companies will select an attractive city and put on a blitz campaign, entering other cities one at a time. Large companies will introduce their product into a whole region and then move to the next region. Companies with national distribution networks, such as car companies, will launch their new models in the national market.

Most companies design new products to sell primarily in the domestic market. If the product does well, the company considers exporting to neighbouring countries or the world market, redesigning if necessary. In choosing roll-out markets, the major criteria are market potential, the company's local reputation, the cost of filling the pipeline, the cost of communication media, the influence of the area on other areas and the strength of competition.

With the Web connecting far-flung parts of the globe, competition is more likely to cross national borders. Companies are increasingly rolling out new products simultaneously across the globe, rather than nationally or even regionally. However, masterminding a global launch poses challenges, and a sequential roll-out across countries may still be the best option.[51]

To whom (target-market prospects)

Within the roll-out markets, the company must adopt a customer relationship approach and target its initial distribution and promotion to the best prospect groups. The company will have profiled these, and ideally they should be early adopters, heavy users and opinion leaders who can be reached at low cost.[52] Few groups have all these characteristics. The company should rate the various prospect groups on these characteristics and target the best group. The aim is to generate strong sales as soon as possible to attract further prospects.

How (introductory market strategy)

The company must develop an action plan for introducing the new product. Because new product launches often take longer and cost more money than expected, many potentially successful offerings suffer from under funding. It is important to allocate sufficient time and resource as the new product gains a foothold in the marketplace.[53]

A master of new product introductions, Apple Computer staged a massive marketing blitz in 1998 to launch the iMac, its re-entry into the computer PC business after a hiatus of 14 years. Five years later, Apple struck gold again with the launch of the iPod.

Breakthrough marketing

Apple iPod

In a few short years, the iPod MP3 music player has truly become a cultural phenomenon. Few people are without one. The iPod exemplified Apple's innovative design skills and looked, felt and operated like no other. The launch of iTunes Music Store, a dynamic duo of legally downloadable music and a cutting-edge portable music player, caused iPod sales to skyrocket. To the delight of Apple (and the chagrin of competitor Sony), the iPod has become 'the Walkman of the 21st century'.

Beyond spurring sales, the iPod has been central in changing the way people listen to and use music. The shuffle feature of iPods helped people make connections between different genres of music. Podcasting enables users to replace radio broadcasts and listen to DJ sets without commercial interruption. The new video, photo and phone features have the potential to change how people interact with those media as well.

Apple reached this impressive state of market domination through a combination of shrewd product innovation and clever marketing. It defined a broad access point for its target market – music lovers who wanted *their* music, whenever and wherever. The marketing effort was designed to appeal to Mac fans as well as people who had not used Apple products in the past. This broader access required a shift in Apple's

channel strategies. Adding 'mass electronic' retailers to Apple's existing channels and company stores resulted in an increase of outlets from 4000 to 21,000.

Besides this enhanced 'push' effort, Apple also developed memorable, creative 'pull' advertising that helped drive the popularity of the iPod. The Silhouettes campaign ran all over the world with a message simple enough to work across cultures, portraying the iPod as cool, but not so cool as to be beyond the reach of anyone who enjoyed music. Television commercials featured people in silhouette listening to iPods and dancing in front of neon backgrounds. Similar images populated print ads, billboards and posters. Advertising text such as 'iPod. Welcome to the digital music revolution. 10,000 songs in your pocket, Mac or PC' told the story of iPod's capabilities in a simple, appealing way.

Apple's campaign also flooded a handful of big cities such as San Francisco and Shanghai with iPod billboards, bus posters, print ads and TV commercials that were intended to spread the message 'iPod is everywhere'. The brand enjoyed exceedingly strong PR, buzz and word of mouth. Apple has continually updated the iPod and released new versions, spawning an 'iPod economy' of third-party accessories and add-ons. Even though some analysts thought sales might slow, consumers have continued to snap up the music players. By April 2007 more than 100 million iPods had been

▶ Breakthrough marketing *(continued)*

The campaign for the Apple iPod was a masterful new product introduction that helped the product quickly achieve a dominant market share.

Source: Justin Sullivan/Getty Images

sold worldwide and the iPod contributed one-third of Apple's corporate revenue. A halo effect from iPod was thought to help explain Apple's increase in market share in retail computers of more than three percentage points in recent years. With a wave of positive buzz and a promising sales start in the summer of 2007, Apple hoped to repeat the success of the iPod with its launch of the iPhone.

Sources: T. Yue Jones (2006) How long can the iPod stay on top? *Los Angeles Times*, 5 March; B. Snyder Bulik (2005) Grab an Apple and a bag of chips, *Advertising Age*, 23 May; J. Parsons (2005) A is for Apple on iPod, *Dallas Morning News*, 6 October; P. Burrows (2004) Rock on, iPod, *BusinessWeek*, 7 June, pp. 130–1; J. Lyman (2004) Mini iPod moving quickly, Apple says, *TechNewsWorld*, 26 February; S. Levy (2004) iPod nation, *Newsweek*, 25 July; www.apple.com; www.effie.org; Apple computer: iPod silhouettes, New York Marketing Association.

Apple continues to set a fast pace and in the summer of 2008 launched their iPhone 2 which is a design leader as well as a technological first that can provide entertainment and business-related features at half the cost of iPhone 1. In the United Kingdom it had a launch price of £100, a saving of 50 per cent on iPhone 1.

To coordinate the many activities involved in launching a new product, management can use network-planning techniques such as **critical path scheduling**. This calls for developing a master chart showing the simultaneous and sequential activities that must take place to launch the product. By estimating how much time each activity takes, the planners estimate completion time for the entire project. Any delay in any activity on the critical path – the shortest route to completion – will cause the project to become overdue.[54]

▽ The consumer adoption process

Adoption is an individual's decision to become a regular user of a product. The *consumer adoption process* is followed by the *consumer loyalty process*, which is the concern of the established producer. Years ago, new product marketers used a *mass market approach* to launch products, which had two main drawbacks: It called for heavy marketing expenditures, and it wasted many exposures. These drawbacks led to a second approach, *heavy-user target marketing*. This approach makes sense, provided that heavy users are identifiable and are early adopters. However, even within the heavy-user group, many heavy users are loyal to existing brands. New product marketers now aim at early adopters and use the theory of innovation diffusion and customer adoption to identify them. Mozilla launched its new Firefox 3 Web browser in the United Kingdom in the summer of 2008 and hopes to build on its encouraging market share in Europe with its new software that is claimed to be more user friendly and adaptable than Microsoft's Internet Explorer's Web browser.

Stages in the adoption process

An **innovation** is any good, service or idea that someone *perceives* as new, no matter how long its history. Innovations take time to spread. Rogers defines the **innovation diffusion process** as 'the spread of a new idea from its source of invention or creation to its ultimate users or adopters'.[55] The consumer adoption process tracks the steps an individual takes from first hearing about an innovation to its final adoption.[56]

Adopters of new products move through five stages:

1 **Awareness**: The consumer becomes aware of the innovation but lacks information about it.

2 **Interest**: The consumer is stimulated to seek information about the innovation.

3 **Evaluation**: The consumer considers whether to try the innovation.

4 **Trial**: The consumer tries the innovation to improve his or her estimate of its value.

5 **Adoption**: The consumer decides to make full and regular use of the innovation.

The new product marketer should facilitate movement through these stages. A portable electric-dishwasher manufacturer might discover that many customers are stuck in the interest stage; they do not buy because of their uncertainty and the large investment cost.[57] But these same customers would be willing to use an electric dishwasher on a trial basis for a small monthly fee. The manufacturer should consider offering a trial-use plan with an option to buy.

Factors influencing the adoption process

Marketers recognise the following characteristics of the adoption process: differences in individual readiness to try new products; the effect of personal influence; differing rates of adoption; and differences in organisations' readiness to try new products. Some researchers are focusing on use-diffusion processes as a complement to adoption process models, to see how consumers actually use new products.[58]

Readiness to try new products and personal influence

Rogers[59] defines a person's level of innovativeness as 'the degree to which an individual is relatively earlier in adopting new ideas than the other members of his social system'. In each product area, there are pioneers and early adopters. Some people are the first to adopt new clothing fashions or new appliances; some doctors are the first to prescribe new medicines; some farmers

Time of adoption of innovations

are the first to adopt new farming methods.[60] People fall into the adopter categories shown in Figure 15.7. After a slow start, an increasing number of people adopt the innovation, the number reaches a peak, and then it diminishes as fewer non-adopters remain. The five adopter groups differ in their value orientations and their motives for adopting or resisting the new product.[61]

- **Innovators**: technology enthusiasts; they are venturesome and enjoy tinkering with new products and mastering their intricacies. In return for low prices, they are happy to conduct alpha and beta testing and report on early weaknesses.
- **Early adopters**: opinion leaders who carefully search for new technologies that might give them a dramatic competitive advantage. They are less price sensitive and willing to adopt the product if given personalised solutions and good service support.
- **Early majority**: deliberate pragmatists who adopt the new technology when its benefits are proven and a lot of adoption has already taken place. They make up the mainstream market.
- **Late majority**: sceptical conservatives who are risk averse, technology shy and price sensitive.
- **Laggards**: tradition bound and resist the innovation until they find that the status quo is no longer defensible.

Each group must be approached with a different type of marketing if the firm wants to move its innovation through the stages of the full product life cycle.[62]

Personal influence is the effect one person has on another's attitude or purchase probability. Its significance is greater in some situations and for some individuals than others, and it is more important in the evaluation stage than the other stages. It has more influence on late adopters than early adopters and is more important in risky situations.

Companies often target innovators and early adopters with product introductions. For Vespa scooters, the Italian company Piaggio has hired models to go around cafés and clubs to publicise the new scooters.[63]

Characteristics of the innovation

Some products are an instant success (rollerblades), whereas others take a long time to gain acceptance (diesel engine cars).[64] Five characteristics influence the rate of adoption of an innovation. These are considered in relation to personal video recorders (PVRs) for home use.

The first characteristic is *relative advantage* – the degree to which the innovation appears superior to existing products. The greater the perceived relative advantage of using a PVR, say for easily recording favourite shows, pausing live TV or skipping commercials, the more quickly it will be adopted. The second is *compatibility* – the degree to which the innovation matches the values and experiences of the individuals. PVRs, for example, are highly compatible with the preferences of avid television watchers. Third is *complexity* – the degree to which the innovation is difficult to understand or use. PVRs are somewhat complex and will therefore take a slightly longer time to penetrate into home use. Fourth is *divisibility* – the degree to which the innovation can be tried on a limited basis. This provides a sizeable challenge for PVRs – sampling can only occur in a retail store or perhaps a friend's house. Fifth is *communicability* – the degree to which the benefits of use are observable or describable to others. The fact that PVRs have some clear advantages can help create interest and curiosity.

Other characteristics that influence the rate of adoption include cost, risk and uncertainty; scientific credibility and social approval. The new product marketer must research all these factors and give the key ones maximum attention in designing the new product and marketing programme.

Organisations' readiness to adopt innovations

The creator of a new teaching method would want to identify innovative schools. The producer of a new piece of medical equipment would want to identify innovative hospitals. Adoption is associated with variables in the organisation's environment (community progressiveness, community income), the organisation itself (size, profits, pressure to change) and the administrators (education level, age, sophistication). Other forces come into play in trying to get a product adopted into organisations that receive the bulk of their funding from the government, such as state schools and hospitals in the United Kingdom. A controversial or innovative new product offering can be seriously damaged by negative public opinion.

▽ SUMMARY

1 Once a company has segmented the market, chosen its target customer groups and identified their needs, and determined its desired market positioning, it is ready to develop and launch appropriate new market offerings. Marketing should participate with other departments in every stage of the development of new value offerings.

2 Successful new product/market offering development requires the company to establish an effective organisation for managing the process. Traditionally companies have chosen to use product managers, new product managers, new product committees, new product departments or new product venture teams. Increasingly companies are adopting cross-functional teams, connecting to individuals and organisations outside the company, and developing multiple market offerings as they accept that the right CPV requires the coordinated effort of all internal and external parties.

3 Eight stages take place in the new product/market offering development process: idea generation, screening, concept development and testing, marketing strategy development, business analysis, product/offer development, market testing and commercialisation. At each stage, the company must determine whether the idea should be dropped or moved to the next stage.

4 The consumer adoption process is the process by which customers learn about new market offerings, try them, and adopt or reject them. Today many marketers are targeting heavy users and early adopters of new products, because both groups can be reached by specific media and tend to be opinion leaders. The consumer adoption process is influenced by many factors beyond the marketer's control, including consumers' and organisations' willingness to try new market offerings.

▽ APPLICATIONS

Marketing debate

Whom should you target with new products? Some new products experts maintain that getting close to customers through intensive research is the only way to develop successful new products. Other experts disagree and maintain that customers can't possibly provide useful feedback on what they don't know and can't provide insights that will lead to breakthrough products.

Take a position: Consumer research is critical to new product development *versus* Consumer research may not be all that helpful in new product development.

Marketing discussion

Think about the last new product you bought. How do you think its success will be affected by the five characteristics of an innovation: relative advantage, compatibility, complexity, divisibility and communicability?

▽ REFERENCES

[1]James Dyson (2002) Business whirl wind, *BBC Business News*, 5 February; P. Marsh (2006) Dyson keeps its wash day hopes alive, *Financial Times*, 27 June.

[2]Sir James Dyson and family (2008) *The Sunday Times* online, 27 April.

[3]For some scholarly reviews, see P. Drucker (2001) *The Essential Drucker*, Oxford: Butterworth-Heinemann; E. Dahan and J. R. Hauser (2002) Product development: managing a dispersed process, in B. Weitz and R. Wensley (eds) *Handbook of Marketing*, London: Sage, 179–222; D. Jain (2001) Managing new-product development for strategic competitive advantage, in D. Iacobucci (ed.), *Kellogg on Marketing*, New York; John Wiley & Sons, Ch. 6, 130–48.

[4]P. Cameron (2007) Innovation and new product development: Sky+ – a mini case study, *Marketing Review*, 7(4), 313–23; S. J. Carson (2007) What to give up control of outsourced new product development, *Journal of Marketing*, January, 71(1), 49–66.

[5]Don't laugh at gilded butterflies, *The Economist*, 24 April 2004, 71. For some academic discussion of the effects of new product introduction on markets, see H.J. Van Heerde, C. F. Mela and P. Manchanda (2004) The dynamic effect of innovation on market structure, *Journal of Marketing Research*, 41 (May), 166–83.

[6]S. Min, M. U. Kalwani and W. T. Robinson (2006) Market pioneer and early follower survival risks: a contingency of new versus incrementally new-product markets, *Journal of Marketing*, 70 (January), 15–33; C. P. Moreau, A. B. Markman and D. R. Lehmann (2001) What is it? Category flexibility and consumers' response to really new products, *Journal of Consumer Research*, 27 (March), 489–98.

[7]S. Wuyts, S. Dutta and S. Stremersch (2004) Portfolios of interfirm agreements in technology-intensive markets: consequences for innovation and profitability, *Journal of Marketing*, 68 (April), 88–100; A. Rindfleisch and C. Moorman (2001) The acquisition and utilization of information in new product alliance: a strength-of-ties perspective, *Journal of Marketing*, 65 (April), 1–18.

[8]S. Hoeffler (2003) Measuring preferences for really new products, *Journal of Marketing Research*, 40 (November), 406–20; P. Lych and T. O'Toole (2006) Involving external users and third parties in the new product development process, *Irish Marketing Review*, 18 (1/2), 29–37.

[9]A. Sood and G. J. Tellis (2005) Technological evolution and radical innovation, *Journal of Marketing*, 69 (July), 152–68.

[10]For more discussion see J. Mohr (2005) *Marketing of High-technology Products and Innovations*, 2nd edn, Upper Saddle River, NJ: Prentice Hall.

[11]S. Hamm (2006) Speed demons, *BusinessWeek*, 27 March, 69–76.

[12]C. Passariello (2006) Brand new bag: Louis Vuitton tries modern methods on factory lines, *Wall Street Journal*, 9 October.

[13]The world's fifty most innovative companies (2007) Special Report, *BusinessWeek*, 9 May.

[14]B. Weiners (2004) Gore-Tex tackles the great indoors, *Business 2.0*, April, 32; A. Harrington (2003) Who's afraid of a new product?, *Fortune*, 10 November, 189–92; W.L. Gore & Associates, *The Times* online, 11 March.

[15]R. Varadarajan (2007) Business insight (a Special Report); Think small: every company wants to hit it big with market-shattering innovations, but the little changes can make a huge difference, *Wall Street Journal*, 2 March.

[16]C. M. Christensen (1977) *The Innovator's Dilemma: When New Technologies Cause Great Firms to Fail*, Boston, MA: Harvard University Press.

[17]Dahan and Hauser (2002) op. cit.

[18]R. G. Cooper and E. Kleinschmidt (1990) *New Products: The Key Factors in Success*, Chicago, IL: American Marketing Association.

[19]S. Ogama and F.T. Pillar (2006) Reducing the risks of new-product development, *MIT Sloan Management Review*, Winter, 65–71; S. Muller (1991) *Die Psyche des Managers als Determinante des Exporterfolges : Eine kulturvergleichende Studie zur Ausland-sorientierung von Managern aus 6 Landen*, Stuttgart: M&P Verlag.

[20]T. N. Burton (2004) By learning from failures Lilly keeps drug pipelines full, *Wall Street Journal*, 21 April.

[21]N. Byrnes (2007) Xerox's new design team customers, *BusinessWeek*, 7 May, 71.

[22]D. Sabbagh (2008) Blu-ray delivers fatal sting to rival in battle of high definition DVD, *The Times*, 19 February.

[23]B. S. Blichfeldt (2005) On the development of brand and line extensions, *Journal of Brand Management*, 12(3), 177–90.

[24]D. Sacks, C. Salter, A. Deutschmann and S. Kirsner (2007) Innovation Scouts, *Fast Company*, May, 90.

[25]R. Sethi, D. C. Smith and C. W. Park (2001) Cross-functional product development team, creativity, and the innovativeness of new consumer products, *Journal of Marketing Research*, 38 (February), 73–85.

[26]R. G. Cooper (1990) Stage-gate systems: a new tool for managing new products, *Business Horizons*, May–June, 44–54.

[27]R. G. Cooper (1998) *Product Leadership: Creating and Launching Superior New Products*, New York: Perseus Books.

[28]An alternative approach to the funnel process advocates 'rocketing'. See D. Nichols, *Return on Ideas*, Chichester: John Wiley & Sons.

[29]J. Hauser, G. J. Tellis and A. Griffin (2006) Research on innovation: a review and agenda for Marketing Science, *Marketing Science*, 25, November–December, 687–717.

[30]H. Chesbrough (2006) *Open Business Models: How to Thrive in the New Innovation Landscape*, Boston, MA: Harvard University Press; E. Von Hipple (2005) *Democratizing Innovation*, Cambridge, MA: MIT Press; B. Helm (2005) Inside a white-hot idea factory, *BusinessWeek*, 15 January, 72–1; C. K. Prahalad and V. Ramaswamy (2004) *The Future of Competition*: Co-Creating Unique Value with Customers, Boston, MA: Harvard University Press.

[31]A. J. Griffin and J. Hauser (1993) The voice of the customer, *Marketing Science*, Winter, 1–27.

[32]P. C. Hoenbein and R. F. Cammarano (2006) Customers at work, *Marketing Management*, January–February, 26–31.

[33]P. Seybold (2007) Customer-controlled innovation: collaboration with customers is transforming product-development strategies and unlocking new ways for companies to innovate, *Optimize*, 6(2), 26.

[34]*BusinessWeek* (2007) op. cit.

[35]D. W. Dahl and P. Moreau (2002) The influence and value of analogical thinking during new-product ideation, *Journal of Marketing Research*, 39 (February), 47–60; M. Goodman (1995) *Creative Management*, Hemel Hempstead: Prentice Hall International.

[36]See www.smokinggun.com.

[37]O. Toubia and L. Flores (2007) Adaptive idea screening using consumers, *Marketing Science*, 26 (May–June), 342–60.

[38]S. Hoeffler (2003) op. cit.; Dahl and Moreau (2002) op. cit.; J. Sharan, J. Kamel and M. Jamil (2007) A multibrand concept-testing methodology for new product strategy, *Journal of Product Management*, 24(1), 34–51.

[39]For additional information see D. Bakken and C. L. Frazier (2006) Conjoint analysis: understanding consumer decision making, in R. Grover and M. Vriens (eds) *The Handbook of Marketing Research*, Thousand Oaks, CA: Sage; V. T. Rao and J. R. Hauser (2004) Conjoint analysis, related modeling and application, in Y. Wind and P. E. Green (eds) *Market Research and Modeling: Progress and Prospects – A Tribute to Paul Green*, New York: Springer, 141–68.

[40]P. N. Golder and G. J. Tellis (1997) Will it ever fly? Modeling the takeoff of really new durables, *Marketing Science*, 16(3), 256–70.

[41]The present value (V) of a future sum (I) to be received t years from today and discounted at the interest rate (r) is given by $V = I_t/(1 + r)^t$. Thus €4,716,000/(1.15)^5 = €2,345,000.

[42]See L. R. Guinta and N. C. Praizler (1993) *The QFD Book: The Team Approach to Solving Problems and Satisfying Customers Through Quality Function Deployment*, New York: AMACOM.

[43]T. Peters (1997) *The Circle of Innovation*, New York: Alfred A Knopf; K. Zheng Zhou, Y. Chi Kin and D. K. Tse (2005) The effects of strategic orientations on technology and market-based breakthrough innovations, *Journal of Marketing*, 2, 42–60.

[44]M. Iansiti and A. MacCormack (1997) Developing products on Internet time, *Harvard Business Review*, September–October. 108–17.

[45]T. Peters (1997) op. cit., 96.

[46]K. J. Clancy, P. C. Krieg and M. M. Wolf (2005) *Marketing New Products Successfully: Using Simulated Test Marketing Methodology*, New York: Lexington Books.

[47]E. Biyalogorski, W. Boulding and R. Staelin (2006) Stuck in the past: why managers persist with new-product failures, *Journal of Marketing*, 70 (April), 108–21.

[48]R. Chandy, B. Hopstaken, O. Narasimhan and J. Prabhu (2006) From invention to innovation: conversion in product development, *Journal of Marketing Research*, 43 (August), 404–508.

[49]R. Prins and P. C. Verhoef (2007) Marketing communication drivers of adoption timing of a new e-service among existing customers, *Journal of Marketing*, 71 (April), 169–83.

[50]For further discussion see Y. Wu, S. Balasubramanian and V. Mahajan (2004) When is a pre-announced new product likely to be delayed?, *Journal of Marketing*, 68 (April), 104–13; R. Srinivasan, G. L. Lilien and A. Rangaswamy (2004) First in first out? The effects of network externalities on pioneer survival, *Journal of Marketing*, 68 (January), 41–58; B. L. Bayus, S. Jain and A. Rao (2001) Consequences: an analysis of truth or vaporware and new-product announcements, *Journal of Marketing Research*, February, 3–13.

[51]K. Gielens and J.-B. E.M. Steenkamp (2007) Drivers of consumer acceptance of new packaged goods: an investigation across products and countries, *International Journal of Research in Marketing*, 97–111.

[52]P. Kotler and G. Zaltman (1976) Targeting prospects for a new product, *Journal of Advertising Research*, February, 7–20; E. Gummesson (1998) Implementation requires a relationship marketing paradigm, *Journal of the Academy of Marketing Science*, 26(3), 242–9.

[53]M. Leslie and C. A. Holloway (2006) The sales learning curve, *Harvard Business Review*, July–August, 114–23.

[54]For details see K. G. Lockyer (1984) *Critical Path Analysis and Other Project Network Techniques*, London: Pitman. Also see A. Rangasway and G. L. Lilien (1997) Software tools for new-product development, *Journal of Marketing Research*, February, 177–84.

[55]The following discussion is based on E. M. Rogers (1962) *Diffusion of Innovations*, New York: Free Press. Also see the 3rd edn published in 1973.

[56]C. P. Moreau, D. R. Lehmann and A. B. Markman (2001) Entrenched knowledge structures and consumer response to new products, *Journal of Marketing Research*, 38 (February), 14–29.

[57]J. T. Gourville (2006) Eager sellers and stony buyers, *Harvard Business Review*, June, 99–106.

[58]C.-F. Shih and A. Ventkatesh (2004) Beyond adoption: development and application of a use-diffusion model, *Journal of Marketing*, 68 (January), 59–72.

[59]E. M. Rogers (1962) *Diffusion of Innovations*, New York: The Free Press, 1962; see also his 3rd edn published in 1983.

[60]M. Hertzenstein, S. S. Posavac and J. J. Brakuz (2007) Adoption of new and really new products: the effects of self regulation systems and risk salience, *Journal of Marketing Research*, 44 (May), 251–60; C. Van den Bulte and Y. V. Joshi (2007) New-product diffusion with influentials and imitators, *Marketing Science*, 26, May–June, 400–21; S. Hoeffler (2003) op. cit.

[61]Rogers (1962) op. cit. 192; G. A. Moore (1999) *Crossing the Chasm: Marketing and Selling High-tech Products to Mainstream Customers*, New York: HarperBusiness.

[62]A. Parasuraman and C. L. Colby (2001) *Techno-ready Marketing*, New York: Free Press; Mohr (2001) op. cit.

[63]M. M. Hall, Selling by stealth, *Business Life*, November, 51–55.

[64]B. Kamrad, S. S. Lele, A. Siddique and R. J. Thomas (2005) Innovation diffusion uncertainty, advertising and pricing policies, *European Journal of Operational Research*, 164(3), 829–50; G. B. Voss, M. Montoya-Weiss and Z. G. Voss (2006) Aligning innovation with market characteristics in the non-profit professional theatre industry, *Journal of Marketing Research*, 43(2), 296–302; M. J. Brand and E. K. R. E. Hurzingh (2008) Into the drivers of innovation adoption: What is the impact of the current level of adoption?, *European Journal of Innovation Management*, 11(1), 5–21; A. Murray and D. Demick (2006) Wine retailing in Ireland: the diffusion of innovation, *International Journal of Wine Marketing*, 18(3); G. Yaleinkaya (2008) A culture-based approach to understanding the adoption and diffusion of new products across countries, *International Marketing Review*, 25(2), 202–14.

Chapter 16

▽ Developing and managing pricing strategies

IN THIS CHAPTER, WE WILL ADDRESS THE FOLLOWING QUESTIONS:

1 How do consumers process and evaluate prices?
2 How should a company initially set prices for products or services?
3 How should a company adapt prices to meet varying circumstances and opportunities?
4 When should a company initiate a price change?
5 How should a company respond to a competitor's price change?

Price is the one element of the marketing mix that produces revenue; the other elements produce costs. Prices are perhaps the easiest element of the marketing programme to adjust; product features, channels, and even promotion take more time. Price also communicates to the market the company's intended value positioning of its product or brand. A price may even cause intensive public debate.

Consider Tesco.

Tesco's low-priced chickens have caused intensive public debate.
Source: Marco Secchi/Rex Features

Understanding pricing

Setting the price

Adapting the price

Initiating and responding to price changes

W hat is the price of a chicken? Even though it was warned that it would make it harder to improve the welfare of factory-farmed animals, British supermarket chain Tesco decided to reduce the price of a whole chicken to £1.99 (€2.50) in early 2008. Tesco said that it aimed to help families on tight budgets, adding that at the same time it had doubled its order for higher-welfare chicken. Weeks of publicity and debate followed the price cut with the animal welfare group, Compassion in World Farming (CIWF), saying that the arrival of a £1.99 bird was 'depressing'. However, according to Tesco the price reduction should be seen as a part of the supermarket chain's strategy of offering customers a variety of choices and good value. Jonathan Church, Tesco's spokesman, said:

> We have been working hard for a while to increase the amount of higher-welfare chicken we sell and the recent debate in the media about chickens has helped raise awareness of the choice available. But our investment in premium chicken should not be seen as a move away from providing more affordable options. No one should feel guilty for buying a chicken just because it is good value. The only reduction we make is in the price, not the welfare.[1]

The Tesco example reveals the power of pricing. Pricing decisions are clearly complex and difficult, however, and many marketers neglect their pricing strategies[2] and the effect they might have on the market and on the public. Holistic marketers must take into account many factors in making pricing decisions – the company, the customers, the competition and the marketing environment. Pricing decisions must be consistent with the firm's marketing strategy and its target markets and brand positionings.

In this chapter, we provide concepts and tools to facilitate the setting of initial prices and adjusting prices over time and markets.

▽ Understanding pricing

Price is not just a number on a tag. Price comes in many forms and performs many functions. Rent, tuition, fares, fees, rates, tolls, wages and commissions all may in some way be the price you pay for some good or service. Price is also made up of many components. If you buy a new car, the sticker price may be adjusted by rebates and dealer incentives. Some firms allow for payment through multiple forms, such as €120 plus 25,000 frequent flier miles from an airline loyalty programme.[3]

Throughout most of history, prices were set by negotiation between buyers and sellers. Bargaining is still a sport in some areas and countries. Setting one price for all buyers is a relatively modern idea that arose with the development of large-scale retailing in the second half of the nineteenth century. European department stores such as Le Bon Marche (France), Delaney's New Mart (Ireland), Whiteleys (England), and others introduced fixed-price policies (accompanied by guarantees allowing exchanges and refunds), because they carried so many items and supervised so many employees.

Traditionally, price has operated as one of the major determinants of buyer choice. Consumers and purchasing agents have more access to price information and price discounters. Consumers and competition put pressure on retailers to lower their prices. Retailers put pressure on manufacturers to lower their prices. The result is a marketplace characterised by heavy discounting and sales promotion.

A changing pricing environment

Pricing practices have changed significantly in recent years. Many firms are bucking the low-price trend and have been successful in trading consumers up to more expensive products and services by combining unique product formulations with engaging marketing campaigns. Even products in fiercely competitive supermarket categories have been able to enjoy price hikes for the right new offerings. Examples include DeWitt, which markets Clinomyn toothpaste for smokers at a 50 per cent premium over other premium toothpastes, and L'Oréal Paris's skin care line Derma Genesis, which is usually priced around 30 per cent higher than other premium supermarket skin care brands (rivalling the lower end of department store brands). Also, Unilever has struck gold with Axe deodorants, which have pushed prices in the category to over €5.

Today the Internet is also partially reversing the fixed pricing trend. As one industry observer noted, 'We are moving toward a very sophisticated economy. It's kind of an arms race between merchant technology and consumer technology.'[4] Here is a short list of how the Internet allows sellers to discriminate between buyers and buyers to discriminate between sellers.[5]

Buyers can:

- **Get instant price comparisons from thousands of vendors**: Customers can compare the prices offered by over two dozen online bookstores by just clicking mySimon.com. PriceScan.com lures thousands of visitors a day, most of them corporate buyers. Intelligent shopping agents

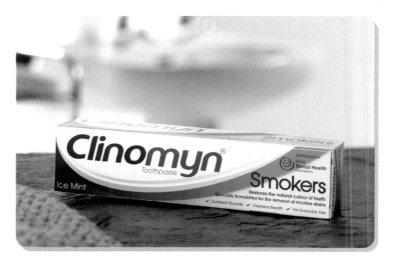

Among the marketers attempting to swim against the trend towards low prices is Clinomyn toothpaste for smokers.

Source: Courtesy of E.C. Dewitt & Company Limited

('bots') take price comparison a step further and seek out products, prices and reviews from hundreds if not thousands of merchants.

- **Name their price and have it met**: On Priceline.com, the customer states the price s/he wants to pay for an airline ticket, hotel or rental car, and Priceline checks whether any seller is willing to meet that price. Volume-aggregating sites combine the orders of many customers and press the supplier for a deeper discount.
- **Get products free**: Open Source, the free software movement that started with Linux, will erode margins for just about any company creating software. The biggest challenge confronting Microsoft, Oracle, IBM and virtually every other major software producer is: how do you compete with programs that can be had for free? 'Marketing insight: Giving it all away' describes how different firms have been successful with essentially free offerings.

Sellers can:

- **Monitor customer behaviour and tailor offers to individuals**: The (Journal Storage) JSTOR project, a non-profit venture that makes available electronic versions of archived issues of scholarly journals, monitors usage data to determine prices to individual customers. More than 2000 international educational institutions, including those from most European countries, have become participants in the project.[6] Educational institutions are charged prices based on the value to the school, not the number of copies sold. So, a large institution where users view articles many times pay more.
- **Give certain customers access to special prices**: CD WOW!, an online vendor of music albums, emails certain buyers a special website address with lower prices. Business marketers are already using extranets to get a precise handle on inventory, costs and demand at any given moment in order to adjust prices instantly.
- **Let customers decide the price**: In 2007, British rock band Radiohead began to distribute its album, *In Rainbows,* on the band's website applying an 'honesty box' principle. Consumers were given the choice of how much they wanted to pay for Radiohead's new album – anything between nothing at all and £100 (€130).[7] An Internet survey of 3000 people who downloaded the album found that most paid an average of £4 (€5), although there was a hardcore of 67 fans who thought that the record was worth more than £10 (€13) and a further 12 who claimed to have paid more than £40 (€50).[8]

Both buyers and sellers can:

- **Negotiate prices in online auctions and exchanges**: Want to sell hundreds of excess and slightly worn widgets? Post a sale on eBay. Want to purchase vintage baseball cards at a bargain price? Go to www.baseballplanet.com.

How companies price

Companies do their pricing in a variety of ways. In small companies, prices are often set by the boss. In large companies, pricing is handled by division and product line managers. Even here, top management sets general pricing objectives and policies and often approves the prices proposed by lower levels of management. In industries where pricing is a key factor (aerospace, railways, oil companies), companies will often establish a pricing department to set or assist others in determining appropriate prices. This department reports to the marketing department, finance department or top management. Others who exert an influence on pricing include sales managers, production managers, finance managers and accountants.

Executives complain that pricing is a big headache – and one that is getting worse by the day. Many companies do not handle pricing well and throw up their hands with 'strategies' such as this: 'We determine our costs and take our industry's traditional margins.' Other common mistakes are: not revising price often enough to capitalise on market changes; setting price independently of the rest of the marketing mix rather than as an intrinsic element of market-positioning strategy; and not varying price enough for different product items, market segments, distribution channels and purchase occasions. Setting the price 'correctly' will not only bring satisfactory returns but will also help strengthen sales and accurately

Marketing insight

Giving it all away

Giving away products for free via sampling has been a successful marketing tactic for years. Estée Lauder gave free samples of cosmetics to celebrities, and organisers at awards shows to this day like to lavish winners with extensive free items or gifts known as 'swag'. Other manufacturers, such as Gillette and HP, have built their business model around selling the host product essentially at cost and making money on the sale of necessary supplies, such as razor blades and printer ink.

With the advent of the Internet, software companies began to adopt similar practices. Adobe gave away PDF Reader for free in 1994, as did Macromedia with its Shockwave player in 1995. More recently, a number of Internet start-ups such as Blogger Weblog publishing tool, Flickr online photo management and sharing application, MySpace online community, Facebook, and Skype Internet phone calls have all achieved some success with a 'freemium' strategy – free online services with a premium component. Venture capitalists and entrepreneurs believe that successful online freemium strategies of this kind depend on a number of factors (see Figure 16.1).

Offline, other firms are also adopting freemium-type strategies. In Europe, profits for discount air carrier Ryanair have been high thanks to its revolutionary business model. The secret? Founder Michael O'Leary thinks like a retailer, charging for almost everything but the seat itself:

1 A quarter of Ryanair's seats are free. O'Leary wants to double that within five years, with the ultimate goal of all seats for free. Passengers pay only taxes and

1 **Have a product or service that truly stands out**. Its performance, ease of use and reliability should be superior to those of current offerings.

2 **Know your up-selling plan from the beginning**. Before you even go into beta, make sure you have at least one paid, add-on premium service up your sleeve. Better yet, have more than one.

3 **Once you've decided that a product will be given away for free, don't change your mind**. 'The fundamental "what's for free" and "what's for pay" divide needs to be set early,' says Adeo Ressi, CEO of Game Trust, a start-up that hosts 45 free games and sells enhancements online. If you make changes, Ressi says, you risk alienating customers accustomed to getting your product for free.

4 **Access to your product should be just one click away**. The fewer time-consuming plug-ins, downloads and registration forms required, the better. Otherwise people may get bored or frustrated and abort.

5 **Make sure the major bugs have been exterminated**. Your product can be in beta, Rimer (Danny Rimer, co-founder of Index Ventures) says, but not 'so much in beta that it doesn't work well'.

6 **Harness the collective intelligence of your users**. Mårten Mickos, CEO of MySQL (the world's most popular open-source database software, with over 100 million copies of its software downloaded or distributed throughout its history), says customer suggestions can help speed up product improvements or inspire ideas for premium services.

7 **Keep improving the product to give users more reasons to stick with it**. 'The reality is that offering a product for free can be far riskier than if you actually charged for your product,' says Howard Anderson, a lecturer at the MIT Entrepreneurship Center. 'Only one in ten companies will succeed at pulling this off.'

8 **Identify a range of revenue sources**. Companies such as Epocrates, Vidal (in France), IFAP Mobile (in Germany) and Medimecum (in Spain) offer medical professionals both free and premium access to drug reference databases via PDAs, yet they don't charge just for the premium information. Epocrates, for example, also charges fees to pharmaceutical firms for surveys it conducts of its customers.[i] Similarly, MySQL makes money from customer service as well as from fees charged to firms that redistribute the software.

9 **Timing is everything**. Make sure that revenue from your premium service soon covers the cost of your free service. Otherwise, cut your losses and move on to the next start-up.

Figure 16.1 Guidelines for a successful freemium strategy

Source: K. Heires (2006) Why it pays to give away the store, *Business 2.0*, October, 36–7.

fees of about €7–16, with an average one-way fare of roughly €35.

2 Passengers pay extra for basically everything else on the flight: checked luggage (€6 per bag); snacks (€4 for a hot dog, €3 for chicken soup and €2.50 for water); and bus or train transportation into town from the far-flung airports that Ryanair uses (€16).

3 Flight attendants sell a variety of merchandise, including digital cameras (€95) and iPocket MP3 players (€110). On-board gambling and a mobile phone service are projected new revenue sources.

4 Seats don't recline, window shades and seat-back pockets have been removed, and there is no entertainment. Seat-back trays now carry ads, and the exteriors of the planes are giant billboards for Vodafone Group, Jaguar, Hertz and others.

5 More than 98 per cent of tickets are sold online. Ryanair's website also offers travel insurance, hotels, ski packages and car rentals.

6 Only Boeing 737–800 jets are flown to reduce maintenance, and flight crews buy their own uniforms.

The formula works for Ryanair's customers, and the airline flies 42 million passengers annually to 127 cities. All the extras add up to 15 per cent of revenue. Ryanair enjoys net margins of 18 per cent, which are more than double the 7 per cent margins Southwest has achieved. Some industry pundits even refer to Ryanair as 'Wal-Mart with Wings'! European discount carrier easyJet has adopted many of the same practices. Other European – as well as US – airlines have

Ryanair wants to earn revenue on everything but the seats on its aeroplanes. In addition to charging passengers for baggage and snacks and eliminating frills such as entertainment and reclining seats, the carrier sells ad space on the interior and exterior of its planes. This Ryanair Boeing 737 is painted in a special sponsored Vodafone colour scheme.

Source: Steven May/Alamy

now taken notice. Fellow discount carrier Spirit Airlines has begun to charge for checking bags and all drinks; and even non-discount carriers such as SAS, Flybe, Sterling Airways, American, Northwest and Delta have begun to charge extra for headsets and snacks.

Sources: P. J. Howe (2007) The next pinch: fees to check bags, *Boston Globe*, 8 March; K. Heires (2006) Why it pays to give away the store, *Business 2.0*, October, 36–7; K. Capel (2006) Wal-Mart with wings, *BusinessWeek*, 27 November, 44–5; M. Maier (2006) A radical fix for airlines: make flying free, *Business 2.0*, April, 32–4; G. Stoller (1996) Would you like some golf balls with that ticket, *USA Today*, 30 October.

reflect the value provided to customers. Not surprisingly, that ideal price cannot be identified only by focusing on the cost of doing business or at competitors' pricing decisions. Rather, developing a pricing strategy should begin with determining the true value of a company's offerings to its customers. There is often a gap between what customers will pay and what a business charges.

There are many ways to find out how much customers value a company's offerings:

● One tactic is to employ researchers to perform so-called discrete choice analysis. In this scenario, customers view different products with different features and are asked to judge the varying prices researchers attach to them. Those findings help a company settle on an attractive mix of features and price them accordingly.

● A simpler, less expensive way to get good pricing information is to ask customers directly. Through qualitative measures, a company can ask customers what they would substitute for a specific product if it did not exist. This will show if customers have alternative options and how good those options are, which reveals the true value of a product or service.

- Another important source of information is company employees. A company's sales force knows a lot about what customers want, need and value in a product, but often they don't have an avenue to share these insights.[9]

Changing a company's pricing strategy often demands a shift in organisational culture. One key to drive such a change in culture is to convince the sales team that low prices or discounts are not always the answer to closing sales, and to ensure that any employee who works directly with customers must be able to explain the value of the product. Ideally, reconsidering pricing will force a company to focus more on its customers' needs and wants.

For any organisation, effectively designing and implementing pricing strategies requires a thorough understanding of consumer pricing psychology and a systematic approach to setting, adapting and changing prices.

Consumer psychology and pricing

Many economists assume that consumers are 'price takers' and accept prices at 'face value' or as given. Marketers recognise that consumers often actively process price information, interpreting prices in terms of their knowledge from prior purchasing experience, formal communications (advertising, sales calls and brochures), informal communications (friends, colleagues or family members), point-of-purchase or online resources, or other factors.[10]

Purchase decisions are based on how consumers perceive prices and what they consider the current actual price to be – *not* the marketer's stated price. Customers may have a lower price threshold below which prices signal inferior or unacceptable quality, as well as an upper price threshold above which prices are prohibitive and seen as not worth the money. The following example helps illustrate the large part consumer psychology plays in determining three different prices for essentially the same item: a black T-shirt.

▽ Armani, Gap, H&M

The black Armani T-shirt for women looks pretty ordinary. In fact, it's not that different from the black T-shirt sold by Gap and by Swedish discount clothing chain H&M. Yet the black Armani T-shirt costs €185.00 whereas the Gap item costs €10.00 and the H&M one €5.30. Customers who purchase the Armani T-shirt are paying for a T-shirt made of 70 per cent nylon, 25 per cent polyester, and 5 per cent Elastine, whereas the Gap and H&M shirts are made mainly of cotton. True, the Armani T is a bit more stylishly cut than the other two and sports a 'Made in Italy' label, but how does it command a €185 price tag? A luxury brand, Armani is primarily known for its suits, handbags and evening gowns that it sells for thousands of euros. In that context, it can hardly sell its T-shirts for €10 or even €70. And because there aren't many takers for €185 T-shirts, Armani doesn't make many, thus further enhancing the appeal for status seekers who like the idea of having a 'limited edition' T-shirt. 'Value is not only quality, function, utility, channel of distribution,' says Arnold Aronson, managing director of retail strategies for Kurt Salmon Associates and former CEO of Saks Fifth Avenue, 'it's also a customer's perception of a brand's luxury connotations'.[11]

Understanding how consumers arrive at their perceptions of prices is an important marketing priority. Here we consider three key topics – reference prices, price–quality inferences and price endings.

Reference prices

Research has shown that although consumers may have fairly good knowledge of the range of prices involved, surprisingly few can accurately recall specific prices of products.[12] When examining products, however, consumers often employ **reference prices**, comparing an observed price

Table 16.1 Possible consumer reference prices

- fair price (what the product should cost)
- typical price
- last price paid
- upper-bound price (reservation price or what most consumers would pay)
- lower-bound price (lower threshold price or the least consumers would pay)
- competitor prices
- expected future price
- usual discounted price.

Source: Adapted from R. S. Winer (1988) Behavioral perspectives on pricing: buyers' subjective perceptions of price revisited, in T. Devinney (ed.) *Issues in Pricing: Theory and Research*, Lexington, MA: Lexington Books, pp. 35–57. Copyright © 1988 Lexington Books. Reproduced with permission.

to an internal reference price they remember or to an external frame of reference such as a posted 'regular retail price'.[13]

All types of reference prices are possible (see Table 16.1), and sellers often attempt to manipulate them. For example, a seller can situate its product among expensive competitors to imply that it belongs in the same class. Department stores will display women's apparel in separate departments differentiated by price; dresses found in the more expensive department are assumed to be of better quality.[14] Marketers also encourage reference-price thinking by stating a high manufacturer's suggested price, or by indicating that the product was priced much higher originally, or by pointing to a competitor's high price.[15]

▽ Consumer electronics

On electronics corporation JVC's website, the manufacturer's suggested retail price often bears no relationship to what a retailer would charge for the same item. For instance, in the Spring of 2007, for the GR-D370 model of a mini digital video camcorder, JVC suggests a retail price of €220.00, but Amazon.com was selling it through its RitzCamera merchant associate for €165.00 and eBay was selling a 'like new' version at a 'buy it for now' price of €99.00. Compared with other consumer items, from clothing to cars and furniture to toothbrushes, the gap between the prices routinely quoted by manufacturer and retailer in consumer electronics is large. 'The simplest thing to say is that we have trained the consumer electronics buyer to think he is getting 20 per cent or 30 per cent or 40 per cent off,' said Robert Atkins, a vice-president at Mercer Management Consulting. Olympus, primarily known for its cameras, defends the practice by saying that the manufacturer's high suggested retail price is a psychological tool, a reference price that makes people see they are getting something of value for less than top price.[16]

High reference prices in the consumer electronics industry have trained consumers to gravitate towards 'sale' prices.

Source: Jeff Greenberg/Alamy

When consumers evoke one or more of these frames of reference, their perceived price can vary from the stated price.[17] Research on reference prices has found that 'unpleasant surprises' – when perceived price is lower than the stated price – can have a greater impact on purchase likelihood than pleasant surprises.[18] Consumer expectations can also play a key role in price response. In the case of Internet auction sites such as eBay, when consumers know similar goods will be available in future auctions, they will bid less in the current auction.[19]

Clever marketers try to frame the price to signal the best value possible; for example, a relatively more expensive item can look less expensive if the price is broken down into smaller units. A €350 annual membership may look more expensive than 'under €30 a month' even if the totals are the same.[20]

Price–quality inferences

Many consumers use price as an indicator of quality. Image pricing is especially effective with ego-sensitive products such as perfumes, expensive cars and Armani T-shirts. A €100 bottle of perfume might contain €10 worth of scent, but gift givers pay €100 to communicate their high regard for the receiver.

Price and quality perceptions of cars interact.[21] Higher-priced cars are perceived to possess high quality. Higher-quality cars are likewise perceived to be higher priced than they actually are. Table 16.2 shows how consumer perceptions about cars can differ from reality. When alternative information about true quality is available, price becomes a less significant indicator of quality. When this information is not available, price acts as a signal of quality.

Some brands adopt exclusivity and scarcity as a means to signify uniqueness and justify premium pricing. Luxury-goods makers of watches, jewellery, perfume and other products often emphasise exclusivity in their communication messages and channel strategies. For luxury-goods customers who desire uniqueness, demand may actually increase with higher prices, as they may believe that fewer other customers will be able to afford to purchase the product.[22]

Table 16.2 Consumer perceptions versus reality for cars

Wall Street firm Morgan Stanley used J.D. Power and Associates' 2003 Vehicle Dependability Study, which tracks reliability over three years, and CNW Market Research's Perceived Quality Survey to find out which car brands were potentially over- and undervalued.

Overvalued: brands whose perceived quality exceeds actual quality by percentage

Land-Rover	75.3
Kia	66.6
Volkswagen	58.3
Volvo	36.0
Mercedes	34.2

Undervalued: brands whose actual quality exceeds perceived quality by percentage

Mercury	42.3
Infiniti	34.1
Buick	29.7
Lincoln	25.3
Chrysler	20.8

Source: D. Kiley (2004) U.S. automakers get a bum rap, *USA Today*, 15 January, p. B5. Copyright © 2004 USA Today. Reprinted with permission.

▽ Tiffany & Company

For its entire history, Tiffany's name has connoted diamonds and luxury. Yet, in the late 1990s during the stock market boom, there emerged the notion of 'affordable luxuries'. Tiffany seized the moment by creating a line of cheaper silver jewellery, and its 'Return to Tiffany' silver bracelet became a must-have item for some teenagers. Sales skyrocketed after the introduction of the Return to Tiffany collection, rising 67 per cent from 1997 to 2002, with earnings more than doubling over the same time. But the rise in sales of cheaper silver jewellery brought on both an image and a pricing crisis for the company: what if all those teens who bought Tiffany charm bracelets grew up to think of Tiffany's only as a place where they got the jewellery of their girlhood? Starting in 2002, the company began hiking prices again. (The Return to Tiffany bracelet has gone from €75 to €120 – a price increase of 60 per cent from 2001.) At the same time, the company launched higher-end collections, renovated stores to feature expensive items that would appeal to more mature buyers, and expanded agressively into new cities and shopping centres. When the slowdown came in 2005 – with earnings and the stock price plunging – sales of items over €15,000 and €35,000 began growing and now lead the company in terms of growth. Still, the firm must be ever careful about diluting its high-end appeal. As one customer says of Tiffany's jewellery, 'You used to aspire to be able to buy something at Tiffany, but now it's not that special anymore'.[23]

For years the link between price and quality was what made Tiffany special. The luxury jeweller has recently tried to broaden its appeal to ever-younger consumers but must safeguard its high-end image.

Source: Kazuhiro Nogi/AFP/Getty Images

Price endings

Many sellers believe prices should end in an odd number. Customers see an item priced at €299 in the €200 rather than the €300 range. Research has shown that consumers tend to process prices in a 'left-to-right' manner rather than by rounding.[24] Price encoding in this fashion is important if there is a mental price break at the higher, rounded price.

Another explanation for the popularity of '9' endings is that they convey the notion of a discount or bargain, suggesting that if a company wants a high-price image, it should avoid the odd-ending tactic.[25] One study even showed that demand was actually increased one-third when the price of a dress *rose* from €34 to €39 but was unchanged when the price increased from €34 to €44.[26]

Prices that end with 0 and 5 are also common in the marketplace; they are thought to be easier for consumers to process and retrieve from memory.[27] 'Sale' signs next to prices have been shown to spur demand, but only if not overused. Total category sales are highest when some, but not all, items in a category have sale signs; past a certain point sale signs may cause total category sales to fall.[28]

Pricing cues such as sale signs and prices that end in 9 become less effective the more they are employed. They are more influential when consumers' price knowledge is poor, when they purchase the item infrequently or are new to the category, and when product designs vary over time, prices vary seasonally or quality or sizes vary across stores.[29] Limited availability (for example, 'three days only') also can spur sales among consumers actively shopping for a product.[30]

▽ Setting the price

A firm must set a price for the first time when it develops a new product, when it introduces its regular product into a new distribution channel or geographical area, and when it enters bids on new contract work. The firm must decide where to position its product on quality and price.

Most markets have three to five price points or tiers. Operating in nearly 100 countries, French Accor Hotels is a European leader. Accor Hotels is good at developing different brands for different price points: Sofitel luxury hotels (highest price), Pullman Hotels and Resorts (high price), Novotel (high–medium price), Mercure (medium–high price), Suitehotel (medium price), Ibis (medium–low price), and Etap and Formule 1 (low price). Consumers often rank brands according to these price tiers in a category.[31]

A firm must consider many factors in setting its pricing policy.[32] Let's look in some detail at a six-step procedure: (1) selecting the pricing objective; (2) determining demand; (3) estimating costs; (4) analysing competitors' costs, prices and offers; (5) selecting a pricing method; and (6) selecting the final price.

Step 1: selecting the pricing objective

The company first decides where it wants to position its market offering. The clearer a firm's objectives the easier it is to set a price. Five major objectives are: survival, maximum current profit, maximum market share, maximum market skimming, and product-quality leadership.

Survival

Companies pursue *survival* as their major objective if they are plagued with overcapacity, intense competition or changing consumer wants. As long as prices cover variable costs and some fixed costs, the company stays in business. Survival is a short-run objective; in the long run, the firm must learn how to add value or face extinction.

Maximum current profit

Many companies try to set a price that will *maximise current profits*. They estimate the demand and costs associated with alternative prices and choose the price that produces maximum current profit, cash flow or rate of return on investment. This strategy assumes that the firm has knowledge of its demand and cost functions; in reality, these are difficult to estimate. In emphasising current performance the company may sacrifice long-run performance by ignoring the effects of other marketing-mix variables, competitors' reactions and legal restraints on price.

Maximum market share

Some companies want to *maximise their market share*. They believe that a higher sales volume will lead to lower unit costs and higher long-run profit. They set the lowest price, assuming the market is price sensitive. Texas Instruments practised this **market-penetration pricing** for years. TI would build a large plant, set its price as low as possible, win a large market share, experience falling costs, and cut its price further as costs fell.

The following conditions favour adopting a market-penetration pricing strategy: (1) the market is highly price sensitive and a low price stimulates market growth; (2) production and distribution costs fall with accumulated production experience; and (3) a low price discourages actual and potential competition.

▽ IKEA

IKEA is using market-penetration pricing to get a lock on China's surging market for home furnishings. When the Swedish home furnishings giant opened its first store in Beijing in 2002, shoppers would come in mainly to take advantage of the air-conditioning and the decorating ideas on display. Outside the store, shops were selling copies of IKEA's furniture designs at a fraction of IKEA's prices. The only way for IKEA to lure China's price-sensitive and frugal customers was to drastically slash its prices. By stocking its Chinese stores with Chinese-made products, IKEA has been able to slash prices as low as 70 per cent below its own prices outside China. The move has worked. Customers are taking their low-priced goods to the checkout counters in droves, and IKEA is building its largest store in the world – aside from the flagship store in Stockholm – in Beijing. Western brands in China usually price products such as make-up and running shoes 20–30 per cent higher than in their other markets, both to make up for China's high import taxes and to give their products added cachet. But with 43 per cent market share in China's homewares segment alone, IKEA is proving that it pays to buck a pricing trend.[33]

Maximum market skimming

Companies unveiling a new technology favour setting high prices to *maximise market skimming*. Sony is a frequent practitioner of **market-skimming pricing**, in which prices start high and slowly drop over time. When Sony introduced the world's first high-definition television (HDTV) to the Japanese market in 1990, it had a price corresponding to €29,000. So that Sony could 'skim' the maximum amount of revenue from the various segments of the market, the price dropped steadily over the years – a 28-inch Sony HDTV cost just over €4000 in 1993 and a 40-inch Sony HDTV about €800 in 2008.

This strategy can be fatal, however, if a worthy competitor decides to price low. When Philips, the Dutch electronics manufacturer, priced its videodisc players to make a profit on each player, Japanese competitors priced low and succeeded in building their market share rapidly, which in turn pushed down their costs substantially.

Market skimming makes sense under the following conditions: (1) a sufficient number of buyers have a high current demand; (2) the unit costs of producing a small volume are not so high that they cancel the advantage of charging what the traffic will bear; (3) the high initial price does not attract more competitors to the market; (4) the high price communicates the image of a superior product.

Product-quality leadership

A company might aim to be the *product-quality leader* in the market. Many brands strive to be 'affordable luxuries' – products or services characterised by high levels of perceived quality, taste and status with a price just high enough not to be out of consumers' reach. Brands such as Starbucks coffee, Aveda shampoo, Victoria's Secret lingerie, BMW cars and Viking ranges have been able to position themselves as quality leaders in their categories, combining quality, luxury and premium prices with an intensely loyal customer base.[34] Grey Goose and Absolut carved out a superpremium niche in the essentially odourless, colourless and tasteless vodka category through clever on-premise and off-premise marketing that made the brands seem hip and exclusive.[35]

Other objectives

Non-profit and public organisations may have other pricing objectives. A university aims for *partial cost recovery*, knowing that it must rely on private gifts and public grants to cover its remaining costs. A non-profit hospital may aim for full cost recovery in its pricing. A non-profit theatre company may price its productions to fill the maximum number of theatre seats. A social service agency may set a service price geared to client income.

Whatever the specific objective, businesses that use price as a strategic tool will profit more than those which simply let costs or the market determine their pricing. For art museums, which earn only an average of 5 per cent of their revenues from admission charges, pricing can send a message that affects their public image and the number of donations and sponsorships they receive.

Vodka has no taste or odour to differentiate brands, but Absolut has used classy advertising to position itself as a superpremium brand.

Source: Reproduced under permission of V&S Vin & Sprit AB (publ)

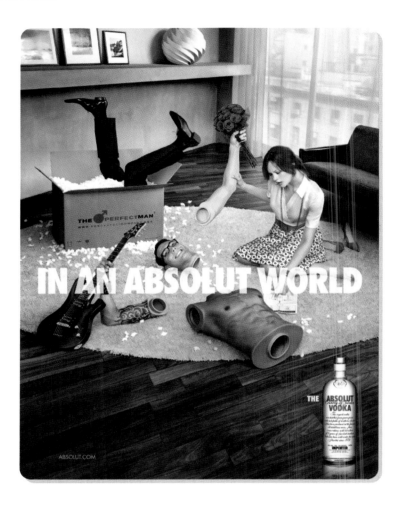

▽ Museums in France

Should art museums be free? This question arose when it was found that two-thirds of all visitors to French national museums such as the Louvre and the Musée d'Orsay are foreign tourists, and that three-quarters of visitors are between the ages of 18 and 25. With a view to persuading more French people to visit their museums, the French government is considering following the British and Danish examples of allowing free access to the permanent collections of major museums. Attendance at British museums has doubled since free admission was introduced in 2001. And the diversity of visitors has increased, with the number of young people and people of ethnic minorities on the rise. Temporary shows, for which ticket prices can exceed €13, have also benefited from the free access given to permanent collections.

Still, a number of French museum experts are sceptical that free admission will in fact attract people who never set foot in museums in the first place. France's minister of culture, Christine Albanel, says: 'The question has been asked for 30 years. Is free access the best solution? Or is it to have more free visiting hours or more attractive prices for different age groups?' These are some of the questions that the French government hopes to find answers to in an initial experiment in which free access is offered to a small number of national and provincial museums.[36]

Figure 16.2 Inelastic and elastic demand

Step 2: determining demand

Each price will lead to a different level of demand and will therefore have a different impact on a company's marketing objectives. The relationship between price and demand is captured in a demand curve (see Figure 16.2). In the normal case, the two are inversely related: the higher the price, the lower the demand. In the case of prestige goods, the demand curve sometimes slopes upward. One perfume company raised its price and sold more perfume rather than less! Some consumers take the higher price to signify a better product. However, if the price is too high, the level of demand may fall.

Price sensitivity

The demand curve shows the market's probable purchase quantity at alternative prices. It sums the reactions of many individuals who have different price sensitivities. The first step in estimating demand is to understand what affects price sensitivity. Generally speaking, customers are less price sensitive to low-cost items or items they buy infrequently. They are also less price sensitive when: (1) there are few or no substitutes or competitors; (2) they do not readily notice the higher price; (3) they are slow to change their buying habits; (4) they think the higher prices are justified; and (5) price is only a small part of the total cost of obtaining, operating and servicing the product over its lifetime.

A seller can charge a higher price than competitors and still get the business if it can convince the customer that it offers the lowest *total cost of ownership* (TCO). Marketers often do not realise the value they actually provide but think only in terms of product features. They treat the service elements in a product offering as sales incentives rather than as value-enhancing augmentations for which they can charge. In fact, pricing expert Tom Nagle believes the most common mistake manufacturers have made in recent years has been to offer all sorts of services to differentiate their products without charging for them in any way.[37]

Of course, companies prefer customers who are less price sensitive. Table 16.3 lists some characteristics associated with decreased price sensitivity. On the other hand, the Internet has the potential

Table 16.3 Factors leading to less price sensitivity

- The product is more distinctive.
- Buyers are less aware of substitutes.
- Buyers cannot easily compare the quality of substitutes.
- The expenditure is a smaller part of the buyer's total income.
- The expenditure is small compared to the total cost of the end product.
- Part of the cost is borne by another party.
- The product is used in conjunction with assets previously bought.
- The product is assumed to have more quality, prestige or exclusiveness.
- Buyers cannot store the product.

Source: Adapted from T. T. Nagle and R. K. Holden (2001) *The Strategy and Tactics of Pricing*, 3rd edn, Upper Saddle River, NJ: Prentice Hall, Chapter 4. Copyright © 2001 Pearson Education, Inc. Reproduced with permission.

to *increase* price sensitivity. Research has found that in some established, fairly big-ticket categories such as car retailing and term insurance, consumers pay lower prices as a result of the Internet. Car buyers use the Internet to gather information and to use the negotiating clout of an online buying service.[38] But customers must visit multiple sites to realise these savings, and they don't always do so. Targeting only price-sensitive consumers may in fact be 'leaving money on the table'.

Estimating demand curves

Most companies make some attempt to measure their demand curves, using several different methods:

- **Surveys** can explore how many units consumers would buy at different proposed prices, although there is always the chance they might understate their purchase intentions at higher prices to discourage the company from setting higher prices.
- **Price experiments** can vary the prices of different products in a shop or charge different prices for the same product in similar territories to see how the change affects sales. Another approach is to use the Internet. An ebusiness could test the impact of a 5 per cent price increase by quoting a higher price to every 40th visitor to compare the purchase response. However, it must do this carefully and not alienate customers.[39]
- **Statistical analysis** of past prices, quantities sold and other factors can reveal their relationships. The data can be longitudinal (over time) or cross-sectional (from different locations at the same time). Building the appropriate model and fitting the data with the proper statistical techniques calls for considerable skill.

Advances in database management have improved marketers' abilities to optimise pricing. A large retail chain uncovered a new strategy by analysing its data. It sold three similar power drills: one for about £45 (€57), a purportedly better one at £60 (€76) and a top-tier one at £65 (€82). The higher the price, the more the store profited. But while drill know-it-alls flocked to the £65 model and price fretters grabbed its £45 cousin, shoppers often ignored the middle one. After analysing an array of variables, including sales history and competitors' prices, the retailer cut the middle drill to £55 (€70). Drill aficionados still chose the £65 option and sales of that drill did not change. However, now that the £45 version seemed less of a bargain, the store sold 4 per cent fewer low-end drills – and 11 per cent more of the mid-range model. As a result, profits rose.[40] Table 16.4 displays some other examples of successful price-optimisation analyses.

Table 16.4 Price optimisation to boost sales and profits

Type of retailer	Before	After
Chemist	The shop was selling tooth-whitening chewing gum with all the other gum.	By putting the whitening gum with the whitening toothpaste and strips, the chemist sold more whitening gum because it was in close proximity to other products that were often in the same basket.
Electronics retailer	The retailer sold four tiers of 27-inch televisions, with Toshiba as the priciest, then Philips, Sharp and Sansui.	The retailer increased the price of Sansui and slightly lowered the price of Sharp, and demand rose for Sharp, the more expensive (and more profitable) TV set.
Hardware chain	The chain's best-selling item was a £1 (€1.30) paintbrush, but a new discount store offered the same paintbrush for £1, potentially stealing sales.	The chain discontinued the £1 brush but lost no ground in brush sales, and profits went up because sales of paint, not price determined brush sales.

Source: V. Murphy Barret (2006) What the traffic will bear, *Forbes*, 3 July, pp. 69–70. Copyright © 2006 Forbes LLC. Reprinted by permission of *Forbes* Magazine.

In measuring the price–demand relationship, the market researcher must control for various factors that will influence demand.[41] The competitor's response will make a difference. Also, if the company changes other marketing-mix factors besides price, the effect of the price change itself will be hard to isolate.

Price elasticity of demand

Marketers need to know how responsive, or elastic, demand would be to a change in price. Consider the two demand curves in Figure 16.2. In demand curve (a), a price increase from €10 to €15 leads to a relatively small decline in demand from 105 to 100. In demand curve (b), the same price increase leads to a substantial drop in demand from 150 to 50. If demand hardly changes with a small change in price we say the demand is *inelastic*. If demand changes considerably demand is *elastic*.

The higher the elasticity the greater the volume growth resulting from a 1 per cent price reduction. If demand is elastic sellers will consider lowering the price. A lower price will produce more total revenue. This makes sense as long as the costs of producing and selling more units do not increase disproportionately.[42]

Price elasticity depends on the magnitude and direction of the contemplated price change. It may be negligible with a small price change and substantial with a large price change. It may differ for a price cut versus a price increase, and there may be a *price indifference band* within which price changes have little or no effect.

Finally, long-run price elasticity may differ from short-run elasticity. Buyers may continue to buy from a current supplier after a price increase, but they may eventually switch suppliers. Here demand is more elastic in the long run than in the short run, or the reverse may happen: buyers may drop a supplier after being notified of a price increase but return later. The distinction between short-run and long-run elasticity means that sellers will not know the total effect of a price change until time passes.

One comprehensive study reviewing a 40-year period of academic research projects that investigated price elasticity yielded a number of interesting findings:[43]

- The average price elasticity across all products, markets and time periods studied was −2.62.
- Price elasticity magnitudes were higher for durable goods than for other goods, and higher for products in the introduction/growth stages of the product life cycle than in the mature/decline stages.
- Inflation led to substantially higher price elasticities, especially in the short run.
- Promotional price elasticities were higher than actual price elasticities in the short run (although the reverse was true in the long run).
- Price elasticities were higher at the individual item or Stock Keeping Unit (SKU) level than at the overall brand level.

Step 3: estimating costs

Demand sets a ceiling on the price the company can charge for its product. Costs set the floor. The company wants to charge a price that covers its cost of producing, distributing and selling the product, including a fair return for its effort and risk. Yet, when companies price products to cover their full costs, profitability isn't always the net result.

Types of costs and levels of production

A company's costs take two forms: fixed and variable. **Fixed** (also known as **overhead**) **costs** are costs that do not vary with production level or sales revenue. A company must pay bills each month for rent, heat, interest, salaries, and so on regardless of output.

Variable costs vary directly with the level of production. For example, each handheld calculator produced by Texas Instruments incurs the cost of plastic, microprocessor chips and packaging. These costs tend to be constant per unit produced, but they're called *variable* because their total varies with the number of units produced.

Total costs consist of the sum of the fixed and variable costs for any given level of production. **Average cost** is the cost per unit at that level of production; it equals total costs divided by production. Management wants to charge a price that will at least cover the total production costs at a given level of production.

To price intelligently, management needs to know how its costs vary with different levels of production. Take the case in which a company such as TI has built a fixed-size plant to produce 1000 handheld calculators a day. The cost per unit is high if few units are produced per day. As production approaches 1000 units per day the average cost falls because the fixed costs are spread over more units. Short-run average cost (SRAC) *increases* after 1000 units, however, because the plant becomes inefficient: workers must line up for machines, getting in each other's way, and machines break down more often (see Figure 16.3(a)).

If TI believes it can sell 2000 units per day it should consider building a larger plant. The plant will use more efficient machinery and work arrangements, and the unit cost of producing 2000 units per day will be lower than the unit cost of producing 1000 units per day. This is shown in the long-run average cost curve (LRAC) in Figure 16.3(b). In fact, a 3000-capacity plant would be even more efficient according to Figure 16.3(b), but a 4000-daily production plant would be less so because of increasing diseconomies of scale: there are too many workers to manage and paperwork slows things down. Figure 16.3(b) indicates that a 3000-daily production plant is the optimal size if demand is strong enough to support this level of production.

There are more costs than those associated with manufacturing. To estimate the real profitability of selling to different types of retailers or customers, the manufacturer needs to use **activity-based cost (ABC) accounting** instead of standard cost accounting. ABC accounting tries to identify the real costs associated with serving each customer. It allocates indirect costs, such as clerical costs, office expenses, supplies, and so on, to the activities that use them, rather than in some proportion to direct costs. Both variable and overhead costs are tagged back to each customer.

Companies that fail to measure their costs correctly are also not measuring their profit correctly and are likely to misallocate their marketing effort. The key to effectively employing ABC is to define and judge 'activities' properly. One proposed time-based solution calculates the cost of one minute of overhead and then decides how much of this cost each activity uses.[44]

(a) Cost behaviour in a fixed-size plant

(b) Cost behaviour over different-sized plants

Figure 16.3 Cost per unit at different levels of production per period

Figure 16.4 Cost per unit as a function of accumulated production: the experience curve

Accumulated production

Suppose TI runs a plant that produces 3000 handheld calculators per day. As TI gains experience producing handheld calculators, its methods improve. Workers learn shortcuts, materials flow more smoothly and procurement costs fall. The result, as Figure 16.4 shows, is that average cost falls with accumulated production experience. Thus the average cost of producing the first 100,000 handheld calculators is €10 per calculator. When the company has produced the first 200,000 calculators the average cost falls to €9. After its accumulated production experience doubles again to 400,000, the average cost is €8. This decline in the average cost with accumulated production experience is called the **experience curve** or **learning curve**.

Now suppose three firms compete in this industry, TI, A and B. TI is the lowest-cost producer at €8, having produced 400,000 units in the past. If all three firms sell the calculator for €10, TI makes €2 profit per unit, A makes €1 per unit, and B breaks even. The smart move for TI would be to lower its price to €9. This will drive B out of the market, and even A may consider leaving. TI will pick up the business that would have gone to B (and possibly A). Furthermore, price-sensitive customers will enter the market at the lower price. As production increases beyond 400,000 units, TI's costs will drop still further and faster and will more than restore its profits, even at a price of €9. TI has used this aggressive pricing strategy repeatedly to gain market share and drive others out of the industry.

Experience-curve pricing nevertheless carries major risks. Aggressive pricing might give the product a cheap image. The strategy also assumes that competitors are weak followers. It leads the company into building more plants to meet demand, but a competitor may choose to innovate with a lower-cost technology. The market leader is now stuck with the old technology.

Most experience-curve pricing has focused on manufacturing costs, but all costs can be improved on, including marketing costs. If three firms are each investing a large sum of money in marketing, the firm that has used it the longest might achieve the lowest costs. This firm can charge a little less for its product and still earn the same return, all other costs being equal.[45]

Target costing

Costs change with production scale and experience. They can also change as a result of a concentrated effort by designers, engineers and purchasing agents to reduce them through **target costing**.[46] Market research establishes a new product's desired functions and the price at which the product will sell, given its appeal and competitors' prices. Deducting the desired profit margin from this price leaves the target cost the marketer must achieve.

The firm must examine each cost element – design, engineering, manufacturing, sales – and consider different ways to bring down costs so the final cost projections are in the target cost range. If this is not possible, it may be necessary to stop developing the product because it cannot sell for the target price and make the target profit. To hit price and margin targets, marketers of 9Lives® brand of cat food employed target costing to bring their price down to 'four cans for a dollar' through a reshaped package and redesigned manufacturing processes. Even with lower prices, profits for the brand doubled.

Step 4: analysing competitors' costs, prices and offers

Within the range of possible prices determined by market demand and company costs, the firm must take competitors' costs, prices and possible price reactions into account. The firm should first consider the nearest competitor's price. If the firm's offer contains features not offered by the nearest competitor, it should evaluate their worth to the customer and add that value to the competitor's price. If the competitor's offer contains some features not offered by the firm, the firm should subtract their value from its own price. Now the firm can decide whether it can charge more, the same, or less than the competitor.

The introduction of any price or the change of any existing price can provoke a response from customers, competitors, distributors, suppliers, and even government. Competitors are most likely to react when the number of firms are few, the product is homogeneous (i.e., when no important differences between the product and competing products are perceived by buyers), and buyers are highly informed. Competitor reactions can be a special problem when these firms have a strong value proposition. Sony's Blu-ray format was able to exclude market pioneer Toshiba (backed by Microsoft) with its HD DVD format from the market and command a price premium in the process. This was due to the success of the Blu-ray team with winning the backing of the major film studios – after all consumers will buy the technology only if they believe most of the films they want will be available.[47]

How can a firm anticipate a competitor's reactions? One way is to assume the competitor reacts in the standard way to a price being set or changed. Another is to assume the competitor treats each price difference or change as a fresh challenge and reacts according to self-interest at the time. Now the company will need to research the competitor's current financial situation, recent sales, customer loyalty and corporate objectives. If the competitor has a market share objective, it is likely to match price differences or changes.[48] If it has a profit-maximisation objective, it may react by increasing the advertising budget or improving product quality.

The problem is complicated because the competitor can put different interpretations on lowered prices or a price cut: that the company is trying to steal the market, that the company is doing poorly and trying to boost its sales, or that the company wants the whole industry to reduce prices to stimulate total demand.

Step 5: selecting a pricing method

Given the customers' demand schedule, the cost function, and competitors' prices, the company is now ready to select a price. Figure 16.5 summarises the three major considerations in price setting: costs set a floor to the price. Competitors' prices and the price of substitutes provide an orienting point. Customers' assessment of unique features establishes the price ceiling.

Companies select a pricing method that includes one or more of these three considerations. We will examine six price-setting methods: mark-up pricing, target-return pricing, perceived-value pricing, value pricing, going-rate pricing and auction-type pricing.

Mark-up pricing

The most elementary pricing method is to add a standard **mark-up** to the product's cost. Construction companies submit job bids by estimating the total project cost and adding a standard mark-up for profit. Lawyers and accountants typically price by adding a standard mark-up on their time and costs.

Suppose a toaster manufacturer has the following costs and sales expectations:

Variable cost per unit	€10
Fixed costs	€300,000
Expected unit sales	50,000

The manufacturer's unit cost is given by:

Figure 16.5 The three Cs model for price setting

$$\text{Unit cost} = \text{variable cost} + \frac{\text{fixed cost}}{\text{unit sales}} = €10 + \frac{€300,000}{50,000} = €16$$

Now assume the manufacturer wants to earn a 20 per cent mark-up on sales. The manufacturer's mark-up price is given by:

$$\text{Markup price} = \frac{\text{unit cost}}{(1 - \text{desired return on sales})} = \frac{€16}{1 - 0.2} = €20$$

The manufacturer would charge dealers €20 per toaster and make a profit of €4 per unit. The dealers in turn will mark up the toaster. If dealers want to earn 60 per cent on their selling price, they will mark up the toaster 100 per cent to €40. Mark-ups are generally higher on seasonal items (to cover the risk of not selling), speciality items, slower-moving items, items with high storage and handling costs, and demand-inelastic items, such as prescription drugs.

Does the use of standard mark-ups make logical sense? Generally, no. Any pricing method that ignores current demand, perceived value and competition is not likely to lead to the optimal price. Mark-up pricing works only if the marked-up price actually brings in the expected level of sales. Consider what happened at Parker Hannifan.[49]

▽ Parker Hannifan

When Donald Washkewicz took over as CEO of Parker Hannifan, maker of 800,000 industrial parts for the aerospace, transportation and manufacturing industries, pricing was done one way: calculate how much it costs to make and deliver a product and then add a flat percentage (usually 35 per cent). Even though this method was historically well received, Washkewicz set out to get the company to think more like a retailer and charge what customers were willing to pay. Encountering initial resistance from some of the company's 115 different divisions, Washkewicz assembled a list of the 50 most commonly given reasons why the new pricing scheme would fail and announced he would listen only to arguments that were not on the list. With the new pricing scheme, Parker Hannifan's products were put into one of four categories depending on how much competition existed. About one-third fell into niches where Parker offered unique value and there was little competition, and higher prices were appropriate. Each division now has a pricing guru or specialist who assists in strategic pricing. The division making industrial fittings reviewed 2000 different items and concluded that 28 per cent of the parts were priced too low, raising prices anywhere from 3–60 per cent.

Still, mark-up pricing remains popular. First, sellers can determine costs much more easily than they can estimate demand. By tying the price to cost, sellers simplify the pricing task. Second, where all firms in the industry use this pricing method, prices tend to be similar and price competition is minimised. Third, many people feel that cost-plus pricing is fairer to both buyers and sellers. Sellers do not take advantage of buyers when the latter's demand becomes acute, and sellers earn a fair return on investment.

Target-return pricing

In **target-return pricing**, the firm determines the price that would yield its target rate of return on investment. General Motors has priced its automobiles to achieve a 15–20 per cent ROI. Public utilities, which need to make a fair return on investment, can also use this method (see Chapter 22 for more on ROI).

Suppose the toaster manufacturer has invested €1 million in the business and wants to set a price to earn a 20 per cent ROI, specifically €200,000. The target-return price is given by the following formula:

$$\text{Target-return price} = \text{unit cost} + \frac{\text{desired return} \times \text{invested capital}}{\text{unit sales}}$$

$$= €16 + \frac{.20 \times €1,000,000}{50,000} = €20$$

Figure 16.6 Break-even chart for determining target-return price and break-even volume

The manufacturer will realise this 20 per cent ROI provided its costs and estimated sales turn out to be accurate. But what if sales don't reach 50,000 units? The manufacturer can prepare a break-even chart to learn what would happen at other sales levels (see Figure 16.6). Fixed costs are €300,000 regardless of sales volume. Variable costs, not shown in the figure, rise with volume. Total costs equal the sum of fixed costs and variable costs. The total revenue curve starts at zero and rises with each unit sold.

The total revenue and total cost curves cross at 30,000 units. This is the break-even volume. We can verify it by the following formula:

$$\text{Break-even volume} = \frac{\text{fixed cost}}{(\text{price} - \text{variable cost})} = \frac{€300{,}000}{€20 - €10} = 30{,}000$$

The manufacturer, of course, is hoping the market will buy 50,000 units at €20, in which case it earns €200,000 on its €1 million investment, but much depends on price elasticity and competitors' prices. Unfortunately, target-return pricing tends to ignore these considerations. The manufacturer needs to consider different prices and estimate their probable impacts on sales volume and profits. The manufacturer should also search for ways to lower its fixed or variable costs, because lower costs will decrease its required break-even volume.

Perceived-value pricing

An increasing number of companies now base their price on the customer's **perceived value**. Perceived value is made up of several elements, such as the buyer's image of the product performance, the ability to deliver on time, the warranty quality, customer support, and softer attributes such as the supplier's reputation, trustworthiness and esteem. Companies must deliver the value promised by their value proposition, and the customer must perceive this value. Firms use the other marketing-mix elements, such as advertising and sales force, to communicate and enhance perceived value in buyers' minds.[50]

Caterpillar uses perceived value to set prices on its construction equipment. It might price its tractor at €100,000, although a similar competitor's tractor might be priced at €90,000. When a prospective customer asks a Caterpillar dealer why he should pay €10,000 more for the Caterpillar tractor, the dealer answers:

€ 90,000	is the tractor's price if it is only equivalent to the competitor's tractor
€ 7,000	Is the price premium for Caterpillar's superior durability
€ 6,000	is the price premium for Caterpillar's superior reliability
€ 5,000	is the price premium for Caterpillar's superior service
€ 2,000	is the price premium for Caterpillar's longer warranty on parts
€110,000	is the normal price to cover Caterpillar's superior value
€ 10,000	discount
€100,000	final price.

The Caterpillar dealer is able to indicate why Caterpillar's tractor delivers more value than the competitor's. Although the customer is asked to pay a €10,000 premium, he is actually getting €20,000 extra value! He chooses the Caterpillar tractor because he is convinced that its lifetime operating costs will be lower.

Ensuring that customers appreciate the total value of a product or service offering is crucial. For example, Danish online children's clothing store 'mormor.nu' (*mormor.nu* is Danish for grandmother now) employs more than 30 grandmothers from all parts of Denmark who create handmade children's clothing items. Mormor.nu is able to command premium prices because of its skill in bringing the trends of nostalgia, storytelling, authenticity, design, style and uniqueness together in a single concept. The company has a relentless focus on crucial aspects of the customer experience, such as creating handmade quality garments from pure wool, alpaca wool or cotton and adding a sense of uniqueness and authenticity – each piece of clothing comes with a small name-tag signed by the grandmother who made the item. Because of higher perceived quality – making the products meet modern demands for fashionable children's clothing, as well as for old-fashioned quality and honest materials – the higher prices (e.g., €13 for a pair of baby socks or €200 for a baby shawl) come to match the product offer in the mind of the consumer. Mormor.nu even bucks the commoditisation trend by custom-designing clothing items to individual specifications.[51]

Yet even when a company claims that its offering delivers more total value, not all customers will respond positively. There is always a segment of buyers who care only about the price. Other buyers suspect the company is exaggerating its product quality and services. One company installed its software system in one or two plants operated by a customer. The substantial and well-documented cost savings convinced the customer to buy the software for its other plants.

The key to perceived-value pricing is to deliver more value than the competitor and to demonstrate this to prospective buyers. Basically, a company needs to understand the customer's decision-making process. The company can try to determine the value of its offering in several ways: managerial judgements within the company, value of similar products, focus groups, surveys, experimentation, analysis of historical data and conjoint analysis.[52]

Value pricing

In recent years, several companies have adopted **value pricing**. They win loyal customers by charging a fairly low price for a high-quality offering. Value pricing is thus not a matter of simply setting lower prices; it is a matter of re-engineering the company's operations to become a low-cost producer without sacrificing quality, to attract a large number of value-conscious customers.

Among the best practitioners of value pricing are IKEA, airlines such as easyJet and Ryanair, and supermarket chains Tesco and Asda.

MPreis, a chain of supermarket stores in Austria, is taking the trend of 'massclusivity' (exclusivity and luxury for the masses) a step further. Positioning itself as 'The Seriously Sexy Supermarket', the company's stores differentiate themselves by unusual and progressive architecture, sleek cafés and carefully chosen materials. Despite the upgrade in retail experience, however, price levels at MPreis are at/on a par with those of competing stores in the region. For players in the game of value pricing, creating a richer customer experience does not require raising prices.[53]

An important type of value pricing is **everyday low pricing (EDLP)**, which takes place at the retail level. A retailer that holds to an EDLP pricing policy charges a constant low price with little or no price promotions and special sales. These constant prices eliminate week-to-week price uncertainty and the 'high-low' pricing of promotion-oriented competitors. In **high-low pricing**, the retailer charges higher prices on an everyday basis but then runs frequent promotions in which prices are temporarily lowered below the EDLP level.[54] The two different pricing strategies have been shown to affect consumer price judgements – deep discounts (EDLP) can lead customers to perceive lower prices over time than can frequent, shallow discounts (high-low), even if the actual averages are the same.[55]

In recent years, high-low pricing has given way to EDLP at such widely different venues as hardware stores such as Bauhaus (an international chain with more than 220 outlets across Europe and with a head office in Zug, Switzerland) and kitchen companies such as Kvik (part of the Swedish group Ballingslöv); but in European grocery retailing so-called 'hard discounters' such as Aldi, Lidl and Netto have been committed to a long-term strategy of offering everyday low prices on major brands since the beginning of the 1990s. Having enjoyed annual growth of around 7 per cent since 1991, these discounters have come to comprise a major force in European retailing, and now command high market shares in, for example, Germany, Belgium and Austria.[56]

Some retailers have even based their entire marketing strategy around what could be called *extreme* everyday low pricing. Partly fuelled by an economic downturn, and partly by changes in consumer habits (where shoppers reject price premiums yet are willing to pay more where they perceive value), once-unfashionable 'dollar stores' are gaining popularity.

▽ Tiger shops

In recent years, 'Tiger' shops have been breaking the boundaries for what is possible to buy for 10, 20, 50 or 100 Danish kroner (dkk). €1 equals approximately 8 dkk. The word 'tiger' sounds like 'ti'er', which is short for 10 dkk. This ultra-discount chain does not consist of 10 dkk stores in the strict sense of the word – Tiger shops sell many items over 10 dkk, although the highest price is 100 dkk. The Tiger chain has developed a successful formula for drawing in customers: build small, easy-to-navigate stores; keep overheads low by maintaining only a limited inventory; spend sparingly on store decor and get a lot of free word-of-mouth publicity. Sales have grown tremendously since Tiger started to send out a monthly catalogue to more than 1 million households. This has made customers aware that Tiger stocks kitchenware, office ware, beauty aids, make-up, toys, games, films, socks, underwear, reading glasses, spices, candles and many other products. Among these, some are surplus stock of well-known brands, but most of the products are bought directly from the factory to keep costs down. A majority of Tiger shoppers are women, who shop in Tiger for small presents for Christmas stockings, for children's birthday parties, or on impulse. But there are also customers who shop for low-priced everyday necessities – particularly in the provinces. The Tiger chain has 59 shops in Denmark, 4 in Iceland, 2 in England, 1 in Germany and 1 in Sweden.[57]

The most important reason retailers adopt EDLP is that constant sales and promotions are costly and have eroded consumer confidence in the credibility of everyday shelf prices. Consumers also have less time and patience for such time-honoured traditions as watching for supermarket specials and clipping coupons. Yet there is no denying that promotions create excitement and draw shoppers. For this reason, EDLP is not a guarantee of success. As supermarkets face heightened competition from their counterparts and from alternative channels, many find that the key to drawing shoppers is using a combination of high-low and everyday low pricing strategies, with increased advertising and promotions.

Going-rate pricing

In **going-rate pricing**, the firm bases its price largely on competitors' prices, charging the same, more, or less than major competitor(s). In oligopolistic industries (i.e., industries dominated by a small number of sellers) that sell a commodity such as steel, paper or fertiliser, all firms normally charge the same price. The smaller firms 'follow the leader', changing their prices when the market leader's prices change rather than when their own demand or costs change. Some firms may charge a slight premium or slight discount, but they preserve the amount of difference. Thus minor petrol stations usually charge a few pence less per gallon than the major oil companies, without letting the difference increase or decrease.

Going-rate pricing is quite popular. Where costs are difficult to measure or competitive response is uncertain, firms feel the going price is a good solution because it is thought to reflect the industry's collective wisdom.

Auction-type pricing

Auction-type pricing is growing more popular, especially with the growth of the Internet. 'Breakthrough marketing: eBay' describes the ascent of that wildly successful Internet company.

Breakthrough marketing

eBay

Pierre Omidayar, a French-Iranian immigrant, created eBay as a way to help his girlfriend sell and trade her Pez candy dispenser collection. Soon the site grew into a broader auction site where consumers could auction collectables such as baseball cards and Barbie dolls. The momentum continued, and soon small businesses discovered that eBay was an efficient way to reach consumers and other businesses. Large companies saw it as an opportunity to sell bulk lots of unsold stock.

By helping buyers get the best price for their items and letting customers decide the price they want to pay, eBay created a pricing revolution. Customers gain control as they choose the price, and the efficiency and wide reach of the site lets sellers make good margins.

eBay generated US $6 (€4) billion in consolidated new revenues in 36 merchandise categories in 2006. The site has 222 million registered users and receives 43 million unique visitors a month. More than 1 million of its members make their living from the site. Yet eBay itself doesn't buy any inventory or own the products on its site. It earns its money by collecting a fee for the auction listing, plus a commission that ranges from 1–5 per cent when the sale is completed. Merchants report profit margins of 40 per cent. With eBay's expansion into a whole range of other categories – from boats and cars, travel and tickets, to health and beauty, home and garden – collectables now make up only 13 per cent of eBay sales.

Consumer trust is a key element of eBay's success. The company tracks and publishes the reputations of both buyers and sellers on the basis of feedback from each transaction. eBay's millions of passionate users have a voice in all major decisions the company makes through its Voice of the Customer programme. Every few months, eBay brings in as many as a dozen sellers and buyers and asks them questions about how they work and what else eBay needs to do. At least twice a week the company holds hour-long teleconferences to poll users on almost every new feature or policy. The result is that users (eBay's customers) feel like owners, and they have taken the initiative to expand the company into ever-new territory.

Although eBay began as an auction site, it has evolved to also offer a fixed-price 'buy it now' option to those who don't want to wait for an auction and are willing to pay the price set by the seller. For years, buyers and sellers used eBay as an informal guide to market value, until a consumer or businessperson – or even a company with a new product design – who wanted to know the 'going price' for anything from a copier to a new DVD player checked on eBay.

eBay has become the premier auction site on the Web by letting customers choose their price.

Source: Courtesy of eBay, Inc.

Current CEO Meg Whitman believes eBay's acquisitions of PayPal online payment service in 2002 and Skype Internet voice and video communication service in 2005 have synergistically expanded the company's auction capabilities and revenue sources: eBay buyers and sellers can talk over Skype (generating ad revenue for eBay); Skype callers can use PayPal to pay for any calls that require payment; and Skype will facilitate the further global expansion of PayPal's positioning itself to be a global giant – part-international swap meet, part-clearing house for the world's manufacturers and retailers.

Acquisitions of shopping.com, an online comparison shopping service, and rent.com online, an apartment-listing service in 2005, and StubHub online ticket resale service in 2007 provided additional diversification, but due to still more intense competition in the online environment eBay will need to continue to transform the modern electronic marketplace to achieve lasting success.

Sources: A. Lashinsky (2006) Building eBay 2.0, *Fortune*, 16 October, 161–4; M. Creamer (2006) A million marketers, *Advertising Age*, 26 June, pp. 1, 71; C. Thompson, eBay heads east, *Fast Company*, July–August, 87–9; B. Streisand (2004) Make new sales, but keep the old, *U.S. News & World Report*, 16 February, 40; G. L. Urban (2004) The emerging era of customer advocacy, *MIT Sloan Management Review*, Winter, 77–82; R. D. Hof (2003) The eBay economy, *BusinessWeek*, 25 August, 125–8.

There are over 2000 electronic marketplaces selling everything from pigs to used vehicles and cargo to chemicals. One major purpose of auctions is to dispose of excess inventories or used goods. Companies need to be aware of the three major types of auctions and their separate pricing procedures.

- **English auctions (ascending bids)**: one seller and many buyers. On sites such as Yahoo! and eBay, the seller puts up an item and bidders raise the offer price until the top price is reached. The highest bidder gets the item. English auctions (the term commonly used for these kinds of auction – but known also as 'ascending-price' auctions) are used today for selling antiques, cattle, property, and used equipment and vehicles. After seeing eBay and other ticket brokers, scalpers and middlemen reap millions by charging what the market would bear, Ticketmaster Corp. has overhauled the way it sells tickets, including running auctions for 30 per cent of major music tours by popular artists such as Barbra Streisand and Madonna, and allowing some customers to resell their seats at its website.[58]
- **Dutch auctions (descending bids)**: one seller and many buyers, or one buyer and many sellers. In the first kind, an auctioneer announces a high price for a product and then slowly decreases the price until a bidder accepts the price. In the other, the buyer announces something he or she wants to buy, and potential sellers compete to get the sale by offering the lowest price. Each seller sees what the last bid is and decides whether to go lower. FreeMarkets.com – later acquired by Ariba – helped Royal Mail Group plc, the United Kingdom's public postal service company, save approximately £2.5 million in 2003, in part via an auction where 25 airlines bid for its international freight business.[59]
- **Sealed-bid auctions**: would-be suppliers can submit only one bid and cannot know the other bids. Governments often use this method to procure supplies (see Chapter 8). A supplier will not bid below its cost but cannot bid too high for fear of losing the job. The net effect of these two pulls can be described in terms of the bid's *expected profit*. Using expected profit for setting price makes sense for the seller that makes many bids. The seller who bids only occasionally or who needs a particular contract badly will not find it advantageous to use expected profit. This criterion does not distinguish between a €1000 profit with a 0.10 probability and a €125 profit with a 0.80 probability. Yet the firm that wants to keep production going would prefer the second contract to the first.

As more and more firms use online auctions for industrial buying, they need to recognise the possible effects it can have on their suppliers. If the increased savings a firm obtains in an online auction translates into decreased margins for an incumbent supplier, the supplier may feel the firm is opportunistically squeezing out price concessions.[60] Online auctions with a large number of bidders, greater economic stakes and less visibility in pricing have been shown to result in greater overall satisfaction, more positive future expectations and fewer perceptions of opportunism.

Step 6: selecting the final price

Pricing methods narrow the range from which the company must select its final price. In selecting that price, the company must consider additional factors, including the impact of other marketing activities, company pricing policies, gain-and-risk-sharing pricing and the impact of price on other parties.

Impact of other marketing activities

The final price must take into account the brand's quality and advertising relative to the competition. In a classic study, Farris and Reibstein examined the relationships among relative price, relative quality and relative advertising for 227 consumer businesses and found the following:

- Brands with average relative quality but high relative advertising budgets were able to charge premium prices. Consumers were willing to pay higher prices for known products than for unknown products.
- Brands with high relative quality and high relative advertising obtained the highest prices. Conversely, brands with low quality and low advertising charged the lowest prices.

- The positive relationship between high prices and high advertising held most strongly in the later stages of the product life cycle for market leaders.[61]

These findings suggest that price is not as important as quality and other benefits in the market offering. One study asked consumers to rate the importance of price and other attributes in using online retailing. Only 19 per cent cared about price; far more cared about customer support (65 per cent), on-time delivery (58 per cent) and product shipping and handling (49 per cent).[62]

Company pricing policies

The price must be consistent with company pricing policies. At the same time, companies are not averse to establishing pricing penalties under certain circumstances.[63]

Banks charge fees for too many withdrawals in a month or for early withdrawal of a certificate of deposit. Dentists, hotels, car rental companies and other service providers charge penalties for no-shows who miss appointments or reservations. Although these policies are often justifiable, marketers must use them judiciously so as not to unnecessarily alienate customers. (See 'Marketing insight: Stealth price increases.')

Many companies set up a pricing department to develop policies and establish or approve decisions. The aim is to ensure that sales people quote prices that are reasonable to customers and profitable to the company.

Marketing insight

Stealth price increases

With consumers stubbornly resisting higher prices, companies are trying to figure out how to increase revenue without really raising prices. Increasingly, the solution has been through the addition of fees for what had once been free features. Although some consumers abhor 'nickel-and-dime' pricing strategies, small additional charges can add up to a substantial source of revenue. The numbers can be staggering. For instance, overdraft penalty fees for unauthorised overdrafts on a bank account typically ranged from £25 (€32) to £50 (€65) in British banks in 2007. In total, British credit card companies collect more than £300 (€380) million a year in penalty charges.

The telecommunications industry in general has been aggressive at adding fees for set-up, change-of-service, service termination, directory assistance, regulatory assessment, number portability, and cable hook-up and equipment, costing consumers billions of euros.

By charging its customers a mobile roaming fee up to €4.93 when using roaming to make calls outside their home nation, mobile operators have brought in as much as €10 billion a year from 150 million mobile phone customers in the EU.

This explosion of fees has a number of implications. Given that list prices stay fixed, they may understate inflation. They also make it harder for consumers to compare competitive offerings. Although various citizens'

groups have been formed to pressure companies to roll back some of these fees, they don't always get a sympathetic ear from national and local governments, which have been guilty of using their own array of fees, fines and penalties to raise necessary revenue.

Companies justify the extra fees as the only fair and viable way to cover expenses without losing customers. Many argue that it makes sense to charge a premium for added services that cost more to provide, rather than charging all customers the same amount whether or not they use the extra service. Breaking out charges and fees according to the related services is a way to keep basic costs low. Companies also use fees as a means to weed out unprofitable customers or get them to change their behaviour.

Ultimately, the viability of extra fees will be decided in the marketplace, and by the willingness of consumers to vote with their wallets and pay the fees, or vote with their feet and move on.

Sources: K. Chu (2003) Credit card fees can suck you in, *USA Today*, 15 December; M. Arndt (2003) Fees! Fees! Fees!, *BusinessWeek*, 29 September, 99–104; The price is wrong, *The Economist*, 25 May 2002, 59–60; Once more unto the branch, *The Economist*, 2 August 2007; British banks come under fire over fees, *International Herald Tribune*, 6 April 2006; H. Spongenberg (2007) EU clinches deal on roaming prices, *BusinessWeek*, 17 May; EU close to mobile roaming fee cut deal, *BusinessWeek*, 16 March 2007; C. Barker (2006) EU to slash mobile roaming rates, *BusinessWeek*, 29 March; www.euobserver.com.

Gain-and-risk-sharing pricing

Buyers may resist accepting a seller's proposal because of a high perceived level of risk. The seller has the option of offering to absorb part or all the risk if it does not deliver the full promised value. In 2008, aircraft manufacturer Bombardier Aerospace was able to secure a contract for the delivery of 27 regional and turboprop planes to Scandinavian Airlines (SAS), by giving SAS more than €106.4 million in cash and credit compensation for future aircraft orders. The compensation was due to the fact that the year before SAS had to ground the airline's entire fleet of 27 Bombardier Dash 8 Q400 aircraft after suffering three landing accidents.[64]

Impact of price on other parties

Management must also consider the reactions of other parties to the contemplated price.[65] How will distributors and dealers feel about it? If they don't make enough profit, they may not choose to bring the product to market. Will the sales force be willing to sell at that price? How will competitors react? Will suppliers raise their prices when they see the company's price? Will the government intervene and prevent this price from being charged?

Marketers need to know the laws regulating pricing. EU competition law states that sellers must set prices without talking to competitors: price fixing is illegal to protect consumers against deceptive pricing practices. Also, it is illegal to exploit a dominant market position in order to directly or indirectly impose unfair purchase or selling prices or other unfair trading conditions.

Very often companies must take into account the many variations in their surroundings when setting price(s). This is considered in the next section.

▽ Adapting the price

Companies usually do not set a single price, but rather develop a pricing structure that reflects variations in geographical demand and costs, market-segment requirements, purchase timing, order levels, delivery frequency, guarantees, service contracts, and other factors. As a result of discounts, allowances and promotional support, a company rarely realises the same profit from each unit of a product that it sells. Here we will examine several price-adaptation strategies: geographical pricing, price discounts and allowances, promotional pricing and differentiated pricing.

Geographical pricing (cash, countertrade, barter)

In geographical pricing, the company decides how to price its products to different customers in different locations and countries.

▽ Unilever

Unilever, the international manufacturer of leading brands in foods, home care and personal care with headquarters in Rotterdam and London, has long played a major role in the Brazilian market for detergents and laundry soaps, yet Brazil's relatively high per capita income covers large regional differences. In particular, more than half of the population in the north-east of Brazil lives on less than two minimum wages. To meet the needs of this consumer group, where a majority wash clothes by hand in rivers or ponds, Unilever altered their product portfolio to include a low-priced, yet effective, brand detergent named Ala. This new product and pricing initiative was launched to help compete against cheaper local brands while still protecting the value of Unilever's global brands.[66]

Should the company charge higher prices to distant customers to cover the higher shipping costs, or a lower price to win additional business? How should it account for exchange rates and the strength of different currencies?

Another question is how to get paid. This issue is critical when buyers lack sufficient hard currency to pay for their purchases. Many buyers want to offer other items in payment, a practice known as **countertrade**. Countertrade may account for 15–25 per cent of world trade and takes several forms:[67]

- **Barter**: The buyer and seller directly exchange goods, with no money and no third party involved.
- **Compensation deal**: The seller receives some percentage of the payment in cash and the rest in products. A British aircraft manufacturer sold planes to Brazil for 70 per cent cash and the rest in coffee.
- **Buyback arrangement**: The seller sells plant, equipment or technology to another country and agrees to accept as partial payment products manufactured with the supplied equipment. For example, a chemical company builds a plant for an Indian company and accepts partial payment in cash and the remainder in chemicals manufactured at the plant.
- **Offset**: The seller receives full payment in cash but agrees to spend a substantial amount of the money in that country within a stated time period. For example, PepsiCo sells its cola syrup to Russia for rubles and agrees to buy Russian vodka at a certain rate for sale in the United States.

Price discounts and allowances

Most companies will adjust their list price and give discounts and allowances for early payment, volume purchases and off-season buying (see Table 16.5).[68] Companies must do this carefully or find their profits much lower than planned.[69]

Discount pricing has become the modus operandi of a surprising number of companies offering both products and services. Some product categories tend to self-destruct by always being on sale. Sales people, in particular, are quick to give discounts in order to close a sale. But word can get around fast that the company's list price is 'soft', and discounting becomes the norm. The discounts undermine the value perceptions of the offerings.

Table 16.5 Price discounts and allowances

Cash discount:	A price reduction to buyers who pay bills promptly. A typical example is '2/10, net 30', which means that payment is due within 30 days and that the buyer can deduct 2 per cent by paying the bill within 10 days.
Quantity discount:	A price reduction to those who buy large volumes. A typical example is '€10 per unit for fewer than 100 units; €9 per unit for 100 or more units'. Quantity discounts must be offered equally to all customers and must not exceed the cost savings to the seller. They can be offered on each order placed or on the number of units ordered over a given period.
Functional discount:	Discount (also called *trade discount*) offered by a manufacturer to trade-channel members if they will perform certain functions, such as selling, storing and record keeping. Manufacturers must offer the same functional discounts within each channel.
Seasonal discount:	A price reduction to those who buy merchandise or services out of season. Hotels, motels and airlines offer seasonal discounts in slow selling periods.
Allowance:	An extra payment designed to gain reseller participation in special programmes. *Trade-in allowances* are granted for turning in an old item when buying a new one. *Promotional allowances* reward dealers for participating in advertising and sales support programmes.

Some companies with overcapacity are tempted to give discounts or even begin to supply a retailer with a store-brand version of their product at a deep discount. Because the store brand is priced lower, however, it may start making inroads on the manufacturer's brand. Manufacturers should stop to consider the implications of supplying products to retailers at a discount, because they may end up losing long-run profits in an effort to meet short-run volume goals.

Kevin Clancy, chairman of Copernicus, a major marketing research and consulting firm, found that only 15–35 per cent of buyers in most categories are price sensitive. People with higher incomes and higher product involvement willingly pay more for features, customer service, quality, added convenience and the brand name. So it can be a mistake for a strong, distinctive brand to plunge into price discounting to respond to low-price attacks.[70]

At the same time, discounting can be a useful tool if a company can gain concessions in return, such as when the customer agrees to sign a longer contract, is willing to order electronically, thus saving the company money, or agrees to buy in truckload quantities.

Sales management needs to monitor the proportion of customers who are receiving discounts, the average discount, and the particular sales people who are overrelying on discounting. Higher levels of management should conduct a **net price analysis** to arrive at the 'real price' of the offering. The real price is affected not only by discounts but by many other expenses that reduce the realised price (see promotional pricing section). Suppose the company's list price is €3000. The average discount is €300. The company's promotional spending averages €450 (15 per cent of the list price). Co-op advertising money of €150 is given to retailers to back the product. The company's net price is €2100, not €3000.

Promotional pricing

Companies can use several pricing techniques to stimulate early purchase:

- **Loss-leader pricing**: Supermarkets and department stores often drop the price on well-known brands to stimulate additional store traffic. This pays if the revenue on the additional sales compensates for the lower margins on the loss-leader items. Manufacturers of loss-leader brands typically object because this practice can dilute the brand image and bring complaints from retailers who charge the list price. Manufacturers have tried to restrain intermediaries from loss-leader pricing through lobbying for retail price maintenance laws, but these laws have been revoked.
- **Special-event pricing**: Sellers will establish special prices in certain seasons to draw in more customers. Every August, there are back-to-school sales.
- **Cash rebates**: Car companies and other consumer goods companies offer cash rebates to encourage purchase of the manufacturers' products within a specified time period. Rebates can help clear inventories without cutting the stated list price.
- **Low-interest financing**: Instead of cutting its price, the company can offer customers low-interest financing. Car manufacturers have used no-interest financing to try to attract more customers.
- **Longer payment terms**: Sellers, especially mortgage lenders and car manufacturers/dealers, stretch loans over longer periods and thus lower the monthly payments. Consumers often worry less about the cost (the interest rate) of a loan and more about whether they can afford the monthly payment.
- **Warranties and service contracts**: Companies can promote sales by adding a free or low-cost warranty or service contract.
- **Psychological discounting**: This strategy sets an artificially high price and then offers the product at substantial savings; for example, 'Was €359, now €299'. Most governments fight such misleading discount tactics. Discounts from normal prices are a legitimate form of promotional pricing.

Promotional-pricing strategies are often a zero-sum game. If they work, competitors copy them and they lose their effectiveness. If they don't work, they waste money that could have been put into other marketing tools, such as building up product quality and service or strengthening product image through advertising.

Differentiated pricing

Companies often adjust their basic price to accommodate differences in target consumers, products, locations, and so on. Designer Donna Karan creates women's clothes in different price classes. The Donna Karan main line is expensive, but also the ultimate in relaxed chic, whereas the lower-priced line, DKNY, is more affordable. A woman's black dress from the DKNY line may cost €84, while a black dress from the Donna Karan Collection may cost as much as €1175.[71]

Price discrimination occurs when a company sells a product or service at two or more prices that do not reflect a proportional difference in costs. In first-degree price discrimination, the seller charges a separate price to each customer depending on the intensity of his or her demand. In second-degree price discrimination, the seller charges less to buyers who buy a larger volume. In third-degree price discrimination, the seller charges different amounts to different classes of buyers, as in the following cases:

- **Customer-segment pricing**: Different customer groups pay different prices for the same product or service. For example, museums often charge a lower admission fee to students and senior citizens.
- **Product-form pricing**: Different versions of the product are priced differently, but not proportionately to their costs. Evian prices a 48-ounce bottle of its mineral water at €1.50. It takes the same water and packages 1.7 ounces in a moisturiser spray for €4.00. Through product-form pricing, Evian manages to charge €2.50 an ounce in one form and about €.03 an ounce in another.
- **Image pricing**: Some companies price the same product at two different levels based on image differences. A perfume manufacturer can put the perfume in one bottle, give it a name and image, and price it at €10 an ounce. It can put the same perfume in another bottle with a different name and image and price it at €30 an ounce.
- **Channel pricing**: Coca-Cola carries a different price depending on whether the consumer purchases it in a fine restaurant, a fast-food restaurant or a vending machine.
- **Location pricing**: The same product is priced differently at different locations even though the cost of offering it at each location is the same. A theatre varies its seat prices according to audience preferences for different locations.
- **Time pricing**: Prices are varied by season, day or hour. Public utilities vary energy rates to commercial users by time of day and weekend versus weekday. Restaurants charge less to 'early bird' customers, and some hotels charge less on weekends.

The airline and hospitality industries use yield management systems and **yield pricing**, by which they offer discounted but limited early purchases, higher-priced late purchases, and the lowest rates on unsold inventory just before it expires.[72] Airlines charge different fares to passengers on the same flight, depending on the seating class; the time of day (morning or night flight); the day of the week (workday or weekend); the season; the person's employer, past business or status (youth, military, senior citizen); and so on.

That's why on a flight from Oslo to Rome you might have paid €93 and be sitting across from someone who has paid €526. At any given moment the global airline market has more than 7 million prices. And in a system that tracks the difference in prices and the price of competitors' offerings, airlines collectively change 75,000 different prices a day! It's a system designed to punish procrastinators by charging them the highest possible prices.

The phenomenon of offering different pricing schedules to different consumers and dynamically adjusting prices is exploding.[73] Many companies are using software packages that provide real-time controlled tests of actual consumer response to different pricing schedules. Constant price variation, however, can be tricky where consumer relationships are concerned. Research shows it tends to work best in situations where there is no bond between the buyer and the seller. One way to make it work is to offer customers a unique bundle of products and services to meet their needs precisely, making it harder for them to make price comparisons.

The tactic most companies favour, however, is to use variable prices as a reward for good behaviour rather than as a penalty. For instance, Danish mobile operator Sonofon rewards customers who shop online, and thus don't take up time in Sonofon retail stores. The customer gets a €13 discount on Internet orders.[74] Customers are also getting more savvy about how to avoid buyer's remorse from overpaying. They are changing their buying behaviour to accommodate the new realities of dynamic pricing – where prices vary frequently by channels, products, customers and time.

Most consumers are probably not even aware of the degree to which they are the targets of discriminatory pricing. For instance, the Apple ITunes Store prices music downloads differently depending on consumers' geographic location. Apple requires users to shop at the online store tied to the country of their credit card's origin, which leads to different prices for the same music downloads. Customers who live in the euro zone pay only €0.99 cents per song whereas the customers in the United Kingdom, which uses the pound sterling, pay £0.79 (€1.17) per tune and the customers in Denmark, which uses Danish kroner, pay 8 dkk (€1.07) per tune.[75]

Some forms of price discrimination (in which sellers offer different price terms to different people within the same trade group) are illegal. However, price discrimination is legal if the seller can prove that its costs are different when selling different volumes or different qualities of the same product to different retailers. Predatory pricing – selling below cost with the intention of destroying competition – is unlawful.[76] Even if legal, some differentiated pricing may meet with a hostile reaction. Coca-Cola considered using wireless technology to raise its vending machine drinks prices on hot days and lower them on cold days. Customers so disliked the idea that Coke abandoned it.

For price discrimination to work, certain conditions must exist. First, the market must be segmentable and the segments must show different intensities of demand. Second, members in the lower-price segment must not be able to resell the product to the higher-price segment. Third, competitors must not be able to undersell the firm in the higher-price segment. Fourth, the cost of segmenting and policing the market must not exceed the extra revenue derived from price discrimination. Fifth, the practice must not breed customer resentment and ill will. Sixth, of course, the particular form of price discrimination must not be illegal.[77]

While this section has examined several price-adaptation strategies, the next section reviews circumstances where companies may initiate and respond to price changes.

▽ Initiating and responding to price changes

Initiating price cuts

Several circumstances might lead a firm to cut prices. One is *excess plant capacity*: the firm needs additional business and cannot generate it through increased sales effort, product improvement, or other measures. Companies sometimes initiate price cuts in a *drive to dominate the market through lower costs*. Either the company starts with lower costs than its competitors, or it initiates price cuts in the hope of gaining market share and lower costs.

Cutting prices to keep customers or beat competitors often encourages customers to demand price concessions, however, and trains sales people to offer them.[78] A price-cutting strategy can lead to other possible traps:

- **Low-quality trap**: Consumers assume quality is low.
- **Fragile market-share trap**: A low price buys market share but not market loyalty. The same customers will shift to any lower-priced firm that comes along.
- **Shallow-pockets trap**: Higher-priced competitors match the lower prices but have longer staying power because of deeper cash reserves.
- **Price-war trap**: Competitors respond by lowering their prices even more, triggering a price war.

Customers often question the motivation behind price changes.[79] They may assume the item is about to be replaced by a new model; that the item is faulty and not selling well; the firm is in financial trouble; the price will come down even further; or the quality has been reduced. The firm must monitor these attributions carefully.

Initiating price increases

A successful price increase can raise profits considerably. For example, if the company's profit margin is 3 per cent of sales, a 1 per cent price increase will increase profits by 33 per cent if sales volume is unaffected. This situation is illustrated in Table 16.6. The assumption is that a company charged €10 and sold 100 units and had costs of €970, leaving a profit of €30, or 3 per cent on sales. By raising its price by 10 cents (a 1 per cent price increase), it boosted its profits by 33 per cent, assuming the same sales volume.

European low-cost airlines such as Sterling and SAS have different views on their respective future pricing strategies. To learn more, visit www.pearsoned.co.uk/ marketingmanagementeurope

A major circumstance provoking price increases is *cost inflation*. Rising costs unmatched by productivity gains squeeze profit margins and lead companies to regular rounds of price increases. Companies often raise their prices by more than the cost increase, in anticipation of further inflation or government price controls, in a practice called *anticipatory pricing*.

Another factor leading to price increases is *overdemand*. When a company cannot supply all its customers, it can raise its prices, ration supplies to customers, or both. The price can be increased in the following ways, each of which has a different impact on buyers.

- **Delayed quotation pricing**: The company does not set a final price until the product is finished or delivered. This pricing is prevalent in industries with long production lead times, such as industrial construction and heavy equipment.
- **Escalator clauses**: The company requires the customer to pay today's price and all or part of any inflation increase that takes place before delivery. An escalator clause bases price increases on some specified price index. Escalator clauses are found in contracts for major industrial projects, such as aircraft construction and bridge building.
- **Unbundling**: The company maintains its price but removes or prices separately one or more elements that were part of the former offer, such as free delivery or installation. Car companies sometimes add antilock brakes and passenger-side airbags as supplementary extras to their vehicles.
- **Reduction of discounts**: The company instructs its sales force not to offer its normal cash and quantity discounts.

Although there is always a chance that a price increase can carry some positive meanings to customers – for example, that the item is 'hot' and represents unusually good value – consumers generally dislike higher prices. In passing price increases on to customers, the company must avoid looking like a price 'gouger'.[80] Consumer concern and dissatisfaction with high petrol, food and prescription drug prices and Amazon.com's dynamic pricing experiment whereby prices varied by purchase occasion have become front-page news. The more similar the products or offerings from a company, the more likely consumers are to interpret any pricing differences as unfair. Product customisation and differentiation and communications that clarify differences are thus critical.[81]

Generally, consumers prefer small price increases on a regular basis to sudden, sharp increases. Their memories are long, and they can turn against companies they perceive as price gougers. Price hikes without corresponding investments in the value of the brand increase vulnerability to lower-priced competition. Consumers may be willing to 'trade down' because they can no longer justify to themselves that the higher-priced brand is worth it.

Table 16.6 Profits before and after a price increase

	Before	**After**
Price	€10	€10.10 (a 1% price increase)
Units sold	100	100
Revenue	€1,000	€1,010
Costs	− €970	− €970
Profit	€30	€40 (a 331/3% profit increase)

Several techniques help consumers avoid sticker shock and a hostile reaction when prices rise: one is that a sense of fairness must surround any price increase, and customers must be given advance notice so they can do forward buying or shop around. Sharp price increases need to be explained in understandable terms. Making low-visibility price moves first is also a good technique: eliminating discounts, increasing minimum order sizes and curtailing production of low-margin products are some examples; and contracts or bids for long-term projects should contain escalator clauses based on such factors as increases in recognised national price indexes.[82]

Given strong consumer resistance to price hikes, marketers go to great lengths to find alternative approaches that will allow them to avoid increasing prices when they would otherwise have done so. Here are a few popular ones.

- **shrinking the amount of product instead of raising the price**: (Hershey Foods maintained its chocolate bar price but trimmed its size. Nestlé maintained its size but raised the price.);
- **substituting less expensive materials or ingredients**: (Many confectionery companies substituted synthetic chocolate for real chocolate to fight price increases in cocoa.);
- **reducing or removing product features**: (Full-service air carriers such as British Airways have changed their services by simplifying fare structures and introducing ticketless travel);[83]
- **removing or reducing product services**: such as installation or free delivery;
- **using less expensive packaging material or larger package sizes**;
- **reducing the number of sizes and models offered**;
- **creating new economy brands**: (Jewel food stores introduced 170 generic items selling at 10–30 per cent less than national brands).

When setting the price it is important that the company pays attention to competitors' price changes and responds to these when appropriate. How a firm should respond to a price cut initiated by a competitor is considered in the next section.

Responding to competitors' price changes

In general, the best response to competitors' price changes varies with the situation. The company must consider the product's stage in the life cycle, its importance in the company's portfolio, the competitor's intentions and resources, the market's price and quality sensitivity, the behaviour of costs with volume, and the company's alternative opportunities.

In markets characterised by high product homogeneity, the firm can search for ways to enhance its augmented product. If it cannot find any, it may need to meet the price reduction. If the competitor raises its price in a homogeneous product market, other firms might not match it if the increase will not benefit the industry as a whole. Then the leader will need to roll back the increase. In non-homogeneous product markets, a firm has more latitude. It needs to consider the following issues: (1) Why did the competitor change the price? To steal the market, to utilise excess capacity, to meet changing cost conditions, or to lead an industry-wide price change? (2) Does the competitor plan to make the price change temporary or permanent? (3) What will happen to the company's market share and profits if it does not respond? Are other companies going to respond? (4) What are the competitors' and other firms' responses likely to be to each possible reaction?

Market leaders often face aggressive price cutting by smaller firms trying to build market share. Using price, Fuji has attacked Kodak, Schick has attacked Gillette, and AMD has attacked Intel. Brand leaders also face competition from lower-priced, private-label store brands. The brand leader can respond in several ways. 'Marketing memo: How to fight low-cost rivals' highlights some possible responses.

An extended analysis of alternatives may not always be feasible when the attack occurs. The company may have to react decisively within hours or days, especially in those industries where price changes occur with some frequency and where it is important to react quickly, such as the meatpacking, lumber or oil industries. It would make better sense to anticipate possible competitors' price changes and prepare contingent responses.

Marketing memo

How to fight low-cost rivals

London Business School's Nirmalya Kumar spent five years studying 50 incumbents and 25 low-cost businesses to better understand the threats posed by disruptive, low-cost competitors. He notes that successful price warriors, such as Germany's Aldi supermarkets, India's Aravind Eye Hospitals and Israel's Teva Pharmaceuticals, are changing the nature of competition all over the world by employing several key tactics, such as focusing on just one or a few consumer segments, delivering the basic product or providing one benefit

better than rivals do, and backing low prices with super-efficient operations.

Kumar believes ignoring low-cost rivals is a mistake, because they eventually force companies to vacate entire market segments. He doesn't see price wars as the answer either: slashing prices usually lowers profits for incumbents without driving the low-cost entrants out of business. In the race to the bottom, he says, the challengers always come out ahead of the incumbents. Instead, he offers three possible responses that will vary in their success depending on different factors, as outlined in Figure 16.7.

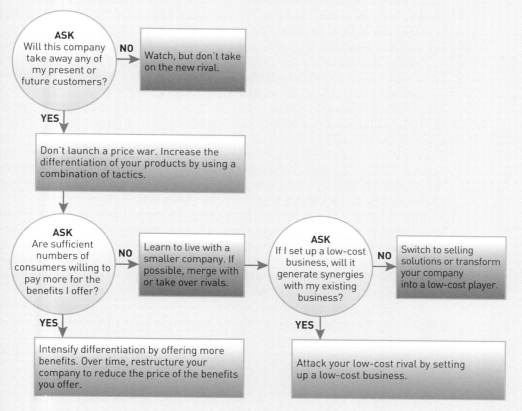

Figure 16.7 A framework for responding to low-cost rivals

Source: N. Kumar (2006) Strategies to fight low-cost rivals, *Harvard Business Review*, December, 86–95. Copyright © 2006 by the President and Fellows of Harvard College. All rights reserved. Reproduced wih permission

The first approach to competing against cut-price players is to differentiate the product or service through various means:

- design 'cool' products (Apple; Bang & Olufsen);
- continually innovate (Gillette; 3M);
- offer unique product mix (Sharper Image; Whole Foods);

- brand a community (Harley-Davidson; Red Bull);
- sell experiences (Four Seasons; Starbucks).

Kumar cautions that three conditions will determine the success of a differentiation response:

1 **Companies must not use differentiation tactics in isolation**. Bang & Olufsen has competed effectively against low-cost electronics manufacturers in part because of its strong design capabilities, but also because the company continually introduces new products, cultivates an upscale brand image, and supports modern-looking retail outlets.

2 **Companies must be able to persuade consumers to pay for added benefits**. Charging a small premium for greater services or benefits can be a powerful defence.

3 **Companies must first bring costs and benefits in line**. HP's resurgence in the PC industry can be attributed in part to its success in cutting Dell's cost advantage from 20 per cent to 10 per cent.

Kumar cautions that unless sizeable numbers of consumers demand additional benefits companies may need to yield some markets to price warriors. For example, British Airways has relinquished some short-haul routes to low-cost rivals easyJet and Ryanair. Kumar also believes strategies that help an incumbent firm coexist with low-cost rivals can work initially, but over the long haul consumers migrate to low-cost options as they become more familiar with them.

Another approach that many companies have tried in responding to low-cost competitors is to introduce a low-cost venture themselves. Citing the failure of no-frills second carriers such as Continental Lite, Delta's Song, KLM's Buzz, SAS's Snowflake, US Airways' MetroJet, and United's Shuttle, however, Kumar asserts that companies should set up low-cost operations only if: (1) the traditional operation will become more competitive as a result; and (2) the new business will derive some advantages that it would not have gained as an independent entity.

A dual strategy succeeds only if companies can generate synergies between the existing businesses and the new ventures, as financial service providers HSBC and ING did. The low-cost venture most likely includes a unique brand name or identity, adequate resources and a willingness to endure some cannibalisation between the two businesses.

If there are no synergies between traditional and low-cost businesses companies should consider two other options. They can switch from selling products to selling solutions, or even convert themselves into low-cost players. In the former approach Kumar believes that by offering products and services as an integrated package, companies can expand the segment of the market that is willing to pay more for additional benefits. Selling solutions requires managing customers' processes and increasing their revenues or lowering their costs and risks.

And if all else fails, the best solution may be reinvention as a low-cost player. After all, as noted above, Ryanair was an unprofitable, high-cost traditional airline before it completely – and quite successfully – transformed itself into a low-cost carrier.

▽ SUMMARY

1 Despite the increased role of non-price factors in modern marketing, price remains a critical element of the marketing mix. Price is the only element that produces revenue; the others produce costs.

2 In setting pricing policy a company follows a six-step procedure. It selects its pricing objective. It estimates the demand curve, the probable quantities it will sell at each possible price. It estimates how its costs vary at different levels of output, at different levels of accumulated production experience and for differentiated marketing offers. It examines competitors' costs, prices and offers. It selects a pricing method. It selects the final price.

3 Companies do not usually set a single price, but rather a pricing structure that reflects variations in geographical demand and costs, market-segment requirements, purchase timing, order levels and other factors. Several price-adaptation strategies are available: (1) geographical pricing; (2) price discounts and allowances; (3) promotional pricing; and (4) discriminatory pricing.

4 After developing pricing strategies firms often face situations in which they need to change prices. A price decrease might be brought about by excess plant capacity, declining market share, a desire to dominate the market through lower costs, or economic recession. A price increase might be brought about by cost inflation or overdemand. Companies must carefully manage customer perceptions in raising prices.

5 Companies must anticipate competitor price changes and prepare contingent responses. A number of

responses are possible in terms of maintaining or changing price or quality.

6 The firm facing a competitor's price change must try to understand the competitor's intent and the likely duration of the change. Strategy often depends on whether a firm is producing homogeneous or non-homogeneous products. A market leader attacked by lower-priced competitors can seek to better differentiate itself, introduce its own low-cost competitor, or transform itself more completely.

▽ APPLICATIONS

Marketing debate

Is the right price a fair price? Prices are often set to satisfy demand or to reflect the premium that consumers are willing to pay for a product or service. Some critics shudder, however, at the thought of €1.50 bottles of water, €150 running shoes and €400 concert tickets.

Take a position: Prices should reflect the value that consumers are willing to pay *versus* Prices should primarily just reflect the cost involved in making a product or service.

Marketing discussion

Think of the various pricing methods described in this chapter – mark-up pricing, target-return pricing, perceived-value pricing, value pricing, going-rate pricing and auction-type pricing. As a consumer, which method do you personally prefer to deal with? Why? If the average price were to stay the same, which would you prefer: (1) for firms to set one price and not deviate; or (2) to employ slightly higher prices most of the year, but slightly lower discounted prices or specials for certain occasions?

▽ REFERENCES

[1] Based on M. Hickman (2008) Tesco hits a new low with arrival of the £1.99 chicken, The *Independent*, 6 February; http://www.independent.co.uk/life-style/food-and-drink/news/tesco-hits-a-new-low-with-arrival-of-the-163199-chicken-778672.html, accessed March 2008.

[2] The price is wrong (2002) *The Economist*, 25 May, 59–60.

[3] X. Dreze and J. C. Nunes (2004) Using combined-currency prices to lower consumers' perceived cost, *Journal of Marketing Research*, 41 (February), 59–72.

[4] M. Menduno (2001) Priced to perfection, *Business 2.0*, 6 March, 40–2.

[5] P. Markillie (2004) A perfect market: a survey of e-commerce, *The Economist*, 15 May, 3–20; D. Kirpatrick (2004) How the open-source world plans to smack down Microsoft, and Oracle, and . . . , *Fortune*, 23 February, 92–100; F. Keenan (2003) The price is really right, *BusinessWeek*, 31 March, 61–7; M. Menduno (2001) Priced to perfection, *Business 2.0*, 6 March, 40–2; A. E. Cortese (1998) Good-bye to fixed pricing?, *BusinessWeek*, 4 May, 71–84. For a discussion of some of the academic issues involved, see F. Zettelmeyer (2000) Expanding to the Internet: pricing and communication strategies when firms compete on multiple channels, *Journal of Marketing*

Research, 37 (August), 292–308; J. G. Lynch Jr. and D. Ariely (2000) Wine online: search costs affect competition on price, quality, and distribution, *Marketing Science*, Winter, 83–103; R. Lal and M. Sarvary (1999) When and how is the Internet likely to decrease price competition?, *Marketing Science*, 18(4), 485–503.

[6] See http://www.jstor.org/about/participants_intl.html, accessed March 2008.

[7] J. Brown (2007) Radiohead album goes live on the Internet, The *Independent*, Music, 11 October, http://www.independent.co.uk/arts-entertainment/music/news/radiohead-album-goes-live-on-the-internet-396544.html, accessed March 2008.

[8] A. Sherwin (2007) How much is Radiohead's online album worth?, *The Times*, 11 October, 10–13.

[9] Based or pricing: the magic number (2006) *BusinessWeek*, Winter, http://www.businessweek.com/magazine/content/06_52/b4015452.htm?chan=search.

[10] For a thorough, up-to-date review of pricing research, see C. Ofir and R. S. Winer (2002) Pricing: economic and behavioral models, in B. Weitz and R. Wensley (eds) *Handbook of Marketing*, London: Sage.

[11]P. Sarkar (2007) Which shirt costs $275? Brand loyalty, bargain hunting, and unbridled luxury all play a part in the price you'll pay for a T-shirt, *Final Edition*, 15 March, C1. Reprinted by permission.

[12]P. R. Dickson and A. G. Sawyer (1990) The price knowledge and search of supermarket shoppers, *Journal of Marketing*, July, 42–53. For a methodological qualification, however, see H. Estalami, A. Holden and Donald R. Lehmann (2001) Macro-economic determinants of consumer price knowledge: a meta-analysis of four decades of research, *International Journal of Research in Marketing*, 18 (December), 341–55.

[13]For a comprehensive review, see T. Mazumdar, S. P. Raj and I. Sinha (2005) Reference price research: review and propositions, *Journal of Marketing*, 69 (October), 84–102. For a different point of view, see C. Janiszewski and D. R. Lichtenstein (1999) A range theory account of price perception, *Journal of Consumer Research*, March, 353–68.

[14]For a discussion of how 'incidental' prices outside the category can serve as contextual reference prices, see J. C. Nunes and P. Boatwright (2004) Incidental prices and their effect on willing-ness to pay, *Journal of Marketing Research*, 41 (November), 457–66.

[15]K. N. Rajendran and G. J. Tellis (1994) Contextual and temporal components of reference price, *Journal of Marketing*, January, 22–34; G. Kalyanaram and R. S. Winer (1995) Empirical generalizations from reference-price research, *Marketing Science*, 14(3), G161–9.

[16]R. Strauss (2002) Prices you just can't believe, *New York Times*, 17 January.

[17]Kalyanaram and Winer (1995) op. cit.

[18]G. E. Mayhew and R. S. Winer (1992) An empirical analysis of internal and external reference-price effects using scanner data, *Journal of Consumer Research*, June, 62–70.

[19]R. Ziethammer (2006) forward-looking buying in online auctions, *Journal of Marketing Research*, 43 (August), 462–76.

[20]J. T. Gourville (1998) Pennies-a-day: the effect of temporal reframing on transaction evaluation, *Journal of Consumer Research*, March, 395–408.

[21]G. M. Erickson and J. K. Johansson (1985) The role of price in multi-attribute product-evaluations, *Journal of Consumer Research*, September, 195–9.

[22]W. Amaldoss and S. Jain (2005) Pricing of conspicuous goods: a competitive analysis of social effects, *Journal of Marketing Research*, 42 (February), 30–42. A. Chao and J. B. Schor (1998) Empirical tests of status consumption: evidence from women's cosmetics, *Journal of Economic Psychology*, 19(4), 107–31.

[23]E. Byron (2007) Fashion victim: to refurbish its image, Tiffany risks profits; after silver took off, Jeweler raises prices to discourage teens, *Wall Street Journal*, 10 January, A1. Reprinted by permission of Dow Jones via Copyright Clearance Center.

[24]M. Stiving and R. S. Winer (1997) An empirical analysis of price endings with scanner data, *Journal of Consumer Research*, June, 57–68.

[25]E. T. Anderson and D. Simester (2003) Effects of $19 price endings on retail sales: evidence from field experiments, *Quantitative Marketing and Economics*, 1(1), 93–110.

[26]E. Anderson and D. Simester (2003) Mind your pricing cues, *Harvard Business Review*, September, 96–103.

[27]R. M. Schindler and P. N. Kirby (1997) Patterns of rightmost digits used in advertised prices: implications for nine-ending effects, *Journal of Consumer Research*, September, 192–201.

[28]Anderson and Simester (2003) op. cit.

[29]Ibid.

[30]D. J. Howard and R. A. Kerin (2006) Broadening the scope of reference-price advertising research: a field study of consumer shopping involvement, *Journal of Marketing*, 70 (October), 185–204.

[31]R. C. Blattberg and K. Wisniewski (1989) Price-induced patterns of competition, *Marketing Science*, 8 (Fall), 291–309.

[32]S. Dutta, M. J. Zbaracki and M. Bergen (2003) Pricing process as a capability: a resource-based perspective, *Strategic Management Journal*, 24(7), 615–30.

[33]Mei Fong (2006) IKEA hits home in China: the Swedish design giant, unlike other retailers, slashes prices for the Chinese, *Wall Street Journal*, 3 March, B1. Reprinted by permission of Dow Jones via Copyright Clearance Center.

[34]M. Silverstein and N. Fiske (2003) *Trading Up: The New American Luxury*, New York: Portfolio.

[35]C. Lawton (2003) A liquor maverick shakes up industry with pricey brands, *Wall Street Journal*, 21 May.

[36]A. Riding (2007) Seducing France into affairs of the art, *International Herald Tribune*, 23 July.

[37]T. Aeppel (2007) Seeking perfect prices, CEO tears up the rules, *Wall Street Journal*, 27 March.

[38]F. Zettelmeyer, F. S. Morton and J. Silva-Risso (2006) How the Internet lowers prices: evidence from matched survey and automobile transaction data, *Journal of Marketing Research*, 43(May), 168–81; J. R. Brown and A. Goolsbee (2002) Does the Internet make markets more competitive? Evidence from the life insurance industry, *Journal of Political Economy*, 110(5), 481–507.

[39]W. Baker, M. Marn and C. Zawada (2001) Price smarter on the Net, *Harvard Business Review*, February, 122–7.

[40]B. Bergstein (2007) Pricing software could reshape retail, *Forbes*, 27 April.

[41]T. T. Nagle and R. K. Holden (2002) *The Strategy and Tactics of Pricing*, 3rd edn, Upper Saddle River, NJ: Prentice Hall.

[42]For a summary of elasticity studies see D. M. Hanssens, L. J. Parsons and R. L. Schultz (1990) *Market Response Models: Econometric and Time Series Analysis*, Boston, MA: Kluwer, 187–91.

[43]T. H. A. Bijmolt, H. J. Van Heerde and R. G. M. Pieters (2005) New empirical generalizations on the determinants of price elasticity, *Journal of Marketing Research*, 42 (May), 141–56.

[44]Easier Than ABC (2003) *The Economist*, 25 October, 56.

[45]W. W. Alberts (1989) The experience curve doctrine reconsidered, *Journal of Marketing*, July, 36–49.

[46]M. Sivy (1991) Japan's smart secret weapon, *Fortune*, 12 August, 75.

[47]R. Grover and C. Edwards (2007) Next-gen DVDs: advantage, Sony, *BusinessWeek*, 6 December; adapted from R. J. Dolan and H. Simon (1997) Power pricers, *Across the Board*, May, 18–19.

[48]K. L. Ailawadi, D. R. Lehmann and S. A. Neslin (2001) Market response to a major policy change in the marketing mix: learning from Procter & Gamble's value pricing strategy, *Journal of Marketing*, 65(January), 44–61.

[49]Aeppel (2007) op. cit.

[50]Tung-Zong Chang and A. R. Wildt (1994) Price, product information, and purchase intention: an empirical study, *Journal of the Academy of Marketing Science*, Winter, 16–27. See also G. D. Kortge and P. A. Okonkwo (1993) Perceived value approach to pricing, *Industrial Marketing Management*, May, 133–40.

[51]H. J. Larsen (2006) Mormor, http://www.springwise.com, 6 February; http://www.mormor.nu/

[52]J. C. Anderson, D. C. Jain and P. K. Chintagunta (1993) Customer value assessment in business markets: a state-of-practice study, *Journal of Business-to-Business Marketing*, 1(1), 3–29.

[53]M. Meng (2006) Sexy supermarkets, www.springwise.com/retail, 9 May; B. Saporito (1994) Behind the tumult at P&G, *Fortune*, 7 March, 74–82. For empirical analysis of its effects, see Ailawadi et al. (2001) op. cit.

[54]S. J. Hoch, X. Dreze and M. J. Purk (1994) EDLP, Hi-Lo, and margin arithmetic, *Journal of Marketing*, October, 16–27; R. Lal and R. Rao (1997) Supermarket competition: the case of everyday low pricing, *Marketing Science*, 16(1), 60–80.

[55]J. W. Alba, C. F. Mela, T. A. Shimp and J. E. Urbany (1999) The effect of discount frequency and depth on consumer price judgments, *Journal of Consumer Research*, September, 99–114.

[56]M. Duff (2005) European retailers reckon with hard discounters' formidable potential, *DSN Retailing Today*, 10 January.

[57]J. E. Rasmussen (2006) Succes ved en tilfældighed, *Erhverv og Økonomi*, 6 March.

[58]E. Smith and S. Silver (2006) To protect its box-office turf, Ticketmaster plays rivals' tune, *Wall Street Journal*, 12 September.

[59]Royal Mail drives major cost savings through free markets (2003) Free Markets press release, 15 December.

[60]S. D. Jap (2007) The impact of online reverse auction design on buyer–supplier relationships, *Journal of Marketing*, 71, January, 146–59; S. D. Jap (2003) An exploratory study of the introduction of online reverse auctions, *Journal of Marketing*, 67 (July), 96–107.

[61]P. W. Farris and D. J. Reibstein (1879) How prices, expenditures, and profits are linked, *Harvard Business Review*, November–December, 173–84. See also M. Abe (1995) Price and

advertising strategy of a national brand against its private-label clone: a signaling game approach, *Journal of Business Research*, July, 241–50.

[62]J. P. Morgan Report (2000) E-tailing and the five Cs, March.

[63]E. H. Fram and Michael S. McCarthy (1999) The true price of penalties, *Marketing Management*, October, 49–56.

[64]Airline SAS gets 1 billion kronor in compensation from Bombardier, Associated Press, 10 March.

[65]J. E. Urbany (2001) Justifying profitable pricing, *Journal of Product and Brand Management*, 10 (3), 141–57; C. Fishman (2003) The Wal-Mart you don't know, *Fast Company*, December, 68–80.

[66]http://faculty.insead.edu/chandon/personal_page/Documents/ Case-Unilever%20Brazil%201997-2007-w.pdf http://www. trendwatching.com/trends/SACHET_MARKETING.htm.

[67]P. N. Agarwala (1991) *Countertrade: A Global Perspective*, New Delhi: Vikas; M. Rowe (1989) *Countertrade*, London: Euromoney Books; C. M. Korth (ed.) (1987) *International Countertrade*, New York: Quorum Books.

[68]For an interesting discussion of a quantity surcharge see D. E. Sprott, K. C. Manning and A. Miyazaki (2003) Grocery price settings and quantity surcharges, *Journal of Marketing*, 67 (July), 34–46.

[69]M. V. Marn and R. L. Rosiello (1992) Managing price, gaining profit, *Harvard Business Review*, September–October, 84–94. See also K. L. Ailawadi, S. A. Neslin and K. Gedenk (2001) Pursuing the value-conscious consumer: store brands versus national-brand promotions, *Journal of Marketing*, 65 (January), 71–89; G. J. Tellis (1995) Tackling the retailer decision maze: which brands to discount, how much, when, and why?, *Marketing Science*, 14(3), 271–99.

[70]K. J. Clancy (1997) At what profit price?, *Brandweek*, 23 June.

[71]L. Smith (1990) Donna Karan's fashions hit London, *The Times*, 20 February.

[72]R. Deesiraju and S. M. Shugan (1999) Strategic service pricing and yield management, *Journal of Marketing*, 63 (January), 44–56; R. E. Weigand (1999) Yield management: filling buckets, papering the house, *Business Horizons*, September–October, 55–64.

[73]C. Fishman (2003) Which price is right?, *Fast Company*, March, 92–102; B. Tedeschi (2002) E-commerce report, *New York Times*, 2 September; F. Keenan (2003) The price is really right, *BusinessWeek*, 31 March, 62–7; P. Coy (2000) The power of smart pricing, *BusinessWeek*, 10 April, 160–4. For a review of recent and seminal work linking pricing decisions with operational insights, see M. Fleischmann, J. M. Hall and D. F. Pyke (2004) Research brief: smart pricing, *MIT Sloan Management Review*, Winter, 9–13.

[74]http://www.sonofon.dk/privat/mobiltelefoner/vejledning/ ofte_stillede_spoergsmaal/

[75]H. Spongenberg (2007) Brussels to grill Apple on iTunes pricing, *BusinessWeek*, 19 September.

[76]M. France (1998) Does predatory pricing make Microsoft a predator?, *BusinessWeek*, 23 November, 130–2. Also see J. P. Guiltinan and G. T. Gundlack (1996) Aggressive and predatory pricing: a framework for analysis, *Journal of Advertising*, July, 87–102.

[77]For more information on specific types of price discrimination that are illegal see H. Cheesman (2007) *Business Law*, 6th edn, Upper Saddle River, NJ: Prentice Hall.

[78]B. Donath (2003) Dispel major myths about pricing, *Marketing News*, 3 February, 10.

[79]For a classic review, see K. B. Monroe (1973) Buyers' subjective perceptions of price, *Journal of Marketing Research*, February, 70–80. See also Z. J. Zhang, F. Feinberg and A. Krishna (2002) Do we care what others get? A behaviorist approach to targeted promotions, *Journal of Marketing Research*, 39 (August), 277–91.

[80]M. C. Campbell (1999) Perceptions of pricing unfairness: antecedents and consequences, *Journal of Marketing Research*, 36 (May), 187–99.

[81]Lan Xia, K. B. Monroe and J. L. Cox (2004) The price is unfair! A conceptual framework of price fairness perceptions, *Journal of Marketing*, 68 (October), 1–15.

[82]E. Mitchell (1990) How not to raise prices, *Small Business Reports*, November, 64–7.

[83]R. Collis (2002) The frequent traveler: getting frills for the cost of a no-frills ticket, *International Herald Tribune*, 5 July.

Delivering value

Video documentary for Part 6

Go to **www.pearsoned.co.uk/marketingmanagementeurope** to watch the video documentary that relates to Part 6 and consider the issues raised below.

Once a company has researched and then developed an attractive value package, it is important to ensure that it reaches customers in the market-place quickly and efficiently.

Part 6: Delivering Value explores three important themes:

1 selecting and managing channels;

2 analysing channel members; and

3 charting the rise of new channels.

Different national markets and different target markets require many companies to design, develop and operate multichannel distribution networks. This provides a real challenge to marketing management of maintaining their corporate brand values.

The rapid growth in digital marketing techniques has helped to speed up order placement, processing and physical delivery logistics as well as opening up new markets and new intermediaries.

When watching the video documentary that accompanies Part 6, consider how the companies being interviewed either seek to do as much as possible 'in-house', or take care to build loyal value chains before moving finished value packages as efficiently as possible to their customers. As distribution channel members are in direct contact with trading customers (their intermediaries) or the final customer, they are in an ideal position to gather and communicate important customer information that has a bearing on the perceived value of the branded offering. Attention to the constant improvement of the customer interface with the supply and delivery network is a vital management concern in competitive market places.

Hear a variety of top marketing executives from a wide range of organisations offer their own interesting and varied perspectives on the key themes of Part 6 including: Josephine Rydberg-Dumont, President, IKEA Sweden (top); Mats Ronne, European Media Director, Electrolux (centre); and Royal Enfield, the Indian-based manufacturer of motorcycles (bottom).

Chapter 17

Designing and managing supply networks

IN THIS CHAPTER, WE WILL ADDRESS THE FOLLOWING QUESTIONS:

1 What are supply networks and channels of distribution?

2 How should marketers design supply networks and channels of distribution?

3 How can marketers select channels members?

4 What are the challenges of managing distribution channels?

5 What are the impacts of digital/information and communication technologies?

We live in a networked global world with marketing managers having to manage increasingly more complex and demanding local and global supply networks operating both online and offline. Previously known as logistics or distribution, marketing managers now realise the importance of managing their supply network for customer satisfaction and profitability. Supply chains can be viewed as networks of entities all working together for a company goal and each company has to decide where they are in the network.

Take the Smart Car.

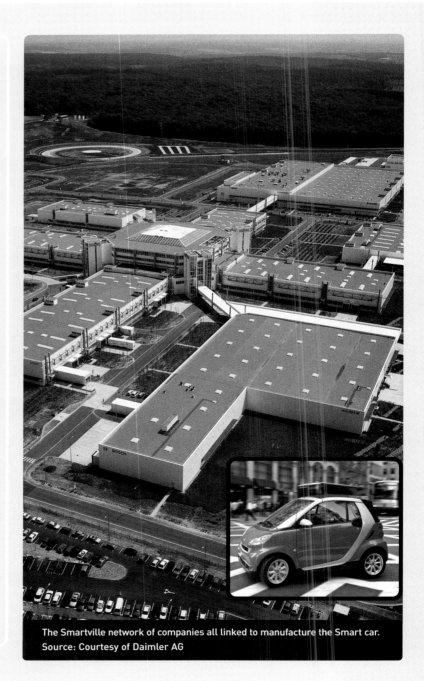

The Smartville network of companies all linked to manufacture the Smart car.
Source: Courtesy of Daimler AG

CHAPTER JOURNEY

Supply networks
and channels of
distribution

Channel
management and
channel design

Selecting channels
members

Understanding
the impact of
technology

Managing
distribution
channels

The Smart car, named after Swatch, Mercedes and Art, was the brainchild of Nicolas Hayek, perhaps better known as CEO of Swatch, the watch company. Hayek's dream was the Swatchmobile, which would do for the small car what he had done for the watch, a car that would be fun, cheap and simple yet environmentally sound, running on hybrid power. The Smart car is managed in a unique network manner.

The Smart car, which is now owned by DaimlerChrysler, the parent company of Mercedes-Benz, was launched in October 1998 and is a two-seater, 2.5 m long by 1.5 m wide car – small enough that two or even three Smart cars can squeeze into a standard parking space. The Smart car is built at one of the most modern car manufacturing network complexes in the world – called Smartville, located at Hambach in Lorraine, France. The car is designed to be highly modular, with modules/parts attached to a rigid integral body frame. Designing the car for assembly and network operations has received particular attention. From a supply chain perspective almost everything is outsourced. The cross-shaped assembly building is surrounded by a number of other buildings housing the main systems suppliers. There are over 1900 people in 11 autonomous but independent companies who work together in a network to build the Smart car.[1] The companies include:

- **Magna**: space frame
- **Magna Uniport (Ymos)**: doors
- **Surtema Eisenmann**: paintshop
- **Bosch**: front powertrain, breaks, lights
- **Mannesmann VDO**: cockpit
- **Dynamit Nobel**: plastic body panels
- **Krupp Automotive Systems**: rear powertrain.

In addition, there are three on-site logistics partners:

- **TNT logistics**: spare part facility
- **Rhenus**: storage for small parts
- **MTL**: moves finished cars to dealers.

The distribution of the Smart car has also been innovative, featuring round transparent towers with Smart cars inside them. Smart was also the first manufacturer to sell cars over the Internet. The Smart small car is very popular in major European cities and has recently been launched in the United States.

Marketing operates within a network. Rather than viewing companies as independent companies, supply chains now compete against supply chains. Instead of limiting their focus to their immediate suppliers, distributors and customers, marketing managers must examine the whole supply network that links raw materials, components and products or service processes and manage every aspect through to the final consumer. Companies are looking at their suppliers' suppliers upstream and at their distributors' customers downstream. They must manage a network of relationships often called value networks. They must look at customer segments and consider a wide range of different possible means to distribute their products and services, both locally and globally. The inclusion of the customer as an integral part of the production or service process rather then simply as the wallet at the end of the chain[2] is also important.

In this chapter we will review how marketers must build and manage continuously evolving and increasingly complex supply networks and channels of distribution. We will begin by discussing the terms and definitions that will be used throughout the chapter and then discuss how to manage and coordinate the supply network right through to the consumer. Technologies including the Internet as a channel of distribution will be explored, reflecting the dominant technology component along supply networks.

▽ What is a supply chain or network?

Company performance is strongly linked to supply networks and distribution excellence.[3] In the new era of networked consumers and digital everything, the economics of distribution are changing rapidly.[4] Companies can improve their supply chain and distribution to reap substantial cost savings, at the same time improving accuracy and service quality. More and more companies are looking to their national or global supply networks for improvements. The ultimate success of a business will depend on the management ability to integrate the company's intricate network of business relationships.[5] As Peter Drucker noted, it is now a network economy with competition between supply networks rather than single companies.[6] Take the image (Figure 17.1) of Diageo's supply network: suppliers, manufacturing sites, distributors and transport companies all over the world have to be managed to ensure a perfect product every time for the consumer.

Managing a global supply network is complex but success means tangible results in increased profitability. There is a perception that management of the networks of relationships is the most crucial aspects of marketing and should be elevated above other aspect of the marketing mix.[7] As Bernard Teiling, Vice-President of Nestlé noted: 'If you are not good at SCM [supply chain management] someone else will be. SCM is both a source of competitive advantage and a lever for profit margin'[8] – see 'Marketing insight: The top supply chain companies in the world', page 616.

The globalisation effect

Supply chains existed in Roman times and between China and Europe with companies such as the Dutch East India Company bringing tea, silk, spices and even opium to Europe in the early seventeenth century. Nowadays the changing pace of global delivery and supply is amazing. So many products and services are moved around the world every minute of every day. UPS, a leading transport company, moves over 13 million items a day and so 2 per cent of the world GNP is on the back of UPS trucks at any given time. At the global hub for FedEx, another transport company, an aircraft lands every 90 seconds and packages are routed along 300 miles of conveyor belts.[9] Take food as an example: French beans from Kenya are flown in refrigerated containers to London. In Beijing and Shanghai consumers enjoy Italian olives, French cheese and Belgian chocolate. Many products have travelled thousands of miles from their origins to where they are consumed. Fish caught in Europe is frozen and sent to China where it is defrosted and filleted before being refrozen and sent back to Europe.[10]

Distribution methods are also changing. We live in a world where fans around the world have downloaded the latest Avril Lavigne CD over 7.3 million times in eight different languages.[11]

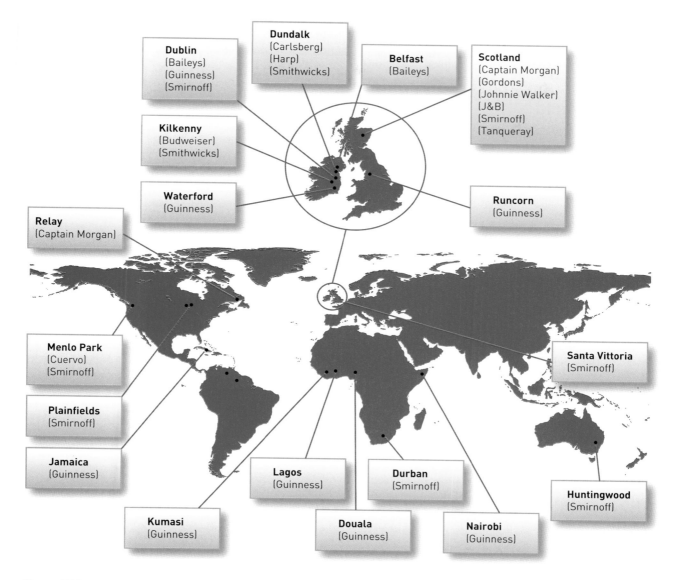

Figure 17.1 Diageo's global supply network

Source: Diageo Ireland, Brands have global reach (see www.diageo.ie/company/global).

Traditional distribution of music featured a trip to a record shop where you brought the physical product: CD, LP or single. Now you can log on to www.iTunes.com and download your choice to your iPod or listen through your computer. A decade ago, Tesco used one distribution outlet – the retail shop. Now you can buy your groceries online with home delivery and use self-service checkouts when in the store. The leading supply network managers are applying new technology, new innovations and process thinking with a customer focus. As Professor Baker of the University of Nottingham notes, 'the distinction between success and failure in competitive markets may be reduced to two basic issues, first an understanding of customer needs and second, the ability to deliver added value'.[12]

Thomas Friedman, author of *The World Is Flat*, notes that technology and fast access to market are levelling the global playing field.[13] Figure 17.2 shows how supplies must be managed globally, coordinating road, rail, sea and air and by technological routes to market such as the Internet. Companies also have to manage a range of relationships, from buying raw materials, managing suppliers, warehousing, operating transport fleets, taking orders, collecting payment,

Marketing insight

The top supply chain companies in the world

Nokia, the Swedish mobile phone company, is the top supply chain company in the world. According to AMR Research 2007, and for the third year in a row, the Supply Chain Top 25 portfolio of companies outperformed the market, this time by a wide margin.[14] The average total return of the Top 25 portfolio for 2007 is 17.89 per cent, compared with returns of 6.43 per cent for the Dow Jones Industrial Average (DJIA) and 3.53 per cent for the S&P 500. Clearly this is a group of companies that excels, strongly, weathering the ups and downs of the market.

The Top 25 is an annual ranking of large manufacturers and retailers that display superior supply chain performance, capabilities and leadership. These are the companies that are furthest along in achieving the ideal of a highly coordinated, demand-driven network that delivers shareholder and community value.

Table 17.1 2007 AMR Research Supply Chain Top 25 stock performance

2007 supply chain top 25 companies	Ticker	29, Dec, 2006 closing price[a]	30 May, 2007 closing price[a]	31 Dec, 2007 closing price[a]	Price change since announced on 31 May (%)	2007 Price change (%)
1 Nokia	NOK	19.87	27.16	38.39	41.35	93.21
2 Apple	AAPL	84.84	118.77	198.08	66.78	133.47
3 Procter & Gamble	PG	62.94	63.18	73.42	16.21	16.65
4 IBM	IBM	95.80	106.18	108.10	1.81	12.84
5 Toyota Motor	TM	134.31	120.05	106.17	−11.56	−20.95
6 Wal-Mart Stores	WMT	45.31	46.67	47.53	1.84	4.90
7 Anheuser-Busch	BUD	48.00	52.00	52.34	0.65	9.04
8 Tesco	TSCDY	23.68	27.41	28.05	2.33	18.45
9 Best Buy	BBY	48.86	46.59	52.65	13.01	7.76
10 Samsung Electronics[b]			n/a			
11 Cisco Systems	CSCO	27.33	26.39	27.07	2.58	−0.95
12 Motorola	MOT	20.32	18.12	16.04	−11.48	−21.06
13 The Coca-Cola Company	KO	47.04	52.09	61.37	17.82	30.46
14 Johnson & Johnson	JNU	64.37	62.41	66.70	6.87	3.62
15 PepsiCo	PEP	61.27	67.49	75.90	12.46	23.88
16 Johnson Controls	JCI	28.27	36.07	36.04	−0.08	27.48
17 Texas Instruments	TXN	28.54	34.82	33.40	−4.08	17.03
18 Nike	NKE	48.84	55.17	64.24	16.44	31.53
19 Lowe's	LOW	30.88	32.12	22.62	−29.58	−26.75
20 GlaxoSmithkline	GSK	50.78	51.67	50.39	−2.48	−0.77
21 Hewlett-Packard	HPQ	40.91	45.45	50.48	11.07	23.39
22 Lockheed Martin	LMT	90.76	97.51	105.26	7.95	15.98
23 Publix Super Markets[c]			n/a			
24 Paccar	PCAR	41.96	56.20	54.48	−3.06	29.84
25 AstraZeneca	AZN	51.89	52.80	42.82	−18.90	−17.48
Average total return from the supply chain top 25					**6.00**	**17.89**
DJIA	^DJI	12,463.15	13,633.08	13,264.82	−2.70	6.43
S&P 500	^GSPC	1,418.30	1,530.23	1,468.36	−4.04	3.53

Notes:
[a] All prices adjusted for splits and dividends.
[b] Samsung is not included because it is not traded on a U.S. stock exchange.
[c] Publix is not included because it is a private company.

Source: D. Hofman and K. O'Marah (2008) The AMR Research supply chain top 25 blows away market with 17.89% return, AMR Research, 10 January (www.amrresearch.com/content/view.asp?pmillid=21042). Data from AMR Research and Yahoo! Copyright © 2008 AMR Research, Inc. Reproduced with permission.

▶ **Marketing insight** *(continued)*

Within the consumer product section three European companies, The Danone Groupe, Unilever and Heineken performed well – see Table 17.2.[15]

Four characteristics distinguish the higher performance of these companies:

1 There is an 'outside-in' marketing focus – that is, everything starts with the customer and then looks back into the organisation.

2 Supply chains extend out to customers and suppliers.

3 Innovation is embedded in these companies.

4 They have the right attitude towards the management of their supply chain.

Looking towards the future, many of the traditional roles of supply chain members are changing due to outsourcing, green supply chains and the increased use of technology. According to the *Supply Chain Management Review* the top issues in SCM are:

● **Global sourcing**: Not just finding the lowest-cost producer, but the source that makes most sense for the overall business strategy.

● **Technology along the supply chain**: Marketers need to understand and use the range of technologies from data management to radio frequency identification devices and on to self-service technologies.

● **Going green**: The global trend of 'going green', or working to minimise the impact of industrialisation on the environment. Companies are going to feel pressure not only to focus more on their impact on the planet, but also to prove their commitment to a cleaner operation.[16]

Table 17.2 AMR Research Supply Network top performers – consumer products

Company	ROA (%)	Inventory turns	Revenue growth (%)	Composite score
Procter & Gamble	6.40	5.3	20.20	5.43
Anheuser-Busch	12.00	14.6	4.30	4.83
The Coca-Cola Company	17.00	5.0	4.30	4.00
PepsiCo	18.80	8.2	7.90	3.81
Colgate Palmolive	14.80	5.5	7.30	2.50
Unilever	12.90	8.6	4.00	2.37
The Danone Groupe	9.00	11.1	8.10	1.97
Heineken	6.80	11.1	9.50	1.90
Average consumer products	12.20	8.7	8.20	
Median for consumer products	12.40	8.4	7.60	

Source: L. Cecere and D. Hofman (2008) Seven lessons from the AMR Research 2008 supply chain top 25 for consumer products, AMR Research, 23 August (www.amrresearch.com/Content/View.asp?pmillid=21730). Data from AMR Research. Copyright © 2008 AMR Research, Inc. Reproduced with permission.

repairs and even call centre issues. They also have to control for different market needs and requirements. For example, within the European market there are 27 different countries and over 20 official languages. When Hewlett Packard produces printers for the European markets it understands that each country has its own language requirements, with different instructions and software. Many also have different power networks and so power supply cables must be manufactured and distributed to suit each country – that is a challenge for a supply network.

Definitions of terms

The traditional view of a **supply chain** is as: 'a set of three or more entities (organisations or individuals) directly involved in the upstream or downstream flows of product, service, finances and/or information from a source to a customer'.[17] The move to the concept of a supply network

Figure 17.2 Global supply networks: coordinating road, rail, shipping, airlines and the Internet.

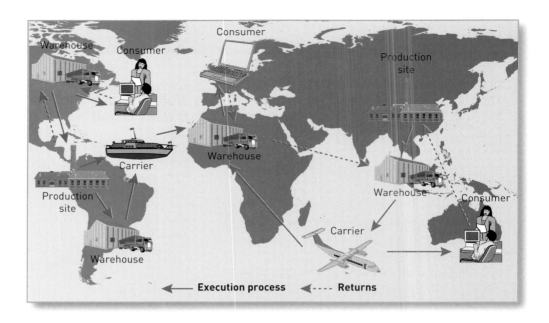

is the idea that these chains are not linear but are more networks and webs of suppliers, distributors, transport companies, customers, and so on. **Logistics** usually focuses on products and is the flow of products from point of origin to end user. It is a subject heavily influenced by operations research, optimisation and modelling and a focus on improving efficiency and speed. The supply network focus is on distribution and channels. There are many **distribution channels** within marketing, from direct to the customer or through a variety of intermediaries, performing a variety of tasks. Today's dynamic markets are forcing companies to design increasingly complex channel strategies involving multiple channels and multichannels to market.[18] An **intermediary** is any channel member that plays some role in bringing the product or service to market.[19] Distribution channels are sets of intermediaries that are usually interdependent organisations involved in the process of making a product or service available for use or consumption. They are the set of pathways a product or service follows after production or service design, culminating in purchase and use by the consumer.

- They can include wholesalers, retailers, distributors, intermediaries, transport companies, and so on as well as the Internet, which is an online route to market. Some intermediaries – such as wholesalers and retailers – buy and resell products; many distributors offer enhanced services such as warehousing and retailing services.
- Brokers, manufacturers' representatives or agents search for customers and may negotiate on the producer's behalf but do not take title to the goods.
- Inventory is the storing of products and services awaiting distribution to final customers.

Supply chain management (SCM) encompasses the planning and management of all activities involved in buying, making, providing and distributing. Importantly, it also includes coordination and collaboration with channel partners, which can be suppliers, intermediaries, third-party service providers and customers. In essence, SCM integrates supply and demand management within and across companies.

A SCM philosophy has the following characteristics:

1. a systems approach to viewing the supply chain as a whole, and to managing the total flow of products or services from the supplier to the ultimate customer;

2. a strategic orientation towards cooperative efforts to synchronise and converge intrafirm and interfirm operational and strategic capabilities into a unified whole; and

3. a customer focus to create unique and individualised sources of customer value, leading to customer satisfaction.[20]

The supply chain is often called a **supply network**, a term that will be intermixed in this chapter. The traditional view of the supply chain is very linear in nature and does not reflect the complexity of the supply networks that marketers must understand. An even broader view sees a company at the centre of a **value chain** or **network** – a system of partnerships and alliances that a firm creates to source, augment and deliver its offerings. A value network includes a firm's suppliers and its suppliers' suppliers and its immediate customers and their end customers.

A definition of a **network** is that it: consists of nodes and relationships with which interaction takes place. It can accommodate movement in any direction . . . it can change into any number of shapes; it is scale-free, it defines stucture but also process and change. Its nodes include people, organisations, machines, events or activitives. We can choose to focus on any of its parts without losing sight of the systemic context. A network can support a strict mode of operation which is cost-effective in mass production but it can equally well be flexible to a customer's individual value-creation.[21]

Figure 17.3 shows how a supply network might look within the health care sector.[22]

As you can see from Figure 17.3 all the members in the network interlink and each member has to reflect or be aware of other members and their needs. Take Nokia. In 2007 Nokia, the Swedish mobile phone company, was ranked number one in the Top 25 supply chains. Nokia excels at supplier collaboration while still pursuing technology and design innovations. Nokia manufactures and delivers mobile phones to almost 1 billion customers worldwide due to its ability to manage complexity, understand consumer needs and really relate to the needs of its market and its network of suppliers and distributors. Nokia insist that

> close cooperation with customers and suppliers is one of our core development principles. It encourages end-to-end efficiency and speed – key success factors for the entire supply chain. Openness and trust are important aspects when working together with suppliers and driving compliance.[23]

Leading companies are jumping ahead of their slower rivals and are establishing positions of dominance, based in large part on their ability to work collaboratively with carefully selected trading partners but also their greater understanding of customer needs and wants and delivering to them when they want and need. Companies such as Zara, Nokia, Heineken and Unilever are examples of firms that focus on their customers and then their supply network. In contrast, some companies still focus their supply network efforts entirely inwardly. They rely on internally

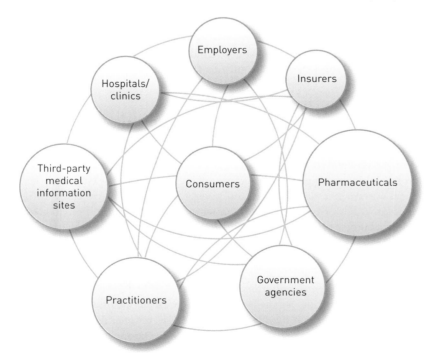

Figure 17.3 The health care network

Source: H. J . Schau, M. F. Smith and P. I. Schau (2005) The healthcare network economy: the role of Internet information transfer and implications for pricing, *Industrial Marketing Management*, 34, 147–56. Reproduced with permission.

generated process improvements aimed at reducing costs in specific functional areas rather than an external focus on what the market needs and wants. Many marketers are still struggling to reach the more advanced stage of supply chain management, in which collaboration and the use of technology links all members[24]– an issue to be explored later in the chapter.

In adopting a network perspective, companies move beyond the one supplier or distributor or even two to the multiparty network of suppliers, distributors, transport companies, and so on. Within these networks the challenge is to balance the interests of so many players in the supply or demand network so that there is *balanced centricity*[25] – a customer and a profit focus. Take the example of transportation companies, many of which are network players in many networks due to their expertise in managing delivery. Third-party suppliers, such as FedEx Logistics Services and TNT, often participate in designing or managing distribution systems. TNT Logistics manages part of BMW's supply network from the moment a part is dispatched by a supplier until its installation in one of the cars on the production site. That means that the fork-lift truck drivers in the BMW factory are actually employees of TNT, not BMW.[26] Take the case of the National Health Service (NHS) in the United Kingdom. DHL has recently entered into a contract worth £1.6 billion with the UK's Department of Health to run a division called NHS supply chain and is responsible for delivering all logistic service and support to 600 hospitals in England. DHL manages key supplier and maintenance contracts, food, bed linen, office equipment, stationery, cleaning products, patients' clothing, medical and surgical equipment.

Figure 17.4 shows the complexity of supply network interactions for Opel Portugal and gives a better perspective on the complexity of relationships and management issues.[27]

The level of network marketing skills needed depends on the complexity of the product or service, the number of available suppliers and customers, the availability of material, distributors, transport companies, and so on. A major decision is what length of a supply chain or network to have and how close a relationship is needed. It would be rare for a firm to participate in only one supply chain or network. Also, companies that are competitors in one area can be partners in another. For example Toyota is a competitor of French carmaker Peugeot Citroën in one area but a partner in another. Toyota has a joint venture with PSA Peugeot Citroën to jointly build small cars in the Czech Republic that will help it to tap local knowledge and also help to control and share investment costs.

Relationsips are hard to manage – think of the relationships you have with your parents, with your friends, and so on. The ability to manage relationships and to colloborate successfully with other firms is a strategic imperative but successful collaborations or relationships do not come easily. Developing close relationships along the supply chain can create superior quality and gain competitive advantage but the barriers to developing and managing these relationships are huge and frequently fail. A recent study found that 50 per cent of interfirm alliances break down prematurely and that significant financial damage is inflicted on both parties in the process.[28]

Designing agile, adaptable, aligned supply networks

Traditionally, most supply chains focused on cost savings first and then on speed. Management's major concern was the total cost of distribution, which can amount to as much as 30–40 per cent of product costs. Taking an example from the grocery industry, changes to its supply network can increase annual operating costs by 10 per cent, translating into billions of euros, by revamping their distribution. A box of breakfast cereal can take 104 days to move through a labyrinth of wholesalers, distributors, brokers and consolidators from factory to supermarket to breakfast table. Within the services sector millions could be saved if processes were improved. Within banking there are over 20 internal processes when a supplier pays an invoice to a customer. A deletion of just one process would result in great savings.

Many companies state their distribution objective as 'getting the right product or service to the right places at the right time for the least cost.' Unfortunately, this objective provides little practical guidance. No system can simultaneously maximise customer service and minimise distribution costs. Maximum customer service implies large inventories, premium transportation and multiple warehouses, all of which raise distribution costs. There has to be a matching of

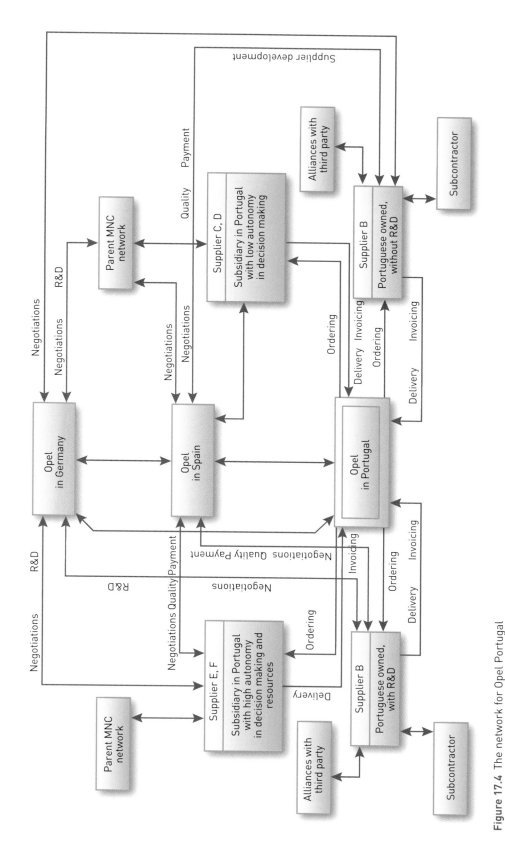

Figure 17.4 The network for Opel Portugal

Source: M. de Lurdes, D.K. Velduo and S. Macbeth (2004) Partnering and relationships within an international network context, *European Journal of Marketing*, 21(2), 142–57.

Figure 17.5
Foundations of Agile
Supply Chains
Source: H. Lee (2004) The
three A's of supply chain
excellence, *Electronics
Supply and Manufacturing*,
1 October. Reproduced
with permission.

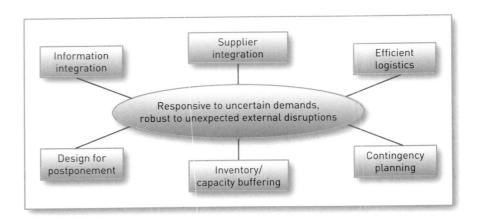

efficiency and customer need. This *customer-centric* view of the supply chain is a new approach for many, an approach that calls for a focus on the customer and his or her needs and must also strive for cost effectivness and speed in the supply networks.

One perspective is to study what has been called the three As – the agility, alignment and adaptability of the supply network.

Agility Supply networks need to be agile to react rapidly, reliably and cost effectively when changes occur. In order to be agile supply networks need:

- strong supplier relationships
- appropriate capacity levels
- parts commonality
- contingency or back-up plans for supply and logistics
- tight integration between all departments within the company.[29]

Nokia demonstrated best practice agility in its response to a fire in a Philips semiconductor factory that had the potential to disrupt Nokia's supply network. This Philips factory supplied a crucial part for Nokia's mobile phone manufacturing process. However Nokia had contingency plans in place and a team trained to react under such circumstances to manage the crisis. It turned to its back-up suppliers and ordered the main parts needed while also modifiying the mobile phone to suit the parts that could be delivered. Ericsson, their main competitor, which sourced parts from the same factory, did not fare so well. It had not developed back-up suppliers and could not cope with the situation, so supply and ultimately sales were damaged by having to scale back production of its mobile phones.[30]

Adaptability When demand or supply conditions change the supply network strategy needs to be re-examined to make sure it is still the best fit. Relocating manufacturing or using different outsourcing resources are some of the options available. The network must be able to adapt to changing times and conditions. Marketers need to study:

- pattern recognition
- preparedness
- supply network/chain structure.

Flextronics, a company headquartered in Singapore, is a leading electronics manufacturing services (EMS) provider focused on delivering complete design, engineering and manufacturing services to car, computing, consumer digital, industrial, infrastructure, medical and mobile original equipment manufacturers. Flextronics helps customers design, build, ship and service electronics products through a network of facilities in 30 countries on four continents and had annual revenues for 2007 of €21.9 billion. It had the contract to manufacture the very success-ful Xboxes for Microsoft. For the European launch it manufactured in Hungary and for the US

Figure 17.6
Foundations of Adaptive Supply Chains

Source: H. Lee (2004) The three A's of supply chain excellence, *Electronics Supply and Manufacturing*, 1 October. Reproduced with permission.

launch manufactured in Mexico since speed and market proximity were crucial. As the product matured, they moved production to China to boost cost efficiency.

Alignment[31] A supply network is only as strong as its weakest link. All members in the network must agree objectives and carry out their side of the bargain. If one member of the supply network simply focuses on their own interests then the network as a whole will suffer. Marketers need to create and manage relationships and align their partners' incentives with their own interests to maximise the chain's overall performance. The roles and functions need to be well defined, as in who is responsible for replenishment, forecasting, order fulfilment, customer service, and so on – see Figure 17.7.

Dimension	Exchanges	Objectives
Information alignment	Information knowledge	Common, shared
Identity alignment	Role, work, responsibility	Efficiency and flexibility
Incentive alignment	Accountability, risks/costs/gains	Equitable and overall performance

Figure 17.7
Foundations of Aligned Supply Chains

Source: H. Lee (2004) The three A's of supply chain excellence, *Electronics Supply and Manufacturing*, 1 October. Reproduced with permission.

Managing a demand-driven chain or network

Marketing should first think of the target market and then design the supply network backwards from that point – this is the concept of *demand-driven* rather than supply-driven networks. This is quite a radical idea because much of the current and traditional view has been supplier centric, a perspective that suits the suppliers rather than the customer. Many companies are in the process of transforming traditional supply networks into what are being called **demand-driven value networks**. There are three steps to moving to a demand-driven philosophy:[32]

1 transforming forecast-based, push-driven supply chains into demand-driven networks;

2 'outside-in' translation of priorities from the point of product or service consumption or usage back into operations and 'inside-out' execution;

3 transforming supply chains into end-to-end, process-oriented value networks that differentiate competitors through joint-value creation activities across the network.

Figure 17.8 Demand-driven supply networks

DDSN is the 21st century supply chain
What's different?

This perspective emphasises what solutions consumers are looking for, not what products or services companies are trying to sell them. Marketers, for their part, have traditionally focused on the customer or towards demand, but too often had little view or control of the supply network. Now they have to increasingly participate in and influence their companies' upstream activities and oversee the management of their network so that it reflects demand needs. Figure 17.8 clearly shows how twenty-first century demand-driven supply networks (DDSN) have moved away from the linear chain model.[33]

The first image shows a linear image of supply to demand while the second image shows supply and demand working together to determine demand. Sometimes it is difficult for companies to know what demand is going to be, particularly for new products or services. Take Toyota.

▽ Toyota

Toyota was convinced that the market for their Prius – the leading hybrid car that can run on petrol or electricity and is very environmentally friendly – would be large. When Toyota launched this car it knew that the market would be different from that for their previous models. The Japanese automobile maker had expertise in tracking trends and geographical preferences but it found it hard to predict how customers were going to react to the Prius. Toyota felt that the car might appeal to environmentalists and conservationists – customer groups which Toyota didn't know much about. It decided to change from its normal practice of product allocation distribution, which was related to sales of previous models. It decided it was wiser not to give the car to its normal car dealer network based on past trends but to await orders – demand from customers. So Toyota decided to keep the car in central locations and wait for the dealer orders to be communicated to the company via the Internet, and then move the car to the dealer. This new distribution system worked well even though Toyota's transportation costs rose, but it customised products to demand and managed the inventory flawlessly.

▽ Supply network management

Traditionally most diagrams focus on a chain aspect and most are product focused even with the increase in services. Figure 17.9 shows a linear product-focused supply chain[34] and Figure 17.10 portrays a service-focused supply chain.[35] The main difference is that the customer becomes part of the process in the service chain. This is discussed in greater detail in Chapter 18.

There are eight key processes that form the core of supply chain management:

1 **Customer relationship management**: The framework for managing customer relationships tailoring the supply chain to customer needs.

2 **Customer service management process**: The customer service management process is the company's face to the customer and is the source of all information, such as product or service availability and order status. This is covered in Chapter 18 in more detail.

3 **Demand management**: This needs to balance the customer's requirements with the firm's supply capability.

4 **Order fulfilment**: Effective order fulfilment requires integration of the company's manufacturing, logistics or distribution and other elements of the marketing mix and the total marketing plan.

Figure 17.9 Supply chain management: integrating and managing business processes across the supply chain from a product perspective

Source: D. Lambert and M. Cooper (2000) Issues in supply chain management, *Industrial Marketing Management*, 29, 65–83. Reproduced with permission.

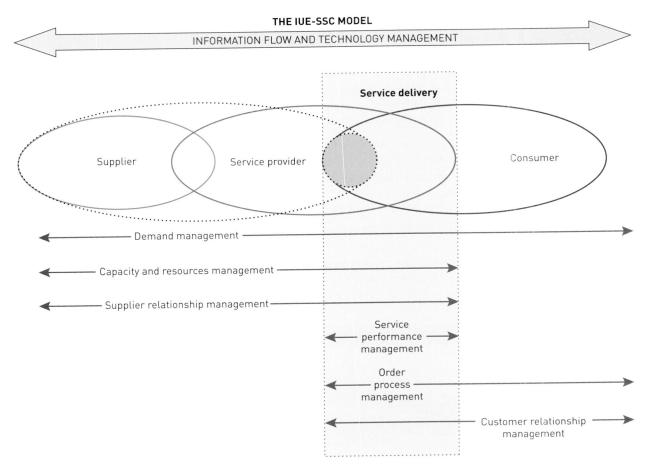

Figure 17.10 The service supply chain

Source: T. Baltacioglu, E. Ada, M. Kaplan, O. Yurt and Y. Kaplan (2007) A new framework for service supply chains, *The Service Industries Journal*, 27(2), 105–24. Reproduced with permission.

5 **Manufacturing or service process flow management**: The manufacturing flow process focuses on designing the product or service process and establishing the manufacturing or service process flexibility needed to serve the target market.

6 **Supplier/distributor/intermediary relationship management**: This process defines how the company interacts with its suppliers/distributors or any intermediaries. It is a mirror image of customer relationship management and shows the importance of managing these relationships.

7 **Product or service development and commercialisation**: Supply chain management includes integrating customers and intermediaries into the product or service development process in order to match needs and to reduce time to market.

8 **Returns**: This is often neglected but is of great importance to assist marketing in understanding the customer processes and how their needs were not met.

These eight key processes also cut across companies within the network. These processes must also operate across all the departmental or functional silos that include the functions at the top of the diagram – R&D, Finance, Production, Purchasing and Logistics/Distribution, and so on. The entire process is often not managed as such but marketers must input into each stage to ensure alignment between the eight aspects and the customer needs and company profitability.

▽ Modelling the service supply chain

Traditionally supply chains have been product focused, assuming a tangible product with a customer at the end of the process. Producers of services and ideas also face the problem of making their output available and accessible to target populations. More and more, supply networks are based on services. For hospitals we have 'health-delivery systems', that is, moving from the patient going to the hospital to remote diagnostics and care in the community as different channels.

Co-creation and prosumers

Figure 17.10 also shows how the consumer often plays a central role in services and the shaded area of the diagram shows how the consumer is often part of the supply network as a **co-creator** or **prosumer**. In 1980, Alvin Toffler introduced the concept of the prosumer as a composite of production, consumer and consumption – to denote the concept that the consumer could be both the producer and the consumer.[36] The dividing line between the supplier and the customer has become blurred or partly erased. The customer is part of the supply chain and not at the end of it. Therefore as we assemble our IKEA furniture we are part of the process and co-create the value of the product for ourselves. Self-service restaurantes and self-care in the medical area where we act as both doctor and patient are other examples. Self-service technologies as the co-creation of value will be discussed later in the chapter.

Customisation can also be seen as the co-creation of products or services. mi adidas has three shoes (one for running, one for soccer and one for tennis) with three areas of customisation; fit (length and width of each foot), performance (outsole and midsole options and seasonal upper materials) and design (choosing from over 100 colour combinations and embroidered lettering). All of this is done by the consumer at adidas shops or online. The challenge is how to amalgamate this into the traditional supply chain. Take Fiat with the Fiat 500 car – customers can now configurate it in 500,000 different ways! By using an online video configurator, you can choose your favourite colour, wheels, fabrics and options, and customise it with a wide variety of accessories and stickers. At the end of the process, you'll have your very own video that you can save in the Fiat 500 video channel and send to your friends. All these requirements must then feed into the production and delivery process for the Fiat 500 and be managed through the process. Co-production and the role of the consumer is covered in more detail in Chapter 18.

▽ Channel management and channel design decisions

A distribution channel is the particular set of channels marketers employ, and decisions about it are among the most critical ones management face. Channel members collectively have earned margins that account for 30–50 per cent of the ultimate selling price. In contrast, advertising typically has accounted for less than 5–7 per cent of the final price.[37] This section moves to a more concentrated focus on the channels of distribution between the company and the consumer and reviews the roles and number of players within the distribution aspect of networks.

Channel levels

The producer or service provider and the final customer are part of every channel. We will use the number of intermediary levels to describe the length of a channel. Figure 17.11(a) illustrates several consumer-goods marketing channels of different lengths and figure 17.11(b) illustrates business to business channels. Many companies operate both.

A **direct channel**, or a **zero-level channel**, consists of a manufacturer or a service provider going directly to the final customer using their own distribution, sales force or other method, such as the Internet. The company controls all aspects of the business itself and this was the traditional view of business before widespread outsourcing and networked companies. The growth of food markets in towns all over Europe are an excellent example of producers going directly to the consumer. Advertising agencies as producers also go directly to their clients.

(a) Consumer Marketing Channels

0-level	1-level	2-level	3-level
Manufacturer	Manufacturer	Manufacturer	Manufacturer
		Wholesaler	Wholesaler
			Jobber
	Retailer	Retailer	Retailer
Consumer	Consumer	Consumer	Consumer

(b) Industrial Marketing Channels

0-level	1-level	2-level	3-level
Manufacturer	Manufacturer	Manufacturer	Manufacturer
		Manufacturer's representative	Manufacturer's sales branch
	Industrial distributors		
Industrial customer	Industrial customer	Industrial customer	Industrial customer

Figure 17.11 Consumer and industrial marketing channels

A *one-level channel* has one intermediary, such as a retailer or a distributor. BMW would be hard pressed to replace all the tasks done by its 8000 car dealers. A *two-level channel* contains two intermediaries. In consumer markets, these are typically a wholesaler and a retailer. Red Bull uses wholesalers and retailers throughout Europe to distribute its product. Red Bull would not find it practical to establish small retail energy drink shops throughout the world or to sell Red Bull over the Internet. A *three-level channel* contains three intermediaries. In Japan, food distribution may include as many as six levels. From the producer's point of view, obtaining information about consumers and exercising control becomes more difficult as the number of channel levels increases.

Figure 17.11(b) shows channels commonly used in business-to-business marketing. An industrial product manufacturer can use its sales force to sell directly to industrial customers; or it can sell to industrial distributors, who sell to the industrial customers. Alternatively it can sell through manufacturer's representatives or its own sales branches directly to industrial customers, or indirectly to industrial customers through industrial distributors.

Different levels of channels in operation at the same time are quite common. For example, Apple has iTunes that sells music for record companies all over the world, while Apple sells computers and other consumer electronics through its own stores and through other electronic retailers. Apple manages a range of channels across a range of products and services. The challenge for marketers is how to manage all these players. See 'Marketing insights: Cadbury's global supply network of channel members', which reflects some of the channel levels and issues for Cadbury's – the UK-based confectionery company.

How to design and manage your supply chain is a crucial decision. Like Apple, more and more companies have multichannels and global networks.

In the highly competitive grocery retailing industry, what's one of the hottest marketing strategies for ensuring success? To learn how San Antonio-based retailer H-E-B has managed to challenge national retailers, visit www.prenhall.com/kotler

The channels chosen affect all other marketing decisions. Channel choices themselves depend on the company's marketing strategy with respect to segmentation, targeting and positioning. The company's pricing depends on whether it uses mass retailers or high-quality boutiques. The company's sales force and advertising decisions depend on how much training and motivation dealers need. In addition, channel decisions include relatively long-term commitments with other firms as well as a set of policies and procedures. When BMW signs up an independent car dealer, it is entering a long-term agreement which both must honour.

Marketing insight

Cadbury's global supply network of channel members

Cadbury's has an extensive global supply network all designed to create one delicious bar of chocolate.

Source: Courtesy of Cadbury plc

The global supply network involved in making a Cadbury's Dairy Milk Fruit & Nut, at Bournville in the United Kingdom, gives a good illustration of how supply networks, and relationships within them, can differ.

Milk – two steps away: The milk that goes into the chocolate bar comes from the United Kingdom. Cadbury's buys it from farmer-run co-operatives and has direct dealings with the co-operatives but not with the individual farmers, which means the farmers who produce the milk are two steps away from the company.

Raisins – two steps away: The raisins come from Turkey. Cadbury's buys the raisins from a family-owned Turkish processing plant near Izmir, which buys its raisins from around 1000 small farmers. The raisins are traceable back to the original farms. The processing plant maintains close relations with the farmers to ensure quality. The company is two steps away from these 1000 small farmers.

Almonds – two steps away: The almonds come from California. Cadbury's buys the almonds from a processor who in turn buys them from the farmer.

Here the company is two steps away from the original producers, the Californian almond growers.

Sugar – two steps away: The sugar comes from the United Kingdom and mainland Europe. The company buys it from sugar processors, which buy sugar beet direct from the farmer. The farmers who grow the sugar beet are therefore two steps away from the company.

Cocoa – three or more steps away: Cocoa is sourced from Ghana. Cadbury's buys cocoa from the Ghanaian Government Cocoa Board (COCOBOD), which controls the cocoa trade in Ghana. Between COCOBOD and the farmer there are licensed buying companies. They buy cocoa from the farmer and transport it to the seaport. Here Cadbury's is three steps or more away from more than half a million farmers.

Distribution: Cadbury's uses wholesalers and distributors and also vending machines at train stations and airports focusing on extensive distribution.

Wholesalers: Cadbury's uses wholesalers to distribute its products.

Retailers: The wholesalers deliver to retailers all over Europe.

The amount of influence Cadbury's can exert on particular supply network members varies. As a major buyer of a product, or where it buys directly from the producer, the company's influence can be great. When it is not a major buyer, or where it is several steps away from the producer, its influence tends to be more limited. Nevertheless it must still recognise its responsibilities for each link in the supply network.

Since its supply chain is so extensive and wide ranging, the number of groups with which Cadbury's can engage, and the degree of engagement, varies according to circumstances. It is also greater where the company believes it can have most effect, for suppliers whose products and services are more central to Cadbury's brands, and for those operating in countries or sectors typically known to face the most significant human and labour rights issues.

To help manage its supply network Cadbury's categorises and prioritises its suppliers into three levels, or tiers, according to risk as well as the importance of the product or service to the company and its brands.[38]

The norm of business operation is to consider which multichannels to market or at the very least to try and understand the many channels available and to choose which one(s) suit your company and customers best. You may have to manage online and offline channels so that the ecommerce channel works with retailers, brokers, agents and other intermediaries as well as phone contact, shops, mail, kiosk or other touch point.

Integrating multichannel systems

Most companies today have adopted multichannel marketing. The UK-based hairdressers Toni & Guy sells its four hair care ranges through three main channels: in Boots chemist stores, in its 402 hair salons in 41 countries, and online from the company's website.

Multichannel marketing occurs when a company uses two or more marketing channels to reach one or more customer segments. There is a real choice between multiple channels and a multi-channel strategy. A **multiple channels** strategy simply provides multiple-channels for the consumer while a multichannel strategy has cross-channel benefits based on the management of the multiple channels. A McKinsey report showed that customers which use multiple channels for purchasing spend two to four times more than the spend of those using one channel. Similarly in banking multichannel customers are 25–50 per cent more profitable than single channel users.[39] A *multi marketing channel strategy* is one in which the strategies and tactics of distribution and sales through one channel reflect the strategies and tactics of distribution and sales through other channels.

Customers want to get products and service when they need them and have these delivered in the many different ways that suit them. To respond to this diversity of needs and situations, marketers need to create multiple points of presence, fully integrated to deliver a seamless customer experience. They need to treat every customer as a unique individual instead of treating all customers alike and discriminating among customers based on the channel they use. Marketers need to ask: am I devoted to my channel or to my customer? At times, it seems, marketers are beholden to their channels but agnostic when it comes to their customers. Remember, a channel is merely a means to an end. What matters isn't the channel through which the customer communicates. Rather, it's the ability to capture, store and track all interactions and transactions with that customer across all touch points to create a seamless, context-rich conversation. As competition intensifies and broadband proliferates, companies need to be everywhere that customers want them to be. They need to market in all the ways that customers want to be reached, in all the ways that customers want to buy, and provide support in all the ways that customers want to be supported.

Customers shouldn't be forced to stay with the channel with which they originated, as if they were driving along a motorway where cars are prohibited from changing lanes. Marketers know that they need to break down the channel walls and allow data that was captured through one channel or customer touch point to instantly migrate to all other channels and touch points. Sometimes customers want to talk to a support rep, at other times they want self-service. Sometimes they want to buy online, other times in a shop. Sometimes they want to return products through UPS, other times at a shopping centre.

Consumers may choose the channels they prefer based on a number of factors: the price, the product or service assortment, the convenience of a channel option, as well as their own particular needs and wants (economic, social or experiential).[40] Segmentation exists, and marketers employing different types of channels must be aware that different consumers have different needs during the purchase process.

Researchers Nunes and Cespedes argue that in many markets, buyers fall into one of four categories.[41]

1   **Habitual shoppers**: Purchase from the same places in the same manner.

2   **High-value deal seekers**: Know their needs and 'channel surf' a great deal before buying at the lowest possible price.

3   **Variety-loving shoppers**: Gather information in many channels, take advantage of high-touch services, and then buy in their favourite channel, regardless of price.

4   **High-involvement shoppers**: Gather information in all channels, make their purchase in a low-cost channel, but take advantage of customer support from a high-touch channel.

A study of 40 grocery and clothing retailers in France, Germany, and the United Kingdom found that retailers in those countries served three types of shoppers:

1   **service/quality customers** who cared most about the variety and performance of products in shops as well as the service provided;

2 **price/value customers** most concerned about spending their money wisely; and

3 **affinity customers** who primarily sought shops that suited people like themselves or the members of groups they aspired to join.

Even the same consumer may choose to use different channels for different aspects of their purchase. For instance, someone may choose to take a test drive at a car dealer before ordering a car online. Consumers may also seek different types of channels depending on the particular types of products or services involved. Some consumers are willing to 'trade up' to retailers offering higher-end products such as TAG Heuer watches or Callaway golf clubs; these same consumers are also willing to 'trade down' to discount retailers to buy own-brand paper towels, washing powder or vitamins from low-cost retailers such as Aldi and Lidl.[42] It is always interesting to note the number of high-value Range Rovers and Mercedes in the car parks of the low cost supermarkets.

Managing your channels as a network rather than as separate but multiple channels to market is the real challenge – see Figure 17.12.

Figure 17.12 Multi-channel shopping behaviour

Source: Adapted from D. Schoenbachler and G. Gordon (2002) Multi-channel shopping: understanding what drives channel choice, *Journal of Consumer Marketing*, 19(1), 42–53. Reproduced with permission.

The multichannel strategy should be customer driven with allocation of resources and investment to the high-value segments. The single channel to market can also be successful, with Dell a great proponent of this strategy. Dell uses a direct channel strategy. Josh Claman, general manager of the Europe, Middle East and Africa channel group, says:

> Our strategy is going to be a simple approach – a one-tier model. The Dell business model lends itself to that. When we went out to the channel and asked them what they wanted, there was very strong feedback that they wanted a direct relationship with Dell.[43]

Space2 – a London-based furniture company that sells online direct to the consumer (www.space2.com): says 'Because we are a manufacturer we cut out the middle-man and the mark-ups, so you can rest assured that the price of space2 furniture is the best around.' Companies that manage multichannels must make sure these channels work well together and match each target customer's preferred ways of doing business.

Channel integration

With the increase in offline and online, customers expect *channel integration*, characterised by features such as:

- the ability to order a product or service online and pick it up at a convenient retail location or have it delivered to your home;
- the ability to return an online-ordered product to a nearby store;
- the right to receive discounts and promotional offers based on total online and offline purchases.

The challenge of integration involves breaking boundaries on two fronts. On the external front, integration means presenting a seamless face to customers, regardless of what they buy, where they buy, and how they choose to interact with the company. It requires breaking outward-facing boundaries that separate the various channels which the company uses to connect with customers and to go to market. On the internal front, integration means creating a unified knowledge system that stores everything the company knows about its customers and offerings. Internal integration requires the breaking of inward-facing boundaries that divide functional departments, product and service divisions, and business units. This can be a real challenge for companies as they try to manage customers within a multichannel system.

▽ Selecting channel members

A marketing channel performs the work of moving products from producers to consumers or providing services. It overcomes the time, place and possession gaps that separate products and services from those who need or want them. Members of the marketing channel perform a number of key functions (see Table 17.3).

You can do away with intermediaries but you can't do away with many of the functions that they perform. Some functions (physical, title, promotion) constitute a *forward flow* of activity from the company to the customer; other functions (ordering and payment) constitute a *backward flow* from customers to the company. Still others (information, negotiation, finance and risk taking) occur in both directions. Five flows are illustrated in Figure 17.13 for the marketing of forklift trucks. If these flows were superimposed in one diagram, the tremendous complexity of even simple marketing channels would be apparent.

The question is not *whether* various channel functions need to be performed – they must be – but rather *who* is to perform them. When the manufacturer shifts some functions to intermediaries, the intermediary must add a charge to cover its work. If the intermediaries are more efficient than the manufacturer, prices to consumers should be lower. If consumers perform some functions themselves, they should enjoy even lower prices but often don't. So even though assembly is handled by the consumer, IKEA does not charge less for its furniture, though it is low cost furniture. The company actually charges you if you would like someone to assemble it for you.

Marketing memo

Different channel designs

There are many channel designs. A conventional marketing channel comprises an independent producer, wholesaler(s) and retailer(s). Each is a separate business seeking to maximise its own profits, even if this goal reduces profit for the system as a whole. No channel member has complete or substantial control over other members.

A **vertical marketing system (VMS)** comprises the producer, wholesaler(s) and retailer(s) acting as a unified system. One channel member, the channel captain, owns the others or franchises them or has so much power that they all cooperate. VMS arose as a result of strong channel members' attempts to control channel behaviour and eliminate the conflict that results when independent members pursue their own objectives. VMSs achieve economies through size, bargaining power and elimination of duplicated services. Business buyers of complex products and systems have been shown to value the extensive exchange of information they can obtain from a VMS.[44] VMSs have become the dominant mode of distribution in many consumer marketplaces, serving between 70 and 80 per cent of the total market. There are three types of VMS: corporate, administered and contractual.

A **corporate VMS** combines successive stages of production and distribution under single ownership. For example, Tesco obtains over 50 per cent of product from companies that it partly or wholly owns. An **administered VMS** coordinates successive stages of production and distribution through the size and power of one of the members. Manufacturers of a dominant brand are able to secure strong trade cooperation and support from resellers. So Germany's Dr Oetker, manufacturer of pizza, yogurt and frozen meals, is able to command high levels of cooperation from its resellers in connection with displays, shelf space, promotions and price policies. A **contractual VMS** consists of independent firms at different levels of production and distribution, integrating their programmes on a contractual basis to obtain more economies or sales impact than they could achieve alone. These have been called 'value-adding partnerships' (VAPs).[45]

Another channel development is the **horizontal marketing system**, in which two or more unrelated companies put together resources or programmes to exploit an emerging marketing opportunity. Each company lacks the capital, know-how, production or marketing resources to venture alone, or it is afraid of the risk. The companies might work with each other on a temporary or permanent basis or create a joint venture company. British mobile operator O2 (which is now owned by Spanish telecoms group Telefonica) and supermarket chain Tesco, launched a joint venture mobile phone operation in 2003 and they now have over 1 million mobile phone customers. Tesco Mobile is equally owned by the two companies and operates as an independent entity.

Channel design

Clearly, marketing managers need to think through their channel designs – how many, who and how (see Marketing memo above). They must determine which channels should perform which function. Figure 17.14 shows a simple grid to help make channel design decisions. The grid consists of major marketing channels (as rows) and the major channel tasks that must be completed (as columns).[46]

The grid illustrates why using only one channel is not efficient. This multichannel design optimises coverage, customisation and control while minimising cost and conflict. Channels should be designed to work together effectively.

Table 17.3 Channel member functions for a product and/or service

- Gather information about potential and current customers, competitors and other channel members and forces in the marketing environment.
- Reach agreements on price and other terms so that transfer of ownership or possession can be effected.
- Develop and disseminate persuasive communications to stimulate purchasing.
- Place orders with manufacturers.
- Acquire the funds to finance inventories at different levels in the marketing channel.
- Assume risks connected with carrying out channel work.
- Provide for the successive storage and movement of physical products.
- Provide for buyers' payment of their bills through banks and other financial institutions.
- Oversee actual transfer of ownership from one organisation or person to another.

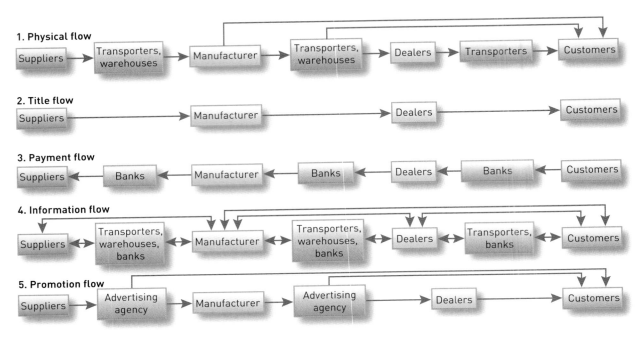

Figure 17.13 Five marketing flows in the marketing channel for forklift trucks

Demand-generation tasks

		Better customer information	Disseminate communication	Reach price agreements	Place orders	Acquire funds for inventories	Assume risks	Facilitate product storage & movement	Facilitate payment	Oversee ownership terms	
Marketing channels and methods — **VENDOR**	Internet										**CUSTOMER**
	National account management										
	Direct sales										
	Telemarketing										
	Direct mail										
	Retail stores										
	Distributors										
	Dealers and value-added resellers										
	Manufacturers' own store										

Figure 17.14 Planning channel architecture

Source: Adapted from R. T. Moriarty and U. Moran (1990) Marketing hybrid marketing systems, *Harvard Business Review*, November–December, 150. Copyright © 1990 by the President and Fellows of Harvard College. All rights reserved. Reproduced with permission.

Designing a marketing channel system requires:

- analysing customers' needs;
- establishing channel objectives and constraints;
- deciding on the number of intermediaries;
- terms and responsibilities of channel members;
- selecting channel members: evaluating the major alternatives.

Analysing customers' needs

In designing the marketing channel, the marketer must understand the service levels its target customers want. This should form a dominant focus but is often overlooked for operational or internal efficiencies. Five service levels need to be studied from the customer perspective:

1 **Quantity of purchase**: The number of units the channel permits a typical customer to purchase on one occasion. In buying cars for its fleet, Hertz prefers a channel from which it can buy a large lot size; a household wants a channel that permits buying a lot size of one car.

2 **Waiting and delivery time**: The average time customers of that channel wait for delivery of the product or service. Customers often prefer faster and faster delivery channels though they are prepared to wait. The ultimate answer to carrying *near-zero inventory* is to build for order, not for stock. Sony calls it SOMA, 'sell one, make one'. Dell, for example, gets the customer to order a computer and pay for it in advance. Then Dell uses the customer's money to pay suppliers to ship the necessary components and parts to make the computer. Many furniture retailers do not order until the product is sold to a customer and then the customer will wait from six weeks to three months for delivery. As long as customers do not need the item immediately, this can save money on storing products waiting for them to sell, but you need to be sure of customers' acceptance of the delay.

3 **Convenience**: The degree to which the marketing channel makes it easy for customers to purchase the product or avail themselves of its service. A convenient channel may also allow the customer to do the work themselves in their own time. So the customer is happy to do online banking at home rather than use the branch network.

4 **Product and service variety**: This is assortment breadth provided by the marketing channel. Normally, customers prefer a greater assortment because more choices increase the chance of finding what they need, though consumers can struggle with the range of choices available.[47]

5 **Service backup**: The add-on services (credit, delivery, installation, repairs) provided by the channel. The greater the service back-up, the greater the work provided by the channel.[48] In many cases if something goes wrong in these areas it is the customer who suffers. In a 2005 study it was found that a customer had to wait 220 minutes for a car to be repaired, of which only 35 minutes was value-creating or repair-focused work.[49]

The marketing channel designer knows that providing greater service outputs also means increasing channel costs and raising prices for customers. Different customers have different service needs. That is why we have first or business class on aeroplanes; though the success of discount airlines indicates that many consumers are willing to accept less service if they can save money.

Establishing channel objectives and constraints

Channel objectives vary with product or service characteristics. Perishable products require more direct channels to market. Bulky products, such as building materials, require channels that minimise the shipping distance and the amount of handling. Non-standard products, such as custom-built machinery and specialised business forms, are sold directly by company sales representatives. Products requiring installation or maintenance services, such as heating and cooling systems, are usually distributed and maintained by the company or by franchised dealers. High-unit-value products such as generators and turbines are often sold through a company sales force rather than intermediaries. Low-value, fast-moving consumer goods are usually distributed through retailers.

Table 17.4 List of channel alternatives for a mobile phone manufacturer

- They could distribute their mobile phones directly to the customer.
- They could sell their mobile phone to retail stores such as Orange, O2 and Vodafone.
- They could sell their mobile phones through mail order catalogues.
- They could distribute directly through the Internet on their own site.
- They could link to other sites and sell their phones through Internet intermediaries.
- The company could sell its mobile phones through major retailers such as Sainsbury's or Carrefour.

A channel alternative is described by three elements:

1 the types of available business intermediaries;
2 the number of intermediaries needed; and
3 the terms and responsibilities of each channel member.

Types of intermediaries

Marketers needs to identify the types of intermediaries available to carry on its channel work. Table 17.4 lists channel alternatives available to a mobile phone manufacturer.

Deciding on the number of intermediaries

Marketing managers have to decide on the number of intermediaries to use at each channel level. Three strategies are available: exclusive distribution, selective distribution and intensive distribution.

1 **Exclusive distribution**: Severely limiting the number of intermediaries. It's appropriate when the company wants to maintain control over the service level and outputs offered by the resellers, and it often includes *exclusive dealing* arrangements. Exclusive distribution requires a closer partnership between seller and reseller and is used in the distribution of new cars, some major appliances (e.g., the Dyson vacuum cleaner) and some women's clothing brands. We do not expect Rolex watches to be available in all locations, but only through its exclusive distribution arrangements at stores such as Harrods and Les Galleries Lafayette in Paris.

2 **Selective distribution**: Reliance on more than a few but less than all of the intermediaries being willing to carry a particular product or service. It makes sense for established companies and for new companies seeking distributors. The company does not have to worry about too many outlets; it can gain adequate market coverage with more control and less cost than intensive distribution.

3 In **intensive distribution**: The company places the product or services in as many outlets as possible. This strategy is generally used for items such as snack foods, soft drinks, newspapers, sweets, fast food restaurants and products or services that consumers seek to buy frequently or in a variety of locations. Convenience stores such as Spar or shops linked to petrol stations have prospered by selling items that provide just that – location and time convenience.

It can be tempting to move from exclusive or selective distribution to more intensive distribution to increase coverage and sales. This strategy may help in the short term, but it can hurt long-term performance. Intensive distribution increases product and service availability but may also encourage retailers to compete aggressively. Price wars can then erode profitability, potentially dampening retailer interest in supporting the product and harming brand equity. Some firms avoid intensive distribution and do not want to be sold everywhere. When the legendary Italian designer label Gucci found its image severely tarnished by overexposure from licensing and discount stores, it decided to end contracts with third-party suppliers, control its distribution and open its own stores to bring back some of the brand lustre.[50]

Terms and responsibilities of channel members

Each channel member must be treated respectfully and given the opportunity to be profitable.[51] The main elements in the management of channel members are price policies, conditions of sale, territorial rights and specific services to be performed by each party.

- **Price policy**: relates to the establishment of a price list and schedule of discounts and allowances that intermediaries see as equitable and sufficient.

- **Conditions of sale**: refers to payment terms and guarantees.
- **Distributors' territorial rights**: defines the distributors' territories and the terms.
- **Mutual services and responsibilities**: must be carefully spelt out, especially in franchised and exclusive agency channels.

Selecting channel members: evaluating the major alternatives

Each channel selection needs to be evaluated against economic, control and adaptive criteria. To customers, the channels are the company. Consider the negative impression customers would get of Mercedes-Benz if one of its dealers was dirty, inefficient or unpleasant. To facilitate channel member selection, marketers should determine what characteristics distinguish the better intermediaries. They should evaluate the number of years in business, other lines carried, growth and profit record, financial strength, cooperativeness, and service reputation. If the intermediaries are distributors, marketers should evaluate the number and character of other lines carried and the size and quality of the sales force. If the intermediaries are department stores that want exclusive distribution, the marketing manager should evaluate locations, future growth potential and type of clientele.

From an economic perspective

Each channel alternative will produce a different level of distribution, sales and costs. Figure 17.15 shows how six different channels compare in terms of the value added per sale and the cost per transaction. For example, in the sale of industrial products costing between €2000 and €5000, the cost per transaction has been estimated at €500 (field sales), €200 (distributors), €50 (telesales), and €10 (Internet). In retail banking services, a Booz, Allen, Hamilton worldwide study shows the average transaction of a full-service branch: it costs €0.69 cents to handle a transaction in a bank branch, about €0.35 cents on the phone, €0.16 cents through an ATM, and just €0.1 cent on the Internet.[52] The interesting point is that the use of multiple channels has increased customer contact. So though they may have lower-cost channels such as ATMs and the Internet, customers use these channels to interact with the organisation more often.

Marketing managers often try to align customers and channels to maximise demand at the lowest overall cost. This is a strategy to watch because it can also damage relationships and profitability. Within the banking sector, banks are finding that their high-value customers are on the Internet and the low-value customer is visiting the branch! Clearly, replacing high-cost channels with low-cost channels can have major repercussions. Going online for the airlines meant that companies could discontinue using expensive travel agents' channels, but the price transparency for the customer meant that prices dropped and continue to drop as customers can shop around for best prices by comparing prices quickly on the Internet.

Figure 17.15 The value adds versus the costs of different channels

Marketing memo

Understanding outsourcing

Outsourcing has become very popular for everything, from design to manufacturing to services being outsourced, often to the four corners of the globe or specifically to the BRIC countries of Brazil, Russia, India and China. Managing outsourcing is a crucial marketing management skill and is also one of the reasons for the need to understand global supply chains. Nestlé is one company that outsources much of its supply networks. Nestlé, the world's largest food company, sells almost nothing directly to customers and does no farming! Outsourcing means relinquishing some control, but companies can often gain in effectiveness and efficiency by outsourcing to other companies that can perform the task better and cheaper. Through their contacts, experience, specialisation and scale of operation, outsourcing (or offshoring as it is sometimes called) usually offers the company more than it can achieve on its own.[53] Outsourcing has become a major part of most organisations, with a recent Stanford University report noting that most companies which outsource show a return that is more than double their annual investment. Despite this there has been some evidence of companies taking operations back in-house.

The negatives to outsourcing are:

- There is an increased risk of poor quality control.
- A company may lose its core competency.
- Outsourcing can lead to low staff morale or loyalty, as well as a confused strategic focus.

FisherPrice, which outsourced its manufacturing to China, found that it had quality issues and had to remove toys from shelves after problems with the paint used by a Chinese manufacturer. Monitoring and control can be crucial in outsourcing.

▽ Managing distribution channels

After a marketing manager has chosen a channel system he or she must select, train, motivate and evaluate individual intermediaries for each channel. He or she must also modify channel design and arrangements over time. There are four issues:

1 training and motivating channel members;

2 gaining cooperation: channel power;

3 evaluating channel members;

4 modifying channel design and arrangements.

Training and motivating channel members

A company needs to view its intermediaries in the same way it views its customers. Being able to stimulate channel members to top performance starts with understanding the intermediaries' needs and wants. The company should plan and implement careful training programmes, market research programmes, and other capability-building programmes to improve intermediaries' performance. Porsche and Volkswagen pride themselves on their training of dealers and issue certification when they have completed their dealer training course. Marketing must constantly communicate its view that the channel members are partners in a joint effort to satisfy end users of the product or service.

Gaining cooperation and channel power

Most marketers see gaining intermediaries' cooperation as a huge challenge. **Channel power** is the ability to alter channel members' behaviour so that they take actions they would not have taken otherwise.[54] Marketing managers can draw on the following types of power to elicit cooperation:

- **Reward power**: The marketing manager can offer intermediaries an extra benefit for performing specific acts or functions. Reward power typically produces better results than coercive power. The intermediaries may come to expect a reward every time the marketer wants a certain behaviour to occur.

- **Coercive power**: Marketing can threaten to withdraw a resource or terminate a relationship if intermediaries fail to cooperate. This power can be effective, but its exercise produces resentment and can generate conflict and lead the intermediaries to organise countervailing power.
- **Legitimate power**: The marketing manager requests a behaviour that is warranted under the contract. As long as the intermediaries view the manufacture or service provider as a legitimate leader, legitimate power works.
- **Expert power**: The marketing manager has special knowledge of what the intermediaries value. Once the intermediaries acquire this expertise, however, expert power weakens. The marketing manager must continue to develop new expertise so that the intermediaries will want to continue cooperating.
- **Referent power**: The marketing manager is so highly respected that intermediaries are proud to be associated with him or her. Companies such as BMW, SAP and Porsche have high referent power.[55]

Coercive and reward power are objectively observable; legitimate, expert and referent power are more subjective and depend on the ability and willingness of parties to recognise them.

Most companies see gaining intermediaries' or buyer supplier cooperation as a huge challenge.[56] They often use positive motivators, such as higher margins, special deals, premiums, cooperative advertising allowances, display allowances and sales contests. At times they will apply negative sanctions, such as threatening to reduce margins, slow down delivery or terminate the relationship. The weakness of some of these approaches is that the marketer is using crude, stimulus-response thinking. In many ways you need to work within the network to try and have win–win situations.

New channels of information and distribution can change power bases and opportunities.

▽ European car dealers

Many issues have arisen in relation to European car dealers and the use of the Internet channel by consumers. Many of the policies are designed to protect the channel rather than to focus on consumer needs. Car dealers now have multiple channels to market: customers can use car dealers, agent websites, the telephone, the companies' or dealers own Internet sites. The Internet could give car dealers and customers new opportunities to take advantage of differential pricing across Europe but this can also damage business within countries. For example, there has been an increasing trend of car exports from Germany and the Netherlands into the United Kingdom. Manufacturers felt that they had to alter their policies to try and block this, to try and manage the situation and to ensure that prices stayed high in the United Kingdom! The following changes were made:

- Factory manufacturing times for cars, ordered by continental dealers, were increased from 4–6 weeks for popular models and to 26 weeks or more for all UK left-hand drive models!
- One European car company requires that when ordering a UK model one must enter a specific UK code that automatically increases prices to UK levels.
- Car manufacturers' websites have been altered to provide less information to UK customers wishing to make price comparisons.[57]

Evaluating channel members

Marketers must regularly evaluate intermediaries' performance against such standards as sales-quota attainment, average inventory levels, customer delivery time, treatment of damaged and lost products and cooperation in promotional and training programmes. Marketers will occasionally discover that it is paying a particular intermediary too much for what they are actually doing. One review showed that though a distributor was being compensated for holding inventory, the company was actually storing it in a public warehouse and charging the company for this. Marketers need to ensure that there are contracts in place which have agreed functional discounts in which they pay specified amounts for the channel member's performance on each agreed upon service. Under-performers need to be counselled, retrained, motivated or terminated.

▽ Apple shops

Within the European market, Apple opened its first retail shop in London in November 2004 and its largest shop inside the FNAC Digital store on the chic Boulevard Saint Germain in central Paris in 2007.[58] With 99 retail locations worldwide, Apple stores have hosted more than 51 million visitors since the first shops opened in May 2001.[59] These new channels were opened because of the company's frustration with its poor retail presentation by its chosen intermediaries. The shops sell Apple products exclusively and target tech-savvy customers with in-store product presentations and workshops; a full line of Apple products, software and accessories; and a 'Genius Bar' staffed by Apple specialists who provide technical support, often free of charge. When Apple stores were launched many critics questioned their prospects and *BusinessWeek* published an article entitled, 'Sorry Steve, here's why Apple Stores won't work'.[60] They have actually been a great success. The typical Apple retail location sells about 21 Mac computers every day versus under 2 for many less specialised electronics shops. This amounts to about 8000 Macs per store per year and played a crucial role in expanding the Mac's appeal. It is estimated that about two-thirds of store revenues came from the computers and earned Apple the lion's share of its converts. Bernstein Research senior analyst Sacconaghi says that 'We estimate that the stores, which collectively represent just 2.5 per cent of the Mac's global distribution points, drove more than one-third of its market share gain during the year'.[61] Although the move upset existing retailers, Apple has worked hard to smooth relationships with its intermediaries, in part justifying the decision to add its own shops as a natural evolution of its already existing online sales channel.[62]

To preserve its channel relationships, Apple has justified the opening of hundreds of its own retail stores as a natural extension of its online channel. The stores have proven extremely profitable too. The London shop pictured opened in 2004.

Source: Justin Kase/zthreez/Alamy

Modifying channel design and arrangements

Marketing must periodically review and modify its channel design and arrangements. It will want to modify them when the distribution channel is not working as planned, consumer buying patterns change, the market expands, new competition arises, innovative distribution channels emerge, and/or the product or service moves into later stages in the life cycle. Early buyers might be willing to pay for high-value-added channels, but later buyers will switch to lower-cost channels. Small office photocopiers were first sold by the manufacturers' direct sales forces, later through office equipment dealers, and still later through mass retailers and Internet sites.

In competitive markets with low entry barriers, the optimal channel structure will inevitably change over time. The change could mean adding or dropping individual channel members, adding or dropping particular market channels, or developing a totally new way to deliver products or services.

Adding or dropping individual channel members requires an incremental analysis. What would profits look like with and without this intermediary? A marketer may drop any intermediary whose sales drop below a certain level. Increasingly more detailed customer information stored in databases and the sophisticated means to analyse that data can provide guidance in those decisions.[63] More analytics are used nowadays before deciding on channel members.

▽ Understanding the impact of technology

You have now studied many of the management aspects of supply networks and managing relationships. This section explores various channels of distribution including the Internet, mobile phones and self-service technologies. As the Internet and other technologies advance, service industries such as banking, insurance and travel are operating through new channels. Kodak offers its customers four different ways to print their digital photos where they can avail themselves of their own minilabs in retail outlets, home printers or online services with the Kodak-owned Ofoto website, and self-service kiosks.

The Internet as a channel of distribution

As Chris Anderson, author of *The Long Tail* notes 'the Internet absorbs each industry it touches, becoming the shop, the theatre and broadcaster at a fraction of the cost'.[64] Online distribution has changed the balance of power in many networks and has changed how products and service are distributed with software, music, newspapers, video games, films, tickets, information and advice and much much more delivered via voice, text, data or images being sent to computers or downloaded to mobiles or on to iPods or PDAs. In 2006 over 100 million European online shoppers spent an average of €1000 each, and drove online retail sales past the €100 billion mark. Online retail sales in Europe will more than double in the next five years, to €263 billion in 2011, according to Forrester Research. The number of online shoppers is expected to grow to 174 million. The leading online purchase categories are travel, clothes, groceries and consumer electronics, all above the €10 billion per year mark. Jaap Favier, Research Director Consumer Markets at Forrester Research, comments:

> The number of Europeans shopping online has increased by 37 per cent in the past two
> years. At the end of 2003, 48 per cent of Europeans went online at least once per month, and
> 19 per cent had shopped online. Two years later, these numbers had soared to 54 per cent
> and 26 per cent, respectively. Total European on line sales grew 50 per cent in two years.

European Visa cardholders spent over €2.6 billion on the Internet, with over 31 million transactions processed in total. In 2007, 58 per cent of European Internet users shopped online, with the United Kingdom, Sweden and Germany far above the EU average.[65]

It's easy to see why. Online retailers can predictably provide convenient, informative and personalised experiences for vastly different types of consumers and businesses. By not having to bear the cost of maintaining retail floor space, staff and inventory and having a global presence

Service innovation in distribution: co-production with the customer across many channels, including a photoframe which plays digital photos.

Source: Courtesy of Kodak Ltd (UK)

if you wish, companies can sell and distribute to more customers than a physical presence often allows. Online retailers compete among themselves in terms of three key aspects of a transaction: (1) How customers enjoy the interaction on the website; (2) delivery of the product and service; and (3) ability to address problems when they occur.[66]

Companies must set up and operate their websites carefully. Customer service is critical. Often, online shoppers select an item for purchase but fail to complete the transaction. The conversion rate of Internet shoppers is only 5 per cent compared to the norm from similar customers using traditional channels, but that is because users visit online sites more often than the physical

Breakthrough marketing

Amazon and Marks & Spencer unite on the Internet

Marks & Spencer have a multichannel strategy to market that includes their retail shops, a call centre and the Internet. Marks & Spencer, the UK-based retailer, which sells products including clothing, home furnishings, food and wine, selected an Amazon-hosted Internet platform to support a single ordering system for its three channels. The company is hoping to double online sales from £100 million in 2007 to £200 million in 2008. 'Marks & Spencer already has a successful website with over 24 million visits every year, but our ecommerce and customer ordering capabilities have yet to reach their full potential,' says Steven Sharp, Director of Marketing and ecommerce at Marks & Spencer.

The single cross-channel ordering system, replacing three separate systems in use today, will let customer service reps respond with information about orders regardless of which channel a customer shopped on. 'With Amazon, we'll be able to track customer orders from in-store to the web to the call centre'.[67] The site navigation and feature filtering has been improved and makes intuitive browsing of the site and product comparison easy. This is useful for customers who need 'help to choose' – those who arrive at a site with few criteria upon which to base their purchasing decision. M&S has also improved delivery options, with a range of choices depending on how quickly you want your items, as well as the ability to track the progress of your deliveries.[68,69]

The Internet is a challenge for many retailers who now have an extra channel of distribution that must be integrated into their channel decisions.

Source: © Marks & Spencer plc

shop.[70] Worse, only 1.8 per cent of visits to online retailers lead to sales, compared with 5 per cent of visits to department stores.

Consumer surveys suggest that the most significant inhibitors of online shopping are the absence of pleasurable experiences, social interaction and personal consultation with a company representative.[71] Marketers need to manage this. Many online shoppers bolt when they're just a click or two away from finishing the checkout process. Maybe it's a security concern, or a worry in relation to returns? Whatever the reason, one study found that as many as 60 per cent of online shoppers flee, making shopping-cart abandonment a huge and costly problem for any business selling on the Web. The great frustration for online businesses is that a salesperson can't just walk over to you and offer help.[72]

Marketing managers choose techniques to overcome these issues. These can include incentives to purchase immediately: sometimes on Amazon a flash appears that says if the consumer purchases the item within a certain number of hours they are entitled to free shipping/delivery. Similarly on Amazon, it is possible to pre-order an item for your shopping basket, so that Amazon will inform you when a hard-to-find item has become available. Ritz Camera and others use live online chat to give potential customers immediate advice about products for sale on their websites. Another benefit of providing live sales assistance is the ability to sell additional items. Investments in website design and processes can help reassure customers sensitive to online risk.[73] Online retailers are also trying new technologies, such as blogs, social networks and mobile marketing to attract new shoppers – all of which were discussed in Chapter 4.

Business-to-business

Ecommerce business-to-business sites are changing the supplier–customer relationship in profound ways. Firms are using B2B auction sites, spot exchanges, online product catalogues, barter sites and other online resources to obtain better prices. The purpose of B2B sites is to make markets more efficient. In the past, buyers had to exert a lot of effort to gather information on worldwide suppliers. With the Internet, buyers have easy access to a great deal of information. They can get information from: (1) *supplier websites*; (2) *infomediaries*, third parties that add value by aggregating information about alternatives; (3) *market makers*, third parties that create markets linking buyers and sellers; and (4) *customer communities* websites where buyers can swap stories about suppliers' products and services. One of the largest of the B2B market makers is Chinese.

▽ Alibaba

The brainchild of 42-year-old Jack Ma, Alibaba, Asia's most popular online auction site, has become the world's largest online B2B marketplace and with its acquisition of Yahoo! it is the twelfth most popular website in the world. At its heart are two B2B websites, alibaba.com and china.alibaba. The former is a marketplace for companies around the globe to buy and sell in English, and the latter is a domestic Chinese marketplace. While Alibaba's rivals, such as Commerce One, were confronted with the challenge of slashing procurement costs, the Chinese powerhouse has a more nationalist agenda: to build markets for China's vast number of small and medium-sized businesses. Alibaba enables them to both trade with each other and link to global supply chains. Alibaba's B2B net has set up a system by which businesses can easily establish trust. When membership in Alibaba's B2B exchange was free, members complained, 'I don't trust this guy!' says Jack Ma. So he set up TrustPass, in which users pay Alibaba a fee to hire a third party that verifies them. Users need to have five people vouch for them and provide a list of all their certificates/business licences. Finally, anyone on Alibaba who has done business with a user is encouraged to comment on the firm, in the same way buyers comment on sellers in Amazon's or eBay's marketplace. Businesses are even starting to print 'TrustPass' on their business cards, a true sign of Alibaba's B2B credibility.[74]

Mobile phones as a channel of distribution

The mobile phone is another technology area that can impact on distribution – an area which is sometimes called mcommerce. It is growing in popularity, with many marketers reviewing the role of mobiles to distribute information and deliver data to the customer; for example, many airlines now text customers in relation to flight information. In the United Kingdom and Ireland when customers order a product at Argos it sends a text message when the product is ready for collection. Many service providers such as hairdressers and dentists send a text reminder so that they can manage their supply. This also helps to build a relationship with the customer.

▽ PayPal Mobile

Paypal Mobile has signed up EMI, Twentieth-Century Fox, Oxfam and Maxim magazine as its first text-to-buy partners in the United Kingdom. The service enables users to buy things instantly by sending specific product codes via text message. The company will then send the product to the user's address as listed in its PayPal account. The company says it already has 10 million PayPal account holders residing in the United Kingdom. As an extension to mobile services, The Walt Disney Company has signed a deal with Channel 4, a UK-based TV channel, to download clips of forthcoming episodes of *Lost* and *Desperate Housewives* to be shown online on the Channel 4 website and via the broadcaster's mobile phone portal. Another example is that charitable organisations such as Unicef and Amnesty have a 'text to give' feature where you can commit to giving a certain amount of money to the charity of your choice over your mobile phone.[75]

Children in Need, which is one of the largest charities helping disadvantaged children in the United Kingdom, raised over £37 million in 2007.[76] People can donate in a myriad of ways: online donations; by cheques through banks, building societies and post offices; by phone with a credit card; via the red button on digital satellite TV by PayPal; and on the *Children in Need* TV show by mobile phone.

Sources: L. Story (2007) New form of impulse: shopping via text message, *New York Times*, 16 April, C6; T. Wasserman (2006) Publishers test out text-to-buy feature, *Brandweek*, 20 November, 4; http://www. mmaeuropeblog.com/2006; PayPal to offer paying by text message, Reuters, 28 March 2006.

Mobile phone Internet connections are also growing in popularity and will herald major changes. While on the move we can connect to the Internet to check stock prices, the weather and sports scores; send and receive email messages; and place online orders, read bank balances, look up medical advice, and so on.[77]

Self-service technologies

Along with an internal focus for managing the supply network, there are many self-service options that have arisen through advances in technology. Many customers now opt to use technology-based systems to interact with the company and particularly for distribution – see Figure 17.16.

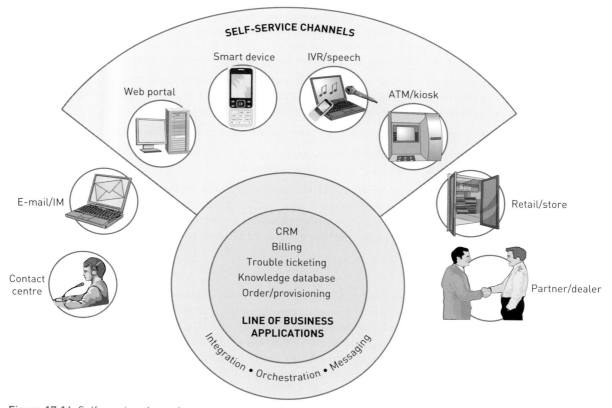

Figure 17.16 Self-service channels

Source: Adapted from Microsoft Corporation (2007) Microsoft® Customer Care Framework 2008: Redefining Customer Experience (retrieved from http://download.microsoft.com/download/b/d/2/bd2a14b8-b64b-4191-a2d5-311d0dc9f0ce/ CCF_08_Brochure_web.pdf). Copyright © Microsoft Corporation. Reproduced with permission.

Much of self-service technology has been connected to **disintermediation**. This is the elimination of channel intermediaries by product or service providers. Ryanair replaced travel agent bookings with online Internet bookings only. Therefore it displaced the traditional intermediaries serving the customer. It is now considered normal to book all flights over the Internet. Another example is the music industry, where high-speed digital distribution channels are replacing retail outlets. Artists today can produce and distribute their own work without the input of a record company. There is also a huge market for downloading music without paying royalties by cutting out the record company. Much disintermediation can change the balance of power in channels. Madonna released her latest album with Justin Timberlake through her MySpace site.

Marketers need to recognise the importance of technology and self-service technology in multichannels to market. The move to self-service technology offers challenges for marketers and consumers but the benefits for both parties can be great. The complexity of service offering can also be great and many services have moved to self-service or online.

▽ FNAC

FNAC, the leading French bookshop, is also the number one distributor of entertainment tickets in France. It has a selection of more than 6000 cultural events and a total of almost 50,000 individual performances a year. The Billetel software solution used by FNAC was launched in 1990. Today it is installed in all 350 FNAC ticket offices in France, Belgium and Switzerland, and also controls the company's direct sales via the Web and by telephone. Billetel is also the software solution used by Carrefour and Geant supermarkets.

Billetel booking is a centralised system, providing real-time management of all activity in the in-store ticket offices as well as telephone and Internet purchases. It makes tickets immediately available through any sales point, regardless of payment method. The feature-rich Billetel information system is behind the sale of over 12 million tickets per year and is subject to a set of demanding operational requirements, including:

* **scalability**: when new events go onsale, attracting a very large number of users at once;
* **performance**: the sales process must be quick and smooth, even under high loads;
* **uptime**: to ensure online sales remain available 24 hours per day.

The computerised ticketing management system has two main missions:

1 Sell and print tickets while managing the inventory of available seats.
2 Interface with the disparate software systems used by venues and event promoters.

When planning the modernisation of the Billetel system, the challenge was to guarantee system flexibility to show events information, put tickets on sale more quickly, and to tackle affordably the scalability issues of activity peaks due to new events going on sale, all the while managing an increased number of new events, venues and tickets added every year.[78]

Many new software and technological advances have enabled companies to optimise distribution and production planning, inventory management, warehousing and transportation systems. Nonetheless, the warehouses of many large companies still operate with 20-year-old technology, producing incomplete and unintegrated information flows and resulting in higher costs, higher inventory, impaired supplier relations and declining customer service. Many companies are still trying to work with finance or production-oriented IT systems that do not reflect the reality of a dynamic, agile supply network and well-managed relationships.[79]

Technology is often the weak link in the supply chain.[80] Figure 17.17 shows a range of technologies that are used in global supply chains that must be considered across the supply network.[81] The range of information systems, technologies and applications, as can be seen in Figure 17.17, play a critical role in managing channel members and networks.

Technology used to advance SCM
(Per cent citing technology)

Technology	Per cent
Enterprise resource planning	63
Inventory planning and optimisation	53
Web-based applications	52
Advanced planning and scheduling	48
e-procurement systems	47
Warehouse management systems	42
Business-to-business exchanges	41
Transportation management systems	30
Customer relationship management	26
CPFR	24
Event management	21
Supplier relationship management	21
Collaborative product design	13
Enterprise application integration	13

Figure 17.17 Technology used to advance supply networks

Source: C. Poirier and F. J. Quinn (2003) Calibrating supply chain management: findings from a survey jointly conducted by Computer Services Corporations (CSC) and *Supply Chain Management Review* magazine.

The technology enabling automated warehouses has modernised much of the distribution area.
Source: Redlink/Corbis

Information is the major resource of companies. Information allows you to make a promise such as 'the product will be at your premises at 10 am tomorrow', and control that promise through information. A major problem with supply chain management is bad data. If a customer is buying peach, orange and strawberry yogurts at the same prices and the cashier swipes one of the yogurts, say peach, three times, then the inventory system misreports the flavours of yogurts sold and thus demand and supply chain inefficiencies can result.[82]

Marketing should implement the best solutions with the best information systems, equipment, policies and procedures. Many firms that have bought leading-edge *supply* chain information systems acknowledge that they use only a fraction of the software's functionality and an even smaller fraction of the promised capability. The CEO of an industrial equipment manufacturer admitted that her company had fallen into one such classic trap:

> We spent $18 million (€13 million) getting an ERP package up and running in our company, and all we did was bring more modern technology to bear on *supply* chain processes that are 40 years out of date. I expected this technology to bring *supply* chain costs down dramatically, and nothing has changed. My mistake was expecting technology to solve a process challenge.[83]

Technology can, if used properly, ensure that there is a communications hub for everyone in the supply network. The system should allow for real-time access to demand plans, inventory levels and the transportation status of various different deliveries – information that in turn can be coordinated with demands from supply chain customers and inbound materials from supply chain providers. Anyone in the supply chain can have read-only access to the real-time data, but only selected individuals have the right to make changes to forecasts, plans and deliveries. This system, which sits atop the *supply* chain processes developed jointly by the company and its *supply* chain partners, is fully exploited as a competitive tool to deliver product faster and cheaper than rivals' *supply* chains do. In essence, sharing information with *supply* chain partners creates breakthrough improvements in performance.[84] 'Marketing memo: A network of technology-based communications' showcases an intranet-based network of the Finnish steel manufacturing industry.

Marketing memo

A network of technology-based communications

The Finnish steel manufacturing industry provides an example on how Internet-based computing and communications may assist company partners in dealing with complex issues. A group of small and medium-sized companies, all located in northern Finland, operate in cooperation with a large steel producer with a turnover of €2900 million. Before going into the Internet-based communications project, information exchange between companies was limited to mail, email, phone calls and company visits. The market demand for steel plate components is expected to increase rapidly – led by buoyant activity in Asian markets[85] – and this volume increase required efficiency improvements (e.g., reducing delivery lead time, reducing production and logistics costs) in the whole network. To facilitate this aim, a new digital business design – the SteelNet system – was created (see Figure 17.18).[86]

The SteelNet system can easily communicate with the partners' own planning systems. The SteelNet system can transmit mutually agreed information and can be used via a Web browser. Each of the participating companies has equal rights and responsibilities in the system. Moreover, company representatives from a broad range of company functionalities (e.g., manufacturing, management and transportation) can communicate and collaborate within the system and with representatives from other companies through the Internet, and relevant information is timely and accurately available to all SteelNet members. Metcalfe's Law[87] states that, 'the value of any communication technology is proportional to the square of the number of users of the system'. Thus, creating the SteelNet enhances the possibility of reaping the full benefits of ebusiness.

Source: Based on P. Iskanius and H. Kilpala (2006) One step closer towards e-business: the implementation of a supporting ICT system, *International Journal of Logistics: Research and Applications*, 9(3), 289; J. Hendler and J. Golbeck, Metcalfe's Law, Web 2.0, and the semantic Web, available at http://www.cs.umd.edu/~golbeck/downloads/ Web20-SW-JWS-webVersion.pdf, accessed March 2008.

► **Marketing memo** *(continued)*

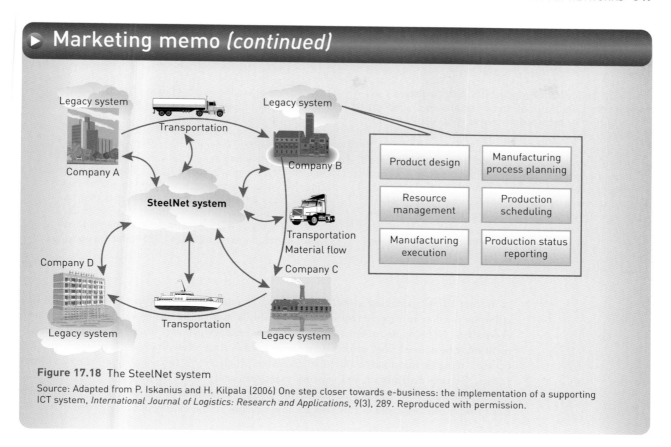

Figure 17.18 The SteelNet system

Source: Adapted from P. Iskanius and H. Kilpala (2006) One step closer towards e-business: the implementation of a supporting ICT system, *International Journal of Logistics: Research and Applications*, 9(3), 289. Reproduced with permission.

Technology can increase efficiency particularly in operations or logistics but it can also create barriers to relationships and change the power relationships within the network. There are also emerging technologies that can provide real-time and context-specific information continuously flowing from the product or service tagged to the company – see 'Marketing insight: Using RFID for real-time information along supply networks'.

Marketing insight

Using RFID for real-time information along supply networks

Radio frequency identification devices systems are made up of 'smart' tags – which have microchips attached to tiny radio antennas – and electronic readers. Chips are about the size of a dot. The tags allow companies to read out of line of sight and to gather a range of information including temperature, position and surroundings. The smart tags can be embedded in products or people, stuck on labels or worn by a person. Legoland in Denmark is looking at introducing RFID armbands for all children similar to those used by Disney in the United States. Alton Towers in England uses RFID to track visitors through the park in order to be able to make DVDs of their visit should they wish to have them. Many toll roads use RFID on their easy pass systems to allow cars to drive through at speed and download payment automatically from the Internet.

When the RFID tag is near a reader the tag transmits a unique identifying number to its computer database. The use of RFIDs has been exploding, with 2.16 billion tags to be sold in 2008 versus 1.74 billion in 2007 and 1.02 billion in 2006. Retailers should use approximately 325 million RFID labels in 2008.[88]

Radio-tagging products allow retailers to alert manufacturers before shelves go bare, and consumer goods manufacturers can further perfect their supply chain so they don't produce or distribute too few or too many goods.

Marketing insight *(continued)*

The ability to link product IDs with databases containing the life histories and whereabouts of products or equipment or even people makes RFID useful for all sorts of marketing along with preventing counterfeiting and even ensuring food and drug safety. Although a potential boon to marketers, smart tags raise issues of consumer privacy. Take tagged medications. Electronic readers in office buildings might detect the type of medication carried by employees – an invasion of privacy. Or what about RFID-enabled customer loyalty cards that encode all sorts of personal and financial data? Already a group of more than 40 public interest groups has called for strict public notification rules, the right to demand deactivation of the tag when people leave shops, and overall limits on the technology's use until privacy concerns have been better addressed.[89]

Radio frequency identification devices could offer many benefits along supply networks. Gillette is using smart tags to improve logistics and shipping from factories. RFID technology enabled Gillette to get the new Fusion razor on store shelves 11 days faster than its normal turn-around time. Gillette forecasts a 25 per cent return on its RFID investment over the next ten years, through increased sales and productivity savings.

In conclusion, managing global and local supply and demand networks and channels of distribution is a core marketing requirement to avoid the trap of the 3Es – everything, to everyone, everywhere. Network management, information technology use and channel design and management must be derived from marketing strategies rather than solely from cost considerations. The network must be information intensive and establish electronic links among all the significant parties. Getting distribution and network management right can have a big pay-off. Managing channel members and all the elements of the supply network well will reap rewards. The decisions that marketers make in this area are among many of the most crucial they have to make.

▽ SUMMARY

1 Marketing channel decisions are among the most critical decisions facing management. The company's chosen channel(s) profoundly affect all other marketing decisions.

2 Many networks are moving to demand-driven networks with agile, adaptable and aligned networks with all members working together.

3 Designing channels focuses on many issues including multiple or multichannel strategies that reflect a co-ordinated approach across all distribution options from retail to Internet, to self-service and even mobile phones.

4 Selecting channel members means understanding that each member is part of the value network and must work together.

5 Conflict among channel members needs to be avoided or at least managed.

6 Technologies play a greater role then ever before both externally, with consumer use of the Internet and self-service technologies and internally, with the use of intranets, information systems, automated warehousing and more innovative technologies such as RFID.

▽ APPLICATIONS

Marketing debate

Think of some of your favourite products and services. How are they delivered to you? Debate the different technology *versus* non technology based methods of distribution.

Marketing discussion

Pretend that you are marketing manager for a fast-moving consumer goods company based in Estonia with a large network of suppliers and distributors throughout Europe and Asia. What are the major challenges that you encounter in trying to manage your supply network?

▽ REFERENCES

[1]P. Kuhn (2002) The world according to Smart. A Presentation by Paul Kuhn of DaimlerChrysler at the Les Amis L'Ecole d'Paris (www.ecole.org).

[2]F. Frei (2006) Breaking the trade off between efficiency and service, *Harvard Business Review*, 84(11), 93–101.

[3]H. Lee (2004) The three As of supply chain excellence, *Harvard Business Review*, October, 102–12.

[4]C. Anderson (2006) *The Long Tail, The new Economics of Culture and Commerce, How Endless Choice Is Creating Unlimited Demand*, London: Random House. M. Brady and M. R. Fellenz (2007) The Service paradox: Supporting Service Supply Chains with product-oriented ICT, IEEE/informs Soli Int. Conference on Service Operations, Logistics and Informatics, Philadelphia, august.

[5]D. Lambert and M. Cooper (2000) Issues in supply chain management, *Industrial Marketing Management*, 29, 65–83.

[6]R. Achrol and P. Kotler (1999) Marketing in the network economy, *Journal of Marketing*, 63, 146–63.

[7]E. Gummesson (2007) Exit services marketing – enter service marketing, *Journal of Consumer Behaviour*, 6(2), 113–41.

[8]B. E. Rosenthal (2001) Supply chain management: Nestle is quick to adopt eprocurement, *Outsourcing Journal*, March (www.outsourcing-information-technology.com/supply.html).

[9]The physical Internet, *The Economist*, 15 June 2006.

[10]S. Murray (2007) *Moveable Feasts: From Ancient Rome to the 21st Century – the Incredible Journeys of the Food We Eat*, New York: St Martin's Press.

[11]See www.fashiontrendsetter.com/content/press/2008/Kohls-Partners-with-Rocker-Avril-Lavigne.html.

[12]M. Baker (2001) (ed.) *Critical Perspectives on Business and Management*, London: Routledge, and Guest lecture at Trinity College Dublin, 2006.

[13]T. L. Freidman (2005) *The World Is Flat: A Brief History of the Twenty-first Century*, New York: Farrar, Straus and Giroux.

[14]D. Hofman and K. O'Marah (2008) The AMR Research supply chain top 25 blows away market with 17.89% return, 10 January (www.amrresearch.com/content/view.asp?pmillid=21042).

[15]L. Cecere and D. Hofman (2008) Seven lessons from the AMR Research 2008 supply chain top 25 for consumer products, AMR Research, 23 August (www.amrresearch.com/Content/View.asp?pmillid=21730). Data from AMR Research.

[16]Hofman and O'Marah (2008) op. cit.

[17]G. Gripsrud, M. Jahre and G. Persson (2006) Supply chain management: back to the future? *International Journal of Physical Distribution & Logistics Management*, 36(8), 643–51.

[18]T. L. Webb (2002) Managing channels of distribution in the age of electronic commerce, *Industrial Marketing Management*, 31(2), 95–102.

[19]A. T. Coughlan, E. Anderson, L. W. Stern and A. I. El-Ansary (2001) *Marketing Channels*, 6th edn, Upper Saddle River, NJ: Prentice Hall.

[20]S. Min and J. T. Mentzer (2004) Developing and measuring supply chain management concepts, *Journal of Business Logistics*, 25(1), 63–99.

[21]Gummesson (2007) op. cit.

[22]H. J. Schau, M. F. Smith and P. I. Schau (2005) The healthcare network economy: the role of Internet information transfer and implications for pricing, *Industrial Marketing Management*, 34, 147–56.

[23]See http://www.nokia.com/A4252213.

[24]M. R. Fellenz and M. Brady (2008) Managing the Innovative deployment of Information and Communication Technology (ICT) for global service organisations, International Journal of Technology Marketing, 3(1), 39–55. C. C. Poirier and F. J. Quinn (2003) A survey of supply chain progress, from the September/October 2003 issue of *Supply Chain Management Review*, 1 September, 7(5), 40–9.

[25]Gummesson (2007) op. cit.

[26]Gripsrud, Jahre and Persson (2006) op. cit.

[27]M. de Lurdes, D. K. Velduo and S. Macbeth (2004) Partnering and relationships within an international network context, *European Journal of Marketing*, 21(2), 142–57.

[28]M. Fielding (2008) Building relationships, *Marketing Management*, January-February, 4–11.

[29]Lee (2004) op. cit.

[30]Lee (2004) op. cit.

[31]Lee (2004) op. cit.

[32]R. Martin (2008) The 2008 supply chain: demand-driven reality, *Supply Chain Management Review*, 12(1), 1–10. (www.scmr.com/article/CA6518149.html).

[33]Ibid.

[34]D. Lambert and M. Cooper (2000) Issues in supply chain management, *Industrial Marketing Management*, 29, 65–83.

[35]T. Baltacioglu, E. Ada, M. Kaplan, O. Yurt and Y. Kaplan (2007) A new framework for service supply chains, *The Service Industries Journal*, 27(2), 105–24.

[36]A. Toffler (1980) *The Third Wave*, New York: Bantam Books.

[37]L. W. Stern and B. A. Weitz (1997) The revolution in distribution: challenges and opportunities, *Long Range Planning*, 30(6), 823–29.

[38]See http://csr2006.cadburyschweppes.com/ethical/supply-chain.html.

[39]C. Yulinsky (2000) Multi-channel marketing, making 'bricks and clicks' stick, McKinsey Marketing Practice Series.

[40]J. S. Thomas and U. Y. Sullivan (2005) Managing marketing communications, *Journal of Marketing*, 69 (October), 239–51; E. J. Fox, A. L. Montgomery and L. M. Lodish (2004) Consumer shopping and spending across retail formats, *The Journal of Business*, 77(2), S25–60; S. Balasubramanian, R. Raghunathan and V. Mahajan (2005) Consumers in a multichannel environment: product utility, process utility and channel choice, *Journal of Interactive Marketing*, 19(2), 12–30; A. Ansari, C. F. Mela and S. A. Neslin (2008) Customer channel migration, *Journal of Marketing Research*, 45(1), 60–76.

[41]P. F. Nunes and F. V. Cespedes (2003) The customer has escaped, *Harvard Business Review*, November, 96–105.

[42]J. Helyar (2003) The only company Wal-Mart fears, *Fortune*, 24 November, pp. 158–66; see also M. Silverstein and N. Fiske (2003) *Trading Up: The New American Luxury*, New York: Portfolio Books.

[43]Dell banks on single-tier strategy for UK partners, December 2007, http://techtaxi.blogspot.com/2007/12/dell-banks-on-single-tier-strategy-for.html

[44]S. Wuyts, S. Stremersch, C. Van Den Bulte and P. H. Franses (2004) Vertical marketing systems for complex products: a triadic perspective, *Journal of Marketing Research*, 41 (November), 479–87.

[45]R. Johnston and P. R. Lawrence (1988) Beyond vertical integration: the rise of the value-adding partnership, *Harvard Business Review*, July–August, 94–101; see also J. A. Siguaw, P. M. Simpson and T. L. Baker (1998) Effects of supplier market orientation on distributor market orientation and the channel relationship: the distribution perspective, *Journal of Marketing*, July, 99–111; N. Narayandas and M. U. Kalwani (1995) Long-term manufacturer–supplier relationships: do they pay off for supplier firms?, *Journal of Marketing*, January, 1–16; A. Bovik and G. John (2000) When does vertical coordination improve industrial purchasing relationships, *Journal of Marketing*, 64 (October), 52–64.

[46]Based on R. T. Moriarty and U. Moran (1990) Marketing hybrid marketing systems, *Harvard Business Review*, November–December, 146–55.

[47]W. Nelson (2002) All power to the consumer? Complexity and choice in consumer lives, *Journal of Consumer Behaviour*, 2(2), 185–95.

[48]Coughlan, Anderson, Stern, and El-Ansary (2006) op. cit.

[49]J. Womack and D. Jones (2005) Lean consumption, *Harvard Business Review*, March, 2–13.

[50]Trouser suit, *The Economist*, 24 November 2001, p. 56.

[51]For more on relationship marketing and the governance of marketing channels see J. B. Heide (1994) Interorganizational governance in marketing channels, *Journal of Marketing*, January, 71–85.

[52]R. K. Heady (1999) Online bank offers best rates, *South Florida Sun-Sentinel*, 22 November, p. 22; D. Fairlamb (1999) Online banks invade Europe: bricks-and-mortar players are caught off guard, *BusinessWeek* (International Edition), 25 October (www.businessweek.com/1999/99_43/b3652200.htm).

[53]Coughlan, Anderson, Stern, and El-Ansary (2006) op. cit.

[54]E. Anderson and A. Coughlan (2006) Channel management: structure, governance, and relationship management, in A. Coughlan, E. Anderson, L. W. Stern, A. El-Ansary (2006) *Marketing Channels*, 6th edn, Upper Saddle River, NJ: Prentice Hall, pp. 223–47.

[55]These bases of power were identified in J. R. P. French and B. Raven (1959) The bases of social power, in D. Cartwright (ed.) *Studies in Social Power*, Ann Arbor, MI: University of Michigan Press, pp. 150–67.

[56]B. Rosenbloom (1995) *Marketing Channels: A Management View*, 5th edn, Hinsdale, IL: Dryden.

[57]G. Wootten (2003) Channel conflict and high involvement Internet purchases – a qualitative cross cultural perspective of policing parallel importing, *Qualitative Market Research: An International Journal*, 6(1), 38–47.

[58]P. Sayer (IDG News Service) (2007) Apple opens largest European store-in-store, *PCWorld*, 29 June.

[59]See www.apple.com/pr/library/2004/nov/18store.html.

[60]C. Edwards (2001) Sorry Steve, here's why Apple stores won't work, *BusinessWeek*, 21 May (www.businessweek.com/magazine/content/01_21/b3733059.htm?chan=search).

[61]See www.appleinsider.com/articles/08/01/07/report_apple_stores_mac_sales_beat_pc_stores_by_10_to_1.html.

[62]T. Elkin (2001) Apple gambles with retail plan, *Advertising Age*, 24 June; N. Wingfield (2006) How Apple's store strategy beat the odds, *Wall Street Journal*, 17 May, B1, B10; J. Useem (2007) Simply irresistible, *Fortune*, 19 March, 107–12.

[63]T. H. Davenport and J. G. Harris (2007) *Competing on Analytics: the New Science of Winning*, Boston, MA: Harvard Business School Press.

[64]Anderson (2006) op. cit.

[65]C. Ramirez (2007) European online holiday retail sales hit €51 billion, *Forrester Research*, 24 October.

[66]J. C. Collier and C. C. Bienstock (2006) How do customers judge quality in an e-tailer, *MIT Sloan Management Review*, Fall, 35–40.

[67]See www.internetretailer.com/internet/marketing-conference/92487-amazon-moves-into-europe-first-e-commerce-services-deal.html.

[68]See www.e-consultancy.com/news-blog/362943/m-s-launches-new-amazon-powered-website.html.

[69]E. West (2004) Who's next?, *Potentials*, February, 7–8; C. Taylor (2003) Smart library, *Time*, 17 November, p. 68; R. D. Hof (2006) Jeff Bezos' risky bet, *BusinessWeek*, 13 November (www.businessweek.com/magazine/content/06_46/b4009001.htm); R. D. Hof (2004) The wizard of web retailing, *BusinessWeek*, 20 December, 18; E. Schonfield (2005) The great giveaway, *Business 2.0*, April, 80–6; Click to download, *The Economist*, 19 August 2006, pp. 57–8.

[70]Nielsen/NetRatings (2005) Online retail report card, Press Release, 7 April.

[71]A. K. J. Barlow, N. Q. Siddiqui and M. Mannion (2004) Development in information and communication technologies for retail marketing channels, *International Journal of Retail and Distribution Management*, 32 (March), 157–63; G&J Electronic Media Services (2001) 7th wave of the GfK-Online-Monitor, Hamburg, Germany: GfK Press.

[72]See http://money.cnn.com/2007/12/14/technology/sloan_upsellit.fortune/index.htm?postversion=2007121705

[73]H. Green (2002) Lessons of the cyber survivors, *BusinessWeek*, 22 April, p. 42.

[74]A. E. Schlosser, T. Barnett White and S. M. Lloyd (2006) Converting web site visitors into buyers: how web site investment increases consumer trusting beliefs and online purchase intentions, *Journal of Marketing*, 70 (April), 133–48; China's pied piper, *The Economist*, 23 September 2006, p. 80; see also www.alibaba.com.

[75]See www.paymentsnews.com/2006/04/paypal_mobile_t.html.

[76]See www.bbc.co.uk/pudsey/fundraising/faq.shtml#1.

[77]D. Lamont (2001) *Conquering the Wireless World: The Age of M-Commerce*, New York: Wiley; M. Weingarten (2002) The medium is the instant message, *Business 2.0*, February, pp. 98–9; V. Kasturi Rangan (2006) *Transforming Your Go-to-Market Strategy: The Three Disciplines of Channel Management*, Boston, MA: Harvard Business School Press.

[78]http://www.mysql.com/news-and-events/press-release/release_2006_31.html

[79]Fellenz and Brady (2008) op. cit; M. Brady, M. R. Fellenz and M. Cholakova (2007) Towards an IT-enabled Customer Centric Service Supply Chain, academy of Marketing Conference (UK) Kingston University, July; R. E. Slone, J. T. Mentzer and J. P. Dittmann (2007) Are you the weakest link in your company's supply chain?, *Harvard Business Review*, 85(9), 116–27.

[80]Ibid.

[81]C. Poirier and F. J. Quinn (2006) CSC-SCMR Survey Says: Solid Gains, *Supply Chain Management Review*, 1 January; See also www.csc.com/ features/2003/images/Chart-05.gif and www.csc.com/ solutions/supplychainmanagement/news/ uploads/5948_1.pdf.

[82]For further information see A. Raman, R. E. Slone, K. Ferdows, M. A. Lewis, J. A.D. Machuca, J. K. Liker, T. Y. Choi, D. M. Lambert, A. M. Knemeyer, V. G. Narayanan, H. L. Lee (2008) The 21st century supply chain, *Harvard Business Review Collection*, Special Issue.

[83]J. Mentzer (2007) What are the critical skills of supply chain leaders, *Industry Week*, 24 December (www.industryweek. com/ReadArticle.aspx?ArticleID=15520).

[84]M. R. Fellenz and M. Brady (2008) RFID and Data capture technologies in global service supply chains: Meeting the Information Management Challenge, Communications of the IBIMA, 4(5), 41–49; Slone, Mentzer and Dittmann (2007) op. cit.

[85]See www.oecd.org/document/10/0,3343,de_2649_201185_39732042_1_1_1_1,00.html [accessed May 2008].

[86]Adapted from P. Iskanius and H. Kilpala (2006) One step closer towards e-business – the implementation of a supporting ICT system, *International Journal of Logistics: Research and Applications*, 9(3), 282–92, diagram 289.

[87]See J. Hendler and J. Golbeck (in press) Metcalfe's law, web 2.0, and the semantic web, available at http://www.cs.umd.edu/~golbeck/downloads/Web20-SW-JWS-webVersion.pdf [accessed March 2008].

[88]IDTechEx RFID market projections 2008 to 2018, IDTechEx, 4 February 2008 (www.idtechex.com/ research/articles/ idtechex_rfid_market_projections_2008_to_2018_00000813.asp).

[89]D. Anderson (2006) RFID technology getting static in New Hampshire, *Brandweek*, 23 January , p. 13.

Chapter 18

Managing the service process and the consumer interface

IN THIS CHAPTER, WE WILL ADDRESS THE FOLLOWING QUESTIONS:

1 How is the service process designed and managed?

2 What are the people management issues (both staff and consumers) during the service process?

3 What are the challenges for managing technologies and particularly self-service technologies within the service process?

4 What are the issues in creating and managing the physical evidence and service experience environment?

This chapter focuses on how to manage the creation or co-creation of value with the customer during the service process, including all aspects of the service environment. Having studied the global supply network in the previous chapter we now look at the role of service process, people and physical evidence in the provision of service to customers.

Swiss (Swiss International Airline) exemplifies each of these areas.

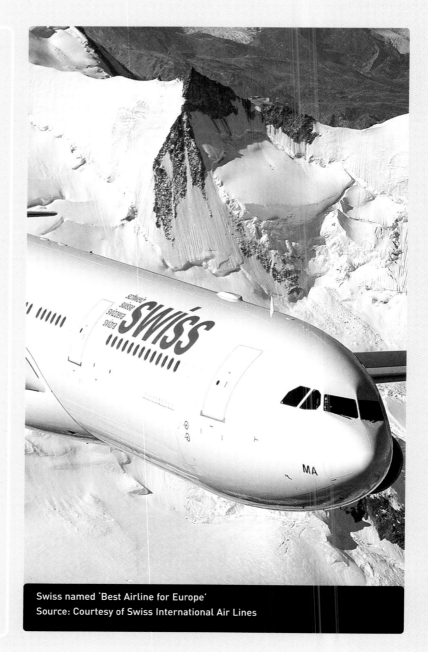

Swiss named 'Best Airline for Europe'
Source: Courtesy of Swiss International Air Lines

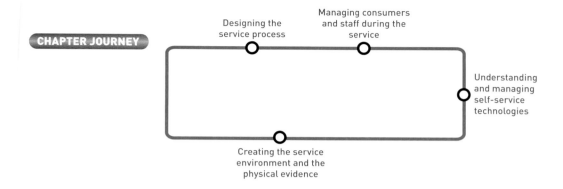

Designing the
service process

Managing consumers
and staff during the
service

Understanding
and managing
self-service
technologies

Creating the service
environment and the
physical evidence

The Swiss (formerly known as SwissAir) story is of a brand that manages its service process, people and physical environment. Swiss was voted 'Best Airline for Europe 2007 for Business Travellers'. Alexander Arafa, Swiss's head of sales and marketing Europe, who collected the prestigious award on behalf of all Swiss personnel at a ceremony in Frankfurt said that

> Our top placings confirm to us that we are delivering on our promise of making our customers feel at home whenever they're aboard. Personal care, quality in every detail and typical Swiss hospitality: these are the values that our staff embody and convey day in, day out. And it's to their tremendous work and commitment that we owe our success.[1]

For Swiss everything counts. The process of boarding the plane, the colour and the texture of the seats, the style of the staff uniform, the music that is piped in and even the greeting from the pilot, are all designed to make the customer feel welcome and safe with Swiss. All of these aspects of marketing need to be managed. If the pilot was wearing jeans and a T-shirt or the music was loud rap a different impression would be created for the customer.

It is amazing in a world so focused on service that there is so much poor service, lip service and disservice. Take airlines, restaurants, discos, banks, museums, hotels, retail stores, and so on, many customer experiences are not necessarily successful ones. In a recent Bain & Co survey only 8 per cent of customers described their experience with companies as 'superior', while 80 per cent of the companies believed that the service they were supplying was superior.[2] There is a large disparity between what the customer wants as service and what companies provide. Many companies find that what should be transparent, customer-centric strategies for delivering value to their customers have become company centric, unhelpful and damaging strategies for extracting value from customers.[3] This chapter focuses on service process, the environment of the service, any physical evidence aligned to the service and the people who perform the service, be they service personnel or customers. Shops such as Spain's Zara, Sweden's H&M, Spain's Mango and Britain's Topshop have thrived in recent years, as they understand the role of service process and environment. Zara in particular uses its store front and service process as core marketing strategies rather than an over focus on advertising.

Companies have spent the last decade re-engineering or changing their business processes but have largely ignored their service processes. A recent study shows that 68 per cent of American customers feel that they are ignored by companies. We can assume that similar findings would result if the study was carried out in Europe. The service era means that customers demand a quality service instantaneously when they touch a button or make a request.

▽ Service process design and management

Service process is the way in which the service system operates. How customers board an aircraft, how they queue in a bank, how you get food in the university canteen, all make up the service process or the process of how we avail ourselves of or perform a service. The range of encounters that customers have with service personnel on a daily basis are immense, and the number of service processes that customers become part of are limitless. The encounters include bus drivers, shop assistants, coffee shop staff, security staff, cinema attendants, waitresses, cashiers, air stewards, repair personnel (from carpenters to plumbers), hairdressers – and the list goes on. In some of the service processes we play a minor role – as in dropping off a jacket to the dry cleaners – and in others we play a major role impacting on the service process and on other customers – eating out at a restaurant or dancing at a disco. Managing the service process is exciting and challenging for marketers and an often overlooked aspect of marketing that is growing in importance.

Service process activity can be viewed as an *activity* or an *output* of a system. When understood as an activity a service is performed for others, usually the customers. As an output a service is 'a deed', 'a performance', 'an offering or 'a benefit'.[4]

Designing a service process that matches the operational demands of service delivery and customer needs is a skill. Marketing managers must design a service that works for the company to meet customer needs without squandering their own or the customer's time, effort and resources.[5] The service process is an important part of marketing, and the design and operation of the service must ensure that service is delivered consistently, on time and over time. Think about going to a top-class restaurant, such as the Restaurante La Dorada in Madrid or the Stella Marina in Vienna. As you walk in the door the process is designed to make you feel special, comfortable and cocooned.

A satisfactory outcome is one when the customer was satisfied with their service and their interactions with a company. In other words the process worked and the customer received the quality of service they expected. There are five issues to be aware of:

1   Avoid dissatisfaction.

2   Try to create satisfaction.

3   Monitor how satisfaction and dissatisfaction are linked: for example making one customer satisfied but by doing so leaving another customer dissatisfied.

4   Try to involve the customer.

5   Try to create a feeling of achievement on the part of the customer.[6]

Satisfied customers will not only visit the service again but also act as a service ambassador, encouraging other customers to use the service and so the profit of the service organisation rises.

You were introduced to the challenges of managing services, service quality and service expectations in earlier chapters. Service quality as perceived by customers has two dimensions, which must be managed: a *technical* (what was received, outcome) and *functional* (how it was received, interactions, process) quality.[7] Taking a restaurant experience as an example, there is the good food (technical) and also timely, friendly staff (functional); all in a pleasant atmosphere. This does not happen by accident. From having clean pots in the kitchen for the chef to cook with, to having enough staff to greet and serve you, to having staff to take your bill and give you your coats on the way out – all of this service process needs to be managed.

> To learn about how Haier became the preferred household appliance manufacturer in China by implementing successful service strategies, visit www.pearsoned-asia.com/marketingmanagementchina

Service process design

Constructing a service process necessitates a number of decisions to be made within key areas highlighted in Figure 18.1.[8]

There are five issues in service process design:

1   **The degree of technology utilised**: How much human and how much technological interaction is there? This will be explored later in the chapter.

Figure 18.1 Service process design

Source: H. Kasper, P. van Helsdingen and M. Gabbott (2006) *Services Marketing Management: A Strategic Perspective*, 2nd edn, Chichester, England: John Wiley & Sons. Copyright © 2006 John Wiley & Sons. Reproduced with permission.

2   **The degree of visibility:** How much of the service is customer or front office (what the customer can see) and how much is operations or back office (hidden from the customer)? Figure 18.2 shows how marketing can move the front and back office activities around. Technology can play a major role in this area. Take booking a ticket on an aeroplane. Doing this online is part of the back office processes that the customer now engages with – from booking the ticket to choosing the seat and even printing the boarding card – all online.[9]

3   **The degree of customisation:** This is dependent on the degree of complexity for the customer (the number of steps involved in the process) and the degree of process divergence (the amount of variety in the process).[10] Only sometimes is it possible to allow customisation of some or all of the service; for example, it would not be possible to allow train passengers to decide what time the train left.

4   **The degree of accessibility:** Accessibility is the degree of ease with which the customer can get to or avail themselves of a service. Once the customer is present accessibility refers to how the service is laid out, where the queues are and how the service environment is designed.

5   **The degree of integration:** This refers to who conducts the service, on a continuum from totally the customer (as in kiosks or vending machines) to service personnel interacting with the customer (as in hairdressing or professional services such as doctors and solicitors).

Figure 18.2 Managing the service process: from operation to customers

Source: R. Johnston and C. Graham (2005) *Service Operations Management: Improving Service Delivery*, 2nd edn, Harlow, England: Prentice Hall. Copyright © 2005 Pearson Education Ltd. Reproduced with permission.

There are three issues in the service process delivery:

1 **Duration**: This relates to the time it takes to provide the service and there are five key elements:

- task time
- total process time
- customer contact time
- thoughput time
- waiting time.

Time is usually connected to queues, which means not just the physical queue but also the queues for computer load time or call waiting for a call centre. Managing waiting can be a core element of service design. Marketing managers can schedule customers to try and control this or operate on a first-come first-served basis and let the customer manage the time. In general the more waiting there is the lower customers rate the service experience.

2 **Efforts of employees**: This will be discussed later in the chapter but the service personnel's ability to interact well with the customer is very important. Whether they smile and how pleasant they are correlate highly with how customers perceive service, whether face to face or over the phone.

3 **Reliability**: Customers like to receive expected outcomes. Reliability links to the consistency, integrity and dependability of the process. Does the customer receive the service promised? If a restaurant says there will be a table in ten minutes was there a table within or before that time? Sometimes it is better to underpromise and overdeliver than overpromise and underdeliver.

Figure 18.3 A service process blueprint for a visit to a bar

Source: R. Fisk, S. Grove and J. John (2004) *Interactive Service Marketing*, Boston, MA: Houghton Mifflin.
Copyright © 2004 South-Western, a part of Cengage Learning, Inc. Reproduced with permission.

Understanding service process design

A service blueprint is a pictorial map of the essential components of the service performance. It identifies the customers, the service personnel (both front and back office) the points of interaction between the customer and the company and any other evidence, processes or activities. Most importantly the blueprint shows how these combine to create the service performance. Designing a blueprint can be very complicated depending on the complexity and amount or flexibility and variability desired. (These issues will be discussed later in the chapter.) Figure 18.3 shows a service process blueprint for a visit to a bar.[11]

The four key steps in preparing a service blueprint are as follows:

1 **Sequencing**: This is deciding on the number of steps or the complexity of the service process.

2 **Visibility**: Deciding how much of the process is revealed to the customer.

3 **Timing**: Many blueprints include timings for each stage of the process. Figure 18.4 shows a blueprint for a more complex visit to – a hospital.

4 **Tolerance**: The best-case scenario, when everything works well, but also the process for what happens when something goes wrong. These are the tolerance levels for how long the customer is prepared to wait.

Designing service processes

Designing and managing these service processes is not easy as there are as many variations of service as there are service organisations. *Process designs* describes and prescribes the procedures to be followed in service delivery and also how the service will use or interact with other resources such as technology and equipment.[12] The whole interrelated chain of processes needs to be carefully designed, managed and controlled to deliver value to customers and the organisation. Nowadays many waitresses have handheld computers that transfer orders straight to the kitchen and also to the cash register for payment. The process needs to be designed, managed and aligned with both the human and the technological aspects.

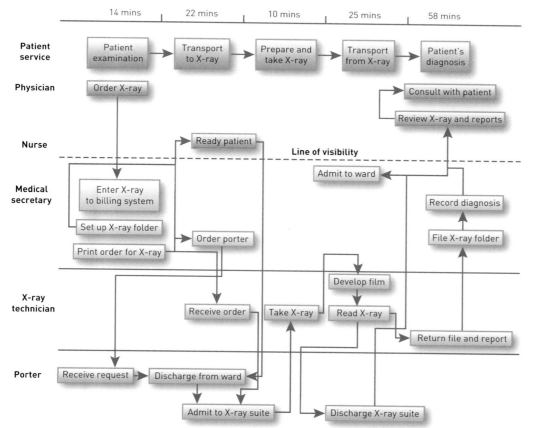

Figure 18.4 A more complex blueprint for a service, with suggested timings

Source: H. Kasper, P. van Helsdingen and M. Gabbott (2006) *Services Marketing Management: A Strategic Perspective*, 2nd edn, Chichester, England: Wiley. Copyright © 2006 John Wiley & Sons. Reproduced with permission.

The Mircosoft Surface can improve the service in a restaurant or café. The customer can select their meal from the images and send the order through to the kitchen by using a 'send' button.

Source: David Paul Morris/ Getty Images

Some services are *extremely flexible* and allow the customer to choose how and when they avail themselves of the service. For online shopping or banking you can send your order or sort out your bank balance at any time of the day or night. Some clothes shops allow customers to enter, roam and browse in their own time. Other service processes are much more *rigid and closely defined* in order to achieve benefits of consistency and efficiency. So in a call centre, the caller is welcomed by a standard greeting that the call centre employee is reading off a screen and much of what they say is standardised to manage the call. Other service processes *depend a lot on the skills, knowledge and expertise* of the service provider, such as medical doctors or ski instructors. All three of these options can make greater or lesser use of technology and customer roles.

Microsoft has recently introduced the Microsoft Surface, which can be used personally or in restaurants, hotels and cafés – see the photograph above. There are many uses, for example, it can be used as an interactive table that allows customers to select what they want from the screen and send the order straight to the kitchen.

Modelling the service process

A good way to view the service is to use the service process model shown in Figure 18.5. This model highlights not just the contact personnel and the customer and other customers within the service process but also the servicescape – the service environment or surroundings. It also shows the broader environment, which internally includes the support staff and management and externally includes competitors, infrastructure and society in general.

Figure 18.5 A services process model showing relationships and interactions between service providers and customers

Source: E. Gummesson (2002) *Total Relationship Marketing*, 2nd edn, London: Elsevier, p. 68. Copyright © 2002 Elsevier. Reproduced with permission.

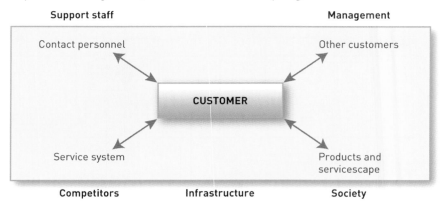

Measuring service efficiency

Within manufacturing measuring efficiency is quite easy. How many products were manufactured in a given period of time? The inputs are the raw material and the output is usually a product. Measuring efficiency is more difficult in services when compared to product producing factories. How many customers did you serve? Customers have very different service skills, motivation, knowledge and expectations, and can be very different personally.[13] Therefore the service delivery system has to be flexible enough to cope with variability in (customer) inputs and also to understand that customers often want different outputs. Two customers can have very different experiences of the service process and both be content. Consider two dining experiences in the same restaurant – one group arrives with three children for a quick meal; the other is a romantic couple hoping for a three-hour meal. Both parties might be satisfied with the output, even if the objective time measurement is quite different.[14]

Marketers often try to use objective manufacturing or automational measures for efficiency in services, which can cause potential pitfalls. They try to automate the service task in a similar way to the manufacturing process. Take a help desk or call centre – measuring average call times would probably not be a measure of satisfied customers. Shorter calls may just be a reflection of staff who hurried the customer off the line, whereas measuring problems solved in a call (no callers returning with the same problem) might be a better measure, even if calls took longer.

▽ Fujitsu Services and British Midlands

Headquartered in Tokyo, Fujitsu Limited is one of the largest providers of IT services in Europe, the Middle East and Africa, with 15,400 employees in 30 countries and revenues of €25.8 billion. It has the account to handle all calls to the BMI (British Midlands) call centre. Normal practice would be that the more calls staff answered the more money the company would be paid. Fujitsu views its call centre operation very differently, and rather than answer as many complaint calls as possible they try to reduce the number of such calls. Fujitsu asked whether, instead of being paid for each call handled, it could receive a set fee on the *potential* number of calls. Staff focus on the content of *all* the calls and try to find the root causes of the problems.

Within the British Midland account one of the main problems (26 per cent of total) was the malfunction of printers when checkout staff were issuing tickets. Fujitsu convinced BMI senior managers to invest in new printers, and calls in relation to malfunctioning printers were cut by 80 per cent in 18 months. Answering complaint calls does not improve the service process. Understanding what the real problem is, sorting out that problem – that is providing real service for customers and employees.

Service quality, productivity and profitability relates to customers' perceived quality, mainly focusing on customer satisfaction surveys. Quality and productivity in the service process are relatively new ideas, whereas product quality has been an ongoing focus. Quality, productivity and profitability should be studied together.[15] It is crucial that marketers understand the profitability of their service process design choices and that they measure precisely the financial consequences of these choices. It is easier to manage profitability when you can manage all the inputs, as can be achieved in the manufacturing area. Within services, profitability is harder to manage. Customer behaviour can greatly affect the level of profit. The average annual profit for a retail bank customer is €150, while the average cost for a single customer visit to a bank is €10. You can easily see how customers' behaviour can influence the profitability of the service.[16] If a customer visited their bank over 15 times a year all their profitability would be gone.

Judging service process quality

It is often very hard for customers to judge how well a service worked. Customer assessment of service process effectiveness and efficiency often relies on their perceived or subjective assessment – how a customer felt about the service rather than on the actual experience or objective assessment, which is the exact measures of what occurred.[17] Hospitals may have delays in accident and emergency but if they ultimately cure your pain you may feel that the service was excellent.[18]

How customers evaluate service quality relates to the five issues below:

1 **Reliability**: the ability to perform the service dependably, accurately and consistently. Reliability is performing the service right the first time. This component has been found to be the most important to consumers.

2 **Responsiveness**: the ability to provide prompt service. Examples of responsiveness include calling the customer back quickly, serving lunch urgently to someone who is in a hurry, or emailing an order confirmation immediately.

3 **Assurance**: the knowledge and courtesy of employees and their ability to convey trust. Skilled employees who treat customers with respect and make customers feel that they can trust the company exemplify assurance.

4 **Empathy**: caring, individualised attention to customers. Firms whose employees recognise customers, smile at them, and learn their customers' specific requirements are providing empathy.

5 **Tangibles**: many services are intangible by nature – you cannot drop them on your foot – so the physical evidence of the service can be used to judge the service. The tangible parts of a service are the physical aspects, including furniture and equipment, the colour of the carpet and the type of wallpaper. Tangibles aspects of services are often judged as part of the service.

In the 1990s Zeithaml, Berry and Parasuraman identified a zone of tolerance for customers and recent research confirms that it still exists and is crucial for customers.[19]

Customers have a range of service expectations Customers have an ideal and a desired level of service. At the top is what they believe the company can and will deliver and adequate service – the minimum they are willing to accept – at the bottom.[20] This is the **zone of tolerance**. If the service has better than desired levels the customer will see it as very good and be delighted. If the service falls *below* the zone of tolerance the customer will be disgusted and look elsewhere.

Zones of tolerance can vary across customers (reflecting different priorities in their service expectations) and also across occasions or contexts (reflecting different potential drivers of expectations). Customers' service expectations can be greatly influenced by what is promised, both explicitly and implicitly. Overpromising can be very dangerous. There can be explicit promises in, for example, service level agreements – which are formal service contracts between companies – that will be hard to reach in some circumstances and difficult to monitor.

Implicit or more intangible or vague service promises are more difficult to address. In addition, customers' personal needs could affect their service expectations. Word-of-mouth communications and recommendations are also powerful determinants of service expectations. The perception of the alternative services that are available to customers will also affect their view of the services offered. Sometimes service levels can be affected by situational factors, which are factors beyond the service provider's control (e.g., a power failure). When service customers are made aware of such situational factors they are often willing to be more understanding and to widen their zones of tolerance.

▽ Virgin Mobile

Virgin Mobile, the UK-based mobile phone provider, was able to break into the US market by making its process simple and transparent. It introduced a simple 'pay as you go' mobile phone service, with no hidden fees, no time or day restrictions and no contract. This was straightforward and the service that the customer wanted. So in a market where there were already major players and growth was slowing, Virgin Mobile was able to get into the market and capture 5 million customers in one year by making its service process simple. Virgin's customers' satisfaction rating has been in the

90 per cent percentile since the service launched and many customers act as goodwill ambassadors for the brand. In 2007 more than two-thirds of customers had recommended it to a friend. Virgin Mobile did all this with low brand recognition and an advertising budget of €50 million, which was less than one-tenth of the major players in the market.[21] It focused on the service process and making it simple to follow. It also made it easy to leave the service, with no cancellation fee. Many little process improvements make the process easy and fun for the customer, resulting in big profits for the company.

▽ Managing people (staff and consumers) during the service process

Many companies forget how important their staff are to them. The organisational chart needs to be turned on its head. So instead of everything focusing on the managing director at the top of the chart, the *staff* should be at the top and everything should be oriented towards them and how to help them achieve the required service levels. The important point is that all staff members must see others, and particularly top management, behaving in ways that they need to copy.

Staff are particularly important in services where, in the absence of clues from tangible products, the customer will form an impression of the company and service through the behaviour and attitude of its staff. Any staff member that customers see or encounter can be classed as a contact person and forms part of the perception of the service. Throughout this chapter we will refer to them as service personnel.

All service personnel interacting with customers must be trained. Some bus companies view their drivers as part of the service; others just train them to provide the technical part of their role – driving a bus. Seeing service providers as part of the overall service can be crucial. The taxi service in the city of Glasgow is considered to be one of the most important aspects of its tourism marketing. Glasgow City Council trains its taxi people to be ambassadors for the city, realising that they are often the first people visitors meet – and we all know that first impressions last.

The people aspect of the service process and the understanding of how to manage personal interactions – what has been referred to as the **moment of truth** – is crucial in service design. Moments of truth or touch points are any occasion on which a customer encounters the brand – from actual experience to personal experience or seeing a promotion to casual observation. For a hotel, the touch points include reservations, check in and check out, frequent-stay programmes, room service, business services, exercise facilities, laundry service, restaurants, bars, and so on. There are so many touch points and so many people.

With services *everyone matters*. Many processes and departments within an organisation must be coordinated in order for the customer to receive service. This is what is referred to as operations management. Everyone must understand their role, no matter how small. In a hotel, the doorman must greet the customer, the receptionist must look after them, housekeeping needs to have their rooms clean and the restaurant needs to be ready to serve them. Marketing managers need to be able to manage across many departments – an issue also called internal marketing that is discussed in Chapter 21.[22]

As seen in Chapter 17, as global supply networks and channels of distribution change more and more service contacts will take place outside the company's control. Marketers need to be aware of and control all company/customer interactions well, even when they are not directly responsible for the staff. This is particularly relevant nowadays when, due to the increase in online purchasing, often the only person that a consumer actually interacts with is the delivery person from TNT, UPS or FedEx. Is the delivery person helpful, friendly and nice?

Failure of the service process

Due to the inseparability between the company and the customer, where services failures occur they often occur in real time while the customer is present and involved in the interaction. Failure means that the service did not meet the customer's expectation.[23] In services, it is the customer contact people who have to both notice the service failure and the unsatisfied customer (if possible) and repair the failure – immediately (if possible). The picture gets complicated for management for several reasons:

- Customers may blame themselves for the failure (not wanting to complain).
- The cause for the failure may be the contact people charged with noticing and repairing the failure (causing potential role conflicts).
- Fixing a service is also different, due to intangibility and perishability. A broken TV can be brought back to working condition. How can you give back to the customer time lost waiting in a queue?
- Compensations that customers are willing to accept and perceive as fair will vary.[24]

The customer as service provider

Marketers need to study the role of the customer in the service process and help to manage and encourage this. In many services the customer is the co-creator of the value they will get from the service. The presence of the customer (and fellow customers) in the service (production) process is a major challenge. This is also a difference when compared to a product production process. Customer participation must be accommodated, planned and designed into the service process.[25] Can you imagine how a manufacturing company would operate if customers were walking around the factory all the time and changing things? Customers often want to do it their way, not necessarily the way the company wants them to do it. As customers provide varied inputs to the service process, service personnel cannot necessarily rely on past procedures and ways of doing things. They must be able to generate novel and appropriate solutions to customer requests. Customers are human and so by nature are different. Watch customers queuing – many try to jump the queue; many jump from queue to queue, always looking for the fastest queue; while others are model consumers and just wait their turn.

'A service is a time-perishable, intangible experience performed for a customer acting in the role of co-producer.'[26] The customer often provides part of the service for themselves. The distinct roles of the customer and the company need to be explored and understood by marketing managers.[27] In many cases the customer performs most of the service process. Take any visit to a Carrefour supermarket in France, an Albert Hein in the Netherlands or a Spar in the United Kingdom. In a supermarket you, as the customer, do a lot of work. You park your car, you find a trolley (with wheels that work!) you go along the aisle, you select products you want and load them into the trolley. You then go to the cash register and load your products on to the conveyor belt and then, when the cashier has scanned them, you put them all back into the trolley. There are now self-service options available, which means that you can also perform the scanning operation yourself. You then push the trolley to the car and load all your products into the boot. You, as the customer, really do a lot of the work in this service process.

Co-creation of value

Co-creation or customer creation is now normal behaviour for many consumers with social networking, gaming and the virtual world as core examples – all discussed in Chapter 4. Take Wikipedia, which was solely developed from consumer inputs. Social networking sites only work if students and young people design and post what is called 'user-generated content'. From eBay to YouTube there is a battle of content between professional companies posting information to the Internet and user content from what could be called amateurs. Customers co-create value when they log on to the EuroDisney site and design their agenda for their trip. Prahalad and Ramaswamy, leading authors in this area, suggest that co-creation is a core part of marketing today. They note: 'high-quality interactions that enable an individual customer to co-create unique experiences with the company are the key to unlocking new sources of competitive advantage'.[28] Co-creation relates to **prosumers**, a word coined by futurist Alan Toffler in 1980, which is a play on the words producer, consumer and consumption or a co-creator of value. In many cases the customer (either through accident or design) performs much of the service themselves. Take IKEA.

▽ IKEA

IKEA, the Swedish furniture store, sees the customer as an integral part of the service process. Customers self-assemble the furniture in their own homes. This is an extreme version of the traditional DIY concept. Interestingly, the IKEA concept of self-service and build-your-own-furniture is partly coincidental. Back in the early days insurance companies were complaning that too many of the IKEA furniture deliveries were damaged when they reached their final destination (IKEA customers). So IKEA designed self-assembly furniture – which was stronger and could not be damaged in transport. In relation to self-service, when IKEA opened its first showroom (IKEA was originally a mail order firm) an overwhelming number of customers showed up. There were too many for store personnel to handle and therefore customers were allowed to go to the storeroom and find the furniture themselves. And so these two winning service process strategies were born. IKEA has managed both of these very well and has created an award winning co-creation process out of necessity.

Service providers and level of relationship

The dividing line between the company and customer can blur in relation to who provides what service and also in regard to the relationships that can develop. Successful service provision relates to the completion of the core service but also the personal aspects of the service. The service process can move through professional, casual, personal to even friendship. In many cases the service provider and the customer can form an emotional attachment, seeking personal advice and even socialising.[29] We can see this occurring with pop stars or film stars as they form friendships with their hairdressers. 'Posh' Spice has said that her two closest friends are her hairdresser and make-up artist[30] – both service providers. Building relationships, whether personal or professional, is always difficult, and the personal touch matters. Financial and health care relationships are viewed as professional, while hair care can be perceived as friendly.[31]

Variability and customer involvement

Customers add variability into the service process. In manufacturing the focus is on eliminating variability but in services the customer often judges the service on the amount of variability that is allowed. As Evert Gummesson, Professor of Marketing at Stockholm University said, 'Customers co-create the value of the service to the benefit of themselves and the service provider. Unfortunately the providers may not see the contribution of this involvement and fail to support it'.[32]

Coping with variability and the various requests and needs of customers in the service process is challenging. Unlike in manufacturing there is no one solution, but there are multiple ways to combat the effects of variability. What is needed is a systematic approach to diagnose problems and design and fine tune interventions to ensure effectiveness of the service. There are five forms of variability:[33]

1 **Arrival variability**: Customers like to arrive at different times, and the classic way to control this is to insist on reservations. There are some services that cannot be foreseen or pre-booked, such as car breakdowns or accident and emergency. When times *can* be controlled waiting time analysis and waiting time standards can be used by marketers. Dominos Pizza states that if you wait for longer than 30 minutes for delivery you get a free pizza. There is also a tracking feature on the company's website that allows you to track your pizza. Many call centres tell you how long you will be kept waiting and also use the call-back facility. Airlines are particularly focused on 'on-time' arrival and many pride themselves on this feature. Czech Airlines (CSA) was Europe's

best airline in on-time departures in 2007 and ranked sixth in terms of on-time arrivals among 26 European airlines, according to the Association of European Airlines (AEA).[34]

2   **Request variability**: Consumers' need for their own unique experience is growing. The fact that customers' desires are not along standard lines can pose problems for services. Travel brochures and menus are a means to reduce request variability. Companies such as Expedia or Trip Advisor allow customers to design their own holidays. Take Café Java or any local café – there are now up to 6000 permutations of the type of coffee or tea customers can order. In a restaurant customers can request how they would like their meat cooked. There was an incident where the head chef at a Michelin-starred restaurant in Dublin reportedly threw out a customer for asking for chips with his dinner and then not eating them.[35] The head chef showed his anger at having to provide a varied request by insisting that the customer eat the chips, allegedly saying, 'They were cooked specially for you, so you eat them.' Not agreeing to special orders reduces the complexity of the service, but agreeing to them can increase the service experience.

3   **Capability variability**: Customers themselves have different levels of understanding and ability. Some customers perform tasks easily and others need to be managed through the process. How well a patient is able to describe their illness or how efficient they are at filling in forms can both affect service levels.

4   **Effort variability**: Customers will decide how much effort they are prepared to give to a service. In the gym, do you wipe down the machine and return the weights or do you expect the gym staff or another customer to do that? To manage this many marketers offer incentives. Customers who return a trolley at an airport or supermarket get their money back.

5   **Subjective preference variability**: Personal preferences of the customer are important. This means that different customers will experience the same service differently. In a bank one customer likes being called by their first name while another may think that it is intrusive.

The less variability the easier it is to manage. Marketers can use either accommodation or reduction to manage variability.

●   **Accommodation**: Allow variability and manage it (focus on service). Employees often judge the level of service required and provide it. So there is a big greeting from the bank manager for certain customers and just a nod and a wave to others. The company bears the cost of the variability strategy.

●   **Reduction**: Reduce variability (focus on operations). This can often be equated with price consciousness. So low-cost airlines and cinema attendance in the afternoon are all priced lower for less service. Marketing opts to reduce the service level and charge less and customers accept this.

There are four techniques for managing customer-introduced variability including classic accommodation, classic reduction, low-cost accommodation and uncompromised reduction. Examples of each appear in Table 18.1. The more innovative companies will manage the situation without damaging the service experience or lowering quality.

Customers of companies such as eBay, iTunes and YouTube expect to perform a lot of the services themselves and that means they can manage the timing and the variability themselves. Other customers are used to companies providing service for them and have to be persuaded to change. Think of petrol pumps. Traditionally there was an attendant and you could stay in your car for the whole process. Nowadays, for much of Europe, the customer has to provide self-service and then pay in the shop. Automated payment at the pump avoids the need to go into the shop.

Training customer service personnel

Customer involvement creates uncertainty and service personnel have to bear most of it. Marketing must develop methods to help them carry the burden. Service personnel have to have **task competency**. They have to be competent in the task. They have to provide guidance and help throughout the process and act as advisers, for example when a waiter is asked to recommend a dish or a repair engineer to suggest which product to buy. Being able to do the job is not enough. They must also have **behaviour skills,** to be able to interact with the customer. Employee selection needs to focus on customer relationship skills. A service company needs to hire for service

Table 18.1 Strategies for managing customer-introduced variability

Once a company has determined which type of customer-introduced variability is creating operational difficulties, it must choose which of four basic strategies to pursue. The chart outlines tactics that have proven to be effective in each category.

	Classic accommodation	Low-cost accommodation	Classic reduction	Uncompromised reduction
Arrival	• Make sure plenty of employees are on hand	• Hire lower-cost labour • Automate tasks • Outsource customer contact • Create self-service options	• Require reservations • Provide off-peak pricing • Limit service availability	• Create complementary demand to smooth arrivals without requiring customers to change their behaviour
Request	• Make sure many employees with specialised skills are on hand • Train employees to handle many kinds of requests	• Hire lower-cost specialised labour • Automate tasks • Create self-service options	• Require customers to make reservations for specific types of service • Persuade customers to compromise their requests • Limit service breadth	• Limit service breadth • Target customers on the basis of their requests
Capability	• Make sure employees are on hand who can adapt to customers' varied skill levels • Do work for customers	• Hire lower-cost labour • Create self-service options that require no special skills	• Require customers to increase their level of capability before they use the service	• Target customers on the basis of their capability
Effort	• Make sure employees are on hand who can compensate for customers' lack of effort • Do work for customers	• Hire lower-cost labour • Create self-service options with extensive automation	• Use rewards and penalties to get customers to increase their effort	• Target customers on the basis of motivation • Use a normative approach to get customers to increase their effort
Subjective preference	• Make sure employees are on hand who can diagnose differences in expectations and adapt accordingly	• Create self-service options that permit customisation	• Persuade customers to adjust their expectations to match the value proposition	• Target customers on the basis of their subjective preferences

attitude and train for skills. Manufacturing companies tend to hire for skills only. Training in task only or in behaviour only will not result in good service. If the service personnel are really nice, but completely ineffectual at their task, the service encounter (though pleasant) is not effective. Both are needed.

Service personnel need to display initiative, cope with stress (and other emotions), be interpersonally flexible and sensitive and be more cooperative than manufacturing staff. Correct expressions and body language have an effect on the customer experience. This can be draining and stressful on the service personnel and has to be managed.[36] The marketing manager has to instil norms, values and a culture that focuses on the desired behaviour of the service personnel so that each time they behave in ways which reflect the brand image of the service provider.[37] Porters in hotels are trained to be friendly, doctors are trained to listen and waitresses are trained to be polite. Human beings by nature are ever changing and have moods and humours that ebb and flow throughout the day. This can impact on the service provision that the customer will receive. In EuroDisney, staff are asked to monitor their own humour when they start work and throughout the day to ensure that the customer always gets a smile and a happy greeting.

Hiring service personnel

Hiring of service personnel is an often overlooked feature of marketing. This must be explored with the human resources department. Marketing needs to be part of the process to ensure that the staff hired match the values of the brand. Marketing needs to ensure explicitly and systematically that people are hired who genuinely embrace the organisation's values.

What you have to do is create an employment offering that attracts the right people – what is referred to as talent management. To attract and maintain the best staff companies need to be 'a place where people not only get paid "their due" but also get to initiate and execute great things.'[38] If you want to hire young, cheerful and happy staff then you need to create an environment where they would like to work. Take Google and their offices in Zurich, which are an exercise in lateral-thinking, creativity-run-wild interior design. Google's offices have a slide, a games room, a library in the style of an English country house, a 'chill-out' aquarium where overworked Googlers can lie in a bath full of red foam and stare at fish. Google Zurich also provides free food for all staff. Meeting 'pods' are in the style of Swiss chalets and igloos; firefighter poles are used to allow easy access between floors – all part of the design of Google's new European engineering headquarters. 'From our flexible, project-based approach to corporate structure to our innovative perks and benefits, we do everything we can to make sure our employees not only have great jobs, but great lives.'[39] The building was designed for – and partly by – the 300 engineers who will work there.

A Google rest pod.

Source: Erin Siegal/ Reuters

Level of service

Marketers need to understand that there are different levels of service that they can provide and different levels required by customers. VIP sections in clubs and restaurants are a clear example of this higher service level. Customers have to decide on the level of service they want, for example – do they want full airline service from Air France-KLM or are they prepared to pay less and receive the low-cost, no frills service of Ryanair? Problems arise when the service level desired and the service level paid for do not equate in the customer's mind. Michael O'Leary, the chief executive of Ryanair, states 'They get the service they paid for.' A €1 flight does not give business-class service.

Within the retail environment different levels of service are required and retailers position themselves as offering one of four levels:

1 **Self-service**: Self-service is the cornerstone of most retail operations. Many customers are willing to carry out their own locate-compare-select process to save money.

2 **Self-selection**: Customers find their own products, although they can ask for assistance.

3 **Limited service**: These retailers carry more shopping products, and provide services such as credit and product-return privileges. Customers need more information and assistance.

4 **Full service**: Sales people are ready to assist in every phase of the locate-compare-select process. Customers who like to be waited on prefer this type of shop. The high staffing costs, along with the higher proportion of speciality products and services, result in high-cost retailing.

By combining these different service levels with different assortment breadths, we can distinguish the four broad positioning strategies available to retailers, as shown in Figure 18.6.

1 **Harrods**: Shops that feature a broad product range and high value added pay close attention to store design, product quality, service, and image. Their profit margin is high, and if they have high enough volume they will be very profitable.

2 **Tiffany**: Shops that feature a narrow product assortment and high value added cultivate an exclusive image and operate on high margin and low volume.

3 **Sunglass Hut**: Shops that feature a narrow line and low value added keep costs and prices low by centralising buying, merchandising, advertising and distribution.

4 **Tesco**: Shops that feature a broad line and low value added focus on keeping prices low and have the image of a place for good buys. High volume makes up for low margin.

Carrefour, the world's second-largest retailer and the largest in Europe with over 12,500 shops and over 500,000 employees, operates four main grocery shop formats: hypermarkets, supermarkets, hard discount and convenience shops – all with different service levels.

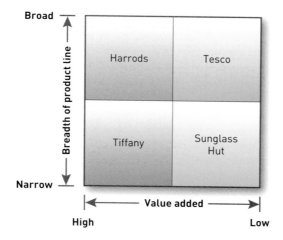

Figure 18.6 Retail positioning map

Source: Adapted from W. T. Gregor and E. M. Friars (1982) *Money Merchandising: Retail Revolution in Consumer Financial Service*, Cambridge, MA: The MAC Group. Reproduced with permission.

Customer-to-customer interactions

Much of the focus in the service process was centred on employees and managing their behaviour. Nowadays there is a greater focus on managing the customers' behaviour within the process. While the customers of manufacturing firms interact at a distance from the company, within service operations the customers are directly involved with operational activities and their behaviour can really impact on the quality, productivity and profitability of the service.[40]

Customer-to-customer interactions are often overlooked but they can make or break the service experience. The other people availing themselves of the service are often crucial to the creation of the service and the levels of satisfaction with the service.

▽ Sziget music festival in Hungary

Music festivals are a core part of the culture of young people all over Europe; for example, the Sziget music festival in Hungary attracts over 50,000 visitors. This festival takes place in a tented city on the Danube in Budapest. It is a huge service process, with innumerable stages featuring mainstream and other bands. The Sziget festival kicks off with one concert (Iron Maiden) on 'Zero Day', followed by five days of bands such as 2007's headliners The Killers, Gogol Bordello, Nine Inch Nails and Pink.[41] The success of these and other festival extravaganzas of camping, food and fun with thousands of other festival goers is very dependent on the other customers. How much fun you have relates to the other people at the concert as much as the bands or the venue. At a music concert the other people help to create the atmosphere and also the enjoyment.

Many positive and negative outcomes can arise from **customer-to-customer encounters**. When you are in hospital other patients can help you to feel that you are not the only person who is unwell. There is always someone who is more ill than you. A UK case study by Harris and Baron found that conversations between train passengers really helped their mood, particularly when there were delays.[42] The study also found that in the absence of service personnel the passengers themselves often gave each other information in relation to timetables and platforms. Customers could be viewed as unsalaried part-time employees.

Managing customers within the service process

There are many techniques that can be used to manage the customer within the service process. This implies customers can be trained. This can be as simple as physical cues such as direction or operational signs, for example 'Please wait to be seated' signs in a restaurant, 'Please queue to the right', or Please take one'. All these indications inform and guide the customer.

Two main customer management techniques which have been suggested are **normative behaviour** and **instrumental control**.[43]

Normative behaviour focuses on the emotional rather than the rational and involves shame, blame or pride. It uses peer pressure, norms of behaviour and other social influences to shape behaviour in the service environment. Think of the cleaning of Ryanair planes. You are asked by the stewards to collect all rubbish and tidy the plane. As your co-passengers rummage around collecting rubbish you do too. eBay is another good example of a customer-to-customer domain where the customers are both the 'sellers' and the 'buyers' of online auction goods. Customer perception of the service level provided by other customers is a matter of public record. There is a rating scale for eBay customers and this influences behaviour. Both buyers and sellers found that there were consequences to their actions. For eBay this is a very low-cost policing method. Online communities often have their own norms of behaviour in relation to what is acceptable. Normative behaviour is best when a foundation of trust exists between the firm and the customer; when customer interdependence makes customer community a viable option and when customers understand that their actions matter.

Directional signs are used to show customers how to process through the service encounter.

Source: © Mike Baldwin/ Cornered/CartoonStock Ltd

Instrumental controls are specific tangible costs and rewards designed to induce desired behaviour. Behavioural theory has long acknowledged two basic tools for influencing human behaviour – reward and punishment. Therefore banks asks customers to keep a certain balance in their account and if customers don't the banks punish them for being overdrawn. There is an argument that banks shouldn't let the person overdraw but this is where the banks make their money. Charging more or less money to promote behaviour that serves the company's interests is very common. This discourages behaviour that unintentionally increases the cost or decreases the quality of a service. Supermarkets have long had the policy of rewarding you with your money back for replacing the trolley in the trolley bay. This shows a lack of trust in relation to expected behaviour. Actually a payment for undesired behaviour does not always work. When a crèche introduced a fee for parents who were late collecting their children, parents were happier and happy to pay. They felt that their guilt was allayed – they could be late and just pay extra.

Sometime both techniques can be used. Take the use or non-use of yellow box junctions while driving. This can be influenced by normative behaviour – pressure from other drivers – but there can also be instrumental control if you are spotted by the police and receive a fine.

Managing the global service process

We live in a multicultural global society. Customers can expect to receive services that are geographically and also culturally diverse; for example, companies have set up call centres all over the world. If you call Hertz Car Hire you are linked through to their call centre in Ireland; if you call Dell you are linked through to their call centre in India. In Ireland call centres employ over 6000 people who carry out many key service processes, ranging from handling customer queries, taking orders and providing technical support, to actively pursuing business on a pan-European level. These multilingual centres provide services to clients across Europe and around the world 24 hours a day, 365 days a year. A list of the companies with call centres in Ireland includes many global service brands including IBM, Citibank, Hertz, Radisson Hotels, Best Western, American Airlines, UPS, Lufthansa Airlines, Korean Airlines and ITT Sheraton.

Service process management on a global scale

We expect that when we go on holidays – anywhere in the world – that we can still avail ourselves of the ATM for banking, still be able to phone home on our mobile phones and also check the news at home by logging on to the Internet. Services are now managed on a local and a global scale. In retailing there are outlets all over the world, and even a Starbucks in China – the home of tea. Many marketers try to manage their operations to be exactly the same all over the world, while others try to change to suit the local customs and habits, which can vary by country. Retailers that have largely stuck to the same formula regardless of geography, such as Marks & Spencer and Wal-Mart, have sometimes encountered trouble in entering new markets.[44]

▽ Wal-Mart in Germany

When superstore giant Wal-Mart entered the German market it was eager to implement traditional US service processes. Wal-Mart tried to get its German staff to have the same enthusiasm as their US employees.[45] It just didn't work, and customers didn't like it either. According to an article in the *New York Times* 'Wal-Mart stopped requiring sales clerks to smile at customers – a practice that some male shoppers interpreted as flirting – and scrapped the morning Wal-Mart chant by staff members. People found these things strange; Germans just don't behave that way'.[46] Cultural differences mean that the organisation's expectations of employee and customer behaviour often need to be changed in new markets. In July 2006, after losing hundreds of millions of euros and a decade in the market, Wal-Mart announced that it was pulling out of Germany.

▽ Managing technology and particularly self-service technologies within the service process

Technology allows service to be delivered at a geographical or physical distance from the company. Much of service process has moved to self-service technologies, from booking flights online at home to using the check-in kiosks at the airport. We can even print out our boarding card at home and go straight to security. Another example is banking. The options now available are ATM, online banking over the Web or phone banking, credit cards and debit cards, all of which are called touch points for banking. There are over 787 million credit cards in Europe. Six countries account for more than 80 per cent of cards in Europe, with the United Kingdom the largest with 181 million cards. Germany is second with 127 million cards. Following in card numbers are France, Spain, Turkey and Italy. At the other end of the scale, Finland, Austria, Denmark and Ireland all have fewer than 10 million cards. ATMs are one of the most successful self-service technologies.

As more and more technology becomes available to customers, they will increasingly opt to handle routine problems themselves, or choose software to help them. In a 2006 survey two-thirds of teenagers and 62 per cent of adults questioned for grocery think tank IGD's report wanted self-scanning systems at checkouts.[47] Interesting for service provision, and on a more low-tech note, 61 per cent of adults and 57 per cent of teenagers wanted staff to pack their bags in shops.[48]

More and more technology is being used in the service process, enabling customer-to-company and customer-to-customer interactions. Chapter 4 introduced many of these technologies and this section focuses on their management by exploring self-service technologies and also technologies used by companies to improve or communicate with the customer during the service process. The role of technologies in service provision is growing and will continue to grow over time.

Self-service technologies offer many benefits but also associated problems. Questions need to be asked. Take the situation of grocery shopping online:

- How does this affect the overall marketing operation?
- What are the costs connected with this level of service process – the 'picking' and the delivery carried out by the company?
- Does this stop impulse purchases, which are a core part of any supermarket's revenues? Recognising that much of the service process is going online demands that marketers understand and manage this process.

The substitution of self-service for labour is often used to reduce costs. For example, self-service kiosks, which are popping up in airports around the world, save the industry as much as €2.50 per check-in, while improving customer service.[49] Furthermore, modern consumers have actually come to appreciate the control they have over the self-service process.

Self-service technologies are not new. The first known use of vending machines was probably about 200 BC when Hero of Alexandria described a coin-operated device designed to vend holy water in an Egyptian temple. The traditional service delivery method was person to person but now the level and range of self-service technologies make this a core area for marketing managers.

Self-service technologies may contribute to the building of an informational wall, a situation of electronic anonymity between the customer and the company.[50] This must be managed by marketing. By offering virtually all services online or through automated phone/ATM centres, many banks unknowingly distanced themselves from their customers and rendered the interaction of the customers with the bank purely transactional. Sensing this as a problem, Dutch ING Direct – a hugely successful, entirely online banking service – has set up ING Direct cafés where existing and potential customers can browse the Internet for free, sip coffee, and learn more about other services on offer.[51]

Self-service technology can often move much of the work to the customer. The skills for self-service technology vary from the technology native to the technology immigrant. There can be a lot of work in completing Web forms, providing all contact details and actually navigating sites and automated technologies. For online self service, customers must purchase all the equipment needed, which at a minimum would be a computer, broadband connection and printer.

Designing the service process online

Marketing now faces a new challenge, as service encounters increasingly take place on the Internet or in 'cyberspace' as opposed to the physical marketspace.[52] Designing and planning the virtual environment so as to 'control', show empathy and create optimal experiences for browsers is therefore as important in cyberspace as in real space. First, there is a need to focus and target site content at particular user groups. Designers and publishers cannot expect to satisfy a wide and diverse audience with single sites. Second, there is a need to offer vividness, providing most notably a depth of sensory information. This provides 'presence', a factor also enhanced by interactivity. Interactivity should also allow the browser a sense of control. This may come from both allowing the browser to match skills with challenges and also to structure the flow of information. Another important point here is the need to understand well the target audience's expectation so as to avoid negative disconfirmation and frustration.[53]

To increase the entertainment and information value and customer satisfaction from Web-based shopping experiences, some firms are employing *avatars*, graphical representations of virtual, animated characters that can act as company representatives. Avatars can provide a more interpersonal shopping experience by serving as identification figures, as personal shopping assistants, as website guides, or as conversation partners. Research has shown that avatars can enhance the effectiveness of a Web channel, especially if they are seen as expert or attractive.[54] See Marketing insights on the next page.

Mobile communication and text messaging The use of mobile phone calls and text messages as part of the service process will continue to grow. For many companies the use of text messaging and mobile calls has improved the service delivered and their relationship with their customers. Many hairdressers and other service providers confirm appointments by text.

There are nearly 1.8 billion mobile customers worldwide. Text messaging is most popular in Europe and Asia, where 70 per cent of mobile phone customers use it. Reality television shows

Marketing insight

Selling to avatars – and to their creators

Online virtual worlds offer untapped marketing potential for real-world products and services, particularly because of their ability to generate sustained consumer engagement with a brand. This occurs through interactions with 'avatars', the beings users create as representations of themselves and through which they live and relate to others in these worlds.

The stage for real-world marketing has been set in virtual worlds like *Second Life*. There, residents run businesses that sell virtual products and services priced in *Second Life*'s, Linden dollars, which are convertible into real-world currency on various Internet exchanges. In one example, Dominus Motors promotes a limited Eleanor edition (named after a famous 1960s muscle car) of its Shadow model that seats five avatars and can be driven through the world at speeds of up to 210 miles an hour.

Wells Fargo bank operates a virtual world called *Stagecoach Island*, designed to educate teens about money matters through games and social activities. At in-world ATMs, players take a financial quiz in order to withdraw virtual cash for activities such as sky-diving and games of paintball.

Coke Studios is a teen-oriented virtual world run by Coca-Cola. In this world, users' avatars interact – that's conversation in the text boxes – and accumulate points through primarily music-related activities. For example, you get five decibels for each thumbs-up from a fellow avatar for your selection of dance music in your role as virtual DJ in one of the public studios. You can use these points to buy furniture and accessories for your own studio, where you can hold events for avatar friends.

Source: P. Hemp (2006) Avatar-based marketing, *Harvard Business Review*, June, 407–58.

---

such as *Big Brother*, which allow viewers to text in their votes, have also given the medium a boost. Companies, banks and government agencies are looking for ways to expand their use of text messaging. eBay allows its customers to receive text alerts when they are outbid for an auction item. They can also rebid via text message. Google has begun using text messaging to deliver search results over mobile phones. Airlines offer text message alerts about flights.[55]

In Japan, millions of teenagers carry DoCoMo mobile phones to order products and services. Each month, users receive a bill from NTT listing the monthly fee, the usage fee and the cost of all their purchases. The person can then pay the bill at the nearest 7-11 store.

The potential market opportunities for **location-based services** are enormous. This is a new form of service that delivers location-dependent (it depends where you are) and context-sensitive (what your particular needs are) information to mobile users. Imagine some not-too-distant possibilities:

- Buying a Red Bull or any other soft drink by pointing and clicking your mobile phone at a vending machine. The bottle drops down and an appropriate amount is deducted from your bank account.
- Using your mobile phone to search for a nearby restaurant that meets the criteria you entered.
- Watching stock prices on your mobile phone while sitting in the restaurant and deciding to place a stock purchase order.
- Clicking your mobile phone to pay the bill for your meal.

More and more payment is moving to technology. As discussed in Chapter 4, new technologies will move towards a touch and wave system or payment through the mobile phone – see the picture opposite. This development will change the payment part of the service process.

Tracking services can also operate with mobile phones. Some see positive benefits, such as locating people making emergency calls or checking on the whereabouts of children late at night. There are privacy issues but, generationally, many people accept this as normal. As with so many new technologies, location-based services have potential for good or ill, and ultimately will warrant public scrutiny and regulation as they develop.

Vending machines or kiosks Automatic vending offers a variety of products and services including impulse items such as call credit, stamps, soft drinks, coffee, sweets, newspapers,

Using mobile phones to pay for products and services.

Source: Masatoshi Okauchi/Rex Features

magazines and other products – cosmetics, hot food and paperbacks. The expectation is that vending machines expenditure will continue to grow as shown in Figure 18.7.

Besides airline check-in, consumers would like to see automated multipurpose kiosks that let them renew drivers' licences or vehicle registration, checking the status of items ordered online, purchasing airline tickets, making photocopies and ordering flowers, books and other items.[56]

Vending machines are found in factories, offices, large retail shops, petrol stations, hotels, restaurants, and many other places. They offer 24-hour self-service. Japan has the most vending machines per person – Coca-Cola has over 1 million machines there and annual vending sales of €318 billion – twice that in the United States. Vending machines that can talk to customers are also slowly appearing.

Other advances in service vending, where the vending machine removes the need for a service provider, are becoming popular. Take three services that we equate with person-to-person contact at some level: hairdresser, doctor and pizza delivery. All now have vending machine versions that change the service process.

- For hairdressing, customers can use the GHD (good hair day) machine in cloakrooms to perfect their hair in minutes.
- Want to check on your health? Kiosks are available to allow you to do just that. You put your finger on a button, look at the screen and the machine reads your retina, heart rate and other factors and gives you a health printout.
- There are even pizza vending machines – see the picture on the next page.

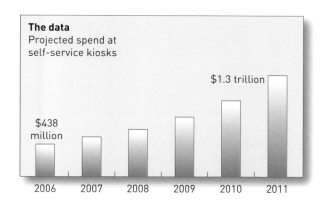

The data
Projected spend at self-service kiosks

$1.3 trillion

$438 million

2006   2007   2008   2009   2010   2011

Figure 18.7 Projected spending on self service kiosks

Source: Adapted from L. Holman and G. Buzek (2008) *North American Self-Service Kiosks Market Study*, Franklin, TN: IHL Group. Reproduced with permission.

Traditional services are now moving to self-service – even pizzas in Italy.

Source: Phil Yeomans/ Rex Features

RFID in the service process Radio frequency identification devices systems (as discussed in Chapter 17) are 'smart' tags that can be read in real time and at a distance. Though normally focused on products these smart tags can be embedded within the service process. Throughout Europe car owners can purchase toll cards with RFID chips that they put on their windscreens; these are read at the toll booth, allowing them fast passage through the booths with the money deducted from their online accounts automatically. The same system is used on trams in Portugal and Ireland. An interesting example of this technology comes from its use in a Spanish disco.

▽ The Baja Beach Club in Barcelona

VIP customers of this nightclub have microchips implanted in their bodies to avoid queues and to make paying easier.[57] On entrance to the club, and each time they order drinks from the bar, customers simply wave their arm over a microchip scanner. This automatically deducts the amount from their bank account. Customers pay €125 to have the chips implanted. They are programmed with a ten-digit number that can be linked to the customer's bank account. Clearly these consumers are not worried about the lack of privacy entailed in this practice. Whatever they buy can be traced, and of course their presence in the club is recorded. The service provision and the customer are tightly intertwined.[58]

The radio tagging of products allows retailers to improve their service process by alerting manufacturers or their warehouses before shelves go bare. Coca-Cola is embedding RFID readers in 200,000 of its 1 million vending machines in Japan to allow consumers to buy a Coke using wallet phones with RFID chips. Dutch bookseller Selexyz is tagging every title it stocks after a pilot study showed a 25 per cent increase in sales. RFID-tagged books make for easier inventory control, consumer search and checkout at the register. This service could improve if we were able to track and trace both people, objects and products. RFID tags in a shopping carts could automatically bill consumers' accounts (cards would no longer be needed to link purchases to individuals), if RFID chips were in fridges they could report their contents to the supermarket for re-ordering, and interactive televisions with RFID could select advertisements based on the contents of a person's fridge.

The future of self-service technology

Much of technology replaces the human input. The Metro example belows shows how the service process could become both more automated and also reliant on self-service technologies. We are nearing the day when we can shop and, as we walk out of a store, a scanner will read all the RFID chips on our groceries and then take payment straight out of our bank account through the mobile phone chip. No stopping, or really shopping, at all.

The Metro Store – Germany's largest retailer and the fifth largest retailer in the world – has opened a future store in Rheninberg in Germany that reflects future technology and also some of the challenges which marketing will face from a service process perspective.

▽ Metro

Metro have opened a Future Store that is a high-tech heaven. The intelligent Scale, using IBM Veggie Vision software, can identify items by sight. In key sections such as baby care, hair colour, wine and meats, touch screen terminals provide in-depth information on the product or suggestions for other uses. They also provide personal shopping assistants (PSAs), which are small Wincor Nixdorf table computers, clipped to the shopping trolley and activated with a loyalty card. Type 'ice cream' on the touch screen and you are directed to the correct aisle – floor plan included. Regular purchases show up on a favourites list with price and location. Special offers are flagged as you move from section to section. If you write a shopping list online you can automatically download it to the PSA. The integrated scanner gives you a running total of your shopping and fast-track treatment at the checkout. The shop's shelves sport 30,000 wireless electronic price labels that can be changed at the push of the button.

With its network of ICT systems, Metro, the German retail shop, is a leading innovator in this area.
Source: Ulrich Baumgarten/vario images/Alamy

▽ Creating and managing the physical evidence or experience environment

The physical evidence and the experience or servicespace of the service encounter must be managed. **Servicescape** is the impact on customer and employee behaviour of a firm's physical surroundings or environment.[59] The servicescape model recognises that the unique characteristics of services mean that the surroundings or physical environments where the service takes place are likely to affect customers and employees alike. Both respond emotionally and physiologically to the perceived environment, and these responses ultimately impact upon behaviour. Some service environments can work for the customer and not for the employee and vice versa.

There are two main emotional impacts: pleasure–displeasure and degree of arousal. Pleasant environments are likely to be ones that people want to spend longer in and to return to. Conversely, unpleasant ones are avoided. Similarly, arousing environments (a lot of stimulation) are viewed positively and customers like to be there, unless of course arousal is accompanied by unpleasantness.[60]

The servicescape or physical environment may assume a variety of strategic roles in services marketing and management:

1 The servicescape provides a visual metaphor for an organisation's total offering.

2 The servicescape can assume a facilitator role by either helping or hindering the ability of customers and employees to carry out their respective activities.

3 The servicescape can serve as a differentiator in signalling the intended market segment, positioning the organisation, and conveying distinctiveness from competitors.

To secure strategy advantages from the servicescape, the needs of ultimate users and the requirements of various company departments must be incorporated into environmental design decisions. Figure 18.8 shows the areas of influence of the experience space.[61]

EuroDisney is very clear that customers enter another world when they enter EuroDisney – the world of Disney. When customers visit the Ritz Carlton in Paris they are embraced by the sounds, vision, feel and smell of luxury, of expense and of elitism.

The environment influences customer perception of the service. Have you ever been in hospital? Was the furniture nice, was there a quiet place to sit, and was the wallpaper attractive? Was there soft lighting and sights and sounds that encouraged peace and calm or was it frantic and stressed? Physical evidence can assist in creating the 'environment' and 'atmospheres' in which a service is bought or performed and can help shape customer perception of a service. Buildings, furnishing, layout, colour, packaging, signs, uniforms and products associated with the service such as carrier bags, tickets, brochures, labels, etc. all combine to create the brand image desired. Many of the physical elements have a rational function, like escalators and directional signs; while others have a more symbolic mission, like wigs on judges or gowns on lecturers.

Figure 18.8 The experience space

Source: C. K. Prahalad and V. Ramaswamy (2003) The new frontier of experience innovation, *MIT Sloan Management Review*, 44(4), 12–18. Copyright © 2003 Massachusetts Institute of Technology. All rights reserved. Reproduced with permission.

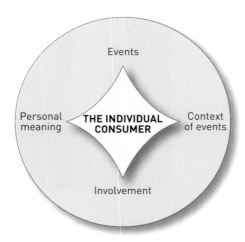

A sporting event is packed full of physical evidence. Your tickets have your team's logo printed on them, and players are wearing team colours. The stadium itself could be impressive and have an electrifying atmosphere. You travelled there and parked quickly nearby, and your seats are comfortable and close to toilets and refreshments. All you need now is for your team to win. This relates to what are called Hygiene or Motivators factors:[62]

- **Motivators factors** come from the experience itself – such as entertainment or education – what you actually get; while the
- **Hygiene factors** can cause dissatisfaction if missing but do not necessarily motivate if increased. In a restaurant the quality of the seating, the toilets or even the car park could be hygiene factors. Customers expect the toilets to be clean and will notice if they are not. Research in 2007 showed that visitors to a zoo in Denmark rated the hygiene factors as more important leading to dissatisfaction with the service than the motivators, as in the actual visit to the zoo.[63]

Service atmosphere

Atmosphere is a major marketing element. Service operations such as shops, supermarkets, hotels, restaurants, clubs, doctors' waiting rooms, hospitals and so on have a 'look', and a physical layout that makes it hard or easy to move around (see 'Marketing memo: Helping stores to market'). Many department stores use a floor plan modelled along the lines of a racetrack. Designed to convey customers smoothly past all the products in the shop, an eight-foot-wide main aisle moves customers in a circle around the store. The design also includes a middle aisle that hurried shoppers can use as a short cut. The racetrack loop yields higher spending levels than many other layouts.[64] Here's how Safeway increased profits by thoroughly reinventing the look of its store:[65]

- **Walls**: replaced plain old white walls with earthy tones to convey freshness and wholesomeness.
- **Lighting**: replaced bright glaring lights with warm accent lights that direct attention to products and departments.
- **Signage**: added big pictures of healthy food, as well as display stations throughout the store to suggest meal ideas for time-starved shoppers.
- **Produce department**: enlarged organic section, moving it from against the wall to wooden crates at centre of floor space, suggesting a farmer's market.
- **Floors**: installed hardwood floors in perishables department to provide a natural feel.
- **Bakery**: knocked down walls to show off bread baking in wood-fired oven. Added island in centre of department that offers custom bread slicing.

Store activities and experiences

The growth of online purchasing has forced a rethink of the physical environment. In addition to their natural advantages, such as products that shoppers can actually see, touch and test, real-life customer service, and no delivery lag time for small or medium-sized purchases, retail shops also provide a shopping experience as a strong differentiator.[66] The Mall of the Emirates in Dubai has a ski slope in the desert shopping centre – an interesting attraction for shoppers used to 50-degree heat.

The retail environment is adopting practices as simple as calling each shopper a 'guest' and as grandiose as building an indoor amusement park. The store atmosphere should match the basic motivations of the shopper – if target consumers are more likely to be in a task-oriented and functional mindset, then a simpler, more restrained in-store environment may be better.[67] Consistent with this reasoning, some retailers of experiential products are creating in-store entertainment to attract customers who want fun and excitement. Other services are also changing. Virgin Atlantic have created a flagship £11 million Heathrow Clubhouse lounge. This lounge is more than double the size of the previous one and sets a whole new standard for business class travellers. It includes a myriad of features ranging from a long bar, a deli, a brasserie, a poolside

Marketing memo

Helping stores to market

In the pursuit of higher sales volume, retailers are studying their store environments for ways to improve the shopping experience. Paco Underhill is managing director of the retail consultant Envirosell, Inc. whose clients include Citibank, McDonald's, Starbucks, Estée Lauder, Blockbuster, The Gap and Burger King. He offers the following advice for fine tuning retail space in order to keep shoppers spending:

- **Attract shoppers and keep them in the shop** The amount of time shoppers spend in a shop is perhaps the single most important factor in determining how much they will buy. To increase shopping time, give shoppers a sense of community; recognise them in some way, manner or form; give them ways to deal with their 'accessories' (such as husbands and children); and keep an environment that is both familiar and fresh each time they come in. IKEA, for example, has a crèche at the entrance and a restaurant half-way through its shops.

- **Honour the 'transition zone'** On entering a shop, people need to slow down and sort out the stimuli, which means they will most likely be moving too quickly to respond positively to signs, products, service personnel or sales people in the area they cross before making that transition. Make sure there are clear sight lines. Create a focal point for information within the shop.

- **Don't make them hunt** Put the most popular products up front to reward busy shoppers and encourage leisurely shoppers to look more.

- **Make products available to the reach and touch** It is hard to overemphasise the importance of customers' hands. A shop can offer the finest, cheapest or sexiest product, but if the shopper cannot reach it or pick it up, much of the appeal can be lost.

- **Note that men do not ask questions** Men always move faster than women through a shop's aisles. In many settings it is hard to get them to look at anything they had not intended to buy. Nor do men like asking where things are. If a man cannot find the section he is looking for, he will look about once or twice, then leave the shop without ever asking for help.

- **Remember women need space** A shopper, especially a woman, is far less likely to buy an item if she is brushed up against, even lightly, by another customer when she is looking at a display. Keeping aisles wide and clear is crucial.

- **Make checkout easy** Be sure to have the right high-margin products near cash registers to satisfy impulse shoppers. Some people love to buy sweets when they checkout – to satisfy their sweet tooth. Be aware that mothers with children do not like to have to battle about sweets while at the cash register. Asda, the UK supermarket chain, has introduced sweet-free checkouts for parents who were seeking refuge from the pestering of their children while grocery shopping.

Some of Paco Underhill's additional words of wisdom for modern retailers include: (1) develop expertise in the mature market; (2) sell both to and through your customer; (3) localise your presence; (4) extend your brand – use your history better; (5) build on the Internet-to-phone-to-shop connection; (6) find your customers where they are; (7) refine the details of each point of sale; and (8) go undercover as your reality check.

Sources: P. Underhill (1999) *Why We Buy: The Science of Shopping*, New York: Simon & Schuster; P. Underhill (2004) *Call of the Mall: The Geography of Shopping*, New York: Simon & Schuster; K. Hammonds (1999) How we sell, *Fast Company*, November, 294; K. Hein, Shopping guru sees death of detergent aisle, *Brandweek*, 27 March, 11; B. Parks (2006) 5 rules of great design, *Business 2.0*, March, 47–9; Monday keynote: why they buy, *Loupe Online*, 15 (Fall), envirosell.com; H. McGavin (2003) Parents pressure supermarket chain to try 'sweet-free checkouts' for children, *The Independent*, 5 December.

lounge, a library and a rooftop garden through to a spa that houses four massage bays, a sauna, six steam-shower rooms, suntan booths and, for those fancying a quick dip before flying, a hydro-pool.

Managing the five senses to create the service environment

Marketing is often about seduction. Just as in personal relations, the best marketers are those that use all five sensual dimensions – sight, sound, touch, taste and smell – to woo you. Retailers and other service providers must consider all the senses in shaping the customer's experience. Supermarkets have found that varying the tempo of music affects average time spent in the store and average expenditure. Retailers are adding fragrances to stimulate certain moods.

SonyStyle stores are seasoned with a specially designed subtle vanilla and mandarin orange fragrance. Every surface in a SonyStyle store is also designed to be touchable, from etched glass with bevelled edges on countertops to silk paper and maple panelling. Bloomingdales uses different essences in different departments: baby powder in the baby store; suntan lotion in the bathing suit area; lilacs in lingerie; and cinnamon and pine scent during the Christmas season.[68]

As consumers we like all our senses to be engaged. As Gummesson noted, 'We are not buying products and services but experiences and dreams.'[69] Martin Lindstrom, a Dutch branding expert, noted that only 10 per cent of the world's top 200 brands use all five senses.

Marketing often overlooks the fact that 75 per cent of day-to-day emotions are influenced by smell, and there can be a 65 per cent chance of a mood change when exposed to a positive sound.[70] Managing the sensory experience makes good sense. Though this is focused on services it also relates to product and brand image creation. If we put on a blindfold we can recognise a Coke bottle or a Barbie doll just from feel.[71]

Sight

Sight or vision is our primary sense. This is connected to how customers see service, the environment and particularly the interior design of the company when the customer visits it. For business class passengers Air France-KLM have leather seats and plush carpets, leading to an impression of luxury and comfort, while Ryanair — the low cost airline — has plastic seats with blue and yellow as the dominant colours reinforcing the cheap, low cost, no-frills focus of the company.

The setting where the service is simultaneously produced and consumed has a significant effect on the customer's service experience. Compare the experience of a meal at the best restaurant in Europe, elBulli, a three Michelin-starred restaurant on the Costa Brava in Catalonia, Spain. The small restaurant overlooks the Cala Monjoi bay, and the head chef has been described as 'the most imaginative generator of haute cuisine on the planet'. ElBulli has subdued lighting and expensive art deco, in contrast to the fast food sector that uses bright colours and bright lights to discourage customers from sitting around and occupying seating needed by the next customers. We actually move from chairs that are brightly coloured and are more inclined to stay on chairs which are neutral in colour. The management and updating of the interior design is an important element of marketing that can easily be overlooked.

Vision and uniforms For many service encounters staff wear uniforms which suggest their role in the organisation and how the interaction should occur. We immediately react to police officers, fire personnel and many others because the uniform is reflective of their positions and authority. So doctors wear white coats and often a stethoscope around their neck, which provides a perception of professionalism and authority. Sometimes a lot of thought goes into designing these uniforms. For example Air Italia have uniforms designed by Giorgio Armani, while Air France used Christian Lacroix and British Airways used Julian McDonald, all helping to create the air of luxury for these brands. In Asian and Islamic countries the airline uniforms are a mix of fashion and modesty to reflect the culture of those countries.

Sound

Sound is an often overlooked part of marketing. We are familiar with piped music in shops and also music in aircraft to calm passengers before the flight. In a recent study the effect of music (tempo and type) on customer perceptions and behavioural outcomes in women's fashion retailing was tested.[72] The results revealed that customers who liked the music being played were more likely to feel happy and to rate highly the quality of service and products on offer. On music *type*, when classical music or slow songs from the Top 40 were played, shoppers had a higher perception of service quality and pleasure than when the music was fast. Music tempo can also suggest the nature of a restaurant — fast food or upmarket.

More and more companies are patenting sounds. Kelloggs has patented the crackle sounds that you get when you open a bag of cornflakes and Mercedes-Benz the sound of the car door

Uniforms are a core marketing feature and are designed to support the brand image of the company. McDonald's in the United Kingdom have staff uniforms designed by fashion designer Bruce Oldfield.

Source: Rex Features

as it opens and closes.[73] That 'cluck' sound has been shown to be an effective criterion that customers use to judge the quality of a car. Children on aeroplanes can really disturb other passengers and in recent research some customers suggested that children should be seated in a separate area.

Smells and the service process

Our sense of smell is one of our strongest senses and one that can trigger dormant memories and associations. A study by Millward Brown revealed that 83 per cent of all brand communication is focused on two senses: what we hear and what we see. In sharp contrast, 75 per cent of our emotions are generated by what we smell.[74] A smell can have long-lasting associations that are cognitive, behavioural and also emotional. The poet Diane Ackerman noted that 'hit a tripwire of smell and memories explode at once'.[75]

Customers often equate the newness of a car with its smell, which by the way is a manufactured smell and does not exist. Rolls-Royce found that the sales of their new car increased after it created and sprayed the same distinctive fragrance as they had used for their 1965 Silver Cloud, into their new cars.[76]

Presence of smells Customers expect to smell coffee in a coffee shop; a hospital or a dentist or doctor wants to convey cleanliness so customers expect an antiseptic lemony smell. Customers expect what is called the ambient smell or a smell that creates an ambience. Many supermarkets smell of freshly baked bread. It is not that they are baking all day but the smell is piped into the shop as the smell of fresh bread has positive connotations and also promotes hunger, which can encourage people to buy more! Other examples:

- Some Barclays Bank branches in the United Kingdom offer freshly-brewed coffee so that the customer has the sense that they are at home in the bank.
- Thomas Pink, which has branches in the United Kingdom, Ireland, France and Turkey sprays the smell of fresh laundry and cotton in its shops to create that 'fresh' ambience.
- Singapore Airlines has developed a signature scent called Stefan Floridian Waters, which is sprayed in all their aeroplanes, worn by their staff and also sprayed on the hot towels handed out to passengers during flights.

Pleasantness of the smell A pleasant or unpleasant smell will reflect either positively or negatively on the service. A German study for Nike trainers found that 85 per cent of respondents preferred trainers displayed in a room with a slight light smell over the exact same shoe displayed in a room with no smell – and also were prepared to spend more to buy them.[77] Casinos have also noted an increase in gambling if there is a citrus smell.[78]

Touch

Customers like to touch, to feel, to experience for themselves. In a recent survey of mobile phone purchasers 35 per cent of consumers stated that the feel of the phone was more important than the look. In a similar study in the United States, 46 per cent of consumers said that the weight of the phone was more important than the look.[79] When customers touch fabrics or furniture they create images in their minds. The touch or texture can trigger connections to quality, as in the fine cotton dining cloth in a restaurant, or the opposite – a fast food outlet with a plastic table top.

Taste

Taste is also important, though the weakest of the five senses. Customers experience thousands of tastes as the tongue and the roof of the mouth are covered with thousands of tiny taste buds. These probably play the most important part in helping us enjoy the many flavours of food. Customers use their taste buds to recognise four basic kinds of taste: sweet, salty, sour and bitter.

Using all the senses in the service environment

Marketing managers need to manage all the senses. Take the Ritz Hotel, where the sound is kept subdued and quiet. Noise from other hotel guests can really impact on other guests' enjoyment. The texture of the bedclothes and the towels are all of the highest quality to reflect the brand image of luxury. All the decor and imagery in the hotel is designed for the refined taste of the clientele. All the food is fine dining with a focus on exquisite tastes. The smell within the hotel is complemented by fresh flowers on all floors. All the senses are managed well to create the image of luxury.

Marketing insight

Martin Lindstrom, *Brand Sense*

Dutchman Martin Lindstrom is one of the world's leading experts on branding and the senses. He is the author of *Brand Sense: How to Build Powerful Brands through Touch, Taste, Smell, Sight, and Sound*. He has always been a freethinker and entrepreneurial. He developed a LEGO house when he was young that attracted hundreds of visitors and also the attention of LEGO, which hired him. At the ripe old age of 12 he founded his first advertising agency and started to explore the lack of use of senses in branding and marketing. He suggests a six-step process to crafting a sensory brand across all touch points:

1 synergy across sensory touch points
2 innovative sensory thinking ahead of competitors
3 sensory consistency
4 sensory authenticity
5 positive sensory ownership
6 constant progress across sensory touch points.

If you would like to use your senses why not listen to Martin Lindstrom talk about and show you how our senses interact as we shop, as we play and as we grow. Log onto www.brandsenses.com. Unfortunately there is no smell!

▽ SUMMARY

1 Identifying and managing the service process, design and delivery to create value for the company and the customer is a core marketing requirement. Service process design uses a blueprint of the service process including all issues of relevance to the service.

2 The people element of the marketing mix is crucial. Managing service personnel and customers during the process to create a service level and expected service provision demands skill.

3 Customer-to-customer interactions need to be explored as they will have an effect on each other.

4 Understanding the role of technology and particularly the growing self-service technology within the service process (including the Internet, cyberspace, mobile phones and RFID) is important.

5 Creating and managing the service environment and the physical evidence relies on understanding how customers use their five senses to experience the service environment, and how each element of the physical evidence can help to form the brand image of the company.

▽ APPLICATIONS

Marketing debate

Should all service experiences use all five senses? Explore and debate this issue in relation to options in service experience design.

Marketing discussion

Discuss a blueprint for the service process for a service you are familiar with. Explore the level of variability and accommodation you will allow within the service process design.

▽ REFERENCES

[1]Swiss named 'Best Airline for Europe' *eTurboNews*, 21 January 2008 (www.eturbonews.com/946/swiss-named-%E2%80%9Cbest-airline-europe%E2%80%9D).

[2]C. Meyer and A. Schwager (2007) Understanding customer experience, *Harvard Business Review*, 85(2), 116–26.

[3]M. Brady, M. R. Fellenz and M. Cholakova (2007) Towards an IT enabled Customer Centric Service Supply Chain, academy of Marketing Conference (UK) Kingston University, July; G. McGovern and Y. Moon (2007) Companies and the customers who hate them, *Harvard Business Review*, June, 2–7.

[4]C. Gronroos (2000) Creating a relationship dialogue, *The Marketing Review*, 1(1), 5–14.

[5]J. Womack and D. Jones (2005) Lean consumption, *Harvard Business Review*, March, 2–13.

[6]B. D. Gelb (1987) How marketers of intangibles can raise the odds for consumer, *The Journal of Services Marketing*, 1(1), 11–18.

[7]C. Gronroos (2000) The perceived service quality concept: a mistake? *Managing Service Excellence*, 5(4), 46–8.

[8] H. Kasper, P. van Helsdingen and M. Gabbott (2006) *Services Marketing Management: A Strategic Perspective*, 2nd edn, Chichester, England: John Wiley & Sons.

[9]R. Johnston and G. Clark (2005) *Service Operations Management: Improving Service Delivery*, 2nd edn, Harlow, England: Prentice Hall.

[10]G. L. Shostack (1987) Service positioning through structural change, *Journal of Marketing*, 54(1), 34–44.

[11]R. Fisk, S. Grove and J. John, (2004) *Interactive Service Marketing*, Boston, MA: Houghton Mifflin.

[12]Johnston and Clark (2005) op. cit.

[13]J. Bowen and R. C. Ford (2002) Managing service organizations: does having a 'thing' make a difference?, *Journal of Management*, 28(3), 447–69.

[14]Ibid.

[15]E. Gummesson (2007) Exit service marketing: enter services marketing, *Journal of Consumer Behaviour*, 6(3), 113–41.

[16]F. Frei and A. Edmondson (2006) Influencing customer behavior in service operations, Harvard Business School Case Study 9-606-061, March, 1–7.

[17]Bowen and Ford (2002) op. cit.

[18]Bowen and Ford (2002) op. cit.

[19]V. A. Zeithaml, L. L. Berry and A. Parasuraman (1996) The behavioral consequences of service quality, *Journal of Marketing*, 60, 31–46.

[20]Ibid.

[21]McGovern and Moon (2007) op. cit.

[22]Bowen and Ford (2002) op. cit.

[23]Bowen and Ford (2002) op. cit.

[24]Bowen and Ford (2002) op. cit.

[25]J. A. Fitzsimmons and M. J. Fitzsimmons (2001) *Service Management: Operations, Strategy and Information Technology*, New York: McGraw Hill.

[26]C.K. Prahalad and V. Ramaswamy (2003) The new frontier of experience innovation, *MIT Sloan Management Review*, 44(4), 12–18.

[27]C. Robin and M. Ligas (2004) A typology of customer-service provider relationships: the role of relational factors in classifying customers, *Journal of Services Marketing*, 18(6), 482–93.

[28]Prahalad and Ramaswamy (2003) op. cit.

[29]Robin and Ligas (2004) op. cit.

[30]Victoria comes to America . . . they're welcome to her, Posted by Zara Rabinowicz on www.startrip.tv/2007/07/victoria-comes-.html, 18 July 2007.

[31]Robin and Ligas (2004) op. cit.

[32]Gummesson (2007) op. cit.

[33]F. Frei (2006) Breaking the trade off between efficiency and service, *Harvard Business Review*, 84(11), 93–101.

[34]J. Knadler (2007) World's most on-time airlines, *Forbes Traveler*, 17 December (www.forbestraveler.com/jets-planes/most-on-time-airlines-story-2.html).

[35]K. Foley (2007) Sunday Times: Kevin Thornton, posted by Kathey Foley on http://kathyfoley.net/2007/03/11/sunday-times-kevin-thornton/, 11 March.

[36]Bowen and Ford (2002) op. cit.

[37]Bowen and Ford (2002) op. cit.

[38]T. Peters (2006) *Reimagine! Business Excellence in a Disruptive Age*, London: DK Adult.

[39]See www.google.ch/intl/en/jobs/index.html.

[40]Frei and Edmondson (2006) op. cit.

[41]See www.wikipedia.org/wiki/Di%cs-Alksiget.

[42]K. Harris and S. Baron (2004) Consumer-to-Consumer conversations in service settings, *Journal of Service Research*, 6(3), 287–303.

[43]Frei (2006) op. cit.

[44]P. Child, S. Heywood and M. Kilger (2002) Do retail brands travel?, *The McKinsey Quarterly*, 1, 11–13.

[45]M. Lander and M. Barbaro (2006) Wal-Mart finds that its formula doesn't fit every culture, *New York Times*, 2 August (www.nytimes.com/2006/08/02/business/worldbusiness/02walmart.html?scp=2&sq=wal-mart&st=nyt).

[46]Ibid.

[47]Young shoppers want to pay with chip in skin, *Daily Mail*, 11 October 2006 (www.dailymail.co.uk/news/article-409867/Young-shoppers-want-pay-chip-skin.html).

[48]Ibid.

[49]Adapting to survive: an industry overview, *airport-technology.com*, 1 March 2006 (www.airport-technology.com/features/feature565/).

[50]M. R. Fellenz and M. Brady (2008) Managing the innovative deployment of Information and Communication Technologies (ICTs) for Global Service Organisations, International Journal of Technology Marketing, 3(1), 39–55. B Meyronin (2004) ICT: the creation of value and differentiation in services. *Managing Service Quality*, 14(2/3), 216–25.

[51]D. Shah, R. T. Rust, A. Parasuraman, R. Staelin and G. S Day (2006) The path to customer centricity, *Journal of Service Research*, 9(2), 113–25.

[52]R. Williams and M. Dargel. (2004) From servicescape to 'cyberscape', *Marketing Intelligence & Planning*, 22(2/3), 310–20.

[53]Ibid.

[54]M. Holzwarth, C. Janiszewski and M. M. Newmann (2006) The influence of avatars on online consumer shopping behavior, *Journal of Marketing*, 70 (October), 19–36.

[55]M. Feltner (2008) Sign up for airline email or text message alerts, *SmarterTravel.com*, 11 September (www.smartertravel.com/travel-advice/sign-up-for-airline-email-or-text-message-alerts.html?id=2652996).

[56]E. Morphy (2008) Self-service kiosks: bane or boon?, *CRM Buyer*, 28 July (www.crmbuyer.com/story/63949.html).

[57]G. Keeley (2006) Now we can start paying by chip in skin, *London Evening Standard*, 11 October, p. 22.

[58]Ibid.

[59]B. Booms and M. Bitner (1982) Marketing services by managing the environment, *The Cornell Hotel and Restaurant Administration Quarterly*, 23(1), 35–40.

[60]M. Bitner, B. Booms and M. Tetrault (1990) The service encounter: diagnosing favorable and unfavorable incidents, *Journal of Marketing*, 54(1), 71–84.

[61]M. Jo Bitner (1992) Servicescape: the impact of physical surroundings on customers and employees, *Journal of Marketing*, 56, 57–71.

[62]J. Møller Jensen (2007) The relationships between, hygiene factors, motivators, satisfaction and response among visitors to zoos and aquaria, *Tourism Review International*, special issue on zoos, aquaria and other captive wildlife attractions, 11(3), 307–16.

[63]Ibid.

[64]C. Coleman (2000) Kohl's retail racetrack, *Wall Street Journal*, 1 March.

[65]J. Hibbard (2006) Put your money where your mouth is, *BusinessWeek*, 18 September, 61–3.

[66]K. T. Rosen and A. L. Howard (2000) E-tail: gold rush or fool's gold?, *California Management Review*, 1 April, 72–100; M. Cotlier (2001) Census releases first e-commerce report, *Catalog Age*, 1 May; Associated Press (2001) Online sales boomed at end of 2000, *Star-Tribune of Twin Cities*, 17 February; Reinventing the store, *The Economist*, 22 November 2003, 65–8.

[67]V. D. Kaltcheva and B. Weitz (2006) When should a retailer create an exciting store environment, *Journal of Marketing*, 70 (January), 107–18.

[68]M. Fetterman and J. O'Donnell (2006) Just browsing at the mall? that's what you think, *USA Today*, 1 September, 1B, 2B.

[69]Gummesson (2007) op. cit.

[70]M. Lindstrom (2005) *Brand Sense: Build Powerful Brands through Touch, Taste, Smell, Sight, and Sound* (foreword by Philip Kotler), New York: The Free Press.

[71]Ibid.

[72]J. C. Sweeney and F. Wyber (2002) The role of cognition and emotions in the music-approach-avoidance behaviour relationship, *Journal of Services Marketing*, 16(1), 51–69.

[73]Lindstrom (2005) op. cit.

[74]See www.ameinfo.com/82230.html.

[75]L. Goldkuhl and M. Styven (2007) Sensing the scent of service success, *European Journal of Marketing*, 41(11/12), 1297–1305.

[76]Lindstrom (2005) op. cit.

[77]Goldkuhl and Styven (2007) op. cit.

[78]Lindstrom (2005) op. cit.

[79]Lindstrom (2005) op. cit.

▽ Communicating value

Video documentary for Part 7

Go to **www.pearsoned.co.uk/marketingmanagementeurope** to watch the video documentary that relates to Part 7 and consider the issues raised below.

Value packages need to be effectively and efficiently communicated to targeted audiences and this is achieved by a mix of promotional tools that are usually termed the marketing communications mix.

Part 7: Communicating Value explores four important themes:

1 managing advertising;

2 managing direct marketing;

3 managing sponsorship; and

4 exploring the potential of word-of-mouth.

Marketing communications are tailored to resonate with national cultures and value sets. When watching the video documentary for Part 7, consider how Royal Enfield's tag line 'Everyone makes way for the bullet' is appropriate for the Indian market but inappropriate for other markets where emphasis on heritage and the low cost of ownership carry more meaning. Advertising seeks to achieve 'top of the mind awareness' according to IKEA and can feature a variety of media (press, the Internet, posters, TV and radio). The rise of web-based advertising has caused a significant shift from traditional 'pull strategies' to modern 'push strategies', as web-based activities facilitate a customer 'call to action'.

An important tool in a modern marketing communications mix is sponsorship activity as this brings a company's value offerings directly into the real theatres of targeted customer's lives.

However, many would agree the best form of advertising is word-of-mouth with its implied third party recommendation.

Hear a variety of top marketing executives from a wide range of organisations offer their own interesting and varied perspectives on the key themes of Part 7 including: Vicky Starnes, Head of Marketing, VSO (top); Acme Whistles, an SME facing fierce global competition (centre); and Marketing Birmingham manage a brand that is constantly changing (bottom).

Chapter 19

Designing and managing marketing communications

Modern marketing calls for more than developing a good market offering, pricing it attractively and making it accessible. Companies must also communicate with present and potential customers, stakeholders and the general public. For most, therefore, the question is not whether to communicate but rather what to say, how and when to say it, to whom, and how often. However, communication becomes progressively more difficult as more companies clamour to attract an increasingly empowered consumer's divided attention. Consumers are taking a more active role in the communication process. They are deciding what communications they want to receive and how they want to communicate to others about the market offerings they choose to

The 'Evolution' advertising video, transforming an ordinary-looking woman's face into the image of a supermodel, was just one of the creative marketing communications that sparked Dove's recent shift in marketing strategy.
Source: Used by permission of Unilever

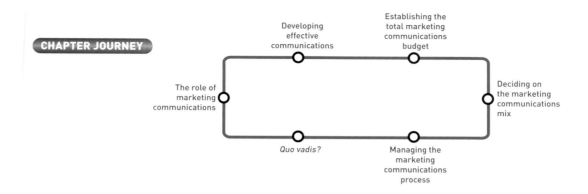

The role of marketing communications

Developing effective communications

Establishing the total marketing communications budget

Deciding on the marketing communications mix

Quo vadis?

Managing the marketing communications process

purchase and use. To reach and influence target markets effectively, holistic marketers are creatively employing multiple forms of communications.

Dove has been a Unilever stalwart for decades, backed by traditional advertising emphasising the brand's benefit of one-quarter moisturising cream and exhorting women to take the seven-day Dove test to discover its effects. A significant shift in strategy occurred for Dove in 2003 with the launch of the Real Beauty campaign, which celebrates 'real women' of all shapes, sizes, ages and colours. The campaign arose from research revealing that only 2 per cent of women *worldwide* considered themselves beautiful. It featured candid and confident images of curvy, full-bodied women – not traditional models. The advertisements promoted Dove skin products such as Intensive Firming Cream, Lotion, and Body Wash. The multimedia campaign was thoroughly integrated. Traditional TV and print advertisements were combined with all forms of new media, such as real-time voting for models on mobile phones and tabulated displays of results on giant billboards. PR was scaled up; paid media was scaled down. The Internet was crucial for creating a dialogue with women. A website was launched and supplemented with advertising videos. The Dove 'Evolution' video showed a rapid-motion view of an ordinary-looking woman transformed by make-up artists, hairdressers, lighting and digital retouching to look like a model. When it was uploaded to YouTube by Dove's advertising agency Ogilvy & Mather, it was an instant hit, drawing 2.5 million views. A subsequent advertisement, 'No Age Limit', featuring older, nude women, also aimed for a primarily online audience. Although the campaign sparked much debate, it was credited with boosting Dove sales and share in every country in which it was launched.[1]

Carried out correctly, marketing communications are hugely valuable. This chapter describes how communications work, discusses the importance of word-of-mouth marketing and demonstrates what marketing communications can achieve for a company. It also addresses how holistic marketers combine and integrate marketing communications. Chapter 20 examines the different forms of mass (non-personal) communications (advertising, sales promotion, events and experiences, and public relations and publicity) and the different forms of personal communications (direct and interactive marketing and personal selling).

▽ The role of marketing communications

Marketing communications are the means by which firms attempt to inform, persuade and remind customers – directly or indirectly – about the brands they market. In a sense, marketing communications represent the 'voice' of the company and its brands and are the ways in which it can establish a dialogue and build relationships with customers.

Marketing communications also perform many functions for customers. They can inform or show customers how and why a market offering is used, by what kind of person, and where and when. Customers can discover who develops and supplies the market offering and judge the reputation of the company's brand. There could also be an incentive or reward for trial or usage. Marketing communications allow companies to link their brands to other people, places, events, brands, experiences, feelings and things. They can contribute to brand equity – by establishing the brand in long-term memory and creating a brand image – as well as drive sales and affect shareholder value.[2]

The changing marketing communication environment

Although marketing communications can play a number of crucial roles, they must do so in an increasingly difficult environment. Technology and other factors have profoundly changed the way customers process information, and even whether they choose to process it at all. The rapid diffusion of powerful broadband Internet connections, advertising-skipping digital video recorders, multipurpose mobile phones, and portable music and video players have forced marketers to

Go forth and tell: the importance of effective communication.
Source: Serif

rethink a number of their traditional practices.[3] These dramatic changes have eroded the effectiveness in terms of impact and use of the traditional marketing communication tools.

Two forces have caused the demise of TV advertising, which used to be the most powerful means of communicating effectively with customers. One is the fragmentation of target audiences and the other is the advent of digital technology and the Internet. As a result prime-time TV advertisement ratings and press advertisement circulations have shown a downward trend since the 1970s.

What *is* new is the proliferation of media and entertainment options – from hundreds of cable and satellite TV and radio stations and thousands of magazines and webzines to numerous websites, blogs, video games and mobile phone screens. Consumers not only have a wider selection of media to use, they also have a choice about whether and how they want to receive commercial content. Additionally, digital or personal video recorders (DVR/PVRs) are part of the second force that is lessening the effectiveness of the 30-second TV advertising spot. DVRs/PVRs allow consumers to eliminate commercials with the push of a fast-forward button.

However, as some marketers flee the traditional media options they still encounter challenges. Commercial *clutter* (i.e., confusion or *noise* caused by multiple messages in multiple media), is rampant. As consumers become increasingly selective both in their choice of media and in the messages that appeal marketers are continually being challenged in their attempts to gain consumers' attention. The average city dweller is now exposed to between 3000 and 5000 advertising messages a day. Advertisements are on the back of bus tickets, parking vouchers and plastic carrier bags. Brand logos are designed to be worn on the outside of clothing or shoes (e.g., the Timberland logo and Nike's swoosh). Advertisements in almost every medium and form have been on the ascendancy and some consumers feel they are becoming increasingly invasive.[4]

Marketing communications, brand equity and sales

In this new communications environment, although advertising is often a central element of a marketing communications programme it is usually not the only one – or even the most important one – in terms of building brand equity and boosting sales.

Marketing communications mix

The **marketing communications mix** consists of eight major modes of communication:[5]

1 **Advertising**: Any paid form of non-personal presentation and promotion of ideas, goods or services by an identified sponsor.

2 **Sales promotion**: A variety of short-term incentives to encourage trial or purchase of a product or service (market offering).

3 **Events and experiences**: Company-sponsored activities and programmes designed to create daily or special brand-related interactions.

4 **Public relations and publicity**: A variety of programmes designed to promote or protect a company's image or its individual market offerings.

5 **Direct marketing**: Use of mail, telephone, fax, email or the Internet to communicate directly with or solicit response or dialogue from specific customers and prospects.

6 **Interactive marketing**: Online activities and programmes designed to engage customers or prospects and directly or indirectly raise awareness, improve image or elicit sales of market offerings (value packages, i.e., combinations of products and service attributes).

7 **Word-of-mouth marketing**: People-to-people oral, written or electronic communications that relate to the merits or experiences of purchasing and consuming market offerings.

8 **Personal selling**: Face-to-face interaction with one or more prospective purchasers for the purpose of making presentations, answering questions and procuring orders.

Table 19.1 lists numerous communication platforms. Company communication goes beyond those specific platforms. The market offering's styling and price, the shape and colour of the package, the salesperson's manner and dress, the store decor, the company's stationery – all communicate value that can be perceived by buyers. Every brand contact delivers an impression that can strengthen or weaken a customer's view of the company.[6] So wise firms carefully develop their brands to reflect these customer-perceived values (see Chapter 11).

Table 19.1 Common communication platforms

Advertising	Sales promotion	Events & experiences	Public relations & publicity	Direct & interactive marketing	Word-of-mouth marketing	Personal selling
Print and broadcast ads	Contests, games, sweepstakes, lotteries	Sports	Press kits	Catalogues	Person to person	Sales presentations
Packaging – outer	Premiums and gifts	Entertainment	Speeches	Mailings	Chatrooms	Sales meetings
Packaging inserts	Sampling	Festivals	Seminars	Telemarketing	Blogs	Incentive programmes
Motion pictures	Fairs and trade shows	Arts	Annual reports	Electronic shopping		Samples
Brochures and booklets	Exhibits	Causes	Charitable donations	TV shopping		Fairs and trade shows
Posters and leaflets	Demonstrations	Factory tours	Publications	Fax		
Directories	Coupons	Company museums	Community relations	Email		
Reprints of ads	Rebates	Street activities	Lobbying	Voicemail		
Billboards	Low-interest financing		Identity media	Blogs		
Display signs	Entertainment		Company magazine	Websites		
Point-of-purchase displays	Trade-in allowances					
Audiovisual material	Continuity programmes					
Symbols and logos	Tie-ins					
Videotapes						

As Figure 19.1 shows, marketing communications activities contribute to brand equity and drive sales in many ways: by creating awareness of the brand; linking the right associations to the brand image in consumers' long-term memory; eliciting positive brand judgements or feelings; and/or facilitating a stronger consumer–brand connection.

Marketing communication effects

The manner in which brand associations are formed is unimportant. Some consumers may have a strong, favourable, and unique brand association of Land-Rover with the concepts of 'outdoors', 'active', and 'rugged', because of exposure to a TV advertisement that shows the car driving over rugged terrain at different times of the year. Others may prefer a Land Rover as they seek a comfortable vehicle for country roads.

These marketing communications activities must be integrated to deliver a consistent message and to achieve the appropriate strategic positioning (see Chapter 10). The starting point in planning marketing communications is an audit of all the potential interactions that customers in the target market may have with the company and all its market offerings. For example, someone interested in purchasing a new laptop computer might talk to others, see television advertisements, read articles, look for information on the Internet and look at laptops in a local computer dealership.

Marketers need to assess which experiences and impressions will have the most influence at each stage of the buying process. This understanding will help them allocate the budget for communications more efficiently and design and implement the right communications programmes. Armed with these insights, marketers can judge marketing communications according to their ability to affect experiences and impressions, build brand equity and drive brand sales. For example,

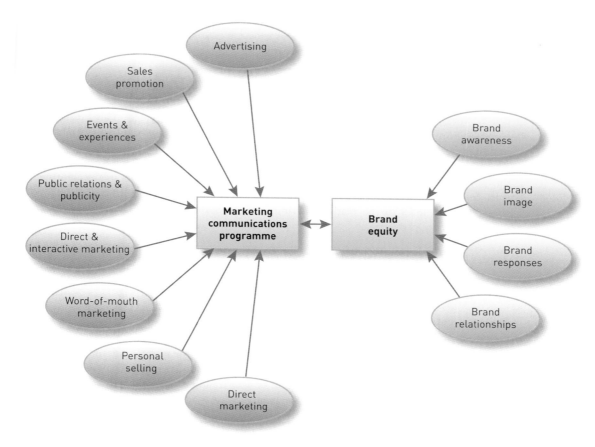

Figure 19.1 Integrating marketing communications to build brand equity

Driving on the edge!

Source: Courtesy of Land Rover

how well does a proposed advertising campaign contribute to awareness or to creating, maintaining or strengthening brand associations? Does sponsorship cause customers to have more favourable brand judgements and feelings? To what extent does a sales promotion encourage consumers to buy more of a market offering?

From the perspective of building brand equity, marketers should be 'media neutral' and evaluate *all* the different possible communication options according to *effectiveness* criteria (how well does it work?) as well as *efficiency* considerations (how much does it cost?). This broad view of brand-building activities is especially relevant when marketers are considering strategies to improve brand awareness.

Anything that causes the consumer to notice and pay attention to the brand – such as sponsorship and advertising – can increase **brand awareness**, at least in terms of brand recognition. To enhance brand recall, however, more intense and elaborate processing may be necessary, so that stronger brand links to the market offering, category or customer needs are established to improve memory performance.

The communications process models

Marketers should understand the fundamental elements of effective communications. Two models are useful: a macro- and a micromodel.

Macromodel of the communications process

Figure 19.2 shows a communications macromodel with nine elements. Two represent the major parties in a communication – *sender* and *receiver*. Two represent the major communication tools – *message* and *media*. Four represent major communication functions – *encoding, decoding, response* and *feedback*. The last element in the system is *noise* (random and competing messages that may interfere with the intended communication).

The model emphasises the key factors in effective communication. Senders must know what audiences they want to reach and what responses they want to achieve. They must encode their messages so the target audience can decode them; then transmit the message through media that reach the target audience and develop feedback channels to monitor the responses. The more the sender's field of experience overlaps that of the receiver, the more *effective* the message is likely to be. Note that selective attention, distortion and retention processes – concepts first introduced in Chapter 7 – may be operating during communication.

Micromodel of consumer responses

Micromodels of marketing communications concentrate on customers' specific responses to communications. Figure 19.3 summarises four classic *response hierarchy models.*

All these models assume that the buyer passes through a cognitive, affective and behavioural stage, in that order. This 'learn-feel-do' sequence is appropriate when the audience has high involvement with a product category perceived to have high differentiation, such as a car or house. An alternative sequence, 'do-feel-learn', is relevant when the audience has high involvement but perceives little or no differentiation within the product category, such as an airline ticket or personal computer. A third sequence, 'learn-do-feel', is relevant when the audience has low involvement and perceives little differentiation within the market offering category, such as salt or batteries. By choosing the right sequence the marketer can fine tune marketing communications.[7]

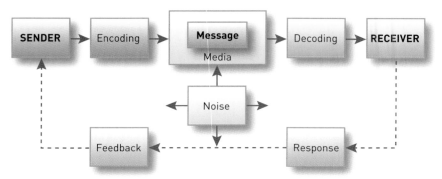

Figure 19.2 Elements in the communication process

Models

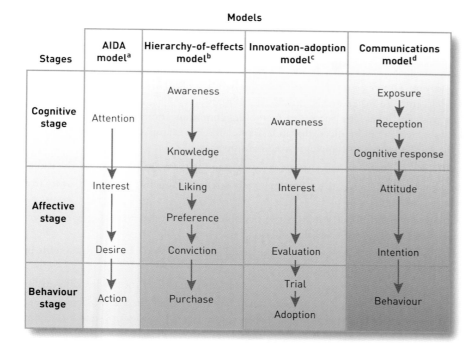

Stages	AIDA model[a]	Hierarchy-of-effects model[b]	Innovation-adoption model[c]	Communications model[d]
Cognitive stage	Attention	Awareness → Knowledge	Awareness	Exposure → Reception → Cognitive response
Affective stage	Interest → Desire	Liking → Preference → Conviction	Interest → Evaluation	Attitude → Intention
Behaviour stage	Action	Purchase	Trial → Adoption	Behaviour

Figure 19.3 Response hierarchy models

Sources: [a]E. K. Strong (1925) *The Psychology of Selling*, New York: McGraw-Hill, p. 9; [b]R. J. Lavidge and G. A. Steiner, (1961) A model for predictive measurements of advertising effectiveness, *Journal of Marketing*, October, 61; [c]E. M. Rogers (1962) *Diffusion of Innovation*, New York: Free Press, pp. 79-86; [d]Various sources.

Assuming that the buyer has high involvement with the market offering category and perceives a high differentiation within it the *hierarchy-of-effects model* (in the second column of Figure 19.3) sheds valuable light on the development of a marketing communications campaign for a small university named Logos.

- **Awareness**: If most of the target audience is unaware of the object, the communicator's task is to build awareness. Suppose Logos seeks applicants from Europe but has no name recognition there. There are many thousand potential students in Europe who may be interested in studying at Logos. The university might set the objective of making 70 per cent of these students aware of its name within one year by an emarketing campaign.

- **Knowledge**: The target audience might have brand awareness but not know much more. Logos may want its target audience to know that it is a prestigious institution with excellent programmes in English, foreign languages and history. It needs to learn how many people in the target audience have little, some or much knowledge about the university. If knowledge is weak, Logos may decide to select brand knowledge as its main communications objective.

- **Liking**: If target members know the brand, how do they feel about it? If the target audience looks unfavourably on Logos, the communicator needs to find out why. If the unfavourable view is based on real problems the university will need to attend to these and then communicate its renewed quality. Good public relations call for 'good deeds followed by good words'.

- **Preference**: The target audience might quite like Logos but not prefer it to other universities. In this case, the communicator must try to build consumer preference by comparing quality, value (see CPV section in Chapter 11), performance and other features where it can claim to beat likely competitors.

- **Conviction**: A target audience might prefer a particular market offering but not develop a conviction about buying it. The communicator's job is to build conviction and purchase intent among students interested in studying at Logos.

- **Purchase**: Finally, some members of the target audience might have conviction but not quite get around to making the purchase. The communicator must lead these potential consumers to take the final step, perhaps by employing 'below-the-line' marketing activity such as press and public relations. Logos might invite selected potential students to visit the campus and attend some classes, or it might offer partial scholarships to deserving students.

To show how fragile the whole communications process is, assume that the probability of *each* of the six steps being successfully accomplished is 50 per cent. The laws of probability suggest that the probability of *all* six steps occurring successfully (assuming they are independent events) is

$$.5 \times .5 \times .5 \times .5 \times .5 \times .5$$

which equals 1.5625 per cent. If the probability of each step occurring was, on average, a more moderate 10 per cent, then the joint probability of all six events occurring would be 0.0001 per cent – in other words, only 1 in 1,000,000!

To increase the odds for a successful marketing communications campaign, marketers must attempt to increase the likelihood that *each* step occurs. For example, from an advertising standpoint, the ideal advertising campaign would ensure that:

1 The right customer is exposed to the right message at the right place and at the right time.

2 The advertisement causes the customer to pay attention to it but does not distract from the intended message.

3 The advertisement properly reflects the customer's level of understanding and appreciation of the value of the branded market offering.

4 The advertisement correctly positions the brand in terms of desirable and deliverable points-of-difference and points-of-parity.

5 The advertisement motivates consumers to consider purchase of the market offering.

6 The advertisement creates strong brand associations with all these stored communications effects so that they can have an impact when consumers are considering making a purchase.

▽ Developing effective communications

Effective communications should accomplish four things: establish a *connection,* promise a *reward*, inspire *action* and stick in the *memory.* The Cillit Bang campaign (see Chapter 15) provides a good example of effective communication. Figure 19.4 shows the eight key steps in developing effective communications: identifying the target audience, determining the objectives, designing the communications, selecting the channels, establishing the budget, deciding on media mix, measuring results, managing integrated marketing communications.

Identify the target audience

The process must start with a clear target audience in mind: potential buyers of the company's market offerings, current users, deciders or influencers; individuals, groups, particular publics or the general public. The target audience is a critical influence on the communicator's decisions about what to say, how, when, where, and to whom.

It is often useful to identify the target audience in terms of any of the market segments identified in Chapter 10 in terms of usage and loyalty. Is the target new to the category or a current user? Is the target loyal to the brand, loyal to a competitor, or someone who switches between brands? If a brand user, is he or she a heavy or light user? Communication strategy will differ depending on the answers. An *image analysis* can provide further insight, by profiling the target audience in terms of brand knowledge.

Determine the communications objectives

Marketers can set marketing communications objectives at any level of the hierarchy-of-effects model. Rossiter and Percy identify four possible objectives, as follows:[8]

1 **Category need:** Establishing a product or service (market offering) category as necessary to remove or satisfy a perceived discrepancy between a current motivational state and a desired emotional state. A new-to-the-world item such as electric cars would always begin with a communications objective of establishing category need.

2 **Brand awareness:** Ability to identify (recognise or recall) the brand within the category in sufficient detail to make a purchase. Recognition is easier to achieve than recall. Brand recall is important outside the store; brand recognition is important inside the store. Brand awareness provides a foundation for brand equity.

Figure 19.4 Steps in developing effective communications

3 **Brand attitude**: Evaluating the brand with respect to its perceived ability to meet a currently relevant need. Relevant brand needs may be negatively oriented (problem removal, problem avoidance, incomplete satisfaction, normal depletion) or positively oriented (sensory gratification, intellectual stimulation or social approval). Household cleaning products often use problem solution; food products, on the other hand, often use sensory-oriented advertisements emphasising appetite appeal.

4 **Brand purchase intention**: Self-instructions to purchase the brand or to take purchase-related action. Promotional offers in the form of coupons or two-for-one deals encourage consumers to make a mental commitment to buy a product. However, many consumers do not have an expressed category need and may not be in the market when exposed to an advertisement, so they are unlikely to form purchase intentions. For example, in any given week, only about 20 per cent of adults may be planning to buy detergent; only 2 per cent may be planning to buy a carpet cleaner; and only 0.25 per cent may be planning to buy a car.

In most cases companies are intent on achieving multiple communications objectives.

Design the communications

Formulating the communications to achieve the desired response will require solving three problems: what to say (message strategy), how to say it (creative strategy), and who should say it (message source).

Message strategy

In determining message strategy, management searches for appeals, themes or ideas that will tie in to the brand positioning and help to establish points-of-parity or points-of-difference. Some of these may be related directly to product or service performance (the quality, economy or value of the brand), whereas others may relate to more extrinsic considerations (the brand as being contemporary, popular or traditional).

Buyers expect one of four types of reward from a market offering: rational, sensory, social, or ego satisfaction.[9] Buyers might visualise these rewards from results-of-use experience, product-in-use experience or incidental-to-use experience. Crossing the four types of rewards with the three types of experience generates 12 types of messages. For example, the appeal 'gets clothes cleaner' is a rational-reward promise following results-of-use experience. The phrase 'real beer taste in a great light beer' is a sensory-reward promise connected with product-in-use experience.

Creative strategy

Communications effectiveness depends on how a message is being expressed, as well as on the content of the message itself. If a communication is ineffective, it may mean the wrong message was used, or the right one was just poorly expressed. *Creative strategies* are the way marketers translate their messages into a specific communication. They can be broadly classified as either *informational* or *transformational appeals*. These two general categories each cover several different specific creative approaches.

Informational appeals An **informational appeal** elaborates on market offering quality and payment attributes or benefits. Examples in advertising are advertisements that provide a solution (Nurofen stops the toughest headache pain), demonstrate a clear benefit (use Cillit Bang 'and the dirt is gone'), offer product comparison (Sky TV offers the best satellite programmes), and testimonials from unknown or celebrity endorsers such as famous film stars or sports personalities. (Jane Fonda recommending the use of L'Oréal's anti-ageing creams – see Chapter 11.) Informational appeals assume very rational processing of the communication on the part of the consumer. Logic and reason rule.

Hovland's research has shed much light on informational appeals and their relationship to such issues as conclusion drawing, one-sided versus two-sided arguments, and order of argument presentation. Some early experiments supported stating conclusions for the audience. Subsequent research, however, indicates that the best advertisements ask questions and allow readers and viewers to form their own conclusions.[9] Some stimulus ambiguity can lead to a broader market definition and more spontaneous purchases.

It would be logical to assume that presentations which praise a market offering would be more effective than two-sided arguments that also mention shortcomings. Yet two-sided messages may be more appropriate, especially when negative associations must be overcome. Listerine (mouth wash) said 'Listerine tastes bad twice a day.' Two-sided messages are more effective with more educated audiences and those who are initially opposed.[10]

Finally, the order in which arguments are presented is important.[11] In a one-sided message, presenting the strongest argument first has the advantage of arousing attention and interest. This is important in media where the audience often does not attend to the whole message. With a captive audience, a climactic presentation might be more effective. In the case of a two-sided message, if the audience is initially opposed, the communicator might start with the other side's argument and conclude with his or her strongest argument.

Transformational appeals A **transformational appeal** elaborates on a non-market offering-related benefit or image. It might depict what kind of person uses a brand. Renault presents the Clio model as being attractive to female drivers and their Megane model (with its celebrated derrière) to male drivers. Transformational appeals often attempt to stir up emotions that will motivate purchase.

Communicators use negative appeals such as fear, guilt and shame to get people to do things (brush their teeth, have an annual health check-up) or stop doing things (smoking, alcohol abuse, overeating). Fear appeals work best when they are not too strong, when source credibility is high, and when the communication promises to relieve, in a believable and efficient way, the fear it arouses. Messages are most persuasive when they are moderately discrepant with what the audience believes. Stating only what the audience already believes at best only reinforces beliefs, and if the messages are too discrepant, audiences will counter argue and disbelieve them.[12]

Communicators also use positive emotional appeals such as humour, love, pride and joy. Motivational or 'borrowed interest' devices – such as the presence of cute babies, frisky puppies (such

Michelin's use of the Michelin Man brand character in its advertising helps to break through the clutter and reinforce the brand's key safety and trust messages.

Source: Used by permission of Michelin, North America, Inc.

as in the Andrex advertisements – see Chapter 20), popular music or provocative sex appeals – are often employed to attract consumer attention and raise their involvement with an advertisement. Borrowed-interest techniques are thought to be necessary in the tough new media environment characterised by low-involvement consumer processing and much competing advertisement and programming clutter.

Although these borrowed-interest approaches can attract attention and create more liking and belief in the sponsor, they may also detract from comprehension, wear out their welcome fast and overshadow the product.[13] Benetton, a retailer of colourful and fashionable clothes, attracted much attention (but much of it negative) when it posted a series of shocking images featuring graphic scenes of new-born babies, oil-infested seabirds, a man dying of Aids and copulating horses. Attention-getting tactics are often *too* effective and distract from brand claims. The advertisements were considered to be notoriously insensitive and damaged the company's brand image. A real challenge in arriving at the best creative strategy is working out how to 'break through the clutter' or 'noise' in the marketplace to attract the attention of consumers – and still deliver the intended message effectively.

The magic of advertising is to bring concepts on a piece of paper to life in the minds of the target customer. In a print advertisement, the communicator must decide on headline, copy, illustration and colour.[14] For a radio message, the communicator must choose words, voice qualities and vocalisations. If the message is to be carried on television or in person, all these elements plus body language (non-verbal clues) must be planned. Presenters need to pay attention to facial expressions, gestures, dress, posture and hairstyle. If the message is carried by the market offering or its packaging, the communicator must pay attention to colour, texture, scent, size and shape.

Message source

Many communications do not use a source beyond the company itself. Others use known or unknown people. Messages delivered by attractive or popular sources can achieve higher attention and recall, which is why advertisers often use celebrities as spokespeople. Celebrities are likely to be effective when they are credible or personify a key market offering attribute. The retired England international footballer and current BBC TV presenter, Gary Lineker, has for years successfully advertised Walkers Crisps. The actress Annette Crosbie is currently advertising Vodafone in the United Kingdom. Tesco, on the other hand, is running TV advertisements that feature a variety of well-known names and voices to boost their image.

What *is* important is the spokesperson's credibility. What factors underlie source credibility? The three most often identified are expertise, trustworthiness and likeability.[15] *Expertise* is the specialised knowledge the communicator possesses to back the claim. *Trustworthiness* is related to how objective and honest the source is perceived to be. Friends are trusted more than strangers or sales people, and those who are not paid to endorse a market offering are viewed as more trustworthy than those who are.[16] *Likeability* describes the source's attractiveness. Qualities such as candour, humour and naturalness make a source more likeable.

▽ Gary Lineker and Jamie Oliver present for Walkers and Sainsbury's

Gary Lineker is regarded by many as being a typical Mr Nice Guy. He has successfully promoted Walkers Crisps for over a decade. For a time the company used his name to promote a sub-brand – Walkers Salt 'n Lineker (salt and vinegar flavoured crisps). His endorsement greatly helped the company to sell an additional 1.4 billion bags of crisps in seven years. The celebrity chef, Jamie Oliver has promoted Sainsbury's supermarkets in the United Kingdom since 2000. The association increased sales by £1 billion in the first two years and increased Sainsbury's gross profits by £200 million. Jamie has also successfully campaigned in a TV series to persuade the UK government to improve the quality of school meals.[17]

Business-to-business financial services marketer Accenture found all these qualities and more in golf professional Tiger Woods.

▽ Accenture

What better symbol for high performance than Tiger Woods, the world's number one golfer? That's why business consulting firm, Accenture, was persistent in seeking to use the golfer as the main focus for its rebranding campaign. Enter Tiger Woods and the new tagline 'High Performance Delivered'. Accenture's message is that it can help client companies become 'high-performing business leaders', like the ones featured on its website. The Woods endorsement drives home the importance of high performance, just as Woods drives home in yet another tournament. The campaign includes advertisements in 27 countries, capitalising on Tiger Woods' international appeal; events and sponsorships that are aligned with the idea of high performance, such as the World Golf Championships; and an interactive website that users can personalise to get information and regular updates relevant to their industry. Accenture has also teamed up with the *Wall Street Journal* to produce a series of articles that explore different facets of high-performance business, written by seasoned journalists and featuring Accenture client companies.

Sources: www.accenture.com; M. E. Podmolik (2004) Accenture turns to tiger for global marketing effort, *BtoB*, 89(12), 25 October; S. Callahan (2003) Tiger tees off in new accenture campaign, *BtoB*, 88(11), 13 October.

The most highly credible source would score high on all three dimensions – candour, humour and naturalness. Pharmaceutical companies want doctors to testify about product benefits because doctors have high credibility. The boxer George Foreman achieved fame in his promotion of healthy grills. 'Marketing insight: Celebrity endorsements as a strategy' focuses on the use of testimonials.

Salton and George Foreman

Salton was a little-known manufacturer of oddball appliances that gained temporary fame in the 1950s with its Salton Hot Tray, an essential item for every wedding list at the time. In the early 1990s, the company introduced an indoor grill that seemed

George Foreman recommends fat-free grilled food.
Source: Salton Europe

destined for obscurity until two-time heavyweight boxing champion George Foreman chose not only to endorse it, but to join up with the company to sell it. Foreman and his Lean, Mean, Fat-Reducing Grilling Machine was a great success.[18]

If a person has a positive attitude towards a source and a message, or a negative attitude towards both, a state of *congruity* is said to exist. What happens if the person holds one attitude towards the source and the opposite one towards the message? Suppose a customer hears a likeable celebrity praise a brand she dislikes. Osgood and Tannenbaum argue that *attitude change will take place in the direction of increasing the amount of congruity between the two evaluations.*[19] The consumer will end up respecting the celebrity somewhat less or respecting the brand somewhat more. If a person encounters the same celebrity praising other disliked brands, he or she will eventually develop a negative view of the celebrity and maintain negative attitudes towards the brands. The **principle of congruity** implies that communicators can use their good image to reduce some negative feelings towards a brand but in the process might lose some esteem with the audience.

Recent research at the University of Bath in the United Kingdom suggests that celebrity endorsements are becoming less effective for many market offerings.[20] Another study has shown that both endorser image and brand image serve as mediators in the equity and creation process of celebrity market offering endorsement.[21] UK supermarkets are shifting their advertising strategies away from campaigns featuring celebrities in favour of price promotions. Asda has frozen its spend at £51 million, and will not commission any more celebrity advertisements that feature the actresses Victoria Wood and Julie Walters and the ex-Arsenal football pundit Ian Wright after its current (2008) campaign is over. Tesco also seems to be cooling its interest.

Marketing insight

Celebrity endorsements as a strategy

To reinforce its prestigious image, Chanel signed up Nicole Kidman to add a quality mystique to its famous No.5 perfume.

The choice of the celebrity is critical. The celebrity should have high recognition, high positive affect and high appropriateness to the product. Paris Hilton, Kate Moss and Britney Spears have high recognition but negative affect among many groups. Robbie Williams has high recognition and high positive affect but might not be appropriate for advertising a World Peace Conference. The TV actor Hugh Laurie (of the US soap *House*) and model Claudia Schiffer could successfully advertise a large number of products because they have extremely high ratings for familiarity and likeability (known as the Q factor in the entertainment industry). Hugh Grant is currently promoting the Marie Curie Cancer Care Great Daffodil Appeal to show his gratitude for the care they gave to his late mother.[22]

Celebrities show up everywhere in the advertising of market offerings to children. Familiar cartoon characters are widely used on cereal packets and children's soft drinks. This lasting attraction can be given a boost by the inclusion of celebrity endorsements even though the young audience does not always know who the celebrity is.[23]

Athletes commonly endorse athletic products, beverages and clothing. One of the premier athletic endorsers has been the US cyclist Lance Armstrong, who battled and beat testicular cancer on his way to winning six consecutive Tour de France championships. He has endorsed a number of bicycle and sports products and companies, including Trek, PowerBar and Nike. Armstrong's improbable 'against all odds' success story also enabled him to win multimillion-dollar endorsement contracts from companies not affiliated with sports, such as Bristol-Myers Squibb pharmaceuticals, Coca-Cola, Subaru and 24 Hour Fitness.

Celebrities can play a more strategic role for their brands, not only endorsing a product but also helping design, position and sell merchandise and services. Since signing Tiger Woods in 1996, Nike has seen its share of the golf ball market grow steadily. Woods has played a key role in developing a series of golf products and apparel that Nike has periodically altered to reflect his changing personality and design tastes.

Using celebrities poses certain risks. The celebrity might demand a larger fee at contract renewal time or withdraw. In common with some films and CDs, celebrity campaigns can sometimes be expensive failures. T-Mobile axed the film actress Catherine Zeta-Jones citing celebrity fatigue due to her overexposure in the United States. The celebrity might lose popularity or, even worse, get caught in a scandal or embarrassing situation as did the English film star Hugh Grant and more recently the pop star Amy Winehouse.

Global adaptations

Multinational companies wrestle with a number of challenges in developing global communications programmes. They must decide whether the market offering is appropriate for a country. They must make sure the market segment they address is both legal and customary. They must decide whether the style of the advertisement is acceptable, and whether advertisements should be created at headquarters or be locally specific.[24]

1 **Product**: Many items are restricted or forbidden in certain parts of the world. Beer, wine and spirits cannot be advertised or sold in many Muslim countries. Tobacco products are subject to strict regulation in many countries.

2 **Market segment**: In Norway and Sweden, for example TV advertisements may not be directed at children under 12. Sweden lobbied hard to extend that ban to all EU member countries in 2001 but failed. To play it safe, McDonald's advertises itself as a family restaurant in Sweden.

3 **Style**: Comparative advertisements, acceptable and even common in the United States and Canada, are less commonly used in the United Kingdom, unacceptable in Japan, and illegal in India and Brazil. The EU seems to have a very low tolerance for comparative advertising, with a Comparative Advertising Directive that prohibits criticising rivals in advertisements.

4 **Local or global**: Today, more and more multinational companies are attempting to build a global brand image by using the same advertising in all markets.

Companies that sell their products to different cultures or in different countries must be prepared to vary their messages. In advertising its hair care products in different countries, Helene Curtis adjusts its messages. Middle-class British women wash their hair frequently, whereas the opposite is true among Spanish women. Japanese women avoid washing their hair too often for fear of removing protective oils. Car advertisements screened on UK TV often feature cars that are left-hand drive and so risk reducing the impact and positive recall.

Select the communications channels

Selecting efficient means to carry the message becomes more difficult as channels of communication become more fragmented and cluttered. Think of the challenges in the pharmaceutical industry. The industry has had to expand its range of communications channels to include advertisements in medical journals, direct mail (including audio and videotapes), free samples and even telemarketing. Pharmaceutical companies sponsor clinical conferences in which physicians are paid to spend a weekend listening to leading colleagues extol the virtues of their drug portfolios. Pharmaceuticals use all these channels in the hope of building physician preference for their branded therapeutic agent. They are also using new technologies to reach doctors through handheld devices, online services and videoconferencing equipment.[25]

Communications channels may be personal and non-personal and in each category there are many subchannels. The best advice is to focus on connecting the company's cause to their targeted audience's values rather than telling people to value the company's cause – and reach people when they are in the best place, time and state of mind to get the best impact for the marketing communications budget. Put another way a successful mantra is *concentrate and inundate* rather than *spray and pray*.

Personal communications channels

Personal communications channels let two or more persons communicate face-to-face, person-to-audience, over the telephone or through email. Instant messaging and independent sites to collect consumer reviews are another channel and one of growing importance in recent years. Personal communication channels derive their effectiveness through individualised presentation and feedback.

A further distinction can be made between advocate, expert and social communications channels. *Advocate channels* consist of company sales people contacting buyers in the target market. *Expert channels* consist of independent experts making statements to target buyers. *Social channels* consist of neighbours, friends, family members and associates talking to target buyers. In a study of 7000 consumers in seven European countries, 60 per cent said they were influenced to use a new brand by family and friends.[26]

Marketers have discovered that one influential person's word of mouth tends to affect the buying attitudes of two other people, on average. That circle of influence, however, jumps to eight online. Considerable consumer-to-consumer communication takes place on the Web on a wide range of subjects. Online visitors also increasingly create product information, not just consume it. They join Internet interest groups to share information, so that 'word of Web' is joining 'word of mouth' as an important buying influence. Word about good companies travels fast; word about bad companies travels even faster. As one marketer noted, 'You don't need to reach 2 million people to let them know about a new product – you just need to reach the right 2000 people in the right way and they will help you reach 2 million.'[27]

Personal influence carries an especially great weight in two situations. One occurs when items are expensive, risky or purchased infrequently. The other arises when purchases may suggest something about the user's status or taste. People often ask others for a recommendation for a doctor, plumber, hotel, lawyer, accountant, architect, insurance agent, interior decorator or financial consultant. If they have confidence in the recommendation, they normally act on the referral. In such cases, the recommender has potentially benefited the service provider as well as the service seeker. Service providers clearly have a strong interest in building referral sources. Research indicates that 30–50 per cent of all brand switching occurs as a result of personal recommendation, as against 20 per cent for advertising, promotions and personal search.[28]

Word of Mouth

Word-of-mouth (WOM) has been defined as an interpersonal communication of products and services (market offerings) where the receiver regards the communicator as impartial. Both positive and negative word of mouth has been shown by research to have a substantial impact on firms' fortunes and should be measured by them.[29] Markets can be regarded as conversations. The London School of Economics and Political Science and The Listening Company Agency found in a 2005 survey of a random sample of 1256 adult consumers in the United Kingdom that WOM advocacy was a significant predictor of annual sales growth. Companies earning higher levels of WOM advocacy, such as HSBC, Asda, O2 and Honda returned higher growth in the research period than their less fortunate competitors. Companies returning poor WOM scores at the time included Lloyds-TSB, Fiat and T-Mobile.[30]

Social networks, such as MySpace and Facebook, have become an important force in both business-to-consumer and business-to-business marketing. A key aspect of social networks is word of mouth and the number and nature of conversations and communications between different parties. Although many are media and entertainment items such as films, TV shows, publications, food items, travel offers and retail stores many other types of offer are often mentioned. Although mega-networks such as MySpace and Facebook can provide the most exposure, niche social networks have the potential to spread the message more effectively to a targeted market segment.

Companies are becoming increasingly aware of the potential of word of mouth. Brands such as Hush Puppy shoes, Pret A Manger and the feature film *The Passion of Christ* benefited considerably through strong WOM, as have the reputations of Amazon, The Body Shop and Red Bull. In some cases word of mouth happens naturally with little support advertising, but in many cases it is managed and facilitated. It is particularly effective for smaller businesses with whom customers may develop a more personal relationship. To facilitate goodwill many companies are seeking to form online virtual communities to forge and strengthen customer relationships.

Buzz and viral marketing

Some marketers highlight two particular forms of word of mouth – buzz and **viral marketing**. (See also Chapter 4.)

Buzz marketing generates excitement, creates publicity and conveys new relevant brand-related information through unexpected or even outrageous means. The advertiser reveals information about the market offering (product or service package) to only a few 'knowing' people in the target audience. By purposely seeking out one-to-one conversations with those who heavily influence their peers, buzz marketers create a sophisticated word-of-mouth campaign where consumers are flattered to be included in the elite group of those 'in the know' and willingly spread the word to their friends and colleagues.

Viral marketing is another form of word of mouth or 'word-of-mouse', that encourages consumers to pass on company-developed impressions of company offers to others online.[31] By exploiting the power of peer-to-peer advertising, brands are able to raise their awareness and achieve valuable dwell time through attracting the full attention of their audience for minutes rather than seconds. This is undoubtedly a major strength of advertising online, when compared with most other traditional media.

The success of viral marketing is often based on the concept of 'cool' – if a recipient enjoys the content of an email they will pass it on to their friends or colleagues. Furthermore if something is seen as particularly informative or useful the same rule applies. A buzz can be created around a new product or service at a relatively low cost, by distributing a cleverly constructed campaign to a specific and targeted database of Internet users. These can include funny videos, entertaining microsites, games, special offers, interesting stories or images that are passed around the online community.

If a viral campaign is based on offensive or controversial content, advertisers must be aware that this can damage brands. Essentially, what makes a successful viral campaign is intelligently created and delivered content in keeping with the values and tone of a brand's communications strategy. The classic example of successful viral marketing is MSN's Hotmail free email service. The company gave away free email addresses. At the end of every message they added the tag 'Get your private, free email at http://www.hotmail.com/'.

Opinion leaders

Communication researchers propose a social structure view of interpersonal communication. They see society as consisting of *cliques,* small groups whose members interact frequently. Clique members are similar and their closeness facilitates effective communication but also insulates the clique from new ideas. The challenge is to create more openness so that cliques exchange information with others in society. This can be helped by people who function as *liaisons* and connect two or more cliques without belonging to either, and *bridges*, people who belong to one clique and are linked to another. Companies can take several steps to stimulate personal influence channels to work on their behalf. 'Marketing memo: How to start a buzz fire' describes some techniques.

Marketing memo

How to start a buzz fire

Marketers can take a number of positive steps to increase the likelihood of securing positive word-of-mouth advantages.

- **Identify influential individuals and companies and devote extra effort towards them**: Purchase influencers such as checkout counter staff and user focus groups can be contacted. In business-to-business markets large corporate customers, industry analysts and journalists can be encouraged to spread the word.

- **Supply key 'influencers' with samples**.

- **Work with local influencers such as radio presenters and TV journalists**.

- **Develop word-of-mouth referral channels to build business**: Businesses can encourage customers to recommend them to others by offering incentives such as a saving on their next purchase.

- **Provide compelling information that customers want to tell friends and professional communities**.

Sources: S. Moldavan, J. Goldenberg and A. Chattopadhyay (2006) What drives word of mouth? the roles of product quality and usefulness, MSI Report No. 06-111, Cambridge, MA: Marketing Science Institute. Also consider M. Hughes (2005) *Buzzmarketing: Get Your People to Talk About Your Stuff*, published by Penguin/Portfolio.

Blogs

Regularly updated online journals or diaries have become an important outlet for word of mouth. They vary widely – some are personal for close friends and families, others are designed to appeal to and reach a large audience. Internet users are increasingly reading blogs but many still regard market offer information from corporate websites as being more trustworthy. Procter & Gamble are noteworthy users of this digital channel and using it to encourage users to participate in the development of its portfolio of brands.[32] (See also Chapter 4.)

Non-personal communications channels

Non-personal channels are communications directed to more than one person and include media, sales promotions, events and experiences, and public relations.

- **Media**: consist of print media (newspapers and magazines); broadcast media (radio and television); network media (telephone, cable, satellite, wireless); electronic media (audiotape, videotape, videodisk, CD-ROM, Web page); and display media (billboards, signs, posters). Most non-personal messages come through paid media.
- **Sales promotions**: consist of consumer promotions (such as samples, coupons and premiums); trade promotions (such as advertising and display allowances); and business and sales force promotions (contests for sales representatives).
- **Events and experiences**: include sports, arts, entertainment and 'good cause' events as well as less formal activities that create novel brand interactions with consumers.
- **Public relations**: include communications directed internally to employees of the company or externally to consumers, other firms, the government and media.

Billboards can capture the attention of large audiences.
Source: Chris P. Batson/Alamy

Much of the recent growth of non-personal channels has taken place through events and experiences. A company can build its brand image by creating or sponsoring events. Events marketers who once heavily favoured sports events are now using other venues such as art museums, zoos or ice shows to entertain clients and employees. HSBC and IBM sponsor symphony performances and art exhibits; Visa is an active sponsor of the Olympics; and Harley-Davidson sponsors annual motorcycle rallies.

Companies are searching for better ways to quantify the benefits of sponsorship and demanding greater accountability from event owners and organisers. They are also creating events designed to surprise the public and create a buzz. Many amount to guerrilla marketing tactics. But if not done properly, they can backfire and have unintended consequences.

Guerrilla marketing – getting noticed

Guerrilla marketing is an unconventional approach originally intended to assist small businesses to get them noticed in markets where the conventional media are cluttered. It is now increasingly being used by large businesses to achieve an instant impact. People in Parliament Square in London were either amused or shocked one night in 1999 when they saw that a 60-foot high image of the actress Gail Porter's bare backside had been projected on to the Houses of Parliament. The deed was perpetrated by the magazine *FHM* to promote its poll to find the sexiest women in town. Although of short duration the stunt was successful, leading to increased sales of the magazine and boosting advertising revenue. Less outrageous have been the attention-seeking activity of firms such as First Group, National Van Rental and Thameslink.

Whilst the *FHM* magazine stunt amused many, Unilever suffered some bad WOM as a result of an Internet guerrilla attack. Raunchy images from a commercial for its Lynx body spray were sliced into a Dove video urging parents to protect girls from negative images of women.[33]

The increased use of attention-getting events is a response to the fragmentation of media: consumers can turn to hundreds of cable channels, thousands of magazine titles and millions of Internet pages. Events can create attention, although whether they have a lasting effect on brand awareness, knowledge or preference will vary considerably, depending on the quality of the product, the event itself, and its execution.

Integration of communications channels

Although one-to-one communication is often more effective than mass communication, mass media is the major means of communicating to large target audiences. Mass communications affect personal attitudes and behaviour through a two-step process. Ideas often flow from radio, television and print to opinion leaders, and from these to the less media-involved population groups. This two-step flow has several implications. First, the influence of mass media on public opinion is not as direct, powerful and automatic as marketers have supposed. It is mediated by opinion leaders, people whose opinions others seek, or who carry their opinions to others. Second, the two-step flow challenges the notion that consumption styles are primarily influenced by a 'trickle-down' or 'trickle-up' effect from mass media. People interact primarily within their own social groups and acquire ideas from opinion leaders in their groups. Third, two-step communication suggests that mass communicators should direct messages specifically to opinion leaders and let them carry the message to others.

▽ Establishing the total marketing communications budget

One of the most difficult marketing decisions is determining how much to spend on promotion. Industries and companies vary considerably in how much they spend on promotion. Expenditure might be 40–45 per cent of sales in the cosmetics industry and 5–10 per cent in the industrial equipment industry. Within a given industry, there are low- and high-spending companies. How do companies decide on the promotion budget? The most common methods are briefly described below.

Affordable method

Many companies set the promotion budget at what they think the company can afford. The affordable method completely ignores the role of promotion as an investment and the immediate impact of promotion on sales volume. It leads to an uncertain annual budget, which makes long-range planning difficult.

Percentage-of-sales method

Many companies set promotion expenditures at a specified percentage of sales (either current or anticipated) or of the sales price. Car manufacturers typically budget a fixed percentage for promotion based on the planned car price. Oil companies set the appropriation at a small fraction of a euro for each litre of petrol sold under their own label.

Supporters of the percentage-of-sales method see a number of advantages. First, promotion expenditures will vary with what the company can afford. This satisfies financial managers, who believe expenses should be closely related to the movement of corporate sales over the business cycle. Second, it encourages management to think of the relationship between promotion cost, selling price and profit per unit. Third, it encourages stability when competing firms spend approximately the same percentage of their sales on promotion.

In spite of these advantages, the percentage-of-sales method has little to justify it. It views sales as the determiner of promotion rather than as the result. It leads to a budget set by the availability of funds rather than by market opportunities. It discourages experimentation with countercyclical promotion or aggressive spending. Dependence on year-to-year sales fluctuations interferes with long-range planning. There is no logical basis for choosing the specific percentage, except what has been done in the past or what competitors are doing. Finally, it does not encourage building the promotion budget by determining what each product and territory deserves.

Competitive parity method

Some companies set their promotion budget to achieve share-of-voice parity with competitors. There are two supporting arguments. One is that competitors' expenditures represent the collective wisdom of the industry. The other is that maintaining competitive parity prevents promotion wars. Neither argument is valid. There are no grounds for believing that competitors know better. Company reputations, resources, opportunities and objectives differ so much that promotion budgets are hardly a guide. Furthermore there is no evidence that budgets based on competitive parity discourage promotion wars.

Objective-and-task method

The objective-and-task method calls upon marketers to develop promotion budgets by defining specific objectives, determining the tasks that must be performed to achieve these objectives, and estimating the costs of performing these tasks. The sum of these costs is the proposed promotion budget.

For example, suppose a company wants to introduce a new market offering, they need to:[34]

1 Establish the market share goal.
2 Determine the percentage of the market that should be reached.
3 Determine the percentage of aware prospects that should be persuaded to try the brand.
4 Determine the number of advertising impressions per 1 per cent trial rate.
5 Determine the number of gross rating points that would have to be purchased.
6 Determine the necessary advertising budget on the basis of the average cost of buying a gross rating point.

The objective-and-task method has the advantage of requiring management to declare its assumptions about the relationship between the amount spent, exposure levels, trial rates and regular usage.

A major question is how much weight marketing communications should receive in relationship to alternatives such as market offering improvement, lower prices or better service. The answer depends on where the company's market offerings/products are in their life cycles (see Chapter 11), whether they are commodities or highly differentiable products, whether they are routinely needed or must be 'sold', and other considerations. Marketing communications budgets tend to be higher when there is low channel support, much change in the marketing programme over time, many hard-to-reach customers, more complex customer decision making, differentiated products and non-homogeneous customer needs, and frequent product purchases in small quantities.[35]

Other methods focus on financial considerations.

Modelling

This uses a variety of econometric and simulation techniques to model how various spend levels will affect performance in terms of awareness rating, revenue flow, and profitability. An example is provided by Unilever's AMTES market-testing model.

Payback period

Calculates the amount of exposure time needed to redeem the budgeted cost of the marketing communications.

Profit optimisation

This seeks to track the point at which the marginal revenue from the spend exceeds the marginal costs. While fine in theory this approach is very difficult to implement in highly competitive markets although hindsight can provide important lessons.

Ideally and in theory marketing managers should establish the total communications budget so that the marginal profit from the last communication euro just equals the marginal profit from the last euro in the best communication cases. Implementing this principle, however, is virtually impossible as customers' responses are influenced by a host of dynamic variables, many of which are beyond the control of marketing management.

▽ Deciding on the marketing communications mix

Companies must allocate the marketing communications budget over the eight major modes of communication – advertising, sales promotion, public relations and publicity, events and experiences, direct marketing, interactive marketing, word-of-mouth marketing, and the sales force. Within the same industry, companies can differ considerably in their media and channel choices. The Avon cosmetics company concentrates its promotional funds on personal selling, whereas Revlon spends heavily on advertising. Electrolux spent heavily on a door-to-door sales force for years, whereas Hoover has relied more on advertising. 'Breakthrough marketing: Ocean Spray' shows how that company has used a variety of communication vehicles to turn their sales fortunes around.

Companies are always searching for ways to gain efficiency by replacing one communications tool with others. Many companies are replacing some field sales activity with advertisements, direct mail and telemarketing. The substitutability among communications tools explains why marketing functions need to be coordinated.

Characteristics of the marketing communications mix

Each communication tool has its own unique characteristics and costs. These are briefly reviewed here and discussed in more detail in Chapter 20.

Advertising

Advertising reaches geographically dispersed buyers. It can build up a long-term image for a product (Cadbury's Dairy Milk advertisements) or trigger quick sales (the DFS furniture upholstery advertisements in the United Kingdom). Certain forms of advertising such as TV can require a large budget, whereas other forms such as newspaper do not. Just the presence of advertising might have an effect on sales: consumers might believe that a heavily advertised brand

Breakthrough marketing

Ocean Spray

Ocean Spray faced a tough situation in 2004. Domestic sales had been flat for five years and sales in the juice category as a whole suffered from concerns over sugar, increased competition from other types of beverages that were adding juice, and growing consumer interest in consumption of other beverages such as water and sports drinks. Cranberry juice was known among women as an effective way to keep the urinary tract healthy – not necessarily a product benefit with broad appeal.

Ocean Spray, an agricultural cooperative of growers of cranberries in the United States, decided to make use of expert marketing consultancy to arrest the decline in sales. The cranberry was repositioned as a 'surprisingly versatile little fruit that supplies modern-day benefits', through a true '360-degree' campaign that used all facets of marketing communications to reach consumers in a variety of settings. The intent was to support the full range of market offerings – cranberry sauce, fruit juices, and dried cranberries in different forms.

The advertising strategy promoted the unique DNA of the Ocean Spray Cooperative and the realisation that the heart of the brand was born in the cranberry bogs and remained there still. The agency decided to focus on the bog to tell an authentic, honest and perhaps surprising story dubbed 'Straight from the Bog'. The campaign was designed to also reinforce two key brand benefits – that Ocean Spray products tasted good and were good for you.

PR played a crucial role. Miniature bogs were brought to New York and were featured on a local TV (*NBC Today*) show morning segment. The event reached over 23 million people through related media pick-up. A 'Bogs across America Tour' brought the experience to Los Angeles, Chicago, and even London. Television and print advertising featured two natural-looking and natural-sounding growers (depicted by actors) standing waist deep in a bog talking, often humorously, about what they did. The advertisements were the highest rated ever for Ocean Spray and improved both awareness and persuasion for the two key benefits.

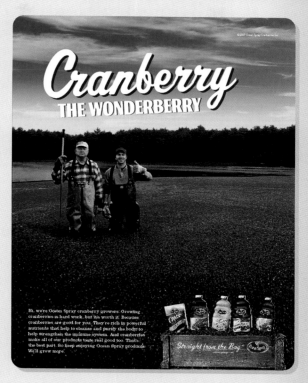

Despite a decline in sales of the entire fruit juice category, Ocean Spray's inventive campaign grew sales of all its cranberry products by a remarkable 10 per cent.

Source: Used by permission of Ocean Spray Cranberries, Inc.

The campaign also included a website, in-store displays and external events for consumers as well as internal ones for members of the growers' cooperative itself. The campaign hit the mark, lifting sales by 10 per cent despite continued decline in the fruit juice category.

Sources: L. Peterson (2006) Breakaway brands: Ocean Spray tells it straight from the bog, *MediaPost*, 9 October; F. J. Kelly III and B. Silverstein (2005) *The Breakaway Brand*, New York: McGraw-Hill.

---

must offer 'good value'.[36] Because of the many forms and uses of advertising, it is difficult to make generalisations about it.[37] Yet a few observations are worthwhile:

1 **Pervasiveness**: Advertising permits the seller to repeat a message many times. It also allows the buyer to receive and compare the messages of various competitors. Large-scale advertising says something positive about the seller's size, power and success.

2 **Amplified expressiveness**: Advertising provides opportunities for dramatising the company and its products through the artful use of print, sound and colour.

3 **Impersonality**: The audience does not feel obligated to pay attention or respond to advertising. Advertising is a monologue in front of, not a dialogue with, the audience.

Sales promotion

Companies use sales promotion tools – coupons, contests, premiums, and so on – to draw a stronger and quicker buyer response, including short-run effects such as highlighting product offers and boosting sagging sales. Sales promotion tools offer three distinctive benefits:

1 **Communication**: They gain attention and may lead the consumer to the product.

2 **Incentive**: They incorporate some concession, inducement or contribution that gives value to the consumer.

3 **Invitation**: They include a distinct invitation to engage in the transaction now.

Public relations and publicity

Marketers tend to underuse public relations, yet a well-thought-out programme coordinated with the other communications mix elements can be extremely effective, especially if a company needs to challenge consumers' misconceptions.

▽ Dove: comedy tour

The Lexis PR agency was retained to energise the UK launch of Dove's new body wash range. Building on research carried out by the Dove campaign's advertising agency Lexis focused on the finding that many women felt uncomfortable with the reality of their bodies. To boost potential consumer confidence Lexis decided to promote the notion of a female-only comedy tour so that women could unite, laugh at themselves and celebrate their diversity. The tour had three stages – invitation, activation and post-tour activation. During the invitation stage consumers were made aware of a programme of events featuring direct marketing, PR, on-pack, radio and TV. The tour itself (activation) involved comedians including Arabella Weir and Julia Morris appearing at ten comedy venues around the United Kingdom over a two-month period. The final stage (post-tour activation) took the form of PR reportage to secure views on how well the tour was received.

The tour was a great success with both the media and consumers. The PR platform generated PR coverage from 13 national sources, 57 regional sources, 6 women's consumer titles, 5 advertorials, 18 competitions, 59 pieces of broadcast coverage and 25 pieces of online coverage. Consumers who attended the events were given samples (2500). The news value of the campaign created further post-tour 'talkability' in the media.

Source: http://www.lexispr.com/case/show/52.

The appeal of public relations and publicity is based on three distinctive qualities:

1 **High credibility**: News stories and features are more authentic and credible to readers than advertisements.

2 **Ability to catch buyers off guard**: Public relations can reach prospects who prefer to avoid sales people and advertisements.

3 **Dramatisation**: Public relations has the potential for dramatising a company or product.

Events and experiences

There are many advantages to events and experiences, among which are:

1 **Relevance**: A well-chosen event or experience can be seen as highly relevant because the consumer gets personally involved.

2 **Involvement**: Given their live, real-time quality, events and experiences are more actively engaging for consumers.

3 **Implicitness**: Events are an indirect 'soft sell'.

Direct and interactive marketing

Direct and interactive marketing takes many forms – over the phone, online or in person. They share three distinctive characteristics. Direct and interactive marketing messages are:

1 **Customised**: The message can be prepared to appeal to the addressed individual.

2 **Up to date**: A message can be prepared very quickly.

3 **Interactive**: The message can be changed depending on the person's response.

Word-of-mouth marketing

Word of mouth also takes many forms online or offline. Three noteworthy characteristics are:

1 **Credible**: Because people trust others they know and respect, word of mouth can be highly influential.

2 **Personal**: Word of mouth can be a very intimate dialogue that reflects personal facts, opinions and experiences.

3 **Timely**: It occurs when people want it to and when they are most interested, and it often follows noteworthy or meaningful events or experiences.

Personal selling

Personal selling is the most effective tool at later stages of the buying process, particularly in building up buyer preference, conviction and action. Personal selling has three distinctive qualities:

1 **Personal interaction**: Personal selling creates an immediate and interactive episode between two or more persons. Each party is able to observe the other's reactions.

2 **Cultivation**: Personal selling also permits all kinds of relationships to spring up, ranging from a matter-of-fact selling relationship to a deep personal friendship.

3 **Response**: The buyer feels under some obligation following the sales talk.

Factors in setting the marketing communications mix

Companies must consider several factors in developing their communications mix: type of market offering, consumer readiness to make a purchase, and stage in the traditional product life cycle. Also important is the company's market ranking.

Type of product market

Communications mix allocations vary between consumer and business markets. Consumer marketers tend to spend comparatively more on sales promotion and advertising; business marketers tend to spend comparatively more on personal selling. In general, personal selling is used more with complex, expensive and risky goods and in markets with fewer and larger sellers (hence, business markets).

Although marketers use advertising less than sales calls in business-to-business markets, advertising still plays a significant role:

- Advertising can provide an introduction to the company and its products.

- If the product has new features, advertising can explain them.

- Reminder advertising is more economical than sales calls.

- Advertisements offering brochures and carrying the company's phone number are an effective way to generate leads for sales representatives.

- Sales representatives can use copies of the company's advertisements to legitimise their company and products.
- Advertising can remind customers how to use the product and reassure them about their purchase.

A number of studies have underscored advertising's role in business markets. Advertising combined with personal selling can increase sales over what would have resulted if there had been no advertising. Corporate advertising can improve a company's reputation and improve the sales force's chances of obtaining a favourable first hearing and early adoption of the product.[38] It can also help to position or reposition a business-to-business market offering.

▽ Jato Dynamics

Jato Dynamics, supplier of information to the automotive industry, had not refreshed its brand image since it launched in the United Kingdom in 1984. Since then the business had grown significantly, and now has offices in 45 countries. Going forwards, it wanted to think more about its key customer markets and tailoring its communications and literature to suit each of these as it strove to drive new business.

There is a general perception that if there's a choice of 'evolution' or 'revolution' then branding companies will go for the less risky visual 'revolution'. Classic examples of the suitability of both are the visual histories of BP and Shell. BP's one big change triggered by merger and repositioning, and Shell's nine visual updates since 1990 (an average of one every two years) symbolise a reaction to change. Both could argue they're right.

Source: C. Weekes (2007) Jato Dynamics needed to rev up its image and show its motor industry customers that it was moving with the times, B2B Marketing online, 14 May.

Personal selling can also make a strong contribution in consumer goods marketing. Some consumer marketers use the sales force mainly to collect weekly orders from dealers and to see that sufficient stock is on the shelf. Yet an effectively trained company sales force can make four important contributions:

1 **Increased stock position**: Sales representatives can persuade dealers to take more stock and devote more shelf space to the company's brand.
2 **Enthusiasm building**: Sales representatives can build dealer enthusiasm by dramatising planned advertising and sales promotion back-up.
3 **Missionary selling**: Sales representatives can sign up more dealers.
4 **Key account management**: Sales representatives can take responsibility for growing business with the most important accounts.

Buyer readiness stage

Communication tools vary in cost effectiveness at different stages of buyer readiness. Figure 19.5 shows the relative cost effectiveness of three communication tools. Advertising and publicity play the most important roles in the awareness-building stage. Customer comprehension is primarily affected by advertising and personal selling. Customer conviction is influenced mostly by personal selling. Closing the sale is influenced mostly by personal selling and sales promotion. Reordering is also affected mostly by personal selling and sales promotion, and somewhat by reminder advertising.

Product life cycle stage

Communication tools also vary in cost effectiveness at different stages of the product life cycle (see Chapter 14). In the introduction stage advertising, events and experiences, and publicity

Figure 19.5 Cost effectiveness of three different communication tools at different buyer readiness stages

have the highest cost effectiveness, followed by personal selling to gain distribution coverage and sales promotion and direct marketing to induce trial. In the growth stage, demand has its own momentum through word of mouth. In the maturity stage advertising, events and experiences, and personal selling all become more important. In the decline stage sales promotion continues strong, other communication tools are reduced, and sales people give the product only minimal attention.

Measuring communication results

Senior managers want to know the *outcomes* and *revenues* resulting from their communications investments. Too often, however, their communications directors supply only *outputs* and *expenses*: press clipping counts, numbers of advertisements placed and media costs. In fairness, the marketing communications directors try to translate outputs into intermediate outputs such as reach and frequency, recall and recognition scores, persuasion changes and cost-per-thousand calculations. Ultimately, behaviour change measures capture the real pay-off.

After implementing the marketing communications plan, the marketing communications director must measure its impact on the target audience. Members of the target audience are asked whether they recognise or recall the message, how many times they saw it, what points they recall, how they felt about the message, and their previous and current attitudes towards the product and the company. The communicator should also collect behavioural measures of audience response, such as how many people bought the product, liked it and talked to others about it.

Figure 19.6 provides an example of good feedback measurement. In this case 80 per cent of the consumers in the total market are aware of brand A, 60 per cent have tried it, and only 20 per cent who have tried it are satisfied. This indicates that the marketing communications programme is effective in creating awareness, but the market offering fails to meet consumer expectations. In contrast, 40 per cent of the consumers in the total market are aware of brand B, and

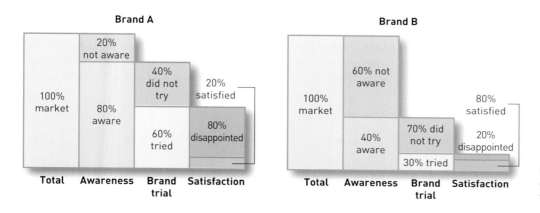

Figure 19.6 Current consumer states for two brands

only 30 per cent have tried it, but 80 per cent of those who have tried it are satisfied. In this case, the marketing communications programme needs to be strengthened to take advantage of the brand's power.

▽ Managing the integrated marketing communications process

As defined by the American Association of Advertising Agencies, **integrated marketing communications (IMC)** is a concept of marketing communications planning that recognises the added value of a comprehensive plan. Such a plan evaluates the strategic roles of a variety of communications disciplines – for example general advertising, direct response, sales promotion and public relations – and combines these disciplines to provide clarity, consistency and maximum impact through the seamless integration of messages. Nike have adopted the IMC concept and their vice-president for global and category management has gone on record saying that, 'We create demand for our brand by being flexible about how we tell the story. We do not rigidly stay with one approach . . . We have an integrated marketing model that involves all elements of the marketing mix'.[39]

Unfortunately, many companies still rely on one or two communication tools. This practice persists in spite of the fragmenting of mass markets into a multitude of minimarkets, each requiring its own approach; the proliferation of new types of media; and the growing sophistication of consumers. The wide range of communication tools, messages and audiences makes it imperative that companies move towards integrated marketing communications. However, despite its potential many firms seem to be slow to accept it seriously.[40] Companies must adopt a '360-degree view' of themselves and consumers to fully understand all the different ways that communications can affect consumer behaviour and so benefit their businesses.

Media companies and advertising agencies are expanding their capabilities to offer multi-platform deals for marketers. For example, newspapers and magazines have been frantically formulating digital strategies, such as adding videos to their homepages, to increase advertising revenue. In the United Kingdom the *Daily Telegraph* and *Financial Times*, for instance, offer online video segments on their websites carrying topic, news and advertising material. These expanded capabilities make it easier for marketers to assemble various media properties in an integrated communication programme.

Coordinating media

Media coordination can occur across and within media types, but marketers should combine personal and non-personal communications channels to achieve maximum impact. Imagine a marketer using a single tool in a 'one-shot' effort to reach and sell to a prospect. An example of a *single-vehicle, single-stage campaign* is a one-time mailing offering a cookware item. A *single-vehicle, multiple-stage campaign* would rely on successive mailings to the same prospect. Magazine publishers, for example, send about four renewal notices to a household before giving up. A more powerful approach is the *multiple-vehicle, multiple-stage campaign*. Consider the sequence in Figure 19.7.

Multiple media deployed within a tightly defined time frame can increase message reach and impact. This strategy is commonly seen in the marketing of financial services. Research has also shown that promotions can be more effective when combined with advertising.[41] The awareness

Figure 19.7 Example of a multiple-vehicle, multiple-stage communication campaign

and attitudes created by advertising campaigns can improve the success of more direct sales pitches. Many companies are coordinating their online and offline communications activities. Listing Web addresses in advertisements (especially print ones) and on packages allows people to more fully explore a company's wares, find store locations and get market offering information. For example, Danone makes it a priority to drive traffic to its Danone Yogurt homepage, so the company can benefit from the twin paybacks of (1) forging direct relationships with customers; and (2) building a database of its best customers, whose loyalty can be strengthened with more targeted coupon and direct mail promotional efforts.[42] When Dutch financial services firm ING Group launched its brand into other European countries, it paired TV and print advertisements with online advertisements.

> To learn how Indian businesses and government leaders put together an elaborate marketing and PR effort to showcase India as an attractive place for business, go to www.prenhall.com/kotler

Implementing IMC

Integrated marketing communications has been slow to take hold for several reasons. Large companies often employ several different communications specialists who may know comparatively little about the other communication tools.[43] Further complicating matters is that many global companies use a large number of advertising agencies located in different countries and serving different divisions, resulting in uncoordinated communications and image diffusion. One company that has managed to coordinate the integrated marketing effort of a number of agencies and internal departments is British Gas.

▽ British Gas

British Gas holds twice-monthly planning meetings with all the agencies working on various aspects of an integrated marketing campaign – from the advertising agency to the PR agency to the company's own internal communications department. These different factions are 'integrated' because British Gas retains them on a project basis and assigns a budget to a specific business initiative rather than to a media channel. Bringing planners from various disciplines together in an open forum to discuss their views shatters their preconceptions. In a recent British Gas campaign around energy efficiency, the company used this collaborative approach and logged 1 million responses from people who wanted to learn more about the issue. A spokesperson commented 'We all got behind the single objective and message, starting with advertising, and followed by direct and online marketing. But integration is not just about marketing communications. It is about everything from PR to the service experience to internal communications.'

Source: S. Bashford (2006) Collaboration is imperative, *Marketing*, 13 December, 4.

Today, however, a few large agencies have substantially improved their integrated offerings. To facilitate one-stop shopping, major advertising agencies have acquired promotion agencies, public relations firms, package-design consultancies, website developers and direct mail houses. These agencies are redefining themselves as *communications companies* that assist clients to improve their overall communications effectiveness by offering strategic and practical advice on many forms of communication. Many international clients have opted to put a substantial portion of their communications work through one full-service agency. An example is IBM turning all its advertising over to Ogilvy to attain uniform branding. The result is integrated and more effective marketing communications at a much lower total communications cost.

Integrated marketing communications can produce stronger message consistency and help to build brand equity and create greater sales impact.[44] It forces management to think about every way the customer comes into contact with the company, how the company communicates its positioning, the relative importance of each vehicle, and timing issues. It gives someone the responsibility – where none existed before – to unify the company's brand images and messages as they progress through a host of company activities. IMC should improve the company's ability to reach the right customers with the right messages at the right time and in the right place.[45]

▽ *Quo vadis?*

In today's buyers' markets consumers expect quality and price attributes offered by companies to meet and – preferably – exceed their CPV requirements (see Chapter 11). They expect firms to deliver a desirable customer experience by integrating information technology, branding, communications and entertainment. The progression from the traditional FMCG marketing and branding approach toward *experiential marketing* is a key theme that is discussed in Chapter 21.

'Marketing memo: How integrated is your IMC programme?' provides some guidelines.

Marketing memo

How integrated is your IMC programme?

In assessing the collective impact of an IMC programme, the marketer's overriding goal is to create the most effective and efficient marketing communications programme possible. The following six criteria can help determine whether marketing communications are truly integrated:

1 **Coverage** Coverage is the proportion of the audience reached by each communication option employed, as well as how much overlap exists among communication options. In other words, to what extent do different communication options reach the designated target market and the same or different consumers making up that market?

2 **Contribution** Contribution is the inherent ability of a marketing communication to create the desired response and communication effects from consumers in the absence of exposure to any other marketing communication option. How much does marketing communication affect consumer processing and build awareness, enhance image, elicit responses and induce sales?

3 **Commonality** Commonality is the extent to which *common* associations are reinforced across communication options, that is, the extent to which information conveyed by different marketing communication options share meaning. The consistency and cohesiveness of the brand image is important because it determines how easily existing associations and responses can be

recalled and how easily additional associations and responses can become linked to the brand in memory.

4 **Complementarity** Marketing communication options are often more effective when used in tandem. Complementarity relates to the extent to which *different* associations and linkages are emphasised across marketing communication options. Different brand associations may be most effectively established by capitalising on those marketing communication options best suited to eliciting a particular consumer response or establishing a particular type of brand association.[46]

5 **Versatility** In any integrated marketing communication programme, when consumers are exposed to a particular marketing communication, some will already have been exposed to other marketing communications for the brand, and some will not have had any prior exposure. Versatility refers to the extent to which a marketing communication option is robust and 'works' for different groups of consumers. The ability of a marketing communication to work at two levels – effectively communicating to consumers who have or have *not* seen other communications – is critically important.

6 **Cost** Marketers must weigh evaluations of marketing communications on all these criteria against their cost to arrive at the most effective *and* efficient communications programme.

▽ SUMMARY

1 Modern marketing calls for more than developing a good product, pricing it attractively and making it accessible to target customers. Companies must also communicate with present and potential stakeholders and with the general public.

2 The marketing communications mix consists of eight major modes of communication: advertising, sales promotion, public relations and publicity, events and experiences, direct marketing, interactive marketing, word-of-mouth marketing and personal selling.

3 The communications process consists of nine elements: sender, receiver, message, media, encoding, decoding, response, feedback and noise. To get their messages through, marketers must encode their messages in a way that takes into account how the target audience usually decodes messages. They must also transmit the message through efficient media that reach the target audience and develop feedback channels to monitor response to the message.

4 Developing effective communications involves eight steps: (1) identify the target audience; (2) determine the communications objectives; (3) design the communications; (4) select the communications channels; (5) establish the total communications budget; (6) decide on the communications mix; (7) measure the communications results; and (8) manage the integrated marketing communications process.

5 In identifying the target audience, the marketer needs to close any gap that exists between current public perception and the image sought. Communications objectives may involve category need, brand awareness,

brand attitude or brand purchase intention. Formulating the communication requires solving three problems: what to say (message strategy), how to say it (creative strategy), and who should say it (message source). Communications channels may be personal (advocate, expert and social channels) or non-personal (media, atmospheres and events). The objective-and-task method of setting the promotion budget, which calls upon marketers to develop their budgets by defining specific objectives, is the most desirable.

6 In deciding on the marketing communications mix, marketers must examine the distinct advantages and costs of each communication tool and the company's market rank. They must also consider the type of product market in which they are selling, how ready consumers are to make a purchase, and the product's stage in the product life cycle. Measuring the effectiveness of the marketing communications mix involves asking members of the target audience whether they recognise or recall the communication, how many times they saw it, what points they recall, how they felt about the communication, and their previous and current attitudes toward the product and the company.

7 Managing and coordinating the entire communications process calls for integrated marketing communications: marketing communications planning that recognises the added value of a comprehensive plan which evaluates the strategic roles of a variety of communications disciplines and combines these disciplines to provide clarity, consistency and maximum impact through the seamless integration of discrete messages.

▽ APPLICATIONS

Marketing debate

Has TV advertising lost power? Long deemed the most successful medium, television advertising has received increased criticism for being too expensive and, even worse, no longer as effective as it used to be. Critics maintain that consumers tune out too many advertisements and that it is difficult to make a strong impression. The future, claim some, is with online advertising. Supporters of TV advertising disagree, contending that the multisensory impact of TV is unsurpassed and that no other media option offers the same potential impact.

Take a position: TV advertising has faded in importance *versus* TV advertising is still the most powerful advertising medium.

Marketing discussion

Pick a brand and go to its website. Locate as many forms of communication as you can find. Conduct an informal communications audit. What do you notice? How consistent are the different communications?

▽ REFERENCES

[1]R. Rothenberg (2007) Dove effort gives packaged-goods marketers lessons for the future, *Advertising Age*, 5 March; T. Howard (2005) Ad campaign tells women to celebrate who they are, *USA Today*, 8 July; J. Neff (2004) In Dove ads, normal is the new beautiful, *Advertising Age*, 27 September; www.campaignforrealbeauty.com.

[2]X. Luo and N. Donthu (2006) Marketing's credibility: a longitudinal investigation of marketing communication productivity and shareholder value, *Journal of Marketing*, 70 (October), 70–91.

[3]D. Kiley (2005) Hey advertisers, TiVo is your friend, *BusinessWeek*, 17 October, pp. 97–8; L. Kaplan Thaler and R. Koval (with Delia Marshall) (2003) *Bang! Getting Your Message Heard in a Noisy World*, New York: Currency.

[4]L. Story (2007) Anywhere the eye can see, it's likely to see an ad, *New York Times*, 15 January; L. Petrecca (2006) Product placement: you can't escape it, *USA Today*, 11 October.

[5]Some of these definitions are adapted from P. D. Bennett (ed.) (1995) *Dictionary of Marketing Terms*, Chicago: American Marketing Association.

[6]T. Duncan and S. Moriarty (2006) How integrated marketing communications 'touch points' can operationalize the service-dominant logic, in R. F. Lusch and S. L. Vargo (eds.) *The Service-Dominant Logic of Marketing: Dialog, Debate, and Directions*, Armonk, NY: M.E. Sharpe; T. Duncan (2005) *Principles of Advertising and IMC*, 2nd edn, New York: McGraw-Hill/Irwin.

[7]D. Vakratsas and T. Ambler (1999) How advertising works: what do we really know? *Journal of Marketing*, 63(1), 26–43.

[8]This section is based on the excellent text, J. R. Rossiter and L. Percy (1997) *Advertising and Promotion Management*, 2nd edn, New York: McGraw-Hill.

[9]J. F. Engel, R. D. Blackwell and P. W Minard (2001) *Consumer Behavior*, 9th edn, Fort Worth, TX: Dryden.

[10]C. I. Hovland, A. A. Lumsdaine and F. D. Sheffield (1948) *Experiments on Mass Communication*, Princeton, NJ: Princeton University Press, Volume 3, Chapter 8; H. E. Crowley and W. D. Hoyer (1994) An integrative framework for understanding two-sided persuasion, *Journal of Consumer Research*, March, 561–74. For an alternative viewpoint see G. E. Belch (1983) The effects of message modality on one and two-sided advertising messages, in R. P. Bagozzi and A. M. Tybout (eds.) *Advances in Consumer Research*, Ann Arbour, MI: Association for Consumer Research, pp. 21–6.

[11]C. P. Haugtvedt and D. T. Wegener (1994) Message order effects in persuasion: an attitude strength perspective, *Journal of Consumer Research*, June, 205–18: H. R. Unnava, R. E. Burnkrant and S. Erevelles (1994) Effects of presentation order and communication modality on recall and attitude, *Journal of Consumer Research*, December, 48–90.

[12]M. R. Solomon, *Consumer Behavior*, 7th edn, Upper Saddle River, NJ: Prentice Hall.

[13]Some recent research on humour in advertising, for example, includes H. Shabbir and D. Thwaites (2007) The use of humor to mask deceptive advertising: it's no laughing matter, *Journal of Advertising*, 36 (Summer), 75–85; T. W. Cline and J. J. Kellaris (2007) The influence of humor strength and humor message relatedness on ad memorability: a dual process model, *Journal of Advertising*, 36 (Spring), 55–67; H. Shanker Krishnan and D. Chakravarti (2003) A process analysis of the effects of humorous advertising executions on brand claims memory, *Journal of Consumer Psychology*, 13(3), 230–45.

[14]R. Pieters and M. Wedel (2004) Attention capture and transfer in advertising: brand, pictorial, and text-size effects, *Journal of Marketing*, 68 (April), 36–50.

[15]H. C. Kelman and C. I. Hovland (1953) Reinstatement of the communication in delayed measurement of opinion change, *Journal of Abnormal and Social Psychology*, 48 (July), 327–35.

[16]D. J. Moore, J. C. Mowen and R. Reardon (1994) Multiple sources in advertising appeals: when product endorsers are paid by the advertising sponsor, *Journal of the Academy of Marketing Science*, Summer, 234–43.

[17]www.celebrityendorsements.co.uk; A. Byrne, M. Whitehead, S. Breen (2003) The naked truth of celebrity endorsement, *British Food Journal*, 105(4/5), 288–96; R. Adams and J. Finch (2003) Take one celebrity chef, *The Guardian*, 1 January.

[18]J. Sloane (2003) Gorgeous George, *Fortune Small Business*, June, 36.

[19]C. E. Osgood and P. H. Tannenbaum (1995) The principles of congruity in the prediction of attitude change, *Psychological Review*, 62 (January), 42–55.

[20]Celebrity endorsements less effective for many products, says research, Press Release, 27 February 2007, Bath, England: University of Bath (www.bath.ac.uk/news/2007/2/27/celebrity-ads.html).

[21]M. Callow and L. Schiffman (2002) Implicit meaning in visual print advertisements: a cross-cultural examination of the contextual communication effect, *International Journal of Advertising*, 21(2), 259–77; D. Seno and B. A. Lukas (2007) The equity effect of product endorsement by celebrities: a conceptual framework, from a co-branding perspective, *European Journal of Marketing*, 41(1/2), 121–34.

[22]L. Carter (2008) Hugh Grant backs Marie Curie cancer case appeal in his mother's memory, *The Daily Telegraph*, 25 February.

[23]A. Sherwin (2004) It's crunch time for cartoon adverts, *The Times*, 23 july.

[24]EU to try again on tobacco advertising ban, *Associated Press*, 9 May 2001; R. C. Morais (1998) Mobile mayhem, *Forbes*, 6 July, p. 138; Working in harmony, *Soap Perfumery & Cosmetics*, 1 July, p. 27; R. Harrabin (1998) A commercial break for parents, *Independent*, 8 September, p. 19; N. Donthu (1998) A cross-country investigation of recall of and attitude toward comparative advertising, *Journal of Advertising*, 27 (June), 111; R. Snoddy (2004) WPP brings local touch to global operations, *The Times*, 12 January; L. Eagle, P. J. Kitche and S. Bulmer (2007) Insights into interpreting integrated marketing communications: a town-nation qualitative comparison, *European Journal of Marketing*, 41(7/8), 956–70.

[25]Rebirth of a salesman, *The Economist*, 14 April 2001.

[26]M. Kiely (1993) Word-of-mouth marketing, *Marketing*, September, 6. See also E. M. Rodger (2003) *Diffusion of Innovation*, 5th edn, New York: Free Press; A. Rindfleisch and C. Moorman (2001) The acquisition and utilization of information in new product alliances: a strength-of-ties perspective, *Journal of Marketing*, April, 1–18; R. East, K. Hammond, W. Lomax and H. Robinson (2005) What is the effect of a recommendation?, *The Marketing Review*, 5(2), 145–57.

[27]I. Mount (2001) Marketing, *Business 2.0*, August–September, 84.

[28]P. R. Smith and J. Taylor (2004) *Marketing Communications: An Integrated Approach*, 4th edn, London: Kogan Page, 590.

[29]D. Stokes and W. Lomax (2002) Taking control of word of mouth marketing: the case of an entrepreneurial hotelier, *Journal of Small Business and Enterprise Development*, 9(4), 349–57; F. F. Reichheld (2003) The one number you need to grow, *Harvard Business Review* (December), 47–54.

[30]J. Kirby and P. Marsden (2005) *Connected Marketing: The Viral Buzz and Word of Mouth Revolution*, London: Butterworth-Heinemann.

[31]A good working definition of viral marketing can be found in A. Vilpponen, S. Winter and S. Sundqvist (2006) Electronic word-of-mouth in online environments: exploring referral network structure and adoption behaviour, *Journal of Interactive Advertising*, 6(2), 71–86.

[32]G. Silverman (2006) How can I help you?, *Financial Times*, 4 February, pp. 16–21.

[33]C. Mortished (2007) Internet guerrilla attack exposes Unilever's 'hypocrisy' of Dove girls and dirty dancers, *The Times*, 3 December.

[34]Adapted from G. Maxwell Ule (1957) A media plan for 'sputnik' cigarettes, *How to Plan Media Strategy*, American Association of Advertising Agencies, Regional Convention, pp. 41–52.

[35]T. C. Kinnear, K. L. Bernhardt, and K. A. Krentler (1995) *Principles of Marketing*, 6th edn, New York: HarperCollins.

[36]K. Sridhar Moorthy and S. A. Hawkins (2005) Advertising repetition and quality perceptions, *Journal of Business Research*, 58 (March), 354–60; A. Kirmani and A. R. Rao (2000) No pain, no gain: a critical review of the literature on signaling unobservable product quality, *Journal of Marketing*, 64 (April), 66–79; A. Kirmani (1990) The effect of perceived advertising costs on brand perceptions, *Journal of Consumer Research*, 17 September, 160–71; A. Kirmani and P. Wright (1989) Money talks: perceived advertising expense and expected product quality, *Journal of Consumer Research*, 16 (December), 344–53.

[37]D. Vakratsas and T. Ambler (1999) How advertising works: what do we really know?, *Journal of Marketing*, 63(1), 26–43.

[38]T. Levitt (1965) *Industrial Purchasing Behavior: A Study in Communication Effects*, Cambridge, MA: Harvard University, Division of Research, Graduate School of Business; J. M. T. Balmer and S. A. Greyser (2006) Corporate marketing: integrating corporate identity, corporate branding, corporate communications, corporate image and corporate reputation, *European Journal of Marketing*, 40(7/8), 730–41; G. O'Malley (2006) Who's leading the way in web marketing? it's Nike, of course, *Advertising Age*, October, D3.

[39]Strategic Direction (2006) The importance of marketing strategy: gaining the competitive edge with integrated marketing communications, General Review, *Strategic Direction*, 22(8), 23–25; A. Gronstedt (2002) *The Customer Century: Lessons from World Class Companies in Integrated Communications*, London: Routledge.

[40]P. A. Naik and K. Raman (2003) Understanding the impact of synergy in multimedia communications, *Journal of Marketing Research*, 40 (November), 375–88; see also P. A. Naik, Kalyan Raman and R. S. Winer (2005) Planning marketing-mix strategies in the presence of interaction effects, *Marketing Science*, 24 (January), 25–34; G. Hughes and C. Fill (2007) Redefining the nature and format of the marketing communications mix, *Marketing Review*, 7(1), 45–57.

[41]S. Neslin (2002) *Sales Promotion*, MSI Relevant Knowledge Series, Cambridge, MA: Marketing Science Institute.

[42]G. Khermouch (2003) The top 5 rules of the ad game, *BusinessWeek*, 20 January, 72–3.

[43]T. Duncan and F. Mulhern (eds.) (2004) A white paper on the status, scope, and future of IMC, New York: McGraw-Hill; O. Holm (2006) Integrated marketing communication: from tactics to strategy, *Corporate Communications: An International Journal*, 11(1), 23–33; P. J. Kitchen (2005) New paradigm: IMC under fire, *Competitiveness Review: An International Journal of Global Competitiveness*, 15(1), 72–80; L. T. Christenson, S. Torp, A. F. Fuat (2005) Integrated marketing communication and postmodernity: an odd couple, *Corporate Communications: An International Journal*, 10(2), 156–67.

[44]S. Madhavaram, V. Badrinarayanan and R. E. McDonald (2005) Integrated marketing communication (IMC) and brand identity as critical components of brand equity strategy, *Journal of Advertising*, 34 (Winter), 69–80; M. Reid, S. Luxton and F. Mavondo (2005) The relationship between integrated marketing communication, market orientation, and brand orientation, *Journal of Advertising*, 34 (Winter), 11–23.

[45]D. E. Schultz and H. Schultz (2003) *IMC, The Next Generation: Five Steps for Delivering Value and Measuring Financial Returns*, New York: McGraw-Hill; D. E. Shultz, S. I. Tannenbaum and R. F. Lauterborn (1992) *Integrated Marketing Communications: Putting It Together and Making It Work*, Lincolnwood, IL: NTC Business Books.

[46]B. Janoff (2006) State Farm asks, 'now what?', *Brandweek*, 8 August; D. L. Vance (2007) Better coverage, *Marketing News*, 15 January, 13–14.

▽ Managing mass and personal communications

Looking out for the family.

The iconic Andrex labrador retriever puppy has been the focus of the Andrex brand's mass and personal communications since 1972, designed to emphasise the attractiveness of Andrex's super-soft luxury toilet tissue.

Source: The Advertising Archives

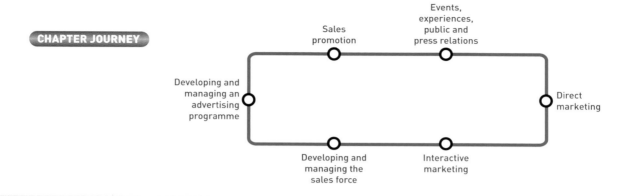

6   How can companies practise effective interactive marketing?

7   What decisions do companies face in designing and managing a sales force?

8   How can sales people improve their selling, negotiating and relationship marketing skills?

Although there has been an increase in the use of personal communications by marketers in recent years (due to the rapid penetration of the Internet and other factors) mass media, if used correctly, can still dramatically improve the fortunes of a brand or company.[1] Today, marketing communications increasingly occur as a kind of personal dialogue between the company and its customers. Companies must ask not only 'How should we reach our customers?' but also 'How should our customers reach us?' and even 'How can our customers reach each other?' Technological advances allow people and companies to communicate with each other through the Internet, fax machines, mobile phones, pagers and wireless appliances. By increasing communication effectiveness and efficiency new technologies have encouraged companies to move from mass communication to more targeted, two-way communications. Consumers now play a much more participatory role in the marketing process.

Kimberly-Clark, the owner of the leading Andrex brand, is the world's largest toilet tissue manufacturer. Since 1972 Andrex has featured an iconic Labrador Retriever puppy in its mass and personal marketing communications strategy. The memorable image of the puppy has been used to convey key value attributes. The luxury two-ply tissue is soft, strong and very long. In addition it is family friendly. According to a poll published in September 2007 the Andrex puppy has become the UK's favourite TV advertising animal. The appeal of the bouncy, friendly puppy has enabled Kimberly-Clark over the years to develop a powerful sales promotion programme. The puppy has its own website, which offers a collection of items including fridge magnets, shoulder bags, toys, a calendar, mouse mat, screen saver, and competitions and interactive games. Over one and a half a million rolls of Andrex are used every day in the United Kingdom. Kimberly-Clark invested £2.5 million in 2007 on the launch of an even longer toilet tissue. The new Longer Lasting toilet tissue branded Andrex Quilts is the only quilted roll on the market and features three plush white layers made into a light and airy quilt that combines the quality attributes of the regular Andrex toilet tissue with 50 per cent more sheets. The Andrex puppy icon has been embossed on to every sheet of Andrex toilet tissue since 2004 to make sure that the icon enjoys maximum exposure. Such is the popularity of the Andrex puppy that in September 2007 it was inducted into the famous London Wax Museum of Madame Tussauds.[2]

Some firms have had great success with advertising, but other marketers are trying to master how best to use mass media in the new communication environment.[3] This chapter examines the nature and use of four mass communication tools – advertising, sales promotion, events and experiences, and public relations and publicity – and how companies personalise their marketing communications. Personalising communications and creating dialogues by saying and doing the right thing to the right person at the right time is critical for marketing. The main elements of the personal communications mix are direct and interactive marketing, personal selling and the sales force.

▽ Developing and managing an advertising programme

Advertising is any paid form of non-personal presentation and communication of products (in the value package sense – see Chapter 11) by an identified sponsor. Its realistic task is not to change what people think about your brand, which is always hard to achieve, but to have them think *about* your brand. As Dr Johnson said almost 300 years ago, 'Men more frequently require to be reminded than informed'. Advertisements are a cost-effective way to communicate messages. Even in today's challenging media environment, good advertisements can generate sales. Advertisements for Olay Definity anti-ageing products and Head & Shoulders Intensive Treatment shampoo helped both brands enjoy double-digit sales gains in recent years.

In developing an advertising programme marketing managers must always start by identifying the target market and buyer motives. Then they can make the five major decisions, known as 'the five Ms': *Mission*: What are our advertising objectives? *Money*: How much can we spend? *Message*: What message should we send? *Media*: What media should we use? *Measurement*: How should we evaluate the results? These decisions are summarised in Figure 20.1 and described in the following sections.

Setting objectives

The advertising objectives must flow from prior decisions on target markets (see Chapter 10) and brand positioning (see Chapter 11).

An **advertising goal** (or objective) is a communication targeted at a preselected audience at a specific time to stimulate increased sales. Advertising objectives can be classified according to whether their aim is to inform, persuade, remind or reinforce. These goals correspond to different stages in the *hierarchy-of-effects* discussed in Chapter 19.

• **Informative advertising** aims to create brand awareness and knowledge of new products/market offerings or upgraded existing product/market offerings.

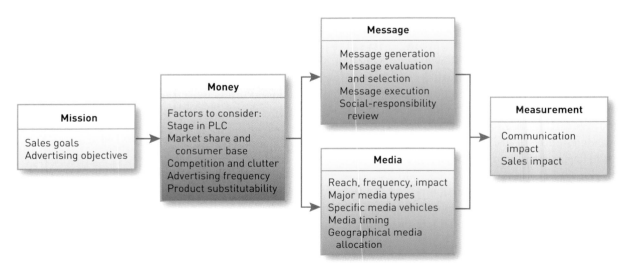

Figure 20.1 The five Ms of advertising

- **Persuasive advertising** aims to create liking, preference, conviction and purchase of a market offering. Some persuasive advertising uses comparative advertising, which makes an explicit comparison of the attributes of two or more brands. The UK supermarket Asda ran a TV advertisement in which they claimed to offer more and better price reductions than a rival supermarket (Morrison's). However comparative advertising is not favoured by the EU authorities.
- **Reminder advertising** aims to stimulate repeat purchase of market offerings. Expensive, four-colour cosmetic advertisements in magazines such as the UK's *Radio Times* and the Sunday newspaper supplements are intended to remind people to purchase such items as skin creams and invite them to 'love the skin you are in' (Olay).
- **Reinforcement advertising** aims to convince current purchasers that they made the right choice. Advertisements for cars often depict satisfied customers enjoying special quality and cost attributes of their new car.

The advertising objective should emerge from studying the current marketing situation. If the market offering/product class is mature, the company is the market leader, and brand usage is low, the objective is to stimulate more usage. If the market offering/product class is new, the company is not the market leader, but the brand is superior to the leader, then the objective is to convince the market of the brand's superiority.

Deciding on the advertising budget and developing the advertising campaign

John Wanamaker, a celebrated nineteenth-century department store magnate, once quipped 'Half my advertising is wasted. I just don't know which half.'[4] How does a company know it is spending the right amount? Large consumer-packaged-goods firms tend to overspend on advertising as a form of insurance against not spending enough. On the other hand, business-to-business companies tend to underspend as they underrate the power of advertising as a means to boost their images.

Although advertising is often treated as a current expense, it is really an investment in building brand equity and customer loyalty. When a company spends €5 million on capital equipment, it may treat the equipment as a five-year depreciable asset and write off only one-fifth of the cost in the first year. When it spends €5 million on advertising to launch a new market offering it is common for management to want to write off the entire cost in the first year.

Factors affecting budget decisions

Here are five specific factors to consider when *setting* the advertising budget.

1 **Stage in the product life cycle**: New market offerings typically merit large advertising budgets to build awareness and to gain consumer trial. Established brands are usually supported with lower advertising budgets, measured as a ratio to sales.

2 **Market share and consumer base**: High-market-share brands usually require less advertising expenditure as a percentage of sales to maintain share. To build share by increasing market size requires larger expenditures.

3 **Competition and clutter**: In a market with a large number of competitors and high advertising spending, a brand must advertise more heavily to be noticed. Even simple distractions ('noise') from advertisements not directly competitive to the brand creates a need for heavier advertising.

4 **Advertising frequency**: The number of repetitions needed to convey the brand's message to consumers has an obvious impact on the advertising budget.

5 **Product substitutability**: Brands in less-well-differentiated or commodity-like classes such as beer, soft drinks, banks and airlines require heavy advertising to establish a differential image.

In one study of budget allocation, Low and Mohr found that managers allocated less to advertising as brands moved to the more mature phase of the product life cycle; when a brand was well differentiated from the competition; when managers were rewarded on short-term results; as retailers gained more power; and when managers had less experience with the company.[5]

Advertising elasticity

The predominant response function for advertising is often concave but can be S-shaped. When consumer response is S-shaped, some positive amount of advertising is necessary to generate any sales impact, but sales increases eventually flatten out.[6]

One classic study found that increasing TV advertising budgets had a measurable effect on sales only half the time. The success rate was higher on new market offerings or line extensions than on established brands, and when there were changes in copy or in media strategy (such as an expanded target market). When advertising was successful in increasing sales, its impact lasted up to two years after peak spending. Moreover, the long-term incremental sales generated were approximately double the incremental sales observed in the first year of an advertising spending increase.[7]

Other studies reinforce these conclusions. In a 2004 Information Resource Incorporated (IRI) study of 23 brands, advertising often did not increase sales for mature brands or categories in decline. A review of academic research found that advertising elasticities were estimated to be higher for new (.3) than for established products (.1).[8]

In designing and evaluating a campaign, marketers need to combine both art and science creatively to develop the *message strategy* or positioning of an advertisement: *what message* it conveys about the brand, its *creative strategy* and *how* the brand claims are expressed in it. Advertisers typically take three steps: message generation and evaluation; creative development and execution; and social-responsibility review.

Message generation and evaluation

Many advertisements for cars today have a sameness about them – a car drives at high speed on a curved mountain road or across a desert. The result is that only a weak link forms between the brand and the message. Advertisers are always seeking 'the big idea' that connects with consumers rationally and emotionally which sharply distinguishes the brand from competitors, and is broad and flexible enough to translate to different media, markets and time periods. Fresh insights are important for avoiding using the same appeals and positioning as competitors.

A good advertisement normally focuses on one or two core selling propositions. As part of refining the brand positioning, the advertiser should conduct market research to determine which appeal works best with its target audience and then prepare a *creative brief*. This is a development of the *positioning statement* (see Chapter 10) and includes: the key message, target audience, communications objectives (to do, to know, to believe), key brand benefits, supports for the brand promise, and media.

How many alternative themes should the advertiser create before making a choice? The more themes explored, the higher the probability of finding a highly successful one. The use of computers has substantially reduced the costs of advertisement development. Many alternative approaches can be created in a short time by drawing still and video images from computer files. Marketers can also cut costs dramatically by using consumers as their creative team, a strategy sometimes called 'open-source' or 'crowd-sourcing'. However, this technique can be either pure genius or a regrettable failure. Other marketers caution that the open-source model does not work for every company or every market offering. Chanel spent nearly £18 million on a three-minute prestigious TV commercial for their Chanel No. 5 brand featuring Nicole Kidman that was screened in the United Kingdom in late 2007.

Creative development and execution

According to Leo Burnett, founder of the famous Chicago-based advertising agency, 'The secret of all effective originality in advertising is not the creation of new and tricky words and pictures, but one of putting familiar words and pictures into new relationships' (www.leoburnett.com). Visual images, sound and motion can be combined to affect viewers' emotions and senses. The advertisement's *impact* depends not only on what it says, but particularly on *how* it says it. Execution can be decisive. Every advertising medium has advantages.

Television advertisements TV is generally acknowledged as the most powerful advertising medium and reaches a broad spectrum of consumers. The wide *reach* translates to low cost per exposure. TV advertising has two particularly important strengths. First, it can be an effective

Chanel No. 5 can make you look and feel like Nicole Kidman.

Source: The Advertising Archives

means of vividly demonstrating market offering attributes and persuasively explaining their corresponding consumer benefits. Second, it can dramatically portray user and usage imagery, brand personality and other intangibles.

Because of its fleeting nature, however, and the distracting creative elements often found in advertisements, it can sometimes fail to impact effectively. Moreover, the high volume of advertising and non-programming material on TV creates *clutter* ('noise') and advertisements can easily be forgotten or ignored. Despite high production and placement costs research has shown that the number of viewers who said they paid attention to TV advertisements has dropped significantly in the past decade. Nevertheless, properly designed and executed TV advertisements can improve brand equity and affect sales and profits. A highly inspirational and professional TV commercial is still a powerful marketing tool.

Print advertisements Print media offer a stark contrast to broadcast advertisements. Magazines and newspapers can provide detailed market offering/product information and effectively communicate user and usage imagery. However, the static nature of the visual images in print media makes dynamic presentations or demonstrations difficult. The two main print media – magazines and newspapers – share many advantages and disadvantages. Although newspapers are timely and pervasive, magazines are typically more effective at building user and usage imagery. Although advertisers have some flexibility in designing and placing newspaper advertisements, poor reproduction quality and short shelf-life can diminish their impact.

Format elements such as size, colour and illustration also affect a print advertisement's impact. Larger ones gain more attention, though not necessarily by as much as their difference in cost. Four-colour illustrations increase both effectiveness and cost. New electronic eye-movement studies show that consumers can be led through an advertisement by the strategic placement of dominant elements. These are devices to focus the eye on the core values of the offering, such as the softness and length of the Andrex toilet tissue featured in the opening vignette.

Researchers studying print advertisements report that the *picture, headline* and *copy* matter in that order. The picture must be interesting enough to draw attention. The headline must reinforce the picture and lead the person to read the copy. The copy must be engaging and the brand's name sufficiently prominent. Even then, less than 50 per cent of the exposed audience will notice even a really outstanding advertisement. About 30 per cent might recall the headline's main point; about 25 per cent the advertiser's name; and fewer than 10 per cent will read most of the body copy. Many advertisements fail to achieve even these results.

▽ **Nissan doodles all over London's entertainment pages as part of a press campaign to back its Qashqai model**

Getting audience attention before a print advertising campaign.

Source: Courtesy of Nissan / Agency: TBWA London

Nissan introduced the Qashqai as a competitor to the traditional hatchback with the 'personality of a 4 × 4' to engage a young, urban target audience. The agency art director created the freehand drawings, which embellished images of the Nissan Qashqai with doodles to emphasise individual features. The 2007 campaign was part of an innovative approach to press advertisements for cars that usually featured big glossy advertisements with standard information about the vehicle and its specification. Each of the four double-page advertisements told a different story about the vehicle's design, handling or technology. The pen illustrations were focused on a shot of the car embedded in the editorial, while the main body copy of the advertisement was in the right-hand corner of the page and handwritten to draw attention to the doodle. The advertisements appeared on London Underground hoardings and *Time Out* magazine before the main press campaign was rolled out across the United Kingdom.

Source: N. Sandison (2008) Brand Republic, 4 March.

Some clear implications emerge for marketers on how consumers process print advertisements and these are summarised in 'Marketing memo: Print advertisement evaluation criteria'.

Radio advertising Radio is a pervasive medium. Perhaps its main advantage is flexibility – stations are highly targeted in terms of – demographic, psychographic and geographic segmentation – and advertisements are relatively inexpensive to produce. Radio is a particularly effective medium at morning and evening commuting times. It can be especially useful for small local businesses and can assist larger national and international firms to achieve a balance between broad and localised market coverage.[9]

The obvious disadvantages of radio are the lack of visual images and the relatively passive nature of the consumer processing that results.[10] Nevertheless, radio advertisements can be extremely creative. Some see the lack of visual images as a plus because they feel the clever use of music, sound and other creative devices can tap into the listeners' imagination to create powerfully relevant, well-liked and consequently easily recalled images.

Legal and social issues

Advertisers and their agencies must be sure advertising does not infringe social and legal norms. Public policy makers have developed a substantial body of laws and regulations to govern advertising. The problem is how to tell the difference between deception and exaggerations, which are not meant to be believed, and that are permitted by law.

Marketing memo

Print advertisement evaluation criteria

In judging the effectiveness of a print advertisement, in addition to considering the communication strategy (target market, communications objectives, message and creative strategy), marketers should be able to answer 'yes' to the following questions about the practical elements:

1 Is the message clear at a glance? Can you quickly tell what the advertisement is all about?

2 Is the benefit in the headline?

3 Does the illustration support the headline?

4 Does the first line of the copy support or explain the headline and illustration?

5 Is the advertisement easy to read and follow?

6 Is the market offering easily identified?

7 Is the brand or sponsor clearly identified?

Source: Adapted from P. W. Burton and S. C. Purvis (2002) *Which Ad Pulled Best*, 9th edn, Lincolnwood, IL: NTC Business Books.

To be socially responsible, advertisers must be careful not to offend the general public as well as any ethnic groups, racial minorities or special interest groups.[11] After choosing the message, the advertiser's next task is to choose media to carry it. The key steps are deciding on desired reach, frequency and impact; choosing among major media types; selecting specific media vehicles; deciding on media timing; and deciding on geographical media allocation. Then the marketer evaluates the results of these decisions.

Managing media matters

Media selection is finding the most cost-effective media to deliver the desired number and type of exposures to the target audience. The advertiser seeks a specified advertising objective and response from the target audience – for example, a target level of customer trial. This level depends on, among other things, level of brand awareness. Suppose the rate of customer trial increases at a diminishing rate with the level of audience awareness, as shown in Figure 20.2(a). If the advertiser seeks a product trial rate of T^*, it will be necessary to achieve a brand awareness level of A^*.

The next task is to find out how many exposures, E^*, will produce a level of audience awareness of A^*. The effect of exposures on audience awareness depends on the exposures' reach, frequency and impact:

- **Reach (R)**: the number of different persons or households exposed to a particular media schedule at least once during a specified time period;
- **Frequency (F)**: the number of times within the specified time period that an average person or household is exposed to the message;
- **Impact (I)**: the qualitative value of an exposure through a given medium (thus a food advertisement in the UK's *Good Housekeeping* magazine would have a higher impact than in the UK's *Radio Times* magazine).

Figure 20.2(b) shows the relationship between audience awareness and reach. Audience awareness will be greater the higher the exposures' reach, frequency and impact. The relationship between reach, frequency and impact is captured in the following concepts:

- **Total number of exposures (E)** – This is the reach times the average frequency; that is, $E = R \times F$, also called the gross rating points (GRP). If a given media schedule reaches 80 per cent of homes with an average exposure frequency of 3, the media schedule has a GRP of 240 (80 × 3). If another media schedule has a GRP of 300, it has more weight, but it is not possible to tell how this weight breaks down into reach and frequency.
- **Weighted number of exposures (WE)** – This is the reach times average frequency times average impact; that is $WE = R \times F \times I$.

Reach is most important when: launching new market offerings, extensions of well-known brands or infrequently purchased brands, prospecting an undefined target market. Frequency is most important where there are strong competitors, a complex story to tell, high consumer

Figure 20.2
Relationship among trial, awareness, and the exposure function

(a) Relationship between product trial rate and audience awareness level

Trial

T^*

A^*

Awareness

(b) Relationship between audience awareness level and exposure reach and frequency

Awareness

Frequency = 5, Impact = 1.5

Frequency = 5, Impact = 1

Frequency = 3, Impact = 1

A^*

E^*

Reach

resistance or a frequent-purchase cycle. Many advertisers believe a target audience needs a large number of exposures. Others believe that after people see the same advertisement a few times they act on it, get irritated by it or stop noticing it. Think of an advertisement that has recently irritated you. Was the advertisement effective? How would you change it if you had the opportunity to advise the client company? Another reason for repetition is forgetting. The higher the forgetting rate associated with a brand market offering message, the higher the warranted level of repetition. However, advertisers should not rest on a tired advertisement but insist on fresh effort from their advertising agency.[12]

The media planner must also know the capacity of the major advertising media types to deliver reach, frequency and impact. The major advertising media along with their costs, advantages and limitations are profiled in Table 20.1.

Media planners make their choices by considering the following variables:

- **Target audience media habits**: Radio and television are the most effective media for reaching teenagers.
- **Product characteristics**: Media types have different potential for demonstration, visualisation, explanation, believability and colour. Women's dresses are best shown in colour magazines, but high-tech products requiring dynamic presentation such as digital cameras, printers or mobile phones are best demonstrated on television.
- **Message characteristics**: Timeliness and information content will influence media choice. A message announcing a major sale tomorrow will require radio, TV or newspaper advertising. A message containing a great deal of technical data might require specialised magazines or mailings.
- **Cost**: Television is very expensive, whereas newspaper advertising is relatively inexpensive. What counts is the cost per thousand exposures.

Given the abundance of media, the planner must first decide how to allocate the budget to the major media types. Consumers are increasingly time starved. Attention is a scarce currency,

Table 20.1 Profiles of major media types

Medium	Advantages	Limitations
Newspapers	Flexibility; timeliness; good local market coverage; broad acceptance; high believability	Short life; poor reproduction quality; small 'pass-along' audience
Television	Combines sight, sound, and motion; appealing to the senses; high attention; high reach	High absolute cost; high clutter; fleeting exposure; less audience selectivity
Direct mail	Audience selectivity; flexibility; no ad competition within the same medium; personalisation	Relatively high cost; 'junk mail' image
Radio	Mass use; high geographic and demographic selectivity; low cost	Audio presentation only; lower attention than television; nonstandardized rate structures; fleeting exposure
Magazines	High geographic and demographic selectivity; credibility and prestige; high-quality reproduction; long life; good pass-along readership	Long ad purchase lead time; some waste circulation; no guarantee of position
Outdoor	Flexibility; high repeat exposure; low cost; low competition	Limited audience selectivity; creative limitations
Yellow Pages	Excellent local coverage; high believability; wide reach; low cost	High competition; long ad purchase lead time; creative limitations
Newsletters	Very high selectivity; full control; interactive opportunities; relative low costs	Costs could run away
Brochures	Flexibility; full control; can dramatise messages	Overproduction could lead to runaway costs
Telephone	Many users; opportunity to give a personal touch	Relative high cost unless volunteers are used
Internet	High selectivity; interactive possibilities; relatively low cost	Relatively new media with a low number of users in some countries

A billboard advertise-
ment with a difference!

Source: Gareth
Cattermole/Getty Images

and advertisers need strong devices to capture it.[13] In recent years researchers have noticed a reduced effectiveness for television due to increased commercial clutter, increased 'zipping and zapping' of commercials aided by the arrival of PVRs such as TiVo, and lower viewing owing to the growth in cable and satellite TV and DVDs/VCRs.

Place advertising

Place advertising, or **out-of-home advertising,** is a broad category including many creative and unexpected forms to capture consumers' attention. The rationale is that it is more effective to reach people where they work, play and, of course, shop. The main options include ambient advertising, billboards, public spaces, point of purchase and transport advertising.

Billboards Billboards have been transformed and now use colourful, digitally produced graphics, backlighting, sounds, movement, and unusual – even three-dimensional – images. In Belgium, eBay posted 'Moved to eBay' stickers on empty storefronts; and in Germany imaginary workers toiling inside vending machines, ATMs and photo booths were justification for a German job-hunting website to proclaim, 'Life is Too Short for the Wrong Job'.

▽ BBC World

The Best Show winner at the OBIE awards sponsored by the Outdoor Advertising Association of America was the BBC World television channel and its advertising agency BBDO. The BBC World Voting Campaign featured interactive digital billboards designed to introduce BBC World to the US market. The interactive units showed images and headlines that reflected current events. Members of the public were then asked to use Bluetooth technology to select one of two available opinions, and a running tally was displayed.[14]

Public spaces or ambient advertising Advertisers are placing advertisements in unconventional places such as cinemas, airlines and lounges, as well as sports arenas, office and hotel lifts, and other public places. Billboard-type poster advertisements are appearing everywhere. Advertisements on buses, subways and metro and commuter trains have become valuable ways to reach consumers. 'Street furniture' – bus shelters, kiosks and public areas – is another fast-growing option.

Advertisers can buy space in stadia, arenas and on rubbish bins, bicycle racks, parking meters, airline snack packages, airport luggage carousels, lifts and petrol pumps. Volkswagen has used fuel pump nozzles to communicate the fuel efficiency of their Golf TDI model.

▽ **British Airports Authority**

Advertising agency JCDecaux has worked alongside the British Airports Authority (BAA) and architects to build advertising into the very foundation of London Heathrow's new Terminal 5. Rather than advertising clutter to besiege the weary traveller, only a small number of advertising sites carry messages, but they will be massive, including light boxes larger than four double-decker buses. Over 300 digital advertising sites were installed in the terminal – taking up 50 per cent of the airport's advertising 'real estate', and departing from the usual B2B or corporate branding campaigns to introduce a whole range of consumer goods – from chocolates and clothing to perfumes and cosmetics. The intensive use of digital images also means that messages can be targeted to different audiences, locations, and times of day. Advertisements can even appear in different languages to greet arriving and departing flights. BAA director of media, Duncan Tolson, says Terminal 5 is just the beginning: 'Terminal 5 will mark the start of a new generation of airport advertising. It will act as a blueprint for the future, and we are looking forward to rolling it out across all BAA airports.'[15]

Product placement

Product placement has been threatening to expand from films to all types of TV shows. Marketers pay high fees so that their goods will make cameo appearances in films and on television. Sometimes placements are the result of a larger network advertising deal, but at other times they are the work of small product-placement shops that maintain ties with prop masters, set designers and production executives. 7-UP, Aston Martin, Finlandia, Visa and Omega all initiated major promotional campaigns based on product-placement tie-ins with the James Bond film *Die Another Day*. With over US$100 million paid for product-placement rights, some critics called the film 'Buy Another Day'. Product placements also featured strongly in *Sex in the City* released in May 2008.

Some firms (such as Chanel and Louis Vuitton) get product placement at no cost by supplying their products to the film company. Nike, too, often supplies shoes, jackets, bags, etc.[16]

Marketers are finding inventive ways to advertise during real-time television broadcasts. Sports fans are familiar with virtual logos networks added digitally to the playing field. Invisible to spectators at the event, these advertisements look just like painted-on logos to viewers at home. **Advertorials** are print advertisements that offer editorial content reflecting favourably on the brand and are difficult to distinguish from newspaper or magazine content.[17] Many companies include advertising inserts in monthly bills. Some companies send CDs or DVDs to prospects.

Point of purchase

There are many ways to communicate with consumers at the **point of purchase (P-O-P)**. In-store advertising includes advertisements on shopping trolleys, aisles and shelves, as well as promotion options such as in-store demonstrations and live sampling. P-O-P radio provides FM-style programming and commercial messages to many stores and shops. Programming includes a store-selected music format, consumer tips and commercials. The appeal of point-of-purchase advertising lies in the fact that in many product categories consumers make the bulk of their final brand decisions in the store.

Evaluating alternative media

Advertisements now appear virtually anywhere. The main advantage of non-traditional media is that they can often reach a very precise and captive audience in a cost-effective manner. The message must be simple and direct. In fact, outdoor advertising is often called the '15-second sell'. It is more effective at enhancing brand awareness or brand image than creating new brand associations.

The challenge with non-traditional media is demonstrating its reach and effectiveness through credible, independent research. Unique advertising placements designed to break through clutter may also be perceived as invasive and obtrusive. Consumer backlash often results when people see advertisements in traditionally advertisement-free spaces, such as in dentists' and doctors' waiting rooms.

Not everyone is turned off by the proliferation of advertising. Branded merchandise is so much a part of teenagers' lives they don't think twice about it. Perhaps because of its sheer pervasiveness, some consumers seem to be less bothered by non-traditional media now than in the past.

However, consumers must be favourably affected in some way to justify the marketing expenditures for non-traditional media. There will always be room for creative means of placing the brand before consumers. The possibilities are endless: 'Marketing insight: Playing games with brands' describes the emergence of yet another new media trend.

The media planner must search for the most cost-effective vehicles within each chosen media type. These choices are critical as it can cost as much to run an advertisement once on network TV as to make it! In making choices, the planner must rely on measurement services that provide estimates of audience size, composition and media cost. Audience size has several possible measures:

- **Circulation**: The number of physical units carrying the advertising.
- **Audience**: The number of people exposed to the vehicle. (If the vehicle has pass-on readership, then the audience is larger than circulation.)
- **Effective audience**: The number of people with target audience characteristics exposed to the vehicle.
- **Effective advertising-exposed audience**: The number of people with target audience characteristics who actually saw the advertisement.[18]

Media planners calculate the cost per thousand persons reached by a vehicle. The media planner ranks each magazine by cost per thousand and favours magazines with the lowest cost per thousand for reaching target consumers. The magazines themselves often put together a 'reader profile' for their advertisers, summarising the characteristics of the magazine's readers with respect to age, income, residence, marital status and leisure activities.

Marketers need to apply several adjustments to the cost per thousand measure. First, they should adjust the measure for *audience quality*. For a baby lotion advertisement, a magazine read by 1 million young mothers has an exposure value of 1 million; if read by 1 million teenagers, it would have an exposure value of almost zero. Second, adjust the exposure value for the *audience-attention*

Marketing insight

Playing games with brands

Advergaming, the practice of incorporating an advertising message into an online game, is becoming an effective way to reach target audiences.

The central concept of advergaming is that if the game is fun, consumers are more likely to remember not just the brand or product itself, but to associate specific brand attributes with it. If the game is popular, players will challenge friends to try it or simply add it to their blogs.

Studies suggest that 50 per cent of recipients play the advergame for an average of 25 minutes and 90 per cent of players who receive a challenge from a friend to play the game, respond back with their score or statistics.

At Web 2.0 websites like Multigames.com, users upload their own free flash games to the site, as users do with videos to sites such as YouTube. Once uploaded, the games are provided with embed codes, which can also accommodate Facebook features and other social bookmarking tools that encourage viral spread of the game.

'One of our most popular games is actually an advergame for Guitar Hero 2 by Red Octane', explains Multigames CEO Christian Lovstedt. 'It's a simplified version of the real Guitar Hero game that you play with your computer keyboards. This advergame is also the game that is being embedded the most so it's a very effective word of mouth communicator for Guitar Hero 2.'

'I am not sure if marketing departments are using the full potential of viral spread of advergames yet. The common set up is that a promotion site is launched with an advergame and the advertising company will spend time trying to drive traffic to that specific site. But you can attract a lot of attention to your product by letting the game "transport itself" virally over the internet. We hope to see more of Advergames on our site in the future' says Lovstedt.

The advergame industry is expected to generate US $312.2 million by 2009, up from US $83.6 million in 2004, according to Boston research firm Yankee Group.

Source: C. Lovstedt, Multigames Sweden AB (www.multigames.com).

probability. Readers of *Vogue* may pay more attention to advertisements than do readers of *The Economist.* Third, adjust for the magazine's *editorial quality* (prestige and trustworthiness). People are more likely to believe a TV or radio advertisement and to become more positively disposed towards the brand when the advertisement is placed within a programme they like. Fourth, adjust for the magazine's *advertising placement policies and extra services* (such as regional or occupational editions and lead-time requirements).

Media planners are increasingly using more sophisticated measures of effectiveness and employing them in mathematical models to arrive at the best media mix. Many advertising agencies use a computer program to select the initial media and then make further improvements based on subjective factors.

In choosing media, the advertiser faces both a macroscheduling and a microscheduling problem. The *macroscheduling problem* involves scheduling the advertising in relationship to seasons and the business cycle. Suppose 70 per cent of a product's sales occur between June and September. The firm can vary its advertising expenditures to follow the seasonal pattern, to oppose the seasonal pattern, or to be constant throughout the year.

The *microscheduling problem* calls for allocating advertising expenditures within a short period to obtain maximum impact. Suppose the firm decides to buy 30 radio spots in the month of September. Figure 20.3 shows several possible patterns. The left side shows that advertising messages for the month can be concentrated ('burst' advertising), dispersed continuously throughout the month, or dispersed intermittently. The top side shows that the advertising messages can be beamed with a level, rising, falling or alternating frequency.

The most effective pattern depends on the communications objectives in relationship to the nature of the market offering, target customers, distribution channels and other marketing factors. The timing pattern should consider three factors. *Buyer turnover* expresses the rate at which new buyers enter the market; the higher this rate, the more continuous the advertising should be. *Purchase frequency* is the number of times during the period that the average buyer buys the product; the higher the purchase frequency, the more continuous the advertising should be. The *forgetting rate* is the rate at which the buyer forgets the brand; the higher the forgetting rate, the more continuous the advertising should be.

In launching a new market offering, the advertiser must choose among continuity, concentration, flighting and pulsing.

- **Continuity** means exposures appear evenly throughout a given period. Generally, advertisers use continuous advertising in expanding market situations, with frequently purchased items, and in tightly defined buyer categories.
- **Concentration** calls for making the advertising spend in a single period. This makes sense for seasonal purchases such as fruit, vegetables, holidays, Christmas presents.

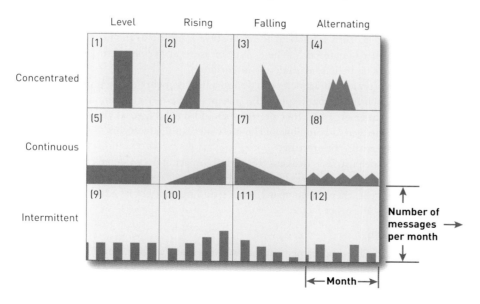

Figure 20.3
Classifications of marketing timing patterns

- **Flighting** calls for advertising for a period, followed by a period with no advertising, followed by a second period of advertising activity. It is useful when funding is limited, the purchase cycle is relatively infrequent, or items are seasonal.
- **Pulsing** is continuous advertising at low-weight levels reinforced periodically by waves of heavier activity. It draws on the strength of continuous advertising and flights to create a compromise scheduling strategy. Those who favour pulsing believe the audience will learn the message more thoroughly, and at a lower cost to the firm.

A company must decide how to allocate its advertising budget over space as well as over time. The company makes 'national buys' when it places advertisements on national TV networks or in nationally circulated magazines. It makes 'spot buys' when it buys TV time in just a few markets or in regional editions of magazines. These markets are called *areas of dominant influence* (ADIs) or *designated marketing areas* (DMAs). Advertisements reach a market 40–60 miles from a city centre. The company makes 'local buys' when it advertises in local newspapers, on radio or at outdoor sites.

Evaluating advertising effectiveness

Most advertisers try to measure the communication effect of an advertisement – that is, its potential effect on awareness, knowledge or preference. They would also like to measure the advertisement's sales effect.

Communication-effect research

Communication-effect research, called *copy testing*, seeks to determine whether an advertisement is communicating effectively. Marketers should perform this test both before an advertisement is put into media and after it is printed or broadcast.

There are three major methods of pre-testing. The *consumer feedback method* asks consumers questions such as these:

1 What is the main message you get from this advertisement?
2 What do you think they want you to know, believe or do?
3 How likely is it that this advertisement will influence you to undertake the action?
4 What works well in the advertisement and what works poorly?
5 How does the advertisement make you feel?
6 Where is the best place to reach you with this message?

Portfolio tests ask consumers to view or listen to a portfolio of advertisements. Consumers are then asked to recall all the advertisements and their content, aided or unaided by the interviewer. Recall level indicates an advertisement's ability to stand out and to have its message understood and remembered.

Laboratory tests use equipment to measure physiological reactions to an advertisement; or consumers may be asked to turn a knob to indicate their moment-to-moment liking or interest while viewing sequenced material.[19] These tests measure attention-getting power but reveal nothing about impact on beliefs, attitudes or intentions.[20]

Pre-test critics maintain that agencies can design advertisements which test well but may not necessarily perform well in the marketplace. Proponents of pre-testing maintain that useful diagnostic information can emerge and that pre-tests should not be used as the sole decision criterion. Widely acknowledged as being one of the most successful advertisers, Nike is notorious for doing very little advertising pre-testing.

Many advertisers use post-tests to assess the overall impact of a completed campaign. If a company hoped to increase brand awareness from 20 per cent to 50 per cent and succeeded in increasing it to only 30 per cent, then the company is not spending enough, its advertisements are poor, or it has overlooked some other factor.

Sales-effect research

What sales are generated by an advertisement that increases brand awareness by 20 per cent and brand preference by 10 per cent? The fewer or more controllable additional factors such as features and price are, the easier it is to measure advertising's effect on sales. The sales impact is easiest to measure in direct marketing situations and hardest in brand or corporate image-building advertising.

Figure 20.4
Formula for measuring sales impact of advertising

Companies are generally interested in finding out whether they are overspending or under-spending on advertising. A company's *share of advertising expenditures* produces a *share of voice* (proportion of company advertising of that product to all advertising of that product) that earns a *share of consumers' minds and hearts* and, ultimately, a *share of market*.

Researchers try to measure the sales impact through analysing historical or experimental data. The *historical approach* involves correlating past sales to past advertising expenditures using advanced statistical techniques. Other researchers use an *experimental design* to measure advertising's sales impact.

Information Resources, Inc.

A growing number of researchers are striving to measure the sales effect of advertising expenditures instead of settling for communication-effect measures.[21] Millward Brown International has conducted tracking studies for years to help advertisers decide whether their advertising is benefiting their brand.[22] Another research pioneer, Nielsen, has begun tracking commercials electronically.[23]

▽ Sales promotion

Sales promotion is a key ingredient in the marketing communications mix. Strictly speaking it should be termed *sales promotion* and not *promotion* as the latter is a collective term for the complete marketing communications mix. It consists of a collection of incentive tools, mostly short term, designed to stimulate quicker or greater purchase of particular market offerings by consumers or the trade.[24]

Whereas advertising offers a *reason* to buy, sales promotion offers an *incentive* to buy. Sales promotion includes tools for *consumer promotion* (samples, coupons, cash refund offers, money off, premiums, prizes, patronage rewards, free trials, warranties, tie-in promotions, cross-promotions, point-of-purchase displays and demonstrations); *trade promotion* (money off, advertising and display allowances, and free goods); and *business* and *sales force promotion* (trade shows and conventions, sales force contests, and speciality advertising).

Setting objectives

Sales promotion tools vary in their specific objectives. A free sample stimulates consumer trial, whereas a free management advisory service aims at cementing a long-term relationship with a retailer. Sellers use incentive-type promotions to attract new users, to reward loyal customers and to increase the repurchase rates of occasional users. Sales promotions often attract brand switchers, who are primarily looking for low price, good perceived value or premiums. If some of them would not otherwise have tried the brand, sales promotion can yield long-term increases in market share.[25]

Sales promotions in markets of high brand similarity can produce a high sales response in the short run but little permanent gain in brand preference over the longer term. In markets of high brand dissimilarity, they may be able to alter market shares permanently. In addition to brand switching, consumers may engage in stockpiling – purchasing earlier than usual (purchase acceleration) or purchasing extra quantities.[26] However, sales may then hit a post-sales-promotion dip.[27]

A number of sales promotion benefits flow to manufacturers and consumers. Manufacturers can adjust to short-term variations in supply and demand and test how high a list price they can charge, because they can always discount it. Promotions induce consumers to try new products and lead to more varied retail formats, such as everyday low pricing and promotional pricing. For retailers, promotions may increase sales of complementary categories (cake mix promotions may drive cake decoration sales) as well as induce store switching. They promote greater consumer awareness of prices. They help manufacturers and service providers (i.e., all market offering providers) sell more than normal at the list price and adapt programmes to different consumer segments.

Advertising versus sales promotion

A decade ago, the advertising-to-sales-promotion ratio was about 60:40. Today, in many consumer-packaged-goods companies, sales promotion accounts for 75 per cent of the combined budget (roughly 50 per cent is trade promotion and 25 per cent is consumer promotion). Sales promotion expenditures increased as a percentage of budget expenditure annually for almost two decades, although its growth has slowed down in recent years.

Several factors contributed to this rapid growth, particularly in consumer markets. Promotion became more accepted by top management as an effective sales tool; the number of brands increased; competitors used promotions frequently; many brands were seen as similar; consumers became more price value oriented; the trade demanded more deals from manufacturers; and advertising efficiency declined.

However the rapid growth of sales promotion created clutter. Incessant price reductions, coupons, deals and premiums may devalue the product in buyers' minds. It is risky to overuse sales promotion for a well-known brand on promotion over 30 per cent of the time.[28] Dominant brands offer deals less frequently, because most deals subsidise only current users.

Loyal brand buyers tend not to change their buying patterns as a result of competitive promotions. Advertising appears to be more effective at deepening brand loyalty, although added-value promotions can be distinguished from price promotions. Certain types of sales promotions may actually be able to enhance brand image.

▽ Harveys Furniture Store

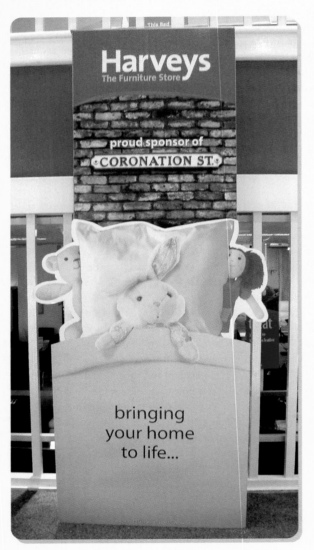

Harveys the UK furniture group, now part of the German Steinhoff Group, which sponsors the long-running UK TV soap *Coronation Street*, is offering discount vouchers to viewers visiting its dedicated area of the soap opera's interactive TV service. The sales promotion, created by the Eagle Eye Solutions agency, will encourage viewers to text in to receive an eight-digit short code to their mobile phone, which can be redeemed against discounts in selected Harveys stores.

Source: G. Jones (2008) ITV signs up Harveys to SMS voucher service, *Marketing*, 4 March (www.brandrepublic.com/News/787797/ITV-signs-Harveys-SMS-voucher-service).

Harveys is the proud sponsor of the long-running UK TV soap *Coronation Street*.

Source: Reproduced with kind permission of Harveys Darlington.

▽ Ford Motor Company

As well as the time-honoured devices of price promotions and two for the price of one offers (BOGOFs), Ford of Britain conducted an unbranded survey of about 150,000 sporty male prospects in 2006 that they had identified as a prospective target audience for the launch of their new S-MAX MPV across Europe. Recipients were incentivised with vouchers that appealed to their lifestyle, such as those for the outdoor retailer Snow+Rock. The response rate of 25,000 was greatly in excess of their expectations and 16,000 turned out to be 'hot' prospects for the new vehicle launch.

Source: C. Foss (2007) Ford car maker targets sporty males, *Marketing Direct*, 2 October (www.brandrepublic.com/News/742978/Ford-car-maker-targets-sporty-males/).

Price promotions may not build permanent total category volume. One study of more than 1000 promotions concluded that only 16 per cent were successful.[29] Small market share competitors find it advantageous to use sales promotion, because they cannot afford to match the market leaders' large advertising budgets. Neither can they obtain shelf-space without offering trade allowances or stimulate consumer trial without offering incentives. The result is that many consumer-packaged-goods companies feel they are forced to use more sales promotion than they wish. They blame the heavy use of sales promotion for decreasing brand loyalty, increasing consumer price sensitivity, brand-quality-image dilution, and a focus on short-run marketing planning.

Major decisions

In using sales promotion a company must establish its objectives; select the tools; develop the programme; pre-test, implement and control it; and evaluate the results.

Establishing objectives

Sales promotion objectives derive from broader promotion objectives, which draw from more basic marketing objectives for the product/market offering. For consumers, objectives include encouraging purchase of larger-sized units, building trial among non-users and attracting switchers away from competitors' brands. Ideally, promotions with consumers would have short-run sales impact as well as long-run brand equity effects. For retailers, objectives include persuading retailers to carry new items and higher levels of inventory, encouraging off-season buying, encouraging stocking of related items, offsetting competitive promotions, building brand loyalty and gaining entry into new retail outlets. For the sales force, objectives include encouraging support of a new market offering or model, encouraging more prospecting and stimulating off-season sales.[30]

Selecting consumer promotion tools

The promotion planner should take into account the type of market, sales promotion objectives, competitive conditions, and each tool's cost effectiveness. The main consumer promotion tools are summarised in Table 20.2. *Manufacturer promotions* are, for instance in the motor industry, rebates, gifts to motivate test drives and purchases, and high-value trade-in credit. *Retailer promotions* include price cuts, feature advertising, retailer coupons and retailer contests or premiums.[31]

A distinction can also be made between sales promotion tools that are *consumer franchise building* and those that are not. The former impart a selling message along with the offer, such as free samples, frequency awards, coupons when they include a selling message and premiums when they are related to the market offering/product. Sales promotion tools that typically are *not* brand building include 'money-off' packs, consumer premiums not related to a product, contests and sweepstakes, consumer refund offers, and trade allowances. Consumer franchise-building promotions offer the best of both worlds – they build brand equity and generate sales.

Selecting trade promotion tools Manufacturers use a number of trade promotion tools. Manufacturers award money to the trade: (1) to persuade the retailer or wholesaler to carry the brand; (2) to persuade the retailer or wholesaler to carry more units than the normal amount;

Table 20.2 Major consumer promotion tools

Samples: Offer of a free amount of a product or service delivered door to door, sent in the mail, picked up in a store, attached to another product or featured in an advertising offer.

Coupons: Certificates entitling the bearer to a stated saving on the purchase of a specific product: mailed, enclosed in other products or attached to them, or inserted in magazine and newspaper ads.

Cash refund offers (rebates): Provide a price reduction after purchase rather than at the retail shop: consumer sends a specified 'proof of purchase' to the manufacturer who 'refunds' part of the purchase price by mail.

Price packs (money-off deals): Offers to consumers of savings off the regular price of a product, flagged on the label or package. A *reduced-price pack* is a single package sold at a reduced price (such as two for the price of one). A *banded pack* is two related products banded together (such as a toothbrush and toothpaste).

Premiums (gifts): Merchandise offered at a relatively low cost or free as an incentive to purchase a particular product. A *with-pack premium* accompanies the product inside or on the package. A *free in-the-mail premium* is mailed to consumers who send in a proof of purchase, such as a box top or bar code. A *self-liquidating premium* is sold below its normal retail price to consumers who request it.

Frequency programme: Programme providing rewards related to the consumer's frequency and intensity in purchasing the company's products or services.

Prizes (contests, sweepstakes, games): *Prizes* are offers of the chance to win cash, trips or merchandise as a result of purchasing something. A *contest* calls for consumers to submit an entry to be examined by a panel of judges who will select the best entries. A *sweepstake* asks consumers to submit their names to a draw. A *game* presents consumers with something every time they buy – bingo numbers, missing letters – that might help them win a prize.

Patronage awards: Values in cash or in other forms that are proportional to patronage of a certain vendor or group of vendors.

Free trials: Inviting prospective purchasers to try the product without cost in the hope that they will buy.

Product warranties: Explicit or implicit promises by sellers that the product will perform as specified or that the seller will fix it or refund the customer's money during a specified period.

Tie-in promotions: Two or more brands or companies team up on coupons, refunds and contests to increase pulling power.

Cross-promotions: Using one brand to advertise another, non-competing brand.

Point-of-purchase (P-O-P) displays and demonstrations: P-O-P displays and demonstrations take place at the point of purchase or sale.

---

(3) to induce retailers to promote the brand by featuring display and price reductions; and (4) to stimulate retailers to push the product.

The growing power of large retailers has increased their ability to demand trade promotion at the expense of consumer promotion and advertising.[32] The company's sales force and its brand managers are often at odds over trade promotion. The sales force says local retailers will not keep the company's products on the shelf unless they receive more trade promotion money, whereas brand managers want to spend the limited funds on consumer promotion and advertising.

Manufacturers face several challenges in managing trade promotions. First, they often find it difficult to persuade retailers to do what they agreed. Manufacturers are increasingly insisting on proof of performance before paying any allowances. Second, some retailers are *forward buying* – that is, buying a greater quantity during the deal period than they can immediately sell. In the light of these problems many manufacturers feel that trade promotions have become a nightmare. They contain several offers, are complex to administer, and often lead to lost revenues.

Selecting business and sales force promotion tools Companies are increasingly spending on business and sales force promotion tools such as sales contests and speciality advertising to gather business leads, impress and reward customers, and motivate the sales force to greater effort. Typically they develop budgets for tools that remain fairly constant from year to year. For many new businesses that want to attract a targeted audience, especially in B2B markets, trade shows are an important tool, but the cost per contact is the highest of all communication options.

Developing the programme

In planning sales promotion programmes marketers are increasingly blending several media into an integrated marketing communications campaign concept.

In deciding to use a particular incentive, marketers must first determine the *size* of the incentive. A certain minimum is necessary if the promotion is to succeed. Second, the marketing manager must establish *conditions* for participation. Incentives might be offered to everyone or to select groups. Third, the marketer must decide on the *duration* of the promotion. Fourth, the marketer must choose a *distribution vehicle*. A money-off coupon can be distributed in the package, in stores, by mail or in advertising. Fifth, the marketing manager must establish the *timing* of promotion. Finally, the marketer must determine the *total sales promotion budget*.

Pre-testing, implementing, controlling and evaluating the programme

Although most sales promotion programmes are designed on the basis of experience, pre-tests can determine whether the tools are appropriate, the incentive size optimal, and the presentation method efficient. Consumers can be asked to rate or rank different possible deals, or trial tests can be run in limited geographic areas.

Marketing managers must prepare implementation and control plans that cover lead time and sell-in time for each individual promotion. *Lead time* is the time necessary to prepare the programme prior to launching it. *Sell-in time* begins with the promotional launch and ends when approximately 95 per cent of the deal merchandise is in the hands of consumers.

Manufacturers can evaluate the programme using sales data, consumer surveys and experiments. Sales (scanner) data helps analyse the types of people who took advantage of the promotion, what they bought before the promotion, and how they behaved later towards the brand and other brands. Sales promotions work best when they attract competitors' customers who then switch. *Consumer surveys* can uncover how many recall the promotion, what they thought of it, how many took advantage of it, and how the promotion affected subsequent brand choice behaviour. *Experiments* vary such attributes as incentive value, duration and distribution media; for example, coupons can be sent to half the households in a consumer panel. Scanner data can track whether the coupons led more people to buy the product and when.

Additional costs beyond the cost of specific promotions include the risk that promotions might decrease long-run brand loyalty. Second, promotions can be more expensive than they appear. Some are inevitably distributed to the wrong consumers. Third are the costs of special production runs, extra sales force effort, and handling requirements. Finally, certain promotions irritate retailers, who may demand extra trade allowances or refuse to cooperate.

▽ Events, experiences, public and press relations

Setting objectives

Sponsorships of sporting events, arts festivals, fairs, and annual and charity events are becoming part of a personally relevant moment in consumers' lives that can broaden and deepen a company's relationship with the target market.

▽ British Telecom sponsor Isle of Wight Festival

British Telecom (BT) marked a strategic change in their sponsorship activity when they signed up to support the popular 'globally recognised' Isle of Wight Festival in June 2008. The event organiser agreed to BT advertising its association with the festival via its voice, broadband and Vision products and to display its branding across the 250-acre site. BT also issued tickets to the sold-out event that featured big acts including NERD, Kaiser Chiefs and The Police.

Source: A. Odoi (2008) *Marketing*, 3 March.

▽ **Red Bull**

Wing away and discover adventure with Red Bull's Flugtag evening.

Source: Gaspar Risko/Getty Images

Cool wings

Red Bull is an energy drink that was launched in the United Kingdom in 1995. It is targeted at the young, such as sportspeople, students and clubbers and has achieved a dominant market share by developing an effective integrated marketing communication programme. The opening TV advertising featured whimsical cartoons and ended with the tag line 'Red Bull gives you wings'. The IMC promotes an adventure/fun brand mystique message. The IMC mix includes whacky TV advertising, sponsorship of a number of high-profile events, such as UK athletics and the £60 million (€84 million) purchase of the Formula One Jaguar racing team. Red Bull also runs a variety of fun events such as the *Flugtag* (where amateur 'pilots' attempt to launch home-made flying machines); and the Art of Can featuring sculptures using Red Bull's distinctive blue and silver cans. It is identified by its target market as a 'cool drink' but has also attracted some adverse publicity when the ethics of its mystique have been challenged. However, it has successfully managed to generate and sustain high levels of added value thus enabling it to be positively differentiated from rivals' products – a strategic focus in itself.

Source: C. J. Simmons and K. L. Becker-Olse (2006) Achieving marketing objectives through social sponsorships, *Journal of Marketing*, 70(4), 154–69; N. Clark (2005) Red Bull eyes sporting chance, *Marketing*, 27 July, 14–15; www.redbull.co.uk.

Daily encounters with brands may also affect consumers' brand attitudes and beliefs. *Atmospheres* are 'packaged environments' that create or reinforce leanings towards market offering purchase. Law offices decorated with Oriental rugs and oak furniture communicate 'stability' and 'success'.[33] A five-star hotel will feature elegant chandeliers, marble columns and other tangible signs of luxury. Small brands, of necessity, are more likely to take less obvious and less expensive paths in sponsorship and communications.

Marketers report a number of reasons to sponsor events:

1 **To identify with a particular target market or lifestyle**: Customers can be targeted geographically, demographically, psychographically or behaviourally according to events (see Chapters 10 and 11).

2 **To increase awareness of company or product name**: Sponsorship often offers sustained exposure to a brand, a necessary condition to build brand recognition and enhance brand recall.

3 **To create or reinforce perceptions of key brand image associations**: Events themselves have associations that help to create or reinforce brand associations.[34]

4 **To enhance corporate image**: Sponsorship can improve perceptions that the company is likeable and prestigious.

5 **To create experiences and evoke feelings**: The feelings engendered by an exciting or rewarding event may indirectly link to the brand.

6 **To express commitment to the community, green or social issues**: Cause-related marketing sponsors non-profit organisations and charities. Ben & Jerry's (ice cream, now owned by Unilever) has been a consistent champion of green and social issues.

7 **To entertain key clients or reward key employees**: Many events include lavish hospitality tents and other special services or activities for sponsors and their guests only. These engender goodwill and establish valuable business contacts. From an employee perspective, events can also build participation and morale or be used as an incentive.

8 **To permit merchandising or promotional opportunities**: Many marketers include contests or sweepstakes, in-store merchandising, direct response or other marketing activities in an event.

Despite these potential advantages, the success of an event can still be unpredictable and beyond the control of the sponsor. Although many consumers will credit sponsors for providing the financial assistance to make an event possible, some may resent the commercialisation of events.

Major sponsorship experiences

Successful sponsorships require choosing the appropriate events, designing the optimal sponsorship programme and measuring the effects of sponsorship. Professional advice on sponsorship is available in most European countries.

Choosing events

Because of the number of opportunities and their huge cost, many marketers are becoming more selective about choosing sponsorship events.

The event must meet the marketing objectives and communication strategy defined for the brand. The audience must match the target market. The event must have sufficient awareness, possess the desired image and be capable of creating the desired effects. Consumers must see favourable attributions for the sponsor's engagement. An ideal event is unique, lends itself to ancillary marketing activities and reflects or enhances the sponsor's brand or corporate image.

More firms are also using their names to sponsor the arenas, stadiums and other venues that hold the events. In the United Kingdom the Premier League football club Arsenal play at the Emirates stadium in London and Bolton football club play at the Reebok stadium in Bolton.

Designing sponsorship programmes

Many marketers believe it is the marketing programme accompanying an event sponsorship that ultimately determines its success. At least two to three times the amount of the sponsorship expenditure should be spent on related marketing activities.

Event creation is a particularly important skill in publicising fund-raising drives for non-profit organisations. Fund-raisers have developed a large repertoire of special events, including anniversary celebrations, art exhibitions, auctions, benefit evenings, bingo games, book and cake sales, contests, dances, dinners, fairs, fashion shows, parties in unusual places, 'phonathons', jumble sales, tours and 'walkathons'. No sooner is one type of event created, such as a 'walkathon', than competitors spawn new versions, such as 'readathons', 'bikeathons', and 'jogathons'.

Measuring sponsorship activities

As with public relations, measurement of events is difficult. The *supply-side* measurement method focuses on potential exposure to the brand by assessing the extent of media coverage, and the *demand-side* method focuses on reported exposure from consumers.

Supply-side methods approximate the amount of time or space devoted to media coverage of an event, for example the number of seconds the brand is clearly visible on a television screen or column inches of press clippings covering an event that mentions the brand. These potential 'impressions' translate into an equivalent value in advertising expenditure according to the fees associated in actually advertising in the particular media vehicle. Some industry consultants have estimated that 30 seconds of TV logo exposure during a televised event can be worth 6 per cent, 10 per cent or as much as 25 per cent of a 30-second TV advertisement.

Although supply-side exposure methods provide quantifiable measures, equating media coverage with advertising exposure ignores the content of the respective communications. The advertiser uses media space and time to communicate a strategically designed message. Media coverage and telecasts only expose the brand and don't necessarily embellish its meaning in any direct way. Although some public relations professionals maintain that positive editorial coverage can be worth 5–10 times the equivalent advertising value, sponsorship rarely provides such favourable treatment.

The demand-side method identifies the effect sponsorship has on consumers' brand knowledge. Marketers can survey event spectators to measure sponsor recall of the event as well as resulting attitudes and intentions towards the sponsor:

1 **direct tracking of sponsorship-related promotions**: (Web data, call centre data, online event statistics, other consumer engagements);

2 **qualitative research**: (on-site/in-market, pre/post and participant/non-participant, using a proprietary model for brand equity transfer and subsequent impact on purchase intent);

3 **quantitative analysis**: (analysis to link sponsorship to brand awareness, sales and retention and to optimise tactics in sponsorship activation that maximise ROI).

Creating experiences

A large part of local marketing is experiential marketing, which not only communicates features and benefits but also connects a market offering with unique and interesting experiences. 'The idea is not to sell something, but to demonstrate how a brand can enrich a customer's life.'[35] 'Marketing insight: Experiential marketing' describes the concept of customer experience management.

Marketing insight

Experiential marketing

Bernd Schmitt has developed the concept of *customer experience management* (CEM) – the process of strategically managing a customer's entire experience with a market offering or company.[36] According to Schmitt, brands can help to create five different types of experiences: sense, feel, think, act and relate. In each case, Schmitt distinguishes between hard-wired and acquired experiential response levels. He maintains that marketers can provide experiences for customers through a set of experience providers:

1 **Communications**: advertising, public relations, annual reports, brochures, newsletters and magalogues (a combination of a magazine and a catalogue);

2 **Visual/verbal identity**: names, logos, signage and transportation vehicles;

3 **Product presence**: product design, packaging and point-of-sale displays;

4 **Co-branding**: event marketing and sponsorships, alliances and partnerships, licensing, and product placement in films or on TV;

5 **Environments**: retail and public spaces, trade booths, corporate buildings, office interiors and factories;

6 **Websites and electronic media**: corporate sites, product or service sites, CD-ROMs, automated emails, online advertising and intranets;

7 **People**: sales people, customer service representatives, technical support or repair providers, company spokespersons, and CEOs and other executives.

The CEM framework is made up of five basic steps:

1 **Analysing the experiential world of the customer**: gaining insights into the socio-cultural context of consumers or the business context of business customers.

2 **Building the experiential platform**: developing a strategy that includes the positioning for the kind of experience the brand stands for ('what'), the value proposition of what relevant experience to deliver ('why') and the overall implementation theme that will be communicated ('how').

3 **Designing the brand experience**: implementing their experiential platform in the look and feel of logos and signage, packaging, and retail spaces, in advertising, collaterals, and online.

4 **Structuring the customer interface**: implementing the experiential platform in the dynamic and interactive interfaces including face to face, in stores, during sales visits, at the check-in desk of a hotel, or the ecommerce engine of a website.

5 **Engaging in continuous innovation**: implementing the experiential platform in new product development, creative marketing events for customers and fine tuning the experience at every point of contact.

Schmitt cites Pret A Manger, the UK-based sandwich company, as an example of an attractive brand experience, customer interface and ongoing innovation:

The Pret A Manger brand is about great tasting, handmade, natural products served by amazing people who are passionate about their work. The sandwiches and stores look appealing and attractive. The company hires only 5 per cent of those who apply and only after they have worked for a day in the shop. This process ensures good fit and good teamwork.

He also offers Singapore Airlines, Starbucks and Amazon.com as outstanding providers of customer experiences.

Sources: www.exgroup.com; B. Schmitt (2003) *Customer Experience Management: A Revolutionary Approach to Connecting with Your Customers*, New York: John Wiley and Sons; B. Schmitt, D. L. Rogers and K. Vrotsos (2003) *There's No Business That's Not Show Business: Marketing in an Experience Culture*, Upper Saddle River, NJ: Prentice Hall; B. Schmitt (1999) *Experiential Marketing: How to Get Companies to Sense, Feel, Think, Act, and Relate to Your Company and Brands*, New York: Free Press; B. Schmitt and A. Simonson (1997) *Marketing Aesthetics: The Strategic Management of Brands, Identity, and Image*, New York: Free Press.

Pine and Gilmore argue that marketers are on the threshold of the 'experience economy' (see also Chapter 22), a new economic era in which all businesses must orchestrate memorable events for their customers.[37] They assert:

- If you charge for stuff, then you are in the *commodity business*.
- If you charge for tangible things, then you are in the *goods business*.
- If you charge for the activities you perform, then you are in the *service business*.
- If you charge for the time customers spend with you, then and only then are you in the *experience* business.

Citing a range of companies from Disney to AOL, Pine and Gilmore maintain that saleable experiences come in four varieties: entertainment, education, aesthetic and escapist.

One survey showed that 80 per cent of respondents found participating in a live event more engaging than all other forms of communication. The vast majority also felt experiential marketing gave them more information than other forms of communication and would make them more likely to tell others about participating in the event and be receptive to other marketing for the brand.[38]

Companies can even create a strong image by inviting prospects and customers to visit their headquarters and factories. Cadbury's, Denby and Nissan all sponsor excellent company tours that draw many visitors a year. Companies such as the Dundee Sweet factory, Lakeland Pencils, Poole Pottery and Walkers Crisps have all built corporate museums at their headquarters that display their history and the drama of producing and marketing their products.

Major decisions in marketing and public relations

Not only must the company relate constructively to customers, suppliers and dealers, it must also relate to a large number of interested publics. A **public** is any group that has an actual or potential interest in or impact on a company's ability to achieve its objectives. **Public relations (PR)** includes a variety of programmes to promote or protect a company's image or individual products.

> To learn how an American Burger King franchise was started in Western Australia by a Canadian and grew to 210 outlets by 2003 before being consolidated under 'Happy Jacks', visit www.pearsoned.com.au/marketingmanagementaustralia

The wise company takes concrete steps to manage successful relationships with its key publics. Most companies have a public relations department that monitors the attitudes of the organisation's publics and distributes information and communications to build goodwill. The best PR departments counsel top management to adopt positive programmes and eliminate questionable practices so that negative publicity doesn't arise in the first place. They perform the following five functions:

1 **Press relations**: presenting news and information about the organisation in the most positive light.

2 **Goods/market offering publicity**: sponsoring efforts to publicise specific marketing offerings.

3 **Corporate communications**: promoting understanding of the organisation through internal and external communications.

4 **Lobbying**: dealing with legislators and government officials to promote or defeat legislation and regulation.

5 **Counselling**: advising management about public issues and company positions and image during good times and bad.

As 'Marketing insight: Managing a brand crisis' explains, sometimes PR must spearhead marketing communication efforts to help when a brand gets into trouble.

Furthermore, the more sincere the firm's response – public acknowledgment of the impact on consumers and willingness to take whatever steps are necessary to solve the crisis – the less likely that consumers will form negative views.

Marketing insight

Managing a brand crises

Marketing managers must assume that, at some point in time, some kind of brand crisis will arise. Famous brands such as BP, Cadbury's, Nestlé and Perrier have all experienced a potentially crippling brand crisis. These may be particularly damaging if there are widespread repercussions: (1) a loss in sales; (2) reduced effectiveness of marketing activities; (3) an increased sensitivity to rival firms' marketing activities; and (4) reduced effectiveness of its marketing activities on the sales of competing, unaffected brands.

In general, the more strongly brand equity and corporate image have been established – especially corporate credibility and trustworthiness – the more likely it is that the firm can weather the storm. Careful preparation and a well-managed crisis management programme, however, are also critical. As with Perrier's mineral water contamination crisis, the key to managing a crisis is that consumers see the response by the firm as both *swift* and *sincere*. Customers must feel an immediate sense that the company truly cares. Listening is not enough.

The longer it takes a firm to respond the more likely it is that consumers can form negative impressions from unfavourable media coverage or word of mouth. Perhaps worse, consumers may find they do not really like the brand after all and permanently switch brands or products.

In 1994 Perrier was forced to halt production worldwide and recall all existing product when traces of benzene, a known carcinogen, were found in excessive quantities in its bottled water The brand never recovered and eventually was taken over by Nestlé SA. More recently British Airways had a difficult time minimising the damage to its reputation over the alledged price-fixing collusion with Virgin Atlantic. BP used PR techniques to damp down the damage it suffered after a large oil spillage off the Shetland Islands. Nestlé had to confront a worldwide PR crisis when it unwittingly supplied baby-formula to Aftrican mothers unaware that they would dilute the powder in local lakes that were often infested with dangerous bugs.

In 2006 Cadbury's was forced to suspend a key advertising contract on UK independent TV stations as it sought to keep a low profile in the wake of a salmonella scare. The company had to recall seven varieties of Cadbury's Dairy Milk chocolate items. The crisis damaged Cadbury's brand reputation and is estimated to have cost £30 million in profit. The company were also severely criticised by the UK government for seeking to disguise the salmonella outbreak for six months and by the UK Advisory Committee on the Microbiological Safety of Food for failing to keep up with modern risk assessment methods.

Sources: N. Klein and S. A. Greyser (2007) The Perrier recall: a source of trouble, Harvard Business School Case #9-590-104 and N. Klein and S. A. Greyser (2007) The Perrier relaunch, Harvard Business School Case #9-590-130; H. Van Heerde, K. Helsen and M. G. Dekimpe (2007) The impact of a product-harm crisis on marketing effectiveness, *Marketing Science* 26, 230–45; M. L. Roehm and A. M. Tybout (2006) When will a brand scandal spill over and how should competitors respond?, *Journal of Marketing Research* 43, 366–73; J. Klein and N. Dawar (2004) Corporate social responsibility and consumers' attributions and brand evaluations in a product-harm crisis, *International Journal of Research in Marketing*, 21(3), 203–17; R. Ahluwalia, R. E. Burnkrant and H. Rao Unnava (2000) consumer response to negative publicity: the moderating role of commitment, *Journal of Marketing Research*, 37, 203–14; N. Dawar and M. M. Pillutla (2000) The impact of product-harm crises on brand equity: the moderating role of consumer expectations, *Journal of Marketing Research*, 37, 215–26; R. Alsop (1989) Enduring brands hold their allure by sticking close to their roots, *Wall Street Journal Centennial Edition*, 23 June; J. Wiggins (2006) Cadbury seeks a low profile after product recall, *Financial Times*, 9 July.

Marketing public relations

Many companies are turning to **marketing public relations (MPR)** to support corporate or market offering/product promotion and image making. MPR, as do financial PR and community PR, serves a special constituency.

The old name for MPR was **publicity**, the task of securing editorial space – as opposed to paid space – in print and broadcast media to promote or 'hype' a product, service, idea, place, person or organisation. MPR goes beyond simple publicity and plays an important role in the following tasks:

- **Launching new products**: The amazing commercial success of toys such as Nintendo's DS and Wii owes a great deal to strong publicity.
- **Repositioning a mature product**: Glasgow had extremely bad press until the 'Glasgow – Smiles Better' campaign.
- **Building interest in a product category**: Companies and trade associations have used MPR to rebuild interest in declining commodities such as eggs, milk, beef and potatoes and to expand consumption of such products as tea, pork and orange juice.

- **Influencing specific target groups**: Supermarkets throughout Europe sponsor special local events to build goodwill.
- **Defending products that have encountered public problems**: PR professionals must be adept at managing crises, such as the crisis suffered by Cadbury's in 2006 when one of its UK factories became contaminated.
- **Building the corporate image in a way that reflects favourably on its brand offerings**: Sir Richard Branson's activities have helped to create an innovative image for the Virgin Group.

As the power of mass advertising weakens, marketing managers are turning to MPR to build awareness and brand knowledge for both new and established lines. MPR is also effective in blanketing local communities and reaching specific groups and can be more cost effective than advertising. Nevertheless, it must be planned jointly with advertising.[39] Marketing managers need to acquire more skill in using MPR resources.

Clearly, creative public relations can affect public awareness at a fraction of the cost of advertising. The company does not pay for media space or time but only for staff to develop and circulate the stories and manage certain events. An interesting story picked up by the media can be worth more than an advertising spend. Some experts say consumers are five times more likely to be influenced by editorial copy than by advertising.

Major decisions in marketing press relations

In considering when and how to use MPR, management must establish the marketing objectives, choose the PR messages and vehicles, implement the plan carefully and evaluate the results. The main tools of MPR are described in Table 20.3.[40]

Establishing objectives

MPR can build *awareness* by placing stories in the media to bring attention to a product, service, person, organisation or idea. It can build *credibility* by communicating the message in an editorial context. It can help boost sales force and dealer *enthusiasm* with stories about a new product

Table 20.3 Major tools in marketing PR

Publications: Companies rely extensively on published materials to reach and influence their target markets. These include annual reports, brochures, articles, company newsletters and magazines, and audio-visual materials.

Events: Companies can draw attention to new products or other company activities by arranging special events such as news conferences, seminars, outings, trade shows, exhibits, contests and competitions, and anniversaries that will reach the target publics.

Sponsorships: Companies can promote their brands and corporate name by sponsoring sports and cultural events and highly regarded causes.

News: One of the major tasks of PR professionals is to find or create favourable news about the company, its products and its people and to get the media to accept press releases and attend press conferences.

Speeches: Increasingly, company executives must field questions from the media or give talks at trade associations or sales meetings, and these appearances can build the company's image.

Public service activities: Companies can build goodwill by contributing money and time to good causes.

Identity media: Companies need a visual identity that the public immediately recognises. The visual identity is carried by company logos, stationery, brochures, signs, business forms, business cards, buildings, uniforms and dress codes.

Breakthrough marketing

Virgin group

Virgin, the brainchild of the UK's Richard Branson, vividly illustrates the power of strong traditional and non-traditional marketing communications. Branson emerged in the 1970s with his innovative Virgin Records. He signed unknown artists no one would touch and began a marathon of publicity that continues to this day. He has since sold Virgin Records (to Thorn-EMI for nearly US $1 billion in 1992) but created over 200 companies worldwide whose combined revenues exceed US $5 billion.

The Virgin name – the third most respected brand in Britain – and the Branson personality help to sell diverse products and services such as planes, trains, finance, soft drinks, music, mobile phones, cars, wine, publishing, even bridal wear. Clearly Branson can create interest in almost any business he wants by simply attaching the name 'Virgin' to it. Virgin Mobile exemplifies this strategy. Branson supplies the brand and a small initial investment and takes a majority control, and big-name partners come up with the cash.

Some marketing and financial critics point out that he is diluting the brand, that it covers too many businesses. Branson has had some fumbles: Virgin Cola, Virgin Cosmetics and Virgin Vodka have all but disappeared. But despite the diversity all the lines connote value for money, quality, innovation, fun, and a sense of competitive challenge. The Virgin Group looks for new opportunities in markets with underserved, overcharged customers and complacent competition. Branson called these customer-hostile competitors 'big bad wolves'. 'Wherever we find them, there is a clear opportunity area for Virgin to do a much better job than the competition. We introduce trust, innovation, and customer friendliness where they don't exist,' Branson said. And once Virgin finds an opportunity, its vaunted marketing expertise kicks in.

A master of the strategic publicity stunt, Branson took on stodgy, overpriced British Airways by wearing World War I-era flying gear to announce the formation of Virgin Atlantic in 1984. The first Virgin flight took off laden with celebrities and media and equipped with a brass band, waiters from Maxim's in white tie and tails, and free-flowing champagne. The airborne party enjoyed international press coverage and millions of dollars' worth of free publicity. Branson knew that photographers have a job to do and they'd turn up at his events if he gave them a good reason.

Although Branson eschews traditional market research he stays in touch through constant customer contact. When he first set up Virgin Atlantic he called 50 customers every month to chat and get their feedback. He appeared in airports to rub elbows with customers, and if a plane was

Canny marketing and public relations has helped Sir Richard Branson build an empire of successful brands under the Virgin name.

Source: Shawn Thew/epa/Corbis

delayed he handed out gift certificates to a Virgin Megastore or discounts on future travel. Virgin's marketing campaigns include press and radio advertisements, direct mail and point-of-sale material. Virgin Mobile, for example, rolled out a postcard advertising campaign offering consumers discounts on new phones.

To identify where listeners to Virgin's Web-based Virgin Radio reside, the company created a VIP club. Listeners join the club by giving their post code, which then lets Virgin Radio target promotions and advertising to specific locations, just as a local radio station would. Once known as the 'hippie capitalist', Sir Richard Branson continues to look for new businesses and to generate publicity in his characteristic charismatic style. Remembering a friend's advice about publicity – 'If you don't give them a photograph that will get them on the front page, they won't turn up at your next event' – Branson always gives them a reason.

Sources: P. Elkind (2007) Branson gets grounded, *Fortune*, 5 February, 13–14; A. Deutschman (2006) The enlightenment of Richard Branson, *Fast Company*, September, 49; A. Serwer (2005) Do Branson's profits equal his joie de vivre?, *Fortune*, 17 October, 57; www.virgin.com; D. H. Silver and B. Austad (2004) Factors predicting the effectiveness of celebrity endorsement advertisements, *European Journal of Marketing*, 38(11/12), 1509–26; http://news.bbc.co.uk/1/hi/business/6936235.stm; http://news.bbc.co.uk/1/hi/business/7083517.stm; www.bbc.co.uk/consumer/tvandradio/watchdog/reports/services/services20071010.shtml.

before it is launched. It can hold down *promotion cost* because MPR costs less than direct mail and media advertising.

Whereas PR practitioners reach their target publics through the mass media, MPR is increasingly borrowing the techniques and technology of direct-response marketing to reach target audience members one to one.

Choosing messages and vehicles

Suppose a relatively unknown college wants more visibility. The MPR practitioner will search for stories. Do any faculty members have unusual backgrounds, or are any working on unusual projects? Are any new and unusual courses being taught? Are any interesting events taking place on campus? If there are no interesting stories, the MPR practitioner should propose newsworthy events the college could sponsor. Here the challenge is to create news. PR ideas include hosting major academic conventions, inviting expert or celebrity speakers, and promoting news conferences. Each event is an opportunity to develop a multitude of stories directed at different audiences. The following is a good example of reaching different audiences.

▽ Vattenfall AB

From its humble roots as a local royal institution and Sweden's electrical company founded in 1909, Vattenfall has become an international brand with 33,000 employees and is now Europe's largest heating firm and fourth-largest electricity firm. This transformation was challenging because it meant mergers and acquisitions with local brands from Germany, Poland, Finland and Denmark, some as old as from the 1880s. Overcoming suspicion, lack of awareness and other obstacles required a number of marketing actions, but events and PR played a crucial role. Vattenfall's joint sponsorship and event strategy concentrated in three areas (with themes) – sports (outdoor life and teamwork), human care (life of future generations) and environment (sustainable development and wildlife). These sponsorships and events were set in local markets as well as across all markets. Broader sponsorship included the National Geographic Society and the World Childhood Foundation. Vattenfall garnered much publicity by also sponsoring a number of local events, such as Brandenburg Gate commemorations in Germany, heated bus stops in Poland, and the 2006 European Athletics (track and field) Championships in Gothenburg, Sweden. Through focused and highly integrated activities, Vattenfall was able to enjoy high public awareness, a competitive local image, top financial market performance and a huge increase in customer satisfaction.[41]

A wide variety of integrated promotions helped Sweden's Vattenfall, a large heating and electricity supplier, reach an equally broad spectrum of audiences and improve its financials.
Source: Lowe Brindfors AB

Implementing the plan and evaluating results

MPR's contribution to the bottom line is difficult to measure, because it is used along with other promotional tools.

The easiest measure of MPR effectiveness is the number of *exposures* carried by the media. Publicists supply the client with a clippings book showing all the media that carried news about the firm's items and a summary statement.

This measure is not very satisfactory because it contains no indication of how many people actually read, heard or recalled the message and what they thought afterwards; nor does it contain information about the net audience reached, because publications overlap in readership. Publicity's goal is reach, not frequency, so it would be more useful to know the number of unduplicated exposures.

A better measure is the *change in product awareness*, *comprehension or attitude* resulting from the MPR campaign (after allowing for the effect of other promotional tools). For example, how many people recall hearing the news item? How many told others about it (a measure of word of mouth)? How many changed their minds after hearing it?

▽ Direct marketing

Setting objectives

Direct marketing is the use of consumer-direct (CD) channels to reach and market offerings to customers without using marketing middlemen. Direct marketers can use a number of channels to reach individual prospects and customers: direct mail, catalogue marketing, telemarketing, interactive TV, kiosks, websites and mobile devices. They often seek a measurable response, typically a customer order, through **direct-order marketing**.

Today, many direct marketers build long-term relationships with customers. Thirty-nine airlines, hotels and other businesses build strong customer relationships through frequency reward programmes and club programmes.[42]

Direct marketing has been a fast-growing mode for serving customers, partly in response to the high and increasing costs of reaching business markets through a sales force. Sales produced through traditional direct marketing channels (catalogues, direct mail and telemarketing) have been growing rapidly, along with direct mail sales, which include sales to the consumer markets, business-to-business, and fund-raising by charitable institutions.[43,44]

The benefits of direct marketing

Market demassification has resulted in an ever-increasing number of market niches. Time-poor consumers appreciate free-phone numbers, websites available 24 hours a day and seven days a week, and direct marketers' commitment to customer service. The growth of next-day delivery by companies such as DHL has made ordering fast and easy. In addition, many chain stores have dropped slower-moving speciality items, creating an opportunity for direct marketers.

Sellers benefit as well. Direct marketers can buy a mailing list containing the names of almost any group. They can customise and personalise messages and build a continuous relationship with each customer.

Direct marketing[45] can reach prospects at the right moment and be read by more interested prospects. It lets marketers test alternative media and messages to find the most cost-effective or efficient approach. Direct marketing also makes the direct marketer's offer and strategy less visible to competitors. Finally, direct marketers can measure responses to their campaigns to gauge which have been the most profitable.

Direct marketing must be integrated with other marketing communications and distribution activities. Successful direct marketers ensure that customers can contact the company with questions and view a customer interaction as an opportunity. These marketers make sure they know enough about each customer to customise and personalise offers and messages and develop a plan for lifetime marketing to each valuable customer, based on knowledge of life events and transitions. They also carefully integrate each element of their campaigns.

▽ **Guinness**

The Direct Marketing Association's top Diamond ECHO award in 2006 went to Target Marketing for its multimedia/integrated media campaign, 'Guinness Relationship Marketing', on behalf of Diageo Ireland. A campaign was designed to maximise the value of the relationship between consumers and pub owners, build brand loyalty, and cross-sell cans of Draught Guinness to consumers who switched brands when drinking at home. Guinness sales representatives gave pub owners The Big Black Book, with information about the campaign. Pint vouchers brought consumers back to the pub. Western-themed posters asked, 'Are you one of the Guinness most wanted?' The campaign also tied in with football events, offering home kit boxes for consumers.[46]

Overview of the direct marketing mix

Here are some of the key issues that characterise different direct marketing channels.

Direct mail

Direct mail marketing means sending an offer, announcement, reminder or other item to an individual consumer. Using highly selective mailing lists, direct marketers send out millions of letters, flyers, foldouts, etc. each year. Some send CDs, DVDs and computer diskettes to prospects and customers.

Direct mail is a popular medium because it permits target market selectivity, can be personalised, is flexible, and allows early testing and response measurement. Although the cost per thousand people reached is higher than with mass media, the people reached are much better prospects. The success of direct mail, however, has also become its liability – so many marketers are sending out direct mail that consumers pay little attention to it. One of the biggest users of direct mail, the financial services industry, has seen its response rates from campaigns drop significantly in recent years.[47] In constructing an effective direct mail campaign, direct marketers must decide on their objectives, target markets and prospects; offer elements; means of testing the campaign; and measures of campaign success.

Objectives

Most direct marketers judge a campaign's success by the number of orders received. An order-response rate of 2 per cent is normally considered good, although this number varies with product category, price, and the nature of the offering. Direct mail can also produce prospect leads, strengthen customer relationships, inform and educate customers, remind customers of offers, and reinforce recent customer purchase decisions.

Target markets and prospects

Most direct marketers apply the RFM formula (recency, frequency, monetary amount). They select customers according to how much time has passed since their last purchase, how many times they have purchased, and how much they have spent since becoming a customer. Points are established for varying RFM levels; the more points, the more attractive the customer.

Marketers also identify prospects on the basis of age, sex, income, education, previous mail order purchases, and occasions. New students will buy laptop computers, backpacks and compact refrigerators; newlyweds look for housing, furniture, appliances and bank loans. Another useful variable is consumer lifestyle or 'passions' such as computers, cooking and the outdoors.

The company's best prospects are customers who have bought its products in the past. The direct marketer can also buy names from list brokers, but these often have problems, including name duplication, incomplete data and obsolete addresses. Better lists include overlays of demographic and psychographic information. Direct marketers typically buy and test a sample before buying more names from the same list. They can build their own lists by advertising a free offer and collecting responses.

Offer elements

The offer strategy has five elements – the *product*, the *offer*, the *medium*, the *distribution method* and the *creative strategy*.[48] Fortunately, all can be tested. The direct mail marketer needs to pay careful attention to five components of the mailing itself: the outside envelope, sales letter, circular, reply form and reply envelope.

1 The outside envelope should contain an illustration, preferably in colour, or an incentive to open it.

2 The sales letter, brief and on good-quality paper, should use a personal salutation and start with a headline in bold type. A computer-typed letter usually outperforms a printed letter, and a pithy PS increases response rate, as does the signature of someone whose title is important.

3 A colourful circular accompanying the letter usually increases the response rate by more than its cost.

4 Direct mailers should feature a free-phone number and a website where recipients can print coupons.

5 A postage-free reply envelope will dramatically increase the response rate.

Direct mail should be followed up by an email, which is less expensive and less intrusive than a telemarketing call.

Testing elements

One of the great advantages of direct marketing is the ability to test, under real marketplace conditions, different elements of an offer strategy, such as products, product features, copy platform, mailer type, envelope, prices, or mailing lists.

Response rates typically understate a campaign's long-term impact. Suppose only 2 per cent of the recipients who receive direct mail advertising Samsonite luggage place an order. A much larger percentage became aware of the product (direct mail has high readership), and some percentage may have formed an intention to buy at a later date (either by mail or at a retail outlet). Furthermore, some may mention luggage to others as a result of the direct mail piece. To better estimate a promotion's impact, some companies measure the impact of direct marketing on awareness, intention to buy and word of mouth.

Measuring campaign success: lifetime value

By totalling the planned campaign costs, the direct marketer can determine the needed breakeven response rate which needs to be net of returned merchandise and bad debts.

Even when a specific campaign fails to break even in the short run, it can still be profitable in the long run if customer lifetime is factored in (see Chapter 7). Calculate the average customer longevity, average customer annual expenditure and average gross margin, minus the average cost of customer acquisition and maintenance (discounted for the opportunity cost of money).[49]

Catalogue marketing

In catalogue marketing, companies may send full-line merchandise, speciality consumer and business catalogues, usually in print form but also sometimes in CDs, videos or online format. For example, Avon sells cosmetics, Coopers sells home interest items, IKEA sells furniture and Lakeland Ltd sells household products, crafts and food items through catalogues. Many direct marketers find combining catalogues and websites an effective way to sell. Thousands of small businesses also issue speciality catalogues. Large businesses send catalogues to business prospects and customers.

Catalogues generate a considerable amount of business. The success of a catalogue business depends on managing customer lists carefully to avoid duplication or bad debts, controlling inventory carefully, offering quality merchandise so returns are low, and projecting a distinctive image. Some companies add literary or information features, send swatches of materials, operate a special hotline to answer questions, send gifts to their best customers, and donate a percentage of profits to good causes.

Business marketers are making inroads as well. Putting their entire catalogue online provides better access to global consumers than ever before, saving printing and mailing costs.

Telemarketing

Telemarketing is the use of the telephone and call centres to attract prospects, sell to existing customers, and provide service by taking orders and answering questions. Telemarketing helps companies increase revenue, reduce selling costs and improve customer satisfaction. Companies use call centres for *inbound telemarketing* – receiving calls from customers, and *outbound telemarketing* – initiating calls to prospects and customers.

Although telemarketing is a major direct marketing tool, its sometimes intrusive nature led to legislation in many European countries that protects the right of consumers to refuse to receive direct marketing telephone calls. It is increasing in business-to-business marketing. Raleigh Bicycles for example, uses telemarketing to reduce personal selling expense in contacting its dealers. Effective telemarketing depends on choosing the right telemarketers, training them well, and providing performance incentives.

Other media for direct response marketing

Direct marketers use all the major media. Newspapers and magazines carry abundant print advertisements offering books, articles of clothing, appliances, holidays, and other goods and services that individuals can order via free-phone numbers. Radio advertisements present offers 24 hours a day. Some companies prepare 30- and 60-minute *infomercials* to combine the sell of television commercials with the draw of information and entertainment. Infomercials promote products that are complicated or technologically advanced, or which require a great deal of explanation (Mercedes, Microsoft, Philips Electronics, Universal Studios, and online financial and employment agencies).[50] Some at-home shopping channels are dedicated to selling goods and services on a free-phone number for delivery within 48 hours.

Public and ethical issues in direct marketing

Direct marketers and their customers usually enjoy mutually rewarding relationships. Occasionally, however, a darker side emerges:

- **Irritation**: Many people are irritated by the large number of hard-sell, direct marketing solicitations. Especially annoying are calls at dinnertime or late at night, poorly trained callers and computerised calls by auto-dial recorded-message players.
- **Unfairness**: Some direct marketers take advantage of impulsive or less sophisticated buyers or prey on the vulnerable, especially the elderly.
- **Deception and fraud**: Some direct marketers design mailings and write copy intended to mislead. They may exaggerate product size, performance claims or the 'retail price'.
- **Invasion of privacy**: It seems that almost every time consumers order products by mail or telephone, apply for a credit card, or take out a magazine subscription their names, addresses and purchasing behaviour may be added to several company databases. Critics worry that marketers may know too much about consumers' lives, and that they may use this knowledge to take unfair advantage.

People in the direct marketing industry are addressing the issues. They know that, left unattended, such problems will lead to increasingly negative consumer attitudes, lower response rates, and calls for greater regulation. In the final analysis, most direct marketers want the same thing consumers want: honest and well-designed marketing offers targeted only to those who appreciate hearing about the offer.

▽ Interactive marketing

(See also Chapter 4)

The newest channels for communicating and selling directly to customers are electronic. The Internet provides marketers and consumers with opportunities for much greater *interaction* and *individualisation*. Few marketing programmes are considered complete without some type of prominent online component, which is gaining ground at the expense of traditional advertising agencies.

Interactive marketing offers unique benefits. Companies can send tailored messages that engage consumers by reflecting their special interests and behaviour. The Internet is highly accountable and its effects can easily be traced. Online, advertisers can gauge response instantaneously by noting how many unique visitors or 'UVs' click on a page or advertisement, how long they spend with it, where they go afterwards, and so on.[51]

The Web offers the advantage of *contextual placement* and buying advertisements on sites that are related to the marketer's offerings. Marketers can also place advertising based on keywords from search engines, to reach people when they've actually started the buying process. Light consumers of other media, especially television, can be reached online. The Web is especially effective at reaching people during the day.

Using the Web also has disadvantages. Consumers can effectively screen out most messages. Marketers may think their advertisements are more effective than they are if bogus clicks are generated by software-powered websites. Advertisers lose some control over what consumers will do with their online messages. However, many feel the advantages outweigh the disadvantages, and the Web is attracting marketers of all kinds.

To capitalise on advertisers' interest, firms are rushing online services and other support to marketers. Microsoft has invested in a broad range of businesses for placing advertisements on the Web, videogames and mobile phones alongside Internet search results. 'Breakthrough marketing: Yahoo!' describes that company's online efforts.

For marketers of cars, financial services, personal computers and telecommunications, marketing activities on the Web have become crucial. However, others are quickly following. Although beauty

Breakthrough marketing

Yahoo!

Since its foundation in 1994 Yahoo! has grown into a powerful force in Internet media, attracting Microsoft to make a bid for it in 2007. Yahoo! has worked hard to be more than just a search engine. The company proudly proclaims it is 'the only place anyone needs to go to find anything, communicate with anyone, or buy anything'. Its wide range of Web services includes email, news, weather, music, photos, games, shopping, auctions, travel, and more.

Yahoo! sees one of its main advantages over rival Google as its vast array of original content. Yahoo! has alliances with hundreds of premier content providers to offer a personalisation option in My Yahoo!, which enables users to specify their favourite Yahoo! features and content to fit a single page. With a database of information about where its millions of registered users live and what their interests are, Yahoo! can present users with both more relevant search results and more relevant advertising. Each month more than 475 million

people worldwide visit one of its myriad sites, with billions of page views each day.

A large percentage of revenue comes from advertising, but the company continues to supplement its revenues through subscription sources such as online personal advertisements, premium email products and services for small businesses. In February 2007 Yahoo! launched a new search advertising system, Panama, to increase the quality of its search results as well the advertising revenue it generates from searches.

Sources: C. Holahan (2007) Yahoo!'s bid to think small, *BusinessWeek*, 26 February, 94; B. Elgin (2006) Yahoo!'s boulevard of broken dreams, *BusinessWeek*, 13 March, 76–7; J. Hibbard (2006) How Yahoo! gave itself a face-lift, *BusinessWeek*, 9 October, 74–7; K. J. Delaney (2006) As Yahoo! falters, executive's memo calls for overhaul, *Wall Street Journal*, 18 November; Yahoo!'s personality crisis, *The Economist*, 13 August, 49–50; F. Vogelstein 92005) Yahoo!'s brilliant solution, *Fortune*, 8 August, 42–55.

pioneer Estée Lauder said she relied on three means of communication to build her cosmetics business – 'telephone, telegraph, and tell a woman' – she would now have to add the Web, which helps to support Estée Lauder brands. Consumer packaged-goods giants such as Danone, Nestlé and Lindt are also significantly increasing their online budgets. Pepsi spent between 5 per cent and 10 per cent of its overall marketing communications budget online in 2006, compared to just 1 per cent in 2001, because of its cost effectiveness.[52]

Marketers must go where the customers are, and increasingly that's online. Customers define the rules of engagement, however, and insulate themselves with the help of agents and intermediaries if they so choose. Customers define what information they need, what offerings they're interested in, and what they're willing to pay (see Chapter 11). Online advertising was estimated at a little less than 6 per cent of global marketing communication spending in 2006, but is expected to jump to 10 per cent by 2010. Helping fuel that growth is the emergence of media advertisements that combine animation, video and sound with interactive features.

Placing advertisements and promotions online

A company chooses which forms of interactive marketing will be most cost effective in achieving communication and sales objectives.

Websites

Companies must design websites that embody or express their purpose, history, products and vision.[53] A key challenge is designing a site that is both attractive and interesting enough to encourage repeat visits.[54] Rayport and Jaworski propose that effective sites feature seven design elements they call the 7Cs (see Figure 20.5).[55] To encourage repeat visits, companies must pay special attention to context and content factors and embrace another 'C' – constant change.[56]

Visitors will judge a site's performance on ease of use and physical attractiveness. Ease of use has three attributes: (1) the site downloads quickly; (2) the first page is easy to understand; and (3) it is easy to navigate to other pages that open quickly. Physical attractiveness is determined by these factors: (1) individual pages are clean and not crammed with content; (2) typefaces and font sizes are very readable; and (3) the site makes good use of colour (and sound). Websites must also be sensitive to national characteristics,[57] security and privacy protection issues.

Microsites

A **microsite** is a limited area on the Web managed and paid for by an external advertiser/company. Microsites are individual Web pages or cluster of pages that function as supplements to a primary site. They are particularly relevant for companies selling low-interest products. People rarely

---

- **Context:** Layout and design
- **Content:** Text, pictures, sound and video the site contains
- **Community:** How the site enables user-to-user communication
- **Customisation:** Site's ability to tailor itself to different users or to allow users to personalise the site
- **Communication:** How the site enables site-to-user, user-to-site or two-way communication
- **Connection:** Degree that the site is linked to other sites
- **Commerce:** Site's capabilities to enable commercial transactions

Figure 20.5 Seven key design elements of an effective website

Source: J. F. Rayport and B. J. Jaworksi (2001) *e-commerce*, New York: McGraw-Hill, p. 116. Copyright © 2001 McGraw-Hill Companies. Reproduced with permission.

visit an insurance company's website, but the company can create a microsite on used-car sites that offers advice for buyers of used cars and insurance at the same time. Some microsites have become huge online hits.

Search advertisements

A hot growth area in interactive marketing is **paid-search** or **pay-per-click advertisements**.[58] The search terms trigger relevant links to market offerings alongside search results from Google, MSN, Tiscali and Yahoo! Advertisers pay only if people click on the links. However, marketers believe consumers have already expressed an interest by clicking on the links and are good prospects.

Some believe the Internet is moving from the era of search to the era of discovery, thanks to recommender sites and systems such as Amazon's 'getting to know you suggestions'. In February 2008 Brent Hoberman, who used to run Lastminute.com, launched Mydeco in the United Kingdom. The action centres on state-of-the-art technology that enables people to upload the dimensions of a room, add windows, doors and fireplaces and then choose from more than 20,000 items of furniture and accessories to see how they will look in the space. Once arranged prospective customers can view a 3-D view of the room – and then buy it all over the Internet.

Display advertisements

Display advertisements or **banner ads** are small, rectangular boxes containing text and perhaps a picture that companies pay to place on relevant websites. The larger the audience, the more the placement costs. Some banners are accepted on a barter basis.[59]

Display advertisements still hold great promise compared to popular search advertisements. Given that Internet users spend only 5 per cent of their time online actually searching for information, there are many opportunities to reach and influence consumers while they surf the Web. However, advertisements need to be more attractive and influential, better targeted and more closely tracked.[60]

The emergence of behavioural targeting is allowing companies to track the online behaviour of target customers to find the best match between advertisement and prospect. For example, if a person clicks on three websites related to car insurance, then visits an unrelated site for sports or entertainment, car insurance advertisements may show up on that site, in addition to the car insurance sites. This practice ensures that advertisements are readily apparent for a potential customer likely to be in the market. Although critics worry about companies knowing too much about customers, Microsoft claims behavioural targeting can increase the likelihood a visitor clicks an advertisement by as much as 76 per cent.

Interstitials

Interstitials are advertisements, often with video or animation that pop up between changes on a website. Many consumers find pop-up advertisements intrusive and distracting, so most ISPs now offer their subscribers a blocking option.

Internet-specific advertisements and videos

With user-generated content sites such as YouTube, MySpace Video and Google Video, consumers and advertisers can upload advertisements and videos to be shared virally by millions of people.

Sponsorships

Many companies appear on the Internet by sponsoring special content on websites that carry news, financial information, and so on. **Sponsorships** are best placed in well-targeted sites that offer relevant information or service. The sponsor pays for showing the content and in turn receives acknowledgment as the sponsor of that particular service on the site.

A popular vehicle for sponsorship is the *podcast*, digital media files created for playback on portable MP3 players, laptops or PCs. Although the costs are higher than for popular radio shows, podcasts are able to reach very specific market segments so analysts expect their popularity to grow.

Alliances

When one Internet company works with another, they end up advertising each other through alliances and affiliate programmes. AOL has created many successful alliances. Amazon has almost 1 million affiliates that post its banners on their websites. Companies can also undertake guerrilla marketing actions to publicise their site and generate word of mouth.

Online communities

Many companies sponsor online communities whose members communicate through postings, instant messaging and chat discussions about special interests related to the company's products and brands. These communities can provide companies with useful, hard-to-get information. A key for success of online communities is to create individual and group activities that help form bonds among members.

Email

Email uses only a fraction of the cost of a 'd-mail', or direct mail, campaign. Consumers are besieged by emails however, and many employ spam filters. Following are some important guidelines for productive email campaigns, followed by pioneering email marketers:[61]

- **Give the customer a reason to respond**: Offer powerful incentives for reading email pitches and online advertisements, such as email trivia games, scavenger hunts and instant-win sweepstakes.
- **Personalise the content of your emails**: IBM's iSource is distributed directly to customers' office email each week, delivering only 'the news they choose' in Announcements and Weekly Updates. Customers who agree to receive the newsletter select from topics listed on an interest profile.
- **Offer something the customer can't get via direct mail**: Because email campaigns can be carried out quickly, they can offer time-sensitive information such as the availability of last-minute cheap airfares and holiday vacancies.
- **Make it easy for customers to 'unsubscribe'**: Online customers demand a positive exit experience. According to a Burston-Marsteller and Roper Starch Worldwide study, the top 10 per cent of Web users who communicate much more often online typically share their views by email with 11 friends when satisfied, but contact 17 friends when dissatisfied.[62]

Mobile

(See also Chapters 17 and 18)
Mobile is an emerging mode which is likely to benefit from the new generation of dual-mode phones that will make it increasingly easy to blend mobile phones with wireless Internet service. The popularity of mobile phones is increasing marketers' interest in mobile marketing, especially as messages can be personalised. However there is some doubt about how consumers will react to such advertisements.

▽ Developing and managing the sales force

Setting objectives and strategy

The original and oldest form of direct marketing is the field sales call. Today most business-to-business companies rely heavily on a professional sales force to locate prospects, develop them into customers and grow the business, or they hire manufacturers' representatives and agents to carry out the direct selling task. In addition, many consumer companies such as Avon, Merrill Lynch, Anne Summers and Tupperware use a direct selling force. Hospitals and museums, for example, use fund-raisers to contact and solicit donations. For many firms, sales force performance is critical.

Although no one debates the importance of the sales force in marketing programmes, companies are sensitive to the high and rising costs of maintaining one. The term *sales representative* covers six positions, ranging from the least to the most creative types of selling:[63]

1 **Deliverer**: a salesperson whose major task is the delivery of a product (water, fuel, oil);

2 **Order taker**: an inside order taker (standing behind the counter) or outside order taker (calling on the supermarket manager);

3 **Missionary**: a salesperson not expected or permitted to take an order but rather to build goodwill or educate the actual or potential user (the medical 'detailer' representing an ethical pharmaceutical house);

4 **Technician**: a salesperson with a high level of technical knowledge (the engineering salesperson who is primarily a consultant to client companies);

5 **Demand creator**: a salesperson who relies on creative methods for selling tangible products (vacuum cleaners, cleaning brushes, household products) or intangibles (insurance, advertising services, education);

6 **Solution vendor**: a salesperson whose expertise is solving a customer's problem, often with a system of the company's products and services (for example computer and communications systems).

In designing the sales force, the company must consider the development of sales force objectives, strategy, structure, size and compensation (see Figure 20.6).

Companies need to define specific sales force objectives. For example, a company might want its sales representatives to spend 80 per cent of their time with current customers and 20 per cent with prospects, and 85 per cent of their time on established market offerings and 15 per cent on new offerings. The specific allocation depends on the kind of offerings and customers. Irrespective of the context, sales people will have one or more of the following specific tasks to perform:

- **Prospecting**: searching for prospects, or leads;
- **Targeting**: deciding how to allocate their time among prospects and customers;
- **Communicating**: communicating information about the company's products and services;
- **Selling**: approaching, presenting, answering questions, overcoming objections and closing sales;
- **Servicing**: providing various services to the customers – consulting on problems, rendering technical assistance, arranging financing, expediting delivery;
- **Information gathering**: conducting market research and doing intelligence work;
- **Allocating**: deciding which customers will get scarce products during product shortages.

Figure 20.6 Designing a sales force

Most companies are choosing a *leveraged sales force* that focuses representatives on selling the company's more complex and customised offerings to large accounts and uses inside sales people and Web ordering for small customers. Tasks such as lead generation, proposal writing, order fulfilment and after-sales support are assigned to others. Sales people handle fewer accounts and are rewarded for key account growth. This is far different from expecting sales people to sell to every possible account, the common weakness of geographically based sales forces.[64]

Companies must deploy sales forces strategically so they call on the right customers at the right time in the right way. Today's sales representatives act as 'account managers' who arrange fruitful contact between people in the buying and selling organisations. Selling increasingly calls for teamwork and the support of others, such as *top management*, especially when national accounts or major sales are at stake; *technical people*, who supply information and service before, during or after product purchase; *customer service representatives*, who provide installation, maintenance and other services; and an *office staff*, consisting of sales analysts, order expediters and assistants, as they all have a vital part to play in the customer-perceived value offerings that companies bring to market.

To maintain a market focus, sales people should know how to analyse sales data, measure market potential, gather market intelligence and develop marketing strategies and plans. Sales representatives, especially at the higher levels of sales management, need analytical marketing skills. Marketers believe sales forces are more effective in the long run if they understand that they are an integral part of the marketing team (see Chapter 22).[65]

Once the company chooses an approach, it can use a direct or a contractual sales force. A **direct (company) sales force** consists of full- or part-time paid employees who work exclusively for the company. Inside sales personnel conduct business from the office using the telephone and receive visits from prospective buyers, and field sales personnel travel to visit customers. A **contractual sales force** consists of manufacturers' representatives, sales agents and brokers, who earn a commission based on sales.

Sales force management issues

The sales force strategy has implications for its structure. A company that offers one product line offering to one end-using industry with customers in many locations would use a territorial structure. A company that sells many product offerings to many types of customers might need a product or market structure. Some companies need a more complex structure. Established companies need to revise their sales force structures as market and economic conditions change.

Figure 20.7 shows how a company must focus on different aspects of its sales force structure over the life cycle of the business.[66] 'Marketing insight: Major account management' discusses a specialised form of sales force structure.

Sales force size

Once the company establishes the number of customers it wants to reach, it can use a *workload approach* to establish sales force size. This method has five steps:

1　Group customers into size classes according to annual sales volume.

2　Establish desirable call frequencies (number of calls on an account per year) for each customer class.

3　Multiply the number of accounts in each size class by the corresponding call frequency to arrive at the total workload for the country, in sales calls per year.

Marketing insight

Major account management

Marketers usually pay special attention to major accounts (also called key, national, global or house accounts). A major account manager (MAM) usually reports to the national sales manager and supervises field representatives calling on customer plants within their territories. Large accounts are often handled by a strategic account management team with cross-functional personnel to cover all aspects of the customer relationship.

Some firms are creating cross-functional strategic account teams that integrate new product development, technical support, supply chain, marketing activities and multiple communication channels. Major account management is growing. As buyer concentration increases through mergers and acquisitions, fewer buyers account for a larger share of a company's sales. Many are centralising their purchases for certain items, which gives them more bargaining power. As market offerings become more complex, more groups in the buyer's organisation participate in the purchase process.

In selecting major accounts, companies look for those that purchase a high volume (especially of more profitable offerings), purchase centrally, require a high level of service in several geographic locations, may be price sensitive, and may want a long-term partnering relationship. Major account managers are responsible for delivering the required level of customer-perceived value offerings (see Chapter 11).

Many major accounts look for perceived added value more than a price advantage. They appreciate having a dedicated single point of contact; single billing; special warranties; EDI links; priority shipping; early information releases; customised products; and efficient maintenance, repair and upgraded service.

Sources: C. Doyle, B. McPhee and I. Harris (2005) Marketing, sales, and major account management: managing enterprise customers as a portfolio of opportunities, talk at Marketing Science Institute's *Marketing, Sales, and Customers* conference, 7 December; S. Sherman, J. Sperry and S. Reese (2003) *The Seven Keys to Managing Strategic Accounts*, New York: McGraw-Hill; J. Neff (2003) Bentonville or bust, *Advertising Age*, 24 February; N. Capon (2001) *Key Account Management and Planning: The Comprehensive Handbook for Managing Your Company's Most Important Strategic Asset*, New York: Free Press. More information can be obtained from NAMA (National Account Management Association) at www.nasm.com.

	Business life cycle stage			
	Start-Up	Growth	Maturity	Decline
Emphasis				
Role of sales force and selling partners	⇨⇨⇨⇨	⇨⇨	⇨	⇨⇨⇨
Size of sales force	⇨⇨⇨	⇨⇨⇨⇨	⇨⇨	⇨⇨⇨⇨
Degree of specialisation	⇨	⇨⇨⇨⇨	⇨⇨⇨	⇨⇨
Sales force resource allocation	⇨⇨	⇨	⇨⇨⇨⇨	⇨
Underlying customer strategy				
	Create awareness and generate quick product uptake	Penetrate deeper into existing segments and develop new ones	Focus on efficiently serving and retaining existing customers	Emphasise efficiency, protect critical customer relationships, exit unprofitable segments

Figure 20.7
The four factors for a successful sales force

Source: A. Zoltners, P. Sinha and S. E. Lorimer (2006) Match your sales-force structure to your business life cycle, *Harvard Business Review*, July–August, 81–9. Copyright © 2006 by the President and Fellows of Harvard College. All rights reserved. Reproduced with permission.

4 Determine the average number of calls a sales representative can make per year.

5 Divide the total annual calls required by the average annual calls made by a sales representative, to arrive at the number of sales representatives needed.

Sales force compensation

To recruit top-quality sales representatives the company must develop an attractive compensation package. Several policies and procedures guide the firm in recruiting, selecting, training, supervising, motivating and evaluating sales representatives (see Figure 20.8).

Recruiting and selecting representatives

At the heart of any successful sales force is a means of selecting effective representatives.[67] Selection procedures can vary from a single informal interview to prolonged testing and interviewing. Although scores from formal tests are only one factor in a selection procedure, tests have been weighted quite heavily by IBM, Prudential and Procter & Gamble. Gillette claims tests have reduced turnover and scores correlated well with the progress of new representatives.

Training and supervising sales representatives

Today's customers expect sales people to have a sound company and offer product knowledge, to add ideas to improve the customers' operations, and to be efficient and reliable. These demands have required companies to make a much higher investment in sales training.

Companies vary in how closely they supervise sales representatives. Representatives paid mostly on commission generally receive less supervision. Those who are salaried and must cover definite accounts are likely to receive substantial supervision. With multilevel selling, used by Endsleigh Insurance, Virgin and others, independent distributors are also in charge of their own sales force selling company products. These independent contractors or representatives are paid a commission not only on their own sales but also on the sales of people they recruit and train.

Figure 20.8 Managing the sales force

Norms for prospect calls

Companies often specify how much time representatives should spend prospecting for new accounts.

Using sales time efficiently

The best sales representatives manage their time both effectively and efficiently. Companies constantly try to improve sales force productivity. To cut costs, reduce time demands on their outside sales force, and take advantage of computer and telecommunications innovations, many have increased the size and responsibilities of their internal sales staff (technical support people, sales assistants and telemarketers).

One of the most valuable electronic tools for the sales representative are prospective companies' websites, which can provide much useful information. At the same time the representative's own company website can provide an introduction to self-identified potential customers and might even receive the initial order. For more complex transactions, the site provides a way for the buyer to contact the seller. Selling over the Internet supports relationship marketing by solving problems that do not require live intervention and thus allows more time to be spent on issues that are best addressed face to face.

Motivating sales representatives

The majority of sales representatives require encouragement and special incentives. Many companies set annual sales quotas (developed from the annual marketing plan) on sales revenue, unit volume, margin, selling effort or activity, or market offering/product type. Compensation is often tied to the degree of quota fulfilment.

Setting sales quotas can create problems. If the company underestimates and the sales representatives easily achieve their quotas, it has overpaid them. If the company overestimates sales potential, the sales people will find it very hard to reach their quotas and be frustrated or leave. Another disadvantage is that quotas can drive representatives to get as much business as possible – often ignoring the ability of the company to successfully deliver the full customer-perceived value offering. The company then gains short-term results at the cost of long-term customer satisfaction.

▽ Ford of Britain

As a sales incentive Ford ran a conference at the Palmeraie Golf Palace in Marrakesh for dealer sales managers to maintain sales momentum in and the end of 2007. The location was specially selected as it echoed a product placement in the Bond film *Casino Royale*. The programme included film clips and captured the enthusiasm of the audience who were well travelled and not always that easy to please.

Source: Brandrepublic, 12 November 2007

Evaluating sales representatives

So far the *feed-forward* aspects of sales supervision – how management communicates what the sales representatives should be doing and motivates them to do it – has been discussed. However, good feed-forward requires good *feedback*, which means getting regular information from customers to assess the performance of the sales force.

Sources of information

The most important source of information about representatives is sales reports. Additional information comes through personal observation, salesperson self-reports, customer letters and complaints, customer surveys, and conversations with other sales representatives.

Formal evaluation

The sales force's reports along with other observations supply the raw materials for evaluation. If effective in producing sales, the representative may not be highly rated by customers. Success may come because competitors' sales people are inferior, the representative's company market offer is better, or new customers are found to replace those who dislike the representative. Managers can gather customer opinions of their sales people's performances by email and postal questionnaires or telephone calls.

Key principles of personal selling

Effective sales people today have more than instinct; they are trained in methods of analysis and customer management. Companies train sales people to transform them from passive order takers into active order winners. Representatives are taught methods such as the SPIN system to build long-term relationships with questions such as:[68]

1 **Situation questions**: These ask about facts or explore the buyer's present situation. For example, 'What system are you using to invoice your customers?'

2 **Problem questions**: These deal with problems, difficulties and dissatisfactions the buyer is experiencing. For example, 'What parts of the system create errors?'

3 **Implication questions**: These ask about the consequences or effects of a buyer's problems, difficulties or dissatisfactions. For example, 'How does this problem affect your people's productivity?'

4 **Need-payoff questions**: These ask about the value or usefulness of a proposed solution. For example, 'How much would you save if our company could help reduce the errors by 80 per cent?'

Most sales training programmes agree on the major steps involved in any effective sales process and these are shown in Figure 20.9; their application to business-to-business selling is discussed below.[69]

Figure 20.9 Major steps in effective selling

The six steps of selling

1 **Prospecting and qualifying**: The first step in selling is to identify and qualify prospects.

2 **Pre-approach**: The salesperson needs to learn as much as possible about the prospect company (what it needs, who is involved in the purchase decision) and its buyers (personal characteristics and buying styles).

3 **Presentation and demonstration**: The salesperson tells the company/market offering 'story' to the buyer, using a *features, advantages, benefits* and *value* approach (FABV). Features describe physical characteristics of a market offering, such as chip-processing speeds or memory capacity. Advantages describe why the features provide an advantage to the customer. Benefits describe the economic, technical, service and social benefits delivered by the offering. Value explains the offering's worth in terms of CPV attributes (see Chapter 10). Sales people often spend too much time on product features and not enough time stressing the prospective CPV of a market offering.

4 **Overcoming objections**: Customers typically pose objections. *Psychological resistance* includes resistance to interference, preference for established supply sources or brands, apathy, reluctance to giving up something, unpleasant associations created by the sales representative, predetermined ideas, dislike of making decisions, and neurotic attitude towards money. *Logical resistance* might be objections to the price, delivery schedule, offering or company characteristics. To handle these objections, the salesperson should maintain a positive and professional approach and seek ways to satisfy the customer's perceived value requirements.

5 **Closing**: Closing signs from the buyer include physical actions, statements or comments, and questions. Representatives can ask for the order, recapitulate the points of agreement, offer to help write up the order, ask whether the buyer wants A or B, get the buyer to make

minor choices such as colour or size, or indicate what the buyer will lose by not placing the order now. The salesperson might offer specific inducements to close, such as a special price, an extra quantity or a token gift.[70]

6 **Follow-up and maintenance**: Follow-up and maintenance are necessary to ensure customer satisfaction and repeat business. Immediately after closing, the salesperson should agree any necessary details about delivery time, purchase terms and other matters important to the customer. The salesperson should schedule a follow-up call after delivery to ensure proper installation, instruction and servicing and to detect any problems, assure the buyer of the salesperson's interest, and reduce any cognitive dissonance. Finally, the salesperson should develop an account maintenance and growth plan.

Relationship marketing (RM)

The principles of personal selling and negotiation are typically transaction oriented because their purpose is to close a specific sale. However, in today's buyers' markets companies should be mindful of the need to actively seek and develop long-term supplier–customer relationships. The reason is simple – in buyers' markets (as opposed to sellers' markets) – customers are in short supply. Furthermore, they will be keen to regard suppliers as being trusted members of their value chains. This is because in highly competitive markets wise companies are striving to gain a market edge by formulating and delivering customer-perceived value offerings that are superior to those of their competitors. So they prefer suppliers who can deliver a coordinated set of CPV offerings (comprised of core products and services to many locations); who can quickly solve problems in different locations; and who can work closely with customer teams to improve CPV offerings and process issues.

When a relationship management programme is properly implemented, the organisation will focus on supplying what CPV offerings are wanted by its customers (market effectiveness in today's business environment) and on managing the development and supply of suitable CPV packages with due regard to its resources (efficiency) and which customers will respond profitably to relationship management. For further discussion of RM see Chapter 21.

▽ SUMMARY

1 Advertising is any paid form of non-personal presentation and promotion of ideas, goods or services by an identified sponsor. Advertisers include not only business firms but also charitable, non-profit and government agencies.

2 Developing an advertising programme is a five-step process: (1) set advertising objectives; (2) establish a budget; (3) choose the advertising message and creative strategy; (4) decide on the media; and (5) evaluate communication and sales effects.

3 Sales promotion consists of a diverse collection of incentive tools, mostly short term, designed to stimulate quicker or greater purchase of particular products or services by consumers or the trade. Sales promotion includes tools for consumer promotion, trade promotion, and business and sales force promotion (trade shows and conventions, contests for sales representatives and speciality advertising). In using sales promotion a company must establish its objectives, select the tools, develop the programme, pre-test the programme, implement and control it, and evaluate the results.

4 Events and experiences are a means to become part of special and more personally relevant moments in consumers' lives. Involvement with events can broaden and deepen the relationship of the sponsor with its target market, but only if managed properly.

5 Public relations (PR) involves a variety of programmes designed to promote or protect a company's image or its individual products. Many companies today use marketing public relations (MPR) to support the marketing department in corporate or product promotion and image making. MPR can affect public awareness at a fraction of the cost of advertising and is often much more credible. The main tools of PR are publications, events, news, speeches, public service activities and identity media.

6 Direct marketing is an interactive marketing system that uses one or more media to effect a measurable response or transaction at any location. Direct marketing, especially electronic marketing, is showing explosive growth.

7 Direct marketers plan campaigns by deciding on objectives, target markets and prospects, offers and prices. This is followed by testing and establishing measures to determine the campaign's success.

8 Major channels for direct marketing include face-to-face selling, direct mail, catalogue marketing, tele-marketing, interactive TV, kiosks, websites and mobile devices.

9 Interactive marketing provides marketers with opportunities for much greater interaction and individualisation through well-designed websites, as well as online advertisements and promotions and other approaches.

10 Two notable forms of word-of-mouth marketing are buzz marketing, which seeks to get people talking about a brand by ensuring that a product or service or how it is marketed is out of the ordinary, and viral marketing, which encourages people to exchange information related one way or another to a product or service online.

11 Sales personnel serve as a company's link to its customers. The sales rep *is* the company to many of its customers, and it is the representative who brings back to the company much-needed information about the customer.

12 Designing the sales force requires decisions regarding objectives, strategy, structure, size and compensation. Objectives may include prospecting, targeting, communicating, selling, servicing, information gathering and allocating. Determining strategy requires

choosing the most effective mix of selling approaches. Choosing the sales force structure entails dividing territories by geography, product or market (or some combination of these). Estimating how large the sales force needs to be involves estimating the total workload and how many sales hours (and hence sales people) will be needed. Compensating the sales force entails determining what types of salaries, commissions, bonuses, expense accounts and benefits to give, and how much weight customer satisfaction should have in determining total compensation.

13 There are five steps involved in managing the sales force: (1) recruiting and selecting sales representatives; (2) training the representatives in sales techniques and in the company's products, policies and customer-satisfaction orientation; (3) supervising the sales force and helping representatives to use their time efficiently; (4) motivating the sales force and balancing quotas, monetary rewards and supplementary motivators; (5) evaluating individual and group sales performance.

14 Effective sales people are trained in the methods of analysis and customer management, as well as the art of sales professionalism. No approach works best in all circumstances, but most trainers agree that selling is a six-step process: (1) prospecting and qualifying customers; (2) pre-approach; (3) presentation and demonstration; (4) overcoming objections; (5) closing; and (6) follow-up and maintenance.

▽ APPLICATIONS

Marketing debate

Should marketers test advertising? Advertising creatives have long lamented advertisement pre-testing. They believe that it inhibits their creative process and results in much sameness in commercials. Marketers, on the other hand, believe that pre-testing provides necessary checks and balances as to whether an advertising campaign is being developed in a way that will connect with consumers and be well received in the marketplace.

Take a position: Advertisement pre-testing is often an unnecessary waste of marketing spend *versus* Advertisement pre-testing provides an important diagnostic function for marketers as to the likely success of an advertising campaign.

Are great sales people born or made? One debate in sales is about the impact of training versus selection in developing an effective sales force. Some observers maintain

the best sales people are born that way and are effective due to their personalities and interpersonal skills developed over a lifetime. Others contend that application of leading-edge sales techniques can make virtually anyone a sales star.

Take a position: The key to developing an effective sales force is selection *versus* The key to developing an effective sales force is training.

Marketing discussion

What are some of your favourite TV advertisements? Why? How effective are the message and creative strategies? How are they building brand equity?

▽ REFERENCES

[1]P. F. Nunes and J. Merrihue (2007) The continuing power of mass advertising, *Sloan Management Review*, Winter, 63–9.

[2]*Marketing*, 11 July 2007; *Marketing*, 7 November 2007; Andrex puppy voted tops, *Manchester Evening News*, 2 September 2007; Andrex puppy inducted into Madam Tussauds, *K9 Magazine*, 2 September 2007; www.andrexpuppy.co.uk.

[3]D. V. Thompson and R. W. Hamilton (2006) The effects of information processing on consumers' responses to comparative advertising, *Journal of Consumer Research*, 32 (March), 530–40; D. Grewal, S. Kavanoor and J. Barnes (1997) Comparative versus noncomparative advertising: a meta-analysis, *Journal of Marketing*, October, 1–15.

[4]A popular saying attributed to John Wanamaker. See http://en.wikipedia.org/wiki/John_Wanamaker.

[5]See G. S. Low and J. J. Mohr (1998) Brand managers' perceptions of the marketing communications budget allocation process, Cambridge, MA: Marketing Science Institute, *Report*, No. 98-105, March; and their The advertising sales promotion trade-off: theory and practice, Cambridge, MA: Marketing Science Institute, *Report*, No. 92-127, October. Also see G. J. Beihal and D. A. Sheinen (1998) Managing the brand in a corporate advertising environment: a decision-making framework for brand managers, *Journal of Advertising*, 17, 22 June, 99.

[6]D. Vakratsas, F. M. Feinberg, F. M. Bass and G. Kalyanaram (2004) The shape of advertising response functions revisited: a model of dynamic probabilistic thresholds, *Marketing Science*, 23(1), 109–19.

[7]L. M. Lodish, M. Abraham, S. Kalmenson, J. Livelsberger, B. Lubetkin, B. Richardson and M.-E. Stevens (1995) How TV advertising works: a meta-analysis of 389 real-world split cable TV advertising experiments, *Journal of Marketing Research*, 32 (May), 125–39.

[8]G. Allenby and D. Hanssens (2005) Advertising response, Marketing Science Institute, *Special Report*, No. 05-200; J. Neff (2004) TV doesn't sell package goods, *Advertising Age*, 24 May, 1, 30.

[9]www.stateofthenewsmedia.org/2007/narrative_newspapers_intro.asp?media=3.

[10]D. Ogilvy (1983) *Ogilvy on Advertising*, New York: Vintage Books. Also consider L. Percy, J. Rossiter and R. Elliott (2002) *Strategic Advertising Management*, Oxford: Oxford University Press.

[11]K. B. Sheehan (2003) *Controversies in Contemporary Advertising*, Thousand Oaks, CA: Sage.

[12]P. Malaviya (2007) The moderating influence of advertising context on ad repetition effects: the role of amount and type of elaboration, *Journal of Consumer Research*, 34 (June), 32–40.

[13]T. H. Davenport and J. C. Beck (2000) *The Attention Economy: Understanding the New Currency of Business*, Boston, MA: Harvard Business School Press.

[14]www.oaaa.org/.

[15]B. Archer (2007) Outdoor media: digital formats – weblinks: airport advertising flies into the future, the *Guardian*, 25 June, 2.

[16]J. Lippman and R. Brooks (2000) Hot holiday flick pairs FedEx, Hanks, *Wall Street Journal*, 11 December; J. Lipman (1991) Product placement can be free lunch, *Wall Street Journal*, 25 November.

[17]W. Berger (2003) That's advertainment, *Business 2.0*, March, 91–5.

[18]For more on other media context effects, see J. Wang and B. J. Calder (2006) Media transportation and advertising, *Journal of Consumer Research*, 33 (September), 151–62.

[19]J. L. C. M. Woltman Elpers, M. Wedel and R. G. M. Pieters (2003) Why do consumers stop viewing television commercials? Two experiments on the influence of moment-to-moment entertainment and information value, *Journal of Marketing Research*, 40 (November), 437–53.

[20]See, for example, A. G. Chessa and J. M. J. Murre (2007) A neurocognitive model of advertisement content and brand-name recall, *Marketing Science*, 26 (January–February), 130–41.

[21]G. J. Tellis, R. K. Chandy and P. Thaivanich (2000) Which ad works, when, where, and how often? Modeling the effects of direct television advertising, *Journal of Marketing Research*, 37 (February), 32–46.

[22]N. Hollis (2004) The future of tracking studies, *Admap*, October, 151–3.

[23]L. Petrecca and T. Howard (2006) Nielsen wants to track who watches commercials, *USA Today*, 11 July.

[24]From R. C. Blattberg and S. A. Neslin, *Sales Promotion: Concepts, Methods, and Strategies*, Upper Saddle River, NJ: Prentice Hall. This text provides the most comprehensive and analytical treatment of sales promotion to date. An extremely up-to-date and comprehensive review of academic work on sales promotions can be found in S. Neslin (2002) Sales promotion in B. Weitz and R. Wensley (eds), *Handbook of Marketing*, London: Sage, 310–38. Also consider, J. Cummins and R. Mullin (2004) *Sales Promotion: How to Create, Implement and Integrate Campaigns that Really Work*, London: Kogan Page.

[25]K. Ailawadi, K. Gedenk and S. A. Neslin (1999) Heterogeneity and purchase event feedback in choice models: an empirical analysis with implications for model building, *International Journal of Research in Marketing*, 16, September, 177–98. See also K. L. Ailawadi, K. Gedenk, C. Lutzky and S. A. Neslin (2007) Decomposition of the sales impact of promotion-induced stockpiling, *Journal of Marketing Research*, 44 (August), 297–308; E. T. Anderson and D. Simester (2004) The long-run effects of promotion depth on new versus established customers: three field studies, *Marketing Science*, 23(1), 4–20; L. Wathieu, A. V. Muthukrishnan and B. J. Bronnenberg (2004) The asymmetric effect of discount retraction on subsequent choice, *Journal of Consumer Research*, 31 (December), 652–65; P. Kopalle, C. F. Mela and L. Marsh (1999) The dynamic effect of discounting on sales: empirical analysis and normative pricing implications, *Marketing Science*, 18 (Summer), 317–32.

[26]C. Mela, K. Jedidi and D. Bowman (1998) The long-term impact of promotions on consumer stockpiling, *Journal of Marketing Research*, 35(2), 250–62.

[27]H. J. Van Heerde, S. Gupta and D. Wittink (2003) Is 75% of the sales promotion bump due to brand switching? No, only 33% is, *Journal of Marketing Research*, 40 (November), 481–91; H. J. Van Heerde, P. S. H. Leeflang and D. R. Wittink (2000) The estimation of pre- and postpromotion dips with store-level scanner data, *Journal of Marketing Research*, 37(3), 383–95.

[28]AutoVIBES (2004) *AutoBeat Daily*, 3 March, K. Lundegaard and S. Freeman (2004) Detroit's challenge: weaning buyers from years of deals, *Wall Street Journal*, 6 January.

[29]M. M. Abraham and L. M. Lodish (1990) Getting the most out of advertising and promotion, *Harvard Business Review*, May–June, 50–60. See also S. Srinivasan, K. Pauwels, D. Hanssens and M. Dekimpe (2004) Do promotions benefit manufacturers, retailers, or both?, *Management Science*, 50(5), 617–29.

[30]For a model for setting sales promotions objectives, see D. B. Jones (1994) Setting promotional goals: a communications relationship model, *Journal of Consumer Marketing*, 11(1), 38–49.

[31]K. L. Ailawadi, B. A. Harlam, J. Cesar and D. Trounce (2006) Promotion profitability for a retailer: the role of promotion, brand, category, and store characteristics, *Journal of Marketing Research*, 43 (November), 518–36.

[32]K. L. Ailawadi and B. Harlam (2004) An empirical analysis of the determinants of retail margins: the role of store brand share, *Journal of Marketing*, 68 (January), 147–66; K. L. Ailawadi (2001) The retail power-performance conundrum: what have we learned? *Journal of Retailing*, 77(3), 299–318; P. W. Farris and K. L. Ailawadi (1992) Retail power: monster or mouse?, *Journal of Retailing*, Winter, 351–69; K. Pauwels (in press). How retailer and competitor decisions drive the long-term effectiveness of manufacturer promotions, *Journal of Retailing*.

[33]P. Kotler (1973–4) Atmospherics as a marketing tool, *Journal of Retailing*, Winter, 48–64.

[34]B. Cornwell, M. S. Humphreys, A. M. Maguire, C. S. Weeks and C. Tellegen (2006) Sponsorship-linked marketing: the role of articulation in memory, *Journal of Consumer Research*, 33 (December), 312–21; A. M. Grey and K. Shildum-Reid (2003) *The Sponsorship Seeker's Toolkit*, Maidenhead, England: McGraw-Hill.

[35]P. Post (2000) Beyond brand: the power of experience branding, *ANA/Advertiser*, October–November.

[36]B. Schmitt (1999) *Experiential Marketing: How to Get Customers to Sense, Feel, Think, Act, Relate*, New York: Free Press.

[37]B. J. Pine and J. H. Gilmore (1999) *The Experience Economy: Work Is Theatre and Every Business a Stage*, Cambridge, MA: Harvard University Press.

[38]2006 experiential marketing study, www.jackmorton.com

[39]Do we have a story for you! (2006) *The Economist*, 21 January, 57–8 A. Ries and L. Ries (2002) *The Fall of Advertising and the Rise of PR*, New York: HarperCollins; P. Baines, J. Egan and F. Jefkins (2003) *Public Relations: Contemporary Issues and Techniques*, Oxford: Butterworth-Heinemann.

[40]For further reading on cause-related marketing, see P. R. Varadarajan and A. Menon (1988) Cause-related marketing: a co-alignment of marketing strategy and corporate philanthropy, *Journal of Marketing*, July, 58–74; S. Adkins (1999) *Cause-related Marketing: Who Cares Wins*, Oxford: Butterworth-Heinemann.

[41]S. Nurpin (2007) From brand out of mind to brand in hand: brand unification by icons, totems, and titans, talk given at International Energy Group's 24th Annual Sponsorship Conference, 13 March.

[42]The terms *direct-order marketing* and *direct-relationship marketing* were suggested as subsets of direct marketing by Stan Rapp and Tom Collins (1990) in *The Great Marketing Turnaround*, Upper Saddle River, NJ: Prentice Hall. See also B. Thomas and M. Housden (2002) *Direct Marketing in Practice*, Oxford: Butterworth-Heinemann; R. Mullin (2003) *A Step-by-Step Guide to Effective Planning and Targeting* (Marketing in Action Series), London: Kogan Page; M. Stone, A. Band and E. Blake (2003) *The Definitive Guide to Direct and Interactive Marketing: How to Select, Reach and Retain the Right Customers*, London: Financial Times Prentice Hall.

[43]R. Kivetz and I. Simonson (2003) The idiosyncratic fit heuristic: effort advantage as a determinant of consumer response to loyalty programs, *Journal of Marketing Research*, 40 (November), 454–67; R. Kivetz and I. Simonson (2002) Earning the right to indulge: effort as a determinant of customer preferences toward frequency program rewards, *Journal of Marketing Research*, 39 (May), 155–70.

[44]M. McCarthy (2002) Direct marketing gets Cannes do spirit, *USA Today*, 17 June.

[45]DMA's 2006 'Power of direct marketing' Reports (2007) *Direct Marketing Association*, 5 June; Direct marketing's growth rate to cushion cooling US economy (2006) *Direct Marketing Association*, 17 October; C. Krol (2005) Direct hits it big, *BtoB*, 10 October, 29–31.

[46]See www.the-dma.org.

[47]On the mat (2005) *The Economist*, 26 November, 78.

[48]E. L. Nash (2000) *Direct Marketing: Strategy, Planning, Execution*, 4th edn, New York: McGraw-Hill.

[49]The *average customer longevity* (N) is related to the *customer retention rate* (CR). Suppose the company retains 80 per cent of its customers each year. Then the average customer longevity is given by: $N = 1/(1-CR) = 1/.2 = 5$.

[50]J. Edwards (2001) The art of the infomercial, *Brandweek*, 3 September, 14–19.

[51]E. Steel (2007) Advertising's brave new world, *Wall Street Journal*, 25 May; J. L. Roberts (2006) How to count eyeballs, *Newsweek*, 27 November, 42.

[52]K. J. Delaney (2006) Once-wary industry giants embrace Internet advertising, *Wall Street Journal*, 17 April.

[53]P. Kotler (2005) *According to Kotler*, New York: American Management Association.

[54]P. J. Danaher, G. W. Mullarkey and S. Essegaier (2006) Factors affecting web site visit duration: a cross-domain analysis, *Journal of Marketing Research*, 43 (May), 182–94.

[55]J. F. Rayport and B. J. Jaworski (2001) *e-commerce*, New York: McGraw-Hill, 116.

[56]B. Tedeschi (2002) E-commerce report, *New York Times*, 24 June.

[57]J.-B. E. M. Steenkamp and I. Geyskens (2006) How country characteristics affect the perceived value of web sites, *Journal of Marketing*, 70 (July), 136–50.

[58]Prime clicking time (2003) *The Economist*, 31 May, 65; B. Elgin (2003) Search engines are picking up steam, *BusinessWeek*, 24 March, 86–7.

[59]P. Manchanda, J.-P. Dubé, Khim Yong Goh and P. K. Chintagunta (2006) The effects of banner advertising on Internet purchasing, *Journal of Marketing Research*, 43, February, 98–108; Pay per sale (2005) *The Economist*, 1 October, 62.

[60]P. Sloan (2007) The quest for the perfect online ad, *Business 2.0*, March, 88–93; C. Holahan (2007) The promise of online display ads, *BusinessWeek*, 1 May.

[61]S. Godin (1999) *Permission Marketing: Turning Strangers into Friends and Friends into Customers*, New York: Simon & Schuster.

[62]C. R. Schoenberger (2002) Web? What web?, *Forbes*, 10 June, 132.

[63]Adapted from R. N. McMurry (1961) The mystique of super-salesmanship, *Harvard Business Review*, March–April, 114. Also see W. C. Moncrief III (1986) Selling activity and sales position taxonomies for industrial sales forces, *Journal of Marketing Research*, August, 261–70.

[64]L. G. Friedman and T. R. Furey (1999) *The Channel Advantage: Going to Marketing with Multiple Sales Channels*, Oxford: Butterworth-Heinemann.

[65]P. Kotler, N. Rackham and S. Krishnaswamy (2006) Ending the war between sales and marketing, *Harvard Business Review*, July–August, 68–78; T. M. Smith, S. Gopalakrishna and R. Chaterjee (2006) A three-stage model of integrated marketing communications at the marketing-sales interface, *Journal of Marketing Research*, 43 (November), 546–79.

[66]M. Copeland (2004) Hits and misses, *Business 2.0*, April, 142.

[67]S. Albers (2002) Sales-force management: compensation, motivation, selection, and training, in B. Weitz and R. Wensley (eds), *Handbook of Marketing*, London: Sage, 248–66; D. Jobber and G. Lancaster (2000) *Selling and Sales Management*, Harlow: Prentice-Hall.

[68]N. Rackham (1988) *SPIN Selling*, New York: McGraw-Hill. Also see his *The SPIN Selling Fieldbook* (1996), New York: McGraw-Hill; J. Lardner (2002–3) Selling salesmanship, *Business 2.0*, December–January, 66; S. D. Morgen (1999) *Selling with Integrity: Reinventing Sales through Collaboration, Respect, and Serving*, New York: Berkeley Books; N. Rackham and J. De Vincentis (1996) *Rethinking the Sales Force*, New York: McGraw-Hill.

[69]Some of the following discussion is based on W. J. E. Crissy, W. H. Cunningham and I. C. M. Cunningham (1977) *Selling: The Personal Force in Marketing*, New York: John Wiley & Sons, 119–29.

[70]G. R. Franke and J.-E. Park (2006) Salesperson adaptive selling behaviour and customer orientation: a meta-analysis, *Journal of Marketing Research*, 43 (November), 693–702; R. G. McFarland, G. N. Challagalla and T. A. Shervani (2006) Influence tactics for effective adaptive selling, *Journal of Marketing*, 70 (October), 103–17.

▽ Managing marketing implementation and control

Video documentary for Part 8

Go to **www.pearsoned.co.uk/marketingmanagementeurope** to watch the video documentary that relates to Part 8 and consider the issues raised below.

In addition to their responsibilities to their companies to ensure that the marketing spend is measured and seen to be productive, marketing managers also have a number of challenges that are contextually and socially important.

Part 8: Managing Marketing Implementation and Control explores two important themes:

1   selecting suitable marketing spends and monitoring their effectiveness; and

2   responding to broader contextual and social challenges.

Marketing expenditure, as with any other company activity, needs to be budgeted and result in a measurable return. Marketing activities are being professionally costed and attempts made to judge the effectiveness of different elements within the marketing budget.

However, the application of management accounting methods to assess the precise contribution of any specific marketing activity is difficult to achieve, as many of the sub-budgets within the responsibility of a marketing manager, are attempting to meet revenue targets that are highly dynamic. Inevitably, marketing management is part intuition, part creative flare and part science but nonetheless dependent crucially on the development and professional use of marketing metrics.

When watching the video documentary that accompanies Part 8, consider how the marketing managers being interviewed measure the effectiveness of their marketing spend, as well as rising to the challenge of ethical and social issues, including the implementation of environmentally sustainable practises.

Hear a variety of top marketing executives from a wide range of organisations offer their own interesting and varied perspectives on the key themes of Part 8 including: Henrik Otto, Senior Vice-President of Global Design, Electrolux (top); Julian Whitehead, Director of Sustainability and Social Responsibility, Land Rover (centre); and St Paul's Cathedral requires marketing support to raise the money needed to stay open (bottom).

▽ Implementing marketing management

Healthy long-term growth for a brand requires that the marketing organisation be managed properly. Holistic marketers must engage in a host of carefully planned, inter-connected marketing activities and satisfy an increasingly broader set of constituents. They must also consider the wider range of effects of their actions. Corporate social responsibility and sustainability have become a priority as organisations grapple with the short- and long-term effects of their marketing. Some firms have embraced this new vision of corporate enlightenment and made it the very core of what they do.

Consider Unilever and Reckitt Benckiser.

Sense and sensibility overcome pride and prejudice as a marketing executive from an underperforming company seeks advice from a marketing consultant.
Source: Serif

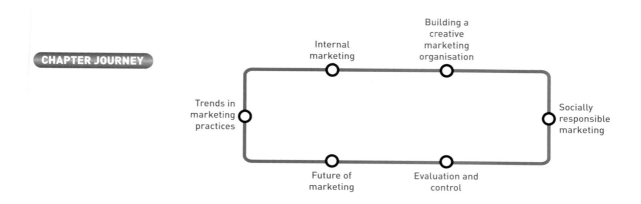

Internal marketing

Building a creative marketing organisation

Trends in marketing practices

Socially responsible marketing

Future of marketing

Evaluation and control

magine, for a second, that Unilever's latest turnaround plan does not work. Chief executive Patrick Cescau has slimmed down management, cut costs, shed some underperforming assets, and so far delivered three years of steady, if gradual, improvement in company performance. An expensive restructuring plan is designed to increase margins. But if the consumer goods giant trips up, perhaps on rising raw material prices, calls for more radical action will be heard. What might plan B look like?[1]

One option could be to try to import wholesale the culture from a smaller and more nimble rival. Reckitt Benckiser, which has been able to grow sales in developed markets where Unilever largely stagnates, leaps to mind. The UK household goods group was itself created in 1999 when the management of Benckiser effectively took control of the larger, but struggling, Reckitt & Colman. The combination of beer makers Interbrew and AmBev in 2004, where the latter's cost-cutting experts took the reins at the newly created InBev, offers a similar precedent.

Other brands such as Ben & Jerry's, Timberland and the Virgin Group have embraced similar philosophies and practices. Successful holistic marketing requires effective relationship marketing, integrated marketing, internal marketing and performance marketing. Preceding chapters addressed the first two topics and the strategy and tactics of marketing.[2] This chapter considers the latter two topics and how to conduct marketing responsibly. The discussion addresses how firms organise, implement, evaluate and control marketing activities and the increased importance of social responsibility. The chapter begins by examining changes in how companies conduct marketing today.

▽ Trends in marketing practices

As a consequence of the paradigm change in the business environment from sellers' to buyers' markets, together with important changes in the marketing macroenvironment such as globalisation, deregulation and technological advances, many companies have or are in the process of restructuring their affairs by:

- **Re-engineering:** appointing teams to manage customer-value-building processes and break down walls between departments;
- **Outsourcing:** buying more goods and services from outside domestic or foreign vendors as they seek to convert traditional supply chains into value chains;
- **Benchmarking:** studying 'best practice companies' to improve performance;
- **Supplier partnering:** partnering with fewer but better value-adding suppliers;
- **Customer partnering:** working more closely with customers to add value to their operations;
- **Merging:** acquiring or merging with firms in the same or complementary industries to gain economies of scale and scope;
- **Globalising:** increasing efforts to 'think global' and 'act local';
- **Flattening:** reducing the number of organisational levels to get closer to the customer;
- **Focusing:** determining the most profitable businesses and customers and focusing on them;
- **Accelerating:** designing the organisation and setting up processes to respond more quickly to changes in the environment;
- **Empowering:** encouraging and empowering personnel to produce more ideas and take more initiative.

The role of marketing in the organisation is also changing.[3] Traditionally marketers have played the roles of middlemen, charged with understanding customer needs and transmitting the voice of the customer to various functional areas in the organisation. In today's markets companies need to take a holistic view of the underlying philosophy of marketing – bring to the marketplace customer-perceived value offerings that will satisfy and delight customers. Thus marketing needs to be regarded as more than a functional activity. A company's output is determined by both the corporate marketing philosophy and the result of the coordination of internal functions as well as those external ones that make up the value chain.

> To find out why Paris-based L'Oréal, the world's biggest cosmetics group, acquired The Body Shop, the UK-based retailer of toiletries and cosmetics well known for its distinctive management approach, visit www.pearsoned.co.uk/marketingmanagementeurope

▽ Internal marketing

The term internal marketing was first used in the 1970s and was initially associated with the marketing of services. However, over the years it has come to emphasise the importance in buyers' markets for a company to adopt a holistic attitude towards the concepts and goals of marketing and engage in choosing, providing and communicating customer-perceived value (see Chapter 11). The provision of CPV involves a coordinated effort spread across the whole company and is no longer seen as a strictly sales department responsibility.[4]

▽ BenQ ready to signal its Siemens solution

When BenQ, the Taiwanese electronics maker with a brand created less than four years ago, announced in early June 2005 that it would take over the mobile handset business of Siemens, one of Europe's most traditional household names, many analysts reacted with scepticism.

The question most frequently asked was: 'How can two laggards become a leader by just joining together?' Siemens had been losing market share because of its 'uncool' handsets. BenQ was failing to sustain a forceful push up the global handset market rankings due to its lack of proprietary technology. Both were losing money. Chief marketing officer Jerry Wang is one of the Taiwanese executives who will help lead BenQ Mobile, the new company with headquarters in Munich. He identified Siemens' conservative, rigid group structure as the main reason why the German company's handset business was underperforming, and expressed confidence that joining BenQ would change its fortunes. 'The business is strangled by standards set in accordance with Siemens' mostly non-consumer operations,' he said. 'Products suffer from over-engineering, a lack of speed in response to market trends, and restrictions put on the brand image by the needs of other group businesses.' BenQ rolled out an internal marketing campaign to boost morale. 'Everybody has to embrace and love the brand,' said Wang.[5]

Marketing is about presenting a unified approach to the customer. If a brand's employees are not engaged by its marketing or, worse still, they do not understand it, any new sales targets will suffer. That is why internal marketing of brand strategy and activity can be one of the most powerful tools a marketing executive can employ. However, in general, internal marketing is underestimated and underutilised. Yet it theoretically has the potential to deliver many tangible benefits to both the company and the brand.

On a very basic level, it can help ease some of the frustrations non-marketing people sometimes have with their marketing colleagues: 'Why do we have to have a brand campaign? Can't you just spend more of your unimaginably large budget on promoting our products?' Most marketers recognise this question and often become irritated at the inference that there is no relationship between brand and sales. However, the question around brand and market offering is valid, as is the answer. The most powerful brands are created when the external marketing reflects the internal culture. British Airways' 'World's Favourite Airline' proposition started life as an internal expression of identity for the airline's own staff.

Holding up a mirror to the organisation and then using the reflection to establish the brand proposition is one of the most effective and credible ways to market. 'This is who we are and this is what we stand for', as opposed to 'This is what we offer' gives consumers and staff alike a much greater insight into a company's brand.

Tesco, with 'Every little helps', and Apple Macintosh with 'Different' are two other brands whose *cri de cœur* works as well internally as it does externally. Indeed, these propositions simply could not work unless both audiences bought into them. Whichever direction a brand takes, if the internal community understands and owns the marketing, a bond is forged, spirits are high and advocates are created. If it does not, there is a pretty good chance that consumers won't either. The *Guardian* reported Sir Richard Branson as saying that 'the best internal marketing tool has been a desk calendar distributed to staff worldwide'. The CEO of Fortis, the Belgian/Dutch bank and insurance company, gave all its 56,000 employees a Rubik's cube style gadget inscribed with 14 imperatives such as 'Deliver results', 'Team spirit' and 'Develop results'. He wanted to encourage a common language and culture across his sprawling company.[6]

A company can have an excellent marketing department on paper, however, and fail to perform effectively. Much depends on how *other* company departments view customers. They must adopt the holistic view of marketing. Only when *all* employees realise their job is to create, serve and satisfy customers does the company become an effective marketer.[7] The 'Marketing memo: Characteristics of company departments that are truly customer driven' presents a tool that evaluates which company departments are truly customer driven.[8]

Critique of internal marketing

Sceptics regard the concept of internal marketing as being based on a false premise that employees can be treated like external customers. In Europe there is little empirical evidence of its detailed and widespread company adoption. The concept is simple: use basic marketing approaches to communicate to employees in the same way that these methods can raise awareness, interest, intent and action with consumers.

The explanation for the revival of internal marketing is also simple. Marketing directors are increasingly delivering a range of internal communication tasks. The logic is that if an organisation

Marketing memo

Characteristics of company departments that are truly customer driven

R&D	– They spend time meeting customers and listening to their problems. – They welcome the involvement of marketing, manufacturing and other departments on each new project. – They benchmark competitors' products and seek 'best of class' solutions. – They solicit customer reactions and suggestions as the project progresses. – They continuously improve and refine the product on the basis of market feedback.
Purchasing	– They proactively search for the best suppliers rather than choose only from those who solicit their business by offering the lowest prices. – They build long-term relationships with fewer but more reliable high-quality suppliers, thereby developing a sustainable value chain.
Manufacturing	– They invite customers to visit and tour their plants. – They visit customer factories to see how they use the company's products. – They willingly work overtime when it is important to meet promised delivery schedules. – They continuously search for ways to produce goods faster and/or at lower costs. – They continuously improve product quality, aiming for zero defects. – They meet customer requirements for 'customisation' where this can be done profitably.
Marketing	– They study customer needs and wants in well-defined market segments. – They allocate marketing effort in relation to the long-run profit potential of the targeted segments. – They develop winning offerings for each target segment. – They measure company image and customer satisfaction on a continuous basis. – They continuously gather and evaluate ideas for new products, product improvements and services to meet customers' needs. – They influence all company departments and employees to be customer centred in their thinking and practice.
Sales	– They have specialised knowledge of the customer's industry. – They strive to give the customer 'the best solution'. – They make only promises they can keep. – They feed back customers' needs and ideas to those in charge of product development. – They serve the same customers for a long period of time.
Logistics	– They set a high standard for service delivery time and they meet this standard consistently. – They operate a knowledgeable and friendly customer-service department that can answer questions, handle complaints and resolve problems in a satisfactory and timely manner.
Accounting	– They prepare periodic 'profitability' reports by product, market segment, geographic areas (regions, sales territories), order sizes and individual customers. – They prepare invoices tailored to customer needs and answer customer queries courteously and quickly.
Finance	– They understand and support marketing expenditures (e.g., image advertising) that represent marketing investments which produce long-term customer preference and loyalty. – They tailor the financial package to the customers' financial requirements. – They make quick decisions on customer creditworthiness.
Public relations	– They disseminate favourable news about the company and they 'damage control' unfavourable news. – They act as an internal customer and public advocate for better company policies and practices.
Other customer-contact personnel	– They are competent, courteous, cheerful, credible, reliable and responsive.

is trying to deliver a differentiating customer experience, then who better to get employees lined up than the people responsible for defining the customer experience? The fact that the marketing function often has greater influence than do internal communications adds weight to the idea. With the importance and power of brand rising rapidly on the corporate agenda, the case is compelling. However, there is a basic problem with the whole idea. The nature of the employment relationship is essentially different from a consumer relationship. The psychological, emotional and rational processes at play in joining, working within and leaving a complex social system, where one spends at least one-third of one's adult life, are more complicated than the processes at play in considering even a significant investment such as a car or a home – let alone a snack, an Individual Savings Account (ISA), a mobile phone or a university education.

This is not to say that some of the methods, practices and tools that prove valuable in marketing do not have an important place in an effective internal communication effort. In fact, internal communication people can learn a lot from marketing approaches such as developing 'the big idea', defining the essence of a brand or value proposition, identifying, prioritising and segmenting stakeholders, and being more creative and inspirational in their overall approach. However, the internal marketing approach generally fails to consider important parts of the equation – for example the human capital, organisational development and behaviour change elements. Probably most importantly, marketers have only recently realised the importance and power of interactivity and active listening in a world where consumer power is paramount.

Most marketing practice is based on crafting a message, packaging it and delivering it to an audience – and then gauging what happens and modifying the next round of activity accordingly. Internal communication, at its best, goes beyond so-called 'two-way' communication models, and creates an ongoing dialogue that both reflects and shapes the place where this conversation occurs. 'Internal marketers' can learn a lot from their internal communication, human resource and engagement colleagues. For example, internal communicators are now able to draw a line between their efforts, the effect of these efforts on the customer experience and the resulting financial impact. Their marketing colleagues have yet to make this link between their efforts and consumer behaviour.

While internal marketing may well be based on a false premise, the emerging truth is that no organisational silo – marketing, human resources, internal communications or IT – owns the whole solution. Best practice engagement is about making sure that these disciplines work together in a complementary manner to deliver the right result for the organisation.

At this point it is appropriate to look at how marketing departments are being organised, how they can work effectively with other departments, and how firms can foster a creative marketing culture within the entire organisation.

Organising the marketing department

Modern marketing departments can be organised in a number of different, sometimes overlapping ways:[9] functionally, geographically, by product or brand, by market, or in a matrix (see also Chapters 3 and 15).

Functional organisation

The most common form of marketing organisation, as adopted by Ford and General Motors, consists of functional specialists reporting to a senior marketing executive who coordinates their activities. Figure 21.1 shows five specialists. Additional specialists might include a customer

Figure 21.1 Functional organisation

service manager, a marketing planning manager, a market logistics manager, a direct marketing manager and a digital marketing manager.

The main advantage of a functional marketing organisation is its administrative simplicity, although it can be quite a challenge to develop smooth working relationships.[10] This form can also lose its effectiveness as the number of products and markets increases. For some retailers and fast-moving consumer goods companies such as Procter & Gamble, a functional organisation often leads to inadequate planning for specific products and markets. Then, each functional group competes with others for budget and status. The senior marketing executive constantly weighs the claims of competing functional specialists and faces a difficult coordination problem.

Geographic organisation

A company selling in a national market often organises its sales force (and sometimes other functions, including marketing) along geographic lines. Many food, beverage, car and pharmaceutical companies use this model of organisation. The national sales manager may supervise four regional sales managers, who each supervise six zone managers, who in turn supervise eight district sales managers, who each supervise ten sales people. If companies seek to market effectively in international markets then it is necessary to appoint *area market specialists* (e.g., EU states and non-EU states, the Middle East, etc.). Each country that is entered requires its own local specialist managers to advise headquarters staff of the variations in marketing mix that are required across regions and countries.

▽ Fortis

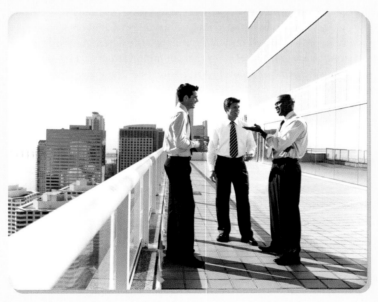

Fortis in the Netherlands: companies generate a wealth of different assets. Protecting these assets is a principle of good business. However, protecting corporate assets is just part of the big picture. What else is at stake? Managing risk, ensuring compliance – thinking of *every* scenario that can impact on the business. Corporate services exist to help companies reduce the burden of responsibility. In this regard, Fortis Intertrust is the reliable, professional partner: to start-ups, to mid-sized companies and to multinationals and to all who face profound changes in the corporate life cycle: expansion, new markets, restructurings and tax issues. This is the territory that Fortis Intertrust handles.

Source: PunchStock/Digital Vision

Fortis is the leading private bank and insurer in Belgium and also, since its foundation in 1990, a noteworthy company in the Netherlands following a cross-border merger. While enjoying a strong presence in its local markets it is very much a bit player in the finance and insurance markets of Europe and the United States. The company has therefore embarked on an expansion programme and its first significant move was to acquire the Turkish Disbank organisation for c. €1 billion in January 2006.

Product- or brand-management organisation

Companies producing a variety of market offerings and brands often establish a product- (or brand-) management organisation along the lines of the model originally developed by Procter & Gamble. It is important to realise that the traditional term 'product' should be interpreted as meaning a suitable customer-perceived market offering. The product-management organisation does not replace the functional organisation, but serves as another layer of management. A product manager supervises product category managers, who in turn supervise specific product and brand managers.

A product-management organisation makes sense if the company's products are quite different, or if the sheer number of products is beyond the ability of a functional organisation to handle. Kraft has used a product-management organisation in its Post division, with separate product category managers in charge of cereals, pet food and beverages. Within the cereal product group, Kraft has had a separate subcategory of managers for nutritional cereals, children's pre-sweetened cereals, family cereals and miscellaneous cereals.

Product and brand management is sometimes characterised as a **hub-and-spoke** system. The brand or product manager is figuratively at the centre, with spokes emanating out to various departments (see Figure 21.2). Some tasks that product or brand managers may perform include the following:

- developing a long-range and competitive strategy for the product;
- preparing an annual marketing plan and sales forecast;
- working with advertising and merchandising agencies to develop copy, programmes and campaigns;
- increasing support of the market offerings among the sales force and distributors;

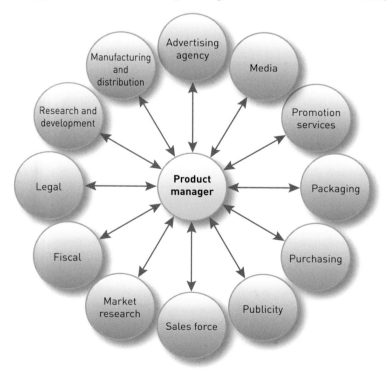

Figure 21.2 The product manager's interactions

- gathering continuous intelligence on the offer performance, customer and dealer attitudes, and new problems and opportunities;
- initiating offer improvements to meet changing market needs.

The product-management organisation lets the product manager concentrate on developing a cost-effective marketing mix and react more quickly to new products in the marketplace; it also gives the company's smaller brands a product advocate. However, this organisation also has disadvantages:

- Product and brand managers may lack sufficient authority to carry out their responsibilities.
- Product and brand managers become experts in their product area but rarely achieve functional expertise.
- The product-management system often turns out to be costly. One person is appointed to manage each major product or brand, and soon more are appointed to manage even minor products and brands.
- Brand managers normally manage a brand for only a short time. Short-term involvement leads to short-term planning and fails to build long-term strengths.
- The fragmentation of markets makes it harder to develop a national strategy. Brand managers must please regional and local sales groups, transferring power from marketing to sales.
- Product and brand managers focus the company on building market share rather than the customer relationship.

A second alternative in a product-management organisation is *product teams*. There are three types of structures: the vertical product team, triangular product team and horizontal product team (see Figure 21.3).

The triangular and horizontal product-team approaches let each major brand be run by a **brand-asset management team (BAMT)** consisting of key representatives from functions that affect the brand's performance. The company is made up of several BAMTs that periodically report to

(a) Vertical product team

(b) Triangular product team

(c) Horizontal product team

PM = product manager
APM = associate product manager
PA = product assistant
R   = market researcher
C   = communication specialist
S   = sales manager
D   = distribution specialist
F   = finance/accounting specialist
E   = engineer

Figure 21.3 Three
types of product teams

a BAMT directors committee, which itself reports to a chief branding manager. This is quite different from the way brands have traditionally been handled.

A third alternative for a product-management organisation is to eliminate product manager positions for minor products and assign two or more products to each remaining manager. This is feasible where two or more products appeal to a similar set of needs. A cosmetics company has no need for product managers for each product because cosmetics serve one major need – beauty. A toiletries company needs different managers for headache remedies, toothpaste, soap and shampoo, because these products differ in use and appeal.

A fourth alternative is to introduce *category management*, in which a company focuses on product categories to manage its brands. Procter & Gamble, pioneers of the brand-management system, and several other leading firms including Colgate-Palmolive, Kraft and Unilever, made a significant shift to category management.[11] P&G cites a number of advantages. By fostering internal competition among brand managers, the traditional brand-management system created strong incentives to excel, but also much internal competition for resources and a lack of coordination. The new scheme was designed to ensure that all categories would be able to receive adequate resources.

Another rationale for category management is the increasing power of the trade. Because the retail trade has tended to think of profitability in terms of product categories, P&G felt it only made sense to deal along similar lines. Retailers and regional grocery chains such as Asda and Carrefour, respectively, have embraced category management as a means to define a particular product category's strategic role within the store and address logistics, the role of private-label products and the trade-offs between product variety and inefficient duplication.

Category management is not a panacea. It is still a product-driven system. Colgate has moved from brand management (Colgate toothpaste) through category management (toothpaste category) to a new stage called 'customer-need management' (mouth care). This last step finally focuses the organisation on a basic customer need.[12]

Market-management organisation

Many companies operate in different markets. Canon sells fax machines to consumer, business and government markets. Corus markets steel to the railway, construction and public utility industries. When customers fall into different user groups with distinct buying preferences and practices, a **market-management organisation** is desirable. Market managers supervise several market-development managers, market specialists or industry specialists and draw on functional services as needed. Market managers of important markets might even have functional specialists reporting to them.

Market managers are staff (not line) people, with duties similar to those of product managers. They develop long-range and annual plans for their markets. Their performance is judged by their market's growth and profitability. This system shares many advantages and disadvantages of product-management systems. Its strongest advantage is organising marketing activity to meet the needs of distinct customer groups rather than focusing on marketing functions, regions or products. Many companies are reorganising along market lines and becoming **market-centred organisations**. Xerox has converted from geographic selling to selling by industry, as have IBM and Hewlett-Packard.

In a **customer-management organisation**, companies can organise themselves to understand and deal with individual customers rather than with the mass market or even market segments.[13] When a close relationship is advantageous, such as when customers have diverse and complex requirements and buy an integrated bundle of products and services, customer-management organisations should prevail. IBM's Global Services are organised in this way because of their need to interact closely with customers. One study showed that companies organised by customer groups reported much higher accountability for the overall quality of relationships and employees' freedom to take actions to satisfy individual customers.[14]

Matrix-management organisation

Companies that produce many products for many markets may adopt a matrix organisation. This enables them to gain cost economies of scale and adapt their market offerings to suit local requirements. Some provide the context in which a matrix can thrive – flat, lean team organisations focused around business processes that cut horizontally across functions.[15] DuPont was a pioneer in developing the matrix structure (see Figure 21.4).

Figure 21.4
Product/management
matrix system

Market managers

	Menswear	Women's wear	Home furnishings	Industrial markets
Rayon				
Acetate				
Nylon				
Orlon				
Dacron				

Product managers

▽ DuPont

Before it was spun off, DuPont's textile fibres department consisted of separate product managers for Rayon, Acetate, Nylon, Orlon and Dacron; and separate market managers for menswear, women's wear, home furnishings and industrial markets. The product managers planned sales and profits for their respective fibres. They asked market managers to estimate how much of their fibre they could sell in each market at a proposed price. Market managers, however, were generally more interested in meeting their market's needs than pushing a particular fibre. In preparing their market plans, they asked each product manager about the fibre's planned prices and availabilities. The final sales forecast of the market managers and the product managers should have added up to the same grand total.

Companies such as DuPont and Courtaulds can go one step further and view the market managers as the main marketers, and their product managers as suppliers. The menswear market manager, for example, would be empowered to buy textile fibres from DuPont's product managers or, if DuPont's price is too high, from outside suppliers, forcing DuPont product managers to become more efficient. If a DuPont product manager was not able to match the '**arm's-length pricing**' levels of competitive suppliers, then perhaps DuPont should not produce that fibre.

A matrix organisation seems desirable in a multiproduct, multimarket company. The disadvantage is that it is costly and often creates conflicts. There is the cost of supporting all the managers, and questions about where authority and responsibility for marketing activities should reside – at headquarters or in the division? Some corporate marketing groups assist top management with overall opportunity evaluation, provide divisions with consulting assistance on request, help divisions that have little or no marketing, and promote the marketing concept throughout the company.

▽ Getting it together

Matrix management is essentially a mindset first and an organisational form second. Many complex organisations, such as British Telecom and Citibank, benefit substantially from this management approach, which has caught the interest of many other organisations both large and small and is operating in both private and public enterprise businesses. Fortis, the dominant bank and insurer in Belgium and, since their formation in 1990 in one of Europe's first cross-border mergers, also a sizeable player in the Netherlands, has adopted a matrix approach to consolidate its business. Meanwhile, since 2005 in the Republic of Ireland, Enterprise Ireland, faced with the challenge of fostering innovation and market knowledge with a view to boosting small and medium-sized enterprises' export opportunities, has moved from a 'cellular structure' to a 'matrix structure'.

Relations with other departments

Under the marketing concept, all departments need to 'think customer' and work together to satisfy customer needs and expectations. The marketing department must drive this point home. The marketing director has two tasks: (1) to coordinate the company's internal marketing activities; and (2) to coordinate marketing with finance, operations and other company functions to serve the customer.

Yet there is little agreement on how much influence and authority marketing should have over other departments. Departments define company problems and goals from their viewpoint, so conflicts of interest and communication problems are unavoidable. Typically, the marketing director must work through persuasion rather than authority. To develop a balanced orientation in which marketing and other functions jointly determine what is in the company's best interests, companies can provide joint seminars to understand each other's viewpoints, joint committees and liaison personnel, personnel exchange programmes, and analytical methods to determine the most profitable course of action.[16]

Many companies now focus on key processes rather than departments, because departmental organisation can be a barrier to the smooth performance of fundamental business processes. They appoint process leaders, who manage cross-disciplinary teams that include marketing and sales people. As a result, marketing personnel may have a solid-line responsibility to their teams and a dotted-line responsibility to the marketing department.

▽ Building a creative marketing organisation

Many companies realise they are not yet really market and customer driven – they are product and sales driven. General Motors and Shell for example are attempting to transform themselves into true market-driven companies. This requires:

1 developing a company-wide passion for customers;

2 organising around customer segments instead of products;

3 understanding customers through qualitative and quantitative research.

The task is not easy, it is not simply a matter of the CEO making speeches and urging every employee to 'think customer'. However the pay-offs can be considerable.[17] See 'Marketing insight: The marketing CEO' for actions a CEO can take to improve marketing capabilities.

Persuading the company to embrace a customer-oriented philosophy is a *necessary* but not a *sufficient* condition for success. The organisation must also foster and sustain a creative culture. Companies today copy each other's advantages and strategies with increasing speed. Differentiation gets harder to achieve, let alone maintain, and margins fall when firms become more alike. The only answer is to build a capability in strategic innovation and idea generation to develop a succession of customer-perceived value offerings (see 'Marketing memo: Fuelling strategic innovation'). This capability comes from assembling tools, processes, skills and measures that let the firm generate more and better new ideas than its competitors.[18]

Taking the creative approach

There are two main applications for creativity. The first is to do what the company already does but in a 'better way'. This may mean doing it faster, at less cost, with less waste; raising customer-perceived quality standards or performing more cost effectively. All these options generally rely on – or at least benefit from – new ideas. The second use of creativity is to do better things. This entails coming up with new market offerings that have additional customer-perceived value. Best results, of course, are obtained when companies practise both approaches. Despite the best of intentions some companies often fail to fully embrace the importance of the creative approach to marketing.

A common reason for this is a failure to understand what creativity is really all about. Essentially creative thinking is a process that brings into being a new approach that can break through constraints imposed by habit and tradition, so making it possible to find new solutions to problems.

Marketing insight

The marketing CEO

What steps can a CEO take to create a market- and customer-focused company?

1 **Convince senior management of the need to become customer focused**: The CEO personally exemplifies strong customer commitment and rewards those in the organisation who do likewise. For example, former CEOs Jack Welch of GE, Lou Gerstner of IBM and Sir John Harvey-Jones of ICI are said to have spent 100 days a year visiting customers, in spite of their many strategic, financial and administrative burdens; current Starbucks CEO Jim Donald visits 10–20 stores a week to go behind the counter and talk to store partners (employees) and customers.

2 **Appoint a senior marketing officer and marketing task force**: The marketing task force should include the CEO; the directors of sales, R&D, purchasing, manufacturing, finance and human resources; and other key individuals.

3 **Get outside help and guidance**: Consulting firms have considerable experience in helping companies move towards a marketing orientation.

4 **Change the company's reward measurement and system**: As long as purchasing and manufacturing are rewarded for keeping costs low, they will resist accepting some costs required to serve customers better. As long as finance focuses on short-term profit, it will oppose major investments designed to build satisfied, loyal customers.

5 **Hire strong marketing talent**: The company needs a strong marketing director who not only manages the marketing department but also gains respect from and influence with the other functional directors. A multidivisional company will benefit from establishing a strong corporate marketing department.

6 **Develop strong in-house marketing training programmes**: The company should design well-crafted marketing training programmes for corporate management, divisional general managers, marketing and sales personnel, manufacturing personnel, R&D personnel, and others. Accenture, Bosch, Electrolux and VW run these programmes.

7 **Install a modern marketing planning system**: The planning format will require managers to think about the marketing environment, opportunities, competitive trends and other forces. These managers then prepare strategies and sales-and-profit forecasts for specific products and segments and are accountable for performance.

8 **Establish an annual marketing excellence recognition programme**: Business units that believe they've developed exemplary marketing plans should submit a description of their plans and results. Winning teams should be rewarded at a special ceremony and the plans disseminated to the other business units as 'models of marketing thinking'. The finance/insurance giant Accenture follows this strategy.

9 **Shift from a department focus to a process-outcome focus**: After defining the fundamental business processes that determine its success, the company should appoint process leaders and cross-disciplinary teams to re-engineer and implement these processes.

10 **Empower the employees**: Progressive companies encourage and reward their employees for coming up with new ideas and empower them to settle customer complaints to retain the customers' business. IBM, for example, lets its frontline employees spend up to US$5000 to solve a customer problem on the spot.

Creative thinking can refer to all aspects of the marketing management domain. For example it can be used to:

• generate new ideas that customers will perceive as having value;
• develop innovative marketing communications;
• operate new forms of distribution;
• come up with ingenious pricing initiatives.

Companies must watch trends and be ready to capitalise on them. Motorola was 18 months late in moving from analogue to digital mobile phones, giving Nokia and Ericsson a big lead. Nestlé was late seeing the trend towards coffee houses such as Starbucks. Coca-Cola was slow to pick up beverage trends towards fruit-flavoured drinks such as Snapple, energy drinks such as Red Bull, and designer mineral water brands. They were also slow to see the emerging market for large pack sizes for colas, thus presenting their rival Pepsi with a way to creatively challenge their hitherto accepted symbol of advantage – the hour-glass shaped bottle. Market leaders tend to miss trends when they are risk averse, obsessed about protecting their existing markets and physical resources, and more interested in efficiency than innovation.[19]

Marketing memo

Fuelling strategic innovation

Professor Stephen Brown of Ulster University has challenged a number of fundamental assumptions underlying the marketing concept. He thinks marketers make too much of researching and satisfying consumers, and they risk losing marketing imagination and significant consumer impact. How can companies build a capability for strategic innovation? Here are some approaches he advocates:

- Hire marketers who are unusually creative to counterbalance the majority who practise marketing by the textbook. These people may be unconventional – rule breaking, risk taking, and even more argumentative, but their ideas will at least present a challenge.

- Train employees in the use of creativity techniques, for groups (brainstorming, Synectics) and individuals (visualisation, attribute listing, forced relationships, morphological analysis, mind mapping).

- Note trends such as longer working hours, single parenting and new lifestyles, and tease out their implications for the firm.

- List unmet customer needs and imagine new offerings or solutions: how to help people lose weight, stop smoking, relieve stress, meet others.

- Run a 'best idea' competition once a month. Give a cash reward, extra holiday or travel awards to those who come up with the best ideas.

- Have senior managers take small sets of employees out to lunch or dinner once a week to discuss ideas for improving the business. Visit new settings, such as a football match, a shopping centre.

- Set up groups of employees to critique the company's and competitors' products and services. Let them critique the company's cherished beliefs and consider turning them upside down.

- Occasionally hire creative resources from outside the firm. Many large advertising agencies, such as Leo Burnett, run a creativity service for clients.

Sources: For more on Brown's views see S. Brown (2001) *Marketing: The Retro Revolution*, Thousand Oaks, CA: Sage. For more on creativity see P. Fallon and F. Senn (2006) *Juicing the Orange: How to Turn Creativity Into a Powerful Business Advantage*, Boston, MA: Harvard Business School Press; B. Schmetterer (2003) *Leap: A Revolution in Creative Business Strategy*, Hoboken, NJ: John Wiley & Sons; J.-M. Dru (2002) *Beyond Disruption: Changing the Rules in the Marketplace*, Hoboken, NJ: John Wiley & Sons; M. Michalko (1998) *Cracking Creativity: The Secrets of Creative Genius*, Berkeley, CA: Ten Speed Press; J. M. Higgins (1994) *101 Creative Problem-Solving Techniques*, New York: New Management Publishing; and all the books by Edward DeBono.

Building a creative culture

Creativity is a property of thought process that can be acquired and improved through instruction and practice. In this context, individual creativity mechanisms refer to activities undertaken by individual employees within an organisation to enhance their capability for developing something, which is meaningful and novel within the work environment. Organisational creativity mechanisms refer to the extent to which the organisation has instituted formal approaches and tools, and provided resources to encourage meaningfully novel behaviours within the organisation. It is not enough for organisations to opt for a 'quick fix' by hiring creative people while making mainly cosmetic changes to their dominant modus operandi. Successful creative marketing requires both an organisational culture change and the training of existing and new staff. It is a TEAM approach. Football players are encouraged to work creatively as a unit and coaches frequently use the word 'team' as a mnemonic – Together Everyone Achieves More. The managers of successful football teams are acutely aware of the importance of both the intrinsic and extrinsic aspects of the creativity driver as they seek competitive success for their clubs.

Creativity – a mystical gift for some or something for all?

For the first time in history creativity is largely understood. The logical basis of how the brain works is understood. From such an understanding it is possible to derive the deliberate tools of lateral thinking, of solving problems by circumventing traditional methods. These tools can be learned and used. As with any skill, some people will become more skilful than others but everyone can learn to be creative.[20] Most companies are confident to invest for the short term but many become more hesitant when faced with investing in the medium to longer term. Continuous creative marketing requires a long-term commitment because creativity and innovation are crucial elements in a competitive world. Something can be done about creativity; it is not just a magic talent. Businesses should take heart for they can always find new ways to add value.[21]

▽ Gaining momentum – the 'Larreche prescription'

Professor Larreche, who holds the Heineken chair in marketing at INSEAD, maintains that *momentum* is something that can be created by companies and, once achieved, can be maintained by pursuing a creative marketing approach. He cites the examples of Toyota, Apple, Nintendo and Skype that have all entered the virtuous circle of continuous growth – 'the momentum effect'. Lasting competitive advantages are the result of getting certain fundamental aspects of business right. What Larreche terms 'value creation' – spotting what customers want and working hard to provide it – is where momentum starts to develop. A company 'that systematically places customers at the centre of its thinking and that strives to attain ambitious goals will be able to harness the power of the momentum and deliver the exceptional growth it provides'.

Professor Larreche takes a nuanced view of customers and argues that they are not always strictly rational. 'Their perception is their reality, and it may be quite different from the "rational" perspective of product-design engineers.' 'Momentum-deficient' businesses suffer from 'transaction myopia': failing to understand, for example, that the lifetime value of a customer is far more important than any short-term revenue 'hit'. Customer retention 'offers an extraordinary acceleration of profitable growth by exceptionally increasing average customer lifetime and, as a result, knowing customer acquisition costs'.

The concept of momentum does offer a big, unifying theory and the success stories referred to by Larreche do seem to share it. However, chance, the mistakes of competitors and sometimes sheer serendipity all play a part in highly competitive markets.

Source: J.-C. Larreche (2008) *The Momentum Effect: How to Ignite Exceptional Growth*, London: Financial Times Series; S. Stern (2008) An elusive concept for staying on a roll, *Financial Times*, 1 May.

Maintaining momentum

Delivering success is a team effort that extends to all management as they all have a contribution to make to the final offering that is presented to customers. The resulting coordinated corporate offering is much harder for a competitor to imitate than new technology and products. Professor Hamel, of the London Business School,[22] believes that for many companies real 'momentum' has slowed down because 'real innovation in management operations has slowed to a crawl'. Professor Hamel believes that, whereas previous advances in management focused on production processes, the management innovators of today must concentrate on people. Companies need to learn how to harness what he calls individual and group 'employee imagination'. In addition to the companies cited by Professor Larreche as good examples of his 'momentum effect' include Danish Toymaker LEGO which, according to Professor Torben Pedersen of the Copenhagen Business School, has expanded its creative and innovative team to include customers for years.

IBM provides proof that some of the biggest companies can innovate in search of 'momentum'. In January 2006, the company launched its 'Innovation Jam', posting dozens of white papers and internal documents online and inviting comment. 'Everyone got involved in discussing IBM's strategy,' according to Professor Hamel, and this included customers, suppliers, employees and family members of employees. The result was ten initiatives and hundreds of millions of US dollars of investment.

However, the majority of companies are failing to develop creative marketing approaches as most managers are not taught to think of themselves as being people whose job it is to be part of a team that aspires to create and invent.

Marketing implementation

Table 21.1 summarises the characteristics of a great marketing company, great not for 'what it is', but for 'what it does'. **Marketing implementation** is the process that turns marketing plans into action assignments and ensures they accomplish the plan's stated objectives.

A brilliant strategic marketing plan counts for little if it is not implemented properly. Strategy addresses the *what* and *why* of marketing activities; implementation addresses the *who, where, when* and *how*. They are closely related: one layer of strategy implies certain tactical implementation assignments at a lower level. For example, top management's strategic decision to 'harvest' a product must be translated into specific actions and assignments.

Companies today are striving to make their marketing operations more efficient and their return on marketing investment more measurable. Marketing costs can amount from 20–40 per cent of a company's total operating budget. Marketers need better templates for marketing processes, better management of marketing assets, and better allocation of marketing resources. Certain repetitive processes can be automated under such names as *marketing resource management* (MRM), *marketing investment management* (MIM), *enterprise marketing management* (EMM) and *marketing automation systems* (MAS).[23]

Marketing resource management software provides a set of Web-based applications that automate and integrate such activities as project management, campaign management, budget management, asset management, brand management, customer relationship management and knowledge management. The knowledge management component consists of process templates, how-to wizards and best practices.

Software packages are Web hosted and available to users with passwords. They add up to what some have called *desktop marketing* and give marketers whatever information and decision structures they need on computer screens. MRM software lets marketers improve spending and investment decisions, bring new products to market more quickly, and reduce decision time and costs.

Leadership

Ideas, however persuasive they may be in workplace discussion, need to be championed by a committed leader if they are to make a real difference to company performance in the marketplace. Effective and sustained creative marketing demands a subtle blending of the knowledge systems of leadership, creativity and innovation. A study completed by Manchester Business School identified nine themes that provide a revealing picture of the insights and skills of creative leaders.[24]

1 **Leadership, learning and knowledge systems**: Absorptive capacity resource-based models and cognitive framing are promising ways of integrating knowledge and leadership studies.

2 **Empowerment and delegated leadership**: Self-managed teams and distributed leadership systems are based on a facilitative or empowering leadership style. Cross-functional teams are necessary for required integration within projects. The collaborative paradigm within networks is also relevant.

Table 21.1 Characteristics of a great marketing company

Percentage of 13–25 year olds who say they:	
Feel personally responsible for making a difference in the world	61
Feel companies should join in the effort to make a difference in the world	75
Are likely to switch brands (given equal price and quality) to support a cause	89
Are more likely to pay attention to messages of companies deeply committed to a cause	74
Consider a company's social commitment when deciding where to shop	69
Consider a company's social commitment when recommending products	64

Source: Cone Inc./AMP Insights survey of 1800 13–25 year olds as reported in *BusinessWeek*, 6 November 2006, 13.

3 **Creative problem-solving leadership**: Creative leadership (in and beyond formalised structures to stimulate creativity) is widely associated with a facilitative or process-oriented style. Person–environment fit (contingency) theories seem relevant too.

4 **Innovation and entrepreneurial leadership**: Roles in technological innovation generally are assumed to operate within a rational model of strategic change.

5 **Crisis leadership**: The theme concerns the concept of managing/leading in uncertain or turbulent environments.

6 **Change-centred leadership**: Change-centred leadership differentiates older and new leadership thinking.

7 **Creating the right environment for creativity to grow and flourish**: Ekvall and Amabile with co-workers are regarded as key sources to work on climate and environment studies. Action research often seeks change by survey feedback of perceived blocks or barriers to change.

8 **Strategic planning leadership**: Resource-based theories help model global innovation.

9 **Evaluation of creativity**: This looks at the most appropriate ways to evaluate creativity (interpretative or social constructivist).

Methodology and madness – the importance of leaving room for creativity

Rigorous marketing training has traditionally been the preserve of companies such as Procter & Gamble and Unilever, which have long been acknowledged as excellent training grounds for marketers. However, now they are being joined by other companies that aspire to make marketing a more potent management activity. As companies strive to find that 'market edge' so there is an increasing need to think outside the traditional marketing toolbox. Creative approaches can bring spectacular success. The problem for many companies is that it can mean taking a risk and can run counter to culture of traditional marketing methodology. Forward thinking firms are beginning to lower their risk ceilings, back their creative thinking and not become too reliant on methodology as they seek to make a difference. They fully accept that being seen to be mad by their competitors can in fact make a difference!

Creative marketing

The creative approach to marketing makes a case that creativity in marketing theory is largely absent and that an alternative way forward for marketing is to apply a creative point of view. According to Ian Fillis (University of Stirling) and Ruth Rentschler (Deakin University),[25] creative marketing 'is used as an umbrella term to capture concepts from marketing and creativity'. Creativity writers in management and organisational studies include Teresa Amabile, Gareth Morgan, Howard Gardner and Richard Florida. Kotler's influence pervades marketing practice: on the bad side, he helped to establish the current marketing management mindset that critics view as prescriptive and formulaic; on the good side, he was an earlier advocate that the concept of marketing ought to be broadened. In this regard, creative marketing is part of the contemporary marketing landscape aligned with the 'critical' approach associated with Stephen Brown. Marketing is a broad church.

New approaches are certainly welcome. Fillis and Rentschler's core message is that

Inspiration for the creative marketing paradigm comes from the imagination of the entrepreneurial marketing practitioner, from both within the conventional notion of the business world and from the arts. It is drawn from the creative ability to bypass everyday thinking and make tangible the intangible. Insight into creative ideas can be gained by examining many aspects of the artistic realm.

As such, they draw from the experiences of artists such as Picasso and Diaghilev, present a definition of creativity based on 6Ps (place, people, property, process, practice and product), and conclude by proffering their creative marketing manifesto as 'a focal point for further discussion and theory construction'.

Is there a threat that creativity will be institutionalised as it serves the interests of marketers? Areas of interest include the nature of creativity; the differences between creativity and innovation and the relationship between the two; different models of the creative process; the conditions which stifle or stimulate creativity; the circumstances that lead from creativity to innovation; the role of risk in creativity and innovation; the value of creativity to business, the economy and society; and changes in how society understands creativity and values innovation in a knowledge economy.[26]

▽ Unilever steps out and trusts market intuition

Observers believe that Unilever is benefiting from a more risk-taking marketing culture than its rival Procter & Gamble. It has been increasingly seeking new creative big ideas for its advertising campaigns. Top Unilever brands such as Dove, Persil and Lynx have all been associated with creativity, dynamism, innovation and energy in recent surveys, in contrast to the ratings of Procter & Gamble brands that are well known for their risk aversion. Nowhere has the new approach been more apparent than with the performance of Unilever's Dove brand, which is now a major contributor to the firm's profits.

Since early 2004 Dove's 'campaign for real beauty' has featured advertisements that have set out to challenge the stereotypical images of female glamour. Similar unorthodox creative marketing has benefited the performance of Persil with the strap line 'Dirt is good' and the creation of a fantasy female-staffed airline for male teenagers who buy Lynx cosmetics.[27]

Much traditional (theoretical) marketing often seems to pass people by. If asked to name five TV commercials that they have viewed recently surprisingly many people are unable to do so effortlessly. Perhaps TV commercials are becoming too much like innocuous wallpaper. Curiously enough, while creative marketing when apparent is recalled easily – for example the Citroën Transformer commercials, the quirky Skoda cake, the mythical Guinness screenings – and annoying advertisements such as Cillit Bang are the ones that people remember.

▽ Socially responsible marketing

Effective marketing must be matched by a strong sense of ethics, values and social responsibility.[28] A number of forces are driving companies to practise a higher level of corporate social responsibility. These include rising customer expectations, evolving employee goals and ambitions, tighter government legislation and pressure, developing investor interest in social criteria, relentless media scrutiny, and changing business procurement practices.[29] The commercial success of ex-US Vice-President Al Gore's 2006 documentary, *An Inconvenient Truth*, shows how the general public has become more concerned about environmental issues.

Corporate social responsibility

The European Commission defines corporate social responsibility (CSR) as enterprises' contribution to sustainable development. Some companies, such as BP, British Telecom, McDonald's and Maersk, have responded positively to the CSR challenge. McDonald's, for example, with its Ronald McDonald House initiative in Norway, has sought to build a corporate brand reputation by means of community involvement.[30] Many others like to be regarded as 'talking the talk'.[31] However, the recent spate of corporate scandals, accounting frauds, allegations of executive greed and dubious business practices has led many to adopt mixed attitudes to CSR and regard it as a sham. Some observers have even dubbed it 'cynical social responsibility' and many have all but abandoned it for 'sustainability'.[32]

Raising the level of socially responsible marketing calls for making a three-pronged attack that relies on bona fide legal, ethical and social responsibilities.

Legal

Organisations must ensure that every employee knows and observes relevant laws. For example, sales people's statements legally must match advertising claims. They should not offer bribes to purchasing agents or others influencing a business-to-business sale. They may not obtain or use competitors' technical or trade secrets through bribery or industrial espionage. Finally, they must not disparage competitors or their products by suggesting things that are not true. Every sales representative should know the law and act accordingly.[33]

Ethical

Business practices come under attack because commercial situations routinely pose tough ethical dilemmas. It is not easy to draw a clear line between normal marketing practice and that which is unethical. Some issues sharply divide critics. Though Walkers Crisps reacted quickly and positively and reduced the salt content of their snack items and Procter & Gamble reduced the sugar content of their orange drink Sunny Delight, some watch groups felt that was not enough.

At the same time, certain business practices are clearly unethical or illegal. These include bribery, theft of trade secrets, false and deceptive advertising, exclusive dealing and tying agreements, quality or safety defects, false warranties, inaccurate labelling, price fixing or undue discrimination, barriers to entry and predatory competition. Companies must adopt and disseminate a written code of ethics, build a company tradition of ethical behaviour, and hold people fully responsible for observing ethical and legal guidelines.[34] Companies that do not perform ethically or well are at greater risk of being exposed, thanks to the Internet. In the past, a disgruntled customer might criticise a firm to 12 other people; today he or she can reach thousands. Microsoft, for example, has attracted scores of anti-Microsoft sites, including Hate Microsoft and Boycott Microsoft.

Striking a socially defensible balance between seeking to improve profits (efficiency) and marketing effectively in the light of the experienced environment can present companies with serious ethical dilemmas. Marketing ethics can be viewed as a continuum that stretches from *caveat emptor* (let the buyer beware) to *caveat venditor* (let the seller beware). Strictly speaking the emphasis should be moving towards *caveat venditor* if the providers fully sign up to the underlying philosophy of the relationship marketing paradigm.[35] So why do food companies 'build bulk' by injecting water into meat? Why do supermarkets incur huge carbon footprints as they transport greengroceries across the oceans of the world? Why do some clothing companies import cheap merchandise from underdeveloped countries and turn a blind eye to the conditions which the workforces have to endure in these countries?

There are many questions surrounding the interpretation of ethical marketing that can result in corporations, divisions and individual brands finding their position on the *caveat emptor–caveat venditor* scale. The matter is not one of right or wrong or of white or black – real life is more complex than this – but it is a matter of conscience. So what does 'ethics' really mean in management activities? Is it a word full of promise but paradoxically also full of unfulfilled promises?[36] Most would agree that an ethical approach to marketing management is desirable in principle. So how can this opportunity be grasped?[37]

Smith proposes the maxims in 'Marketing memo: Key steps in assessing marketing ethics standards' to guide companies as to whether or not they are marketing ethically.

Social responsibility

Individual marketers must practise a 'social conscience' in specific dealings with customers and stakeholders. Increasingly, people want information about a company's record on social and environmental responsibility to help decide which companies to buy from, invest in, and work for.[38]

Deciding how to communicate corporate social responsibility can be difficult. Once a firm airs an environmental initiative it can become a target for criticism. Many well-intentioned marketing initiatives attract unforeseen negative consequences. Palm oil was hailed as a renewable

Marketing memo

Key steps in assessing marketing ethics standards

- The golden rule: do unto others as you would be done by.
- The media test: would members of the marketing team be embarrassed in front of colleagues/family/friends, if marketing decisions were published in the media for all to see?
- The invoice test: are payments being requested that might not meet with the approval of internal and external auditors?

- Good ethics is good business practice: the practised belief that sellers should regard integrity as being in the best long-term interest of the business.
- The professional test: would marketing decisions be regarded as ethical by professional peers in other companies?
- When in doubt, reconsider proposed actions.

Source: Adapted form N. C. Smith (1999) Marketing ethics, in M. J. Bakers (ed.) *Encyclopaedia of Marketing*, London: International Thomson Business Press, 924.

fuel for food companies looking to find a solution to a trans-fat ban, until its use was linked to the potential extinction of the orang-utan and the sun bear.

Corporate philanthropy also can pose problems as the motives of organisations can be misunderstood.[39]

Sustainability

Sustainability – the importance of meeting humanity's needs without harming future generations – has risen to the top of many corporate agendas. Major corporations now outline in great detail how they are trying to improve the long-term impact of their actions on communities and the environment. As one sustainability consultant put it, 'There is a triple bottom line – people, planet, and profit – and the people part of the equation must come first. Sustainability means more than being eco-friendly; it also means you are in it for the long haul.'[40]

Many CEOs believe embracing sustainability can avoid the negative consequences of environmental disasters, political protests, and human rights or workplace abuses. Often a target of environmental criticism in the past, DuPont has moved through two phases of sustainability in the past 15 years: first, drastically reducing the emission of greenhouse gases, release of carcinogens and discharge of hazardous wastes; and second, embracing sustainability as a strategic goal via the introduction of alternative biofuels and energy-saving materials such as its new bio-PDO fibre.[41]

Investors are demanding ever more concrete information about what firms are doing to achieve sustainability. Sustainability ratings exist, although there is little agreement about what the appropriate metrics might be.[42]

▽ Innovest

Founded in 1995, Innovest studies firms on 120 different factors, such as energy use, health and safety records, litigation, employee practices, regulatory history, and management systems for dealing with supplier problems. It uses these measures to assign 2200 listed companies grades ranging from AAA to CCC, much like a bond rating. Companies scoring well include Nokia Corp. and Ericsson, which excel at tailoring products for developing nations, and banks such as HSBC Holdings and ABN-AMRO, which study the environmental impact of projects they help finance. Although Hewlett-Packard and Dell both rate AAA, Apple gets a middling BBB rating on the grounds of weaker oversight of offshore factories and lack of a 'clear environmental business strategy'.

Some feel companies that score well on sustainability factors typically exhibit high levels of management quality in that 'they tend to be more strategically nimble and better equipped to compete in the complex, high-velocity, global environment.'[43]

Many companies in diverse industries beyond edible food products are embracing organic offerings that avoid the use of chemicals and pesticides to stress ecological preservation. Apparel and other non-food items make up the second-fastest growth category. Organic cotton grown by farmers who fight boll weevils with ladybirds, weed their crops by hand, and use manure for fertiliser has become a hot retail attraction. Sustainability is becoming more mainstream, and consumers are increasingly willing to pay more to support the environment.[44]

▽ Levi's

Innovation delivers the first sustainable Levi's® jean launch in Europe.
Source: Ross Haily/Fort Worth Star Telegram/MCT/NewsCom

Levi Strauss Europe launched its Levi's® eco jeans in October 2006. This was believed to be the first fully sustainable jean from a major denim brand, made using 100 per cent certified organic cotton, and sustainable product components and production processes. Levi Strauss Europe was granted an 'EKO sustainable textile' certification for the Levi® eco jeans from Control Union Certifications, a leading worldwide inspection and certification body for organic production and products. Even the garment tags and packaging are made of organic fabric or recycled paper and printed with soy-based ink.

Source: Media Office, Levi Strauss Europe.

Many firms have decided to take a more active, strategic role with corporate responsibility. Even banana producer Chiquita, which once had a poor reputation for exploiting farm workers, contaminating water and destroying rain forest, has improved workers' conditions, significantly reduced pesticide use, reduced erosion and chemical run-off and even implemented a major recycling programme on its farms.[45]

Such a belief in the value of social responsibility has not been in evidence in the past. In 1776 the English economist Adam Smith proclaimed, 'I have never known much good done by those who profess to trade for the public good.' Legendary US economist Milton Friedman famously declared social initiatives 'fundamentally subversive' because he felt they undermined the profit-seeking purpose of public companies and wasted shareholders' money. Some critics worry that important business investment in areas such as research and development could suffer as a result of a focus on social responsibility.

These critics are in the minority. Many now believe that satisfying customers, employees and other stakeholders and achieving business success are closely tied to the adoption and implementation of high standards of business and marketing conduct. Firms are finding that one benefit of being seen as a socially responsible company is the ability to attract employees. The most admired – and increasingly most successful – companies in the world abide by a code of serving people's interests as well as their own.

Firms of endearment

Researchers Sisodia, Wolfe and Sheth believe humanistic companies make great companies. They define 'Firms of Endearment' as those that have a culture of caring and serve the interests of their stakeholders. Stakeholders are defined in terms of the acronym SPICE: society, partners, investors, customers and employees. Firms of Endearment create a love affair with stakeholders. Their senior managers run an open-door policy, are passionate about customers, and their compensation is modest. They pay more to their employees, relate more closely to a smaller group of excellent suppliers, and give back to the communities in which they work. The researchers assert that Firms of Endearment actually spend less on marketing as a percentage but yet earn greater profits. It appears that the customers who love the company do most of the marketing. The authors see the twenty-first-century marketing paradigm as being essentially about firms creating value for all stakeholders and being recognised as socially responsible organisations.[46]

'Breakthrough marketing: Starbucks' describes the practices of a highly rated endearment firm. However, many smaller firms excel too.

Socially responsible business models

The future holds a wealth of opportunities.[47] Technological advances in solar energy, online networks, cable and satellite television, biotechnology and telecommunications promise to change the world as we know it. At the same time, forces in the socio-economic, cultural and natural environments will impose new limits on marketing and business practices. Companies that innovate solutions and values in a socially responsible way are the most likely to succeed.[48]

Many companies, such as BASF, Bayer, Ben & Jerry's, Kwik-Fit, Marks & Spencer, Michelin and The Body Shop, are giving social responsibility a more prominent role. BASF has funded a research laboratory at Nottingham University in the United Kingdom after the company withdrew from chemical research in the city. Michelin is lending money to worthy manufacturing start-ups to give something back to the community.

Corporate philanthropy as a whole is on the increase. More firms are realising that corporate social responsibility in the form of cash donations, in-kind contributions, cause marketing and employee volunteer programmes is not just the 'right thing' but also the 'smart thing'[49] to do. Coutts, the London based top-person's bank, is receiving more enquiries than ever from clients interested in setting up charitable trusts and foundations. 'Marketing insight: New views on corporate social responsibility' offers two high-profile perspectives on how to make progress in that area.

Breakthrough marketing

Starbucks

Starbucks opened in Seattle in 1971 when coffee consumption in the United States had been declining for a decade. Rival coffee brands were also using cheaper coffee beans to compete on price. Starbucks' founders decided to experiment with a new concept: a store that would sell only the finest imported coffee beans and coffee-brewing equipment. The original store didn't sell coffee by the cup, only beans.

Howard Schultz came to Starbucks in 1982. While in Milan on business, he walked into an Italian coffee bar and had a flash of inspiration with his espresso. 'There was nothing like this in America. It was an extension of people's front porch. It was an emotional experience,' he said. He knew right away that he wanted to take this concept to the United States. Schultz set about creating an environment for Starbucks coffee houses that would reflect Italian elegance melded with US informality. He envisioned Starbucks as a 'personal treat' for its customers, a 'Third Place' – a comfortable, sociable gathering spot bridging the workplace and the home.

From its launch in Seattle, Starbucks' expansion throughout the United States was carefully planned. The management team agreed that all stores would be owned and operated by the company, ensuring complete control to cultivate an unparalleled image of quality. Starbucks employed a 'hub' expansion strategy, in which coffee houses entered a new market in a clustered group. Although this deliberate saturation often cannibalised 30 per cent of one store's sales by introducing a store nearby, any drop in revenue was offset by efficiencies in marketing and distribution costs, and the enhanced image of convenience. A typical customer would stop by Starbucks in the United States as many as 18 times a month.

Part of the success of Starbucks undoubtedly lies in its market offerings, and its relentless commitment to providing customers with the richest possible sensory experiences. But another key is the enlightened sense of responsibility that manifests itself in a number of different ways.

Schultz believes that in order to exceed the expectations of customers it is first necessary to exceed the expectations of employees. As far back as 1990 Starbucks provided comprehensive health care to all employees, including part timers. Health insurance now costs Starbucks more each year than coffee. The firm also introduced a stock option plan called 'Bean Stock', which allows Starbucks' employees to participate in the company's financial success.

Starbucks believes that by focusing and aligning the giving priorities of Starbucks Coffee Company with The Starbucks Foundation, a separate charitable organisation, its contributions will have greater impact and provide more benefit to communities around the world. The Starbucks Foundation celebrated its ten-year anniversary in 2007 with the announcement of Starbucks About Youth, a global philanthropic endeavour focused on supporting educational initiatives and youth leadership in Starbucks retail markets around the world.

Source: Used by permission of Starbucks Corporation

The company donates large sums of money to charities via The Starbucks Foundation, created in 1997 with proceeds from the sale of Schultz's book. The mission of the foundation is to 'create hope, discovery, and opportunity in communities where Starbucks partners [employees] live and work.' The primary focus of the foundation has been on improving young people's lives by supporting literacy programmes for children and families. By 2007, the foundation had provided over US$12 million to more than 700 youth-focused organisations in the United States and Canada. Starbucks has also donated 5 cents of every sale of its Ethos bottled water to improving the quality of water in poor countries as part of a five-year US$10 million pledge.

Starbucks also promotes 'fair trade' export practices with third-world coffee bean producers and pays its producers in those countries an average of 23 per cent above market price. It took the company ten years of development to create the world's first recycled

▶ Breakthrough marketing *(continued)*

beverage cup made from 10 per cent post-consumer fibre, conserving 5 million pounds of paper or approximately 78,000 trees a year.

Howard Schultz stepped down as CEO in 2000, and assumed the role of chairman and 'Chief Global Strategist'. Following a recent slide in the company's fortunes Schultz has taken back the reins of the company. Starbucks currently has over 12,400 stores worldwide, with 115,000 employees and almost US$8 billion in revenue. The company hopes to expand to 40,000 outlets, cafés and kiosks worldwide, half of them outside the United States. No matter what the growth trajectory, Schultz believes Starbucks must retain a passion for coffee and a sense of humanity, to remain small even as it gets big, and to always treat workers as individuals.

_____

Sources: H. Schultz (2006) Dare to be a social entrepreneur, *Business 2.0*, December, 87; E. Iwata (2006) Owner of small coffee shop takes on java titan starbucks, *USA Today*, 20 December; Staying pure: Howard Schultz's formula for Starbucks, *The Economist*, 25 February 2006, p. 72; D. Anderson (2006) Evolution of the eco cup, *Business 2.0*, June, 50; B. Horovitz (2006) Starbucks nation, *USA Today*, 19 May; T. Howard (2005) Starbucks takes up cause for safe drinking water, *USA Today*, 2 August; H. Schultz and D. Jones Yang (1997) *Pour Your Heart into It: How Starbucks Built a Company One Cup at a Time*, New York: Hyperion; see also www.starbucks.com.

Marketing insight

New views on corporate social responsibility

Two of management's most renowned thinkers have turned their attention to corporate social responsibility, offering some unique perspectives that builds on their past management research and thinking.

Michael Porter

Harvard's Michael Porter and Mark Kramer, managing director of FSG Social Impact Advisors, believe good corporate citizenship can be a source of opportunity, innovation and competitive advantage, as long as firms evaluate it using the same frameworks and concepts that guide their core business strategies. They feel corporate social responsibility must mesh with a firm's strengths, capabilities and positioning. They assert that *strategic corporate social responsibility* results when firms: (1) transform value chain activities to benefit society while reinforcing strategy; and (2) engage in strategic philanthropy that leverages capabilities to improve salient areas of competitive context.

According to the authors, firms should select causes that intersect their particular businesses to create shared value for the firm and society. For example, Toyota addressed public concerns about automotive emissions by creating a competitively strong and environmentally friendly hybrid vehicle, the Prius, and French banking giant Crédit Agricole differentiated itself through specialised environmentally friendly financial products.

Porter and Kramer note that,

> By providing jobs, investing capital, purchasing goods, and doing business every day, corporations have a profound and positive influence on society. The most important thing a corporation can do for society, and for any community, is to contribute to a prosperous economy.

Although companies can address hundreds of social issues, only a handful offer the opportunity to build focused, proactive and integrated social initiatives that link with core business strategies to make a real difference to society and create a competitive advantage in the marketplace.

Clayton Christensen

Harvard's Clayton Christensen, along with his research colleagues, advocates *catalytic innovations* to address social sector problems. Like Christensen's disruptive innovations – which challenge industry incumbents by offering simpler, good enough alternatives to an underserved group of customers – catalytic innovations offer good enough solutions to inadequately addressed social problems. Catalytic innovators share five qualities:

1 They create systemic social change through scaling and replication.

2 They meet a need that is either overserved (because the existing solution is more complex than many people require) or not served at all.

▶

> ► Marketing insight *(continued)*

3 They offer simpler, less costly products and services that may have a lower level of performance, but that users consider to be good enough.

4 They generate resources, such as donations, grants, volunteer manpower or intellectual capital, in ways that are initially unattractive to competitors.

5 They are often ignored, disparaged or even encouraged by existing players for whom the business model is unprofitable or otherwise unattractive and who therefore avoid or retreat from the market segment.

To find organisations that are creating a catalytic innovation for investment or other purposes, Christensen and his colleagues offer some guidelines:

1 **Look for signs of disruption in the process**: Although not necessarily easily observed, pre-existing catalytic innovators may already be present in a market.

2 **Identify specific catalytic innovations**: Apply the five criteria listed.

3 **Assess the business model**: Determine whether the organisation can effectively introduce the innovation and scale it up and sustain it.

Sources: M. F. Porter and M. R. Kramer (2006) Strategy & society, *Harvard Business Review*, December, 78–82; C. M. Christensen, H. Baumann, R. Ruggles and T. M. Stadtler (2006) Disruption innovation for social change, *Harvard Business Review*, December, 94–101. See also: R. Steckel, E. Ford, C. Hilliard and T. Sanders (2004) *Cold Cash for Warm Hearts: 101 Best Social Marketing Initiatives*, Homewood, IL: High Tide Press.

Cause-related marketing

Many firms blend corporate social responsibility initiatives with marketing activities.[50] **Cause-related marketing** links the firm's contributions to a designated cause to customers' engaging directly or indirectly in revenue-producing transactions with the firm.[51] Cause marketing is part of *corporate societal marketing* (CSM), which Drumwright and Murphy define as marketing efforts 'that have at least one economic objective related to social welfare and use the resources of the company and/or of its partners'.[52] They also include other activities such as traditional and strategic philanthropy and volunteerism as part of CSM.

Tesco, a leading UK retailer, has created a 'Computers for Schools' programme: customers receive vouchers for every £10 spent, which they can donate to the school of their choice and the school can exchange the vouchers for new computer equipment. British Airways too has a particularly successful and highly visible programme.

▽ British Airways

British Airways partnered with UNICEF and developed a cause-marketing campaign called 'Change for Good'. Passengers on British Airways flights are encouraged to donate left-over foreign currency from their travels. The scheme is simple: passengers deposit their surplus currency in envelopes provided by British Airways, which collects the deposits and donates them directly to UNICEF. British Airways advertises its programme during an in-flight video, on the backs of seat cards and with in-flight announcements. The company also developed a television advertisement that featured a child thanking British Airways for its contribution to UNICEF. Because 'Change for Good' can be directly targeted to passengers and can produce immediate results, it does not require extensive advertising or promotion and is highly cost efficient. Since 1994 it has distributed almost US$45 million around the world.[53]

Cause-marketing benefits and costs

A successful cause-marketing programme can improve social welfare; create differentiated brand positioning; build strong consumer bonds; enhance the company's public image with government officials and other decision makers; create a reservoir of goodwill; boost internal morale and galvanise employees; drive sales; and increase the market value of the firm.[54]

Customers may develop a strong, unique bond with the firm that transcends normal marketplace transactions.[55] Specifically, cause marketing can: (1) build brand awareness; (2) enhance brand image; (3) establish brand credibility; (4) evoke brand feelings; (5) create a sense of brand community; and (6) elicit brand engagement. Cause marketing has a particularly interested audience in civic-minded 13–25-year-old millennial customers.[56]

The danger, however, is that a cause-related marketing programme could misfire if customers question the link between the product and the cause and see the firm as self-serving and exploitative as was the case with Cadbury Schweppes.[57]

▽ Cadbury Schweppes PLC

Cadbury's 'Sports for Schools' promotion offered sports and fitness equipment for schools in exchange for tokens. The problem was the public and media saw a perverse incentive for children to eat more chocolate, a product associated with obesity. As Britain's The Food Commission, a non-governmental organisation, said, 'Cadbury wants children to eat 2 million kilograms of fat – to get fit.' The commission estimated that to generate the 90 tokens to purchase a £5 netball would require spending £38 on Cadbury's confectionery and consuming more than 20,000 calories and over 1000 grams of fat. The product and the cause seemed to be at war. Cadbury Schweppes quickly discontinued the token programme, but it continued its 'Get Active' campaign offering teachers tips for sporty games in conjunction with the Youth Sport Trust and sponsored events such as Get Active Day with British sports stars. Putting a positive spin on the bad press, a Cadbury spokesperson insisted, 'The ensuing debate was very welcome. We have been trying to promote Get Active for two months. I don't think there can be anyone in the country who hasn't heard of it this week.'

Sources: N. C. Smith (2007) Out of left field, *Business Strategy Review*, 18(2), 55–9; A. Jones (2003) Choc horror over Cadbury tokens, *Financial Times*, 3 May, 14.

The knowledge, skills, resources and experiences of a top firm may be even more important to a non-profit or community group than funding so they must be clear about what their goals are, communicate clearly what they hope to accomplish and have an organisational structure in place to work with different firms. Developing a long-term relationship with a firm can take a long time.

Firms must make a number of decisions in designing and implementing a cause-marketing programme, such as how many and which cause(s) to choose and how to brand the cause programme.

Choosing a cause

Some experts believe the positive impact of cause-related marketing is reduced by sporadic involvement with numerous causes. For example, Gillette's director of civic affairs states: 'When you're spreading out your giving in fifty-dollar to one-thousand-dollar increments, no one knows what you are doing . . . It doesn't make much of a splash.'[58] Many companies choose to focus on one or a few main causes to simplify execution and maximise impact. One such focused marketer is McDonald's. Ronald McDonald Houses in more than 27 countries offer more than 6000 rooms each night to families needing support while their child is in hospital. The Ronald McDonald

House programme has provided a 'home away from home' for nearly 10 million family members since its beginning in 1974.

Limiting support to a single cause, however, may limit the pool of consumers or other stakeholders who can transfer positive feelings from the cause to the firm. In addition, many popular causes already have numerous corporate sponsors. Over 300 companies, including Avon, Ford, Estée Lauder, Revlon, Lee Jeans, Polo Ralph Lauren, Yoplait, Saks, BMW and American Express, have associated themselves with breast cancer as a cause.[59] As a consequence, the brand may find itself 'lost in the shuffle'. Opportunities may be greater with 'orphan causes' – diseases that afflict fewer than 200,000 people,[60] or with overlooked diseases, such as pancreatic cancer. Most firms choose causes that fit their corporate or brand image and which matter to their employees and shareholders.

Social marketing

Cause-related marketing supports a cause. **Social marketing** has been defined by French and Blair-Stevens as 'the systematic application of marketing alongside other concepts and techniques, to achieve specific goals, for a social good', often by non-profit or government organisations. Typical campaigns encourage consumers to 'Say No to Drugs' or 'Exercise More and Eat Better'.[61] Social marketing goes back many years. In the 1950s, India started family planning campaigns. In the 1970s, Sweden ran social marketing campaigns to turn the country into a nation of non-smokers and non-drinkers; the Australian government ran 'Wear Your Seat Belt' campaigns; and the Canadian government launched campaigns to 'Say No to Drugs', 'Stop Smoking' and 'Exercise for Health'. In the 1980s, the World Bank, World Health Organization, and Centres for Disease Control and Prevention started to use the term and promote interest in social marketing. A number of different types of organisation conduct social marketing in most European countries.

Choosing the right goal or objective for a social marketing programme is critical. Should a family-planning campaign focus on abstinence or birth control? Should a campaign to fight air pollution focus on car sharing or public transport? Social marketing campaigns may have

Marketing memo

Key features of social marketing

The key features and concepts for understanding social marketing according to the UK's National Social Marketing Centre are:

Customer or consumer orientation: A strong 'customer' orientation with importance attached to understanding where the customer is starting from, their knowledge, attitudes and beliefs, along with the social context in which they live and work.

Behaviour and behavioural goals: Clear focus on understanding existing behaviour and key influences on it, alongside developing clear behavioural goals, which can be divided into actionable and measurable steps or stages, phased over time.

'Intervention mix' and 'marketing mix': Using a range (or 'mix') of different interventions or methods to achieve a particular goal. When used at the strategic level this is commonly referred to as the 'intervention mix', and when used operationally it is described as the 'marketing mix' or 'social marketing mix'.

Audience segmentation: Clarity of audience focus using 'audience segmentation' to target effectively.

'Exchange': Use and application of the 'exchange' concept – understanding what is being expected of 'the customer', the 'real cost to them'.

'Competition': Use and application of the 'competition' concept – understanding factors that impact on the customer and that compete for their attention and time.[62]

objectives related to changing people's cognitions, values or actions. The following examples illustrate the range of possible objectives:

Cognitive campaigns
- Explain the nutritional value of different foods.
- Explain the importance of conservation.

Action campaigns
- Attract people for mass immunisation.
- Motivate people to vote 'yes' on a certain issue.
- Motivate people to donate blood.
- Motivate women to go for breast screening.

Social campaigns
- Discourage cigarette smoking.
- Discourage usage of hard drugs.
- Discourage excessive consumption of alcohol.

Value campaigns
- Alter ideas about abortion.
- Change attitudes of bigoted people.

Social marketing uses a number of different tactics to achieve its goals.[63] The planning process follows many of the same steps as for traditional products and services (see Table 21.2). Some key success factors in developing and implementing a social marketing programme include the following:

- Study the literature and previous campaigns.
- Choose target markets that are most ready to respond.
- Promote a single, do-able behaviour in clear, simple terms.
- Explain the benefits in compelling terms.

Table 21.2 Social marketing planning process

Where are we?

- Determine programme focus.
- Identify campaign purpose.
- Conduct an analysis of strengths, weaknesses, opportunities and threats (SWOT).
- Review past and similar efforts.

Where do we want to go?

- Select target audiences.
- Set objectives and goals.
- Analyse target audiences and the competition.

How will we get there?

- Product: design the market offering.
- Price: manage costs of behaviour change.
- Distribution: make the product available.
- Communications: create messages and choose media.

How will we stay on course?

- Develop a plan for evaluation and monitoring.
- Establish budgets and find funding sources.
- Complete an implementation plan.

- Make it easy to adopt the behaviour.
- Develop attention-grabbing messages and media.
- Consider an education-entertainment approach.

Social marketing programmes are complex; they take time and may require phased programmes or actions. For example, recall the steps in discouraging smoking: raising taxes on cigarettes to pay for antismoking campaigns, cancer reports, labelling of cigarettes, banning cigarette advertising, education about secondary smoke effects, no smoking in aeroplanes and restaurants.

Social marketing organisations should evaluate programme success in terms of objectives. Criteria might include incidence of adoption, speed of adoption, continuance of adoption, low cost per unit of adoption, and absence of counterproductive consequences.[64]

Ethnic marketing

The ethnic minority population in some European countries, such as France, Germany and the United Kingdom, is sizeable and represents a viable and untapped market segment. In today's fragmented and increasingly turbulent markets, ethnic marketing offers a new strategic focus for market/offering (product/market) development and, in many respects, companies that ignore this do so at their own competitive peril. Companies wishing to do business with ethnic minority groups will fundamentally have to review the basic premises of their marketing plans to take account of the growing market pluralism and the emergent multiethnic reality of European countries.[65]

Marketing as a concept pays a great deal of attention to the individual market transactions, often ignoring the impact of marketing practices on society at a macrolevel. In multicultural marketplaces, marketers and consumers of different ethnic backgrounds coexist, interact and adapt to each other. In doing so, consumers act as skilled navigators who frequently engage in culture swapping to sample the many tastes, themes and sounds of different cultures and values. Marketing facilitates this culture swapping and contributes towards tolerance and acceptance of lifestyle among consumers. However, traditional racial or ethnic segmentation could become problematic due to the fact that consumers no longer conform either individually or as a group to any one specific segment or category.[66]

Green marketing

From the earliest of times humankind has been aware of the importance of the environment. Natural climatic and weather conditions have marked the passage of the seasons. Human activity such as political, population and profit pursuits have all interacted with the rhythm of the natural order but have essentially been subservient to it. In the early decades of the twenty-first century there is mounting evidence that the environment is changing and that much of the cause of this change can be ascribed to human activity. As a result there is a growing concern about the natural changes that are occurring and those that are the direct result of the activity of humans.

As a consequence of these concerns the term 'green marketing' came into prominence in the last two decades of the twentieth century. It has been defined by the American Marketing Association as 'the marketing of products that are presumed to be environmentally safe'. For marketers this has many implications. Market offerings will require modification so that their use does not damage the environment. Material extraction, preparation and production processes will need rethinking. Conventional packaging approaches will need re-evaluating. Many companies are using recycled materials but many are not. In the United Kingdom non-degradable plastic bags have suddenly been declared undesirable. Marketing communications will have to become less profligate in their use of resources.

Such is the complexity of the environmental challenge facing humankind that while there is a general recognition of the existence of the problem there is no commonly accepted creed. Hence the existence of terms such as 'environmental marketing' and 'ecological marketing' that all emphasise different aspects of the matter. Not surprisingly, there is little general agreement as to what private and public enterprise should do about it.

▽ **At-a-glance: The UK government Stern Review**

The world has to act now on climate change or face devastating economic consequences, according to a report by Sir Nicholas Stern for the UK government.

Here are the key points of the review written by the former chief economist of the World Bank.

Temperature

- Carbon emissions have already pushed up global temperatures by half a degree Celsius.
- If no action is taken on emissions, there is more than a 75 per cent chance of global temperatures rising between two and three degrees Celsius over the next 50 years.
- There is a 50 per cent chance that average global temperatures could rise by five degrees Celsius.

Environmental impact

- Melting glaciers will increase flood risk.
- Crop yields will decline, particularly in Africa.
- Rising sea levels could leave 200 million people permanently displaced.
- Up to 40 per cent of species could face extinction.
- There will be more examples of extreme weather patterns.

Economic impact

- Extreme weather could reduce global GDP by up to 1 per cent.
- A two to three degrees Celsius rise in temperatures could reduce global economic output by 3 per cent.
- If temperatures rise by five degrees Celsius, up to 10 per cent of global output could be lost. The poorest countries would lose more than 10 per cent of their output.
- In the worst case scenario global consumption per head would fall 20 per cent.
- To stabilise at manageable levels, emissions would need to stabilise in the next 20 years, and fall between 1 per cent and 3 per cent after that. This would cost 1 per cent of GDP.

Source: At a glance: the Stern Review, *BBC News*, 30 October 2006 (http://news.bbc.co.uk/1/hi/business/6098362.stm).

Approaching a green marketing response

The plurality of environmental beliefs hinders a concerted response to examining these beliefs and thus evaluating their impact on marketing activity. Peattie and Crane concluded that much of what has been commonly referred to as green marketing has not been underpinned by either a marketing or an environmental philosophy.[67] D'Souza et al.[68] suggested that green firms should pay particular regard to:

- the need to build a strong green and competitive advantage for their market offerings;
- the need to develop and project a green consumer profile based on demographic segmentation, targeting and positioning;
- the need to meet customers' expectations by acting genuinely as well as being recognised as demonstrably environmentally responsible.

Practical advice on how to introduce a green philosophy and the functional activities needed to support it must, argues Grant,[69] be a central feature of company strategy. He stresses that it is not a matter of cosmetically 'green theming' and provides a road map to facilitate both the adoption and practical introduction of green marketing.

Existing firms

In many respects the task is harder for existing than for new firms. Cynics often argue that few companies pay more than lip-service to green marketing in terms of real acceptance and hence resource allocation but are quite happy to gain some PR advantage from time to time. This is, on the whole, a harsh view as companies such as IKEA, LEGO, Marks & Spencer, O2, SUT (Swedish broadcaster), Sky, Tesco, Toyota and the Virgin Group are all making progress. This is highly commendable and represents a real start but the jury is still out as to whether this is a lasting commitment. The Body Shop and Ben & Jerry's were pioneers in green marketing and it is hoped that the Unilever Group will continue this tradition after acquiring these companies.

▽ B&Q rebuilds its image to top the eco-friendly shoppers' chart

M&S, Homebase and IKEA are left trailing as the home improvement group wins plaudits for its credentials on green and social issues. B&Q, Britain's biggest home improvement chain, has finally won over the hearts and minds of environmentally conscious shoppers, an exclusive survey for *The Times* revealed. Nearly two decades after B&Q's former marketing director was forced to admit that he did not know the source of the chain's timber, the company has been voted top of the class in its sector on green and social issues. It comes less than a month after the retailer announced a number of initiatives to boost its eco-credentials, including the phasing out of controversial patio heaters and a new partnership with the World Wide Fund for Nature on sustainability.

The UK do-it-yourself chain B&Q provides practical environmental advice and service.

Source: Courtesy of B&Q / Agency: The Red Consultancy

A Populus survey compiled for *The Times* showed that B&Q had a higher standing among customers than Homebase, Marks & Spencer, John Lewis or IKEA when it came to social and environmental issues. However, nearly two-thirds of the 1600 people surveyed felt that these large retailers were still not doing enough and carbon emissions remained one of the highest concerns. Eighty per cent were either 'very concerned' or 'quite concerned' about the level of CO_2 emissions associated with the manufacture and transportation of products designed for our homes and gardens.

Patio heaters have become the number one enemy of environmentalists in the past year after a surge in demand for them following the introduction of the smoking ban. The Energy Savings Trust calculated that a propane-fuelled heater emitted 34.9 kg of carbon dioxide before running empty – the equivalent amount of energy used to make 5200 cups of tea. Friends of the Earth described the heaters as 'carbon-belching monstrosities'.

Ian Cheshire, at the time the chief executive of B&Q, said: 'A quarter of the UK's total carbon emissions come from the home and, as the largest home improvement retailer, we are uniquely placed to make a difference.' Nearly 70 per cent of the group's timber now has to come from well-managed or recycled sources.

Other stores are matching B&Q's efforts. IKEA has sold energy-saving light bulbs for ten years and launched a 'Bag the Plastic Bag!' programme designed to cut plastic bag usage by 50 per cent to 35 million. Marks & Spencer aims to become carbon neutral by 2012 under its much-lauded environmental scheme. However, the Populus survey showed that tackling the environment may not be enough. Just as high up the list of consumers' concerns as CO_2 emissions comes the use of child labour by suppliers and the potential health dangers of chemicals used in products. Giles Gibbons, founder of Good Business, the green campaigner, says: 'The social and environmental impact of a product can [now] act to curtail its market growth.'

Source: Adapted from S. Hawkes (2008) B&Q rebuilds its image to top the eco-friendly shoppers' chart, *The Times*, 28 February. Copyright © 2008 NI Syndication Ltd. Reproduced with permission.

New firms

New firms have the advantage of being in a position to build in a green marketing approach from the start.

▽ See the green light and go!

When Anya Pearson was forging a high-flying career working for high street clothing retailers, she noticed a lot of things about the fashion industry that she did not like. So two years ago she decided to take matters into her own hands and start a fashion label of her own, called Frank and Faith (Frankandfaith.com). Frank and Faith, which is based in Dorset, makes ethical clothing from sustainable sources for men, women and children, with all items made in Britain from organic cotton and prices similar to those on the high street.

'Over 20 years of working in the fashion industry I have seen a lot of sweatshops. I wanted to have everything made in Britain so I would know 100 per cent that nothing was made by children or abused workers,' she said. 'Being made in Britain means that our clothes are locally sourced and completely traceable.'

After much searching, Pearson found a specialist knitwear maker in Leicester, one of the last of its kind in Britain. It costs more than using a factory in China, but Pearson is happy with her choice. 'The only reason people are able to buy clothes at such low prices is because somebody else is losing out. It is the four-year-old Bangladeshi kid who should be in school who is losing out.' Instead of using sweatshop labour to keep costs down, Pearson has chosen to keep her prices competitive by reducing her own profit margins. As a result, business is booming and – something Pearson is pleased to note – not just from consciously green consumers:

> The main core of shoppers is the people who can't afford ethical designer wear so this is my way of trying to get people in and trying to educate them in what it's all about. I want them to understand why clothing has become so cheap and throw-away in the past ten years. It is because of these hideous issues of sweatshop manufacturing and the complete disregard for the environment.

Pearson is one of a growing number of fledgling entrepreneurs who have decided that going green is not just something to be aware of, but is integral to the way they run their business. By incorporating sustainable, green ethics when they form their business, they create a strategy that places green values throughout the company. Furthermore larger companies, such as Marks & Spencer, were increasingly insisting that their small suppliers should become more sustainable in their operations. Many big companies want to move towards a green value chain.

Source: R. Bridge (2008) Green means go for new firms, *The Sunday Times*, 9 March; The Carbon Trust, carbontrust.co.uk: Green Energy 360, greenenergy360.org.

The key challenge for green marketers is to strengthen individuals' perception of the individual benefits to be gained from 'going green' by adding more and stronger emotional values to green brands. Future green market research should extend its analysis to the emotional values and benefits associated with environmentally responsible consumption behaviour.[70]

Companies are increasingly working with public interest groups to avoid perceptions of 'greenwashing' – insincere, phoney efforts to appear more environmentally sensitive than they really are. Alliances with environmentalists can achieve more satisfying solutions that both address public concerns and increase the firm's image and profits. DuPont once viewed Greenpeace as an enemy; the firm now uses Greenpeace's former head as a consultant. Greenpeace has also worked with McDonald's and others to stop farmers cutting down the Amazon rainforest to grow soybeans. When Greenpeace called out Coca-Cola on the eve of the 2000 Sydney Olympics for using a potent greenhouse gas in its nearly 10 million coolers and vending machines, Coca-Cola, along with PepsiCo, Unilever and McDonald's, invested US$30 million in a less damaging system that now displays a 'technology approved by Greenpeace' banner.[71]

▽ Evaluation and control

In spite of the need to monitor and control marketing activities, many companies have inadequate control procedures. Table 21.3 lists four types of required marketing control: annual-plan control, profitability control, efficiency control and strategic control. We consider each.

Annual-plan control

Annual-plan control ensures the company achieves its planned sales, profits and other goals. There are four steps (see Figure 21.5). First, management sets monthly or quarterly goals. Second, management monitors its performance in the marketplace. Third, management determines the causes of serious performance deviations. Fourth, management takes corrective action to close gaps between goals and performance.

Keeping a close eye on company progress.
Source: Serif

Table 21.3 Types of marketing control

Type of control	Prime responsibility	Purpose of control	Approaches
1 Annual-plan control	Top management Middle management	To examine whether the planned results are being achieved	• Sales analysis • Market share analysis • Sales-to-expense ratios • Financial analysis • Market-based scorecard analysis
2 Profitability control	Marketing controller	To examine where the company is making and losing money	Profitability by: • product • territory • customer • segment • trade channel • order size
3 Efficiency control	Line and staff management Marketing controller	To evaluate and improve the spending efficiency and impact of marketing expenditures	Efficiency of: • sales force • advertising • sales promotion • distribution
4 Strategic control	Top management Marketing auditor	To examine whether the company is pursuing its best opportunities with respect to markets, products and channels	• Marketing effectiveness rating instrument • Marketing audit • Marketing excellence review • Company ethical and social responsibility review

Figure 21.5 The control process

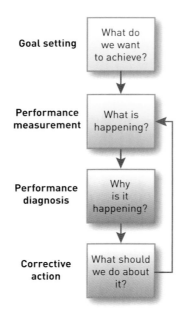

Goal setting — What do we want to achieve?

Performance measurement — What is happening?

Performance diagnosis — Why is it happening?

Corrective action — What should we do about it?

This control model applies to all levels of the organisation. Top management sets annual sales and profit goals; each product manager, regional district manager, sales manager and sales representative is committed to attaining specified levels of sales and costs. Each period, top management reviews and interprets the results.

Marketers today have better marketing metrics for measuring the performance of marketing plans (see Table 22.1 on page 828 for some sample ones).[72] They can use four tools to check on plan performance: sales analysis, market share analysis, marketing expense-to-sales analysis and financial analysis.

Sales analysis

Sales analysis measures and evaluates actual sales in relationship to goals. Two specific tools make it work.

Sales-variance analysis measures the relative contribution of different factors to a gap in sales performance. Suppose the annual plan called for selling 4000 widgets in the first quarter at €10 per widget, for total revenue of €40,000. At quarter's end, only 3000 widgets were sold at €8 per widget, for total revenue of €24,000. How much of the sales performance gap is due to the price decline, and how much to the volume decline? This calculation answers the question:

$$\text{Variance due to price decline} = (€10 - €8)(3000) = €\ \ 6000 \quad 37.5\%$$
$$\text{Variance due to volume decline} = (€10)(4000 - 3000) = \underline{€10,000} \quad \underline{62.5\%}$$
$$€16,000 \quad 100.0\%$$

Almost two-thirds of the variance is due to failure to achieve the volume target. The company should look closely at why it failed to achieve expected sales volume.

Microsales analysis looks at specific products, territories, and so forth that failed to produce expected sales. Suppose the company sells in three territories, and expected sales were 1500 units, 500 units and 2000 units, respectively. Actual volumes were 1400 units, 525 units, and 1075 units, respectively. Thus territory 1 showed a 7 per cent shortfall in terms of expected sales; territory 2, a 5 per cent improvement over expectations; and territory 3, a 46 per cent shortfall! Territory 3 is causing most of the trouble. Maybe territory 3's sales representative is underperforming; a major competitor has entered this territory; or business is in a recession there.

Market share analysis

Company sales do not reveal how well the company is performing relative to competitors. For this purpose, management needs to track its market share in one of three ways.

Overall market share expresses the company's sales as a percentage of total market sales. **Served market share** is sales as a percentage of the total sales to the market. The **served market** is all the buyers able and willing to buy the product, and served market share is always larger than overall market share. A company could capture 100 per cent of its served market and yet have a relatively small share of the total market. **Relative market share** is market share in relationship to the largest competitor. A relative market share over 100 per cent indicates a market leader. A relative market share of exactly 100 per cent means the company is tied for the lead. A rise in relative market share means a company is gaining on its leading competitor.

Conclusions from market share analysis, however, are subject to certain qualifications:

- The assumption that outside forces affect all companies in the same way is often not true.
- The assumption that a company's performance should be judged against the average performance of all companies is not always valid.
- If a new firm enters the industry, every existing firm's market share might fall.
- Sometimes a market share decline is deliberately engineered to improve profits.
- Market share can fluctuate for many minor reasons.[73]

A useful way to analyse market share movements is in terms of four components:

$$\begin{array}{c}\text{Overall}\\\text{market share}\end{array} = \begin{array}{c}\text{Customer}\\\text{penetration}\end{array} \times \begin{array}{c}\text{Customer}\\\text{loyalty}\end{array} \times \begin{array}{c}\text{Customer}\\\text{selectivity}\end{array} \times \begin{array}{c}\text{Price}\\\text{selectivity}\end{array}$$

where:

Customer penetration	Percentage of all customers who buy from the company
Customer loyalty	Purchases from the company by its customers as a percentage of their total purchases from all suppliers of the same products
Customer selectivity	Size of the average customer purchase from the company as a percentage of the size of the average customer purchase from an average company
Price selectivity	Average price charged by the company as a percentage of the average price charged by all companies.

Now suppose the company's market share falls during the period. The overall market share equation provides four possible explanations: the company lost some customers (lower customer penetration); existing customers are buying less from the company (lower customer loyalty); the company's remaining customers are smaller in size (lower customer selectivity); or the company's price has slipped relative to competition (lower price selectivity).

Marketing expense-to-sales analysis

Annual-plan control requires making sure the company isn't overspending to achieve sales goals. The key ratio to watch is *marketing expense-to-sales*. In one company, this ratio was 30 per cent and consisted of five component expense-to-sales ratios: sales force-to-sales (15 per cent); advertising-to-sales (5 per cent); sales promotion-to-sales (6 per cent); marketing research-to-sales (1 per cent); and sales administration-to-sales (3 per cent).

Fluctuations outside normal range are cause for concern. Management needs to monitor period-to-period fluctuations in each ratio on a *control chart* (see Figure 21.6). This chart shows the advertising expense-to-sales ratio normally fluctuates between 8 per cent and 12 per cent, say 99 out of 100 times. In the 15th period, however, the ratio exceeded the upper control limit. One of two hypotheses can explain why: (1) the company still has good expense control, and this situation represents a rare chance event; (2) the company has lost control over this expense and should find the cause. If there is no investigation, the risk is that some real change might have occurred, and the company will fall behind. An investigation may also uncover nothing and be a waste of time and effort.

Managers should watch the number of successive observations even within the upper and lower control limits. Note in Figure 21.6 that the level of the expense-to-sales ratio rose steadily from the 9th period onwards. The probability of encountering six successive increases in what should be independent events is only 1 in 64.[74] This unusual pattern should have led to an investigation sometime before the 15th observation.

Figure 21.6 The control-chart model

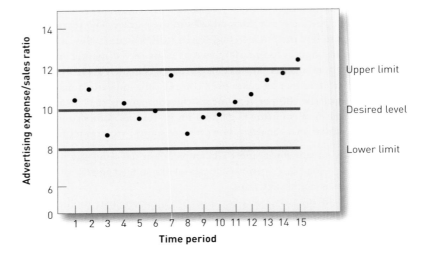

Figure 21.7 Financial model of return on net worth

Financial analysis

Marketers should analyse the expense-to-sales ratios in an overall financial framework to determine how and where the company is making its money. They can, and are increasingly, using financial analysis to find profitable strategies beyond building sales.

Management uses financial analysis to identify factors that affect the company's *rate of return on net worth*.[75] The main factors are shown in Figure 21.7, along with illustrative numbers for a large chain-store retailer. The retailer is earning a 12.5 per cent return on net worth. The return on net worth is the product of two ratios, the company's *return on assets* and its *financial leverage*. To improve its return on net worth, the company must increase its ratio of net profits to assets, or increase the ratio of assets to net worth. The company should analyse the composition of its assets (cash, accounts receivable, inventory, and plant and equipment) and see whether it can improve its asset management.

The return on assets is the product of two ratios, the *profit margin* and the *asset turnover*. The profit margin in Figure 21.7 seems low, whereas the asset turnover is more normal for retailing. The marketing executive can seek to improve performance in two ways: (1) increase the profit margin by increasing sales or cutting costs; and (2) increase the asset turnover by increasing sales or reducing assets (inventory, receivables) held against a given level of sales.

Profitability control

Companies can benefit from deeper financial analysis and should measure the profitability of their products, territories, customer groups, segments, trade channels and order sizes. This information can help management determine whether to expand, reduce or eliminate any products or marketing activities.

Marketing profitability analysis

Consider the following example: the marketing director of a lawnmower company wants to determine the profitability of selling through three types of retail channels: hardware stores, garden supply shops and department stores. The company's profit-and-loss statement is shown in Table 21.4.

Step 1: identifying functional expenses Assume the expenses listed in Table 21.4 are incurred to sell the product, advertise it, pack and deliver it, and bill and collect for it. The first task is to measure how much of each expense was incurred in each activity.

Suppose most of the salary expense went to sales representatives and the rest to an advertising manager, packing and delivery help, and an office accountant. Let the breakdown of the €9300 be €5100, €1200, €1400, and €1600, respectively. Table 21.5 shows the allocation of the salary expense to these four activities.

Table 21.5 also shows the rent account of €3000 allocated to the four activities. Because the sales reps work away from the office, none of the building's rent expense is assigned to selling. Most of the expenses for floor space and rented equipment are for packing and delivery. The supplies account covers promotional materials, packing materials, fuel purchases for delivery and home office stationery. The €3500 in this account is reassigned to functional uses of the supplies.

Step 2: assigning functional expenses to marketing entities The next task is to measure how much functional expense was associated with selling through each type of channel. Consider the selling effort, indicated by the number of sales in each channel. This number is in the selling column of Table 21.6. Altogether, 275 sales calls were made during the period. Because

Table 21.4 A simplified profit-and-loss statement

Sales		€60,000
Cost of goods sold		39,000
Gross margin		€21,000
Expenses		
Salaries	€9300	
Rent	3000	
Supplies	€3500	
		15,800
Net profit		€5200

Table 21.5 Mapping natural expenses into functional expenses

Natural accounts	Total	Selling	Advertising	Packing and delivery	Invoicing and collecting
Salaries	€9300	€5100	€1200	€1400	€1600
Rent	3000	—	400	2000	600
Supplies	3500	400	1500	1400	200
	€15800	€5500	€3100	€4800	€2400

Table 21.6 Bases for allocating functional expenses to channels

Channel type	Selling	Advertising	Packing and delivery	Invoicing and collecting
Hardware	200	50	50	50
Garden supply	65	20	21	21
Department stores	10	30	9	9
	275	**100**	**80**	**80**
Functional expense ÷ No. of units	€5500	€3100	€4800	€2400
	275	100	80	80
Equals	**€ 20**	**€ 31**	**€ 60**	**€ 30**

the total selling expense amounted to €5500 (see Table 21.6), the selling expense averaged €20 per call.

Advertising expense can be allocated according to the number of ads addressed to different channels. Because there were 100 advertisements altogether, the average advertising cost €31.

The packing and delivery expense is allocated according to the number of orders placed by each type of channel. This same basis was used for allocating invoicing and collection expense.

Step 3: preparing a profit-and-loss statement for each marketing entity A profit-and-loss statement for each type of channel can now be prepared (see Table 21.7). Because hardware stores accounted for half of total sales (€30,000 out of €60,000), charge this channel with half the cost of goods sold (€19500 out of €39,000). This leaves a gross margin from hardware stores of €10,500. From this we deduct the proportions of functional expenses hardware stores consumed. According to Table 21.6, hardware stores received 200 of 275 total sales calls. At an imputed value of €20 a call, hardware stores must bear a €4000 selling expense. Table 21.6 also shows hardware stores were the target of 50 advertisements. At €31 an advertisement, the hardware stores are charged with €1550 of advertising. The same reasoning applies in computing the share of the other functional expenses. The result is that hardware stores gave rise to €10,050 of the total expenses (see Table 21.7). Subtracting this from gross margin, we find the profit of selling through hardware stores is only €450.

Repeat this analysis for the other channels. The company is losing money in selling through garden supply shops and makes virtually all its profits through department stores. Notice that gross sales is not a reliable indicator of the net profits for each channel.

Table 21.7 Profit and loss account for channels

	Hardware	Garden supply	Dept stores	Whole company
Sales	€30,000	€10,000	€20,000	€60,000
Cost of goods sold	19,500	6,500	13,000	39,000
Gross margin	€10,500	€3,500	€7,000	€21,000
Expenses				
Selling (€20 per call)	€4,000	€1,300	€200	€5,500
Advertising (€31 per advertisement)	1,550	620	930	3,100
Packing and delivery (€60 per order)	3,000	1,260	540	4,800
Invoicing (€30 per order)	1,500	630	270	2,400
Total expenses	€10,050	€3,810	€1,940	€15,800
Net profit or loss	€450	€(310)	€5,060	€5,200

Determining corrective action

It would be naive to conclude the company should drop garden supply shops and possibly hardware stores so that it can concentrate on department stores. The following questions need to be answered first:

- To what extent do consumers buy on the basis of type of retail outlet versus brand?
- What are the trends with respect to the importance of these three channels?
- How good are the company marketing strategies directed at the three channels?

On the basis of the answers, marketing management can evaluate five alternatives:

1 Establish a special charge for handling smaller orders.
2 Give more promotional aid to garden supply shops and hardware stores.
3 Reduce the number of sales calls and the amount of advertising going to garden supply shops and hardware stores.
4 Do not abandon any channel entirely, but only the weakest retail units in each channel.
5 Do nothing.

In general, marketing profitability analysis indicates the relative profitability of different channels, products, territories or other marketing entities. It does not prove that the best course of action is to drop the unprofitable marketing entities, nor does it capture the likely profit improvement if these marginal marketing entities are dropped.

Direct versus full costing

As with all information tools, marketing profitability analysis can lead or mislead marketing executives, depending on how well they understand its methods and limitations. The lawnmower company showed some arbitrariness in its choice of bases for allocating the functional expenses to its marketing entities. It used 'number of sales calls' to allocate selling expenses, generating less record keeping and computation, when in principle 'number of sales working hours' is a more accurate indicator of cost.

Far more serious is another judgemental element affecting profitability analysis – whether to allocate full costs or only direct and traceable costs in evaluating a marketing entity's performance. The lawnmower company sidestepped this problem by assuming only simple costs that fit in with marketing activities; however in the real-world this would be unwise. Three types of costs can be distinguished:

1 **Direct costs**: These can be attributed directly to the proper marketing entities. Sales commissions are a direct cost in a profitability analysis of sales territories, sales representatives or customers. Advertising expenditures are a direct cost in a profitability analysis of products to the extent that each advertisement promotes only one product. Other direct costs for specific purposes are sales force salaries and travelling expenses.

2 **Traceable common costs**: Traceable common costs can only be assigned indirectly, but on a plausible basis, to the marketing entities. In the example, rent was charged this way.

3 **Non-traceable common costs**: Common costs whose allocation to the marketing entities is highly arbitrary are non-traceable common costs. To allocate 'corporate image' expenditures equally to all market offerings would be arbitrary, because they do not all benefit equally. To allocate them proportionately to the sales of the various market offerings would be arbitrary, because relative sales reflect many factors besides corporate image making. Other examples are top management salaries, taxes, interest, and other overheads.

No one disputes the inclusion of direct costs in marketing cost analysis. There is some controversy about including traceable common costs, which consolidate costs that would and would not change with the scale of marketing activity. If the lawnmower company drops garden supply shops, it would probably continue to pay the same rent. In this event, its profits would not rise immediately by the amount of the present loss in selling to garden supply shops (€310).

The major controversy is about whether to allocate the non-traceable common costs to the marketing entities. Such allocation is called the *full-cost approach*, and its advocates argue that all costs must ultimately be imputed in order to determine true profitability. However, this argument confuses the use of accounting for financial reporting with its use for managerial decision making. Full costing has three major weaknesses:

1   The relative profitability of different marketing entities can shift radically when one arbitrary way to allocate non-traceable common costs is replaced by another.

2   The arbitrariness demoralises managers, who feel their performance is judged adversely.

3   The inclusion of no traceable common costs could weaken efforts at real cost control.

Operating management is most effective in controlling direct costs and traceable common costs. Arbitrary assignments of no traceable common costs can lead managers to spend their time fighting cost allocations instead of managing controllable costs well.

Companies show growing interest in using marketing profitability analysis, or its broader version, activity-based cost accounting, to quantify the true profitability of different activities.[76] Managers can then reduce the resources required to perform various activities, make the resources more productive, acquire them at lower cost or raise prices on products that consume heavy amounts of support resources. The contribution of ABC is to refocus management's attention away from using only or material standard costs to allocate full cost, and towards capturing the actual costs of supporting individual products, customers and other entities.

Efficiency control

Suppose a profitability analysis reveals the company is earning poor profits in certain products, territories or markets. Are there more efficient ways to manage the sales force, advertising, sales promotion and distribution in connection with these marketing entities?

Some companies have established a *marketing controller* position to calculate work out of the controller's office and to specialise in improving marketing efficiency. Sophisticated companies such as Bosch, Danone and IKEA perform a sophisticated financial analysis of marketing expenditures and results. They examine adherence to profit plans, help prepare brand managers' budgets, measure the efficiency of promotions, analyse media production costs, evaluate customer and geographic profitability, and educate marketing personnel on the financial implications of marketing decisions.[77] They can examine the efficiency of the channel, sales force, advertising, or any other form of marketing communication.

For example, in assessing channel efficiency, management needs to search for distribution economies in inventory control, warehouse locations and transportation modes. It should track such measures as:

* logistics costs as a percentage of sales;
* percentage of orders filled correctly;
* percentage of on-time deliveries;
* number of invoicing errors.

Management should strive to reduce stocks while at the same time speeding up the order-to-delivery cycle. Dell Computers shows how to do both simultaneously.

▽ Dell

A customer-customised computer ordered from Dell's website at 9 am on Wednesday can be on the delivery van by 9 pm on Thursday. In that short period, Dell electronically orders the computer components from its suppliers' warehouses. Equally impressively, Dell gets paid electronically within 24 hours, whereas Compaq, supplying its computers to retailers, receives payment days later.

Strategic control

Each company should periodically reassess its strategic approach to the marketplace with a good marketing audit. Companies can also perform marketing excellence reviews and ethical/social responsibility reviews.

The marketing audit

In buyers' markets companies can lose several of their customers in five years, several employees in four years, and many investors as the stock markets fluctuate. Wise companies carry out regular marketing audits.[78] A **marketing audit** is a comprehensive, systematic, independent and periodic examination of a company's or business unit's marketing environment, objectives, strategies and activities, with a view to determining problem areas and opportunities and recommending a plan of action to improve the company's marketing performance.

A marketing audit should be:

1 **Comprehensive**: The marketing audit covers all the major marketing activities of a business, not just a few troublespots. It would be called a functional audit if it covered only the salesforce, pricing, or some other marketing activity. Although functional audits are useful, they sometimes mislead management. Excessive sales force turnover, for example, could be a symptom not of poor sales force training or compensation but of weak company products and promotion. A comprehensive marketing audit is usually more effective in locating the real source of problems.

2 **Systematic**: The marketing audit is an orderly examination of the organisation's macro- and micromarketing environments, marketing objectives and strategies, marketing systems, and specific activities. The audit indicates the most-needed improvements, incorporating them into a corrective action plan with short- and long-run steps to improve overall effectiveness.

3 **Independent**: Marketers can conduct a marketing audit in six ways: self-audit, audit from across, audit from above, company auditing office, company task-force audit, and outsider audit. Self-audits, in which managers use a checklist to rate their own operations, lack objectivity and independence. Generally speaking, however, the best audits come from outside consultants who have the necessary objectivity, broad experience in a number of industries, some familiarity with the industry being audited, and undivided time and attention.

4 **Periodic**: Typically, firms initiate marketing audits only after sales have turned down, sales force morale has fallen, and other problems have occurred. Companies are thrown into a crisis partly because they failed to review their marketing operations during good times. A periodic marketing audit can benefit companies in good health as well as those in trouble.

A marketing audit starts with a meeting between the company officer(s) and the marketing auditor(s) to work out an agreement on the audit's objectives, coverage, depth, data sources, report format and time frame. It includes a detailed plan of who is to be interviewed, the questions to be asked, and where and when to minimise time and cost. The cardinal rule in marketing auditing is: do not rely solely on company managers for data and opinions. Ask customers, dealers, and other outside groups. Many companies do not really know how their customers and dealers see them, nor do they fully understand customer needs.

The marketing audit examines six major components of the company's marketing situation. Table 21.8 lists the major questions.

The marketing excellence review

The three columns in Table 21.9 distinguish among poor, good and excellent business and marketing practices. Management can place a checkmark to indicate its perception of where the business stands. The profile that results from this marketing excellence review exposes weaknesses and strengths, highlighting where the company might make changes to become a truly outstanding player in the marketplace.

As customers can usually choose from a number of companies in contemporary buyers' markets (see Chapter 10) effective marketing activity needs to be practised with appropriate sensitivity to society. The concluding section in this chapter highlights the important sensitivities that marketing management needs to take into account.

Table 21.8 Components of a marketing audit

Part 1 Marketing environment audit

Macroenvironment

A. Demographic	What major demographic developments and trends pose opportunities or threats to this company? What actions has the company taken in response to these developments and trends?
B. Economic	What major developments in income, prices, savings and credit will affect the company? What actions has the company been taking in response to these developments and trends?
C. Environmental	What is the outlook for the cost and availability of natural resources and energy needed by the company? What concerns have been expressed about the company's role in pollution and conservation, and what steps has the company taken?
D. Technological	What major changes are occurring in product and process technology? What is the company's position in these technologies? What major generic substitutes might replace this product?
E. Political	What changes in laws and regulations might affect marketing strategy and tactics? What is happening in the areas of pollution control, equal employment opportunity, product safety, advertising, price control, and so forth, that affects marketing strategy?
F. Cultural	What is the public's attitude towards business and towards the company's products? What changes in customer lifestyles and values might affect the company?

Task environment

A. Markets	What is happening to market size, growth, geographical distribution and profits? What are the major market segments?
B. Customers	What are the customers' needs and buying processes? How do customers and prospects rate the company and its competitors on reputation, product quality, service, sales force and price? How do different customer segments make their buying decisions?
C. Competitors	Who are the major competitors? What are their objectives, strategies, strengths, weaknesses, sizes and market shares? What trends will affect future competition and substitutes for the company's products?
D. Distribution and dealers	What are the main trade channels for bringing products to customers? What are the efficiency levels and growth potentials of the different trade channels?
E. Suppliers	What is the outlook for the availability of key resources used in production? What trends are occurring among suppliers?
F. Facilitators and marketing firms	What is the cost and availability outlook for transportation services, warehousing facilities and financial resources? How effective are the company's advertising agencies and marketing research firms?
G. Publics	Which publics represent particular opportunities or problems for the company? What steps has the company taken to deal effectively with each public?

Part 2 Marketing strategy audit

A. Business mission	Is the business mission clearly stated in market-oriented terms? Is it feasible?
B. Marketing objectives and goals	Are the company and marketing objectives and goals stated clearly enough to guide marketing planning and performance measurement? Are the marketing objectives appropriate, given the company's competitive position, resources and opportunities?
C. Strategy	Has the management articulated a clear marketing strategy for achieving its marketing objectives? Is the strategy convincing? Is the strategy appropriate to the stage of the product life cycle, competitors' strategies and the state of the economy? Is the company using the best basis for market segmentation? Does it have clear criteria for rating the segments and choosing the best ones? Has it developed accurate profiles of each target segment? Has the company developed an effective positioning and marketing mix for each target segment? Are marketing resources allocated optimally to the major elements of the marketing mix? Are enough resources or too many resources budgeted to accomplish the marketing objectives?

Table 21.8 (*Continued*)

Part 3 Marketing organisation audit

A. Formal structure	Does the marketing vice-president have adequate authority and responsibility for company activities that affect customers' satisfaction? Are the marketing activities optimally structured along functional, product, segment, end user and geographical lines?
B. Functional efficiency	Are there good communication and working relationships between marketing and sales? Is the product management system working effectively? Are product managers able to plan profits or only sales volume? Are there any groups in marketing that need more training, motivation, supervision or evaluation?
C. Interface efficiency	Are there any problems between marketing and manufacturing, R&D, purchasing, finance, accounting and/or legal that need attention?

Part 4 Marketing systems audit

A. Marketing information system	Is the marketing intelligence system producing accurate, sufficient and timely information about marketplace developments with respect to customers, prospects, distributors and dealers, competitors, suppliers and various publics? Are company decision makers asking for enough marketing research, and are they using the results? Is the company employing the best methods for market measurement and sales forecasting?
B. Marketing planning system	Is the marketing planning system well conceived and effectively used? Do marketers have decision support systems available? Does the planning system result in acceptable sales targets and quotas?
C. Marketing control system	Are the control procedures adequate to ensure that the annual plan objectives are being achieved? Does management periodically analyse the profitability of products, markets, territories and channels of distribution? Are marketing costs and productivity periodically examined?
D. New product development system	Is the company well organised to gather, generate and screen new product ideas? Does the company do adequate concept research and business analysis before investing in new ideas? Does the company carry out adequate product and market testing before launching new products?

Part 5 Marketing productivity audit

A. Profitability analysis	What is the profitability of the company's different products, markets, territories and channels of distribution? Should the company enter, expand, contract or withdraw from any business segments?
B. Cost-effectiveness analysis	Do any marketing activities seem to have excessive costs? Can cost-reducing steps be taken?

Part 6 Marketing function audits

A. Products	What are the company's product line objectives? Are they sound? Is the current product line meeting the objectives? Should the product line be stretched or contracted upwards, downwards, or both ways? Which products should be phased out? Which products should be added? What are the buyers' knowledge and attitudes towards the company's and competitors' product quality, features, styling, brand names, and so on? What areas of product and brand strategy need improvement?
B. Price	What are the company's pricing objectives, policies, strategies and procedures? To what extent are prices set on cost, demand and competitive criteria? Do the customers see the company's prices as being in line with the value of its offer? What does management know about the price elasticity of demand, experience-curve effects, and competitors' prices and pricing policies? To what extent are price policies compatible with the needs of distributors and dealers, suppliers and government regulation?

(Continued)

Table 21.8 *(Continued)*

Part 6 Marketing function audits

C. Distribution	What are the company's distribution objectives and strategies? Is there adequate market coverage and service? How effective are distributors, dealers, manufacturers' representatives, brokers, agents and others? Should the company consider changing its distribution channels?
D. Marketing communications	What are the organisation's advertising objectives? Are they sound? Is the right amount being spent on advertising? Are the ad themes and copy effective? What do customers and the public think about the advertising? Are the advertising media well chosen? Is the internal advertising staff adequate? Is the sales promotion budget adequate? Is there effective and sufficient use of sales promotion tools such as samples, coupons, displays and sales contests? Is the public relations staff competent and creative? Is the company making enough use of direct, online and database marketing?
E. Sales force	What are the sales force's objectives? Is the sales force large enough to accomplish the company's objectives? Is the sales force organised along the proper principles of specialisation (territory, market, product)? Are there enough (or too many) sales managers to guide the field sales representatives? Do the sales compensation level and structure provide adequate incentive and reward? Does the sales force show high morale, ability and effort? Are the procedures adequate for setting quotas and evaluating performance? How does the company's sales force compare to competitors' sales forces?

Table 21.9 The marketing excellence review: best practices

Poor	Good	Excellent
Product driven	Market driven	Market driving
Mass-market oriented	Segment oriented	Niche oriented and customer oriented
Product offer	Augmented product offer	Customer solutions offer
Average product quality	Better than average	Legendary
Average service quality	Better than average	Legendary
End-product oriented	Core-product oriented	Core-competency oriented
Function oriented	Process oriented	Outcome oriented
Reacting to competitors	Benchmarking competitors	Leapfrogging competitors
Supplier exploitation	Supplier preference	Supplier partnership
Dealer exploitation	Dealer support	Dealer partnership
Price driven	Quality driven	Value driven
Average speed	Better than average	Legendary
Hierarchy	Network	Teamwork
Vertically integrated	Flattened organisation	Strategic alliances
Stockholder driven	Stakeholder driven	Societally driven

▽ The future of marketing

The marketing manager's key tasks

The first two decades of the twenty-first century pose several exceptional challenges to marketers. Many markets in developed countries are oversupplied with most market offerings, leading to fierce competition that is of global proportions. The rapid rate of technological advance, increasingly sophisticated and demanding customers and new market regulations suggest that their functional activity will become of paramount importance to their companies. There are four key tasks for contemporary marketing managers, as outlined in 'Marketing memo: Key tasks of marketing managers'.

Marketing memo

Key tasks of marketing managers

1 Develop a detailed and deep understanding of current and prospective customers. Much of this should come from regular direct contact with customers and from programmed ad hoc research to reveal new trends in customer preferences. Suitable customer-perceived value offerings should then be developed and introduced into the market as quickly as possible to gain or maintain a sustainable competitive advantage.

2 Develop a detailed and deep understanding of existing and emerging competitors by regarding expenditure on suitable market research as an investment decision rather than a cost sign-off.

3 Develop a detailed and deep understanding of how markets are changing. This needs to be communicated clearly by regular briefing reports to all functional managers to facilitate a holistic approach to marketing in the company. Update topics might include the state of key markets (context); distribution and marketing communications issues.

4 Develop a strategic marketing approach to support corporate strategy. Seek to become a 'market driver' rather than be a company that is 'market-driven'.[79]

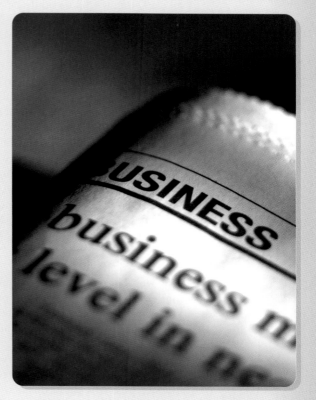

The holistic approach to marketing management.
Source: Serif

A holistic approach to marketing management

In January 2008 Deloitte & Touche LLP published a report on the role of marketing in driving business growth among European countries. The findings revealed the existence of a paradox. While 81 per cent of chief executives interviewed believed that marketing was a key factor for growth and 85 per cent said it was crucial to developing strategy, the report also suggested that not all CEOs felt that the involvement of senior marketers in the overall direction of the business was an assurance of growth for the organisation.[80] These findings reveal a disturbing picture of the current state of marketing management. Marketing thought and practice has evolved over the past 100 years from a philosophy of taking things to market to a philosophy of market(ing) to customers and, increasingly today, to a philosophy of market(ing) in social settings with customers.[81] So why has it lost its way? In view of the generally accepted value of marketing it is alarming that relatively few marketers in the United Kingdom are acting CEOs.

The nature of marketing

To address this question it is useful to consider two important aspects of marketing. It is both a philosophical holistic concept and a functional activity. The Deloitte & Touche LLP report indicates that the connection between these aspects lacked some joined-up thinking. In theory senior marketing executives should greatly assist the overall growth performance of organisations. Marketing is a word that in English ends in 'ing'. This implies that it is a doing word; skill and action within a social context are required to perform it. Another view of the malaise of marketing was dramatically exposed by Egan[82] when his researches found that marketing had, to all intents and purposes, been sidelined in many organisations.

Egan surveyed eight senior relationship-oriented marketing executives who were in top organisations representing business-to-business, conglomerate, energy, non-profit, service and technological companies. Regarding the holistic approach to marketing it was felt that marketers appeared to have a non-structured view of business and so fitted poorly in the corporate world. They did not have a sufficient understanding of financial data and corporate metrics. Marketing tended to be seen as a cost and not as an investment that would generate income. Marketers took too many risks and were not sufficiently accountable for their expenditure. Marketers seemed to have little power to influence senior management. In the light of the fact that 70 per cent of the CEOs in the FTSE 100 listing in May 2007 were accountants it is perhaps not surprising that marketers were considered to be lightweight and misunderstood.

As the slowing buyers' markets became evident many companies started to question the role of marketers. There was a reluctance to sanction large expenditure on marketing with little indication of what and when the return on investment would result. CEOs and finance managers sought to reduce costs. Marketers seemed to have fallen from grace.

Marketing myopia

The world of business had become confused between the holistic and functional understanding of marketing. The shifting paradigm from sellers' to buyers' markets that is evident in developed economies focused interest on customers. They were now the scarce resource. How might they be attracted and retained in the face of mounting competition? Chapter 10 discussed the impact of the paradigm change and stressed the importance of the subtle transformation that occurred in the concept of value. In buyers' markets value was a concept that was determined greatly by buyer perceptions. If the customer-centric philosophy of marketing was accepted how could this new value concept be delivered? Some felt that it was a holistic matter and a concern of all and others that it was a strictly functional issue for the marketers. Some theorists argued that non-customer relationship issues were outside the domain of marketing.

First things first

Many companies accept that in principle marketing makes sense as a philosophy. Many, too, are aware of the traditional functional tasks of marketers. A useful starting point in any attempt to indicate how marketing might be managed in the future is to address the issue of how a company thinks in the boardroom. Current buyers' markets place pressure on firms to promise and deliver the right market offering. This should be seen as a holistic response that will require the input of functional skills within the company and those of external parties such as the supply (or rather value) chain and interested stakeholders. Thus real teamwork is needed. The CEO must ensure that the task is fully understood and all players cooperate to provide the required customer-perceived value (see Chapter 11) offering for a targeted customer. In this sense the role of the CEO is similar to that of the conductor of an orchestra. The players in the respective sections such as brass, percussion, strings and woodwind are to apply their individual and group skills, in tune. This implies that they must have an appreciation of the nature of each other's functional skills.

Remember TEAM? Together everyone achieves more. This is the prime responsibility of the CEO. Next the CEO must answer the question: Who owns the customer? Is it the marketing department? The sales department? Or is it the accounts department? Worse still is the confusion evident here. The paradigm change from sellers' to buyers' markets has led loyal customers to become highly prized. Repeat business for the company's offerings signifies success is the essence of a good BRAND. The next section explores customer relationship activity.

Relationship activity

Relationship marketing

(See also Chapter 1.)

Relationship marketing was seen by many as the new way forward and has been very much 'in vogue' recently among both academics and practitioners. It became the 'hot topic' of marketing in the 1990s and was heralded as a breakthrough that would replace the traditional marketing mix model. In a world where premium paying customers were highly valued all marketed offers should seek to build lasting relationships with customers and a good way to do this was to promise and deliver desirable CPV offerings.

Despite the general adherence to the philosophy embedded in RM there is little evidence to reflect its success for companies that expressed interest in its execution in the opening decade of the twenty-first century. Few marketers rose to the CEO's chair. Mounting frustration of the perceived inability of functional marketers to deliver the RM promise resulted in mounting pressures to classify non-customer relationships as residing outside the marketing domain. The myopia here was the failure to appreciate that RM must translate into the promise and delivery of the right CPV packages. This requires coordinating company inputs rather than just independent functional contributions that are bundled together at the market gate.

Customer relationship marketing

The result was the birth of a new way forward that was termed customer relationship marketing (CRMk). A new resolve was born as many companies sought to talk to their suppliers and customers to create CPV packages. CRMk it was claimed was a distinct concept that was well suited to managing customer relationships in mass markets. It was under the control of general management and the marketing input was viewed as functional. With little real adoption of the TEAM requirement for holistic marketing CRMk soon became dominated by general management's push for the most profit at the least cost with the least risk in the shortest period of time. Relationship building soon largely became confined to mechanised offers and sales promotions. Customer focus became subservient to the supplier or transactional marketing dyad. In many cases customers became digits and were classified according to their present worth to the company. Furthermore many firms were tempted to overuse technology and adopt too great a reliance on managing customer relations with digital methods such as CRMk software and Internet programming. Cynics termed CRMk 'technology-enabled RM'. It was oversold and it seems to have failed to live up to expectations – a philosophic manifesto but without a suitable accompanying organisational toolkit. Overdigitisation, that is, the progressive loss of the human interface, flies in the face of the holistic approach to marketing. While programmed phones and the Internet 'help' pages have their place they need to be carefully integrated into a people-friendly interface. Too much digital technology and consumers start to feel like numbers and robots. Successful relationships often seem to occur when companies carefully research what customers want, promise it and then successfully deliver it.

Customer-perceived value marketing

As more and more academics and practitioners have begun to realise the importance of customer-perceived value, of promising and delivering what customers want, so another concept – that of customer – perceived value *marketing* (CPVM) has appeared. This requires firms to develop an organisational structure that is top down, bottom up and side to side. The top management empowers TEAM players. Players at the customer interface are supported by top management. Marketers (or designated functional players) seek to co-create value with customers, the value chain and stakeholder interests. Figure 21.8 presents a matrix that charts the routes that companies are following and exploring to build a sustainable corporate advantage in the surplus microeconomic conditions of buyer's markets.

Figure 21.8 Key
company market
cultures
Source: M.R.V. Goodman,
Durham University, UK.

For many the journey began with transactional marketing (TM), which was very much in evidence during the post-Second World War sellers' markets. The functional activity was focused around the traditional 4P (product, price, place and promotion) marketing mix. As the service industries assumed an ever-greater importance so an additional 3Ps were added (*people, process and physical evidence*), as the original mix was felt by academics to be wanting. However, did these additional Ps really help?

Henry Ford of automotive fame was a major pioneer of mass production and once quipped that customers could 'have any colour they liked as long as it was black'. Clearly he had a *product* (the car); a *price* (the purchase cost); made his cars available (*place*) and communicated to interested parties (*promotion*).

Service marketers, on the other hand, were seen as being differentiated as their offerings were for *people*, involved *processes* and resulted in *physical evidence* that the service had been rendered. The ordinary man in the street might quip that Ford intended its cars for *people*, rolled out real cars from the end of the production line (*physical evidence*) and used a production *process* to build the cars.

The halcyon days of **TM** placed an emphasis on the supplier–customer dyad and in many cases relied heavily on the price and promotion tools of the marketing mix. When the roaring sellers' markets started to turn inexorably into today's buyers' markets from the late 1980s onwards so companies began to focus on customer satisfaction and loyalty.

Enter, stage left, the new concept of relationship marketing (RM). This was greatly in fashion during the 1990s but failed to perform satisfactorily for several reasons, mainly from abundant confusions concerning the interaction between functional and holistic marketing. Also there was a tendency for academics to concentrate too much on the positive aspects of **RM** and to under-research customer dissatisfaction.[83] At the turn of the millennium RM went through a process of metamorphism and customer relationship marketing emerged. For similar reasons as RM, CRMk has so far failed to live up to expectations.

The 1990s saw an awakening of interest in the concept of market-perceived value. Or as Kotler terms it customer-perceived value (see Chapter 11). This approach demands that to be effective in markets where customer choice is very much in evidence, companies should provide customers with what they want, not necessarily what companies would rather place on the market. It is a suitable philosophy on which to build an organisation that is well fitted to respond to the needs of the experience economy. However, it requires a deep and lasting commitment to managing organisational change.

As buyers' markets in the developed world start to lose their impetus, due to a complex factor set, including climate warming, increasing inflation in the leading nations of the underdeveloped world (primarily China and India), 'the credit crunch' and increased pressure on the world's material and energy resources many markets will become very price sensitive. Add to this social problems caused by the failure of many poor economies to feed their people and the effects of the declining developed economies and the world is in turmoil. The effect of this could be to increasingly energise a new paradigm change away from CRM and CPV.

Many observers of the marketing scene are sensing that companies are consciously or unconsciously beginning to move away from the theories and concepts that have been formulated to assist in the management of customer relationships. The pressing requirement of many companies to return short-term profits places strong pressure on CEOs to favour the customer–supplier dyad, that is return to TM at the expense of customer relationship concerns. This will make building a market-oriented value culture more difficult for all key players and greatly reduce the chances of the theory behind internal marketing being evident in practice. For marketers to achieve and hold down CEO status they will need to challenge the underlying general management traditions and win the case for discovering, promising and delivering CPV offerings. The task in the twenty-first century is not easy for marketers and the challenge is real. The marketing profession has much to offer companies but it needs to become less intuitive and adopt a more scientific approach and adopt metrics that are a crucial part of the language of business.

Market research

Change is in the air and will remain so for the foreseeable future. Companies need to be sure that they are reading their operating environment effectively. This requires them to keep up to date with the latest developments and trends affecting their markets, customers, competitors, costs, channels and company response options. So expenditure on market research must be seen as an investment rather than an expenditure. As the developed economies seem to be lurching towards less affluent times marketers need to be on their guard to detect a possible major paradigm shift back to sellers' market conditions. However, such a paradigm change is unlikely to happen overnight and will also occur at different rates in different markets.

New product development

Current buyers' market conditions encourage investment and rapid development of new products (meaning market offerings) as long as they mainly cater for previously researched customer needs (see Chapter 15). Jam today – and more, and juicier, jam tomorrow. Innovation promises sweet rewards but there is no easy-to-follow recipe for developing market-leading products and services (offerings) that guarantee attractive profits. New product development is costly to sustain and often flies in the face of conventional general management thinking. It is by nature highly creative, qualitative and to many appears to rely on chance and serendipity. This is partially true, but companies that have achieved recognised success as innovators subscribe to Edison's dictum that 'genius is 1 per cent inspiration, 99 per cent perspiration'.

Marketing communications activity

Modern technological advances have already changed and will further change the traditional approach to marketing communications. TV advertising is likely to become highly interactive. More effort will be put into integrated marketing communications (IMC) to maximise customer reach, recall and capture. However, IMC should not be used to advance false messages and promises. Rather confusingly referred to as promotion in the traditional 4P marketing mix, marketing communications should not by default become the only live instrument of the 4P toolbox.

▽ Getting started

The mission of this text is to provide readers with the following:
1   an understanding of marketing management;
2   an appreciation of the main methods used by marketers to capture marketing insights;
3   an overview of the ways in which marketers connect with customers;
4   an insight into how marketing practitioners shape the market offering;
5   an understanding of how marketers deliver value in global and local supply networks;
6   an appreciation of the methods by which marketers communicate value;

Marketing memo

Getting to grips with the practice of marketing

1 Study the **contextual factors** that impact on the marketplace:

- Is the market domestic or international? (Each national market will need a separate application of this toolbox.)
- Political, economic, socio-cultural and technological factors.
- Is the market a sellers' or a buyers' market?
- If a buyers' market, then the concept of CPV will be relevant.

2 Study the **customer factors**, such as:

- Segmentation, targeting and positioning.
- Product/market offering value circles (quality and price attributes).
- Branding activity.
- New product development.
- Branding.

3 Study the **competition**:

- Perceived product/market offering expertise.
- Breadth and width of product/market offering portfolio.

- NPD skills.
- Market share.
- Profitability.

4 Study the **cash/cost matters**:

- Invest in market research to make informed decisions on key market characteristics (context, customers, competition, channels).
- Pay careful attention to the development of revenue forecasts.

5 Study **channel factors** to achieve effective and efficient use of funds.

6 Examine the **underlying company philosophy and practice**:

- Is it mainly TM, RM, CRM or CVP?

Source: Adapted from K. Kashani and D. Turpin (1999) *Marketing Management: An International Perspective,* International Institute for Management Development (IMD), Lausanne, London: Macmillan Business, 3–15.

---

7 an overview of how marketers manage brands;

8 an insight into how marketing management approaches issues of implementation and control.

Additionally readers are encouraged to try their hand at some 'hands-on' experience. Marketing is a discipline that requires know-what (knowledge) and is developed and fine tuned by practice (know-how). The 'Marketing memo: Getting to grips with the practice of marketing' is offered as a guide to getting under way. For further guidance on developing a marketing plan see Chapter 3, the Euromart sample marketing plan.

▽ SUMMARY

1 The modern marketing department has evolved through the years from a simple sales department into an organisational structure where marketing personnel work mainly on cross-disciplinary teams.

2 Modern marketing departments can be organised in a number of ways. Some companies are organised by functional specialisation, whereas others focus on geography and regionalisation. Still others emphasise product and brand management or market-segment management. Some companies establish a matrix organisation consisting of both product and market managers. Finally, some companies have strong corporate marketing, others have limited corporate marketing, and still others place marketing only in the divisions.

3 Effective modern marketing organisations are marked by a strong cooperation and customer focus among the company's departments: marketing, R&D, engineering, purchasing, manufacturing, operations, finance, accounting and credit.

4 A brilliant strategic marketing plan counts for little if it is not implemented properly. Implementing marketing plans calls for skills in recognising and diagnosing a problem, assessing the company level where the problem exists and evaluating results.

5 The marketing department must monitor and control marketing activities continuously. Marketing plan control involves analysis to ensure that the company achieves the sales, profits and other goals established in its annual plan. The main tools are sales analysis, market share analysis, marketing expense-to-sales analysis, and financial analysis of the marketing plan. Profitability control seeks to measure and control the profitability of various products, territories, customer groups, trade channels and order sizes. An important part of controlling for profitability is assigning costs and generating profit-and-loss statements. Efficiency control focuses on finding ways to increase the efficiency of the sales force, advertising, sales promotion and distribution. Strategic control entails a periodic reassessment of the company and its strategic approach to the marketplace using the tools of the marketing effectiveness and marketing excellence reviews, as well as the marketing audit.

6 Companies must practise social responsibility through their legal, ethical and social words and actions. Cause marketing can be a means for companies to productively link social responsibility to consumer marketing programmes. Social marketing is done by a non-profit or government organisation to directly address a social problem or cause.

7 Achieving marketing excellence in the future will require new challenges and oppportunities. The resulting marketing imperatives will require a new set of skills and competencies.

▽ APPLICATIONS

Marketing debate

Is marketing management an art or a science? Some marketing observers maintain that good marketing is more of an art and does not lend itself to rigorous analysis and deliberation. Others strongly disagree and contend that marketing management is a highly disciplined enterprise that has much in common with other business disciplines.

Take a position: Marketing management is largely an artistic exercise and therefore highly subjective *versus* Marketing management is largely a scientific exercise with well-established guidelines and criteria.

Marketing discussion

How does cause or corporate societal marketing affect your personal consumer behaviour? Do you ever buy or not buy products or services from a company because of its environmental policies or programmes? Why or why not?

▽ REFERENCES

[1] Unilever and Reckett, *Financial Times*, 15 March 2008.

[2] For additional updates on the latest academic thinking on marketing strategy and tactics, see D. Iacobucci and B. Calder (eds.) (2003) *Kellogg on Integrated Marketing*, New York: John Wiley & Sons; and D. Iacobucci (ed.) (2001) *Kellogg on Marketing*, New York: John Wiley & Sons.

[3] F. E. Webster Jr, A. J. Miller and S. Ganescan (2003) Can marketing regain its seat at the table?, Marketing Science Institute Report No. 03–113, Cambridge, MA: Marketing Science Institute.

[4] For a broad historical treatment of marketing thought see D. G. B. Jones and E. H. Shaw, (2002) A history of marketing thought, in B. A. Weitz and R. Wensley (eds.) *Handbook of Marketing*, London: Sage, pp. 39–65; J. Pervaiz (2005) *Internal Marketing*, Butterworth-Heinemann; for public sector setting see also M. T. Ewing, A. Carvana (1999) An internal marketing approach to public sector management: the marketing and human resources interface, *Journal of Public Sector Management*, 12(1), 17–19.

[5] K. Hille (2005) BenQ ready to signal its Siemens solution, *Financial Times*, 19 September.

[6] S. Laitner and P. Thai Larsen (2006) Bid to rouse Belgium's sleeping beauty, *Financial Times*, 31 January; J. Chimhanzi (2002) The impact of marketing/HR interactions on marketing strategy implementation, *European Journal of Marketing*, 38(1/2), 73–98; S. N. Sheth and R. S. Sisodia (2006) *Does Marketing Need Reform? Fresh Perspectives on the Future*, New York: M. E. Sharp.

[7] H. Pringle and W. Gordon (2001) *Beyond Manners: How to Create the Self-Confident Organisation to Live the Brand*, Chichester, England: John Wiley & Sons; F. E Webster Jr (1992) The changing role of marketing in the corporation, *Journal of Marketing*,

October, 1–10; see also J. P. Workman Jr, C. Homburg and K. Gruner (1998) Marketing organization: an integrative framework of dimensions and determinants, *Journal of Marketing*, July, 21–41; R. S. Achrol (1991) Evolution of the marketing organization: new forms for turbulent environment, *Journal of Marketing*, October, 77–93; for some contemporary perspectives see Special Issue 1999 of *Journal of Marketing Fundamental Issues and Directions for Marketing*; D. Ballantyne (2003) A relationship-mediated theory of internal marketing, *European Journal of Marketing*, 37(9), 1242–60; P. K Ahmed, M. Rafiq (2003) Internal marketing issues and challenges, *European Journal of Marketing*, 37(9), 1177–86; M. Kelemen and I. Papasoloou (2007) Internal marketing: a qualitative study of culture change in the UK banking sector, *Journal of Marketing Management*, 23(7/8), 745–67.

[8]For an excellent account of how to convert a company into a market-driven organization, see G. Day (1989) *The Market-Driven Organization: Aligning Culture, Capabilities, and Configuration to the Market*, New York: Free Press.

[9]F. E. Webster Jr (2002) The role of marketing and the firm, in B. A. Weitz and R. Wensley (eds.) *Handbook of Marketing*, London: Sage, pp. 39–65.

[10]F. V. Cespedes (1996) *Managing Marketing Linkages: Text, Cases, and Readings*, Upper Saddle River, NJ: Prentice Hall; F. V. Cespedes (1995) *Concurrent Marketing: Products, Sales, and Service*, Boston, MA: Harvard Business School Press.

[11]M. J. Zenor (1994) The profit benefits of category management, *Journal of Marketing Research*, May, 202–13; G. Khermouch (1994) Brands overboard, *Brandweek*, 22 August, 25–39; Z. Schiller (1988) The marketing revolution at Procter & Gamble, *BusinessWeek*, 25 July, 72–6.

[12]For further reading see R. Dewar and D. Shultz (1998) The product manager, and idea whose time has gone, *Marketing Communications*, May, 28–35; G. S. Low and R. A Fullerton (1994) Brands, brand management, and the brand manager system: a critical historical evaluation, *Journal of Marketing Research*, May, 173–90; M. J. Zanor (1994) The profit benefits of category management, *Journal of Marketing Research*, May, 202–13.

[13]L. Selden and G. Colvin (2003) *Angel Customers & Demon Customers*, New York: Portfolio.

[14]For an in-depth discussion of issues around implementing a customer-based organization on which much of this paragraph is based see G. S. Day (2006) Aligning the organization with the market, *MIT Sloan Management Review*, Fall, 41–9.

[15]R. E Anderson (1994) Matrix Redux, *Business Horizons*, November–December, 6–10.

[16]B. P. Shapiro (1977) Can marketing and manufacturing coexist?, *Harvard Business Review*, September–October, 104–14; see also R. W. Ruekert and O. C. Walker Jr (1987) Marketing's interaction with other functional units: a conceptual framework with other empirical evidence, *Journal of Marketing*, January, 1–19.

[17]E. Brynjolfsson and L. Hitt (1996) The customer counts, *InformationWeek*, 9 September.

[18]G. Hamel (2000) *Leading the Revolution*, Boston, MA: Harvard Business School Press; S. Brown (2002) Vote, vote, vote for Philip Kotler, *European Journal of Marketing*, 36(2), 313–24; M. Goodman (2004) Managing in times of change: avoiding management myopia in A. Ghobadian, N. O'Regan, D. Gallear

and H. Viney (eds.) *Strategy and Performance*, Basingstoke, England: Palgrave Macmillan, Chapter 9, pp. 185–210; P. A. Titus (2007) Applied creativity: the creative marketing breakthrough model, *Journal of Marketing Education*, 29(3), 262–72.

[19]E. De Bono (2004) Creativity is an option for business, *Financial Times*, 6 July.

[20]J. N. Sheth (2007) *The Self-Destructive Habits of Good Companies . . . And How to Break Them*, Upper Saddle River, NJ: Wharton School Publishing.

[21]M. Witzel, Managers who use a little imagination for big rewards, *Financial Times*, 6 May 2008.

[22]G. Hamel, *Leading the Revolution* (Boston: Harvard Business School Press, August 2000).

[23]C. Marcus, Marketing Resource Management; Key Components, *Gartner Research Note*, 22 August 2001.

[24]W. M. Cohen and D. A. Levinthal (1990) Absorptive capacity: a new perspective on learning and innovation, *Administrative Science Quarterly*, 35, 28–52; D. K. Banner (1993) Self-managed work teams: an idea whose time has come?, *Creativity and Innovation Management*, 2(1), 27–36; C. C. Manz and H. P. Sims Jr (1987) Leading workers to lead themselves: the external leadership of self-managing work teams, *Administrative Science Quarterly*, 32, 106–28; C. C. Manz and H. P. Sims Jr (2001) *Superleadership: Leading others to lead themselves*, Englewood Cliffs, NJ: Prentice Hall; M. B. Pinto, J. K. Pinto and J. E. Prescott (1993). Antecedents and consequences of project team cross-functional cooperation, *Management Science*, 39(10), 1281–97; S. J. Parnes (1997) *Sourcebook for Creative Problem-solving*, Buffalo, NY: Creative Education Foundation Press; M. R. V. Goodman (1995) *Creative Management*, Harlow, England; J. Tidd, J. Bessant and K. Pavitt (2001) *Managing Innovation: Integrating Technological, Market, and Organizational Change*, 2nd edn, Chichester, England: John Wiley & Sons; S. Bharadwaj and A. Menon (2000) Making innovation happen in organizations: individual creativity mechanisms, organizational creativity mechanisms or both?, *Journal of Product Innovation Management*, 17(6), 424–34; E. C. Martins and F. Trerblanche (2003) Building organizational culture that stimulates creativity and innovation, *European Journal of Innovation Management*, 6(1), 64–74; K. M. Eisenhart (1989) Making fat strategic decisions, *Academy of Management Journal*, 32, 543–76; M. R. V. Goodman (2000) The frustration of talent: a study in scarlet, *Creativity and Innovation Management*, 9(1), 46–53; A. Bryman (1997) Leadership in organizations, in S.R Clegg, C. Hardy and W. A. Nord (eds.) *Handbook of organization studies*, London: Sage, 276–92; G. Ekvall (1993) Creativity in project work: a longitudinal study of a product development project, *Creativity and Innovation Management*, 2(1), 17–26; G. Ekvall (2000) Management and organizational philosophies and practices as stimulants or blocks to creative behaviour: a study of engineering, *Creativity and Innovation Management*, 9(2), 94–9; T. M. Amabile and R. Conti (1999) Changes in the work environment for creativity during downsizing, *Academy of Management Journal*, 42, 630–40; D. J. Teece, G. Pisano and A. Shuen (1997) Dynamic capabilities and strategic management, *Strategic Management Journal*, 18, 509–34; K. D. Elsbach and R. M. Kramer (2003) Assessing creativity in Hollywood pitch meetings: evidence for a dual-process model of creativity judgments, *Academy of Management Journal*, 46(3), 283–302.

[25]D. A. Pitta, V. R. Wood and F. J. Franzak (2008) Nurturing an effective creative culture within a marketing organization,

Journal of Consumer Marketing, 25(3), 137–48; I. F. Fillis and R. Rentschler (2006) *Creative Marketing: An Extended Metaphor in a New Age,* Basingstoke, UK: Palgrave Macmillan.

[26]A. O'Driscoll (2008) Exploring paradox in marketing: managing ambiguity towards synthesis, *Journal of Business and Industrial Marketing*, 23(2), 95–104.

[27]C. Grande (2007) Bearing rivals when it comes to risk-taking, *Financial Times*, 16 May.

[28]Special Report: Corporate Social Responsibility *Economist* (14 December 2002); 62–63; W. L. Wilkie and E. S. Moore (2002) Marketing's relationship to society, in B. A. Weitz and R. Wensley (eds.) *Handbook of Marketing*, London: Sage, pp. 1–38.

[29]J. Alsever (2006) Chiquita cleans up its act, *Business 2.0*, August, 56–8.

[30]P. S. Bronn (2006) Building corporate brands through community involvement: is it exportable? The case of the Ronald McDonald House in Norway, *Journal of Marketing Communications*, 2(4), 309–20.

[31]I. Carrasco (2007) Corporate social responsibility, values and cooperation, advances in economic research, 12(4), 454–60; B. Grow, S. Hamin and L. Lee (2005) The debate over doing good, *Business Week*, 5 August; C. Kamp (2008) Be seen to talk the talk: how national perception can influence a company's CSR strategy, *Strategic Direction*, 24(1), 25–27.

[32]M. Skapinker (2008) Corporate responsibility is not quite dead, *Financial Times,* 12 February.

[33]S. D. Hunt and S. Vitell (1992) The general theory of marketing ethics: a retrospective and revision, in J. Quelch and C. Smith (eds.) *Ethics in Marketing*, Chicago: Irwin.

[34]M. Schultz, Y. M. Antorini and F. F. Csaba (2005) *Corporate Branding: Purpose, People and Process*, Koge, Denmark: Copenhagen Business School Press; R. J. Alsop (2004) *The 18 Immutable laws of Corporate Reputation: Creating, Protecting, and Repairing Your Most Valuable Asset*, New York: Free Press; M. Gunther (2003) Tree huggers, soy lovers, and profits, *Fortune*, 23 June, 98–104; R. J. Alsop (2002) Perils of corporate philanthropy, *Wall Street Journal*, 16 January.

[35]I. Szmigin, M. Carrigan and D. O'Loughlin (2007) Integrating ethical brands into your consumption lives, *Journal of Brand Management*, 14(5), 396–409.

[36]E. Baccarini (2008) What does ethical behaviour mean in management activities?, *The TQM Journal*, 20(2), 154–65.

[37]J. Hall (2007) The ethical opportunity, *Journal of Brand Management*, 4(5), 365–7.

[38]M. Frazier (2007) Going green? plant deep roots, *Advertising Age*, 30 April, 1, 54–5.

[39]D. H. Deane (2002) Associating the corporation with a charitable event through sponsorship: measuring the effects on corporate community relations, *Journal of Advertising*, Winter, 77–87.

[40]S. O'Loughlin (2007) The wearin'o'the green, *Brandweek*, 23 April, 26–7. For a critical response see also J. R. Ehrenfield (2006) Feeding the beast, *Fast Company*, December–January, 42–3.

[41]N. Varchaver (2007) Chemical reaction, *Fortune*, 2 April, 53–8.

[42]P. Engardio (2007) Beyond the green corporation, *BusinessWeek*, 29 January, 50–64.

[43]Ibid.

[44]K. Hein (2006) The world on a platter, *Brandweek*, 23 April, 27–8; M. Johnson (2006) Hard sell for a soft fabric, *Forbes*, 30 October, 73–80.

[45]B. Grow, S. Hamin and L. Lee (2005) The debate over doing good, *Business Week*, 15 August.

[46]R. Sisodia, D. B. Wolfe and J. Sheth (2007) *Firms of Endearment: How World-Class Companies Profit from Passion and Purpose*, Upper Saddle River, NJ: Wharton School Publishing.

[47]See P. Kotler and N. Lee (2005) *Corporate Social Responsibility: Doing the Most Good for Your Company and Your Cause*, New York: John Wiley & Sons.

[48]L. Upshaw (2007) *Truth: The New Rules for Marketing in a Skeptical World*, New York: Amacon; C. Dahle (2007) A more powerful path, *Fast Company*, December–January, 68–81.

[49]R. Berner (2005) Smarter corporate giving, *BusinessWeek*, 28 November, 68–76; C. N. Smith (2003) Corporate social responsibility: whether or how?, *California Management Review*, 45(4), 52–76.

[50]L. Chiagouris and I. Ray (2007) Saving the world with cause-related marketing, *Marketing Management*, July-August, 48–51; H. Pringle and M. Thompson (1999) *Brand Spirit: How Cause-Related Marketing Builds Brands*, New York: John Wiley & Sons; S. Adkins (1999) *Cause-Related marketing: Who Cares Wins*, Oxford, England: Butterworth-Heinemann; Marketing corporate social initiatives, and the bottom line, Marketing Science Institute Conference Summary, MSI Report No. 01-106, 2001; M. K. File and A. R. Price (2006) Cause related marketing and corporate philanthropy in the privately held enterprise, *Journal of Business Ethics*, 63(2), 1529–39; S. L. Grau and J. A. Garretson (2007) Cause related marketing (CRM), *Journal of Advertising*, 36(4), 19–33; C. Peters, J. Thomas and H. Tolson (2007) An exploratory study of cause-related retailing, *International Journal of Retail and Distribution Management*, 35(11), 895–911.

[51]R. Varadarajan and A. Menon (1988) Cause-related marketing: a co-alignment of marketing strategy and corporate philanthropy, *Journal of Marketing*, 52 (July), 58–74.

[52]M. Drumwright and P. E. Murphy (2001) Corporate societal marketing in P. N. Bloom and G. T. Gundlach (eds.) *Handbook of Marketing and Society*, Thousand Oaks, CA: Sage, 162–83; see also M. Drumwright (1996) Company advertising with a social dimension: the role of noneconomic criteria, *Journal of Marketing*, 60 (October), 71–87.

[53]See www.britishairways.com.

[54]X. Luo and C. B. Bhattacharya (2006) Corporate social responsibility, customer satisfaction and market value, *Journal of Marketing*, 70 (October), 1–18; P. Auger, T. Devinney and J. J. Louviere (2003) What will consumers pay for social product features?, *Journal of Business Ethics*, 42 (February), 281–304.

[55]D. B. Arnett, S. D. German and S. D. Hunt (2003) The identity salience model of relationship marketing success: the case of nonprofit marketing, *Journal of Marketing*, 67 (April), 89–105; C. B. Bhattacharya and S. Sen (2003) Consume-company identification: a framework for understanding consumers; relationships with companies, *Journal of Marketing*, 67 (April), 76–88; S. Sen and C. B. Bhattacharya (2001) Does doing good always lead to doing better? Consumer reactions to corporate social responsibility, *Journal of Marketing*, 38(2), (May), 225–44.

[56]P. N. Bloom, S. Hoeffler, K. L. Keller and C. E. Basurto (2006) How social-cause marketing affects consumer perceptions, *MIT Sloan Management Review*, Winter, 49–55; C. J. Simmons and K. L. Becker-Olsen (2006) Achieving marketing objectives through social sponsorships, *Journal of Marketing*, 70 (October), 154–69; G. Berens, C. B. M. van Riel and G. H. van Bruggen (2005) Corporate associations and consumer product responses: the moderating role of corporate brand dominance, *Journal of Marketing*, 69 (July), 35–48; D. R. Lichtenstein, M. E. Drumwright and B. M. Braig (2004) The effect of social responsibility on customer donations to corporate-supported nonprofits, *Journal of Marketing*, 68 (October), 16–32; S. Hoeffler and K. L. Keller (2002) Building brand equity through corporate societal market-ing, *Journal of Public Policy and Marketing*, 21(1), 78–89. See also: 2003 Special issue: corporate responsibility, *Journal of Brand Management*, 10(2), 4–5.

[57]M. R. Forehand and S. Grier (2003) When is honesty the best policy? The effect of stated company intent on consumer skepticism, *Journal of Consumer Psychology*, 12(3), 349–56; D. H. Dean (2002) Associating the corporation with a charita-ble even through sponsorship: measuring the effects on corporate community relations, *Journal of Advertising*, 31(4), 77–87.

[58]R. J. Alsop (2006) *The Immutable Laws of Corporate Reputation: Creating, Protecting, and Repairing Your Most Valuable Asset*, London: Kogan Page, 125.

[59]S. Orestein (2003) The selling of breast cancer, *Business 2.0*, February, 88–94; H. Meyer, (1999) When the cause is just, *Journal of Business Strategy*, November-December, 27–31.

[60]C. Bittar (2002) Seeking cause and effect, *Brandweek*, 11 November, 18–24.

[61]J. French and C. Blair-Stevens (2005) *Social Marketing Pocket Guide*, 2 edn, National Society Marketing Centre for Excellence (www.nsms.org.uk); P. Kotler, N. Roberto and N. Lee, (2002) *Social Marketing; Improving the Quality of Life*, Thousand Oaks, CA: Sage; M. L. Rothschild (1999) Carrots, sticks, and promises: a conceptual framework for the man-agement of public health and social issue behaviors, *Journal of Marketing*, 63 (October), 24–37; D. Luck (2006) Customer relationship marketing and corporate social responsibility: not just ethical standpoints or business strategies, *Social Responsibility Journal*, 21(1), 83–7.

[62]A fuller explanation of the key features and concepts is available from the National Social Marketing Centre in the UK (www.nsms.org.uk).

[63]M. Katsiolondes, J. Grant and D. S. Mckechnie (2007) Social marketing: strengthening company-customer bonds, *Journal of Business Strategy*, 28(3), 55–64; J. DeGruchy and D. Coppel (2008) Listening to reason: a social marketing stop-smoking campaign in Nottingham, *Social Marketing Quarterly*, 14(1), 5–17; S. Bird and A. Tapp (2008) Social marketing and the meaning of cool, *Social Marketing Quarterly*, 14(1), 18–29; M. Stead, R. Gordon, K. Angus and L. McDermott (2007) A systematic review of social marketing effectiveness, *Health Education*, 107(2), 126–91.

[64]G. Arulmari and A. Abdulla (2007) Capturing the ripples: addressing the sustainability of the impact of social marketing, *Social Marketing Quarterly*, 13(4), 84–107; C. T. Donegan, (2008) Social marketing: implications for contemporary practices classification scheme, *Journal of Business and Industrial*

Marketing, 2(2), 135–41; A. Thorpe, R. Merritt, D. McVey and A. Truss (2008) What next for social marketing: developing 'superman' or a sustainable system?, *Social Marketing Quarterly*, 14(1), 63–71.

[65]D. Burton (2002) Incorporating ethnicity into marketing intelli-gence and planning, *Marketing Intelligence and Planning*, 20(7), 442–57.

[66]A. Jamal (2003) Marketing in multicultural world: the interplay of marketing, ethnicity and consumption, *European Journal of Marketing*, 37(1/2), 1599–1620.

[67]K. Peattie and A. Crane (2005) Green marketing: legend, myth or prophesy? *Qualitative Market Research: An International Journal*, 8(4), 357–70; J. Rivera-Comino (2007) Re-evaluating green marketing strategy: a stakeholder perspective, *European Journal of Marketing*, 41(11/12), 1328–58.

[68]C. D'Souza, M. Taghian and R. Khosla (2007) Examination of environmental beliefs and its impact on the influence of price, quality and demographics with respect to green pur-chases, *Journal of Targeting Measurement and Analysis*, 15(2), 69–78.

[69]J. Grant (2007) *The Green Manifesto*, Chichester: John Wiley & Sons.

[70]P. Hartmann and V. A. Ibanez (2006) Green value added, *Marketing Intelligence and Planning*, 24(7), 673–80.

[71]J. Pickard (2007) National news: property company 'green' group to be set up, *Financial Times*, 27 February.

[72]For other examples, see P. W. Ferris, N. T. Bendle, P. E. Pfeifer and D. J. Reibstein (2006) *Marketing Metrics 50+ Metrics Every Executive Should Master*, Upper Saddle River, NJ: Wharton School Publishing; M. Debruyne and K. Hubbard (2000) Marketing metrics, working paper series, Conference Summary, Marketing Science Institute Report No. 00-119.

[73]A. R. Oxenfeldt (1969) How to use market-share measurement, *Harvard Business Review*, January-February, 59–68.

[74]There is a one-half chance that successive observation will be higher or lower. Therefore, the probability of finding six successively higher value is given by (1/2) to the sixth, or 1/64.

[75]Alternatively companies need to focus on factors affecting shareholder value. The goal of marketing planning is to increase shareholder value, which is the present value of the future income stream created by the company's present actions. Rate-of-return usually focuses on one year's results only. See A. Rapport (1997) *Creating Shareholder Value*, Revised Edition, New York: Free Press.

[76]For additional reading on financial analysis see Chapter 22 of this text.

[77]R. C. Cooper and R. S. Kaplan (1991) Profit priorities from activity-based costing, *Harvard Business Review*, May-June, 130–5.

[78]S. R. Goodman (1982) *Increasing Corporate Profitability*, New York: Ronald Press, Chapter 1. See also: B. J. Jaworski, V. Stathakopoulos and S. Krishman (1993) Control combinations in marketing: conceptual framework and empirical evidence, *Journal of Marketing*, January, 57–69.

[79]M. R. V. Goodman (2001) Marketing quo vadis? *Eclectic: The Banking and Finance Faculty Magazine*, 5 (summer), 21–6.

[80]T. Ambler (2008) Marketing 2008: discipline in crisis, *Marketing*, 16 January, 26–8.

[81]R. Lusch (2007) Marketing's evolving identity: defining our future, *Journal of Public Policy & Marketing*, 2, 261–8.

[82]E. Gummesson (1987) The new marketing: developing long term interactive relationships, *Long Range Planning*, 20(4), 10–20; C. Gronroos (1994) From marketing mix to relationship marketing: towards a paradigm shift in marketing, *Management Decision*, 32(2), 4–20; J. Egan (2006) Sidelined? The future of marketing in the contemporary organisation, *The Irish Journal of Management*, 27(2), 99–118.

[83]E. Kasabov (2007) Towards a contingent, empirically validated and power cognisant relationship marketing, *European Journal of Marketing*, 14(1/2), 94–120.

Chapter 22

Managing marketing metrics

IN THIS CHAPTER, WE WILL ADDRESS THE FOLLOWING QUESTIONS:

1 What are marketing metrics?
2 What is the need for marketing metrics?
3 What are useful marketing metrics?
4 What are the key marketing metrics?
5 What metrics do companies use?
6 What is a marketing dashboard?

To stay in business a company needs positive cash flows, which in turn are generated from the company's ability to create value. Since value is defined by customers, marketing makes a fundamental contribution to long-term business success. Recognising that evaluating marketing performance is a key task for management, marketing metrics are concerned with calculating the value of marketing activity in a company.

What you can't measure, you can't manage – this is the true marketing metrics philosophy.
Source: Curt Pickens/iStockphoto

The need
for marketing
metrics

Measuring
marketing
performance
and productivity

The
balanced
scorecard
approach

Marketing
dashboards

Brands spend large amounts of marketing money and the brand owners and their agencies need to be accountable for this money, and how it is spent. There is a constant need to create growth and thus prioritise spend behind campaigns, and media that are more effective, to get a 'bigger bang for our buck'. But you only know what is more effective if you measure and monitor the effect properly. BrandScience – a specialist unit within OmnicomMediaGroup – is a global network of econometric and marketing analysis experts specialising in delivering state-of-the-art, 100 per cent tailor-made brand, business and communication evaluation by quantifying and measuring properly what matters to businesses. Advanced statistical modelling methods are employed on hard data on the brand's sales, marketing and communications history, competitors and economic context in order to identify significant drivers of the businesses, separate the effects of different drivers and isolate and quantify the contribution from marketing both on a short-, medium- and long-term basis.[1]

Marketing managers are increasingly being held accountable for their investments and must be able to justify marketing expenditures to senior management.[2] Marketing metrics provide valuable data points against which the marketing organisation can track its progress, demonstrate accountability and allow marketers to better know, act upon and align efforts.[3] This chapter explores how companies can measure and improve their marketing performance by applying marketing metrics.

▽ The need for marketing metrics

In the modern business environment, companies to an increasing degree derive substantial and sustained competitive advantage from intangible assets such as brand equity, knowledge, networks and innovative capability. Measuring the return on both tangible (fixed assets, e.g., land, buildings and machinery) and intangible (assets that have no physical substance, e.g., brand names, copyrights and patents, strong channel relationships, etc.) assets has therefore now become imperative for managers.[4] Without metrics to track performance, marketing and business plans are ineffective.

Marketing metrics are the set of measures that help firms to quantify, compare and interpret their marketing performance. In 2005 the American Marketing Association (AMA) established the following definition of marketing accountability: 'The responsibility for the systematic management of marketing resources and processes to achieve measurable gains in return on marketing investment and increased marketing efficiency, while maintaining quality and increasing the value of corporation.' A number of factors have elevated the importance of measuring marketing performance:[5]

- **Corporate trend for greater accountability of value added**: Companies that want to measure the return on marketing need to treat marketing expenditures as an investment instead of just a short-term expense. The investment perspective allows managers to compare marketing to other assets and thus enables companies to be financially accountable. Being financially accountable is also necessary when a company wants to be cost effective and/or wants to reduce costs. Moreover, marketing is generating a stream of revenue (through sales), and therefore it should be possible to pay for marketing activities by their results.[6]
- **Discontent with traditional metrics**: Conventional methods (e.g., balance sheets, income statements, gross margins) of productivity and return are often historical and say little about the future long-term performance of a company. In a competitive and highly dynamic company environment, past performance is a poor and almost useless predictor of future performance. In compliance with treating marketing as an investment, marketing metrics should be forward looking and should also involve a long-term performance perspective.
- **Availability of ICT and Internet infrastructure**: The development of ICT and the Internet has facilitated the development of new methods for marketing metrics. In addition, the prevalence of enterprise resource planning software, supply chain management software and customer relationship management software enable the use of more advanced and forward looking marketing metrics.

Unfortunately, however, while many companies may be aware of the opportunities associated with marketing metrics, the reality is that many still rely on traditional historic metrics[7] such as balance sheets, gross margins, and so on.

What marketing metrics should do

More than ever, marketers are being pressured to deliver hard data on how their efforts increased the company's bottom line. This trend seems to be global.[8] A focus on metrics can mean the difference between a marketing department that is considered highly valuable and one on the brink of extinction. For example, research giant IDC surveyed senior marketing executives in IT companies to determine their priorities for the coming year. Measuring and justifying their efforts and steering marketing initiatives towards tangible results were at the top of their lists.[9]

To find out more about how the Stockholm based Ericsson Group, a world-leading telecommunications company, utilises a portfolio of metrics to monitor both operating efficiency and market effectiveness of their marketing activities, go to www.pearsoned.co.uk/marketingmanagementeurope

Recently, researchers Seggie, Cavusgil and Phelan[10] have formulated seven themes, or dimensions, that together define the capabilities of the 'ideal marketing metrics' – and at the same time also provide guidelines on how existing marketing metrics may be improved.

1 Marketing metrics should be financial. By speaking the same financial language as the rest of the company, senior management can obtain a greater understanding of marketing initiatives, intervene when necessary and take appropriate remedial action.

2 You cannot drive a car, or a company, by looking in the rearview mirror. Companies wanting to survive intense competition have to be at the forefront of environmental development and also need to be able to forecast the future results of actions taken today. In order to be forward, rather than backward looking, metrics should not just be projecting past results inflated by an uplift (an adjustment) factor.

3 Marketing actions may have both short- and long-term effects. By regarding marketing as an expense, the short-term perspective has been emphasised at the expense of the long-term perspective. However, the view of marketing as an investment introduces the long-term perspective necessary for the purpose of comparing the real benefits of marketing activities.

4 Looking only at aggregated, or average, tendencies among customers may mask important shifts among customer segments or even individual customers. Sufficient marketing metrics should therefore be capable of transforming data at the macrolevel into microlevel data.

5 Independent metrics should be moved from separate measures to causal chains, thereby facilitating the direct measure of marketing activities as evaluated by their effect on the bottom line. Intermediate variables such as consumer attitudes and market share should be taken into account.

6 No company exists in a vacuum and value is most often reached in competition with company rivals. Reflecting this, marketing metrics should also be relative – not just absolute – to allow managers to contrast performance with that of the company's competitors.

7 Marketing metrics should be able to deliver objective data, which can be used for comparisons with other companies and with other company activities – and that can facilitate accountability.

Marketing researchers Rust, Ambler, Carpenter, Kumar and Srivastava[11] propose that there are three challenges to the measurement of marketing productivity. The first challenge is relating marketing activities to long-term effects. The second is the separation of individual marketing activities from other actions. Third, the use of purely financial methods has proved inadequate for justifying marketing investments.

Non-financial metrics are needed, for example metrics that relate to innovations or employees. Since the late 1990s the economy has increasingly recognised that intangible (market-based) assets are the drivers of value.[12] A company's tangible or balance sheet assets (e.g., factories, raw materials, financial assets) have traditionally been seen as its most vital resource. However, in the modern market economy investors increasingly view intangible assets (e.g., brands, company knowledge, reputation, skills) as the key to superior business processess.[13]

London Business School's Tim Ambler suggests that if companies think they are already measuring marketing performance adequately they should ask themselves five questions:[14]

1 Do you routinely research consumer behaviour (retention, acquisition, usage) and why consumers behave that way (awareness, satisfaction, perceived quality)?

2 Do you routinely report the results of this research to the board in a format integrated with financial marketing metrics?

3 In those reports, do you compare the results with the levels previously forecast in the business plans?

4 Do you also compare them with the levels achieved by your key competitor using the same indicators?

5 Do you adjust short-term performance according to the change in your marketing-based asset(s)?

Ambler believes firms must give priority to measuring and reporting marketing performance through marketing metrics. He believes evaluation can be split into two parts: (1) short-term results; and (2) changes in brand equity. Short-term results often reflect profit-and-loss

Table 22.1 Sample marketing metrics

1 External	2 Internal
Awareness	Awareness of goals
Market share (volume or value)	Commitment to goals
Relative price (market share value/volume)	Active innovation support
Number of complaints (level of dissatisfaction)	Resource adequacy
Consumer satisfaction	Staffing/skill levels
Distribution/availability	Desire to learn
Total number of customers	Willingness to change
Perceived quality/esteem	Freedom to fail
Loyalty/retention	Autonomy
Relative perceived quality	Relative employee satisfaction

Source: T. Ambler (2001) What does marketing success look like?, *Marketing Management*, Spring, 13–18. Reproduced with permission.

concerns as shown by sales turnover, shareholder value, or some combination of the two. Brand-equity measures could include customer awareness, attitudes and behaviours; market share; relative price premium; number of complaints; distribution and availability; total number of customers; perceived quality; and loyalty and retention.[15] DoubleClick, Inc., which places roughly 200 billion ads a month for clients, offers 50 different types of metrics, such as pauses, restarts, average view times and full screen views for video ads, to monitor campaigns.[16]

Companies can also monitor an extensive set of metrics internal to the company, such as innovation; for example, 3M tracks the proportion of sales resulting from its recent innovations. Ambler also recommends developing employee measures and metrics, arguing that 'end users are the ultimate customers, but your own staff are your first; you need to measure the health of the internal market'. Table 22.1 summarises a list of popular internal and external marketing metrics from Ambler's survey in the United Kingdom.[17]

To date, marketing metrics results have been largely internal to the firm, although it has been argued that they should also be communicated to shareholders, subject to commercial confidentiality.[18]

The chain of marketing productivity

Regarding marketing as investment implies that the marketing assets in which the company invests should be identified. Also, it should be understood that these assets contribute to profits in the short run and provide potential for growth and sustained profits in the long run. Emphasis is not on underlying products, pricing or customer relationships but on marketing expenditures such as marketing communications, promotions and other activities, and how these expenditures influence marketplace performance.[19] Marketing expenditures may influence, for example, customers' beliefs, attitudes, feelings and behaviour, which in turn may impact on the financial performance of the company, such as profit and shareholder value. Marketing actions both create and leverage market-based assets; for example, an advertising effort may improve, or build, brand equity. Brand equity may in turn be leveraged to improve short-term productivity – advertising in combination with stronger brands is usually more productive. Figure 22.1 illustrates 'the chain of marketing productivity'.[20]

The chain of marketing productivity is concerned with marketing activities that require expenditures. Companies' strategies might include promotion strategy, product strategy, or any

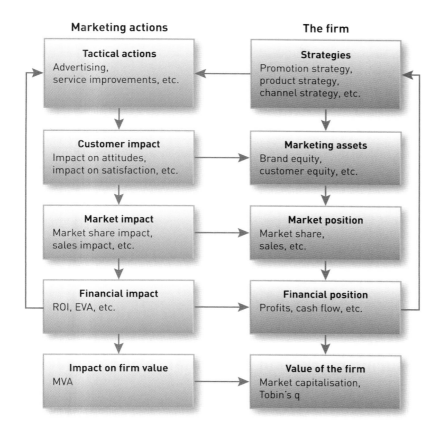

Marketing actions

Tactical actions
Advertising,
service improvements, etc.

Customer impact
Impact on attitudes,
impact on satisfaction, etc.

Market impact
Market share impact,
sales impact, etc.

Financial impact
ROI, EVA, etc.

Impact on firm value
MVA

The firm

Strategies
Promotion strategy,
product strategy,
channel strategy, etc.

Marketing assets
Brand equity,
customer equity, etc.

Market position
Market share,
sales, etc.

Financial position
Profits, cash flow, etc.

Value of the firm
Market capitalisation,
Tobin's q

Figure 22.1 The chain of marketing productivity

Source: Adapted from R. T. Rust, T. Ambler, G. S. Carpenter, V. Kumar and R. K. Srivastava (2004) Measuring marketing productivity: current knowledge and future directions, *Journal of Marketing*, 68, October, 77. Copyright © 2004 American Marketing Association. Reproduced with permission.

other marketing or company strategy. These strategies lead to tactical marketing actions taken by the firm, such as advertising campaigns, service improvement efforts, branding initiatives, loyalty programmes, or other specific initiatives designed to have a marketing impact. The tactical actions in turn impact customer satisfaction and attitude, and other customer-centred elements. Such customer-centred elements represent marketing assets to a company such as brand equity and customer equity. Customer behaviour influences may change market share and sales and thereby the market position of a company. The changes in market share, sales, etc., may have financial impact in terms of, for example, return on investment and economic value added (EVA), that is, net operating profit after taxes less the money cost of capital. Net operating profit after taxes (NOPAT) and cost of capital are considered in subsequent sections of this chapter. Return on investment (ROI) and EVA in turn influence the financial position of the company. The financial impacts have consequences for firm value in terms of MVA (market value added), which together with the financial position of the firm influences the value of the firm. 'Marketing insight: What metrics do companies use?' provides some insight on what metrics are used by companies.

Effectiveness versus efficiency

The company should distinguish between the 'effectiveness' and the 'efficiency' of marketing actions.[21] For example, price cuts can be efficient in that they deliver short-term revenues and cash flows. However, to the extent that they invite competitive actions and destroy long-term profitability and brand equity, they may not be effective. Businesses also need to know which success factors require measuring, and they must understand the differences between measurements (the raw outcomes of quantification), metrics (ideal standards for measurement) and benchmarks (the standards by which all others are measured).[22]

Marketing insight

What metrics do companies use?

Marketing metrics include all internal and external measurements related to marketing and market position, which are believed to be linked to short- and long-term financial performance.[23] Barwise and Farley[24] have recently studied adoption of six metrics in the top five global markets: the United States, Japan, Germany, the United Kingdom and France. The six metrics were market share, perceived product or service quality, customer loyalty or retention, customer or segment profitability, relative price and actual or potential customer/segment lifetime value.

Most businesses in these five countries said that they now report one or more of the six metrics to the board, with market share (79 per cent) and perceived

product/service quality (77 per cent) the most used. Least used (40 per cent) was customer/segment lifetime value. Germany was above average for all six metrics, especially market share (97 per cent) and relative price (84 per cent). Japan was below average on all metrics. The US and UK samples were fairly close to average, while France was high on both market share and customer/segment lifetime value. No significant differences related to industry use of metrics were found. Some systematic firm-related differences were found in that multinational subsidiaries and larger firms tended to use more metrics.

Source: Based on P. Barwise and J. U. Farley (2004) Marketing metrics: status of six metrics in five countries, *European Management Journal*, 22(3), 257–62.

▽ Measuring marketing performance and productivity

Marketing performance and productivity is multidimensional and therefore different metrics should be seen as complements rather than substitutes.[25] Marketing has the main responsibility for achieving profitable revenue growth and this is done by finding, keeping and growing the value of profitable customers.[26] Taking this perspective, marketing metrics must relate to finding customers (customer acquisition), keeping customers (consumer retention) and growing customer value (monetisation). This approach[27] connects marketing to essential business outcomes, customer acquisition to market share, customer retention to lifetime value and monetisation to customer/brand equity and shareholder value. We divide these marketing metrics into three dimensions: (1) counting-based (or activity) metrics; (2) accounting-based (or operational) metrics; and (3) outcome metrics. All three dimensions may comprise both external and internal company metrics.

Counting-based metrics

Counting-based metrics include, for example, number of complaints, sales, headcounts, number of customers, number of orders and new hires. In principle, any internal and external factor that can be counted may serve as a counting-based metric.

Accounting-based metrics

ROI and ROA

Most marketing research on company performance has relied on accounting-based ratio measures, such as return of investment and return on assets (ROA).[28] The formula for calculating ROI is:

$$\text{ROI}\% = \frac{\text{Net income before tax} \times 100}{\text{investment}}$$

ROI is usually calculated for a specific activity or campaign at a specific point in time. Consider a company that invests €1,500,000 on marketing a new product where the company expects to earn a net profit of €200,000 the first year. ROI% can then be calculated as:

$$\text{ROI}\% = \frac{€200,000 \times 100}{€1,500,000} = 13.3\%$$

The investment profitability rate of 13.3 per cent is here reported before taxes – but sometimes it is reported after taxes in comparing geographical areas where taxes vary substantially.[29]

The formula for calculating ROA is:

$$ROA\% = \frac{\text{Net income before tax} \times 100}{\text{total assets}}$$

Total assets are the invested capital in the company, comprising both debt and equity. The major disadvantage of ROA is that the invested assets have multiple ways of being measured, including historical costs, book values, appraisal value, market value, and so on.[30] ROA tells how effectively the company converts invested capital into net income, usually before taxes. Thus if net income is €1,500,000 and assets are €10,000,000, the ROA% is 15 per cent. ROA can vary substantially across industries.

The ROI and ROA measures are both limited by two deficiencies.[31] First, the cost of capital is not considered. The company needs to set a standard for acceptable performance at a level above the company's cost of capital. If the cost of capital is 10 per cent, the estimated ROI or ROA must be higher to make the investment. Second, the measures may lead to potential dysfunctional decision making by unit managers. Some marketing managers acting in self-interest may choose to estimate ROI on the high side to get money for the project or on the low side to discourage undertaking a project.

Another limitation is that ROI and ROA do not fully measure impact. Studies by the advertising agency Young & Rubicam suggest that only one-third of a brand's impact is realised in current sales and operating earnings, while two-thirds of its influence is obtained via future financial performance. Thus, while ROI analyses may provide some insight into the short-term financial performance of marketing activities they may capture only one-third of the total value creation of the marketing programme. Net present value (NPV) is a method that explicitly deals with the expected future cash flows as a result of company marketing activity.

NPV

Having €1000 in your hand today is better than having €1000 in five years from now. The reason is that over five years that €1000 that you have today would have a chance to grow by investing it. To calculate the net present value we discount the anticipated cash inflows with an acceptable discount rate.[32] NPV is the sum of all such discounted cash flows associated with a project.[33] NPV is calculated as:[34]

$$NPV = \sum_{t=0}^{n} \frac{C_t}{(1 + i)^t}$$

where

t = the time of the cash flow

n = the total time of the project

i = the discount rate

C_t = the net cash flow at time t.

The discount rate is usually arrived at as a weighted average cost of capital. The company may also choose to use variable discount rates, for example by using higher discount rates for riskier projects. Using an appropriate discount rate assures that the company only accepts projects where the expected cash flows add value to the company.

Outcome metrics

Marketing accountability also means that marketers must more precisely estimate the effects of different marketing investments. *Marketing-mix models* analyse data from a variety of sources, such as retailer scanner data, company shipment data, pricing, media, and promotion spending data, to understand more precisely the effects of specific marketing activities.[35] To deepen understanding, marketers can conduct multivariate analyses to sort through how each marketing element influences marketing outcomes such as brand sales or market share.[36]

Figure 22.2 Sales decomposition – obtained through advanced econometric modelling

Source: Sales modelling carried out by BrandScience. Copyright © Omnicom Media Group Reproduced with permission.

Advanced econometric modelling methods enable BrandScience to separate the effects of the different drivers and to isolate and quantify the contribution from marketing. Figure 22.2 shows a sales decomposition conducted for a European financial services brand, where the weekly number of credit card activations has been modelled and the significant drivers and their changing influence over time identified.

The blue dotted line represents the actual number of activations that has been decomposed via econometric modelling. The light blue base is the 'worst case sales' if all marketing activities had not occurred. In the base the following effects have been aggregated in order to show the impact from marketing more clearly: the base line, seasonality, internal structural changes and increased brand awareness. At the end of the period the uncompetitiveness (lack of competiveness) has prevented the company from realising the actual sales potential illustrated with the untapped dark blue area above the blue dotted *actual* line.

Four outcome metrics – shareholder value, customer lifetime value, brand equity measures and balanced scorecard are described and discussed.

Marketing metrics and shareholder value

Metric researcher Peter Doyle maintains that 'the real objective of marketing in the business enterprise is to develop and implement customer-led strategies that create shareholder value'.[37] **Shareholder value** is the value of the firm minus the future claims (future claims are also known as debts):

$$\text{Shareholder value} = \text{company value} - \text{debts}$$

where

$$\text{company value} = (\text{present value of all future cash flows} + \text{value of non-operating assets})$$

Non-operating assets are assets that are not essential to the ongoing operations of a business, but may still generate income or provide a return on investment – for example, a company may own some property that generates a yearly income.[38] While the shareholder value can be used to estimate the value of the shareholders' stake in a company or business unit, it can also be used to formulate and evaluate marketing decisions.[39] Consider the illustration opposite.

▽ Launching an advertising campaign for a French women's fragrance: the impact on shareholder value

The marketing department of a French producer of exclusive women's fragrances considers launching a €5 million advertising campaign in upmarket women's magazines such as *Elle* and *Vogue* in order to further promote its already popular series of fragrances.

The advertising campaign will run for five years with €1 million invested each year; the marketing department estimates that sales will increase by 5 per cent each year as a result. The company wants to estimate how the advertising campaign might affect the company's shareholder value. The calculations are shown in Table 22.2.

We assume an operating margin of 10 per cent. **Operating margin** is the ratio of operating profit divided by net sales. In year 1 the operating margin is obtained as: 10.5 (operating profits)/105 (sales) = 0.10. Since operating margin is 10 per cent this means that operating costs are 90 per cent of sales – for example in year 1: 94.5/105 = 0.90. Also, we assume that taxes are 25 per cent. Taxes are paid out of operating profits.

In Table 22.2 NOPAT is a company's after-tax operating profit. It is defined as follows:

$$\text{NOPAT} = \text{Operating profits} \times (1 - \text{tax rate})$$

Following this definition year 2 NOPAT is obtained as NOPAT $= 11.0 \times (1 - 0.25) = 8.25$, which we round off to €8.3 million.

The opportunity cost of capital is the return the capital could obtain if it was invested elsewhere in projects/activities of similar risk.[40] We estimate the opportunity cost of

How will an advertising campaign for a women's fragrance impact on shareholder value?

Source: The Advertising Archives

Table 22.2 Advertising campaign: calculating cash flow and shareholder value (€ million)

	Year					
	0	**1**	**2**	**3**	**4**	**5**
Sales	100.0	105.0	110.3	115.8	121.6	127.6
Operating costs	90.0	94.5	99.2	104.2	109.4	114.9
Operating profits	10.0	10.5	11.0	11.6	12.2	12.8
Tax (25%)	2.5	2.6	2.8	2.9	3.0	3.2
NOPAT	7.5	7.9	8.3	8.7	9.1	9.6
Advertising campaign		1.0	1.0	1.0	1.0	1.0
Cash flow		6.9	7.3	7.7	8.1	8.6
Discount factor (10%)		0.909	0.826	0.751	0.683	0.621
Net present value of cash flow		6.3	6.0	5.8	5.5	5.3
Cumulative net present value		6.3	12.3	18.1	23.6	28.9
Net present of value of cash flows after planning horizon						59.6
Value of company operation (including advertising campaign)						88.5
Initial shareholder value (before advertising campaign)						75.0
Shareholder value added from advertising campaign						13.5

capital (the discount factor), i, to be 10 per cent. The *annual* discount factor is calculated as:

$$\text{Annual discount factor} = 1/(1 + i)^t \text{ where } t = 1, 2, \ldots \text{ is the year}$$

For example, the annual discount factor for year 3 ($t = 3$) is:

$$\text{Annual discount factor, year 3} = 1/(1 + 0.10)^3 = 0.751$$

By multiplying the year 3 cash flow, which is €7.7 million, with the year 3 annual discount factor, which is 0.751, we get €5.8 million (the net present value of cash flow in year 3). Similar calculations can be carried for years 1, 2, 4 and 5. NPV of cash flows during planning horizon is now obtained as the cumulative present value in year 5: €6.3 + €6.0 + €5.8 + €5.5 + €5.3 = €28.9 million.

In principle, cash flows for all future years beyond the planning period (year 6, year 7, year 8, etc.) should be estimated in a similar way in order for the value of the advertising campaign to be accurately determined. However, a short-cut approach is often used in practice.[41] Here the NPV of cash flows after the planning horizon is calculated by the standard perpetuity model, which is the year 5 NOPAT/i multiplied by the year 5 discount factor (= 0.621). Thus, the perpetuity method simply assumes that beyond the five-year planning period competition will drive down profits to a level such that new investments just earn the company's cost of capital.[42] The year 5 NOPAT is €9.6 million (Table 22.2) and the discount factor, i, is 10 per cent. Thus we can now calculate NPV of cash flows after planning horizon as 9.6/0.10 × 0.621 = €59.6 million.

Future cash flows have thus been divided into two time periods: those that occur during the planning horizon, and those that occur after the planning horizon. We add the cash flows from these two time periods and get the value of company operation: €28.9 + €59.6 = €88.5 million

The perpetuity method can also be used for calculating the initial shareholder value of the company. The company's initial shareholder value before the advertising campaign is €75 million. This is estimated by dividing the year 0 NOPAT (= €7.5 million) by the cost of capital: €7.5/0.10 = €75 million. The expected shareholder value added from the advertising campaign is then the 'value of company operation' (including advertising campaign) less the 'company's initial shareholder value': €88.5 − €75 = €13.5 million.

Taking a shareholder perspective may enhance the opportunity of making marketing recognised as a significant corporate value driver. Lukas, Whitwell and Doyle have emphasised five contributions of a shareholder value approach to marketing:[43]

1 **A shareholder value approach helps marketing properly define its objective**: To the extent that the governing business objective of a company is to maximise shareholder value, marketing should focus on contributing to this objective.

2 **A shareholder value approach provides the language for integrating marketing more effectively with the other functions of the company**: Shareholder value analysis is rooted in the discipline of finance, which is also the most common language in the boardroom. Unless marketing learns to speak this language its influence will be limited.

3 **A shareholder value approach allows marketing to demonstrate the importance of its assets**: Many marketing assets are intangible (e.g., brand equity, customer loyalty). By relating these assets to shareholder value marketing has the potential to increase its strategic influence in the company.

4 **A shareholder value approach protects marketing budgets from profit-maximisation policies**: Taking a shareholder value approach may prevent cuts in marketing budgets. Fundamentally a shareholder approach is long term, with an explicit disdain for short-term solutions. Moreover, the shareholder approach emphasises that marketing assets should be considered as investments, which in turn emphasises that short-term, profit-driven marketing budgets may destroy rather than build company value.

5 **A shareholder value approach puts marketing in a pivotal role in the strategy formulation process**: Creating shareholder value is essential for creating a competitive advantage. Marketing provides the tools for creating such a competitive advantage.

The shareholder perspective should not be confused with the stakeholder perspective. The stakeholder perspective regards the purpose of a company to create value for all involved parties. Advocates say that this is even more likely to produce higher profits for the shareholders because the other parties will be more productive and better rewarded.

Customer lifetime value

As modern economies become predominantly service based, companies increasingly derive revenue from the creation and sustenance of long-term relationships with their customers. In such an environment marketing serves the purpose of maximising customer lifetime value. The case for maximising long-term customer profitability is captured in the concept of customer lifetime value.[44] Customer lifetime value is rapidly gaining acceptance as a metric to acquire, grow and retain the 'right' customers in customer relationship management.[45]

The CLV approach assumes that customers who stay with a company for a long period generate more profits as compared with customers who only stay for a short period. It is more cost effective to deal with established customers whose needs and wants are known, and satisfied customers are also more likely to increase their purchases and to recommend the company to other customers. CLV can be seen as the series of transactions between a company and a customer over the period of time that the customer remains with the company.[46] CLV can be measured as the present value of the future net cash flows that are expected to be received over the lifetime of a customer, consisting of the revenue obtained from the customer less the cost of attracting, serving and satisfying the customer.[47] A key decision is what time horizon to use for estimating CLV. Typically, three to five years is reasonable.

The formula for estimating customer lifetime value is:

$$CLV = \sum_{t=0}^{T^*} \frac{(p_t - c_t)}{(1 + i)^t} - AC,$$

where

p_t = price paid by a consumer at time t

c_t = direct cost of servicing the customer at time t

i = discount rate

t = expected lifetime of a customer

AC = acquisition cost

The formula can be applied for an individual customer and for segments of customers. CLV is a suitable metric for both business and consumer markets.

For example, a company may invest €10,000 in attracting a business customer. This acquisition cost (AC) consists of the costs associated with convincing a consumer to buy your product or service, including marketing, advertising costs, negotiating expenses in terms of human resources and travelling, conducting research and preparing various analyses on how to serve the customer in the best way, and so on. The customer stays with the company for three years, each year generating a €5000 NOPAT to the company. The company estimates the opportunity cost of capital, i, to be 10 per cent. The annual discount factor for year 1 is calculated to be 0.909, for year 2 it is calculated to be 0.826, and for year 3 it is calculated to be 0.751. The lifetime value of the customer can now be calculated as CLV $= -10,000 + 5000/1.10 + 5000/1.10^2 + 5000/1.10^3 =$ €2434.

We find the lifetime value of this customer to be €2434. Since the lifetime value is larger than zero, this customer is expected to contribute positively to the value of the company.

It is useful for a company to find out what types of customers are the most profitable, how much it should spend on them and what product offerings should be made. The service and repair company Midas uses customer lifetime value as a tool for its direct marketing effort in several European countries. Midas tracks cars based on vehicle mileage and contacts customers to remind them of service and brake opportunities over the life of their vehicle.[48]

By comparing CLV with different types of customers, service activities and product offerings, the company can obtain highly useful knowledge and may also estimate **customer equity**. Customer equity (CE) is defined as the lifetime value of current and future customers.[49] CLV and CE focus on the long-term rather than the short-term profit or marketshare. Therefore, maximising CLV, and hence CE, is effectively maximising the long-term profitability and financial health of a company.[50]

▽ Variations in customer lifetime value

Customers may vary dramatically in their overall value to a company. Niraj, Gupta and Narasimhan[51] recently studied the drivers of current customer profitability in a supply chain for a large distributor with a heterogeneous client base. They found that a small percentage of customers contributes to a large percentage of total profits, and that a substantial percentage (32 per cent of total) of customers is unprofitable.

An important question relating to CLV is whether shareholder value would benefit from changing the level of marketing investment in a certain customer. Spending too much on an individual customer, or a segment of customers, can have a damaging impact on shareholder value. Some bankers are known for lavish dinners or rounds of golf with VIPs, long-term customers who are probably unlikely to switch to another bank. On the other hand, insufficient spending can also decrease shareholder value because an underserved customer may defect to a competitor or reduce spending volume.[52]

Companies wanting to take advantage of the CLV measurement should build individual-level customer databases. Without such data true longitudinal data analysis of customers' behavioural responses to marketing actions – and related costs – cannot be implemented.[53]

Brand equity and financial performance

Brand equity is probably the most prized measure for many companies of the value of the marketing asset.[54] Brand equity we conceptualise as 'the added value endowed to products and services' by the brand name. This value may be reflected in how consumers think, feel and act with respect to the brand. Brand equity is an important intangible asset that has psychological and financial value to the company. Positive equity is likely to be associated with behaviour that benefits the brand through purchase frequency, brand loyalty, price insensitivity and willingness to recommend.[55]

There are two primary perspectives related to brand equity, one based on financial outcomes for the company and the other on softer, consumer-based perceptions of company performance. Most studies have focused on the consumer-based perspective. Also, much of the data necessary to test the financially based brand equity perspective are confidential and not available to marketing researchers.[56]

In the consumer-based brand equity (CBBE) perspective, the power of a brand lies in what customers have learned, thought, felt, seen and heard about the brand as a result of their experiences over time.[57]

There is a direct and an indirect approach to measure CBBE. The indirect approach requires measuring potential sources of brand equity by identifying and tracking consumer brand knowledge structures. The direct approach requires experiments in which one group of customers responds to an element in the marketing programme when it is attributed to the brand, and another group of customers responds to the same element when it is attributed to a fictitiously named or unnamed version of the product or service. 'Blind tests' constitute an example of the direct approach.[58] The indirect approach is concerned with detecting the causes of brand equity, whereas the direct approach is concerned with assessing the added value of the brand.

Examples of operationalising direct measures include price premiums for brand switching and purchase intention, while examples of indirect measures include unaided and aided recall (awareness), familiarity, brand image favourability and rating of beliefs of associations (brand image strength). No single concept or dimension can be applied for measuring CBBE since it is a multidimensional construct.

One view suggests that brand equity arises from the strength and favourability of the two components of consumer-based brand knowledge structures: brand awareness and brand image. Brand awareness relates to the strength of a brand in memory, and the likelihood and ease with which the brand will be recognised or recalled under various conditions. Brand image is defined as 'perceptions about the brand as reflected by the brand associations held in consumer memory'.[59] Netemeyer and his colleagues[60] found that in the fast food industry the dimensions 'perceived brand quality' and 'perceived brand value for the cost' (these dimensions were collapsed into one dimension) and brand uniqueness are highly relevant in predicting customer-based brand equity.

Brand equity was operationalised (measured) as the willingness to pay a price premium for a brand. This operationalisation included four measurement items:

1 The price of (brand name) would have to go up quite a bit before I would switch to another brand of (product).

2 I am willing to pay a higher price for the (brand name) brand of (product) than for other brands of (product).

3 I am willing to pay X per cent more for the (brand name) brand over other brands of (product): 0 per cent, 5 per cent, 10 per cent, 15 per cent, 20 per cent, 25 per cent, 30 per cent, or more.

4 I am willing to pay a lot more for the (brand name) than for other brands of (product category).

Items were measured on seven-point 'strongly disagree' to 'strongly agree' scales.

Higher levels of brand awareness and positive brand image are thought to increase the probability of brand choice, as well as produce greater customer loyalty and decrease vulnerability to marketing actions.[61] Some researchers have suggested that brand equity measures should also rely on market-based, objective measures because consumer attitude and preference measures are inherently subjective. Silverman, Sprott and Pascal[62] have explored the relationship between customer-based and financial/market-based brand equity measurements. They found only small, but positive, relationships between brand awareness – assessed by familiarity, usage and favourability – and market-based outcomes of brand value – measured by annual sales and Financial World brand ratings (see www.financialworld.co.uk).

Advertising agency Young & Rubicam has developed a model of brand equity called brand asset valuator, which can be accessed on its website – http://www.yrbav.com/. BAV measures brand value by applying four broad factors:[63] (1) differentiation (the ability of a brand to stand apart from its competitors); (2) relevance (consumers' actual and perceived importance of the brand); (3) esteem (consumers' perceived brand quality together with their assessment of the popularity of the brand); and (4) knowledge (consumers' brand awareness together with their understanding of the brand's identity).

Recently Young & Rubicam[64] has investigated to what extent BAV contributes to a company's financial performance.[65] Using unanticipated change in stock price as the dependent variable (i.e., financial measure), the relative contribution of individual brand components to changes in stock price was explored. The results revealed that energised brand strength (a combination of energy, differentiation and relevance) demonstrates a significant relationship with market value. BAV's energised brand strength was found to be 81 per cent as effective as sales growth in explaining changes in market value.

▽ The balanced scorecard approach

Kaplan and Norton developed and advocated a balanced scorecard approach (BSC) on the grounds that purely financial metrics may tell the wrong story about a company. Consider the following racing car metaphor offered by Andra Gumbus.[66]

▽ The need for both financial and non-financial metrics

Organisations that focus solely on financial measures can be compared to a racing car driver who only monitors his or her speed during a race. Suppose you are a driver in Formula 1 and are monitoring your car by looking at the RPM (revolutions [of the engine] per minute) gauge on your dashboard. You are not noticing the MPG (miles per gallon of fuel), nor the MPH (miles per hour, or speed your car is travelling), nor the temperature gauge. You might win the race, but you are putting yourself and your car at risk by not monitoring *all* the gauges while focusing exclusively on the RPM dial. You might run out of fuel, overheat the engine, crash into another car and make other errors in navigating the course.

Installing BSC in a company requires active participation from top management and sustaining the practice over time.[67] BSC provides a systematic tool that combines financial and non-financial performance metrics in one coherent measurement system. Metrics are constructed according to a predefined strategy, and the company's processes are aligned towards this strategy. BSC systematically measures the company in four areas:[68]

1 The *financial perspective* uses traditional accounting measures in order to evaluate a firm's short-term financial results. Metrics include ROI, cash flow analyses and return on equity.

2 The *customer perspective* measures relate to customer satisfaction of identified target groups and is generally marketing focused. Metrics include delivery performance to customers, customer satisfaction rate and customer retention.

3 The *internal business process perspective* is based on the concept of the (firm-internal) value chain, including the process (or steps) needed to realise the intended product or service. Metrics include opportunity success rates, number of activities and defect rates.

4 The final dimension comprises the *innovation and learning perspective* that is inherent in a company by measuring various human resources-focused effects as well as learning systems support effectiveness. Metrics include illness rate, internal promotions in per cent and employee turnover.

By combining these four measures, Kaplan and Norton establish the BSC as a representation of a company's shared vision (see Figure 22.3).

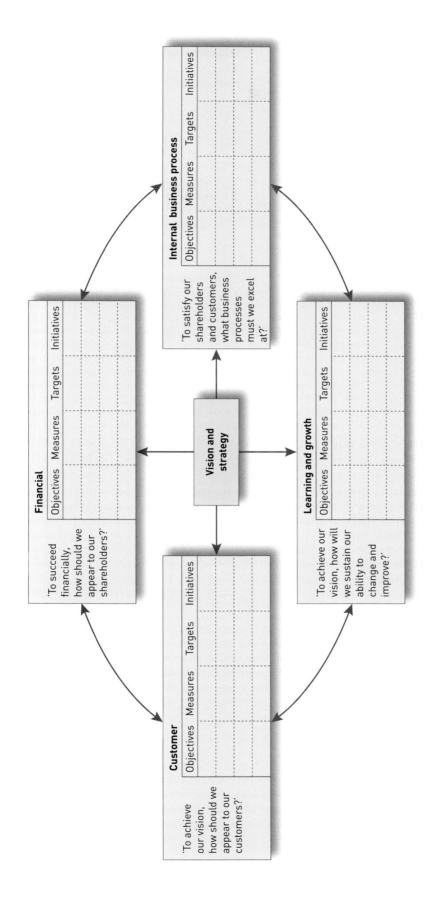

Figure 22.3 Translating vision and strategy: four perspectives

Figure 22.4 Managing strategy: four processes

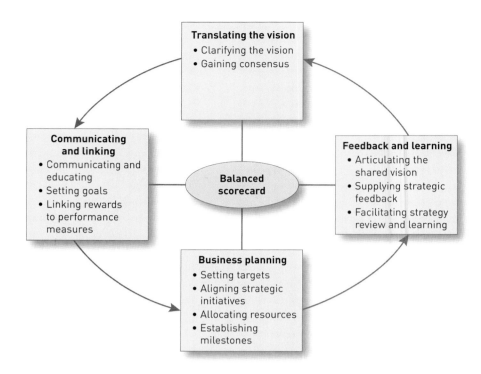

BSC is not only a tool for measurement, but also a tool for strategic management.[69] BSC has not been developed to serve strategy formulation, but to implement strategy. BSC can be regarded as a tool for translating a company's strategy into measurable goals, actions and performance measures. According to Kaplan and Norton the set of measures gives top managers a fast but comprehensive view of the business. Kaplan and Norton[70] have developed four management processes that contribute to linking long-term strategic objectives with short-term actions (see Figure 22.4).

- **The first process**: *translating the vision* – assists managers to build a consensus around the company's vision and strategy. For example, a top management vision that the company wants to be the 'number one supplier' offers by itself little guidance on how to operationalise that vision.
- **The second process**: *communicating and linking* – assists managers to communicate their strategy up and down the organisation and link it to objectives at the departmental and individual level, for example by linking rewards to performance measures.
- **The third process**: *business planning* – assists companies to integrate their business and financial plans, for example by setting targets and allocating sufficient resources.
- **The fourth process**: *feedback and learning* – enables companies to achieve strategic learning. The feedback and learning process facilitates feedback on all four perspectives (financial performance, customers, internal business processes, and learning and growth).

Accounting professor Erkki K. Laitinen argues that it is difficult to identify the relative importance of and the trade-offs between the suggested four perspectives of the approach.[71] Moreover, it is also difficult to identify the links between financial and non-financial performance measures. Kaplan and Norton acknowledge this criticism to a certain degree when stating that 'accumulating sufficient data to document significant correlations and causation among balanced scorecard measures can take a long time – months or years'.[72] Such data may enable a company to establish correlations between the various measures from the four perspectives.

▽ Marketing dashboards

Firms can assemble a summary set of relevant internal and external measures in a *marketing dashboard* for synthesis and interpretation. Marketing dashboards are like the instrument panel in a car or plane, visually displaying real-time indicators to ensure proper functioning. They are only as good as the information on which they are based, but sophisticated visualisation tools are helping bring data alive to improve understanding and analysis.[73]

Some companies are also appointing marketing controllers to review budget items and expenses. Increasingly, these controllers are using business intelligence software to create digital versions of marketing dashboards that aggregate data from disparate internal and external sources.

As input to the marketing dashboard, companies should include two key market-based scorecards that reflect performance and provide possible early warning signals.

1 A **customer-performance scorecard** records how well the company is doing year after year on such customer-based measures as those shown in Table 22.3. Management should set norms for each measure and take action when results get out of bounds.

2 A **stakeholder-performance scorecard** tracks the satisfaction of various constituencies who have a critical interest in and impact on the company's performance: employees, suppliers, banks, distributors, retailers and stockholders. Again, management should take action when one or more groups register increased or above-norm levels of dissatisfaction.[74]

Some executives worry that they'll miss the big picture if they focus too much on a set of numbers on a dashboard. Others are concerned about privacy and the pressure the technique places on employees. But most experts feel the rewards offset the risks.[75] 'Marketing insight: Marketing dashboards to improve effectiveness and efficiency' provides practical advice about the development of these marketing tools.

Table 22.3 Sample customer-performance scorecard measures

- percentage of new customers to average number of customers;
- percentage of lost customers to average number of customers;
- percentage of win-back customers to average number of customers;
- percentage of customers falling into very dissatisfied, dissatisfied, neutral, satisfied, and very satisfied categories;
- percentage of customers who say they would repurchase the product;
- percentage of customers who say they would recommend the product to others;
- percentage of target market customers who have brand awareness or recall;
- percentage of customers who say that the company's product is the most preferred in its category;
- percentage of customers who correctly identify the brand's intended positioning and differentiation;
- average perception of company's product quality relative to chief competitor;
- average perception of company's service quality relative to chief competitor.

Marketing insight

Marketing dashboards to improve effectiveness and efficiency

Marketing consultant Pat LaPointe sees marketing dashboards as providing all the up-to-the-minute information necessary to run the business operations for a company – such as sales versus forecast, distribution channel effectiveness, brand equity evolution and human capital development. According to LaPointe, an effective dashboard will focus thinking, improve internal communications and reveal where marketing investments are paying off and where they aren't.

LaPointe observes four common measurement 'pathways' marketers are pursuing today (see Figure 22.5).

- The *customer metrics pathway* looks at how prospects become customers, from awareness to preference to trial to repeat purchase. Many companies track progression through a 'hierarchy of effects' model to follow the evolution of broad market potential to specific revenue opportunities.

- The *unit metrics pathway* reflects what marketers know about sales of product/service units – how much is sold by product line and/or by geography; the marketing cost per unit sold as an efficiency yardstick; and where and how margin is optimised in terms of characteristics of the product line or distribution channel.

- The *cash-flow metrics pathway* focuses on how well marketing expenditures are achieving short-term returns. Programme and campaign ROI models measure the immediate impact or net present value of profits expected from a given investment.

- The *brand metrics pathway* tracks the development of the longer-term impact of marketing through brand equity measures that assess both the perceptual health of the brand from customer and prospective customer perspectives as well as the overall financial health of the brand.

LaPointe emphasises that a marketing dashboard can present insights from all the pathways in a graphically related view that helps management see subtle links between them. A well-constructed dashboard can have a series of 'tabs' that allow the user to toggle easily between different 'families' of metrics

Figure 22.5 Marketing measurement pathways

Source: Adapted from D. Schultz (2005) Chapter 13 in P. Kotler and A. Tybout (ed.) *Kellogg on Branding: The Marketing Faculty of the Kellogg School of Management*, New York: John Wiley & Sons. Copyright © 2005 John Wiley & Sons, Inc. Reproduced with permission.

▶ **Marketing insight** *(continued)*

Figure 22.6 The marketing dashboard

Source: Adapted from P. LaPointe (2005) *Marketing by the Dashboard Light – How to Get More Insight, Foresight, and Accountability from Your Marketing Investments.* Copyright © 2005 Patrick LaPointe. Reproduced with permission.

organised by customer, product, brand, experience, channels, efficiency, organisational development or macroenvironmental factors. Each tab presents the three or four most insightful metrics, with data filtered by business unit, geography or customer segment based upon the users' needs (see Figure 22.6 for an example).

Ideally, the number of metrics presented in the marketing dashboard would be reduced to a handful of key drivers over time. Importantly, the process of developing and refining the marketing dashboard will undoubtedly raise and resolve many key questions about the business.

▽ SUMMARY

1 Marketers must be able to justify marketing expenditures to company management. Marketing metrics is the set of measures that helps firms to quantify, compare and interpret their marketing performance.

2 Good marketing metrics are financial, forward-looking and capture both short-term and long-term effects.

3 Marketing performance and productivity is multidimensional and therefore different metrics should be seen as complements rather than substitutes. Marketing has the main responsibility for achieving profitable revenue growth and this is done by finding, keeping and growing the value of profitable customers.

4 Marketing metrics are divided into three dimensions: (1) counting-based (or activity) metrics;

(2) accounting-based (or operational) metrics; and (3) outcome metrics. All three dimensions comprise both external and internal metrics.

5 While ROI analyses may provide some insight into the financial performance of marketing activities, they may at the same time capture only one-third of the total value creation of the marketing programme. Net present value is a method that explicitly deals with the expected future cash flows as a result of company marketing activity.

6 Marketing should develop and implement customer-led strategies that create shareholder value. Taking a shareholder perspective enhances the opportunity of making marketing recognised as a significant corporate value driver.

7 Customer lifetime value is the net profit or loss to a company from a customer flowing from the lifetime of that customer's transactions with the company. CLV assumes that customers who stay with a company for a long period of time generate more profits as compared to customers who stay for only a short period of time.

8 There are two primary perspectives related to brand equity, one based on financial outcomes for the company and one based on softer, consumer-based perceptions of company performance. Marketing performance during a period will be judged by whether brand equity has risen, is static, or has declined.

9 The balanced scorecard approach provides a systematic tool that combines financial and non-financial performance metrics in one coherent measurement system. Metrics are constructed according to a predefined strategy, and the company's processes are aligned towards this strategy. BSC systematically measures the company from four perspectives: the financial perspective, the customer perspective, the internal business process perspective, and the innovation and learning perspective.

10 A marketing dashboard provides up-to-the-minute information necessary to run the business operations for a company – such as sales versus forecast, distribution channel effectiveness, brand equity evolution and human capital development.

▽ APPLICATIONS

Marketing debate

Take a position: For any marketing activity there should be an established link between the activity and its measurement in terms of cash flow, ROI, effect on shareholder value, and so on. Otherwise that activity should not be carried out *versus* Marketing activities are often based on feelings, experiences, and so on, which are difficult to quantify. Therefore the outcome of a marketing activity need not be measurable for the marketing activity to be carried out.

Marketing discussion

What marketing activities need to be measured? Why? Which ones do not? What metrics should be used in relation to what companies and in relation to what activities?

▽ REFERENCES

[1] Based on dialogue with BrandScience; www.brandsciencenetwork.com.

[2] J. McManus (2004) Stumbling into intelligence, *American Demographics*, April, 22–5.

[3] L. Patterson (2007) MP 'classic truths': if you don't measure, you can't manage – the best metrics for managing marketing performance, *MarketingProfs*, 23 October.

[4] S. H. Seggie, E. Cavusgil and S. E. Phelan (2007) Measurement of return on marketing investment: a conceptual framework and the future of marketing metrics, *Industrial Marketing Management*, 36, 834–41.

[5] Ibid.

[6] M. Uncles (2005) Marketing metrics: a can of worms or the path to enlightenment?, editorial to *Brand Management*, 12(6), 412–18.

[7] T. Ambler, F. Kokkinaki and S. Puntoni (2004) Assessing marketing performance: reasons for metric selection, *Journal of Marketing Management*, 29(3/4), 475–98; P. Barwise and J. U. Farley (2004) Marketing metrics: status of six metrics in five countries, *European Management Journal*, 22(3), 257–62; Seggie et al. (2007) op. cit.

[8] Barwise and Farley (2004) op. cit.

[9] Marketing metrics: where to get them? Which ones work?, *Advertising & Marketing Review*, http://www.ad-mkt-review.com/public_html/docs/fs059.html, accessed December 2007.

[10] Seggie et al. (2007) op. cit.

[11] R. T. Rust, T. Ambler, G. S. Carpenter, V. Kumar and R. K. Srivastava (2004) Measuring marketing productivity: current knowledge and future directions, *Journal of Marketing*, 68 (October), 76–89.

[12] AMI (2004) 'What value marketing? A position paper on marketing metrics in Australia', Australian Marketing Institute, Sydney, 1, available at http://www.ami.org.au.

[13] P. Doyle (2001) Shareholder-value-based brand strategies, *Brand Management*, 9(1), 20–30.

[14] T. Ambler (2003) *Marketing and the Bottom Line: The New Methods of Corporate Wealth*, 2nd edn, Harlow, England: Pearson Education.

[15] K. L. Ailawadi, D. R. Lehmann and S. A. Neslin (2003) Revenue premium as an outcome measure of brand equity, *Journal of Marketing*, 67 (October), 1–17.

[16] S. Baker (2006) Wiser about the Web, *BusinessWeek*, 27 March, 53–7.

[17] Ambler (2003) op. cit.

[18] T. Ambler, P. Barwise and C. Higson (2001) *Market Metrics: What Should We Tell the Shareholders?*, Institute of Chartered Accountants in England and Wales, Centre for Business Performance, London; Barwise U. Farley (2004) op. cit.

[19] T. Rust et al. (2004) op. cit.

[20] Ibid.

[21] Ibid.

[22] Patterson (2007) op. cit.

[23] Ambler (2003) op. cit.

[24] Barwise and Farley (2004) op. cit.

[25]Ibid.

[26]P. Kotler (1999) *Kotler on Marketing: How to Create, Win, and Dominate Markets*, New York: Free Press.

[27]L. Patterson (2007) Case study: taking on the metrics challenge, *Journal of Targeting, Measurement and Analysis for Marketing*, 15(4), 270–6.

[28]E. W. Anderson, C. Fornell and S. K. Mazvancheryl (2004) Customer satisfaction and shareholder value, *Journal of Marketing*, 68, 172–85.

[29]http://en.wikipedia.org/wiki/Return_on_investment.

[30]R. D. Dillon and J. E. Owers (1997) EVA® as a financial metric: attributes, utilization, and relationship to NPV, *Financial Practice and Education*, Spring/Summer, 32–40.

[31]Ibid.

[32]http://moneyterms.co.uk/discount-rate/.

[33]http://www.smartcapitalist.com/blog_36.shtml.

[34]http://en.wikipedia.org/wiki/Net_present_value.

[35]G. J. Tellis (2006) Modeling marketing mix, in R. Grover and M. Vriens (eds) *Handbook of Marketing Research*, Thousand Oaks, CA: Sage.

[36]J. Neff (2004) P&G, Clorox rediscover modeling, *Advertising Age*, 29 March, 10.

[37]P. Doyle (2000) Valuing marketing's contribution, *European Management Journal*, 18(3), 233–45.

[38]http://www.investopedia.com/terms/n/nonoperatingasset.asp.

[39]S. Cooper and M. Davies (2004) Measuring shareholder value: the metrics in *Maximising Shareholder Value Achieving Clarity in Decision-making, CIMA Technical Report*, London: The Chartered Institute of Management Accountants, November, 10–15.

[40]Doyle (2000) op. cit.

[41]Cooper and Davies (2004) op. cit.

[42]Doyle (2000) op. cit.

[43]B. A. Lukas, G. J. Whitwell and P. Doyle (2005) How can a shareholder value approach improve marketing's strategic influence?, *Journal of Business Research*, 58(4), 414–22.

[44]S. Gupta, D. Hanssens, B. Hardie, W. Kahn, V. Kumar, N. Lin and N.R.S. Srinam (2006) Modeling Customer Lifetime Value, *Journal of Service Research*, 19(2), 139–55.

[45]R. Venkatesan and V. Kumar (2004) A customer lifetime value framework for customer selection and resource allocation strategy, *Journal of Marketing*, 68, 106–25.

[46]D. Jain and S. S. Singh (2002) Customer lifetime value research in marketing: a review and future directions, *Journal of Interactive Research*, 16(4), 34–46.

[47]R. H. Chenhall and K. Langfield-Smith (2007) Multiple perspectives of performance measures, *European Management Journal*, 25(4), 266–82.

[48]R. Baran, C. Zerres and M. Zerres Customer relationship management, free-learning summary in cooperation with www.ventus.dk; www.midas.com.

[49]S. Gupta and V. Zeithaml (2006) Customer metrics and their impact on financial performance, *Marketing Science*, 25(6), 718–39.

[50]Ibid.

[51]R. Niraj, M. Gupta and C. Narasimhan (2001) Customer profitability in a supply chain, *Journal of Marketing*, 65, July, 1–16.

[52]G. Cokins (2006) Measuring customer value: how BPM supports better marketing decisions, *Business Performance Management*, February, 13–18.

[53]Rust et al. (2004) op. cit.

[54]T. Ambler and Wang Xiucun (2003) Measures of marketing success: a comparison between China and the United Kingdom, *Asia Pacific Journal of Management*, 20, 267–81.

[55]T. J. Reynolds and C. B. Phillips (2005) In search of true brand equity metrics: all market share ain't created equal, *Journal of Advertising Research*, June, 171–86.

[56]S. A. Taylor, G. L. Hunter and D. L. Lindberg (2007) Understanding (customer-based) brand equity in financial services, *Journal of Services Marketing*, 21(4), 241–52; K. L. Keller (1993) Conceptualizing, measuring, and managing customer-based brand equity, *Journal of Marketing*, 57(1), 1–23.

[57]K. L. Keller (2003) *Strategic Brand Management: Building, Measuring and Managing Brand Equity*, 2nd edn, Englewood Cliffs, NJ: 2003 Prentice-Hall, E. Atilgan, S. Aksoy and S. Akinci (2005) Determinants of the brand equity: a verification approach in the beverage industry in Turkey, *Marketing Intelligence & Planning*, 23(3) 237–48.

[58]Keller (1993) op. cit.; Hong-bumm Kim, Woo Gon Kim and Jeong A. An (2003) The effect of consumer-based brand equity on firms' financial performance, *Journal of Consumer Marketing*, 20(4), 335–51.

[59]Keller (1993) op. cit.

[60]R. G. Netemeyer, B. Krishnan, C. Pullig, G. Wang, M. Yagci, D. Dean, J. Ricks and F. Wirth (2004) Developing and validating measures of facets of customer-based brand equity, *Journal of Business Research*, 57, 209–24.

[61]Keller (1993) op. cit.

[62]S. N. Silverman, D. E. Sprott and V. J. Pascal (1999) Relating consumer-based sources of brand equity to market outcomes, *Advances in Consumer Research*, 26, 352–8.

[63]http://www.valuebasedmanagement.net/methods_brand_asset_valuator.html.

[64]In collaboration with Robert Jacobson from the University of Washington School of Business and Natalie Mizik from the Columbia Graduate School of Business.

[65]J. Gerzema (Young & Rubicam Brands), E. Lebar (BrandAsset® Valuator, Worldwide), M. Sussman (Y&R, North America) and J. Gaikowski (Young & Rubicam Brands) (2007) Energy: igniting brands to drive enterprise value, *International Journal of Market Research*, 49(1), 25–45.

[66]A. Gambus (2005) Introducing the balanced scorecard: creating metrics to measure performance, *Journal of Management Education*, 29(4), 617–30.

[67]Ibid.

[68]S. C. Voelpel, M. Leibold, R. A. Eckhoff (2006) The tyranny of the balanced scorecard in the innovation economy, *Journal of Intellectual Capital*, 7(1), 43–60; R. S. Kaplan and D. P. Norton (1992) The balanced scorecard: measures that drive performance, *Harvard Business Review*, 70(1), 71–85.

[69]Voelpel et al. (2006) op. cit.

[70]R. S. Kaplan and D. P. Norton (2007) Using the balanced scorecard as a strategic management system, *Harvard Business Review*, July–August, 150–61.

[71]E. K. Laitinen (2006) A constant growth model of the firm: empirical analysis of the balanced scorecard, *Review of Accounting and Finance*, 5(2), 140–73.

[72]Citation from Kaplan and Norton (2007) op. cit., 160.

[73]J. Zabin (2006) Marketing dashboards: the visual display of marketing data, *Chief Marketer* 26 June.

[74]R. S. Kaplan and D. P. Norton (1996) *The Balanced Scorecard*, Boston, MA: Harvard Business School Press.

[75]S. Ante (2006) Giving the boss the big picture, *BusinessWeek*, 13 February, 48–50.

▽ Digitel marketing plan and exercises

▽ The marketing plan: an introduction

As a marketing practitioner, you will need a good marketing plan to provide direction and focus for your brand, product or company. With a detailed plan, any business will be better prepared to launch an innovative new product or increase sales to current customers. Non-profit organisations also use a marketing plan to guide their fundraising and outreach activity. Even government agencies put together marketing plans for initiatives such as building public awareness of healthy eating and road safety.

▽ The purpose and content of a marketing plan

A marketing plan has a more limited scope than a business plan which offers a broad overview of the entire organisation's vision, mission, objectives, strategy, and resource allocation. The marketing plan documents how the organisation's strategic objectives will be achieved through specific marketing strategies and tactics, with the customer as the starting point. It is also linked to the plans of other organisational departments. Suppose a marketing plan calls for selling 200,000 units annually. The production department must gear up to make that many units, finance must arrange funding to cover the expenses, human resources must be ready to hire and train staff, and so on. Without the appropriate level of organisational support and resources, no marketing plan can succeed.

Although the exact length and layout varies from company to company, a marketing plan usually adopts a similar approach to that described in Chapter 3 and Chapter 21. Smaller businesses may create shorter or less formal marketing plans, whereas corporations require highly structured marketing plans. To guide implementation effectively, every part of the plan must be described in considerable detail. Sometimes a company will post its marketing plan on an internal website so managers and employees in different locations can consult specific sections and collaborate on additions or changes.

▽ The role of research

To develop innovative products, successful strategies, and action programmes, marketers need up-to-date information about the environment, the competition, and the selected market segments. Often, analysis of internal data is the starting point for

Figure A.1

assessing the current marketing situation, supplemented by marketing intelligence and research investigating the overall market, customers, the competition, cost and revenue implications, channel matters and company strategic issues. As the plan is implemented, marketers use research to monitor developments in their markets; to measure objectives and to identify areas for improvement if results fall short of expectations.

Finally, marketing research helps marketers learn more about their customers' requirements, expectations, perceptions, satisfaction, and loyalty. This deeper understanding provides a foundation for building competitive advantage through well-informed segmenting, targeting, and positioning decisions. Thus, the marketing plan should outline what marketing research will be conducted and when, as well as how the findings will be applied.

▽ The role of relationships

Although the marketing plan shows how the company will establish and maintain profitable customer relationships, it also affects both internal and external relationships. First, it influences how marketing personnel work with each other and with other departments to deliver value and satisfy customers. Second, it affects how the company works with suppliers, distributors and partners to achieve the plan's objectives. Third, it influences the company's dealings with other stakeholders, including government regulators, the media, and the community at large. All these relationships are important to the organisation's success and must be considered when developing a marketing plan.

▽ From marketing plan to marketing action

Most companies create yearly marketing plans, although some plans cover a longer period. Marketers start planning well in advance of the implementation date to allow time for marketing research, analysis, management review, and coordination between departments. Then, after each action programme begins, marketers monitor ongoing results, investigate any deviation from the projected outcome, and take corrective steps as needed. Some marketers also prepare contingency plans for implementation if certain conditions emerge. Because of inevitable and sometimes unpredictable environmental changes, marketers must be ready to update and adapt marketing plans at any time.

For effective implementation and control, the marketing plan should define how progress towards objectives will be measured. Managers typically use budget, schedules and marketing metrics for monitoring and evaluating results. With budgets, they can compare planned expenditures with actual expenditures for a given period. Schedules allow management to see when tasks were supposed to be completed and when they were actually completed. Marketing metrics track the actual outcomes of marketing programmes to see whether the company is moving forward towards its objectives.

▽ Sample marketing plan for Digitel

This section takes you inside the sample marketing plan for Digitel, a hypothetical start-up company. The company's first product is the Digitel 1000, a multimedia, cellular/Wi-Fi-enabled personal digital assistant (PDA), also known as a handheld computer. Digitel will be competing with Palm, Hewlett-Packard, Motorola, Apple, and other well-established rivals in a crowded, fast-changing marketplace where smart phones and many other electronic devices have PDA functionality as well as entertainment capabilities. The annotations explain more about what each section of the plan should contain.

1. Executive summary

This section summarises market opportunities, marketing strategy, and marketing and financial objectives for senior managers who will read and approve the marketing plan.

Digitel is preparing to launch a new multimedia, dual-mode PDA product, the Digitel 1000, in a mature market. We can compete with both PDAs and smart phones because our product offers a unique combination of advanced features and functionality at a value-added price. We are targeting specific segments in the consumer and business markets, taking advantage of the growing interest in a single device with communication, organisation, and entertainment benefits.

The primary marketing objective is to achieve a first year European market share of 3 per cent with unit sales of 240,000. The primary financial objectives are to achieve first-year sales revenues of €60 million, keep first-year losses to less than €10 million, and break-even early in the second year.

2. Situation analysis

The situation analysis describes the market, the company's capability to serve targeted segments, and the competition.

Digitel, founded 18 months ago by two entrepreneurs with telecommunications experience, is about to enter the now mature PDA market. Multifunction cell phones, email devices and wireless communication devices are increasingly popular for both personal and professional use, with more than 5 million PDAs and 22 million smart phones sold worldwide each year. Competition is increasingly intense even as technology evolves, industry consolidation continues, and pricing pressures squeeze profitability. Palm, a PDA pioneer, is one of several key players having difficulty adapting to the smart-phone challenge. To gain market share in this dynamic environment, Digitel must carefully target specific segments with valued features and plan for a next-generation product to keep brand momentum going.

2.1 Market summary Market summary includes size, needs, growth and trends. Describing the targeted segments in detail provides context for marketing strategies and programmes discussed later in the plan.

Digitel's market consists of customers and business users who prefer to use a single device for communication, information storage and exchange, organisation, and entertainment on the go. Specific segments being targeted during the first year include professionals, corporations, students, entrepreneurs, and medical users. Table A.1 shows how the Digitel 1000 addresses the needs of targeted customers and business segments.

Table A.1 Needs and corresponding features/benefits of Digitel PDA

Targeted segment	Customer need	Corresponding feature/benefit
Professionals	Stay in touch while on the go	Wireless email to conveniently send and receive messages from anywhere; cell phone capability for voice communication from anywhere
	Record information while on the go	Voice recognition for no-hands recording
Students	Perform many functions without carrying multiple gadgets	Compatible with numerous applications and peripherals for convenient, cost-effective functionality
	Express style and individuality	Case wardrobe of different colours and patterns allows users to make a fashion statement
Corporate users	Input and access critical data on the move	Compatible with widely available software
	Use for proprietary tasks	Customisable to fit diverse corporate tasks and networks
Entrepreneurs	Organise and access contacts, schedule details	No-hands, wireless access to calendar and address book to easily check appointments and connect with contacts
Medical users	Update, access and exchange medical records	No-hands, wireless recording and exchange of information to reduce paperwork and increase productivity

PDA purchasers can choose between models based on several different operating systems, including systems from Palm, Microsoft, and Symbian, plus Linux variations. Digitel licenses a Linux-based system because it is somewhat less vulnerable to attack by hackers and viruses. Storage capacity (hard drive or flash drive) is an expected feature for PDAs, so Digitel is equipping its first product with an ultra-fast 20-gigabyte drive that can be supplemented by extra storage. Technology costs are decreasing even as capabilities are increasing, which makes value-priced models more appealing to private customers and to business users with older PDAs who want to trade up to new, high-end multifunction units.

2.2 Strengths, weaknesses, opportunities and threat analysis Digitel has several powerful strengths on which to build, but our major weakness is lack of brand awareness and image. The major opportunity is demand for multifunction communication, organisation, and entertainment devices that deliver a number of valued benefits. We also face the threat of ever-higher competition and downward pricing pressure.

Strengths

Strengths are internal capabilities that can help the company reach its objectives. Digitel can build on three important strengths:

1 **Innovative product**: The Digitel 1000 offers a combination of features that would otherwise require customers to carry multiple devices, such as speedy, hands-free dual-mode cell/Wi-Fi telecommunications capabilities, and digital video/music/TV programme storage/playback.

2 **Security**: Our PDA uses a Linux-based operating system that is less vulnerable to hackers and other security threats that can result in stolen or corrupted data.

3 **Pricing**: Our product is priced lower than competing multifunction PDAs – none of which offer the same bundle of features – which gives us an edge with price-conscious customers.

Weaknesses

Weaknesses are internal elements that may interfere with the company's ability to achieve its objectives. By waiting to enter the PDA market until considerable consolidation of competitors has occurred, Digitel has learned from the successes and mistakes of others. Nonetheless, we have two main weaknesses:

1 **Lack of brand awareness**: Digitel has no established brand or image, whereas Palm, Apple, and others have strong brand recognition. We will address this issue with a professional marketing communications plan.

2 **Heavier and thicker unit**: The Digitel 1000 is slightly heavier and thicker than most competing models because it incorporates many multimedia features and offers far more storage capacity than the average PDA. To counteract this weakness, we will emphasise our product's benefits and value-added pricing, two compelling competitive strengths.

Opportunities

Opportunities are areas of buyer need or potential interest in which the company might perform profitably. Digitel can take advantage of two major opportunities:

1 **Increasing demand for multimedia devices with communication functions**: The market for multimedia, multifunction devices is growing much faster than the market for single-use devices. Growth is accelerating as dual-mode capabilities become mainstream, giving customers the flexibility to make phone calls over mobile phone or Internet connections. PDAs and smart phones are already commonplace in public, work, and educational settings; in fact, users who bought entry-level models are now trading up.

2 **Lower technology costs**: Better technology is now available at a lower cost than ever before. Thus, Digitel can incorporate advanced features at a value-added price that allows for reasonable profits.

Threats

Threats are challenges posed by an unfavourable trend or development that could lead to lower sales and profits. We face three main threats at the introduction of the Digitel 1000:

1 **Increased competition**: More companies are offering devices with some but not all of the features and benefits provided by the Digitel 1000 PDA. Therefore, Digitel's marketing communications must stress our clear differentiation and value-added pricing.

2 **Downward pressure on pricing**: Increased competition and market share strategies are pushing PDA prices down. Still, our objective of seeking a 10 per cent profit on second-year sales of the original model is realistic, given the lower margins in the PDA market.

3 **Compressed product life-cycle**: PDAs have reached the maturity stage of their life-cycle more quickly than earlier technology products. Because of this compressed life-cycle, we plan to introduce a media-oriented second product during the year following the Digitel 1000's launch.

2.3 Competition This section identifies key competitors, describes their market positions, and provides an overview of their strategies.

The emergence of new multifunction smart phones, including the Apple iPhone, has increased competitive pressure. Dell has already left the PDA market; the remaining competitors are continually adding features and sharpening price points. Competition from specialised devices for text and email messaging, such as Blackberry devices, is another major factor. Key competitors:

Palm: As the PDA market leader, with 34 per cent share, Palm has excellent distribution in multiple channels and alliances with a number of European telecommunications carriers. However, Palm's smart-phone share is well below that of Nokia and other handset marketers. Palm products use either the proprietary Palm operating system or Windows.

Hewlett-Packard: HP holds 22 per cent of the PDA market and targets business segments with its numerous iPAQ Pocket PC devices. Some of its PDAs can send documents to Bluetooth-equipped printers and prevent data loss if batteries run down. For extra security, one model allows access by fingerprint match as well as by password. HP enjoys widespread distribution and offers a full line of PDAs at various price points.

Motorola: Motorola sold 100 million of its RAZR clamshell phones worldwide in three years and now offers the RAZR2, smaller and lighter than earlier models and with two operating system options. The Motorola Q targets professionals and business users with PDA and email functions, a tiny keyboard, Bluetooth connections, multimedia capabilities, and more.

Apple: The iPhone, a smart phone with a 3.5 inch colour screen, has been designed with entertainment enthusiasts in mind. It's well equipped for music, video, and Web access, plus calendar and contact management functions. Apple initially partnered in the UK with O_2.

Samsung: Value, style, function: Samsung is a powerful competitor, offering a variety of smart phones and Ultra mobile PCs for consumer and business segments. Some of its smart phones are available for specific telecommunications carriers and some are 'unblocked', ready for any compatible telecommunications network.

Despite strong competition, Digitel can serve out a definite image and gain recognition among targeted segments. Our voice-recognition system for hands-off operation is a critical point of differentiation for competitive advantage. Our second product will have PDA functions but will be more media-oriented to appeal to segments where we will have strong brand recognition. Table A.2 shows a sample of competitive products and process.

Table A.2 Selected PDA products and pricing

Competitor	Model	Features	Price
PalmOne	Tungsten C	PDA functions, wireless capabilities, colour screen, tiny keyboard, wireless capabilities	€499
PalmOne	M 130	PDA functions, colour screen, expandable functionality	€199
Handspring	Treo 270	PDA and cell phone functions, colour screen, tiny keyboard, speakerphone capabilities; no expansion slot	€499
Samsung	i500	PDA functions, cell phone functions, mp3 player, colour screen, video capabilities	€599
Dell	Axim X5	PDA functions, colour screen, email, voice recorder, speaker, expandable	€199
Sony	Clie PEG-NX73V	PDA functions, digital camera, tiny keyboard, games, presentation software, MP3 player, voice recorder	€499

2.4 Product offerings This section summarises the main features of the company's various products. The Digitel 1000 offers the following standard features:

- voice recognition for hands-free operation;
- organisation functions, including calendar, address book, synchronisation;
- built-in dual cell phone/Internet phone and instant calling facility;
- digital music/video/television recording, wireless downloading, and instant playback;
- wireless Web and email, text messaging, instant messaging;
- three-inch colour screen;
- ultra-fast 20-gigabyte drive and expansion slots;
- four megapixel camera with flash and photo editing/sharing tools.

First-year sales revenues are projected to be €60 million, based on sales of 240,000 of the Digitel 1000 model at a wholesale price of €250 each. Our second-year product will be the Digitel All Media 2000, stressing multimedia communication, networking, and entertainment functions with PDA capabilities as secondary features. The Digitel All Media 2000 will include Digitel 1000 features plus:

- built-in media beaming to share music, video, television files with other devices;
- web cam for instant capture and uploading to popular video websites;
- voice-command access to popular social networking websites;
- integrated eight megapixel camera, flash, and photo editing/sharing tools.

2.5 Distribution Distribution explains each channel for the company's products and mentions new developments and trends.

Digitel-branded products will be distributed through a network of retailers in the top European markets. Among the most important channel partners being contacted are:

- office supply superstores;
- computer stores;
- electronics specialty stores;
- online retailers.

3. Marketing strategy

3.1 Objectives Objectives should be defined in specific terms so management can measure progress and take corrective action to stay on track.

We have set aggressive but achievable objectives for the first and second years of market entry.

First-year objectives: We are aiming for a 3 per cent share of the European PDA market through a unit sales volume of 240,000

Second-year objectives: Our second-year objective is to achieve break-even on the Digitel 1000 and launch our second model.

3.2 Target markets All marketing strategies start with segmentation, targeting and positioning. Digitel's strategy is based on a positioning of product differentiation. Our primary customer target for the Digitel 1000 is middle-to upper-income professionals who need one device to co-ordinate their busy schedule, stay in touch with family and colleagues, and be entertained on the go. Our secondary customer target is senior school pupils and undergraduate and post graduate university students who want a multimedia, dual-mode device. This segment can be described demographically by age (16-39) and education status. Our Digitel All Media 2000 will be aimed at teens and twenty-somethings who want a device with features to support social networking and heavier entertainment media consumption.

The primary business target for the Digitel 1000 is mid- to large-sized companies that want to help their managers and employees stay in touch and input or access critical data when away from work. This segment consist of companies with more than €25 million annual sales and more than 100 employees. A secondary target is entrepreneurs and small business owners. Also we will target medical users who want to update or access patients' medical records.

Each of the marketing-mix strategies conveys Digitel's differentiation to these target market segments.

3.3 Positioning Positioning strategy includes decisions about setting initial prices in response to opportunities and competitive challenges.

Using product differentiation, we are positioning the Digitel PDA as the most versatile, convenient, value-added model for personal and professional use. Our marketing will focus on the hands-free operation of multiple communication use, entertainment, and information capabilities differentiating the Digitel 1000.

3.4 Strategies

Product

Product strategy includes decisions about product mix, lines, brands, packaging, labelling and warranties.

The Digitel 1000, including all the features described in the earlier Product Review section, will be sold with a one-year warranty. We will introduce the Digitel All Media 2000 during the following year, after we have established our Digitel brand. The brand and logo (Digitel's distinctive lightening streak) will be displayed on our products and packaging as well as in all marketing campaigns.

Pricing

Pricing strategy covers decisions about setting initial prices and adapting processes in response to opportunities and competitive challenges.

The Digitel 1000 will be introduced at €250 wholesale/€350 estimated retail price per unit. We expect to lower the price of this model when we expand the product line by launching the Digitel All Media 2000, to be priced at €350 wholesale per unit. These prices reflect strategy of (1) attracting desirable channel partners and (2) taking market share from established competitors.

Distribution

Distribution strategy includes selection and management of channel relationships to deliver value to customers.

Our distribution strategy is to be selective, marketing Digitel PDAs through well-known stores and online retailers. During the first year, we will add distribution partners until we have a coverage in all major European markets and the product is featured in the major electronics catalogues and websites. We will also investigate distribution through call-phone outlets maintained by major carriers. In support of distribution partners, we will provide demonstration products, detailed specification handouts, and full-colour photographs and displays featuring the product. Finally, we plan to arrange special payment terms for retailers that place volume orders.

Marketing communications

Marketing communication strategy covers all efforts to communicate to target audiences and channel members.

By integrating all messages in all media, we will reinforce the brand name and the main points of product differentiation. Research about media consumption patterns will help our advertising agency choose appropriate media and timing to reach prospects before and during product introduction. Thereafter, advertising will appear on a pulsing basis to maintain brand awareness and communicate various differentiation messages. The agency will also coordinate public relations efforts to build the Digitel brand and support the differentiation message. To generate buzz, we will host a user-generated video contest on our website. To attract, retain, and motivate channel partners for a push strategy, we will use trade sales promotions and personal selling. Until the Digitel brand has been established, our communications will encourage purchases through channel partners rather than from our website.

3.5 Marketing mix The Digitel 1000 will be introduced in February. Here are summaries of action programmes we will use during the first six months to achieve our stated objectives.

January

We will launch a €200,000 trade sales promotion campaign and participate in major industry trade shows to educate dealers and generate distribution support for the product launch in February. Also, we will create buzz by providing samples to selected product reviewers, opinion leaders, influential bloggers, and celebrities. Our training staff will work with retail sales personnel at major chains to explain the Digitel 1000's features, benefits and advantages.

February

We will start an integrated print/radio/Internet campaign targeting professionals and private users. The campaign will show how many functions the Digitel PDA can perform and emphasise the convenience of a single, powerful handheld device. This multimedia campaign will be supported by point-of-sale signage as well as online-only advertisements and video tours.

March

As the multimedia advertising campaign continues, we will add private user sales promotions such as a contest in which users post videos on our website, showing how they use the Digitel in creative and unusual ways. We will also distribute new point-of-purchase displays to support our retailers.

April

We will hold a trade sales contest offering prizes for the salesperson and retail organisation that sells the most Digitel PDAs during the four week period.

May

We plan to roll out a new national advertising campaign this month. The radio advertisements will feature celebrity voices telling their Digitel PDAs to perform functions such as initiating a phone call, sending an email, playing a song or video, and so on. The stylised print and online advertisements will feature these celebrities holding their Digitel PDAs. We plan to reprise this theme for next year's product launch.

June

Our radio campaign will add a new voice-over tag line promoting the Digitel 1000 as a graduation gift. We will provide retailers with new competitive comparison handouts as a sales aid. In addition, we will analyse the results of customer satisfaction research for use in future campaigns and product development efforts.

3.6 Marketing research This section shows how marketing research will support the development, implementation and evaluation of marketing strategies and programmes.

Using research, we will identify specific features and benefits our target market segments value. Feedback from market tests, surveys and focus groups will help us develop and fine-tune the Digitel All Media 2000. We are also measuring and analysing customers' attitudes toward competing brands and products. Brand awareness research will help us determine the effectiveness and efficiency of our messages and media. Finally, we will use customer satisfaction studies to gauge market reaction.

4. Financial matters

These include budgets and forecasts to plan for marketing expenditure, scheduling and operations.

Total first-year sales revenue for the Digitel 1000 is projected at €60 million, with an average wholesale price of €250 per unit and variable cost per unit of €150 for unit sales volume of 240,000. We anticipate a first-year loss of up to €10 million. Break-even calculations indicate that the Digitel will become profitable after the sales volume exceeds 267,500

Figure A.2 Digitel's marketing department

during the product's second year. Our break-even analysis assumes per-unit wholesale revenue of €250 per unit, variable cost of €150 per unit, and estimated first-year fixed costs of €26,750,000.

5. Controls

Controls help management measure results and identify any problems or performance variations that need corrective action.

Controls are being established to cover implementation and the organisation of our marketing activities.

5.1 Implementation We are planning tight control measures to closely monitor quality and customer service satisfaction. This will enable us to react very quickly in correcting any problems that may occur. Other early warning signals that will be monitored for signs of deviation from the plan include monthly sales (by segment and distribution outlet) and monthly expenses.

5.2 Marketing organisation The marketing department may be organised by function, as in this sample, or by geography, product, customer, or some combination of these.

Digitel's marketing director, Jill Gilbey, holds overall responsibility for all of the company's marketing activities. Figure A.2 shows the structure of the seven person marketing department. Digitel has retained the Global Marketing agency to handle sales campaigns, trade and customer sales promotions and public relations activity.

▽ Sample marketing plan chapter assignments

Chapter 3

As assistant to Jill Gilbey, Digitel's marketing director, you've been assigned to draft a mission statement for top management's review. This should cover the competitive spheres within which the firm will operate and your recommendation of an appropriate generic competitive strategy. Using your knowledge of marketing and the information you have about Digitel, answer the following questions.

- What should Digitel's mission be?
- In what markets (consumer and business) should Digitel operate?
- Which of Porter's generic competitive strategies would you recommend Digitel follow in formulating overall strategy?

As your instructor directs, enter your answers and supporting information in a written marketing plan. Follow the format given at the end of Chapter 3 or at the beginning of this Appendix.

Chapter 4

Your next task will require you to consult Nina Van Piercy, the Market Research Manager, Abi Jeffrey, the Advertising Manager and David Henry, the Promotion Manager. Jill has asked you to draft a memo to report on how Digitel could best use information communication technology (ICT) in their market research and marketing communications. She has asked you to address the following questions.

- How can Digitel best use ICT in its market research activity?
- How might Digitel use ICT to gain a competitive advantage in advertising activity?
- How can Digitel use ICT to boost its promotional activities?

Chapter 5

Jill Gilbey asks you to scan Digitel's external environment for early warning signals of new opportunities and emerging threats that could affect the success of the Digitel 1000 PDA.

Using the Internet or library sources, locate information to answer these questions about key areas of the macroenvironment.

- What demographic changes are likely to affect Digitel's targeted segments?
- What economic trends might influence buyer behaviour in Digitel's targeted segments?
- How might the rapid pace of technological change alter Digitel's competitive position?

Enter your answers about Digitel's environment in the appropriate sections of a written marketing plan.

Chapter 6

Your next task is to consider how marketing research can help Digitel support its marketing strategy. Jill Gilbey also asks you how Digitel can measure results after the marketing plan is implemented. She wants you to answer the following three questions.

- What surveys, focus groups, observation, behavioural data, or experiments will Digitel need to support its marketing strategy? Be specific about the questions or issues that Digitel needs to resolve using market research.
- Where can you find suitable secondary data about total demand for PDAs over the next two years? Identify at least two sources (online or offline), describe what you plan to draw from each source, and indicate how the data would be useful for Digitel's marketing planning.
- Recommend three specific marketing metrics for Digitel to apply in determining marketing effectiveness and efficiency.

Enter this information in the marketing plan you've been writing.

Chapter 7

You are responsible for researching and analysing the consumer market for Digitel's PDA product. Look again at the data you have already entered about the company's current situation and macroenvironment, especially the markets being targeted. Now answer these questions about the market and buyer behaviour.

- What cultural, social and personal factors are likely to most influence customer purchasing of PDAs? What research tools would help you better understand the effect on buyer attitudes and behaviour?
- Which aspects of customer behaviour should Digitel's marketing plan emphasise and why?
- What marketing activities should Digitel plan to coincide with each stage of the customer buying process?

After you have analysed these aspects of consumer behaviour, consider the implications for Digitel's marketing efforts to support the launch of its PDA. Finally, document your findings and conclusions in your written marketing plan.

Chapter 8

You have been learning more about the business market for Digetel's PDA. Jill Gilbey has defined this market as mid- to large-sized corporations that want their employees to stay in touch and be able to input or access data from any location. Respond to the following three questions based on your knowledge of Digitel's current situation and business-to-business marketing.

- What types of businesses appear to fit Gilbey's market definition? How can you research the number of employees and find other data about these types of businesses?
- What type of purchase would a Digitel PDA represent for these businesses? Who would participate in and influence this type of purchase?
- Would demand for PDAs among corporate buyers tend to be inelastic? What are the implications for Digitel's marketing plan?

Your answers to these questions will affect how Digitel plans marketing activities for the business segments to be targeted. Take a few minutes to note your ideas in a written marketing plan.

Chapter 9

Digitel is a new entrant in an established industry characterised by competitors with relatively high brand identity and strong market positions. Use research and your knowledge of how to deal with competitors to consider three issues that will affect the company's ability to introduce its first product successfully:

- What factors will you use to determine Digitel's strategic group?
- Should Digitel select a class of competitor to attack on the basis of strength versus weakness, closeness versus distance, or good versus bad? Why is this appropriate in the PDA market?
- As a start-up company, what competitive strategy would be most effective as Digitel introduces its first product?

Take time to analyse how Digitel's competitive strategy will affect its marketing strategy and tactics. Now summarise your ideas in a written marketing plan.

Chapter 10

Identifying suitable market segments and selecting targets are critical to the success of any marketing plan. As Jill Gilbey's assistant, you are responsible for market segmentation and targeting. Study the market information, buyer behaviour data, and competitive details and answer the following questions.

- Which variables should Digitel use to segment its consumer and business markets?
- How can Digitel evaluate the attractiveness of each identified segment? Should Digitel market to one consumer customer segment and one business consumer segment or target more than one in each market? Why?
- Should Digitel pursue full market coverage, market specialisation, product specialisation, selective specialisation, or single-segment concentration? Why?

Next consider how your decisions about segmentation and targeting will affect Digitel's marketing efforts. Depending on your instructor's directions summarise your conclusions in a written marketing plan.

Chapter 11

Digitel has decided to focus on total customer satisfaction as a way of encouraging brand loyalty in a highly competitive marketplace. With this in mind, you have been assigned to analyse three specific issues as you continue working on Digitel's marketing plan.

- How (and how often) should Digitel monitor customer satisfaction?
- To which customer touch points should Digitel pay particularly close attention, and why?

Consider your answers in the context of Digitel's current situation and the objectives it has set. Then enter your latest decisions in the written marketing plan.

Chapter 12

Digitel is a new brand with no prior brand associations, which presents a number of marketing opportunities and challenges. Jill Gilbey has given you responsibility for making recommendations about three brand equity issues that are important to Digitel's marketing plan.

- What brand elements would be most useful for differentiating the Digitel brand from competing brands?
- How can Digitel sum up its brand promise for the new PDA?
- Should Digitel add a brand for its second product or retain the Digitel name?

Be sure that your brand ideas are appropriate in the light of what you have learned about your targeted segments and the competition. Then add this information to your written marketing plan.

Chapter 13

As before, you are working with Jill Gilbey on Digitel's marketing plan for launching a new PDA. Now you are focusing on Digitel's positioning and product life-cycle strategies by answering three specific questions.

- In a sentence or two, what is an appropriate positioning statement for the Digitel 1000 PDA?
- Knowing the stage of Digitel's PDA in the product life-cycle, what are the implications for pricing, promotion, and distribution?
- In which stage of its evolution does the PDA market appear to be? What does this mean for Digitel's marketing plans?

Document your ideas in a written marketing plan. Note any additional research you may need to determine how to proceed after the Digitel 1000 has been launched.

Chapter 14

Introducing a new product entails a variety of decisions about product strategy, including differentiation, ingredient branding, packaging, labelling, warranty and guarantee. Your next task is to answer the following questions about Digitel's product strategy.

- Which aspect of product differentiation would be most valuable in setting Digitel apart from competitors, and why?
- Should Digitel use ingredient branding to tout the Linux-based operating system that it says makes its PDA more secure than PDAs based on some other operating systems?
- How can Digitel use packaging and labelling to support its brand image and help its channel partners sell the PDA product more effectively?

Once you have answered these questions, incorporate your idea into the marketing plan you have been writing.

Chapter 15

Knowing that the PDA market is not growing as quickly as the market for multimedia, multifunction communication devices, Jill Gilbey wants you to look ahead at how Digitel can develop new products outside the PDA market. Review the competitive situation and the market situation before you continue working on the Digitel marketing plan.

- List three new-product ideas that build Digitel's strengths and the needs of its various target segments. What criteria should Digitel use to screen these ideas?
- Develop the most promising idea into a product concept and explain how Digitel can test this concept. What particular dimensions must be tested?

- Assume that the most promising idea tests well. Now develop a marketing strategy for introducing it, including: a description of the target market; the product positioning; the marketing budget you will recommend for this new product introduction. If possible, estimate Digitel's costs and conduct a break-even analysis.

Document all the details of your new-product development ideas in the written marketing plan.

Chapter 16

You are in charge of pricing Digitel's product for its launch early next year. Review its strengths and weaknesses. Check on Digitel's competitive environment, targeting strategy and product positioning. Now continue working on your marketing plan by responding to the following questions.

- What should Digitel's primary pricing objective be? Explain your reasoning.
- Are PDA customers likely to be price sensitive? What are the implications for your pricing decisions?
- What price adaptations (such as discounts, allowances and promotional pricing) should Digitel include in its marketing plan?

Make notes about your answers to these questions and then document the information in a written plan.

Chapter 17

The next task you have been asked to tackle is to develop a suitable distribution channel model for the new Digitel 1000 PDA. On the basis of your knowledge of integrated distribution networks answer these questions.

- Jill Gilbey has intimated that she wants to move to an integrated demand driven network. Do you think that this would be wise? Explain your reasoning.
- The selection of distribution channel members should support each part of the value network (chain). How do you think Digitel can avoid conflicts in their selected distribution network?
- What technologies should be considered for the launch of the Digitel 1000 PDA?

Check that your distribution channel ideas support the product positioning and are consistent with the goals that Digitel have set. Record your responses in a written marketing plan.

Chapter 18

Imagine that you have been asked to plan the customer support services for Digitel's new PDA. Review what you know about your target market and its needs; also think about what Digitel's competitors are offering. Then respond to the questions about designing and managing a suitable services support.

- What service process design blueprint will customers need in support of the launch of Digitel's new PDA?
- How should Digitel manage staff and customers to support the service process?
- What role should technology play in the development and functioning of a successful service environment?

Think through how your service process design will support Digitel's overall marketing activity. Summarise you recommendations in a written marketing plan.

Chapter 19

Jill Gilbey has asked you to liaise with Abi Jeffrey, the Advertising Manager and David Henry, the Promotion Manager to formulate an integrated marketing communications plan for

Digitel's new PDA. Review your written marketing plan so far before you answer the following questions.

- What communications objectives are required for Digitel's new PDA launch?
- How can Digitel use the eight major modes of the communications mix to best advantage?
- Which communication tools would you use to boost sales of the Digitel 1000 PDA six months after launch?

Check that your marketing communications plans are consistent with Digitel's overall marketing activities and record your work in a written marketing plan.

Chapter 20

The art/science of marketing communications lies in the subtle integration of affordable mass and personal communications vehicles. Jill Gilbey now wants you to further develop your communications mix ideas in detail with Abi Jeffrey and David Henry and to discuss them with Hans Larson, the Sales Manager. Then respond to the following questions to continue the process of developing Digitel's final marketing communications plan.

- What is the best way to thematically integrate Digitel's advertising and sales promotion activities?
- How can Digitel's exploit direct marketing and digital marketing activities such as viral marketing, mobile phone advertising and interactive TV advertising to boost sales?
- What decisions will need to be taken to ensure that the sales force is informed and managed effectively?

Document your ideas in your written marketing plan.

Chapter 21

As Jill Gilbey's assistant with the complete marketing plan now in place, you are now required to make recommendations as to how Digitel's marketing activities can be effectively and efficiently managed.

- What are the key trends in marketing practice? How should social responsibility feature in Digitel's marketing operations?
- How can Digitel build a creative marketing organisation to develop and sustain its reputation for developing and delivering highly valued offerings to its target customers?
- What general tools are available to help Digitel monitor and improve its marketing activities?

Chapter 22

Now that you have been a member of the Digitel marketing team and drafted an integrated marketing plan Jill Gilbey has invited you to a meeting of her department to discuss how the company can measure its performance as the plan is implemented. In addition to adopting a set of sales targets Jill has reminded you that it is vitally important to apply metrics to the cost side of the business. Before she finally drafts the agenda for the departmental meeting Jill has asked you to respond to the following questions.

- What do you understand by the term 'marketing metrics'?
- What are the key dimensions of marketing metrics?
- How can qualitative and quantitative factors be balanced to produce a sound marketing dashboard for Digitel?

To finish your work convey your responses to Jill and draft an executive summary of the plan's highlights to take to the meeting.

Glossary

A

activity-based cost (ABC) accounting procedures that can quantify the true profitability of different activities by identifying their actual costs.

administered VMS coordinates successive stages of production and distribution through the size and power of one of the members.

adoption an individual's decision to become a regular user of a product or service.

advertising any paid form of non-personal presentation and promotion of ideas, goods, or services by an identified sponsor.

advertising goal (or advertising objective) is a communication targeted at a pre-selected audience at a specific time to stimulate increased sales.

advertorials print advertisements that offer editorial content reflecting favourably on the brand and are difficult to distinguish from newspaper or magazine content.

anchoring and adjustment heuristic when consumers arrive at an initial judgement and then make adjustments of their first impressions based on additional information.

arm's-length pricing the price charged by other competitors for the same or a similar product or service.

aspirational groups groups a person hopes or would like to join.

associative network memory model a conceptual representation that views memory as consisting of a set of nodes and interconnecting links where nodes represent stored information or concepts and links represent the strength of association between this information or concepts.

attitude a person's enduring favourable or unfavourable evaluation, emotional feeling, and action tendencies towards some object or idea.

augmented product a product that includes features that go beyond consumer expectations and differentiate the product from competitors.

availability heuristic when consumers base their predictions on the quickness and ease with which a particular example of an outcome comes to mind.

available market the set of consumers who have interest, income, and access to a particular offer.

average cost the cost per unit at a given level of production; it is equal to total costs divided by production.

B

backward invention reintroducing earlier product forms that can be well adapted to a foreign country's needs.

banner ads (Internet) small, rectangular boxes containing text and perhaps a picture to support a brand.

banner advertisements see display advertisements.

basic product what specifically the actual product is.

behaviour skills how people interact with others. For example are they good at helping others and deciding that others might need help.

belief a descriptive thought that a person holds about something.

brand a name, term, sign, symbol, or design, or a combination of them, intended to identify the goods or services of one companie or group of companies and to differentiate them from those of competitors. To learn more about **corporate branding**, go to www.pearsoned.co.uk/marketingmanagementeurope for additional commentary from the authors.

brand-asset management team (BAMT) consists of key representatives from functions that affect the brand's performance.

brand associations all brand-related thoughts, feelings, perceptions, images, experiences, beliefs, attitudes, and so on that become linked to the brand node.

brand audit a consumer-focused exercise that involves a series of procedures to assess the health of the brand, uncover its sources of brand equity, and suggest ways to improve and leverage its equity.

brand awareness consumers' ability to identify the brand under different conditions, as reflected by their brand recognition or recall performance.

brand contact any information-bearing experience a customer or prospect has with the brand, the product category, or the market that relates to the marketer's product or service.

brand culture is the values and beliefs that people have about a brand in their hearts and minds.

brand development index (BDI) the index of brand sales to category sales.

brand dilution when consumers no longer associate a brand with a specific product or highly similar products or start thinking less favourably about the brand.

branded entertainment using sports, music, arts, or other entertainment activities to build brand equity.

branded variants specific brand lines uniquely supplied to different retailers or distribution channels.

brand elements those trademarkable devices that serve to identify and differentiate the brand such as a brand name, logo, or character.

brand equity the added value endowed to products and services.

brand extension a company's use of an established brand to introduce a new product or service.

brand image the perceptions and beliefs held by consumers, as reflected in the associations held in consumer memory.

branding endowing products and services with the power of a brand.

branding strategy the number and nature of common and distinctive brand elements and marketing programme applied to the different products and services sold by the firm.

brand knowledge all the thoughts, feelings, images, experiences, beliefs, and so on that become associated with the brand.

brand line all products, original as well as line and category extensions, sold under a particular brand name.

brand mix the set of all brand lines that a particular company makes available to buyers.

brand personality the specific mix of human traits that may be attributed to a particular brand.

brand portfolio the set of all brands and brand lines a particular company offers for sale to buyers in a particular category.

brand promise the marketer's vision of what the brand must be and do for consumers.

brand valuation an estimate of the total financial value of the brand.

brand value chain a structured approach to assessing the sources and outcomes of brand equity and the manner in which marketing activities create brand value.

breakeven analysis a means by which management estimates how many units of the product the company would have to sell to break even with the given price and cost structure.

brick-and-click existing companies that have added an online site for information and/or e-commerce.

business database complete information about business customers' past purchases; past volumes, prices, and profits.

business market all the organisations that acquire goods and services used in the production of other products or services that are sold, rented, or supplied to others. To learn more about **business markets**, go to www.pearsoned.co.uk/marketingmanagementeurope for additional commentary from the authors.

C

capital items long-lasting goods that facilitate developing or managing the finished product.

captive products products that are necessary to the use of other products, such as razor blades or film.

category extension Using the parent brand to brand a new product or service outside the product category currently served by the parent brand.

category membership the products or sets of products with which a brand competes and which function as close substitutes.

cause-related marketing marketing that links a firm's contributions to a designated cause to customers' engaging directly or indirectly in revenue-producing transactions with the firm.

channel advantage when a company successfully switches its customers to lower-cost channels, while assuming no loss of sales or deterioration in service quality.

channel conflict when one channel member's actions prevent the channel from achieving its goal.

channel coordination when channel members are brought together to advance the goals of the channel, as opposed to their own potentially incompatible goals.

channel power the ability to alter channel members' behaviour so that they take actions they would not have taken otherwise.

club membership programme a tool used by to attract and retain customers and to build long-term brand loyalty for their products or services.

clustered preferences result when natural market segments emerge from groups of customers with shared preferences.

co-branding also called dual branding or brand bundling, two or more well-known brands are combined into a joint market offering or marketed together in some fashion.

co-creation an open, ongoing collaboration between a company and their customers to define and create products, services, experiences, ideas and information together.

cohorts groups of individuals who are born during the same time period and travel through life together.

communication adaptation changing marketing communications programmes for each local market.

communication-effect research determining whether an ad is communicating effectively.

company demand the company's estimated share of market demand at alternative levels of company marketing effort in a given time period.

company sales forecast the expected level of company sales based on a chosen marketing plan and an assumed marketing environment.

company sales potential the sales limit approached by company demand as company marketing effort increases relative to that of competitors.

competitive advantage is a company's ability to perform in one or more ways that competitors cannot or will not match.

conformance quality the degree to which all the produced units are identical and meet the promised specifications.

conjoint analysis a method for deriving the utility values that consumers attach to varying levels of a product's attributes.

conjunctive heuristic the consumer sets a minimum acceptable cutoff level for each attribute and chooses the first alternative that meets the minimum standard for all attributes.

consumer behaviour the study of how individuals or groups buy, use, and dispose of goods, services, ideas, or experiences to satisfy their needs and wants.

consumer involvement the level of engagement and active processing undertaken by the consumer in responding to a marketing stimulus.

consumerist movement an organised movement of citizens and government to strengthen the rights and powers of buyers in relation to sellers.

consumption system the way the user performs the tasks of getting and using products and services.

containerisation putting the goods in boxes or trailers that are easy to transfer between two transportation modes.

content-target advertising links ads not to keywords but to the contents of Web pages.

contractual sales force manufacturers' reps, sales agents, and brokers, who are paid a commission based on sales.

contractual VMS consists of independent firms at different levels of production and distribution integrating their programmes on a contractual basis to obtain more economies or sales impact than they could alone.

convenience goods goods the consumer purchases frequently, immediately, and with a minimum of effort.

convenience items item that sell in high volume but receive less promotion. These items can carry higher margins.

conventional marketing channel an independent producer, wholesaler(s), and retailer(s).

core benefit the service or benefit the customer is really buying.

core competency attribute that (1) is a source of competitive advantage in that it makes a significant contribution to perceived customer benefits, (2) has applications in a wide variety of markets, (3) is difficult for competitors to imitate.

core product offering items that produce high sales volume and are heavily promoted but with low margins because they are viewed as undifferentiated commodities.

core values the belief systems that underlie consumer attitudes and behaviour, and that determine people's choices and desires over the long term.

corporate culture the shared experiences, stories, beliefs, and norms that characterise an organisation.

corporate retailing corporately owned retailing outlets that achieve economies of scale, greater purchasing power, wider brand recognition, and better-trained employees.

corporate VMS combines successive stages of production and distribution under single ownership.

countertrade exchanging items that are paid for, in whole or part, with other items.

critical path scheduling a network-planning technique that calls for developing a master chart showing the simultaneous and sequential activities that must take place to launch a product or service.

cues stimuli that determine when, where, and how a person responds.

culture the fundamental determinant of a person's wants and behaviour.

customer-based brand equity the differential effect that brand knowledge has on a consumer response to the marketing of that brand.

customer churn rate of customer defection.

customer consulting data, information systems, and advice services that the seller offers to buyers.

customer database an organised collection of comprehensive information about individual customers or prospects that is current, accessible, and actionable for marketing purposes.

customerisation see customisation

customer lifetime value (CLV) the net present value of the stream of future profits expected over the customer's lifetime purchases.

customer mailing list a set of names, addresses, and telephone numbers.

customer-management organisation where companies organise marketing activity to understand and deal with individual customers rather than with the mass market or even market segments.

customer-perceived value (CPV) the difference between the prospective customer's evaluation of all the benefits and all the costs of an offering and the perceived alternatives.

customer-perceived value analysis a review of a company's strengths and weaknesses relative to those of various competitors.

customer-performance scorecard how well the company is doing year after year on particular customer-based measures.

customer profitability analysis (CPA) a means of assessing and ranking customer profitability through accounting techniques such as Activity-Based Costing (ABC).

customer relationship management the process of carefully managing detailed information about individual customers and their encounters or interaction with the brand or product to maximise customer loyalty.

customer-to-customer interactions/encounters direct or indirect, face-to-face or technology-mediated, active or passive interaction between two or more customers in the service setting or outside the service setting, which may or may not involve verbal communication.

customer training training the customer's employees to use the vendor's equipment properly and efficiently.

customer value analysis report of the company's strengths and weaknesses relative to various competitors.

customer value hierarchy five product levels that must be addressed by marketers in planning a market offering.

customisation combination of operationally driven mass customisation with customised marketing in a way that empowers consumers to design the product and service offering of the choice.

D

dashboards are on screen easy to read summaries of key marketing metrics. A marketing dashboard is a personalised view of all relevant marketing information to a specific job and role.

database marketing the process of building, maintaining, and using customer databases and other databases for the purpose of contacting, transacting, and building customer relationships.

data mining the extracting of useful information about individuals, trends, and segments from the mass of data.

data warehouse a collection of current data captured, organised, and stored electronically, designed to facilitate reporting and analysis.

delivery how well the product or service is delivered to the customer.

demand chain planning the process of designing the supply chain based on adopting a target market perspective and working backwards.

design mix of features that affect how a market offering looks, feels and functions in terms of customer requirements.

diffused preferences exist when customers' preferences vary greatly in their requirements.

direct channel consists of the manufacturer or service organisation going directly to the final consumer.

direct marketing the use of consumer-direct (CD) channels to reach and deliver goods and services to customers without using marketing middlemen.

direct-order marketing marketing in which direct marketers seek a measurable response, typically a customer order.

direct product profitability (DDP) a way of measuring a product's handling costs from the time it reaches the warehouse until a customer buys it in the retail store.

direct (company) sales force full- or part-time paid employees who work exclusively for the company as sales representatives.

disclaimant groups groups to which a person belong but whose values, norms or behaviour an individual seeks to avoid.

discrimination the process of recognising differences in sets of similar stimuli and adjusting responses accordingly.

disintermediation the elimination of channel intermediaries by product or service providers.

display advertisements (or banner advertisements) small, rectangular boxes containing text and perhaps a picture that companies pay to place on relevant websites or in other media.

dissociative groups those groups whose values or behaviour an individual rejects.

distribution channels sets of dependent or independent organisations involved in the process of making a product or service available for use or consumption.

distribution programming building a planned, professionally managed, vertical marketing system that meets the needs of both manufacturer and distributors.

drive a strong internal stimulus impelling action.

dual adaptation adapting both the product and the communications to the local market.

dumping situation in which a company charges either less than its costs or less than it charges in its home market, in order to enter or win a market.

durability a measure of a product's expected operating life under natural or stressful conditions.

durable goods product offerings that have a longer use lifetime, e.g. refrigerators and machine tools.

E

ebusiness the use of electronic means and platforms to conduct a company's business.

ecommerce a company or site offers to transact or facilitate the selling of products and services online.

elimination-by-aspects heuristic situation in which the consumer compares brands on an attribute selected probabilistically, and brands are eliminated if they do not meet minimum acceptable cutoff levels.

emarketing company efforts to inform buyers, communicate, promote, and sell its products and services over the Internet.

emotional branding engaging the consumer on the level of senses and emotions; forging a deep, lasting, intimate emotional connection to the brand that transcends material satisfaction; it involves creating holistic experience that delivers an emotional fulfilment so that the customer develops a special bond with and unique trust in the brand.

emotions mental and physiological states associated with a wide variety of feelings, thoughts and behaviour.

environmental threat a challenge posed by an unfavourable trend or development that would lead to lower sales or profit.

epurchasing purchase of goods, services, and information from various online suppliers.

events and experiences company-sponsored activities and programmes designed to create daily or special brand-related interactions.

everyday low pricing (EDLP) in retailing, a constant low price with few or no price promotions and special sales.

exchange the process of obtaining a desired product or service from someone by offering something in return. To learn more about **exchange**, go to www.pearsoned.co.uk/marketingmanagementeurope for additional commentary from the authors.

exclusive distribution severely limiting the number of intermediaries, in order to maintain control over the service level and outputs offered by resellers.

expectancy-value model consumers evaluate products and services by combining their brand beliefs – positive and negative – according to their weighted importance.

expected product a set of attributes and conditions buyers normally expect when they purchase this product.

experience curve (learning curve) a decline in the average cost with accumulated production experience as an individual or an organisation gets more experienced at a task they usually become more efficient at it.

experimental research is designed to capture cause-and-effect relationships by eliminating competing explanations of the observed findings.

F

fad a craze that is unpredictable, short-lived and intense.

family brand situation in which the parent brand is already associated with multiple products through brand extensions.

family of orientation parents and siblings.

family of procreation spouse and children.

features things that enhance the basic function of a product.

financial value refers to the monetary value of a company.

fixed (overhead) costs costs that do not vary with production or sales revenue.

flexible market-market perceived value offering (1) a naked solution containing the product and service elements that all segment members value, and (2) discretionary options that some segment members value.

focus group a gathering of six to ten people who are carefully selected based on certain demographic, psychographic, or other considerations and brought together to discuss various topics of interest.

forecasting the art of anticipating what buyers are likely to do under a given set of conditions.

form the size, shape or physical structure of a product.

forward invention creating a new product to meet a need in another country.

frequency programme (FPs) designed to provide rewards to customers who buy frequently and in substantial amounts.

G

global community where people around the world view themselves as potential partners or even family members in a vast increasingly interconnected human family.

global firm a firm that operates with multi-national branches and captures R&D, production, logistical, marketing, and financial advantages in its costs and reputation that are not available to purely domestic competitors.

global industry an industry in which the strategic positions of competitors in major geographic or national markets are fundamentally affected by their overall global positions.

globalisation has been described as the decoupling of space and time, emphasising that with instantaneous communications, knowledge and culture can be shared around the world simultaneously. To learn more about **globalisation**, go to www.pearsoned.co.uk/marketingmanagementeurope for additional commentary from the authors.

goal formulation the process of developing specific goals for the planning period.

going-rate pricing price based largely on competitors' prices.

gray market branded products diverted from normal or authorised distributions channels in the country of product origin or across international borders. It is the trade of something legal through unofficial, unauthorised or unintended distribution channels.

H

hedonic bias the phenomenon that people have a general tendency to attribute success to themselves and failure to external causes.

heuristics rules of thumb or mental shortcuts in the decision process.

high-low pricing charging higher prices on an everyday basis but then running frequent promotions and special sales.

holistic marketing a concept based on the development, design and implementation of marketing programmes, processes, and activities that recognises their breadth and interdependencies.

homogeneous preferences exists when all customers have roughly the same preferences.

horizontal marketing system two or more unrelated companies at the same level put together resources or programmes to exploit an emerging market opportunity.

hub-and-spoke system a system of marketing organisation where the brand or product manager is figuratively at the centre, with spokes emanating out to various departments.

hybrid channels use of multiple channels of distribution to reach customers in a defined market.

I

image the set of beliefs, ideas, and impressions a person holds regarding an object.

industry a group of firms that offer a product or service or class of products or services that are close substitutes for one another.

informational appeal an appeal that elaborates on market offering quality and payment attributes or benefits.

ingredient branding a special case of co-branding that involves creating brand equity for materials, components, or parts that are necessarily contained within other branded products.

innovation any good, service, or idea that is perceived by someone as new.

innovation diffusion process the spread of a new idea from its source of invention or creation to its ultimate users or adopters.

installation the work done to make a product operational in its planned location.

institutional market schools, hospitals, nursing homes, prisons, and other institutions that must provide goods and services to people in their care.

instrumental controls specific tangible costs and rewards designed to induce desired behaviour. Behaviourial theory has long acknowledged two basis tools for influencing human behaviour – reward and punishment.

integrated logistics systems (ILS) materials management, material flow systems, and physical distribution, supported by information technology (IT).

integrated marketing mixing and matching marketing activities to maximise their individual and collective efforts.

integrated marketing communications (IMC) a concept of marketing communications planning that recognises the added value of a comprehensive plan in order to integrate and coordinate it's message and media to deliver clear and reinforcing communication.

intensive distribution the manufacturer placing the goods or services in as many outlets as possible.

interactive marketing online and offline activities and programmes designed to engage customers or prospects and directly or indirectly raise awareness, improve image, or elicit sales of market offerings by moving from a transaction based effort to a conversation or interaction with the customer.

intermediary any channel member that plays some role in bringing the product or service to market.

internal branding activities and processes that help to inform and inspire employees.

interstitials advertisements, often with video or animation, that pop up between changes on a website.

J

joint venture a company in which multiple investors share ownership and control.

L

learning changes in an individual's behaviour arising from experience.

lexicographic heuristic consumer choosing the best brand on the basis of its perceived most important attribute.

licensed product or service one whose brand name has been licensed to other manufacturers who actually make the product or to another service provider.

life-cycle cost the product's purchase cost plus the discounted cost of maintenance and repair less the discounted salvage value.

lifestyle a person's pattern of living in the world as expressed in activities, interests and opinions.

line extension the parent brand is used to brand a new product or service that targets a new market segment within a product category currently served by the parent brand.

line stretching a company lengthens its product or service line beyond its current range.

location-based services new forms of mobile service, which are delivered location dependent (it depends on where you are) and context sensitive (related to what you are doing or your particular needs), to mobile users.

logistics the flow of products from point of origin to end user.

long-term memory (LTM) a permanent repository of information.

loyalty a commitment to re-buy or re-patronise a preferred product or service.

M

maintenance and repair the service programme for helping customers keep purchased products in good working order.

market-buildup method identifying all the potential buyers in each market and estimating their potential purchases.

market-centred organisations where companies organise marketing activity to meet the needs of distinct customer groups rather than focusing on marketing functions, regions or products.

market demand the total volume of a product or service that would be bought by a defined customer group in a defined geographical area in a defined time period in a defined marketing environment under a defined marketing programme.

marketer someone who seeks a response (attention, a purchase, a vote, a donation) from another party, called the prospect.

market forecast the market demand corresponding to the level of industry marketing expenditure.

marketing process of planning and executing the conception, pricing, promotion, and distribution of ideas, goods and services to create exchanges that satisfy individual and organisational goals.

marketing audit a comprehensive, systematic, independent, and periodic examination of a company's or business unit's marketing environment, objectives, strategies and activities.

marketing channels sets of interdependent organisations involved in the process of making a product or service available for use or consumption.

marketing channel system the particular set of marketing channels employed by a firm.

marketing communications the means by which firms attempt to inform, persuade, and remind consumers – directly or indirectly – about products, services and brands that they sell.

marketing communication mix consists of eight major modes of communication: advertising, sales promotion, events and experiences, public relations and publicity, direct marketing, interactive marketing, word-of-mouth marketing and personal selling.

marketing dashboard see dashboard.

marketing decision support system (MDSS) a coordinated collection of data, systems, tools, and techniques with supporting software and hardware by which an organisation gathers and interprets relevant information from business and the environment and turns it into a basis for marketing action.

marketing implementation the process that turns marketing plans into action assignments and ensures that such assignments are executed in a manner that accomplishes the plan's stated objectives.

marketing information system (MIS) people, equipment, and procedures to gather, sort, analyse, evaluate, and distribute information to marketing decision makers.

marketing insights provide diagnostic information about how and why we observe certain effects in the marketplace, and what that means to marketers.

marketing intelligence system a set of procedures and sources managers use to obtain everyday information about developments in the marketing environment.

marketing management the art and science of choosing target markets and getting, keeping, and growing customers through creating, delivering, and communicating superior customer value.

marketing metrics the set of measures that helps firms to quantify, compare, and interpret their marketing performance.

marketing mix is the marketing activities used to create, communicate and deliver value to the customer. There were originally four marketing mix variables expanded to seven to include the product/service, price, place, promotion, process, physical evidence and people.

marketing network the company and its supporting stakeholders, with whom it has built mutually profitable business relationships.

marketing opportunity an area of buyer need and interest in which there is a high probability that a company can profitably satisfy that need.

marketing plan written document that summarises what the marketer has learned about the marketplace, indicates how the firm plans to reach its marketing objectives, and helps direct and coordinate the marketing effort.

marketing public relations (MPR) publicity and other activities that build corporate or brand image to facilitate marketing goals.

marketing research the systematic design, collection, analysis, and reporting of data and findings relevant to a specific marketing situation facing the company.

market logistics planning the infrastructure to meet demand, then implementing and controlling the physical flows or materials and final goods from points of origin to points of use, to meet customer requirements at a profit.

market-management organisation where companies organise marketing activity based to meet the needs of customers who fall into different user groups with distinct buying preferences and practices.

market mavens consumers possessing a broad expertise concerning many different products and decisions related to the marketplace.

market offering/product-mix pricing a set of prices that maximises profits on the total mix of products.

market opportunity analysis (MOA) system used to determine the attractiveness and probability of success.

market partitioning the process of investigating the hierarchy of attributes consumers examine in choosing a brand if they use phased decision strategies.

market penetration index a comparison of the current level of market demand to the potential demand level.

market-penetration pricing pricing strategy where prices start low to drive higher sales volume from price-sensitive customers and produce productivity gains.

market potential the upper limit to market demand whereby increased marketing expenditures would not be expected to stimulate further demand.

market share the proportion of the available market that is being serviced by a company.

market-skimming pricing pricing strategy where prices start high and are slowly lowered over time to maximise profits from less price-sensitive customers.

mark-up pricing an item by adding a standard increase to the product's cost.

mass customisation is the ability of a company to meet each customer's requirements – to prepare on a mass basis individually designed products, services, programmes and communications.

mass marketing is when a seller engages in the mass production, distribution and promotion of one item for all buyers.

materials and parts goods that enter the manufacturer's product completely.

media selection finding the most cost-effective media to deliver the desired number and type of exposures to the target audience.

megamarketing the strategic coordination of economic, psychological, political, and public relations skills, to gain the cooperation of a number of parties in order to enter or operate in a given market.

megatrends large social, economic, political, and technological changes that are slow to form, and once in place, have an influence for seven to ten years or longer.

membership groups groups having a direct influence on a person.

memory encoding how and where information gets into memory.

memory retrieval how and from where information gets out of memory.

mental accounting the manner by which consumers code, categorise, and evaluate financial outcomes of choices.

microsales analysis examination of specific products and territories that fail to produce expected sales.

microsite a limited area on the Web managed and paid for by an external advertiser/company.

mission statements statements that organisations develop to share with managers, employees, and (in many cases) customers.

mixed bundling the seller offers goods both individually and in bundles.

moment of truth an instance of contact or interaction between a customer and a company which gives the customer an opportunity to form or change their impression about the company.

motive what drives consumers to act in order to reach a desired goal.

multiple channels or **multichannel marketing** when a marketer opts to uses multiple channels but does not have a multichannel strategy across the channels. Multichannel occurs when a single firm uses two or more channels to reach one or more customer segments and has cross-channel benefits based on the management of the multiple channels.

multitasking doing two or more things at the same time.

N

net price analysis analysis that encompasses company list price, average discount, promotional spending, and co-op advertising to arrive at net price.

network a network interlinks diverse members and each member has to reflect or be aware of other members and their needs.

network economy complex interacting sets of markets linked through exchange processes and driven by a dynamic and knowledge-rich technology dominant environment.

non-compensatory models in consumer choice, when consumers do not simultaneously consider all positive and negative attribute considerations in making a decision.

non-durable goods offerings, usually termed fast-moving consumer goods (fmcgs), that are normally consumed in one or a few uses, e.g. beer and soap.

normative behaviour focuses on the emotional rather then the rational behaviour and involves shame, blame or pride. It uses peer pressure, norms of behaviour and other social influence to shape behaviour in the service environment.

O

online alliances and affiliate programs when one Internet company works with another one and they advertise each other.

operating margin the ratio of operating profit divided by net sales.

opinion leader the person in informal, product- or service-related communications who offers advice or information about a specific product or product category.

ordering ease how easy it is for the customer to place an order with the company.

organisation a company's structures, policies and corporate culture.

organisational buying the decision-making process by which formal organisations establish the need for purchased products and services and identify, evaluate and choose among alternative brands and suppliers.

out-of-home advertising see place advertising.

outsourcing subcontracting a part of a company's operations such as product manufacturing, to a third-party company. The decision to outsource is often made in the interest of lowering costs as companies can often gain in effectiveness and efficiency by outsourcing to companies who can perform that task better and cheaper.

overall market share the company's sales expressed as a percentage of total market sales.

P

packaging all the activities of designing and producing the container for a product or market offering.

paid-search advertisements (or pay-per-click advertisements) search terms that trigger relevant links to market offerings alongside search results from Google, MSN, Tiscali and Yahoo!. Advertisers pay only if people click on the links.

parent brand an existing brand that gives birth to a brand extension.

partner relationship management (PRM) activities the firm undertakes to build mutually satisfying long-term relations with key partners such as suppliers, distributors, ad agencies and marketing research suppliers.

pay-per-click advertisements see paid-search advertisements.

penetrated market the set of consumers who are buying a company's product or service.

perceived value the value promised by the company's value proposition and perceived by the customer.

perception the process by which an individual selects, organises, and interprets information inputs to create a meaningful picture of the world.

performance quality the level at which the product's or service's primary characteristics operate.

performance value the level at which the market offering's primary characteristic attributes operate.

personal communications channels two or more persons communicating directly face-to-face, person-to-audience, over the telephone, or through email.

personal influence the effect one person has on another's attitude or purchase probability.

personality a set of distinguishing human psychological traits that lead to relatively consistent responses to environmental stimuli.

personal selling face-to-face interaction with one or more prospective purchasers for the purpose of making presentations, answering questions and procuring orders.

place advertising (also out-of-home advertising) ads that appear outside of home and where consumers work and play.

point-of-purchase (POP) the location where a purchase is made, typically thought of in terms of a retail setting.

points-of-difference (PODs) attributes or benefits consumers strongly associate with a brand, positively evaluate, and believe they could not find to the same extent with a competing brand.

points-of-parity (POPs) associations consumers make that are not unique to a brand and may be shared with other brands.

positioning is the act of designing a company's offering and image to occupy a distinctive place in the minds of the target market.

potential market the set of consumers who profess a sufficient level of interest in a market offer.

potential product all the possible augmentations and transformations the product or offering might undergo in the future.

price discrimination a company sells a product or service at two or more prices that do not reflect a proportional difference in costs.

price escalation an increase in the price of a product or service due to added costs of selling it in different countries.

primary groups groups with which a person interacts continuously and informally, such as family, friends, neighbours and co-workers.

principle of congruity psychological mechanism that states that consumers like to see seemingly related objects as being as similar as possible in their favourability.

private label brand brands that retailers and wholesalers develop and market.

product anything that can be offered to a market to satisfy a want or need and consists of a set of attributes, including physical goods, services, experiences, events, persons, places, properties, organisations, information and ideas.

product adaptation altering the product to meet local conditions or preferences.

product assortment the set of all products and items a particular seller offers for sale.

product invention creating something new via product development or other means.

product map shows which competitors' items are competing against company X's items.

product mix see product assortment.

product penetration percentage the percentage of ownership or use of a product or service in a population.

product system a group of diverse but related items that function in a compatible manner.

profitable customer a person, household, or company that over time yields a revenue stream that exceeds by an acceptable amount the company's cost stream of attracting, selling and servicing that customer.

prospect theory when consumers frame decision alternatives in terms of gains and losses according to a value function.

prosumers where the consumer moves from a passive role to an active role and becomes involved in the design and manufacture of products or services. This word is formed by linking the word producer with the word consumer.

psychographics is the science of using psychology and demographics to better understand consumer market consumers.

public any group that has an actual or potential interest in or impact on a company's ability to achieve its objectives.

public relations (PR) a variety of programmes designed to promote or protect a company's image or its individual products or services.

publicity the task of securing editorial space – as opposed to paid space – in print and broadcast media to promote something.

pull strategy when the manufacturer uses advertising and promotion to persuade consumers to ask intermediaries for the product or service, thus inducing the intermediaries to order it.

purchase probability scale a scale to measure the probability of a buyer making a particular purchase.

pure bundling a firm only offers its products as a bundle.

pure-click companies that have launched a website without any previous existence as a firm.

push strategy when the manufacturer uses its sales force and trade promotion to induce intermediaries to carry, promote and sell the product and service to end users.

Q

questionnaire consists of a set of questions that are presented to a number of respondents.

R

reference groups all the groups that have a direct or indirect influence on a person's attitudes or behaviour.

reference prices pricing information a consumer retains in memory which is used to interpret and evaluate a new price.

relational equity the cumulative value of the firm's network of relationships with its customers, partners, suppliers, employees and investors.

relationship marketing building mutually satisfying long-term relationships with key parties, in order to earn and retain their business.

relative market share market share in relation to a company's largest competitor.

reliability a measure of the probability that a product will not malfunction or fail within a specified time period.

repairability a measure of the ease of fixing a product when it malfunctions or fails.

representativeness heuristic when consumers base their predictions on how representative or similar an outcome is to other examples.

retromarketing a return to the past where products and services and marketing techniques from 50 and even 100 years ago are now popular.

risk analysis a method by which possible rates of returns and their probabilities are calculated by obtaining estimates for uncertain variables affecting profitability.

role the activities a person is expected to perform.

S

sales analysis measuring and evaluating actual sales in relation to goals.

sales budget a conservative estimate of the expected volume of sales, used for making current purchasing, production and cash flow decisions.

sales promotion a variety of short-term incentives to encourage trial or purchase of a product or service (market offering).

sales quota the sales goal set for a product or service, company division, or sales representative.

sales-variance analysis a measure of the relative contribution of different factors to a gap in sales performance.

satisfaction a person's feelings of pleasure or disappointment resulting from comparing perceived performance or outcome in relation to his or her expectations.

scenario analysis developing plausible representations of a firm's possible future that make different assumptions about forces driving the market and include different uncertainties.

search-related ads ads in which search terms are used as a proxy for the consumer's consumption interests and relevant links to product or service offerings are listed alongside the search results.

secondary groups groups which tend to be more formal and require less interaction than primary groups, such as religious, professional, and trade-union groups.

selective attention the mental process of screening out certain stimuli while noticing others.

selective distortion the tendency to interpret information in a way that fit consumer perceptions.

selective distribution the use of more than a few but less than all of the intermediaries who are willing to carry a particular product or service.

selective retention the process of remembering only a small part of what a person is exposed to. People remember more accurately messages that are close to their interests, views and beliefs.

served market all the buyers who are able and willing to buy a company's product or service.

served market share a company's sales expressed as a percentage of the total sales to its served market.

service any act or performance that one party can offer to another that is essentially intangible, is a process rather than a unit of output, a focus on dynamic resources such as skill or knowledge and an understanding of value as a collaborative process between providers and customers.

service process the way in which the service system operates.

service quality the perception the customer has of the level of service received. In general the customer compares the perceived service with the expected service.

services traditionally viewed as intangible, inseparable, variable, and perishable offerings, e.g. haircuts, legal advice and appliance repairs.

servicescape the impact on customer and employee behaviour of a service firm's physical surroundings or environment. It emphasises the importance of the physical environment in which a service process takes place.

shareholder value the value of the firm minus the future claims.

share penetration index a comparison of a company's current market share to its potential market share.

shopping goods goods that the consumer, in the process of selection and purchase, characteristically compares on such bases as suitability, quality, price and style.

short-term memory (STM) a temporary repository of information.

social classes homogeneous and enduring divisions in a society, which are hierarchically ordered and whose members share similar values, interests and behaviour.

social marketing marketing done by a non-profit or government organisation to further a cause, such as 'say no to drugs'.

speciality goods goods that have unique characteristics or brand identification for which a sufficient number of buyers are willing to make a special purchasing effort.

specialties items with lower sales volume but might be highly promoted or might generate income for services.

sponsorships financial support of an event or activity in return for recognition and acknowledgment as the sponsor.

stakeholder-performance scorecard a measure to track the satisfaction of various constituencies who have a critical interest in and impact on the company's performance.

staples items with lower sales volume and no promotion that yield a somewhat higher margin.

status one's position within his or her own hierarchy or culture.

straight extension introducing a product or service in a foreign market without any change in the product or service.

strategic brand management the design and implementation of marketing activities and programmes to build, measure, and manage brands to maximise their value.

strategic business units (SBUs) a single business or collection of related businesses that can be planned separately from the rest of the company, with its own set of competitors and a manager who is responsible for strategic planning and profit performance.

strategic group firms pursuing the same strategy directed to the same target market.

strategic marketing plan laying out long-term decisions, like the target markets, market position and the value proposition that will be offered, based on analysis of the best market opportunities.

strategy a company's game plan for achieving its goals.

style a product's look and feel to the buyer.

sub-brand a new brand combined with an existing brand.

subculture subdivisions of a culture that provide more specific identification and socialisation, such as nationalities, religions, racial groups, and geographical regions.

subliminal perception receiving and processing subconscious messages that affect behaviour.

supersegment a set of segments sharing some exploitable similarity.

supplies and business services short-term goods and services that facilitate developing or managing the finished product.

supply chain set of three or more entities (organisations or individuals) directly involved in the upstream or downstream flows of product, service, finances and /or information from a source to a customer.

supply chain management (SCM) procuring the right inputs (raw materials, components, and capital equipment); converting them efficiently into finished products or services; and dispatching them to the final destinations.

supply network a system of partnerships and alliances that a firm creates to source, augment and deliver its offerings.

total customer cost the bundle of costs customers expect to incur in evaluating, obtaining, using, and disposing of the given market offering, including monetary, time, energy and psychic costs.

total customer value the perceived monetary value of the bundle of economic, functional and psychological benefits customers expect from a given market offering.

total market potential the maximum amount of sales that might be available to all the firms in an industry during a given period, under a given level of industry marketing effort and environmental conditions.

total quality management (TQM) an organisationwide approach to continuously improving the quality of all the organization's processes, products and services.

tracking studies collecting information from consumers on a routine basis over time.

transaction a trade of values between two or more parties: A gives X to B and receives Y in return.

transfer in the case of gifts, subsidies and charitable contributions: A gives X to B but does not receive anything tangible in return.

transfer price the price a company charges another unit in the company for goods it ships to foreign subsidiaries.

transformational appeal an appeal that elaborates on a non-market offering-related benefit or image.

trend a direction or sequence of events that has some momentum and durability.

two-part pricing a fixed fee plus a variable usage fee.

tying agreements agreement in which producers of strong brands sell their products to dealers only if dealers purchase related products or services, such as other products in the brand line.

T

tactical marketing plan is related to the first year of the strategic plan and so is short term and gives specific actions. It is a highly detailed, heavily researched and, well written report that forces internally in order to fully understand the results of past marketing decisions; forces externally in order to fully understand the market in which they operate; sets future goals and provides direction for future marketing efforts that everyone within the organisation should understand and support and is a key component in obtaining funding to pursue new initiatives.

target costing deducting the desired profit margin from the price at which a market offering will sell, given its appeal and competitors' prices.

target market the part of the qualified available market the company decides to pursue.

target-return pricing determining the price that would yield the firm's target rate of return on investment (ROI).

task competency having the skills required for a specific job/role.

telemarketing the use of telephone and call centres to attract prospects, sell to existing, customers, and provide service by taking orders and answering questions.

total customer benefit is the perceived monetary value of the bundle of economic, functional and psychological benefits customers expect from a given market offering because of the products, services, personnel and image involved.

total costs the sum of the fixed and variable costs for any given level of production.

U

unsought goods those the consumer does not know about or does not normally think of buying, like smoke detectors.

V

value chain or **value network** a company's supply of partnerships and alliances and how the company partners with specific suppliers, distributors, manufacturers and so on to source, create, augment and deliver products and services to the market. At each activity along the chain or within the network the product or service gains either tangible or intangible value.

value delivery system all the expectancies the customer will have on the way to obtaining and using the offering.

value pricing winning loyal customers by charging a fairly low price for a high-quality offering.

value proposition the whole cluster of benefits the company promises to deliver.

variable costs costs that vary directly with the level of production.

venture team a cross-functional group charged with developing a specific product or business.

vertical integration situation in which manufacturers try to control or own their suppliers, distributors or other intermediaries.

vertical marketing system (VMS) producer, wholesaler(s), and retailer(s) acting as a unified system.

viral marketing any form of advertising and/or communication that spreads with like a virus and is passed on from consumer to consumer and market to market. The use of the internet (particularly social networking sites) and the internet increases the speed and geographic coverage of these communications.

W

warranties formal statements of expected product/market offering performance by the manufacturer.

Weber's law a rule saying that people are more likely to notice stimuli whose deviations are large in relationship to the normal size of the stimuli.

word-of-mouth marketing people-to-people oral, written, or electronic communications that relate to the merits or experiences of purchasing and consuming market offerings.

Y

yield pricing situation in which companies offer (1) discounted but limited early purchases, (2) higher-priced late purchases, and (3) the lowest rates on unsold inventory just before it expires.

Z

zero-level channel a manufacturer selling directly to the final customer.

zone of tolerance a range where a service dimension would be deemed satisfactory anchored by the minimum level consumers are willing to accept and the level they believe can and should be delivered.

Index

Name index

Organisation and brand index

Subject index